CORPORATE FINANCE

ASPEN CASEBOOK SERIES

CORPORATE FINANCE

Robert J. Rhee

John H. and Marylou Dasburg Professor of Law

University of Florida Levin College of Law

Printed in the United States of America.

1 2 3 4 5 6 7 8 9 0

ISBN 978-1-4548-7028-9

Library of Congress Cataloging-in-Publication Data

Names: Rhee, Robert J.
Title: Corporate finance / Robert J. Rhee, John H. and Marylou Dasburg
   Professor of Law, University of Florida Levin College of Law.
Description: New York : Wolters Kluwer, 2016. | Series: Aspen casebook series
   | Includes index.
Identifiers: LCCN 2015049569 | ISBN 9781454870289
Subjects: LCSH: Corporations–Finance–Law and legislation–United States. |
   Securities–United States. | Corporation law–United States. | LCGFT:
   Casebooks.
Classification: LCC KF1428 .R48 2016 | DDC 338.6/04102434–dc23 LC record
available at http://lccn.loc.gov/2015049569

For Nicki, Piers, and Blake

SUMMARY OF CONTENTS

CONTENTS

Contents

Contents

PREFACE

governance & economic rights embedded in financial Instruments

Corporate Finance is important. It is not an esoteric course. It should be a standard course in a rigorous business law curriculum. Along with Business Associations and Securities Regulation, Corporate Finance should be the foundational course to prepare for corporate and business transactional practice. Business Associations introduces students to different business organizational forms and provides an overview of the duties and powers of directors and officers, governance rights, shareholder litigation, and a bit of securities regulation. This introduction to corporations covers only a portion of the types of problems seen in business law practice.

Financings are routine corporate transactions. Every financing transaction triggers the consideration of two spheres of law. The first is the public law regulating securities issuances and trading, which is Securities Regulation. The second is the mostly private law dealing with the private ordering of the bundles of governance and economic rights embedded in financial instruments; this is the field of Corporate Finance. Business lawyers should have grounding in both the spheres of law. Corporate Finance is a transaction-oriented course. It is fundamentally the study of the legal and economic nature of financial instruments that corporations issue to service their financing needs.

When an author undertakes the work of writing a book, he or she should answer two questions.

Why write it? Although Corporate Finance is a practical subject, there is not a broader selection of casebooks in legal education. There are several wonderful books authored by some of the most distinguished scholars and teachers in the field, but there is not the type of broad selection seen in Business Associations or Corporation Law or even Securities Regulation. There may be reasons for this thin menu. Corporate Finance is difficult. Financial transactions can be factually and conceptually complex. Corporate Finance is an interdisciplinary study. Law, finance, transaction economics, and accounting are intertwined in financing transactions and their documentation. This casebook provides more options in this important field of business law and professional practice.

How is this book different? With the above considerations in mind, I sought to distinguish this casebook from several other fine books in the field in four ways.

1. *This book is interdisciplinary in nature.* I provide essential coverage of the basic concepts of accounting and finance needed for a business lawyer to understand deal economics. Lawyers should not compartmentalize legal issues from business, economic, accounting, and financial issues. They should be more than caretakers of boilerplate contracts and wordsmith functionaries. A corporate lawyer should understand financial transactions as clients and financial advisors do. Essential accounting and financial concepts are comprehensively covered, at the basic level, in clear expository text, including: financial statements, financial statement analysis, time value of

money, cost of capital, securities valuation, capital structure, market efficiency, and derivatives.

2. *This book facilitates ease of learning and teaching.* I tried to make this book accessible. I avoided excerpting technically dense academic writings in finance and economics, which can intimidate students and teachers alike. There is no hiding the ball or gratuitous academic-speak. I wrote the materials in the plainest way I could to convey essential ideas. Some ideas are difficult, but they should be readily accessible to all if written in clear exposition.

3. *This book provides a basic understanding of financial instruments to prepare students for corporate practice.* I highlighted contractual contents of financial instruments and transaction documents taken from various sources, including: model indentures and debt contracts, SEC filings, legal and financial advisor opinion letters, and corporate charter provisions. Economics and business needs drive corporate transactions, but deals are enabled by law and memorialized in legal transactional documents. Students should begin to see and read financial contracts and documents within the constraint of publication page limits.

4. *This book takes a business and transactional perspective.* I included several case studies, which will give students the opportunity to analyze legal problems in the context of business transactions. These case studies go beyond the specific legal issues and present opportunities to consider more broadly the transaction from business and economic perspectives.

I packaged the materials in this book with a specific course goal in mind. After finishing the course using this book, students should have foundational knowledge of the legal and economic structure of major classes of financial instruments used in financing the corporate enterprise, and such knowledge encompasses a basic understanding of the business, economic, and accounting contexts and the sources of law and documents used in corporate finance transactions. If a student can acquire this knowledge, the book will have served its purpose.

Robert J. Rhee, J.D., M.B.A.

John H. and Marylou Dasburg Professor of Law
University of Florida Levin College of Law
Gainesville, Florida

December 2015

NOTE ON CASE EDITING AND ANNOTATION

The editing of cases is an important feature of this book. Case opinions have been heavily edited, and so full disclosure is required. The single purpose of editing a casebook is easier, efficient reading for students without compromising the essential substance and law in the opinion. With this sole purpose in mind, I used the following editorial and stylistic conventions throughout this book, some of which are atypical for a law school casebook.

Annotations and other author supplied materials. In actual practice, transactions are schematized; tables of data are created; information is packaged in visual form if it will facilitate better communication. In addition to word processing software, PowerPoint and Excel are heavily used in business practice. However, judicial opinions are written in prose, making the task of understanding facts and transactions more difficult. When complex data, information, or transactions are presented in prose, and when appropriate, I embedded in the opinions "Author's Case Annotation," which are diagrams, charts, and data summaries.

No use of ellipses or brackets. Editing necessarily changes the style and substance of the original case. As with all case editing, the most prominent editorial changes to the original text are deletions of certain sections of opinions. Where materials have been deleted, they have not been indicated with ellipses (". . ." or "* * *"). When capitalization has been supplied due to deletions of the sentence beginning, no brackets [ ] have been used. These standard conventions of legal writing are visually distracting and pedagogically unnecessary.

Choices on deletion and retention of citations to authority. Some casebooks keep most citations in opinions and others delete the majority of them. This book follows the latter convention. I preserved case citations mostly when the excerpted cases cite to each other. These cross-citations among the selected cases illustrate the collective body of case law bound by common substantive principles and efforts to achieve interpretive consistency among common law courts.

Emphases added for contract terms. Contract terms in financial instruments or corporate charters are frequently boilerplate language that can be lengthy, abstruse, artfully drafted, and difficult to read. Some case opinions do not sufficiently highlight or emphasize important contract language. Important terms may be buried in a footnote or in a long paragraph in the prose of judicial opinions. When needed, important contractual terms have been indented, emphasized, or moved from footnote and to text.

Citation formatting and other minor editorial changes. When an edited opinion contains an incomplete citation fragment or uses unconventional citation methods, I took the liberty of completing or standardizing the citation. Some portions of the citations may have been edited out: for example, "cert. denied" or parallel citations to multiple reporters. I diligently made other nonsubstantive, minor editorial changes—edits in the nature of: rewriting "$.6" to "$0.6," supplying or deleting headings, changing "mm" denoting million to "m," or deleting unnecessary text, words, phrases, and parentheticals within sentences to streamline the reading to the essential points of analysis and law.

The accumulation of these editing and annotation conventions over the course of the entire book will make a material impact on the reading and learning experience. A casebook is not a primary legal source; it is an educational tool. This textbook was not a brief writing exercise. The editorial process strove for visual appeal, superior presentation of complex information, and easier reading with an eye toward advancing student learning of a complex area of law and business without losing or altering substance. The complete, unaltered case opinions are readily available in the law reporters.

Acknowledgments

Drafts of this book were assigned to my students over the years, and their comments have been informative. I thank the students who took Corporate Finance with me at the University of Maryland Carey School of Law (Fall 2013), the Georgetown University Law Center (Fall 2013), and the University of Florida Levin College of Law (Spring and Fall 2015).

I would also like to thank the following authors and publishers for kindly granting permission to reproduce excerpts of the following material:

Ad Hoc Committee for Revision of the 1983 Model Simplified Indenture, "Revised Model Simplified Indenture," 55 Business Lawyer 1115 (2000). Copyright © 2000 by the American Bar Association. Reprinted with permission. All rights reserved. This information or any or portion thereof may not be copied or disseminated in any form or by any means or stored in an electronic database or retrieval system without the express written consent of the American Bar Association.

Brealey, Richard A., Stewart C. Myers, and Franklin Allen, *Principles of Corporate Finance*. Copyright © 2013 McGraw-Hill Education. Reprinted with permission of McGraw-Hill Global Education Holdings, LLC.

Broughton, Philip Delves, *Ahead of the Curve: Two Years at Harvard Business School*. Copyright © 2008 by Philip Delves Broughton. Used by permission of Penguin Press, an imprint of Penguin Publishing Group, a division of Penguin Random House LLC.

Buxbaum, Richard M., "Preferred Stock—Law and Draftsmanship," 42 Cal. L. Rev. 243 (1954). Copyright © 1954 by California Law Review, Inc. Reprinted with permission of the California Law Review.

Coates IV, John C., Jesse M. Fried & Kathryn E. Spier, "What Courses Should Law Students Take? Lessons from Harvard's BigLaw Survey," 64 Journal of Legal Education 443 (2015). Copyright © 2015 Association of American Law Schools (AALS). Reprinted with permission of AALS and the authors.

Cohan, William D., *House of Cards: A Tale of Hubris and Wretched Excess on Wall Street*. Copyright © 2009, 2010 by William D. Cohan. Used by permission of Doubleday, an imprint of the Knopf Doubleday Publishing Group, a division of Penguin Random House LLC. All rights reserved.

Committee on Trust Indentures and Indenture Trustees, "Model Negotiated Covenants and Related Definitions," from *Business Lawyer*, Vol. 61, No. 4 (August 2006). Copyright © 2006 by the American Bar Association. Reprinted with permission. All rights reserved. This information or any or portion thereof may not be copied or disseminated in any form or by any means or stored in an electronic database or retrieval system without the express written consent of the American Bar Association.

Frock, Roger J., *Changing How the World Does Business: FedEx's Incredible Journey to Success—The Inside Story*. Published by Berrett-Koehler Publishers. Copyright © 2006 Roger J. Frock. Used by permission.

Shiller, Robert J., *Irrational Exuberance*, Copyright © 2015 Robert J. Shiller. Republished with permission of Princeton University Press. Permission conveyed through Copyright Clearance Center, Inc.

TriBar Opinion Committee, "Third-Party 'Closing' Opinions: A Report of the TriBar Opinion Committee," from *The Business Lawyer*, Vol. 53, February 1998. Copyright © 1998 by the TriBar Opinion Committee. Reprinted with permission by the TriBar Opinion Committee.

Uniform Fraudulent Transfer Act, Copyright © 2013 by the National Conference of Commissioners on Uniform State Laws. Reprinted with permission of the Uniform Law Commission.

CORPORATE FINANCE

Sources

(1) Financial
    Contract

(2) State
    Corporation
    Statute

(3)

INTRODUCTION

A. WHAT IS CORPORATE FINANCE?

Corporate Finance is the field of law dealing with the legal rights and economic benefits of the holders of financial instruments. It continues the study of corporation and contract laws dealing specifically with financing the corporate enterprise. From an economic perspective, corporations are legal entities facilitating the financing of business endeavors by potentially diffused groups of mostly private investors, each seeking a particular financial return. The ownership of a financial instrument issued by the corporation grants the investor a bundle of legal rights and economic benefits.

When a corporation issues financial instruments, two distinct spheres of law are triggered. The first is the public law regulating securities, which is covered in Securities Regulation. This is the regulatory aspect of issuing and trading securities and disclosure of information by issuers. The regulation of securities does not mandate specific substantive terms of financial contracts. The underlying philosophy is that market actors will negotiate the economic and governance terms of securities. Regulation of securities is fundamentally concerned with registration, disclosure, and the process of securities issuance and trading. These rules are complex and fundamentally procedural in nature.

The second sphere of law is the mostly private law dealing with the private ordering of the substantive terms of financial instruments, those being the bundle of economic and governance rights embedded in financial instruments. Corporate Finance examines the rights and benefits of creditors, preferred stockholders, common stockholders, and holders of derivatives, and their legal and economic relationships with not just the corporate issuer, but also with each other. Corporate lawyers should have a solid grounding in both the public law and private law facets of financing transactions.

In drafting or reading financial contracts, lawyers should understand that there are four broad sources of law that interact with each other. The first source is the financial contract itself, which may be found in the credit or derivatives contract (such as a bond indenture or credit default swap), or the corporate charter for preferred and common stocks. The second source of law is the state corporation statute, which enables the creation of the corporation and thus its stock. Corporation law principally applies to equity instruments, but it also affects creditors as well. The third source of law is a collection of mostly statutes that may have particular application to a financial instrument or class of capital investors. For example, the Trust Indenture Act of 1939

1

and fraudulent transfer statutes protect bondholders and creditors. The fourth source of law is case law. Courts interpret contracts, apply statutory corporation law and other statutes, and make common law. The whole analysis can be complicated.

In thinking about financial contracts, lawyers should understand the importance of boilerplate contract terms. Many cases turn on detailed analyses of contractual language. In practice, lawyers do not write financial contracts word-for-word from scratch. The market practice in commercial transactions, including corporate financings, depends on the use of standardized terms and form documents; they are then tailored by the lawyer for the individual transaction. Repeat transactions in the market call for efficient drafting and document production processes. Boilerplate terms and form documents incorporate many generations of market customs and common understandings, as well as judicial opinions interpreting their meanings. Continued legal innovations in financing over time have resulted in a set of boilerplate terms and form documents that have taken on consistent, uniform meaning, which have resulted in greater efficiencies in the market. The advice of famed lawyer Paul D. Cravath, the namesake of a prestigious New York corporate law firm, should be well taken.

> The provisions of the modern reorganization agreement and the modern corporate mortgages are the result of the experience and prophetic vision of a great many able lawyers. Every new provision is suggested either by some decision of the courts or by an actual experience or by some lawyer's conception of a possible exigency. Ordinarily in drafting a document a lawyer must draw chiefly upon his own experience and the results of his own observation, but corporate mortgages and reorganization agreements are public documents so that each lawyer can have the benefit of the experience of many others. . . . I advise you adhere to precedent and, in most cases, you will find the long reorganization agreement based on precedent much safer than the agreement half as long drawn by your neighbor who scorns precedents.*

Lastly, the lessons learned in Corporate Finance are not just restricted to transactions involving corporations. The universe of business organizations can be broadly categorized into corporations and noncorporate limited liability entities. While important distinctions separate these forms, they also share common attributes. With respect to debt, lessons concerning the rights of corporate creditors and debtholders apply in the noncorporate context. With respect to equityholders, the concept of freedom of contracts is a significant principle in the laws of noncorporate entities. *See, e.g.,* Delaware Limited Liability Company Act, 6 Del.C. §18-1102(b) ("It is the policy of this chapter to give the maximum effect to the principle of freedom of contract and to the enforceability of limited liability company agreements."). Like corporations, which can create different classes of stock, noncorporate entities can create different classes of equityholders with different bundles of financial and governance rights. Some statutes explicitly recognize this specific aspect of financial contracting. Consider New York's Limited Liability Company Act §418(a): "The articles of organization of a limited liability company may provide for classes or groups of members having such relative rights, powers, preferences and limitations as the operating agreement of such limited liability company may provide." This provision borrows

---

* Paul D. Cravath, Reorganization of Corporations in Some Legal Phases of Corporate Financing, Reorganization and Regulation 153, 178 (1917).

from corporate statutes permitting different classes of stock with unique bundles of financial and governance rights, such as preferred stock. *See, e.g.*, Delaware General Corporation Law §151(a) ("classes or series [of stock] may have . . . such designations, preferences and relative, participating, optional or other special rights, and qualifications, limitations or restrictions thereof, as shall be stated and expressed in the certificate of incorporation. . . ."). The lessons concerning the structuring of financial rights among different economic claimants can be applied to noncorporate entities. *See, e.g.*, In re Nantucket Associates Ltd. Partnership Unitholders Litigation, 810 A.2d 351 (Del.Ch. 2002) (case involving "preferred units" of a limited partnership, resembling priority rights of preferred stock in corporations). Thus, Corporate Finance teaches broadly applicable principles in the entire field of business organizations.

B. WHAT IS THE RELEVANCE OF CORPORATE FINANCE TO PRACTICE?

Financings are a major part of a corporate transactional lawyer's work. Finance and capital are the lifeblood of the corporate enterprise. Financings are frequent corporate transactions in the market. Before engaging in any meaningful operations, a corporation will need to be capitalized with equity capital and perhaps other forms of financing as well. Over time, this initial funding may not provide the necessary capital to engage in new investments and activities. As a going concern, many corporations will have ongoing financial needs. They may wish to build a billion dollar factory, acquire a competitor firm, expand existing operations, diversify into other businesses, or replenish capital after losses. The circumstances necessitating financing are many. There is no guarantee that a corporation can fund its operations through recurring profits: Profits may not be had, they may not be enough, or they may have been distributed to shareholders. Most sophisticated business enterprises routinely engage in financing transactions over the course of their lifecycle. Such transactions require financial and legal advisors. In any major corporate transaction, lawyers perform three principal functions: They advise corporate managers on legal issues related to the transaction; they facilitate the regulatory aspects of the transaction; and, they draft the transactional documents.

Corporate Finance is an important area of business practice because lawyers advise corporate clients on the legal and economic implications of financing, draft and negotiate the terms of the financial instruments, and litigate financial disputes. The importance of Corporate Finance is seen in a 2013 Harvard Law School (HLS) survey of 124 practicing lawyers at major law firms.* The survey revealed the importance of business methods and business knowledge. The surveyed lawyers were asked to rank business methods courses and skill sets. The following are the survey results.

---

* John C. Coates IV, Jesse M. Fried & Kathryn E. Spiers, *What Courses Should Law Students Take? Lessons from Harvard's BigLaw Survey*, 64 Journal of Legal Education 443 (2015).

Question #1, Rating Business Methods Courses: "For each of the following existing HLS classes, please indicate how useful the course would be for an associate to have taken." (1 = Not at all Useful; 3 = Somewhat Useful; 5 = Extremely Useful)

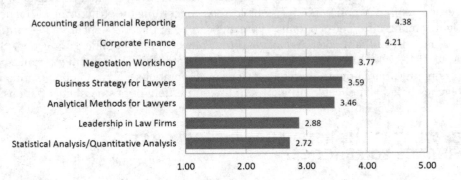

Question #2, Ranking Business Methods Courses: "If you were advising an HLS student about which business methods class (or classes) to take, which three of the above classes would you suggest?"

Question #3, Rating Knowledge/Skills Bases: "Please indicate how important the following knowledge bases/skills are for your associates." (1 = Not at all Useful; 3 = Somewhat Useful; 5 = Extremely Useful)

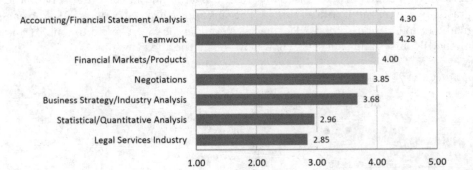

The survey reveals that practicing business lawyers at major law firms believe that Corporate Finance—the study of how corporations finance their enterprise and the financial instruments they issue to do so—is important. The survey also suggests the importance of knowledge in accounting, financial statement analysis, and financial markets. This collective opinion of practicing lawyers doing sophisticated business work should reinforce the practical idea that business lawyers should know something about business.

The importance of foundational business concepts is the reason why Chapters 1 through 4 are devoted to providing basic knowledge in financial statements, principles of finance, valuation of securities, financial management, and capital markets. Although little "law" is covered in Chapters 1 through 4, these chapters provide the foundational knowledge that frames the financial instruments in their accounting, business, financial, and market context. This context is necessary for a business lawyer to see capital market transactions through the prism of business necessity and economic circumstance, which is the perspective of the corporate client. Once the foundation is laid, the remainder of the book explores the major categories of financial instruments. The order of study in Chapters 5, 6, and 7 is from the riskiest security to the least, which is the order of common stock, preferred stock, and debt. Chapter 8 covers hybrid securities, which are convertible securities. Finally, Chapter 9 introduces derivatives, which are not used to raise capital the way that debt and equity instruments are, but which are instead used by corporations for financial management including the hedging of risk.

Author's Note on Case Annotations

Some cases in the field are complicated with respect to transaction structure and facts. Most judicial opinions describe transactions in the prose of lawyers, and sometimes reading prose makes the task of understanding the facts and transaction more difficult. In practice, even among lawyers, there is much use of diagrams and charts to map out complex transactions and organize data. In some case opinions, there are author-supplied annotations in the form of diagrams, charts, and data summaries as the transactions are described in the case opinions, and these annotations are embedded directly in the judicial opinions as comprehension aids for the purpose of facilitating analysis. This aspect of case editing is not typically seen in other casebooks. Annotations are clearly marked "**Author's Case Annotation**."

FINANCIAL STATEMENTS

Corporate Finance transactions are recorded under the rules of accounting. Accounting standardizes the production of financial data under accounting rules and standards called "generally accepted accounting principles" (GAAP). Accounting is important in corporate transactions. Investors cannot provide debt or equity capital unless they know the issuer corporation's expected income, assets, and liabilities, among other financial measures. Corporate managers cannot analyze whether to raise new financing in equity or debt unless they understand financial analysis. Boards cannot approve a financing or business transaction unless they understand the accounting implications. Lawyers cannot understand financial contracts unless they understand basic accounting inputs.

Accounting is the starting point for understanding applied finance, including financial analysis and valuation of firms and securities. Accounting inputs are also directly written into the terms, conditions, and covenants of financial contracts such as debt and preferred stock instruments. The engagement of business requires an accurate tally of revenue, expenses, cash flow, assets, and liabilities, which are accountings of the different economic components of the business. Accounting is the study of keeping track of money and things reducible to money. Accounting is indispensable in business. It is important that business lawyers have a proficient understanding of the basic concepts of accounting.

Major corporations will have audited financial statements, and public companies report to the Securities and Exchange Commission (SEC) by filing, among other things, financial reports called Form 10-K (audited annual reports) and Form 10-Q (unaudited quarterly reports). Investors rely heavily on these financial statements, containing detailed information about the company's financial performance, accounting policies, and auditor's and management's reports and certifications. At the heart of financial statements are four accounting statements that summarize essential financial attributes of the company:

- Balance sheet
- Income statement
- Cash flow statement
- Statement of shareholder equity

These four specific statements are typically presented in four pages (one page per statement), but the complete financial statements are often very lengthy (some Form 10-Ks and 10-Qs are several hundred pages long). Much of the remainder of financial statements provides essential information supporting the data presented in these four financial statements.

Being able to proficiently read these four financial statements is a minimum requirement of a transactional lawyer. Such knowledge is required to understand the transaction holistically as opposed to only the legal aspects of the deal, which limits the lawyer's effectiveness. Accounting terms and concepts are frequently incorporated into the terms and conditions of financial contracts.

A. BALANCE SHEET

1. FUNDAMENTAL BALANCE SHEET EQUATION

The balance sheet provides an accounting of the firm's assets and liabilities. An _asset_ is defined as a probable future economic benefit obtained or controlled by a particular entity as a result of past transactions or events: for example, property, plant, and equipment (PP&E), intellectual property, and cash. A _liability_ is defined as a probable future sacrifice of economic benefits arising from present obligations of a particular entity to transfer assets or to provide services to another entity in the future as a result of past transactions or events: for example, debt provided by banks and bondholders, taxes owed, and unpaid short-term obligations. _Equity_ is the difference between assets and liabilities—this is the residual claim of the corporation's shareholders.

The concept of equity has different terms. In the generic use, the terms "net worth" and "net assets" are used synonymously with equity. Net worth is worth net of liabilities; net assets are assets net of liabilities. In the context of different forms of business organizations, the equity in an entity has specific terms. In a partnership, equity is called "partner's capital"; in a limited liability company, equity of members is called "member's interest." In a corporation, equity is called _shareholder's equity_.

Assets and liabilities change daily as transactions are made and recorded. A day's business may bring in cash, create liabilities, and earn profit. A balance sheet is a one-day picture of the firm's assets and liabilities, and this snapshot is taken at the end of the fiscal year, which does not necessarily correspond with the calendar year: For example, the fiscal year of The Walt Disney Company runs from October to September. Sophisticated firms keep internal managerial accounts that track assets and liabilities contemporaneous, and some firms, including public companies, produce quarterly unaudited financial statements.

The most important point about a balance sheet is that it must balance. This means that assets must _always_ equal liabilities plus equity.

$$\text{Assets} = \text{Liabilities} + \text{Equity}$$

Through simple algebraic manipulation of subtracting "Equity" from each side of the equation, we can rearrange this equation to state that equity is the difference between assets and liabilities:

$$\text{Assets} - \text{Liabilities} = \text{Equity}$$

This equation states that equity is assets net of liabilities (thus, sometimes equity is called "net assets"). We can picture the balance sheet equation as:

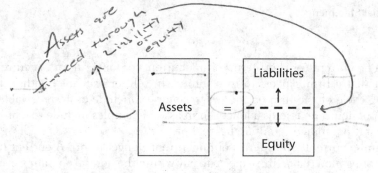

Assets are financed through liability or equity

The proportion between liabilities and equity can shift up and down (see the dotted line inside the box), but liabilities plus equity must always equal assets. A basic concept of the balance sheet is the principle that all assets must be funded by some mix of liabilities and equity. Another way to say this is that all assets are claimed by some mix of creditors and equityholders.

Although assets must equal liabilities plus equity, this does not mean that assets must always be at least equal to liabilities. There are times when liabilities are greater than assets: (Assets < Liabilities). Consider a toy manufacturer that had assets of $10 and no liabilities, but subsequently incurs a financial judgment on a product liability class action of $20: (Asset $10 < Liabilities $20). If liabilities exceed assets, how can the fundamental balance sheet equation (Assets = Liabilities + Equity) hold true? Since the fundamental balance sheet equation must always hold true, the equity must be negative in an amount equal to liabilities in excess of assets. This is the case of "negative equity" (or "negative net worth" or "negative book value").

The following example illustrates the principle. Assume the following: Assets have a value of A, and liabilities have a value of $(A + B)$. If so, equity must be $-B$.

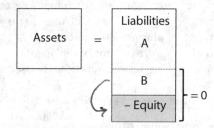

Negative equity simply means that the value of the equity is "under water" by the negative difference between assets and liabilities. The creditors who are owed the liabilities have a prior claim against the assets of the firm. If there are not sufficient assets to satisfy the creditor claims, whether creditors can claim the difference against equityholders depends on whether the rule of limited liability applies. In the case of corporations, shareholders are protected against personal liability. The negative difference between assets and liabilities constitutes the creditors' loss. In the toy manufacturer example, the tort creditor can recover $10 of the amount owed through the assets, but if the market value of these assets are in fact only $10 as stated in the books, then it cannot collect on the balance of $10. Of course, shareholders have also lost their $10 investment when the corporation paid the tort creditor $10.

2. DIVISION BETWEEN WORKING CAPITAL AND CAPITAL ASSETS

Assets, liabilities, and equity can be categorized by duration, and the duration indicates an important split in understanding the corporation's operations and financing.

An asset can be current (or short term) or noncurrent (or longer term). A current asset is an asset that a firm expects to turn into cash, sell, or exchange within the normal operating cycle of the firm or one year. Examples include cash, receivables, and inventory. A noncurrent asset is a longer-term asset. Examples include real property, physical plant, equipment, and intellectual property.

A liability can be current (short term) or noncurrent (longer term). A current liability is a debt or obligation that a firm expects to pay within the normal operating cycle of the firm or one year, such as a utility bill or monthly employee wages that have yet to be paid. In the case of financing, short-term debt such as commercial paper and loans maturing in less than one year are forms of current liabilities. A noncurrent liability is a longer-term debt or obligation. Examples include a loan with a 5-year maturity, and bonds that mature in 20 years.

Equity is always long-term capital because it generally has no maturity; that is, in most cases the corporation has no fixed date obligation to repurchase the common stock, though some preferred stocks have mandatory or optional redemption dates. In the case of any debt instrument, the corporation has a fixed date obligation to repay the principal.

Short-term assets and liabilities are a part of the corporation's *working capital*. Working capital embodies the basic idea that a business needs to get paid and pay its bills to keep operations going on a short-term basis. These are current assets (such as cash and receivables from customers when they have not yet paid), and current liabilities (such as payables when the corporation has incurred an expense but has not paid yet).

Most businesses need long-term assets, called *capital assets* because their purchase must be financed by capital. Think about an automobile manufacturer such as Hyundai. It needs a factory to manufacture cars, and such factories can cost in excess of over a billion dollars. A restaurant operator such as McDonald's needs real estate, building, and heavy kitchen equipment. A pharmaceutical company needs a portfolio of drugs, the development of which may require billions of dollars in research and development. These are just a few examples of long-term assets that are used to generate income on a long-term basis.

The traditional balance sheet equation (Assets = Liabilities + Equity) divides the balance sheet vertically: assets on the left side, and liabilities and equity on the right side.

Assets	Liabilities
	Equity

However, with duration in mind, the balance sheet can be conceptually divided horizontally, as between (1) current assets and liabilities on the top side, and (2) noncurrent assets and liabilities, and equity on the bottom side. This is the division between working capital and capital assets and their respective financing.

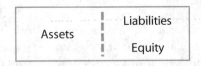

Current Assets	Current Liabilities
Noncurrent Assets	Noncurrent Liabilities
	Equity

Two aspects of the firm's operations are gleaned by horizontally splitting the balance sheet into working capital and capital assets. Working capital concerns the funds needed to operate the business on a current basis. The chief financial officer (CFO) of a corporation is responsible for all aspects of the company's finance, and within the financial operations under her control the treasury operations of the finance department manages the corporation's cash position and liquidity function. While important, this aspect of the corporate business is principally financial management. While lawyering may be required for contracting and regulatory compliance issues, there is less need for corporate transactional lawyers (unless there is a liquidity and solvency crisis and the company cannot meet its current obligations, in which case transactional lawyers, including bankruptcy lawyers, figure prominently).

On the other hand, capital assets concern the assets used to generate income on a long-term basis. Clearly, capital assets are not free; their purchase requires capital. Since capital assets are long-term assets, they must be financed by long-term capital—either long-term debt or equity or a combination of both.

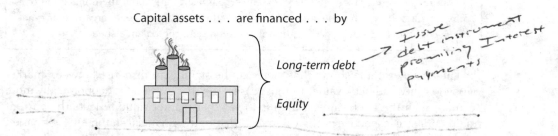

Capital assets . . . are financed . . . by

Long-term debt

Equity

→ Issue debt instrument promising Interest payments

The purchase of these assets requires the corporation to raise capital in the form of longer-term debt (such as bonds and debentures) or equity capital (such as common and preferred stock). In capital raising transactions, corporate and securities lawyers are indispensable advisors on transactions. Corporate finance transactions are below the horizontal division in the balance; that is, they are transactions involving longer-term liabilities and equity. Below the horizontal line is where corporate finance transactions occur involving the proverbial "stocks and bonds" of the corporation that constitute the long-term capital of a corporation.

3. DIFFERENCE BETWEEN BOOK VALUE AND MARKET VALUE

An important accounting concept is that items in the balance sheet are generally recorded on a *historical cost* basis. This means that most items in the balance sheet are recorded at their original acquisition cost, and generally are not adjusted for their fair market value.* The implication is that values recorded in the balance sheet do not necessarily correspond to market values. This general rule reflects a conservative

---

* There are exceptions under the accounting rules. An exception to the historical cost method of recording assets and liabilities is called *marked-to-market*. Under this method, assets and liabilities are marked to fair market value and their values are adjusted per changing market value. Accounting principles allow some assets and liabilities to be recorded under changing market values.

bias, which has served the accounting profession well but which also highlights accounting's limitations.

EXAMPLE

Market Cap Versus Book Value

As of December 31, 2010, McDonald's Corporation has 1.053 billion shares outstanding (shares issued and held by shareholders). On this day, the share price closed at $76.76 per share. What is the market value of shareholder's equity in McDonald's?

1.053 billion shares x $76.76 per share = $80.8 billion market value

However, in the balance sheet, the book value of equity is stated as $14.6 billion. The ratio of market value ($80.8 billion) to book value ($14.6 billion) is 5.5x. This ratio is called the *price-to-book* (or P/B) ratio, and we will study these kinds of multiples later.

The disparity between market value and book value seen in the valuation of McDonald's is commonly seen for many publicly traded companies. Think about the implication of a 5.5x P/B ratio. It says that the fair market value of the equity is 5.5 times greater than what the accountants have recorded as the value of equity in the balance sheet.

The above example shows that there can be significant disparity between market value of equity and book value. In most cases, the market value is economically more accurate than the book value, which is to say that market value reflects the current trading prices irrespective of the value recorded in the financial statements. If market value is generally more accurate, what accounts for the disparity between market and accounting values? There are three main reasons.

1. Much of accounting is based on recording historical acquisition cost, and not changing the figures based on day-to-day changes in market values. A building located in midtown Manhattan in 1929 might have cost $100,000, but it may be worth $100 million in 2015. Generally, the balance sheet will not reflect changing market values.

2. The accounting profession has certain limitations when it comes to recording assets and liabilities. For example, a company's goodwill and human capital are not recorded in the balance sheet. Think about the true value of a law firm. The law firm's balance sheet will record the physical assets and liabilities: for example, books, computers, and office furniture. But the equity value may not reflect the talent of its lawyers. Think about the intangible value of the brand names "The Coca-Cola Company" or "The Walt Disney Company." The balance sheet does not recognize the goodwill of a company, no matter how apparent it is, unless the goodwill has been purchased in a purchase transaction. Thus, if Pepsi bought Coke, then Pepsi may recognize the purchase of goodwill, if any, in the purchase transaction and the goodwill will be seen on the post-transaction balance sheet of Pepsi. However, as long as Coca-Cola remains an independent company, the goodwill in the brand "Coke" will not be recognized on Coca-Cola's balance sheet.

3. Accountants and the marketplace value equity differently. Accountants note equity as the simple arithmetic deduction from an equation: For example,

equity is assets minus liabilities, which are generally recorded at the historical cost of past transactions. The financial markets value equity based on how much a firm will generate income in the future. A firm may have zero book value because assets equal liabilities, but if these assets and liabilities have a combined positive future earning potential, then the market will assign a positive equity value irrespective of the fact that the net assets are zero in the books. Therefore, accountants record the value of equity based on *past transactions*, but the marketplace, such as the stock markets and private economic actors, values equity based on *future prospect*.

These disparities between the book values of assets and equity and the market values are not so unusual. The crucial take-home lesson is that financial statements do not necessarily reflect market value, fair value, or economic truth.

4. PERSPECTIVES ON THE BALANCE SHEET

The balance sheet equation is deceptively simple: Assets = Liabilities + Equity. A lawyer must understand three important concepts about the balance sheet.

The balance sheet is a statement of ownership. This concept says that every asset is owned by two types of owners—the corporation's creditors and shareholders. Therefore, the purchase of capital assets by the corporation must be financed by creditors and shareholders, or some combination of both.

The balance sheet is a statement of risk. Because of the priority that creditors have in terms of their payment of interest and principal ahead of payments to shareholders, creditors and equityholders are investors holding different forms of risk. By taking a subordinate position as residual claimants, equityholders are taking greater risk than creditors.

A balance sheet equation must be seen in terms of book value and market value. This concept says that there are two balance sheet equations with potentially different values assigned to the assets, liabilities, and equity. After issuance, the values of both debt instruments and shares fluctuate and are not tied to the original issue price or the values stated in the balance sheet.

The following case involves an interpretation of an accounting-related term "net worth" found in the corporate charter of Merrimack Pharmaceutical, Inc. A little background on the company may be helpful in understanding the business context for the legal dispute.

In March 2012, Merrimack conducted an initial public offering (IPO), a process in which it issues common stock to the public at large. It raised $100 million by offering 14.3 million shares at $7 per share to the public. The IPO prospectus provides the following information.

> We are a biopharmaceutical company discovering, developing and preparing to commercialize innovative medicines paired with companion diagnostics for the treatment of serious diseases, with an initial focus on cancer. Our mission is to provide patients, physicians and the healthcare system with the medicines, tools and

information to transform the approach to care from one based on the identification and treatment of symptoms to one focused on the diagnosis and treatment of illness through a more precise mechanistic understanding of disease. . . .

We currently have no commercial products, and we have not received regulatory approval for, nor have we generated commercial revenue from, any of our products. . . .

We have incurred significant losses since our inception and will need substantial additional funding. We expect to incur losses for the foreseeable future and may never achieve or maintain profitability. Our net loss was $61.5 million for the nine months ended September 30, 2011, $50.2 million for the year ended December 31, 2010, $49.1 million for the year ended December 31, 2009 and $45.6 million for the year ended December 31, 2008. As of September 30, 2011, we had an accumulated deficit of $332.7 million.

As you read the case below, think about the various sources the court references in attempting to define the term "net worth."

Bolt v. Merrimack Pharmaceuticals, Inc.
503 F.3d 913 (9th Cir. 2007)

O'SCANNLAIN, Circuit Judge:

We are called upon to interpret a corporation's articles of organization to decide whether it has an obligation to redeem certain shares of its stock.

Albert Bolt owns 52,488 shares of Series A Redeemable Preferred Stock issued by Merrimack Pharmaceuticals, Inc., a biotechnology company organized under the laws of Massachusetts. Bolt now wants to redeem those shares.

The relevant redemption provision of Merrimack's Restated Articles of Organization provides:

At any time from and after December 31, 1997, if the *net worth* of the Corporation, determined in accordance with generally accepted accounting principles and as shown on the balance sheet of the Corporation as of the end of the fiscal quarter then most recently ended, equals or exceeds five million dollars ($5,000,000), then upon the request of the holder of [the Series A] Preferred Stock, the Corporation shall redeem at the Redemption Price any and all shares of [the Series A] Preferred Stock which such holder, by such request, offers to the Corporation for redemption.

The following statement provides a snapshot of Merrimack's balance sheet as of December 31, 2001:

Assets	
Total assets	11,331,070
Liabilities, Preferred Stock and Stockholders' Deficit	11,331,070
Total liabilities	1,270,230
Series A redeemable preferred stock	548,380
Series B convertible preferred stock	11,915,267
Total stockholders' deficit	(2,402,807)
[Total Preferred Stock and Shareholders' Deficit]	10,060,840]

PricewaterhouseCoopers LLP audited Merrimack's financial statements, and opined that Merrimack's balance sheet referred to above "presents fairly, in all material respects, the financial position of Merrimack Pharmaceuticals, Inc. at December 31, 2001 in conformity with accounting principles generally accepted in the United States of America."

During 2001, Merrimack had issued 3,315,201 shares of Series B Redeemable Convertible Preferred Stock with a book value of $11,915,267. The Series B Stock is redeemable at the option of the holder upon a "deemed liquidation," defined as (1) a merger with another company, after which the Merrimack stockholders would no longer hold a majority of the voting power, or (2) the sale of Merrimack's business assets. The Series B Stock appears in the "mezzanine" of the balance sheet, between the liabilities section and the stockholders' deficit (equity) section.

Bolt sent written requests to Merrimack for the redemption of his shares of Series A Stock. Merrimack rejected Bolt's demands for redemption. Bolt filed suit in federal district court seeking a declaratory judgment that Merrimack's net worth exceeded $5 million as of December 31, 2001. On cross-motions for summary judgment, the district court granted summary judgment for Bolt, concluding that Merrimack's net worth exceeded $5 million as of that date.

We must first determine the meaning of the term "net worth," the threshold yardstick to determine whether Merrimack has an obligation to redeem the Series A Stock as Bolt requests. Merrimack's Restated Articles of Organization fail to define that term. Nor does GAAP define that term. And no item on Merrimack's balance sheet is specifically labeled "net worth."

Merrimack is organized under Massachusetts law, and therefore we apply that state's body of law here. Moreover, because articles of organization are contractual in nature, we look to Massachusetts general contract principles. "Where the language of a contract is not ambiguous," we are instructed to give words "their plain meaning, or their well established meaning."

The common and well-established meaning of the term "net worth" is the difference between a corporation's total assets and its total liabilities. Merrimack's total assets and total liabilities, as shown on its December 31, 2001 balance sheet, equal $11,331,070 and $1,270,230, respectively. Accordingly, employing the well-established meaning, Merrimack's net worth equals $10,060,840, well in excess of the $5 million threshold set by the Restated Articles of Organization.

Merrimack suggests that net worth is sometimes referred to as stockholders' equity. This reference is often accurate because a balance sheet generally involves only three basic accounting elements—assets, liabilities, and equity—and equity by definition equals the residual interest in the assets after subtracting liabilities. Yet, under this reasoning, Merrimack's net worth would still exceed $5 million.

But Merrimack goes further, arguing that the definition of net worth for purposes of its Restated Articles of Organization equals *only* Merrimack's total stockholders' deficit of $2,402,807, excluding Merrimack's total redeemable convertible preferred stock of $12,463,647. Merrimack contends that limiting the meaning of net worth to this amount is appropriate here because the Restated Articles of Organization point to net worth "as shown on the balance sheet" and call for no further calculations. While this argument has surface appeal, we ultimately are unpersuaded. The Restated Articles of Organization indeed point us to "net worth . . . *as shown* on the balance sheet." But there is no item so labeled on the balance sheet involved here. Thus, such an interpretation of net worth is "shown" on the balance sheet only to the extent that we accept an additional premise necessary to connect it to the net worth reference in the Restated Articles of Organization. Either we accept Merrimack's premise that net worth is limited to total stockholders' equity (deficit) on the balance sheet, or we accept Bolt's premise that net worth is commonly defined as the difference between total assets and liabilities. Regrettably, the Restated Articles of Organization provide no further guidance as to the proper definition of the term. Given the common and well-established meaning of the term "net worth" as the difference between total assets and total liabilities, we cannot accept that the document reflects an intentionally narrower, more nuanced definition of that term that would equal only total stockholders' equity (deficit) simply because it employed the phrase "as shown on the balance sheet." We therefore decline to adopt Merrimack's definition here.

Nevertheless, our analysis does not end with our construction of the term "net worth." The Restated Articles of Organization specify that the balance sheet relied upon must be determined in accordance with GAAP. If the balance sheet incorrectly reports total assets or total liabilities under GAAP, our determination of net worth necessarily would be affected.

To determine whether the balance sheet is prepared in accordance with GAAP, we do not take off our judicial black robes and reach for the accountant's green eyeshade. Rather, because "'generally accepted accounting principles' are far from being a canonical set of rules that will ensure identical accounting treatment of identical transactions[, and] tolerate a range of 'reasonable' treatments," we generally defer to the professional judgment of the accountant who audited or prepared the financial statements, unless a GAAP authority *demands* a contrary accounting treatment.

Merrimack argues on appeal that the Series B Stock, which is presented in the mezzanine section of the balance sheet, is akin to a liability under GAAP authorities. Of course, if the Series B Stock were considered a liability, Merrimack's net worth would not equal or exceed $5 million. But Merrimack's balance sheet does not show the Series B Stock to be part of total liabilities. Nor do we believe that GAAP requires such accounting classification.

First, Merrimack claims to find support in Regulation S-X* of the SEC, which requires certain stock to be presented on the balance sheet under the caption "redeemable preferred stock" and expressly prohibits including such stock under a general caption "stockholders' equity" or combined in a total with non-redeemable preferred stocks, common stocks, or other stockholders' equity. That regulation applies to any class of stock with the following characteristics:

> (1) it is redeemable at a fixed or determinable price on a fixed or determinable date or dates, whether by operation of a sinking fund or otherwise; (2) it is redeemable at the option of the holder; or (3) *it has conditions for redemption which are not solely within the control of the issuer,* such as stocks which must be redeemed out of future earnings. Amounts attributable to preferred stock which is not redeemable or is redeemable solely at the option of the issuer shall be included under §210.5-02.29 unless it meets one or more of the above criteria.

---

* Author's note: Regulation S-X is the SEC rule that regulates the specific format and the content of financial disclosures in certain SEC filings.

The parties do not dispute on appeal that Merrimack's Series B Stock falls within the scope of Regulation S-X and therefore is presented properly in the mezzanine section of the balance sheet. Merrimack, however, places great weight on the fact that Regulation S-X requires such stock to be presented "outside" of stockholders' equity, implicitly suggesting, Merrimack urges, that it should be considered akin to a liability for purposes of determining net worth.

In our view, Merrimack reads too much into Regulation S-X, which only requires that the Series B stock be *presented* in a separate caption in the mezzanine section of the balance sheet, not that such stock be *classified* as part of total liabilities. Indeed, in Accounting Series Release No. 268, the SEC expressly emphasized that these "rules are intended to highlight the future cash obligations attached to redeemable preferred stock through appropriate balance sheet *presentation* and footnote disclosure. *They do not attempt to deal with the conceptual question of whether such security is a liability.*" Accordingly, we are not persuaded that Regulation S-X requires the Series B Stock to be classified as part of total liabilities on the balance sheet for purposes of calculating net worth.

The parties also direct us to FASB's Concept No. 6. But we do not believe the conceptual definitions found therein require a conclusion that the Series B Stock must be classified as part of total liabilities, contrary to the presentation on Merrimack's balance sheet. Concept No. 6 defines "liabilities" as "probable future sacrifices of economic benefits arising from present obligations of a particular entity to transfer assets or provide services to other entities in the future as a result of past transactions or events," and "equity" as "the residual interest in the assets of an entity that remains after deducting its liabilities." Moreover, and more importantly, Concept No. 6 recognizes the conceptual difficulties with classifying certain hybrid securities like the Series B Stock at the nub of this case,[9] and instructs in such cases that the conceptual definitions are the starting point and "provide a basis for assessing, for example, the extent to which a particular application meets the qualitative characteristic of *representational faithfulness, which includes the notion of reporting economic substance rather than legal* form."

Merrimack argues that the Series B Stock should not be considered equity pursuant to Concept No. 6 because that stock is not a "residual interest." We appreciate, as do the parties, that the Series B Stock has a number of hybrid characteristics: Series B stockholders have (1) a right to vote, together with the common stock as a single class, on all actions to be taken by the stockholders; (2) a right to elect one board member; (3) a dividend of four percent per annum of purchase price; (4) a liquidation preference before common stock, but after debts and liabilities and the Series A Stock preference; (5) a cash redemption right upon a "deemed liquidation" and at the election of the holder; (6) a right to convert such stock into common stock at any time according to a specified formula; (7) covenants and restrictions on certain actions by

---

9. Elements of Financial Statements, Statement of Fin. Accounting Concepts No. 6, §55, at 23-24 ("Although the line between equity and liabilities is clear in concept, it may be obscured in practice. Applying the definitions to particular situations may involve practical problems because several kinds of securities issued by business enterprises seem to have characteristics of both liabilities and equity in varying degrees or because the names given some securities may not accurately describe their essential characteristics. . . . Preferred stock [for example] often has both debt and equity characteristics, and some preferred stocks may effectively have maturity amounts and dates at which they must be redeemed for cash.").

Merrimack; and (8) a preemptive right. However, while recognizing that the Series B Stock does not fit neatly into either the definition of liabilities *or* equity under Concept No. 6, we are unpersuaded that Merrimack's balance sheet, by not classifying that stock as part of total liabilities, is contrary to GAAP.

In sum, [the court found] no GAAP authority that requires classifying Merrimack's Series B Stock as part of total liabilities.

Merrimack has an obligation to redeem Bolt's Series A Stock if its net worth equals or exceeds $5 million. Because we conclude that the term "net worth" for purposes of the Restated Articles of Organization should be given its well-established meaning as the difference between total assets and total liabilities, and because Merrimack's total assets and total liabilities equaled $11,331,070 and $1,270,230, respectively, as shown on the December 31, 2001 balance sheet calculated in conformity with GAAP, Merrimack's net worth exceeded $5 million. Accordingly, the district court's grant of summary judgment in favor of Bolt is affirmed.

QUESTIONS

1. According to the court, what is the well-established, generally understood meaning of "net worth"?
2. How much was Merrimack's "net worth" as of December 31, 2001?
3. In hindsight, how could the drafter of the Articles of Organization have prevented the ambiguity giving rise to this legal dispute?
4. In venture capital deals, Series A preferred stock is typically the first round of financing from external capital providers, typically venture capital firms. In this case, what was the purpose and economic rationale of the redemption right in the Series A preferred stock?
5. Why did the Series A preferred stockholder seek redemption?
6. Note that Merrimack has relatively little debt. Why is Merrimack mostly equity financed?

B. INCOME STATEMENT

A business entity sells goods or services. It takes inputs and produces outputs. A beverage company like The Coca Cola Company purchases various ingredients and labor (inputs) and manufactures Coke (output); a delivery service like FedEx uses planes and trucks driven by employees (inputs) and provides delivery service (output). If a firm sells its outputs for more money than the cost of its inputs, it earns an accounting profit. These activities are tracked by the income statement. Like the balance sheet, the income statement has a simple equation:

$$\text{Revenue} - \text{Expenses} = \text{Net Income}$$

Revenue is also sometimes called sales. *Revenue* is formally defined in accounting as the increase in the equity (in the balance sheet) caused by services rendered or the sale of goods. In other words, after deducting expenses, the remaining revenue (which is called net profit or net income) adds to the equity in the balance sheet. Expenses are all expenses that the corporation incurs. These include the direct cost of production, the indirect costs of overhead expenses, interest expense on debt, and tax payments.

The net difference of revenue minus expense is net income (if there is a positive difference) or net loss (if expenses are greater than revenue).

If there are preferred shareholders, they are typically entitled to a fixed dividend. They have priority over common stockholders on the net income with respect to dividend payments. After the dividends are paid to preferred stockholders from net profit, the profit remaining is called net profit available to common stockholders.

In a competitive free market, there is no guarantee that a firm will make any kind of profit. There could be a loss. In such a case, the nomenclature changes from "profit" to "loss," such as "operating loss" or "net loss." The net loss is then recognized in the balance sheet as a reduction of shareholders' equity since shareholders bear this loss.

Why is a corporation's income statement so important? The income statement provides the outcome of the company's business activities. Did it make a profit? Obviously, profit is very important to all constituents, not the least of which are the corporation's creditors and shareholders.

1. ORGANIZATION OF INCOME STATEMENT

Let's break down the income statement further. The components in the income statement can be categorized into the following items, though the labeling of these items in individual income statements may vary significantly.

Operation	Revenue	Sales of goods and services
	– Cost of goods sold	Called "COGS," including the direct cost of the production of the goods of the goods or services, including supplies and payroll attributable to the direct production of the goods or services
	Gross profit	Revenue minus COGS
	– Sales, general & administrative	Called "SG&A," operating expenses not connected to the direct production of specific goods and services, including overhead and administrative expenses (sometimes also called "G&A")
	Operating profit (income)	Operating income is reveue minus operating expenses (COGS + SG&A)
Debt	– Interest expense	Expense from the payment of interest to creditors (lenders)
	Pretax profit	Taxable income
Tax	– Tax expense	Money paid to the government in tax (Uncle Sam gets its slice of the economic pie!)
Equity	Net profit (or loss)	Residual income after deduction of all expenses from revenue

The income statement is organized in a way that the claims on the operating side (COGS and SG&A) are deducted first. This results in gross profit and operating profit, which are measures of profitability before the claims of the creditors (interest expense) and government (tax expense). Note that with respect to financing, there is a queue of financiers. Creditors are paid interest on debt first, then tax is collected, and whatever remains after taxes is net income, which belongs to shareholders.

There is an intuitive logic to the income statement. Like the balance sheet, there is a priority among economic claims. Let's see what that queue looks like.

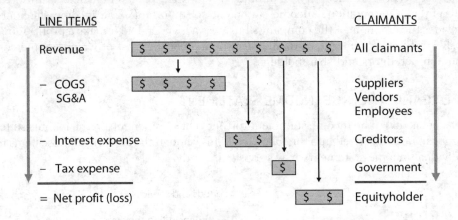

2. DEPRECIATION

It is natural to think about revenue and expenses (a firm's economic inflow and outflow) in cash. However, the inflow or outflow of cash can be delayed for a number of reasons such as: when a customer has contracted to purchase a good or service but has yet to pay (account receivable); when the firm owes money for the receipt of a good or service (account payable); or when a tax liability does not need to be paid at the time (deferred tax liability). Ultimately, the firm expects to monetize its receivables or payables. However, sometimes expenses are simply noncash items. This does not mean that the expenses are somehow fictitious or phantom in nature. They are very real, but they just are not incurred (recognized) in cash.

Many assets simply do not hold their value in a constant manner. Some assets may increase or decline in value due to various economic factors, for example, securities such as stocks or bonds or commodities such as gold or oil. For many other assets, however, the arrow of value only points downward over time due to various economic factors. For example, money decreases in value over time due to inflation. Other assets decrease in value over time simply from use (wear and tear), *e.g.,* cars, computers, equipment, and factories. Other assets may become obsolete, *e.g.,* software, patents, and computers. These diminishments in value are real expenses (costs) of running a business, and they must be recognized, even though the company is not paying for the expense in the form of cash payments akin to wages, utility bills, and insurance premiums.

Depreciation is the diminishment of value of *tangible assets* such as physical plant, property, or equipment. *Amortization* is the diminishment of value of *intangible assets* such as patents and goodwill. *Depreciation and amortization* (D&A) connote a common idea of a gradual loss of value in an asset. D&A are noncash expenses, meaning that the company does not "pay" in cash the expense as it pays, for example, employee wages. D&A are costs that are recognized as expenses in the income statement. The "payment" of D&A by the company occurs through the gradual loss of value of the assets, which is a form of a cost to the business.

D&A is not a separate line item in the income statement such as COGS and SG&A. One will typically not find a separate line on the income statement labeled "depreciation" or "depredation and amortization" (though in the Alcoa Inc. income statement, *infra,* depreciation is separately broken out as a line expense item). For most firms, D&A are embedded in the COGS and SG&A lines of the income statement. However, D&A are always stated in the cash flow statement of the financial statements.

D&A is important in financial analysis because it is related to the company's cash flow. As an expense, D&A reduces a firm's profit. However, because it is a *noncash* expense, the firm's profit *understates* the amount of cash flow it generates from its business. The firm's cash flow exceeds its profit by at least the amount of the D&A. D&A is important because cash is important. This explains why EBITDA (earnings before interest, taxes, depreciation, and amortization) is such an important measure of profitability. It is EBIT plus D&A, which is an approximation of the cash flow of the firm's business operation.

Importantly, accounting principles allow various methods to depreciate or amortize assets. With respect to depreciation policy, they may allow a firm and its accountant to choose the best or most appropriate methods. There are several ways in which depreciation is calculated. Straight-line depreciation is a method in which the asset is depreciated by a fixed amount over its life. Accelerated depreciation is a method in which the asset is depreciated in its earlier years, rather than the later years. Unit-of-activity depreciation is a method in which depreciation is calculated as a percentage of used life of the asset for each year.

EXAMPLE

Straight-Line Depreciation

Assume that a commercial-duty computer mainframe was bought for $50,000 and has a useful life of five years with no residual value due to rapid obsolescence in computer technology. Under a *straight-line method*, the firm's depreciation expense is $10,000 per year for the next five years.

YEAR	BOOK VALUE (BV) A	×	DEPRECIATION RATE B	=	DEPRECIATION EXPENSE C	ACCUMULATED DEPRECIATION D	BV (NET) (A − D)
1	50,000	×	20%	=	(10,000)	(10,000)	40,000
2	50,000	×	20%	=	(10,000)	(20,000)	30,000
3	50,000	×	20%	=	(10,000)	(30,000)	20,000
4	50,000	×	20%	=	(10,000)	(40,000)	10,000
5	50,000	×	20%	=	(10,000)	(50,000)	0

In each of the years 1 through 5, the income statement will recognize $10,000 in depreciation expense. Note that the items "accumulated depreciation" and "book value (net)" are balance sheet items.

EXAMPLE

Declining-Balance Method

Under the *declining-balance method*, the asset is depreciated by a constant percentage of the purchase cost of the asset adjusted each subsequent year for depreciation. Consider depreciation of the computer mainframe in which it is depreciated by 40 percent of the net book value each year with the last year depreciating the asset to zero residual value.

YEAR	STARTING BOOK VALUE (BV) (NET) A	×	DEPRECIATION RATE B	=	DEPRECIATION EXPENSE C	ACCUMULATED DEPRECIATION D	ENDING BV (NET) (A − D)
1	50,000	×	40%	=	(20,000)	(20,000)	30,000
2	30,000	×	40%	=	(12,000)	(32,000)	18,000
3	18,000	×	40%	=	(7,200)	(39,200)	10,800
4	10,800	×	40%	=	(4,320)	(43,520)	6,480
5	6,480				(6,480)	(50,000)	0

The declining-balance method is an accelerated depreciation method as compared to the straight-line method. Depreciation is greater in the early years than in the later years. Compare year 1 depreciation of $20,000 with year 2 depreciation of $12,000.

EXAMPLE

Unit-of-Activity Method

Under the *unit-of-activity method,* the depreciation is calculated on a per unit of production basis. As production of units varies, the depreciation expense varies as well. Suppose the computer mainframe has a total utility of 100,000 "bits" and these total bits are consumed yearly according to this schedule: 30,000 (year 1), 20,000 (year 2), 20,000 (year 3), 20,000 (year 4), and 10,000 (year 5). The depreciation schedule under the unit-of-activity method would be the following:

YEAR	BOOK VALUE (BV)		"BITS" USED		TOTAL "BITS"		DEPRECIATION EXPENSE	ACCUMULATED DEPRECIATION	BV (NET)
	A	×	B	÷	C	=	D	E	(A − E)
1	50,000	×	30,000	÷	100,000	=	15,000	(15,000)	35,000
2	50,000	×	20,000	÷	100,000	=	10,000	(25,000)	25,000
3	50,000	×	20,000	÷	100,000	=	10,000	(35,000)	15,000
4	50,000	×	20,000	÷	100,000	=	10,000	(45,000)	5,000
5	50,000	×	10,000	÷	100,000	=	5,000	(50,000)	0

The straight-line, declining-balance, and unit-of-activity methods produced different depreciation expenses. The following is a summary of the above calculations.

YEAR	STRAIGHT LINE	DECLINING BALANCE	UNIT-OF-ACTIVITY
1	10,000	20,000	15,000
2	10,000	12,000	10,000
3	10,000	7,200	10,000
4	10,000	4,320	10,000
5	10,000	6,480	5,000
Total	50,000	50,000	50,000

Therefore, the income statement will produce different yearly profit figures depending on the method of depreciation used.

3. INTEREST TAX SHIELD

Pretax profit is EBIT minus interest expense. This is the taxable profit, *i.e.,* the profit that is taxed at the appropriate tax rate by the government. Notice that interest expense reduces the profit from which taxes are taken. This is a benefit of carrying debt— the interest expense paid to creditors lowers the tax liability by reducing the taxable profit. This benefit is called the *interest tax shield* (and this concept is covered again in greater detail later in the finance sections).

Interest expense affects tax expense because it reduces taxable profit, thus reducing tax liability. The *interest tax shield* is the tax benefit provided when interest expense is deductible from taxable income. This tax policy reduces the effective cost of debt by shielding some of the firm's profit from tax liability.

23

EXAMPLE

Effect of Interest Tax Shield

Let's see how the interest tax shield works by comparing two income statements. Assume common financial inputs: (1) revenue $1,000 and operating expense $400, (2) interest expense of $200 representing a rate of 8% on debt of $2,500, and (3) tax rate of 25%.

WITH TAX SHIELD		WITHOUT TAX SHIELD	
Revenue	1,000	Revenue	1,000
Operating expense	(400)	Operating expense	(400)
Interest expense	(200)		
		Pretax profit	600
		Taxes at 25%	(150)
Pretax profit	400		
Taxes at 25%	(100)	After-tax profit	450
		Interest expense	(200)
Net income	300	Net income	250

By deducting the interest expense from taxable (pretax) income, there is less tax liability. Less money going to the government means more profit. Thus, the interest tax shield is a government subsidy that promotes the use of debt.

4. KEY PROFIT MEASURES

"Profit" is not one measure or definition. There are different kinds of profit. This is seen in industry usage of terms. "Earnings" and "profit" and "net profit" are synonymous with net income. However, when these terms are modified they do not refer to net income. For example, important financial measures in valuation and financial contracting are earnings before interest and tax and operating profit. These items, though referencing the terms "earnings" and "profit," are not the same as net income. The loose use of these terms can be confusing, but these jargon-driven distinctions are important because knowledgeable professionals understand these differences and assume others do as well. The following are important profit measures.

Net profit—This is the residual income claimed by the equityholders after all expenses are paid to other claimants including employees, vendors, creditors, and the government. Net income can be distributed to shareholders in the form of a dividend, which is a cash payment to shareholders. If it is not distributed to shareholders but is instead retained by the company, it is recorded in the balance sheet as retained earnings under equity. Since the balance sheet must always balance, an increase in retained earnings must also correspond to an increase in assets. In this case, cash or accounts receivable increases since the company now has more assets representing the profit made. Note that the residual is not always a profit. No firm is guaranteed a profit. If revenue is smaller than the claims on it, there is a net loss. Of course, the equityholder must assume this net loss.

Earnings before interest and tax—EBIT is synonymous with operating profit in most cases, except that EBIT may include special or one-off (nonrecurring) revenue or expense items not associated with core operations.

operating profit = earnings before interest + taxes

24

Operating profit—This is profit from core operations and would not include special or nonrecurring revenue or expenses. If there are none, then operating profit and EBIT are the same.

Earnings before interest, tax, depreciation, and amortization—EBITDA is EBIT plus depreciation and amortization (D&A), which are noncash expense items. EBITDA is a rough approximation of the amount of cash flow generated by the company's operations.

Net profit, operating profit, EBIT, and EBITDA are important in corporate finance for two reasons. First, these accounting items are typically the accounting inputs to important valuation metrics (which are discussed in *infra* Chapter 3). The corporation and its capital providers are keenly interested in the value of the corporation's financial instruments. Second, accounting items are frequently used in financial contracts. The covenants of debt instruments may use these accounting measures to define conditions or rights. The corporate charter may provide that dividends may only be paid from net income.

C. CASH FLOW STATEMENT

Cash is important. Cash is the blood flow within a business. Without cash, a firm— even a good one from the perspective of management and business model—can be in danger of insolvency. Many companies become insolvent because they are bad businesses. But not all insolvent companies are bad businesses. Some great businesses can become insolvent because they run out of cash.

Financial statements are generally prepared under an accounting convention called accrual accounting. Under this convention, there are many kinds of transactions where revenue, expenses, and net profit are recognized but are not perfectly correlated to cash inflows and outflows. For example, a customer may have purchased a good from the corporation, but may not have paid for it yet (this is called a receivable). The corporation may have purchased items from a trade creditor, but may not have paid for it yet (this is called a payable). Depreciation expense may have been recognized in the income statement, but this expense is a noncash expense. Despite the potential decoupling of cash from the recognition of the transaction, accrual accounting provides the principal benefit of matching transactions to the economic and legal event.

However, since cash is so important, the cash flow statement keeps track of all cash that is circulating throughout the firm during the fiscal year. Cash flow can be categorized into three activities: (1) operations, (2) investing, and (3) financing. These categories recognize the three main activities of a firm that raise or consume cash. Let's examine each of these categories separately.

1. CASH FLOW FROM OPERATIONS

Cash flow from operations is all cash flow attributable to the operational aspect of the business. The firm's operations are the activities associated directly with the provision of products or services that the firm sells. If the firm is Nike, the operations consist of the factory production, distribution, and sales of shoes. If the firm is FedEx, the operations consist of running planes and trucks, and delivering packages.

Cash flow from operations is simply calculated. Start with net income. Assume that net income is all cash, but of course this assumption is wrong. Net income is not always perfectly correlated to the cash receipts and disbursements. The corporation and its customers may be paying their respective bills later. Also, depreciation is an expense, but there is no cash outlay.

Since not all transactions are executed in cash, adjustments will need to be made. There can be many adjustments, but there are three primary adjustments that are commonly seen:

1. *D&A*—Add back depreciation and amortization because they are expenses reducing net income, but they are noncash expenses.
2. *Receivables*—Adjust for the difference in receivables from the prior year because it has been recognized as revenue and thus flows down to net income, but the customer has yet to pay. A lower receivable amount from the previous year means that, absent default, customers have paid off their receivables, and thus cash increased (and vice versa).
3. *Payables*—Adjust for the difference in payables from the prior year because it has been recognized as an expense and thus flows down to net income, but the firm has yet to pay. A lower payables amount than the previous year means that the corporation paid its obligations, and thus cash decreased (and vice versa).

Cash flow from operations can be calculated as the following adjustments to net income:

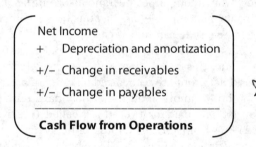

Net Income
+ Depreciation and amortization
+/− Change in receivables
+/− Change in payables

Cash Flow from Operations

2. CASH FLOW FROM INVESTING

Cash flow from investing is all cash flow attributable to investing activities. A firm must invest to make a profit. Nike may invest in a new factory in China. Walmart may invest in a new superstore in Kansas. Goldman Sachs may invest in a new headquarters building on Wall Street. McDonald's may invest in new restaurants.

Cash flow from investing is simply calculated. Investments made are recorded as negative cash flow. Divestitures of investment are recorded as positive cash flow. Typically, investments are in the form of property, plant, or equipment (PP&E) and investments in securities or other companies. Cash flow from investing can be calculated as the following:

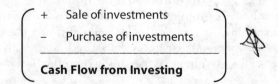

+ Sale of investments
− Purchase of investments

Cash Flow from Investing

3. CASH FLOW FROM FINANCING

Cash flow from financing is all cash flow attributable to financing activities. A firm must be financed. This means that it must raise funds necessary to engage in business activities. Pfizer must have funds to do research in promising new drugs. FedEx must have funds to buy new airplanes. Recall that all assets must have a claim against them. As discussed, capital assets such as factories and airplanes generate profit. These assets must be financed, either by creditors or equityholders.

Cash flow from financing is simple to calculate. Funds raised by the issuance of stocks or bonds are recorded as cash inflow. Funds used to pay off bonds or purchase the company's own stock in the open market are recorded as cash outflow. Also, funds used to pay dividends are recorded as cash outflow. Cash flow from financing can be calculated as the following:

```
+   Issuance of stock or debt
-   Repayment of debt
-   Stock buyback
-   Payment of dividends
_____
Cash Flow from Financing
```

4. NET CASH FLOW

The three cash flow statements are added together to determine whether the firm generated cash inflow or outflow for the year. They also indicate how the company has managed its cash and the cash activities of the fiscal year. The net cash amount is then added to the previous year's cash balance to calculate the current year's cash balance.

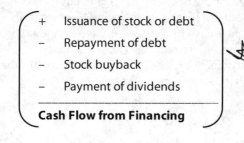

Cash Flow Statement (Year 2)	**Balance Sheet** (Year 1)
Cash flow from operations	ASSETS
+ Cash flow from investing	Cash $100
+ Cash flow from financing	
Year 2 Net Cash	
	Balance Sheet (Year 2)
+ $100 (Cash from Year 1)	ASSETS
New Cash Balance ⇒	New Cash Balance

27

D. STATEMENT OF SHAREHOLDERS' EQUITY

The statement of shareholders' equity is relevant because the most important item for shareholders is their equity in the corporation. The statement of shareholders' equity provides a detailed breakdown of how shareholders' equity changes from year to year. It breaks down all factors contributing to a change in shareholders' equity.

1. ADJUSTMENTS TO EQUITY

There are two large items that affect shareholders' equity. Retained earnings increase shareholders' equity. If the corporation incurs a net loss, the amount of the loss sub- tracts from the retained earnings account.

Stock issuances increase shareholders' equity. A corporation receives cash (assets increase on the left side of the balance sheet), and equity increases by a corresponding amount (the right side of the balance sheet). Stock repurchases decrease shareholders' equity; a corporation pays cash (a decrease in assets), and it takes stock out of circula- tion (a decrease in shareholders' equity). The stock bought back goes into an account- ing item called treasury stock, which is seen as a negative number in the balance sheet in the equity section (thus, decreasing equity).*

2. NORMATIVE VIEWS ON EQUITY

There is a temptation to believe that an increase in shareholders' equity is a good thing, and a decrease a bad thing. We should reject this thinking. Even in broad generalities, these intuitions may not hold true.

Consider a key component of shareholders' equity—retained earnings. Obviously, if the corporation suffers net losses, which reduces shareholders' equity, this is a bad thing. However, suppose there are profits. There is the question of whether profits should be retained or distributed to shareholders. This involves a whole set of consid- erations in financial management. If distribution is the better route, then an increase in shareholders' equity through retained earnings is not necessarily a good thing.

Consider another key component of shareholders' equity—stock. It is not neces- sarily a good thing for a company to hold lots of stock. A corporation should only hold the capital that it needs, and not more. If the contrary were true, corporations would seek to raise the maximum gross amount of capital rather than limiting a capital raise to some defined value.

Consider a stock repurchase program that reduces the amount of stock, thus redu- cing the shareholders' equity account. A corporation will buy back its stock, thus reducing its equity, if it believes that the transaction would result in a net benefit.

Try to avoid the generality that an increase in shareholders' equity is always a good thing. If all other accounting variables and policies are held constant, it is generally true that net losses, reducing shareholders' equity, are bad; and net profits, increasing shareholders' equity, are good. However, it does not follow that an increase in share- holders' equity is always a good thing. The amount of equity held and the ratio mix of

---

* In technical accounting terms, the negative number is called a "debit" to equity.

debt and equity are individualized financial decisions. Each situation is different. The subject of capital structure is discussed later in Chapter 4 of this book.

E. FINANCIAL STATEMENT ANALYSES

The accounting data in financial statements can be used to conduct simple but informative financial analyses. These analyses are simple ratios that provide an understanding of the firm's profitability, liquidity, and leverage. Most of these ratios are expressed as percentages or multiples that are convenient to benchmark against peers. There are three sets of measurements: (1) profitability, (2) liquidity, and (3) leverage.

1. PROFITABILITY ANALYSES

Profitability analyses measure the profitability of a company, expressed as a ratio of the different kinds of profit to (1) revenue, (2) assets, and (3) equity. Assume that a corporation made a net profit of $100 million. Is this good or bad? We can't answer this question in the abstract. A $100 million profit from revenue of $100 billion may not be considered very profitable—a puny margin compared to revenues. A $100 million profit for General Electric may be very disappointing (in fiscal year 2010, it generated $150.2 billion in revenue, and earned $12.1 billion in net income), but it may be a stunning return for an Internet startup whose business plan was put together on the back of a pizza box. To answer the question "how profitable is the firm?" we need more information.

The gross profit margin measures gross profit profitability against revenue as the benchmark.

$$\text{Gross Profit Margin} = \frac{\text{Gross Profit}}{\text{Revenue}}$$

The operating profit margin measures operating profit profitability against revenue as the benchmark.

$$\text{Operating Profit Margin} = \frac{\text{Operating Profit}}{\text{Revenue}}$$

The net income margin measures net profit profitability against revenue as the benchmark.

$$\text{Net Income Margin} = \frac{\text{Net Income}}{\text{Revenue}}$$

Profitability can be measured against the balance sheet items. Profitability can be measured against assets and equity.

$$\text{Return on Assets (ROA)} = \frac{\text{Net Income}}{\text{Average Total Assets}}$$

$$\text{Return on Equity (ROE)} = \frac{\text{Net Income}}{\text{Average Total Equity}}$$

Average total assets and average total equity can be calculated by averaging last year's assets and equity with this year's figures. ROA and ROE answer the questions: What is the profit yield from assets? What is the profit yield from equity?

EXAMPLE

Margin Comparisons

McDonald's and Burger King are competitors. The following are their fiscal year 2010 profitability measures (year ended December 31 for McDonald's and June 30 for Burger King).

($ MILLION)	MCDONALD'S	BURGER KING
Revenue	$ 24,074	$ 2,502
Gross profit	9,637	887
Gross profit margin	*40%*	*35%*
Operating profit	7,473	332
Operating profit margin	*31%*	*13%*
Net profit	4,946	186
Net profit margin	*21%*	*7%*

The following are ROA and ROE measures for fiscal year 2010.

($ MILLION)	MCDONALD'S	BURGER KING
Net income	$ 4,946	$ 186
Assets (2009)	30,224	2,707
Assets (2010)	31,975	2,747
Average assets	31,100	2,727
ROA	*16%*	*7%*
Equity (2009)	14,033	974
Equity (2010)	14,634	1,128
Average equity	14,334	1,051
ROE	*35%*	*18%*

Based on these profitability measures, which company performs better?

Profit belongs to shareholders. A shareholder would want to know how much profit is attributable to each share. This information is called *earnings per share (EPS)*.

$$EPS = \frac{\text{Net Income Attributable to Common Stock}}{\text{Average Common Shares Outstanding}}$$

Net income attributable to common stockholders is net income after payment of dividends to preferred stockholders. Preferred stock is a form of stock wherein the stockholder is entitled to a fixed dividend (similar to the way that creditors are entitled to a fixed interest rate). Preferred stock is a form of equity for reasons discussed *infra* Chapter 6, but they stand in priority to common stockholders. Dividends to preferred stockholders must be paid before common stockholders can claim against the remaining profit. EPS tells a common shareholder how much profit can be ascribed to each share she purchases.

In one sense, EPS by itself, without other information, is an arbitrary number because it depends on the number of shares outstanding. For example, suppose there are 10 shares outstanding. The corporation has $100 of net income attributable to common stockholders. The EPS is $10 per share. Assume you own 1 share, which is 10 percent of the company. Your portion of the net income is $10. Assume now that the corporation splits the shares on a 2-for-1 basis. There are now 20 shares outstanding. The EPS is now $5 per share. Your portion of the net income is still $10 since you now own 2 shares at EPS of $5 per share.

Despite this aspect of arbitrariness, EPS is an important measure of a firm's profitability on a per share basis when it is considered in conjunction with the stock price (as explained later).

EXAMPLE

EPS of McDonald's Corporation

Because EPS is a measure of earnings, it is also an important factor in the value of a company. The value of a company is frequently expressed as multiples of its various financial outputs: for example, net income, EBIT, EBITDA, and book value.

In the fiscal year ended December 31, 2010, McDonald's earned $4.946 billion in profit. It had average shares outstanding (basic) of 1.066 billion. This produced an EPS (basic) of $4.64 per share. The company's share price and market cap on December 31 were $76.76 per share and $80.828 billion based on the year end shares outstanding of 1.053 billion shares (or $81.826 billion if 1.066 billion average shares outstanding is used). Share price and market capitalization can be expressed as multiples of earnings, called *price-to-earnings* (P/E) multiple.

$$P/E = \frac{\text{Share Price}}{\text{EPS}} = \frac{\$76.76}{\$4.64} = 16.5x$$

Note that the P/E multiple can be expressed as a multiple of market cap to net income. The ratios are the same. Why?

$$P/E = \frac{\text{Market Cap}}{\text{Net Income}} = \frac{\$81.828\text{ B}}{\$4.946\text{ B}} = 16.5x$$

These multiples can be used as valuation metrics. Suppose there was another restaurant company, Philly Cheesesteak Inc., that wanted to know its market value, and suppose the value of McDonald's is a fair comparable. McDonald's P/E multiple can be used as a valuation metric to value Philly Cheesesteak. For example, if Philly Cheesesteak earned $10 million, then its implied market valued based on the McDonald's multiple would be $165 million.

Profitability measures are useful for three reasons related to financial management, benchmarking against peers, and valuation:

1. Margin analyses are used internally for financial management purposes. For example, suppose that the gross profit margin is 15 percent, which is in line with the industry average, but the operating profit margin is 0 percent (there is no operating profit). This means that SG&A is consuming 15 percent of revenue, which is clearly unsustainable. Margin analysis can provide the company's managers valuable information on various aspects of the company's financial performance. Also, margin analyses are helpful in forecasting financial performance. Many people, including investors and managers, are interested in the future performance of the company. Of course, everyone understands that past performance is not a guarantee of the future. However, past performance levels provide information which can be used to make projections of the future.

2. Margin analyses are important to compare comparable companies. For example, companies A, B, and C are direct competitors and make widgets. The net profit margins are: A, 10 percent; B, 13 percent; and C, 16 percent. Which company is better? At least on this metric, company C is more profitable. Of course, there are many other metrics. The point of margin analysis is that it provides a way to compare peer companies.

3. Margin analyses provide important inputs in the process of valuation. Benchmarking against peers indicates whether the subject company is better or worse than its peers, which is relevant to a valuation. The market price of shares can be expressed as a ratio of EPS, which provides a metric for gauging the market value of shares.

2. LIQUIDITY AND SOLVENCY ANALYSES

Liquidity concerns the ability of a firm to convert assets into cash. Liquidity ratios measure the short-term, operational ability of the firm to pay its current obligations through the measurement of current assets and current liabilities. Current noncash assets are assets that are presumed to be highly liquid, and thus capable of servicing current liabilities. A firm must be able to pay its bills. If the company cannot pay its ongoing obligations, then its operations can be severely disrupted—employees will stop working, utility companies will stop providing utility services, trade creditors will stop providing materials and inventory, and so forth. Cash is needed. The need is measured by the amount of short-term liabilities, and the ability to pay is measured by the available cash and assets that can be readily liquidated into cash.

Working capital analysis focuses on the company's ability to pay all of its current (short-term) obligations. Recall back to the lesson of the balance sheet where we distinguished current (short-term) assets and liabilities, and capital assets and long-term financing (*i.e.*, the horizontal division of the balance sheet). Working capital concerns the top half of this horizontal division. Thus, working capital analyzes balance sheet items (current assets and current liabilities).

An important working capital analysis is net working capital, which is defined as:

$$\text{Net Working Capital} = \text{Current Assets} - \text{Current Liabilities}$$

Current assets are cash and other assets that the company reasonably expects to convert to cash or use up within one year. Current liabilities are obligations that a company reasonably expects to pay within one year. For most companies, cash and receivables constitute the bulk of current assets, and payables constitute the bulk of current liabilities. If the company's current liabilities cannot be satisfied through payment, creditors can throw it into insolvency. Note that even good companies can occasionally run into a cash crunch. Thus, working capital is important.

Net working capital measures the funds available to operate the firm's daily business. In operating a business, a firm has to be able to pay its current liabilities, such as utility bills and payroll. Otherwise, it faces a liquidity crisis wherein it cannot pay its bills. Expenses are paid with cash or assets that can be quickly converted to cash. Clearly, a positive net working capital is superior to a negative one. The more positive the difference between current assets and current liabilities, the better is the company's ability to meet its current obligations.

Another way to express the amount of working capital is the *current ratio*, which is expressed as a ratio.

$$\text{Current Ratio} = \frac{\text{Current Assets}}{\text{Current Liabilities}}$$

Negative working capital means that current liabilities are greater than current assets. This could be a problem.

The *quick ratio* is another form of an acid test on liquidity. It differs from the current ratio because it excludes inventory from the current assets. (not liquid)

$$\text{Quick Ratio} = \frac{\text{Cash} + \text{Marketable Securities} + \text{Receivables}}{\text{Current Liabilities}}$$

Why exclude inventory from the current assets? The quick ratio measures the ability to pay current obligations with the most liquid (easily converted to cash) assets, which are cash, marketable securities, and receivables. Inventory is less liquid because it needs to be sold and this may take time. On the other hand, receivables are more liquid as there are many financial purchasers.

Solvency concerns the ability of the firm to remain solvent, which requires the ability to pay creditors and other obligations.

EXAMPLE

Enron's Solvency Crisis

The death of Enron is a complicated corporate murder story with a chain of causal acts and events contributing to the dramatic death of a public corporation. The final event in this chain was a solvency crisis—Enron ran out of cash because no one lent it short-term money to operate as a going concern. Credit is important to consumers and corporations alike. If cash is akin to blood in a human body, Enron bled to death. There was no more cash circulating in the corporate body. On October 23, 2001, a few days after it publicly announced its accounting problems, Enron's financial structure collapsed. Its short-term loans in the commercial paper market were not rolling over (renewing). Creditors were taking the cash from maturing loans and not buying new commercial paper. As a result, Enron could not finance its ongoing operations, a situation that quickly led to insolvency and the demise of the company.

Debt service analysis examines the ability of the company to pay interest on debt. The ability to pay principal and interest is called "debt service" or "service of debt." Debt service analysis thus concerns the interest of a specific kind of creditors, *i.e.,* lenders. Unlike working capital analysis which looks to balance sheet items, debt service analysis looks to income statement items.

The interest cover ratio measures the amount of funds available to pay interest payments due to creditors. The funds from operations are net income plus interest expense paid, and tax expense.

$$\text{Interest Cover} = \frac{\text{Net Income} + \text{Interest Expense} + \text{Tax Expense}}{\text{Interest Expense}}$$

Tax expense is added back because interest expense is paid before taxes. The sum of net income, interest expense, and tax expense constitute the funds available to pay the interest expense.

The higher the interest cover ratio, the more the firm has the ability to pay interest on its debts.

The EBITDA coverage ratio is a ratio of EBITDA to interest expense. As with interest cover ratio, a higher ratio means the firm has a greater ability to pay interest on its debts.

$$\text{EBITDA Cover} = \frac{\text{EBITDA}}{\text{Interest Expense}}$$

Why EBITDA? Recall from the discussion of the income statement that EBITDA is an approximation of cash flow. For the most part, operating profit is expected to result in cash or assets readily reducible to cash (receivables), and depreciation and amortization (D&A) are noncash expenses. Cash flow is important because debt service is done with cash.

EXAMPLE

Consolidated EBITDA and Leverage Coverage Ratios

Financial ratios are frequently used in debt contracts. For example, Section 4.04, "Limitation on Indebtedness," in *Model Negotiated Covenants and Related Definitions,* 61 Business Lawyer 1439 (2006), provides a model term for the limitation on the amount of debt that a debtor can undertake as a condition to the provision of credit by a creditor.

> The Company shall not, and shall not permit any Restricted Subsidiary to, Incur, directly or indirectly, any Indebtedness; provided, however, that the Company [and its Restricted Subsidiaries] [and its Guarantors] shall be entitled to Incur Indebtedness if, on the date of such Incurrence and after giving effect thereto on a pro forma basis, no Default has occurred and is continuing and the *Consolidated Coverage Ratio* exceeds _____ to 1.0 [the *Consolidated Leverage Ratio* would be less than _____ to 1.0.] [if such Indebtedness is Incurred prior to [date], _____ to 1.0, or _____ to 1.0 if such Indebtedness is Incurred thereafter].

The definition of "Consolidated Coverage Ratio" is:

> the ratio of (x) the aggregate amount of Consolidated EBITDA for the period of the most recent four consecutive fiscal quarters ending at least 45 days prior to the date of such determination to (y) Consolidated Interest Expense for such four fiscal quarters [which is the following equation]

$$\text{Consolidated Coverage Ratio} = \frac{\text{Consolidated EBITDA}}{\text{Consolidated Interest Expense}}$$

The definition of "Consolidated Leverage Ratio" is:

> the ratio of (x) the aggregate amount of Indebtedness of the Company and its Restricted Subsidiaries as of such date of determination to (y) Consolidated EBITDA for the most recent four consecutive fiscal quarters ending at least 45 days prior to such date of determination

$$\text{Consolidated Leverage Ratio} = \frac{\text{Indebtedness}}{\text{Consolidated EBITDA}}$$

Commentary

The foregoing is the basic debt incurrence test allowing for "ratio debt." If the Company on a trailing twelve month basis, and on a pro forma basis after giving effect to the incurrence of the proposed indebtedness, has enough cash flow (or "Consolidated EBITDA") in relation to its interest expense (typically a minimum ratio of 2 to 1 or higher), then the Company can incur such indebtedness. For example, assume the Company has outstanding $100 million of debt bearing interest at 5 percent per annum and has Consolidated EBITDA of $30 million for the trailing twelve months. Assume further that the Company wants to incur an additional $100 million in debt with an interest rate of 9 percent. With those numbers, pro forma Consolidated Interest Expense (assuming no other debt or preferred stock) would be $14 million. If the required minimum Consolidated Coverage Ratio is 2:1, the Company would be permitted to incur that additional debt;

the Consolidated Coverage Ratio would be \$30 million divided by \$14 million or 2.14.

* * *

Under Section 4.04, "Limitation on Indebtedness," both the Consolidated Coverage Ratio and the Consolidated Leverage Ratio are based on a baseline ratio of 1.0. Why is 1.0 the baseline ratio?

3. LEVERAGE ANALYSES

Leverage means the extent to which the firm is debt financed (as opposed to equity financed). As a general term, "leverage" connotes debt: for example, "to lever" a firm, means to increase its debt load. Leverage is meaningful for two reasons. First, as we will learn in the finance section, there is a theoretically and practically optimal ratio of debt and equity financing. Second, and perhaps of more immediate concern, leverage is directly related to bankruptcy risk. Creditors can force the company into bankruptcy; equityholders do not have this option. If they are unhappy, they can either gain control of the company by taking a controlling stake (if they have the funds and the will to do this) or they can attempt to exit the investment by selling their shares (if there is a liquid market for the shares). Leverage measures provide a sense of the debt-to-equity mix.

An important clarification should be explicitly made: When we say "debt," we specifically mean noncurrent debt. Current obligations such as accounts payable are legal obligations and specifically recognized in the balance sheet as current liabilities. However, they are working capital items. Leverage ratios concern the right side of the balance below the horizontal division between current and noncurrent liabilities. The debt that matters for the following leverage calculations is medium-term and long-term debt. For example, if the item is a "note payable" and is categorized as a noncurrent liability, this is a longer-term debt and is a part of the capital structure of the firm.

The leverage ratio is defined as assets divided by equity.

$$\text{Leverage Ratio} = \frac{\text{Assets}}{\text{Equity}}$$

The leverage ratio measures how much of assets are funded by equity. This ratio is particularly important to financial institutions.

The debt-to-equity ratio is long-term debt divided by equity.

$$\text{Debt to Equity Ratio} = \frac{\text{Longterm Debt}}{\text{Equity}}$$

The long-term debt-to-equity ratio measures the ratio of long-term financing. It answers the questions: How are the firm's long-term capital requirements funded? What is the mix of debt and equity?

The following financial statements are from the 2013 Form 10-K of Alcoa Inc. The financial statements have been accurately reprinted, except that for convenience of presentation, some relatively minor items in terms of dollar value that were presented separately in the actual financial statement have been consolidated with other lines.

* * *

ALCOA INC. STATEMENT OF CONSOLIDATED OPERATIONS

IN MILLIONS EXCEPT PER SHARE DATA, YEAR ENDED DECEMBER 31	2013	2012	2011
Sales	**$ 23,032**	**$ 23,700**	**$ 24,951**
Cost of goods sold (exclusive of expenses below)	19,286	20,401	20,480
Selling, general administrative, and other expenses	1,008	997	1,027
Research and development expenses	192	197	184
Depreciation, depletion, and amortization	1,421	1,460	1,479
Impairment of goodwill	1,731	–	–
Restructuring and other charges	782	172	281
Interest expense	453	490	524
Other operating (income) expense, net	(25)	(341)	(87)
Total costs and expenses	**24,848**	**23,376**	**23,888**
Income/(loss), continuing operations before taxes	**(1,816)**	**324**	**1,063**
Provision for income taxes	428	162	255
Income/(loss) from continuing operations	(2,244)	162	808
Loss from discontinued operations	–	–	(3)
Less: Net income/(loss) attributable to noncontrolling interest	41	(29)	194
Net income/(loss) attributable to Alcoa	**$ (2,285)**	**$ 191**	**$ 611**
EPS attributable to Alcoa common shareholders			
Basic	$ (2.14)	$ 0.18	$ 0.57
Diluted	$ (2.14)	$ 0.18	$ 0.55

ALCOA INC. CONSOLIDATED BALANCE SHEET

IN MILLIONS EXCEPT PER SHARE DATA, AS OF DECEMBER 31	2013	2012
ASSETS		
Current assets		
Cash and equivalents	$ 1,437	$ 1,861
Receivables	1,818	1,739
Inventories	2,705	2,825
Prepaid expenses and other current assets	1,009	1,275
Total current assets	6,969	7,700
Property, plant, and equipment, at cost	17,639	18,947
Goodwill	3,415	5,170
Investments	1,907	1,860
Deferred taxes	3,184	3,790
Other noncurrent assets	2,628	2,712
Total noncurrent assets	28,773	32,479
Total assets	**$ 35,742**	**$ 40,179**
LIABILITIES		
Current liabilities		
Accounts payable	$ 2,960	$ 2,702
Accrued compensation and retirement costs	1,013	1,058
Other current liabilities	2,132	2,182
Total current liabilities	6,105	5,942
Long-term liabilities		
Long-term debt	7,607	8,311
Accrued pension and other retirement benefits	5,537	6,325
Other noncurrent liabilities	2,971	3,078
Total noncurrent liabilities	16,115	17,714
Total liabilities	**$ 22,220**	**$ 23,656**
SHAREHOLDERS' EQUITY		
Preferred stock, Class A $100 par value, issued shares 546,024 (in 2013 and 2012)	55	55
Common stock, $1.00 par value, issued shares 1,177,906,867 (2013) and 1,177,906,557 (2012)	1,178	1,178
Additional capital	7,509	7,560
Retained earnings	9,272	11,689
Treasury stock	(3,762)	(3,881)
Accumulated other comprehensive loss	(3,659)	(3,402)
Noncontrolling interests	2,929	3,324
Total shareholders' equity	**13,522**	**16,523**
Total liabilities and shareholders' equity	**$ 35,742**	**$ 40,179**

ALCOA INC. STATEMENT OF CONSOLIDATED CASH FLOWS

IN MILLIONS, YEAR ENDED DECEMBER 31	2013	2012	2011
OPERATING ACTIVITIES			
Net income/(loss)	$ (2,244)	$ 162	$ 805
Adjustments to reconcile to net income/(loss)			
Depreciation, depletion, and amortization	1,422	1,462	1,481
Deferred income taxes	178	(99)	(181)
Equity income, net of dividends	77	2	(26)
Impairment of goodwill	1,731	-	-
Restructuring and other charges	782	172	281
Net gain on investment activities	(10)	(321)	(41)
Stock-based compensation	71	67	83
Other adjustments	4	62	44
Changes in assets and liabilities:			
(Increase)/decrease in receivables	(141)	104	(115)
(Increase)/decrease in inventory	25	96	(339)
Increase/(decrease) in accounts payable	326	(12)	394
Increase/(decrease) in accrued expenses	(418)	(166)	(16)
Increase/(decrease) in taxes	(43)	15	115
Pension contributions	(462)	(561)	(336)
(Increase)/decrease in noncurrent assets	(153)	9	(154)
Increase/(decrease) in noncurrent liabilities	442	570	125
Cash provided by operations	**1,578**	**1,497**	**2,193**
FINANCING ACTIVITIES			
Net change in short-term borrowings and commercial paper	5	(234)	193
Additions to debt, net of issuance costs	1,849	967	1,239
Payment on debt	(2,317)	(1,489)	(1,194)
Proceeds from exercise of employee stock options	13	12	37
Excess tax benefit on stock-based compensation	–	1	6
Dividends paid to shareholders	(132)	(131)	(131)
Distributions to noncontrolling interests, net of contributions	(97)	76	(88)
Cash used for financing activities	**(679)**	**(798)**	**62**
INVESTING ACTIVITIES			
Capital expenditures	(1,193)	(1,261)	(1,287)
Acquisitions, net of cash acquired	-	-	(240)
Proceeds from the sale of assets and businesses	13	615	38
Additions to investments	(293)	(300)	(374)
Sale of investments	-	31	54
Other adjustments	183	156	(43)
Cash used for investing activities	**(1,290)**	**(759)**	**(1,852)**
Effects of exchange rates on cash and equivalents	(33)	(18)	(7)
Cash and equivalents increase (decrease)	**(424)**	**(78)**	**396**
Cash and equivalents at beginning of year	1,861	1,939	1,543
Cash and equivalent at end of year	**$ 1,437**	**$ 1,861**	**$ 1,939**

ALCOA INC. STATEMENT OF CHANGES IN CONSOLIDATED EQUITY

	PREFERRED STOCK	COMMON STOCK	ADDITIONAL CAPITAL	RETAINED EARNINGS	TREASURY STOCK	OTHER LOSSES	NONCONTROLLING INTERESTS	TOTAL EQUITY
Balance at Dec. 31, 2011	55	1,178	7,561	11,629	(3,952)	(2,627)	3,351	17,195
Net income				191			(29)	805
Other loss						(775)	(73)	(1,181)
Cash dividends								
Preferred at $3.75 per share				(2)				(2)
Common at $0.12 per share				(129)				(129)
Stock-based compensation			67					22
Common stock issued			(68)		71			
Distributions							(95)	(257)
Contributions							171	167
Other							(1)	(1)
Balance at Dec. 31, 2012	55	1,178	7,560	11,689	(3,881)	(3,402)	3,324	16,523
Net income				(2,285)			41	(2,244)
Other loss						(257)	(338)	(848)
Cash dividends								
Preferred at $3.75 per share				(2)				(2)
Common at $0.12 per share				(130)				(130)
Stock-based compensation			71					71
Common stock issued			(122)		(119)			(3)
Distributions							(109)	(109)
Contributions							12	12
Other							(1)	(1)
Balance at Dec. 31, 2013	55	1,178	7,509	9,272	(3,762)	(3,659)	2,929	13,522

CHAPTER

2

FINANCE PRINCIPLES

A. RISK AND RETURN

To understand finance, we begin with this simple but keen insight from a seminal academic paper: "We next consider the rule that the investor does (or should) consider expected return a desirable thing and variance of return an undesirable thing. This rule has many sound points, both as a maxim for, and hypothesis about, investment behavior."*

The idea that investors like economic return is obvious: 10 percent is better than 5 percent. Modern finance is built on the connection between the return investors receive and the risk they take to achieve that return. Most people are risk averse, and this means that, all else being the same (that is, the rate of return), they prefer the less risky choice. One is exposed to risk when one faces the possibility of two or more different outcomes. The possibility of two or more outcomes in the future creates uncertainty, and people don't like uncertainty when a potential future outcome can be negative. Most people prefer certain outcomes. This is the reason why people buy insurance: They would rather part with a fixed, small sum of money each year than risk the possibility, however small, of a large loss.**

Accordingly, an investor has these sentiments: (1) When the corporation puts her capital at risk, she does not like it; (2) she provides the capital to get an economic return; and (3) she accepts the fact that to get a return, her capital must be put at risk. A corporation needs capital to pursue a business enterprise, but when that capital is put to use it is subject to risk. Investors must be compensated to bear that risk. The

---

* Harry Markowitz, *Portfolio Selection*, 7 J. Fin. 77, 77 (1952). This paper arguably marked the beginning of modern finance. For his work on portfolio theory, which also led to the development of the capital asset pricing model, Markowitz was awarded the Nobel Prize in economics.

** "Risk-averse people will pay to avoid risk, as they do when they buy insurance knowing that an insurance premium includes a loading charge (that is, a fee to compensate the insurance company for its administrative expenses) on top of the estimate of the loss to the insured, discounted by the probability that the loss will occur. That discounted loss would be the actuarial value of the policy, and a risk-neutral person would pay no more. In fact he would never buy insurance, because there is always a loading charge." *Steinman v. Hicks*, 352 F.3d 1101, 1104 (7th Cir. 2003) (Posner, J.). The typical loading charge for an insurance company is between 10 percent to 50 percent, constituting a part of the premium in excess of the actuarial value of the expected loss. Policyholders are willing to pay quite a hefty amount in excess of the actuarial value of their future loss to the insurance company to eliminate their risk. The existence of a large insurance market is explained only if we understand that most people are risk averse.

corporation must provide a suitable return. The greater the risk, the greater must be the return.

We can formalize these intuitions. In finance and business, the concept of "risk" means an uncertainty as to future economic outcome. An investment of X, such as the purchase of stock, is made today, and we do not know how this investment may turn out. On an ex ante perspective, the future has multiple paths. Consider these two probability density distributions.

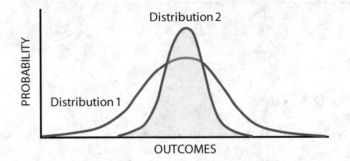

The x-axis represents the number of potential different outcomes, ranging from terrible result (a loss of the entire investment) to fabulous result (a tremendous rise in the stock price), and everything in between. The y-axis represents a probability for a particular outcome. The outcomes under Distribution 1 are more spread out than the outcomes for Distribution 2, which are much more tightly clustered. Risk is the measure of this dispersion. Distribution 1 is more risky than Distribution 2. If the expected returns for Distribution 1 and Distribution 2 are the same, then an investment represented in Distribution 2 is superior to an investment in Distribution 1—the same return is achieved but less risk is taken.

Consider a simple numeric example of the above concept. Distributions 1 and 2 have the following probabilities and outcomes.

	Distribution 1			Distribution 2	
Outcome	Probability of Outcome	Expected Value	Outcome	Probability of Outcome	Expected Value
400	10%	40	200	25%	50
225	20%	45	150	50%	75
125	40%	50	100	25%	25
75	20%	15			
0	10%	0			
	100%	**150**		100%	**150**

The expected values of both distributions are the same (150). Yet Distribution 1 is much more variable, ranging from an "outstanding return" (let's call it) of 400 to a "terrible return" of 0. Distribution 2 is much tighter in possibilities, ranging from a "good return" of 200 to something like "not bad" of 100. We say that Distribution 1 is more risky than Distribution 2. If Distribution 2 narrows to only one possible outcome (e.g., 100 percent probability of a 150 return), we say that the investment is risk-free.

If people don't like risk, they must be compensated to take risk. Consider the provision of a loan. The credit risks associated with lending money to the U.S. government and to one's neighbor are qualitatively different. One may charge 5 percent to the U.S. government, but perhaps 10 percent to some company. These different interest rates reflect the simple fact that there is a tradeoff between risk and return. The compensation for risk can be graphically represented. The following chart shows that as risk increases, the expected return must increase as well.

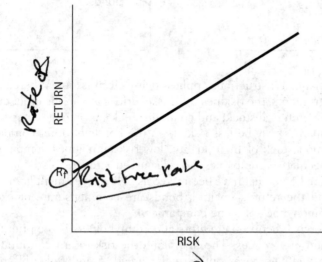

The point R_f on the y-axis represents the risk-free rate, which is the rate of return on an investment that carries no risk. An investment in U.S. government debt, typically called Treasury securities or Treasuries, is considered a benchmark for a risk-free investment.* By purchasing Treasuries, an investment is lending the U.S. government money for the rate of return R_f. The assumption of the risk-free rate is that the U.S. government carries no credit risk; an investment is free of risk as to principal and interest. Accordingly, the expected return is low compared to investments in other securities such as corporate bonds.

A corporation issues various financial instruments to raise capital for needed projects. On a basic level, we can order these financial instruments along the risk-return horizon. From the least risky to the most risky for the capital providers, the order of financial instruments is corporate bonds, preferred stock, and common stock for a given issuer.

---

* In 2011, one of the two major credit rating agencies, Standard & Poor's, downgraded the U.S. debt from AAA (the highest credit rating) to AA+ (the next level down), which was the first time that the creditworthiness of the U.S. government has been less than a perfect AAA. *United States of America Long-Term Rating Lowered to 'AA+' on Political Risks and Rising Debt Burden; Outlook Negative*, Standard & Poor's (August 5, 2011). However, based on the yields on Treasuries subsequent to the downgrade, the market seems to believe that U.S. government debt is risk-free. Moreover, credit rating agencies have previously exhibited instances of bad judgment. *See* Robert J. Rhee, *On Duopoly and Compensation Games in the Credit Rating Industry*, 108 Nw. U. L. Rev. 85 (2013).

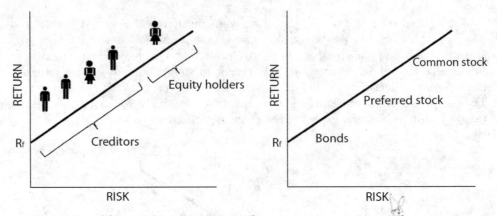

This order of financial instructions applies to any given issuer. When a company issues financial instruments, the riskiness of the securities are, in the order of increasing riskiness: bonds, preferred stock, and common stock. As among issuers, common stock of some companies may be less risky than the bonds of other companies: for example, the common stock of high-quality, low-risk companies compared to the "junk" bonds of speculative companies. (As discussed later in this book, "junk" or "high yield" bonds are bonds that have been rated as below investment grade by credit rating agencies, and the returns on junk bonds are commensurate or exceed the returns on the common stock of some companies.)

A principal difference between creditors and equityholders is the priority in payment and liquidation preferences. The line along the risk-return continuum represents a line of investors who have contractually agreed to undertake different risks. Creditors take less risk and get less return; equityholders take greater risk for greater return. Remember that equity is a concept that connotes the residual economic claim. Because equityholders stand last in the financial queue for distribution from the income statement and the balance sheet, they bear the greatest economic risk. If so, they must be compensated the most. Accordingly, equityholders should earn greater returns than R_f or creditors.

Risk and return are conjoined twins. As risk increases, investors demand more return and thus the investment must yield a greater return, and vice versa. There is a direct relationship between risk and return.

There is always a tradeoff between risk and return. Because people are risk averse, a more risky investment opportunity must incentivize an investor by providing a greater prospect of return. Investors will not take financial risks for free. However, greater risk means that an investor is exposed to increased potential for bad things to happen—that is the definition of risk.

EXAMPLE

Analysis of Bernie Madoff's Ponzi Scheme

In 2008, Bernie Madoff was arrested for operating the world's largest Ponzi scheme. He pled guilty to the charges. Before his arrest, he marketed his investment advisory services to wealthy clients and hedge funds that invested their funds with him. Below are the purported returns of one such hedge fund as indexed and compared to the S&P 100 market index. The hedge fund's marketing document shows that the fund averaged

12% yearly return, net of large hedge fund fees, for many years, and there were no losses in any year dating back to 1990.

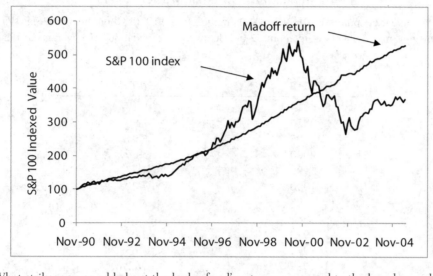

What strikes you as odd about the hedge fund's returns compared to the broader market index? Is it plausible that someone can consistently make a profit (average of 12%) year-in, year-out? Should we expect to see some variance in the return? Indeed, in the 174 months in the time period 1990 to 2005, there were only 7 months of negative returns, and the largest loss was −0.55%, which means that a fund balance of $100,000 would have suffered a loss of $550 for the month. This was the allure of an investment with Bernie Madoff: You can get 12% on your investment, which consistently beats the long-term market return on stocks (about 10%) with no risk. Guaranteed riskless profit that beats the risk-free rate is like the power to print money, isn't it?

B. TIME VALUE OF MONEY

Another core principle of finance is the concept of time value of money. We must learn the meaning of present value, future value, annuity value, and perpetuity value. These concepts are bound together by precise mathematical relationships. The math required is simple algebra, but the dry, abstract math is pregnant with meaning.

Before getting to the "fun" of the math, start with the fact that the money in your pocket has a present value. It does not take much persuasion to convince you that the dollar bill in your pocket is worth exactly $1.00 today. If someone were to trade $0.99 for that dollar bill, you would balk; if the same person offered $1.01, you would be delighted (well, maybe not at the prospect of earning one penny, but add a few zeroes to the transaction, and we would quickly be talking about real money). The point is that a dollar is worth a dollar today. However, the same nominal currency does not have constant value over time. The dollar bill in your pocket would have had much greater purchasing power 100 years ago than today. If you have a net worth of $100,000 and could take that money back in time 100 years, you would have been a very wealthy person, whereas the same cannot be said today. Travel forward in time to the year 2115, and maybe the same $100,000 can buy you a nice business suit.

EXAMPLE

Inflation and the Price of Movie Tickets

Let's make these points still a little more concrete. In the 1970s when the movie *Star Wars* came out, movie tickets were about $2.00. Below is historic data for the average cost of a movie ticket.

YEAR	PRICE
2014	8.17
2010	7.89
2005	6.41
2000	5.39
1995	4.35
1990	4.22
1985	3.55
1980	2.69
1975	2.03
1971	1.65
1967	1.22
1963	0.86
1958	0.68
1954	0.49

Source: National Association of Theatre Owners

The nominal price of movie tickets increased almost 300% from the 1970s (from $2.03 in 1975 to $8.17 in 2014). This is primarily attributable to the fact that inflation decreases the value of money. The true value of the film experience did not increase threefold for the average moviegoer. Moviegoers probably enjoyed the movie experience in the 1970s about the same as they do now and pay accordingly. The increase in the nominal price is mostly attributable to inflation. Inflation has increased the nominal price of a movie ticket, but concomitantly the wages of the average worker have increased. Thus, dollar values from different periods of time must be adjusted from "nominal" values (the unadjusted numeric values of price and money) to "real" values, which account for inflation and the time value of money.

Money has a time value. Imagine that you are a time traveler. When you travel, you take all of your money with you, which is a single $1.00 bill. As you travel through Einstein's space-time continuum, you are subject to a number of weird and exotic phenomena. In addition to the strange visual sensation of traveling almost at the speed of light, you also notice that even the $1.00 bill in your pocket displays magical properties: Although its physical form (a $1.00 paper note) remains the same, the money changes in value as you travel through time. When you go back in time, you discover that it has greater value; and when you travel into the future, you find that the same note has less value. Time travel is weird in physics, and it is weird in finance as well.

When we say that money has a time value, it means that the value of the nominal dollar is not constant over time, but instead it changes and the direction of the change is known: *Money decreases in value as it moves forward in the future*. This is why savers who have cash today will invest that money in assets that yield a rate of return such that the cash today earns a return to make a profit or at least not lose value. It is dumb not to invest savings over a long-term period, though "going to cash" over transitory periods may make sense.

Consider another more earthly example. The U.S. government wants to borrow $1,000 from you, and it will return this principal in 10 years. Assume that the U.S. government's promise is risk-free (there is no credit risk). Would you lend the government your hard-earned $1,000 at no interest since you will certainly get it back 10 years later? Of course not!

Two major factors contribute to the time value of money. First, money depreciates in value. This is called inflation, which is the economic phenomenon where the price of goods and services increase relative to the same nominal dollar. Second, money also has time value because by not spending the money today, one is delaying consumption until the future. Since consumption is a benefit, its delay is a detriment and the investor must be given a financial return. As the old adage goes, "Good things come to those who wait." Delayed gratification must be compensated.

1. FUTURE VALUE

If money has a time value, we must be able to calculate the future value. Future value is the amount of money one expects to receive on a specific future date given a specified rate of return on the money.

EXAMPLE

The Power of Compounding

1. You deposit $100 in an interest-bearing account that earns 5%. At the end of one year, how much will you have in your account?

$$\$100.00 \ \text{x} \ (1 \ + \ 5\%) \ = \ \$105.00$$

2. You are thrifty, and you leave the money in the account for another year. At the end of the second year, how much will you have in your account?

$$\$105.00 \ \text{x} \ (1 \ + \ 5\%) \ = \ \$110.25$$

At an interest rate of 5%, the depositor earned $10.25 on a deposit of $100 at the end of two years. This is a 10.25% total return for two years.

3. Why isn't the return simply 10% (= 2 x 5%), or $10.00 instead of $10.25?

The additional $0.25 is the additional 5% return on the $5 earned in the first year ($5 x 5% = $0.25). Therefore, at the end of the second year, the total return is: $5 first year interest, $0.25 interest on $5 interest, and $5 second year interest. This is the power of compounding.*

---

* For those of you who are rusty in algebra, multiplying a value by itself is represented as an exponent. For example, $(1 + 5\%) \ \text{x} \ (1 + 5\%) = (1 + 5\%)^2$ and $(1 + 5\%) \ \text{x} \ (1 + 5\%) \ \text{x} \ (1 + 5\%) = (1 + 5\%)^3$ and so forth. The exponential growth is the compounding effect.

We can generalize the above example to calculate future value. Future value is expressed as:

$$FV = PV \times (1 + R)^T$$

where PV = present value, R = rate of return, and T = time. Future value calculates a sum that an investor would have at some future point in time T given an initial investment PV and an investment rate R. The term $(1 + R)^T$ captures the compounding effect of time. For example, in the above bank account hypothetical, we can write:

$$\$110.25 = \$100 \times (1 + 5\%)^2$$

The future value equation says that the future value is the present value multiplied by the multiple representing the rate of return and time. Notice that: (1) As the rate of return increases, the future value increases, and vice versa; and (2) as the time increases, the future value increases, and vice versa. The future value multiple is this term.

$$\text{Future Value Multiple} = (1 + R)^T$$

For instance, the following are the calculations for future value multiples:

$$
\begin{aligned}
&\text{3 years at 20\%:} &&\Rightarrow &&(1+20\%)^3 &&= 1.728 \\
&\text{5 years at 15\%:} &&\Rightarrow &&(1+15\%)^5 &&= 2.011 \\
&\text{10 years at 10\%:} &&\Rightarrow &&(1+10\%)^{10} &&= 2.594 \\
&\text{20 years at 5\%:} &&\Rightarrow &&(1+5\%)^{20} &&= 2.653
\end{aligned}
$$

Since there are two variables, R and T, the future value multiple can be presented in convenient tabular format. The following is a future value multiple table.

Future Value Table

				TIME			
	3	4	5	$\cdots$	10	$\cdots$	20
20%	1.728	2.074	2.488	$\cdots$	6.192	$\cdots$	38.338
$\cdots$	$\cdots$	$\cdots$	$\cdots$	$\cdots$	$\cdots$	$\cdots$	$\cdots$
15%	1.521	1.749	2.011	$\cdots$	4.046	$\cdots$	16.367
$\cdots$	$\cdots$	$\cdots$	$\cdots$	$\cdots$	$\cdots$	$\cdots$	$\cdots$
10%	1.331	1.464	1.611	$\cdots$	2.594	$\cdots$	6.727
$\cdots$	$\cdots$	$\cdots$	$\cdots$	$\cdots$	$\cdots$	$\cdots$	$\cdots$
5%	1.158	1.216	1.276	$\cdots$	1.629	$\cdots$	2.653
$\cdots$	$\cdots$	$\cdots$	$\cdots$	$\cdots$	$\cdots$	$\cdots$	$\cdots$
1%	1.030	1.041	1.051	$\cdots$	1.105	$\cdots$	1.220

(RETURN RATE shown along the left side of the table)

𝒩 **QUESTIONS**

1. You deposit $100 in Investment A, which is an interest-bearing account that earns 98 percent. At the end of one year, how much is in your account?
2. You deposit $100 in Investment B, which is an interest-bearing account that earns 5 percent. At the end of 14 years, how much is in your account?
3. As between Investments A and B, which is a better proposition?
4. What is the future value of $1,000 earning a rate of 15 percent for 10 years? Use the future value table to find the multiple.
5. What is the future value of $1,500 earning a rate of 5 percent for five years? Use the future value table to find the multiple.

2. PRESENT VALUE

Present value and future value are related. Present value is the future value discounted to the value equal to today's (present) value. Think about a principal payment on a $100,000 bond that matures 10 years in the future. The $100,000 principal expected to be received 10 years in the future is not equivalent to $100,000 today. If a dollar tomorrow is always worth less than a dollar today, the $100,000 principal must be discounted to calculate the equivalent present value.

We can calculate the present value of a future value. In other words, given a future value, what is its present value? This requires a present value calculation. With algebraic manipulation of the future value formula, present value can be defined. Start with the formula for future value.

$$FV = PV \times (1 + R)^T$$

Multiply each side of the future value equation by the term $\dfrac{1}{(1+R)^T}$ so that we can algebraically isolate PV on the left side of the equation.*

$$PV \times (1+R)^T \times \left[\frac{1}{(1+R)^T}\right] = FV \times \left[\frac{1}{(1+R)^T}\right]$$

$$PV \times \cancel{(1+R)^T} \times \left[\frac{1}{\cancel{(1+R)^T}}\right] = FV \times \left[\frac{1}{(1+R)^T}\right]$$

This equation simplifies to the expression:**

---

* Multiplying each side of an equation by the same number or term keeps the equation true. For example, if A = A, then multiplying each side by 3 keeps the equation true: 3A = 3A.
** The term $[(1 + R)^T \times 1/(1 + R)^T]$ is simply the number 1. For example, 3 x 1/3 = 3/3 = 1.

$$PV = \frac{FV}{(1+R)^T}$$

Thus, the present value is defined as the future value discounted by an appropriate discount rate and time.

EXAMPLE

Discounting Investments to Present Value

You have the choice of two investments. Investment A requires $100 and will pay $500 at the end of five years. Investment B requires $100 and will pay $700 at the end of nine years. You are indifferent to the timing of the future payout, and you are only concerned with maximizing the rate of return. Assume that the discount rate applicable to both investments is 10%. Which investment do you make?

$$PV(\text{Investment A}) = \frac{500}{(1+10\%)^5} = 310.46$$

$$PV(\text{Investment B}) = \frac{700}{(1+10\%)^9} = 296.87$$

Thus, Investment A is superior to Investment B because the present value is slightly higher.

The important lesson is that the present value and the future value formulas (which are the same) are a way to convert values into a like-for-like comparison. The future value of an anticipated return cannot be compared to the present value of a cash investment outlay without a conversion to present value. Apples must be compared to apples, and present value must be compared to present value. With time value of money as a fact, it makes no sense to compare present value to future value without discounting the latter back to present value. This is important because, as mentioned, the purchase of a security instrument represents the sacrifice of present value of cash for economic rights to future returns.

Present value is the value of a future sum of money expressed as a present dollar equivalent. Because money today is always worth more than its dollar value tomorrow, a future value (or a past value) cannot be compared to the present dollar value unless it is converted to a present value equivalent.

The present value equation says that the present value is the discounted future value. Discount rate is the term R, used to perform a present value calculation. It is the rate at which the future value is discounted to derive the present value. Notice that as the discount rate increases, the present value decreases, and vice versa. The discount factor is the term that discounts the future value.

$$\text{Discount Factor} = \frac{1}{(1+R)^T}$$

For instance, the following are the calculations for the discount factors:

$$1 \text{ year at } 20\%: \quad \Rightarrow \quad \frac{1}{(1+20\%)^1} = 0.833$$

$$3 \text{ years at } 10\%: \quad \Rightarrow \quad \frac{1}{(1+10\%)^3} = 0.751$$

$$5 \text{ years at } 5\%: \quad \Rightarrow \quad \frac{1}{(1+5\%)^5} = 0.784$$

$$10 \text{ years at } 1\%: \quad \Rightarrow \quad \frac{1}{(1+1\%)^{10}} = 0.905$$

Since there are two variables, R and T, the discount factors can be presented in convenient tabular format. The following is a present value discount factor table.

Present Value Table

DISCOUNT RATE	TIME 1	2	3	4	5	...	10
20%	0.833	0.694	0.579	0.482	0.402	...	0.162
...	...	...	...	...	...	...	...
15%	0.870	0.756	0.658	0.572	0.497	...	0.247
...	...	...	...	...	...	...	...
10%	0.909	0.826	0.751	0.683	0.621	...	0.386
...	...	...	...	...	...	...	...
5%	0.952	0.907	0.864	0.823	0.784	...	0.614
...	...	...	...	...	...	...	...
1%	0.990	0.980	0.971	0.961	0.951	...	0.905

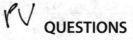

QUESTIONS

1. You deposited $100 in an interest-bearing account that earns 5 percent. At the end of one year, your account will have a future value of $105. At the end of two years, it will have a future value of $110.25. Calculate the present value of these future values.
2. Your rich uncle Charles leaves you $100,000 in a trust fund that matures in 10 years. Assume that the discount rate is 10 percent. What is the present value of this future value?
3. A plaintiff suffered injury fairly valued at $100,000. The defendant offers a structured settlement. The defendant offers to pay $20,000 now, and will pay $120,000 five years from now. Assume that the appropriate discount rate is 10 percent. Should the plaintiff accept this settlement offer?

4. What is the present value of $1,000 at a discount rate of 10 percent in 10 years? Use the present value table to find the discount factor.
5. What is the present value of $1,500 at a discount rate of 15 percent in five years? Use the present value table to find the discount factor.

3. ANNUITY VALUES

An annuity value is the present value of a fixed payment made over a fixed period of time. The formula for calculating an annuity is as follows:

$$PV = \frac{A}{(1+R)^1} + \ldots \ldots + \frac{A}{(1+R)^N}$$

where A is the fixed annuity amount, and N is the time period in years.

An annuity is nothing more than a series of present value calculations made on a fixed future value and discount rate, but over a defined period of time. For example, consider the following series of calculations:

$$\text{5 years at 10\%:} \Rightarrow \frac{A}{(1+10\%)^1} + \frac{A}{(1+10\%)^2} + \frac{A}{(1+10\%)^3} + \frac{A}{(1+10\%)^4} + \frac{A}{(1+10\%)^5}$$

This calculation produces a multiple (in this case 3.791) that we apply to the annuity amount A to get the present value of the sum of the annuity stream ($A_1 \ldots A_5$). Thus, if the annuity amount is $1,000, the present value of the annuity is $3,791.

Given a discount rate R and annuity term T, there is an annuity multiple. These calculations can be presented in convenient tabular format. The following is an annuity table providing annuity multiples.

Annuity Table

	TIME						
	5	⋯ 10	⋯ 15	⋯ 20	⋯ 25	⋯	50
20%	2.991	4.192	4.675	4.870	4.948	⋯	4.999
⋯	⋯	⋯	⋯	⋯	⋯	⋯	⋯
15%	3.352	5.019	5.847	6.259	6.464	⋯	6.661
⋯	⋯	⋯	⋯	⋯	⋯	⋯	⋯
10%	3.791	6.145	7.606	8.514	9.077	⋯	9.915
⋯	⋯	⋯	⋯	⋯	⋯	⋯	⋯
5%	4.329	7.722	10.380	12.462	14.094	⋯	18.256
⋯	⋯	⋯	⋯	⋯	⋯	⋯	⋯
1%	4.853	9.471	13.865	18.046	22.023	⋯	39.196

DISCOUNT RATE

QUESTIONS

1. What is the present value of a 50-year $500 annuity discount rate of 20 percent? Use the annuity table to find the multiple.
2. What is the present value of a 50-year $500 annuity discount rate of 5 percent? Use the annuity table to find the multiple.
3. Investment A yields a 50-year $1,000 annuity discounted at a 20 percent rate. Investment B yields a 10-year $1,000 annuity discounted at a 15 percent rate. What are the gross future payments from each investment? Which annuity has greater value?

4. PERPETUITY VALUES

A perpetuity value is the present value of a perpetual stream of a fixed sum. Think about this question: "Assume that you can live in perpetuity, and you are given the right to receive $1 each year in perpetuity. How much is this perpetual annuity worth?" Before dismissing this question as pure fancy, think again—the assumption of perpetual life is not so unrealistic for a corporation. Corporate earnings and cash flows are easily conceptualized as annuity and perpetuity payments. The financial proposition is clearly worth more than $0. But is it worth an infinite amount (∞) since a corporation is providing an infinite stream of $1? The answer is "no." Somewhere in between zero and infinity $(0, \infty)$ is the correct answer.

The formula to calculate the value is the following, where A is the annuity amount.

$$PV = \frac{A}{R}$$

Note that if $R = 0$, then $PV = \infty$ (because any positive value divided by zero is an infinite value). This is intuitively apparent. If $R = 0$, a dollar in the future is worth the same as a dollar today; if a corporation is providing a dollar for every year in perpetuity, the stream of cash must be worth an infinite amount and thus the corporation would be worth an infinite value.

However, if $R > 0$, then $PV \neq \infty$. It must be some finite value. The proposition that a dollar tomorrow is always worth less than a dollar today means that the discount rate R must be greater than 0. If so, the present value of any perpetual stream of income must have a finite value.

A variation of the perpetuity formula is the growth perpetuity formula. If the annuity is expected to grow at a constant rate in perpetuity, an unrealistic assumption in many cases (what earnings grow in perpetuity?), the growth perpetuity formula to calculate the present value is the following, where g is the growth rate.

$$PV = \frac{A}{R - g}$$

EXAMPLE

Perpetuity Value

1. We know that the discount rate R cannot be zero because a fundamental principle of finance is that a dollar tomorrow is *always* worth less than a dollar today. If so, the present value of the infinite stream of $1 cannot be an infinite sum. Assume that the discount rate is 10%. What is the value of a perpetual stream of $1?

$$PV = \frac{\$1}{10\%} = \$10$$

   Therefore, if a corporation is expected to generate $1 in cash flow in perpetuity and its discount rate is 10%, the value of that corporation must be $10.

2. If the $1 annuity is expected to grow at a 5% rate with the same discount rate, what is the present value?

$$PV = \frac{\$1}{(10\% - 5\%)} = \$20$$

3. What if the growth rate was 9%?

$$PV = \frac{\$1}{(10\% - 9\%)} = \$100$$

Note that growth assumptions can dramatically affect the present value. An aggressive growth assumption can result in high present value.

Very few things involving economic transactions have perpetual existence, including people and corporations. However, as long as the life of an asset is long-lived, the assumption of perpetual existence is not grave error. Since most of the present value is captured within a specific duration, the use of a perpetuity formula provides a reasonably approximate value for a long-lived asset even if it is overstated.

QUESTIONS

1. A corporation is expected to receive $10 per year for the remainder of its perpetual life. Assume that the discount rate is 10 percent. What is the present value of this perpetual annuity?
2. A corporation is expected to receive $10 per year for the next 50 years, and then per its charter it will terminate its business and dissolve. Assume that the discount rate is 10 percent. What is the present value of this 50-year annuity? We can discount all 50 cash flows individually.
3. A corporation is expected to receive $10 next year, and this sum is expected to grow at a constant 2 percent rate. Assume that the discount rate is 10 percent. What is the present value of this perpetual growth annuity?
4. Investment A produces a 25-year annuity of $1,000 discounted at a 15 percent rate. Investment B produces a perpetuity annuity of $1,000 discounted at a 15 percent rate. How much greater in value is Investment B?

5. IMPLICATIONS OF TVM FOR CORPORATE FINANCE

What's the point of this math? Why do lawyers need to understand this?

The above mathematical exercises seem abstract and dry (and perhaps tedious), but the math is rich in meaning. Time value of money is the critical concept in the value of assets, such as corporations. In economics and business, the value of an asset, such as a corporation or the economic value of a person, is the amount of cash flow it is expected to generate *in the future.* Notice that this is very different from the accounting concept of recording value from past transactions.

Let's first think about the value of an asset more intuitively, and outside the context of dry finance. Suppose that you are the general manager (GM) of the Chicago Bears. What is your ultimate goal? Easy, you want to win the Super Bowl. Why? Easy, winning will make the Bears a more valuable enterprise. Suppose that the team needs a top quarterback to make a successful run for the Super Bowl. Joe Q. Starr is the best free agent in the market, but he commands an annual salary of $20 million per year for the next five years. Starr has been the league's most valuable player (MVP) for the past two years; over an eight-year NFL career he has accumulated incredible statistical success with his old team; and he won the Heisman Trophy as a Gator at the University of Florida. As the GM, you want to sign Starr to be the starting quarterback of the Bears. You are willing to pay $20 million per year. Why? Let's be clear in what you are not paying for. You are not paying for the two MVP awards, the incredible statistical success of the past, or the Heisman Trophy. You don't care because the past success was enjoyed by Starr's previous teams. Those benefits will never inure to the benefit of the Bears. You are willing to pay $100 million over five years because you are expecting future success with Starr. Past performance only supports the expectation of future performance. Starr only has value to a football team for what he is *expected* to do in the future, the next game, the next season, or the next five years of the contract.

Conceptually, a corporation is no different from Joe Q. Starr. A corporation is an asset, and its investors expect a future return when they invest in the *present* dollar value in the asset. Notice the problem: A dollar in the present and the future is not the same. Investors pay in present value (a dollar today), but their return is expected in the future (a dollar tomorrow). On a gross unadjusted basis, these dollar values are not the same and cannot be compared on a like-for-like basis. They must be equalized on a like-for-like basis.

Most investors pay for a security (such as a bond) in cash. By paying cash today, an investor is trading cash in his pocket today for an economic right to a future value. For example, when an investor buys a bond for $1,000 with a maturity in 10 years and an interest rate of 10 percent, the investor is giving up $1,000 of present value for the promise of future values, which are $100 for the next 10 years and the principal repayment of $1,000 in the tenth year. The trade between present value and future value is conceptually the same for a shareholder who purchases a share of stock. The shareholder pays cash, which is a present value, for the implicit expectation of future economic benefits to be gained by the corporation through its business activities.

The discount rate is both a rate of return and a measure of riskiness in the investment. In other words, since investors do not like taking risk, increased riskiness in the investment requires a greater rate of return, and thus a greater discount rate. To understand this intuition, compare two contractual rights: the U.S. government's obligation to pay $100 five years in the future; General Motors' obligation to pay

$100 five years in the future. How should a potential buyer value these contractual rights? We intuit several propositions.

1. A buyer would pay less than $100 irrespective of the debtor's creditworthiness. A dollar five years from now is always worth less than a dollar today.
2. A buyer would not be able to get the contract for nothing because the obligations are not worthless. The present value of the obligations are worth somewhere in the range of $0 to $100.
3. The U.S. government's obligation to repay the $100 is worth more than General Motors'. There is some chance that General Motors will not be able to pay the obligation, but no real chance that the U.S. government will not be able to pay.

Therefore, the present value of the U.S. government obligation to pay $100 in the future should be worth more than the present value of General Motors' obligation. All else being the same, would you rather own the promise of payment from the U.S. government or from General Motors?

Financiers are only concerned about the relationship between the present value and future value. Why the future? The answer is simple (*The value of securities represents the present value of the expected future cash flows*) The relationship between the present and future is defined in terms of the expected future return and the riskiness of that expected return. In the most abstract sense, a security instrument is an economic right of an investor to a future payment in return for the rent of capital needed to pursue the opportunity to earn economic profit—*it is fundamentally a swap between present value and future value.*

Time value of money is not simply rote math calculations. The mathematical process and its underlying concept have deep significance in understanding the value of corporations and business transactions. Clients always think in terms of value and wealth creation. The economic value of an asset, such as a corporation, is measured by the amount of money that the corporation is expected to pay to its capital providers in the future. If so, the future values must be discounted to present value to figure out the value of the security instrument entitling the holder to the benefit of the future payments, which is the value that he pays in the present.

The following case involves the valuation of a substantial asset. To ascertain value, the bankruptcy court conducted a discounted cash flow analysis, which is a complex series of time value calculations. Valuation was the critical issue in the case, and the court and the litigating attorneys were deeply involved in the minutia of the present value calculations.

In re Vanderveer Estates Holding, LLC
293 B.R. 560 (Bkr. E.D.N.Y. 2003)

CRAIG, Bankruptcy Judge.

The matter before this Court is the determination of the value of the property known as Vanderveer Estates ("Vanderveer" or the "Property"), a multi-family low-income housing project which is the principal asset of Vanderveer Estates Holding LLC (the "Debtor"). Vanderveer consists of 59 contiguous apartment buildings containing 2,496 apartment units located in the East Flatbush section of Brooklyn. Vanderveer was placed under the control of a receiver prior to the commencement of this case and the receiver has continued in control of the Property with the Debtor's consent pursuant to §543(d) of the Bankruptcy Code.

The purpose of this valuation is to fix the value of Vanderveer in connection with consideration of the Debtor's Fourth Amended Plan of Reorganization (the "Debtor's Plan") and the reorganization plan proposed by VE Apartments LLC ("VE"), the debtor's principal secured creditor.

The valuation of Vanderveer plays a pivotal role in this Court's consideration of the plans proposed in this case. [The Debtor's Plan to pay off VE depends on a future refinancing, which further depends on the value of Vanderveer.]

One of VE's principal objections to confirmation of this Plan is that it is not feasible. VE contends that, at the end of the initial ten years, assuming a valuation of Vanderveer of approximately $81 million at that time, Debtor would be unable to secure refinancing to pay off the $68 million balloon payment because an institutional lender would only lend a maximum of $57.2 million [which suggests that a lender will loan 70% of the value of asset, called "loan-to-value," which is calculated as $57.2m ÷ $81m].

VE and Debtor have each submitted appraisals into evidence and have cross-examined each other's appraisers. Not surprisingly, the appraisal each offers serves its own purposes, and the two diverge significantly in their conclusions as to value.

[The court found the Debtor's expert, his assumptions, and valuation methodology not credible, and instead found credible VE's expert, Von Ancken.]

VE's appraiser, Von Ancken, employed the discounted cash flow method, which estimates the net cash flow of a property over 10 years and then discounts that amount by an appropriate discount rate to the present value.[3] It then estimates the reversion value of the Property, by predicting the value of the Property in the eleventh year and discounting that number to present value. The reversion value is then added to the discounted cash flow to arrive at a final value. VE contends that the discounted cash flow method is appropriately used in this case in order to account for fluctuations in income resulting from the fact that certain sources of income will change over the course of a ten-year holding period.

At least as important as the methodology employed at arriving at market value is the "quality and reasonableness of the assumptions which are plugged into [the valuation methodology]." Moreover, evaluation of those assumptions is critical to determining the appropriate appraisal methodology.

Von Ancken appropriately employed the discounted cash flow method which provides a more precise valuation of a property (such as Vanderveer) with a changing income stream. Von Ancken explained:

> [The discounted cash flow method] is more precise and it's used in most of the appraisals of commercial buildings, such as office buildings and shopping centers because they have leases that fluctuate and there are differences going on in the expected income.
>
> It's used in cases for apartment buildings where you expect changes in the income system.

---

[3] "Discounting" is a general term used to describe the process of converting future cash flows into a present value. The discount rate represents the interest rate used for the discounting process, and takes into account risk and time value of money.

[It's] the only method that I could use here to measure the fall off of the rents in net operating income over a three year period.

Many of the banks insist now for apartment buildings that you also include the discounted cash flow analysis. If you have a situation when you know that the income side is going to change over a period of time, then you should use this discounted cash flow analysis since it's the only appraisal tool that measures the actual value of a property where there is a change happening.

For all of the foregoing reasons, this Court finds that the value of Vanderveer is approximately $78,902,062. [The court supported this value with the discounted cash flow method analysis shown in the case Appendix.]

APPENDIX

Calculation of Modification to Net Operating Income (NOI)

The following table sets out the modified NOI for each year.

Net Operating Income Table

YEAR 1	YEAR 2	YEAR 3	YEAR 4	YEAR 5	
$9,502,596	$9,037,920	$8,134,011	$7,002,652	$7,192,696	

YEAR 6	YEAR 7	YEAR 8	YEAR 9	YEAR 10	YEAR 11
$7,387,523	$7,587,241	$7,791,957	$8,001,783	$8,216,829	$8,534,210

Calculation of the *Present Value* (PV) of a 10-year Cash Flow

The Court applied a discounted cash flow analysis, projected over a ten-year period, to determine what the present value of future cash flows generated by the modified NOI at Vanderveer would be. "Discounting" is a procedure used to convert cash flows and reversions into present value; based on the concept that benefits received in the future are worth less than the same benefits received today. "A future payment is discounted to present value by calculating the amount that, if invested today, would grow with compound interest at a satisfactory rate to equal the future payment." The standard formula for discounting future value to present value is:

$$Present\ Value = \frac{Future\ Value}{(1 + i)^n}$$

where i is the rate of return on capital per period (or the discount rate) that will satisfy the investor and n is the number of periods that the payment will be deferred. If a series of future payments is expected (as in the instant case), each payment is discounted with the standard formula, and the present value of the payments is the sum of all the present values. The yield formula is expressed as:

$$PV = \frac{CF}{(1 + Y)} + \frac{CF_2}{(1 + Y)^2} + \frac{CF_3}{(1 + Y)^3} + \ ... \ + \frac{CF_n}{(1 + Y)^n}$$

where PV = present value; CF = the cash flow for the period specified; Y = the appropriate period yield rate; and n = the number of periods in the projection.

Using the above yield formula, this Court calculated the present value of the projected ten-year cash flow of Vanderveer, incorporating the modified NOI, and using a discount rate of 11.5%, as did Von Ancken, as expressed in the following formula:

$$PV = \frac{\$9,502,596}{(1+11.5\%)} + \frac{\$9,037,920}{(1+11.5\%)^2} + \frac{\$8,134,011}{(1+11.5\%)^3} + \ldots + \frac{\$8,216,829}{(1+11.5\%)^{10}}$$

By calculating the present value of the proposed cash flow for each separate year, and then adding them all together, pursuant to the above PV formula, this Court arrives at an estimated PV of a 10–year cash flow of $46,782,319. The following table shows the present value of the modified NOI for each year:

PV of a 10-year Discounted Cash Flow

YEAR 1	YEAR 2	YEAR 3	YEAR 4	YEAR 5
$8,522,507	$7,271,053	$5,868,694	$4,529,529	$4,174,518

YEAR 6	YEAR 7	YEAR 8	YEAR 9	YEAR 10
$3,843,664	$3,540,476	$3,261,597	$3,003,672	$2,766,609

Calculation of Reversion Value of the Property

Income-producing properties, such as Vanderveer, provide two types of financial benefits to the investor, which are added together to arrive at a final value of the property: 1) the periodic income or the present value of the cash flow generated from the property (as calculated in Section B above) and 2) the future value obtained from a hypothetical sale of the property at the end of the holding period (at the end of the 10-year projection period), otherwise known as the reversion value. In order to estimate a property reversion, appraisers typically use a capitalization rate, the "terminal capitalization rate" to convert income the NOI of the property for the year following the last year in the forecast period (which would be the 11th year in the present model) into an indication of the anticipated value of the property at the end of the holding period. In essence, the terminal capitalization rate is used to determine the resale value of the property using direct capitalization, using the following standard formula:

$$\text{Reversion Value} = \frac{\text{Net Operating Income}}{\text{Terminal Cap. Rate}}$$

After calculating the reversion of the property, the appraiser will typically deduct the selling expense of the property (the transaction costs) to arrive at the net proceeds of the hypothetical resale. The reversion is often a major portion of the total benefit to be received from an investment in income-producing property. In the present case, the Court applied a terminal capitalization rate of 9.5% (as used by Von Ancken) to the projected NOI of the 11th year, which was estimated to be $8,534,210 to arrive at a gross reversion of approximately $89,833,789. This equation is expressed as:

$$\text{Gross Reversion} = \frac{\$8,534,210}{9.5\%} = 89,833,789$$

Next, the Court deducted Von Ancken's transaction costs of 4.25% from the gross reversion [$89,833,789 x 4.25% = $3,817,936] to arrive at the net proceeds of the hypothetical resale of Vanderveer in the 10th year of approximately $86,015,853. Next, in order to determine what the present value of this reversion is, the Court simply applied the present value formula to the reversion of $86,015,853 as shown below:

$$\text{PV of Reversion} = \frac{\$86,015,853}{(1 + 11.5\%)^{10}}$$

Using the above formula, the Court arrived at a present value of the reversion (PV of Reversion) of approximately $28,961,566.

Calculation of Final Value

Von Ancken explained at trial that he took into account both the present value of the income stream generated by Vanderveer, as well as the present value of the reversion of Vanderveer derived from a hypothetical sale of Vanderveer in the 10th year, and added these values together to arrive at a final value. Using this method, this Court arrived at a value of Vanderveer of approximately $75,743,885, as expressed in the formula below:

Total Present Value = Present Value of Reversion
+ Present Value of a 10-year cash flow

where   Present Value of Reversion is estimated at $28,961,566
Present Value of a 10-year cash flow is estimated at $46,782,319
[The sum total is $75,743,885.]

In order to arrive at the final value of Vanderveer, the Court then deducted the immediate necessary repair costs, in the amount of $1,168,250, from the Total Present Value and added the Present Value of the J–51 Tax Benefits, in the amount of $4,326,427, as Von Ancken did in his final valuation. [The tax benefit net of repair costs is $3,158,177.] In this way, the Court arrived at an estimated final value of the Property of $78,902,062.

QUESTIONS

1. What is the theory of the value of Vanderveer properties?
2. Assume that debt to VE is $68 million, which the debtor plans to pay off through a refinancing, and that the limit of refinancing is 70 percent loan-to-value. What

asset value is needed to achieve the planned refinancing and payoff to VE from the refinancing?

3. Assume that the projections of the net operating income found in the opinion are the most credible projections. However, based on the credibility of conflicting expert testimony, the court believes that the discount rate should be 8 percent rather than 11.5 percent. All other assumptions in the valuation model are the same, including: (1) 9.5 percent terminal capitalization rate is used to calculate the gross reversion; (2) the 4.25 percent transaction cost is deducted from the gross reversion; and (3) the $3,158,177 is the tax benefit net of repair costs. Under these assumptions, can the $68 million debt to VE be paid off by a refinancing at 70 percent loan-to-value?

C. COST OF CAPITAL

A business enterprise, such as a corporation, rents capital from capital providers. "Rent" means that the corporation does not "own" its capital in the economic sense, and thus it is charged an economic fee for the use of capital. This economic fee is easily understood in the context of debt because creditors have a legal contractual entitlement to the payment of an interest rate. However, shareholders also charge an economic fee for providing equity capital, though this "charge" is more abstract in nature. It should come as no surprise that shareholders and creditors provide capital with the expectation of earning a return. Financial instruments have certain contractual benefits entitling their holders to specific financial claims against the corporation. A corporation *must* provide the contractual obligation of the return to creditors, lest there be *legal* consequences; a corporation *should* provide the expected return to common stockholders, lest there be *market* consequences.

The cost of capital is the rate of return required by each capital provider in order to provide capital to the business enterprise. Different capital providers of the same corporation will have different rates of return even though they are providing capital to the same corporation. The reason for this common phenomenon is that capital providers do not rent their capital under the same terms. Stocks and bonds, for example, have fundamentally different terms under which shareholders and bondholders are providing capital. Since the economic value of financial instruments depends on their terms, we would expect that the cost of each form of capital would be different as well.

A corporation's cost of capital is the rate of return a corporation must provide to its capital providers. Conceptually, the value of a corporation is the sum of all future cash flow that is claimed by its capital providers after payment of all other expenses and charges, such as taxes and wages. If a corporation issues financial instruments that constitute different claims on the expected economic benefit, the future economic benefit must be discounted to the present value in order to assign a present value of the financial instrument. This requires a present value calculation. Therefore, the discount rate R in this present value calculation is the cost of capital that discounts the future returns, expected to be generated by the corporation, by the investors' expected rate of return for the rent of their capital.

The cost of capital is simply the corporation's unique discount rate used to discount its expected returns to investors. The rate discounts future values at the level providing the corporation's investors the rate of return on their investments.

EXAMPLE

Rate of Return on the "Rent" of Capital

1. Let's keep the facts simple and stylized. Suppose a corporation is capitalized through the issuance of only 1 share of stock. This is the only capital that the corporation will need. After 10 years, the corporation will dissolve and upon windup it is expected to return net assets to its sole shareholder of $5,000. Given the nature of the risk to be undertaken by the corporation, the shareholder will "rent" equity capital only for a 15% rate. The shareholder understands that if the corporation has creditors at the end of year 10, it must pay off creditors first before she is entitled to the net assets. She may not get anything at all if creditors' claims in the end consume all of the assets. This is a risk, but she believes that the risk is embedded in the 15% she implicitly "charges" to the corporation. If she believes that this was a risk-free venture, like lending to the U.S. government, she may only get 5%. Given the cost of capital, how much should the shareholder pay for the 1 share of stock?

$$PV = \frac{\$5,000}{(1 + 15\%)^{10}} = \frac{\$5,000}{4.056} = \$1,236$$

   This means that if the shareholder pays $1,236 today, and the corporation returns $5,000 in year 10, the shareholder will have earned a 15% compounded rate of return. The future value expected to inure to the shareholder is discounted by the cost of capital such that the present payment for the share of stock equals a rate of return that meets the cost of capital.

2. Suppose the corporation balks at the suggested 15% rate, and instead offers a 10% rate of return to the shareholder. After looking at all other investment opportunities, the shareholder believes that a 10% rate is a suitable return given her other opportunities and the risk taken. She accepts the 10% rate. How much should she pay for the 1 share of stock?

$$PV = \frac{\$5,000}{(1 + 10\%)^{10}} = \frac{\$5,000}{2.594} = \$1,928$$

   The cost of capital—the rate of return charged to the corporation by the market and valuation processes—is important to price financial instruments that a corporation issues to capital providers.

The concept of cost of capital is crucial to valuation of corporations and financial instruments. It is simply the discount rate used when expected (future) corporate earnings or cash flows are discounted back to present value. Embedded in the discount rate is the investor's expected return.

The cost of capital incorporates these fundamental finance principles: (1) Money in the future is always worth less than today's money; (2) financial instruments, containing discrete economic claims on a corporation's future benefits, are paid for by today's money; and (3) since investors must be compensated to bear risk, the riskier the investment, the greater should be the expected return that the capital provider charges to the corporation. The value of an asset is the expected future return discounted by *time* and *risk*. The cost of capital incorporates the risk inherent in the financial instrument, and thus charges a rate of return suitable for the risk taken by the investor.

Since a corporation can issue different kinds of securities with different terms and benefits—including debt, preferred stock, and common stock—the cost of capital of each security will be different and calculated differently.

1. CALCULATING THE COSTS OF DEBT AND PREFERRED STOCK

The *cost of debt* is the rate of return required by creditors to provide debt financing, which is a cost to the firm to use debt capital. A charge for credit is intuitive enough. What is the interest charged by the creditor? However, there are two important nuances.

The first nuance is that the cost of debt must account for the benefit of the interest tax shield. The government subsidizes the use of debt capital by allowing interest expense to be deductible from taxable income. Recall from the previous chapter on financial statements that "interest expense" is subtracted from operating income, and the difference is the resulting pretax profit from which the tax rate is applied. This tax policy reduces the effective cost of debt by shielding some of the firm's profit from tax liability. Taking into account the benefit of the tax shield, the cost of debt is defined as:

$$\text{Cost of debt} = R \times (1 - T)$$

where R is the interest rate and T is the tax rate. This equation says that the cost of debt is the interest rate on debt, net of tax benefit, which is captured in the term $(1 - T)$.

The second nuance is that R is not the stated interest rate on the debt instrument (also known as the coupon rate). Instead, it is the cost of borrowing as determined by the yield on the debt. For example, suppose a corporation issued a $1,000 face value, 20-year bond at the stated coupon rate of 10 percent. That was ten years ago. Currently, the bond trades today at a value of $1,250. What is the company's current cost of borrowing on a 10-year term? Based on the market trading values, the company can issue a 10-year bond today at a face value of $1,250 with an interest payment of $100 per year. This implies that the company's cost of debt today is not the 10 percent coupon on the face of the bond, but it is instead the 8 percent yield on the bond, which is calculated as $(8\% = \$100 \div \$1,250)$.

The cost of the preferred stock is the dividend yield on the preferred stock. Like a bond, most preferred stocks pay a regular payment called a dividend that is a fixed percentage rate on the face value of the preferred stock: for example, 8 percent of the $1,000 face value. However, like the market price of bonds, the market value of preferred stock can fluctuate in the market. Thus, the cost of issuing preferred stock must take into account the current yield on the preferred stock.

$$\text{Cost of preferred stock} = \frac{\text{Dividend Amount}}{\text{Market Price of Preferred}}$$

2. CALCULATING THE COST OF EQUITY AND THE CAPM

Most people intuitively understand the concept of the cost of debt because we are familiar with paying interest payments on loans, whether they are home mortgages, credit cards, or student loans. We pay interest in cash, and we notice cash inflows and outflows. However, the cost of equity is not intuitive. It is a difficult concept to grasp at first because it does not involve cash transfers akin to interest payments. Neither corporate law nor the typical corporate charter requires any cash payment or other direct compensation to common shareholders. In fact, many companies do not pay dividends. Dividends are paid at the rational discretion of the board of directors. Unlike creditors, shareholders cannot throw the company into default for failure to pay dividends and the disappointed shareholders' sole remedy, in the vast majority of cases, is to exercise the "Wall Street rule" (*i.e.*, sell the shares of stocks that disappoint expectations).

Think about this: A corporation can issue stock to shareholders, take their money in exchange for giving them paper that says they own stock, and never have a legal obligation to pay dividends or repurchase the shares. Because of the separation of ownership and control, the typical shareholder will also have little say in the matter. A corporation can take shareholders' money and not have any obligation to provide a return. Therefore, equity capital must be free, right? Our intuition says this is wrong. Equity capital cannot be "free" even if shareholders are not legally entitled to dividends or any other form of direct compensation from the company. In fact, equity capital must be expensive since shareholders are the residual claimants, standing last in the financial queue and taking greater risk than creditors.

So what does it mean when we say that equity has a capital cost just the way debt has a cost of debt? To rent equity capital from shareholders, the firm must compensate them. But a corporation generally does not have a legal obligation to return cash to shareholders. How, then, are shareholders "compensated"? The cost of equity must reflect the shareholders' expectation of return. Thus, the short answer to the question is that *the cost of equity is the shareholders' expected return commensurate with the specific risk associated with the firm, and shareholders are compensated in the process of valuation of the stock, which can be monetized through the capital markets.* Let's unpack this difficult concept step by step.

We start the analysis by noting the range of an investor's opportunities. What can an investor do with her savings? She can stuff it under her pillow and leave it there, but this would be irrational. Aside from the risk of fire and thieves, she would earn no return on her money. She can invest the money in various ways: for example, buy gold, invest in real estate, or invest in a friend's pizza shop. These may be fine investments. She can also invest in the capital markets—lend money to institutional borrowers such as governments and corporations, or invest in the equity of corporations through the purchase of stock. If she invests her money this way, she is a seller of capital in the capital markets. In this marketplace, she has a number of investment options: (1) risk-free government bonds, (2) stock in individual companies, or (3) a diversified portfolio of stocks that mirror market returns.

On the safest end of the spectrum are risk-free investments, which are federal government debt instruments. Since there is no risk, the return on the risk-free rate is comparatively low. The capital markets operate under the assumption that there is a risk-free rate. A risk-free investment is an investment in U.S. government debt instruments, called Treasury bills, notes, and bonds (the terms denote differences in the length of maturity and are collectively called Treasury securities or Treasuries). Many investors invest in Treasuries, including retail investors, pension funds, insurance companies, and foreign governments. These investors are creditors of the U.S. government. Treasury securities are considered risk-free because the assumption is the U.S. government will not default on its loans.

If a risk-free rate is undesirable because it pays too little, the other option is to invest in the stock of any given company. There is a qualitative difference in the riskiness of a loan to the U.S. government and a stock investment in any given company, even seemingly safe companies. If an investor chooses to invest in the equity of a corporation, she undertakes the "firm specific" or "unique risk" associated with that company. Firm-specific risk is any risk that is unique to the firm, and it may include risks associated with management competence, business strategy, and competitive position. A number of bad things can happen to any given firm. If the investment is the Walt Disney Co., perhaps tomorrow Mickey Mouse will cease to be popular with children. If it is McDonald's Corp., perhaps tomorrow consumer preferences in the fast food market will shift. If it is Eastman Kodak Co., perhaps one day the firm's leading technology in paper-and-pulp film processing will be made obsolete by digital cameras and computer imaging technology. If it is the Enron Corp., perhaps one day the senior executives of the company will orchestrate one of the largest accounting frauds in business history and destroy the company. An investment in stock of a specific company is always subject to the unique risk (sometimes also called "unsystematic risk") associated with that company.

Individual investments in stock are risky. Imagine that you have come across an inheritance of $1,000,000—a princely sum. Would you feel comfortable investing the entire sum in shares of General Electric? To be sure, GE is the company that "brings good things to life" (the company's slogan); it is a world-class company and a most admirable company. But many people would still be uneasy with putting all one million eggs in one basket, particularly if this represents the only investment of one's assets.

If an all-in investment in one firm is undesirable, an investor can diversify away firm-specific risk by investing in a diversified portfolio of stocks. A diversified portfolio can eliminate the unique risk of an investment in any one company. As Antonio in Shakespeare's *The Merchant of Venice*, advised, "My ventures are not in one bottom trusted, Nor to one place; nor is my whole estate Upon the fortune of this present year." Antonio was well diversified, and thus he was not sad when misfortune fell upon one of his many investments. In a diversified portfolio, one firm's implosion would certainly affect the return on the portfolio. A diversified portfolio may have some laggards (and scoundrels), but for every laggard there may be a star. If Enron was in the basket of stocks, perhaps a company like Google would have been in the basket as well. A diversified portfolio would smooth out the ups and downs of individual stock movements, and thus eliminate the unique risks associated with any individual company in the basket. If well diversified, a portfolio will mirror the return on the broader market.

EXAMPLE

Enron's Unique Risk

Before its collapse in late 2001, Enron was one of the most lauded companies in Corporate America. Among other plaudits, *Fortune* magazine named Enron "The Most Innovative Company in America," and *CFO* magazine named Andrew Fastow, the architect of the massive accounting fraud, "CFO of the Year."

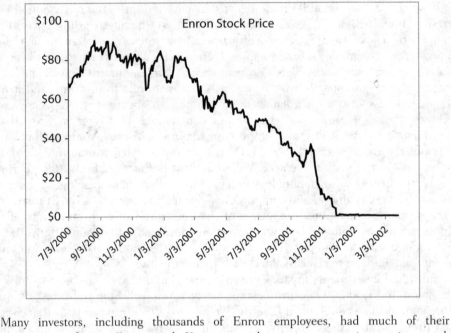

Enron Stock Price

Many investors, including thousands of Enron employees, had much of their investment tied up in Enron stock. You can see that an investment in any given stock is very risky.

One should not confuse diversification with the elimination of all risk. Only risk-free investments are free of risk. Diversification only eliminates exposure to firm-specific risk of investing in a particular company, *i.e.*, the risk of bad things happening to a specific investment due to the unique circumstance of that specific company. An investment in the market is still risky. The market moves. It can go up, down, and sideways. Diversification cannot eliminate the risk inherent in an investment in a market portfolio. This risk is called "market risk" (sometimes called "systematic risk").

EXAMPLE

Market Risk

In thinking about the risks of investing in the stock market, consider the stock market crash of 1929, which precipitated the Great Depression, and the crash of 2008, which precipitated what is dubbed the Great Recession.

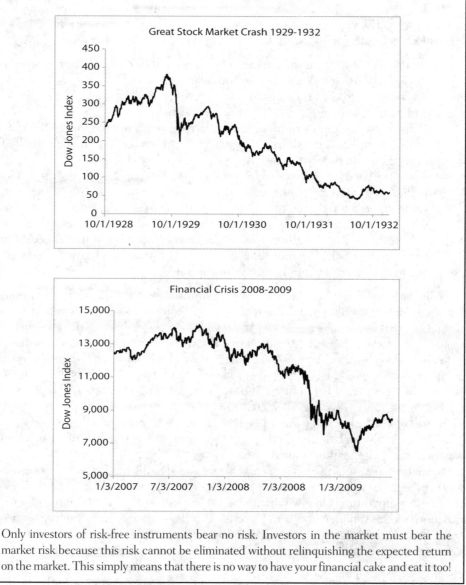

Only investors of risk-free instruments bear no risk. Investors in the market must bear the market risk because this risk cannot be eliminated without relinquishing the expected return on the market. This simply means that there is no way to have your financial cake and eat it too!

With this background on the range of investment opportunities, we can embark on a rigorous analysis of how investors set the expectation of return in a specific stock. The conventional and generally accepted way of calculating the cost of equity is the

Capital Asset Pricing Model, which was developed by, among others, William Sharpe, a Nobel Prize–winning financial economist.[*] CAPM states:

$$\text{Cost of equity} = \beta \, (R_m - R_f) + R_f$$

where β = beta, R_m = market return, and R_f = risk-free rate.

CAPM is a part of the discount rate used to discount the corporation's future cash flows, which is the process of valuing the corporation's equity (it is the R in the time value of money calculation). CAPM has an elegant logic, which goes like this:

1. An investor always has the opportunity to invest in risk-free instruments and get R_f (the risk-free rate), and she would bear no risk.
2. An investor also has the opportunity to invest in a diversified market portfolio and get R_m, and she would bear the market risk.
3. If an investor chooses to invest in the market portfolio and forego the opportunity to invest in a risk-free rate, she must be compensated additionally for bearing the market risk: thus, $R_m > R_f$.
4. The difference is measured as $(R_m - R_f)$, called the *equity risk premium*, which is the additional compensation that an investor requires to forego the opportunity to earn a risk-free return and bear the market risk.
5. Thus far, we have focused on the difference between the market rate and the risk-free rate. The investor also has the option to forego a market return and invest in the stock of an individual company. This risk must be measured so that the investor can be appropriately compensated.

This last step (5) is where beta becomes relevant. Beta is the measure of covariance between the market return and the return on the company's stock. In plain English, this means that beta is the sensitivity of a company's stock return to the movement of the market return. A beta of 1.0 means that the stock return is correlated one-for-one with the market return. Assume a market return of 11 percent. The return on the company's stock would be: +22 percent for a beta of 2.0; +11 percent for a beta of 1.0; +5.5 percent for a beta of 0.5; and –11 percent for a beta of –1.0.

Beta is the measure of the stock's risk relative to the market risk. Why a comparison to market risk? Market risk cannot be eliminated. An investor in a diversified market portfolio must always bear the market risk. Accordingly, the measure of a stock return is compared to the market return.

Since beta measures the riskiness of a stock relative to the market risk, there is now a way to ascertain the compensation needed to incentivize an investment in the stock given the investor's opportunity to invest in the market or a risk-free rate. Keep in mind that risk is defined as the variance of return. A return that is more variable is considered more risky. The principle of risk and return says this: The more variance in an investment, the more the investor must be compensated because she is assuming more risk.

Bearing more risk means more return must be given. Beta is the measure of risk, which is used to calculate the necessary return. The market risk premium $(R_m - R_f)$ is multiplied by beta to calculate the premium above the risk-free rate required to

---

[*] John Lintner, *The Valuation of Risk Assets and the Selection of Risky Investments in Stock Portfolios and Capital Budgets*, 47 Rev. Econ. & Stat. 13 (1965); William F. Sharpe, *Capital Asset Prices: A Theory of Market Equilibrium under Conditions of Risk*, 19 J. Fin. 425 (1964).

incentivize an investment in the specific company. Once this equity premium is calcu-lated, we add back the risk-free rate since it is the baseline return from which different investment opportunities in the market portfolio and individual stocks are measured.

Through these logical steps, we have a way to calculate the cost of equity as the discount rate used to value the firm's equity.

1. The greater the risk, the greater is the beta.
2. The greater the beta, the greater is the discount rate.
3. The greater the discount rate, the less is the equity value.
4. The less the equity value, the more that the investor's dollar can purchase equity ownership of the firm, and as a result earn an increased rate of return.

In this way, the investor is compensated through the process of equity valuation vis-à-vis cash payments akin to interest payments on debt.

EXAMPLE

Applying Beta 2.0

Think about what a beta of 2.0 means. If the market return is $+R_m$, the particular stock return would be $+2R_m$; and if the market return is $-R_m$, the stock return would be $-2R_m$. It is correlated with the market movement at twice the sensitivity.

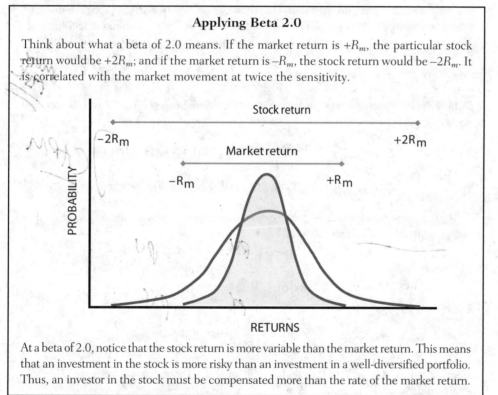

At a beta of 2.0, notice that the stock return is more variable than the market return. This means that an investment in the stock is more risky than an investment in a well-diversified portfolio. Thus, an investor in the stock must be compensated more than the rate of the market return.

It is useful to know certain market benchmarks. For the long-term period 1900–2008, the following are important market benchmarks.*

- Market return R_m: The average return on common stocks is about 11 percent.
- Risk-free return R_f: The average return on Treasury bills is about 4 percent.

---

* Richard A. Brealey, Stewart C. Myers & Franklin Allen, Principles of Corporate Finance, 158 (concise 2d ed., 2011).

- Market risk premium: $R_m - R_f = 7\%$
- Inflation: The average inflation is about 3 percent.

It is important to note that these are long-term averages, and in any given year the market return and the risk-free rates can vary. For instance, on December 31, 2007, the S&P 500 index closed at 1,411.63, and on December 29, 2008, it closed at 903.25, which is a decline of 36 percent. Any investment in the stock market is a risky proposition.

EXAMPLE

How Shareholders Are Compensated, and Why Equity Is Not "Free"

Assume two corporations Acme and Zulu. Corporations are valued based on (1) how much free cash flow they generate in the future (2) discounted by the riskiness of that cash flow (we will study the Discounted Cash Flow method of valuation in the next section). If Acme and Zulu are assumed to exist in perpetuity, we can use the perpetuity formula to discount the free cash flow.

Acme and Zulu have no debt such that their cost of equity is the appropriate discount rate (the cap rate). Both firms have 100 outstanding shares of common stock. Both are expected to generate $1,200 in free cash flow in perpetuity. Assume the following:

$$R_m = 11\% \qquad R_f = 4\% \qquad \beta_{Acme} = 0.86 \qquad \beta_{Zulu} = 1.57 \quad \text{more risk}$$

Zulu is almost twice as risky as Acme as measured by beta. Under CAPM, the cost of equity for each firm is:

Acme $\qquad 0.86 \times (11\% - 4\%) + 4\% = 10\%$

Zulu $\qquad 1.57 \times (11\% - 4\%) + 4\% = 15\%$ CAPM

Using the perpetuity formula and the cost of equity as the capitalization rate, we calculate the present value of all free cash flow as:

$$\text{Acme} = \frac{1,200}{10\%} = 12,000$$

$$\text{Zulu} = \frac{1,200}{15\%} = 8,000$$

Each firm has 100 outstanding shares, and thus the share prices are: Acme $120 per share, and Zulu $80 per share. Why is Zulu share price lower?

Assume that a shareholder has $720 to invest in either Acme or Zulu. The $720 buys the following choices:

Acme $\Rightarrow$ 6 shares at $120 per share, which is 6% of the total equity

Zulu $\Rightarrow$ 9 shares at $80 per share, which is 9% of the total equity

It is important to reiterate that both Acme and Zulu are expected to generate *the same level of free cash flow of $1,200 per year in perpetuity*. Yet with the same $720, the shareholder

---

can buy more Zulu shares than Acme shares. Why? Because Zulu is more risky, as measured by beta. The shareholder must be compensated more for choosing Zulu over Acme. If the investor holds the stock in perpetuity, the investor will get, per the valuation method, the following *gross* payouts (*i.e.*, not discounted):

Acme   ⟹ $72 per year in perpetuity (which is 6% of $1,200 per year)

Zulu   ⟹ $108 per year in perpetuity (which is 9% of $1,200 per year)

Thus, the shareholder is additionally compensated through the valuation process by investing in the more risky Zulu stock. This is what we mean when we say that *the cost of equity is embedded in the company's stock valuation*. The investor is not compensated in cash like an interest payment (because neither corporate law nor the typical corporate charter requires cash payment to shareholders), but instead the shareholder is compensated in the form of valuation, allowing him to purchase more or less of the company for the same dollar depending on the riskiness of that company. Of course, the investment can be converted to cash by selling shares in the market.

Note that a drop in the share price increases the return to prospective *new* shareholders who would get more stock for the same money, thus increasing returns. Obviously, *old* shareholders who bought at a higher price pay the penalty for making a bad stock selection.

Assume that the share price of a company falls on a sustained basis; day-to-day market prices may be volatile, but over a sustained period the share price is falling. Should the company's management be worried? What can an investor do? She can obviously exercise the Wall Street rule and sell the shares, which may decrease the share price more. Alternatively, if she has significant purchasing power, she can acquire more shares. Why might a rational, wealth-maximizing investor want to purchase more shares in a stock that is underperforming? If an investor gains control of the corporation, what can she do?

3. WEIGHTED AVERAGE COST OF CAPITAL

To finance its enterprise, a firm can use a combination of debt, preferred stock, and common stock. Debt and equity are simply means of financing, and an enterprise can use any proportional mix with at least a residual claim. Each form of capital has its own cost as determined by the risk undertaken by the capital provider. This implies that the firm has an average cost of capital that must be weighted for the different forms of capital it deploys, which is the *weighted average cost of capital* (WACC). WACC is the average cost of capital given a firm's capital structure.

$$\text{WACC} = \frac{D}{V} C_d (1 - T) + \frac{P}{V} C_p + \frac{E}{V} C_e$$

Where   V   =   firm value (total debt, preferred and common stock)
            D   =   value of debt
            P   =   value of preferred stock
            E   =   value of common stock (market cap)

C_d = cost of debt (which must be adjusted for the tax shield)
C_p = cost of preferred stock
C_e = cost of equity (as calculated by CAPM)

EXAMPLE

Calculating WACC

Acme Inc. has a firm value of 1,000, which is composed of: 250 debt, 300 preferred stock, and 450 common stock. The interest rate on the debt is 8%. The annual cumulative dividend rate on preferred stock is 9%, which is the cost of the preferred stock. Based on the application of CAPM, the cost of equity is 12%. The tax rate is 35%. What is Acme's WACC?

$$WACC = \frac{250}{1,000} \, 8\% \, (1 - 35\%) + \frac{300}{1,000} \, 8\% + \frac{450}{1,000} \, 12\%$$

$$WACC = 1.3\% + 2.7\% + 5.4\% \quad = \quad 9.4\%$$

Based on Acme's capital structure, its weighted average cost of capital is 9.4%. This is the discount rate that would be used to discount the future free cash flow Acme is expecting. And, the sum of the discounted free cash flow is the theoretical value of the company.

Note that the cost of debt is 5.2% because interest expense is tax deductible, and thus the cost of debt is net of the interest tax shield. However, the cost of the preferred stock is 9% because dividends are paid from net profit and they do not create a tax benefit for the issuing company.

---

4. IMPLICATIONS OF COST OF CAPITAL

The cost of capital is not just an abstract number derived from finance theory. It is a practical tool in the exercise of valuation. Under the discounted cash flow (DCF) method, which is discussed in greater detail in the next chapter, the theoretical value of a corporation is the sum of the future stream of free cash flow available to capital providers that a corporation is expected to generate, discounted by its cost of capital. Conceptually, a DCF analysis is simply a present value calculation. Any present value problem has two variables: What is the expected future return? What is the discount rate R? In a DCF valuation, these variables are: (1) What is the future stream of free cash flow? (2) What is the cost of capital?

WACC is used as the discount rate in the process of valuing a corporation's free cash flow. Valuation is an important part of a business transaction for obvious reasons. A key aspect of any corporate finance transaction is: How much? The values of the stock, debt, assets, and ultimately the corporation are fundamental issues in capital raisings, restructurings, or M&A (mergers and acquisitions) transactions. In the valuation process, the discount rate used to value the corporation's earnings or cash flow is one of the most important inputs.

Outside of any specific transactional context, WACC is important internally to the corporate manager because it is the internal hurdle rate. A corporation rents capital from capital providers. This capital has a cost, which is the expected return of each capital provider. If a corporate manager chooses to put capital to use, then that project must provide sufficient return to meet the cost of the capital.

The cost of capital is an important concept. It tells a manager how much the firm must earn to meet the expectations of its capital providers given that they have other investment opportunities. In the long term, the share price will adjust to meet the expectations of shareholders: *i.e.*, the value of bad companies will decline, and that of good companies will rise. That is the business side of financial management.

What relevance does cost of capital have for a lawyer? It is relevant in several ways. First, the client's concerns must be the lawyer's. Business clients are always seeking ways to enhance value and create wealth, and lawyers help to do this. Second, cost of capital may be central to many corporate transactions for which lawyers will be hired as advisors. Third, valuation is always a critical issue in both capital raisings and mergers and acquisitions. This is true on the transactional side and, for mergers and acquisitions (M&A) specifically, including the litigation practice associated with M&A transactions, because dissenting shareholders are legally entitled under corporate law to an appraisal of their shares if they don't like the consideration offered in a merger or acquisition. The cost of capital is not just an abstract number derived from finance theory. It is a practical tool in the exercise of valuation.

The following case is an appraisal proceeding involving the valuation of the dissenting shareholder's common stock. The litigation lasted several decades, and it was extraordinarily complex and convoluted. The trial court's opinion below was appealed, and on appeal, *Cede & Co. v. Technicolor, Inc.*, 884 A.2d 26 (Del. 2005) ("*Technicolor VI*"), the Delaware Supreme Court noted:

> This is the sixth appeal by Cinerama relating either to its statutory appraisal proceeding or its shareholder rescissory damages lawsuit for fraud and unfair dealing. As the Court of Chancery correctly noted, the history of this 'sempiternal appraisal action' is thoroughly recorded in the annals of Delaware corporate law. *See Cede & Co. v. Technicolor, Inc.,* 542 A.2d 1182 (Del. 1988) ("*Technicolor I*"); *Cede & Co. v. Technicolor, Inc.,* 634 A.2d 345 (Del. 1993), *modified,* 636 A.2d 956 (Del. 1994) ("*Technicolor II*"); *Cinerama, Inc. v. Technicolor, Inc.,* 663 A.2d 1156 (Del. 1995) ("*Technicolor III*"); *Cede & Co. v. Technicolor, Inc.,* 684 A.2d 289 (Del. 1996) ("*Technicolor IV*"); *Cede & Co. v. Technicolor, Inc.,* 758 A.2d 485 (Del. 2000) ("*Technicolor V*").

The ultimate question in any appraisal proceeding is the value of the asset being appraised. To ascertain the value of common stock, the court, working with the litigating parties, their lawyers and experts, engages in a rigorous valuation exercise.

Cede & Co. v. Technicolor, Inc.
2003 WL 24700218 (Del. Ch. 2003)

CHANDLER, Chancellor.

This case involves the appraisal of 201,200 shares [4.4% of common stock] of Technicolor, Inc. owned by Cinerama, Inc. The litigation began in 1983. There

73

have been five remands by the Supreme Court and two appraisal trials before two different trial judges. The second appraisal trial was completed in May 2003. This is the Court's decision, following the May 2003 trial and post-trial briefing.

For the reasons that follow, I conclude that the per share going concern value of Technicolor at the time of the merger, taking into account the implementation of the so-called Perelman plan, is $21.98 per share. Cinerama is entitled to $21.98 per share, or $4,422,376.

Only a brief review of the facts will be given since the history of this action is thoroughly recorded in the annals of Chancery litigation. In the early 1980s, MacAndrews and Forbes Group ("MAF"), through a wholly-owned subsidiary, sought to purchase Technicolor. On December 31, 1982, MAF closed a public cash tender offer at $23.00 per share for up to all of the Technicolor common stock. All but 17.81% of the outstanding stock was tendered. On January 24, 1983, a cash-out merger occurred, converting all common stock not owned by MAF into the right to receive $23.00 in cash. Cinerama, Inc., a beneficial shareholder that owned 201,200 Technicolor shares through its nominee, Cede & Co., dissented from the merger and sought judicial appraisal of its stock under 8 Del. C. §262.

[To conduct the appraisal under DGCL §262, the court conducted a highly detailed DCF analysis based on fact-finding related to projections of financial performance and the calculation of free cash flows. In the final step of the DCF analysis, the court calculated the WACC, which became the discount rate used to discount the free cash flow.]

Now that the forecasted cash flows are determined, I need to discount those cash flows to their present value. The Weighted Average Cost of Capital ("WACC") is used to determine the discount rate based on Technicolor's cost of capital. WACC is equal to the sum of: (1) the percentage of the capital structure financed with equity multiplied by the cost of equity capital; and (2) the percentage of the capital structure financed with debt multiplied by the after-tax cost of debt.* Each of these inputs will be determined to establish Technicolor's WACC.

Capital Structure
Long-Term Debt

To determine Technicolor's debt-to-equity capital structure, I must first determine Technicolor's outstanding long-term debt at the time of the merger. The only financial statement available to determine Technicolor's debt is the Macanfor consolidated statement dated December 31, 1982. Macanfor was created solely to merge with Technicolor. Therefore, the debt listed on that financial statement is limited to the debt used to purchase Technicolor and the debt attributable to Technicolor itself. All but $21.3 million is attributable to the purchase of Technicolor. The debt used to acquire the company cannot be figured into the calculation when determining Technicolor's long-term debt. Since all the remaining debt is Technicolor's, the resulting long-term debt of Technicolor is $21.3 million.

Cinerama asserts that only $19.9 million should be attributable to long-term debt because this is the figure that appears on MAF's 1983 10-K Annual Report filed with

---

* Author's note: The company did not have preferred stock.

74

the SEC. This figure reflects MAF's bank loan agreement, that called for all outstanding, pre-existing Technicolor debt to be repaid by January 24, 1983, subject to a limitation that the debt *could not exceed $20 million*. Appropriately, the MAF 10-K stated that the $19.9 million in Technicolor pre-existing debt was repaid to the bank on January 24, 1983. The MAF 10-K, however, is not the best evidence available, as it merely reports the payment of Technicolor debt that was capped at $20 million and, therefore, was not necessarily an accurate reflection of the true outstanding Technicolor debt.

Debt-to-Equity Capital Structure

It seems hardly necessary to state that the capital structure of Technicolor at the time of the merger is the best indication of the capital structure of the company in determining its future value.

I estimate Technicolor's capitalization by using the purchase price at the time of the merger—$105.1 million. Using the long-term debt of $21.3 million, the total capital is $126.4 million. Therefore, of the total capital, 16.9% [= 21.3 ÷ 126.4] was debt and 83.1% [= 105.1 ÷ 126.4] was equity.

Cost of Equity Capital

The cost of equity capital is the risk-free rate of return plus Technicolor's risk under the Perelman plan. Risk is determined by multiplying Technicolor's beta[315] by the equity risk premium. The required inputs to be determined are (1) the risk-free rate of return; (2) Technicolor's beta; and (3) the equity risk premium.

Risk-free Rate

Cinerama uses a risk-free rate of 10.37%, based on U.S. Treasury Bonds with greater than ten years to maturity without citing to any source. Technicolor uses a risk-free rate of 10.88% based on the 30-Year Total Constant Maturity Yield as of January 24, 1983, citing the Federal Reserve's website as its source. According to the Federal Reserve, the risk-free rate never dropped below 10.39% the entire month of January 1983, and varied between 10.39% and 10.99% for that month. I think it is reasonable to adopt the risk-free rate on the closing date of the merger, which was 10.88%.

Technicolor's Beta

Beta measures the relative risk of a company. Torkelsen [Cinerama expert] does not calculate a beta specific to Technicolor, but instead makes an *assumption* that it should be around one without any verifiable reason other than his own opinion. Easton [Technicolor expert] lists the various betas for Technicolor from January 1980 through December 1982, listing separate periods with varying betas. Five different sources are used for the historical betas. Easton then averages Technicolor

---

315. Beta measures the relative risk of a company. Beta is "a measure of systematic risk of a security; the tendency of a security's returns to correlate with swing in the broad market." Shannon P. Pratt et al., Valuing a Business, Appendix A at 912 (4th ed. 2000). For example, a beta of 1 indicates that the security's price will rise and fall with the market. A beta greater than 1 indicates that its price will be more volatile than the market. And a beta less than 1 means that it will be less volatile than the market.

beta from January 1980 through December 1982, ending with a *pre-Perelman plan beta* of 1.43.

Since I am required to evaluate Technicolor under the Perelman plan, and not the Kamerman plan,[*] I am concerned that using the two-year historical beta created under the Kamerman plan would be viewed as an error by the Supreme Court. Thus, I will use the average beta for December 1982 (after the Perelman plan became the guiding force for Technicolor) as the appropriate beta. That beta, which is equal to 1.60, is appropriate because it incorporates the risks of the Perelman plan, as is indicated by the increase in Technicolor's post-offer, pre-Perelman beta (1.57) to the post-Perelman beta (1.60). It thus takes account of the market's perception of the changing riskiness of an investment in Technicolor after the tender offer, and for that reason is the most appropriate beta.

It is standard to use the derivable beta from market information when valuing a public company. As stated earlier in this opinion, Technicolor was in a highly competitive industry with a small customer base. It had already lost its United Artists contract, and was facing increased competition. The videocassette business was suspect in its potential, and there was no guarantee as to the sale or purchase price of the divisions Perelman sought to sell. Coupled with a new business plan, the Technicolor beta of 1.60 in December 1982, *as actually reflected by the market*, is the most accurate indication for purposes of valuing the company. Accordingly, I use a beta equal to 1.60 for my calculation.

Equity Risk Premium

Cinerama uses the average equity risk premium for long-term market risk in 1982, which is 8.3%. Cinerama states that the arithmetic mean of the differences between returns on common stock and the risk-free rate is most commonly used. Technicolor lists both the geometric and arithmetic means, but comes up with a slightly different number of 7.2% for the arithmetic mean.

Easton, however, uses a different equity risk premium for his discount rate calculation. In his review of the previous trial he found an equity risk premium equal to 4.6%. He did not independently verify this number, but yet deems it reliable for his use. Since my mandate was to hold a completely new trial, I choose not to use an unverified equity risk premium from the first trial. Instead, I agree with Cinerama's assertion that the arithmetic mean of the differences is the best source for the equity risk premium. Cinerama's arithmetic mean is based on 1982 historical averages. Technicolor's is based on the mean at the time of the merger. Recognizing the differences between the two experts, I find that Technicolor's arithmetic mean at the time of the merger is the more appropriate value to determine Technicolor's cost of capital. Accordingly, the equity risk premium is 7.2%.

---

[*] Author's note: The Perelman plan was the set of financial projections assuming a corporate strategy developed by the acquirer Perelman of MAF. The Kamerman plan was management's competing strategy. Previously, the Delaware Supreme Court held that the Perelman plan "was the operative reality on the date of the merger," and thus in an appraisal proceeding the value must be based on the going concern as represented in the Perelman plan at the time of the merger. *Cede & Co. v. Technicolor, Inc.*, 684 A.2d 289, 299 (Del. 1996).

Conclusion *equity risk premium (Rm - Rf)*

Using the formula that Technicolor's cost of equity capital equals the risk-free rate added to the product of beta multiplied by the equity risk premium, I find this value to be 22.4% (*i.e.,* 10.88% + (1.60) x (7.2%) = 22.4%). *Cost of capital / equity*

After-tax Cost of Debt

The after-tax cost of debt is equal to the cost of debt multiplied by the difference of one minus the tax rate (*i.e.,* (cost of debt) x (1—tax rate)). The cost of debt is the borrowing cost of Technicolor at the valuation date. Cinerama does not analyze any borrowing cost, but simply assumes that the prime rate should be the borrowing cost. Technicolor evaluates the borrowing cost as equivalent to the rate paid in acquiring Technicolor. Macanfor had a credit facility at 13.0% and a note payable to its parent at 15.625%. Easton weighted the interest in proportion to the balance of each debt to obtain a borrowing cost of 13.96%. I find this to be a more accurate borrowing cost than the prime rate since it accurately reflects the rate at which Technicolor would borrow under the Perelman plan. Using the 46% tax rate agreed upon by both experts, the resulting after-tax cost of debt is 7.54% (*i.e.,* (13.96%) x (1—46%) = 7.54%). *p. 43*

Technicolor's Cost of Capital

Using all of the above inputs, I obtain the resulting discount rate:

WACC λ =   (cost of equity capital) x (percentage of equity capital structure) +
              (after-tax cost of debt) x (percentage of debt capital structure)

=   (22.40) x (0.831) + (7.54) x (0.169) = 19.89 %.

The Final Valuation of Technicolor Under the Perelman Plan

[Using the WACC, the court calculated the present value of the projected free cash flows of the retained and sold businesses.] To determine the final valuation of Technicolor per share, I sum the value of the retained businesses and the sold businesses, subtract the value of the outstanding debt, and divide by the number of outstanding shares.

$$\frac{\text{Total Equity Value} \quad \$100,412,374}{\text{Shares Outstanding} \quad 4,567,491} = \$21.98 \text{ per share}$$

QUESTIONS

1. The court used 10.88 percent as the risk-free rate. This seems very high compared to the yields on Treasuries in the 2014–2015 economic environment. For example, on Friday, November 28, 2014, the yield on the 30-year Treasury bond closed at 2.91 percent. What generally accounts for the approximately 8 percent difference?
2. If the corporate tax rate was 35 percent, what would be the WACC based on the court's calculations?

NOTES

1. Because there were numerous proceedings over two decades of litigation, there were significant established facts constituting the law of the case. On appeal, the Delaware Supreme Court reversed the trial court's finding of 19.89 percent WACC and corporate debt of $21.3 million based on the doctrine of the law of the case. *Cede & Co. v. Technicolor, Inc.*, 884 A.2d 26, 38-41 (Del. 2005). The court held that based on the law of the case the proper WACC was 15.28 percent and corporate debt was $19.9 million. Based on these figures, it held that the fair value per share was $28.41. *Id.* at 30.

2. Based on the court's calculation of $28.41 per share, the implied total equity value was $129,762,419. This is a difference of $29.3 million. Since the difference in the debt amounts are not significant ($21.3 million versus $19.9 million), most of this amount is attributable to the difference in the cost of capital of 4.71 percent. The court's use of a lower discount rate resulted in an increase in the value of the corporation by approximately $29 million. Do you see why the discount rate in any present value calculation is so important?

D. SECURITY MARKET LINE

The concept of beta—that stocks can be empirically measured in their sensitivity to the market return—leads to a very simple idea: All stocks rest on a sloping line called the security market line. The security market line says that as risk increases, the expected return must also increase in a precise mathematical relationship such that stocks literally "line up" on the security market line. The security market line starts from the risk-free rate and slopes upward along the risk-return continuum.

Consider the following example. The risk-free rate is the yield on Treasury bills. A diversified portfolio has a beta of 1.0, which means that the portfolio's return mimics the market's movements and earns the average return on the market of R_m. Security A returns R_f with a beta of 0.5. Security B returns R_{2m} with a beta of 1.5.

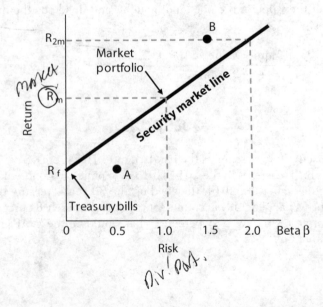

Can a stock lie below the security market line such as Stock A? No. For a beta of 0.5, the investor in Stock A gets a return of R_f. For this rate, she can simply buy Treasuries and assume no risk. If she seeks to assume the risk of a beta 0.5, she can get greater returns through an alternative investment. With the same amount of money, she can invest in a 50/50 mix of Treasury bills and a market portfolio which creates a return resting on the security market line with a beta of 0.5. The return would be $(R_m + R_f)/2$, which is more than simply R_f. Thus, if Stock A really sits below the security market line, its share price would drop until the return to the shareholder increases to $(R_m + R_f)/2$.

Can a stock lie above the security market line such as Stock B? No. If such opportunity exists, other investors would soon see an arbitrage opportunity (a chance to make *abnormal* profit). Remember the market is full of bad *and* good investors. The "smart money" would buy Stock B, increasing its price until the return on the stock declines, in accordance to the risk—return continuum of the security market line.

In essence, the security market line says that there is a perfect risk-return continuum in which riskier securities should earn greater return in a precise linear manner.

CHAPTER

3

VALUATION

In most corporate finance transactions, valuation is *the* most important issue. In capital raisings, issuers want the highest value for stock and the lowest interest rate for bonds, both of which depend on the value and the financial quality of the company. Mergers and acquisition transactions hinge on an acceptable acquisition price; and if the merger consideration is in the securities of the acquirer, valuation becomes doubly important. In a bankruptcy or restructuring, the ability of the debtor to get financing depends on its value. At the most basic level, corporate transactions are market transactions between buyers and sellers and there must be an agreed price. Valuation sets the price of things (securities and business assets), and prices are fundamental to economic transactions.

Valuation provides a value to the currency of exchange in many business transactions. The currency of cash is easily understood and fairly incontestable: In present value, a dollar is a dollar. However, many business transactions are not in cash, for example: (1) A company buys an asset or another company by issuing its stock; (2) a company takes a stake in a joint venture by contributing a vital asset; or (3) a company buys back its shares from a significant shareholder by distributing a business unit. Valuation provides a basis for doing business deals.

Lawyers will not be asked to conduct valuations of companies. Investment bankers typically do this work. However, lawyers should know the foundational concepts of valuation because it is important to understand the deal economics and the legal documentation in many corporate transactions discuss or analyze valuation. These documents include fairness opinions, merger proxies, securities prospectuses, offering letters, and term sheets. Valuation is important in the process of fulfilling a board's fiduciary duty, judicial appraisal proceedings, and securities litigation. Furthermore, it is not uncommon for modern lawyers to become board members or business managers rising as high as the CEO level.* Lawyers are also entrepreneurs who start their own businesses, and they frequently advise entrepreneurial firms on general business

---

* In a 2014 survey, the top 25 law schools placed a total of 1,299 JD graduates serving as officers or directors of U.S. public companies. Robert Anderson, *JDs in the Boardroom*, Witnesseth: Law, Deals, & Data (Dec. 1, 2014) (ranking based on per capita number of graduates), available at *http://witnesseth.typepad.com/blog/2014/12/jds-in-the-boardroom-2014-edition.html*. There are approximately 200 accredited law schools. Based on this list of only the top 25 schools, we can infer that there are many thousands of lawyers serving as directors and officers in U.S. public companies. Furthermore, public companies are only a subset of business corporations. There are privately held corporations for which there are no public disclosures. We can infer that there are many more thousands of lawyers serving as officers, directors, and business managers of private corporations.

issues. A business lawyer must understand the foundational concepts in valuation not because they will be asked to do it, but because valuation is always on the client's mind.

Value can be thought of in a number of ways. There is not a single concept or number associated with value. Liquidation value is the value of the assets net of liabilities in a windup. Book value is the value of the equity as stated in the balance sheet. These values may diverge greatly from the *market value* and the *theoretical intrinsic value* of the company. Financial statements do not always reflect economic reality, and the circumstance of liquidation may yield values of assets that may be different from their values as a part of a going concern. This chapter focuses on economic value of a corporation as a going concern based on market and theoretical valuations.

A. MARKET MULTIPLES

1. HOW MULTIPLES WORK

Multiples are useful because they communicate the value of a firm. Some uninformed people believe that stock price communicates the value of a firm. This is wrong. The stock price is, among other things, a function of the number of shares outstanding, and in this sense it is an arbitrary number. It has one function: The stock price tells us how much an investor must pay to buy one share of stock in the company. The stock price, in and of itself, communicates no other information. The value of a company is gleaned from the multiples of financial benchmarks the company is trading. Multiples tell us the quality of a firm's market valuation—whether the company is valued high or low.

What are market multiples? They are ratios of the trading value of the company to some selected financial benchmarks. The typical benchmarks used are revenue, EBIT, EBITDA, net income, and book value.

EXAMPLE

Comparing Google and McDonald's

Google and McDonald's are entirely unrelated businesses. It makes no sense to compare their financial performances (*e.g.*, did McDonald's earn more profit than Google?). However, we can compare their valuations for the purpose of answering whether the financial market values Google more than McDonald's, or whether innovative tech companies are valued more than innovative fast-food companies. The answers may give us relevant insights. The information below is relevant to making a comparison of valuation between Google and McDonald's.

(AS OF DEC. 31, 2010)	GOOGLE	MCDONALD'S
Share price	$593.97	$76.76
Earnings per share (EPS)	$26.69	$4.64
Price-to-earnings ratio (P/E)	22.3x	16.5x
Net income	$8.505 billion	$4.946 billion
Shares outstanding	0.321 billion	1.053 billion
Market cap	$191 billion	$81 billion

Google share price is 7.74x more than McDonald's share price. Does this mean that Google is 7.74x more valuable?

No. The share price, *in and of itself*, is an arbitrary number. It simply indicates how much money is required to purchase one share of stock. If Google split its stock 2-for-1 (each shareholder trades in 1 old share and gets 2 new shares) such that the shares outstanding would increase from 0.321 to 0.642 billion shares, then Google share price would decrease to $296.99 per share. Similarly, McDonald's can do a reverse stock split 1-for-7.74 (each shareholder trades in 7.74 old shares and gets 1 new share), and increase McDonald's share price from $76.76 to $593.97 at that exact moment.

Google earned 1.72x more net income than McDonald's. Does this mean that Google is 1.72x more valuable?

No. Net income is simply an indication of how much quantity of profit a firm generated. The number *alone* is not a measure of value.

How do we compare the value of Google and McDonald's?

One comparison is the P/E multiple. The P/E multiple says that Google's equity value is 22.3x its net income, whereas McDonald's equity value is 16.5x its net income. Thus, the market is valuing Google at a higher level than McDonald's by assigning a market multiple that is higher than that of McDonald's.

2. ENTERPRISE VALUE MULTIPLES

The first set of commonly used market multiples are multiples of enterprise value (or sometimes called firm value) to revenue, EBIT, and EBITDA.

$$\text{Revenue Multiple} = \frac{\text{Enterprise Value}}{\text{Revenue}}$$

$$\text{EBIT Multiple} = \frac{\text{Enterprise Value}}{\text{EBIT}}$$

$$\text{EBITDA Multiple} = \frac{\text{Enterprise Value}}{\text{EBITDA}}$$

Enterprise value (EV) is the market value of all securities issued by the company.

$$\text{Enterprise Value} = \text{Net Debt} + \text{Market Value of Equity}$$

The market capitalization of equity is the market values of preferred stock (if any) and common stock. Net debt is debt net of cash in excess of working capital requirements. The implication of net debt is that excess cash can be used to pay off debt.

Why are revenue, EBIT, and EBITDA used as the financial benchmarks, but not net income? Revenue, EBIT, and EBITDA are *above* the tax line, and thus are financial outputs claimed by *all* capital providers (creditors and shareholders). Net income is a financial claim exclusive to shareholders. Creditors do not share in the net income because they have already been paid above the tax line as "interest expense." Therefore, it would make no sense to derive multiples of enterprise value to net income. Similarly, it would make no sense to derive multiples of market capitalization (the market value of equity securities) to revenue, EBIT, and EBITDA, because these financial benchmarks are shared by all capital providers and not just shareholders. Doing so would be akin to using Celsius as the temperature unit when the cooking instructions direct that the temperature is measured in Fahrenheit.

3. EQUITY VALUE MULTIPLES

Multiples of only equity value can be calculated. The first prominently used multiple is the price-to-earnings (P/E) ratio, which is the ratio of market price of stock to net income.

$$\text{Price/Earnings Ratio} = \frac{\text{Market Cap}}{\text{Earnings}} = \frac{\text{Stock Price}}{\text{EPS}}$$

The P/E multiple says that the market value of the company's equity can be measured as a multiple of its earnings. A larger multiple indicates greater value.

Another prominently used equity value multiple is the price-to-book (P/B) ratio, which is the ratio of market price of stock to book value.

$$\text{Price/Book Ratio} = \frac{\text{Market Cap}}{\text{Book Value}}$$

The P/B ratio measures the ratio of market value of stock to the book value. Recall that the value of equity can be stated as either an accounting value, or as a market value. Book value is equity stated in the balance sheet, which is a value assigned by accountants. The P/B ratio measures the degree of deviation between the market and book values of equity.

Why are net income and book value compared to market cap? Market cap is the market value of *equity*. Net income is the claim of equityholders after creditors are paid. Book value is the equity in the financial statements. Thus, P/E and P/B are multiples measured on a like-for-like metric.

EXAMPLE

> **Market Value Versus Book Value**
>
> Let's work through some numbers to illustrate the difference between market cap and book value.
>
> A significant disparity between book and market values is not so unusual. Compare the market capitalizations, book values, and P/B ratios of the companies below as of the date of their balance sheets.

AS OF 12/31/2010	NO. SHARES ($m)		SHARE PRICE		MARKET CAP ($m)		BOOK VALUE ($m)		P/B RATIO
Coca Cola	[2,292	x	$65.77	=	150,744]	÷	31,317	=	4.81x
McDonald's	[1,053	x	$76.76	=	80,828]	÷	14,634	=	5.52x
United Technologies	[921	x	$78.72	=	72,501]	÷	22,332	=	3.25x

Another illustration of the difference between market and book values is the case of Ford Motor Co. In its 2010 annual report, Ford reported the following balance sheet information (as of year ended December 31 and in $millions).

- Assets: $164,687
- Liabilities: 165,329
- Equity: (642)

Ford had 3.707 billion common shares outstanding, and the stock price closed on December 31, 2010, at $16.79. Thus, the market capitalization of Ford's common stock was $62 billion. The accountants said that Ford had a negative net worth of $642 million, but the market said that Ford's equity was worth $62 billion.

The important lessons here are: (1) It is not so unusual to find a company with negative book value, and (2) the fact that there is a negative book value does not necessarily mean that the company is troubled or is a bad company, but one must understand the entire circumstance including the market value of the company.

4. COMPARABLE COMPANIES ANALYSIS

Multiples are useful in valuing and assessing companies. In some sense, it is not particularly useful to compare companies like McDonald's and Google. They have very little in common, and the only thing that we can say about their multiples is that at a particular moment in time Google seems to be valued higher than McDonald's. On the other hand, a comparison of McDonald's to Wendy's or Burger King would be highly relevant because they are comparable companies. Relative valuation among peers is important. If Burger King is valued lower than McDonald's, its management and board would need to know why and attempt to at least achieve parity with McDonald's (its shareholders would demand it).

Multiples are also useful to conduct a comparable companies valuation. Suppose a company is privately held and there are no trading market values of its securities, yet it engages in corporate transactions where the value of its stock must be assessed. These transactions can be, for example, private capital raisings or a sale of the company. A comparable companies analysis is a valuation based on a comparison to the market multiples of peer companies. This analysis uses market values of peer companies that are publicly to calculate the implied value of the company in question. The most important facet of this analysis is to select the most appropriate comparables. Proverbially speaking, it makes no sense to compare apples to oranges.

By using the multiples of publicly traded comparable companies, an analyst can calculate the implied value of the subject company's enterprise and equity values.

EXAMPLE

Advising In-N-Out Burger on Strategic Alternatives

If you are an aficionado of hamburgers and have lived in Western states like Arizona and California, you may know that In-N-Out Burger makes wonderful fast food. In-N-Out is a private company, and its stock is owned by the Snyder family. Suppose the family is "exploring strategic alternatives," which is a signal that the company is considering some major corporate transaction: perhaps either selling shares to the public or selling the entire company to an acquirer like McDonald's. A deal team of investment bankers, lawyers, and accountants is assembled. An important consideration is the value of In-N-Out.

Step 1: What are reasonable comparables for In-N-Out Burger?

McDonald's and Burger King are very good comparables. McDonald's is a public company. On October 19, 2010, Burger King was acquired by an affiliate of 3G Capital, and ceased to be a publicly traded company (a transaction called "going private"). However, significant data exists because it was a public company. Other comparables are Wendy's and Arby's, two smaller fast-food chains operated by Wendy's Arby's Group, Inc., a public company. From this rich set of data, we can construct a comparable companies analysis. (This example assumes 2010-2011 period.)

Step 2: Construct a comparable companies analysis for McDonald's, Burger King, and Wendy's Arby's (data as of each company's fiscal year end).

(IN $MILLIONS)	MCDONALD'S	BURGER KING	WENDY'S	AVERAGE
Values of securities				
Market cap	80,874	2,237	1,919	NA
Long-term debt	11,497	667	1,553	NA
Enterprise value	92,371	2,904	3,472	NA
Financial data				
Book value	14,634	1,128	2,163	NA
Net income	4,946	186	(4.3)	NA
EBIT	7,431	332	132	NA
EBITDA	8,607	443	314	NA
Multiples				
P/B	5.5x	2.0x	0.9x	2.8x
P/E	16.4x	12.0x	−446.3x (na)	14.2x
EV/EBIT	12.4x	8.7x	26.3x (na)	10.1x
EV/EBITDA	10.7x	6.6x	11.1x (na)	8.7x

Note: The average P/E and EV multiples used only McDonald's and Burger King as the figures for Wendy's are unreliable because of financial problems at the company. These kinds of ad hoc adjustments in valuation studies are common, which suggests that valuation is as much based on subjective judgment as it is on the science of economics.

The accounting and financial data communicate much information about the fast-food industry. It says that McDonald's is the clear market leader, judging by the combination of size and premium valuation relative to its competitors. Making a profit in the restaurant business may be hard (see the experience of Wendy's).

Step 3: Derive valuation of In-N-Out using the company's financial data.

If we were actually advising In-N-Out, we would get private information on the firm. Because that information is not publicly available, the following analysis uses hypothetical numbers for In-N-Out's financial performance.

(IN $MILLIONS)	BOOK VALUE	NET INCOME	EBIT	EBITDA
In-N-Out's financial data	110	25	40	50
	x	x	x	x
Multiple	2.8	14.2	10.1	8.7
	=	=	=	=
Equity value	308	355		
Enterprise value			404	435
In-N-Out's debt	___	___	40	40
Implied equity value	308	355	364	395

The valuation range for In-N-Out is from about $300 to $400 million based on this multiples analysis. This is a broad range, but such ranges are not unusual. Valuation is part science and part art. This range also leaves much to be negotiated in a transaction with interested parties, and lawyers may be major players.

Parenthetically, note that if In-N-Out's true comparable is not the average multiples of publicly traded fast-food companies, which includes McDonald's, but is instead Burger King, the multiples used would be lower and thus In-N-Out's value range would be lower as well. The multiples themselves are subject to negotiations.

This is only a hypothetical. As of 2011, a sale of the company was not in the immediate future: "In-N-Out remains privately owned and the Snyder family has no plans to take the company public or franchise any units." *http://www.in-n-out.com/history.asp* (as of June 14, 2011). Since then, there is no public comment on the company's website concerning its intent to remain private (last visited December 7, 2014).

The following case provides an example of how a court uses a multiples-based valuation analysis to value the common stock in question.

Agranoff v. Miller
734 A.2d 1066 (Del. Ch. 1999)

STRINE, Vice Chancellor.

[The defendant unlawfully acquired warrants to purchase shares of EMS Corp. as part of a deceptive scheme to take over the company. The right to purchase these warrants, which are company issued options to purchase its shares, belonged to the plaintiffs. The court held that the remedy required a determination of the hypothetical price at which the plaintiffs could have purchased the warrants. This required a valuation of EMS's principal asset, which was a 62 percent stake in Express Messenger Systems, Inc. The court determined that the fair market value of the warrants was $41.02, and it used a market multiple analysis to calculate this value.]

The parties both utilized highly qualified experts in support of their positions regarding valuation. For his part, Miller proffered the testimony of Professor Donald Puglisi, the MBNA America Business Professor and Professor of Finance at the University of Delaware. The plaintiffs submitted the testimony of Morton Mark Lee, a recently retired partner of KMPG LLP and now a senior managing director at Sutter Securities, a professional with thirty years of experience in valuing businesses. Both experts provided the court with helpful testimony.

As a frame for valuing EMS however, Puglisi's analysis is the preferable one. The Puglisi analysis focused on three variations of the comparable companies method of valuation, involving multiples based on EMS's revenues (the "Revenues Analysis"), earnings before interest and taxes ("EBIT"), and earnings before interest, taxes, depreciation, and amortization ("EBITDA"). The Puglisi analysis was also very user-friendly, and enabled the reader to follow the steps he used in computing his comparable companies valuation. Puglisi's report also acknowledged that a discounted cash flow ("DCF") approach would have been viable, had reliable projections of EMS's performance for the relevant time period been available. But Puglisi considered the projections that EMS had to be wildly unreliable and overly optimistic. Thus, he believed that a reliable DCF valuation was not possible.

· Lee used a wider variety of valuation methods. Although Lee also believed that EMS's projections were unreliable, he purported to base a DCF analysis on a substantial negative revision of those projections that he came up with after discussions with EMS managers after the valuation date. That is, Lee discussed the projections for the years following 1998 with managers who knew what the actual results of those later years were. Based on these conversations, Lee developed revised projections that he plugged into a DCF model.

I refuse to give any weight to this technique and therefore to Lee's DCF analysis. The possibility of hindsight bias and other cognitive distortions seems untenably high. Consider this analogy. Suppose there was an interview with Sir George Martin from 1962 in which he opined as to how many number one songs he thought would be released by his new protégés, the Beatles. Could one fast-forward to 1971, interview Martin, and revise Martin's earlier projection in some reliable way, recognizing that Martin would have known the correct answer as of that date? How could Martin provide information that would not be possibly influenced in some way by his knowledge of the actual success enjoyed by the Beatles and his recollection of his earlier projection? The parties have approached this valuation exercise with the mutual understanding that they could not consider the actual results for EMS past the valuation date of October 1998. Lee's DCF analysis seems like an unreliable way to have those actual results influence the court's valuation in an indirect manner that is not susceptible to fair evaluation. Nor have the plaintiffs provided finance literature supporting the acceptance of Lee's approach to projection modification. Likewise, I also give no weight to Lee's valuations that are based solely on equity, rather than entity, valuation techniques. These techniques do not consider the different capital structures of corporations.

Instead, I choose to focus on the three variations of the comparable companies method of valuation that both Puglisi and Lee agree are appropriate tools to value EMS: analyses based on multiples of Revenues, EBIT and EBITDA. The comparable companies method of valuation determines the equity value of the company by: (1) identifying comparable publicly traded companies; (2) deriving appropriate valuation multiples from the comparable companies; (3) adjusting those multiples to account for the differences from the[1] company being valued and the comparables; and (4) applying those multiples to the revenues, earnings, or other values for the company being valued. Comparable companies analyses are frequently calculated on a debt free basis, to derive the fair market value of the company's market value of invested capital ("MVIC"). The company's equity value is derived by subtracting the company's interest bearing debt from the company's MVIC.

[The court noted various objections and problems with the experts' analyses and methods.]

With these objections out of the way, the court can display its valuation of EMS—putting aside for a moment the question of whether a premium should be added because the BT Warrants constituted a substantial block of EMS voting power and whether a marketability discount should be subtracted because EMS shares were not traded on public markets. In coming to this intermediate step, I use Puglisi's approach of giving equal weight to the Revenues, EBIT, and EBITDA approaches and adopt his EBIT and EBITDA multiples. This analysis yields a value of $41.02 for the Warrants Shares, computed as follows:

	With Selected Revenue Multiple	With Selected EBITDA Multiple	With Selected EBIT Multiple	Average of Three Approaches
Express Revenues, EBITDA, EBIT ($000)	$50,313	$1,520	$960	N/A
EV/Multipliers	0.28	5.97	9.70	N/A
Express Enterprise Value ($000)	$14,088	$9,074	$9,312	$10,825
Less Express Net Debt ($000)	$1,951	$1,951	$1,951	$1,951
Plus Value of Express NOL Carryfoward[1] (thousands)	$1,938	$1,938	$1,938	$1,938
Value of Common Stock ($000)	$14,075	$9,061	$9,299	$10,812
EMS Ownership of Express	[62%]	[62%]	[62%]	[62%]
Value of EMS Holding of Express Common Stock ($000)	$8,727	$5,618	$5,765	$6,703
Number of Shares of EMS Common Stock	163,403	163,403	163,403	163,403
Value per Share of EMS Common Stock	$53.40	$34.38	$35.28	$41.02

---

1. NOL carryfoward is net operating loss that may be carried forward as a tax deduction against future earnings. It is a tax benefit, and thus has value.

[Note: EMS was a holding company for 62 percent of the stock of an operating company called Express Messenger Systems, Inc. ("Express"). EMS's value constituted 62 percent of Express. Accordingly, Express is the real subject of the valuation.]

QUESTIONS

1. Which multiple in the court's analysis produced the greatest value?
2. In calculating the equity value, why is net debt subtracted from the enterprise value?
3. Why did the court not use a DCF analysis as another method of valuation in addition to the comparable companies analysis?
4. Why was the average of the three multiples used?

B. DISCOUNTED CASH FLOW ANALYSIS

The discounted cash flow (DCF) method is a valuation model that produces a theoretical value of the firm. What is the value of a corporation? It has no aesthetic value like art. Owning stock does not give us inherent pleasure like a hug from a loved one. There is only one measure of value: How much cash will the corporation generate after payment to everyone else?

The DCF calculates the sum of the future stream of free cash flow available to all capital providers discounted by the firm's cost of capital. A properly conducted DCF analysis is a very complex study requiring expert hands. Lawyers will not be asked to conduct such analysis, but they should understand the basic concept.

Conceptually, a DCF analysis is nothing more than a present value calculation. Any present value problem has two large variables: the expected future value, and the discount rate. In a DCF valuation, these variables are: (1) the future stream of free cash flow, and (2) the firm's cost of capital. An investor pays dollars today (a cash outflow) in the purchase of a financial instrument for the promise of dollars tomorrow. The value of a corporation is the sum of the future stream of free cash flow discounted by the firm's cost of capital.

A going concern is a firm that operates indefinitely into the future, resulting in the expectation of free cash flow (FCF) in perpetuity. The typical DCF model is divided into two time periods: (1) a forecast period constituting the first several years of projections; and (2) a perpetuity period constituting the remaining time in perpetuity. The typical forecast period of modeling is anywhere from 5 to 20 years (practices by professionals can vary). The value attributable to the perpetuity period, called the terminal (or continuing or residual) value, constitutes the perpetuity stream of cash flow after the final year of the forecast period. The terminal value is typically calculated under the perpetuity formula or its cousin, the growth perpetuity formula, using WACC as the capitalization rate.

$$\text{Terminal Value} = \frac{\text{FCF (Final Year)}}{\text{WACC} - g}$$

(The value g represents the perpetual growth rate of the FCF.)

Once the forecast of the free cash flow is made, the last step in the DCF analysis is to discount the free cash flow using the firm's WACC. The illustration below summarizes the DCF analysis. The free cash flows ($FCF_1 \ldots FCF_N$) are the free cash flows for the forecast period ($1 \ldots N$), and the free cash flows ($FCF_{(N+1)} \ldots FCF_\infty$) are the free cash flows for the perpetuity period. Together, these cash flows constitute the entire stream of free cash that the firm is expected to generate and that is available to all capital providers. This stream of cash must be discounted in a way that reflects its riskiness, which is the firm's WACC.

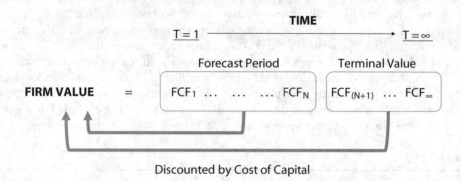

Discounted by Cost of Capital

1. FREE CASH FLOW

The first task in conducting a DCF analysis is to make financial projections. This requires a robust financial model, including projections of income statement, balance sheet, and cash flow statement. Depending on the circumstance and the necessity, this can be done internally by management or by external advisors such as accountants, investment bankers, consultants, or expert witnesses. If an external analyst is doing this work, he or she will typically obtain past financial data and other information relevant to making projections from the company's managers. Lawyers will not be doing this type of work.

The next step in the analysis is to project free cash flow from the financial projections. "Free cash flow is the after-tax cash flow available to *all* investors: debt holders and equity holders. Unlike 'cash flow from operations' reported in a company's financial statement, free cash flow is independent of financing and nonoperating items."* Free cash flow is defined as:

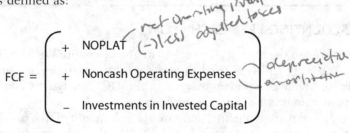

---

* Tim Koller, Marc Goedhart & David Wessels, Valuation: Measuring and Managing the Value of Companies 164 (4th ed., Wiley 2005).

Noncash operating expenses are depreciation and amortization. Investments in invested capital are capital expenditures and investments in working capital (as a going concern, a company must continuously purchase capital assets and manage its working capital).

NOPLAT is net operating profit less adjusted taxes. It is the after-tax operating income that is available to all capital providers of the firm. It differs from the accountant's income statement in the following ways. First, it is operating profit only. It does not include any nonoperating income or expense (income or expense not related to core operation). Also, operating profit is *before* the interest expense deduction; thus it is income available to creditors and equityholders. Second, "adjusted taxes" are calculated on the basis of operating income, and not pretax profit based on the income statement. We start from the reported tax liability in the income statements, add back the tax shield on interest expense, and remove taxes paid for nonoperating income.

Conceptually, free cash flow is cash that is available to all capital providers from core operations of the firm after payment of all operating expenses, taxes on operations, and continuing investments in capital assets and working capital. For a going concern, it is the cash that remains (cash that is free) to all capital providers.

EXAMPLE

Income Statement Versus NOPLAT

This example illustrates the difference between the income statement, which provides the inputs to a projection of free cash flow, and NOPLAT.

INCOME STATEMENT		NOPLAT	
Revenue	1,000	Revenue	1,000
Operating expense	(700)	Operating expense	(700)
Depreciation	(100)	Depreciation	(100)
Operating profit	200	Operating profit	200
Interest expense	(50)	Operating taxes at 25%	(50)
Nonoperating income	10	NOPLAT	150
Pretax profit	160		
Taxes at 25%	(40)		
Net income	120		

2. DISCOUNTING FREE CASH FLOW

The next step in the analysis is to calculate the discount rate used. The capital assets pricing model (CAPM) is used to calculate the cost of equity, and the WACC is calculated. While complex in execution, the DCF analysis is conceptually nothing more than a time value of money problem.

The variables affecting firm value are (1) the amount of free cash flow in the future (the measure of expected return), and (2) the discount rate (the measure of risk). Obviously, the more free cash flow in the future, the greater would be the value, and vice versa. Obviously as well, the greater the discount rate used, the less would be the value, and vice versa. These two variables ultimately determine firm value. The table below summarizes these effects.

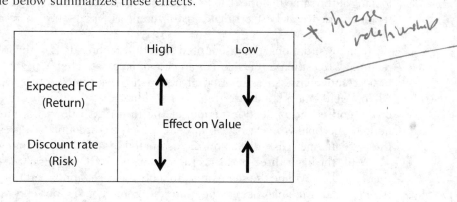

The following case is an earlier case in the convoluted *Cede* litigation. In the appraisal proceeding, the court applies the DCF valuation. The opinion is very long and complicated. Excerpted below is only a small portion of the full opinion. The DCF valuations of two competing experts were complicated and produced widely divergent outcomes. The wide range of valuation well illustrates the point that valuation is part science and a large part art. Much judgment goes into a valuation, which means that reasonable minds may differ quite a bit and the concept of reasonable becomes elastic in litigation. The opinion also shows that investment bankers, financial analysts, and economists are not the only people who are fluent in the concept of valuations.

Cede & Co. v. Technicolor, Inc.
1990 WL 161084 (Del. Ch. 1990)

ALLEN, Chancellor.

[MacAndrews & Forbes Group (MAF) completed a leverage buyout of Technicolor Inc., a film processing company. Cinerama Inc. owned 4.4 percent of the common stock, and it dissented from the merger and sought an appraisal. The valuation centered around expert testimony. Each expert employed a DCF analysis of Technicolor, but significant methodological and input differences yielded radically different estimates of value. The plaintiff's expert, John Torkelsen, opined that the statutory fair value of Technicolor was $62.75 per share. The defendant's expert, Professor Alfred Rappaport, opined that the statutory fair value of Technicolor was $13.14 per share. The court concluded that "the dynamics of litigation no doubt contribute to this distressingly wide difference."]

For the reasons set forth below I conclude, attempting to consider all pertinent factors as of the date of the merger, exclusive of elements of value arising from the expectation or accomplishment of the merger, and acting within the confines of the record created by the parties at trial, that the fair value of a share of Technicolor stock for purposes of appraisal was $21.60.

93

In this case the expert opinions on value cover an astonishing range. Two experts looking at the same historic data and each employing a discounted cash flow valuation technique arrive at best estimates as different as $13.14 per share and $62.75 per share.[15]

In many situations, the discounted cash flow technique is in theory the single best technique to estimate the value of an economic asset. The DCF model entails three basic components: an estimation of net cash flows that the firm will generate and when, over some period; a terminal or residual value equal to the future value, as of the end of the projection period, of the firm's cash flows beyond the projection period; and finally a cost of capital with which to discount to a present value both the projected net cash flows and the estimated terminal or residual value.

While the basic three-part structure of any two DCF models of the same firm, as of the same date, will be the same, it is probably the case (and is certainly true here) that the details of the analysis may be quite different. That is, not only will assumptions about the future differ, but different methods may be used within the model to generate inputs. This fact has a significant consequence for the way in which this matter is adjudicated. Sub-part of the DCF models used here are not interchangeable. With certain exceptions, each expert's model is a complex, interwoven whole, no part of which can be removed from that model and substituted into the alternative model.

An appraisal action is a judicial, not an inquisitorial, proceeding. The statutory command to determine fair value is a command to do so in a judicial proceeding. The court must decide which of the two principal experts has the greater claim overall to have correctly estimated the intrinsic value of Technicolor stock at the time of the merger. Having decided that question, it will be open to me to critically review the details of that expert's opinion in order to determine if the record will permit, and judicial judgment require, modification of any inputs in that model. What the record will not permit is either a completely independent judicially created DCF model[17] or a pastiche composed of bits of one model and pieces of the other.

The estimation of the fair value as of January 24, 1983, of Technicolor of Professor Rappaport is, in my considered opinion, a more reasonable estimation of statutory fair value than is the alternative valuation of petitioner's expert.

---

15. A significant part of this difference is accounted for by the differing discount rates used in the DCF models. If one substitutes the higher discount rate used by respondent's principal expert for the lower rate used by petitioner's expert and makes no other adjustment to either DCF model the difference reduces from $49.61 a share to $20.86.

17. For good reasons aside from technical competence, one might be disinclined to do so. Simply to accept one experts' view or the other would have a significant institutional or precedential advantage. The DCF model typically can generate a wide range of estimates. In the world of real transactions (capital budgeting decisions for example) the hypothetical, future-oriented, nature of the model is not thought fatal to the DCF technique because those employing it typically have an intense personal interest in having the best estimates and assumptions used as inputs. In the litigation context use of the model does not have that built-in protection. On the contrary, particularly if the court will ultimately reject both parties DCF analysis and do its own, the incentive of the contending parties is to arrive at estimates of value that are at the outer margins of plausibility-that essentially define a bargaining range. If it is understood that the court will or is likely to accept the whole of one witnesses testimony or the other, incentives will be modified. While the incentives of the real world applications of the DCF model will not be replicated, at least the parties will have incentives to make their estimate of value appear most reasonable. This would tend to narrow the range of estimates, which would unquestionably be a benefit to the process.

The following statement of the reasoning leading to this conclusion is in three principle parts reflecting the tripartite structure of the DCF model used by each witness. [PART 1] The first part treats the generation of net cash flows for the forecast period for the various Technicolor businesses and a particular legal question relating to cash flow projection upon which the parties divide. [PART 2] The second aspect of the DCF model [is] the terminal or residual value of the company at the conclusion of the forecast period. It is in connection with that aspect of the model that the methodological differences between the DCF methodology of Mr. Rappaport and that of Mr. Torkelsen will be treated. [PART 3] Finally, the selection of an appropriate cost of capital/discount rate will be discussed.

[PART 1: Projection of Net Cash Flows by Line of Business]

[The court meticulously analyzes various lines of Technicolor's businesses, which are valued separately, including the core business of film processing. Below is the discussion on the valuation of another business segment: One Hour Photo, a chain of stores that would provide consumers rapid "one hour" photo printing services. This was a new business for Technicolor, and the experts disagreed on its value. The court observed: "Technicolor's plan for One Hour Photo was an ambitious one. It was risky, not only because of the large capital investment it required, but also because of the nature of the One Hour Photo business."]

[A predicate legal question is whether in valuing Technicolor the court should assume the business plan that MacAndrews & Forbes (the acquirer) had for Technicolor (called the "Perelman plan"), or whether valuation should be premised on the company as a going concern under current management (called the "Kamerman plan"), *i.e.*, as if the company was never acquired by MacAndrews & Forbes. The plaintiff's expert, Mr. Torkelsen, valued the business based on the Perelman plan. Professor Rappaport valued it based on the Kamerman plan. The difference in assumptions led to these differences in valuation.]

	Torkelsen's Assumed Sale Value	Rappaport's Assumed Going Concern Value	Difference
One Hour Photo	$8m	–$7.7m	$15.8m

Thus, very roughly estimated, the question of which assumption is legally appropriate with respect to sales of assets accounts for about $4.50 per share of the difference between Rappaport's $13.14 valuation and Torkelsen's $62.75 valuation.

For the following reasons I conclude, in these circumstances, that value added to the corporation by the implementation or the expectation of the implementation of Mr. Perelman's new business plan for the company is not value to which, in an appraisal action, petitioner is entitled to a pro rata share, but is value that is excluded from consideration by the statutory exclusion for value arising from the merger or its expectation.

Our statute and a long line of cases that focus our inquiry on "going concern" value recognize that the value that is relevant in an appraisal is the value of the assets in the way they are deployed in the corporation from which the shareholder will exit.

When value is created by substituting new management or by redeploying assets "in connection with the accomplishment or expectation" of a merger, that value is not, in my opinion, a part of the "going concern" in which a dissenting shareholder has a legal (or equitable) right to participate.

Thus, in my view, petitioner's entitlement in this action to fair value, exclusive of value created by or in anticipation of the merger, means he is entitled to a pro rata share of the going concern value of the enterprise and that the going concern here was the business, as of the merger date, subject to the business plan of the Kamerman management. That view is inconsistent with adoption of Mr. Torkelsen's valuation of One Hour Photo and consistent with acceptance of Professor Rappaport's valuation method and opinion. Mr. Torkelsen did not value One Hour Photo as a going concern. Rather, on the assumption that as of January 24, 1983, the controlling shareholder (MAF) intended to sell that business, he valued One Hour Photo as an $8 million ($1.75 per share) asset to be liquidated by July 1983.

Professor Rappaport valued One Hour Photo as a going concern. He concluded that it would continue to be a persistent money loser and that it was likely that the company would ultimately be forced to sell it by the end of 1984. He opined that One Hour Photo had a negative $7.7 million value (-$1.69 per share).

Professor Rappaport generated two projections of net cash flows for One Hour Photo. The first was based upon optimistic management long-term plans. These plans appear to be the only long-term plans the company generated; they are, in several respects, unlike the year-to-year plans that were used by Professor Rappaport in connection with valuing film processing. Most importantly, those planners had a record of creating good year-to-year forecasts. In addition they were only year-to-year plans and thus would be inherently more reliable.

The management plan for One Hour Photo was prepared in February 1982. It predicated a rapid annual growth rate for photofinishing (10.3%) and an emerging large share of that business (25%) going to the new on-site development processors (minilabs). Management assumed it could capture 15% to 25% of this market and generate between $882 million and $1.47 billion in revenue by 1989. This vision called for 960 Technicolor stores in place by 1986. Professor Rappaport estimated the net present value of Technicolor One Hour Photo under the management plan to be $75.1 million.

In his second, "base case" forecast, Professor Rappaport accepted management's February 1982 projections of fixed and variable cost structures, depreciation, administration, and start-up expenses. Instead, of management's revenue forecast, however, he estimated Technicolor's One Hour Photo revenue to equal the average revenue per minilab (i.e. photofinishing store) in 1982 multiplied by the number of Technicolor minilabs in operation during each year of the forecast period. Professor Rappaport assumed annual growth in revenues equal to the rate of inflation (5%). The base scenario predicted heavy operating losses for each year of the seven-year forecast period. Professor Rappaport, however, assumed that the substantial losses in the first two forecast years would convince management to cut their losses and exit the One Hour Photo business.

Professor Rappaport assumed that at the end of 1984, Technicolor would sell each minilab for $125,000. The net present value of One Hour Photo under the base forecast was negative 16.9 million.

To estimate the value of One Hour Photo at the time of the merger, Professor Rappaport used a weighted average of the two scenarios. Professor Rappaport concluded that the base forecast more reasonably estimated the value of One Hour Photo in January 1983 than did the management plan. Accordingly, he assigned only a 10% weight to the management scenario and a 90% weight to the base scenario. The result was an estimated negative 7.7 million value to One Hour Photo at the time of the merger.

Estimating the value of One Hour Photo in 1983 is a difficult task. At that time, Technicolor was a newcomer to the industry which was itself in its infancy. In comparing the competing models in their treatment of the business, two factors seemed critical. First, Mr. Torkelsen's assumption that Technicolor would sell the One Hour Photo division in 1983 is contrary to the record testimony concerning Mr. Kamerman's plan for the business. It is the value of Technicolor under that plan that is at issue in this case. Second, Professor Rappaport's weighted valuation of the business seems reasonable. For the reasons discussed below, I am convinced that management's forecast was overly optimistic and that Professor Rappaport's base scenario is the most reliable valuation of the business and therefore deserves greater weight than the management forecast.

I do not lightly criticize management's One Hour Photo forecast. As a general rule, I am of the view that management projections done for real-world purposes are deserving of substantial weight. The following reasons, however, lead me to conclude that Professor Rappaport was reasonable in heavily discounting the management plan.

1. Management had no experience in the One Hour Photo business and no track record of forecasting the businesses' prospects.

2. The industry itself was in its infancy and faced uncertainty and risk.

3. Management's plan for store openings in 1982 was far off the mark. The plan, prepared in February 1982 was thus unable to include consideration of the problems the company would face as a result of its failure to establish the strong foothold in the industry that had been anticipated. That strong, rapid accumulation of locations was viewed by Mr. Kamerman and the market as critical to success in the business. Had management prepared its report in January 1983, an entirely different estimate may have resulted.

4. Management's poor forecast of store openings in 1982 suggests that the management scenario was not accurate.

5. The stock market reaction to the announcement of Technicolor's One Hour Photo venture was strongly negative.

6. The management scenario implies a value of One Hour Photo approximately $75 million (or $16 per share). A reasonable person in 1983 would not have valued this struggling start-up business at that price.

[PART 2: Methodology and Residual Values]

The most basic conceptual difference in the two DCF models used is this: Professor Rappaport assumes (and Mr. Torkelsen does not) that for every company its particular set of comparative advantages establish, as of any moment, a future period of same greater or lesser length during which it will be able to earn rates of return that exceed its cost of capital. Beyond that point, the company (as of the present moment of valuation) can expect to earn no returns in excess of its cost of capital and therefore, beyond that point, no additional shareholder value will be created. Professor Rappaport calls this period during which a company's net returns can be predicted to exceed its costs of capital, the company's "value growth duration," which is a coined term. While Professor Rappaport has copyrighted some software that employs this concept, the basic idea is not unique to him. It is an application of elementary notions of neo-classical economics: profits above the cost of capital in an industry will attract competitors, who will over some time period drive returns down to the point at which returns equal the cost of capital. At that equilibrium point no new competition will be attracted into the field. The leading finance text includes a reference to this concept of a future period beyond which there is no further value created. The existence of such a point in time does not mean that there is no value attributed to the period beyond that point, but rather that there is no further value growth.

I accept as sound the methodology of Professor Rappaport. Mr. Rappaport's method is in most respects conceptually similar to that employed by Mr. Torkelsen.

In the final analysis, however, Professor Rappaport used a period to project Technicolor's most important net cash flows similar to that employed by Mr. Torkelsen (5 years). Therefore, the practical significance of this conceptual difference between the DCF model used by Rappaport and that used by Torkelsen is in connection with what each does with cash flows at the end of the projection period, that is how each creates the terminal or residual value component of his DCF analysis. To estimate residual value Rappaport capitalizes a constant (last forecasted year) cash flow; he assumes no new value creation beyond the forecast period (but nevertheless much of his total value is attributed to the residual value). In creating his estimation of residual value Torkelsen, on the other hand, increases the last forecasted year's net cash flows by 5% each year (for inflation) into infinity, before capitalizing those flows. The result—and this is the practical gist of this theoretical difference between the experts—is that Mr. Torkelsen assumes that Technicolor net profits (along with all other aspects of its cash flow) and its value will increase every year in perpetuity, while Professor Rappaport assumes there will come a time when, while it may make profits, Technicolor will not be increasing in value.

The absolute difference in the residual value of each model is large. That difference is attributable not simply to methodology but to three differences in the assumptions of the models: differing discount rates, the differing estimates of cash flows in the last year projected and the assumption by PVR of a net cash flow that is perpetually increasing at 5%, a stipulated rate of inflation. It is this last assumption that most pointedly relates to the differing DCF methodology of the witnesses. PVR's assumption of a 5% growth rate in cash flows after the projection period is striking when one recalls that PVR projects growth during the 5 year explicit forecast period in the critical film processing business at 2.3%. This 5% growth assumption adds very substantial additional value to the discounted present value of a share of Technicolor stock. That assumption alone contributes $16.56 in per share value (making all other assumptions PVR makes).

In estimating residual value, Professor Rappaport, capitalizes a constant (the last forecast year) cash flow, not a perpetually growing one. He asserts that this is consistent with an inflating (or deflating) future world because he posits that whatever the value of money and indeed whatever the size of the company's cash flows, the most reasonable assumption about the future is that there will be a future time at which the firm will not earn returns in excess of its cost of capital. That is if, after that point, one posits increases cash flows, due to inflation (or decreases due to deflation) his model stipulates off-setting increases (or decreases) in the firms overall cost of capital.

[PART 3: Discounting With the Cost of Capital]

The cost of capital supplies the discount rate to reduce projected future cash flows to present value. The cost of capital is a free-standing, interchangeable component of a DCF model. It also allows room for judicial judgment to a greater extent than the record in this case permits in other areas of the DCF models.

Professor Rappaport used two cost of capital rates. For most of the cash flows (notably film processing and videocassette) he used a weighted cost of capital of 20.4%; for One Hour Photo and two small related businesses he used 17.3%.

Professor Rappaport used the Capital Asset Pricing Model (CAPM) to estimate Technicolor's costs of capital as of January 24, 1983. That model estimates the cost of company debt (on an after tax basis for a company expected to be able to utilize the tax deductibility of interest payments) by estimating the expected future cost of borrowing; it estimates the future cost of equity through a multi-factor equation and then proportionately weighs and combines the cost of equity and the cost of debt to determine a cost of capital.

The CAPM is used widely (and by all experts in this case) to estimate a firm's cost of equity capital. It does this by attempting to identify a risk-free rate for money and to identify a risk premium that would be demanded for investment in the particular enterprise in issue. In the CAPM model the riskless rate is typically derived from government treasury obligations. For a traded security the market risk premium is derived in two steps. First a market risk premium is calculated. It is the excess of the expected rate of return for a representative stock index (such as the Standard & Poor 500 or all NYSE companies) over the riskless rate. Next the individual company's "systematic risk"—that is the nondiversified risk associated with the economy as a whole as it affects this firm-is estimated. This second element of the risk premium is, in the CAPM, represented by a coefficient (beta) that measures the relative volatility of the subject firm's stock price relative to the movement of the market generally. The higher that coefficient (i.e., the higher the beta) the more volatile or risky the stock of the subject company is said to be. Of course, the riskier the investment the higher its costs of capital will be.

The CAPM is widely used in the field of financial analysis as an acceptable technique for estimating the implicit cost of capital of a firm whose securities are regularly traded. It is used in portfolio theory and in capital asset budgeting decisions. It cannot, of course, determine a uniquely correct cost of equity. Many judgments go into it. The beta coefficient can be measured in a variety of ways; the index rate of return can be determined pursuant to differing definitions, and adjustments can be made, such as the small capitalization premium, discussed below. But the CAPM methodology is certainly one of the principal "techniques or methods . . . generally considered acceptable [for estimating the cost of equity capital component of a discounted cash flow modeling] in the financial community . . ."

In accepting Professor Rappaport's method for estimating Technicolor's costs of capital, I do so mindful of the extent to which it reflects judgments. That the results of the CAPM are in all instances contestable does not mean that as a technique for estimation it is unreliable. It simply means that it may not fairly be regarded as having claims to validity independent of the judgments made in applying it.

With respect to the cost of capital aspect of the discounted cash flow methodology (in distinction to the projection of net cash flows and, in most respects, the terminal value) the record does permit the court to evaluate some of the variables, used in that model chosen as the most reasonable of the two (i.e., Professor Rappaport's) and to adjust the cost of capital accordingly. I do so with respect to two elements of Professor Rappaport's determination of costs of equity for the various Technicolor divisions. These businesses were all (excepting One Hour Photo, Consumer Photo Processing and Standard Manufacturing) assigned a cost of equity of 22.7% and a weighted average cost of capital of 20.4%. The remaining businesses were assigned a cost of equity of 20.4% and a weighted average cost of capital of 17.3%.

In fixing the 22.7% cost of equity for film processing and other businesses Professor Rappaport employed a 1.7 beta which was an estimate published by Merrill Lynch, a reputable source for December 1982. That figure seems intuitively high for a company with relatively stable cash flows. Intuition aside, however, it plainly was affected to some extent by the striking volatility in Technicolor's stock during the period surrounding the announcement of MAF proposal to acquire Technicolor for $23 per share. Technicolor stock rapidly shot up to the $23 level from a range of $9 to $12 in which it traded for all of September and the first week of October. Technicolor stock was thus a great deal more volatile than the market during this period. Applying the same measure of risk—the Merrill Lynch published beta—for September yields a significantly different beta measurement: 1.27. Looking at other evidence with respect to Technicolor betas I conclude that 1.27 is a more reasonable estimate of Technicolor's stock beta for purposes of calculating its cost of capital on January 24, 1983, than 1.7, even though that latter figure represents a December 1982 estimation.

The second particular in which the record permits and my judgment with respect to weight of evidence requires a modification of Mr. Rappaport's cost of capital calculation relates to the so-called small capitalization effect or premium. This refers to an unexplained inability of the capital asset pricing model to replicate with complete accuracy the historic returns of stocks with the same historic betas. The empirical data show that there is a recurring premium paid by small capitalization companies. This phenomena was first noted in 1981 and has been confirmed. The greatest part of the additional return for small cap companies appears to occur in January stock prices. No theory satisfactorily explaining the phenomena has been generally accepted.

Thus, in summary, I find Professor Rappaport's calculation of a cost of capital follows an accepted technique for evaluating the cost of capital; it employs that technique in a reasonable way and, except for the two particulars noted above, in a way that is deserving of adoption by the court. Applying these adjustments they lead to a cost capital of 15.28% for the main part of Technicolor's cash flow and 14.13% for the One Hour Photo related cash flows.

QUESTIONS

1. Explain generally how two experts of financial analysis and valuation, applying the same valuation technique, can produce an "astonishing" difference in valuation outcomes.
2. What specific point of difference between Torkelsen and Rappaport accounted for much of the "astonishing" difference?
3. At the end of Part 1, the court states: "5. The stock market reaction to the announcement of Technicolor's One Hour Photo venture was strongly negative." What is the significance of the stock market's reaction to the court's reasoning to accept Rappaport's discounting of the management plan?
4. What was the court's reasoning in adjusting the WACC from Rappaport's calculation?

NOTES

1. This case was an earlier proceeding in the complicated and convoluted *Cede* litigation. It preceded the opinion in *supra* Chapter 2, and it established the law of the case for a 15.28 percent cost of capital (see the last paragraph).
2. On appeal, the Delaware Supreme Court reversed the trial court's use of the Kamerman plan rather than the Perelman plan. *Cede & Co. v. Technicolor, Inc.*, 684 A.2d 289, 299 (Del. 1996) ("*Technicolor IV*"). The supreme court concluded that the trial court found that the Perelman plan "was the operative reality on the date of the merger," and held that the trial court's determination not to value Technicolor as a going concern on the date of merger under the Perelman plan was legal error. *Id.* at 299.
3. The "small capitalization effect" that the court references is a well-observed financial phenomenon in which historically small cap stocks have produced greater long-term returns than larger cap stocks. From 1926 to 2011, the average annual difference between the largest and smallest capitalization stocks has been 3.6 percent, a distinct difference in returns.[*] This suggests that historically and over the longterm investors thought that small cap stocks were riskier and thus demanded higher returns. The small cap effect undermines CAPM somewhat because CAPM says that beta is the only reason for differences in expected returns. CAPM does not account for size effect on the cost of equity, but empirical observations suggest that there is one.

3. EFFECTS OF CAPITAL STRUCTURE ON BETA AND CAPM

The beta of any company will depend on the capital structure. The beta of debt is typically lower than that of equity. Different companies, therefore, may have different betas depending on the capital structure. Financial analysis may require calculation of the unlevered beta: that is, the beta of the underlying assets. There are reasons to unlever the beta. First, a company may wish to find out what the WACC may be with a different capital structure. Second, a company may be a private company and its cost of capital must be inferred from public comparables. If so, the comparable companies may have different capital structures, and thus the unlevered beta provides a basis to calculate the cost of equity based on the subject company's capital structure.

$$\beta_A = \beta_D \frac{D}{V} + \beta_E \frac{E}{V}$$

The following case applies the above technique of calculating the beta of the assets to strip out the effect of different capital structures of the peer companies.

[*] Richard A. Brealey, Stewart C. Myers & Franklin Allen, Principles of Corporate Finance 203 (11th ed. 2014).

In re Pullman Const. Indus. Inc.

107 B.R. 909 (Bkrp. N.D. Ill. 1989)

SCHMETTERER, Bankruptcy Judge.

[The court conducted a DCF valuation of the debtor in bankruptcy, Pullman Construction Industries, Inc. Since Pullman was a private company, it did not have publicly traded stock, and thus no measurable stock returns in relation to market returns. To calculate the cost of equity, Pullman's beta had to be implied from a group of 18 publicly traded peer companies. Since these companies had different capital structures, the court calculated the beta of the assets, which were then relevered to Pullman's capital structure.]

Beta statistics for each company in the Peer Group were calculated by Ernst & Whinney, utilizing a linear regression technique. The linear regression methodology calculates the relationship between monthly returns on the peer company stock and monthly returns on a weighted New York Stock Exchange portfolio of stocks during the period January, 1983 through December, 1987. A calculated beta of 1.0 generally indicates that the volatility or risk of an investment in a stock is equal to the volatility or risk of the market as a whole; that is, a one percent change in the value of the market portfolio is accompanied by a one percent change in the value of the stock. Betas above 1.0 indicate stocks that are more volatile (risky) than the market, while betas less than 1.0 indicate stocks that are less volatile (risky).

The betas calculated by this linear regression method for all Peer Group companies are equity or stock betas, which measure the risk of an investment in the equity of a company. Such equity returns are affected by the level of debt, or leverage, that the company carries. In order to estimate the risk of the *business* rather than the risk of an investment in the *equity* of the business, an asset beta is calculated which adjusts to eliminate the financial risk of leverage. The asset beta for each Peer Group company was calculated from its equity beta, using the following formula (referred to as "unlevering the beta"):*

$$\text{Beta(a)} = [\text{Beta(d)} \times (1 - Tc) \times (D/V)] + [\text{Beta(e)} \times (E/V)]$$

where | Beta(a) | = | asset beta
|---|---|---|
| Beta(e) | = | beta of the company's equity, as calculated |
| Beta(d) | = | beta of the company's debt, assumed to be .195 |
| E | = | market value of equity |
| D | = | market value of debt |
| V | = | market value of capital (i.e., D + E) |

---

* The original opinion contained a typographical error. In reciting the formula, the court wrote: Beta(a) = [Beta(d) x (1 − Tc) x (D/V)] = [Beta(e) x (E/V)]. The second "=" should actually be "+". The formula in the text above fixes this typo.

The appropriate market values of debt and equity for the above equation were estimated as follows:

- The market value of debt was derived from an analysis of the 10–K annual reports filed by each Peer Group company and a survey of Moody's Bond Record to obtain prices on publicly-traded debt.
- The market value of equity was derived by extending the number of shares outstanding by the share price derived from the Wall Street Journal and/or public databases.
- The debt/capital and equity/capital ratios were calculated for each of the peer company's three fiscal years ending before June 29, 1988 (where market information for all three years was available).
- The average of the debt/capital and debt/equity ratios calculated for each year was used in the equation to "unlever" the beta.

Once the asset betas were calculated for each Peer Group company, the Peer Group asset beta was calculated as the average of the asset betas for each company in the Peer Group.

NOTES

1. The court took into account the interest tax shield of debt in calculating the beta contribution of the debt. While the effective cost of debt must take into account the tax shield, there is no reason to discount the beta of the debt, a measure of the covariance of the debt to the market return, by the tax rate. Presumably, if the tax rate affects the variance of return, the beta of the debt would have incorporated this factor. The proper formula for unlevered beta is: $\beta_A = \beta_D (D/V) + \beta_E (E/V)$. Richard A. Brealey, Stewart C. Myers & Franklin Allen, Principles of Corporate Finance 437, 493 (11th ed. 2014).

C. VALUATION OF BONDS

The value of bonds depends on two factors (1) the borrower's credit rating, and (2) the prevailing interest rate environment.

Credit rating is intuitively understood because most adults have an individual credit rating that determines how much one can borrow and at what rate. Corporations too have credit ratings, and they are determined by credit rating agencies, such as Moody's, Standard & Poor's (S&P), and Fitch. If the credit rating changes, one expects that the change would affect the bond price.

The prevailing interest rate environment is a complex economic factor that no single person or institution has ultimate control over. Real interest rates are subject to the law of supply and demand. Real rates are determined by the willingness of people to save money (the supply of capital) and the needs and opportunities of businesses and institutions (the demand for capital). For example, investors may move money from the stock markets to the bond markets, thus decreasing the price of stock and increasing the price of bonds. Or, the credit market may become "tight" due to some large exogenous event, such as the default on sovereign bonds of a major country that triggers a flight from sovereign bonds. There are many reasons why interest rates move. If there is abundant supply of capital but less demand, interest rates will decline. If there is less supply of capital but greater demand, interest rates will increase.

All investments are ultimately benchmarked against the risk-free rate. Recall that in calculating the cost of equity, the CAPM benchmarks the stock return against the market return and the risk-free rate. For debt instruments, the risk-free rate is important because a firm's cost of debt is calculated as a risk premium above the risk-free rate. The risk-free rate is not fixed, but instead depends on broader economic factors. For example, below is a chart indicating the yields on different Treasuries from 1996 to 2009. Note how, like stocks, the yields on debt instruments are subject to variance.

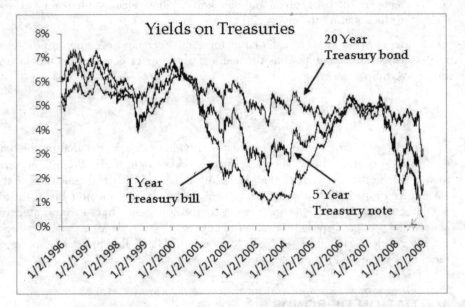

These changing yields over time suggest that the market prices of Treasuries are changing over time. The contract for a typical debt instrument has a fixed rate, a fixed principal payment, and a fixed maturity date. If so, how can the price of bonds change when the economic terms are fixed? The interest payment is contractually fixed, and cannot be changed absent renegotiation. However, the implied rate of return can change with a fixed interest payment by changing the trading price of the bond. If the bond price falls below the face value, the rate of return increases even when the coupon is fixed, and vice versa.

A bond will be issued with a principal amount F sometimes called the *face value*, *par value*, or *maturity value* (all synonymous); an interest rate called the coupon rate C; and a maturity T. These simple factors seem to suggest that the rate of return on a bond is the stated interest payment C. For example, if the coupon on the bond is 8 percent, the bondholder is getting paid a rate of 8 percent. This is correct only at the time of issuance, at which a bond investor will typically pay the face value of the bond. However, the value of a bond (its price) does not remain fixed at the face. Think about it this way: Suppose a corporation issues stock at $100 per share. Will the stock price remain fixed at $100 as time passes and it is traded in the market? Obviously not. If this is so obvious, why should we expect the value of bonds, another form of a corporation's securities, to behave any differently? The price of the bond fluctuates in the market. As interest rates move with time and economic development and as the corporation's financial status changes, the bond price must also adjust.

The value of a bond will change with time, and this means that the bond's real interest rate—the rate at which bondholders are being paid—will also change. But how can the value of a bond change when F and C are contractually fixed? In other words, an 8 percent coupon C off of a $100 face F cannot change as a matter of contract (absent renegotiation between the issuer and bondholders). This is true, but what can change is the market (trading) value of the bond. For the return on the bond to change, the trading price of the bond must change. The trading value is a determinant of the market and not of the contract. If the bond price falls below the face value, the rate of return on the bond increases even when the coupon is fixed. For example, if the above bond's price falls from $100 to $80, the effective interest rate is no longer 8 percent, but is 10 percent ($8/$80).

Like the DCF analysis, the value of a bond is fundamentally a present value problem. A bond is a security instrument that provides a stream of future cash flow. If so, the market value of a bond must be:

$$PV(bond) = PV(annuity\ of\ coupons) + PV(face\ value)$$

By the terms of the contract, the following information is known: the annuity of coupons C, the time remaining to maturity T, and the principal amount F. Only one variable is needed in the present value problem to calculate the price of the bond—that is, the discount rate.

The rate of return on a bond is called the bond's *yield-to-maturity*. The yield-to-maturity incorporates the market rate of return given the prevailing interest rates for bonds of similar quality and duration. The bond price must reflect the yield-to-maturity to provide the appropriate rate of return on the bond. The formula to calculate the yield is:

$$P = \frac{C}{(1+y)^1} + \frac{C}{(1+y)^2} + \ldots + \frac{C+F}{(1+y)^T}$$

where
P	=	market price of bond
C	=	coupon interest
F	=	face value (principal)
y	=	yield-to-maturity

This formula is a present value calculation. The bond represents a stream of future cash flow constituting the interest and principal payments. The discount rate (the yield-to-maturity) reflects the market's judgment of the appropriate rate of return on the bond.

EXAMPLE

Bond Valuation

At the beginning of Year 0, Acme Inc. issued a $1,000 face value Bond A with a fixed interest rate of 8% and a maturity at Year 5. The coupon rate reflected the issuer's credit rating, and a 4% risk premium (or credit spread) from the risk-free rate of 4%.

At the beginning of Year 1, Acme issues another $1,000 face value Bond B with a maturity at Year 5 and the same terms as Bond A. Assume that the company's credit rating remains the same, but in the ensuing year the risk-free rate increased to 6%. The credit spread is still the same. Bond B is issued with a coupon rate of 10%. The coupon for Bond A has already been paid out in Year 0. The expected cash flow for both bonds for Years 1 through 5 looks like this:

	YR. 1	YR. 2	YR. 3	YR. 4	YR. 5
Bond A	$80	$80	$80	$80	$1,080
Bond B	$100	$100	$100	$100	$1,100

At the start of Year 1, Bonds A and B are economically the same. They are issued by the same company with the same credit rating and contract terms, suggesting that the credit spread should be the same, and the bonds should mature at the same time in Year 5. Yet based on the payouts of C and F, Bond B is preferable. Since C and F for Bond A cannot change as a matter of contract, what must happen to make Bonds A and B the same?

The market value of Bond A must adjust in a way that the rate of return (called yield-to-maturity) becomes the same as that of Bond B. In this case, the new discount rate is 10%, which is the rate at which Acme issued Bond B. If so, the new price for Bond A can be calculated as this:

$$P = \frac{80}{(1 + 10\%)^1} + \frac{80}{(1 + 10\%)^2} + \frac{80}{(1 + 10\%)^3} + \frac{80}{(1 + 10\%)^4} + \frac{80 + 1000}{(1 + 10\%)^5}$$

$$P = 924.18$$

The price of Bond A must fall from $1,000 (face value) to $924.18, a difference of $75.82. This difference must equal the present value of the additional future payments given to Bond B holders under the terms of debt contract discounted at 10%.

$$75.82 = \frac{20}{(1 + 10\%)^1} + \frac{20}{(1 + 10\%)^2} + \frac{20}{(1 + 10\%)^3} + \frac{20}{(1 + 10\%)^4} + \frac{20}{(1 + 10\%)^5}$$

Holders of Bond B are given $75.82 present value in additional coupon payments. Since Bond A coupon payments are contractually fixed, purchasers of Bond A must be given a $75.82 discount on the price of the bond. Thus, Bonds A and B are made equal through a repricing of Bond A through the discounting process in a way that yields the new interest rate of 10%. In other words, Bond A priced at $924.18 with a coupon of 8% and Bond B priced at $1,000 with a coupon of 10% maturing in Year 5 will produce an identical 10% rate of return (yield-to-maturity).

Bond A issued by the company provided these cash flows (80 . . . 80 . . . 80 . . . 80 . . . 1,080), and Bond B with the same terms provided these cash flows (100 . . . 100 . . . 100 . . . 100 . . . 1,100) in the same time period. The two bonds are the same, and thus Bond A must equal Bond B. But the cash flows are different. Therefore, Bond A must be priced at a discount that equals the discounted value of the increased cash flow from Bond B, thus making the bonds equal in price.

Of course, old holders of Bond A (the original purchasers) would lose because they bought the bond at $1,000 and now the bond is worth only $924.18. But this is the risk that a bondholder takes—that interest rates would increase such that the value of their bonds decreases. The market value of Bond A is $924.18 such that any potential buyer will earn a 10% rate of return.

EXAMPLE

Zero Coupon Bonds

There are special forms of bonds called zero coupon bonds, in which the issuer will issue the bond at a discount to the face value. It does not pay interest. At maturity, the bond is paid at face value.

1. For example, an investor pays $750 for Bond Z and will get $1,000 in payment in Year 5.

	YR. 0	YR. 1	YR. 2	YR. 3	YR. 4	YR. 5
Bond Z cash flow	($750)	$0	$0	$0	$0	$1,000

What is the interest rate on a zero coupon bond? It is the yield on the bond. The yield is the implied rate of return. In other words, it is the internal rate of return (IRR) on the investment.

$$750 = \frac{1000}{(1 + y)^5} \quad \Rightarrow \quad y = 5.9\%$$

In other words,

$$750 \times (1 + 5.9\%)^5 = 1000$$

Thus, we can calculate the implied interest rate of zero coupon bonds, and compare it to other bonds that pay periodic interest rates.

2. A zero coupon bond is a bond that pays no interest payment while the bond is outstanding, but pays a lump sum interest and principal at the same time upon maturity. Bond A is a three-year zero coupon bond. It requires a payment of $1,000, and at the end of three years the holder will receive a payment of $1,250. Bond B is a five-year zero coupon bond. It requires a payment of $1,000, and at the end of five years the holder will receive a payment of $1,400. Assume that you are only interested in maximizing your rate of return. There are no other considerations. Which investment is better?

$$1,000 \ (A) = \frac{1,250}{(1 + y)^3} \quad \Rightarrow \quad y = 7.7\%$$

Check for correctness: $1,000 \times (1.077)^3 = 1,250$ . . . meaning that $1,000 invested at an annual rate of 7.7% for three years will produce a future value of $1,250.

$$1,000 \ (B) = \frac{1,400}{(1 + y)^5} \quad \Rightarrow \quad y = 7.0\%$$

Check for correctness: $1,000 \times (1.07)^5 = 1,400$.

It would be wrong to say that Bond B is superior because it produces $400 in gross return whereas Bond A produces only $250. The real measure of return is the yield over time. Clearly, a bond that yields 7.7% (A) is better than a bond that yields 7.0% (B).

D. VALUATION PROCESS AND STUDIES

1. JUDGMENT IN VALUATION

Valuations are typically performed by financial advisors or investment bankers. The process of valuation encompasses gathering relevant market information including stock price history, dividend payment history, capital structure, financial projections, strategic analysis, and other information. Market comparables are prepared. Finally, a DCF analysis, or some variant of it, is conducted.

Intrinsic value is impossible to determine as a precise, single value derived from a deductive, scientific process. The typical valuation study performed for a transaction uses different methods, for example: (1) analysis of historical stock price performance; (2) comparative companies analysis using various ratios and financial inputs such as earnings, book value, revenue, EBIT, and EBITDA; (3) comparative transactions analysis, which is multiples analysis for transactions; and (4) theoretical value under the DCF. Such a study produces a range of reasonable values.

Valuation requires technical competence and quantitative rigor in analysis. However, it also requires subjective judgment on many variables that materially affect the results. Valuations typically produce a range of values. Assumptions and subjective judgments matter. Don't be dazzled or intimidated by the seemingly scientific nature of the inquiry. Consider this passage from a business school student learning the uncertainties of the practical side of finance:*

> There seemed to come a point in every class involving the use of numbers when the professor would say, "This is an art not a science." And there always seemed to be a note of regret in his voice. Valuing companies, for all the sweat and effort people put into it, always ran into immeasurable uncertainties. . . .
>
> . . . [Valuations] make no claim to be exactly right. They are negotiating tools. If you spent any time at a bank you would see that all these techniques and models just serve the political needs of the bankers and their clients. If the bankers come up with one valuation and the client says, can't we make that a little higher or lower, the bankers will go back to their model and adjust it to get it where the client wants it. And the more complex-seeming the model, the more tricks there are to pull. You should never mistake what they do for objective science. All that matters is the assumptions, and anyone can have a discussion about them, regardless of how much finance they know. The main thing is understanding the business in question.

---

* Philip Delves Broughton, Ahead of the Curve: Two Years at Harvard Business School 101-102 (2008).

This observation of a student of finance has a ring of truth to it. Unless you are the one doing it, valuation is presented in neat Excel spreadsheets and impressive-looking PowerPoint presentations, but one may not get the full sense of uncertainty involved in the selection of the variables that materially affect the outcomes—such as the group of peers for comparable company analysis, the assumptions used to generate projections, and other judgment calls that were made.

If you think valuation is a precise science, a methodology that will produce ontological truth, you are deluding yourself. If you are intimidated by the scientific-looking nature of the exercise, you are shortchanging yourself. If one assumes the correct and nonfraudulent application of a valuation methodology by a financial analyst working in good faith, the key to understanding the valuation of the firm or asset is to understand the business and the underlying assumptions derived therefrom.

EXAMPLE

Sensitivity to Assumption in DCF Analysis

The DCF model, like all time value of money problems, is highly sensitive to the discount rate. The truth is that economic and financial forecasting is subject to a high degree of uncertainty. Accordingly, financial models should be subject to a range of variables. Such an analysis is called a sensitivity analysis, and it produces a range of value.

This example is a stylized DCF analysis. It shows the sensitivity of the valuation to the discount rate, the relationship between the terminal value and the discount rate, and the effect of assumptions on the valuation. The DCF analysis has three case scenarios: Optimistic, Base, and Pessimistic. The performance of such multiple scenario analyses is typical in actual practice because there is a large component of subjectivity and uncertainty. The free cash flows are modeled on the assumption of a growth rate. The terminal value is calculated per the growth perpetuity formula based on the Year 7 FCF, and then is discounted by the Year 7 discount factor because the terminal value is the gross sum of the perpetual cash as of Year 7.

Assumptions	Optimistic	Base	Pessimistic
Growth rate	3%	1%	0%
Discount rate	10%	12%	14%
Terminal growth	3%	1%	0%

Output ($000)	1	2	3	4	5	6	7	Terminal	Total	%
Optimistic Model										
Free cash flow (FCF)	1,250	1,288	1,326	1,366	1,407	1,449	1,493	21,322		
Discount factor	0.909	0.826	0.751	0.683	0.621	0.564	0.513			
PV of FCF (1-7)	1,136	1,064	996	933	874	818	766	→	6,587	38%
PV of FCF (Terminal)								10,942 →	10,942	62%
Total value									**17,529**	100%
Base Model										
Free cash flow (FCF)	1,250	1,263	1,275	1,288	1,301	1,314	1,327	12,063		
Discount factor	0.893	0.797	0.712	0.636	0.567	0.507	0.452			
PV of FCF (1-7)	1,116	1,006	908	818	738	666	600	→	5,853	52%
PV of FCF (Terminal)								5,457 →	5,457	48%
Total value									**11,309**	100%

Pessimistic Model

Free cash flow (FCF)	1,250	1,250	1,250	1,250	1,250	1,250	1,250	8,929		
Discount factor	0.877	0.769	0.675	0.592	0.519	0.456	0.400			
PV of FCF (1-7)	1,096	962	844	740	649	569	500	→ 5,360		60%
PV of FCF (Terminal)								3,568 → 3,568		40%
Total value								**8,929**		100%

The difference between the Pessimistic and Optimistic scenarios is $8.6 million. Notice that even seemingly small changes in assumptions—a percent or two in the discount rate or growth rate assumptions—have a large impact on the valuation. Such wide variations in litigation and transactional practices are not so unusual. There is a lot of money at stake; judgment is frequently subjective (and often not improperly so); the future is uncertain.

Notice also the effect of the discount rate on the proportion between value assigned to the forecast period and the terminal value. Consider this in light of the fact that the nearer the future, the more accurate the projections will be. In other words, the projections for next year are probably more accurate than the projections for ten years in the future.

EXAMPLE

Judgment in Comparable Companies Analysis

The selection of comparable companies can make a substantial difference in the valuations produced. Let's just consider as an example one metric, the P/E. Assume that the following are candidates for selection as comparables to Company Zeta, which is the subject of the valuation.

Company A	12x		Company F	17x
Company B	12x		Company G	17x
Company C	13x		Company H	19x
Company D	14x		Company I	20x
Company E	14x		Company J	22x

For various reasons, each of these companies differs from one another in nontrivial ways. As we can see, the selection of comparables matters quite a bit. Assume that Company Zeta has earnings of $100. If Companies A through E are the comparables, the average P/E multiple is 13x. If Companies F through J are the comparables, the average P/E multiple is 19x. If Companies A through J are the comparables, the average P/E multiple is 16x. If Company A is the only comparable, the P/E multiple is 12x. If Company J is the only comparable, the P/E multiple is 22x. To summarize, the following are the implied equity values of Company Zeta based on the following selection of multiples:

Average Companies A through E:	13 x $100 = $1,300
Average Companies F through J:	19 x $100 = $1,900
Average Companies A through J:	16 x $100 = $1,600
Company A:	12 x $100 = $1,200
Company J:	22 x $100 = $2,200

The range produced by the different selections of comparables is $1,200 to $2,200. This is a broad range, but in practice this type of a range may not be so unusual. We see that the selection of comparables is an important part of the valuation process—and the negotiation process in the business transaction.

Valuation is part science and part art: Science because rigorous economic reasoning provides the method, and art because judgment is required in applying the method. Valuation is ultimately art created under the methods of a particular discipline. If you understand this aspect, you will have a sophisticated understanding of the proper uses and application of valuation, and the limits of valuation. The fact that valuation has limits and depends on subjective judgment does not mean that we should be cynical to the point of nihilism. The reality is that valuation must be performed in earnest because a deal requires a firm price.

Valuation requires technical competence and quantitative rigor in analysis. However, it also requires subjective judgment on many variables that materially affect the results. Valuations typically produce a range of values. Assumptions and subjective judgments matter. Don't be dazzled or intimidated by the seemingly scientific nature of the inquiry.

The following case provides a perspective on how a Delaware chancellor views the valuation exercise.

Cede & Co. v. Technicolor, Inc.
2003 WL 23700218 (Del. Ch. 2003)

CHANDLER, Chancellor.

Although 8 Del. C. §262 requires this Court to determine "the fair value" of a share of Technicolor on January 24, 1983, it is one of the conceits of our law that we purport to declare something as elusive as *the* fair value of an entity on a given date, especially a date more than two decades ago. Experience in the adversarial, battle of the experts' appraisal process under Delaware law teaches one lesson very clearly: [valuation decisions are impossible to make with anything approaching complete confidence. Valuing an entity is a difficult intellectual exercise, especially when business and financial experts are able to organize data in support of wildly divergent valuations for the same entity. For a judge who is not an expert in corporate finance, one can do little more than try to detect gross distortions in the experts' opinions. This effort should, therefore, not be understood, as a matter of intellectual honesty, as resulting in *the* fair value of a corporation on a given date. The value of a corporation is not a point on a line, but a range of reasonable values, and the judge's task is to assign one particular value within this range as the most reasonable value in light of all of the relevant evidence and based on considerations of fairness.]

NOTES

1. Chancellor Chandler's admonition applies equally in the transactional context. Valuation in the transactional context also involves inherent uncertainties. There is not a discussion of "the" value, but usually a range of reasonable values. In mergers and acquisitions transactions where an investment banker delivers a fairness opinion, the opinion never states that the consideration is "the" precise

intrinsic value of the stock, but instead the investment banker opines that the consideration is "fair from a financial point of view."

2. Like Chancellor Allen's earlier opinion in *Cede*, Chancellor Chandler noted in another portion of the above opinion the "battle of the experts' appraisal" and the "wildly divergent valuations." Like most fact-finding in trial proceedings, the question came down to credibility. The court found the plaintiff (dissenting shareholders) expert's analysis "unpersuasive and demonstrably inaccurate" and the defendant's expert "more reliable and persuasive." Among other things, the plaintiff expert rejected wholesale the management's forecasts while the defendant expert adopted them. The court found that "Technicolor management was in the best position to project the short-term prospects of the company, as they created projections *ex ante*, based upon information gleaned from their particular customers . . . [and] that management forecasts for Technicolor were historically accurate and, therefore, the best evidence regarding the short-term prospects of Technicolor."

2. VALUATION STUDIES

Valuation studies are routinely performed in the course of many different kinds of corporate transactions. The typical transactions requiring valuation studies are mergers and acquisitions (M&A), restructurings, and capital raisings. In M&A deals, valuations are required to assess the acquisition consideration, to advise the board of directors as to their fiduciary duty with respect to the fairness of the transaction to shareholders from a financial point of view, and possibly an appraisal proceeding for dissenting shareholders. In a restructuring, valuation is important in such issues as the disposal of assets, terms of refinancing from new capital providers, and the compromise and exchange of securities with respect to the value of the firm. In capital raisings, valuation is crucial because it determines the price at which securities can be issued.

Lawyers will not be asked to conduct valuation studies, but they will use such studies. Corporate managers will sometimes conduct valuations, particularly when they are used for internal management purposes. In corporate transactions, however, an external valuation is typically required. In the typical M&A, restructuring, or capital raising transaction, financial advisors are hired. In the transactional context, investment bankers conduct valuations. In the litigation context of, for example, corporate appraisals, bankruptcy proceedings, or securities litigation, each side typically hires an expert witness who may be an accountant, a financial analyst, an economist, or an academic.

Although lawyers would be incompetent to perform a valuation study, they would be less competent in the performance of lawyerly work if they do not understand valuation or facilitate the valuation process (as is the case in judicial proceedings, such as merger appraisal and bankruptcy proceedings, where the court must directly work with valuations). Legal work requires a working knowledge of valuation for the purpose of, among other things, understanding the economics of transactions, discussing transactions with clients and other professionals, drafting transaction documents, and working with expert witnesses.

The typical valuation study contains different valuation methods, including many different forms of market multiples and a DCF analysis. In M&A deals, transaction comparables, which are multiples of transaction price, are also considered along with data on merger premiums. In addition to valuation, analyses of historical stock price, dividends, and share liquidity may also be considered.

Financial advisors typically do not require much input from corporate managers to perform multiples analyses and transaction comparables. The data are broadly available in the market. The technical aspects of culling the data and crunching the numbers are fairly straightforward. The only difficult aspect of these forms of analyses is the judgment required to determine what companies and transactions are true comparables. With respect to a DCF analysis, however, corporate managers typically provide significant data or input. Investment bankers are less familiar with the internal details and strategy of the company, and corporate managers are really the experts on their business. Therefore, they provide much of the assumptions, strategic considerations driving the projections, and sometimes the projections themselves.

The following case is the same case from the previous discussion on calculating the beta of the assets. That discussion was a part of a valuation exercise. The important issue was the value of the assets as they related to the interest of a secured creditor. The bankruptcy court undertook a comprehensive valuation study, including market multiples and DCF analysis and sensitivity analysis.

In re Pullman Const. Indus. Inc.

107 B.R. 909 (Bkrp. N.D. Ill. 1989)

SCHMETTERER, Bankruptcy Judge.

On May 1, 1987 ("Petition Date"), Pullman Construction Industries, Inc., Pullman Sheet Metal Works, Inc., Preferred Piping, Inc., and Mid–City Architectural Iron Co. (collectively referred to as "Debtors" or "Pullman") filed petitions for relief under Chapter 11 of the Bankruptcy Code, 11 U.S.C. §101 *et seq.*

Debtors are incorporated under the laws of Illinois, and have their principal place of business in Chicago, Illinois. Pullman Construction Industries, Inc. ("PCI") is the parent Corporation of three wholly-owned subsidiaries: Pullman Sheet Metal Works, Inc., Preferred Piping, Inc., and Mid–City Architectural Iron Co. The stock of PCI is owned by Lester and Norma Goldwyn.

Wells Fargo Collateral and Claim

Wells Fargo has a first priority, properly perfected security interest in and to all assets of the Debtors, including, without limitation, accounts, accounts receivable, contracts, contract rights, inventory, goods, raw material, work in process, patents, machinery and equipment, vehicles, fixtures, improvements, general intangibles and proceeds thereof (the "Collateral"). Wells Fargo also has a first priority, properly perfected security interest in, and lien upon, all shares of Stock issued by the Debtors.

On August 19, 1988, the Court approved a Settlement Agreement, signed by both Debtors and Wells Fargo, that provided that "Wells Fargo shall have a finally allowed secured claim against the Pullman Companies, and property of the Pullman Companies' bankruptcy estates, in the amount of $8,038,138.95 . . ."

Wells Fargo has a lien on all assets of the Debtors' existing estates.

The Dispute as to Going Concern Value

Debtors and Wells Fargo cannot agree upon the going concern value of Wells Fargo's collateral for purposes of establishing the secured portion of Wells Fargo's allowed claim under 11 U.S.C. §506(a). Since Wells Fargo has a lien on all of Debtors' assets, Wells Fargo's allowed secured claim is equal to the going concern value of Debtors' assets or estate. The Plan must provide Wells Fargo with payments having a present value equal to the going concern value of Wells Fargo's collateral. The Plan proposes to satisfy Wells Fargo's Class 4 secured claim as follows:

Representing cash payments / transfers to Wells Fargo	$732,000
Representing the proceeds from the settlement of the "Sheraton Claim"	$687,000
Cash payment upon confirmation	$1,855,000
TOTAL	$3,274,000

The factual issue to be resolved is this: Whether the Debtors' proposed $1,855,000 cash payment at confirmation, or the lesser amount suggested by the Committee, is equal to the going concern value of Wells Fargo's presently existing collateral? For reasons stated below, the Court finds that the answer is no.

This Court previously has found as of the Petition Date that the forced liquidation value of Debtors' cash, accounts receivable, machinery and equipment and inventory was $3,182,500. However, this Court has not previously determined the going concern value of Wells Fargo's collateral.

Theories and Evidence as to Valuation

Pullman's going concern valuation expert witnesses relied primarily upon a discounted cash flow analysis and have concluded that the appropriate discount rate for Pullman is 18 percent. In reaching this conclusion they employed numerous valuation models and techniques to determine the appropriate discount rate, including: (i) Capital Asset Pricing Model ("CAPM") alternatives; (ii) weighted average cost of capital analyses, (iii) arbitrage pricing theory, and (iv) a survey of selected current investment yields. As additional confirming measures for their valuation results, they also reviewed price/earnings comparisons, earnings before interest and taxes ("EBIT") comparisons, earnings before depreciation, interest and taxes ("EBDIT")* comparisons, book value comparisons and dividend capitalization model analyses. They agreed on an 18 percent discount rate which, when applied to the anticipated future cash flows set forth in Pullman's Business Plan, produces what they found to be the most likely net present value of Pullman's future cash flows. This is one component of Pullman's aggregate reorganization value, the other being excess cash or non-operative assets.

Pullman's expert witnesses on this issue were Harold Sullivan, Jr. of Ernst & Whinney and Dr. Robert Hamada. Sullivan utilized the CAPM as well as several other valuation methodologies discussed herein below, while Hamada used only his refinement of the CAPM approach to validate and corroborate Ernst & Whinney's conclusion that Pullman's cost of capital, or the property discount rate, is eighteen percent (18%).

---

* The court's use of EBDIT is the same as EBITDA, which is a more commonly used acronym for earnings before interest, taxes, and depreciation and amortization.

Sullivan testified on behalf of the Debtors that the "most likely value" of the Debtors' "present value of free cash flows," based on his use of a discounted cash flow analysis, is $3,411,000. This analysis was based upon an 18% discount rate. The $3,411,000 net present value of free cash flows excluded consideration of $2,136,000 of "Non–Operating Items."

To calculate the most likely aggregate value of the Debtors' estate, Sullivan added "Non–Operating Items" totaling $2,136,000 to his most likely net present value of free cash flows of $3,411,000. Sullivan then concluded that the most likely aggregate value of Debtors' existing estate is $5,547,000. This is the value "available to pay administrative and pre-petition priority and secured claims."

Professor Alfred Rappaport defines "corporate value" as the sum of "present value of cash flow from operations during the forecast period plus residual value plus marketable securities." This definition was essentially followed by experts for both sides. Debtors claim corporate value of $5,547,000 comports with this definition as follows: (a) present value of cash flow from operations during the forecast period—$1,354,000 (present value of free cash flows 1989 through 1993); plus, (b) residual value—$2,057,000 (present value of free cash flows after forecast period); plus, (c) marketable securities—$2,136,000 (non-operating items). Sullivan testified that these items have a strong or identical correlation to Professor Rappaport's definition of corporate value.

The following is a discussion of each of the valuation approaches utilized by Debtors' witnesses to determine the most likely value of Pullman's Aggregate Estate.

Discounted Cash Flow

The discounted cash flow method presents value as the sum of a stream of free cash flows from the Plan's Effective Date into perpetuity. The present value of the cash flows is dependent on the time value of money and the risk of producing the projected cash flows. The projected cash flows are based on Pullman's Business Plan. Those cash flows include both the projection period through 1993 and the perpetuity period beginning in 1994. Pullman's experts prepared detailed projections through 1993 because they assumed that by that time Pullman would regain its historical market share and achieve its growth projections. It is found below that if Debtor were reorganized in 1989, they would gain their maximum market share by 1993. After that, they will be unable to grow further in value because of the competitive nature of the construction industry and the historical inverse relationship between Debtors' revenues and margins. The evidence does not demonstrate that Pullman can make additional investments after 1993 that will generate returns in excess of its cost of capital.

After gaining its maximum market share, Pullman will not experience further economic growth, even though it may grow in size. The addition of years of projections after 1993 does not demonstrate any real value for purposes of a present valuation. Instead, the residual value of Pullman's cash flows from 1994 into perpetuity can be determined by the perpetuity method. As Rappaport explained it,

> Using the perpetuity method, the present value (at the end of the forecast period) is therefore calculated by dividing a "perpetuity cash flow" by the cost of capital:

$$\text{Residual value} = \frac{\text{Perpetuity cash flow}}{\text{Cost of capital}}$$

Keep in mind that the perpetuity method for estimating residual value is not based on the assumption that all future cash flows will actually be identical. It simply reflects the fact that the cash flows resulting from future investments will not affect the value of the firm because the overall rate of return earned on those investments is equal to the cost of capital.

Pullman's value is properly calculated discounting each projected annual cash flow through 1993 by the cost of capital and calculating the value of the cash flows thereafter by the perpetuity method as described by Rappaport.

Once the annual cash flows have been projected, the other important component to be determined is Pullman's cost of capital or discount rate. Pullman's experts utilized several methodologies in forming their opinion as to the appropriate discount rate. These methods, which rely in varying degrees upon analyses of publicly-held companies in the construction industry are:

Capital Asset Pricing Model ("CAPM")—The CAPM methodology measures a company's risk relative to the stock market as a whole. Risk is measured as the variability of a stock price relative to a market portfolio. The average historical annual premium of an investment in the market portfolio relative to an investment in an estimated risk-free instrument is adjusted by the variability of the individual stock price relative to the market portfolio (*i.e.*, an estimate of the riskiness of the particular stock or its "beta"). This estimate is added to the current risk-free rate to estimate the rate of return an investor would require on such an investment.

Here, an equally weighted New York Stock Exchange portfolio was analyzed as the "market portfolio" in order better to reflect the performance of both smaller and larger publicly-held companies. A value weighted portfolio (the S&P 500) was also analyzed and adjusted for a small stock premium. The use of CAPM methodology is described below.

Weighted Average Cost of Capital ("WACC")—WACC is the weighted average of the after-tax cost of debt (*i.e.*, the marginal rate at which a company can borrow funds) and the company's cost of equity. The cost of debt is tax-effected because of the tax deductions associated with interest payments. Cost of equity has been based on analysis of potential peer companies. The costs are weighted respectively by the ratios of the market values of debt and equity to the market value of total capital (debt plus equity) to derive a weighted average. The results were very similar to those obtained using CAPM methodology.

Peer Group Multiple Analyses

In order to confirm their discounted cash flow valuation findings, Pullman's experts analyzed certain multiples of financial data for other companies. Although this analysis was not performed in the same depth as the discounted cash flow analysis, and it is not entitled to the same weight because of its reliance on accounting-based numbers, it serves to corroborate results of the cash flow analysis. This multiple analysis, which was performed on publicly-held companies in the construction industry, included:

Price–Earnings Multiple ("P/E")—"Earnings" is defined as operating earnings after taxes. The respective median P/E multiples for the Peer Group were estimated to be 11.79 and 9.86. These multiples were applied to Pullman's actual 1988 and projected 1989 operating earnings to calculate a range of potential values.

EBIT Multiple—"EBIT" is earnings before interest and taxes. The median Peer Group EBIT multiple was estimated to be 6.06. This multiple was applied to PCI's 1988 actual earnings before interest and taxes to calculate a potential value.

EBDIT Multiple—"EBDIT" is earnings before depreciation, interest and taxes. The median EBDIT multiple for the Peer Group was 5.03. This multiple was applied to PCI's 1988 earnings before depreciation, interest and taxes to calculate a potential value.

Book Value Multiple—Book value is the excess of the net book value of the assets over the net book value of the liabilities (*i.e.,* stockholder's equity). The Peer Group companies' median book value multiple was estimated to be 1.38. Pullman's net book value was calculated both before and after the new equity investments, and those figures were multiplied by the median book value multiple to estimate potential values.

All of these multiple analyses were adjusted by reconciling items to make estimates of Pullman's gross reorganization value.

Dividend Capitalization

Another confirming technique employed was the dividend capitalization model, which assumes that dividends are a constant stream of cash flows to equity investors. The present value of a stream of equal cash flows, or an annuity, is the cash flow divided by the discount rate. The discount rate is calculated as described above in the Discounted Cash Flow Approach Summary. Items were added to this calculated value to reconcile to the reorganization value.

The Synthesis of the Various Techniques Used

In addition to these confirming techniques, Pullman's experts considered certain other factors, including the following: (i) Pullman is privately-held and does not have access to public capital markets; (ii) achieving the Business Plan's objectives is dependent on the continued involvement of a few key managers; (iii) Pullman has been in bankruptcy; (iv) the construction industry is very dependent upon personal relationships and a substantial portion of Pullman's good will and value resides in the Goldwyns; and (v) Pullman operates in a single localized market, not a regional or national market. Finally, Pullman's experts weighed the strengths and weaknesses of each of the methodologies employed in forming their opinions that 18% is the appropriate discount rate and that the most likely gross value of Pullman's aggregate estate is $5,547,000.

Application of the various confirming techniques produced the following range of values of Pullman's Aggregate Estate:

Price/earnings multiple on forecasted 1989 earning	$4,490,000
Book value multiple before new equity investment	$4,693,000
Dividend capitalization model	$4,803,000
Price/earnings multiple on EBIT	$4,815,000
Price/earnings multiple on EBDIT	$4,882,000
Book value multiple after new equity investment	$5,390,000
Price/earnings multiple on pre-confirmation 1988 earnings	$5,663,000

CAPM Methodology

The principal technique employed by both Ernst & Whinney and Dr. Hamada to determine the discount rate was CAPM. CAPM methodology recognizes that different investments have different levels of risk and, therefore, should produce different returns to investors. The CAPM method measures the risk associated with a specific investment relative to the risk of a portfolio of investments, and prices or values that investment relative to the return on the portfolio. The general CAPM cost of capital equation is summarized as follows:

$$R(c) = R(f) + B(a) \times [R(m) - R(f)]$$

where
$R(c)$ = the CAPM cost of capital
$R(f)$ = the after-tax risk-free rate of return
$B(a)$ = the beta, or risk, of the asset
$R(m)$ = the return on the market portfolio
$R(m) - R(f)$ = the market risk premium

The derivation of each of the components of the CAPM equation used in calculating Pullman's cost of capital is as follows:

The after-tax risk-free rate of return is first calculated. This is the rate of return an investor could expect to receive by investing in a risk-free asset, after paying taxes on the investor's return. One year Treasury Bills, backed by the full faith and credit of the United States Government, are generally considered to be the best proxy for the risk-free rate. Pullman's before-tax risk-free rate was assumed to be equal to the yield, as of April 11, 1989, on one-year Treasury Bills due April 12, 1990. That rate is 9.72 percent. Using the same forty percent (40%) assumed corporate tax rate that was used in developing the "free cash flows" in Pullman's Business Plan and Projected Financial Statements, the after-tax risk-free rate was calculated as follows:

Before-tax risk-free rate	9.72%
Less: taxes at 40%	(3.89%)
After-tax risk-free rate	5.83%

The "beta" coefficient measures the risk of an investment in Pullman's business relative to the risk of the market as a whole. Since Pullman is not publicly traded, it is impossible to measure changes in the return on Pullman's common stock over time against a portfolio of market securities. Accordingly, a group of publicly-traded companies in the construction industry was selected in order to measure the risk of the special trade contracting industry against the risk of the entire market. This group of companies was used as Pullman's "Peer Group." These comparable publicly-traded companies were selected through an analysis of publicly-traded companies in the special trade contracting and non-residential general contracting businesses.

Ernst & Whinney initially identified 108 publicly-traded companies having either primary or secondary business lines within Standard Industrial Codes in the 1,700 series ("Special Trade Contractors") or 1,540 series ("Non–Residential Building Contractors"). Ninety of these companies were excluded as potential peers because they were not deemed to be comparable to Pullman. The reasons for exclusion were as follows:

- Certain companies were excluded because their primary SIC Code was not in the 1,540 or 1,700 series;
- Certain companies were excluded because their lines of business are not comparable to Pullman's business;
- Certain companies were excluded because they were in bankruptcy proceedings at sometime during 1985–1987;
- Certain companies were excluded because they operate primarily outside of the United States;
- One company was excluded because it was privately held until August, 1987;
- Certain companies were excluded because of thin trading of their securities on regional stock markets; and
- Certain companies were excluded because their beta coefficient was not statistically significant.

After these exclusions, the following eighteen companies formed Pullman's "Peer Group": Abrams Industries, Acmat, Apogee Enterprises, Comstock Group, Fischback, GMX, CH Heist, Insituform East, Insituform Gulf South, Insituform Southeast, JWP, LVI Group, Maxco, MMR Holding, Morrison Knudsen, Perini, Turner, and Williams Industries.

The eighteen companies making up the Peer Group were then further analyzed and divided into three separate "Cases." Case I includes all eighteen companies in the Peer Group; Case II includes only eleven companies in the Peer Group; and Case III includes sixteen of the original eighteen companies in the Peer Group. Two deletions were made from the Case I companies to arrive at the Case III group of companies. One company was deleted because it provided maintenance services only, a business line markedly different than Pullman's. The other company was excluded because it had significant units in the business of manufacturing and distributing auto parts, auto paints and industrial supplies.

Next, the market risk premium was calculated. This is defined as the premium which investors demand over the risk-free rate in order to compensate them for investments in common stock. The market risk premium for the stock market as a whole was calculated as follows:

- The Center for Research in Security Prices ("CRSP") calculates a monthly equal-weighted market return on the New York Stock Exchange portfolio of securities for each month from 1926 through 1987. These monthly NYSE portfolio returns were downloaded from CRSP by Ernst & Whinney, and comparable annual returns were calculated from these monthly returns.
- The average monthly return on Treasury Bills was also downloaded from the CRSP database. Comparable annual returns were calculated from these monthly returns. The top marginal tax rate in each year from 1926 through 1987 was applied to the calculated annual Treasury Bill returns to determine the after-tax return on Treasury Bills, *i.e.*, the after-tax risk-free rate.
- The market risk premium between the equal weighted NYSE portfolio and the after-tax risk-free rate was calculated by Ernst & Whinney for each year from 1926

to 1987. The average of these annual premiums, 14.98% was used as the market risk premium in the CAPM equation.

The CAPM cost of capital for each of the three Cases was calculated using the risk-free rate (5.83%), the market risk-premium (14.98%) and the applicable asset betas (.80 for Case I, .85 for Case II, and .82 for Case III) as follows:

	Case I	Case II	Case III
After-tax market risk premium	14.98%	14.98%	14.98%
Peer group asset beta	0.80	0.85	0.82
	11.94%	12.72%	12.24%
Add: after-tax risk-free rate	5.83%	5.83%	5.83%
Derived discount rate	17.77%	18.55%	18.07%

Pullman and Wells Fargo experts concluded that 18% is the proper rate applicable here.

The Court's Conclusions as to Value from all the Evidence

Considering the foregoing evidence and arguments, the Court concludes that Debtors' approach and computation as to valuation was correct in the main and generally adequate to enable this Court to find the appropriate value. As many other judges have found, this Court recognizes that all valuations of going business value are only educated estimates in the absence of one or more buyers ready, willing and able to purchase the business. Given the two years of bankruptcy wherein no buyer appeared, the closely held nature of a business in which its president is a key and perhaps irreplaceable leader, and the inherent uncertainties of future business in the construction industry, an arms' length outside buyer is not foreseeable and was not obtained. Consequently, based on expert evidence and historic results, this Court must fix a value through the use of imperfect theories, formulas, and assumptions. Some of the assumptions are uncertain (e.g. use of the "Peer Group" of companies to formulate a capitalization rate despite many differences between those companies and the Debtors.) However, use of uncertain assumptions are inherent in this process. While this underlines the inherently uncertain quality of the analysis, economic assumptions that all experts agreed on provide persuasive evidence even where they are uncertain.

However, the Court need not and does not accept one assumption that came from the Debtors and is more a wild leap of faith than a reasoned but uncertain assumption. That is the projection by Debtors of future "large commercial construction" business to be obtained by it in the years following its hoped-for confirmation.

Debtors project that revenue from that source will rise from $6,964,000 in 1988 to $7,268,000 in 1989, and then jump to a whopping $10,037,000 in 1990 after confirmation. That projects an increase of more than one-third in one year. This projection as a major component in the valuation of cash flow. However, it is based almost entirely on an anticipated "bounce" from the hoped-for reorganization. No firm evidence of actual specific new jobs and customers support this projection which is therefore a mere hope.

Wells Fargo sought a finding of value even higher than that proposed by Debtors, so it did not question the projection by Debtors for large commercial projects. The

Committee and this Court does. Based on historic data (and Debtors' prior short-falls in revenues predicted in prior hearings before this Court), it is doubtful that revenues from large commercial construction will be as high as projected. The Debtors' exaggerated projection inflates its computation of value. A five percent shortfall from Debtors' projections is likely. This reduces the Debtor's total valuation computation of $5,547,000 by $516,000.

Rounding off the result recognizes that valuation here is only an informed approximation. The Court finds the going concern value of Debtors to be $5,000,000.

QUESTIONS

1. Since Pullman was a private company and thus there is no beta of the company, how did the court calculate the discount rate? *mkt comparables*
2. Other than a "wild leap of faith" about some aspect of the projections, what other factor found in the case opinion might have led the court to reduce the valuation from $5,547,000 to $5 million?

In 2010, Berkshire Hathaway, Warren Buffett's investment company, acquired Burlington Northern Santa Fe Corporation ("BNSF") for a mixed cash and stock consideration of over $26 billion. In Berkshire Hathaway's registration statement in connection with the issuance of its stock, it informed its shareholders that BNSF hired two investment bankers, Goldman Sachs and Evercore, to advise BNSF's board of directors on the fairness of the acquisition consideration from a financial point of view. This advice required a thorough valuation study. Below are: (1) the complete excerpt of the section of the registration statement summarizing Evercore's valuation study, and (2) a complete reproduction of Goldman Sachs' letter to the board opining on the fairness of the transaction (each investment banker performed an independent valuation and provided a separate fairness opinion letter).

Form S-4 of Berkshire Hathaway Inc.

Registration Statement Related to the Acquisition of BNSF (Nov. 25, 2009)

OPINION OF EVERCORE

On November 2, 2009, at a meeting of the BNSF Board, Evercore delivered to the BNSF Board an oral opinion, which opinion was subsequently confirmed by delivery of a written opinion dated November 2, 2009, to the effect that, as of that date and based on and subject to assumptions made, matters considered and limitations on the scope of review undertaken by Evercore as set forth therein, the merger consideration was fair, from a financial point of view, to the holders (other than Berkshire and its affiliates) of the shares of BNSF common stock entitled to receive such merger consideration.

The full text of Evercore's written opinion, dated November 2, 2009, which sets forth, among other things, the procedures followed, assumptions made, matters considered and limitations on the scope of review undertaken in rendering its opinion, is attached as Annex D to this proxy statement/prospectus and is incorporated by reference in its entirety into this proxy statement/prospectus. You are urged to read Evercore's opinion carefully and in its entirety. Evercore's opinion was directed to the BNSF Board and addresses only the fairness, from a financial point of view, of the merger consideration to the holders (other than Berkshire and its affiliates) of the shares of BNSF common stock entitled to receive such merger consideration. The opinion does not address any other aspect of the proposed merger and does not constitute a recommendation to any holder of BNSF common stock as to how such stockholder should vote or act with respect to any matters relating to the merger. Evercore's opinion does not address the relative merits of the merger as compared to other business or financial strategies that might be available to BNSF, nor does it address the underlying business decision of BNSF to engage in the merger.

In connection with rendering its opinion, Evercore, among other things:

- reviewed certain publicly available business and financial information relating to BNSF and Berkshire that it deemed to be relevant, including publicly available research analysts' estimates;
- reviewed certain non-public historical financial and operating data relating to BNSF prepared and furnished to it by management of BNSF;
- reviewed certain non-public projected financial and operating data relating to BNSF under alternative business assumptions prepared and furnished to it by management of BNSF;
- discussed the past and current operations, financial projections and current financial condition of BNSF with management of BNSF (including management's views on the risks and uncertainties of achieving such projections) and discussed the past and current operations, current financial condition and certain forward-looking information of Berkshire with management of Berkshire;
- reviewed the reported prices and the historical trading activity of BNSF common stock and Berkshire Class A common stock;
- compared the financial performance of BNSF and Berkshire and their respective stock market trading multiples with those of certain other publicly traded companies and indices that it deemed relevant;
- compared the financial performance of BNSF and the valuation multiples relating to the merger with those of certain other transactions that it deemed relevant;
- reviewed the merger agreement; and
- performed such other analyses and examinations and considered such other factors that it deemed appropriate.

For purposes of its analysis and opinion, Evercore assumed and relied upon, without undertaking any independent verification of, the accuracy and completeness of all of the information publicly available, and all of the information supplied or otherwise made available to, discussed with, or reviewed by Evercore, and Evercore assumed no liability therefor. With respect to the projected financial data relating to BNSF referred to above and approved for Evercore's use by BNSF, Evercore assumed that such projected financial data had been reasonably prepared on bases reflecting the best currently available assumptions, estimates and good faith judgments of management of BNSF as to the future financial performance of BNSF. Management of BNSF had informed Evercore that the 2011 Recovery Case was the most likely of the forecasts provided to Evercore. Evercore expressed no view as to any projected financial data relating to BNSF or the assumptions on which such projected financial data was based. Management of Berkshire did not provide Evercore with any forecasts or projections for Berkshire and Evercore's discussions with Berkshire's management with respect to potential future forecasts and projections were therefore limited to discussions of certain forward-looking information.

For purposes of rendering its opinion, Evercore assumed, in all respects material to its analysis, that the representations and warranties of each party contained in the merger agreement were true and correct, that each party would perform all of the covenants and agreements required to be performed by it under the merger agreement and that all conditions to the consummation of the merger would be satisfied without material waiver or modification thereof. Evercore further assumed that all governmental, regulatory or other consents, approvals or releases necessary for the consummation of the merger would be obtained without any material delay, limitation, restriction or condition that would have an adverse effect on BNSF or the consummation of the merger or reduce the benefits to the holders of BNSF common stock of the merger in any respect material to its opinion.

Evercore did not make or assume any responsibility for making any independent valuation or appraisal of the assets or liabilities of BNSF, nor was Evercore furnished with any such appraisals. Evercore did not evaluate the solvency or fair value of BNSF under any state or Federal laws relating to bankruptcy, insolvency or similar matters. Evercore's opinion was necessarily based upon information made available to it as of the date of its opinion and financial, economic, market and other conditions as they existed and as could be evaluated on the date of its opinion. It should be understood that subsequent developments may affect Evercore's opinion and that Evercore has no obligation to update, revise or reaffirm its opinion.

Evercore was not asked to pass upon, and expressed no opinion with respect to, any matter other than the fairness, from a financial point of view, of the merger consideration to the holders (other than Berkshire and its affiliates) of the shares of BNSF common stock entitled to receive such merger consideration. Evercore did not express any view on, and its opinion did not address, the fairness of the proposed transaction to, or any consideration received in connection therewith by, the holders of any other securities, creditors or other constituencies of BNSF, nor the fairness of the amount or nature of any compensation to be paid or payable to any of the officers, directors or employees of BNSF, or any class of such persons, whether relative to the merger consideration or otherwise. Evercore assumed that any modification to the structure of the transaction would not vary such structure in any respect material to its analysis. Evercore's opinion did not address the relative merits of the merger as compared to other business or financial strategies that might be available to BNSF, nor did Evercore's opinion address the underlying business decision of BNSF to engage in the merger. In arriving at its opinion, Evercore was not authorized to solicit, and did not solicit, interest from any third party with respect to the acquisition of any or all of the BNSF common stock or any business combination or other extraordinary transaction involving BNSF. Evercore expressed no opinion as to the price at which shares of BNSF or Berkshire will trade at any time. Evercore's opinion noted that Evercore is not a legal, regulatory, accounting or tax expert and that Evercore had assumed the accuracy and completeness of assessments by BNSF and its advisors with respect to legal, regulatory, accounting and tax matters.

Except as described above, the BNSF Board imposed no other instructions or limitations on Evercore with respect to the investigations made or the procedures followed by Evercore in rendering its opinion. Evercore's opinion was only one of many factors considered by the BNSF Board in its evaluation of the merger and should not be viewed as determinative of the views of the BNSF Board or BNSF management with respect to the merger or the merger consideration payable in the merger.

Set forth below is a summary of the material financial analyses reviewed by Evercore with the BNSF Board on November 2, 2009 in connection with rendering its opinion. The following summary, however, does not purport to be a complete description of the analyses performed by Evercore. The order of the analyses described and the results of these analyses do not represent relative importance or weight given to these analyses by Evercore. Except as otherwise noted, the following quantitative information, to the extent that it is based on market data, is based on market data as it existed on or before October 30, 2009 (the last trading day prior to November 2, 2009, the date on which the BNSF Board adopted a resolution to approve the merger), and is not necessarily indicative of current market conditions.

The following summary of financial analyses includes information presented in tabular format. These tables must be read together with the text of each summary in order to understand fully the financial analyses. The tables alone do not constitute a complete description of the financial analyses. Considering the tables below without considering the full narrative description of the financial analyses, including the methodologies and assumptions underlying the analyses, could create a misleading or incomplete view of Evercore's financial analyses.

BNSF Financial Analysis

Historical Share Price Analysis. Evercore considered historical data with regard to the closing stock prices of BNSF common stock as of October 30, 2009 and over the ten-year, five-year, one-year, six-month, three-month, one-month and ten-day periods prior to and including October 30, 2009, and the average closing stock price for each such period. During the one-year period prior to and including October 30, 2009, the closing stock price of BNSF common stock ranged from a low of $51.20 to a high of $91.60 per share, with an average closing stock price of $73.07. The foregoing historical share price analysis was presented to the BNSF Board to provide it with background information and perspective with respect to the relative historical share price of BNSF common stock.

	HISTORICAL CLOSING STOCK PRICE		
	LOW	*HIGH*	*AVERAGE*
1 Day (October 30, 2009)	$75.32	$75.32	$75.32
10 Days	75.32	86.40	80.34
1 Month	75.32	86.50	81.20
3 Months	75.32	86.50	82.13
6 Months	68.09	86.50	79.07
1 Year	51.20	91.60	73.07
5 Years	41.67	114.56	74.63
10 Years	19.25	114.56	51.46

Historical Exchange Ratio Analysis. Evercore compared the historical per share prices of BNSF common stock and Berkshire Class A common stock over the ten-year, five-year, one-year, six-month, three-month, one-month and ten-day periods prior to and including October 30, 2009 in order to determine the low, high and average implied exchange ratio that existed for each such period.

HISTORICAL EXCHANGE RATIO

	LOW	HIGH	AVERAGE
1 Day (October 30, 2009)	0.00077x	0.00077x	0.00077x
10 Days	0.00076x	0.00086x	0.00080x
1 Month	0.00076x	0.00086x	0.00081x
3 Months	0.00076x	0.00086x	0.00082x
6 Months	0.00076x	0.00088x	0.00082x
1 Year	0.00065x	0.00093x	0.00078x
5 Years	0.00049x	0.00100x	0.00073x
10 Years	0.00032x	0.00100x	0.00057x

Research Analyst Price Targets. Evercore analyzed research analyst estimates of potential future value for shares of BNSF common stock, commonly referred to as "price targets," based on publicly available equity research published with respect to BNSF. Evercore observed that, as of October 30, 2009, research analyst one-year forward price targets for shares of BNSF common stock ranged from $70 to $103 per share, with an average price target of $91 per share. Evercore then discounted the price targets twelve months at an assumed discount rate of 11%, derived by taking into consideration, among other things, a cost of equity calculation, resulting in a present value ranging from $63.06 to $92.79 per share.

Peer Group Trading Analysis. In order to assess how the public market values shares of similar publicly traded companies, Evercore reviewed and compared specific financial and operating data relating to BNSF to that of a group of selected peer companies that Evercore deemed to have certain characteristics that are similar to those of BNSF. As part of its peer group trading analysis, Evercore calculated and analyzed the multiple of current stock price to estimated 2009 and 2010 earnings per share (commonly referred to as a "price earnings multiple," or "P/E") for BNSF and each member of its peer group. Evercore also calculated and analyzed the multiple of enterprise value to estimated 2009 and 2010 earnings before interest, taxes, depreciation and amortization ("EBITDA") (commonly referred to as an "EBITDA multiple") for BNSF and each member of its respective peer group. The enterprise value of each company was obtained by adding its short and long term debt to the sum of the market value of its common equity and the book value of any minority interest, and subtracting its cash and cash equivalents and book value of unconsolidated investments. The companies that Evercore deemed to have certain characteristics similar to those of BNSF were Canadian National Railway Company, Canadian Pacific Railway Limited, CSX Corporation, Norfolk Southern Corporation and Union Pacific Corporation.

The analysis of current stock price to earnings per share indicated that, for the selected peer group, the current stock price as a multiple of estimated 2009 earnings per share ranged from 14.8x to 17.7x with a mean of 16.1x, and the current stock price as a multiple of estimated 2010 earnings per share ranged from 12.9x to 13.7x with a mean of 13.4x. This compared to a current stock price to estimated 2009 earnings per share multiple of 15.4x for BNSF and a current stock price to estimated 2010 earnings per share multiple of 13.6x for BNSF, in each case based on publicly available research estimates. Evercore noted that, with respect to the merger, the implied price as a multiple of BNSF estimated 2009 and 2010 earnings per share, in each case based on publicly available research estimates, was 20.4x and 18.1x, respectively.

Based on the above analysis, Evercore then applied a range of current stock price as a multiple of estimated 2009 earnings per share of 15.0x to 17.0x and a range of current stock price as a multiple of estimated 2010 earnings per share of 13.0x to 14.0x to the mean of BNSF's consensus publicly available earnings per share research estimates for 2009 and 2010, respectively. This analysis indicated implied per share equity reference ranges for BNSF common stock of $73.52 to $83.32 and $71.97 to $77.50 based on the mean of BNSF consensus publicly available earnings per share research estimates for 2009 and 2010, respectively. Evercore also applied such ranges of multiples to the respective BNSF 2009 and 2010 earnings per share estimates under each of the BNSF management 2010 Recovery Case, the BNSF management 2011 Recovery Case, the BNSF management No Recovery Case and the BNSF management Deeper Recession Case; such analysis indicated implied per share equity reference ranges for BNSF common stock of $71.55 to $81.09 and $49.66 to $70.56 for 2009 and 2010, respectively. Management of BNSF had informed Evercore that the 2011 Recovery Case is the most likely of the forecasts provided to Evercore.

The analysis of financial multiples indicated that, for the selected peer group, enterprise value as a multiple of estimated 2009 EBITDA ranged from 7.0x to 9.5x with a mean of 8.1x, and enterprise value as a multiple of estimated 2010 EBITDA ranged from 6.4x to 8.3x with a mean of 7.2x. This compared to an enterprise value to estimated 2009 EBITDA multiple of 7.4x and an enterprise value to estimated 2010 EBITDA multiple of 6.7x for BNSF, based on publicly available research estimates. Evercore noted that, with respect to the merger, the implied enterprise value as a multiple of BNSF estimated 2009 and 2010 EBITDA, in each case based on publicly available research estimates, was 9.2x and 8.4x, respectively.

Based on the above analysis, Evercore then applied a range of enterprise value as a multiple of estimated 2009 EBITDA of 7.0x to 8.5x and a range of enterprise value as a multiple of estimated 2010 EBITDA of 6.5x to 8.0x to the mean of BNSF's consensus publicly available EBITDA research estimates for 2009 and 2010, respectively. This analysis indicated implied per share equity reference ranges for BNSF common stock of $70.14 to $90.91 and $71.73 to $94.46 based on the mean of consensus publicly available EBITDA estimates for 2009 and 2010, respectively. Evercore also applied such ranges of multiples to the respective BNSF 2009 and 2010 EBITDA estimates, under each of the BNSF management 2010 Recovery Case, the BNSF management 2011 Recovery Case, the BNSF management No Recovery Case and the BNSF management Deeper Recession Case; such analysis indicated implied per share equity reference ranges for BNSF common stock of $69.53 to $90.17 and $56.04 to $90.61 for 2009 and 2010, respectively. Management of BNSF had informed Evercore that the 2011 Recovery Case is the most likely of the forecasts provided to Evercore.

Evercore selected the peer companies identified above because their respective businesses and operating profiles are reasonably similar to that of BNSF. However, because of the inherent differences between the businesses, operations and prospects of BNSF, on the one hand, and the businesses, operations and prospects of the selected peer companies on the other, no company is exactly the same as BNSF.

Discounted Cash Flow Analysis. Evercore performed a discounted cash flow analysis of BNSF in order to derive implied per share equity reference ranges for BNSF based on the implied present value of projected future cash flows of BNSF. In this analysis, Evercore calculated implied per share equity reference ranges for BNSF under each of the BNSF management 2010 Recovery Case, the BNSF management 2011 Recovery Case, the BNSF management No Recovery Case and the BNSF management Deeper Recession Case based on the sum of the (i) implied present values, using discount rates ranging from 8.0% to 10.0% derived by taking into consideration, among other things, a weighted average cost of capital calculation, of BNSF's projected unlevered free cash flows for calendar years 2010 through 2014 and (ii) implied present values, using discount rates ranging from 8.0% to 10.0%, of the terminal value of BNSF's future cash flows beyond calendar year 2014 calculated by applying a range of EBITDA terminal multiples of 6.75x to 8.25x derived from the selected peer companies as described in "Peer Group Trading Analysis" above to BNSF's calendar year 2014 projected EBITDA. This analysis indicated implied per share equity reference ranges for BNSF common stock of $91.50 to 124.47 under the BNSF management 2010 Recovery Case, $81.53 to $112.12 under the BNSF management 2011 Recovery Case, $54.16 to $76.92 under the BNSF management No Recovery Case, and $46.56 to $67.70 under the BNSF management Deeper Recession Case. Management of BNSF had informed Evercore that the 2011 Recovery Case is the most likely of the forecasts provided to Evercore.

Present Value of Future Stock Price Analysis. Evercore performed a present value of illustrative future stock price analysis of BNSF based on the BNSF management projections provided to Evercore. In this analysis, Evercore calculated future prices per share and equity values of BNSF under each of the BNSF management 2010 Recovery Case, the BNSF management 2011 Recovery Case, the BNSF management No Recovery Case and the BNSF management Deeper Recession Case for calendar years 2010 through 2014 by applying a multiple of 13.5x (representing the mid-point of the range of current stock price as a multiple of estimated 2010 earnings per share for the BNSF group of selected peer companies as described in "Peer Group Trading Analysis" above) to BNSF's projected earnings per share for each of those years. These illustrative future stock prices were discounted to present value as of December 31, 2009 using discount rates of 10.0% to 12.0%, taking into consideration, among other things, a cost of equity calculation, and were increased to reflect the present value of the future dividend projected to be paid by BNSF. With reference to the median discount rate of 11.0%, this analysis indicated ranges of implied value per share of BNSF common stock of $68.04 to $103.73 under the BNSF management 2010 Recovery Case, $59.54 to $89.41 under the BNSF management 2011 Recovery Case, $50.05 to $58.00 under the BNSF management No Recovery Case, and $40.98 to $51.57 under the BNSF management Deeper Recession Case. Management of BNSF had informed Evercore that the 2011 Recovery Case is the most likely of the forecasts provided to Evercore.

Premiums Paid Analysis. Evercore performed a premiums paid analysis of BNSF in order to derive implied per share equity reference ranges for BNSF based on the premiums paid in selected transactions. In this analysis, using publicly available information, Evercore reviewed the premiums paid in the 20 largest transactions (based on transaction value) involving U.S. corporations that were announced between January 15, 1999 and January 26, 2009, which transactions are listed below:

Acquiror	**Target**
• Vodafone Group PLC	• AirTouch Communications, Inc.
• AT&T Corp.	• MediaOne Group Inc.
• Qwest Communications Int'l, Inc.	• US WEST Inc.
• Viacom Inc.	• CBS Corp.
• Pfizer Inc.	• Warner-Lambert Co.
• America Online Inc.	• Time Warner, Inc.
• JDS Uniphase Corp.	• SDL Inc.
• Chevron Corp.	• Texaco Inc.
• Pfizer Inc.	• Pharmacia Corp.
• Bank of America Corp.	• FleetBoston Financial Corp.
• JPMorgan Chase & Co.	• Bank One Corp.
• Cingular Wireless LLC	• AT&T Wireless Services Inc.
• Sprint Corp.	• Nextel Communications Inc.
• The Procter & Gamble Company	• The Gillette Company
• Bank of America Corp.	• MBNA Corp.
• AT&T Inc.	• BellSouth Corp.
• The Blackstone Group L.P.	• Equity Office Properties Trust
• InBev NV	• Anheuser-Busch Cos., Inc.
• Roche Holding AG	• Genentech Inc.
• Pfizer Inc.	• Wyeth

Evercore reviewed the premiums paid in the selected transactions referenced above based on the value of the per share consideration received in the relevant transaction relative to the closing stock price of the target company one day, one week and four weeks prior to the announcement date of the transaction.

IMPLIED PREMIUMS FOR SELECTED TRANSACTIONS

	1 DAY	1 WEEK	4 WEEKS
Mean	26%	27%	33%
Median	23%	27%	30%
High	69%	54%	69%
Low	0%	2%	1%
Mean Since 2008	23%	26%	34%

Based on the above analysis, Evercore then applied low and high selected premiums of 20% and 30% derived from the selected transactions to the closing price of BNSF common stock on October 30, 2009, the last trading day prior to the date on which the BNSF Board adopted a resolution approving the merger agreement. This analysis indicated an implied per share equity reference range for BNSF of $90.38 to $97.92.

Precedent Transactions Analysis. Evercore performed an analysis of selected transactions to compare multiples paid in other transactions to the multiples implied in the merger. Evercore identified and analyzed a group of six merger and acquisition transactions that were announced (but not necessarily completed) between 1994 and 1999. Although, in Evercore's opinion, none of those transactions are by themselves directly comparable to the merger, each could be considered similar to the merger (although not necessarily to each other) in certain limited respects. In assessing the quantitative results of the precedent transactions analysis, Evercore noted and made qualitative judgments concerning the small number of potentially comparable transactions and the differences between the nature and characteristics of the merger and such transactions (specifically, rail network transactions occurring between 1994 and 1999 involving strategic parties and projected to generate substantial synergies). For each of the selected transactions, Evercore calculated enterprise value as a multiple of last twelve months ("LTM") EBITDA and enterprise value as a multiple of LTM revenue.

The selected transactions are set forth below:

DATE ANNOUNCED	ACQUIROR	TARGET
12/20/99	BNSF	Canadian National Railway Co.
02/10/98	Canadian National Railway Co.	Illinois Central Corp.
04/08/97	CSX Corp./Norfolk Southern Corp.	Consolidated Rail Corp.
08/03/95	Union Pacific Corp.	Southern Pacific Rail Corp.
03/10/95	Union Pacific Corp.	Chicago & North Western Transportation
06/30/94	BNSF	Santa Fe Pacific Corp.

Based on these transactions, Evercore selected a range of implied enterprise value to LTM EBITDA multiples between 7.0x and 10.0x LTM EBITDA, yielding an implied price per share of BNSF common stock that ranged from $74.39 to $117.76. Evercore noted that the implied enterprise value to LTM EBITDA multiple of the merger was 8.8x relative to the range of implied multiples of 6.8x to 12.5x determined with reference to LTM EBITDA and also noted that the implied enterprise value to LTM revenue multiple of the merger was 2.98x relative to the range of implied multiples of 1.73x to 4.29x determined with reference to LTM revenue.

Berkshire Financial Analysis

Historical Share Price Analysis. Evercore considered historical data with regard to the closing stock prices of Berkshire Class A common stock for the three-month, one-year and five-year periods prior to and including October 30, 2009. During these periods, the closing stock prices of Berkshire Class A common stock ranged from a low of $95,250 to a high of $108,100 per share in the three-month period, a low of $72,400 to a high of $118,400 per share in the one-year period, and a low of $72,400 to a high of $149,200 per share in the five-year period, in each case prior to and including October 30, 2009, the last trading day prior to the date on which the BNSF Board adopted a resolution approving the merger agreement. The foregoing historical share price analysis was presented to the BNSF Board to provide it with background information and perspective with respect to the relative historical share prices of Berkshire Class A common stock.

Research Analyst Price Targets. Evercore analyzed research analyst estimates of potential future value for shares of Berkshire Class A common stock, commonly referred to as "price targets," based on publicly available equity research published with respect to Berkshire. Evercore observed that two research analyst one-year forward price targets for shares of Berkshire Class A common stock ranged from $96,000 to $133,000 per share, with an average price target of $114,500 per share. Evercore then discounted the price targets twelve months at an assumed discount rate of 11.5%, derived by taking into consideration, among other things, a cost of equity calculation, resulting in a present value range from $86,108 to $119,295 per share.

Book Value Analysis. Using publicly available information, Evercore analyzed the multiple of closing stock price per share to last reported book value per share for Berkshire for each of the seven and one-half year, five-year, three-year, one-year, six-month, three-month and one-month periods prior to and including October 30, 2009. Evercore then compared the results of such analysis to the multiples derived from the same analysis for the S&P 500. Based on reference to the median of the upper and lower quartiles of the multiple of closing stock price per share to last reported book value per share for Berkshire for each of the seven and one-half year, five-year, three-year, one-year, six-month, three-month and one-month periods prior to and including October 30, 2009, Evercore selected a range of market price to book value per share multiples of 1.3x to 1.7x, yielding an implied price per share of Berkshire Class A common stock that ranged from $95,948 to $125,471 per share. Evercore also selected and applied a discount range of 30% to 45% discount to the S&P 500 market price to book value per share multiple as of October 30, 2009, yielding an implied price per share of Berkshire Class A common stock that ranged from $88,740 to $112,941 per share.

Forward Price Analysis. Using publicly available research estimates and other publicly-available information, Evercore analyzed the multiple of closing stock price to the next fiscal year mean earnings per share estimate for Berkshire Hathaway for each of the seven and one-half year, five-year, three-year, one-year, six-month, three-month and one-month periods prior to and including October 30, 2009. Evercore then compared the results of such analysis to the multiples derived from the same analysis for the S&P 500. Based on reference to the median of the upper and lower quartiles of the multiple of closing stock price per share to the next fiscal year mean earnings per share estimate for Berkshire for each of the seven and one-half year, five-year, three-year, one-year, six-month, three-month and one-month periods prior to and including October 30, 2009, Evercore selected and applied a premium range of 10% to 40% to the S&P 500 closing stock price to next fiscal year mean earnings per share estimate multiple as of October 30, 2009, yielding an implied price per share of Berkshire Class A common stock that ranged from $85,134 to $108,352.

General

In connection with the review of the merger by the BNSF Board, Evercore performed a variety of financial and comparative analyses for purposes of rendering its opinion. The preparation of a fairness opinion is a complex process and is not necessarily susceptible to partial analysis or summary description. Selecting portions of the analyses or of the summary described above, without considering the analyses as a whole, could create an incomplete view of the processes underlying Evercore's opinion. In arriving at its fairness determination, Evercore considered the results of all the analyses and did not attribute any particular weight to any factor or analysis considered by it. Rather, Evercore made its determination as to fairness on the basis of its experience and professional judgment after considering the results of all the analyses. In addition, Evercore may have deemed various assumptions more or less probable than other assumptions, so that the range of valuations resulting from any particular analysis described above should therefore not be taken to be Evercore's view of the value of BNSF or Berkshire or their respective common stocks. No company used in the above analyses as a comparison is directly comparable to BNSF or Berkshire, and no transaction used is directly comparable to the transactions contemplated by the merger agreement. Further, in evaluating comparable transactions, Evercore made judgments and assumptions with regard to industry performance, general business, economic, market and financial conditions and other matters, many of which are beyond the control of BNSF, Berkshire and Evercore, such as the impact of competition on BNSF and Berkshire and their respective industries generally, industry growth and the absence of any material adverse change in the financial condition of BNSF and Berkshire or in the markets generally.

Evercore prepared these analyses for the purpose of providing an opinion to the BNSF Board as to the fairness, from a financial point of view, of the merger consideration to the holders (other than Berkshire and its affiliates) of the shares of BNSF common stock entitled to receive such merger consideration. These analyses do not purport to be appraisals or to necessarily reflect the prices at which the business or securities actually may be sold. Analyses based upon forecasts of future results are not necessarily indicative of actual future results, which may be significantly more or less favorable than suggested by these analyses. Because these analyses are inherently subject to uncertainty and are based upon numerous factors, assumptions with respect to industry performance, general business and economic conditions and other matters or events beyond the control of BNSF, Berkshire and Evercore, none of BNSF, Berkshire or Evercore assumes responsibility if future results are materially different from those forecast. The merger consideration to be received by the holders of the shares of BNSF common stock pursuant to the merger agreement was determined through arm's-length negotiations between BNSF and Berkshire and was approved by the BNSF Board. Evercore did not recommend any specific merger consideration to the BNSF Board or that any given merger consideration constituted the only appropriate merger consideration.

Pursuant to its engagement letter, a fee of $11.5 million becomes payable to Evercore promptly upon consummation of the transaction. Furthermore, BNSF has agreed to reimburse Evercore for its reasonable expenses incurred in connection with the engagement and to indemnify Evercore for certain liabilities arising out of its engagement.

The BNSF Board engaged Evercore as its financial advisor because it is an internationally recognized investment banking and advisory firm that has substantial experience in transactions similar to the merger. Evercore, as part of its investment banking business, is continuously engaged in the valuation of businesses and their securities in connection with mergers and acquisitions, competitive biddings and valuations for corporate, estate and other purposes. In the ordinary course of its business, Evercore and its affiliates may, from time to time, trade in the securities or the indebtedness of BNSF, Berkshire and their affiliates or any currencies or commodities (or derivative thereof) for its own account, the accounts of investment funds and other clients under the management of Evercore and for the accounts of its customers and, accordingly, may at any time hold a long or short position in such securities, indebtedness, currencies or commodities (or derivative thereof) for any such account. Evercore may provide financial or other services to BNSF or Berkshire in the future and in connection with any such services Evercore may receive compensation.

* * *

[FAIRNESS OPINION LETTER OF GOLDMAN SACHS]

November 2, 2009

Board of Directors
Burlington Northern Santa Fe Corporation
2650 Lou Menk Drive
Fort Worth, TX 76131-2830
Ladies and Gentlemen:

You have requested our opinion as to the fairness from a financial point of view to the holders (other than Berkshire Hathaway Inc. ("Berkshire Hathaway") and its affiliates) of the outstanding shares of common stock, par value $0.01 per share (the "Shares"), of Burlington Northern Santa Fe Corporation (the "Company") of the Stock Consideration and the Cash Consideration (each as defined below) to be paid to such holders, taken in the aggregate, pursuant to the Agreement and Plan of Merger, dated as of November 2, 2009 (the "Agreement"), by and among Berkshire Hathaway, R Acquisition Company, LLC, a wholly owned subsidiary of Berkshire Hathaway ("Merger Sub"), and the Company. Pursuant to the Agreement, the Company will be merged with and into Merger Sub (the "Merger") and holders of outstanding Shares (other than Dissenting Shares (as defined in the Agreement) and Shares owned by Berkshire Hathaway, the Company or their respective direct or indirect wholly owned subsidiaries (collectively, "Excluded Shares")) may elect to receive that number of shares (or fraction thereof) of Class A Common Stock, par value $5.00 per share (the "Berkshire Hathaway Class A Common Stock"), of Berkshire Hathaway equal to the Class A Exchange Ratio (as defined in the Agreement); provided that, if after applying the calculation with respect to all Stock Election Shares (as defined in the Agreement) held by a particular holder, that holder would become entitled to receive a fraction of a share of Berkshire Hathaway Class A Common Stock, in lieu of receiving such fractional share, the holder will receive that number of shares of Class B Common Stock, par value $0.1667 per share (the "Berkshire Hathaway Class B Common Stock"), of Berkshire Hathaway equal to the Class B Exchange Ratio (as defined in the Agreement); and provided further that, if such holder would then become entitled to receive a fraction of a share of Berkshire Hathaway Class B Common Stock, in lieu of such fractional share, the holder will receive a cash payment equal to the product of (x) such fraction and (y) the Average Parent Class B Stock Price (as defined in the Agreement) (collectively, the "Stock Consideration"). Holders of Shares (other than Excluded Shares) may elect, with respect to all or a portion of their Shares, to convert such Shares into the right to be paid $100 per Share in cash (the "Cash Consideration"), subject to proration and certain other procedures and limitations contained in the Agreement with respect to Stock Election Shares, Cash Election Shares (as defined in the Agreement) and No Election Shares (as defined in the Agreement), as to which procedures and limitations we express no opinion.

Goldman, Sachs & Co. and its affiliates are engaged in investment banking and financial advisory services, commercial banking, securities trading, investment management, principal investment, financial planning, benefits counseling, risk management, hedging, financing, brokerage activities and other financial and non-financial activities and services for various persons and entities. In the ordinary course of these activities and services, Goldman, Sachs & Co. and its affiliates may at any time make or hold long or short positions and investments, as well as actively trade or effect transactions, in the equity, debt and other securities (or related derivative securities) and financial instruments (including bank loans and other obligations) of third parties, the Company, Berkshire Hathaway and any of their respective affiliates or any currency or commodity that may be involved in the transaction contemplated by the Agreement (the "Transaction") for their own account and for the accounts of their customers. We have acted as financial advisor to the Company in connection with, and have participated in certain of the negotiations leading to, the Transaction. We expect to receive fees for our services in connection with the Transaction, all of which are contingent upon consummation of the Transaction, and the Company has agreed to reimburse our expenses arising, and indemnify us against certain liabilities that may arise, out of our engagement. In addition, we have provided investment banking and other financial services to the Company and its affiliates from time to time, including, but not limited to, having acted as joint-lead manager with respect to an offering by the Company of its 6.150% Global Debentures due 2037 (aggregate principal amount $650,000,000) and its 5.650% Global Debentures due 2017 (aggregate principal amount $650,000,000) in April 2007; as a joint bookrunner with respect to an offering by the Company of its 7.00% Notes due 2014 (aggregate principal amount $500,000,000) in November 2008; and as a joint bookrunner with respect to an offering by the Company of its 4.70% Notes due 2019 (aggregate principal amount $750,000,000) in September 2009. We also have extensively provided and are currently providing certain investment banking and other financial services to Berkshire Hathaway and its affiliates and portfolio companies, including, but not limited to, having acted as joint bookrunner with respect to an offering by PacifiCorp, a subsidiary of Berkshire Hathaway, of its 5.75% First Mortgage Bonds due 2037 (aggregate principal amount $600,000,000) in March 2007; as sole bookrunner with respect to an offering by XTRA Finance Corporation, a subsidiary of Berkshire Hathaway, of its 5.150% Senior Notes due 2017 (aggregate principal amount $400,000,000) in March 2007; as sole bookrunner with respect to an offering by Berkshire Hathaway Finance of its 5⅛% Senior Notes due 2012 (aggregate principal amount $750,000,000) in December 2007; as sole bookrunner with respect to an offering by Berkshire Hathaway Finance of its 4.50% Senior Notes due 2013 (aggregate principal amount $500,000,000) and Floating Rate Notes due 2011 (aggregate principal amount $1,500,000,000) in March 2008; and as joint bookrunner with respect to an offering by Berkshire Hathaway Finance of its 4.00% Senior Notes due 2012 (aggregate principal amount $750,000,000) and its 5.40% Senior Notes due 2018 (aggregate principal amount $250,000,000) in March 2009. We also may provide investment banking and other financial services to the Company and Berkshire Hathaway and its portfolio companies and their respective affiliates in the future.

In connection with the above-described services we have received, and may receive, compensation. On October 1, 2008, affiliates of Berkshire Hathaway purchased from The Goldman Sachs Group, Inc. 50,000 shares of 10% Cumulative Perpetual Preferred Stock, Series G of The Goldman Sachs Group, Inc. (aggregate liquidation preference $5,000,000,000) and warrants to purchase 43,478,260 shares of common stock of The Goldman Sachs Group, Inc. at an exercise price of $115 per share.* Goldman, Sachs & Co. and its affiliates also have co-invested with Berkshire Hathaway and its affiliates from time to time and may do so in the future. In connection with this opinion, we have reviewed, among other things, the Agreement; annual reports to stockholders and Annual Reports on Form 10-K of the Company and Berkshire Hathaway for the five fiscal years ended December 31, 2008; certain interim reports to stockholders and Quarterly Reports on Form 10-Q of the Company and Berkshire Hathaway; certain other communications from the Company and Berkshire Hathaway to their respective stockholders; certain publicly available research analyst reports for the Company and Berkshire Hathaway; and certain internal financial analyses and forecasts for the Company prepared by its management, including the Company's 2011 Recovery forecast (the "2011 Recovery Forecast"), which were approved for our use by the Company. The Company has directed us to assume that the 2011 Recovery Forecast is more likely than the Company's other forecasts prepared by its management. As you are aware, the management of Berkshire Hathaway did not make available its forecasts of the future financial performance of Berkshire Hathaway. With your consent, our review of the future financial performance of Berkshire Hathaway was limited to our discussions with the management of Berkshire Hathaway regarding the publicly available estimates of a certain research analyst, as well as current consensus forecasts of Berkshire Hathaway. We also have held discussions with members of the senior managements of the Company and Berkshire Hathaway regarding their assessment of the strategic rationale for, and the potential benefits of, the Transaction and the past and current business operations, financial condition and future prospects of their respective companies. In addition, we have reviewed the reported price and trading activity for the Shares, the shares of Berkshire Hathaway Class A Common Stock and the shares of Berkshire Hathaway Class B Common Stock, compared certain financial and stock market information for the Company and Berkshire Hathaway with similar information for certain other companies the securities of which are publicly traded, reviewed the financial terms of certain recent business combinations in the transportation and rail industry specifically and in other industries generally and performed such other studies and analyses, and considered such other factors, as we considered appropriate.

For purposes of rendering this opinion, we have relied upon and assumed, without assuming any responsibility for independent verification, the accuracy and completeness of all of the financial, legal, regulatory, tax, accounting and other information provided to, discussed with or reviewed by us, and we do not assume any liability for

---

* Author's note: In Chapter 6 discussing preferred stock, this book presents a case study on Berkshire Hathaway's preferred stock and warrants investment in Goldman Sachs referenced here in Berkshire Hathaway's Form S-4.

any such information. In that regard, we have assumed with your consent that the 2011 Recovery Forecast has been reasonably prepared on a basis reflecting the best currently available estimates and judgments of the management of the Company. In addition, we have not made an independent evaluation or appraisal of the assets and liabilities (including any contingent, derivative or off-balance-sheet assets and liabilities) of the Company or Berkshire Hathaway or any of their respective subsidiaries and we have not been furnished with any such evaluation or appraisal. We have assumed that all governmental, regulatory or other consents and approvals necessary for the consummation of the Transaction will be obtained without any adverse effect on the Company or Berkshire Hathaway or on the expected benefits of the Transaction in any way meaningful to our analysis. We also have assumed that the Transaction will be consummated on the terms set forth in the Agreement, without the waiver or modification of any term or condition the effect of which would be in any way meaningful to our analysis. We are not expressing any opinion as to the impact of the Transaction on the solvency or viability of the Company or Berkshire Hathaway or the ability of the Company or Berkshire Hathaway to pay its obligations when they come due. Our opinion does not address any legal, regulatory, tax or accounting matters.

Our opinion does not address the underlying business decision of the Company to engage in the Transaction, or the relative merits of the Transaction as compared to any strategic alternatives that may be available to the Company. We were not requested to solicit, and did not solicit, interest from other parties with respect to an acquisition of, or other business combination with, the Company or any other alternative transaction. This opinion addresses only the fairness from a financial point of view, as of the date hereof, to the holders of Shares (other than Berkshire Hathaway and its affiliates) of the Stock Consideration and the Cash Consideration to be paid to the holders of Shares, taken in the aggregate, pursuant to the Agreement. We do not express any view on, and our opinion does not address, any other term or aspect of the Agreement or Transaction or any term or aspect of any other agreement or instrument contemplated by the Agreement or entered into or amended in connection with the Transaction, including, without limitation, the fairness of the Transaction to, or any consideration received in connection therewith by, the holders of any other class of securities, creditors, or other constituencies of the Company; nor as to the fairness of the amount or nature of any compensation to be paid or payable to any of the officers, directors or employees of the Company, or class of such persons in connection with the Transaction, whether relative to the Stock Consideration and the Cash Consideration to be paid to the holders of Shares, taken in the aggregate, pursuant to the Agreement or otherwise. We are not expressing any opinion as to the prices at which shares of Berkshire Hathaway Class A Common Stock or Berkshire Hathaway Class B Common Stock will trade at any time. Our opinion is necessarily based on economic, monetary, market and other conditions as in effect on, and the information made available to us as of, the date hereof and we assume no responsibility for updating, revising or reaffirming this opinion based on circumstances, developments or events occurring after the date hereof. Our advisory services and the opinion expressed herein are provided for the information and assistance of the Board of Directors of the Company in connection with its consideration of the Transaction and such opinion does not constitute a recommendation as to how any holder of Shares should vote or make an election with respect to such Transaction or any other matter. This opinion has been approved by a fairness committee of Goldman, Sachs & Co.

Based upon and subject to the foregoing, it is our opinion that, as of the date hereof, the Stock Consideration and the Cash Consideration to be paid to the holders of Shares, taken in the aggregate, pursuant to the Agreement is fair from a financial point of view to such holders (other than Berkshire Hathaway and its affiliates).

Very truly yours,

GOLDMAN, SACHS & CO.

E. MARKET MECHANISMS

1. LAW OF ONE PRICE AND ARBITRAGE

If multiples and other valuational metrics are so important to valuation, where do they come from? Why is McDonald's P/E 16.5x and Google's 22.3x? Why aren't these multiples 10.0x or 19.8x or 33.5x? Who assigns these important numbers, or how did they come to be? The capital market—a marketplace where the securities of companies are bought and sold—determines the value of companies just the way that everyday markets for foods, electronics, clothing, and the like determine the price of things. But how does the capital market determine the value of company securities? The short answer is that ultimately the values are anchored by the intrinsic, theoretical value of the companies (keeping in mind that the market isn't perfect). The capital markets are an aggregation of many investors seeking the maximum return for the lowest risk. Many smart investors try to figure out the value of firms by doing detailed analyses of valuation. Their activities of buying and selling based on available information set the market price and value levels.

A core principle of securities pricing is the Law of One Price. Risk and return can be packaged into different securities, including the many varieties of stocks and debt instruments. The Law of One Price is the principle that securities with the same returns and risks must be priced at the same level irrespective of how they are packaged in securities. It embodies the commonsense notion that there must be one price for the same thing. The Law of One Price is enforced by a process called arbitrage.

Arbitrage is the process wherein riskless profit is made by exploiting incorrectly priced securities. While the term *arbitrage* is fancy, Wall Street traders are not the only ones doing it. For example, not infrequently at the start of a semester, law professors are faced with the situation where a student did not do the reading, not because the student deliberately neglected the assignment but because the textbook had not arrived from the online seller. While textbooks are available at campus bookstores, students routinely shop at various places to buy the cheapest book on the market—the students are exploiting price differentials in the market and are arbitrageurs of law textbooks. Arbitrage facilitates efficient pricing. If an arbitrageur spots a mispriced asset and exploits that difference, others will soon follow. This process results in the closing of mispriced assets as quickly as they are discovered. In an efficient, liquid market, arbitrage opportunities are few and they are fleeting.

EXAMPLE

The Law of One Price and Arbitrage

Let's see how the Law of One Price and arbitrage works with some complicated securities. Suppose a bond, Bond B, can be "stripped" of its interest payments such that rights to interest payments and the principal are traded separately as Bond B(I) and Bond B(P). Other than the process of disaggregation, Bond B and its interest and principal components produce the identical cash flows. Under the Law of One Price, the following must be true: Bond B = Bond B(I) + Bond B(P).

Suppose that Bond B has a face value of $1,000 with a coupon rate of 10% with five years remaining to maturity. From the time that it was issued, say 15 years ago, interest rates have increased substantially. As a result, the price of Bond B dropped significantly. Absent a discount on the market price of the bond, no investor will buy it since they have other opportunities to buy similar quality bonds that are providing greater returns consistent with the prevailing interest rates.

Assume that the current yield on Bond B is 20%, which means that based on the fixed interest payments ($100) and relative current market price of the bond, it is producing a 20% rate of return. The price of Bond B is calculated as follows:

	Yr. 1	Yr. 2	Yr. 3	Yr. 4	Yr. 5
Bond B interest payments	$100	$100	$100	$100	$100
Bond B principal payment					$1,000
Discount factor at 20%	0.8333	0.6944	0.5787	0.4823	0.4019
PV of interest payments	$83.33	$69.44	$57.87	$48.23	$40.19
PV of sum of interest payments					$299.06
PV of principal payment					$401.90
Sum PV of bond					$700.96

Thus, Bond B has a market at $700.96. With interest payments of $100 per year and a principal payment of $1,000 at the end of five years, Bond B produces a rate of return of 20%, which is the amount it should be producing based on the higher interest rate environment. We also see that Bond B(I) should trade on the market for $299.06, and Bond B(P) at $401.90. The Law of One Price states that the following must be true:

$$Bond\ B\ =\ Bond\ B(I)\ +\ Bond\ B(P)$$

$$\$700.96\ =\ \$299.06\ +\ \$401.90$$

Assume that Bond B trades at $700.96 and Bond B(P) at $401.90, but that Bond B(I) trades at $300.06 (one dollar more than its theoretical value).

How should an investor arbitrage this price discrepancy?

The investor should sell the overpriced security: sell Bond B(I) at $300.06 and Bond B(P) at $401.90. With the $701.96 proceeds, she should buy Bond B at $700.96. Bond B produces the identical cash flow of the stripped components Bond B(I) and Bond B(P). The investor makes a riskless profit of $1.00.

If enough smart investors figure out this profit opportunity, the opportunity disappears because the price of Bond B(I) will decline as arbitrageurs sell this overpriced stripped bond. The price will eventually decline to its intrinsic value of $299.06, which means that the arbitrage opportunity would disappear. Thus, the Law of One Price and the process of arbitrage impose financial logic and rationality into the valuation of securities.

EXAMPLE

Bernie Madoff's Amazing Scheme of Riskless Profit

Bernie Madoff, the perpetrator of the world's largest Ponzi scheme, represented that his trades consistently produced an average 12% yearly return, net of large hedge fund fees, for many years without any risk (see below). Without the hedge fund fees deducted, his yearly return is about 16%.

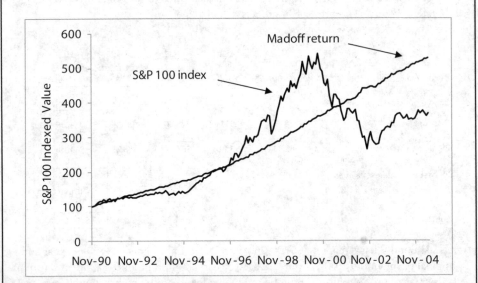

The average long-term returns on a market portfolio is about 11%. The above chart shows that Madoff found a way to make phenomenal riskless profit for many years. Moreover, an investment with Madoff supposedly had a portfolio beta of 0.06. This means that there was almost zero correlation with the market return, as confirmed by the above graph (the market goes up and down, but Madoff's return only goes up). Are Madoff's representations about his trading in the stock market consistent with the Law of One Price and arbitrage?

2. EFFICIENT CAPITAL MARKET HYPOTHESIS

The efficient capital market hypothesis (ECMH) is the hypothesis that the capital markets incorporate information into the price of securities. As a broad thesis, this must be correct. The capital markets incorporate enormous volume of information: *e.g.*, General Motors is short on cash; Enron is embroiled in an accounting scandal; Apple will unveil its new product in two weeks; the CEO of Google resigns; and so forth. Markets assimilate information. The controversy (or at least differences of opinion) concerns the details.

Three forms of ECMH have been asserted. The *weak form* of ECMH states that the market prices of securities incorporate past publicly disclosed information. The *semi-strong* form states that prices quickly incorporate current publicly disclosed information. The *strong form* states that prices incorporate all public and nonpublic information.

The weak form of ECMH must be correct. We can be fairly confident that past public information is already factored into the stock price. For example, McDonald's financial performance in the past fiscal year is surely baked into its current stock price. The capital market may not be perfect, but it is not obtuse either. The validity of the weak form of ECMH means that one cannot achieve abnormal returns by studying past information such as past financial performance and stock price movements because that information is already baked into the current stock price.

We can also be fairly confident that the strong form of ECMH is wrong. As a general proposition, nonpublic information is not factored into stock prices. We know this empirically because upon the announcement of an acquisition with a premium, the share price of the target rises sharply to the level of the acquisition price. These observable events would not occur if the nonpublic information concerning the takeover has already been baked into the stock price at the time of announcement. Studies of insider trading indicate that insiders earn abnormal returns, suggesting that private information is not baked into the stock price. The real abnormal profit opportunity is the reason why criminals risk criminal sanctions. Private information is not substantially baked into the share price.

The controversy concerns the semi-strong form of ECMH. The claim here is that prices are efficient as to all publicly disclosed information. The claim implies that price levels are rational because (1) all past and current public information is incorporated into the stock price, (2) the trades of irrational, stupid, or "noisy" investors are random and so they cancel each other out, and (3) any correlated trading by irrational traders would be subject to arbitrage opportunities by arbitrageurs, who would beat the noisy traders consistently until prices are brought back to a rational level. Thus, prices of securities on the market are efficient, reflecting the accurate value of the securities given the limitation of the public information. The implication of efficient prices is that an investor cannot consistently beat the market.

The claims of the semi-strong form of ECMH are susceptible to challenge because empirical evidence exists to contradict its claims. In the history of the stock market, there have been a number of historic stock market crashes in 1929, 1987, 2000, and most recently 2008. No one can seriously claim that mortgage-backed securities, the stock of financial institutions that heavily invested in them, or the price levels of homes were rationally priced in 2006. If the claim is that the prices of securities are always efficient as to the public information, and thus absent illegal trading on inside information, an investor should have no reason to trade. But there is an enormous amount of trading in the markets. Many investors, smart and stupid, must think that they can beat the market. Moreover, the fact that stock markets have historically gone into periods of bubbles and crashes suggests that markets can be inefficient for sustained periods of time.

As a hypothesis, the semi-strong form of the ECMH will continue to be debated because it cannot be proven. Proof will require a way to confirm the intrinsic value of stocks, and then compare that value to price levels. This would create a paradox: A way to confirm intrinsic value of stock would stop all trading in securities because there would be no reason to trade securities whose value is fundamentally true. This is a hypothetical Gordian knot because intrinsic value cannot be proven: "It is almost impossible to test whether stocks are *correctly valued*, because no one can measure true value with any precision. . . . It may be impossible to *prove* that market levels are, or are not, consistent with fundamentals."[*] In the end, it comes down to one's own belief about the market, and each side can point to some evidence of the correctness of their view.[**]

This economic theory figures very prominently in important legal doctrines of securities laws, particularly on issues of causation and reliance in connection with securities trades (see cases below). In the *transactional* context, the ECMH is not a concept that is routinely invoked in the daily practice of advising corporations or doing corporate transactions. However, the concept finds its way into conversations when clients discuss the value of their shares. Occasionally, clients may express the view that the stock price is "undervaluing" the true or intrinsic value of their companies. Such comments suggest that the client disagrees with the market's assignment of values. The client's statement goes to the core of the ECMH: (1) The market has incorrectly valued the stock in contradiction to the semi-strong form of efficiency; (2) she has private information concerning the value of the company that, being private information, would not have been incorporated into the strong form of efficiency; or (3) possibly, she may be engaging in puffery or wishful thinking consistent with structural bias.

The client may believe that the market price is significantly inaccurate or does not reflect maximized potential, and in this context transactional advisors may be called to assist. If shares are thought to be undervalued, there may be a problem of disclosure and communication to the market; certain transactions such as spinoff of assets may "unlock" value; or there may be a problem in using stock as consideration for a mergers and acquisitions (M&A) deal. If the client thinks that the price is "high," this viewpoint may trigger different sets of considerations in contemplating transactions. Perhaps it is the right time to raise equity capital; or using stock as consideration in an M&A deal makes sense; or it is a better idea to not engage in the stock buyback. The value of the stock price is always an important consideration in the client's mind and thinking, and in the background is the structure of ECMH.

---

[*] Richard A. Brealey, Stewart C. Myers & Franklin Allen, Principles of Corporate Finance 281 (concise 2d ed., 2011).

[**] Frank J. Fabozzi & Franco Modigliani, Capital Markets: Institutions and Instruments 291 (4th ed. 2009) ("Evidence on whether the stock market is price efficient in the semi-strong form is mixed."); William W. Bratton, Corporate Finance: Cases and Materials 36 (7th ed. 2012) ("The number of EMH supporters in the financial economic community has dwindled.").

(ECMH)

The following case is a seminal case in securities regulation. It applies the efficient capital market hypothesis to solve a legal problem related to a fraud-based cause of action. In a fraud, reliance on the fraud is an element of the cause action. The problem is simply stated: In capital markets where most investors are passive and do not actively follow publicly available information (or misinformation), how can it be said that the investor relied on the fraud?

Basic, Inc. v. Levinson
485 U.S. 224 (1988)

Justice BLACKMUN delivered the opinion of the Court.

This case requires us to apply the materiality requirement of §10(b) of the Securities Exchange Act of 1934 and the Securities and Exchange Commission's Rule 10b-5* in the context of preliminary corporate merger discussions. We must also determine whether a person who traded a corporation's shares on a securities exchange after the issuance of a materially misleading statement by the corporation may invoke a rebuttable presumption that, in trading, he relied on the integrity of the price set by the market.

[Basic Inc. was a publicly traded company. In 1976, it entered into confidential discussions to sell itself to Combustion Engineering Inc. During 1977 and 1978, Basic made three public false statements to the media denying that it was engaged in merger negotiations. Subsequently, in December 1978, it publicly announced a sale of the company for $46/share. Former Basic shareholders, who sold their stock after Basic's first public statement of October 21, 1977 and before the merger announcement, brought a class action against Basic and its directors. They asserted that the defendants issued false or misleading public statements about a possible merger in violation of Rule 10b-5. The Sixth Circuit adopted the "fraud-on-the-market theory" creating a rebuttable presumption that respondents relied on petitioners' material misrepresentations.]

We turn to the question of reliance and the fraud-on-the-market theory. Succinctly put:

> The fraud on the market theory is based on the hypothesis that, in an open and developed securities market, the price of a company's stock is determined by the available material information regarding the company and its business. . . . Misleading statements will therefore defraud purchasers of stock even if the purchasers do not directly rely on the misstatements. . . . The causal connection between the defendants' fraud and the plaintiffs' purchase of stock in such a case is no less significant than in a case of direct reliance on misrepresentations.

---

* Rule 10b-5 provides: "It shall be unlawful for any person, directly or indirectly, by the use of any means or instrumentality of interstate commerce, or of the mails or of any facility of any national securities exchange, (a) To employ any device, scheme, or artifice to defraud, (b) To make any untrue statement of a material fact or to omit to state a material fact necessary in order to make the statements made, in the light of the circumstances under which they were made, not misleading, or (c) To engage in any act, practice, or court of business which operates or would operate as a fraud or deceit upon any person, in connection with the purchase or sale of any security."

Our task, of course, is not to assess the general validity of the theory, but to consider whether it was proper for the courts below to apply a rebuttable presumption of reliance, supported in part by the fraud-on-the-market theory.

We agree that reliance is an element of a Rule 10b-5 cause of action. Reliance provides the requisite causal connection between a defendant's misrepresentation and a plaintiff's injury. There is, however, more than one way to demonstrate the causal connection. Indeed, we previously have dispensed with a requirement of positive proof of reliance, where a duty to disclose material information had been breached, concluding that the necessary nexus between the plaintiffs' injury and the defendant's wrongful conduct had been established. Similarly, we did not require proof that material omissions or misstatements in a proxy statement decisively affected voting, because the proxy solicitation itself, rather than the defect in the solicitation materials, served as an essential link in the transaction.

The modern securities markets, literally involving millions of shares changing hands daily, differ from the face-to-face transactions contemplated by early fraud cases, and our understanding of Rule 10b-5's reliance requirement must encompass these differences.

> In face-to-face transactions, the inquiry into an investor's reliance upon information is into the subjective pricing of that information by that investor. With the presence of a market, the market is interposed between seller and buyer and, ideally, transmits information to the investor in the processed form of a market price. Thus the market is performing a substantial part of the valuation process performed by the investor in a face-to-face transaction. The market is acting as the unpaid agent of the investor, informing him that given all the information available to it, the value of the stock is worth the market price.

Presumptions typically serve to assist courts in managing circumstances in which direct proof, for one reason or another, is rendered difficult. The courts below accepted a presumption, created by the fraud-on-the-market theory and subject to rebuttal by petitioners, that persons who had traded Basic shares had done so in reliance on the integrity of the price set by the market, but because of petitioners' material misrepresentations that price had been fraudulently depressed. Requiring a plaintiff to show a speculative state of facts, i.e., how he would have acted if omitted material information had been disclosed, or if the misrepresentation had not been made would place an unnecessarily unrealistic evidentiary burden on the Rule 10b-5 plaintiff who has traded on an impersonal market.

Arising out of considerations of fairness, public policy, and probability, as well as judicial economy, presumptions are also useful devices for allocating the burdens of proof between parties. The presumption of reliance employed in this case is consistent with, and, by facilitating Rule 10b-5 litigation, supports, the congressional policy embodied in the 1934 Act. In drafting that Act, Congress expressly relied on the premise that securities markets are affected by information, and enacted legislation to facilitate an investor's reliance on the integrity of those markets:

> No investor, no speculator, can safely buy and sell securities upon the exchanges without having an intelligent basis for forming his judgment as to the value of the securities he buys or sells. The idea of a free and open public market is built upon the theory that competing judgments of buyers and sellers as to the fair price of a security brings about a situation where the market price reflects as nearly as possible a just price. Just as artificial manipulation tends to upset the true function of an open

market, so the hiding and secreting of important information obstructs the operation of the markets as indices of real value.

The presumption is also supported by common sense and probability. Recent empirical studies have tended to confirm Congress' premise that the market price of shares traded on well-developed markets reflects all publicly available information, and, hence, any material misrepresentations. It has been noted that "it is hard to imagine that there ever is a buyer or seller who does not rely on market integrity. Who would knowingly roll the dice in a crooked crap game?" Indeed, nearly every court that has considered the proposition has concluded that where materially misleading statements have been disseminated into an impersonal, well-developed market for securities, the reliance of individual plaintiffs on the integrity of the market price may be presumed. Commentators generally have applauded the adoption of one variation or another of the fraud-on-the-market theory. An investor who buys or sells stock at the price set by the market does so in reliance on integrity of that price. Because most publicly available information is reflected in market price, an investor's reliance on any public material misrepresentations, therefore, may be presumed for purposes of a Rule 10b-5 action.

Justice WHITE, with whom Justice O'CONNOR joins, concurring in part and dissenting in part.

I dissent from the remainder of the Court's holding because I do not agree that the "fraud-on-the-market" theory should be applied in this case.

In general, the case law developed in this Court with respect to §10(b) and Rule 10b-5 has been based on doctrines with which we, as judges, are familiar: common-law doctrines of fraud and deceit. Even when we have extended civil liability under Rule 10b-5 to a broader reach than the common law had previously permitted, we have retained familiar legal principles as our guideposts. The federal courts have proved adept at developing an evolving jurisprudence of Rule 10b-5 in such a manner. But with no staff economists, no experts schooled in the "efficient-capital-market hypothesis," no ability to test the validity of empirical market studies, we are not well equipped to embrace novel constructions of a statute based on contemporary microeconomic theory.[4]

For while the economists' theories which underpin the fraud-on-the-market presumption may have the appeal of mathematical exactitude and scientific certainty, they are—in the end—nothing more than theories which may or may not prove accurate upon further consideration. Even the most earnest advocates of economic analysis of the law recognize this. Thus, while the majority states that, for purposes of reaching its result it need only make modest assumptions about the way in which "market professionals generally" do their jobs, and how the conduct of market professionals affects stock prices, I doubt that we are in much of a position to assess which theories aptly describe the functioning of the securities industry.

---

4. This view was put well by two commentators who wrote a few years ago: "Of all recent developments in financial economics, the efficient capital market hypothesis ('ECMH') has achieved the widest acceptance by the legal culture. . . . Yet the legal culture's remarkably rapid and broad acceptance of an economic concept that did not exist twenty years ago is not matched by an equivalent degree of *understanding*." Ronald J. Gilson & Reinier H. Kraakman, The Mechanisms of Market Efficiency, 70 Va. L. Rev. 549, 549-550 (1984) (emphasis added). While the fraud-on-the-market theory has gained even broader acceptance since 1984, I doubt that it has achieved any greater understanding.

QUESTIONS

1. What is the fundamental legal and policy problem posed by this lawsuit?
2. In what way does *Basic* incorporate the ECMH into the rule of law?
3. What legal problem does the ECMH solve?

NOTES

1. *Basic* was reaffirmed by the Supreme Court in *Halliburton Co. v. Erica P. John Fund, Inc.*, 134 S.Ct. 2398 (2014). The majority opinion by Chief Justice Roberts reaffirmed the fraud-on-the-market doctrine, but permitted challenges to the presumption in the class certification proceeding:

> More than 25 years ago, we held that plaintiffs could satisfy the reliance element of the Rule 10b–5 cause of action by invoking a presumption that a public, material misrepresentation will distort the price of stock traded in an efficient market, and that anyone who purchases the stock at the market price may be considered to have done so in reliance on the misrepresentation. We adhere to that decision and decline to modify the prerequisites for invoking the presumption of reliance. But to maintain the consistency of the presumption with the class certification requirements of Federal Rule of Civil Procedure 23, defendants must be afforded an opportunity before class certification to defeat the presumption through evidence that an alleged misrepresentation did not actually affect the market price of the stock.

Justices Thomas, Scalia and Alito dissented and wrote:

> *Basic* based the presumption of reliance on two factual assumptions. The first assumption was that, in a "well-developed market," public statements are generally "reflected" in the market price of securities. The second was that investors in such markets transact "in reliance on the integrity of that price." In other words, the Court created a presumption that a plaintiff had met the two-part, fraud-on-the-market version of the reliance requirement because, in the Court's view, "common sense and probability" suggested that each of those parts *would* be met.
>
> In reality, both of the Court's key assumptions are highly contestable and do not provide the necessary support for *Basic*'s presumption of reliance. The first assumption—that public statements are "reflected" in the market price—was grounded in an economic theory that has garnered substantial criticism since *Basic*. The second assumption—that investors categorically rely on the integrity of the market price—is simply wrong.

2. What would it mean for securities class actions if, as the dissent advocates, the Supreme Court overrules *Basic*? If the market is not always the semi-strong form of efficient, does this mean that the rule in *Basic* must be overturned?

The following case tests the limits of the fraud-on-the-market theory. It discusses how securities are priced in the market and the factors that move prices.

West v. Prudential Securities, Inc.
282 F.3d 935 (7th Cir. 2002)

EASTERBROOK, Circuit Judge.

According to the complaint in this securities-fraud action, James Hofman, a stockbroker working for Prudential Securities, told 11 of his customers that Jefferson Savings Bancorp was "certain" to be acquired, at a big premium, in the near future. Hofman continued making this statement for seven months (repeating it to some clients); it was a lie, for no acquisition was impending. And if the statement had been the truth, then Hofman was inviting unlawful trading on the basis of material non-public information. He is a securities offender coming or going, as are any customers who traded on what they thought to be confidential information—if Hofman said what the plaintiffs allege, a subject still to be determined. What we must decide is whether the action may proceed, not on behalf of those who received Hofman's "news" in person but on behalf of *everyone* who bought Jefferson stock during the months when Hofman was misbehaving. The district judge certified such a class, invoking the fraud-on-the-market doctrine of *Basic, Inc. v. Levinson*, 485 U.S. 224, 241-49 (1988).

The district court's order marks a substantial extension of the fraud-on-the-market approach. The theme of *Basic* and other fraud-on-the-market decisions is that *public* information reaches professional investors, whose evaluations of that information and trades quickly influence securities prices. But Hofman did not release information to the public, and his clients thought that they were receiving and acting on non-public information; its value (if any) lay precisely in the fact that other traders did not know the news. No newspaper or other organ of general circulation reported that Jefferson was soon to be acquired. As plaintiffs summarize their position, their "argument in a nutshell is that it is unimportant for purposes of the fraud-on-the-market doctrine whether the information was 'publicly available' in the . . . sense that . . . the information was disseminated through a press release, or prospectus or other written format". Yet extending the fraud-on-the-market doctrine in this way requires not only a departure from *Basic* but also a novelty in fraud cases as a class-as another court of appeals remarked only recently in another securities suit, oral frauds have not been allowed to proceed as class actions, for the details of the deceit differ from victim to victim, and the nature of the loss also may be statement-specific.

Causation is the shortcoming in this class certification. *Basic* describes a mechanism by which public information affects stock prices, and thus may affect traders who did not know about that information. Professional investors monitor news about many firms; good news implies higher dividends and other benefits, which induces these investors to value the stock more highly, and they continue buying until the gains are exhausted. With many professional investors alert to news, markets are efficient in the sense that they rapidly adjust to all public information; if some of this information is false, the price will reach an incorrect level, staying there until the truth emerges. This approach has the support of financial economics as well as the imprimatur of the Justices: few propositions in economics are better established than the quick adjustment of securities prices to public information.

No similar mechanism explains how prices would respond to non-public information, such as statements made by Hofman to a handful of his clients. These do not come to the attention of professional investors or money managers, so the price-

145

adjustment mechanism just described does not operate. Sometimes full-time market watchers can infer important news from the identity of a trader (when the corporation's CEO goes on a buying spree, this implies good news) or from the sheer volume of trades (an unprecedented buying volume may suggest that a bidder is accumulating stock in anticipation of a tender offer), but neither the identity of Hofman's customers nor the volume of their trades would have conveyed information to the market in this fashion. No one these days accepts the strongest version of the efficient capital market hypothesis, under which non-public information automatically affects prices. That version is empirically false: the public announcement of news (good and bad) has big effects on stock prices, which could not happen if prices already incorporated the effect of non-public information. Thus it is hard to see how Hofman's non-public statements could have caused changes in the price of Jefferson Savings stock. *Basic* founded the fraud-on-the-market doctrine on a causal mechanism with both theoretical and empirical power; for non-public information there is nothing comparable. ~~does not apply to~~

Because the record here does not demonstrate that non-public information affected the price of Jefferson Savings' stock, a remand is unnecessary. What the plaintiffs have going for them is that Jefferson's stock did rise in price (by about $5, or 20% of its trading price) during the months when Hofman was touting an impending acquisition, plus a model of demand-pull price increases offered by their expert. [The model proposed by Michael Barclay, the plaintiff's expert economist] assumes that some trades are by informed traders and some by uninformed traders, and that the market may be able to draw inferences about which is which. The model has not been verified empirically. Barclay approached the issue differently, assuming that all trades affect prices by raising demand even if no trader is well informed—as if there were an economic market in "Jefferson Savings stock" as there is in dill pickles or fluffy towels. Hofman's tips raised the demand for Jefferson Savings stock and curtailed the supply (for the tippees were less likely to sell their own shares); that combination of effects raised the stock's price. Yet investors do not want Jefferson Savings stock (as if they sought to paper their walls with beautiful certificates); they want monetary returns (at given risk levels), returns that are available from many financial instruments. One fundamental attribute of efficient markets is that information, not demand in the abstract, determines stock prices. There are so many substitutes for any one firm's stock that the effective demand curve is horizontal. It may shift up or down with new information but is not sloped like the demand curve for physical products. That is why institutional purchases (which can be large in relation to normal trading volume) do not elevate prices, while relatively small trades by insiders can have substantial effects; the latter trades convey information, and the former do not. Barclay, who took the view that the market for Jefferson Savings securities is efficient, did not explain why he departed from the normal understanding that information rather than raw demand determines securities prices.

Barclay's report calls into question his belief that the market for Jefferson Savings stock is efficient, the foundation of the fraud-on-the-market doctrine. In an efficient market, how could one ignorant outsider's lie cause a long-term rise in price? Professional investors would notice the inexplicable rise and either investigate for themselves (discovering the truth) or sell short immediately, driving the price back down. In an efficient market, a lie told by someone with nothing to back up the

146

statement (no professional would have thought Hofman a person "in the know") will self-destruct long before eight months have passed. Hofman asserted that an acquisition was imminent. That statement might gull people for a month, but after two or three months have passed the lack of a merger or tender offer puts the lie to the assertion; professional investors then draw more astute inferences and the price effect disappears. That this did not occur implies either that Jefferson Savings was not closely followed by professional investors (and that the market therefore does not satisfy *Basic*'s efficiency requirement) or that something other than Hofman's statements explains these price changes.

The record thus does not support extension of the fraud-on-the-market doctrine to the non-public statements Hofman is alleged to have made about Jefferson Savings Bancorp. The order certifying a class is REVERSED.

QUESTIONS

1. Given that Hofman's "news" never reached the public, in what way did the plaintiff argue that the stock price was improperly affected by Hofman's bad acts?
2. The court reasoned that the ordinary law of supply and demand does not apply to individual stocks. Why not? According to the court, in what way does an investor "want" a share of Google or General Electric or Walt Disney?
3. What fact fundamentally distinguishes *Basic* from *West*?

NOTES

1. A key rationale of the court's decision is this statement: "There are so many substitutes for any one firm's stock that the effective demand curve is horizontal. It may shift up or down with new information but is not sloped like the demand curve for physical products." According to classical economics, most things in the market (*e.g.*, "physical products" referred to in the quotation) are subject to the normal law of supply and demand, which can be graphically represented.

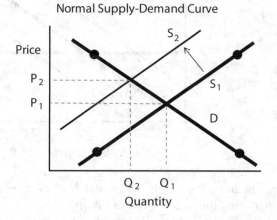

Normal Supply-Demand Curve

For those who have not had basic microeconomics in college or law school, the x-axis represents the quantity of the good, and the y-axis represents the price. The demand curve, denoted as D, slopes downward, and the supply curve, denoted as S, slopes upward. This means that at very high prices, the quantity demanded is low (see the top left point on the demand curve, trace that point horizontally to the y-axis price and vertically to the x-axis quantity), but the quantity desired to be supplied is high (see top right point on the supply curve, and trace similarly). There is not a match of supply and demand as the supply and demand curves do not intersect, which would indicate that demand is matched by supply at the same quantity and price. At very low prices, the quantity demanded is high (see bottom right point on the demand curve), but the quantity desired to be supplied is low (see bottom left point on the supply curve). Again, there is not a match of supply and demand. Based on sloping demand curve D and supply curve S_1, the supply and demand intersect at the price P_1 and quantity Q_1. This normal dynamic of supply and demand is what determines prices of commodity goods and services such as books, homes, and attorney services.

The normal law of supply and demand says that as the supply shrinks (noted by the shifting of the supply curve from S_1 to S_2), the quantity sold decreases to Q_2 and the price increases to P_2. This comports with simple intuition. As the supply of anything desired decreases (and demand being the same), the price of the thing increases. For example, if half of the lawyers in the country retired tomorrow, attorney fees would increase. The above graph simply formalizes this intuition.

However, when the demand curve is horizontal, as asserted by the Seventh Circuit in *West*, the shifting of the supply curve does not affect prices. In *West*, the plaintiffs alleged that the supply curve shifted because Hofman created a shortage of Jefferson Savings stock through his lies.

Horizontal Demand Curve

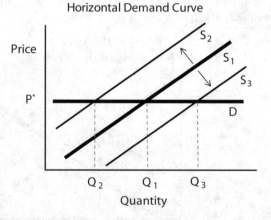

If the demand curve D is horizontal, irrespective of whether the supply decreases (shifting to S_2) or increases (shifting to S_3) resulting in lower quantity Q_2 or higher quantity Q_3 sold, the market clear price is the same P^*. As the court notes, the demand curve "may shift up or down with new information," which would then affect prices: A shift up would increase prices and a shift down would decrease prices irrespective of the supply curve.

2. Whether market prices accurately reflect the value of the firm figures prominently in the context of mergers and acquisitions where an acquirer frequently pays an acquisition premium over the current market price to target shareholders. Some commentators have suggested that investors have heterogeneous demand for stocks, meaning that investors hold different reasons for "wanting" particular stocks, and not just "monetary returns (at given risk levels), returns that are available from many financial instruments" as suggested by the court in *West*. If demand is heterogeneous, this implies that the demand curve is downward shifting. There is significant academic commentary suggesting as such. *See* Reinier Kraakman, *Taking Discounts Seriously: The Implications of "Discounted" Share Prices as an Acquisition Motive*, 88 Colum. L. Rev. 891, 899 n.25 (1988) ("Heterogeneous demand implies downward sloping demand curves for equity rather than the horizontal demand curves predicted by common forms of the efficient capital markets hypothesis."); Lynn A. Stout, *Are Takeover Premiums Really Premiums? Market Price, Fair Value, and Corporate Law*, 99 Yale L.J. 1235, 1239 (1990) ("In contrast to the CAPM, the heterogeneous beliefs model posits that the demand for stocks is downward-sloping."); Richard A. Booth, *Discounts and Other Mysteries of Corporate Finance*, 79 Cal. L. Rev. 1055, 1058 (1991) ("The downward-sloping demand hypothesis predicts that most shareholders value their shares at a price that is higher than the market price.").

In re Polymedica Corp. Sec. Litig.
432 F.3d 1 (1st Cir. 2005)

LIPEZ, Circuit Judge.

In this appeal from an order certifying a class in a securities fraud case, we must decide an issue of first impression in this Circuit: the standard for determining whether a market was "efficient" when applying the fraud-on-the-market presumption of investor reliance. We also address the level of inquiry that a district court may pursue at the class-certification stage when making that efficiency determination. PolyMedica Corporation argues that the district court erred in finding that common questions predominated, by determining that the market was efficient for eight months of the class period, from January 2001 through August 2001 (the "Contested Time Period"). For the reasons set forth below, we vacate the district court's order certifying the class for the Contested Time Period, and remand for further proceedings.

Thomas Thuma is a purchaser of PolyMedica stock, who seeks to represent a class of all purchasers of PolyMedica stock [which traded on NASDAQ and the American Stock Exchange]. Plaintiff alleges that PolyMedica artificially inflated the market price of its stock by misrepresenting sales, revenues, and accounts receivable, and by issuing false press releases, causing Plaintiff and other members of the class to purchase stock at artificially inflated prices. Plaintiff further alleges that when the truth of this fraud became known, PolyMedica's stock lost more than 80% of its value. Plaintiff seeks damages under Section 10(b) of the Securities Exchange Act of 1934 (the "Exchange Act") and Rule 10b-5, and Section 20(a) of the Exchange Act.

Following several years of litigation, Plaintiff moved for class certification, asserting that common questions of law and fact predominated, based on the "fraud-on-the-market" theory. Under the Supreme Court's plurality decision in *Basic, Inc. v. Levinson,* 485 U.S. 224 (1988), this theory obviates the need for a plaintiff to demonstrate individualized reliance on a defendant's misstatement by permitting a class-wide rebuttable presumption of reliance, thereby enabling a securities fraud class action to meet Rule 23(b)(3)'s commonality requirement. PolyMedica opposed the motion, arguing that the fraud-on-the-market presumption of reliance was inapplicable for the Contested Time Period because the market for PolyMedica stock was not "efficient" (a prerequisite for application of the presumption).

The Fraud-on-the-Market Theory

The Supreme Court has described the "basic elements" of a securities fraud action under §10(b) of the Exchange Act and Rule 10b-5 promulgated thereunder as including: (1) "a material misrepresentation (or omission)"; (2) "scienter, i.e., a wrongful state of mind"; (3) "a connection with the purchase or sale of a security"; (4) "reliance"; (5) "economic loss"; and (6) "loss causation." While reliance is typically demonstrated on an individual basis, the Supreme Court has noted that such a rule would effectively foreclose securities fraud class actions because individual questions of reliance would inevitably overwhelm the common ones under Rule 23(b)(3). *Basic,* 485 U.S. at 242.

To avoid this result, the Supreme Court has recognized the fraud-on-the-market theory, which relieves the plaintiff of the burden of proving individualized reliance on a defendant's misstatement, by permitting a rebuttable presumption that the plaintiff relied on the "integrity of the market price" which reflected that misstatement. As the Supreme Court recognized in *Basic,* "the fraud on the market theory is based on the hypothesis that, in an open and developed securities market, the price of a company's stock is determined by the available material information regarding the company and its business," including any available material misstatements. Since investors who purchase or sell stock do so in reliance on "the integrity of the market price," they indirectly rely on such misstatements because they purchase or sell stock at a price which necessarily reflects that misrepresentation. Under the fraud-on-the-market theory, "misleading statements will therefore defraud purchasers of stock even if the purchasers do not directly rely on the misstatements."

Before an investor can be presumed to have relied upon the integrity of the market price, however, the market must be "efficient". Efficiency refers to the flow of information in the relevant market and the effect of that information on the price of the stock. In an efficient market, the defendant's misrepresentations are said to have been absorbed into, and are therefore reflected in, the stock price. Conversely, when a market lacks efficiency, there is no assurance that the market price was affected by the defendant's alleged misstatement at all. Instead, the price may reflect information wholly unrelated to the misstatement.

The fraud-on-the-market presumption of reliance and its relationship to market efficiency can thus be reduced to the following syllogism: (a) an investor buys or sells stock in reliance on the integrity of the market price; (b) publicly available information, including material misrepresentations, is reflected in the market price; and therefore, (c) the investor buys or sells stock in reliance on material misrepresentations. This syllogism breaks down, of course, when a market lacks efficiency, and the market does not necessarily reflect the alleged material misrepresentation. With this understanding as background, we must now decide the appropriate standard for determining whether a market is efficient.

The Meaning of "Market Efficiency"

The efficient market hypothesis began as an academic attempt to answer the following question: Can an ordinary investor beat the stock market, that is, can such an investor make trading profits on the basis of new information? In an efficient market, the answer is "no," because the information that would have given the investor a competitive edge and allowed the investor to "beat" the market is already reflected in the market price. There is, therefore, no "bargain" from which an investor can benefit. Since the stock price fully reflects the information, an investor cannot take advantage of it by either purchasing the stock (if the information indicates the stock is underpriced) or selling the stock (if the information indicates the stock is overpriced).

One way information gets absorbed into the market and reflected in stock price is through arbitrageurs, who obtain and analyze information about stocks from a variety of sources, including from the issuer, market analysts, and the financial and trade press. These arbitrageurs immediately attempt to profit from such information (for instance, through short sales[13]), thereby causing the stock to move to a price which reflects the latest public information concerning the stock, where it is no longer possible to generate profits.[14]

The capacity of arbitrageurs to "seek out new information and evaluate its effects on the price of securities" distinguishes them from ordinary investors, who "lack the time, resources, or expertise to evaluate all the information concerning a security," and are thus "unable to act in time to take advantage of opportunities for arbitrage profits." In an efficient market, then, an ordinary investor "who becomes aware of publicly available information cannot make money by trading on it" because the information will have already been incorporated into the market by arbitrageurs. "An example would be an investor who decides to sell a stock upon the public announcement of a decline in corporate earnings, who finds that by the time she calls her broker, the price has already dropped."

According to the prevailing definition of market efficiency, an efficient market is one in which market price fully reflects all publicly available information. This

---

13. In a short-sale transaction, the seller borrows shares that the seller believes to be overvalued from a broker, and pays the broker a so-called "loan fee" for the right to borrow the shares plus collateral (in cash) for the value of the shares (which is held in an interest-bearing margin account). The seller agrees to return shares of a similar type and amount to the broker at an unspecified date in the future. The seller then sells the borrowed stock. Assuming the price of the stock later decreases, the seller's profit will be the positive difference between the price the seller pays to replace the borrowed shares (a process known as "covering"), and the price at which the seller sold the stock. If the price increases before the seller covers its position, the seller suffers a loss.

14. Plaintiff offers the following example of an arbitrage opportunity. Assume that the price of gold trading on the New York commodities market was $100.50 per ounce, while on the London market, which opened five hours earlier, the price was only $100 per ounce. The arbitrageur could first sell an ounce of gold "short" in New York, receiving $100.50 in return, and then purchase an ounce of gold in London for $100, retaining a profit of $0.50. In an efficient market, the New York market would have swiftly moved to match the London market price as arbitrageurs moved to exploit the imbalance in the two markets.

definition has been adopted by many lower courts as a prerequisite for applying the fraud-on-the-market presumption of reliance. PolyMedica urges us to do likewise, arguing that an "efficient" market is an open and developed one, in which a stock price will move quickly to reflect all publicly available information.

The district court, on the other hand, expressly declined to adopt this prevailing definition of market efficiency. Relying upon language gleaned from the Supreme Court's decision in *Basic,* the district court held that "the 'efficient' market required for [the] 'fraud on the market' presumption of reliance is simply one in which 'market professionals generally consider most publicly announced material statements about companies, thereby affecting stock market prices'"; it "is *not* one in which a stock price rapidly reflects all publicly available material information."

PolyMedica argues that the definition adopted by the district court wrongly focuses on the thought processes of unidentified market professionals and whether stock prices are in some way affected by their consideration of most (but not necessarily all) material public information. The prevailing definition, on the other hand, requires a more searching inquiry into whether stock prices fully reflect all publicly available information.

The Standard for Determining an Efficient Market

While endorsing the fraud-on-the-market presumption of reliance in *Basic,* the Supreme Court did not explicitly address the meaning of an "efficient" market. Poly-Medica points to various passages in *Basic* purportedly showing a preference for the prevailing definition of an efficient market, noting the Supreme Court's statements that "the market is acting as the unpaid agent of the investor, informing him that given *all the information available* to it, the value of the stock is worth the market price," and that "the market price of shares traded on well-developed markets reflects *all publicly available information,* and hence, any material misrepresentations." *Basic,* 485 U.S. at 244, 246 (emphasis added).

Elsewhere, however, the *Basic* decision suggests that something less than "all publicly available information" may be required, noting that an investor's reliance may be presumed "because *most* publicly available information is reflected in market price," *id.* at 247 (emphasis added). In separate footnotes of the decision, the Court further appeared to resist PolyMedica's suggested definition of an efficient market. As pointed out by the district court, the Supreme Court, after listing several academic articles, noted that:

> We need not determine by adjudication what economists and social scientists have debated through the use of sophisticated statistical analysis and the application of economic theory. For purposes of accepting the presumption of reliance in this case, we need only believe that market professionals generally consider most publicly announced material statements about companies, thereby affecting stock market prices.

In addition, the Court noted that by accepting a rebuttable presumption of reliance, it "did not intend conclusively to adopt any particular theory of how quickly and completely publicly available information is reflected in market price."

Given the Supreme Court's disclaimer that it was not adopting any particular economic theory in applying the fraud-on-the-market presumption of reliance, on the one hand, and its embrace of the holdings of cases adopting the prevailing definition of market efficiency on the other hand, the most that can be said of *Basic* is that it did not directly address the meaning of an efficient market, choosing instead to leave the development of that concept to the lower courts. *Basic* is therefore not the benchmark for deriving a definition of market efficiency.

PolyMedica correctly notes that in the wake of *Basic,* many lower courts have accepted a definition of market efficiency which requires that stock price fully reflect all publicly available information.

The precedents from other circuits overwhelmingly favor the definition advanced by PolyMedica. [The court reviewed the precedents.]

On the basis of the authorities and considerations cited, we conclude that the definition of market efficiency adopted by the district court is inconsistent with the presumption of investor reliance at the heart of the fraud-on-the-market theory. By focusing on the general consideration by market professionals of *most* publicly announced material statements about companies, the district court applied the wrong standard of efficiency. For application of the fraud-on-the-market theory, we conclude that an efficient market is one in which the market price of the stock *fully reflects all* publicly available information.

Anticipating the possibility of this definition, Plaintiff complains that it forces him to prove that market price "correctly" reflects a stock's fundamental value before a market will be considered efficient. This argument misconstrues the conclusion that market price must "fully reflect" all publicly available information. The words "fully reflect" have two distinct meanings, each of which points to a different concept of market efficiency.

The first meaning of "fully reflect" focuses on the ability of the market to digest information, thereby preventing trading profits: market price "fully reflects" all publicly available information when "prices respond so quickly to new information that it is impossible for traders to make trading profits on the basis of that information." This is known as "informational efficiency," and is best understood "as a prediction or implication about the speed with which prices respond to information."

"With many professional investors alert to news, markets are efficient in the sense that they rapidly adjust to all public information. . . ." *West v. Prudential Sec., Inc.,* 282 F.3d 935, 938 (7th Cir. 2002). Where the market reacts slowly to new information, it is less likely that misinformation was reflected in market price and therefore relied upon.

Determining whether a market is informationally efficient, therefore, involves analysis of the structure of the market and the speed with which all publicly available information is impounded in price.

The second, and much broader meaning of "fully reflect," focuses on the price of the stock as a function of its fundamental value: market price "fully reflects" all publicly available information when it responds to information not only quickly *but accurately,* such that "market prices mirror the best possible estimates, in light of all available information, of the actual economic values of securities in terms of their expected risks and returns." Stout, *supra,* at 640. This is known as "fundamental value efficiency."

Determining whether a market is fundamental value efficient is a much more technical inquiry than determining informational efficiency. Depending on the method of valuation used, a stock's fundamental value turns on an assessment of various factors, including "present operations, future growth rates, relative risk levels, and the future levels of interest rates."

Courts and commentators often use these two concepts of market efficiency interchangeably. Despite this blurring of concepts, one thing is clear: a market can be information efficient without also being fundamental value efficient. While fundamental value efficiency may be the more comprehensive of the two concepts, encompassing both speed *and* accuracy, "efficiency is not an all-or-nothing phenomenon."

Therefore, by requiring that stock price in an efficient market fully reflect all publicly available information in order to establish the fraud-on-the-market presumption, we do not suggest that stock price must accurately reflect the fundamental value of the stock. This distinction is well-supported by the legal and economic commentary.

Our focus on whether a particular market has absorbed all available information (and misinformation)—such that an ordinary investor cannot beat the market by taking advantage of unexploited profit opportunities—is not a fundamental value inquiry. Investors need only show that the market was informationally efficient. The fraud-on-the-market theory is concerned with whether a market processes information in such a way as to justify investor reliance, not whether the stock price paid or received by investors was "correct" in the fundamental value sense.

For purposes of establishing the fraud-on-the-market presumption of reliance, we adopt the prevailing definition of market efficiency, which provides that an efficient market is one in which the market price of the stock fully reflects all publicly available information. By "fully reflect," we mean that market price responds so quickly to new information that ordinary investors cannot make trading profits on the basis of such information. This is known as "informational efficiency." We reject a second and much broader meaning of "fully reflect," known as "fundamental value efficiency," which requires that a market respond to information not only quickly but accurately, such that the market price of a stock reflects its fundamental value.

QUESTIONS

1. If the market for PolyMedica was not efficient, how does that finding defeat the plaintiff's argument for class certification?
2. In what way is the district court's definition of efficiency more favorable to the plaintiff?
3. What is the difference between informational and fundamental value efficiency? If courts adopt the fundamental value efficiency definition, in what way does this legal standard affect plaintiffs and defendants in a Rule 10b-5 action?

The following excerpt, written by the economist Robert Shiller, describes the ongoing debate on market efficiency. In 2013, the Nobel Prize in economics was awarded to Shiller and Eugene Fama. The joint award was ironic in that Fama is the leading proponent of the idea that markets are efficient while Shiller, as a prominent proponent of behavioral finance, has spent much of his career showing why markets are not always efficient. It seems that the Nobel Committee exercised Solomonic judgment on the academic debate. In the passage below, Shiller describes the idea of market efficiency and explains why, in his view, markets are not always efficient.

Robert J. Shiller, Irrational Exuberance, Chapter 11 (Efficient markets, random walks, and bubbles) at 195-213 (3rd ed. 2015)

EFFICIENT MARKETS, RANDOM WALKS, AND BUBBLES

The theory that financial markets are efficient forms the leading intellectual basis for arguments against the idea that markets are vulnerable to excessive exuberance or bubbles. Extensive academic research has been widely seen as supporting this theory.

The *efficient markets theory* asserts that all financial prices accurately reflect all public information at all times. In other words, financial assets are always priced correctly, given what is publicly known, at all times. Price may *appear* to be too high or too low at times, but, according to the efficient markets theory, this appearance must be an illusion.

Stock prices, by this theory, approximately describe "random walks" through time: the price changes are unpredictable since they occur only in response to genuinely new information, which by the very fact that it is new is unpredictable. The efficient markets theory and the random walk hypothesis have been subjected to many tests using data on stock markets, in studies published in scholarly journals of finance and economics. Although the theory has been statistically rejected many times in these publications, by some interpretations it may nevertheless be described as approximately true. The literature on the evidence for this theory is well developed and includes work of the highest quality. Therefore, whether or not we ultimately agree with it, we must at least take the efficient markets theory seriously.

BASIC ARGUMENTS THAT MARKETS ARE EFFICIENT AND THAT PRICES ARE RANDOM WALKS

The idea of efficient markets is so natural that it has probably been with us for centuries. Although the term *efficient markets* apparently first became widely known through the work of University of Chicago professor Eugene Fama (who was jointly awarded the Nobel Prize in Economic Sciences with me in 2013, despite our different views on some basic issues) in the late 1960s, the theory itself preceded this name by many years. It was clearly mentioned in 1889 in a book by George Gibson titled *The Stock Markets of London, Paris and New York*. Gibson wrote that when "shares become publicly known in an open market, the value which they acquire may be regarded as the judgment of the best intelligence concerning them."

The efficient markets theory has long been a fixture in university economics and finance departments ever since the 1970s. The theory has commonly been offered to justify what seem to be elevated market valuations such as the 1929 stock market peak. Professor Joseph Lawrence of Princeton concluded in 1929 that "the consensus of judgment of the millions whose valuations function on that admirable market, the Stock Exchange, is that stocks are not at present overvalued. . . . Where is that group of men with all-embracing wisdom which will entitle them to veto the judgment of the intelligent multitude?"

The most simple and direct argument for efficient markets theory comes from the observation that it seems to be difficult to make a lot of money by buying low and selling high in the stock market. Many seemingly capable people try but fail to do this with any consistent degree of success. Moreover, one observes that in order to make money one must compete against some of the smartest investors, the so-called "smart money," who trade in financial markets looking for the same opportunities. If one thinks that an asset is either under- or overpriced, one must then reflect on why it remains so despite the efforts of the smart money to make a profitable trade.

If the smart money were able to find ways to make profits by buying low and selling high, then the effect of such smart money would be, according to the efficient markets theory, to drive asset prices to their true values. They would be buying underpriced stocks and thereby tending to bid their prices up. They would be selling overpriced stocks and thereby tending to bid their prices down. Moreover, if there were substantial mispricing of securities, then their profits doing this trading would tend to make the smart money into rich people, thereby increasing their influence on the market and increasing their power to eliminate mispricing.

Unfortunately, this argument for the efficient markets hypothesis does not tell us that the stock market cannot go through periods of significant mispricing lasting years or even decades. The smart money could not make money rapidly by exploiting such a profit opportunity, and there would be considerable uncertainty about when the mispricing would end. If indeed one knew today that the market would do poorly over the next ten or twenty years, but did not know exactly *when* it would begin to do poorly and could not prove one's knowledge to a broad audience, then there would be no way to profit significantly from this knowledge. There is therefore no substantial reason to think that the smart money must necessarily eliminate such stock mispricing.

But this limitation of the efficient markets theory is often overlooked. The assumption is made that the same efficient markets theory that says that it is difficult to predict day-to-day changes implies that one cannot predict *any* changes.

REFLECTIONS ON "SMART MONEY"

At its root, the efficient markets theory holds that differing abilities do not produce differing investment performance. The theory claims that the smartest people will not be able to do better than the least intelligent people in terms of investment performance. They can do no better because their superior understanding is already completely incorporated into share prices.

If we accept the premise of efficient markets, not only is being smart no advantage, but it also follows immediately that being *not so smart* is *not a disadvantage* either. If not-so-smart people could lose money systematically in their trades, then this would suggest a profit opportunity for the smart money: just do the opposite of what the not-so-smart money does. Yet according to the efficient markets theory, there can be no such profit opportunity for the smart money.

Thus, according to this theory, effort and intelligence mean nothing in investing. In terms of expected investment returns, one might as well pick stocks at random—the common metaphor of throwing darts at the stock market listings to choose investments. It is ultimately for this reason that so many people have thought that they do not need to pay any attention at all to whether any given stock is or is not overpriced, and why they have felt they could ignore the unusual valuation of the market at the time of this writing, or at the height of the stock market boom in 2000.

But why should the very smartest people set all prices, as efficient markets theory implies? Many apparently less-intelligent or less well-informed people are buying and selling—why should they not have an impact on prices?

One notion, referred to previously, is that the smartest money has already mostly taken over the market through its profitable trading and has now set prices correctly; the less-intelligent investors are holding so little as to be insignificant forces in the market. This is an easy argument to dismiss. First of all, if this is the reason the smart money dominates, then it must have been the case that there *were* profitable trades for them; otherwise, they could not have used their intelligence to take over the market. But if there *were* profitable trades, then there must *still be* profitable trades, since smart money investors retire from the business and must be replaced. One cannot argue that smart money took over the market 100 years ago and that ever since they have dominated the market, since those smart traders of yore are all dead now.

Another piece of evidence that has been offered in support of the efficient markets theory is that professional investors, institutional money managers, or securities analysts do not seem to have any reliable ability to outperform the market as a whole, and indeed they often seem to underperform the market once account is taken of transactions costs and management fees. This result may seem puzzling, since one would think that professional investors are more educated about investing, more systematic, than individual investors. But perhaps the result is not as puzzling as it at first seems. Individual investors get advice from professional investors, and they can also observe (albeit with some time lag) what professional investors are doing. So there may be no significant difference between the success of professional investors and the market as a whole, even if their analysis is very valuable to others. Individual investors with substantial resources tend to be educated and intelligent people, too. Moreover, some studies have documented that professional analysts' advice is indeed worth something, if it is acted upon swiftly enough.

Ultimately the reason that studies have not found stronger evidence that people who are smarter tend to make more money is that there is no good way to measure how smart investors are. Institutional investors as a group are not necessarily smarter than individual investors as a group. We do not have databases giving the IQ scores of investment managers to enable us to compare their performances with their scores, and even if we did, it is not clear that the available intelligence tests would measure the right abilities.

One study, by Judith Chevalier and Glenn Ellison, did come close to acquiring data about investment managers' intelligence, even though they did not have access to their individual test scores, by tabulating the average Scholastic Aptitude Test (SAT) scores of the colleges the investment managers attended. They did indeed find some evidence that firms whose managers attended higher-SAT colleges performed somewhat better, even after controlling for other factors.

Another approach to testing whether smarter people can make money by trading stocks relies on persistence of investing success. If we have data on individual trades, and if some people are smarter than others at trading, then we should find that some people persistently lose money, while others persistently make money. In effect, we can measure a trader's investing intelligence by his or her own pasts successes, and then see how this compares with subsequent successes.

It has been found that mutual funds trading success is only moderately persistent through time. But mutual funds are organizations, not individuals. The problem has been that, at least until recently, comprehensive databases of trades that identify individual traders through time have not been available.

One recent study, however, was able to use data on all day traders on Taiwan Stock Exchange that consistently identified individuals for a five-year period. The study found substantial persistence of trading success. It also found that most day traders did not make enough money from their trades to offset their trading costs, but a small number of them consistently did. Unsuccessful day traders tended to drop out through time; successful ones tended to trade very heavily.

These studies do not settle the issue of intelligence and investing success. Yet, from the available evidence, I see no reason to doubt the thesis that smarter and more hard-working people will, in the long run, tend to do better at investing.

EXAMPLES OF "OBVIOUS" MISPRICING

Despite the general authority of the efficient markets theory in popular thinking, one often hears examples that seem to offer fragrant evidence against it. There are in fact many examples of financial prices that, it seems, cannot possibly be right. They are regularly reported in the media. In the 1990s stock market boom, many of these examples have been Internet stocks; judging from their prices, the public appears to have held an exaggerated view of their potential.

For example, consider eToys, a firm established in 1997 to sell toys over the Internet. Shortly after its initial public offering in 1999, eToys' stock value was $8 billion, exceeding the $6 billion value of the long-established "brick and mortar" retailer Toys "R" Us. And yet in fiscal 1998, eToys' sales were $30 million, while the sales of Toys "R" Us were $11.2 billion, almost 400 times larger. And eToys' profits were a negative $28.6 million, while the profits of Toys "R" Us were a positive $376 million. In fact, Toys "R" Us, like other established toy retailers, had already created its own website. Despite some initial difficulties getting its site launched, Toys "R" Us was seen by many as having a longer-run advantage over eToys in that dissatisfied purchasers of toys on the Internet could go to one of its numerous retail outlets for returns or advice. In addition, customers who were already shopping at one of those outlets would naturally gravitate to the Toys "R" Us website when making online purchases. Despite these publicly aired doubts, investors loved eToys. But it didn't take long for the doubters to be proven right: eToys.com filed for bankruptcy and was delisted from NASDAQ in March 2001. The final step was the May 2001 sale of the eToys.com web address to KB Toys, which in turn filed for bankruptcy in January 2004.

The valuation the market placed on stocks such as eToys at the peak of the market in 1999 and 2000 appears absurd to many observers, and yet the influence of these observers on market prices does not seem to correct the mispricing. What could they do that would have the effect of correcting it? Those who doubt the value of these stocks could try to sell them short, and some do, but their willingness to do so is limited, partly since there is always a possibility that the stock will be bid up even further by enthusiastic investors. We will see other reasons later. Absurd prices sometimes last a long time.

It seems obvious that investors in these stocks are not thinking very clearly about long-run investment potential, and also that there are no forces in the market to prevent these investors from causing substantial overpricing. Doesn't such evidence clearly speak against market efficiency, at least for some stocks? And if some stocks can be overpriced, then does it not follow that the market as a whole can be overpriced, given that those stocks are part of the market?

SHORT-SALES CONSTRAINTS AND THE PERSISTENCE OF OBVIOUS MISPRICING

There is a reason to think that obvious mispricing really ought to occur, even in a world with huge quantities of smart money searching for mispriced assets. That reason: there are often obstacles to short sales, to borrowing the assets and selling them, thereby in effect holding negative quantities of the assets. Edward Miller, an eccentric professor at the University of New Orleans who has written provocative papers on a wide range of academic disciplines, first pointed this out in a 1977 article in the *Journal of Finance* that seemed to take efficient markets theorists by surprise.

Miller's argument was actually very simple. Suppose a particular stock, or a particular tulip, or whatever, comes into great demand by a small group of zealots, who bid eagerly against one another to buy as much of this investment as they can. Efficient markets theory does not say that there are no zealots, which would be an absurd claim; it says only that somehow the smart money ultimately sets market prices. But if these zealots have really lost their sense, and if they buy so aggressively that they end up being the only people holding these assets, who is to say that these assets won't become wildly overpriced? The smart money, who are not crazy, would like to short the overpriced assets, to profit from the eventual fall in price, but if they cannot find any of the assets to borrow, the only way they can participate is by *buying*. As a result, they must just sit on the sidelines. The market with short-sales constraints can be wildly overpriced, and the smart money knows it, but there is no way for the smart money to use that knowledge.

Short-sales constraints are very real. Some countries' governments do not allow short sales at all. Even in countries where short sales are allowed, the institutions supporting them may not work very well. Part of the reason is that even in these countries, there is a widespread antipathy to short sellers. Short sellers are blamed for all sorts of bad things. The New York Stock Exchange used to have an orderly market for the borrowing and lending of shares, the "loan crowd" on the floor of the exchange, but shut this market down some years after the stock market crash in 1929—a move that was widely blamed on short sellers. Short sellers are commonly targeted as "boogeymen" for fluctuating or falling equity prices, a position echoed by regulators—short sales of financial stocks were temporarily banned in the United States and Europe after the market crash of 2008 in an attempt to stem market declines.

The difficulty of making short sales has played a real role in the mispricing of securities. A good example is the mispricing of the shares sold during the 3Com sale of Palm near the peak of the stock market in March 2000. In this initial public offering, 3Com sold 5% of its subsidiary Palm, a maker of personal digital assistants, to the general public, and announced at the same time that the rest of Palm would be sold later. This initial 5% of Palm went for such a high price in the market that, if one assumed that the other 95% of the Palm shares were worth as much, these shares exceeded the market value of their owner, 3Com. This is obvious mispricing if there ever was such a thing. But the interest cost of borrowing Palm shares grew to extraordinary levels, 35% per year by July 2000, high enough to make it impractical for smart money to profit from knowledge of this mispricing by shorting Palm and buying 3Com.

The Palm example of extreme, but it illustrates the effects of restrictions on short sales. There are many barriers to short selling, not just the explicit interest cost; some of these barriers are bureaucratic, psychological, and social.

STATISTICAL EVIDENCE OF MISPRICINGS

It is difficult to make any solid judgments about market efficiency based on a few anecdotes about alleged extreme mispricing of assets. But, in fact, there is no shortage of systematic evidence that firms that are "overpriced" by conventional measures have indeed tended to do poorly afterward. Many articles in academic finance journals show this, not by colorful examples but by systematic evaluation of large amounts of data on many firms.

Stocks that are difficult to short tend to do relatively poorly as investments, as was shown by Stephen Figlewski in 1981. More generally, stocks that are just overpriced by various measures tend to do poorly relative to stocks that are underpriced. Sanjoy Basu found in 1977 that firms with high price-earnings ratios tend to underperform, and in 1992 Eugene Fama and Kenneth French found the same for stocks with high price-to-book value. Werner De Bondt and Richard Thaler reported in 1985 that firms whose price had risen a great deal over five years tend to go down in price in the next five years, and that firms whose price has declined a great deal over five years tend to go up in price in the succeeding five years. Jay Ritter found in 1991 that initial public offerings tend to occur at the peak of industry-specific investor fads and then to show gradual but substantial price declines relative to the market over the subsequent three years. Thus there is a sort of regression to the mean (or to longer-run past values) for stock prices: what goes up a lot tends to come back down, and what goes down a lot tends to come back up.

These findings, and similar findings by many other researchers, have encouraged an approach to the market called *value investing*, that of picking portfolios of stocks that are underpriced by conventional measures, on the theory that they have been overlooked only temporarily by investors and will appreciate eventually. The other side of this strategy is to sell overpriced stocks short. One might think that the effect on the market of so many value investors would be to reduce, and even possibly eliminate for a time, the relation across stocks between value and subsequent returns. Value investors are after all buying the underpriced assets and bidding up their prices, and also diverting demand away from overpriced assets.

Sometimes value investing strategies will probably cease to work as investors flock to exploit them, yet it certainly does not follow that value investing as a whole will ever be out for good. Certainly avoiding investments that have become so overpriced that only the zealots own them is a sensible strategy. There are many different way to define value, and the market as a whole is not going to find it easy to eliminate all such profit opportunities.

Moreover, even if the effect of value on return *across stocks* disappears, it does not follow that the effect of value on return *over time for the market as a whole* must also disappear. The characteristic strategy of value investors is to pull out of overvalued individual stocks, but not to pull out of the market as a whole when it appears to be overvalued.

EARNINGS CHANGES AND PRICE CHANGES

Another argument that markets are basically efficient, in most global sense, is merely that stock prices roughly track earnings over time—that despite great fluctuations in earnings, price-earnings ratios have stayed within a comparatively narrow range.

Peter Lynch, an investment analyst who appeared frequently in the media during the bull market of the 1990s, was quoted in banner red letters in a 1999 advertisement for Fidelity Investments featuring a full-page photograph of him: "Despite 9 recessions since WWII, the stock market's up 63-fold because earnings are up 54-fold. Earnings drive the market." The ad, first seen just before the peak of the market, appeared to be designed to sell Fidelity's stock mutual funds by convincing readers that price growth is approximately justified by earnings growth. But in fact the numbers were deceptive. When such a long time interval is chosen for comparison, when no inflation correction is made, and since earnings were very low right after World War II, it is not surprising that Lynch could find such a correspondence. But if other examples are chosen, price changes may seem far less justified by earnings growth. Lynch's statement was indicative of a common view that stock price changes are generally justified by earnings changes, and that this proves that stock market price movements are not due to any irrational behavior on the part of investors.

As we have noted, there have been only three great bull markets, periods of sustained and dramatic stock price increase, in U.S. history: the bull market of the 1920s, culminating in 1929; the bull market of the 1950s; and the long bull market running from 1982 to 2000. (One might also add the bull market leading to the peak in 1901, but it was not so dramatic. The Ownership-Society Boom 2003-7 and the New-Normal Boom 2009-14 are even less dramatic in comparison.)

The first great bull market, from 1920 to 1929, was a period of rapid earnings growth. Real S&P Composite earnings doubled over this period, and real stock prices increased almost five-fold. The market change might be viewed as a reaction to the earnings change, albeit an overreaction.

But in the second great bull market, the correspondence between price growth and earnings growth is not so clear. Most of the price growth then occurred in the 1950s, and from January 1950 to December 1959 the real S&P Composite Index almost tripled. But real S&P earnings grew only 16% in total over this entire decade, an earnings performance that was below average by historical standards. In terms of overall economic growth, the 1950s were a little above average, though not as strong as either the 1940s or the 1960s: average real gross domestic product growth was 3.3% a year from 1950 to 1960.

In the third great bull market, real stock prices rose more or less continually from 1982 to 2000, but earnings did not grow at all uniformly. Real S&P Composite earnings were actually lower at the bottom of the recession of 1991 than they were at the bottom of the recession of 1982, but the real S&P Composite Index was almost two and a half times as high. So, for this bull market, price increases cannot be viewed as a simple reaction to earnings increases.

These examples show that earnings growth and price growth do not correspond well at all. One cannot criticize bubble theories by claiming that they do.

DIVIDEND CHANGES AND PRICE CHANGES

Some economists have claimed that there is a good relation between real stock price movements and, if not real earnings movements, at least real dividend movements. Dividend movements may be regarded as indicators of fundamental value, and so, these economists suggest, there is evidence that stock prices are driven by real fundamentals, not investor attitudes.

I think that these economists overstate their case of co-movements between dividends and prices. The wiggles in stock prices do not in fact correspond very closely to wiggles in dividends. Recall that between the stock market peak in September 1929 and the bottom in June 1932, when the stock market fell 81% as measured by the real S&P index, real dividends fell only 11%. Between the stock market peak in January 1973 and the bottom in December 1974, when the stock market fell 54% as measured by the real S&P index, real dividends fell only 6%. And there are many other such examples.

It is also likely that part of the reason for the observed co-movement between real prices and real dividends is the response of dividends to the same factors—possibly including speculative bubbles—that irrationally influence prices. Managers set dividends, and in so doing, they may vary over time the dividend-earnings ratio, that is, the payout rate. The managers are part of the same culture as the investing public, and are therefore probably influenced often enough by the same varying sense of optimism and pessimism that infects the public; they may allow this feeling to influence their decisions on how much of a dividend to pay out. Thus, the mere fact that prices and dividends show some substantial similarity is not inconsistent with the possibility that they are both influenced by fashions and fads.

In sum, stock prices clearly have a life of their own; they are not simply responding to earnings or dividends. Nor does it appear that they are determined only by information about future earnings or dividends. In seeking explanations of stock price movements, we must look elsewhere.

EXCESS VOLATILITY AND THE BIG PICTURE

There is indeed a good deal of evidence about market efficiency in academic finance journals, but it is hard to say that it is evidence *for* efficiency rather than against it. A great many anomalies have been discovered over the years within the efficient markets theory. These anomalies include the January effect (stock prices tend to go up between December and January), the small-firm effect (small firms' stocks tend to have higher returns), the day-of-the-week effect (the stock market tends to do poorly on Mondays), and others. How then can we summarize this literature as supporting market efficiency?

One way of arguing that the literature nevertheless supports market efficiency is to claim that many of these have been small effects, not the stuff of bull or bear markets. Another way is to note that many of these effects diminished after they were discovered, as indeed the January effect weakened after 1995 and the small-firm effect disappeared during the Millennium Boom. This makes it tricky to summarize the literature. On the one hand, the fact that these anomalies persisted for a long time shows that markets are inefficient. On the other hand, the fact that many of them have weakened suggests that there is a basic truth to the theory.

Merton Miller, who was a leading advocate of efficient markets theory, recognized that there are indeed many little anomalies, but he argued that they are inconsequential: "That we abstract from all these stories in building our models is not because the stories are uninteresting but because they may be too interesting and thereby distract us from the pervasive market forces that should be our principal concern." But he did not explain his presumption that the pervasive market forces are rational ones.

Abstracting (as Miller urged us to do) from the little details about day-of-the-week effects and the like, what is the basic evidence that stock markets are efficient in the big-picture sense? Do large changes in stock prices over the years really reflect information about important changes in the underlying companies?

The evidence that there is not much short-run momentum or inertia—that there is not much predictability of day-to-day or month-to-month changes in stock price indices—does not tell us anything about efficiency in the big-picture sense. We already know from simple economic reasoning that day-to-day changes in stock prices cannot be very forecastable, since such forecastability would be too good a profit opportunity to be true; it would be too easy to get rich.

One method for judging whether there is evidence in support of the basic validity of the efficient markets theory, which I published in an article in the *American Economic Review* in 1981 (at the same time as a similar paper by Stephen LeRoy and Richard Porter appeared), is to see whether the very volatility of speculative prices, such as stock prices, can be justified by the variability of dividends over long intervals of time. If the stock price movements are to be justified in terms of the future dividends that firms pay out, as the basic version of the efficient markets theory would imply, then under efficient markets we cannot have volatile prices without subsequently volatile dividends.

In fact, my article concluded, no movement of U.S. aggregate stock prices beyond the trend growth of prices has ever been subsequently justified by dividend movements, as the dividend present value with constant discount rate has shown an extraordinarily smooth growth path. This conclusion, coming at a time when the finance profession was much more attached to the efficient markets theory than it is now, produced a strong reaction. I received more attacks on this work than I could hope to answer. No one questioned the observation that stock prices have been more volatile than the dividend present value—only whether the difference between the two was statistically significant or whether my interpretation of this difference was on target.

Included in my article was a figure showing the real (inflation-corrected) S&P Composite Stock Price Index for 1871-1979 and, on the same figure, the *dividend present value*, the present value for each year of real dividends paid subsequent to that year on the shares making up the index, computed by making an assumption about dividends after the last year. An updated version of that figure, showing both the stock price and the dividend present value through 2003, is shown in Figure 11.2.

The dividend present value is not known with certainty in the year to which it corresponds, since it is determined entirely by dividends after the year, which have yet to be paid. According to the efficient markets model, the dividend present value subsequent to any given year is the (as yet unknown) true fundamental value of the stock market in that year. The actual level of the real stock market in that same year, the stock price shown in 11.2, is supposed to be the optimal prediction, using information available in that year, of one of the dividend present values shown for the same year.

Looking at this figure, we can get a sense of the extent of big-picture, important evidence for the efficiency of the aggregate stock market in the United States. If the dividend present value moved up and down massively over time, and if the actual stock price appeared to move with these movements as if it were successfully forecasting the changes in the dividend present value, then we could say that there was evidence that stock prices were behaving in accordance with the tenets of the efficient markets theory. But we see that none of the present-value series has been more volatile than the price series itself, and, in the past half century, all of the present-value series

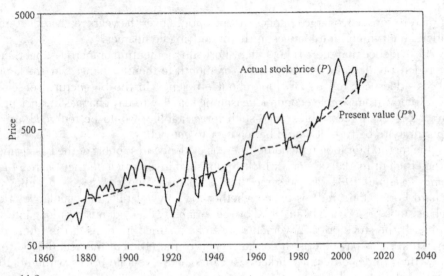

Figure 11.2
Stock Prices and Dividend Present Values, 1871-2004

Real S&P Composite Stock Price Index, 1881-2004 (heavy irregular curve), and present values, 1881-2003, of subsequent real dividends calculated by three different discount rates: a constant discount rate (heavy smooth curve), a discount rate based on market interest rates (this curve), and a discount rate based on per capita consumption expenditure (dashed curve).

has been much less volatile than the price series. Moreover, there is little tendency of the stock prices to forecast any of the dividend present values.

The dividend present value is extremely steady and trend-like, partly because the calculations for present value use data over a range far into the future and partly because dividends have not moved very dramatically. Now that one sees present value plotted over a long range of time, it seems obvious from what some of us (who have thought about it and have good intuitive grasp of quantities) have always known at gut level: the big stock market movements in history were not in fact justified by what actually happened to the businesses of the various companies later. One might try to argue that a little over a century is not a long enough time period to be confident that one *would* expect to see such justification, but the fact still remains that there has been no such justification.

The point I made in 1981 was that stock prices appear to be too volatile to be considered in accord with efficient markets. Assuming that stock prices are supposed to be an optimal predictor of the dividend present value, then they should not jump around erratically if the true fundamental value is growing along a smooth trend. Only if the public could predict the future perfectly should the price be as volatile as the present value, and in that case it should match up perfectly with the present value, and in that case it should match up perfectly with the present value. If the public cannot predict well, then the forecast should move around a lot less than the present value. But that's not what we see in Figure 11.2.

We learn by considering Figure 11.2 that the common interpretation given in the media for stock market fluctuations in terms of the outlook for the short-run business cycle is generally misguided. The prospect that a temporary recession is on the horizon that will lower future dividends should have virtually no impact on stock prices, if the efficient markets theory is correct. Recessions have just been too short and too small historically to justify the stock price movements that are associated with them. Fluctuations in stock prices, if they are to be interpretable in terms of the efficient markets theory, must instead be due to new information about the *longer-run* outlook for real dividends. Yet in the entire history of the U.S. stock market we have never seen such longer-run fluctuations, since dividends have closely followed a steady growth path.

As I argued in my 1981 paper, the only way to reconcile the volatility of stock prices with the efficient markets model without relying on ad hoc assumptions about changing stock market discount rates is to suppose that, one way or the other, the historical fluctuations of dividends around their growth path are not representative of the *potential* fluctuations. That is, one would have to say that the fluctuations observed in market prices were the result of people's legitimate concerns with possible major and lasting dividend movements that just did not chance to happen in the century of data we observe. For example, people might have been concerned about a big, rare event, such as a complete nationalization and confiscation of the stock market by the government, or an enormous technological breakthrough that would make existing companies able to pay many times more dividends.

As noted earlier, my work invited the attention of an army of critics. Most notable among them was Robert C. Merton, a brilliant financial theorist who also was to suffer a major financial loss as a principal in the Long Term Capital Management hedge fund. Merton, with Terry Marsh, wrote an article in the *American Economic Review* in 1986 that argued against my results and concluded, ironically, that speculative markets were not too volatile.

John Campbell and I wrote a number of papers attempting to put these claims of excess volatility on a more secure footing, and we developed statistical models to study the issue and deal with some of the problems emphasized by the critics. We felt that we had established in a fairly convincing way that stock markets do violate the efficient markets model.

Our research has not completely settled the matter, however. There are just too many possible statistical issues that can be raised, and the sample provided by only a little over a century of data cannot prove anything conclusively.

It should also be noted that some substantial fraction of the volatility in financial markets *is* justified by news about future dividends or earnings. The very trend-like behavior of U.S. corporate dividends over the past century was probably partly due to luck, not a law saying that dividends must hug a trend. Taking account of uncertainty about the trend, Campbell and I, in interpreting the results of one of our statistical studies, estimated that 27% of the annual return volatility of the U.S. stock market might be justified in terms of genuine information about future dividends. Campbell and John Ammer, using similar methodology and a more recent (postwar) data set, found that 15% of the variability in monthly returns in the U.S. stock market could be attributed to genuine information about future dividends.

There appears to be less evidence of excess volatility in long-term interest rates and little evidence of excess volatility in the spread between stock price indices. Individual stocks, for which the present value of future dividends is much more volatile than with the aggregate market, show less excess volatility than the market as a whole. Excess volatility due to speculative bubbles is probably just one of the factors that drive speculative markets, and the prominence of this factor varies across markets and over time. We are not always in an excess volatility situation.

But we are in such a situation, or recently have been, in many of our stock markets, housing markets, and even commodity markets. Defenders of the recent high price levels of these markets have had a difficult time making an inspiring case that the sudden increases we have seen in these markets can be interpreted as the rational efficient-markets response to genuine new information.

CAPITAL TRANSACTIONS, STRUCTURE, AND MARKETS

A. CAPITAL TRANSACTIONS

1. REASONS FOR CAPITAL RAISING TRANSACTIONS

Capital is the lifeblood of the company. It funds the capital assets necessary to engage in enterprise over the long term. A corporation can acquire capital through the issuance of debt or equity. Most security instruments fall broadly into three basic categories: debt, preferred stock, and common stock. Within these broad categories, a financial instrument can take as many forms of freedom as a contract allows, which is to say that the diversity of form and terms in a security are driven by the unique needs of issuers and investors.

Before a corporation decides to raise capital, it must answer two questions: (1) Does the corporation have a business need for the capital? and (2) Can the expected use of the capital by the corporation satisfy the financial needs of investors? A firm may raise capital for a number of reasons, but the basic business reason is that the corporation needs money. Business projects require funding. It cannot always be assumed that internal funding—the existing cash flow generated by retained profits— will fund the desired project. Just because a company does not have the capital on hand does not mean that it should forego an opportunity for a profitable project. If so, the corporation requires external capital.

New capital is not raised to simply increase the company's cash reserve. At some point, excess cash (excess of working capital needs) must be deployed toward productive use. It must fund existing or new projects. During the capital raising process, investors will want to know the expected use of the capital. The answer cannot be that the company is losing money and requires capital to fund losses. No rational investor will put up the capital. The answer must be that capital is required to fund existing or new projects that are expected to generate the return expected by all capital providers.

For example, a firm could be a startup company needing capital to start a new business model. It could be an established company needing capital to fund a new project such as expanding business operations in China. It could need money for an acquisition. It could have run out of capital because of bad luck or poor management, but the current projects would be profitable with better luck or management. If capital is needed for whatever reason, and the firm does not have cash on hand to fund itself, it must raise capital.

EXAMPLE

> ### Goldman Sachs Raises Capital in the Nick of Time
>
> During the financial crisis, financial institutions such as commercial banks and investment banks were caught in a liquidity and solvency crisis. The asset values on their balance sheets were declining precipitously with the collapse of the housing market; the assets were illiquid; the banks were heavily leveraged. The confluence of these factors resulted in the small slivers of equity on their balance sheets rapidly evaporating. The banks needed to recapitalize. Some could not due to market conditions or, more likely, lack of confidence in the companies, as may have been the case for Lehman Brothers and Bear Stearns. Others were more fortunate.
>
> In September and October 2008, as Lehman Brothers filed for bankruptcy and Merrill Lynch was sold to Bank of America, Goldman Sachs completed a series of capital raisings, including the sale of preferred stock to Warren Buffett's company Berkshire Hathaway and to the U.S. government under the Troubled Asset Relief Program (TARP). Below is the portion of Goldman Sachs' 2008 annual report describing its various capital raising activities during the nadir of the financial crisis of 2008–2009. The activities described below helped to prevent the firm from collapsing like some of its peers.
>
> * * *
>
> **Stock Offerings.**   In September 2008, we completed a public offering of 46.7 million shares of common stock at $123.00 per share for proceeds of $5.75 billion.
>
> In October 2008, we issued to Berkshire Hathaway Inc. and certain affiliates 50,000 shares of 10% Cumulative Perpetual Preferred Stock, Series G (Series G Preferred Stock), and a five-year warrant to purchase up to 43.5 million shares of common stock at an exercise price of $115.00 per share, for aggregate proceeds of $5.00 billion. The allocated carrying values of the warrant and the Series G Preferred Stock on the date of issuance (based on their relative fair values) were $1.14 billion and $3.86 billion, respectively. The warrant is exercisable at any time until October 1, 2013 and the number of shares of common stock underlying the warrant and the exercise price are subject to adjustment for certain dilutive events.
>
> In October 2008, under the U.S. Treasury's TARP Capital Purchase Program, we issued to the U.S. Treasury 10.0 million shares of Fixed Rate Cumulative Perpetual Preferred Stock, Series H (Series H Preferred Stock), and a 10-year warrant to purchase up to 12.2 million shares of common stock at an exercise price of $122.90 per share, for aggregate proceeds of $10.00 billion. The allocated carrying values of the warrant and the Series H Preferred Stock on the date of issuance (based on their relative fair values) were $490 million and $9.51 billion, respectively. Cumulative dividends on the Series H Preferred Stock are payable at 5% per annum through November 14, 2013 and at a rate of 9% per annum thereafter. The Series H Preferred Stock will be accreted to the redemption price of $10.00 billion over five years. The warrant is exercisable at any time until October 28, 2018 and the number of shares of common stock underlying the warrant and the exercise price are subject to adjustment for certain dilutive events. If, on or prior to December 31, 2009, we receive aggregate gross cash proceeds of at least $10 billion from sales of Tier 1 qualifying perpetual preferred stock or common stock, the number of shares of common stock issuable upon exercise of the warrant will be reduced by one-half of the original number of shares of common stock.

2. LEGAL AUTHORITY FOR ISSUANCE

In a corporate finance transaction, there are important legal questions on: (1) whether the financing transaction is legal as to the power and authority of the corporation to issue the specific securities in question; and (2) whether the issuance of the security conflicts with terms and conditions of existing securities. The first question is answered by reviewing the applicable corporation law and the corporate governance documents, including principally the corporate charter. The second question is answered by reviewing all relevant financial contracts in light of the new issue.

The following case involves the issuance of super-voting preferred stock. The question was whether the board had authority to issue such a stock and, if not, the consequence of an unauthorized issuance.

Waggoner v. Laster
581 A.2d 1127 (Del. 1990)

MOORE, Justice.

In this case we review issues involving the alleged creation of preferred stock with super-majority voting rights. Thomas Waggoner and Patricia Waggoner appeal from a judgment of the Court of Chancery determining that the board of directors of STAAR Surgical Company consists of LaMar Laster, John Ford, Howard Silverman, Peter Utrata, and Thomas Waggoner. Waggoner had attempted to replace the other members of the Board by executing a written consent purporting to vote the preferred stock in question. The Court of Chancery assumed without deciding that the preferred stock held by Waggoner was validly issued, but nonetheless ruled that the super-majority voting rights were void. Accordingly, Waggoner's attempted removal of the other directors was improper. We agree and affirm.

In October, 1982, STAAR was organized by Waggoner as a California corporation to develop, produce, and market patented soft intraocular lenses and related products used primarily in cataract surgery. Later, in April 1986, the company was reincorporated in Delaware. Its common stock has been traded over-the-counter. From its inception, Waggoner has served as STAAR's Chief Executive Officer and President.

By 1987, STAAR faced mounting financial difficulties. It was overdrawn by approximately $1 million on a line of credit with the Bank of New York ("BONY"); BONY was demanding personal guarantees from Waggoner on $3.5 million in corporate debt; and STAAR was overdue on additional debt of nearly $1.8 million.

It became clear that only Waggoner was willing and able to guarantee the corporate debt in the near future and on such short notice. Waggoner agreed to provide personal guarantees and stock pledges for substantially all of STAAR's debt. In return the Board issued convertible preferred stock to Waggoner as compensation for these agreements. Waggoner required that voting control of STAAR be given to him while his personal guarantees were outstanding. He now contends that the preferred stock issued to him contained super-majority voting rights to achieve that end.

STAAR's financial difficulties continued through 1989, at which time the Board sought to raise additional capital by merging with or selling some of its assets to another company. Two companies, Vision Technologies, Inc. ("VTI") and Chiron Corp., made proposals to merge with STAAR or to acquire certain of its assets. The four directors other than Waggoner concluded that VTI's proposal was more viable and terminated negotiations with Chiron. Indeed, the Board unanimously approved a resolution "to proceed expeditiously to attempt to complete the proposed VTI transaction". Waggoner, however, continued to hold discussions personally with Chiron without informing the other directors. Notably, under the Chiron proposal Waggoner would continue to be employed by the successor corporation to STAAR, whereas under the VTI proposal he would be terminated. Moreover, Waggoner had apparently decided that, if necessary, he would remove the other directors using his preferred stock voting rights.

Another director discovered Waggoner conferring with Chiron representatives in STAAR's offices. The Board met the following day to consider removing Waggoner from the Board and stripping him of his positions as President and CEO. Before a vote could be taken, however, Waggoner executed a stockholder's written consent purporting to vote his super-majority voting preferred stock to oust the other directors, to reduce the size of the Board to three members, and named himself and his wife to the new board. Thereafter, Waggoner and his wife held a board meeting at which they purported to remove Laster from his corporate offices and to approve the Chiron transaction.

The plaintiffs brought civil actions in Delaware to determine the lawful members of STAAR's board under 8 *Del.C.* §225 and to enjoin Waggoner from causing STAAR to enter into the Chiron transaction. After expedited discovery and a full trial, the Vice Chancellor concluded that the board lacked authority under STAAR's certificate of incorporation to issue preferred stock to Waggoner with super-majority voting rights. He concluded that Waggoner's attempt to remove the other directors was invalid.

STAAR's Delaware certificate of incorporation expressly authorized the board to issue both common and preferred stock. Article *Fourth* of the Delaware certificate provides:

(a) The Corporation shall be authorized to issue THIRTY MILLION (30,000,000) shares, consisting of TWENTY MILLION (20,000,000) shares of Common Stock, each of the par value of $.01 ("Common Stock") and TEN MILLION (10,000,000) shares of Preferred Stock, each of the par value of $.01 ("Preferred Stock").

(b) The designations and the powers, preferences and rights, and the qualifications or restrictions thereof are as follows:

Except as otherwise required by statute or provided for by resolution or resolutions of the Board of Directors, as hereinafter set forth, the holders of the Common Stock of the Corporation shall possess the exclusive right to vote for the election of directors and for all other corporate purposes.

The Preferred Stock shall each be issued from time to time in one or more series, with such distinctive serial designations as shall be stated and expressed in the resolution or resolutions providing for the issue of such shares from time to time adopted by the Board of Directors; and in such resolution or resolutions providing for the issue of shares of each particular series the Board of Directors is expressly authorized to fix the annual rate or rates of dividends for the particular series and the date from which dividends on all shares of such series issued prior to the record date for the first dividend payment date shall be cumulative; the redemption price or prices for the particular series; the rights, if any, of holders of the shares of the particular series to convert the same into shares of any other series or class or other securities of the Corporation or of any other corporation, with any provisions for the subsequent adjustment of such conversion rights; and to classify or reclassify any unissued Preferred Stock by fixing or altering from time to time any of the foregoing rights, privileges and qualifications.

Notably absent [in] the Delaware certificate was any reference to voting rights or super-majority voting rights.

The primary issue in this case is whether the Court of Chancery correctly concluded that STAAR's board of directors lacked authority under STAAR's certificate of incorporation to issue convertible preferred stock with super-majority voting rights. Without such authority, those voting rights held by Waggoner, which he contends allow him to vote out the other directors, are null and void.

We start with basics. The Delaware General Corporation Law allows corporations to issue preferred stock with special designations. 8 *Del.C.* §151(a), §102(a)(4). Section 151, which outlines the general corporate power to issue stock and dividends, provides:

> Every corporation may issue 1 or more classes of stock . . . which classes . . . may have *such voting powers,* full or limited, or no voting powers, and such designations, preferences and relative, participating, optional or other special rights, and qualifications, limitations or restrictions thereof, *as shall be stated and expressed* in the certificate of incorporation or of any amendment thereto, or *in the resolution or resolutions providing for the issue of such stock adopted by the board of directors pursuant to authority vested in it by the provisions of its certificate of incorporation.*

Section 102(a)(4), which deals specifically with the technical formation of corporations, provides:

> The certificate of incorporation *shall also set forth* a statement of the designations and powers, preferences and rights, and the qualifications, limitations, or restrictions thereof, which are permitted by §151 of this title in respect of any class or classes of stock or any series of any class of stock of the corporation and the fixing of which by the certificate of incorporation is desired, and *an express grant of such authority as it may then be desired to grant to the board of directors to fix by resolution or resolutions any thereof that may be desired but which shall not be fixed by the certificate of incorporation.*

Section 151 specifically includes voting rights among the list of stock attributes that directors may be empowered to set.

STAAR's Delaware certificate of incorporation authorized the board to issue preferred stock. Indeed, it specifically allowed the board to establish certain stock preferences, including dividends, redemption prices, conversion rights, and reclassification rights. It did not, however, expressly authorize the board to establish special voting rights for preferred stock. In light of that omission, and Delaware's statutory requirement that such powers be enumerated in the certificate of incorporation, the Vice Chancellor found that the record was insufficient to establish that STAAR's board was expressly authorized to grant preferential voting rights to certain classes of stock.

Conceding that the Delaware certificate fails to expressly list voting rights among the preferences the Board is authorized to grant, the Waggoners nonetheless argue

171

that one portion of STAAR's Delaware certificate contains the blanket authority sufficient to meet Delaware's statutory requirements. They point to the second paragraph of subsection (b), Article *FOURTH* which provides:

> *Except as otherwise required by statute or provided for by resolutions of the Board of Directors, as hereinafter set forth,* the holders of the Common Stock shall possess the exclusive right to vote for the election of directors and for all other corporate purposes.

A certificate of incorporation is viewed as a contract among shareholders, and general rules of contract interpretation apply to its terms. *Rothschild Int'l Corp. v. Liggett Corp.,* 474 A.2d 133, 136 (Del. 1984). Courts must give effect to the intent of the parties as revealed by the language of the certificate and the circumstances surrounding its creation and adoption. *Goldman v. Postal Telegraph, Inc.,* 52 F.Supp. 763 (D.Del. 1943). Since stock preferences are in derogation of the common law, they must be strictly construed. An express grant of authority to establish stock preferences cannot be conferred by a general reservation clause worded in a nonspecific fashion.

In one of the earliest cases to address this issue, the Court of Chancery stated:

> The power to create preferred stock is granted in §18 [of the certificate], and it is granted upon the terms set forth in that section. To enact that the stock should have such preference as is stated or expressed in the certificate was equivalent to enacting that it should have no other preferences upon the general principle of interpretation that the expression of one thing is the exclusion of another.

Moreover, the court stated:

> It is elementary that the rights of stockholders are contract rights. The mere word "preferred" unless it is supplemented by a definition of its significance conveys no special meaning. The holder of preferred stock must therefore refer to the appropriate language of the corporate contract for the ascertainment of his rights. The nub of the present contention is—where may such appropriate language be found? The exceptants say in the certificate of incorporation and nowhere else. In this I think they are correct.

Subsequently, numerous decisions applying Delaware law have adhered to the rule that stock preferences are to be strictly construed. We think those decisions clearly establish the rule that stock preferences are to be strictly construed in Delaware. We adhere to that view.

Applying the rule of strict construction to the language urged by Waggoner, we find that it is merely a general reservation clause which is insufficient to expressly reserve authority in the board to establish preferences. Such general reservation clauses are commonly found in corporate documents, and we need not impose a strained construction to give the phrase different meaning. The clause is phrased in the negative, and is too general and nonspecific to confer the broad authority suggested by Waggoner. Moreover, the sentence contains the limitation "as hereinafter set forth" which appears to refer to the list of designations, powers, preferences and rights the board was authorized to confer. The power to establish voting rights was conspicuously absent from the enumerated rights and powers granted the board.

While that omission may have been accidental, given the requirements of Delaware law this Court cannot presume so and thereafter supply the missing provisions. Under the rule of strict construction, any ambiguity must be resolved against granting the challenged preferences, rights or powers.

In this action, the Court of Chancery assumed that Waggoner had been issued preferred stock with super-majority voting rights, but it nevertheless concluded that such voting rights were void because the Board lacked authority under STAAR's certificate of incorporation to authorize preferred stock with such special rights. We uphold that determination because the power to establish special voting rights is conspicuously absent from the list of preferences the Board was authorized to confer. No other provision of STAAR's certificate clearly grants the Board such authority.

QUESTIONS

1. How must preferred stock be authorized and issued?
2. Assume that STAAR really wanted to have the option to issue preferred stock with voting rights. Obviously, the failure to mention voting rights in the certificate was the key drafting mistake. In terms of the drafting process, how could this error have been avoided?
3. In what way(s) are the rights of preferred stockholders similar to the rights of creditors?

NOTES

1. If the corporate charter does not authorize the issuance of preferred stock, it must be properly amended to do so. To avoid this, a charter can include a provision to give the board "blank check" authority to create the class or series of shares and establish its terms without shareholder approval. If the board uses its blank check authority to create the class or series, it files a certificate of designation with the secretary of state, which acts as an amendment of the charter and becomes a part of the corporate charter.

To address the concern of investors and their advisors that the transaction is legally binding, the counsel for the issuer customarily issues a legal opinion as to the validity of the transaction. With respect to the issuance of stocks or bonds, the purchaser must have comfort that the issuance is valid as to authority pursuant to laws, the corporate charter, and other sources of or restraints on authority.

The following are illustrative opinion letters. The first document is an actual opinion letter regarding an issuance of debentures in connection with Berkshire Hathaway's acquisition of Burlington Northern Santa Fe Corporation, and the second document is a sample template letter regarding a stock purchase agreement.

Form 8-K of Burlington Northern Santa Fe, LLC

May 12, 2010

ITEM 1.01. ENTRY INTO A MATERIAL DEFINITIVE AGREEMENT.

Burlington Northern Santa Fe, LLC ("BNSF") entered into an underwriting agreement (the "Underwriting Agreement") dated as of May 12, 2010, with Banc of America Securities LLC, Citigroup Global Markets Inc. and J.P. Morgan Securities Inc., as representatives of the several underwriters listed therein (collectively, the "Underwriters"), pursuant to which BNSF agreed to sell and the Underwriters agreed to purchase, subject to and upon terms and conditions set forth therein, $750 million in aggregate principal amount of 5.75% Debentures due May 1, 2040, as described in the prospectus supplement dated May 12, 2010, filed pursuant to BNSF's shelf registration statement on Form S-3, Registration No. 333-166755.

The debentures were issued under the Indenture dated as of December 1, 1995, as supplemented by the Sixth Supplemental Indenture dated as of May 17, 2010, between BNSF and The Bank of New York Mellon Trust Company, N.A. (formerly known as The Bank of New York Trust Company, N.A.), as successor in interest to The First National Bank of Chicago, as trustee, and an officers' certificate providing for the issuance of the debentures. The Underwriters delivered the debentures against payment on May 17, 2010.

EXHIBIT 5.1. OPINION OF SULLIVAN & CROMWELL LLP, AS TO THE VALIDITY OF THE SECURITIES BEING OFFERED.

[Letterhead of Sullivan & Cromwell LLP]

May 17, 2010

Burlington Northern Santa Fe, LLC,
2650 Lou Menk Drive,
Fort Worth, Texas 76131-2830.

Ladies and Gentlemen:

In connection with the registration under the Securities Act of 1933 (the "Act") of $750,000,000 principal amount of 5.75% Debentures due May 1, 2040 (the "Securities") of Burlington Northern Santa Fe, LLC, a Delaware limited liability company (the "Company"), we, as your special counsel, have examined such records, certificates and other documents, and such questions of law, as we have considered necessary or appropriate for the purposes of this opinion.

Upon the basis of such examination, we advise you that, in our opinion, the Securities constitute valid and legally binding obligations of the Company, subject to bankruptcy, insolvency, fraudulent transfer, reorganization, moratorium and similar laws of general applicability relating to or affecting creditors' rights and to general equity principles.

The foregoing opinion is limited to the Federal laws of the United States and the laws of the State of New York and the Delaware Limited Liability Company Act, and we are expressing no opinion as to the effect of the laws of any other jurisdiction.

We have relied as to certain factual matters on information obtained from public officials, officers of the Company and other sources believed by us to be responsible, and we have assumed that the Indenture under which the Securities have been issued and the Sixth Supplemental Indenture thereto have been duly authorized, executed and delivered by the Trustee thereunder, an assumption which we have not independently verified.

Third-Party "Closing" Opinions

53 Bus. Law. 591, 671-72 (1998)

Illustrative Opinion Letter
Outside Counsel: Stock Purchase Agreement

[Law Firm Letterhead]

[DATE]

World Wide Ventures L.P.
Ten World Trade Center
New York, New York 10048

re: Macromoney Corporation
       Sale of Stock Under Stock Purchase Agreement
       dated as of _____

Ladies and Gentlemen:

We have acted as counsel for Macromoney Corporation, a Delaware corporation (the "Company"), in connection with the preparation, execution and delivery of, and sale of stock under, the Stock Purchase Agreement, dated as of _____, between you and the Company (the "Stock Purchase Agreement"). This opinion letter is delivered to you pursuant to Section _____ of the Stock Purchase Agreement. Terms defined in the Stock Purchase Agreement are used herein as therein defined.

For purposes of this opinion letter we have reviewed such documents and made such other investigation as we have deemed appropriate. As to certain matters of fact material to the opinions expressed herein, we have relied on the representations made in the Stock Purchase Agreement and certificates of public officials and officers of the Company [and others]. We have not independently established the facts so relied on.

Based on the foregoing and subject to the other paragraphs hereof, we express the following opinions.

1. The Company is a corporation [duly incorporated and] validly existing under the law of the State of Delaware.

2. The Shares have been duly authorized and validly issued and are fully paid and nonassessable.
3. The Company
   (a) has the corporate power to execute, deliver and perform the Stock Purchase Agreement,
   (b) has taken all necessary corporate action to authorize the execution, delivery and performance of the Stock Purchase Agreement, and
   (c) has duly executed and delivered the Stock Purchase Agreement.
4. The Stock Purchase Agreement is a valid and binding obligation of the Company enforceable against the Company in accordance with its terms.
5. The execution and delivery by the Company of the Stock Purchase Agreement do not, and the performance by the Company of its obligations thereunder will not, result in a violation of the Certificate of Incorporation or By-Laws of the Company.
6. The execution and delivery by the Company of the Stock Purchase Agreement do not, and the performance by the Company of its obligations thereunder will not,
   (a) result in any violation of any law of the United States or the State of New York, or any rule or regulation thereunder, or
   (b) require approval from or any filings with any governmental authority under any law of the United States or the State of New York, or any rule or regulation thereunder.

[Insert any other opinions.]

Our opinions above are subject to bankruptcy, insolvency and other similar laws affecting the rights and remedies of creditors generally and general principles of equity.

[Insert any other exceptions, stated assumptions, etc.]

The opinions expressed herein are limited to the federal law of the United States, the law of the State of New York, and the Delaware General Corporation Law.

This opinion letter is being delivered to you in connection with the above described transaction and may not be relied on by you for any other purpose. This opinion letter may not be relied on by or furnished to any other Person without our prior written consent.

Very truly yours,

3. ACCOUNTING TREATMENT OF CAPITAL RAISE

At the most elemental level, accounting for capital transactions is simple. When a corporation issues a financial instrument to raise capital, assets (cash) increase and, depending on the nature of the financial instrument (whether it is debt or equity), either liabilities or equity increases. The balance sheet gets bigger. When a corporation buys back a financial instrument by either paying off the principal on debt or repurchasing stock, assets (cash) decreases, and again, depending on the nature of the financial instrument, either liabilities or equity decreases. The balance sheet gets smaller.

EXAMPLE

Internal and External Funding

In Year 0, NewCo is formed. It raised $100 by borrowing from a bank and another $100 by issuing 100 shares to shareholders. The bank note is a liability, and the stock issued is the equity. Assume that the par value of the stock is $0.01, and thus the additional paid in capital (APIC) for each share is $0.99. The concept of "par value" is discussed later in Chapter 5 on common stock, but for the purpose of understanding the account we can understand par value as an arbitrary amount set by the company and typically it is a low figure. The most commonly seen par value figure is $0.01. When a corporation issues stock in a jurisdiction that recognizes par value stock (such as Delaware*), the issue price (the price investors pay to buy a share) constitutes two accounting items that are separately noted in the shareholders' equity section of the balance sheet:

$$\text{Issue Price} = \text{Par Value} + \text{Additional Paid in Capital}$$

In this case, since the issue price of the stock is $1/share and the par value is $0.01, APIC is $0.99 per share. There are now 100 shares outstanding, which is noted in the balance sheet as "shares issued" (the shareholders' equity account under the item "Stock" will also note the number of shares "outstanding").

Assets		**Liabilities**	
Cash	200	Note	100
		Equity	
		Stock (100 shares issued)	1
		APIC	99

In Year 1, NewCo earned a profit of 200, received all of the profit in cash, and retained all the cash. The retained earnings are a form of internal funding. The money is an economic claim of shareholders, but the corporation has control of whether to retain it for business purposes or to distribute it in the form of a dividend. The balance sheet looks like this.

Assets		**Liabilities**	
Cash	400	Note	100
		Equity	
		Stock (100 shares issued)	1
		Additional paid in capital	99
		Retained earnings	200

Note the increase in assets from profit and a corresponding increase in equity indicating that the profit is a part of the shareholders' economic claim.

In Year 2, given the profitable previous year and flush with cash from the activities and transactions of Year 0 and Year 1, NewCo decides to repay the bank note and also buy

---

* *See* Delaware General Corporation Law §151(a) ("Every corporation may issue 1 or more classes of stock or 1 or more series of stock within any class thereof, any or all of which classes may be of stock with par value or stock without par value. . . .").

back 50 shares of stock at the price of $2 per share (note that the original issue price was $1 per share). The repurchase is recorded under the cost method, which records the entire repurchase amount as a contra-equity under the label "treasury stock" at the cost of shares repurchased (in nontechnical terms, treasury stock is a subtraction from equity because treasury constitutes a reduction in equity due to payment to shareholders). The cash outflow for the repayment of the bank debt is 100, and NewCo no longer has any liabilities on its balance sheet. The cost of repurchase of shares is 100. The combined cash outflow is 200.

Assets		Equity	
Cash	200	Stock (100 shares issued)	1
		Additional paid in capital	99
		Retained earnings	200
		Treasury stock	(100)

Note the decrease in assets of 200, a decrease in liabilities to 0, and a new line item in the shareholder's equity called "treasury stock," which accounts for the stock buyback. Also, even though NewCo issued 100 shares, the shareholders' equity account will note that the shares outstanding is 50 shares since treasury stock is considered issued but not outstanding ("outstanding shares" simply means that the stock is currently held by shareholders).

B. CAPITAL BUDGETING

Capital is not free. It has a cost. Because capital is not an unlimited resource, there has to be a very good reason for raising capital. Stockpiling cash in the corporate treasury without anticipated use is not a good reason. The cost of capital means that investors always expect managers to provide a suitable return on capital. Managers must budget capital and allocate it to only economically sensible (profitable) projects. Capital must be allocated among different projects, and the choice of potential projects in which capital can be deployed requires investment criteria. Managers must evaluate all projects. How is this evaluation done? Two major analyses are used. The first is net present value (NPV) and the other is internal rate of return (IRR).

1. NET PRESENT VALUE

NPV takes into account the cash inflows and outflows of the investment, and adjusts them by the firm's cost of capital. If the net present value of the project is positive, it means that the project creates value because it met or exceeded the cost of capital. On the other hand, if the net present value is negative, the project has destroyed value because it did not meet the cost of capital.

EXAMPLE

NPV

Consider a firm with a 10% cost of capital, meaning that the corporation must return 10% on its rent of capital. The project requires these capital investments (negative figures) and cash flow returns.

	YEAR 0	YEAR 1	YEAR 2	YEAR 3	YEAR 4	YEAR 5	
Cash	(1,000)	300	300	300	300	300	
Discount factor	1.0000	0.9091	0.8264	0.7513	0.6830	0.6209	NPV
PV	(1,000)	273	248	225	205	186 →	$\boxed{+137}$

This is a positive NPV project. The net present value is +137. Based on a cash expenditure of 1,000, this project returns a 10% rate plus another 137 in positive present value.

Now consider the same project, except that the cost of capital is 16%. The following is the NPV calculation.

	YEAR 0	YEAR 1	YEAR 2	YEAR 3	YEAR 4	YEAR 5	
Cash	(1,000)	300	300	300	300	300	
Discount factor	1.0000	0.8333	0.6944	0.5787	0.4823	0.4019	NPV
PV	(1,000)	250	208	174	145	121 →	$\boxed{-103}$

Notice that while the project returns 1,500 in gross value, the present value of the returns at a 16% discount rate is 897, which is 103 less than the 1,000 investment on a present value basis. Although in accounting terms, the project has profited by 500, the project destroys economic value by 103.

2. INTERNAL RATE OF RETURN

Another basis for evaluating a project is IRR. In many financial or corporate transactions, an investment is made today (resulting in cash outflow) and the payback is received in the future. We need to calculate the implied rate of return, R. Why? Suppose the investor has a "benchmark" or "hurdle" rate that must be met. We must be able to calculate the return rate R so that we can determine whether this business opportunity meets the investment requirement. IRR is the implied rate of return given an investment today and a future payout. In other words, it is the discount rate that satisfies the time value formula given a present value cash outflow and expected future values given a specific time horizon.

The formula below captures this concept (IRR is the discount rate R that satisfies the equation).

$$0 = -PV + \frac{FV}{(1 + R)^T}$$

EXAMPLE

How Venture Capital Firms Evaluate Investment Opportunities

Venture Capital LP ("VC") must consider whether to invest $1,000 in Legal Documents Inc., a company that sells efficient document review services. The financial models indicate that after seven years, the company can do an IPO and sell itself to a larger company, and VC can exit (monetize) the investment at a value of $3,000. The investors of VC have a hurdle rate of 20%, which is their expectation of a return based on the riskiness of venture capital investments (many venture capital investments never pan out and so investors demand a high rate of return). Should VC invest in Legal Documents?

This is a simple time value problem. We are told that we make an investment of $1,000 in present value, and we anticipate a return of $3,000 in future value. We are also given a time horizon, seven years. We are only missing the rate of return R.

$$1,000 = \frac{3,000}{(1 + R)^7}$$

Although formulating the problem is simple, calculating R manually cannot be done because of the complex polynomial term $(1 + R)^7$. Typically, these calculations are done through iterative trial and error, or with a calculator or spreadsheet. When calculated, the IRR is 17%. This means that $1,000 growing at a 17% rate on a compounded basis will yield $3,000 in seven years. Do the math yourself and check.

The investment is expected to produce $2,000 in profit after seven years. But this investment is not profitable enough. The IRR does not meet the hurdle rate of 20%, which is the expectation that investors have given the risks they are taking. This means that VC should pass on the opportunity, even though the opportunity is projected to make $2,000 in profit in seven years. The opportunity is simply *not profitable enough* based on the VC's benchmark to invest.

We can visualize the concept of investment and IRR with this schematic.

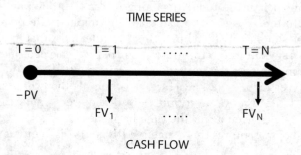

At $T = 0$ (denoting the present time), an investment of PV is made. An investment is a cash outflow, thus −PV. At various times, $T = (1 \ldots N)$, there are corresponding future values $(FV_1 \ldots FV_N)$. The IRR is the discount rate that must be used to discount all future cash flows $(FV_1 \ldots FV_N)$ such that they equal PV.

EXAMPLE

Calculating IRR Using Excel

The spreadsheet Excel easily calculates IRR. The function is "=IRR()." For example, Venture Capital LP's investment in Legal Document Inc.'s business is calculated as:

		COLUMN								
ROW		A	B	C	D	E	F	G	H	I
	1	Year 0	Year 1	Year 2	Year 3	Year 4	Year 5	Year 6	Year 7	
	2									
	3	(1,000)	0	0	0	0	0	0	3,000	=IRR(A3:H3)

The cash flows are laid out as (−1,000 . . . +3,000) in cells A3 to H3, for years Year 0 (now) to Year 7. Excel has a formula "IRR." To use it properly, we type in "=IRR(A3:H3)" which captures the cash flows from Year 0 to Year 7. Excel goes through an iterative process of trial and error until it finds the correct solution, which in this case is 17%, i.e., $1,000 \times (1 + 17\%)^7 = 3,000$.

Assume that Venture Capital's hurdle rate is 20%. The 17% IRR does not meet the hurdle rate. Assume now that further due diligence and financial modeling shows that in addition to the $3,000 exit in Year 7, Legal Documents Inc. can pay a dividend of $75 for Years 1 through 7.

		COLUMN								
ROW		A	B	C	D	E	F	G	H	I
	1	Year 0	Year 1	Year 2	Year 3	Year 4	Year 5	Year 6	Year 7	IRR
	2									
	3	(1,000)	75	75	75	75	75	75	3,075	22.0%

What is the IRR of the investment now? Does the investment meet VC's benchmark rate?

C. CAPITAL STRUCTURE

Capital structure is the structure of the firm's long-term capital—typically some combination of debt, preferred stock, and common stock. Certain industries are regulated as to financial structure. Prominent examples are commercial banks. They hold our savings, and we do not want managers in these companies gambling with our money by taking excessive financial risk in terms of capital structure and solvency. Regulated industries, like banking, must be controlled in terms of putting limits on financial risk. For most companies and industries, however, capital structure is unregulated. A company, like McDonald's, Google, or Apple, may freely elect its capital structure. This means that managers must structure the firm's capital in a way that maximizes value.

The question is whether the mix of debt or equity is arbitrary, or whether the choice is based on rational considerations. The choice of capital structure is not arbitrary. There are theoretical and practical considerations that determine the capital structure. The first step toward understanding capital structure is to reject the idea that having liabilities on the balance sheet is a bad thing. A lawyer may be particularly susceptible to this misguided thought because he or she is trained to think that "liability" is a bad thing. In accounting and finance, however, liability is simply one way of funding assets. In finance, debt is not a bad thing in some normative sense. It is a source of funding. There can be too much debt on the balance sheet, but this simply means that the capital structure is not optimal.

1. MODIGLIANI & MILLER

Given that firms need capital to engage in business, what drives the decision to borrow money from creditors or raise equity from shareholders? Why do some firms have 70% debt and 30% equity, and others are 100% equity financed? Are these decisions random? A good business lawyer must understand the reasons behind a client's decisions because corporate lawyers are essential to executing capital raising transactions.

We start our understanding from the wrong answer: *Capital structure is irrelevant in a world of zero taxes and bankruptcy cost*. Thus capital structure could just as well be random, and no thought need be given to it. This proposition is called the Modigliani and Miller capital structure irrelevance hypothesis, named after its authors, Nobel Prize–winning economists Franco Modigliani and Merton Miller (jointly referred to as M&M).* Everyone, including Modigliani and Miller, knows that this hypothesis is wrong because taxes, along with death, are the only certainties in life,** but the M&M capital structure irrelevance hypothesis helps us to think more formally about how managers construct their firm's capital structure.

Why is capital structure irrelevant if there are no taxes and bankruptcy cost? Think about a firm that raises $1,000 to build a factory, which produces widgets. The firm must pay for the cost of production and thereafter sell the widgets on the market. Does capital structure affect the firm's operations of making and selling widgets? In other words, does the firm operate more efficiently or inefficiently because it is financed in a particular way? How a factory is financed has nothing to do with how that factory is used to make and sell things—the activity that is the core of business.

Modigliani and Miller provided a more formal answer to this intuition. Let's see their logic. Don't be intimidated by the analysis that follows; the math used here is nothing more than addition, subtraction, and multiplication.

Assume a 100 percent equity financed firm such that the firm value (the value of all securities) equals the value of equity: $V = E$. Sally invests x percent in the firm's capital such that her stake is $xV = xE$. The firm generates operating profit P, which belongs to all equityholders. Sally is entitled to xP.

Assume now a firm financed by 50 percent debt and 50 percent equity such that $V = D + E$. Sally invests x percent in both debt and equity capital, such that her capital contribution remains the same: $xV = xD + xE$. The interest rate payment on debt is R. Without bankruptcy cost and interest expense tax shield, the firm would earn the same operating profit P because the mix of capital does not affect how operating profit is made. The operating profit P is divided between the claims by the creditor and the equityholder, where R is the creditor's claim and the remaining $(P - R)$ is the equityholder's claim. Sally is entitled to: $xR + x(P - R) = xP$, which is the same as the shareholder's return in the 100 percent equity financed structure. Under these assumptions, capital structure is irrelevant.

---

* Franco Modigliani & Merton H. Miller, *The Costs of Capital, Corporation Finance and the Theory of Investment*, 48 Am. Econ. Rev. 261 (1958); Franco Modigliani & Merton H. Miller, *Corporate Income Taxes and the Cost of Capital: A Correction*, 53 Am. Econ. Rev. 433 (1963).

** "Our new Constitution is now established, and has an appearance that promises permanency; but in this world nothing can be said to be certain, except death and taxes." Benjamin Franklin letter to Jean-Baptiste Leroy, November 13, 1789.

EXAMPLE

M&M Capital Structure Irrelevance Hypothesis

Let's run through a numeric example to reinforce the point. Assume that an investor takes a 10% ownership stake in the total capital of Firms A and B. Firm A is 100% equity financed. Firm B is equally financed by debt and equity. The cost of debt is 10%. Both firms generate operating income of 300. The firms are identical, except that they are financed with different capital structures.

	FIRM A	FIRM B
Capital		
Equity	2,000	1,000
Debt at 10%	0	1,000
Operating income	300	300
Debt service	0	(100)
Net income	300	200
Investor's 10% of equity claim	30	20
Investor's 10% of debt claim	0	10
Total return to investor	**30**	**30**

This example shows that capital structure is irrelevant to the value a firm creates. If capital structure does not affect operating income (300), how that operating income is divided through financial claims by creditors and equityholders should be irrelevant under unrealistic assumptions of no taxes and bankruptcy cost.

However, in the real world, taxes and bankruptcy costs do exist. Therefore, capital structure must be relevant to the value of the firm. Let's continue the above example. The same assumptions hold, except that we assume a tax rate of 30%.

	FIRM A	FIRM B
Capital		
Equity	2,000	1,000
Debt at 10%	0	1,000
Operating income	300	300
Debt service	0	(100)
Pretax profit	300	200
Taxes at 30%	(90)	(60)
Net income	210	140
Investor's 10% of equity claim	21	14
Investor's 10% of debt claim	0	10
Total return to investor	**21**	**24**

Debt increases value because the interest expense deduction reduces tax liability, and thus capital providers pocket this surplus. The increase in value in Firm B of 30 is the tax shield: $100 \times 30\% = 30$ not paid in taxes due to the interest expense deduction.

The benefit of the tax shield increases firm value. However, it is intuitively obvious that as a firm increases leverage, the risk of bankruptcy increases. Increased bankruptcy risk decreases firm value. The graph below illustrates these antipodal effects.

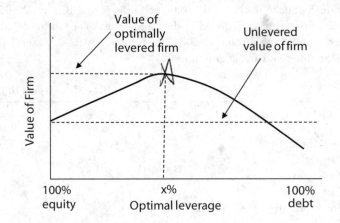

In a world of interest tax shield, as the firm increases leverage, its value increases and reaches an apex. When its capital structure has leverage beyond the optimal ratio of x between debt and equity, the firm value diminishes as the cost of bankruptcy eats into the benefit of leverage. Ultimately, a highly levered firm may be worth less than a firm capitalized by 100 percent equity.

The cost of bankruptcy can be significant. Enron paid $757 million in legal and other professional fees, and the cost of resolving Lehman Brother's bankruptcy are approximately $1.5 billion.* According to several studies, the average cost of bankruptcy has been calculated to be about 3 percent of total book assets, and 10 percent to 20 percent of predistress market value of the firm.** These figures are only the direct costs. There are also indirect costs. Managing a bankruptcy, suboptimal business decisions made in the shadow of bankruptcy, and lost opportunities due to bankruptcy are significant indirect costs that are immeasurable.

2. TRADEOFF AND PECKING ORDER THEORIES

The tradeoff theory of capital structure is premised on the understanding that debt results in offsetting benefit of the interest tax shield and the cost of financial distress. One implication of the tradeoff theory is that safer companies prefer to issue debt because they can capture the interest tax shield while avoiding financial distress, and riskier companies prefer to issue equity. The debt-to-equity ratio cannot be calculated

---

* Richard A. Brealey, Stewart C. Myers & Franklin Allen, Principles of Corporate Finance 458 (11th ed. 2014).

** See L.A. Weiss, *Bankruptcy Resolution: Direct Costs and Violation of Priority of Claims*, 27 J. Fin. Econ. 285 (1990); E.I. Altman, *A Further Investigation of the Bankruptcy Cost Question*, 39 J. Fin. 1067 (1984); G. Andrade & S.N. Kaplan, *How Costly Is Financial (not Economic) Distress? Evidence from Highly Leveraged Transactions That Became Distressed*, 53 J. Fin. 1443 (1998). See also J.B. Warner, *Bankruptcy Costs: Some Evidence*, 26 J. Fin. 337 (1977).

in a manner that is consistent across firms. It may vary from firm to firm because each firm is uniquely situated.

Under the pecking order theory of capital structure, the key distinction is between internal and external funding. A target debt-to-equity ratio is more amorphous and less important than maintaining a preference for internal funding and avoidance of issuing equity securities. The pecking order theory explains and predicts several behaviors of firms. Profitable firms have less debt since they can fund investments through internal cash flow. If there are no investment opportunities, they will pay down debt. Less profitable firms issue debt since they must externally fund investments.

The choice of form of capital to fund a firm's business is subject to a preferred pecking order. Firms prefer to fund their activities in the following pecking order. (1) Firms prefer internal funding over external finance. (2) Firms seek to fund investment through a management of dividend payout ratios, but dividend policy is "sticky" and so firms avoid unexpected changes in dividend payouts. (3) If cash flow is greater than the cash needs of the investment, firms pay off debt or invest in securities. If cash flow is less than the cash needs of an investment, firms draw down on the cash balance or sell securities. (4) If external funding is required, firms prefer to issue the safest securities first and the riskiest securities last—debt first, hybrid securities second, and equity last.

3. DEBT'S ALLURE AND CONSEQUENCES

Leverage has several value enhancing properties. Debt provides a tax benefit in the form of an interest tax shield, which is the deductibility of interest expense from taxable profit, thus reducing tax liability. Debt is cheaper than equity capital up to the point where the marginal (incremental) gain is outweighed by increased bankruptcy cost. Debt can reduce total agency cost. It incentivizes managers to perform because creditors must be paid their interest and principal. The process of securing credit requires the firm to undergo due diligence, a vetting process that monitors the firm and bonds the manager's performance. Thus, debt has a number of salutary properties.

Debt also increases the return on equity. The selection of high leverage by corporate managers illustrates the allure of debt. Leverage "juices up" returns on equity, meaning that the return on equity becomes more profitable. The basic intuition is that an acquirer borrows most of the money from creditors to acquire a firm and only uses a small slice of equity. As long as creditors can be paid back, there is a substantial chance that the equityholder, as the residual claimant, can earn more profit than if the acquirer used 100 percent equity.

A good example of the allure of debt is a leverage buyout (LBO). An LBO is an acquisition of a firm using a substantial amount of debt as the acquisition financing. It is a risky transaction because the firm is heavily levered and interest payments must be

EXAMPLE

LBO Transaction and Leveraging Equity Returns with Debt

Let's consider a simple stylized example of an acquisition. Assume that William Conqueror seeks to acquire UK Inc. for the price of $1,000. UK is expected to generate pretax earnings of 100 for the first five years, and in Years 6 and 7 operational efficiencies gain

---

traction and UK is projected to generate pretax earnings of 150. The effective tax rate is 30%. At the end of Year 7, Conqueror will "exit" the investment by a sale of the shares to the public (an IPO) or a sale of UK to another company. The projected exit value is $2,000, which is the projected firm value of UK at the end of Year 7. The choice of financing may produce different equity returns.

Acquisition Method: 100% equity financed

In an all-equity-financed transaction, the cash flow and IRR are projected below.

	YR. 0	YR. 1	YR. 2	YR. 3	YR. 4	YR. 5	YR. 6	YR. 7
Pretax income		100	100	100	100	100	150	150
Taxes at 30%		(30)	(30)	(30)	(30)	(30)	(45)	(45)
Net earnings		70	70	70	70	70	105	105
Acquisition & exit values	(1,000)							2,000
Returns	(1,000)	70	70	70	70	70	105	2,105

Equity IRR $\boxed{16.3\%}$

The IRR on the $1,000 of equity used to acquire the firm is 16.3% based on the expected returns. Not bad. This is much better than the long-run return on the equity market.

Acquisition Method: 80/20 debt-to-equity financed LBO

Assume, however, that an IRR of 16.3% is an insufficient return for Conqueror. His investors expect a 25% return given the risk they are taking, and so this is the hurdle rate. He seeks to do an LBO using 80% debt. The acquisition financing is thus $800 in debt and $200 of equity. The interest on debt is high: 12% (or $96 per year). Leveraged transactions are inherently risky. The debt matures at the end of Year 7 with a principal payment due of $800. Other operating assumptions remain the same, as well as the exit valuation of UK.

	YR. 0	YR. 1	YR. 2	YR. 3	YR. 4	YR. 5	YR. 6	YR. 7
Operating profit		100	100	100	100	100	150	150
Interest expense		(96)	(96)	(96)	(96)	(96)	(96)	(96)
Pretax profit		4	4	4	4	4	54	54
Taxes at 30%		(1)	(1)	(1)	(1)	(1)	(16)	(16)
Net earnings		3	3	3	3	3	38	38
Debt principal repayment								(800)
Acquisition & exit value	(200)							2,000
Returns	(200)	3	3	3	3	3	38	1,238

Equity IRR $\boxed{31.1\%}$

The IRR on the $200 of equity used to acquire the firm is 31.1% based on the expected returns. The use of 80% debt almost doubled the profitability of equity. How? The basic intuition is that an equityholder uses a little of his money and a lot of his creditor's money to acquire the firm; and, if the firm is successful, he can pay down the debt and keep whatever remains as the residual, which can be quite a lot. In the above scenarios, Conqueror paid $1,000 in equity and received $2,105 in the 100% equity financing. He paid $200 in equity and received $1,238 in the leveraged transaction. There is a significant difference in the return as a percentage of the original investment.

made to creditors, lest there be a default. However, the benefit of an LBO, if it ultimately works, is an enhanced return to equityholders.

(–) The allure of debt is counterbalanced by the specter of bankruptcy. Too much leverage can make a firm very risky. In the above example, the firm is barely able to service its debt ($96 in interest) from operating profit ($100). The firm is barely solvent, and there is a high chance it could default if its business falters. There is little margin for error.

One can make bad decisions on capital structure and such mistakes can have dire consequences. A cautionary tale is the use of debt by investment banks during the years leading up to the financial crisis of 2008–2009. During this period, many financial institutions became distressed. At the center of the maelstrom were investment banks. At the time, there were only five large independent investment banks left after a long period of industry consolidation. During the financial crisis, three of these investment banks collapsed. Lehman Brothers filed for bankruptcy in September 2008. Staring in the face of bankruptcy, Bear Stearns was acquired by JPMorgan Chase in March 2008, and a financially distressed Merrill Lynch was acquired by Bank of America in September 2008. The collapse of these financial institutions, among others, precipitated the financial crisis. The balance sheets of these three firms looked like this.

($ million)	Bear Stearns As of 2/28/09	Lehman Brothers As of 5/31/08	Merrill Lynch As of 6/27/08
Assets	$ 398,995	$ 639,432	$966,210
Liabilities	387,099	613,156	931,432
Equity	11,896	26,276	34,778

What is the fundamental problem with how these investment banks operated? In the several years before the financial crisis of 2008, the major independent investment banks (Goldman Sachs, Morgan Stanley, Merrill Lynch, Lehman Brothers, and Bear Stearns) increased their leverage to enhance profits.[*]

---

[*] Robert J. Rhee, *The Decline of Investment Banking: Preliminary Thoughts on the Evolution of the Industry 1996-2008*, 5 J. Bus. L. & Tech. 75, 80-81 (2010).

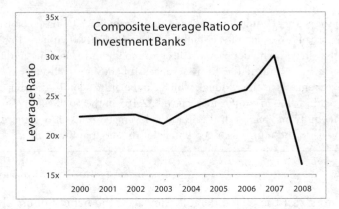

Increased leverage resulted in increased profitability as measured by ROE. Note the declining profitability of investment banks after the dot.com Internet technology bubble burst in 2000, and the sharp increase in profitability corresponding to a sharp increase in leverage, until the housing bubble burst in 2007 and 2008.

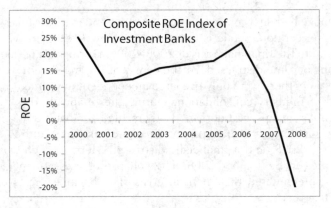

The above chart also shows that the leverage level proved to be too much. The profitability of investment banks declined in 2008. Three firms went insolvent in 2008: Bear Stearns, Merrill Lynch, and Lehman Brothers. The other two firms, Morgan Stanley and Goldman Sachs, barely escaped with their solvency and independence.

4. PERSPECTIVE ON CAPITAL STRUCTURE

There are different theories of capital structure. So, is there a generally accepted single theory of optimal capital structure—something that informs the manager definitively "your capital structure should be x percent debt and y percent equity"? No. There is no single theory that determines the choice of debt and equity to a precise ratio. There are several theories and practices competing as the *grande idée,* but in reality they are useful fragments, and often complementary, in the complex task of managing capital structure in the context of the firm's assets, liabilities, operations, and other circumstances.

In other words, *relax:* Don't waste time searching for a magic formula for the optimal debt ratio. Remember too that most value comes from the left side of the balance sheet, that is, from the firm's operations, assets, and growth opportunities. Financing is less important. Of course, financing can subtract value rapidly if you screw it up, but you won't do that.*

This suggests that the perfect choice of financing is elusive, and that there may be several good and bad choices depending on the circumstances. Consistent with the spirit of the M&M capital structure irrelevance proposition, the operations of a firm are more important to the firm's production than its financing. But let's be clear: Financing *is* consequential. So what are the takeaway lessons on capital structure?

(1) *Capital structure is not arbitrary.* In financing a venture, the choice of capital structure is not a random matter. Thought must be given to the formation and maintenance of capital structure.

(2) *Debt is good until it is bad.* This tautology has some meaning beyond the trite. The interest tax shield and the lower cost of capital of debt are significant benefits of debt. However, debt raises the risk of bankruptcy. Shareholders cannot throw the company into bankruptcy, but creditors can. Bankruptcy imposes significant costs on the firm.

(3) *Capital structure may be determined by industry experience or requirement.* After long experience, some industries or business sectors have found defined ranges of suitable capital structure. For example, there are good reasons why startup ventures or young companies should be wary of debt financing (*see, e.g.*, the capital structure in *Bolt v. Merrimack Pharmaceuticals, Inc., supra* Chapter 1). Also, some industry sectors such as banking and utilities are regulated as to their capital structures.

(4) *Perfect capital structure is elusive.* Capital structure is not based on a "plug and chug" algorithm. It is based on a judgment concerning on the one hand the risk of the capital structure and on the other hand the cheapest cost of capital to the issuer. In practice, corporate managers engage in a multivariate analysis of the choice of capital structure.

EXAMPLE

Berkshire Hathaway 2009 Annual Report at 16-17

In 2010, Berkshire Hathaway, Warren Buffett's investment company, acquired Burlington Northern Santa Fe Corporation ("BNSF") for a mixed cash and stock consideration of over $26 billion. A key feature of this transaction was the issuance of Berkshire Hathaway stock to BNSF shareholders as a part of the consideration. In the annual report to shareholders, Warren Buffett elegantly explains the problems of using equity as consideration and equity dilution upon the issuance of new equity.

* * *

AN INCONVENIENT TRUTH (BOARDROOM OVERHEATING)

Our subsidiaries made a few small "bolt-on" acquisitions last year for cash, but our blockbuster deal with BNSF required us to issue about 95,000 Berkshire shares that amounted to 6.1% of those previously outstanding. Charlie and I enjoy issuing Berkshire stock about as much as we relish prepping for a colonoscopy.

---

* Richard A. Brealey, Stewart C. Myers & Franklin Allen, Principles of Corporate Finance 472 (11th ed. 2014).

The reason for our distaste is simple. If we wouldn't dream of selling Berkshire in its entirety at the current market price, why in the world should we "sell" a significant part of the company at that same inadequate price by issuing our stock in a merger?

In evaluating a stock-for-stock offer, shareholders of the target company quite understandably focus on the market price of the acquirer's shares that are to be given them. But they also expect the transaction to deliver them the *intrinsic* value of their own shares—the ones they are giving up. If shares of a prospective acquirer are selling below their intrinsic value, it's impossible for that buyer to make a sensible deal in an all-stock deal. You simply can't exchange an undervalued stock for a fully-valued one without hurting your shareholders.

Imagine, if you will, Company A and Company B, of equal size and both with businesses intrinsically worth $100 per share. Both of their stocks, however, sell for $80 per share. The CEO of A, long on confidence and short on smarts, offers 1¼ shares of A for each share of B, correctly telling his directors that B is worth $100 per share. He will neglect to explain, though, that what he is giving will cost his shareholders $125 in intrinsic value. If the directors are mathematically challenged as well, and a deal is therefore completed, the shareholders of B will end up owning 55.6% of A & B's combined assets and A's shareholders will own 44.4%.* Not everyone at A, it should be noted, is a loser from this nonsensical transaction. Its CEO now runs a company twice as large as his original domain, in a world where size tends to correlate with both prestige and compensation.

If an acquirer's stock is overvalued, it's a different story: Using it as a currency works to the acquirer's advantage. That's why bubbles in various areas of the stock market have invariably led to serial issuances of stock by sly promoters. Going by the market value of their stock, they can afford to overpay because they are, in effect, using counterfeit money. Periodically, many air-for-assets acquisitions have taken place, the late 1960s having been a particularly obscene period for such chicanery. Indeed, certain large companies were built in this way. (No one involved, of course, ever publicly acknowledges the reality of what is going on, though there is plenty of private snickering.)

In our BNSF acquisition, the selling shareholders quite properly evaluated our offer at $100 per share. The cost to us, however, was somewhat higher since 40% of the $100 was delivered in our shares, which Charlie and I believed to be worth more than their market value. Fortunately, we had long owned a substantial amount of BNSF stock that we purchased in the market for cash. All told, therefore, only about 30% of our cost overall was paid with Berkshire shares.

In the end, Charlie and I decided that the disadvantage of paying 30% of the price through stock was offset by the opportunity the acquisition gave us to deploy $22 billion of cash in a business we understood and liked for the long term. It has the additional virtue of being run by Matt Rose, whom we trust and admire. We also like the prospect of investing additional billions over the years at reasonable rates of return. But the final decision was a close one. If we had needed to use more stock to make the acquisition, it would in fact have made no sense. We would have then been giving up more than we were getting.

---

* Author's note: Assume that A and B each have 100 shares outstanding. A must issue to B's shareholders 125 shares of A. The total shares outstanding of A would be 225 shares. A's shareholders own 100 shares out of 225, which is 44.4% of shares outstanding. B's shareholders (now new A shareholders) would own 125 shares out of 225, which is 55.6%.

The following case involves ratemaking in a regulated utility industry. The court discusses the relationship among capital structure, the utility's risk, and the reasonableness of increasing rates to compensate the utility for the risk inherent in the capital structure.

Missouri Gas Energy v. Public Service Commission
186 S.W.3d 376 (Mo. App. W.D. 2005)

THOMAS H. NEWTON, Judge.

Missouri Gas Energy (MGE), claiming among other matters that it had been unable to earn its Commission-authorized rate of return under prior tariffs and could not therefore compete effectively in capital markets, sought a $44.8 million increase in the rates it charges its Missouri customers for natural gas service. After extensive hearings, the Public Service Commission (Commission) entered an order that gave the public utility a $22.5 million rate increase. The key issue on appeal is whether the Commission's decision results in a confiscatory and unreasonable return on equity. We affirm the Commission's order.

MGE distributes natural gas in Missouri as an operating division of Southern Union Company (Southern Union). It has no separate corporate existence; thus, MGE has no capital structure of its own, and it has no investors in its own right. Southern Union, which owns gas-distribution companies like MGE in a number of states, was characterized during Commission proceedings as a company with an aggressive growth strategy that has for some years operated under a capital structure which includes significantly more debt than equity. Panhandle Eastern Pipeline Company (Panhandle) is an interstate pipeline company that is a separate Southern Union subsidiary. In 2003 the Commission approved a Stipulation and Agreement relating to Southern Union's Panhandle acquisition. Under the terms of that agreement, Panhandle's debt [about $1.2 billion] is non-recourse as to MGE and Southern Union, i.e., MGE and its customers are supposed to be insulated financially in all respects from Panhandle debt.

MGE claims on appeal that the Commission's decisions as to capital structure and return on equity result in a rate of return that is unconstitutionally confiscatory, unreasonable, arbitrary, and capricious, and not supported by the evidence. MGE further contends that the Commission erred in including the Panhandle debt in MGE's capital structure, thus lowering its equity ratio.

Regulatory Finance—Capital Structure and Return on Equity

As we consider the issues raised by this appeal, it is helpful to keep in mind that the cost of capital, or the amount a utility must pay to secure financing from debt and equity investors (shareholders), "is essentially the equivalent of fair rate of return." And rate of return is determined by a calculation that factors in (i) the ratio of debt and equity to total capital, and (ii) the cost and (iii) weighted cost for each of these capital components. While rate of return is the result of a straightforward mathematic calculation, the inputs, particularly regarding the cost of common equity, are not a matter of "precise science," because inferences must be made about the cost of equity, which involves an estimation of investor expectations. In other words, some amount of speculation is inherent in any ratemaking decision to the extent that it is based on capital structure, because such decisions are forward-looking and rely, in part, on the accuracy of financial and market forecasts.

A rate of return is generally considered to be fair if it "covers utility operating expenses, debt service, and dividends, if it compensates investors for the risks of investment, and if it is sufficient to attract capital and assure confidence in the enterprise's financial integrity." That said, "the rate of return should not be higher than is necessary to achieve these goals. Otherwise, utility customers will pay excessive prices, something regulation seeks to prohibit." The United States Supreme Court tells us simply that "the fixing of 'just and reasonable' rates, involves a balancing of the investor and the consumer interests."

According to the Commission, "all else being equal, a capital structure that includes a low percentage of equity and a large percentage of debt will be less costly, resulting in a lower rate of return, and consequently a lower revenue requirement and lower rates to customers." This is so because the cost of debt, or what it costs a corporation to borrow money and pay interest, is usually less than the cost of equity, i.e., issuing stock and paying dividends or a return on investment.

A corollary to this principle is that "a company with a capital structure that includes a high percentage of debt is more risky for shareholders [who] will consequently demand a higher rate of return to compensate them for the increased risk caused by the high level of debt." This is so because the holders of equity are subordinate to the holders of debt and face the greater risk should the enterprise fail. The more equity there is in a company's capital structure, [the more return is necessary which] imposes higher costs on customers, thus increasing a company's cash flow. There is, obviously, a limit to the costs that can be imposed on ratepayers, who may default when the cost is too high, a situation that also runs counter to investor interests.

Justness and Reasonableness

[The court quotes *Bluefield Waterworks & Improvement Co. v. Public Service Commission of West Virginia*, 262 U.S. 679 (1923), which] established a standard for "just and reasonable" public-utility rates as follows:

> The return should be reasonably sufficient to assure confidence in the financial soundness of the utility and should be adequate, under efficient and economical management, to maintain and support its credit and enable it to raise the money necessary for the proper discharge of its public duties.

The capital structure that MGE recommended was characterized by the Commission and several witnesses as a "hypothetical" structure and was based on Southern Union's consolidated capital structure, excluding the Panhandle debt. It contained an overall higher percentage of equity than debt. The recommended ratios of capital components to total capital were 47.49% for long-term debt, 11.49% for preferred stock and 41.14% for common equity. Such ratios are similar to the average ratios for comparable utilities, although the common equity ratio was somewhat lower than the average, and the debt was consequently somewhat higher. Factoring in the costs and weighted costs of these capital components, MGE proposed that the cost of capital/rate of return be calculated at 9.35%, and further recommended a return on equity of 12% for MGE's equity investors.

What MGE seeks is a capital structure with less debt, which would be more in line with national averages, but a higher return on equity—12%, as compared to the 2003 national average of 11.1%. MGE justifies this increase in return on equity over the national average by pointing to the higher risk faced by investors due to the debt in its capital structure, which is somewhat higher than the national average even without inclusion of the Panhandle debt. While MGE argues that Panhandle debt must be excluded from consideration under the stipulation it signed in 2003, it is this debt that causes Southern Union's capital structure to significantly deviate from national averages and raises the risk of investing in the company.[7] Requiring ratepayers to pay an excessive risk premium effectively transfers the risk related to the company's acquisition from its shareholders to its ratepayers, something that the company agreed not to do via stipulation and agreement. In this regard, the stipulation states:

> Southern Union will not recommend an increase or claim Staff should make an adjustment to increase the cost of capital for MGE as a result of the Transaction. Southern Union will ensure that the retail distribution rates for MGE ratepayers will not increase as a result of the Transaction.

And while the capital structure MGE recommended in this proceeding technically excludes the Panhandle "transaction," the risk on which it bases its inflated return-on-equity recommendation cannot be separated from the risk posed by actual market conditions, which reflect the Panhandle debt.

Staff recommended that the Commission use Southern Union's actual consolidated capital structure, including the Panhandle debt. This can also be characterized as a hypothetical structure because, as noted above, MGE does not have its own capital structure. Both recommendations contained a higher percentage of debt than equity. Thus, Staff's recommended ratios of capital components to total capital were 63.61% for long-term debt, 6.40% for preferred stock and 29.99% for common stock. Staff's expert witness further recommended a return on equity in the range of 8.52 to 9.52%. The Commission adopted Staff's recommended capital structure, but increased the value for return on equity to 10.5%, which was the same return on equity adopted when MGE's rates were last approved in 2001.

In effect, the Commission increased Staff's recommended return on equity in recognition of the higher risk to shareholders from the large amount of debt in Southern Union's actual consolidated capital structure. The Commission was also concerned about costs to consumers, who will be facing significantly higher natural gas prices, which are passed directly through to them. So the Commission refused to adopt a return on equity as high as that suggested by MGE. Its decision to do so reflects a careful balance between consumer and shareholder interests (recall that high debt should mean lower rates for consumers and a high rate of return should mean higher rates and better returns for shareholders).

---

7. Wholly owned subsidiaries, like corporate divisions in our case, do not raise capital in the open market and, thus, that the attractiveness of a company as an investment "is dependent on how attractive the parent company is as an investment."

The return on equity approved by the Commission that increases MGE's revenue stream by more than $22 million a year, while higher than that recommended by Staff and lower than that recommended by MGE, is supported by substantial and competent evidence on the whole record.

Methodology

The Commission made specific findings to support its decision to attribute the Panhandle debt to MGE's capital structure and referred to specific testimony to support those findings. In this regard, the Commission stated:

> MGE contends that the use of the consolidated capital structure adjusted to remove the effects of the Panhandle Eastern Pipeline subsidiary is appropriate because that structure most closely approximates the capital structure of Southern Union's natural gas distribution operations, including its MGE division. It does this by removing the equity and debt of the Panhandle Eastern subsidiary from the consolidated capital structure in a manner that it contends is consistent with the requirements of Generally Accepted Accounting Principles (GAAP).
>
> Although Southern Union describes its proposed capital structure as an adjusted actual consolidated capital structure, what it is proposing may more accurately be described as a hypothetical capital structure in that its proposed capital structure clearly does not exist in the real world. Rather, it is the unadjusted consolidated capital structure under which Southern Union actually operates in the marketplace. Southern Union is able to conduct business, finance its operations, and raise capital with an investment grade rating based on that capital structure. When a business analyst such as Moody's or Standard & Poor's examines Southern Union to assess its credit worthiness, it looks to that unadjusted consolidated capital structure to make its determination.
>
> Furthermore, Southern Union's unadjusted consolidated capital structure, with its heavy reliance on debt, results directly from Southern Union's management decision to become highly leveraged to finance the purchase of Panhandle Eastern, as well as earlier acquisitions. Southern Union decided to take on that additional debt because it saw an opportunity to earn greater returns to the benefit of its shareholders. That decision is clearly within Southern Union's management prerogative and the Commission does not wish to criticize or punish Southern Union for that decision. However, Southern Union must operate with the results of its investment decisions and one result of those investment decisions is a capital structure that includes a large amount of debt and relatively low amounts of equity.

These findings, based on evidence in the record, may not be to MGE's liking, but they constitute a sufficient factual basis for the Commission's decision to include the Panhandle debt in MGE's capital structure.

For these reasons we reverse the circuit court and affirm the Commission's Report and Order.

QUESTIONS

1. The court suggested that a highly levered balance sheet is good for consumers because it will result in lower utility bills. On the other hand, having more equity will result in higher utility bills. Why?

2. MGE made an argument that smacked of having one's financial cake and eating it too. As the court notes: "What MGE seeks is a capital structure with less debt, which would be more in line with national averages, but a higher return on equity—12%, as compared to the 2003 national average of 11.1%." Higher levels of equity mean that the company must charge more to provide a sufficient return to shareholders. With less debt, however, the return on equity should be lower because the risk to the equityholder is less. How did MGE justify a higher return on equity on a less levered balance sheet?

3. The court observed that MGE was "a company with an aggressive growth strategy that has for some years operated under a capital structure which includes significantly more debt than equity." The court further wrote: "Requiring ratepayers to pay an excessive risk premium effectively transfers the risk related to the company's acquisition [of Panhandle] from its shareholders to its ratepayers." In what way did MGE seek to have consumers pay for the risk assumed by the company for acquiring Panhandle and more generally its aggressive growth strategy?

D. OVERVIEW OF CAPITAL MARKETS

The capital market is a global marketplace where issuers and investors transact for the rent of capital. Investors are savers who have capital to rent for a return. They have a range of appetite for risk and return. Those unwilling to assume any risk will seek risk-free investments. Other investors will seek higher returns and accept the concomitant increase in risking their capital, and these investments can range from the least risky bonds to most risky equity securities. Issuers are principally corporations and governments that need capital to fund their activities and projects. There are several important aspects of the capital market.

(1) In an era of globalization, many advanced economies in North America, Western Europe, and East Asia, and rising economies in other parts of the world, need capital. BP p.l.c., a UK-based oil company (yes, *that* BP of Deepwater Horizon infamy) lists its stock in the London Stock Exchange, but its American depository receipt (ADR), which is a dollar-denominated certificate representing shares, trades on the New York Stock Exchange. Capital providers (investors) are also located in various parts of the world. The Abu Dhabi Investment Authority is a sovereign wealth fund of the United Arab Emirates, but it invests its capital globally, including investments in the United States. Thus the financial markets are a global marketplace of finance.

(2) Many laypersons associate the capital market with the equity financial markets and stock exchanges where stocks are publicly traded. This is only one aspect of the capital market, and in terms of dollar volume the equity market is a smaller component of the capital markets. The capital markets also include the credit market, which for corporations is equally important to the stock market.

(3) The capital market is extremely complicated and varied across products, participants, and regulatory frameworks. A complex machinery of laws, regulators, financial institutions, and professional advisors serve to match issuers with investors. This process means that the capital markets channel and allocate trillions of dollars of capital to business enterprises.

1. SIZE OF THE CAPITAL MARKET

Although it is common to think of the capital market as synonymous with organized stock exchanges, such as the New York Stock Exchange or the London Stock Exchange, the capital market is much larger than this. It encompasses the entire market for capital, whose transactions constitute the broad range of financial instruments bought and sold in organized exchanges and transaction platforms, and various professional networks among investors, issuers, and intermediaries such as investment banks and other financial institutions. A significant part of the capital market is not publicly traded on organized exchanges, but instead the transactions occur through professional networks.

The capital market constitutes both the equity market and the credit market. These markets reflect the fact that there are two broad kinds of investors: creditors who lend money for a fixed rate over a fixed term, and shareholders who lend money for a variable rate over an indefinite period. The credit market has two components: The bond market constitutes the market for bonds, which are generally liquid and traded security instruments, and the investor is the group of securityholders; the bank loan market constitutes traditional loans to corporations and other debtors, and the lender is typically a bank or a group of banks called a syndicate. Equity investors are shareholders of corporations (other business organizational forms have equityholders such as partners and members, but in corporate finance we are mostly dealing with corporations). Governments only borrow money as debtors (*e.g.*, there are no shares for an equity stake in the U.S. government), but government-sponsored or -affiliated corporations or entities, like purely private business firms, can issue equity securities.

How big is the capital market? According to McKinsey & Company,* as of the Q2 of 2012, the global capital market was $225 trillion. In the graph below, note the significant decline in the global stock market capitalization in 2008, which reflects the stock market losses during the height of the financial crisis of 2008–2009.

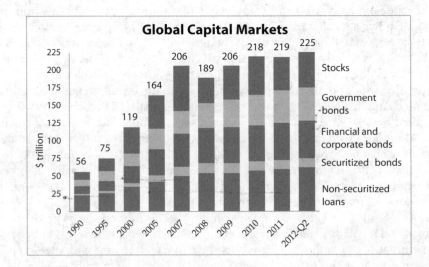

* Susan Lund et al., *Financial globalization: Retreat or reset?: Global capital markets 2013*, at 2, McKinsey Global Institute (March 2013).

When we think of the capital markets, some people erroneously think only of the stock markets. However, as between debt and equity, the stock market is only a small fraction of the total market. The market for fixed income securities is much greater in total volume and number of issuers than the equity market. As of Q2 of 2012, the following is a breakdown of financial asset classes by dollar volume (in $ trillion) and percentage of the total $225 trillion capitalization:

- Equities $50   (22 percent)
- Government bonds $47   (21 percent)
- Financial bonds $42   (19 percent)
- Corporate bonds $11   (5 percent)
- Securitized loans $13   (6 percent)
- Nonsecuritized loans $62   (28 percent)

This breakdown tells us that the credit market is extremely important. It constitutes the majority of the capitalization of the capital markets by dollar volume. Also, there are many more borrowers and a diversity of borrowers than issuers of equity. For the most part, issuers of equity are private, for-profit corporations. Borrowers are governments, other public entities, financial institutions, securitization issuers, and private firms.

The data for capital issuance also shows the relative sizes of the debt and equity markets. The following is data on the amount of capital raised in the financial markets.**

Net of repayments ($ billion)	2000	2004	2006	2008	2011
International bank loans	714	1,343	2,816	(1,279)	185
International bonds and notes	1,148	1,560	2,617	2,436	1,212
International money market instruments	87	61	168	82	(6)
Domestic bonds and notes	865	2,461	2,322	2,282	2,566
Domestic money market instruments	377	774	983	1,462	(611)
International equity issues	318	214	371	392	485
Domestic equity issues	901	593	717	999	617
Total excluding domestic loans	4,410	7,006	9,994	6,374	4,448

The capital market is big, and arguably it is the single most important institution in a well-functioning, modern, sophisticated economy. It is also incredibly complex. Indeed, one of the many revelations to come out of the financial crisis of 2008–2009 is the degree to which everything in the capital market, and the society as a whole for that matter, is financially interconnected. In financing its activities and projects, a corporation will access the capital market by, among other things, taking out loans from banks, issuing bonds or stock, or securitizing its assets into securitized bonds.

** Marc Levinson, Guide to Financial Markets, at 4 (6th edition 2014).

2. FUNCTIONS OF THE CAPITAL MARKET

Formal financial markets perform vital functions necessary to a modern society and economic system.

Capital issuance. The financial markets, and principally the debt and equity markets, provide a forum where firms can raise capital by issuing securities, principally debt and equity securities. Firms will have ongoing capital needs beyond their capability to raise internal funding through retained profits. When external capital is needed, firms will access the financial markets.

Investing. The financial markets allow savers to invest their money in financial assets and instruments to earn returns over a chosen investment time horizon. Investments can be made directly in the debt or equity of firms, or in other financial assets such as derivatives, currencies, or commodities.

Asset valuation and price setting. The financial markets promote the discovery of asset values and pricing of securities. When buyers and sellers of securities and financial assets transact in the primary and secondary markets, they generate information to support such trading. The financial markets incorporate this vast quantity of information, which is then seen in the market prices of securities and assets.

Arbitrage. The financial markets allow traders to engage in arbitrage, which promotes consistent prices and rational values of financial assets.

Commercial transactions. The financial markets promote commercial transactions. Like consumer transactions, commercial transactions are not always settled with cash. Financing is required to fund payroll or the purchase of things such as commercial office buildings, jet engines, and hydroelectric dams.

Risk management. The financial markets, principally the derivatives markets, allow firms and institutions to manage risks.

An important organizational division in the financial markets, and particularly for debt and equity securities, is the primary and the secondary markets. The primary market is the market for newly issued securities in which issuers sell securities to investors. The function of the primary market is to provide issuers access to capital. The secondary market is the trading market for already-issued securities. The issuer is not involved and receives no funds from trading activities. An important function of the secondary market is price discovery. Trading activity in the secondary market provides information to issuers and investors about the value of securities.

3. EQUITY MARKETS

The principal function of the equity markets is to provide a market to raise equity capital. Equity capital can come in various forms of financial instruments such as common stock, preferred stock, warrants, and convertible securities. The greatest portion of the equity markets is the market in common stocks.

a. Public Equity Market

The public equity market is the market for publicly traded stocks. The top five countries or regions, ranked by the capitalization of publicly listed stocks as of May 2013, are: (1) U.S. $21,149 billion, (2) Japan $4,222 billion, (3) China $4,038 billion,

(4) UK $3,603 billion, and (5) Euronext $3,037 billion.* The U.S. equity market is the largest equity market in the world by several orders, and it accounts for over 30 percent of the entire global market capitalization of equities.

The equity markets are not limited to just publicly traded stocks. Publicly traded companies are traded in stock exchanges or in the over-the-counter (OTC) market. The OTC market refers to the informal market for securities where parties trade securities on negotiated terms, as opposed to securities traded on organized exchanges.

Stock exchanges are formal organizations that are regulated by the SEC. Stocks traded on the exchange are called listed stocks. In the United States, the major national stock exchange is the New York Stock Exchange (NYSE) (also called the "Big Board"). There are also regional stock exchanges: the Boston Stock Exchange, the Chicago Stock Exchange, the Philadelphia Stock Exchange, and the Pacific Stock Exchange. Each exchange has its own rules and procedures for trading of listed stocks, and sets standards and criteria for companies that seek to list their stock on the exchange. A listed company must satisfy a stock exchange's listing rules in addition to satisfying federal securities laws.

The *OTC market* is the market for stocks that are not listed on stock exchanges. The Nasdaq stock market is the most prominent OTC market. Nasdaq (National Association of Security Dealers Automated Quote System) is not an exchange with a brick-and-mortar trading floor like the NYSE. It is a virtual, electronic trading platform. It provides an electronic price quotation system for Nasdaq-listed companies through a telecommunications network that links thousands of "market makers" who make markets in stocks by buying and selling. Market makers create liquidity in the market by availing themselves as counterparties to any investor's need to buy or sell a stock.

Although most companies traded on the OTC market are small, the fact that Nasdaq is an OTC market should not be construed as it being small, unimportant, or unsophisticated. Companies like Apple, Intel, Facebook, Microsoft, American Airlines, and Cisco list their stocks on Nasdaq.

b. Private Equity Market

In addition to the public equity markets, there is also a market for private equity. This is the domain of private equity. The concept of private equity encompasses several activities: leveraged buyouts (LBOs), growth and mezzanine capital, and venture capital. These investments are typically made through private equity funds sponsored by private equity firms and invested in by institutional and wealthy individual investors.

Private equity firms raise capital from institutional investors and high net worth individuals for the purpose of investing in private equity and related transactions, which may include investments in the debt and other securities of invested companies as well. They hold a portfolio of investments, and make investments under an articulated investment strategy. These firms are mostly private firms. However, there are a few highly prominent publicly traded firms.

Private equity firms are typically structured as limited partnerships or limited liability companies. These entities are highly suitable for having two classes of

---

* Marc Levinson, Guide to Financial Markets, at 155 (6th edition 2014).

equityholders. General partners or managing members actively manage the portfolio of investments. The largest private equity firm may have as many as 40 general partners. Limited partners are passive investors. They are typically pension funds, banks and asset managers, insurance companies, government-owned entities, endowments and foundations, and high net worth individuals or families. The funds may be capitalized by general partners, but typically most of the capital is provided by limited partners. The partnership agreement sets forth the economic arrangement among the partners. Typically, the general partners receive an annual management fee in the range of 1 percent to 3 percent, and earn 20 percent of the fund's profit, which is called "carried interest", the remainder of the fund's profits is distributed to the limited partners.

Based on time value of money calculations, the returns provided to limited partners depend significantly on the timing of the returns. For example, an original investment of $1,000 with an exit value of $2,000 can be a good investment or a bad one depending on the timing of the exit.

Investment	Exit Value	Exit Year	IRR
(1,000)	2,000	Year 3	26.0%
(1,000)	2,000	Year 7	10.4%

In light of this financial reality, private equity funds are expected to be fully invested within five years and each investment has an expected exit within three to seven years of the original investment. The typical fund is expected to close within 12 years. The successful private equity firm provides suitable risk-adjusted returns to its limited partners, and based on this track record the firm can attract new capital to fund more investments. Successful private equity firms raise new funds to replace and augment retiring funds, which typically means a new fund every three to five years as existing funds become fully invested.

Venture capital is a form of private equity investment activity where the venture capital firm provides equity capital to new or newer businesses ("startups"). Startups cannot access the public capital markets because their business models have not been market tested, have little financial history, and are otherwise highly risky. They need seed money for new and developing businesses. The motivation of venture capitalists is to invest in huge potential payoff projects. For example, not so far in the past, companies like Amazon, eBay, and Google were mere fledging companies started by ambitious entrepreneurs, and now they are Fortune 500 companies.

4. CREDIT MARKETS

The credit market can be broadly categorized into the money market, the bank loan market, and the bond market.

a. Money Markets

The money market is the network of corporations, governments, financial institutions, and investors that deal in the flow of short-term capital, usually debt instruments with a maturity of one year or less at the time of issuance. Businesses and governments need short-term capital to fund ongoing operations. Payments to employees, utilities, and trade creditors need to be made, and cash inflow from revenue does not always match cash outflow. At the same time, investors and corporations have a need to earn return on a short-term basis. Corporations are major investors in the money market because they generate lots of cash that must be invested on a short-term basis, and the job of the corporate treasurer is to manage the cash flow. The market created from these needs is the money market. As of 2012, the money market was around $13 trillion, which is slightly below the $14 trillion level in December 2008.

The money market does not trade in formal exchanges or a formal set of rules under the auspice of one regulator. It is a network of borrowers and lenders connected by business relationships, and money transactions are executed electronically with or without clearinghouse intermediation. At the center of the money market are the central banks of governments that set short-term interest rates. Based on these interest rates, borrowers and lenders transact in the money market and the aggregate outcome of these transactions set the market interest rates in the money market.

The major credit rating agencies rate the short-term debt of issuers. Credit ratings affect the ability of issuers to borrow in the money market. Debt instruments in the money market are generally expected to be safe. Poor (speculative) credit ratings may prohibit the ability to borrow on short term, or increase the cost of borrowing significantly.

There are several significant instruments issued by corporations in the money market. They are: commercial paper, bankers' acceptance, interbank loans, and repurchase agreements.

Commercial paper. Large corporations can also secure short-term financing through the issuance of commercial paper. Commercial paper is an unsecured promissory note issued by a corporation with a maximum potential maturity of 270 days (9 months). It is not underwritten like stocks or bonds, where the issue is registered with the SEC and investment banks manage the issuance process, including some form of commitment to sell the issue to investors in a public offering. Larger corporations sell commercial paper directly to investors, and corporations that do not have this capacity issue paper through a dealer. The 270-day limit exists because longer-duration instruments must be registered with the SEC.* For short-term financings, the registration requirement would be frequent, expensive, and cumbersome. The average maturity on commercial paper is 30 days, and most commercial paper has a maturity of 60 days or less. Commercial paper is typically high grade in creditworthiness, and is mostly issued by high quality companies.

Bankers' acceptance. A bankers' acceptance is a financing method to facilitate commercial trade transactions. It is a letter of credit issued by a bank that accepts the ultimate responsibility to repay a loan to its holder. Acceptance finance is a good method to facilitate import/export commercial transactions because a financial institution accepts the responsibility of repayment of a loan.

Interbank loan. Interbank loans are short-term loans made among banks. Like other businesses, a bank may require short-term loans. The London interbank offering

---

* Section 3(a)(3) of the Securities Act of 1933 exempts commercial paper from the registration requirement of Section 5 of the statute: "Any note, draft, bill of exchange, or banker's acceptance which arises out of a current transaction or the proceeds of which have been or are to be used for current transactions, and which has a maturity at the time of issuance of not exceeding nine months, exclusive of days of grace, or any renewal thereof the maturity of which is likewise limited."

rate (or "LIBOR") is the rate at which banks in the United Kingdom offer short-term loans to each other. Since London is an important financial center and many global financial institutions operate there, LIBOR is an important financial benchmark. In the United States, the Fed funds rate is the rate at which banks with excess reserves can lend to banks requiring short-term financing. The Fed funds rate is indirectly controlled by the Federal Reserve, which sets a target Fed funds rate and seeks to steer that rate to the target rate by changing the money supply.

Repurchase agreement. An important method of raising short-term funding is a repurchase agreement ("repo"). A repo is not an instrument or a security like commercial paper. It is a financing method commonly used by financial institutions, such as investment banks, to fund their operations. In a repo, the borrower sells a security with a commitment to buy the security back from the purchaser at a specified higher price at a designated future date. It is a collateralized loan where the collateral is the security sold.

b. Bank Loan Market

Bank loans and medium-term notes are typically longer duration than money market instruments, but are still short-term financings compared to bonds. If a large corporation has a medium-term financing need, beyond 270 days but typically less than 10 years, it may issue a medium-term note (MTN). MTNs are not underwritten like bonds or debentures, and like commercial paper they can be sold directly or through a dealer. Dealers support a secondary market in MTNs and provide liquidity for these instruments. MTNs straddle the durational gap between commercial paper and bank loans on the short-term of the scale, and bonds and debentures on the long term of the scale.

Bank loans also provide shorter-term debt financings. They may have a maturity for only a few months, such as "bridge loans" which provide temporary financing for an acquisition or purchase of an asset until more permanent financing can be put in place. "Term loans" are longer duration loans, typically four to five years. Shorter-term loans usually have fixed rates, and longer-term loans have *floating rates* that are benchmarked against an interest rate index. The most common interest rate benchmarks are: (1) the London Interbank Offered Rate (LIBOR), which is the rate at which major international banks lend to each other in London; (2) federal funds rate, which is the rate at which banks lend to each other based on excess reserves they hold; and (3) the bank's prime interest rate, which is a benchmark lending rate sent by U.S. banks. Thus, a floating rate of interest is set at, for example, x percent above LIBOR.

Bank loans can be unsecured or secured by collateral. Bank loans are usually secured. All else being the same, collateralized loans have lower interest rates. Collateral can be any asset or thing of value owned by the debtor, such as equipment, real property, receivables, and financial instruments. Issues such as the nature of the collateral, the amount of collateral relative to the loan value, and periodic release of collateral are subject to negotiation.

Corporations typically have lines of credit (sometimes called "revolvers"), which are contractual commitments of a bank to make available and to provide upon a company's request a defined amount of loans over a specific duration. The revolver amount, interest rate, and duration are explicitly negotiated between borrower and creditor. The benefit to the corporation is that it has a contractually guaranteed access to capital; a revolver can be seen as liquidity insurance because in difficult financial or economic times, liquidity is guaranteed up to the amount of the revolver. However, this comfort comes at a cost. In addition to the interest paid on loans taken, the borrowing corporation must also pay a commitment fee of about 0.25 percent (or 25 basis points) on the untapped portion of the revolver.

Bank loans can be very large. If the loan amount is big enough, a single bank might not want to be exposed to this level of credit risk from a single borrower. As a way to spread the risk, the bank loan might be syndicated among a group (syndicate) of banks, which will share in the risk and return. These financings are put together by an arranger, which earns a fee anywhere from 10 basis points for blue-chip companies and much higher for highly leveraged firms or risky transactions. The process of putting a syndicate together includes preparing an information memorandum giving details of the deal, structuring and negotiating the terms, and soliciting and securing commitments from participating banks.

EXAMPLE

Ashland's Use of Bank Loans to Acquire Hercules

In 2008, Ashland, a Kentucky chemical manufacturer, borrowed $1.6 billion to finance the acquisition of Hercules. The following is a description of the deal.*

* * *

Bank of America and Scotia Capital are marketing a $1.6 billion credit facility for Ashland, a Covington, Ky.-based chemical company that makes the resins, polymers and adhesives used in cars. The credit facility consists of a $377 million term loan A that matures in 2013, an $830 million term loan B that matures in 2014, and a $400 million revolver that matures in 2013. Price talk on million term loan A and revolver is at Libor plus 350 bps and includes a 1% fee on any undrawn balance, while talk on the term loan B is at Libor plus 440 bps. Ashland is rated BB- by Standard & Poor's. The bank meeting was held Thursday, an Ashland spokesman confirmed. He declined to provide additional information. The deal has garnered a lot of attention from investors. "All eyes are on [Ashland] right now," a CLO manager said. The proceeds from the credit facility, combined with $650 million in 9.125% senior unsecured notes due 2017, which the company issued on May 19, will be used to repay a $750 million bridge loan it used to acquire Hercules, a Wilmington, Del.-based chemical company that specializes in water-treatment chemicals used in latex paints and printing inks. BofA was the lead underwriter on the bonds. Ashland also has $250 million in 8.8% senior unsecured notes due 2012 outstanding. Hercules has $600 million in subordinated notes outstanding, split into two tranches—$350 million in 6.5% notes due 2029, and $250 million in 6.75% notes due 2029.

Bank loans are typically illiquid and sit on the bank's balance sheet as an asset. However, liquidity can be created in several ways. Loans or whole portfolios of loans can be sold to a buyer that may want to invest in them. Another way to create liquidity

---

* Richard Kellerhals, *Banks Shop $1.6 Billion Facility for Ashland*, Vol. 24, Issue 21, Bank Loan Report (May 25, 2009), available at 2009 WLNR 9960141.

is to engage in a structure finance transaction that converts illiquid loans to liquid bonds called "collateralized debt obligations" (CDOs). Loans are pooled together, and the cash flow generated from the payment of interest and principal from borrowers are packaged as bonds. Typically, a CDO issue will have different tranches of bonds. Each tranche has a different risk and credit rating. Cash flows are tiered such that a senior tranche is entitled to the first layers of cash flow, and so forth to the most junior tranche.

c. Bond Market

If debt financing is preferred and the investment horizon is long term (10 years or more), an issuer would most probably finance its investments and assets with bonds, debentures, and long-term notes. Historically, notes were not issued pursuant to an indenture, whereas bonds and debentures were; bonds were long-term debt securities that were secured by security interest whereas debentures were unsecured debt instruments. While indentures and security interest are certainly important matters, the historic definitional distinctions are frequently ignored in conversation. The term "bond" used in conversation refers to the class of long-term debt instruments including bonds, debentures, and long-term notes.

Duration is a key consideration in whether to issue bonds or some shorter-term debt issue. Bonds are longer-term financing options. Bond issues typically extend beyond the medium term of 5 to 10 years, and they are issued to finance long-term projects or to secure long-term financing needs. Accordingly, bonds are not issued to secure short-term financing needs.

Most bonds are straight bonds, which means that they have a fixed interest rate and maturity with no equity link. However, since bonds are debt contracts, their contractual terms vary quite a bit. There are many kinds of bonds.

- *Interest rate*: Most bonds have fixed coupon rates, but the interest payments on some bonds are variable or adjustable based on a contractually determined formula.
- *Fixed duration*: Most bonds have a fixed maturity, but some bonds are callable by the issuer and others are putable (redeemable) at the option of the investor before the maturity.
- *Security*: Some bonds are secured by collateral, but other bonds (technically called debentures) are unsecured obligations.
- *Seniority and subordination*: If there is more than one class of debt instruments, bonds can have different levels of seniority with respect to liquidation preference.
- *Equity link*: Most bonds are not convertible or have some other equity link like attached warrants, but some bonds are convertible or come with attached warrants.

These different features can be combined into different structures. The only limits on contracting are the needs of the issuer and the investment criteria of investors. The contractual terms must satisfy both the issuer and the investor.

Most bonds are issued in the domestic market by domestic companies. There is also an international bond market in which domestic issuers issue bonds in the international market. "Foreign bonds" are bonds issued outside of the domestic market and denominated in the currency of the country of issuance. "Eurobonds" are bonds issued outside of the domestic market and not denominated in the currency of the country of issuance. For example, a bond issued by a Korean company in London denominated in Swiss francs would be a Eurobond.

There are several reasons why a domestic firm would choose to issue a bond offering internationally. First, the bond is issued in the currency of the project that the bond would finance, and thus currency is kept consistent. Second, the bond may be refinancing a prior debt which is denominated in a foreign currency. Third, for foreign companies, bonds issued in major financial markets like New York and London may offer superior terms with respect to the difference in the domestic and foreign interest rates. Fourth, diversification of financing sources may have benefits in the long term.

There are three basic types of bond issuers: corporations, national and other governments, and securitizations. A major segment of the corporate debt market is the corporate bond market, the principal market studied in this book. The typical issuers of corporate bonds are public utilities, transportation companies, banks and financing companies, and industrial companies. These companies are characterized by mature, stable businesses that generate significant cash flow.

The Treasury market is the market for U.S. government securities. The U.S. government is the largest single issuer of debt in the world. The U.S. Treasury issues Treasury debt instruments (Treasury bills, notes, and bonds) to finance the ongoing cash needs of operating the U.S. government. Treasuries are issued in the primary market. There is an auction process in which primary dealers buy Treasuries from the U.S. government, which are then traded in the secondary market. Because the U.S. government is the largest single debtor in the world, the Treasury market is a highly liquid market. Other sovereign nations issue debt as well. Debt issued by national governments is called sovereign debt. In addition to sovereign debt, municipalities and government agencies can issue debt. Bonds issued by municipalities are called municipal bonds.

The securitization market is the market for asset-backed (ABS) and mortgage-backed (MBS) securities. This market converts illiquid receivables sitting on the balance sheet of originating companies like banks, mortgage originators, and credit card companies, into publicly traded bonds. This market is very large, the largest segments being credit card receivables and mortgage receivables.

5. DERIVATIVES MARKETS

The derivatives markets can be broadly categorized into exchange-traded futures and options markets, and over-the-counter (OTC) derivatives markets. In the exchange-traded market, an exchange serves as the intermediary between buyers and sellers of futures and options contracts. Exchange-traded derivatives are traded under standardized contract terms. In the OTC market, transactions are done directly between two counterparties. OTC derivatives are transactions between parties that can be custom tailored to fit particularized needs.

a. Exchange-Traded Market

Futures contracts are standardized contracts, which make them suitable for trading on exchanges. Contract terms include the following items: contract size, quality, delivery date, price limits, position limits, and settlement. The futures markets owe their heritage to agricultural and commodities trading. Many of the contracts still involve the trade of agricultural products and commodities in physical form. However, the futures market developed into markets for financial futures. There are now two basic types of futures: commodity futures and financial futures. Of these, the financial futures market is now much bigger than the commodity futures market by trading volume.

There are three basic types of physical commodity futures: (1) agricultural futures are contracts for agricultural products, the most popular being soya products, sugar, rubber, corn products, and wheat; (2) metals futures include steel rebar, aluminum, copper, silver, zinc, and gold, which is one of the most heavily traded futures; and (3) energy futures are contracts for natural gas and petroleum products.

Futures contracts in agricultural commodities have not been consolidated to the leading exchanges due to the desire by traders to have contractual variations in agricultural markets. Leading exchanges for agricultural commodities include Chicago Board of Trade and the Chicago Mercantile Exchange. Leading exchanges for metals include London Metal Exchange and New York Mercantile Exchange. Leading exchanges for energy futures include the New York Mercantile Exchange and Multi-Commodity Exchange of India.

There are four basic types of financial futures: (1) interest rate futures are tied to various kinds of interest rates; (2) currency futures are tied to exchange rates; (3) stock index futures are tied to various stock market indices such as the Standard & Poor's 500 Index, the Dow Jones/Euro Stoxx 50 Index, and the Nikkei 225 Index; and (4) stock price futures are futures contracts on the price of individual stocks.

All exchange-traded options are standardized and governed by the exchanges. There are five basic types of exchange-traded options: (1) equity options, which are options on individual stocks; (2) index options, which are options on some form of financial indices; (3) interest rate options, which are options to purchase bonds and options on yields of specified bonds; (4) commodity options, which are options on commodities; and (5) currency options, which are options on currencies. A standard contract size of equity options in most exchanges is the delivery of 100 shares of the stock. The most popular indices on index options are equity market indices such as the Standard & Poor's 500. Any financial index, however, is subject to being traded as options if the exchange develops the contract and there is investment appetite or need for it.

The value of an exchange intermediation is that once the buyer and the seller agree to transact, they have no further obligations to each other. The exchange acts as a buyer for each seller, and as a seller for each buyer. The exchange guarantees the economic exchange between buyers and sellers. There are no counterparty risks such as the failure to execute on an agreed transaction or the insolvency of a counterparty upon closing of the transaction.

The process of intermediating the transaction occurs through the clearing and settlement process that the exchange implements. An important part of this process is the maintenance of margins. Before an investor can transact in an exchange, it is required to maintain a margin account. The required margin depends on the rules of the exchange. As the contracts on the exchange are marked to market, and as the current market values fluctuate, the investor may be required to make more margin deposits or can withdraw deposits per the exchange rules. Requirements to make additional deposits are called margin calls. If the investor does not make the required margin call(s), the exchange liquidates the position.

b. OTC Market

The OTC derivatives market is the market for derivatives outside of exchange inter-mediation. This market is one of the fastest growing markets in the financial markets. The OTC derivatives market is important because it permits investors to custom tailor their financial transactions to their needs and appetites. It is where we will also see "exotic" securities with highly customized and highly complex structures. Derivatives traded on exchanges are standardized contracts and cannot be custom tailored. For example, one option on an individual stock is set at 100 shares, and not 87 shares. If an investor has a need for an option on 87 shares, it must go to the OTC market. Given the complexity of the financial markets and the range of financial needs and appetites, one can see the need for an OTC market.

The size of the OTC derivatives market is large. The notional value is the principal or face value of the derivative. For example, a derivative on $100 million currency swap for euros has a notional value of $100 million. Clearly, the notional value of derivatives is a misleading number in terms of measuring the value of the derivatives contracts, the risks in the derivatives markets, and the amount of actual money that will ultimately change hands upon settlement. The gross market value is the replacement cost of the contract if the contract was purchased on the open market.

Below is a table that summarizes the size of the OTC derivatives market as of December 2012 (in $ billion).*

Type	Notional Value	Gross Value
Foreign currency	67,358	2,304
Interest rate	489,703	18,833
Equity-linked	6,251	605
Commodity	2,587	358
Credit default swaps	25,069	848
Others	41,611	1,792
Total	632,579	24,740

There are three basic categories of OTC derivatives. (1) *Forwards* are contracts establishing a current contract price for the sale and delivery of something in the future. Forward contracts exist because there is a need for contract terms beyond the standardized terms of futures contracts set by exchanges. Nonstandard terms may be the object of exchange (*e.g.*, infrequently traded assets or indices), and the contract duration, which may be longer than most futures contracts. (2) *Options* contain nonstandard contract terms. A common class of OTC options is interest rate options. These options can build in a great variety of customization. For example, interest rate options can include a cap on the maximum interest rate on a floating rate debt, or a floor on the minimum interest rate on a floating rate debt. (3) *Swaps* are contracts to exchange an asset or thing in the future at a current predetermined price. The most common swap is interest rate swaps, and the most common interest rate swap is a swap between floating and fixed rates.

---

* Marc Levinson, Guide to Financial Markets, at 255 (6th edition 2014).

An important class of OTC derivatives is credit derivatives. A credit derivative is a derivative based on the credit of an issuer or credit instrument. The most common credit derivative is the credit default swap (CDS). A CDS defines a "credit event," which is some form of an adverse credit event involving the specified issuer or credit instrument. Upon the trigger of a credit event, the protection seller pays the protection buyer the specified amount. Because a CDS is a custom tailored contract, an investor's exposure to credit risk can be custom tailored as well.

The OTC derivatives market exposes participants to several risks that are not present in the exchange derivatives market. (1) Parties are subject to counterparty risk. In the exchange market, the exchange serves as a counterparty to each buyer and seller, and thus market participants need not worry about getting paid. This is not the case with OTC derivatives where the parties are directly transacting with each other. (2) Related to counterparty risk is settlement risk. Whereas counterparty risk involves the creditworthiness of the counterparty, settlement risk involves the timeliness and the procedures to ultimately settle up. The manner and efficacy of settling up depends on how well the contract is drafted and how well the parties execute the settlement between themselves. (3) Parties are subject to price risk. Most exchange-traded instruments are liquid due to active trading. OTC derivatives are custom tailored, and thus there may be limited numbers of secondary market traders. Some instruments may be so "exotic" that there are no other buyers. The lack of liquidity affects prices if the instruments are sold rather than kept to maturity.

6. ISSUERS AND INVESTORS

Issuers are any private or public entity that requires capital to operate their enterprises and that can issue securities to investors. The two largest classes of issuers are corporations and governments. Companies like General Electric, Walt Disney, Home Depot, Apple, Facebook, Google, Coca Cola, Goldman Sachs, Wells Fargo, and McDonalds (as well as the many countless not commonly known, smaller, or private companies) issue financial instruments to finance their ventures. Without prior and continued financing from investors, these businesses cannot be sustained as going concerns.

When a corporation is created, it is initially capitalized with some capital. If it is simply a shell at the moment, existing on paper in the office of the secretary of state but otherwise inactive, the capitalization can be minimal. However, if it is intended to engage in enterprise, it must have an initial capitalization that meets its funding needs. This real (business-driven) capitalization can be in the form of debt or equity, or a mix of the two. If the corporation is long lived, there is no guarantee over time that this initial capitalization is sufficient to funding continuing activities and investments. Previous debt must be repaid upon maturity. There may not be sufficient ongoing profits to internally fund continuing or new investments and activities. Bad financial results (losses) might have eroded the financial foundation. New activities and investments may require more capital than is required under the old business model. For a myriad of reasons, an existing corporation may be required to access the capital market on a continuing basis during its life.

Investors are savers who have excess money to invest. They are broadly categorized into retail investors and institutional investors. Retail investors are individual bondholders and shareholders, the proverbial "mom and pop" who typically hold and trade securities through accounts held at retail brokerage firms. Institutional investors are institutions having large pools of capital. The range of institutional investors is broad. Major institutional investors can be categorized into these groups: insurance companies, depository institutions, investment banks, corporations, and asset management firms.

Insurance companies invest premiums received from policyholders in principally investment grade fixed income securities. Depository institutions invest in the capital markets chiefly by making loans to borrowers. Given the size of the global insurance and commercial banking sectors, insurance companies and depository institutions are major players in the bond and bank loan markets.

Investment banks are major players in the capital markets because they perform a number of important functions. Among other things, they underwrite and make markets in securities. They act as securities brokers on behalf of clients, and they also act as principal dealers on their own accounts.

The category of asset managers is broad. Asset managers include pension funds, mutual funds, sovereign wealth funds (investment vehicles for foreign governments), university endowments, private equity funds, and hedge funds. These different kinds of funds have different investment strategies, which reflect the investment and risk appetites of the capital providers of the funds.

Pension funds invest the retirement savings of groups of employees (*e.g.*, California public school teachers, automotive workers, state government employees, etc.). The investment strategy is dictated by the fact that the purpose of the fund is to secure the retirement of workers participating in the fund. The goal is sustained long-term growth with minimal exposure to high risk. This goal is similar to that of endowments, which seek to generate earnings without exposing the principal to much risk.

Mutual funds are investment pools drawn from retail investors (the proverbial mom and pop). Each fund may have a particular strategy or focus (*e.g.*, international large capitalization companies, energy sector, commodities, domestic small capitalization companies, etc.). Mutual funds allow professional management of smaller sums of investments, sector investment, and diversification.

At the other end of the risk-return continuum are private equity and hedge funds. Private equity and hedge funds are different, though there is not a formal legal definition separating the two and the two can engage in similar types of investment strategies. Private equity funds pursue a defined strategy of providing equity and debt capital to issuing companies in the hope of realizing capital returns through a turnaround of the business or an exit such as a sale of the company or an IPO. Hedge funds may do these things as well, but they pursue a variety of investment strategies seeking arbitrage opportunities. These investments may go far afield from tradition promising capital investments in startup or mature companies.

Private equity and hedge funds are principally capitalized by institutional players and high net worth individuals. Institutional investors in private equity and hedge funds are insurance companies, investment banks, endowments, pension funds, sovereign wealth funds, and other financial institutions. Even though some of these institutional investors keep an overall lower risk profile in their investment portfolio (*e.g.*, insurance companies and pension funds), they diversify and increase the overall return by investing some funds in high-risk ventures.

7. PROFESSIONAL FIRMS

A broad group of professional firms provides essential services to make the capital market work. However, there are four groups of professionals who are indispensable to the working of the capital market: lawyers, accountants, investment banks, and credit rating agencies.

a. Lawyers

Lawyers are indispensable to the capital markets. Markets are regulated, and transactions require contracts. As noted in this book's introduction, the capital markets are regulated by the laws of securities regulation and administered by government regulators, and the substantive economic and governance terms of the securities and financial instruments are subject to private ordering between issuer and holder.

On the private transaction side, the lawyer must navigate both public and private spheres of law. The public sphere is the law of securities regulation. The private sphere of law is the construction of the financial contract. These contracts can be long and complex, reflecting the underlying complexity of the business transactions. Managing the regulatory process of securities issuance and trading, drafting contracts and regulatory documents, and advising on legal risk are all in the lawyer's domain. Lawyers are needed to perform, among other things, the following tasks:

- Advising on the security issuance process and regulatory hurdles
- Drafting and filing the registration statement and prospectus with the SEC (for a public offering)
- Drafting the terms of the security instrument
- Conducting due diligence on the issuer and the transaction
- Ensuring that the transaction is valid with respect to corporate law, corporate charter, and the rights of other capital providers
- Negotiating with creditors if the terms of existing debt do not permit the new capital raising
- Facilitating a process with other regulators, if they are involved
- Advising the board of legal and fiduciary issues
- Providing opinion letters required or expected in the transaction

In performing monitoring and vetting functions, lawyers are also one of many gatekeepers of the capital market. Little more needs to be said about the importance of lawyers in the capital markets, securities regulation, and corporate finance transactions.

b. Accountants

Accounting firms are vitally important to the capital markets because they provide and audit financial statements. They provide independently verified financial and economic data. The process of financial analysis and valuation begins with financial statements. Additionally, accountants are important in transactional work. Their advice may be needed on the appropriate accounting and tax treatments of a contemplated transaction, and they may be asked to conduct due diligence on the books and records of a transacting company.

There are many large national and international law firms that practice business law. There are also many smaller and boutique firms. Unlike law firms, there are not that many large accounting firms. In the 1980s, there was a group of eight firms called, unimaginatively, the "Big Eight." But through mergers and, in the case of Arthur Andersen, an implosion after the Enron scandal, the eight firms have consolidated to the "Big Four": (1) Deloitte Touche Tohmatsu, (2) PricewaterhouseCoopers, (3) Ernst & Young, and (4) KPMG. Any lawyer working in the transactional field or in large business advisory functions will come across the Big Four firms in the course of many engagements.

c. Investment Banks

Investment banks play a crucial role in the capital markets, though to many people their activities are not well known. Large multiservice investment banks are complex institutions. They provide investment banking, research, and trading services.

Investment banking involves helping companies to raise capital and providing corporate finance advisory services including mergers and acquisitions. In a capital raise, investment banks serve as underwriters of stocks and bonds. The underwriting process includes valuing the securities to be issued, advising the issuer on the best method to sell the securities, gauging investor appetite for the securities, conducting due diligence on the issuer, coordinating the issuance process with accountants, lawyers, exchanges, and regulators, coordinating the sales and trading of the securities, and assuming some of the risk of the issuance by committing to purchase the securities from the issuer with the intent to sell to the ultimate investors. Investment banking also involves providing corporate finance advisory services including advising on mergers and acquisitions. In this capacity, the investment bank is a financial advisor. In an M&A process, the investment banker values the firm, conducts due diligence, coordinates the sale or purchase of the target company, and provides a fairness opinion to the board of directors on the acquisition consideration.

Research involves conducting research on companies and securities, and the investment bank disseminates this research to the investment community. This is called "sell-side" research as the investment bank is considered to be on the "sell-side" of the market because of their underwriting services, which represent original sellers of securities (issuers) and sell newly issued securities to the market. Although this research function has an inherent structural bias, it is important because it serves to disseminate information to the capital market.

Trading involves the trading of securities. Investment banks are also broker-dealers, two distinct roles in trading securities. As a broker, the bank is acting as an agent for an institutional client who seeks to buy or sell securities. As a dealer, it is using its own capital to buy or sell securities on its own account. By trading securities, investment banks provide liquidity in the market.

A brief discussion of the recent history of the investment banking industry is helpful. The Glass-Steagall Act was enacted in response to the stock market crash of 1929 and the Great Depression. It separated investment banks from commercial banks. The thought was that investment banking is inherently risky, and its activities should be separated from commercial banking, which involves the deposit of money into banks by the population at large. In the era of Glass-Steagall, investment banks were smaller firms. In 1999, the Glass-Steagall Act was repealed. As a result of industry consolidation and regulatory changes, investment banks became bigger or were acquired by larger commercial banks.

Before the financial crisis, there were only five large, independent, full-service (also called "bulge bracket") investment banks: Goldman Sachs, Morgan Stanley, Merrill Lynch, Lehman Brothers, and Bear Stearns. "Full service" means that the investment bank provides the full panoply of banking services to corporations: corporate finance advisory work including mergers and acquisitions advisory, securities underwriting for both debt and equity securities, securities research, trading in securities as both broker (agent) and dealer (principal), and market making in securities where the investment bank provides liquidity in securities by acting as buyers and sellers.

During the financial crisis, Bear Stearns became insolvent and was acquired in a fire sale by JPMorgan Chase, a commercial bank with major investment banking operations; Lehman Brothers filed for bankruptcy and portions of the firm were sold to Barclays, a commercial bank with major investment banking operations; and Merrill Lynch teetered on the knife's edge of insolvency and was acquired by Bank of America, a commercial bank with major investment banking operations. The two remaining investment banks, Goldman Sachs and Morgan Stanley, converted to bank holding companies. Today, investment banking is done under the umbrella of large money center banks with enormous balance sheets and international scales of operations. Some of the largest financial institutions doing full-service investment banking business are: Goldman Sachs, Morgan Stanley, JP Morgan Chase, Bank of America Merrill Lynch, Citigroup, UBS, Credit Suisse, Deutsche Bank, and Barclays. With the exception of Goldman Sachs and Morgan Stanley, these financial institutions have roots as large depository institutions, which subsequently acquired global investment banking capabilities. Any lawyer working in the transactional field or in large business advisory functions will come across these investment banks in the course of many engagements.

d. Credit Rating Agencies

Credit rating agencies are vital to the global economy. They assign credit ratings to bond issues and issuers, and most public bonds carry a credit rating, which is a probabilistic assessment of the risk of default. Credit ratings impact the price at which bonds are issued in the primary market and traded in the secondary market, and the assessment of risk in the portfolios of investors. There are only three major credit rating agencies, which collectively dominate the market for credit ratings. They are Moody's Investors Service, Standard & Poor's, and Fitch Ratings.

Publicly traded bonds in the credit market are rated. A rating is necessary because many financial institutions, which are the primary investors of bonds, are limited in the amount of risk they can assume in their portfolios. Creditworthiness is the probability of default of a bond of that rating. A higher ranked issue should have a lower probability of default, and vice versa. A credit places the issue or issuer on an ordinal scale of credit ratings. Among the major rating agencies, their alphanumeric rating scales are very similar.

The major taxonomical division in ratings is between "investment grade" (BBB or Baa and above) and "speculative grade" (below BBB or Baa), and within each are finer divisions of ratings. Speculative grade bonds are called "junk" or "high yield" bonds. These bonds provide higher yields than investment grade bonds. The pejorative "junk"

	Moody's	S&P and Fitch	Description
Investment Grade	Aaa	AAA	Prime rating
	Aa1	AA+	Very high grade
	Aa2	AA	
	Aa3	AA–	
	A1	A+	Upper medium grade
	A2	A	
	A3	A–	
	Baa1	BBB+	Lower medium grade
	Baa2	BBB	
	Baa3	BBB–	
Speculative Grade	Ba1	BB+	Low grade
	Ba2	BB	
	Ba3	BB–	
	B1	B+	Highly speculative
	B2	B	
	B3	B–	

should not be confused with the notion that junk bonds are useless or worthless. They provide a means to do risky transactions, which ex ante may be worthy of doing despite the high risk, such as LBOs.

An investment grade rating is important because many bond investors are regulated financial institutions such as banks, broker-dealers, insurance companies, pension funds, and money market funds. These financial institutions invest heavily in bonds, because relative to stocks and other assets they are safer. Do we want our banks and insurance companies using our deposits and premiums to chase the higher returns of stocks? Thus the use of credit ratings has been pervasive in the regulation of investments. An example is the regulation of bank capital, which among other things employs credit ratings. Another example is Rule 2a-7 of the Investment Company Act, which provides that a money market fund shall "present minimal credit risk" as may be determined by "factors pertaining to credit quality in addition to any rating assigned to such securities." Still another example is the pervasive use of ratings to regulate the liquidity and the investment portfolios of insurance companies. Many financial institutions are restricted from investing in speculative grade bonds. For example, in fiscal year 2011, The Harford, an insurance company, reported that 95.5 percent of its investments in bonds were investment grade and only 4.5 percent were in junk bonds.

E. OVERVIEW OF SECURITIES ISSUANCE

As discussed in the introduction to this book, the manner and procedures used to offer and sell securities is the subject of Securities Regulation. A brief overview of how securities are offered and sold in capital markets may be helpful to put in context the capital markets and securities traded therein.

When a corporation needs external capital, it must seek an investor, who may be a creditor or an equityholder. The company can borrow money through a credit arrangement that does not trigger the securities laws. A commercial paper issuance is such a transaction, as well as perhaps a privately negotiated, short-duration bank loan. However, when substantial, longer-term capital is required, a corporation will typically issue securities. The securities can be debt in the form of a bond or debenture, or equity in the form of preferred or common stock. The issuance of securities triggers a regulatory regime under federal securities laws and the agency authority of the Securities and Exchange Commission.

1. PUBLIC AND PRIVATE OFFERINGS

When an issuer offers securities to investors, the laws of securities regulation make a fundamental distinction between a public offering and a private (or exempt) offering. This distinction arises from Section 5 of the Securities Act of 1933 (codified in 15 U.S.C. §77e):

> (a) *Unless a registration statement is in effect as to a security, it shall be unlawful* for any person, directly or indirectly—
> (1) *to . . . sell such security* through the use or medium of any prospectus or otherwise; or
> (2) to carry or cause to be carried . . . any such security for the purpose of sale or for delivery after sale.
> (b) *It shall be unlawful for any person*, directly or indirectly—
> (1) *to . . . carry or transmit any prospectus* relating to any security with respect to which a registration statement has been filed under this subchapter, unless such prospectus meets the requirements of section 10; or
> (2) to carry or cause to be carried . . . any such security for the purpose of sale or for delivery after sale, unless accompanied or preceded by a prospectus that meets the requirements of subsection (a) of section 10.
> (c) *It shall be unlawful for any person*, directly or indirectly . . . *to offer to sell or offer to buy* through the use or medium of any prospectus or otherwise any security, *unless a registration statement has been filed as to such security*. . . .

Section 5 applies to a "security." Section 2(a)(1) of the Securities Act defines a security broadly and includes, among other things, "any note, stock, . . . bond, debenture, evidence of indebtedness, . . . investment contract." In a seminal case, *SEC v. W.J. Howey Co.*, 328 U.S. 293 (1946), the Supreme Court interpreted the term "investment contract" to mean "a contract, transaction or scheme whereby a person invests his money in a common enterprise and is led to expect profits solely from the efforts of the promoter or a third party." Based on this standard and the subsequent nuances to *Howey*, "investment contract" functionally works as a catch-all provision defining the essential nature of a security, which is then subject to federal securities law. Thus, in addition to stocks, bonds, and debentures (financial instruments that are traditionally recognized as "securities" without much thought), the concept of securities includes less obvious financial instruments that can meet the definition of items listed in Section 2(a)(1).

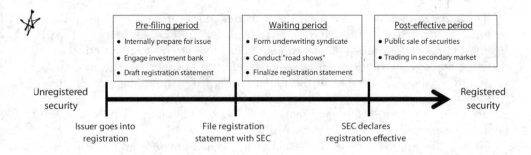

Section 5 provides: "It shall be unlawful . . . to *offer to sell or offer to buy* . . . any security, unless a registration statement has been *filed*" and "Unless a registration statement is *in effect* . . . , it shall be unlawful . . . [to] *sell* such security." The registration process obligates issuers to make public, regulated disclosure of information (the registration statement) administered and approved by the SEC, which then permits the sales transaction in registered securities.

Securities regulations set forth the steps required for registering securities for a public offering. Broadly speaking, the steps can be categorized into three periods: pre-filing, waiting, and post-effective periods.

Before the filing of the registration statement, an issuer is in registration at least from the time the issuer reaches an understanding with the broker-dealer (investment bank) in which the investment bank would act as the managing underwriter. This point begins the pre-filing period. The issuer engages an investment bank to lead the underwriting that will manage the issuance. The working group of the issuer, the investments, and lawyers (the issuer and the underwriters have their separate lawyers) then begins preparing for the issue, including drafting the registration statement. An "offer" of securities cannot be made prior to the filing of the registration statement. Section 2(a)(3) defines an "offer" as "every attempt or offer to dispose of, or solicitation of an offer to buy, a security." An illegal offer in the pre-filing period is called "gun-jumping," and there are various SEC rules setting forth what is and is not gun-jumping.

The process of registering securities is complicated, but the key part is the filing of the registration statement with the SEC. A registration statement is a legal document that contains highly detailed, mandatory disclosure of information on the business and financials of the issuer, as well as the risks associated with the investment, and the security to be offered. It is a thick document, running many dozens of pages, and is chock full of financial data. It is prepared by a cohort of advisors including the issuer's investment bank, accountant, and lawyer. Because it is a legal document and regulatory filing, the lawyer is the primary drafter and custodian of the registration statement.

When the registration statement is filed with the SEC, the waiting period begins. The lead underwriter typically forms the syndicate of investment banks that will, together, sell the issuance. A capital raising can be negotiated directly between issuer and investor, and this is a common process in a private offering of securities. However, a typical public offering is underwritten. Underwriting may be required when the capital raising is complex and risky: For example, it could be a large sum or there could be many investors. In an underwritten deal, the investment bank is the selling intermediary between the issuer and the investor. An underwriting syndicate spreads the risk of the issue, which may be in the hundreds of millions or many billions of dollars.

215

public sec. offering

The underwriting agreement between the issuer and the investment bank provides that the latter will underwrite the issue on a "firm commitment" or "best effort" basis. In a best effort underwriting, the investment bank agrees to make a best effort to sell the issue at a specified price, but does not commit to buying the issue. It does not assume the risks of ownership in the underwriting. In a firm commitment underwriting, the investment bank buys the issue on a short-term basis with the intent to resell the securities in the open market. The investment bank is fully at risk for holding the security.

During the waiting period, the issuer and the investment bank conduct "road shows," where they meet with institutional investors to inform them of the issue. The road show informs investors and is designed to generate interest. It also helps to inform the issuer and the investment bank of the potential range of price that "the market" will bear. At some point, based on the gauging of interest and market conditions, the number of securities offered and the price are both set. Upon filing of the registration statement, the SEC reviews it and may make comments. There may be a back and forth process between the issuer and the SEC about the information contained in the registration statement and any deficiencies thereof.

When the SEC declares the registration statement "effective," it triggers the post-effective period. Investment banks in the syndicate are allotted their shares of the issue, and they begin to distribute the issue by selling to the market of investors. Active trading of the securities begins, and the securities are now publicly traded.

Not all securities offered for sale must be registered. Section 4(a) sets forth a number of exemptions to registration, which are private offerings. For example, Section 4(a)(2) provides that Section 5 does not apply to "transactions by an issuer not involving any public offering," thus creating a route for private offerings. There are various SEC rules permitting private offerings under specifically defined criteria and conditions. An important exemption is Regulation D (encompassing Rules 501 to 508), which, if followed, provides a safe harbor from the registration requirement. The private market for securities is large. For example, venture capital deals involving early investments in startup or young companies are transactions for private equity securities, and foreign issuers can raise capital in the U.S. market through a private placement of debt securities.

In addition to rules exempting securities from the registration requirement, Section 3(a), among other federal securities statutes, provides that certain securities are exempt from registration. An important exemption is Section 3(a)(3)'s exemption of commercial paper: "Any note, draft, bill of exchange, or banker's acceptance which arises out of a current transaction or the proceeds of which have been or are to be used for current transactions, and *which has a maturity at the time of issuance of not exceeding nine months*, exclusive of days of grace, or any renewal thereof the maturity of which is likewise limited." This exemption permits the offer and sale of commercial paper without registration. Corporate issuers routinely use the commercial paper market to seek short-term debt and to manage their working capital. This exemption makes the "money market" (the market for short-term cash) quick, liquid, and cost efficient. Because there is no registration requirement, some corporate issuers directly place commercial paper without the use of a financial intermediary such as an investment bank.

Lastly, the registration process or exemption applies to securities, and not to issuers in some global sense. A company's common stock may be privately held (and thus the company is considered privately held), but nevertheless it can offer registered bonds. A company's common stock may be publicly traded, but nevertheless it can offer securities that are private offerings because they are exempt or the company chooses not to register them. There are various reasons why companies may choose to register securities or not, but it is obvious that two major, competing considerations are: (1) the time and cost of the registration process, and (2) the freedom to offer and sell the securities to the public and the desirability of registered securities to the investor as a result. These are business and financial decisions, but the legal issues and legal advice figures prominently into the decision.

2. INITIAL PUBLIC OFFERING

An initial public offering (IPO) is when a company "goes public" by registering its common stock and selling it to the public. It is the grandest transaction in the capital markets. A company may "go public" and access the public equity capital market through an IPO if it wishes to:

- Create public shares for use in mergers and acquisitions
- Establish a public market value
- Enhance company reputation
- Broaden the shareholder base
- Diversification of holdings of large block owners
- Reduce cost of capital by minimizing the illiquidity discount
- Create exit options for entrepreneurs and venture capitalists
- Avoid expensive debt and increasing cost of debt

An IPO is a strategic decision. Immediate financial considerations may precipitate an IPO, but often larger strategic factors are at work. An IPO is exciting, expensive, and complex.

An IPO is exciting because the company is, proverbially speaking, first introduced to the world. There is increased scrutiny from the media, financial markets, competitors, and regulators. The company may become financially much bigger by issuing new shares to the public. The balance sheet may balloon. The company may be flush with cash, and this means that its business enterprise must ramp up to new levels. Existing shareholders, who may be original entrepreneurs, employees, and early financial investors, may be able to monetize their investment (and perhaps become cash rich). Shares will be traded on exchanges or trading platforms, allowing everyone to follow the changing stock price in real time. The company's officers, directors, and employees may ring the bell to start the trading day at the floor of the New York Stock Exchange on the day of the IPO.

An IPO is expensive because the registration and underwriting processes are very costly. First, there are the direct costs involved in facilitating the process: the time, effort, and opportunity cost of the issuer's internal team (including senior managers), and the fees of professional advisors (including investment bankers, accountants, and lawyers). There is an underwriter's spread (or discount), which is the difference between the price the underwriters pay the issuer for the shares and the price they charge to investors during the sales process. This spread can be as much as the "standard" 7 percent or something negotiated to be less. For example, if the issue amount was $100 million, the issuer would sell this amount to the underwriters for

$93 million. That is a hefty fee.* Second, there is a very large indirect cost in the form of pricing. Historically, investment banks have tended to underprice the issue price. Underpricing occurs when an offer price for the security is discounted from the internal calculation of the intrinsic value. On average, the issue price has been observably lower than the first day's closing trading price. The average underpricing for U.S. IPOs was 14.8 percent from 1990 to 1998, and 12.1 percent from 2001 to 2009.** There are several reasons why the bias may be toward underpricing the deal. Risk aversion of the underwriters who bear the risk of the issue in a firm commitment underwriting partly explains the phenomenon. Another reason is the desire by the issuer and the underwriter to have active post-issue trading indicative of investor demand and liquidity in shares. Whatever the explanation for the underpricing bias, when the underwriter spread and undervalue bias are combined, the average discount from the "fair" value of the stock can be approximately 20 percent or more.

An IPO is a complex transaction. The registration process is complicated and the size of the deal team is very large. The issuer has to put together an internal team comprised of senior officers including the chief executive officer and the chief financial officer. The investment bank puts together a deal team from various parts of the bank including investment bankers who advise on the deal structure, valuations, institutional sales, and securities research. The underwriter and the issuer have their own lawyers. Accountants are involved on matters of financial statements, accounting policies, and accounting data. After the engagement of a "lead manager" investment bank (a major decision in itself), there are a myriad of preliminary issues, including for example:

- What is the issue size and anticipated pricing?
- What are the potential problems—*e.g.*, legal, financial, accounting, governance, owner interests, operations, etc.—that need to be resolved for the purpose of disclosure and generating investor interest?
- With what exchange or trading platform should the company list its stock?
- What are the changes to governance as a result of SEC or stock exchange requirements? For example, must independent directors be added to the board of directors to meet rules of the stock exchange?

The first major task when the company is "in registration" is to draft the registration statement. For most IPO companies, this will be Form S-1. This is a lengthy, highly detailed document governed by SEC rules mandating various items to be disclosed. The issuer's lawyer and senior officers will ordinarily write the first draft because so much detailed information about the company is required. SEC rules require "plain English" writing. Major sections of Form S-1 include:

- Description of the "risk factors" associated with an investment in the company
- "Management's discussion and analysis" of financial condition and results of operations (MD&A)

---

* When the author was working as an investment banker in the late 1990s and early 2000s in New York, a colleague, who shall remain nameless, described an IPO this way: "An IPO is a money tree. You shake it and all this money falls out." The professional and transaction fees associated with an IPO are very hefty.

** Steven Davidoff Solomon, *Why I.P.O.'s Get Underpriced*, N.Y. Times (May 27, 2011) (citing a study by Professor Jay Ritter, University of Florida Warrington College of Business Administration). The article notes that from 1999 to 2000 the average IPO underpricing was 51.4 percent. This is an unusually high number because the period 1999 to 2000 was the height of the Internet "dot.com" bubble and prices were irrational.

- Financial statements, accounting policies, and accounting data
- Descriptions of the company, products, operations, management and their compensation, governance, legal matters, industry in which the company operates, etc.
- Description of the nature of the securities to be offered, including economic and governance rights

As filed with the Securities and Exchange Commission on February 1, 2012

Registration No. 333-

UNITED STATES
SECURITIES AND EXCHANGE COMMISSION
Washington, D.C. 20549

Form S-1
REGISTRATION STATEMENT
Under
The Securities Act of 1933

Facebook, Inc.
(Exact name of Registrant as specified in its charter)

Delaware	7370	20-1665019
(State or other jurisdiction of incorporation or organization)	(Primary Standard Industrial Classification Code Number)	(IRS Employer Identification No.)

Facebook, Inc.
1601 Willow Road
Menlo Park, California 94025
(650) 308-7300
(Address, including zip code, and telephone number, including area code, of Registrant's principal executive offices)

David A. Ebersman
Chief Financial Officer
Facebook, Inc.
1601 Willow Road
Menlo Park, California 94025
(650) 308-7300
(Name, address, including zip code, and telephone number, including area code, of agent for service)

Please send copies of all communications to:

Gordon K. Davidson, Esq.	Theodore W. Ullyot, Esq.	William H. Hinman, Jr., Esq.
Jeffrey R. Vetter, Esq.	David W. Kling, Esq.	Daniel N. Webb, Esq.
James D. Evans, Esq.	Michael L. Johnson, Esq.	Simpson Thacher & Bartlett LLP
Fenwick & West LLP	Facebook, Inc.	2550 Hanover Street
801 California Street	1601 Willow Road	Palo Alto, California 94304
Mountain View, California 94041	Menlo Park, California 94025	(650) 251-5000
(650) 988-8500	(650) 308-7300	

Once the issuer and its lawyers (and maybe other advisors) have completed a draft of the registration statement, the underwriters and their lawyers will review the draft and engage in due diligence of the issuer. Due diligence is practically necessary because it is good market practice to investigate the issuer and issue for accuracy in representations to the investment community. Due diligence is also legally necessary because federal securities laws, principally Section 11 of the Securities Act, impose liability for material misstatements on various parties associated with the issuance and filing processes, and conducting a proper due diligence can be a defense against civil liability. The review of the draft of the registration statement by "all hands on deck" may result in intensive, sometimes frenetic "all day, all night" drafting sessions.

When the waiting period begins with the filing of the registration statement, Section 5(c) no longer applies and thus offers to sell securities can begin. The SEC may review the registration statement or not. In most IPOs, however, it will most likely review the registration statement, and it may issue a "letter of comments" that the issuer must address. The issuer and its advisors will also draft a preliminary prospectus, which is a marketing document that permits potential investors to consider the investment opportunity. However, the prospectus is not a "marketing" document in the sense of a free-for-all puffery. It is a legal document that is largely based on the registration statement. Section 10(a)(1) of the Securities Act provides that a prospectus "shall contain the information contained in the registration statement" subject to certain excludable items. Rule 430 provides guidelines on the submission of a conforming preliminary prospectus. The preliminary prospectus need not disclose an actual offer price, but must disclose a price range (the permissible range is governed by SEC rules). The actual offer price should be determined as close to the sale date as feasible because market conditions always change, and the issuer and underwriters should have the flexibility to adapt to those changes. The preliminary prospectus, sometimes called a "red herring prospectus," is also visually apparent because it has on the front page a bold legend in red font stating something to the effect of:

> "*Information contained herein is subject to completion and amendment. A Registration Statement relating to these securities has been filed with the Securities and Exchange Commission but has not yet become effective. These securities may not be sold nor may offers to buy be accepted prior to the time the Registration Statement becomes effective.*"

Because offers can now be made in the waiting period, the issuer can go on "road shows" to visit potential investors and to discuss the issue. The road show is informational to potential investors, but the issuer and its investment bankers also gain a sense of the level of interest, which is important as the IPO marches toward pricing the deal and the sale of securities.

The post-effective period begins when the registration statement becomes effective. Section 8(a) provides that "the effective date of a registration statement shall be the twentieth day after the filing thereof or such earlier date as the Commission may determine." As a matter of practice, most issuers wait for assurance's sake until the SEC informs the issuer that it has approved the registration statement. Section 5(a)'s prohibition against the sale of securities is lifted. The stock is offered and sold on the public market, and a final prospectus containing price information must be delivered to purchasing investors.

PROSPECTUS (Subject to Completion)
Issued May 3, 2012

337,415,352 Shares

facebook

CLASS A COMMON STOCK

Facebook, Inc. is offering 180,000,000 shares of its Class A common stock and the selling stockholders are offering 157,415,352 shares of Class A common stock. We will not receive any proceeds from the sale of shares by the selling stockholders. This is our initial public offering and no public market currently exists for our shares of Class A common stock. We anticipate that the initial public offering price will be between $28.00 and $35.00 per share.

We have two classes of common stock, Class A common stock and Class B common stock. The rights of the holders of Class A common stock and Class B common stock are identical, except voting and conversion rights. Each share of Class A common stock is entitled to one vote. Each share of Class B common stock is entitled to ten votes and is convertible at any time into one share of Class A common stock. The holders of our outstanding shares of Class B common stock will hold approximately 96.3% of the voting power of our outstanding capital stock following this offering, and our founder, Chairman, and CEO, Mark Zuckerberg, will hold or have the ability to control approximately 57.3% of the voting power of our outstanding capital stock following this offering.

We have applied to list our Class A common stock on the NASDAQ Global Select Market under the symbol "FB."

We are a "controlled company" under the corporate governance rules for NASDAQ-listed companies, and our board of directors has determined not to have an independent nominating function and instead to have the full board of directors be directly responsible for nominating members of our board.

Investing in our Class A common stock involves risks. See "Risk Factors" beginning on page 12.

PRICE $ A SHARE

	Price to Public	Underwriting Discounts and Commissions	Proceeds to Facebook	Proceeds to Selling Stockholders
Per share	$	$	$	$
Total	$	$	$	$

We and the selling stockholders have granted the underwriters the right to purchase up to an additional 50,612,502 shares of Class A common stock to cover over-allotments.

The Securities and Exchange Commission and state regulators have not approved or disapproved of these securities, or determined if this prospectus is truthful or complete. Any representation to the contrary is a criminal offense.

The underwriters expect to deliver the shares of Class A common stock to purchasers on   , 2012.

MORGAN STANLEY   J.P. MORGAN   GOLDMAN, SACHS & CO.

BofA MERRILL LYNCH   BARCLAYS   ALLEN & COMPANY LLC
CITIGROUP   CREDIT SUISSE   DEUTSCHE BANK SECURITIES
        RBC CAPITAL MARKETS   WELLS FARGO SECURITIES

        , 2012

Facebook, Inc.

Nasdaq ticker: FB
IPO issue price: $38 per share

3. RESALE OF SECURITIES

When a security is registered and sold to the public, it is traded in the secondary market. Such trading is permissible under Section 4(a)(1) of the Securities Act of 1933, which provides that the registration requirement of Section 5 shall not apply to "transactions by any person other than an issuer, underwriter, or dealer." This means that once a security has been registered and issued to the public, such as an IPO or secondary offering (public offerings following an IPO), trading in the secondary market between investors is exempt so long as they are not deemed to be an issuer or underwriter. Publicly issued shares can trade in the secondary market.

There are restricted and privately issued securities that are exempt from the registration requirement, such as securities issued under Regulation D. Private companies are, by definition, companies whose common stock is owned privately and not publicly traded. Private securities are resold in the market as well, and SEC rules regulate this process. Two important safe harbor rules apply to the resale of private securities: Rule 144 and Rule 144A.

Rule 144 allows public resale of restricted securities and control securities if a number of conditions are met. Restricted securities are securities acquired in unregistered, private sales from the issuer or an affiliate of the issuer. Restricted securities are typically issued through Regulation D offerings, other private placement offerings, employee stock benefit plans, compensation for professional services, venture capital or private equity investments. Control securities are those held by an affiliate of the issuer, who is a person in a relationship of control with the issuer. Such persons may be a senior executive, director, or financier of the issuer. Control means the power to direct the management and policies of the company in question, whether through the ownership of voting securities, by contract, or otherwise. The security certificate of a restricted security will be stamped with a "restrictive" legend, which indicates that the securities may not be resold in the marketplace unless they are registered with the SEC or are exempt from the registration requirements.* Certificates for control securities usually are not stamped with such a legend.

To sell restricted securities or control securities, the conditions of Rule 144 must be met. (1) There is a holding period condition. Before restricted securities can be sold in the marketplace, the securityholder must have held them for a specific period of time: six months if the issuer is a "reporting company" under the Securities Exchange Act of 1934, and at least one year for nonreporting companies. (2) There is a current public information requirement. There must be adequate publicly available information about the issuer before the sale. For reporting companies, this requirement is met by the periodic reporting requirements and compliance with them. For nonreporting companies, a certain level of information, such as description of the business, management structure, and financial information, must be somehow publicly available. (3) There is a trading volume restriction. If the securityholder is an affiliate, there are limits on the amount that can be traded. The amount cannot exceed the greater of

---

* An example of a legend might be something like this (usually presented in all caps): "The securities represented by this certificate have not been registered under the Securities Act of 1933, as amended. The securities may not be sold or offered for sale or otherwise distributed except in conjunction with an effective registration statement for the securities under the Securities Act, or in compliance with Rule 144 or pursuant to another exemption."

1 percent of the outstanding shares of the same class being sold, or if the class is listed on a stock exchange the greater of 1 percent or the average reported weekly trading volume during the four weeks preceding the filing of a notice of sale.

If the securityholder is not an affiliate and has held the restricted securities for at least one year, it can sell the securities without regard to the above conditions. If the issuer is a reporting company and the securityholder has held the securities for at least six months but less than one year, it may sell the securities as long as it satisfies the current public information condition. Even if a securityholder has met the conditions of Rule 144, it cannot sell restricted securities to the public until it properly removes the restriction legend from the security certificate. Only transfer agents can remove a restrictive legend, but for them to do so the securityholder must obtain the consent of the issuer.

Rule 144A is a nonexclusive safe harbor exemption from the Section 5 registration requirements for resale of certain securities to qualified institutional buyers (called "QIBs"). The SEC promulgated Rule 144A in 1990 to incentivize foreign issuers to issue capital in the U.S. capital markets. The rule provides a safe harbor for resale of exempt securities. It provides that a sale to QIBs in compliance with the rule is not a "distribution" and thus the seller is not an "underwriter" for the purpose of the Section 5 registration process. By creating a safe harbor for the resale of securities, Rule 144A facilitates the issuance of exempt securities. It permits the purchaser of securities from a company in a private placement to resell the securities and thus create a trading market for exempt securities. The rule has four requirements.

1. The resale must be to a QIB. This requirement recognizes that certain institutional investors, being sophisticated institutional market actors, require less regulatory protection and that regulatory policy favors a less regulated capital market within the conditions defined in the rule. QIBs include insurance companies, investment companies, investment advisors, corporations, partnerships, business trusts, and certain entities that, in the aggregate, own and invest on a discretionary basis at least $100 million in securities of unaffiliated issuers. A registered broker-dealer qualifies as a QIB if it owns and invests on a discretionary basis at least $10 million in securities of unaffiliated issuers. Prior to the Jumpstart Our Business Startups Act of 2012 (JOBS Act), offers of securities under Rule 144A were required to be limited to QIBs, which effectively prohibited the use of general solicitation under Rule 144A. However, in response to JOBS Act §201(a) the SEC amended Rule 144A to permit the use of general solicitation, as long as the purchasers are limited to QIBs or to purchasers that the seller and any person acting on behalf of the seller reasonably believe are QIBs.

2. The seller must take "reasonable steps" to make the purchaser aware that the seller is relying on Rule 144A to sell the security. This informs the investors that those securities may only be resold pursuant to an exemption and that the securities will be subject to reduced liquidity. This notice is typically given by placing a legend on the security stating that the securities have not been registered and thus may not be resold absent proper registration or exemption.

Also, the private placement memorandum used in connection with the Rule 144A offering will include a prominent notice to investors.*

3. The securities must not be "fungible" with certain securities that are exchange traded or quoted in an automated interdealer quotation system. The most obvious example of a fungible, traded security is common stock. Thus, although Rule 144A applies equally to equity and debt securities, debt issuances and preferred stock more easily meet the nonfungible requirement: Debt securities have different interest rates, maturities, and other terms; preferred stock are frequently issued in different series with specific preferences and rights to each series. Convertible securities that convert into fungible common stock can also be considered nonfungible, but there must be a specified term before conversion can occur, and the conversion premium (the premium above the current trading price of the common stock at the time of issue) must be at least 10 percent to qualify. This condition on convertibles is imposed to prohibit the gaming of Rule 144A to issue common stock in the guise of a convertible security issuance. The nonfungible condition permits foreign issuers to raise debt capital and thus access to the U.S. capital markets even though they are not listed companies.

4. The issuer must provide certain reasonably current information to a security-holder or a prospective purchaser. This information includes a "very brief statement" of the nature of the business, the issuer's most recent balance sheet, as well as profit and loss and retained earnings statements and similar financial statements for the two preceding fiscal years. This requirement provides an information burden on the issuer, but the issuer also benefits because the information requirement enhances the liquidity of these securities.

---

* The notice will state something to the effect of: "Each purchaser of the securities will be deemed to have represented and agreed that it is acquiring the securities for its own account or for an account with respect to which it exercises sole investment discretion, and that it or such account is a qualified institutional buyer and is aware that the sale is being made to it in reliance on Rule 144A."

CHAPTER

5

COMMON STOCK

There is a spectrum of securities that a corporation can issue ranging from the least to the most risky—from debt to equity. The study of financial instruments starts with the riskiest and indispensable security, which is common stock. It is also the most familiar financial instrument since the introductory corporation law course teaches that the board of directors owes fiduciary duty to stockholders, and two accountability mechanisms are the right to vote and to pursue derivative actions on behalf of the corporation. This chapter does not delve into these facets of stock that have already been covered in prior study.

This chapter focuses on the economic rights of common stockholders. As discussed *supra* Chapter 3, shareholders economically gain by capital appreciation of their stock through the process of market valuation. In addition to potential capital appreciation, shareholders economically gain through distributions of cash, stock, and other assets. However, there are legal and equitable limitations on such distributions.

A. COMMON STOCK FINANCING

1. BASIC CHARACTERISTICS OF COMMON STOCK

When a stock corporation is created, it will issue one class of common stock at issue. "The articles of incorporation must authorize (1) one or more classes or series of shares that together have unlimited voting rights, and (2) one or more classes or series of shares (which may be the same class or classes as those with voting rights) that together are entitled to receive the net assets of the corporation upon dissolution." Model Business Corporation Act (MBCA) §6.01(b). Whereas debt is a choice in the capital structure of issuers (though, in reality, debt is a prominent form of capital for many issuers), at least one class of common stock is the practical necessity of a legal rule. Corporations can have very complex equity capital structures, but in practice most corporations, even large public companies, have just one class of common stock that gives the right to vote and to receive net assets. The equity capital structure is fairly simple. If there are multiple classes of stock (whether preferred and common, or multiple classes of common), there should be a good business, economic, or governance reason.

Common stock has two principal features. The first is the legal right to vote. The voting requirement of corporation statutes like MBCA §6.01(b) reflects the principle that equityholders should logically have the power to vote for directors and certain fundamental transactions since they have the greatest incentive to maximize the residual value. *See Applebaum v. Avaya, Inc.*, 812 A.2d 880, 886 n.7 (De. 2002)

("Shares of stock are issued to provide a verifiable property interest for the residual claimants of the corporation."); *Eliasen v. Itel Corp.*, 82 F.3d 731, 735 (7th Cir. 1986) ("A corporate structure in which the bondholders . . . have all the voting rights, and the shareholders . . . have no voting rights, is anomalous.").

The second principal feature of common stock is the right to the residual earnings and assets of the corporation. In a liquidation, creditors and preferred stockholders have priority over common shareholders, who are the most junior securityholders with respect to distribution of assets. In addition to the liquidation right to net assets, common stock has the residual economic claim on earnings. Common stockholders are the economic claimants to the net income after dividends to preferred stockholders, whether such earnings are distributed to them or retained by the corporation. This benefit is properly called a residual "economic claim" and not a "legal right" because, as we will see, there is not a general legal right to a distribution in common stock instruments; the decision regarding the retention of profit belongs to the business judgment of the board. The claim to profit and net assets is economic in nature. Stockholders benefit from the residual economic claim through market valuation wherein corporate profits or losses are reflected in stock value. Common stock value increases, generally if not perfectly, as the net assets and earnings increase, though control of the assets and earnings resides with managers by virtue of the separation of ownership and control inherent in the corporate system.

Since common stockholders are residual claimants, their rights are not highly particularized through the written contract the way that the rights of bondholders and preferred stockholders are found in indentures and corporate charters. Common stockholders assume the greatest risk among capital providers and generally have the most incentive to maximize firm value. Only when all other claimants are paid—employees, creditors, preferred stockholders—are common stockholders "paid." The residual nature of the common shareholders' claim explains why their interests are often conflated with the best interest of the corporation such that in most ordinary situations the board is said to owe fiduciary duty to the corporation and shareholders. *See, e.g., Smith v. Van Gorkom*, 488 A.2d 858, 872 (Del. 1985) ("In carrying out their managerial roles, directors are charged with an unyielding fiduciary duty to the corporation and its shareholders.").

2. DUAL CLASS STOCKS

The vast majority of corporations have only one class of stock, which is a single class of common stock. However, corporation law permits any classes of shares or series of shares (MBCA §6.01(a); DGCL §151(a)). If a corporation has more than one class of stock, it typically has preferred stock, which may also come in a series. A corporation can also have different classes of common stock. There may be several reasons for dual class common stock. One reason might be related to different dividend or participation rights among common stockholders. A more common reason is related to voting rights. Two classes of stock may have identical economic rights, but voting rights may differ. Such stock arrangements may serve the purpose of giving a particular class of shareholders who are otherwise minority owners control rights, including protection from hostile acquisition.

The holders of superior voting power stock have private benefits, which may include the effective power to designate board seats or separate negotiation leverage in a sale of the company. A small number of public companies have dual class common stock with different voting rights. Although the number of companies are small, some highly prominent companies have dual class stock including Berkshire Hathaway, Ford Motor, Google, and Facebook.

EXAMPLE

Google Inc.'s Dual Class Common Stock

The following are excerpts from Google's Fourth Amended and Restated Certificate of Incorporation, and Form S-1 filed pursuant to the company's IPO. The corporate certificate provides the legal rights of the two classes of common stockholders, and the Form S-1 provides Google's disclosure of the risk related to the dual class stock structure.

* * *

[Certificate of Incorporation]

Section 1. Authorized Shares. This Corporation is authorized to issue nine billion (9,000,000,000) shares of Class A Common Stock, par value $0.001 per share (the "Class A Common Stock"), three billion (3,000,000,000) shares of Class B Common Stock, par value $0.001 per share (the "Class B Common Stock", and together with the Class A Common Stock, the "Common Stock"), three billion (3,000,000,000) shares of Class C Capital Stock, par value $0.001 per share (the "Class C Capital Stock"), and one hundred million (100,000,000) shares of Preferred Stock, par value $0.001 per share. The number of authorized shares of any class or classes of stock may be increased or decreased (but not below the number of shares thereof then outstanding) by the affirmative vote of the holders of at least a majority of the voting power of the issued and outstanding shares of Common Stock of the Corporation, voting together as a single class.

Section 2. Common Stock. A statement of the designations of each class of Common Stock and the powers, preferences and rights and qualifications, limitations or restrictions thereof is as follows:

(a) Voting Rights.
(i) Except as otherwise provided herein or by applicable law, the holders of shares of Class A Common Stock and Class B Common Stock shall at all times vote together as one class on all matters (including the election of directors) submitted to a vote or for the consent of the stockholders of the Corporation.
(ii) Each holder of shares of Class A Common Stock shall be entitled to one (1) vote for each share of Class A Common Stock held as of the applicable date on any matter that is submitted to a vote or for the consent of the stockholders of the Corporation.
(iii) Each holder of shares of Class B Common Stock shall be entitled to ten (10) votes for each share of Class B Common Stock held as of the applicable date on any matter that is submitted to a vote or for the consent of the stockholders of the Corporation.

(b) Dividends. Subject to the preferences applicable to any series of Preferred Stock, if any, outstanding at any time, the holders of Class A Common Stock and the holders of Class B Common Stock shall be entitled to share equally, on a per share basis, in such dividends and other distributions of cash, property or shares of stock of the Corporation as may be declared by the Board of Directors from time to time with respect to the Common Stock out of assets or funds of the Corporation legally available therefor;

provided, however, that in the event that such dividend is paid in the form of shares of Common Stock or rights to acquire Common Stock, the holders of Class A Common Stock shall receive Class A Common Stock or rights to acquire Class A Common Stock, as the case may be, and the holders of Class B Common Stock shall receive Class B Common Stock or rights to acquire Class B Common Stock, as the case may be.

(c) Liquidation. Subject to the preferences applicable to any series of Preferred Stock, if any outstanding at any time, in the event of the voluntary or involuntary liquidation, dissolution, distribution of assets or winding up of the Corporation, the holders of Class A Common Stock and the holders of Class B Common Stock shall be entitled to share equally, on a per share basis, all assets of the Corporation of whatever kind available for distribution to the holders of Common Stock.

(d) Subdivision or Combinations. If the Corporation in any manner subdivides or combines the outstanding shares of one class of Common Stock, the outstanding shares of the other class of Common Stock will be subdivided or combined in the same manner.

(e) Equal Status. Except as expressly provided in this Article IV, Class A Common Stock and Class B Common Stock shall have the same rights and privileges and rank equally, share ratably and be identical in all respects as to all matters. Without limiting the generality of the foregoing, (i) in the event of a merger, consolidation or other business combination requiring the approval of the holders of the Corporation's capital stock entitled to vote thereon (whether or not the Corporation is the surviving entity), the holders of the Class A Common Stock shall have the right to receive, or the right to elect to receive, the same form of consideration, if any, as the holders of the Class B Common Stock and the holders of the Class A Common Stock shall have the right to receive, or the right to elect to receive, at least the same amount of consideration, if any, on a per share basis as the holders of the Class B Common Stock, and (ii) in the event of (x) any tender or exchange offer to acquire any shares of Common Stock by any third party pursuant to an agreement to which the Corporation is a party or (y) any tender or exchange offer by the Corporation to acquire any shares of Common Stock, pursuant to the terms of the applicable tender or exchange offer, the holders of the Class A Common Stock shall have the right to receive, or the right to elect to receive, the same form of consideration as the holders of the Class B Common Stock and the holders of the Class A Common Stock shall have the right to receive, or the right to elect to receive, at least the same amount of consideration on a per share basis as the holders of the Class B Common Stock.

* * *

[Form S-1]

Risks Related to Our Offering

The concentration of our capital stock ownership with our founders, executive officers, employees, and our directors and their affiliates will limit your ability to influence corporate matters.

After our offering, our Class B common stock will have ten votes per share and our Class A common stock, which is the stock we are selling in this offering, will have one vote per share. We anticipate that our founders, executive officers, directors (and their affiliates) and employees will together own approximately 84.8% of our Class B common stock, representing approximately 83.6% of the voting power of our outstanding capital stock. In particular, following this offering, our two founders and our CEO, Larry, Sergey and

Eric, will control approximately 38.1% of our outstanding Class B common stock, representing approximately 37.6% of the voting power of our outstanding capital stock. Larry,
Sergey and Eric will therefore have significant influence over management and affairs and
over all matters requiring stockholder approval, including the election of directors and
significant corporate transactions, such as a merger or other sale of our company or its
assets, for the foreseeable future. In addition, because of this dual class structure, our
founders, directors, executives and employees will continue to be able to control all matters submitted to our stockholders for approval even if they come to own less than 50% of
the outstanding shares of our common stock. This concentrated control will limit your
ability to influence corporate matters and, as a result, we may take actions that our stockholders do not view as beneficial. As a result, the market price of our Class A common
stock could be adversely affected.

3. MECHANICS OF ASSET DISTRIBUTIONS TO SHAREHOLDERS

When a corporation chooses to make a distribution to shareholders, the traditional and
most common way is through a cash dividend. Dividends can be regular cash dividends, where the company creates an expectation that investors can rely on a regular
dividend, though the board ultimately controls the decision to declare a dividend.
Dividends can also be a one-time dividend, which is called a "special dividend" so
as not to create an expectation beyond the one-off transaction.

Another way in which the company returns cash to shareholders is through a stock
repurchase. Reacquired shares are called "treasury stock," which are issued but are no
longer outstanding stock (however, MBCA §6.31 eliminates this terminology).
Repurchases were infrequent up to the mid-1990s, but they became a significant
part of payout policy in the 2000s. In 2007, for example, 28 U.S. corporations
each bought back more than $5 billion in stock, including ExxonMobile $31 billion,
Microsoft $28 billion, IBM $19 billion, and GE $14 billion.

A company can also distribute noncash assets. It can spinoff an entire business
unit or subsidiary or investment through a distribution of the stock of the business
unit, subsidiary, or investment (e.g., infra, Kamin v. American Express Co.). The net
result is that whereas previously shareholders owned the asset indirectly through ownership of the parent company, they now directly own the spunoff asset.

Cash dividends are paid according to the following procedure. A board decides
to pay dividends. An announcement is made of the decision, including the amount
and record date. The record date is the cutoff date on which the shareholder of
record as of the date is entitled to receive dividends. Shares normally trade with
dividends (or *cum dividend*) until two business days before the record date, and then
they are traded without dividend (or *ex dividend*). Ex dividend shares trade at lower
levels because the corporation will be distributing cash and as a result the shareholders' equity will also decrease by the amount of the asset reduction. If an investor
buys an ex dividend share, the purchase is not entered into the company's books
before the record date and thus he is not entitled to the dividend. At some point
after the record date, usually a few weeks, the dividend is paid to shareholders as of
the record date.

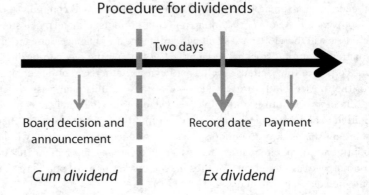

Procedure for dividends

For example, the following was the process that ExxonMobile used to issue its first dividend in 2012.*

- January 5, 2012:   Board declares quarterly dividend of $0.47/share
- February 8, 2012:   Shares trade ex dividend
- February 10, 2012: Record date
- March 9, 2012:   Payment date

4. THEORY AND PRACTICE OF DISTRIBUTIONS

In ordinary circumstances, distribution is a choice and business judgment of the board. The choice raises the question on the criteria for making the decision. A key criterion is whether the choice of dividend or repurchase affects the value of the firm. Stated differently, is there a theoretical basis for preferring distribution over the retainment as a matter of policy? There is not a definitive answer to these questions. There are several theories.

The first theory is that payout policy is irrelevant in perfect capital markets without taxes or transaction costs. Under these conditions, payout policy does not change a shareholder's wealth. To see this, consider the firm Acme Inc., which has the following predistribution balance sheet ($million).

Assets		Equity	
Cash	1.0	Stock (1m shares)	11.0
Fixed assets	10.0		

Share price = $11/share

Assume for simplicity that the share price is equal to the book value per share. Therefore, Acme's share price is $11 per share predistribution: $11 million book value ÷ 1 million shares outstanding.

---

* Richard A. Brealey, Stewart C. Myers & Franklin Allen, Principles of Corporate Finance 402 (11th ed. 2014).

A *Dividend Payout.* Acme decides to distribute $1 million in cash as a dividend. The book value falls to $10 million. We do not expect the valuation multiple (price-to-book) to change because the decline in cash does not affect earnings.

Assets		Equity	
Cash	0.0	Stock (1m shares)	10.0
Fixed assets	10.0		

$$\text{Share price} = \$10/share$$

The market value of its equity must fall to $10 million, and thus share price drops to $10 per share. However, the shareholders' wealth has not changed. In addition to the share, they have received a dividend of $1 million. Post-dividend the shareholders' wealth is still: $11 per share = $10 per share + $1 dividend per share.

B *Repurchase Payout.* Suppose that Acme does not pay a dividend, but instead chooses to use the $1 million in cash to repurchase shares. The number of shares repurchased would be: $1,000,000 ÷ $11/share = 90,909 shares. Although the shares outstanding decrease as a result of the buyback, the share price remains the same because the repurchase was done at book value: $11 per share = $10 million book value ÷ 909,091 shares outstanding.

Assets		Equity	
Cash	0.0	Stock (909,091 shares)	10.0
Fixed assets	10.0		

$$\text{Share price} = \$11/share$$

It is irrelevant whether the shareholder sold back the shares to Acme or retained the shares. The selling shareholder would get $11/share in cash. The nonselling shareholder would have shares worth $11/share.

The payout irrelevance hypothesis depends on the assumption of no taxes and transaction costs. If a shareholder wants to monetize some portion of the investment and dividends are not paid, the shareholder can mimic dividend payout by selling shares fractionally. The shareholder's value remains the same. However, the payout irrelevance hypothesis is limited by its unreal assumptions.

An alternative theory of payout policy considers the real-world possibility that investor behavior may not perfectly mimic the rational wealth optimizer. Some investors may prefer dividends over capital gains or repurchases. This may have something to do with the preferences of some investors who like regular cash payments, as opposed to repurchases that require active choices (selling back to the company) or obtaining needed cash by selling shares. On the last point, selling shares incrementally can replicate cash dividends. But one practical problem with this strategy is that shares are typically alienable in whole units and transactions in shares incur transaction cost.

Another theory of payout policy revolves around differential tax treatment on dividends and capital gains. If the tax rate on dividend distribution is higher than the tax rate on capital gains, the company should minimize dividends and instead make distributions through share repurchase. Different tax benefits always require consideration, but payout policy is not entirely driven by tax considerations. If tax is the primary driver, there should be no reason why companies should ever pay dividends, which would automatically trigger a tax event. Also, taxes on capital gains have been historically lower than taxes on dividends. Holding shares would defer tax liability, and shareholders should elect the time of share sales.

In the real world, payout decisions also communicate information to the market. Managers are reluctant to make downward deviations from prior dividend levels. They prefer "smooth" dividend distributions showing a sustained, predictable, long-term positive trend in dividend payments. They are less concerned about the absolute value of dividends than the relative changes in dividend payments from period to period. This is why investors perceive as good news an increase in dividend payment. Since managers do not want to disappoint market expectations, such an increase communicates the information that the company expects to be able to sustain a new higher level of cash payments.

Since share repurchases are not done with the frequency of dividends, the informational value of share repurchases is weaker. Like an increase in dividends, share repurchases can communicate management's optimism: The future may yield greater cash and managers may feel comfortable with distributing cash; or the future is brighter than the current valuation of stock suggests and thus managers seek to buy-back underpriced shares. A repurchase may ease stockholders' concern that the management will waste excess cash in unprofitable ventures, such as chasing investments that do not earn the company's cost of capital.

The empirical data on payout policy reflects an amalgamation of the theoretical and practical considerations. The following table provides a summary of the payout policies of U.S. corporations from 2001 to 2010:[*]

		Repurchases?	
		Yes	No
Dividends?	Yes	13.9%	19.4%
	No	11.5%	55.1%

During this time period, only 19.4 percent of companies paid dividends as the exclusive way of distributing cash to shareholders, and only 32.4 percent of companies paid dividends. A majority of firms, 55.1 percent, did not distribute any cash to shareholders. Many non-dividend-paying companies are young growth companies, which either need to preserve cash or have significant investment opportunities. But non-dividend companies also include Google, Amazon, and Berkshire Hathaway.

B. LEGAL CAPITAL

Some corporation statutes, including Delaware, require corporations to maintain "legal capital." This is a legal concept of equity capital structure. It is entirely divorced from economic reality and financial purpose. The concept of legal capital is a historical

---

[*] Richard A. Brealey, Stewart C. Myers & Franklin Allen, Principles of Corporate Finance 401 (11th ed. 2014).

vestige that no longer serves an effective modern function: neither effectively setting the minimum value of the stock nor effectively protecting existing shareholders from dilution of the value of their shares. The basic idea of legal capital is that the corporation should hold a minimum, statutorily defined level of equity capital defined by a fixed value of the stock. This statutory amount came to be known as "par value" and "stated value." These values form the legal capital that fixes a minimum stock value and a minimum level of capital required to be held in the corporation.

In the early era of corporation law and corporate finance, a statutorily fixed share value was believed to protect against "watered stock," a practice where consideration for stock was not deemed to be adequate for the stock issued. The stock became "watered," thus believed to be an improper value transfer from existing shareholders to new shareholders through artifice. As the concept of legal capital developed, a statutorily fixed value also came to be seen as a device to protect creditors as well. Legal capital represents the minimum level of capital that the corporation must hold; it represents a layer of equity cushion that cannot be distributed to shareholders, thus purportedly protecting creditors from shareholder opportunism.

The idea was simple, but too simplistic to work effectively since the real value of a corporation's stock is subject to the laws of economics and not the law's fiat. The concept of legal capital only applies when a corporation issues stock, and not subsequent trading of stock by shareholders in the secondary market. Suppose in the trading market, the corporation's stock value falls below the legal value. What would happen if the corporation needed to raise capital, but it cannot sell shares to new shareholders at the legally fixed amount? Why would any prospective shareholder consider an investment in common stock at an artificial price set by legal fiat if the market price is less than the fiat price?

Modern corporation law and corporation law make clear that these earlier ideas of legally defining capital and economic value were misguided. Stock value is not determined by legal standards or the lawyer's pen, but by the market for capital. Attempt to define a useful statutory value also ran into the problem that boards do and should have broad discretion, subject to fiduciary duty and good faith, in determining the value of consideration and the price of stock as determined by the market conditions existing at the time of issuance.

The Model Business Corporation Act §6.21 eliminated the "traditional (but arbitrary)" concept of par value and stated capital. The board must determine that the consideration for stock is adequate, and that determination is deemed to be conclusive insofar as the adequacy of consideration relates to whether the shares are fully paid and thus nonassessable. "Practitioners and legal scholars have long recognized that the statutory structure embodying 'par value and 'legal capital' concepts is not only complex and confusing but also fails to serve the original purpose of protecting creditors and senior security holders from payments to junior security holders." MBCA §6.21, official comment (Dec. 2010).

For jurisdictions that maintain the vestige of legal capital rules, such as Delaware, the "end around" the ineffective notion of legal capital came in the form of discretion to determine the amount of "par value" or "stated capital." If a stock has a par value, shares cannot be issued for less than par value but they can be issued for more than par value. If a stock has no par value, the board determines the amount of the issue that it determines to be the stated capital. These legal constraints are easily circumscribed. Stated capital simply leaves the decision of the amount of legal capital to the board.

Par value can be set at very low values to protect against the possibility that the issue price would fall below the par value. Thus, even when corporation law preserves the vestige of the legal capital system, the original protective intent has been effectively nullified. The modern practice in jurisdictions maintaining legal capital rules is that most boards rationally prefer maximum flexibility in setting the amount of legal capital. Many corporations set an arbitrarily low par value ("arbitrary" from the point of view that the value has no relation to economic reality). A commonly seen par value is $0.01, or even fractions of a penny.*

The accounting for an equity issuance conveys the futility of legal capital. The product of the par value and shares issued is the "capital." Any amount in excess of the par value is "additional paid in capital." For example, suppose the par value is $0.01. The corporation issues 10 million shares at the prevailing market price of $10 per share. The total proceed is $100 million. Only a tiny fraction of this amount ($100,000) is designated as capital and is added ("credited" in accounting speak) to a line item typically labeled in the balance sheet as "common stock" or "stock" or "capital."

$$\text{Common stock} = \$0.01 \text{ per share} \times 10 \text{ million shares} = \$100,000$$

The remaining $99.9 million is credited to a line typically labeled "additional paid-in-capital" (APIC) or simply "paid in capital."

$$\text{APIC} = \$9.99 \text{ per share} \times 10 \text{ million shares} = \$99,900,000$$

An actual example is seen in the 2008 Form 10-K of Goldman Sachs, a Delaware company. The investment bank reported the balance sheet financial status as of November 2008 (in $millions).

- Assets $884,547
- Liabilities   820,178
- Shareholders' equity   64,369

Common stock	7
Additional paid-in-capital	31,071
Preferred stock	16,471
Retained earnings	39,913
Treasury stock	(32,175)
Other equity items	9,082
Total shareholders' equity	64,369

Goldman Sachs had issued 680,953,836 common shares with $0.01 par value. Based on the number of shares issued, the legal capital, labeled above as "common stock,"

---

* Alcoa Inc., whose financials are presented in *supra* Chapter 1, presents a less commonly seen instance where the par value ($1.00) has been set at some value that is substantially more than a penny.

was $7 million (rounded up from $6.8 million), and APIC was $31,071 million. Does the $7 million held as legal capital serve any serious protection to creditors in light of the size of the balance sheet? (As seen later in a case study, *infra* Chapter 6, Warren Buffett's Investment in Goldman Sachs, the above balance sheet reflects over $20 billion of new equity capital (preferred stock with a $0.01 par value), including common stock and preferred stock (issuances to avert a potential collapse of the investment in September and October of 2008.)

The ineffectiveness of legal capital to protect creditors is evinced by the fact that creditors have shown an almost total lack of interest in the subject. *See* Bayless Manning & James J. Hanks, Jr., Legal Capital 95 (4th ed. 2013). They have not lobbied for stricter rules and standards or for the inclusion of the concept into newer business organizational forms such as the limited liability company. Instead, as seen in *infra* Chapter 7, the creditor's most important protection is the ability to contract for their rights.

EXAMPLE

Delaware General Corporation Law

§152. Issuance of stock; lawful consideration; fully paid stock

The consideration, as determined pursuant to §153(a) and (b) of this title, for subscriptions to, or the purchase of, the capital stock to be issued by a corporation shall be paid in such form and in such manner as the board of directors shall determine. The board of directors may authorize capital stock to be issued for consideration consisting of cash, any tangible or intangible property or any benefit to the corporation, or any combination thereof. The board of directors may determine the amount of such consideration by approving a formula by which the amount of consideration is determined. In the absence of actual fraud in the transaction, the judgment of the directors as to the value of such consideration shall be conclusive. The capital stock so issued shall be deemed to be fully paid and nonassessable stock upon receipt by the corporation of such consideration; provided, however, nothing contained herein shall prevent the board of directors from issuing partly paid shares under §156 of this title.

§153. Consideration for stock

(a) Shares of stock with par value may be issued for such consideration, having a value not less than the par value thereof, as determined from time to time by the board of directors, or by the stockholders if the certificate of incorporation so provides.

(b) Shares of stock without par value may be issued for such consideration as is determined from time to time by the board of directors, or by the stockholders if the certificate of incorporation so provides.

(c) Treasury shares may be disposed of by the corporation for such consideration as may be determined from time to time by the board of directors, or by the stockholders if the certificate of incorporation so provides.

(d) If the certificate of incorporation reserves to the stockholders the right to determine the consideration for the issue of any shares, the stockholders shall, unless the certificate requires a greater vote, do so by a vote of a majority of the outstanding stock entitled to vote thereon.

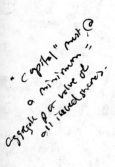

§154. Determination of amount of capital; capital, surplus and net assets defined

Any corporation may, by resolution of its board of directors, determine that only a part of the consideration which shall be received by the corporation for any of the shares of its capital stock which it shall issue from time to time shall be capital; but, in case any of the shares issued shall be shares having a par value, the amount of the part of such consideration so determined to be capital shall be in excess of the aggregate par value of the shares issued for such consideration having a par value, unless all the shares issued shall be shares having a par value, in which case the amount of the part of such consideration so determined to be capital need be only equal to the aggregate par value of such shares. In each such case the board of directors shall specify in dollars the part of such consideration which shall be capital. If the board of directors shall not have determined (1) at the time of issue of any shares of the capital stock of the corporation issued for cash or (2) within 60 days after the issue of any shares of the capital stock of the corporation issued for consideration other than cash what part of the consideration for such shares shall be capital, the capital of the corporation in respect of such shares shall be an amount equal to the aggregate par value of such shares having a par value, plus the amount of the consideration for such shares without par value. The amount of the consideration so determined to be capital in respect of any shares without par value shall be the stated capital of such shares. The capital of the corporation may be increased from time to time by resolution of the board of directors directing that a portion of the net assets of the corporation in excess of the amount so determined to be capital be transferred to the capital account. The board of directors may direct that the portion of such net assets so transferred shall be treated as capital in respect of any shares of the corporation of any designated class or classes. The excess, if any, at any given time, of the net assets of the corporation over the amount so determined to be capital shall be surplus. Net assets means the amount by which total assets exceed total liabilities. Capital and surplus are not liabilities for this purpose. Notwithstanding anything in this section to the contrary, for purposes of this section and §§160 and 170 of this title, the capital of any nonstock corporation shall be deemed to be zero.

C. STATUTORY LIMITATIONS ON DISTRIBUTIONS

Corporation statutes impose certain limits on distributions to common stockholders. The general principle of the limitations on distributions is that a distribution should not result in or jeopardize the solvency of the corporation. Solvency is typically measured from two perspectives: first, the balance sheet perspective in which there is positive equity; second, the cash flow perspective in which there is positive cash flow to meet debt service and other current obligations. Unlike the legal capital requirement, which does nothing for creditors, this limitation has more substance. However, the efficacy of this limitation is bounded as well.

EXAMPLE

Model Business Corporation Act

§6.40. Distributions to shareholders

(a) A board of directors may authorize and the corporation may make distributions to its shareholders subject to restriction by the articles of incorporation and the limitation in subsection (c).

(b) If the board of directors does not fix the record date for determining shareholders entitled to a distribution (other than one involving a purchase, redemption, or other acquisition of the corporation's shares), it is the date the board of directors authorizes the distribution.

(c) No distribution may be made if, after giving it effect:

(1) the corporation would not be able to pay its debts as they become due in the usual course of business; or

(2) the corporation's total assets would be less than the sum of its total liabilities plus (unless the articles of incorporation permit otherwise) the amount that would be needed, if the corporation were to be dissolved at the time of the distribution, to satisfy the preferential rights upon dissolution of shareholders whose preferential rights are superior to those receiving the distribution.

(d) The board of directors may base a determination that a distribution is not prohibited under subsection (c) either on financial statements prepared on the basis of accounting practices and principles that are reasonable in the circumstances or on a fair valuation or other method that is reasonable in the circumstances.

(e) Except as provided in subsection (g), the effect of a distribution under subsection (c) is measured:

(1) in the case of distribution by purchase, redemption, or other acquisition of the corporation's shares, as of the earlier of (i) the date money or other property is transferred or debt incurred by the corporation or (ii) the date the shareholder ceases to be a shareholder with respect to the acquired shares;

(2) in the case of any other distribution of indebtedness, as of the date the indebtedness is distributed; and

(3) in all other cases, as of (i) the date the distribution is authorized if the payment occurs within 120 days after the date of authorization or (ii) the date the payment is made if it occurs more than 120 days after the date of authorization.

(f) A corporation's indebtedness to a shareholder incurred by reason of a distribution made in accordance with this section is at parity with the corporation's indebtedness to its general, unsecured creditors except to the extent subordinated by agreement.

(g) Indebtedness of a corporation, including indebtedness issued as a distribution, is not considered a liability for purposes of determinations under subsection (c) if its terms provide that payment of principal and interest are made only if and to the extent that payment of a distribution to shareholders could then be made under this section. If the indebtedness is issued as a distribution, each payment of principal or interest is treated as a distribution, the effect of which is measured on the date the payment is actually made.

237

EXAMPLE

Delaware General Corporation Law

§160: Corporation's powers respecting ownership, voting, etc., of its own stock; rights of stock called for redemption

(a) Every corporation may purchase, redeem, receive, take or otherwise acquire, own and hold, sell, lend, exchange, transfer or otherwise dispose of, pledge, use and otherwise deal in and with its own shares; provided, however, that no corporation shall:

(1) Purchase or redeem its own shares of capital stock for cash or other property when the capital of the corporation is impaired or when such purchase or redemption would cause any impairment of the capital of the corporation, except that a corporation other than a nonstock corporation may purchase or redeem out of capital any of its own shares which are entitled upon any distribution of its assets, whether by dividend or in liquidation, to a preference over another class or series of its stock, or, if no shares entitled to such a preference are outstanding, any of its own shares, if such shares will be retired upon their acquisition and the capital of the corporation reduced in accordance with §§243 and 244 of this title. Nothing in this subsection shall invalidate or otherwise affect a note, debenture or other obligation of a corporation given by it as consideration for its acquisition by purchase, redemption or exchange of its shares of stock if at the time such note, debenture or obligation was delivered by the corporation its capital was not then impaired or did not thereby become impaired;

(2) Purchase, for more than the price at which they may then be redeemed, any of its shares which are redeemable at the option of the corporation; or

a. In the case of a corporation other than a nonstock corporation, redeem any of its shares, unless their redemption is authorized by §151(b) of this title and then only in accordance with such section and the certificate of incorporation, or

b. In the case of a nonstock corporation, redeem any of its membership interests, unless their redemption is authorized by the certificate of incorporation and then only in accordance with the certificate of incorporation.

(b) Nothing in this section limits or affects a corporation's right to resell any of its shares theretofore purchased or redeemed out of surplus and which have not been retired, for such consideration as shall be fixed by the board of directors.

(c) Shares of its own capital stock belonging to the corporation or to another corporation, if a majority of the shares entitled to vote in the election of directors of such other corporation is held, directly or indirectly, by the corporation, shall neither be entitled to vote nor be counted for quorum purposes. Nothing in this section shall be construed as limiting the right of any corporation to vote stock, including but not limited to its own stock, held by it in a fiduciary capacity.

(d) Shares which have been called for redemption shall not be deemed to be outstanding shares for the purpose of voting or determining the total number of shares entitled to vote on any matter on and after the date on which written notice of redemption has been sent to holders thereof and a sum sufficient to redeem such shares has been irrevocably deposited or set aside to pay the redemption price to the holders of the shares upon surrender of certificates therefor.

---

§170(a). Dividends

(a) The directors of every corporation, subject to any restrictions contained in its certificate of incorporation, may declare and pay dividends upon the shares of its capital stock either:

(1) Out of its surplus, as defined in and computed in accordance with §§154 and 244 of this title; or

(2) In case there shall be no such surplus, out of its net profits for the fiscal year in which the dividend is declared and/or the preceding fiscal year.

If the capital of the corporation, computed in accordance with §§154 and 244 of this title, shall have been diminished by depreciation in the value of its property, or by losses, or otherwise, to an amount less than the aggregate amount of the capital represented by the issued and outstanding stock of all classes having a preference upon the distribution of assets, the directors of such corporation shall not declare and pay out of such net profits any dividends upon any shares of any classes of its capital stock until the deficiency in the amount of capital represented by the issued and outstanding stock of all classes having a preference upon the distribution of assets shall have been repaired. Nothing in this subsection shall invalidate or otherwise affect a note, debenture or other obligation of the corporation paid by it as a dividend on shares of its stock, or any payment made thereon, if at the time such note, debenture or obligation was delivered by the corporation, the corporation had either surplus or net profits as provided in (a)(1) or (2) of this section from which the dividend could lawfully have been paid.

These statutory limitations have a common law analogue. Courts have held that a corporation cannot make distributions to shareholders if they would make the corporation insolvent. "The common law has long restricted a corporation from redeeming its shares when the corporation is insolvent or would be rendered insolvent by the redemption." *SV Investment Partners, LLC v. ThoughtWorks, Inc.*, 7 A.3d 973 (Del.Ch. 2010), *infra* Chapter 8. Thus, for example, the redemption right of a preferred stockholder cannot impair the rights of creditors and cannot be done if the corporation is insolvent or would be rendered insolvent by the redemption. *See* Richard M. Buxbaum, *Preferred Stock-Law and Draftsmanship*, 42 Cal. L. Rev. 243, 264 (1954) ("A contract of compulsory redemption is interpreted to require redemption 'if the company is not insolvent or will not thereby become insolvent' (or harm creditors or impair capital).").

The following case involves a repurchase of shares in connection with the acquisition of the company. The question is whether the company was solvent after a share repurchase that was debt financed.

Klang v. Smith's Food & Drug Centers, Inc.
702 A.2d 150 (Del. 1997)

VEASEY, Chief Justice:

This appeal calls into question the actions of a corporate board in carrying out a merger and self-tender offer. Plaintiff in this purported class action alleges that a corporation's repurchase of shares violated the statutory prohibition against the impairment of capital.

No corporation may repurchase or redeem its own shares except out of "surplus," as statutorily defined, or except as expressly authorized by provisions of the statute not relevant here. Balance sheets are not, however, conclusive indicators of surplus or a lack thereof. Corporations may revalue assets to show surplus, but perfection in that process is not required. Directors have reasonable latitude to depart from the balance sheet to calculate surplus, so long as they evaluate assets and liabilities in good faith, on the basis of acceptable data, by methods that they reasonably believe reflect present values, and arrive at a determination of the surplus that is not so far off the mark as to constitute actual or constructive fraud.

We hold that the Court of Chancery was correct in finding that there was no impairment of capital and there were no disclosure violations. We affirm.

Smith's Food & Drug Centers, Inc. ("SFD") owns and operates a chain of supermarkets in the Southwestern United States. Slightly more than three years ago, Jeffrey Smith, SFD's Chief Executive Officer, began to entertain suitors with an interest in acquiring SFD. At the time, and until the transactions at issue, Smith and his family held common and preferred stock constituting 62.1% voting control of SFD. Plaintiff and the class he purports to represent are holders of common stock in SFD.

SFD entered into an agreement with The Yucaipa Companies, a California partnership also active in the supermarket industry. Under the agreement, the following would take place:

1. Smitty's Supermarkets, Inc. ("Smitty's"), a wholly-owned subsidiary of Yucaipa that operated a supermarket chain in Arizona, was to merge into Cactus Acquisition, Inc. ("Cactus"), a subsidiary of SFD, in exchange for which SFD would deliver to Yucaipa slightly over 3 million newly-issued shares of SFD common stock;

2. SFD was to undertake a recapitalization, in the course of which SFD would assume a sizable amount of new debt, retire old debt, and offer to repurchase up to fifty percent of its outstanding shares (other than those issued to Yucaipa) for $36 per share; and

3. SFD was to repurchase 3 million shares of preferred stock from Jeffrey Smith and his family.

SFD hired the investment firm of Houlihan Lokey Howard & Zukin to examine the transactions and render a solvency opinion. Houlihan eventually issued a report to the SFD Board replete with assurances that the transactions would not endanger SFD's solvency, and would not impair SFD's capital in violation of 8 *Del.C.* §160. In reliance on the Houlihan opinion, SFD's Board determined that there existed sufficient surplus to consummate the transactions, and enacted a resolution proclaiming as much. SFD's stockholders voted to approve the transactions, which closed on that day. The self-tender offer was over-subscribed, so SFD repurchased fully fifty percent of its shares at the offering price of $36 per share.

A corporation may not repurchase its shares if, in so doing, it would cause an impairment of capital, unless expressly authorized by Section 160. Section 160(a) provides:

> (a) Every corporation may purchase, redeem, receive, take or otherwise acquire, own and hold, sell, lend exchange, transfer or otherwise dispose of, pledge, use and otherwise deal in and with its own shares; provided, however, that no corporation shall:

(1) Purchase or redeem its own shares of capital stock for cash or other property when the capital of the corporation is impaired or when such purchase or redemption would cause any impairment of the capital of the corporation, except that a corporation may purchase or redeem out of capital any of its own shares which are entitled upon any distribution of its assets, whether by dividend or in liquidation, to a preference over another class or series of its stock, or, if no shares entitled to such a preference are outstanding, any of its own shares, if such shares will be retired upon their acquisition and the capital of the corporation reduced in accordance with §§243 and 244 of this title.

A repurchase impairs capital if the funds used in the repurchase exceed the amount of the corporation's "surplus," defined by 8 *Del.C.* §154 to mean the excess of net assets over the par value of the corporation's issued stock. Section 154 provides, "Any corporation may, by resolution of its board of directors, determine that only a part of the consideration . . . received by the corporation for . . . its capital stock . . . shall be capital. . . . The excess . . . of the net assets of the corporation over the amount so determined to be capital shall be surplus. Net assets means the amount by which total assets exceed total liabilities. Capital and surplus are not liabilities for this purpose."

Plaintiff asked the Court of Chancery to rescind the transactions in question as violative of Section 160. Plaintiff's position breaks down into two analytically distinct arguments. First, he contends that SFD's balance sheets constitute conclusive evidence of capital impairment. He argues that the negative net worth that appeared on SFD's books following the repurchase compels us to find a violation of Section 160. Second, he suggests that even allowing the Board to "go behind the balance sheet" to calculate surplus does not save the transactions from violating Section 160. In connection with this claim, he attacks the SFD Board's off-balance-sheet method of calculating surplus on the theory that it does not adequately take into account all of SFD's assets and liabilities. Moreover, he argues that the May 17, 1996 resolution of the SFD Board conclusively refutes the Board's claim that revaluing the corporation's assets gives rise to the required surplus. We hold that each of these claims is without merit.

SFD's balance sheets do not establish a violation of 8 Del.C. §160

In a proxy statement, the SFD Board released a pro forma balance sheet showing that the merger and self-tender offer would result in a deficit to surplus on SFD's books of more than $100 million. A balance sheet the SFD Board issued shortly after the transactions confirmed this result. Plaintiff asks us to adopt an interpretation of 8 *Del.C.* §160 whereby balance-sheet net worth is controlling for purposes of determining compliance with the statute. Defendants do not dispute that SFD's books showed a negative net worth in the wake of its transactions with Yucaipa, but argue that corporations should have the presumptive right to revalue assets and liabilities to comply with Section 160.

Plaintiff advances an erroneous interpretation of Section 160. We understand that the books of a corporation do not necessarily reflect the current values of its assets and liabilities. Among other factors, unrealized appreciation or depreciation can render book numbers inaccurate. It is unrealistic to hold that a corporation is bound by its balance sheets for purposes of determining compliance with Section 160. We adhere to the principles allowing corporations to revalue properly its assets and liabilities to show a surplus and thus conform to the statute.

It is helpful to recall the purpose behind Section 160. The General Assembly enacted the statute to prevent boards from draining corporations of assets to the detriment of creditors and the long-term health of the corporation. That a corporation has not yet realized or reflected on its balance sheet the appreciation of assets is irrelevant to this concern. Regardless of what a balance sheet that has not been updated may show, an actual, though unrealized, appreciation reflects real economic value that the corporation may borrow against or that creditors may claim or levy upon. Allowing corporations to revalue assets and liabilities to reflect current realities complies with the statute and serves well the policies behind this statute.

The SFD Board appropriately revalued corporate assets to comply with 8 Del.C. §160.

Plaintiff contends that SFD's repurchase of shares violated Section 160 even without regard to the corporation's balance sheets. Plaintiff claims that the SFD Board was not entitled to rely on the solvency opinion of Houlihan, which showed that the transactions would not impair SFD's capital given a revaluation of corporate assets. The argument is that the methods that underlay the solvency opinion were inappropriate as a matter of law, because they failed to take into account all of SFD's assets and liabilities. We disagree, and hold that the SFD Board revalued the corporate assets under appropriate methods. Therefore the self-tender offer complied with Section 160.

Houlihan released its solvency opinion to the SFD Board, expressing its judgment that the merger and self-tender offer would not impair SFD's capital. Houlihan reached this conclusion by comparing SFD's "Total Invested Capital" of $1.8 billion—a figure Houlihan arrived at by valuing SFD's assets under the "market multiple" approach—with SFD's long-term debt of $1.46 billion. This comparison yielded an approximation of SFD's "concluded equity value" equal to $346 million, a figure clearly in excess of the outstanding par value of SFD's stock. Thus, Houlihan concluded, the transactions would not violate 8 *Del.C.* §160.

Plaintiff contends that Houlihan's analysis relied on inappropriate methods to mask a violation of Section 160. Noting that 8 *Del.C.* §154 defines "net assets" as "the amount by which total assets exceeds total liabilities," plaintiff argues that Houlihan's analysis is erroneous as a matter of law because of its failure to calculate "total assets" and "total liabilities" as separate variables. In a related argument, plaintiff claims that the analysis failed to take into account all of SFD's liabilities, i.e., that Houlihan neglected to consider current liabilities in its comparison of SFD's "Total Invested Capital" and long-term debt. Plaintiff contends that the SFD Board's resolution proves that adding current liabilities into the mix shows a violation of Section 160. The resolution declared the value of SFD's assets to be $1.8 billion, and stated that its "total liabilities" would not exceed $1.46 billion after the transactions with Yucaipa. As noted, the $1.46 billion figure described only the value of SFD's long-term debt. Adding in SFD's $372 million in current liabilities, plaintiff argues, shows that the transactions impaired SFD's capital.

We believe that plaintiff reads too much into Section 154. The statute simply defines "net assets" in the course of defining "surplus." It does not mandate a "facts and figures balancing of assets and liabilities" to determine by what amount, if any, total assets exceeds total liabilities. The statute is merely definitional. It does not require any particular method of calculating surplus, but simply prescribes factors that any such calculation must include. Although courts may not determine compliance with Section 160 except by methods that fully take into account the assets and liabilities of the corporation, Houlihan's methods were not erroneous as a matter of law simply because they used Total Invested Capital and long-term debt as analytical categories rather than "total assets" and "total liabilities."

We are satisfied that the Houlihan opinion adequately took into account all of SFD's assets and liabilities. Plaintiff points out that the $1.46 billion figure that approximated SFD's long-term debt failed to include $372 million in current liabilities, and argues that including the latter in the calculations dissipates the surplus. In fact, plaintiff has misunderstood Houlihan's methods. The record shows that Houlihan's calculation of SFD's Total Invested Capital is already net of current liabilities. Thus, subtracting long-term debt from Total Invested Capital does, in fact, yield an accurate measure of a corporation's net assets.

The record contains, in the form of the Houlihan opinion, substantial evidence that the transactions complied with Section 160. Plaintiff has provided no reason to distrust Houlihan's analysis. In cases alleging impairment of capital under Section 160, the trial court may defer to the board's measurement of surplus unless a plaintiff can show that the directors "failed to fulfill their duty to evaluate the assets on the basis of acceptable data and by standards which they are entitled to believe reasonably reflect present values." In the absence of bad faith or fraud on the part of the board, courts will not "substitute [our] concepts of wisdom for that of the directors." Here, plaintiff does not argue that the SFD Board acted in bad faith. Nor has he met his burden of showing that the methods and data that underlay the board's analysis are unreliable or that its determination of surplus is so far off the mark as to constitute actual or constructive fraud. Therefore, we defer to the board's determination of surplus, and hold that SFD's self-tender offer did not violate 8 Del.C. §160.

QUESTIONS

1. Why is book value not dispositive of whether there is surplus?
2. What is "Total Invested Capital"? What method did Houlihan use to calculate it?
3. Did Houlihan's method involve an independent calculation of assets and liabilities?

The following cases raise the question of whether mergers and acquisitions transactions can implicate corporation law on improper distributions when the acquisition is heavily debt financed, which is the case in LBOs. LBOs expose the basic conflict between creditors and shareholders. Shareholders benefit from a buyout in the transaction, but creditors assume a leverage capital structure that increases the risk of insolvency. The two cases below reach different conclusions on the question of whether an LBO can result in an improper distribution.

In re C-T of Virginia, Inc.

958 F.dd 606 (4th Cir. 1992)

WILKINSON, Circuit Judge:

This case presents the question of whether the leveraged acquisition of a corporation, structured in the form of a cash-out merger and consummated at arm's length, is subject to restrictions on distributions to shareholders under Virginia law. The case involves an action brought by an official committee of unsecured creditors of a corporation now in bankruptcy against the former directors of that corporation. The creditors, suing on behalf of the corporation, claimed that the leveraged acquisition created an illegal distribution to shareholders under the Virginia Stock Corporation Act, Va.Code Ann. §13.1-601 *et seq.* (1989). We agree with the district court that the merger did not create a distribution under Virginia law and therefore affirm its judgment.

The facts underlying this case are not in dispute. C-T of Virginia, Inc. is engaged in the manufacture, wholesale, and mail-order sale of shoes. Prior to the purchase that is the subject of this action, C-T was a publicly owned corporation whose stock was traded on the over-the-counter market. In April 1985, C-T hired a financial adviser, Prudential-Bache Securities, Inc., to study the strategic alternatives available to the company. Prudential recommended that C-T's management pursue a leveraged buyout ("LBO") of the company. Prudential indicated that an LBO would both realize maximum value for C-T's shareholders and maintain the viability of the post-LBO enterprise.

C-T's board of directors accepted Prudential's recommendation and authorized management to explore the possibility of a management-sponsored LBO at $15 per share. (C-T common stock was trading for $14.25 per share when this authorization was announced.)

C-T received an unsolicited offer from HH Holdings, Inc. Holdings is owned by Sidney Kimmel and Alan Salke. Holdings proposed a cash merger in which C-T shareholders would receive $19 per share of common stock. After the directors announced this offer, several owners of substantial amounts of C-T common stock urged that the directors reject the offer and demand $20 per share instead. Holdings agreed to the merger at $20 per share, and an Agreement in Principle was signed.

The parties formalized the transaction in an Agreement and Plan of Merger. The merger agreement structured the purchase in the form of a reverse triangular merger. For purposes of the merger, Holdings formed HH Acquisition, Inc., a wholly owned subsidiary. The merger agreement provided that Acquisition would merge into C-T, leaving C-T as the surviving corporation wholly owned by Holdings. The funds necessary to purchase all outstanding shares of C-T, about $30 million, would be deposited with the exchange agent, Sovran Bank, before or at the closing of the transaction. At the moment that the merger was effected, the outstanding shares of C-T common stock would be automatically canceled, and the former shareholders would receive the right to submit their canceled stock certificates to Sovran for payment of $20 per canceled share. Also at that time, the directors of C-T would resign and be replaced by Salke, John Baker, and Roland Peters.

The financing for the merger was arranged solely by Holdings. Holdings provided about $4 million of its own money. It obtained the balance, approximately $26 million, in the form of bank loans secured by C-T's assets. The pre-merger directors did not solic proposed financing, negotiate the terms of the financing or of the security, or participate in or authorize the encumbering of C-T's assets. The merger agreement did obligate C-T to provide Holdings, Acquisition, and the financing banks access to C-T's properties, personnel, and books and records and to cooperate with Holdings' efforts to secure financing. Further, the pre-merger directors approved the repurchase of C-T's preferred stock, which was a prerequisite to effectuation of the merger.

C-T's board of directors approved the merger agreement and unanimously voted to recommend that the shareholders approve the merger, which they did. The transaction was consummated as planned. The surviving corporation struggled along for about eighteen months, and it filed for bankruptcy under Chapter 11.

The Official Committee of Unsecured Creditors of C-T filed this action in federal court against the pre-merger directors and officers of the corporation. The complaint alleged that the directors and officers breached their fiduciary duties owed to the corporation and that the directors had approved a distribution in violation of Va.Code Ann. §§13.1-653 and 13.1-692 (1989). [The district court granted the defendants' motion to dismiss on both claims.]

[Analysis]

All states now impose limitations on the power of a corporation to make various distributions to its shareholders, and federal courts must pay strict attention to the language of the relevant state statute.

The Virginia statute defines "distribution" as follows:

"Distribution" means a direct or indirect transfer of money or other property, except its own shares, or incurrence of indebtedness *by a corporation to or for* the benefit of *its* shareholders in respect of any of its shares. A distribution may be in the form of a declaration or payment of a dividend; a purchase, redemption, or other acquisition of shares; a distribution of indebtedness of the corporation; or otherwise.

Va.C. §13.1-603. Not all distributions are unlawful. Rather, a distribution is prohibited only if, after it is made, the corporation fails either of two insolvency tests:

No distribution may be made if, after giving it effect: (1) The corporation would not be able to pay its debts as they become due in the usual course of business; or (2) The corporation's total assets would be less than the sum of its total liabilities plus (unless the articles of incorporation permit otherwise) the amount that would be needed, if the corporation were to be dissolved at the time of the distribution, to satisfy the preferential rights upon dissolution of shareholders whose preferential rights are superior to those receiving the distribution.

Va.C. §13.1-653(C)

We now address the central question in this case: whether the merger involved a distribution to shareholders within the meaning of §13.1-603. We conclude that the transaction does not fall within the statutory definition of distribution and, therefore, that the directors cannot be subjected to potential liability.

Appellant argues that the plain meaning of the statute contradicts the district court's conclusion that the merger did not create a distribution under Virginia law. It claims that the purchase of the premerger shareholders' shares in C-T entailed a distribution because the payment of the purchase price of $20 per share was a "transfer of money . . . by a corporation to . . . its shareholders." Since this purchase was funded primarily through loans secured by the assets of C-T, the argument runs, the value of the corporation—and hence the financial position of its creditors—was diminished. According to appellant, it is irrelevant whether the funds that are transferred to shareholders derive from the corporation's capital surplus, retained earnings, or new loans secured by corporate assets, and it is likewise immaterial that the payment resulted from a cash-out merger.

We do not share appellant's view of the statute. The Virginia Stock Corporation Act provides a precise definition of the word "distribution": "a direct or indirect transfer of money or other property, except its own shares, or incurrence of indebtedness by a corporation to or for the benefit of its shareholders in respect of any of its shares." Payment of the merger consideration to C-T's former shareholders simply does not fit within the plain language of this definition. The key language is the requirement that the transfer of money or property be "by a corporation to . . . *its* shareholders." When post-merger C-T transferred $20 per canceled share to C-T's pre-merger shareholders, they were no longer the corporation's—"its"—shareholders, for their ownership interest had been lawfully canceled as of the effective time of the merger.

We must reject appellant's argument that the encumbering of C-T's assets to raise sufficient funds to pay for the merger was a distribution because it represented the "incurrence of indebtedness by a corporation . . . for the benefit of its shareholders." The financing for the merger was negotiated not by C-T's pre-merger directors for the benefit of C-T's pre-merger shareholders, but by the new owners and directors of the corporation. Moreover, the financing closed simultaneously with the closing of the merger. Accordingly, at the time the encumbering was undertaken, the pre-merger shareholders' ownership interests were canceled and, therefore, C-T did not incur debt "for the benefit of *its* shareholders."

Appellant's attempt to shoehorn the payment of merger consideration into the statutory definition of distribution must thus prove unsuccessful, for its argument fails to appreciate the significance of the fact that the transaction at issue represented the arm's-length purchase of C-T by Holdings. The distribution statute is aimed by its terms at actions taken by a corporation to enrich unjustly its own shareholders at the expense of creditors and to the detriment of the continuing viability of the company. It does not cover third-party payments to acquire the stock of a corporation or the encumbering of assets after a change in corporate ownership, and it is not intended to obstruct an arm's-length acquisition of an enterprise by new owners who have their own plans for commercial success. The reason for this distinction is simple: A corporate acquisition, structured as a merger, is simply a different animal from a distribution. Distribution statutes, as noted above, derive from the regulation of corporate dividends and traditionally apply to situations in which shareholders, after receiving the transfer from the corporation, retain their status as owners of the corporation. Distribution statutes have not been applied to wholesale changes in corporate ownership, as is the case here, and C-T has presented no evidence that the Virginia legislature intended the statutory definition to expand the applicability of distribution restrictions beyond their traditional scope.

Appellant insists, however, that the text of the statute does not exclude from the definition of distribution transfers incident to changes in corporate control. Appellant relies on the fact that §13.1-603 states that "a distribution may be in the form of . . . a purchase, redemption, or other acquisition of shares." This language, however, is not nearly as broad as C-T suggests. To begin with, it is subject to the general requirement that the corporation act for the benefit of *its* shareholders. Further, the language functions in this context to prevent a corporation from disguising a distribution in the form of a partial acquisition of shares—*e.g.*, by "purchasing" twenty-five percent of each shareholder's shares, which would have the effect of transferring corporate assets to the shareholders without the corporation receiving any consideration in exchange and without changing the ownership structure in the slightest. The inclusion of purchases, redemptions, and other acquisitions within the ambit of distributions, therefore, is not an indication that the statutory definition applies when all outstanding shares of the corporation are purchased at a market rate in the course of an arm's-length purchase of the corporation.

It is difficult for us to conceive how distribution restrictions would effectively function in the corporate acquisitions context. In determining whether a proposed distribution is legal, directors must apply two sophisticated insolvency tests. In applying these tests, directors must assess the future business prospects and decisions of the company. When, after a distribution, directors continue to operate the company and set its business policy, such a task is manageable and within their competence. In cases involving corporate acquisitions, however, the pre-acquisition directors typically depart their positions in the corporation after the transaction. Not only do they therefore lack any control over the future course of the company's business, but they also may be fully unaware of new management's plans and strategies. Indeed, the primary rationale for a change in corporate ownership and control is the new owners' belief that, by altering the company's business strategy and structure, they can make the company more profitable than it was under old management. In this situation, it seems both unrealistic and perverse to charge the old directors under the distribution statute with knowledge and responsibility for the actions of the new owners. We cannot believe that the legislature intended such a result.

We also do not share appellant's view that non-application of the distribution statute would be unfair to creditors. In this case, it is possible that the leveraged acquisition of C-T hastened or caused the company's downfall. On the other hand, C-T's creditors may have actually benefitted from the acquisition. The infusion of $4 million in new capital and the presence of a more effective management team may have permitted C-T to survive longer than it otherwise would have and may also have increased the chances that the company would survive over the long-term. In other words, it is impossible to conclude *a priori* whether a leveraged transaction such as that here on balance benefits or harms creditors of the target corporation. It is possible to say, however, that a creditor cannot avoid bearing the risk that his debtor will make a bad business decision. Finally, it is important to recognize that, since LBOs are a well-known element in contemporary business life, creditors are well-positioned to protect themselves. "The debtor-creditor relationship is essentially contractual." If a creditor fears the prospect of a future leveraged acquisition of its debtor, it can protect itself by bargaining for security interests or protective provisions in its loan agreements that restrict the ability of its debtor to subject itself to a leveraged acquisition without the creditor's approval.

We note that even if corporate acquisitions are not subject to state distribution restrictions, protection is accorded creditors by the law of creditors' rights, particularly fraudulent conveyance statutes. In contrast to state corporate law, the law of creditors' rights is designed and better equipped to protect creditors in situations such as that presented here. For example, state fraudulent conveyance statutes and federal bankruptcy law, *see* 11 U.S.C. §548(a), enable creditors to recapture transferred funds by attacking the transaction directly. In contrast, distribution restrictions merely impose personal liability on directors, without any provision for a direct recoupment of the distributed assets from the shareholders who received them.

In attacking the transaction here, appellant fails to acknowledge all the risks inherent in it. Holdings' acquisition of C-T was an uncertain financial proposition for C-T's shareholders as well as its creditors. Although the post-merger corporation failed in this case some eighteen months after the leveraged acquisition, it was anything but clear at the time of the transaction that the corporation would enter bankruptcy. Indeed, C-T's new owners were so confident of its future success that they invested $4 million of their own money in it. Thus, had the domestic shoe market rebounded after the acquisition, the market price of a share in C-T may have risen substantially above the $20 that the pre-merger shareholders received. In that situation, the shareholders—not C-T's creditors—would be complaining today. Both this corporate acquisition and the lending of money to pre-merger C-T involved risk—the same risk that inheres in all legitimate business activity. State distribution statutes simply do not authorize courts to rearrange the losses that inevitably result from risks taken in the hope of gains.

In sum, we conclude that Holdings' leveraged acquisition of C-T, accomplished in the form of an arm's-length merger between Holdings' subsidiary Acquisition and C-T, did not create a distribution under Virginia law.

QUESTION

1. Explain how an LBO could be considered in principle to be an improper distribution. In other words, how can an LBO be structured to siphon assets available to unsecured creditors for the benefit of shareholders?

Matter of Munford, Inc.
97 F.3d 456 (11th Cir. 1996)

HATCHETT, Chief Judge:

In this corporate leveraged-buy-out merger case, we affirm the district court's ruling that Georgia's stock distribution and repurchase statutes apply.

In May 1988, the Panfida Group offered to purchase Munford, Inc., a public company on the New York Stock Exchange, through a leverage buy out (LBO) structured as a reverse triangle merger for $18 per share. Under the terms of the proposed merger agreement, the Panfida Group agreed to create Alabama Acquisition Corporation (AAC) and a subsidiary, Alabama Merger Corporation (AMC), and through AAC or AMC deposit the funds necessary to purchase Munford's outstanding stock with Citizens & Southern Trust Company. As evidence of its commitment to purchase Munford, the Panfida Group bought 291,100 of Munford's stock. In June

1988, the Panfida Group also told Munford's board of directors that it, upon the sale of Munford, intended to put additional capital into Munford but would only invest as much as Citibank required to finance the proposed merger.

After consulting its lawyers and financial experts at Shearson Lehman Brothers (Shearson), the board of directors accepted the Panfida Group's offer pending shareholder approval of the purchase agreement. Prior to the directors seeking shareholder approval, the Panfida Group learned that Munford had potential environmental liability. Consequently, the Panfida Group reduced the purchase price from $18.50 a share to $17 a share. The shareholders approved the merger plan. The sale of Munford to the Panfida Group closed. Pursuant to the purchase agreement, the LBO transaction converted each share of common stock into the right to receive the merger price of $17 per share and extinguished the shareholders' ownership in Munford Thirteen months after the merger, Munford filed for Chapter 11 proceedings in bankruptcy court.

Munford brought an adversary proceeding in bankruptcy court on behalf of itself and unsecured creditors pursuant to 11 U.S.C. §§544(b) and 1107(a), seeking to avoid transfers of property, disallow claims and recover damages against former shareholders, officers, directors, and Shearson. Munford asserted that the directors violated legal restrictions under Georgia's distribution and share repurchase statutes in approving the LBO merger. Specifically, Munford asserts that the LBO transaction constituted a distribution of corporate assets that rendered Munford insolvent. The directors moved for summary judgment contending that the Georgia distribution and repurchase statutes did not apply to LBO mergers. The district court denied the directors' motion for summary judgment on Munford's stock repurchase and distribution claim, ruling that Georgia's stock distributions and repurchase restrictions applied to LBO transactions.

The sole issue on appeal is whether the district court erred in ruling that Georgia's stock distribution and repurchase statutes apply to a leverage acquisition of a corporation.

Georgia's capital surplus distribution statute provides, in pertinent part:

(a) The board of directors of a corporation may from time to time distribute to shareholders out of capital surplus of the corporation a portion of its assets in cash or property subject to the following [provision]: (1) No such distribution shall be made at a time when the corporation is insolvent or when such distribution would render the corporation insolvent.

O.C.G.A. §14-2-91. Similarly, Georgia's stock repurchasing statute prohibits directors of a corporation from repurchasing the corporation's shares when such purchase would render the corporation insolvent. O.C.G.A. §14-2-92(e). Under both statutes, directors who vote for or assent to a corporate distribution or stock repurchase in violation of these statutes are jointly and severally liable for the amount distributed or paid to the extent the payments violated the restrictions.

The directors argue that Georgia's distribution and repurchase statutes only apply in circumstances where the directors take assets of the corporation and either distribute them to shareholders or use them to repurchase shares. In both cases, the directors assert, control of the company does not change hands and the directors determine the source of the assets used. The directors note that in this case the Panfida Group owned Munford at the completion of the LBO merger and thereafter ran the company. The directors therefore argue that only Georgia's merger statutes apply to this transaction.

The district court denied the directors' motion for summary judgment adopting the reasoning of the bankruptcy court. The bankruptcy court, in analyzing the LBO merger, considered the substance of the transaction and equated the LBO merger to a stock distribution or repurchase, disregarding the fact that Munford had new owners and stockholders as a result of the merger at the time the shareholders received the LBO payments. The bankruptcy court specifically found that (1) the directors "approved or assented to the underlying merger agreement which structured and required payment to the shareholders"; (2) the merger agreement contemplated the Panfida Group's pledging of "virtually all of Munford's assets as collateral" for the loan that funded the LBO payments made to the shareholders; and (3) the directors knew or should have known "the source, purpose, or use of" Munford's assets prior to or at the time the directors approved the merger plan. Based on these findings, the bankruptcy court concluded that a reasonable jury could conclude that the merger rendered Munford insolvent in violation of Georgia's distribution and stock repurchase statutes.

In reaching its conclusion, the bankruptcy court rejected a Fourth Circuit case that refused to apply Virginia's corporate distribution statute to recapture payments made to shareholders pursuant to an LBO merger. *See C-T of Virginia, Inc. v. Barrett*, 958 F.2d 606 (4th Cir. 1992).

The bankruptcy court, in this case, rejected [*C-T of Virginia*], reasoning that the legislature enacted the distribution and share repurchase statutes of the Georgia Code to protect creditors "by prohibiting transfers at a time when a corporation is insolvent or would be rendered insolvent." Such intent, the bankruptcy court noted, "furthers the longstanding principle that creditors are to be paid before shareholders." We agree with the district court and the reasoning of the bankruptcy court and decline to join the Fourth Circuit in holding that "a corporate acquisition, structured as a merger, is simply a different animal from a distribution." *C-T of Virginia*, 958 F.2d at 611.

We note that the LBO transaction in this case did not merge two separate operating companies into one combined entity. Instead, the LBO transaction represented a "paper merger" of Munford and AMC, a shell corporation with very little assets of its own. To hold that Georgia's distribution and repurchase statutes did not apply to LBO mergers such as this, while nothing in these statutes precludes such a result, would frustrate the restrictions imposed upon directors who authorize a corporation to distribute its assets or to repurchase shares from stockholders when such transactions would render the corporation insolvent. We therefore affirm the district court's ruling that Georgia's restrictions on distribution and stock repurchase apply to LBO.

QUESTION

1. *C-T of Virginia* and *Munford* represent a split in authority. Which case has the better argument?

D. OTHER LIMITATIONS ON DISTRIBUTIONS

In addition to limitations on distributions imposed by corporation statutes, there are legal and equitable limitations on distributions. The problems are highly contextual. A distribution may be a poor business decision or may be motivated by reasons other than a business purpose. Stock instruments may grant different rights to different stockholders that limit the authority of the board to declare and pay dividends (these situations are most commonly seen when a corporation has preferred stock, but there may be different classes of common stock raising the same issue). Different shareholders may be treated differently in a distribution or repurchase. In a repurchase, there may be an obligation to disclose the transaction to shareholders.

1. DIVIDENDS

Dividends are declared and paid at the discretion of the board of directors, subject to certain statutory limitations. Section 6.40 of the Model Business Corporation Act provides: "A board of directors may authorize and the corporation may make distributions to its shareholders subject to restriction by the articles of incorporation and the limitation in subsection (c)." Section 170(a) of the Delaware General Corporation Law provides that a board may declare and pay dividends either out of surplus or out of net profits for the current or preceding fiscal year. In addition to these statutory limitations, there are legal and equitable limitations on the board's decisions on dividends and distributions.

Many students in the introductory Business Associations course may have had the chance to read *Dodge v. Ford*, 170 N.W. 668 (Mich. 1919). In this case, John and Horace Dodge were 10 percent shareholders in Ford Motor Company. Henry Ford was 59 percent controlling shareholder. The company was phenomenally successful. The Dodge brothers invested $10,000, which yielded a total return of approximately $35 million over 13 years (about a 100 percent annualized rate of return). In the previous eight years, the company paid out 40 to 60 percent of profit. In 1916, however, the company earned $60 million and paid out only $3.2 million (5 percent payout ratio). The Dodge brothers sued to force the company to pay dividends. The court approvingly quoted an earlier case stating that the board has the exclusive power to declare dividends "unless it is clearly made to appear that they are guilty of fraud or misappropriation of the corporate funds, or refuse to declare a dividend when the corporation has a surplus of net profits which it can, without detriment to its business, divide among its stockholders, and when a refusal to do so would amount to such an abuse of discretion as would constitute a fraud, or breach of that good faith which they are bound to exercise towards the stockholders." The *Dodge* court held that the board of Ford Motor abused its discretion when it withheld dividends, despite enormous accumulation of profits, based on Henry Ford's stated desire "to employ still more men, to spread the benefits of this industrial system to the greatest possible number, to help them build up their lives and their homes." The court held that this was not a proper business purpose, and then declared the famous proposition on shareholder primacy for which the case is largely recognized today: "A business corporation is organized and carried on primarily for the profit of the stockholders. The powers of the directors are to be employed for that end."

The following cases in this section are modern cases dealing with the question of when a board's decision on distributions is proper and thus subject to the business judgment rule, and when a board has abused its discretion or otherwise acted improperly in making a distribution to shareholders.

Kamin v. American Express Co.
86 Misc.2d 809 (N.Y. Sup. 1976)

GREENFIELD, Justice:

The individual defendants, who are the directors of the American Express Company, move for an order dismissing the complaint for failure to state a cause of action, and alternatively, for summary judgment.

The complaint is brought derivatively by two minority stockholders of the American Express Company, asking for a declaration that a certain dividend in kind is a waste of corporate assets, directing the defendants not to proceed with the distribution, or, in the alternative, for monetary damages. The motion to dismiss the complaint requires the Court to presuppose the truth of the allegations.

The complaint alleges that in 1972 American Express acquired for investment 1,954,418 shares of common stock of Donaldson, Lufkin and Jenrette, Inc. (DLJ), a publicly traded corporation, at a cost of $29.9 million. It is further alleged that the current market value of those shares is approximately $4.0 million. On July 28, 1975, the Board of Directors of American Express declared a special dividend to all stockholders of record pursuant to which the shares of DLJ would be distributed in kind. Plaintiffs contend further that if American Express were to sell the DLJ shares on the market, it would sustain a capital loss of $25 million, which could be offset against taxable capital gains on other investments. Such a sale, they allege, would result in tax savings to the company of approximately $8 million, which would not be available in the case of the distribution of DLJ shares to stockholders.

The crucial allegation alleges: "All of the defendant Directors engaged in or acquiesced in or negligently permitted the declaration and payment of the Dividend in violation of the fiduciary duty owed by them to Amex to care for and preserve Amex's assets in the same manner as a man of average prudence would care for his own property."

There is no claim of fraud or self-dealing, and no contention that there was any bad faith or oppressive conduct. The law is quite clear as to what is necessary to ground a claim for actionable wrongdoing. "In actions by stockholders, which assail the acts of their directors or trustees, courts will not interfere unless the powers have been illegally or unconscientiously executed; or unless it be made to appear that the acts were fraudulent or collusive, and destructive of the rights of the stockholders. Mere errors of judgment are not sufficient as grounds for equity interference, for the powers of those entrusted with corporate management are largely discretionary."

The question of whether or not a dividend is to be declared or a distribution of some kind should be made is exclusively a matter of business judgment for the Board of Directors. "Courts will not interfere with such discretion unless it be first made to appear that the directors have acted or are about to act in bad faith and for a dishonest purpose. It is for the directors to say, acting in good faith of course, when and to what extent dividends shall be declared * * * The statute confers upon the directors this power, and the minority stockholders are not in a position to question this right, so long as the directors are acting in good faith * * *"

A complaint must be dismissed if all that is presented is a decision to pay dividends rather than pursuing some other course of conduct. A complaint which alleges merely that some course of action other than that pursued by the Board of Directors would have been more advantageous gives rise to no cognizable cause of action. Courts have more than enough to do in adjudicating legal rights and devising remedies for wrongs. The directors' room rather than the courtroom is the appropriate forum for thrashing out purely business questions which will have an impact on profits, market prices, competitive situations, or tax advantages.

It is not enough to allege, as plaintiffs do here, that the directors made an imprudent decision, which did not capitalize on the possibility of using a potential capital loss to offset capital gains. More than imprudence or mistaken judgment must be shown. "Questions of policy of management, expediency of contracts or action, adequacy of consideration, lawful appropriation of corporate funds to advance corporate interests, are left solely to their honest and unselfish decision, for their powers therein are without limitation and free from restraint, and the exercise of them for the common and general interests of the corporation may not be questioned, although the results show that what they did was unwise or inexpedient."

The objections raised by the plaintiffs to the proposed dividend action were carefully considered and unanimously rejected by the Board at a special meeting called precisely for that purpose at the plaintiffs' request. The minutes of the special meeting indicate that the defendants were fully aware that a sale rather than a distribution of the DLJ shares might result in the realization of a substantial income tax saving. Nevertheless, they concluded that there were countervailing considerations primarily with respect to the adverse effect such a sale, realizing a loss of $25 million, would have on the net income figures in the American Express financial statement. Such a reduction of net income would have a serious effect on the market value of the publicly traded American Express stock. This was not a situation in which the defendant directors totally overlooked facts called to their attention. They gave them consideration, and attempted to view the total picture in arriving at their decision. While plaintiffs contend that according to their accounting consultants the loss on the DLJ stock would still have to be charged against current earnings even if the stock were distributed, the defendants' accounting experts assert that the loss would be a charge against earnings only in the event of a sale, whereas in the event of distribution of the stock as a dividend, the proper accounting treatment would be to charge the loss only against surplus.

What we have here as revealed both by the complaint and by the affidavits and exhibits, is that a disagreement exists between two minority stockholders and a unanimous Board of Directors as to the best way to handle a loss already incurred on an investment. The directors are entitled to exercise their honest business judgment on the information before them, and to act within their corporate powers. That they may be mistaken, that other courses of action might have differing consequences, or that their action might benefit some shareholders more than others presents no basis for the superimposition of judicial judgment, so long as it appears that the directors have been acting in good faith. The question of to what extent a dividend shall be declared and the manner in which it shall be paid is ordinarily subject only to the qualification that the dividend be paid out of surplus. The Court will not interfere unless a clear case is made out of fraud, oppression, arbitrary action, or breach of trust. The plaintiffs have failed as a matter of law to make out an actionable claim.

QUESTIONS

1. Was the board's decision on the distribution of DLJ shares economically justifiable?
2. What is the standard that applies to the decision of the board as to dividend policy and distribution decisions?
3. The court stated that the case was really "a disagreement [that] exists between two minority stockholders and a unanimous Board of Directors as to the best way to handle *a loss already incurred on an investment.*" Assume a semi-strong efficient capital market where knowledge of the value of DLJ can be fairly inferred in light of public disclosures and knowledge of DLJ's performance as an investment bank. What should have occurred to American Express's share price? Assuming a semi-strong efficient capital market, how should we assess a board decision based on the concern that lower earnings will negatively affect the stock price?

NOTE

1. DLJ eventually became a prominent investment bank in the 1990s. In the era of Wall Street consolidation, it was acquired by Credit Suisse for $11.5 billion in November 2000. Of course, American Express could not have known this in 1975 when it made the decision to divest.

Sinclair Oil Corp. v. Levien
280 A.2d 717 (Del. 1971)

WOLCOTT, Chief Justice.

This is an appeal by the defendant, Sinclair Oil Corporation (hereafter Sinclair), from an order of the Court of Chancery in a derivative action requiring Sinclair to account for damages sustained by its subsidiary, Sinclair Venezuelan Oil Company (hereafter Sinven), organized by Sinclair for the purpose of operating in Venezuela, as a result of dividends paid by Sinven.

Sinclair, operating primarily as a holding company, is in the business of exploring for oil and of producing and marketing crude oil and oil products. At all times relevant to this litigation, it owned about 97% of Sinven's stock. The plaintiff owns about 3000 of 120,000 publicly held shares of Sinven. Sinven, incorporated in 1922, has been engaged in petroleum operations primarily in Venezuela and since 1959 has operated exclusively in Venezuela.

Sinclair nominates all members of Sinven's board of directors. The Chancellor found as a fact that the directors were not independent of Sinclair. Almost without exception, they were officers, directors, or employees of corporations in the Sinclair *h/c conflict of interest*

complex. By reason of Sinclair's domination, it is clear that Sinclair owed Sinven a fiduciary duty. Sinclair concedes this.

The Chancellor held that because of Sinclair's fiduciary duty and its control over Sinven, its relationship with Sinven must meet the test of intrinsic fairness. The standard of intrinsic fairness involves both a high degree of fairness and a shift in the burden of proof. Under this standard the burden is on Sinclair to prove, subject to careful judicial scrutiny, that its transactions with Sinven were objectively fair.

When the situation involves a parent and a subsidiary, with the parent controlling the transaction and fixing the terms, the test of intrinsic fairness, with its resulting shifting of the burden of proof, is applied. The basic situation for the application of the rule is the one in which the parent has received a benefit to the exclusion and at the expense of the subsidiary.

A parent does indeed owe a fiduciary duty to its subsidiary when there are parent-subsidiary dealings. However, this alone will not evoke the intrinsic fairness standard. This standard will be applied only when the fiduciary duty is accompanied by self-dealing—the situation when a parent is on both sides of a transaction with its subsidiary. Self-dealing occurs when the parent, by virtue of its domination of the subsidiary, causes the subsidiary to act in such a way that the parent receives something from the subsidiary to the exclusion of, and detriment to, the minority stockholders of the subsidiary.

The plaintiff argues that, from 1960 through 1966, Sinclair caused Sinven to pay out such excessive dividends that the industrial development of Sinven was effectively prevented, and it became in reality a corporation in dissolution.

From 1960 through 1966, Sinven paid out $108,000,000 in dividends ($38,000,000 in excess of Sinven's earnings during the same period). The Chancellor held that Sinclair caused these dividends to be paid during a period when it had a need for large amounts of cash. Although the dividends paid exceeded earnings, the plaintiff concedes that the payments were made in compliance with 8 Del.C. §170, authorizing payment of dividends out of surplus or net profits. However, the plaintiff attacks these dividends on the ground that they resulted from an improper motive—Sinclair's need for cash. The Chancellor, applying the intrinsic fairness standard, held that Sinclair did not sustain its burden of proving that these dividends were intrinsically fair to the minority stockholders of Sinven.

Since it is admitted that the dividends were paid in strict compliance with 8 Del.C. §170, the alleged excessiveness of the payments alone would not state a cause of action. Nevertheless, compliance with the applicable statute may not, under all circumstances, justify all dividend payments. If a plaintiff can meet his burden of proving that a dividend cannot be grounded on any reasonable business objective, then the courts can and will interfere with the board's decision to pay the dividend.

Sinclair contends that it is improper to apply the intrinsic fairness standard to dividend payments even when the board which voted for the dividends is completely dominated.

We do not accept the argument that the intrinsic fairness test can never be applied to a dividend declaration by a dominated board, although a dividend declaration by a dominated board will not inevitably demand the application of the intrinsic fairness standard. If such a dividend is in essence self-dealing by the parent, then the intrinsic fairness standard is the proper standard. For example, suppose a parent dominates a subsidiary and its board of directors. The subsidiary has outstanding two classes of stock, X and Y. Class X is owned by the parent and Class Y is owned by minority stockholders of the subsidiary. If the subsidiary, at the direction of the parent, declares a dividend on its Class X stock only, this might well be self-dealing by the parent. It would be receiving something from the subsidiary to the exclusion of and detrimental to its minority stockholders. This self-dealing, coupled with the parent's fiduciary duty, would make intrinsic fairness the proper standard by which to evaluate the dividend payments.

Consequently it must be determined whether the dividend payments by Sinven were, in essence, self-dealing by Sinclair. The dividends resulted in great sums of money being transferred from Sinven to Sinclair. However, a proportionate share of this money was received by the minority shareholders of Sinven. Sinclair received nothing from Sinven to the exclusion of its minority stockholders. As such, these dividends were not self-dealing. We hold therefore that the Chancellor erred in applying the intrinsic fairness test as to these dividend payments. The business judgment standard should have been applied.

We conclude that the facts demonstrate that the dividend payments complied with the business judgment standard and with 8 Del.C. §170. The motives for causing the declaration of dividends are immaterial unless the plaintiff can show that the dividend payments resulted from improper motives and amounted to waste. The plaintiff contends only that the dividend payments drained Sinven of cash to such an extent that it was prevented from expanding.

QUESTIONS

1. How do the business judgment rule and the intrinsic fairness standards apply to the board's decision to declare dividends?
2. Suppose the plaintiff was able to prove that the declaration of dividends was an extremely poor decision in light of Sinven's business and financial needs. What would be the result?
3. The court stated that the motive was immaterial unless there was an "improper motive." What is an "improper motive"?

Gabelli & Co. Profit Sharing Plan v. Liggett Group, Inc.
479 A.2d 276 (Del. 1984)

HERRMANN, Chief Justice:

This appeal from the Court of Chancery involves a class action brought by a minority stockholder to compel the payment of a dividend on the theory that the majority stockholder breached its fiduciary duty to the minority stockholders by causing the corporation to refrain from declaring the dividend solely for the purpose of enabling the majority stockholder to obtain the dividend funds for itself after a merger of the corporation with a wholly-owned subsidiary of the majority stockholder and a cash-out of the minority stockholders. The Court of Chancery granted summary judgment in favor of the defendants. We affirm.

In April 1980, the defendant GM Sub Corporation ("GM Sub"), a wholly-owned subsidiary of defendant Grand Metropolitan Limited ("Grand Met") formed to acquire the defendant Liggett Group, Inc. ("Liggett"), commenced a tender offer for "any and all" of Liggett's approximately 8.4 million common shares at [the price of $69 per share]. In the first quarter of 1980, Liggett common stock traded on the New York Stock Exchange in the range of $34.125 to $41.75 per share.

On May 15, Liggett's Board of Directors resolved to approve GM Sub's amended offer of $69 and to recommend that it be accepted by Liggett's shareholders as a fair price.

The Offer to Purchase sent to Liggett stockholders in connection with the tender offer stated that Grand Met and GM Sub intended "as promptly as possible [after the conclusion of the tender offer] to seek to have [Liggett] consummate a merger with [GM Sub] or an affiliate of [GM Sub]." Further, it was stated in the Offer that GM Sub intended to pay the tender offer price of $69 per share in connection with the merger cash-out of shares not tendered.

GM Sub acquired 87.4% of Liggett's outstanding common stock. Gabelli & Co., Inc. Profit Sharing Plan did not tender its 800 shares in response to the offer.

Immediately following consummation of the tender offer, preparations for the merger were commenced. On June 30, the Liggett Board approved the Merger Agreement.

The stockholders' meeting approving the merger was held on August 7, and the merger became effective on that date. The minority shareholders who were merged out in August received the same $69 per share price paid to the shareholders who tendered their shares in June. Gabelli surrendered its shares in the merger cash-out and accepted the $69 price.

Historically, Liggett had paid quarterly dividends to its common shareholders in an amount of $0.625 per share in March, June, September and December of each year. On June 2, 1980, prior to the consummation of the merger and during the pendency of the tender offer, a quarterly dividend of $0.625 per share was paid to the holders of Liggett common stock as of a record date of May 15, 1980. The dividend at issue in this case is a third-quarter dividend, which in prior years had been declared in late July, with a mid-August record date and payment in September. No such dividend was declared or paid to Liggett stockholders for the third quarter of 1980. The merger transaction involved approximately 300 million dollars; the dividends claimed on behalf of the minority stockholders involved approximately $677,000.

Gabelli brought this action to compel Liggett's Board to declare a third-quarterly dividend for 1980. Gabelli there alleged that "Grand Met, by reason of its majority and controlling position in Liggett, owes a fiduciary duty to Liggett's minority share-holders," and that "Grand Met is breaching its fiduciary duty to Liggett's minority shareholders by causing Liggett to eliminate its regular dividend to enable Grand Met to obtain the Liggett dividend money for itself upon the merger of Liggett and Grand Met." The prayer of the complaint was for judgment "requiring that Liggett pay the omitted quarterly dividend of $0.625 per share." The complaint did not seek to enjoin the consummation of the merger or attack the fairness of the price offered.

In our view, this case commenced as, and continues to be, no more nor less than an action to compel the declaration and payment of a dividend by the Board of Directors of Liggett for the benefit of about 13% of its stockholders who were then in the final stages of being cashed-out in a merger transaction for a price conceded to be fair for the acquisition of all of the assets of Liggett.

As so simplified, it is abundantly clear upon the undisputed facts that summary judgment for the defendants was correctly granted.

There is no showing by the plaintiff that, given the extraordinary circumstances existing in Liggett's affairs in late July 1980, the Board of Liggett abused its discretion in the exercise of its business judgment by not declaring a third-quarter dividend in accord with the corporation's dividend history of prior years. In the absence of such showing, the plaintiff may not prevail in this action to compel the dividend.

It is settled law in this State that the declaration and payment of a dividend rests in the discretion of the corporation's board of directors in the exercise of its business judgment; that, before the courts will interfere with the judgment of the board of directors in such matter, fraud or gross abuse of discretion must be shown.

Gabelli has not alleged fraud; and it has made no showing that the failure of Liggett's Board to declare a third-quarter dividend is explicable only on the theory of a gross or oppressive abuse of discretion. Gabelli took no discovery in this case.

On the record before us, the non-payment of a final dividend by the Liggett Board in the final stages of the cash-out merger, is reasonably "explicable" for at least 2 reasons: (1) It would have been unfair to the holders of 87% of the stock, who accepted the tender offer upon the recommendation of the Board, to reward by a "farewell" or "bonus" dividend the holders of the remaining 13% who, for some unannounced reason, declined to accept the tender-offer and held out for the merger cash-out with the risk-free assurance of receiving the same price per share; and (2) It would have been unreasonable to supplement the $69 per share, which had been approved by the Board as a fair price for Liggett and all of its assets, by a last minute dividend declared in the final stages of the merger cash-out process.

Gabelli has summarized the crux of its case as follows: "Simply put, plaintiff does not urge that the Liggett board of directors was necessarily required to pay the July 1980 dividend. Instead, plaintiff claims that Grand Met, for its own gain, wrongfully prevented Liggett from declaring a dividend it would otherwise have declared."

The plaintiff has placed nothing on this record to raise a genuine issue of material fact as to whether (1) Grand Met actually "prevented" the Liggett Board from declaring the dividend; or (2) the Liggett Board actually would have "otherwise" declared the dividend. The undisputed facts before us, and the reasonable inferences to be drawn therefrom, are to the contrary.

Gabelli has attempted to avoid the force and effect of the law governing the declaration of dividends, and to overcome its failure to show any material issue of fact suggesting an abuse of discretion by the Liggett Board, by the claim that Grand Met, in its position as dominant majority stockholder, engaged in self-dealing such as to require that its conduct be subjected to the "intrinsic fairness" test discussed by this Court in *Sinclair Oil Corp. v. Levien*, 280 A.2d 717 (Del. 1971).

The plaintiff rests its entire case upon the statement in *Sinclair* that self-dealing "occurs when the parent, by virtue of its domination of the subsidiary, causes the subsidiary to act in such a way that the parent receives something from the subsidiary to the exclusion of, and detriment to, the minority stockholders of the subsidiary." Upon that basis, Gabelli builds the contention that the conduct of the defendants is not to be tested by the business judgment rule under which a court will not interfere with the judgment of a board of directors unless there is a showing of gross and palpable overreaching, and as to which the plaintiff has the burden of proof; that, by reason of the applicability of the intrinsic fairness test, the burden of proof shifts in this case to the defendants to prove, subject to judicial scrutiny, that the conduct under attack was objectively fair. Gabelli's position is manifestly untenable.

All such contentions are based upon the assumption that, under the law and the facts of this case, Gabelli had a right or entitlement to a third-quarter dividend which Grand Met "usurped," "retained," or "misappropriated."

The record does not justify any such assumption for the following reasons: (1) Gabelli had no right or entitlement to a third-quarter dividend in the absence of a declaration thereof, especially under the extraordinary circumstances of this case; (2) Gabelli was not prevented from tendering its shares and receiving full payment therefor promptly, the tender offer being for "any and all" shares; (3) Gabelli had no valid reason in July to expect extra compensation for its stock, by dividend or otherwise, over and above that paid to the great majority of its fellow stockholders in June; (4) The merger price of $69 per share, conceded here to have been a fair price for all assets of Liggett including cash on hand, fully compensated Gabelli for its shares, including any right to receive any additional dividends.

QUESTIONS

1. What might have been the pragmatic business and legal reason why the board did not declare the third quarter dividend so that the 13 percent of shareholders can get another dividend payment?
2. Suppose Grand Met and the board of Liggett had discussed dividends, and Grand Met had communicated that it did not want Liggett to declare dividends in the third quarter on the view that it preferred that Liggett preserve the cash. Would the plaintiffs necessarily prevail? What standard would apply to the board's decision?
3. Suppose Liggett Group has declared quarterly dividends for the past 20 years. What would be the result?

Wertheim Schroder & Co. Inc. v. Avon
1993 WL 126427 (S.D.N.Y. 1993)

LEISURE, District Judge,

This action arises out of the issuance by defendant Avon Products, Inc. of a new series of preferred stock entitled Preferred Equity–Redemption Cumulative Stock (the "PERCS") in June 1988. Plaintiff Wertheim Schroder & Co., a PERCS holder, alleges in the Amended Complaint that Avon's declaration of two common stock dividends on February 7, 1991, or the subsequent payment of a quarterly dividend on March 1, 1991, triggered the Accelerated Redemption of the PERCS pursuant to the terms upon which the PERCS were issued. [The amended complaint alleges a cause of action for breach of contract under New York law.]

Defendant Avon moves for summary judgment with respect to all claims asserted in the amended complaint. The Court hereby denies Avon's motion for summary judgment as to the breach of contract claim.

Avon is one of the world's leading manufacturers and marketers of beauty products. In 1979, Avon decided to expand beyond its core business and, over the next several years, acquired numerous and diverse businesses such as Tiffany & Co., health care facilities, medical supply companies, drug and alcohol abuse treatment centers, nursing homes, and clothing catalogs. In the late 1980s, Avon began to retreat from this ambitious expansion program. Thus, in 1988, Avon developed a restructuring program with several components: (1) the sale of various health care and related businesses; (2) the expansion of Avon's core beauty products business; and (3) the repayment of debt.

As part of the restructuring program, the Avon board decided that, in an effort to conserve cash needed to retire debt, Avon's annual cash dividend on its common stock would be reduced from $2 to $1 per share. However, Avon's financial adviser, Morgan Stanley & Co., advised Avon that this substantial reduction in the common stock dividend would likely lead to a significant decrease in Avon's stock price. In order to avoid this decrease in the stock price, Morgan Stanley recommended that, at the time Avon announced the dividend reduction, Avon should also announce the issuance of a new class of stock, PERCS, which would provide shareholders with the option of continuing to receive the $2 per share dividend in exchange for a limitation on capital appreciation.

Avon announced (1) that it was cutting the annual dividend on its common stock from $2 to $1 per share, and (2) that it was offering its common shareholders the opportunity to exchange, on a one-to-one basis, up to eighteen million shares (approximately 25 percent) of the common stock for PERCS, an entirely new class of voting stock which would provide investors with a continuation of the $2 per share annual dividend for a limited period of time in exchange for certain limitations on capital appreciation. The PERCS would be issued for a maximum term of a little more than three years, with certain specified conditions for earlier redemption. If the PERCS were not subject to an early redemption, they would automatically be converted back into Avon common stock on a share-for-share basis at the end of their maximum term, referred to as "Final Redemption," which would occur on September 1, 1991.

The key component of the PERCS was the continuation of the prior annual dividend of $2 per year in exchange for a limitation on capital appreciation during this period. Avon effectuated this limitation on capital appreciation by incorporating an Optional Redemption into the terms of the PERCS. The Optional Redemption allowed Avon to redeem the PERCS at any time during their term in accordance with a fixed schedule of prices, known as the "Call Price." The Call Price would be set at levels significantly above the market price of the Avon common stock at the time the PERCS were issued and could be paid in either cash or Avon common stock. Thus, if the market price of the Avon common stock rose above the Call Price, Avon would be able to effect an Optional Redemption of the PERCS prior to the end of their term at a value below the then-current market price of Avon common stock.

The rationale behind the issuance of PERCS was that yield-oriented investors, instead of selling their common stock, would be willing to exchange their shares for PERCS, thereby maintaining the $2 annual dividend in exchange for a limitation on capital appreciation. However, there was a concern that the PERCS would not appeal to investors if there was the potential that they would be excluded from any large dividend payout made on the common stock while the PERCS were outstanding, or would be excluded from the consideration received by common stockholders in a merger involving Avon. In order to alleviate the concern that common stockholders might receive some benefit that the PERCS holders would have received if they had retained their common shares, Avon incorporated an Accelerated Redemption provision into the terms of the PERCS. Under this provision, it was agreed that (1) in the event Avon "shall pay" a common stock dividend at a "cumulative rate per annum equal to or greater than $1.50 per share"; or (2) in the event Avon was involved in a merger, consolidation, or similar extraordinary transaction during this period, the Accelerated Redemption provision would be triggered and PERCS holders would be entitled to a one-for-one exchange for common stock (or cash equivalent), plus the payment of a specified premium and accrued and unpaid dividends.

The precise terms upon which the PERCS were issued were set forth in an Amendment to Article IIIB of Avon's Certificate of Incorporation. Article IIIB provided that there were three ways in which redemption would occur: (1) *Final Redemption*—On September 1, 1991, each share of PERCS would be exchanged for one share of common stock if the PERCS were not redeemed previously under either Optional Redemption or Accelerated Redemption; or (2) *Optional Redemption*—At any time prior to September 1, 1991, Avon could redeem PERCS at certain fixed Call Prices, either in cash or its equivalent common shares; or (3) *Accelerated Redemption*—Prior to September 1, 1991, if Avon increased dividends on the common stock to a rate equal to or greater than $1.50 per share, the PERC holders would be entitled to a one-for-one exchange between the PERCS and common stock (or cash equivalent), plus the payment of a specified premium and accrued and unpaid dividends.

The "Exchange Offer" of common shares for PERCS was fully subscribed. After the expiration of the Exchange Offer on July 1, 1988, the 18 million PERCS which Avon had issued were traded on the New York Stock Exchange. Plaintiff Wertheim Schroder, an investment banking firm, became a substantial investor in PERCS. As of February 6, 1991, Wertheim Schroder held approximately 138,000 PERCS which it had acquired in the open market.

The basis for this lawsuit is plaintiff's claim that Avon triggered the Accelerated Redemption Provision on February 7, 1991, as a result of Avon's declaration of two common stock dividends or, in the alternative, that Avon triggered the provision by the payment of the quarterly dividend on March 1, 1991, at the "new dividend rate" in excess of $1.50 per share. More specifically, on February 7, 1991, Avon declared a first quarter common stock dividend of $0.35 per share payable on March 1. At the same time, Avon declared a special dividend of $3.00 per share to be paid on September 16, 1991 to common shareholders of record on September 4, 1991. In addition, Avon indicated that in the future it would continue to declare and pay regular quarterly common stock dividends at the rate of $0.35. Wertheim Schroder argues that the declaration of the $0.35 quarterly dividend and $3.00 special dividend on February 7, 1991 brought the "cumulative rate per annum" above $1.50 and, thus, required Avon to exercise Accelerated Redemption.

On March 1, 1991, Avon paid the quarterly dividend of $0.35 announced on February 7. The quarterly dividend of $0.35 was paid again on June 1, 1991. On June 3, 1991, Avon exercised the Optional Redemption of all PERCS.

Wertheim Schroder alleges that the redemption of the PERCS by Optional Redemption on June 3, 1991, rather than Accelerated Redemption in February 1991, caused damages to the class of PERCS holders in the range of approximately $232,480,296 to $275,378,506.

Plaintiff Wertheim Schroder alleges that Avon had a contractual duty to plaintiff to redeem the PERCS in accordance with the terms set forth in Article IIIB and the Offering Circular and, by its failure to do so, breached the agreement. It is also alleged that Avon, by its conduct, breached the covenant of good faith and fair dealing implied in the investment agreement. The language of Article IIIB at issue in this summary judgment motion is contained in the Accelerated Redemption provision of the PERCS which states in relevant part:

> In the event . . . the Corporation *shall pay* any regular quarterly cash dividend or any other cash dividend with respect to the shares of its Common Stock *at a cumulative rate per annum equal to or greater than $1.50 per share,* then the Corporation shall redeem all outstanding shares of [the PERCS] . . . on the business day next preceding the date fixed as the record date for the determination of holders of shares of Common Stock entitled to receive such cash dividend.

Having carefully considered the language of the Accelerated Redemption provision in the context of the full terms of the PERCS issuance, the Court finds that there are ambiguities contained in the Accelerated Redemption provision which preclude summary judgment on the issue of whether the declaration of February 7, 1991 and/or the subsequent dividend payment on March 1, 1991 triggered the Accelerated Redemption provision.

The Dividend Payment of March 1, 1991 as the Trigger Event

The Court finds that the language of the Accelerated Redemption provision is ambiguous as to whether the quarterly dividend payment of March 1, 1991 triggered the application of the provision. This ambiguity is based, in large part, on the use of the term "cumulative rate per annum." The provision states that Accelerated Redemption would occur in the event that Avon "shall pay" a dividend on its common stock "at a cumulative rate per annum equal to or greater than $1.50 per share. . . ." Avon argues that the term "cumulative rate per annum" for dividends on common stock would be determined as of March 1, 1991 by multiplying the quarterly dividend paid on that date, namely $0.35 per share, by four. Moreover, Avon contends that the special cash dividend of $3.00 per share, payable on September 16, 1991, would be excluded from the "cumulative rate per annum," even though it was declared on February 1, 1991, because it was not payable until after the date for Final Redemption of the PERCS. If the term "cumulative rate per annum" is given this meaning, the rate as of March 1, 1991 (as well as June 1, 1991) would be $1.40 per share and such a rate would not trigger the provision. Thus, while conceding that special dividends are part of the cumulative rate, Avon contends that the focus of the inquiry must be when the special dividend is paid, rather than when it is declared.

In contrast, plaintiff Wertheim Schroder argues that, at any given time, the calculation of the "cumulative rate per annum" for the common stock dividend would include all declared dividend payments payable in the 12–month period. Thus, Wertheim Schroder contends that the special dividend of $3.00 declared on February 7, 1991 and payable on September 16, 1991, would be included in calculating the "cumulative rate per annum" for the common stock at any point after February 7, 1991. Using this definition, as of February 7, 1991, the "cumulative rate per annum" for 1991 included the announced regular and special dividends and, thus, equaled $4.40 per share. Accordingly, Wertheim Schroder argues that the dividend paid on March 1 was paid at a "cumulative rate per annum" of $4.40 and, as a result, triggered the Accelerated Redemption provision.

The Court finds that, after examining the phrase "cumulative rate per annum" in the context of the PERCS agreement as a whole, it is ambiguous as to whether the declaration of a $3.00 special dividend in February 1991, during the term of the PERCS, allows such dividend to immediately become part of the "cumulative rate per annum" of that particular year even though the payment of the dividend would not take place until September 1991, after the term of the PERCS had expired.

As an initial matter, the Court notes that "cumulative rate per annum" is not defined anywhere in Article IIIB or in the Offering Circular relating to the issuance of the PERCS. Avon argues that no definition was necessary because it is abundantly clear from the language of the provision itself that it is only the payment of a dividend, not the declaration of such dividend, which is relevant for purposes of determining whether the Acceleration Provision has been triggered. However, the Court finds that, according to the language of the provision, it is not simply the payment of the dividend of $1.50 or more that triggers the provision, but rather the provision also includes the payment of a smaller dividend at an annual *rate* of $1.50 or more. Thus, once a payment has been made, it is the method of calculating the *rate per annum* which becomes the pivotal focus of the inquiry.

While Avon argues that until a dividend is paid it cannot be part of the "cumulative rate per annum," the Court finds that the terms of the Accelerated Provision do not unambiguously support this position. By defendant's own interpretation of the contractual language, the calculation of the "cumulative rate per annum" would include future undeclared quarterly dividends. For example, if the first quarter dividend for 1991 was $0.35 and there was no declaration of the special dividend or declaration of other future quarterly dividends, then clearly the "cumulative rate per annum" would be $1.40, even though the rate would be based upon three future quarterly dividends of $0.35 for that year which were undeclared at that point in time.

Avon's real contention is that the payment of the quarterly dividend on February 7, 1991 must be treated separately from the declared, but unpaid, $3.00 special dividend for purposes of calculating the "cumulative rate per annum." In other words, Avon argues that the mere *declaration* of a separate special dividend to be paid at a later date cannot be treated as part of the *payment* of the regular quarterly dividend for purposes of calculating the rate per annum. The reasoning behind this distinction is that the language of the provision states that Accelerated Redemption is triggered when "the Corporation *shall pay* any regularly quarterly cash dividend or any other cash dividend . . . at a cumulative rate per annum equal to or greater than $1.50 per share." Thus, the contention is that the *payment* of a regular quarterly dividend allows for the inclusion of such a dividend in the calculation of the "rate per annum" (by multiplying that dividend by four), but a declared special dividend is a separate consideration that does not become part of the cumulative calculation until it is paid.

While defendant Avon has asserted a reasonable interpretation of the contractual language, the Court finds that it is not the *only* reasonable interpretation of the language of the provision. A reasonable factfinder could conclude, as Wertheim Schroder contends, that there is no basis for allowing projected but *undeclared and unpaid* quarterly dividends to be included in the "cumulative rate per annum," while a simultaneous *declared* but unpaid special dividend is not included. The plain meaning of the terms of the provision does not preclude finding that when a corporation pays a quarterly dividend and also has declared that a special dividend will be paid at a later date during that same year, both dividends immediately become part of the cumulative dividend rate for that year despite the fact that the special dividend has not yet been paid. In other words, a reasonable person could conclude that "cumulative rate per annum" is determined by multiplying the last quarterly dividend by four and adding to that any declared special dividends that would be paid prospectively in the twelve-month period. Thus, the payment of the quarterly dividend can be said to be paid at a rate that includes both the remaining unpaid quarterly payments for that year, as well as any declared, but unpaid, special dividend for that year. Under this interpretation, the March 1, 1991 quarterly dividend of $0.35 was paid out at a "cumulative rate per annum" of $4.40 because of the previous declaration of the $3.00 special dividend on February 7, 1991.

The ability for such an interpretation to survive a summary judgment motion is strengthened by the fact that after the February 7 declaration of the special dividend on the common stock, Avon had a legally binding obligation to pay the special dividend. In its Report to the Avon Board addressing the proposed issuance of the PERCS, the Special Committee of the Board recognized that, once declared, a special dividend could not be rescinded by the Board:

> The Special Committee recommends that Avon declare the special cash dividend immediately. Under New York law, once a dividend is declared it becomes a liability of the company and cannot be rescinded by the Board. This would give the shareholders the maximum possible legal certainty of receiving the dividend.

Given that once Avon declared the special dividend on February 7 it had a legal obligation to pay that dividend on the announced future date, an investor could reasonably conclude that, at the time Avon made its first quarterly dividend payment on March 1, 1991, that the payment was being made at a "cumulative rate" for 1991 which now included not only future quarterly dividends for 1991, but also the mandatory special dividend to paid out on September 16, 1991. Thus, one could reasonably interpret the annual dividend rate, as of March 1, 1991, to be $4.40 per share.

The February 7, 1991 Declaration as the Triggering Event

In addition to alleging that the March 1 payment was the triggering event, plaintiff Wertheim Schroder also argues that, given the ambiguity in the terms of the Accelerated Redemption provision, one could interpret the provision as stating that Accelerated Redemption was triggered by the declaration of the special dividend on February 7. The basis for plaintiff's alternative interpretation is the ambiguity in the term "shall pay." Plaintiff contends that the use of the term "shall pay"—as opposed to language such as "pays" or "has paid"—indicates that the provision is triggered by a future intention or obligation to pay. Thus, plaintiff claims that, since the declaration of a dividend constitutes a future intention or obligation to pay, a reasonable interpretation of the Accelerated Provision is that a dividend becomes part of the "cumulative rate per annum" at the time Avon declares that it "shall pay" such a dividend, rather than at the time the actual payment is made.

The Court finds that this alternative argument can be viewed as a reasonable interpretation of the contractual provision. The word "shall", in its normal usage, is used "to express what is inevitable or what seems to be fated or decreed or likely to happen in the future." *Webster's Third New International Dictionary* 2085 (1981). Given this definition, the term "shall pay" would appear to include a future intention or obligation to pay and, thus, one could reasonably interpret the provision as referring not only to the actual payment of dividends, but also the declaration of dividends. The declaration of a dividend is not only an expressed intention to pay such a dividend but, as noted earlier, is also a binding obligation on the Company at the time of its declaration. Therefore, a reasonable investor could interpret the February 7 declaration of dividends—which involved a $0.35 quarterly dividend payable on March 1 and the $3.00 special dividend payable on September 16—as a statement that Avon "shall pay" a cumulative dividend for 1991 of greater than $1.50 and, as a result, triggered the Accelerated Redemption at the time of the declaration.

If Avon wished to make clear that the Accelerated Redemption was only triggered upon actual payment of an offending dividend, rather than the mere declaration of such a dividend, it could have used language such as "in the event the Corporation pays" or "in the event the Corporation has paid." Accordingly, the Court is unable to conclude that the term "shall pay," used in conjunction with the other language of the Accelerated Redemption provision, is of a definite and precise meaning that is unattended by danger of misconception. Instead, the Court finds that the ambiguity creates a reasonable basis for a difference of opinion as to whether the February 7 declaration triggered Accelerated Redemption.

In sum, the Court is unable to conclude that the Accelerated Redemption provision is of such definite and precise meaning that there is no reasonable basis for a difference of opinion under the facts of the instant case. The terms, on their face, do not dictate a particular result with respect to the instant situation where a dividend is declared months in advance of its payment date, especially when there is the added complication that the dividend was declared during the life of the PERCS, but was paid out after the term of the PERCS expired. Thus, the peculiar circumstances of the instant case render the contractual terms ambiguous and susceptible to several reasonable interpretations. Given this ambiguity, the parties must be given an opportunity to present extrinsic evidence, which each side has gathered, to demonstrate what was intended under this investment agreement.

Good Faith and Fair Dealing

Assuming *arguendo* that Avon did not violate the express terms of the PERCS provisions, Wertheim Schroder contends that Avon's "purposeful manipulation of its dividend to circumvent Accelerated Redemption" was a breach of the covenant of good faith and fair dealing. The covenant of good faith and fair dealing is implied in all contracts governed by New York law. The Second Circuit has noted that the covenant of good faith and fair dealing "precludes each party from engaging in conduct that will deprive the other party of the benefits of their agreement." Thus, the covenant of good faith and fair dealing "is violated when a party to a contract acts in a manner that, although not expressly forbidden by any contractual provision, would deprive the other of the right to receive the benefits under their agreement."

In support of its contention that Avon purposefully manipulated the dividend process to the disadvantage of PERCS investors, plaintiff Wertheim Schroder notes that Avon had never before deferred a dividend payment for such an extended period of time. Plaintiff's expert states that there is no apparent precedent in the industry for such a dividend deferral. Thus, plaintiff argues that Avon's invariable practice of declaring and paying dividends in the normal course was an underlying assumption of the investment agreement and that Avon altered this procedure solely for the purpose of depriving plaintiff of benefits that it reasonably expected to receive under the investment agreement. *See* Report of Avon's Special Committee, at 6 ("In order to avoid paying this premium and to preserve Avon's optional redemption rights, the Special Committee recommends that the special dividend be declared as soon as possible, but made payable to holders of record as of September 4, 1991 (immediately after the final redemption of the PERCS)."). According to plaintiff, this declaration of the extraordinary dividend allowed Avon to boost the common stock price and then choose to pay for the Optional Redemption of the PERCS with common stock whose value was inflated by the declaration of a special dividend which had not yet been paid. The alleged result of this procedure was that PERCS holders received fewer common shares on Optional Redemption than they would have received under an Optional Redemption without the impact of the declaration of the special dividend. Thus, plaintiff contends that "a reasonable investor in PERCS was certainly entitled to presume that the timing between the declaration and payment of a dividend would not purposefully be manipulated to inflate the price of the common stock so that Optional Redemption could be exercised on the least favorable terms for investors in PERCS."

Drawing all inferences in plaintiff's favor, the Court finds that plaintiff has raised genuine issues of material fact as to whether Avon's conduct, with respect to the timing of the declaration of the special dividend and payment of that dividend, improperly deprived plaintiff of benefits which were reasonably expected under the terms of the PERCS and, as a result, constituted a breach of the covenant of good faith and fair dealing.

QUESTIONS

1. How would you rewrite the Accelerated Redemption provision to eliminate the ambiguity in favor of the plaintiff?
2. Assume that the Accelerated Redemption provision as rewritten by Avon was the actual original provision at the time when Avon presented the exchange offer. Could Avon have successfully executed the exchange offer?
3. What specific factors contributed to Schroder's successful argument on the good faith and fair dealing issue?

2. STOCK REPURCHASES

A corporation can repurchase shares from shareholders. Since common stock is ubiquitous but preferred stock is not, the typical repurchase involves common stock. For accounting and nomenclature purposes, some jurisdictions call repurchased shares "treasury stock," which is defined as issued stock but not outstanding. The company can resell treasury stock later if it requires capital. Delaware corporation law recognizes this concept of treasury stock. *See* Delaware General Corporation Law §153(c)

("Treasury shares may be disposed of by the corporation for such consideration as may be determined from time to time by the board of directors, or by the stockholders if the certificate of incorporation so provides."). However, the Model Business Corporation Law has eliminated the concept of treasury stock, and repurchased stock is treated simply as "unissued" shares.

EXAMPLE

Model Business Corporation Act

§6.31. Corporation's acquisition of its own shares

   (a) A corporation may acquire its own shares, and shares so acquired constitute authorized but unissued shares.
   (b) If the articles of incorporation prohibit the reissue of the acquired shares, the number of authorized shares is reduced by the number of shares acquired.

There are four ways in which a corporation repurchases shares from shareholders. The most common method is purchasing shares on the open market like any other investor. A company can privately negotiate a stock purchase from an investor that has a significant block of shares (*e.g., see infra*, *Kahn v. Roberts*). Another method is to make a public self-tender offer for a fixed price (*e.g., infra* Chapter 6, *Eisenberg v. Chicago Milwaukee Corp.*). Public shareholders can always sell in the market, and thus self-tenders incentivize tender by offering a premium to the market price, which is usually about 20 percent above pre-announcement market trading price. Lastly, companies can repurchase shares through a Dutch auction. The company sets a series of prices at which it is willing to buy back shares. Shareholders submit bids on how many shares they are willing to sell at the set prices. Then, the company buys back shares at the lowest cost.

A Dutch auction works like this. Liverpool Inc. offers to purchase 100 shares in a Dutch auction at a price range of $9 to $10 per share. The following institutional shareholders submit these offers to tender 120 shares in total:

- Arsenal: 60 shares at $10.00
- Bournemouth: 50 shares at $9.50
- Chelsea: 10 shares at $9.00

Liverpool would buy the lowest offer prices first: Chelsea's 10 shares at $9.00 and Bournemouth's 50 shares at $9.50. Then Liverpool would need to buy 40 shares at $10.00 from Arsenal. Thus, Liverpool would have repurchased 100 shares at the average purchase price of $9.65 per share (= [10 shares x $9.00 + 50 shares x $9.50 + 40 shares x $10.00] ÷ 100 shares).

Both cash dividends and repurchases are distributions of cash to shareholders. What, then, are the differences? There are several considerations in the selection of repurchase over cash dividends.

Tax effects. Cash dividends and repurchases are ways to distribute cash to shareholders. Dividends are taxed to the shareholder at ordinary income rates. Since a repurchase is a sale of the stock, it triggers capital gains tax rates, which are lower than ordinary income tax rates. Moreover, dividends are involuntary in the sense that the board declares and pays dividends. Shareholders have no choice in the matter, and they become subject to taxes. On the other hand, shareholders can control the timing of their tax liability by deciding whether to tender their shares or not.

Shareholder expectations. Repurchases are not as routine as dividends and thus do not create sticky expectations. Ordinary dividends may create expectations and may send market signals of optimism or pessimism upon an increase or decrease in dividends, respectively. By returning cash to shareholders through a repurchase, a company may signal optimism, but the nonregularity of a repurchase may create weaker expectations.

Liquidity and exit. Dividends can create some liquidity for a shareholder, but all shareholders of the same class of stock must in general be treated equally in a dividend. Differential dividend treatment of shareholders within the same class of stocks would probably not receive the business judgment presumption, and it would likely trigger heightened scrutiny of the unequal policy. On the other hand, a repurchase offer can be made broadly (a self-tender offer) or can be targeted to specific shareholders (a privately negotiated block sale). Moreover, dividends cannot create an exit for a shareholder. However, a repurchase is the sale of the stock and thus can create individualized liquidity and exit for shareholders (*see, e.g., infra, Kahan v. United States Sugar Corp.*).

Takeover defense. A repurchase by a target corporation can bid up the acquirer's price. It can also take out of circulation shares owned by those shareholders who were most likely to sell their shares. This would leave the acquirer with a pool of shareholders who are less inclined to tender their shares. By preemptively taking out "easy" shares and leaving "hard" shares, a target company may make an acquisition more expensive or infeasible: *e.g.*, in *Unitrin, Inc. v. American General Corp.*, 651 A.2d 1361, 1370 (Del. 1995), Unitrin sought to defend against a hostile takeover by American General and engaged in a repurchase program. Its public announcement stated that the purpose of the repurchase was to "increase the percentage ownership of those stockholders who choose not to sell." Consider a company that has 100 shares outstanding with 10 shares held by insiders and 90 shares held by the public. Insiders own 10 percent of shares outstanding. In response to an unsolicited takeover bid, if the company repurchases 40 shares, (1) these shares would become unavailable to the acquirer, and (2) insiders would double their percentage ownership to 20 percent of shares outstanding that would vote against the deal.

Market signal. A repurchase may signal management's opinion that the company's stock is undervalued. Management would not repurchase shares if it believed that the stock price was overvalued; if anything, it would be inclined to issue (sell) shares at overvalued prices. Since it has inside information whereas public shareholders do not, a company's repurchase may communicate management's belief that the shares are undervalued.

Capital structure. By reducing cash, dividends and repurchases similarly reduce equity. The balance sheet gets smaller. A reduction in equity also increases the firm's leverage. For example, assume that a firm has the following balance sheet:

- Assets   120
- Liabilities   60
- Shareholders' equity   60
- Debt-to-equity ratio of   1.0x

If the firm distributes 20 in cash through either cash dividends or repurchase, the firm's balance sheet would be:

- Assets   100
- Liabilities   60
- Shareholders' equity   40
- Debt-to-equity ratio of   1.5x

Cash dividends do not affect the number of shares outstanding, whereas a repurchase reduces this number.

Stock price. Cash dividends reduce stock price because cash is returned, resulting in commensurate reduction in book value per share. However, in a repurchase, the number of shares outstanding is reduced. Assuming no other effects, the share price may remain unaffected. For example, suppose a firm has 110 shares outstanding with earnings of 110 (earnings per share is $1/share). The firm's share price trades at a P/E of 10x, thus $10/share. The company has assets of 1,100 and equity of 1,100, thus a book value per share of $10/share.

- Assets   1,100
- Equity   1,100
- Earnings   110
- Shares outstanding   110
- Share price $10/share
- Earnings per share (EPS) $1/share
- Book value per share $10/share
- Price-to-earnings (P/E)   10x

Assume now that the company repurchases 10 shares at $10/share. Assets and equity are reduced by 100. Shares outstanding are now 100 shares. Let's also assume that earnings are not affected because the reduction in cash is not expected to affect the firm's operating results.

- Assets   1,000
- Equity   1,000
- Earnings   110
- Shares outstanding   100
- Earnings per share (EPS) $1.1/share
- Book value per share $10/share
- Price-to-earnings (P/E)   10x

If the stock was repurchased at the market price, the book value per share would be unaffected. And, if the P/E multiple (or the valuation) remains the same due to the same unaffected earnings expectation, then the share price would increase to $11/share. However, if the repurchase was done at a premium to the current share price, which is often the case, it would tend to reduce the share price given the greater reduction in the book value. The net result of these factors is that a repurchase may not reduce share price in the way that dividends do, and indeed it may increase share price in some cases due to the reduced number of shares outstanding given constant earnings. The different effects on share price between dividends and repurchase may also be significant in executive or employee compensation schemes that are tied to the company's stock price, unless there are mechanisms to offset such effects from the selection (or manipulation) of payout policies.

The following case provides the framework for analyzing fiduciary duty in a repurchase when different shareholders or even different classes of stock are not treated equally. Ordinarily, the decision to repurchase shares is a business decision subject to the presumptive protection of the business judgment rule, but as suggested in *Sinclair Oil Corp. v. Levien* equitable principles may come to bear if different classes of stockholders are treated unequally in a distribution.

Nixon v. Blackwell
626 A.2d 1366 (Del. 1993)

VEASEY, Chief Justice:

In this action we review a decision of the Court of Chancery holding that the defendant directors of a closely-held corporation breached their fiduciary duties to the plaintiffs by maintaining a discriminatory policy that unfairly favors employee stockholders over plaintiffs. The Vice Chancellor found that the directors treated the plaintiffs unfairly by establishing an employee stock ownership plan ("ESOP") and by purchasing key man life insurance policies to provide liquidity for defendants and other corporate employees to enable them to sell their stock while providing no comparable liquidity for minority stockholders. We reverse and remand to the Court of Chancery for proceedings not inconsistent with this opinion. *no breach.*

Plaintiffs are 14 minority [nonemployee] stockholders of Class B, non-voting, stock of E.C. Barton & Co. (the "Corporation"). The individual defendants are the members of the board of directors. The Corporation is also a defendant. Plaintiffs collectively own only Class B stock, and own no Class A stock. Their total holdings comprise approximately 25 percent of all the common stock outstanding.

These directors collectively owned approximately 47.5 percent of all the outstanding Class A shares. The remaining Class A shares were held by certain other present and former employees of the Corporation.

There is no public market for, or trading in, either class of the Corporation's stock. This creates problems for stockholders, particularly the Class B minority stockholders, who wish to sell or otherwise realize the value of their shares. The Corporation purported to address this problem in several ways over the years.

The Corporation established an ESOP designed to hold Class B non-voting stock for the benefit of eligible employees of the Corporation. The ESOP is a tax-qualified profit-sharing plan whereby employees of the Corporation are allocated a share of the assets held by the plan in proportion to their annual compensation, subject to certain vesting requirements. The ESOP is funded by annual cash contributions from the Corporation. Under the plan, terminating and retiring employees are entitled to receive their interest in the ESOP by taking Class B stock or cash in lieu of stock. It appears from the record that most terminating employees and retirees elect to receive cash in lieu of stock [those who take Class B and any subsequent owners become nonemployee Class B stockholders]. Thus, the ESOP provides employee Class B stockholders with a substantial measure of liquidity not available to non-employee stockholders. The Corporation had the option of repurchasing Class A stock from the employees upon their retirement or death. The estates of the employee stockholders did not have a corresponding right to put the stock to the Corporation.

The Corporation also purchased certain key man life insurance policies with death benefits payable to the Corporation. Each executive executed an agreement giving the Corporation a call option to substitute Class B non-voting stock for their Class A voting stock upon the occurrence of certain events, including death and termination of employment, so that the voting shares could be reissued to new key personnel. In return, the Board adopted a resolution creating a non-binding recommendation that a portion of the key man life insurance proceeds be used to repurchase the exchanged Class B stock from the executives' estates at a price at least equal to 80 percent of their ESOP value. The ultimate decision on the use of insurance proceeds for this purpose was left to the discretion of the Corporation's management or the Board.

In 1985 the Corporation purchased eight $300,000 keyman life insurance policies and adopted a plan in connection with its June self-tender. The Corporation's tender offer was for both Class A and Class B stock. The intended use for the proceeds of the keyman life insurance policies was to fund the retirement of any unpaid principal and interest on promissory notes issued in payment for Class A stock acquired in one of the self-tenders. A resolution of the Board facilitating this end was unanimously adopted.

The death benefits of such policies are normally payable to the Corporation and are designed to benefit the Corporation by providing some measure of compensation for the loss of productive corporate executives. Here the two resolutions recited above show a desire to earmark the proceeds. On the death of each individual, the 1985 resolution would apply the proceeds to liquidation of at least part of the corporate debt (i.e., the corporate promissory note issued to the deceased in connection with that employee's previous tender of stock). Certainly that would provide "liquidity" to the employee's estate by paying off a corporate debt, but presumably that obligation was owing in any event and was a liability on the corporate balance sheet. Liquidation of it would improve the corporate balance sheet and would also put cash in the hands of the employee's estate.

Defendants contend that the trial court erred in not applying the business judgment rule. Since the defendants benefited from the ESOP and could have benefited from the key man life insurance beyond that which benefited other stockholders generally, the defendants are on both sides of the transaction. For that reason, we agree with the trial court that the entire fairness test applies to this aspect of the case. Accordingly, defendants have the burden of showing the entire fairness of those transactions.

> When directors of a Delaware corporation are on both sides of a transaction, they are required to demonstrate their utmost good faith and the most scrupulous inherent fairness of the bargain. . . . The requirement of fairness is unflinching in its demand that where one stands on both sides of a transaction, he has the burden of establishing its entire fairness, sufficient to pass the test of careful scrutiny by the courts.

[There are] two aspects of entire fairness, fair price and fair dealing:

> The concept of fairness has two basic aspects: fair dealing and fair price. The former embraces questions of when the transaction was timed, how it was initiated, structured, negotiated, disclosed to the directors, and how the approvals of the directors and the stockholders were obtained. The latter aspect of fairness relates to the economic and financial considerations of the proposed merger, including all relevant factors: assets, market value, earnings, future prospects, and any other elements that affect the intrinsic or inherent value of a company's stock. . . . All aspects of the issue must be examined as a whole since the question is one of entire fairness.

The case before us involves only the issue of fair dealing.

It is often of critical importance whether a particular decision is one to which the business judgment rule applies or the entire fairness rule applies. It is sometimes thought that the decision whether to apply the business judgment rule or the entire fairness test can be outcome-determinative.

> Because the effect of the proper invocation of the business judgment rule is so powerful and the standard of entire fairness so exacting, the determination of the appropriate standard of judicial review frequently is determinative of the outcome of derivative litigation.

Application of the entire fairness rule does not, however, always implicate liability of the conflicted corporate decisionmaker, nor does it necessarily render the decision void.

The entire fairness analysis essentially requires "judicial scrutiny." In business judgment rule cases, an essential element is the fact that there has been a business decision made by a disinterested and independent corporate decisionmaker. When there is no independent corporate decisionmaker, the court may become the objective arbiter.

The trial court in this case, however, appears to have adopted the novel legal principle that Class B stockholders had a right to "liquidity" equal to that which the court found to be available to the defendants. It is well established in our jurisprudence that stockholders need not always be treated equally for all purposes. To hold that fairness necessarily requires precise equality is to beg the question:

> Many scholars, though few courts, conclude that one aspect of fiduciary duty is the equal treatment of investors. Their argument takes the following form: fiduciary principles require fair conduct; equal treatment is fair conduct; hence, fiduciary principles require equal treatment. The conclusion does not follow. The argument depends on an equivalence between *equal* and *fair* treatment. To say that fiduciary principles require equal treatment is to beg the question whether investors would contract for equal or even equivalent treatment.

Frank H. Easterbrook and Daniel R. Fischel, *The Economic Structure of Corporate Law* 110 (1991) (emphasis in original). This holding of the trial court overlooks the significant facts that the minority stockholders were not: (a) employees of the Corporation; (b) entitled to share in an ESOP; (c) qualified for key man insurance; or (d) protected by specific provisions in the certificate of incorporation, by-laws, or a stockholders' agreement.

There is support in this record for the fact that the ESOP is a corporate benefit and was established, at least in part, to benefit the Corporation. Generally speaking, the creation of ESOPs is a normal corporate practice and is generally thought to benefit the corporation. The same is true generally with respect to key man insurance programs. If such corporate practices were necessarily to require equal treatment for non-employee stockholders, that would be a matter for legislative determination in Delaware. There is no such legislation to that effect.

We hold on this record that defendants have met their burden of establishing the entire fairness of their dealings with the non-employee Class B stockholders, and are entitled to judgment. The record is sufficient to conclude that plaintiffs' claim that the defendant directors have maintained a discriminatory policy of favoring Class A employee stockholders over Class B non-employee stockholders is without merit. The directors have followed a consistent policy originally established by Mr. Barton, the founder of the Corporation, whose intent from the formation of the Corporation was to use the Class A stock as the vehicle for the Corporation's continuity through employee management and ownership.

Mr. Barton established the Corporation in 1928 by creating two classes of stock, not one, and by holding 100 percent of the Class A stock and 82 percent of the Class B stock. Mr. Barton himself established the practice of purchasing key man life insurance with funds of the Corporation to retain in the employ of the Corporation valuable employees by assuring them that, following their retirement or death, the Corporation will have liquid assets which could be used to repurchase the shares acquired by the employee, which shares may otherwise constitute an illiquid and unsalable asset of his or her estate. Another rational purpose is to prevent the stock from passing out of the control of the employees of the Corporation into the hands of family or descendants of the employee.

The directors' actions following Mr. Barton's death are consistent with Mr. Barton's plan. An ESOP is normally established for employees. Accordingly, there is no inequity in limiting ESOP benefits to the employee stockholders. Indeed, it makes no sense to include non-employees in ESOP benefits. The fact that the Class B stock represented 75 percent of the Corporation's total equity is irrelevant to the issue of fair dealing. The Class B stock was given no voting rights because those stockholders were not intended to have a direct voice in the management and operation of the Corporation. They were simply passive investors—entitled to be treated fairly but not necessarily to be treated equally. The fortunes of the Corporation rested with the Class A employee stockholders and the Class B stockholders benefited from the multiple increases in value of their Class B stock. Moreover, the Board made continuing efforts to buy back the Class B stock.

QUESTION

1. In what way was the different treatment of the two classes of stock equitable though unequal?

Repurchasing shares in anticipation of a potential hostile takeover is a common takeover defense. The determination of the appropriate standard of judicial review is frequently outcome determinative. Upon application of the presumption of the business judgment rule, a court will decline to review the substance of the transaction unless there is a showing of a breach of fiduciary duty. But where there is a showing of this breach, the presumption is rebutted and a Delaware court will review the entire fairness of the transaction. Ordinarily, the decision to engage in a repurchase, absent a takeover threat or insider dealing, would be subject to the business judgment rule.

When a board responds to a takeover threat, there is an intermediate, enhanced review. The Delaware Supreme Court recognized in *Unocal Corp. v. Mesa Petroleum Co.*, 493 A.2d 946 (Del. 1985) that when a board takes action designed to defeat a threatened change in control of the company, the "omnipresent specter that a board may be acting primarily in its own interests" justifies a two-part, enhanced review: (1) there must be shown some basis for the board to have concluded that a proper corporate purpose was served by implementation of the defensive measure; (2) that measure must be found reasonable in relation to the threat posed by the change in control that instigates the action. Directors in the face of an inherent conflict "must show that they had reasonable grounds for believing that a danger to corporate policy and effectiveness existed because of another person's stock ownership." This standard is a balancing test. "If a defensive measure is to come within the ambit of the business judgment rule, it must be <u>reasonable in relation to the threat posed</u>."

In *Unitrin, Inc. v. American General Corp.*, 651 A.2d 1361 (Del. 1995), the Delaware Supreme Court applied the *Unocal* framework to a target corporation's repurchase of its shares in the face of a takeover threat. The chancery court enjoined the repurchase program of a target corporation on the ground that the program was "unnecessary" to protect against an inadequate offer in light of the board's adoption of other defense mechanisms including the poison pill. The Delaware Supreme Court reversed, ruling that under the *Unocal* standard the repurchase program must fall within a "range of reasonableness." In remanding, the court instructed the lower court to consider whether: "(1) [the repurchase] is a statutorily authorized form of business decision which a board of directors may routinely make in a non-takeover context; (2) it was limited and corresponded in degree or magnitude to the degree or magnitude of the threat; (3) the Board properly recognized that all shareholders are not alike, and provided immediate liquidity to those shareholders who wanted it."

The following case applies the *Unocal* and *Unitrin* framework. The Delaware Supreme Court considered again a repurchase transaction in the possible shadow of a takeover. The case is fact-sensitive and revolves around the question of whether the business judgment rule or an enhanced review should apply, and this question depended on whether or not there was a threat that triggered the *Unocal* and *Unitrin* analysis.

Kahn v. Roberts
679 A.2d 460 (Del. 1996)

WALSH, Justice.

Plaintiff Alan Kahn ("Kahn") appeals the dismissal of his claims of breach of the duties of care and disclosure in connection with a buyback of one-third of the outstanding stock of DeKalb Genetics Corporation ("DeKalb"). Kahn argues that the DeKalb directors' actions do not withstand the judicial scrutiny required under *Unocal Corp. v. Mesa Petroleum Co.*, 493 A.2d 946 (Del. 1985), and that the board violated its duty of disclosure.

The Court of Chancery correctly held that no enhanced judicial scrutiny of the transaction under *Unocal* is required. With respect to the disclosure claim, the Court of Chancery ruled that no duty of disclosure arises where the board of directors undertakes to disclose information in a context wherein shareholder action is not implicated. Since the alleged deficiencies are immaterial in any event, we need not reach the issue of the scope of the duty of disclosure, but hold that lack of materiality of the alleged omissions precludes recovery.

DeKalb engages in the production and marketing of corn and soybean seed product lines, swine and poultry production, and biotechnology research. It has a dual capitalization structure, consisting of Class A and Class B stock. Class A stockholders and Class B stockholders have the same rights to dividends and other distributions, but Class B stockholders have no voting rights other than required by Delaware law. No national securities exchange trades the Class A stock, but Class B trades on the NASDAQ over-the-counter market. For corporate purposes, DeKalb values the Class A stock at the market price of the Class B stock.

In December, 1990, Thomas Roberts, Jr., Thomas Roberts, III and their families collectively owned one-third of the Class A and Class B stock of DeKalb. In the first half of 1990, John Nelson, the executive manager of one of DeKalb's business segments, DeKalb Poultry Research, Inc. ("DPRI"), resigned. Thomas Roberts, III headed the international marketing division and showed interest in succeeding Nelson. Bruce Bickner, who was the chairman of the board, and Richard Ryan, another director, were responsible for selecting Nelson's successor. They chose someone other than Thomas Roberts, III for the position.

This selection process disappointed Thomas Roberts, III and his father Thomas Roberts, Jr. As a result, they suggested to Bickner and Ryan that the Roberts family would "rethink" its position as large DeKalb stockholders.

Thomas Roberts, III faced further disappointment. After the United States Customs Agency audited DPRI's international sales in October, 1990, Bickner requested that Thomas Roberts, III resign because of alleged irregularities. Thomas Roberts, III tendered his resignation shortly thereafter, to be effective March 30, 1991. Despite the severance of the employment relationship, Thomas Roberts, III did not leave his position as a director of DeKalb for more than two years after his resignation.

As a result of its disenchantment with DeKalb, the Roberts family determined to reduce or sever its financial ties with the company.

Thomas Roberts, Jr. approached Charles Roberts and Bickner with a proposal: that DeKalb repurchase the Roberts' family stock. Bickner sought the assistance of Merrill Lynch & Company to evaluate whether DeKalb should sell itself, the status and effectiveness of DeKalb's research, the competitiveness of DeKalb's product line, and the financial future of the company in general. Bickner also retained Shearman & Sterling as legal counsel for DeKalb.

On May 23, 1991, the DeKalb board held a special meeting to discuss the concerns Thomas Roberts, Jr. had originally raised about deficiencies in the seed research program. At the meeting, Thomas Roberts, Jr. expressed his view that these failings ultimately would result in loss of DeKalb's market share and he urged a sale or merger of the company. DeKalb's head of Plant Genetics gave a presentation rebutting Thomas Roberts, Jr.'s concern. Agreeing with the rebuttal presentation, Bickner expressed his view that current policies had been effective and that DeKalb should remain independent. After deliberating, the board rejected Thomas Roberts, Jr.'s recommendation and passed a resolution, by a vote of nine to three, that it was in the best interest of DeKalb and its stockholders to remain independent. Only Thomas Roberts, Jr., Thomas Roberts, III, and Paul Judy voted against the resolution.

After the board's rejection of the proposal to sell the company, Merrill Lynch met with financial advisors and attorneys representing the Roberts family concerning the family's interest in selling their DeKalb Class A and Class B stock.

The full board considered the issue of a possible repurchase of the Roberts family stock at its regular meeting on July 1, 1991. During this meeting, after the Thomas Roberts Defendants departed, the remainder of the board met with Douglas Brown of Merrill Lynch. Brown supported the repurchase of the Roberts family stock. In addition to this recommendation, Merrill Lynch presented the board with several options, including the possibility of generating a sale of the entire company to a "hostile" outsider and the possibility of a "poison pill" to discourage sale of DeKalb. Consistent with its earlier determinations to maintain DeKalb as an independent corporation, the board sought further consideration of a repurchase of the Roberts family's shares. Brown advised the board that a repurchase price of $40 per share for the Class A Stock would be a beneficial transaction for DeKalb.

The Merrill Lynch presentation apparently was sufficiently persuasive to prompt the board to consider seriously the repurchase of the Roberts family stock. To that end, at the July 1 meeting, the board appointed a Special Committee of six outside directors to oversee and to conduct discussions between the Company and the Roberts family. This committee was also responsible for recommending to the full board the terms for any repurchase.

Four days later, the Special Committee conducted a telephonic meeting. All directors except the Thomas Roberts defendants participated. The Special Committee concluded that, should DeKalb go forward with the repurchase, it not pay more than $40 per share for the voting Class A stock. It also determined DeKalb should not purchase the Roberts family's non-voting Class B stock.

On July 7, the board again met by telephone to decide whether to go forward with the repurchase. During that meeting, Merrill Lynch reviewed the materials it had distributed at the regular board meeting and again advised that the repurchase of the Roberts family stock would be a good transaction for DeKalb. At this meeting, the board unanimously adopted a resolution authorizing Bickner to enter into an agreement with the Roberts family to purchase their shares at $40 per share of voting Class A Stock.

In a letter to the shareholders dated July 15, Bickner announced the repurchase of the Roberts family's DeKalb Class A stock for $40 per share. He also stated that bank borrowing would finance the repurchase and made the following statement which became the focus of Kahn's disclosure claim: "We view this repurchase as a positive move. It is a good transaction for the company, and one that allows certain Roberts family members to diversify their holdings and gain the liquidity they sought."

Kahn filed suit alleging violations of the directors' fiduciary duties. Specifically, Kahn claimed that the directors had breached their duty of disclosure by failing to disclose all material facts surrounding the repurchase; approved an excessively high repurchase price; and acted with the intent to entrench themselves in office.

When a board of directors responds to a threat to corporate policy or effectiveness, there is "the omnipresent specter that [it] may be acting primarily in its own interests, rather than those of the corporation and its shareholders." *Unocal Corp. v. Mesa*

Petroleum Corp., 493 A.2d 946, 954 (Del. 1985). Because the directors' fiduciary duty to serve the corporation conflicts with their own self-interest, the presumption of propriety under the business judgment rule does not protect their actions. Instead, the board's actions must withstand enhanced judicial scrutiny.

Kahn argues that such enhanced scrutiny of the stock repurchase is appropriate and dictates a finding that the directors violated their fiduciary duties. His argument is two-pronged. Kahn argues first that the board's actions in buying back the Roberts family's shares were a defensive measure in response to a threat to control of DeKalb. Kahn then asserts that the board's actions cannot withstand *Unocal*'s heightened analysis because there were "no reasonable grounds to believe that the vague assertions purportedly made by Thomas Roberts, Jr. . . . constituted a legally cognizable threat to DeKalb's corporate policy or effectiveness." Kahn made similar arguments before the Court of Chancery.

The Court of Chancery dismissed Kahn's *Unocal* claim because Kahn took contradictory positions in briefing and because from an objective standpoint no threat existed. The Court of Chancery held that, since no threat to corporate control existed, the business judgment rule applied. We concur in the determination that the DeKalb board's actions were not a violation of fiduciary norms under *Unocal* and its progeny.

The business judgment rule normally protects all lawful actions of a board of directors, provided they were taken in good faith, after a reasonable deliberative process and in the absence of conflicts of interest. Where, however, the board takes defensive action in response to a threat to the board's control of the corporation's business and policy direction, a heightened standard of judicial review applies because of the temptation for directors to seek to remain at the corporate helm in order to protect their own powers and perquisites. Such self-interested behavior may occur even when the best interests of the shareholders and corporation dictate an alternative course. Thus, where the board perceives a threat, its response will not be upheld merely because the response serves "any rational business purpose." *Unocal,* 493 A.2d at 954 (quoting *Sinclair Oil Corp. v. Levien,* 280 A.2d 717, 720 (Del. 1971)).

We find that the factual circumstances do not warrant the application of *Unocal* to the repurchase of the DeKalb shares. This is not the case where one-third of the outstanding shares are being sought by a third party, or a self-tender for those shares was made in the face of a third party bid for control. Such situations might bring about a change in control and be closer to the *Unocal* paradigm. Here the corporation sought to repurchase its own shares in a situation where there was no hostile bidder.[6] Nothing in the record indicates that there was a real probability of any hostile acquiror emerging or that the corporation was "in play." Furthermore, the board acted to remove disgruntled shareholders, not in contemplation of an ephemeral threat that could somehow materialize at some point in the future,

> If the actions of the board were motivated by a sincere belief that the buying out of the dissident stockholder was necessary to maintain what the board believed to be proper business practices, the board will not be held liable for such decision, even though hindsight indicates the decision was not the wisest course. On the other hand,

---

6. The result we reach here is consistent with earlier decisions of this Court. We have repeatedly ruled that a board may repurchase the stock of a dissatisfied shareholder without implicating heightened scrutiny.

if the board has acted solely or primarily because of the desire to perpetuate themselves in office, the use of corporate funds for such purposes is improper.

Absent an actual threat to corporate control or action substantially taken for the purpose of entrenchment, the actions of the board are judged under the business judgment rule. Kahn has not presented evidence to overcome the presumption of propriety that accompanies this rule for actions taken in good faith and after reasonable investigation by independent directors. The repurchase was approved after the board established an independent committee, consulted with legal and financial advisors and considered its options over the course of several meetings. Further analysis of the repurchase is unnecessary to sustain the board's decision as a sound exercise of business judgment.

The Court of Chancery held that the director defendants were not under a duty to make any disclosures since a shareholder vote was not being sought. Kahn argues that the trial court erred because "even if defendants were under no initial duty to disclose all information about the repurchase agreement, once they undertook to disclose information about the repurchase, the defendants were obligated to fully and fairly disclose all material information about the repurchase." Even assuming the existence of the duty of disclosure in this case, Kahn has failed to show any material omissions or misstatements.

This Court has held that full disclosure is required when management is seeking stockholder action. Notably, this Court has never stated that full disclosure is required *only when* seeking shareholder action. Because none of the disclosure violations alleged by Kahn are material, we need not and do not reach today the question of whether a duty of disclosure exists absent shareholder action. Even if the duty of disclosure is implicated here, such a duty lacks a factual basis.

Kahn alleges two omitted facts. First, he alleges that the company should have disclosed that the repurchase caused DeKalb to incur $18 million in debt. Second, he contends that DeKalb should have disclosed that the Roberts family sold their investment in DeKalb because they were dissatisfied with company policies which threatened DeKalb's competitiveness.

If there is any duty, it extends only to material factual omissions or misstatements. Since Kahn complains only of non-material deficiencies in the disclosure, he cannot recover.

As to the amount of debt financing for the repurchase, the board did fully disclose the relevant facts. It disclosed that the buyback would be debt financed, the number of shares and the price per share. Simple multiplication would have revealed the allegedly omitted fact. Thus, no material information was withheld and no breach of duty occurred.

Kahn alleges that the letter [to shareholders] was misleading in that it stated that the Thomas Roberts family's motivation was to diversify its holdings when their true reason for selling was DeKalb's decreasing competitiveness. The director defendants' disagreed with the Thomas Roberts defendants' claims that DeKalb was losing its competitive edge. These assertions were speculative and not shared by a majority of the DeKalb board. The director defendants were under no duty to disclose views with which they disagreed and thought were unsupported.

In conclusion, the Court of Chancery correctly granted summary judgment in favor of the defendants. Kahn's contentions on appeal are meritless. He alleges only nonmaterial omissions from the letter to the shareholders describing the repurchase. In addition, the DeKalb directors were not responding to a threat to corporate control in approving the repurchase, so their decision is protected by the business judgment rule. The decision below is therefore affirmed.

QUESTIONS

1. Why did the company repurchase the Roberts' stake? Was there a potential threat posed by the Roberts' stake?
2. Why did the facts not trigger enhanced judicial review?
3. What additional facts, if present, could have triggered enhanced judicial scrutiny?

The following case concerns the board's fiduciary duty relating to disclosure under state corporation law. When there is a public self-tender by the corporation, there must be disclosure to the shareholder on the price and terms of the tender offer. Much of this facet of the transaction, including the regulatory safe-harbor from stock manipulation charges, is governed by federal securities regulation. However, state corporation law also applies to the transaction with respect to the actions of the board.

Kahan v. United States Sugar Corp.
1985 WL 4449 (Del. Ch. 1985)

HARTNETT, Vice Chancellor.
This suit was brought as a class action challenging a leveraged cash tender offer made by United States Sugar Corporation and a trust existing under its Employee Stock Ownership Plan (ESOP) to the corporation's stockholders. A class consisting of those minority public shareholders who tendered their shares in response to the tender offer was certified and a trial was held.

I find that there was a breach of fiduciary duty by the defendants because the disclosures made in the tender offer solicitation materials did not disclose with complete candor all the material facts a stockholder needed to make a fully informed decision as to whether to accept the tender offer. I also conclude that the tender offer was coercive. I further find that it would be impossible to rescind the transaction and that, therefore, an award of damages is the only possible remedy. I find that the amount of damage is $4 per share.

[Reason for Tender Offer]

The named plaintiffs represent the class of minority, public shareholders of U.S. Sugar who tendered their shares in response to the tender offer by U.S. Sugar and the ESOP. Defendants are U.S. Sugar, the ESOP, and the members of the Board of Directors of U.S. Sugar.

At the time of the tender offer U.S. Sugar was a public company with almost 5 million shares outstanding and its shares were held of record by more than 2,000 shareholders. The shares traded on the over-the-counter market, but only 28% of the outstanding shares were held by the public. The other 72% were owned either by charitable organizations established by Charles Stewart Mott, the founder of U.S. Sugar, or by members of the Mott family (collectively, the "Mott Interests").

U.S. Sugar is the largest producer of sugar cane and raw sugar in the United States. It was founded in 1931 and immediately purchased a substantial acreage of muckland in central Florida at a foreclosure sale.

Muckland is a unique type of soil formed from the overflow of Lake Okeechobee in south central Florida. It is so fertile that little fertilizer is needed to produce high yield sugar crops and it is the perfect soil for the raising of sugar cane but has limited other uses.

U.S. Sugar's production process is integrated in nature. Its two sugar mills in the Okeechobee area are powered by use of sugar cane waste by-products. An internal railroad system is used to transport the cane from the fields to the mills and is cheaper to operate than the standard truck transport used by all other sugar cane operations in the area. The superior farm equipment, irrigation system, ditches, canals, roadways, as well as the housing for migrant workers, also contribute to U.S. Sugar's acknowledged efficiency and value.

The tender offer came about because the Mott Interests wished to reduce their holdings in U.S. Sugar but did not wish to relinquish their aggregated ability to exercise majority control over the company. The market price for U.S. Sugar stock was already considered to be depressed due to the world sugar glut and the sale of a substantial block of stock would have likely depressed it still further. It was therefore decided that a leveraged tender offer for 75% of the outstanding shares (over 3.5 million shares) was the best means of facilitating the wishes of the Mott Interests, while not depressing the market. Additionally, this tender offer would allow public shareholders to share in the tender offer and thus take advantage of a premium above market price.

Because the Mott Interests planned to tender a substantial number of shares while still retaining majority control, they had competing desires to both receive the highest possible tender offer price and still leave U.S. Sugar as a viable company not unduly burdened with debt. It is asserted by the defendants that these competing interests would tend to assure that those public shareholders who tendered their shares in response to the tender offer would receive as high a price as feasible for their shares, while also assuring that shareholders who did not choose to tender would not be locked into an overburdened corporation. Be that as it may, although more than 93% of the publicly held shares were tendered, more than 42% of the 2,000 shareholders chose not to be completely cashed out but elected to retain some portion of their holdings.

The ESOP was formed as a part of the tender offer plan. It purchased over one million shares at $68 per share with funds borrowed from U.S. Sugar. It was planned that the ESOP would repay U.S. Sugar from the annual tax deductible contributions made to the ESOP by the company.

There being no independent directors on U.S. Sugar's Board, no independent committee of directors could be appointed to review the tender offer and to negotiate on behalf of the public shareholders. However, the existence of the conflicts of interest was disclosed in the tender offer statement.

The tender offer was not intended to be merely the first step of a two-step elimination of public shareholders because those shareholders who did not tender their shares were not to be cashed out in a merger following the tender offer. A substantial number of shares are presently outstanding and held by public shareholders, and there continues to be a market for the trading of U.S. Sugar shares, although it has been trading at a lesser price than it did before the tender offer.

Prior to the challenged transaction, U.S. Sugar was virtually debt free. Chemical Bank, the corporation's traditional bank, was approached and was requested to advance $300 million, $250 million of which was to be used to finance the tender offer while the remaining $50 million would be used for working capital. Chemical Bank determined that U.S. Sugar would generate sufficient cash flow to service such a loan and that its assets would be sufficient to repay the loan in the event a foreclosure became necessary. Using conservative projections as to sugar yields, number of acres planted, etc., it also decided that sufficient cash would be generated to service the debt. The bank further determined that on a "worse case" basis, assuming a foreclosure sale, the assets would be worth at least $369 million (approximately $75 per share.) Chemical Bank, for its loan purposes, concluded that the current market value of U.S. Sugar's assets indicated a real net worth of more than $400 million (more than $80 per share). The replacement cost of U.S. Sugar's assets was estimated by the corporation in 1983 to be over $631 million ($130 per share).

Plaintiffs assert that U.S. Sugar's management disregarded information it had as to the value of its assets and instead arrived at the proposed tender offer price by considering only the price range which could be paid off by a projected cash flow over ten years. This range was $60 to $70 per share.

While consideration of the tender offer price range was still taking place, U.S. Sugar retained First Boston Corporation to render a fairness opinion on the offering price. It was paid $650,000 for its three weeks of work. Initially First Boston was only informed of the range being considered for the tender offer by the corporation and was not informed of the actual tender offer price of $68 until the Friday before it delivered its opinion on Tuesday, September 13, 1983. In the fairness opinion issued by First Boston it opined that the $68 per share was fair to the public shareholders from a financial point of view.

First Boston was originally engaged to represent the public shareholders, as well as to give an opinion as to fairness. Its representative role was never carried out: it was not asked to recommend an independently arrived at fair price; it did not engage in any negotiations over the offering price with U.S. Sugar; it did not consult with any representatives of the minority shareholders; nor did it solicit outside offers to purchase.

Bear Stearns & Co. was retained to represent the ESOP and U.S. Sugar. It was asked to opine that the price to be offered in the tender offer was reasonable to the ESOP. It was also asked to determine whether after the proposed transaction the fair market value of U.S. Sugar's assets would exceed its liabilities by at least $50 million.

The determination that the corporation's assets had a fair market value which would exceed liabilities by at least $50 million after the tender offer was completed was necessary to allow the Board to make a finding that U.S. Sugar's capital would not be impaired, a finding required by Delaware law. This determination was called for because the distribution to be made under the tender offer would be greater than the net book value of the corporation's assets.

Bear Stearns did negotiate on behalf of the ESOP. It was responsible for the setting of the offering price at $68 rather than the $70 which the officers of U.S. Sugar had originally determined should be the offering price. The $68 price followed Bear

Stearns' decision that the fair price range was between $62 and $68 per share and that any higher price would be unfair to the ESOP.

The Offer to Purchase ("Tender Offering Statement") was sent to the stockholders by U.S. Sugar and the ESOP about September 20, 1983. In response, 1,288,210 shares were tendered by public stockholders. Of the then outstanding publicly held shares only 89,108 were not tendered.

[Disclosure Problem]

Plaintiffs contend that the Tender Offering Statement was misleading or coercive and concealed or buried facts which, if disclosed, might have led stockholders to conclude that the $68 price was inadequate. They suggest that there were three categories of inadequate disclosures: (1) those designed to persuade the public stockholders that the price was fair; (2) those designed to persuade the public stockholders that First Boston had adequately protected their interests by determining independently that $68 per share was a fair price; and (3) those designed to persuade the public stockholders that the consequences of not tendering would be far less pleasant than the consequences of tendering. They claim that the first and second categories of disclosures were misleading while the third was coercive.

Plaintiffs also claim that facts were emphasized in the Tender Offering Statement which would lead the shareholders to conclude that the $68 price was fair, while facts to the contrary were omitted or buried. Omissions cited by plaintiffs include the facts: (1) that U.S. Sugar's market price was depressed so that the premium was less meaningful; (2) that its book value bore no relationship to the fair market value of its assets; (3) that in 1982 its internal real estate department had determined that the fair market value of its fee simple land holdings was in excess of $408 million (approximately $83 per share); (4) that a Cash Flow Terminal Value Study prepared by First Boston had shown values as high as $100.50 per share for the company.

In addition, plaintiffs find fault with the prominent representations as to Bear Stearns' finding that the fair market value of U.S. Sugar's assets would exceed stated liabilities by at least $50 million after the transaction. They assert that it created the impression that Bear Stearns had performed a valuation of the fair market value of the assets when in fact it did not but instead relied upon pre-existing findings of value. They also challenge the omission of information that Bear Stearns had arrived at values of up to $78 per share.

Plaintiffs also assert that the Tender Offering Statement contained disclosures which created the impression that U.S. Sugar's management had arrived at the $68 price based mainly upon the independent valuation opinion of First Boston, that First Boston had been allowed to do a thorough valuation study with no restraints placed upon it, and that the interests of the public shareholders had been adequately represented by First Boston in the process of determining the terms of the offer. These disclosures are claimed to be false and misleading because certain alleged facts were omitted: (1) that U.S. Sugar's management, and not First Boston's, had arrived at the $68 price and that First Boston had never suggested a price which it felt was fair but merely opined as to the fairness of the price suggested by management; (2) that the $68 price was derived from a consideration of the amount which could comfortably be borrowed and repaid rather than from any evaluation of U.S. Sugar's true worth; (3) that management would have paid up to $70 per share if Bear Stearns had not represented that no price above $68 would be reasonable for the ESOP to pay; (4) that

First Boston had accepted a representation that the sale of U.S. Sugar to a third party would not be considered and therefore had made no attempt to solicit outside offers; and (5) that after the meeting of the Board of Directors at which it was unanimously determined that $68 per share was a fair price, Stewart Mott, a director and son of the founder of U.S. Sugar, decided not to tender any of the shares registered in his name.

The tender offer and the disclosures in the Tender Offering Statement are further asserted by the plaintiffs to have been coercive because the shareholders were told that they had a choice between tendering at $68 per share or retaining their stock, which after the transaction would no longer be listed on any exchange, would yield no dividends for a minimum of three years, and would represent ownership in a company burdened by substantial debt.

Plaintiffs claim that the fair value of U.S. Sugar at the time of the tender offer was $122 per share which they claim was the liquidation value of the assets. They claim that the appropriate remedy is an award of money damages measured by the difference between the $68 tender offering price and $122.

I find that the disclosures in the Tender Offer Statement did not fully comply with the requirements for disclosure with complete candor which are mandated by Delaware law.

There was a failure to clearly indicate in the proxy materials that the book value of the land, which was the principal asset of U.S. Sugar, was based primarily on the 1931 acquisition costs of the land and that in 1982 the internal real estate department of the corporation had rendered an informal opinion to management that the fee simple holdings of land was in excess of $408 million ($83 per share). The tender offer proxy materials also failed to adequately disclose that a Cash Flow Terminal Value Study prepared by First Boston had shown estimated values as high as $100.50 per share; that Bear Stearns had made some estimates of value of up to $78 per share; and that First Boston did not actually prepare a thorough valuation study without restraints.

I also find that there was a failure to adequately disclose the methods used to arrive at the $68 tender offer price, especially because it was, for all practical purposes, chosen because that is what the ESOP and the corporation could afford to pay to service the loan obtained to finance the tender offer.

I also find that the method used to select the tender offer price was not likely to assure that the public minority stockholders would receive the true value of their shares and, as will be seen, they did not. The tender offer price, unfortunately, was arrived at by determining how much debt the corporation could safely and prudently assume. The public stockholders had to either accept this price and tender their shares or to hold on to their shares only to find, because of the large loan which was to be used to pay for the shares tendered, that their shares would dramatically decline in value with no prospects for any dividends for at least three years.

In some circumstances a corporation is under no obligation to offer a particular tender offer price. Here, however, because of the highly leveraged nature of the transaction it was coercive and therefore defendants had an obligation to offer a fair price.

I acknowledge that the directors of U.S. Sugar were faced with a most difficult scenario because the majority shareholders desired to sell a substantial portion of their shares and yet insisted on retaining control of the corporation. The only feasible way to accomplish this was for the corporation to buy its own shares by the means of a leveraged tender offer. If the price offered had been fair there would not be any problem.

The price offered, however, was not fair and it should have been selected with a greater emphasis on the true value of the corporation.

I do not, however, find the statements in the proxy statement setting forth the results which would likely occur if a stockholder did not tender to have been inadequate, improper or coercive. The proxy materials merely set forth that which was obvious: the minority stockholders who did not tender their shares would end up owning shares with a greatly diminished value because of the large debt being created to finance the tender offer.

[Damages]

Plaintiffs seek, as damages, the difference between the fair value of the shares and the $68 offering price, plus pre-judgment interest. They correctly point out that it would be impossible now to rescind the transaction.

Most of the testimony adduced at trial relating to value was produced by experts retained by the litigants who expressed their opinion of the fair and intrinsic value of U.S. Sugar's stock at the time of the tender offer. Analyses of U.S. Sugar were performed on behalf of the plaintiffs by Professor James E. Walter and on behalf of the defendants by Francis Schaffer, Stanley Hanson, First Boston and Bear Stearns.

A review of this testimony clearly shows the reason that testimony as to value by experts is of such limited use to a trier of fact.

The valuations expressed by the several expert witnesses were all based on numerous value judgments. While the assumptions had a basis, almost every figure used, whether a base figure or a multiplier, could have just as well been a different figure and the selection of the figure to be used necessarily involved a choice or guess by the witness, who in turn was being handsomely paid by one side or the other. The range between the two sides as to the value of the shares at the time of the tender offer was from a high (expressed by one of the experts called by the plaintiffs) of $121.92 per share and the low (expressed by one of defendants' experts) of $51.82 per share. Supposedly all of the experts were evaluating the same corporation!

[The court described the divergent valuations and methodologies of the expert witnesses.]

The foregoing is but a summary of the testimony of the expert witnesses. It is in hopeless disagreement. Each expert presented impressive credentials. Each expressed an opinion as to value based on dozens of value judgment assumptions. While each assumption was based on some data, almost all of the assumptions were fairly debatable and reasonable men using the same data could conclude that a different percentage multiple, or per acreage figure, etc., should be used.

Quite frankly, there is no rational way that I as the trier of fact could conclude that one expression of value was best. All had flaws, all were based on personal assumptions and opinions and all were expressed by obviously knowledgeable and experienced experts who were retained by one side or the other.

In only one respect did the two sides come close to each other. Professor Walter, who was called by the plaintiffs, relied heavily on land appraisals prepared for defendants. Based on this information he opined that the going concern value of U.S. Sugar was $79.14 per share. Although he also opined that the liquidation value was $104 to $122 per share, the assumptions which he used to arrive at the going concern value were more persuasive than the basis he used for his liquidation value. His $79.14 per share going concern value, while also obviously based on some invalid data and questionable assumptions, was not entirely unreasonable.

The defendants even conceded that Professor Walter's data, if the errors which defendants believe existed are taken into account, established a liquidation value of $62.91 to $72.52 per share. Chemical Bank also arrived at a $75 per share value in one of its evaluations prepared in connection with the loan request.

Although the two investment bankers who were retained by the defendants did not testify as expert witnesses as to the value of U.S. Sugar, they did testify on behalf of the defendants and explained how they arrived at their opinions that the tender offer price of $68 was fair.

First Boston is a leading firm of investment bankers. Robert Cotter was the Vice President in charge of the U.S. Sugar valuation and testified as part of defendants' case. He stated that as part of the valuation process, First Boston engaged in detailed discussions with the management of U.S. Sugar in Florida and New York, examined U.S. Sugar's physical plant, met with real estate appraisers and reviewed comparable appraisals, reviewed sugar industry data, reviewed U.S. Sugar's historical and projected operating results, and reviewed recent acquisitions and cash tender offers seeking control. Three valuation methods were considered: going concern value, acquisition value, and liquidation value.

In determining the going concern value, three analyses were performed using different sets of assumptions with Case I assumed to be the most likely occurrence, Case II being the less likely, and Case III being the least likely to occur. The highest value reached as to Case I was $59.33 per share. The Case II analysis yielded figures from $45.11 to $90 per share but more than two-thirds of the values were below $68 per share. In Case III, which was considered "grossly unrealistic" by Cotter, almost half of the value range was below $68 per share.

In reviewing the acquisition value of U.S. Sugar to a potential acquiror, First Boston compared premiums over market paid in recent acquisitions. The 66% premium offered by U.S. Sugar in its tender offer was significantly higher than the average premium paid in tender offers which First Boston assumed were comparable. First Boston determined that it was unlikely that any third party could be found willing to pay a higher price than $68 per share.

First Boston considered replacement value to be completely unrelated to fair market value and did not consider it in reviewing liquidation value. Their analysis of liquidation value was done merely to check the values suggested by the going concern analysis. It was not as extensive an analysis as that done for the going concern value, but the results were believed by First Boston to support the fairness of the $68 tender offer price.

Bear Stearns' was retained to ensure that the ESOP did not pay an unreasonably high price. It is the second largest investment banking partnership on Wall Street. Its investigations included discussions with U.S. Sugar's management and review of considerable information provided by U.S. Sugar. It also considered companies which it deemed to be comparable and U.S. Sugar's historical and projected operating results.

An evaluation was done to determine earnings per share assuming that all of U.S. Sugar's muckland was put to its highest and best use as sugar cane production ($6.00 to $6.50 per share). A multiple of eight was assumed based on comparison to companies in mature, non-growth industries-other than the sugar industry. They conceded that there is really no sugar producing company which is truly comparable to U.S.

Sugar. They also assumed that the cattle operation could be liquidated for $14 to $16 per share. This resulted in a value range of $62 to $68 per share. Thus, they concluded $68 was the highest price the ESOP could fairly pay.

Notwithstanding that none of the opinions of value expressed by the experts are conclusive or even persuasive, I must establish from the trial record the value of the stock of U.S. Sugar at the time of the tender offer.

The primary assets of U.S. Sugar are its large holdings of the unique muckland which is used primarily for the growing of sugar cane and its capital assets used in the growing, harvesting and processing of the sugar cane. I find that the expressions of value based on estimates of the value of the muckland and its improvements were the most persuasive and accurate, although certain errors of fact were pointed out by cross-examination and the values expressed represented a certain amount of puffing or discounting depending on whether the witness was retained by the plaintiffs or defendants.

After considering and weighing all the conflicting testimony, the many value judgments and assumptions (some of which were invalid), and the credentials and demeanor of the witnesses, I conclude that the fair value of the assets of U.S. Sugar at the time of the tender offer was $72 per share. The damages, therefore, are equal to $4 per share ($72 less the $68 tender offer price).

QUESTIONS

1. How does a leveraged tender offer give the Mott family liquidity but at the same time maintain their control?
2. What were the factors resulting in a finding of fact that the board breached its fiduciary duty?
3. In what way was the tender offer coercive? Why was the coercion wrongful?

NOTES

1. It appears that the damages were calculated as an approximate average of the different valuations: (1) $65, which is the midpoint of Bear Stearns' valuation, (2) $59.33, which is the highest value of the most likely case in the First Boston analysis, (3) $79.14, which is the plaintiff expert's opinion, (4) $75, which is Chemical Bank's evaluation, and (5) $83, which is real estate evaluation. These values constitute the opinions of the participants. The average of these values is $72.29.

E. FRAUDULENT TRANSFER

The federal Bankruptcy Code and state fraudulent transfer statutes limit the ability of a corporation to make distributions to shareholders. These statutes protect creditors: when a corporation seeks to make distributions to shareholders with the intent to hinder, delay, or defraud creditors; or when a corporation receives less than reasonably equivalent value in a transaction after which the corporation is left insolvent. Any corporate transaction meeting the statutory standard may be subject to a determination of fraudulent transfer. Such transactions include distributions to shareholders and leveraged buyouts (LBOs).

EXAMPLE

Fraudulent Transfer Statutes

Bankruptcy Code

11 U.S.C. §548(a)(1), Fraudulent transfers and obligations

The trustee may avoid any transfer (including any transfer to or for the benefit of an insider under an employment contract) of an interest of the debtor in property, or any obligation (including any obligation to or for the benefit of an insider under an employment contract) incurred by the debtor, that was made or incurred on or within 2 years before the date of the filing of the petition, if the debtor voluntarily or involuntarily—

    (A) made such transfer or incurred such obligation with actual intent to hinder, delay, or defraud any entity to which the debtor was or became, on or after the date that such transfer was made or such obligation was incurred, indebted; or

    (B)(i) received less than a reasonably equivalent value in exchange for such transfer or obligation; and (ii)

        (I) was insolvent on the date that such transfer was made or such obligation was incurred, or became insolvent as a result of such transfer or obligation;

        (II) was engaged in business or a transaction, or was about to engage in business or a transaction, for which any property remaining with the debtor was an unreasonably small capital;

        (III) intended to incur, or believed that the debtor would incur, debts that would be beyond the debtor's ability to pay as such debts matured; or

        (IV) made such transfer to or for the benefit of an insider, or incurred such obligation to or for the benefit of an insider, under an employment contract and not in the ordinary course of business.

Uniform Fraudulent Transfer Act

§4, Transfers Fraudulent as to Present and Future Creditors

    (a) A transfer made or obligation incurred by a debtor is fraudulent as to a creditor, whether the creditor's claim arose before or after the transfer was made or the obligation was incurred, if the debtor made the transfer or incurred the obligation:

        (1) with actual intent to hinder, delay, or defraud any creditor of the debtor; or

        (2) without receiving a reasonably equivalent value in exchange for the transfer or obligation, and the debtor: (i) was engaged or was about to engage in a business or a transaction for which the remaining assets of the debtor were unreasonably small in relation to the business or transaction; or (ii) intended to incur, or believed or reasonably should have believed that he [or she] would incur, debts beyond his [or her] ability to pay as they became due.

    (b) In determining actual intent under subsection (a)(1), consideration may be given, among other factors, to whether:

        (1) the transfer or obligation was to an insider;

        (2) the debtor retained possession or control of the property transferred after the transfer;

        (3) the transfer or obligation was disclosed or concealed;

        (4) before the transfer was made or obligation was incurred, the debtor had been sued or threatened with suit;

        (5) the transfer was of substantially all the debtor's assets;

(6) the debtor absconded;

(7) the debtor removed or concealed assets;

(8) the value of the consideration received by the debtor was reasonably equivalent to the value of the asset transferred or the amount of the obligation incurred;

(9) the debtor was insolvent or became insolvent shortly after the transfer was made or the obligation was incurred;

(10) the transfer occurred shortly before or shortly after a substantial debt was incurred; and

(11) the debtor transferred the essential assets of the business to a lienor who transferred the assets to an insider of the debtor.

Uniform Fraudulent Transfer Act

§5, Transfers Fraudulent as to Present Creditors

(a) A transfer made or obligation incurred by a debtor is fraudulent as to a creditor whose claim arose before the transfer was made or the obligation was incurred if the debtor made the transfer or incurred the obligation without receiving a reasonably equivalent value in exchange for the transfer or obligation and the debtor was insolvent at that time or the debtor became insolvent as a result of the transfer or obligation.

(b) A transfer made by a debtor is fraudulent as to a creditor whose claim arose before the transfer was made if the transfer was made to an insider for an antecedent debt, the debtor was insolvent at that time, and the insider had reasonable cause to believe that the debtor was insolvent.

The following case applies the bankruptcy and state statutes on fraudulent conveyance to a transaction in which shareholders were bought out through leverage financing, resulting in the encumbrance of the company's assets to the detriment of unsecured creditors.

Wieboldt Stores, Inc. v. Schottenstein
94 B.R. 488 (N.D. Ill. 1988)

HOLDERMAN, District Judge:

Wieboldt Stores, Inc. filed this action under the federal bankruptcy laws, the state fraudulent conveyance laws, and the Illinois Business Corporation Act. Pending before the court are numerous motions to dismiss this action.

William Wieboldt began operating Wieboldt in Chicago as a dry goods store in 1883. Mr. Wieboldt's business prospered and diversified. In 1907 Wieboldt was incorporated under Illinois law. Wieboldt's business continued to expand. In 1982 Wieboldt's business was operated out of twelve stores and one distribution center in the Chicago metropolitan area. At that time, Wieboldt employed approximately 4,000 persons and had annual sales of approximately $190 million. Its stock was publicly traded on the New York Stock Exchange.

During the 1970's, demographic changes in Wieboldt's markets, increased competition from discount operations, and poor management caused Wieboldt's business to decline. Wieboldt showed no profit after 1979 and was able to continue its operations only by periodically selling its assets to generate working capital. These assets included its store in Evanston, Illinois and some undeveloped land.

Wieboldt brings this action against 119 defendants. These defendants can be grouped into three non-exclusive categories: (1) controlling shareholders, officers and directors [they were Julius and Edmond Trump, Jerome Schottenstein, and their interests]; (2) other shareholders of Wieboldt's common stock who owned and tendered more than 1,000 shares in response to the tender offer (Schedule A shareholders); and (3) entities which loaned money to fund the tender offer.

Wieboldt has included as defendants in this action four of the entities which were involved in these financial transactions: One North State Street Limited Partnership (ONSSLP), State Street Venture (SSV), Boulevard Bank National Association (Boulevard Bank), BA Mortgage and International Realty Corporation (BAMIRCO), and General Electric Credit Corporation (GECC).

By January 1985 Wieboldt's financial health had declined to the point at which the company was no longer able to meet its obligations as they came due. [WSI Acquisition Corporation, a company formed solely for the purpose of acquiring Wieboldt, proposed a possible tender offer for Wieboldt common stock at $13.50 per share.] Schottenstein informed Wieboldt's Board of Directors of the WSI proposal and the Board agreed to cooperate with WSI in evaluating the financial and operating records of the company. WSI proceeded to seek financing from several lenders, including Household Commercial Financial Services (HCFS).

During 1985 it became apparent to Wieboldt's Board that WSI would accomplish its tender offer by means of an LBO [leveraged buyout] through which WSI would pledge substantially all of Wieboldt's assets, including the company's fee and leasehold real estate assets, as collateral. Many of these real estate assets already served as collateral for $35 million in secured loan obligations from Continental Illinois National Bank (CINB) and other bank creditors. Wieboldt was at least partially in default on these obligations at the time of the LBO.

In order to free these assets for use as collateral in obtaining tender offer financing, WSI intended to sell the One North State Street property [main store and executive office in downtown Chicago] and pay off the CINB loan obligations. In furtherance of these efforts, WSI entered into a joint venture with Bennett & Kahnweiler Associates (BKA), a real estate broker. WSI and BKA intended to sell the One North State Street property to a partnership for $30,000,000. The partnership would then mortgage the property to a funding source. Accordingly, BKA applied for and BAMIRCO accepted a first mortgage term loan on the property.

The sale of the One North State Street property did not generate sufficient funds to pay off the CINB loan obligations. Consequently, WSI sought additional funds from GECC through the sale of Wieboldt's customer charge card accounts. GECC agreed to enter into an accounts purchase agreement after WSI acquired Wieboldt through the tender offer. One term of the accounts purchase agreement required Wieboldt to pledge all of its accounts receivable to GECC as additional security for Wieboldt's obligations under the agreement.

Thus, by October, 1985 HCFS, BAMIRCO, and GECC had each agreed to fund WSI's tender offer, and each knew of the other's loan or credit commitments. These

lenders were aware that WSI intended to use the proceeds of the financing commitments to (1) purchase tendered shares of Wieboldt stock; (2) pay surrender prices for
Wieboldt stock options; or (3) eliminate CINB loan obligations.

The Board of Directors was fully aware of the progress of WSI's negotiations. The
Board understood that WSI intended to finance the tender offer by pledging a
substantial portion of Wieboldt's assets to its lenders, and that WSI did not intend
to use any of its own funds or the funds of its shareholders to finance the acquisition.
Moreover, although the Board initially believed that the tender offer would produce
$10 million in working capital for the company, the members knew that the proceeds
from the LBO lenders would not result in this additional working capital.

Nevertheless, in October, 1985 the Board directed William Darrow [a director]
and Wieboldt's lawyers to work with WSI to effect the acquisition. During these
negotiations, the Board learned that HCFS would provide financing for the tender
offer only if Wieboldt would provide a statement from a nationally recognized
accounting firm stating that Wieboldt was solvent and a going concern prior to
the planned acquisition and would be solvent and a going concern after the acquisition. Darrow informed WSI that Wieboldt would only continue cooperating in the
LBO if HCFS agreed not to require this solvency certificate. HCFS acceded to
Wieboldt's demand and no solvency certificate was ever provided to HCFS on Wieboldt's behalf.

On November 18, 1985 Wieboldt's Board of Directors voted to approve WSI's
tender offer, and on November 20, 1985 WSI announced its offer to purchase Wieboldt stock for $13.50 per share.[8] By December 20, 1985 the tender offer was
complete and WSI had acquired ownership of Wieboldt through its purchase of
99% of Wieboldt's stock at a total price of $38,462,164.00. All of the funds WSI
used to purchase the tendered shares were provided by HCFS and were secured
by the assets which BAMIRCO and GECC loan proceeds had freed from CINB
obligations. After the LBO,

1. Wieboldt's One North State Street property was conveyed to ONSSLP as
   beneficiary of a land trust established with Boulevard Bank as trustee;
2. Substantially all of Wieboldt's remaining real estate holdings were subject to
   first or second mortgages to secure the HCFS loans; and
3. Wieboldt's customer credit card accounts were conveyed to GECC and Wieboldt's accounts receivable were pledged to GECC as security under the
   GECC accounts purchase agreement.

In addition, Wieboldt became liable to HCFS on an amended note in the amount
of approximately $32.5 million. Wieboldt did not receive any amount of working
capital as a direct result of the LBO.

---

8. Approximately 1,900 shareholders held the 2,765,574 shares of Wieboldt common stock that were
outstanding on that date. As a result of the offer, Mr. Schottenstein and his affiliates tendered at least 416,958
shares and received $5,628,933.00 from WSI. Trump brothers [tendered] 480,072 shares and received
$6,480,972.00 from WSI. The Schedule A shareholders also tendered their shares at the offer price.

Author's Case Annotation: Structure of Transaction

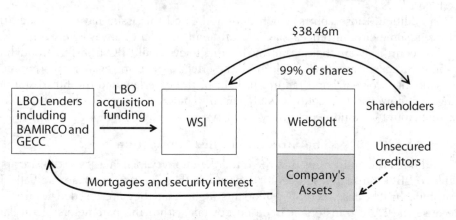

Wieboldt alleges that WSI's tender offer and the resulting LBO was a fraudulent conveyance under the federal bankruptcy statute and the Illinois fraudulent conveyance laws.

The controlling shareholders, insider shareholders, Schedule A shareholders, and the State Street defendants move to dismiss the complaint on the grounds that Wieboldt has failed to state a claim under either the federal or the state fraudulent conveyance laws. In addition, the board of directors seek dismissal of the counts against them because Wieboldt has failed to state a claim for breach of fiduciary duty. Each of these assertions are discussed below.

Applicability of Fraudulent Conveyance Law

Both the federal Bankruptcy Code and Illinois law protect creditors from transfers of property that are intended to impair a creditor's ability to enforce its rights to payment or that deplete a debtor's assets at a time when its financial condition is precarious.

The controlling shareholders, insider shareholders, and some of the Schedule A shareholders argue that fraudulent conveyance laws do not apply to leveraged buy-outs. These defendants argue (1) that applying fraudulent conveyance laws to public tender offers effectively allows creditors to insure themselves against subsequent mismanagement of the company; (2) that applying fraudulent conveyance laws to LBO transactions and thereby rendering them void severely restricts the usefulness of LBOs and results in great unfairness; and (3) that fraudulent conveyance laws were never intended to be used to prohibit or restrict public tender offers.

Although some support exists for defendants' arguments, this court cannot hold at this stage in this litigation that the LBO in question here is entirely exempt from fraudulent conveyance laws. Neither Section 548 of the [Bankruptcy] Code nor the Illinois statute exempt such transactions from their statutory coverage. Section 548 invalidates fraudulent "transfers" of a debtor's property. Section 101(50) defines such a transfer very broadly to include "every mode, direct or indirect, absolute or conditional, voluntary or involuntary, of disposing of or parting with property or with an interest in property, including retention of title as a security interest." Likewise, the Illinois statute applies to gifts, grants, conveyances, assignments and transfers. The language of these statutes in no way limits their application so as to exclude LBOs.

In addition, those courts which have addressed this issue have concluded that LBOs in some circumstances may constitute a fraudulent conveyance.

The court is aware that permitting debtors to avoid all LBO transfers through the fraudulent conveyance laws could have the effect of insuring against a corporation's subsequent insolvency and failure. In light of the case law and the broad statutory language, however, this court sees no reason to hold as a general rule that LBOs are exempt from the fraudulent conveyance laws.

The Structure of the Transaction

Although the court finds that the fraudulent conveyance laws generally are applicable to LBO transactions, a debtor cannot use these laws to avoid any and all LBO transfers. In this case, certain defendants argue that they are entitled to dismissal because the LBO transfers at issue do not fall within the parameters of the laws. These defendants argue that they are protected by the literal language of Section 548 of the Code. They contend, initially, that they did not receive Wieboldt property during the tender offer.

The merit of this assertion turns on the court's interpretation of the tender offer and LBO transactions. Defendants contend that the tender offer and LBO were composed of a series of interrelated but independent transactions. They assert, for example, that the transfer of property from HCFS to WSI and ultimately to the shareholders constituted one series of several transactions while the pledge of Wieboldt assets to HCFS to secure the financing constituted a second series of transactions. Under this view, defendants did not receive the *debtor*'s property during the tender offer but rather received *WSI*'s property in exchange for their shares.

Wieboldt, on the other hand, urges the court to "collapse" the interrelated transactions into one aggregate transaction which had the overall effect of conveying Wieboldt property to the tendering shareholders and LBO lenders. This approach requires the court to find that the persons and entities receiving the conveyance were direct transferees who received "an interest of the debtor in property" during the tender offer/buyout, and that WSI and any other parties to the transactions were "mere conduits" of Wieboldt's property. If the court finds that all the transfers constituted one transaction, then defendants received property from Wieboldt and Wieboldt has stated a claim against them.

Few courts have considered whether complicated LBO transfers should be evaluated separately or collapsed into one integrated transaction.

[In two federal appellate cases, courts] expressed the view that an LBO transfer—in whatever form—was a fraudulent conveyance if the circumstances of the transfer were not "above board." These cases indicate that a court should focus not on the formal structure of the transaction but rather on the knowledge or intent of the parties involved in the transaction.

Applying this principle to defendants' assertions, it is clear that, at least as regards the liability of the controlling shareholders, the LBO lenders, and the insider shareholders, the LBO transfers must be collapsed into one transaction. The complaint alleges clearly that these participants in the LBO negotiations attempted to structure the LBO with the requisite knowledge and contemplation that the full transaction, tender offer and LBO, be completed. The Board and the insider shareholders knew that WSI intended to finance its acquisition of Wieboldt through an LBO and not with any of its own funds. They knew that Wieboldt was insolvent before the LBO and that the LBO would result in further encumbrance of Wieboldt's already encumbered assets. Attorneys for Schottenstein Stores apprised the Board of the fraudulent conveyance laws and suggested that they structure the LBO so as to avoid liability. Nonetheless, these shareholders recommended that Wieboldt accept the tender offer and themselves tendered their shares to WSI.

Wieboldt's complaint also alleges sufficient facts to implicate the LBO lenders in the scheme. HCFS, BAMIRCO and GECC were well aware of each other's loan or credit commitments to WSI and knew that WSI intended to use the proceeds of their financing commitments to purchase Wieboldt shares or options and to release certain Wieboldt assets from prior encumbrances. Representatives of the lenders received the same information concerning the fraudulent conveyance laws as did the Board of Directors. These LBO lenders agreed with WSI and the Board of Directors to structure the LBO so as to avoid fraudulent conveyance liability.

The court, however, is not willing to "collapse" the transaction in order to find that the Schedule A shareholders also received the debtor's property in the transfer. While Wieboldt directs specific allegations of fraud against the controlling and insider shareholders and LBO lenders, Wieboldt does not allege that the Schedule A shareholders were aware that WSI's acquisition encumbered virtually all of Wieboldt's assets. Nor is there an allegation that these shareholders were aware that the consideration they received for their tendered shares was Wieboldt property. In fact, the complaint does not suggest that the Schedule A shareholders had any part in the LBO except as innocent pawns in the scheme. They were aware only that WSI made a public tender offer for shares of Wieboldt stock. Viewing the transactions from the perspective of the Schedule A shareholders and considering their knowledge and intent, therefore, the asset transfers to the LBO lenders were indeed independent of the tender offer to the Schedule A shareholders.

This conclusion is in accord with the purpose of the fraudulent conveyance laws. The drafters of the Code, while attempting to protect parties harmed by fraudulent conveyances, also intended to shield innocent recipients of fraudulently conveyed property from liability. Thus, although Section 550(a) permits a trustee to avoid a transfer to an initial transferee or its subsequent transferee, subsection (b) limits recovery from a subsequent transferee by providing that a trustee may not recover fraudulently conveyed property from a subsequent transferee who takes the property in good faith, for value, and without knowledge that the original transfer was voidable. Subsection (b) applies, however, only to subsequent transferees.

Similarly, the LBO lenders and the controlling and insider shareholders of Wieboldt are direct transferees of Wieboldt property. Although WSI participated in effecting the transactions, Wieboldt's complaint alleges that WSI was a corporation formed solely for the purpose of acquiring Wieboldt stock. The court can reasonably infer from the complaint, therefore, that WSI served mainly as a conduit for the exchange of assets and loan proceeds between LBO lenders and Wieboldt and for the exchange of loan proceeds and shares of stock between the LBO lenders and the insider and controlling shareholders. On the other hand, the Schedule A shareholders are not direct transferees of Wieboldt property. From their perspective, WSI was the direct transferee of Wieboldt property and the shareholders were merely indirect transferees because WSI was an independent entity in the transaction.

In sum, the formal structure of the transaction alone cannot shield the LBO lenders or the controlling and insider shareholders from Wieboldt's fraudulent conveyance claims. These parties were aware that the consideration they received for their financing commitments or in exchange for their shares consisted of Wieboldt assets and not the assets of WSI or any other financial intermediary. The Schedule A shareholders, on the other hand, apparently unaware of the financing transactions, participated only to the extent that they exchanged their shares for funds from WSI. Therefore, based on the allegations in the complaint, the court concludes that: (1) the motions to dismiss filed by the LBO lenders, insider shareholders, and controlling shareholders are denied at this point because these parties received Wieboldt property through a series of integrated LBO transactions; and (2) the Schedule A shareholders' motions to dismiss are granted because these defendants did not receive Wieboldt property through the separate exchange of shares for cash.

As discussed above, the transfers to and between the debtor and the LBO lenders, controlling shareholders, and insider shareholders are subject to the provisions in Section 548(a) of the Code* and Section 4 of the Illinois statute. The court now must determine whether Wieboldt's complaint states sufficient facts to allege the elements of these causes of action.

Section 548(a)(1) — actual fraud

In order to state a claim for relief under Section 548(a)(1) of the Code, a debtor or trustee must allege (1) that the transfer was made within one year before the debtor filed a petition in bankruptcy, and (2) that the transfer was made with the actual intent to hinder, delay or defraud the debtor's creditors. Although defendants do not dispute that the LBO transfers occurred within a year of the date on which Wieboldt filed for bankruptcy, they vigorously assert that Wieboldt has failed to properly allege "intent to defraud" as required by Section 548(a)(1).

"Actual intent" in the context of fraudulent transfers of property is rarely susceptible to proof and "must be gleaned from inferences drawn from a course of conduct." A general scheme or plan to strip the debtor of its assets without regard to the needs of its creditors can support a finding of actual intent. In addition, certain "badges of fraud" can form the basis for a finding of actual intent to hinder, delay or defraud.

Counts I and III of Wieboldt's complaint state a claim under Section 548(a)(1). Count I, which Wieboldt brings against the controlling and insider shareholders, states that these defendants exchanged their shares with the actual intent to hinder, delay or defraud Wieboldt's unsecured creditors. Count III states that the State Street defendants received Wieboldt's interest in One North State Street property with the actual intent to defraud Wieboldt's unsecured creditors. The complaint also states generally that the LBO Lenders and the controlling and insider shareholders structured the LBO transfers in such a way as to attempt to evade fraudulent conveyance liability. These allegations are a sufficient assertion of actual fraud. Defendants' motions to dismiss Counts I and III are therefore denied.

---

* Author's note: For students who are looking up the references in the opinion to Sections 548(a)(1) and 548(a)(2) with the text of the Bankruptcy Code §548(a) as given above, note that the Bankruptcy Code has been renumbered since the date of the opinion. The opinion's reference to §548(a)(1) is the predecessor provision to the current statute §548(a)(1)(A), and the reference to §548(a)(2) corresponds to current §548(a)(1)(B).

Section 548(a)(2) *— Constructive fraud* [handwritten]

Unlike Section 548(a)(1), which requires a plaintiff to allege "actual fraud," Section 548(a)(2) requires a plaintiff to allege only constructive fraud. A plaintiff states a claim under Section 548(a)(2) by alleging that the debtor (1) transferred property within a year of filing a petition in bankruptcy; (2) received less than the reasonably equivalent value for the property transferred; and (3) either (a) was insolvent or became insolvent as a result of the transfer, (b) retained unreasonably small capital after the transfer, or (c) made the transfer with the intent to incur debts beyond its ability to pay.

Defendants argue that Wieboldt's allegation of insolvency is insufficient as a matter of law to satisfy the insolvency requirement in Section 548(a)(2)(B)(i). Section 101(31)(A) of the Code defines "insolvency" as a condition which occurs when the sum of an entity's debts exceeds the sum of its property "at a fair valuation." Wieboldt's complaint alleges that the corporation was insolvent in November, 1985 "in that the fair saleable value of its assets was exceeded by its liabilities when the illiquidity of those assets is taken into account."

Wieboldt's allegations satisfy the "insolvency" requirement of Section 548(a)(2)(B)(i). Defendants' attempt to distinguish Wieboldt's phrase "fair saleable value" from Section 101(31)(A)'s "fair valuation" is, as Wieboldt suggests, "hypertechnical." "Fair valuation" is near enough in meaning to "fair value of saleable assets" to defeat defendants' motion to dismiss. In addition, Wieboldt did not destroy its claim of insolvency by characterizing its assets as "illiquid" at the time of the transfer. In determining "fair valuation," a court must consider the property's intrinsic value, selling value, and the earning power of the property. Assets may be reduced by the value of the assets that cannot be readily liquidated. The complaint meets the financial condition test of Section 548(a)(2)(B)(i).

Finally, defendants claim that Wieboldt cannot state a claim under Section 548(a)(2) because it received "reasonably equivalent value" in the transfer to the shareholders and the conveyance of the One North State Street property. Wieboldt granted a security interest in substantially all of its real estate assets to HCFS and received from the shareholders in return 99% of its outstanding shares of stock. This stock was virtually worthless to Wieboldt. Wieboldt received less than a reasonably equivalent value in exchange for an encumbrance on virtually all of its non-inventory assets, and therefore has stated a claim against the controlling and insider shareholders.

Likewise, the court need not dismiss Wieboldt's Section 548(a)(2) claim against the State Street defendants on the grounds that Wieboldt received reasonably equivalent value in exchange for its One North State Street property. The effect and intention of the parties to the One North State Street conveyance was to generate funds to purchase outstanding shares of Wieboldt stock. Although Wieboldt sold the property to ONSSLP for $30 million, and used the proceeds to pay off part of the $35 million it owed CINB, Wieboldt did not receive a benefit from this transfer. Defendants knew that the conveyance would neither increase Wieboldt's assets nor result in a net reduction of its liabilities. In fact, all parties to the conveyance were aware that the newly unencumbered assets would be immediately remortgaged to HCFS to finance the acquisition. According to the complaint, therefore, Wieboldt received less than reasonably equivalent value for the conveyance of the One North State Street property and has stated a claim against the State Street defendants under Section 548(a)(2).

In sum, Counts II and IV of Wieboldt's complaint state a claim under Section 548(a)(2). Defendants' motions to dismiss these counts are denied.

Illinois Fraudulent Conveyance Law

Under Section 544(b) of the Code, a trustee may avoid transfers that are avoidable under state law if there is at least one creditor at the time who has standing under state law to challenge the transfer. 11 U.S.C. §544(b). Wieboldt utilizes this section to pursue a claim under the Illinois fraudulent conveyance statute.

The Illinois fraudulent conveyance statute is similar to Section 548 of the Code. The statute provides that:

> Every gift, grant, conveyance, assignment or transfer of, or charge upon any estate, real or personal, . . . made with the intent to disturb, delay, hinder or defraud creditors or other person, . . . shall be void as against the creditors, purchasers and other persons.

Ill.Rev.Stat. ch. 59, §4 (1976). Illinois courts divide fraudulent conveyances into two categories: fraud in law and fraud in fact. In fraud in fact cases, a court must find a specific intent to defraud creditors; in fraud in law cases, fraud is presumed from the circumstances.

Count VIII of Wieboldt's complaint purports to state a claim against the insider and controlling shareholders, Schedule A shareholders, and State Street defendants for fraud in law. Fraud in law occurs when a debtor makes a voluntary transfer without consideration, and the transfer impairs the rights of creditors. To state a claim for fraud in law, a plaintiff must allege: (1) a voluntary gift; (2) an existing or contemplated indebtedness against the debtor; and (3) the failure of the debtor to retain sufficient property to pay the indebtedness. Wieboldt's complaint alleges that the LBO transfers were fraudulent because "Wieboldt did not receive fair consideration for the property it conveyed and was insolvent at the time of the conveyance because it was then unable to meet its obligations as they became due."

Wieboldt's complaint clearly alleges the elements of fraud in law. Although Wieboldt's complaint does not specifically allege that it made a "voluntary gift," a transfer for grossly inadequate consideration is deemed to be a "voluntary gift" under Illinois law. As previously discussed, Wieboldt did not receive a benefit from these transfers. Second, Wieboldt clearly was obligated to a number of entities at the time of the transfers and in fact had defaulted on its obligations to CINB. Finally, Wieboldt alleges that the LBO transfers rendered it insolvent. An insolvent corporation does not have sufficient assets to repay its obligations. The complaint therefore satisfies the elements of fraud in law under Section 4.

In sum, the court cannot dismiss Wieboldt's claim under Section 4 of the Illinois statute. Defendants' motion to dismiss Count VIII is denied.

QUESTIONS

1. What was the purpose of the LBO transaction? Who gained? Who lost?
2. What is the relevance of the solvency issue raised by HCFS and Wieboldt's lawyers? Why did HCFS want a solvency opinion? Why did Wieboldt's lawyers object?
3. What is the relevance of the fact that the board knew the acquisition funding from creditors did not include $10 million in working capital?

F. STOCK DIVIDENDS AND SPLITS

Cash is the typical asset distributed in a dividend, but a corporation can also issue its shares as a dividend. A stock dividend effectively acts as a stock split. For example, a corporation with 10 million shares outstanding issues a 10 percent stock dividend, resulting in the issuance of 1 million new shares to current shareholders and a total shares outstanding of 11 million shares. A stock dividend is not an actual distribution of the company's assets in the way that cash dividends, asset distributions, or stock repurchases are. When a company distributes shares of its own stock, it does not affect its financial status: It does not reduce cash or affect the total amount of equity, though there are a few minor accounting adjustments within the equity account. There are simply more shares outstanding.

A stock split is the splitting of a single share into multiple shares. It increases shares outstanding and thus decreases share price. For example, if a corporation has 10 million shares and it executes a 3-for-1 stock split, the company's total shares outstanding would increase to 30 million shares. A reverse stock split combines multiple shares into a single share. For example, a 1-for-2 reverse stock split would decrease the number of shares outstanding from 10 million shares to 5 million shares. A stock dividend or a stock split does not change the value of the corporation, but it changes the stock price. Stock price is determined by the market capitalization divided by shares outstanding. For example, assume that the market capitalization of the company is $100 million, shares outstanding 10 million shares, and thus share price of $10/share. If the stock is split 2-for-1, the share price decreases to $5/share.

$$\frac{\$100m}{10m\ shares} = \$10\ per\ share \quad \rightarrow \quad \frac{\$100m}{20m\ shares} = \$5\ per\ share$$

However, notice that the equity value of the company does not change. After the stock split, the market capitalization is still $100 million (= $5 per share x 20 million shares outstanding).

A reverse stock split has the opposite effect on share price: It increases share price. For example, assume the same market capitalization of $100 million, shares outstanding are 10 million shares, and thus share price is $10/share. If the company executes a 1-for-2 reverse stock split, the share price increases to $20/share.

$$\frac{\$100m}{10m\ shares} = \$10\ per\ share \quad \rightarrow \quad \frac{\$100m}{5m\ shares} = \$20\ per\ share$$

A stock split changes the number of shares outstanding and the share price. One or both effects are the reasons for doing a stock split. Changing the share price is the more common reason why a company executes a stock split. A company's share price may reach such high levels that it may limit investment by retail shareholders. An investor with $5,000 to invest may be discouraged from investing in a company whose shares are trading at $1,000 per share even though she is able to buy 5 shares. Contrarily, a reverse stock split may increase share price, which may benefit perceptions of value or, more importantly, raise share prices to avoid minimum share price requirements of listing standards of stock exchanges.

EXAMPLE

Apple Inc.'s Stock Splits

On June 9, 2014, shares of Apple Inc. split 7-for-1 and closed at $93.70; previously, on June 6, 2014, the stock closed at $645.57. Prior to this most recent stock split, Apple had executed three stock splits, each 2-for-1. This implies an eight-fold reduction in the stock price (8 = 2 x 2 x 2), which suggests that without the three previous stock splits Apple stock would have traded at $5,164.56 unadjusted for any splits (= $645.57 x 8). Without the stock splits, an investment in Apple might have been out of reach of many small investors. Commenting on the reason for doing the most recent 7-for-1 stock split, the CEO of Apple said, "We're taking this action to make Apple stock more accessible to a larger number of investors." But this comment seems to contradict a comment made two years earlier at Apple's shareholder meeting in February 2012, where splitting shares would do "nothing" for shareholders. Steven Russolillo, *What Apple's Stock Split Means for You*, Wall St. J. (June 9, 2014). In fact, the CEO's comments are not necessarily contradictory. In what way are the two comments broadly accurate?

The following case involves a stock split transaction in which the transaction affected shareholders differently. The disparate effects arose from the workings of the technical facets of the stock split transaction.

Applebaum v. Avaya, Inc.
812 A.2d 880 (Del. 2002)

VEASEY, Chief Justice.

In this appeal, we affirm the judgment of the Court of Chancery holding that a corporation could validly initiate a reverse stock split and selectively dispose of the fractional interests held by stockholders who no longer hold whole shares. The Vice Chancellor interpreted Section 155 of the Delaware General Corporation Law to permit the corporation, as part of a reverse/forward stock split, to treat its stockholders unequally by cashing out the stockholders who own only fractional interests while opting not to dispose of fractional interests of stockholders who will end up holding whole shares of stock as well as fractional interests. In the latter instance the fractional shares would be reconverted to whole shares in an accompanying forward stock split.

We hold that neither the language of Section 155 nor the principles guiding our interpretation of statutes dictate a prohibition against the disparate treatment of stockholders, for this purpose. We also hold that the corporation may dispose of those fractional interests pursuant to Section 155(1) by aggregating the fractional interests and selling them on behalf of the cashed-out stockholders where this method of disposition has a rational business purpose of saving needless transaction costs.

A further issue we address is whether, as an alternative method of compensation, the corporation may satisfy the "fair price" requirement of Section 155(2) by paying the stockholders an amount based on the average trading price of the corporation's stock. Here, the Vice Chancellor properly held that the trading price of actively-traded stock of a corporation, the stock of which is widely-held, will provide an adequate measure of fair value for the stockholders' fractional interests for purposes of a reverse stock split under Section 155.

Avaya, Inc. is a Delaware corporation that designs and manages communications networks for business organizations and large non-profit agencies. The enterprise is a descendant of the industry standard-bearer, AT&T. Avaya was established as an independent company in October of 2000 when it was spun off from Lucent Technologies. Lucent itself is a spin-off of AT&T. Because its capital structure is the product of two spin-off transactions, the outstanding stock of Avaya is one of the most widely-held on the New York Stock Exchange. Over 3.3 million common stockholders own fewer than 90 shares of Avaya stock each.

Although a large number of stockholders hold a small stake in the corporation, Avaya incurs heavy expenses to maintain their accounts. Avaya spends almost $4 million per year to print and mail proxy statements and annual reports to each stockholder as well as to pay transfer agents and other miscellaneous fees. Stockholders who own their stock in street names cost Avaya an additional $3.4 million in similar administrative fees.

Since the cost of maintaining a stockholder's account is the same regardless of the number of shares held, Avaya could reduce its administrative burden, and thereby save money for its stockholders, by decreasing its stockholder base. In February of 2001, at the corporation's annual meeting, the Avaya board of directors presented the stockholders with a transaction designed to accomplish this result. The Avaya board asked the stockholders to grant the directors authorization to engage in one of three alternative transactions:

(1) a reverse 1–for–30 stock split followed immediately by a forward 30–for–1 stock split of the Common stock
(2) a reverse 1–for–40 stock split followed immediately by a forward 40–for–1 stock split of the Common stock
(3) a reverse 1–for–50 stock split followed immediately by a forward 50–for–1 stock split of the Common stock.

Regardless of the particular ratio the board chooses, at some future date the Reverse Split will occur at 6:00 p.m., followed by a Forward Split one minute later.

The transaction will cash out stockholders who own stock below the minimum number ultimately selected by the directors for the Reverse/Forward Split pursuant to those three alternative options. Stockholders who do not hold the minimum number of shares necessary to survive the initial Reverse Split will be cashed out and receive payment for their resulting fractional interests (the "cashed-out stockholders" or "targeted stockholders"). Stockholders who own a sufficient amount of stock to survive the Reverse Split will not have their fractional interests cashed out. Once the Forward Split occurs, their fractional holdings will be converted back into whole shares of stock.

Avaya will compensate the cashed-out stockholders through one of two possible methods. Avaya may combine the fractional interests and sell them as whole shares on the open market. In the alternative, the corporation will pay the stockholders the value of their fractional interests based on the trading price of the stock averaged over a ten-day period preceding the Reverse Split.

To illustrate the Proposed Transaction through a hypothetical, assume Stockholder A owns fifteen shares of stock and Stockholder B owns forty-five shares of stock. If Avaya chooses to initiate a Reverse 1–for–30 Stock Split, Stockholder A will possess a fractional interest equivalent to one-half a share of stock. Stockholder B will hold one whole share of Avaya stock and a fractional interest equivalent to one-half a share. Avaya would cash out Stockholder A since he no longer possesses a whole share of stock. Stockholder A would no longer be an Avaya stockholder. Stockholder B will remain a stockholder because Avaya will not cash out the fractional interest held by her. Stockholder B's fractional interest remains attached to a whole share of stock. When Avaya executes the accompanying Forward 30–for–1 Stock Split, Stockholder B's interest in one and one-half shares will be converted into forty-five shares of stock, the same amount that she held prior to the Transaction.

At the annual meeting, Avaya stockholders voted to authorize the board to proceed with any one of the three alternative transactions. Applebaum, a holder of twenty-seven shares of Avaya stock, filed an action in the Court of Chancery to enjoin the Reverse/Forward Split. Under any one of the three alternatives Applebaum would be cashed out because he holds less than thirty shares.

Section 155 Does Not Prevent Avaya from Disposing of Fractional Interests Selectively

Applebaum questions the board's authority to treat stockholders differently by disposing of the fractional interests of some stockholders but not others. Applebaum contends that Avaya will issue fractional shares in violation of Section 155 [which provides].

[Fractions of shares. A corporation may, but shall not be required to, issue fractions of a share. If it does not issue fractions of a share, it shall (1) arrange for the disposition of fractional interests by those entitled thereto, (2) pay in cash the fair value of fractions of a share as of the time when those entitled to receive such fractions are determined or (3) issue scrip or warrants in registered form (either represented by a certificate or uncertificated) or in bearer form (represented by a certificate) which shall entitle the holder to receive a full share upon the surrender of such scrip or warrants aggregating a full share. . . .]

According to [Applebaum's] view of the transaction, during the one minute interval between the two stock splits the corporation will not issue fractional shares to stockholders who possess holdings below the minimum amount. Those stockholders will be cashed out. Stockholders who hold stock above the minimum amount, by contrast, will be issued fractional shares that will be reconverted in the Forward Split into the same number of whole shares owned by those stockholders before the Reverse Split.

Applebaum reads Section 155 to mean that Avaya can employ the cash-out methods provided in Section 155 only if the corporation "does not issue fractions of a share."

We need not reach the merits of Applebaum's interpretation of Section 155 because he has based his argument on the flawed assumption that Avaya will issue fractional shares. Since the Reverse/Forward Split is an integrated transaction, Avaya need not issue any fractional shares. The initial Reverse Split creates a combination of whole *shares* and fractional *interests*. Avaya will use either Section 155(1) or (2) to cash out the fractional interests of stockholders who no longer possess a whole share of stock. Fractional *interests* that are attached to whole *shares* will not be disposed of. Nor will they be represented by fractions of a share. Fractional shares are unnecessary because the surviving fractional interests will be reconverted into whole shares in the Forward Split.

Applebaum correctly notes that Avaya stockholders are not treated equally in the Proposed Transaction. The disparate treatment, however, does not arise by issuing fractional shares selectively. It occurs through the selective disposition of some fractional interests but not others. The provisions of Section 155 do not forbid this disparate treatment. While principles of equity permit this Court to intervene when technical compliance with a statute produces an unfair result, equity and equality are not synonymous concepts in the Delaware General Corporation Law.[9] Moreover, this Court should not create a safeguard against stockholder inequality that does not appear in the statute. Here there is no showing that Applebaum was treated inequitably. From all that appears on this record, the proposed transaction was designed in good faith to accomplish a rational business purpose—saving transaction costs.

Our jurisprudence does not prevent Avaya from properly using Section 155 in a creative fashion that is designed to meet its needs as an on-going enterprise. The subsections listed in Section 155 merely require the corporation to compensate its stockholders when it chooses not to recognize their fractional interests in the form of fractional shares. Based upon this record, we conclude that Avaya is free to recognize the fractional interests of some stockholders but not others so long as the corporation follows the procedures set forth in Section 155.

Section 155(1) Permits Avaya to Sell the Factional Interest on Behalf of the Stockholders

The stockholders have authorized Avaya to compensate the cashed-out stockholders by combining their fractional interests into whole shares and then selling them on the stockholders' behalf. Section 155(1) permits Avaya to "arrange for the disposition of fractional interests by those entitled thereto."

Applebaum claims that Avaya cannot use Section 155(1) because the corporation will sell whole shares rather than "fractional interests." According to this rendition of the transaction, the fractional interests held by the targeted stockholders must be reconverted into whole shares in the Forward Split. Otherwise, their fractional interests will be diluted. Avaya must reconvert the interests back to their initial value as whole shares in order to sell the combined fractional interests. Thus, Avaya would be selling whole shares rather than fractional interests.

Applebaum's argument incorrectly assumes that Avaya must issue fractions of a share in the Proposed Transaction. After the Reverse Split takes place, the stockholders holding shares below the minimum amount will be cashed out. The fractional interests will not be represented as shares and are therefore not involved in the Forward Split. Avaya will then aggregate the fractional interests and repackage them as whole shares which the corporation will sell on the open market. The statute does not mandate any set procedure by which the fractional interests must be disposed of so long as those interests are sold in a manner that secures the proportionate value of the cashed-out holdings.

Applebaum also contends that Avaya cannot sell the fractional interests on behalf of the cashed-out stockholders. If Avaya sells the interests for the stockholders,

---

9. *See Nixon v. Blackwell*, 626 A.2d 1366, 1376 (Del. 1993) ("It is well established in our jurisprudence that stockholders need not always be treated equally for all purposes.").

Applebaum argues that the corporation will not comply with Section 155(1) because the interests are not disposed of by "those entitled thereto."

Applebaum's interpretation also ignores the corporation's responsibility under Section 155(1) to "arrange" for the disposition of fractional interests. Since fractional shares cannot be listed on the major stock exchanges, the corporation must arrange for their aggregation in order to sell them. Aggregation is normally performed by

> affording to the stockholder an election to sell the fractional share or to purchase an additional fraction sufficient to make up a whole share. The elections are forwarded to a trust company or other agent of the corporation who matches up the purchases and sales and issues certificates for the whole shares or checks for payment of the fractional shares. . . ."

The general practice requires the corporation to act as an intermediary to package the fractional interests into marketable shares. If the corporation were not permitted to do so, the fractional interests of the cashed-out stockholders would be dissipated through the transaction costs of finding other fractional holders with whom to combine and sell fractional interests in the market.

The Ten–Day Trading Average by which Avaya Proposes to Compensate the Cashed–Out Stockholders Constitutes "Fair Value" under Section 155(2)

As an alternative to selling the fractional interests on behalf of the stockholders, Avaya may opt to pay the stockholders cash in an amount based on the trading price of Avaya stock averaged over a ten-day period preceding the Proposed Transaction. To do so, Avaya relies on Section 155(2), which provides that a corporation may "pay in cash the fair value of fractions of a share as of the time when those entitled to receive such fractions are determined."

The corporation owes its cashed-out stockholders payment representing the "fair value" of their fractional interests. The cashed-out stockholders will receive fair value if Avaya compensates them with payment based on the price of Avaya stock averaged over a ten-day period preceding the Proposed Transaction. While market price is not employed in all valuation contexts,[28] our jurisprudence recognizes that in many circumstances a property interest is best valued by the amount a buyer will pay for it.[29] The Vice Chancellor correctly concluded that a well-informed, liquid trading market will provide a measure of fair value superior to any estimate the court could impose.

Avaya stock is actively traded on the NYSE. The value of Avaya's stock is tested daily through the purchase and sale of the stock on the open market.

In a related argument, Applebaum contends that the trading price cannot represent fair value because the stock price is volatile, trading at a range of prices from

---

28. See e.g., 8 Del. C. §262(h) ("In determining . . . fair value," in an appraisal proceeding, "the Court shall take into account all relevant factors."); Smith v. Van Gorkom, 488 A.2d 858, 876 (Del.1985) (holding that a decision by the board of directors to approve a merger did not fall within the proper exercise of business judgment because the directors failed to consider the intrinsic worth of the corporation where the stock traded at a depressed market value).

29. Cf. 8 Del. C. §262(b)(1) (denying appraisal rights for stock listed on a national securities exchange, interdealer quotation system by the National Association of Securities Dealers, Inc. or held of record by more than 2,000 holders); Revlon, Inc. v. MacAndrews & Forbes Holdings, 506 A.2d 173, 182 (Del. 1986) (noting that an auction for the sale of a corporation is an appropriate method by which to secure the best price for the stockholders).

$13.70 per share to $1.12 per share over the past year. The volatility in trading does not necessarily mean that the market price is not an accurate indicator of fair value. Avaya stock is widely-held and actively traded in the market. The ten-day average has been recognized as a fair compromise that will hedge against the risk of fluctuation. Corporations often cash out fractional interests in an amount based on the average price over a given trading period.

Applebaum also misunderstands the appropriate context for which a going-concern valuation may be necessary under Section 155(2). A transaction employing Section 155 may warrant a searching inquiry of fair value if a controlling stockholder initiates the transaction. When a controlling stockholder presents a transaction that will free it from future dealings with the minority stockholders, opportunism becomes a concern. Any shortfall imposed on the minority stockholders will result in a transfer of value to the controlling stockholder. The discount in value could be imposed deliberately or could be the result of an information asymmetry where the controlling stockholder possesses material facts that are not known in the market. Thus, a Section 155(2) inquiry may resemble a Section 262 valuation if the controlling stockholder will benefit from presenting a suspect measure of valuation, such as an outdated trading price, or a wrongfully imposed private company discount.

Although the Reverse/Forward Split will cash out smaller stockholders, the transaction will not allow the corporation to realize a gain at their expense. Unlike the more typical "freeze-out" context, the cashed-out Avaya stockholders may continue to share in the value of the enterprise. Avaya stockholders can avoid the effects of the proposed transaction either by purchasing a sufficient amount of stock to survive the initial Reverse Split or by simply using the payment provided under Section 155(2) to repurchase the same amount of Avaya stock that they held before the transaction.

The Reverse/Forward Split merely forces the stockholders to choose affirmatively to remain in the corporation. Avaya will succeed in saving administrative costs only if the board has assumed correctly that the stockholders who received a small interest in the corporation through the Lucent spin-off would prefer to receive payment, free of transaction costs, rather than continue with the corporation. The Transaction is not structured to prevent the cashed-out stockholders from maintaining their stakes in the company. A payment based on market price is appropriate because it will permit the stockholders to reinvest in Avaya, should they wish to do so.

The Meaning of "Fair Value" under Section 155(2) is Not Identical to the Concept of "Fair Value" in Section 262

The Court of Chancery correctly interpreted "fair value" in Section 155 to have a meaning independent of the definition of "fair value" in Section 262 of the Delaware General Corporation Law.[44] Relying on the maxim that the same words used in different sections must be construed to have the same meaning, Applebaum argues that "fair value" under Section 155(2) requires the court to perform a valuation similar

---

44. 8 *Del. C.* §262(a) (providing that "Any stockholder of a corporation of this State who holds shares of stock on the date of the making of a demand pursuant to subsection (d) . . . who continuously holds such shares through the effective date of the merger or consolidation . . . who has neither voted in favor of the merger or consolidation nor consented thereto . . . shall be entitled to an appraisal by the Court of Chancery of the fair value of the stockholder's shares of stock. . . . ").

to an appraisal proceeding. Borrowing from appraisal concepts that require that shares of stock be valued as proportionate interests in a going concern, Applebaum contends that the average trading price would be inadequate because the market price possesses an inherent discount that accounts for the holder's minority stake in the company.

The Delaware General Assembly could not have intended Section 155(2) to have the same meaning as the fair value concept employed in Section 262. The reference to fair value in Section 155 first appeared in 1967. The General Assembly did not place the term fair value in Section 262 until 1976. Furthermore, the case law developing the concept of fair value under the appraisal statute did not acquire its present form until this Court discarded the Delaware block method and underscored the necessity of valuing a corporation as a going concern. This Court has not suggested similar valuation guidelines for the right to receive "fair value" under Section 155(2).

The valuation of a stockholder's interest as a "going concern" is necessary only when the board's proposal will alter the nature of the corporation through a merger. When a corporation merges with another corporation, the dissenting stockholder is entitled to the value of the company as a going concern because the nature of the corporation's future "concern" will be vastly different. In a merger requiring an appraisal, the dissenting stockholder's share must be measured as a proportionate interest in a going concern because the proponents of the merger will realize the full intrinsic worth of the company rather than simply the market price of the stock. Thus, when a minority stockholder is confronted with a freeze-out merger, the Section 262 appraisal process will prevent the proponents of the merger from "reaping a windfall" by placing the full value of the company as a going concern into the merged entity while compensating the dissenting stockholder with discounted consideration.

Avaya will not capture its full going-concern value in the Reverse/Forward Split. As the Vice Chancellor noted, if the cashed-out stockholders were awarded the value of the company as a going concern, they, rather than the corporation, would receive a windfall. The cashed-out stockholders could capture the full proportionate value of the fractional interest, return to the market and buy the reissued stock at the market price, and realize the going concern value a second time should Avaya ever merge or otherwise become subject to a change of control transaction.

The judgment of the Court of Chancery is affirmed.

QUESTIONS

1. What was the business reason for doing this complicated transaction?
2. Why does it matter whether Avaya issued or did not issue fractional shares?
3. What are the meanings of "fair value" under Section 155 and Section 262?
4. What rationale explains the different meaning given to the term "fair value"?

G. CASE STUDY: AIG'S REVERSE STOCK SPLIT

During the years leading up to the financial crisis of 2008-2009, American International Group, Inc. (AIG) was a massive financial institution that provided insurance and financial products and services. It sold traditional insurance products, such as property and casualty insurance policies. It also dealt in derivatives and financial hedging. Specifically, it provided financial hedges on mortgage-related securities held by bond investors and other institutions. The exposure to mortgage-related bonds and financial instruments was massive. As the residential housing market collapsed in 2008, AIG was on the wrong side of the financial bet in a massive way. This is related to the collapse of AIG's share price.

On July 1, 2009, AIG executed a 1-for-20 reverse stock split. The chart below shows the stock price reaction to the reverse stock split.

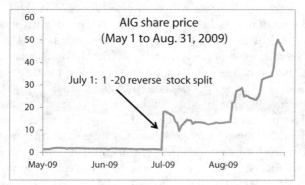

A stock split does not change the value of the company. The AIG of June 30th was the same company on July 1st. The only two things that changed were the number of shares outstanding and the share price resulting from a reverse stock split.

The following are the applicable New York Stock Exchange Listing Rules and AIG's proxy statement disclosure on the contemplated reverse stock split transaction. After reading them, think about these questions:

1. Why did AIG execute the reverse stock split?
2. What might have happened if the reverse stock split was not executed?

* * *

NEW YORK STOCK EXCHANGE LISTED COMPANY MANUAL SECTION 8: SUSPENSION AND DELISTING

802.01C Price Criteria for Capital or Common Stock

A company will be considered to be below compliance standards if the average closing price of a security as reported on the consolidated tape is less than $1.00 over a consecutive 30 trading-day period.

Once notified, the company must bring its share price and average share price back above $1.00 by six months following receipt of the notification. A company is not eligible to follow the procedures outlined in Paras. 802.02 and 802.03 with respect to this criteria. The company must, however, notify the Exchange, within 10 business days of receipt of the notification, of its intent to cure this deficiency or be subject to suspension and delisting procedures. In addition, a domestic company must disclose receipt of the notification by issuing a press release disclosing the fact that it has fallen below the continued listing standards of the Exchange within the time period allotted by SEC rules for the making of a filing with respect to Exchange notification of that event, but no longer than four business days after notification. A non-U.S. company must issue this press release within 30 days after notification. If the company fails to issue this press release during the allotted time period, the Exchange will issue the requisite press release. The company can regain compliance at any time during the six-month cure period if on the last trading day of any calendar month during the cure period the company has a closing share price of at least $1.00 and an average closing share price of at least $1.00 over the 30 trading-day period ending on the last trading day of that month. In the event that at the expiration of the six-month cure period, both a $1.00 closing share price on the last trading day of the cure period and a $1.00 average closing share price over the 30 trading-day period ending on the last trading day of the cure period are not attained, the Exchange will commence suspension and delisting procedures.

Notwithstanding the foregoing, if a company determines that, if necessary, it will cure the price condition by taking an action that will require approval of its shareholders, it must so inform the Exchange in the above referenced notification, must obtain the shareholder approval by no later than its next annual meeting, and must implement the action promptly thereafter. The price condition will be deemed cured if the price promptly exceeds $1.00 per share, and the price remains above the level for at least the following 30 trading days.

Notwithstanding the foregoing, if the subject security is not the primary trading common stock of the company (e.g., a tracking stock or a preferred class) or is a stock listed under the Affiliated Company standard where the parent remains in "control" as that term is used in that standard, the Exchange may determine whether to apply the Price Criteria to such security after evaluating the financial status of the company and/or the parent/affiliated company, as the case may be.

* * *

SCHEDULE 14A DEFINITIVE PROXY STATEMENT (June 5, 2009)

PROPOSAL—To approve Amendment to AIG's Restated Certificate of Incorporation to effect a reverse stock split of outstanding AIG Common Stock

AIG's Board of Directors adopted a resolution declaring it advisable to amend the Restated Certificate of Incorporation to effect a reverse stock split of the outstanding

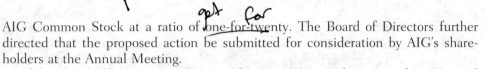

AIG Common Stock at a ratio of one-for-twenty. The Board of Directors further directed that the proposed action be submitted for consideration by AIG's share-holders at the Annual Meeting.

If the shareholders approve the amendment, AIG intends to amend its Restated Certificate of Incorporation to effect a reverse stock split of the shares of issued and outstanding AIG Common Stock at a ratio of one-for-twenty. A reverse stock split results in a proportionate reduction of the number of shares owned by each share-holder in accordance with the ratio, but it has no effect on each shareholder's per-centage ownership of AIG (except to the extent that any shareholder holds only a fractional share interest and receives cash for such interest after the proposed reverse stock split, as discussed below under "Fractional Share Interests in the Reverse Stock Split"). Although the number of issued and outstanding shares of AIG Common Stock will be reduced by a reverse stock split, the number of authorized shares of AIG Common Stock will be unaffected by the reverse stock split and accordingly will remain the same. If the reverse stock split is approved, the number of additional shares of AIG Common Stock to be authorized pursuant to Proposal 3 will be reduced in proportion to the one-for-twenty reverse stock split ratio. The affected text of Article Four of the Restated Certificate of Incorporation as it is proposed to be amended is set forth as Appendix B to this Proxy Statement.

The number of shareholders of record will not be affected by the proposed reverse stock split (except to the extent that any shareholder holds only a fractional share interest and receives cash for such interest after the proposed reverse stock split, as discussed below under "Fractional Share Interests in the Reverse Stock Split"). However, if the proposed reverse stock split is approved, it will increase the number of shareholders who own "odd lots" of less than 100 shares of AIG Common Stock. Brokerage commissions and other costs of transactions in odd lots may be higher than the costs of transactions of more than 100 shares of AIG Common Stock.

If adopted by the shareholders, the change will become effective on the filing of the amendment to the Restated Certificate of Incorporation with the Secretary of State of the State of Delaware.

Amendment of AIG's Restated Certificate of Incorporation for the purposes described in this Proposal 4 requires the affirmative vote of the holders of a majority of the voting power of the outstanding shares of AIG Common Stock and AIG Series C Preferred Stock, voting together as a single class. Failure to vote or to instruct your broker to vote or an abstention will have the same effect as a vote against the proposed amendments.

See Proposal 3 for a table showing the number of shares of AIG Common Stock (1) authorized, (2) issued, (3) reserved but unissued, and (4) authorized but unissued and unreserved in the following scenarios:

- If Proposal 3 is approved, but Proposal 4 is not;
- If Proposal 4 is approved, but Proposal 3 is not; and
- If Proposal 3 and 4 are both approved.

The primary purpose of the reverse stock split is to increase the per share trading price of AIG Common Stock. AIG believes a reverse stock split will increase the price of AIG Common Stock, and thus allow a broader range of institutional investors to invest in AIG Common Stock, increase other investor interest in AIG Common Stock and help ensure the continued listing of AIG Common Stock on the NYSE.

Many investment funds and institutional investors have investment guidelines and policies that prohibit them from investing in, or holding in their portfolios, stocks whose price is below a certain threshold, which, at current AIG Common Stock market prices, reduces the number of potential investors for AIG Common Stock. AIG believes that brokerage firms are reluctant to recommend lower-priced stocks to their clients. Also, other investors may be dissuaded from purchasing lower-priced stocks because the brokerage commissions, as a percentage of the total transaction, tend to be higher for such stocks. The reverse stock split could address these concerns by helping to ensure that the price of AIG Common Stock attains a level that would be viewed more favorably by potential investors.

The share price of AIG Common Stock has declined significantly since the third quarter of 2008, and, during February and March 2009, and occasionally since then, it has closed below $1.00 per share. With the shares trading at this level, small moves in absolute terms in the price per share of AIG Common Stock translate into disproportionately large swings in the price on a percentage basis.

AIG Common Stock currently trades on the NYSE under the symbol "AIG." AIG Common Stock will be quoted on the NYSE at the post-split price on and after the effective date of the amendment. The NYSE has several continued listing criteria that companies must satisfy in order to remain listed on the exchange, including minimum share price requirements. While the NYSE has temporarily suspended the minimum share price requirement, this suspension may be terminated at any time and, in any event, the suspension expires on June 30, 2009. As a result, unless the trading price of AIG Common Stock continues to trade above $1.00 per share, AIG Common Stock could be delisted from the NYSE after June 30, 2009. For further discussion of this risk, see Item 1A. Risk Factors in AIG's 2008 Annual Report on Form 10-K. Although AIG believes that approval of the reverse stock split will help AIG to meet the minimum share price requirements, AIG cannot provide assurance to shareholders that AIG will continue to meet the NYSE's continued listing criteria following the reverse stock split.

In addition, the reverse stock split may not increase the price of AIG Common Stock or may not lead to a sustained increase in the price of AIG Common Stock, which would prevent AIG from realizing some of the anticipated benefits of the reverse stock split. Although AIG's Board of Directors expects that the reverse stock split will increase the market price of AIG Common Stock, the reverse stock split may not result in a stock price that will attract investment funds or institutional investors or satisfy the investment guidelines of investment funds or institutional investors. The market price of AIG Common Stock is primarily driven by factors unrelated to the number of shares outstanding, including AIG's current and expected future performance, the support the NY Fed and the Department of the Treasury have provided to AIG, and the support the NY Fed and the Department of the Treasury may continue to provide to AIG, the status of AIG's asset sales, conditions in the United States and the global economy, conditions in AIG's industries and markets, stock market conditions generally and other factors, many of which are beyond AIG's control. Therefore, it is possible that the per share price of AIG Common Stock after the reverse stock split will not rise in proportion to the reduction in the number of outstanding shares of AIG Common Stock resulting from the reverse stock split, which could cause AIG to fail to realize the anticipated benefits of the reverse stock split.

The effective increase in AIG's authorized and unissued shares as a result of the reverse stock split will not have anti-takeover effects during the time in which the Trust controls more than 50 percent of the voting power of AIG.

Shares of AIG Common Stock after the reverse stock split will be fully paid and non-assessable. This amendment will not change any of the other terms of AIG Common Stock although other amendments proposed in this Proxy Statement, if adopted, would change other terms of AIG Common Stock. The shares of AIG Common Stock after the reverse stock split will have the same voting rights and rights to dividends and distributions and will be identical in all other respects to the shares of AIG Common Stock prior to the reverse stock split.

An overall effect of the reverse stock split of the outstanding AIG Common Stock will be a reduction of the total number of outstanding shares of AIG Common Stock approximately in proportion to the one-for-twenty reverse stock split ratio and therefore an increase in authorized but unissued shares of AIG Common Stock. AIG currently has no plans for these authorized but unissued shares of AIG Common Stock other than those shares previously reserved for issuance under AIG's Equity Units, the Warrants and AIG's employee benefit plans. In the future, these shares may be issued by AIG's Board of Directors in its sole discretion. Any future issuance will have the effect of diluting the percentage of stock ownership and voting rights of the present holders of AIG Common Stock.

Under the Delaware General Corporation Law, AIG's shareholders are not entitled to dissenter's rights with respect to the proposed amendment to AIG's Restated Certificate of Incorporation to effect the reverse stock split.

CHAPTER

6

PREFERRED STOCK

Common stock is not the only form of stock. There is a class of stock called preferred stock, which is also a form of equity. Corporation law permits multiple classes of stock, some of which may have preferences in certain rights over common stock: "The articles of incorporation may authorize one or more classes or series of shares that . . . have preference over any other class or series of shares with respect to distributions, including distributions upon the dissolution of the corporation." Model Business Corporation Act §6.01(c)(4). Stocks that have certain preferences over common stock are called preferred stock. Since they have economic priority in a defined way over common stock, preferred stock is considered less risky than common stock.

Preferred stock is not required, but a corporate charter "may authorize" it. Common stock is ubiquitous, but most corporations, even large public corporations, do not have preferred stock in their capital structure. This is not to say that preferred stock is exotic or rarely seen. It is a routinely used stock instrument that has usefulness in particular situations or industries.

A. PREFERRED STOCK FINANCING

1. BASIC CHARACTERISTICS OF PREFERRED STOCK

Preferred stock sits between debt and common stock in priority and thus riskiness. Because preferred stock is a creature of the corporate charter, its contract terms can be highly variable. The following passage nicely summarizes the nature of preferred stocks.*

> Preferred stock is an anomalous security. It is a debt security when it claims certain absolute rights, especially its right to an accumulated return or to throw the enterprise into receivership for failing to meet its obligations. It is an equity security when it tries to control the enterprise through a practical voting procedure or to share in excess distributions of corporate profits. Of course, a share of preferred stock is actually a composite of many rights. It is entitled to dividends at a set rate which probably accumulate if they are not paid. It is next in line after creditors if the enterprise is liquidated and may share exclusively to a limited amount or participate in any distribution. It is probably subject to redemption and more likely than not has the

---

* Richard M. Buxbaum, *Preferred Stock—Law and Draftsmanship*, 42 Cal. L. Rev. 243 (1954).

supposed benefit of a sinking fund to regulate this redemption. A substantial percentage of contemporary issues are convertible into common stock. It may, but probably does not, have preemptive rights in new stock issues. It probably cannot vote in the election of the corporate management but may have some contingent voting rights for certain proposed actions and upon default in dividend payments. Some of these rights are "inherent;" others are granted by statute; still others are voluntary contractual provisions.

Although preference rights of preferred stock can be highly varied, there are some commonly seen features of preferred stock. The two most common features are preferences in the distribution of dividends and assets in liquidation. In most preferred stock, the holder is entitled to the payment of a fixed dividend that has priority over the dividend to common stock (meaning that preferred stock dividends must be paid before any dividend payment to common stock). Also, in a liquidation, preferred stockholders are paid the stated liquidation value before any distribution to common stockholders.

Throughout this chapter, we will examine an actual preferred stock contract that was purchased by Warren Buffett's investment company, Berkshire Hathaway, from Goldman Sachs.

EXAMPLE

Goldman Sachs' Series G Preferred Stock

During the financial crisis of 2008–2009, Warren Buffett through his investment company Berkshire Hathaway purchased "Series G" preferred stock from Goldman Sachs, which provide the company more equity capital during troubled times. The following provisions in the certificate of designations set forth the preferred stock's limited participation.

* * *

Section 4. Dividends.

  (b) Priority of Dividends. . . . Subject to the foregoing [priority of dividends], such dividends (payable in cash, securities or other property) as may be determined by the Board of Directors . . . may be declared and paid on any securities, including Common Stock and other Junior Stock, from time to time out of any funds legally available for such payment, and the Series G shall not be entitled to participate in any such dividends.

Section 5. Liquidation Rights.

  (c) Residual Distributions. If the Liquidation Preference has been paid in full to all holders of Series G, the holders of other stock of the Corporation shall be entitled to receive all remaining assets of the Corporation (or proceeds thereof) according to their respective rights and preferences.

The dividend to preferred stockholders is paid from net income or from equity, and it is not an expense in the way that interest payments are an expense. Preferred stock does not provide a tax advantage to the issuing corporation in the same way that debt provides an interest tax shield that directly reduces tax liability.

Another basic aspect of preferred stock is that preferred stockholders do not have unbounded participation rights. Most preferred stocks do not participate in the economic value of the corporation beyond the stated contractual rights to dividends, redemption value, or liquidation value. Preferred stockholders are residual claimants of the corporation's earnings and equity but the nature of the residual claim is fixed by contract, whereas common stockholders typically have unlimited participation in the corporation's economic gain. There is no reason why preferred stockholders cannot participate beyond the stated dividend. Participating preferred stocks are paid additionally if certain conditions are met. A common condition is a trigger based on financial performance of the company or a business unit. Additional participation may be in the form of more dividends or some other form of return. However, most preferred stocks are nonparticipating.

Participation can also take an indirect form through a conversion right. Convertible preferred stock permits the conversion of preferred stock at a defined price (or ratio) into common stock. The corporate charter would provide the time-frame for conversion and a conversion formula. The conversion formulas can be complex. Convertible preferred stock is not commonly issued. Most issued preferred stocks are straight preferred stocks, which have cumulative dividends with a liquidation preference. However, convertible preferred stock is commonly issued in high risk venture capital investments because it allows the venture capital firm to sit in priority to the entrepreneurs, but convert to common stock if the business is successful.

2. NATURE OF PREFERRED STOCK

Corporation law permits a corporation to issue preferred stock. Section 151 of the Delaware General Corporation Law is illustrative:*

EXAMPLE

> **Delaware General Corporation Law §151(a), (c), (d), (g)**
>
> **Classes and Series of Stock; Redemption; Rights**
>
> (a) Every corporation may issue 1 or more classes of stock or 1 or more series of stock within any class thereof, any or all of which classes may be of stock with par value or stock without par value and which classes or series may have such voting powers, full or limited, or no voting powers, and such designations, preferences and relative, participating, optional or other special rights, and qualifications, limitations or restrictions thereof, as shall be stated and expressed in the certificate of incorporation or of any amendment thereto, or in the resolution or resolutions providing for the issue of such stock adopted by the board of directors pursuant to authority expressly vested in it by the provisions of its certificate of incorporation. . . .

---

* The Model Business Corporation Act has a comparable provision: "The articles of incorporation may authorize one or more classes or series of shares that . . . have preference over any other class or series of shares with respect to distributions, including distributions upon the dissolution of the corporation." Mod. Bus. Corp. Act §6.01(c)(4).

(c) The holders of preferred or special stock of any class or of any series thereof shall be entitled to receive dividends at such rates, on such conditions and at such times as shall be stated in the certificate of incorporation or in the resolution or resolutions providing for the issue of such stock adopted by the board of directors as hereinabove provided, payable in preference to, or in such relation to, the dividends payable on any other class or classes or of any other series of stock, and cumulative or noncumulative as shall be so stated and expressed. When dividends upon the preferred and special stocks, if any, to the extent of the preference to which such stocks are entitled, shall have been paid or declared and set apart for payment, a dividend on the remaining class or classes or series of stock may then be paid out of the remaining assets of the corporation available for dividends as elsewhere in this chapter provided.

(d) The holders of the preferred or special stock of any class or of any series thereof shall be entitled to such rights upon the dissolution of, or upon any distribution of the assets of, the corporation as shall be stated in the certificate of incorporation or in the resolution or resolutions providing for the issue of such stock adopted by the board of directors as hereinabove provided.

(g) When any corporation desires to issue any shares of stock of any class or of any series of any class of which the powers, designations, preferences and relative, participating, optional or other rights, if any, or the qualifications, limitations or restrictions thereof, if any, shall not have been set forth in the certificate of incorporation or in any amendment thereto but shall be provided for in a resolution or resolutions adopted by the board of directors pursuant to authority expressly vested in it by the certificate of incorporation or any amendment thereto, a certificate of designations setting forth a copy of such resolution or resolutions and the number of shares of stock of such class or series as to which the resolution or resolutions apply shall be executed, acknowledged, filed and shall become effective, in accordance with §103 of this title. . . .

Section 151 further provides that any stock of any class or series "may be made subject to redemption by the corporation at its option or at the option of the holders of such stock or upon the happening of a specified event . . . [and] may be made convertible into, or exchangeable for, at the option of either the holder or the corporation or upon the happening of a specified event." This provision identifies a number of commonly seen features in the preferred stock contract: (1) stated dividend, (2) priority in dissolution, (3) redemption feature, and (4) convertibility.

Dividends and liquidation preferences are simply the most commonly seen preferences. Contract terms and potential preferences and limitations are subject to contracting. Each set of contract terms may satisfy the particular needs of the issuer and holder at the time.

The rights of preferred stockholders are set forth in the corporate charter. If the corporate charter does not authorize the issuance of preferred stock, it must be properly amended by the board or be approved by the shareholders. Where the board has "blank check" authority to create the class or series of shares and establish its terms, pursuant to a provision in the charter authorized by statute, shareholder approval would not be necessary. If the board uses its blank check authority to create the class or series, it files a certificate of designation with the secretary of state, which acts as an amendment of the charter and becomes a part of the corporate charter.

When preferred stock is issued, investors typically seek an opinion from the issuer's counsel that the newly issued preferred stock has been duly authorized and validly issued. A legal opinion letter should include a legal opinion of counsel that:

- The shares are part of a class or series of shares that the issuer has authority to issue under the corporate charter
- When the shares were issued, the issuer had a sufficient number of authorized shares of that class or series available to issue
- The issuer took the proper procedural steps to create the class or series of preferred stock, including amendments to the charter if necessary
- The charter contains all the substantive terms of the class or series of preferred stock including, for example, number of authorized shares, par value, voting rights, and dividend rate   *rights in AOI*
- The issuer has the power under the state corporation statute and its charter to create stock having the rights and preferences of the newly issued preferred stock   *blank check*

When a class or series of preferred stock is authorized or issued by the corporation, the work of the corporate attorney includes the determination of the authority of the corporation to issue the preferred stock under the state corporation statute; the corporate charter; and the rights, powers, and preferences of other securities set therein.

The following case addresses whether the preferred stock contract can eliminate (what would otherwise be) the mandatory right of appraisal for stockholders. Consider the court's answer and analysis in the context of the nature of a preferred stock.

In the matter of the Appraisal of Ford Holdings, Inc. Preferred Stock

698 A.2d 973 (Del.Ch. 1997)

ALLEN, Chancellor.

This is an appraisal proceeding under Section 262 of the Delaware General Corporation Law. It arises from a merger in which Ford Holdings, Inc. ("Holdings"), a subsidiary of Ford Motor Company, merged with Ford Holdings Capital Corporation, its own wholly owned subsidiary. The effect of the merger was to cash-out various types and series of Holdings' preferred stock. In each instance, the holders of preferred were paid the liquidation value of their security, plus a "merger premium" if the certificate creating the preferred called for it, plus any accumulated and unpaid dividends. Holdings asserts that under the various documents creating these securities that is exactly what the holders of the preferred stock are entitled to in the event of a merger. Plaintiffs in this appraisal action are certain holders of preferred stocks of Holdings. They seek a judicial appraisal of the "fair value" of their shares at the time of the merger, which they contend is higher than the amount Holdings calculated as due to them.

Holdings was incorporated to engage in the business of consumer and commercial lending, insurance underwriting, and equipment leasing. All of its common stock is held, directly or indirectly, by Ford Motor Company. Holdings issued twenty series of preferred stock to the public. The preferred shares were of two different types:

315

(1) Flexible Rate Auction Series A through P ("Auction Preferred"), and (2) Cumulative Preferred Series A through D ("Cumulative Preferred"). The specific terms of each series of preferred stock were contained in its Certificate of Designations ("Designations"). All series were nonconvertible and nonredeemable, had cumulative dividends, and had liquidation preferences equal to par plus any accumulated and unpaid dividends. The Certificates of Designations setting forth the terms, preferences, and limitations of the stock were not identical.

Bancorp purchased 100 shares of Auction Preferred Series D shares in the secondary market. The terms of these shares at that time included a five year period and no merger premium. Later, Holdings' board of directors approved a plan to merge Holdings with Ford Holdings Capital Corporation. In the merger, all of Holdings' preferred stock was eliminated and converted to a right to receive cash.

As a holder of Auction Preferred Series D, Bancorp did not accept the merger consideration; it dissented and filed this suit seeking an adjudication of the fair value of its shares. Certain holders of the Cumulative Preferred joined Bancorp's action seeking appraisal rights. Holdings then filed a motion for summary judgment asserting that it is clear from the language of the Designations that the holders of the preferred shares are entitled in the event of a merger to consideration fixed in those documents and not to any other amount.

Bancorp makes two arguments to support its claim that it is entitled to an appraisal proceeding. First, it asserts, that appraisal rights are mandated by statute and cannot be eliminated by provisions in the corporate charter or the Designations. Second, Bancorp alleges that even if it is permissible to contract away one's right to appraisal, the terms of the Designations of the Cumulative Preferred and the Auction Preferred do not specify that petitioners have done so.

The Designations Defining the Security May, In Effect, Eliminate Statutory Appraisal Rights by Clearly Defining Rights of Holders in the Event of a Merger

Delaware's General Corporation Law, like most general laws of incorporation in the twentieth century U.S., is an *enabling statute*. That is, the philosophy that underlies it is that the public good is advanced by the provision of an inexpensive mechanism that allows all individuals to achieve the benefits that the corporate form provides (most importantly, centralized management and entity status, with its characteristics of indefinite duration and separately salable share interests) through establishing management and governance terms that appear advantageous to those designing the organization. Thus, unlike the corporation law of the nineteenth century, modern corporation law contains few mandatory terms; it is largely enabling in character. It is not, however, bereft of mandatory terms. Under Delaware law, for example, a corporation is required to have an annual meeting for the election of directors; is required to have shareholder approval for amendments to the certificate of incorporation; must have appropriate shareholder concurrence in the authorization of a merger; and is required to have shareholder approval in order to dissolve. Generally, these mandatory provisions may not be varied by terms of the certificate of incorporation or otherwise.

Among these mandatory provisions of Delaware law is Section 262, the appraisal remedy. That Section provides in part:

> Any stockholder of a corporation of this State who holds shares of stock on the date of a demand . . . who continuously holds such shares through the effective date of the merger . . . and who has [not] voted in favor of the merger . . . *shall be entitled to an appraisal . . . of the fair value of his stock . . .*

mandatory?

It is this provision upon which petitioners rely. They satisfy each of the statutory conditions to an appraisal of the "fair value" of their shares, they say. They have evidence, they say, that the market price of their securities was greater than the merger consideration. They add that they have a right to present that evidence and for the court to determine the "fair value" of their shares in light of it and other indicia of value as of the merger date.

Defendant asserts that the Designations of the Cumulative Preferred and the Auction Preferred limit the appraisal rights of holders of these shares. Specifically, defendant contends that the Designations define the consideration to which the holders are entitled in the event of a merger. According to defendant, while shareholders may be statutorily entitled to an appraisal of fair value, the instrument creating their security fixes that value.

One question to be resolved then, is whether purchasers of preferred stock can, in effect, contract away their rights to seek judicial determination of the fair value of their stock, by accepting a security that explicitly provides either a stated amount or a formula by which an amount to be received in the event of a merger is set forth. This question is a specification of the general question—which has received a great deal of scholarly attention—whether, as a matter of sound policy, mandatory provisions are ever desirable in corporation law. While this question is of general interest, we need not hazard any speculation on whether mandatory terms are efficient in general, because this case deals only with the appraisal remedy for preferred stock and preferred stock is a very special case. As is well understood, preferred stock can have characteristics of both debt and equity. To the extent it possesses any special rights or powers and to the extent it is restricted or limited in any way, the relation between the holder of the preferred and the corporation is contractual. *H.B. Korenvaes Investments, LP, et al. v. Marriott Corp., et al.,* 1993 WL 205040 (Del.Ch. 1993) ("rights of preferred stock are primarily but not exclusively contractual in nature.") While, as part of that contract, an issuer will owe the limited duty of good faith that one contractual party always owes to the other, with respect to those special preferences, etc., the issuer owes no duty of loyalty to the holders of the preferred. *E.g., H.B. Korenvaes; Jedwab v. MGM Grand Hotels, Inc.,* 509 A.2d 584 (Del.Ch. 1986).

All of the characteristics of the preferred are open for negotiation; that is the nature of the security. There is no utility in defining as forbidden any term thought advantageous to informed parties, unless that term violates substantive law. Particularly, there is no utility in forbidding the parties *creating* a preferred stock (the issuer, its advisors and counsel, and the underwriter and its counsel) from establishing a security that has a stated value (or a value established by a stated formula) in the event of stated contingencies.

The general rule applies as with all contracting parties: that which is a valid contract will be enforced either specifically or through a damages action, unless the contract violates positive law or its non-performance is excused. I cannot conclude that a provision that establishes the cash value of a preferred stock in the event of a cash-out merger would violate the public policy reflected in Section 262, given the essentially contractual nature of preferred stock. Thus, the relevant question in this case is whether the instruments establishing the rights and preferences of these various series of preferred stocks do contractually limit the right of a holder to seek judicial appraisal in the event of a cash-out merger.

I start with a preliminary generality. Since Section 262 represents a statutorily conferred right, it may be effectively waived in the documents creating the security only when that result is quite clearly set forth when interpreting the relevant document under generally applicable principles of construction. Secondly, I note that ambiguity in these matters ought to be construed against the issuer who, as the analysis below certainly indicates, had it within its power clearly to establish the result for which it here contends.

The Series D Cumulative Preferred Shares

The rights of stockholders of the Cumulative Preferred in the event of a merger are clearly stated in the Designations. Paragraph 4(b) of the Designations states:
4. *Rights on Liquidation or Cash–Out Merger.*

> (b) In any merger . . . of [Holdings] with or into any other corporation . . . which . . . provides for the payment of only cash to the holders . . . each holder . . . *shall be entitled to receive an amount equal to the liquidation preference* [which is defined in paragraph 4(a) as $100,000 per share] of shares . . . held by such holder, plus an amount equal to accumulated and unpaid dividends on such shares . . . , *and no more* in exchange for such shares of Series D Preferred Stock. . . .

This provision specifically identifies the consideration that preferred shareholders will receive upon a cash-out merger of the type which occurred between Holdings and Ford Holdings Capital Corporation. It states explicitly that shareholders will be paid the liquidation preference—a specific, pre-determined dollar amount—and accrued and unpaid dividends—also a specifically determinable amount. The last phrase of the provision, stating that the holder is entitled to the consideration specified "and no more", reinforces the conclusion that the shareholders are not entitled to anything additional.

The terms of the Designations of the Cumulative Preferred clearly describe an agreement between the shareholders and the company regarding the consideration to be received by the shareholders in the event of a cash-out merger. There is no ambiguity in paragraph 4 regarding the value to be paid to shareholders if they are forced to give up their shares in a cash-out merger. The shareholders can not now come to this court seeking additional consideration in the merger through the appraisal process. Their security had a stated value in a merger which they have received.

The Auction Preferred Series D

The rights of the Auction Preferred Series D shareholders in the event of a cash-out merger are not as clearly expressed as those of the Cumulative Preferred shares. Most notably, there is no provision specifically governing (and limiting) "Rights on . . . Cash-out Merger." There are two interrelated provisions in the Designations which the corporation claims bear upon the rights of the shareholders to receive money in a cash-out merger.

The provisions state in relevant part:

3. *Dividends.*

> (b)(viii) [T]he Term Selection Agent *may give . . . notice* [shortly before an auction is held to set the terms of the shares for the next period] *specifying* the [length of the] next succeeding Dividend Period . . . and *whether such shares shall be entitled under the circumstances set forth in paragraph 5(d)(iii) to a premium upon . . . [the] merger of [Holdings]* with or into any other corporation ("Merger Premium"). . . .

Preferred Section 5(d)(iii) deals with voting rights. It provides in pertinent part:
5. *Voting Rights.*

> (d)(iii) *Right to Vote in Certain Events.* Without the affirmative vote of the holders of a majority of the Outstanding shares of all series of Auction Preferred, Voting Preferred and Parity Preferred, voting as a single class, . . . [Holdings] may not . . . merge with or into any other corporation unless, in the case of a . . . merger, each holder of shares of Auction Preferred, Voting Preferred and Parity Preferred shall receive, upon such . . . merger, an amount in cash equal to the liquid preference, Merger Premium, if any, and accumulated and unpaid dividends. . . .

Under Holding's interpretation of the Designations, the merger consideration is fixed by the operation of these provisions, just as it was in the case of the Cumulative Preferred shares. I cannot agree, although that may have been the imperfectly expressed intention of the drafter.

Paragraph 5(d)(iii) assures that the preferred shareholders will be able *to vote as a class* to prevent the corporation from engaging in a merger that a majority of holders find disadvantageous, but that the class *loses that power if* the preferred receive specified consideration—the liquidation preference ($100,000), a merger premium, if any is authorized, and accumulated and unpaid dividends. Thus, the provision implies that the class has no need for class vote protection—no risk of exploitation—if the preferred receives in the merger consideration equal to the liquidation value, etc. Such an implication would of course be consistent with an understanding that that consideration was all that the preferred was entitled to receive. While this implication is possible, it is not clear or compelled. The voting provisions are, in the end, voting provisions. The stipulated absence of a class vote is too frail a base upon which to rest the claim that there has been a contractual relinquishment of rights under Section 262 or, to state it differently, that the consideration that acts to remove the rights to a class vote also is conclusively established to be the "fair value."

Clear and direct drafting, of the type found in Section 4 of the Designation of the Cumulative Preferred, can implement a term conclusively fixing merger consideration of preferred. But the court may not cut stockholders off from a statutory right by the level of indirection that the company's argument requires.

Two principles mentioned above support the determination that the "fair value" of Series D Preferred is not contractually limited by the terms of the Designation. The first is the principle that statutory rights should ordinarily be waived only by clear affirmative words or actions. The second is the principle that holds that ambiguity in a contractual document should be construed against the party that had the power to avoid the ambiguity.

QUESTIONS

[handwritten margin note: — they are, but / can be evaded by contracting / around for preferred / stock]

1. Why are not the appraisal rights in DGCL §262 mandatory?
2. What is the relationship between voting rights in a merger transaction and DGCL §262?
3. Is there an argument that if the liquidation preference is offered under §5(d)(iii), the Auction Preferred should be treated exactly as the Cumulative Preferred?

NOTES

1. In *In re Appraisal of Metromedia International Group, Inc.*, 971 A.2d 893 (Del.Ch. 2009), the court relied on *Appraisal of Ford Holding* to state the rule: "Given the contractual nature of preferred stock, a clear contractual provision that establishes the value of preferred stock in the event of a cash-out merger is not inconsistent with the language or the policy of §262. Thus, the most critical question in this action is whether the certificate of designation, which establishes the rights of MIG's preferred shares, contractually establishes the metric for valuing the preferred shares in the event of a merger." The court analyzed the following charter provision and held that the contract provided for a specific merger consideration that precluded an appraisal remedy.

> In case of any capital reorganization or reclassification or other change of outstanding shares of Common Stock (other than a change in par value . . .) or *in case of any consolidation or merger* of the Company with or into another Person . . . *each share of Preferred Stock then outstanding shall, without the consent of any holder of Preferred Stock, become convertible only into* the kind and amount of shares of stock or other securities (of the Company or another issuer) or *property or cash receivable upon such [merger] by a holder of the number of shares of Common Stock into which such share of Preferred Stock could have been converted immediately prior to such [merger]* after giving effect to any adjustment event. The provisions of this Section 8(g) and any equivalent thereof in any such certificate similarly shall apply to successive [mergers]. *The provisions of this Section 8(g) shall be the sole right of holders of Preferred Stock in connection with any [merger]* and such holders shall have no separate vote thereon.

3. USES OF PREFERRED STOCK

Most corporations do not use preferred stock. However, preferred stock has utility in some circumstances. The most important point to understand about preferred stock is that it has hybrid qualities. Some aspects of preferred stock look like debt, and other aspects like equity. This hybrid nature of preferred stock gives it its utility.

Although preferred stock dividends are not tax deductible to the issuer, the tax case for preferred stock is more nuanced. If the preferred stockholder is a corporation, the holder gets a tax benefit under I.R.C. §243. If an investor corporation is a non-affiliate corporation, 70 percent of the dividend received from the issuer corporation is deductible for the holder. If an investor corporation owns at least 20 percent of the issuer corporation, 80 percent of the dividend income is deductible. For example, if the corporation has a corporate tax rate of 35 percent and it receives $100 of preferred stock dividend, and assuming the 20 percent threshold is not met, the investor corporation is taxed on the $30 of dividend income at the 35 percent rate, which is $10.50. Thus, the effective tax rate on the $100 of dividend income is 10.5 percent (which compares favorably to the 35 percent corporate tax rate). Since corporate investors have a special tax advantage, most preferred stockholders are corporate institutional investors.

A corporate investor has a significant tax advantage, whereas the interest income earned by a creditor corporation is taxed as ordinary income. The tax advantage of preferred stock has an indirect benefit to the issuer corporation because the issuer considers the tax effects when it prices the preferred stock dividend rate. Knowing that the preferred stockholder has a tax benefit, the issuer corporation can issue preferred stock at lower dividend rates. The different tax treatments of dividends for issuers and investors suggest that some set circumstances are more conducive for the issuance of preferred stock than others. Specifically, the issuer corporation has a low effective tax rate such that the interest tax shield does not inure sufficient benefits, and the investor corporation has a high effective tax rate such that the dividend tax shield on investment income is beneficial.*

Preferred stock may be useful for regulated industries. Some industries, like banking and financial institutions, are regulated as to capital structure. Preferred stock can be considered equity capital in regulatory assessment of capital structure. Since the payout to straight (nonconvertible) preferred stockholders is fixed like the payout to debtholders, the company can issue equity and yet protect the economic interest of common stock from dilution. If equity is the preferred or required choice of capital, preferred stock is a cheaper form of equity than common stock.

Preferred stock may be used as a device of governance, or as a way to grant voting rights without diluting the economic rights of common stockholders. Voting preferred stock may serve to maintain or transfer voting control. This may be useful in mergers and acquisitions or in situations where voting rights are negotiated among a few principal participants of the company.

Preferred stock may also be useful in a bankruptcy or restructuring in which debt is exchanged for preferred stock. Unlike interest on debt, dividends on preferred stock are not mandatory (interest must be paid or else there is a default). The discretion to pay dividends gives the issuer greater financial flexibility. Why would debtholders agree to such a swap? Such exchange of securities is a common part of the bargaining process during the restructuring (*see, e.g., Eliasen v. Itel Corp.* and *Katz v. Oak Industries Inc., infra* Chapter 7). Despite the uncertainty over dividend payments, perhaps an equity investment may ultimately yield greater returns. One possible enticement may be a convertibility feature in the preferred stock that would allow the prior debtholder to convert to common stock at some point.

Also, convertible preferred stock is a useful security in venture capital investments. It does not have the rigorous cash flow demands of debt service, and dividends are subject to the more risky or lumpy cash flow of a new or young business. The preferred stock is superior in liquidation to common stock, which may be issued to the entrepreneur, managers, and employees. The convertibility of the preferred stock then allows the investor to convert to the common, thus becoming residual claimants.

---

* *See* I. Gooladi & G. Roberts, *On Preferred Stock*, J. Fin. Research 319 (Winter 1986); A.L. Houston Jr. & C.O. Houston, *Financing With Preferred Stock*, 19 Fin. Management 42 (Autumn 1990).

Equity-Like Characteristics	Debt-Like Characteristics
• Payment of dividends are subject to board discretion, unlike interest payments on debt, though dividends may cumulate into the forward year as dividends owed • Preferred stockholders cannot throw the issuer into bankruptcy for dividend arrearage, though they may have contractual remedies if dividends are not paid • The board of directors owe fiduciary duty to preferred stockholders • Preferred stockholders may have voting rights and an entitlement to designate board seats • Preferred stocks are often treated as equity for accounting and tax purposes	• Preferred stock has fixed dividend payments, which resembles periodic interest payments • Preferred stockholders have liquidation preference ahead of common stockholders • Rights of preferred stockholders are contract based, flowing largely from the express terms of the corporate charter • Absent a convertibility feature or participation rights, preferred stockholders do not have a potential for unbounded economic return

B. COMMON TERMS OF PREFERRED STOCK

1. DISTRIBUTIONS AND ARREARAGE

An important attribute of preferred stock is the right to dividends. The dividend preference provides that dividends cannot be paid to common stockholders unless they are first paid to preferred stockholders. This is a dividend priority, but dividends are not mandatory in the same way interest payment on debt has a ticktock regularity. The board has discretion to issue dividends, including dividends on preferred stock. The preferred stock contract takes away the discretion to pay dividends to common stockholders if preferred stockholders have not been paid. The failure to pay dividends may have market consequences because it will be considered adverse news pertaining to the issuer.

The typical preferred stock has a fixed dividend right based off the face value of the stock (*e.g.*, 7 percent off $1,000 face value per annum, payable every quarter). Again, this is the typical contractual term, but it is not a mandatory rule of preferred stock. Dividends along with other preferences are subject to freedom of contract. Like interest rates on debt, dividends can be floating or adjustable. The dividends on adjustable-rate preferred stocks are pegged to some moving benchmark such as other securities or interest rates. A variation of the adjustable-rate preferred stock is the auction-rate preferred stock, in which the dividend is determined through a Dutch auction between holders of preferred stock who seek to sell and investors who submit auction bids for particular yields at which they will buy the stock.

Most preferred stocks are "cumulative" preferreds. Any dividend not paid in the current year is carried forward as a dividend owed in the subsequent year. The accumulation of unpaid dividends is called arrearage. Cumulative means that all past dividends, accrued and unpaid, must be paid first before the common stockholders can be paid any dividends. The cumulative aspect of preferred stock dividends makes dividend payments practically mandatory. A corporation does not pay cumulative dividends only if that legal power to withhold dividends is exercised out of business necessity or if legal power cannot be exercised due to statutory and common law prohibitions against distributions causing insolvency. If dividends are noncumulative, any dividend not paid in the year is not carried forward. The risk of nonpayment on dividends is on the preferred stockholder.

Cumulative preferred stock puts significant pressure on the board of directors to pay dividends since common stockholders will also want to be paid dividends, or at least the possibility of being paid if the board wishes. If a cumulative nonconvertible preferred stock is trading well above its face value, then one reason might be that there is an accumulation of unpaid dividends and an expectation that dividends will be paid. Noncumulative preferred stock means that if dividends have not been paid, the right to past dividends is extinguished. Clearly, from the stockholder's perspective this is an undesirable feature of a noncumulative preferred stock, and its existence can be explained by the unique circumstances under which the security was issued or the stock has other preference rights that compensate for a less sure right to dividends.

EXAMPLE

Goldman Sachs' Series G Preferred Stock

Section 4. Dividends

(a) **Rate**. Holders of Series G shall be entitled to receive, on each share of Series G, out of funds legally available for the payment of dividends under Delaware law, cumulative cash dividends . . . at a per annum rate of 10% on (i) the amount of $100,000 per share of Series G and (ii) the amount of accrued and unpaid dividends on such share of Series G, if any. . . .

(b) **Priority of Dividends**. So long as any share of Series G remains outstanding, no dividend shall be declared or paid on the Common Stock or any other shares of Junior Stock . . . , and no Common Stock, Junior Stock or Parity Stock shall be purchased, redeemed or otherwise acquired for consideration by the Corporation, directly or indirectly . . . , unless all accrued and unpaid dividends for all past Dividend Periods . . . on all outstanding shares of Series G have been declared and paid in full. . . .

First priority of dividends

The following case interprets the distribution rights of preferred stock as set forth in the charter. It involves a noncumulative dividend preferred stock and discusses the implication when a preferred stock is clearly expressed as noncumulative.

Guttman v. Illinois Central R. Co.
189 F.2d 927 (2d Cir. 1951)

FRANK, Circuit Judge.

The trial court's findings of facts establish that the directors acted well within their discretion in withholding declarations of dividends on the non-cumulative preferred stock up to the year 1948. In so holding, we assume, arguendo, that, as plaintiff insists, the standard of discretion in weighing the propriety of the non-declaration of dividends on such preferred stock is far stricter than in the case of non-declaration of dividends on common stock. We think the directors, in not declaring dividends on the preferred in the years 1937-1947, adopted a reasonable attitude of reluctant but contingent pessimism about the future, an attitude proper, in the circumstances, for persons charged, on behalf of all interests, with the management of this enterprise.

The issue, then, is whether the directors could validly declare a dividend on the common stock in 1950 without directing that there should be paid (in addition to preferred dividends on the preferred for that year) alleged arrears of preferred dividends, the amount of which had been earned in 1942-1947 but remained undeclared and unpaid. To put it differently, we must decide whether (a) the directors had the power to declare such alleged arrears of dividends on the preferred and (b) whether they "abused" their discretion in declaring any dividend on the common without ordering the payment of those alleged arrears.

Our lode-star is *Wabash Railway Co. v. Barclay*, 280 U.S. 197 (1930), which dealt with the non-cumulative preferred stock of an Indiana railroad corporation.

In *Wabash*, plaintiffs, holders of non-cumulative preferred stock, sought an injunction preventing the defendant railroad company from paying dividends on the common stock unless it first paid dividends on the non-cumulative preferred to the extent that the company, in previous years, had had net earnings available for that payment and that such dividends remained unpaid. The Court decided against the plaintiffs. It spoke of the fact that, in earlier years, "net earnings that could have been used for the payment were expended upon improvements and additions to the property and equipment of the road"; it held that the contract with the preferred meant that "if those profits are justifiably applied by the directors to capital improvements and no dividend is declared within the year, the claim for that year is gone and cannot be asserted at a later date."

Plaintiff, however, seeks to limit the effect of the *Wabash* ruling to instances where the net earnings, for a given year, which could have been paid to the non-cumulative preferred, have once been expended justifiably for "capital improvements" or "additions to the property or equipment." He would have us treat the words "non-cumulative" as if they read "cumulative if earned except only when the earnings are paid out for capital additions." He argues that *Wabash* has no application when net earnings for a given year are legitimately retained for any one of a variety of other corporate purposes, and when in a subsequent year it develops that such retention was not necessary. We think the attempted distinction untenable. We do not believe that the Supreme Court gave the contract with the preferred such an irrational interpretation. It simply happened that in *Wabash* the earnings had been used for capital additions, and that, accordingly, the court happened to mention that particular purpose. Consequently, we think that the Court, in referring to that fact, did not intend it to have any significance.

Here we are interpreting a contract into which uncoerced men entered. Nothing in the wording of that contract would suggest to an ordinary wayfaring person the existence of a contingent or inchoate right to arrears of dividends. The notion that such a right was promised is, rather, the invention of lawyers or other experts, a notion stemming from considerations of fairness, from a policy of protecting investors in those securities. But the preferred stockholders are not—like sailors or idiots or infants—wards of the judiciary. As courts on occasions have quoted or paraphrased ancient poets, it may not be inappropriate to paraphrase a modern poet, and to say that "a contract is a contract is a contract." To be sure, it is an overstatement that the courts never do more than carry out the intentions of the parties: In the interest of fairness and justice, many a judge-made legal rule does impose, on one of the parties to a contract, obligations which neither party actually contemplated and as to which the language of the contract is silent. But there are limits to the extent to which a court may go in so interpolating rights and obligations which were never in the parties" contemplation. In this case we consider those limits clear.

In sum, we hold that, since the directors did not "abuse" their discretion in withholding dividends on the non-cumulative preferred for any past years, (a) no right survived to have those dividends declared, and (b) the directors had no discretion whatever to declare those dividends subsequently.

QUESTIONS

1. What is the holding of this case? Under what circumstances can a board of directors withhold dividends on noncumulative preferred stock? Under what circumstances may its decision be suspect?
2. Given the holdings in cases like *Guttman* and *Wabash*, one wonders why an investor would purchase noncumulative preferred stock. What could be some reasons why rational, presumably wealth-maximizing investors purchase noncumulative preferred stock?

The following case also interprets the distribution priority of preferred stock as set forth in the charter. A key advantage of preferred stock is the priority of distribution as set forth in the charter. This case involves a drafting oversight, at least an error in hindsight, in placing limits on distributions to common stockholders.

In re Sunstates Corp. Shareholders' Litigation
788 A.2d 530 (Del. Ch. 2001)

LAMB, Vice Chancellor.

Count II of the Amended Complaint is brought as a class action on behalf of the owner of shares of Sunstates Corporation $3.75 Preferred Stock. The complaint alleges that, between 1991 and 1993, and in violation of its certificate of incorporation, Sunstates purchased shares of its common and Preferred Stock when it was in arrears on the Preferred Stock dividend.

The defendants have moved for summary judgment on this claim. They concede the existence of the special limitation in the charter. But they deny its applicability because, as a matter of fact, Sunstates, itself, made no share repurchases. Rather, all reacquired shares were purchased by one or more of Sunstates's subsidiary corporations. Because the Sunstates certificate does not prohibit (although it might have) share repurchases by subsidiaries when the parent is in arrears on its Preferred Stock dividend, defendants argue that they are entitled to judgment in their favor as a matter of law.

Plaintiffs respond that it would render the protective provision of the charter nugatory and illusory if I interpreted it literally to apply only to share repurchases by the corporation itself, since the limitation could so easily be avoided. In a similar vein, they argue that the doctrine of good faith and fair dealing in contracts requires that I interpret the special limitation more broadly to reach the activity of Sunstates's subsidiaries. Finally, they suggest that I should ignore the separate corporate existence of the subsidiaries and treat them as mere agents of the parent corporation for this purpose.

The pertinent facts are easily stated. Sunstates Corporation is a Delaware corporation having a number of subsidiaries incorporated in various jurisdictions. Article IV, Section 4.3 of the Sunstates certificate of incorporation creates the $3.75 Preferred Stock. Paragraph 3 thereof specifies the dividend rights of that stock and provides that, unless Sunstates is current in its payment of dividends on the Preferred Stock:

> The Corporation shall not (i) declare or pay or set apart for payment any dividends or distributions on any stock ranking as to dividends junior to the $3.75 Preferred Stock (other than dividends paid in shares of such junior stock) or (ii) *make any purchase . . . of . . . any stock ranking as to dividends junior or* pari passu *to the $3.75 Preferred Stock . . .*

Paragraph 4(e) of section 4.3 similarly proscribes all non-pro rata purchases of shares of Preferred Stock when dividends are in arrears, as follows:

> In the event that any semiannual dividend payable on the $3.75 Preferred Stock shall be in arrears and until all such dividends in arrears shall have been paid or declared and set apart for payment, the Corporation shall not . . . purchase or otherwise acquire any shares of $3.75 Preferred Stock except in accordance with a purchase offer made by the Corporation on the same terms to all holders of record of $3.75 Preferred Stock for the purchase of all outstanding shares thereof.

Article I, section 1.1 of the certificate defines the "Corporation" to mean Sunstates Corporation. Nothing in the certificate expressly provides that the "Corporation" includes anything but Sunstates Corporation.

In 1991, Sunstates fell into arrears in the payment of the Preferred Stock dividend. Over the next two years, subsidiary corporations controlled, directly or indirectly, by Sunstates bought shares of both common stock and Preferred Stock. The Preferred Shares were not acquired in compliance with the "any and all" tender offer requirement of paragraph 4(e). The repurchases of common stock amounted, over a three year period, to nearly 70 percent of the total outstanding common stock. The Preferred Stock repurchased equaled nearly 30 percent of the total number outstanding.

Section 151(a) of the Delaware General Corporation Law allows Delaware corporations to issue stock having such "special rights, and qualifications, limitations or restrictions" relating thereto "as shall be stated and expressed in the certificate of incorporation or of any amendment thereto. . . ." Thus, the law recognizes that the existence and extent of rights of preferred stock must be determined by reference to the certificate of incorporation, those rights being essentially contractual in nature.[6]

---

6. *Warner Communications, Inc. v. Chris-Craft Industries, Inc.*, 583 A.2d 962, 966 (Del.Ch. 1989).

Plaintiffs advance no construction of the certificate of incorporation that would permit me to read the word "Corporation" to refer to any corporation other than Sunstates. This is hardly surprising since the language at issue is clear in its meaning and there is nothing within the four corners of the certificate suggesting a broader or different interpretation. Thus, as a matter of simple contract interpretation, there is no basis on which to apply the special limitation against share repurchases to any entity other than Sunstates.

The legal flaw in the [plaintiff's] agency argument is fundamental. For the purposes of the corporation law, the act of one corporation is not regarded as the act of another merely because the first corporation is a subsidiary of the other, or because the two may be treated as part of a single economic enterprise for some other purpose. Rather, to pierce the corporate veil based on an agency or "alter ego" theory, "the corporation must be a sham and exist for no other purpose than as a vehicle for fraud."

Plaintiffs fare no better in arguing that Sunstates violated the implied covenant of good faith and fair dealing by its subsidiaries' share repurchases. It is true, that, as a general matter, the implied covenant of good faith and fair dealing exists in all contracts. Nevertheless, the circumstances in which it is relied on to find a breach of contract are narrow. As this court has said before:

> the duty arises *only* where it is clear from what the parties expressly agreed, that they would have proscribed the challenged conduct as a breach of contract . . . had they thought to negotiate with respect to the matter.

In this case, the only evidence of what the parties "expressly agreed" is found in the prohibition against certain conduct by the "Corporation." That does not provide a reasonable basis to infer that "the parties would have proscribed" share purchases by Sunstates's subsidiaries "had they thought to negotiate with respect to the matter."

On the contrary, the law of this State has clearly stated for many decades that special rights or preferences of preferred stock must be expressed clearly and that nothing will be presumed in their favor. Thus, there is no basis to infer that any person negotiating the terms of the Sunstates certificate of incorporation could have reasonably believed that the limitation of share repurchases found in Article IV, section 4.3, paragraphs 3 and 4, would preclude repurchase activity by any party other than Sunstates. Indeed, it is more readily inferred that whoever negotiated the Sunstates certificate of incorporation knew and understood the scope of the limitations contained therein.[14]

In the final analysis, plaintiffs' arguments run counter to both the doctrine of strict construction of special rights, preferences and limitations relating to stock and the doctrine of independent legal significance. The situation is not unlike that confronted in *Rothschild Int'l Corp. v. Liggett Group, Inc.* There, the plaintiffs owned preferred shares that were entitled to a liquidation preference. To avoid paying this preference,

---

14. Moreover, "the implied duty to perform in good faith does not come into play" where the topic is either expressly covered in the contract or intentionally omitted therefrom. Here, the subject of the scope of the special limitation sued upon is expressly covered in the written contract by the prohibition against the Corporation (defined elsewhere as Sunstates) from making certain share purchases when the Preferred Stock dividend is in arrears.

the defendant companies structured a combined tender offer and reverse cash-out merger that eliminated the preferred shares for a price substantially lower than the liquidation preference. The Supreme Court concluded that the charter provision only operated in the case of a liquidation and that there had been no liquidation. Applying the doctrine of independent legal significance, the Supreme Court reiterated "that action taken under one section of [the Delaware General Corporation Law] is legally independent, and its validity is not dependent upon, nor to be tested by the requirements of other unrelated sections under which the same final result might be attained by different means."

The defendants' motion for partial summary judgment as to Count II of the Amended Complaint will be granted.

QUESTIONS

1. Why does the argument based on the doctrine of good faith and fair dealing in contracts not apply in this case?
2. In hindsight, what was the drafting mistake from the perspective of the preferred stockholders?
3. In what way is the doctrine of veil-piercing relevant for the purpose of analyzing this situation?

NOTES

1. The job of the drafter of the preferred stock contract (the certificate of incorporation and the certificate of designation) is akin to the game "whack-a-mole," in which the "moles" are unforeseen circumstances and possible end-arounds the unstated assumptions and implicit understandings. This is not a problem that is unique to financial contracting, but is a common problem in contracting in general. Contracts are incomplete. Like most contracting processes, ambiguity and unforeseen circumstances loom. The following passage from a footnote in the court's opinion is apropos: "Fifty years ago, the fallacy of plaintiffs' argument was recognized in the seminal law review article by Richard M. Buxbaum, *Preferred Stock-Law and Draftsmanship*, 42 Cal. L. Rev. 243, 257 (1954). In discussing problems in drafting financial restriction clauses in preferred stock contract, Professor Buxbaum stated as follows: 'As to all these clauses, *it is vital that all payments, distributions, acquisitions, etc. include those of the subsidiaries; otherwise the provisions can be totally avoided*'."

2. LIQUIDATION PREFERENCE

The liquidation preference provides that, after payment to creditors in a liquidation, preferred stockholders have priority over common stockholders in the distribution of assets. The corporate charter will provide the liquidation value of the preferred stock, which must be paid first before any distribution of assets to common stockholders.

EXAMPLE

> **Goldman Sachs' Series G Preferred Stock**
>
> **Section 5. Liquidation Rights.**
>
>   (a) **Voluntary or Involuntary Liquidation**. In the event *or merger or acquisition* of any liquidation, dissolution or winding up of the affairs of the Corporation, whether voluntary or involuntary, holders of Series G shall be entitled to receive for each share of Series G, out of the assets of the Corporation or proceeds thereof (whether capital or surplus) available for distribution to stockholders of the Corporation, and after satisfaction of all liabilities and obligations to creditors of the Corporation, before any distribution of such assets or proceeds is made to or set aside for the holders of Common Stock and any other stock of the Corporation ranking junior to the Series G as to such distribution, payment in full in an amount equal to the sum of (i) $100,000 per share and (ii) the accrued and unpaid dividends thereon (including, if applicable as provided in Section 4(a) above, dividends on such amount), whether or not declared, to the date of payment.

The following case involves an amendment of the charter that adversely changed the liquidation preference to suit a business need. Consider how the preferred stockholders could have ex ante contracted to protect against the type of contingency seen in this case.

Goldman v. Postal Telegraph
52 F. Supp. 763 (D. Del. 1943)

LEAHY, District Judge.

The occasion has never arisen for the Delaware courts to determine where a certificate of incorporation provides a preference stock is to be paid $60 per share upon liquidation before any distribution is to be made to the common stockholders whether an amendment under Sec. 26 of the Delaware Corporation Law which attempts to provide that such preferred stockholder shall receive on dissolution less than the stated figure of $60 a share is valid.

Postal Telegraph, Inc., incorporated under the laws of Delaware, agreed to transfer to Western Union Telegraph Company, another Delaware corporation, all its assets. At the time of the agreement plaintiff owned 500 shares of non-cumulative preferred stock of Postal which, by the terms of Postal's certificate of incorporation, entitled all preferred stockholders to a payment of $60 a share on liquidation before any distribution could be made to its common stockholders. Defendant Postal proposed to its stockholders three resolutions authorizing (1) the sale of all its assets to Western Union, conditioned upon the approval by Postal's stockholders of an amendment to its certificate of incorporation; (2) the amendment of Postal's certificate of incorporation so as to provide that the holders of defendant's non-cumulative preferred stock would receive in lieu of $60 per share on liquidation one share of Western Union B stock; and (3) formal dissolution of Postal. At the stockholders' meeting,

329

these resolutions were passed by a requisite vote over plaintiff's express objection. This suit followed.

Prior to the amendment under Sec. 26, the provisions of Postal's certificate of incorporation with respect to the liquidating rights of the non-cumulative preferred stock provided:

> (e) In the event of any liquidation, dissolution or winding up of the affairs of the Corporation, whether voluntary or involuntary, the holders of shares of the Non-Cumulative Preferred Stock, $60 per share plus all unpaid dividends thereon to the extent that the same shall be deemed to have been earned, as provided in subdivision (a) hereof, to the date of payment. In the event that at such date of payment the amount, if any, of the dividends deemed to have been earned on the shares of the Non-Cumulative Preferred Stock for the period between the dividend payment date next preceding such date of payment and such date of payment cannot be determined, dividends on the shares of Non-Cumulative Preferred Stock shall be deemed to have been earned at the full rate of $2.40 per share per annum for such period.
>
> After the making of such payment to the holders of the Non-Cumulative Preferred Stock, the remaining assets and funds of the Corporation shall be distributed among the holders of the Common Stock and of all other classes of stock ranking junior to the Non-Cumulative Preferred Stock according to their respective rights and shares. If, upon any such liquidation, dissolution or winding up of the affairs of the Corporation, whether voluntary or involuntary, the assets of the Corporation shall not be sufficient to provide payment in full of the amounts to which the holders of the Non-Cumulative Preferred Stock shall be so entitled, the amount distributable to the holders of all shares of the Non-Cumulative Preferred Stock shall be apportioned among them ratably, in proportion to the amounts to which they are respectively entitled.

The certificate of incorporation as amended provides:

> (e) In the event of any liquidation, dissolution or winding up of the affairs of the Corporation whether voluntary or involuntary, the holders of shares of the Non-Cumulative Preferred Stock shall be entitled to be paid, before any distribution or payment shall be made to the holders of the Common Stock or of any other class of stock ranking junior to the Non-Cumulative Preferred Stock, $60 per share plus all unpaid dividends thereon to the extent that the same shall be deemed to have been earned, as provided in subdivision (a) hereof, to the date of payment. In the event that at such date of payment the amount, if any, of the dividends on the shares of Non-Cumulative Preferred Stock shall be deemed to have been earned at the full rate of $2.40 per share per annum for such period.
>
> *Provided, however, that notwithstanding the provisions of the next preceding paragraph in this subdivision (e) contained, if substantially all of the assets of the Corporation or of its operating subsidiaries are sold to the Western Union Telegraph Company then upon any liquidation, dissolution or winding up of the affairs of the Corporation the holders of shares of the Non-Cumulative Preferred Stock shall be entitled to receive for each share out of the assets of the Corporation (in lieu of the cash payments in said next preceding paragraph specified) one share of the Class B Stock of The Western Union Telegraph Company before any distribution or payment shall be made to the holders of shares of Common Stock; but they shall be entitled to no further or other participation in any distribution or payment.*
>
> After the making of such payment to the holders of the Non-Cumulative Preferred Stock, the remaining assets and funds of the Corporation shall be

distributed among the holders of the Common Stock and of all other classes of stock ranking junior to the Non-Cumulative Preferred Stock according to their respective rights and shares. If, upon any such liquidation, dissolution or winding up of the affairs of the Corporation, whether voluntary or involuntary, the assets of the Corporation shall not be sufficient to provide payment in full of the amounts to which the holders of the Non-Cumulative Preferred Stock shall be so entitled, the amount distributable to the holders of all shares of the Non-Cumulative Preferred Stock shall be apportioned among them ratably, in proportion to the amounts to which they are respectively entitled.

The Postal-Western Union agreement provides that for the transfer of all the assets of Postal to Western Union, Postal will receive as part consideration 308,124 shares of Class B stock of Western Union. The entire amount of Class B stock to be received from Western Union will have a value substantially less than the aggregate liquidation preference of the preferred stock of Postal. Consequently, under its certificate of incorporation Postal's common stockholders—whose equity is deeply under water— would be entitled to receive nothing if ordinary liquidation occurred. Subject to various adjustments which do not have my immediate attention, Western Union will assume approximately $10,800,000 of Postal's liabilities. Postal's economic position is shown by its steady losses, aggregating over $13,500,000 from February 1, 1940, to May 31, 1943. These losses have been financed, in part, by advances from the Reconstruction Finance Corporation. In facing further corporate existence, two courses were open to Postal: (a) To submit to government ownership or (b) to seek some type of merger with or absorption by Western Union.

In order to complete the proposed transfer of assets to Western Union, the vote of a majority of the outstanding stock of Postal was required under the Delaware law. Postal's outstanding preferred was 256,769 and the number of shares of common was 1,027,076. Hence, if all the preferred voted in favor of the plan, it would still be necessary to obtain the affirmative vote of approximately 400,000 shares of common. In order to obtain such vote, Postal's directors determined it advisable that the preferred's rights on liquidation be modified so as to provide that out of the 308,124 shares of Class B stock of Western Union to be received by Postal, 256,770 shares would be distributed share for share for each of Postal's preferred and the balance of the Class B—51,354 shares—would be distributed to Postal's common stockholders, which was to be in the ratio of 1/20 of a share of Class B Western Union stock for each share of common stock of Postal.

Plaintiff here seeks to enforce the liquidating rights which he contends are secured to him by the certificate of incorporation of Postal prior to the adoption of the resolution to amend it under Sec. 26. Defendant moved to dismiss on the ground that the complaint failed to state a cause of action.

[The issue is whether] the amendment of Postal's certificate of incorporation is authorized under Sec. 26 of the Delaware Corporation Law.

Defendant's certificate of incorporation provides that, in the event of liquidation or dissolution, the holders of preferred stock are entitled to be paid $60 per share, plus all unpaid dividends (of which there are none), before any distribution is made to the holders of the common or junior stock. Sec. 26 provides that an amendment to a certificate of incorporation may alter or change "preferences" theretofore provided for a preferred stock, if the vote of a requisite majority is had. Because at common law, in the absence of agreement to the contrary, all shares of stock, by whatever name they may be known, stand upon an equal footing, preferences, being in derogation of the common law rule, must be strictly construed. Historically, preferential rights consist generally of two classes of preferences: (1) preferences as to dividends and (2) preferences in distribution of assets upon liquidation, or winding-up.

As the right of the preferred stockholder here involved is a preferential right within the meaning of the Delaware Corporation Law (i.e., the stock is preferred on dissolution), I hold such right is subject to the amendment here involved under the particular language of Sec. 26.

In the case at bar, I see no reason why a Delaware corporation cannot agree to sell its assets conditioned upon the seller corporation amending its certificate of incorporation as a part of the transaction. In fact, such a condition may well become a part of the urgent necessities of a particular transaction. Here, for example, 256,770 shares of preferred, if entitled to $60 a share on dissolution, would be entitled to receive approximately $15,000,000 on liquidation. The present value of the Class B stock of Western Union to be received by Postal in exchange for its assets, at about $19 a share, admittedly amounts to only $4,888,000. If the preferential right of $60 a share remains unaltered, it would be impossible in this case to obtain the vote of the common stockholders in favor of the sale and dissolution, because there could not possibly be any rational basis, under the circumstances, for the common stock voting in approval. One thing is certain. Nothing can be accomplished, either in law or in life by calling the recalcitrants names. The reality of the situation confronting Postal's management called for some inducement to be offered the common stockholders to secure their favorable vote for the plan. The fact is something had to induce the common stockholders to come along. This court and the Delaware courts have recognized the strategic position of common stock to hamper the desires of the real owners of the equity of a corporation, and the tribute which common stock exacts for its vote under reclassification and reorganization.

QUESTIONS

1. If the equity in the common stock was "deeply under water," why not just liquidate the company and distribute the assets to the preferred stockholders?
2. What did the court mean when it wrote "Nothing can be accomplished, either in law or in life by calling the recalcitrants names"? From the perspective of the preferred stockholders, what "names" (pejoratives) come to mind when thinking about the common stockholders?
3. Why should the common stockholders get anything at all in the asset sale? What was the "hold up" problem for the board of directors?
4. As a general proposition of contract law, can contracts be amended by contracting parties as the business or economic situation changes during the course of the contract?
5. What kind of a term or mechanism in the original charter could have protected the complaining preferred stockholder?

The following case interprets the meaning of "liquidation" with respect to the rights of preferred stockholders. Since preferred rights are contractual in nature and since liquidation preference is a common seen right of preferred stockholders, the term "liquidation" must be clearly defined.

Rothschild International Corp. v. Liggett Group Inc.
474 A.2d 133 (Del. 1984)

HORSEY, Justice.

This appeal is from a summary judgment Order of the Court of Chancery dismissing a purported class action filed by the owners of 7% cumulative preferred stock in Liggett Group, Inc., a Delaware corporation. The suit arises out of a combined tender offer and reverse cash-out merger whereby the interests of the 7% preferred shareholders were eliminated for a price of $70 per share, an amount $30 below the liquidation preference stated in Liggett's certificate of incorporation. Plaintiff asserts claims for breach of contract and breach of fiduciary duty based on the non-payment of the $30 premium.

Rothschild International Corp. filed a class action on behalf of 7% cumulative preferred stockholders of Liggett against defendants Liggett [and] Grand Metropolitan Limited ("GM"). The class was to consist of those 7% shareholders who tendered their preferred stock for $70 per share in response to GM's tender offer and those who did not so tender and were cashed out for the same per share price in the subsequent merger of [GM's acquisition subsidiary] into Liggett.

Plaintiff contends that the takeover of Liggett via the combined tender offer and merger in essence effected a liquidation of the company thus warranting payment to the holders of the 7% preferred stock of the $100 liquidation value set forth in Liggett's charter. Plaintiff's breach of contract and breach of fiduciary duty claims are premised on a single assertion—that GM's plan of acquisition was equivalent to a liquidation. However, as we view the record, the transaction did not involve a liquidation of Liggett's business. Hence, we must affirm.

There is no dispute of facts. Liggett's certificate of incorporation provided that

> In the event of any liquidation of the assets of the Corporation (whether voluntary or involuntary) the holders of the 7% Preferred Stock shall be entitled to be paid the par amount of their 7% Preferred shares and the amount of any dividends accumulated and unpaid thereon. . . .

Under the terms of Liggett's charter, each share of the 7% security carried a $100 par value. Plaintiff makes two interrelated arguments: (1) that the economic effect of the merger was a liquidation of Liggett's assets "just as if [Liggett] were sold piece meal to Grand Met"; and (2) that any corporate reorganization that forcibly liquidates a shareholder's *interests* is tantamount to a liquidation of the *corporation* itself. From this, plaintiff argues that it necessarily follows that defendants' failure to pay the preferred shareholders the full liquidation price constituted a breach of Liggett's charter. We cannot agree with either argument.

Preferential rights are contractual in nature and therefore are governed by the express provisions of a company's certificate of incorporation. Stock preferences must also be clearly expressed and will not be presumed.

Liggett's charter stated that the $100 liquidation preference would be paid only in the event of "any liquidation of the assets of the Corporation. The term "liquidation", as applied to a corporation, means the "winding up of the affairs of the corporation by getting in its assets, settling with creditors and debtors and apportioning the amount of profit and loss." W. Fletcher, *Corporations* §7968 (1979). *See Sterling v. Mayflower Hotel Corp.,* 93 A.2d 107, 112 (Del. 1952).

Our view of the record confirms the correctness of the Chancellor's finding that there was no "liquidation" of Liggett within the well-defined meaning of that term. Clearly the directors and shareholders of Liggett determined that the company should be integrated with GM, not that the corporate assets be liquidated on a "piece meal" basis. The fact is that Liggett has retained its corporate identity. Having elected this plan of reorganization, the parties had the right to avail themselves of the most effective means for achieving that result, subject only to their duty to deal fairly with the minority interests.

We must construe Liggett's liquidation provision as written and conclude that the reverse cash-out merger of Liggett did not accomplish a "liquidation" of Liggett's assets. Only upon a liquidation of its assets would Liggett's preferred shareholders' charter rights to payment of par value "spring into being."

Sterling v. Mayflower Hotel Corp. is in point on this issue. There, this Court held that a merger is not equivalent to a sale of assets. In so holding, the Court followed the well-settled principle of Delaware Corporation Law that "action taken under one section of that law is legally independent, and its validity is not dependent upon, nor to be tested by the requirements of other unrelated sections under which the same final result might be attained by different means."

It is equally settled under Delaware law that minority stock interests may be eliminated by merger. And, where a merger of corporations is permitted by law, a shareholder's preferential rights are subject to defeasance. Stockholders are charged with knowledge of this possibility at the time they acquire their shares. *Federal United Corp. v. Havender,* 11 A.2d 331, 338 (Del. 1940).

Plaintiff claims that reliance on *Sterling* and *Havender* for a finding that Liggett was not liquidated is misplaced. To support this claim, plaintiff variously argues: (1) that as *Sterling* and *Havender* pre-dated cash mergers, they are not dispositive as to whether a Liggett-like takeover could constitute a liquidation; (2) that the relied-on authorities viewed a merger as contemplating the continuance of a stockholder's investment in the corporate enterprise; and (3) that because of the *Sterling/Havender* view of a merger and the unique features of the 7% preferred stock, the 7% shareholders could reasonably expect to be paid the $100 liquidation preference in any circumstance effecting a total elimination of their investment in Liggett.

The short answer to plaintiff's arguments is that, as a matter of law, stock issued or purchased prior to the Legislature's authorization of cash mergers does not entitle the stockholder to any vested right of immunity from the operation of the cash merger provision. Further, it is settled that the State has the reserved power to enact laws having the effect of amending certificates of incorporation and any rights arising thereunder. As plaintiff is charged with knowledge of the possible defeasance of its stock interests upon a merger, plaintiff cannot successfully argue for relief on the basis of the uniqueness of the 7% stock and the stockholders' "reasonable expectations" theory.

We find that the Chancellor did not err as a matter of law in granting defendants' motion for summary judgment.

QUESTIONS

1. What is the definition and concept of "liquidation" in the context of determining the preferred shareholder's liquidation preference?
2. The court states: "the measure of 'fair value' is not 'liquidation value.'" What does this mean?

NOTES

1. In light of cases like *Rothchild*, which require that preference rights be highly specific in description, such rights are contractual and thus can be drafted to include a merger or acquisition as a liquidation event triggering the payment of a liquidation value. *See, e.g., In the matter of the Appraisal of Ford Holdings, Inc. Preferred Stock*, 698 A.2d 973 (Del.Ch. 1997). Such a provision would define the consideration for preferred stockholders in the event of a merger or acquisition.
2. Additionally, a separate class vote on proposed amendments to the articles of incorporation affecting the stockholder can protect preferred stockholders. *See, e.g.,* Model Business Corporation Act §10.04 cmt. ("The right to vote as a separate voting group provides a major protection for classes or series of shares with preferential rights, or classes or series of limited nonvoting shares, against amendments that are especially burdensome to that class or series."). However, there are countervailing considerations to providing a separate class vote. Such votes may present a "hold up" situation by one class as seen in *Goldman v. Postal Telegraph*, or such provisions themselves can be subject to amendment, *see infra, Gradient OC Master, Ltd. v. NBC Universal, Inc.*

3. REDEMPTION

Like common stocks, some preferred stocks do not have a fixed maturity. Preferred stock that has no mandatory redemption date is called perpetual preferred stock. In a redeemable preferred stock, the contract terms would specify a redemption price at which shares will be redeemed, and the redemption price may include a redemption premium to the face value of the preferred stock. The redemption may also be optional, which permits the issuer to call the preferred stock at a time of its choosing. Since the right to redeem shares is an option held by the issuer, the redemption premium can be seen as an option premium paid to preferred stockholders for the issuer's redemption right.

There may be a number of reasons why preferred stocks may have redemption or call features. The preferred stock may be needed only for a specific time, for example when a company needs to boost its equity capital for a set duration. An issuer may exercise optional redemption if interest rates are forecast to decline. Although preferred stock is equity, its value is connected to interest rates since they are paid periodic dividends and have debt-like features. With declining rates, the corporation can finance at cheaper rates, and thus it would have incentive to call higher rate preferred stock.

Redemption can work in reverse. Preferred stockholders can negotiate a right to force the issuer to redeem the stock (which is an option "to put" the shares to the company). For example, they can negotiate a put right that is triggered by a failure to pay dividends or a certain amount of dividend arrearage.

335

EXAMPLE

> ### Goldman Sachs' Series G Preferred Stock
>
> **Section 6. Redemption.**
>
> (a) **Optional Redemption**. The Corporation, at its option, subject to the approval of the Board of Governors of the Federal Reserve System, may redeem, in whole at any time or in part from time to time, the shares of Series G at the time outstanding, upon notice given as provided in Section 6(c) below, at a redemption price equal to the sum of (i) $110,000 per share and (ii) the accrued and unpaid dividends thereon(including, if applicable as provided in Section 4(a) above, dividends on such amount), whether or not declared, to the redemption date, *provided* that the minimum number of shares of Series G redeemable at any time is the lesser of (i) 10,000 shares of Series G and (ii) the number of shares of Series G outstanding. The redemption price for any shares of Series G shall be payable on the redemption date to the holder of such shares against surrender of the certificate(s) evidencing such shares to the Corporation or its agent. Any declared but unpaid dividends payable on a redemption date that occurs subsequent to the Dividend Record Date for a Dividend Period shall not be paid to the holder entitled to receive the redemption price on the redemption date, but rather shall be paid to the holder of record of the redeemed shares on such Dividend Record Date relating to the Dividend Payment Date as provided in Section 4 above. An exchange of Series G for Spinco Preferred (as defined in the Securities Purchase Agreement, dated as of September 29, 2008, between the Corporation and Berkshire Hathaway Inc. (the "SPA")) pursuant to Section 4.7 of the SPA, shall not be deemed to be a redemption for purposes of this Section 6.

The following case considers fiduciary obligations of and equitable limitations on the board in connection with its decision to redeem preferred stock. Ordinarily, the decision to redeem preferred stock is a point of contract and a business decision, but determining the propriety of conduct in light of fiduciary obligations and equity is a highly contextual scrutiny.

Eisenberg v. Chicago Milwaukee Corp.
537 A.2d 1051 (Del. Ch. 1987)

JACOBS, Vice-Chancellor.

On October 28, 1987, Chicago Milwaukee Corp., a Delaware corporation ("CMC") commenced a self-tender offer (the "Offer") for any and all shares of its $5 Prior Preferred Stock ("the Preferred"), at an offering price of $55 per share cash.

The plaintiff, a Preferred stockholder of CMC, commenced this class action against CMC and its directors. He attacks the validity of the Offer and seeks a preliminary injunction to prevent its consummation.

CMC's principal assets presently consist of approximately $300 million in cash, plus real estate (including 66,000 acres of timberland) appraised at $90 million. As of September 30, 1987, the common stockholders' equity approximated $369 million.

CMC has two classes of stock. Approximately 2.5 million shares of common stock, and 463,946 shares of the Preferred, are issued and outstanding. As of October 27, 1987 the Preferred shares were held of record by 591 Preferred stockholders. Both the common and Preferred are listed and publicly traded on the New York Stock Exchange (NYSE), and are registered under the Securities Exchange Act of 1934.

The rights of the Preferred stock are limited. The Preferred has a $5 per year dividend right, but payable only "when and as declared by the Board of Directors". The dividend is noncumulative. The Preferred also has a liquidation preference of $100 per share, and may be redeemed at a value of $100 per share plus up to $7.50 of unpaid dividends per share. However, CMC is not obligated to redeem the shares or to liquidate CMC at any time.

CMC's Certificate of Incorporation prohibits the payment of a dividend on the common stock in any given period, unless the Preferred dividend is paid first. But there is no requirement that any dividend be paid, and, in fact, no dividends have ever been paid on either the Preferred or the common stock since 1971. The Preferred stockholders may vote, along with common stockholders, for the eight regular members of the Board of Directors. However, if Preferred stock dividends are not paid for three semi-annual dividend payment dates, the Preferred, voting as a class, becomes entitled to elect two additional special directors. In 1985 [two directors] were elected as the special Preferred directors, and presently serve in that capacity.

The Company has declined to pay dividends on the Preferred. Although CMC has abundant liquidity (almost $300 million of cash) and although a relatively small percentage of that liquidity (approximately $2.32 million) would be required to pay the $5 dividend, CMC's management has adopted a "no-dividend" policy for the stated purpose of conserving assets for an acquisition. At CMC's most recent annual stockholder meeting held in June of 1987, several Preferred stockholders complained about CMC's refusal to pay dividends on (or to redeem) the Preferred. After the meeting, other Preferred stockholders wrote to CMC to voice similar protests.

CMC's directors do not own any appreciable amount of Preferred shares. The record does indicate, however, that CMC's directors, and the "Schedule 13D" shareholder group with which certain of those directors are affiliated, own a significant percentage of the common stock. As of August 6, 1987, directors and the Schedule 13D Group owned collectively 41% of CMC's common stock. Because Preferred dividends are noncumulative, CMC's policy of retaining earnings rather than paying dividends, operates to benefit the common stockholders generally, and the directors individually, because the directors own significant amounts of common stock.[1]

The trading price of the Preferred has fluctuated widely over the past decade. After the Railroad filed for bankruptcy, the Preferred traded as low as $10. Once the Railroad emerged from bankruptcy in 1985, the market price of the Preferred traded from a low of $55 to a high of $80.25. In 1986, the price fluctuated from a low of $57 to a high of $88.50. For the first three quarters of 1987, the price fluctuated from $53 to $78.50. From early 1987 to October 16, 1987, the price moved gradually downward, from a high of $78.50 in March, 1987, to a low of $52.50 on October 16, 1987.

---

1. Because dividends on the Preferred do not cumulate, the nonpayment of each Preferred dividend operates to increase the retained earnings of CMC, thereby increasing the common stockholders' equity.

On October 19, 1987, the stock market phenomenon popularly described as "Black Monday" occurred. On that date the Dow Jones Industrial Average as reported by the NYSE declined by 508 points [a 22.6% decline in the index], causing a sudden, significant decline in the market price of many listed securities, including CMC. The record shows that Black Monday was the originating force that motivated the decision to conduct the tender offer presently under challenge. On October 19 the Preferred stock price dropped another ten points, and by October 20, it had fallen to $42 per share. On October 27, the day before the Offer was announced, the Preferred closed at $41.50 per share.

The tender offer documents represented that "the movement in the market price of the [Preferred] Shares immediately prior to the commencement of the Offer was one of several considerations in the Company's decision to make the Offer." The record evidence indicates, however, that that $41.50 market price level—the lowest price at which the Preferred had traded since early 1983—was the predominant, if not the sole, factor motivating the directors' decision to make the Offer. Before Black Monday, CMC had never considered making a tender offer for the Preferred.

On October 20, defendant Edwin Jacobson, CMC's President, telephoned defendant Jack Nash, a fellow director, and suggested that CMC make a tender offer for the Preferred, since the stock price had declined substantially. Mr. Nash agreed and suggested that the Executive Committee consider the matter. A meeting by telephone took place on the following day, October 21, 1987. At that meeting the Executive Committee decided to authorize Mr. Jacobson to retain legal counsel and investment bankers to advise the CMC Board. The Committee also decided that a special meeting of the Board of Directors would be held on October 27, 1987, six days later.

On October 23, Mr. Jacobson retained PaineWebber as financial advisor to evaluate and recommend an offering price that would be fair and would maximize the offer's chances of success. PaineWebber performed its entire financial analysis over a three-day period, (the weekend and the following Monday, October 24, 25, and 26). The statistical data supporting PaineWebber's conclusions were presented to the Board for the first time at the scheduled October 27 meeting.

As part of its valuation study, PaineWebber analyzed other securities "comparable" to the Preferred, to determine the yield and an appropriate price for those securities. PaineWebber relied upon certain public financial data and upon management's representations that CMC had no present intention to pay dividends or to redeem the Preferred shares. Based upon its analysis, PaineWebber concluded that the "intrinsic" or "fair" value of the Preferred was between $20 and $30—a value significantly lower than the current trading price.[4] Given that valuation, PaineWebber concluded that an offer at the current market price ($41.50) would be fair. PaineWebber recognized, nonetheless, that for a tender offer to succeed, it would have to be at a premium above market. Its study of other self-tenders revealed that the average premium paid in those transactions was 14% above market. On that basis, PaineWebber recommended that

---

4. PaineWebber's low "intrinsic" valuation presumably flowed from the fact that the Preferred carries with it no guaranteed right to dividends or to redemption that would enable a shareholder to receive a certain return on his investment.

CMC offer at least a comparable (14%) premium, that is, an offering price of $48 per share.

Although CMC's directors received no written materials before the October 27 special meeting, PaineWebber's representatives did present their reasoning and conclusions orally at that meeting. When the 1 1/2 hour meeting concluded, the Board approved an "any and all" cash tender offer for the Preferred within a price range of $50 to $55 per share, delegating to the Executive Committee the task of selecting a specific offering price. There is no evidence that at that meeting the Board considered or discussed the need to "delist" or "deregister" the Preferred, the effect of delisting or deregistration upon the Preferred shareholders' investment, or the need to reduce CMC's administrative and bookkeeping costs (including costs of communication) relating to the Preferred stockholders.

In a short meeting held later that same afternoon, the Executive Committee fixed the offering price at $55 per share. The following day, the Offer was formally commenced, and CMC disseminated to all Preferred stockholders an Offer to Purchase bearing that same date. Although the Offer to Purchase disclosed the opinion of both PaineWebber and the Board of Directors that the $55 offering price was fair, that document also admonished that neither CMC nor its directors were making any recommendation as to whether or not the Preferred shareholders should tender.

The plaintiff's motion for injunctive relief rests primarily upon two grounds. He first contends that the defendants violated their fiduciary duty to disclose with entire candor all material facts relating to the Offer. Second, he argues that the defendants violated their fiduciary duty of loyalty by structuring the Offer so as to impermissibly coerce the Preferred stockholders to tender their shares.

The Court concludes that the plaintiff's motion must prevail, and that the Offer should be preliminarily enjoined during the time required to allow its deficiencies to be cured.

By its very nature and form, a tender offer is normally regarded as a voluntary transaction. Unlike a cash-out merger where public stockholders can be involuntarily eliminated from the enterprise, in a properly conducted tender offer the stockholder-offerees may freely choose whether or not to tender. That choice will normally depend upon each stockholder's individual investment objectives and his evaluation of the merits of the offer. Moreover, tender offers often afford shareholders a unique opportunity to sell their shares at a premium above market price. For those reasons, a tender offer that is voluntary (and that otherwise satisfies applicable legal requirements) will not be enjoined.

However, a tender offer—particularly one made by a corporation for its own shares—may be voluntary in appearance and form but involuntary as a matter of reality and substance. Thus far two classes of situations have arisen that have been found to deprive a tender offer of its voluntary character: (i) cases involving materially false or misleading disclosures made to shareholders in connection with the offer, and (ii) cases where the offer, by reason of its terms or the circumstances under which it is made, is wrongfully coercive. If either circumstance exists, preliminary injunctive relief will follow.

The Claim of Improper Disclosure

The standard applicable to the plaintiff's disclosure claims is well established. Corporate directors owe a fiduciary duty to their stockholders to disclose all facts material to the transaction in an atmosphere of entire candor. *Smith v. Van Gorkom,* 488 A.2d 858, 890 (Del. 1985). That standard requires:

> A showing of substantial likelihood that under all the circumstances, the omitted fact would have assumed actual significance in the deliberations of the reasonable shareholder. Put another way, there must be a substantial likelihood that the disclosure of the omitted fact would have been viewed by the reasonable investor as having significantly altered the "total mix" of information available.

Where a corporation tenders for its own shares, the exacting duty of disclosure imposed upon corporate fiduciaries is even "more onerous" than in a contested offer. That is because in a self-tender, the disclosures are unilateral and not counterbalanced by opposing points of view.

A related reason for requiring the strictest possible standard of disclosure is that corporate self-tenders, by their very nature, involve built-in conflicts of interest between the fiduciaries responsible for conducting the offer and the stockholders to whom the offer is directed. The interest of the corporate offeror (*qua* buyer) is to pay the lowest price possible; the interest of the stockholders (*qua* sellers) is to receive as high a price as possible. The directors are acting both as the representatives of the corporate offeror and as fiduciaries for the shareholder-offerees. That dual role necessarily gives rise to a potential conflict of the directors, which calls for procedural protections for the stockholders whose interests may not be adequately represented.

Disclosures Relating to the Purpose of the Offer

The Offer to Purchase, on the first page, recites three separate purposes for the Offer. These are:

> (i) to acquire the Shares at a price which the Company believes makes the Shares an attractive investment for the Company at this time;
>
> (ii) to reduce the number and aggregate market value of the outstanding publicly held Shares and the number of Preferred Stockholders of record in order to effect the delisting of the Shares from the NYSE and the deregistration of the Shares under the Securities Exchange Act of 1934, as amended (the "Exchange Act"), which should reduce the administrative and bookkeeping costs attributable to the Company's communication and other activities with its Preferred Stockholders; and

The Offer to Purchase conveys the clear impression that the second (delisting/deregistration) purpose is a separate purpose, of coordinate importance with the first purpose, and of equal dignity. That impression is reinforced by the disclosure that if, as a result of the Offer, the Preferred shares no longer meet the requirements for continued listing on the NYSE,[10] ". . . the company intends to request delisting of the shares from the NYSE." The Supplement also discloses that "the movement in the market price of the Shares immediately prior to the commencement of the Offer was *one of the several considerations* in the Company's decision to make the Offer."

---

10. According to the Offer to Purchase, the NYSE's published guidelines indicate that the NYSE "would consider delisting the Shares if (i) the aggregate market value of publicly held Shares should fall below $2 million or (ii) the number of publicly held Shares would fall below 100,000 shares." That document also discloses that registration under the 1934 Exchange Act may be terminated upon certification by CMC to the Securities and Exchange Commission that there are fewer than 300 record holders of Preferred Shares.

These disclosures of the Offer's purported delisting/deregistration purpose are misleading. They clearly suggest that the Offer had a business-oriented, cost-saving, rationale, separate from and unrelated to the first Offer's purpose, which is to enable CMC to acquire the Preferred at an attractive price. Those disclosures further suggest that CMC's directors made a considered business judgment, unrelated to considerations of stock market price, to conduct the Offer in order to effect corporate cost savings.

Neither impression is accurate. The record shows that the Offer is not being made to effect cost savings. Its purpose, plainly and simply, is to enable CMC to take advantage of the unprecedented "Black Monday" market crash that drove down the price of the Preferred to its lowest level in five years. The $55 offering price for the Preferred is attractive, because it is far less than the cost of redeeming the stock ($100 per share), and because the Offer, if successful, would eliminate the only legal barrier to the payment of dividends on the common stock. There was no consideration or discussion at any of the directors meetings of cost savings that would result from delisting or deregistering the Preferred, and any such cost savings would be minimal. In short, cost savings played either no role in the directors' decision to make the offer, or were at best a factor of minimal significance. In either event, it was materially misleading to portray cost savings as being a "purpose" of the Offer.

The shareholder-offerees are entitled to an accurate, candid presentation of why the self-tender offer is being made. There is nothing *per se* improper in a corporation deciding to make a noncoercive tender for its own stock to take advantage of a decline in stock market prices, so long as the shareholders are fully, candidly and accurately informed of all material facts. The disclosures relating to the cost-savings "purpose" served not to enlighten but to obscure the real reasons motivating the Offer.

Disclosures Relating to the Fairness of the Price

The plaintiff next contends that the $55 offer price is unfair and that the disclosures relating to that price were calculated to, and did, obscure and divert attention from that fact. If that were the case, the disclosures would clearly be defective. Shareholders are entitled to be informed of information in the fiduciaries' possession that is material to the fairness of the price.

That portion of the Offer to Purchase which relates to the "Fairness of the Offer" discloses that (i) "the Board of Directors of the Company believes that the Offer, including the price to be paid per Share to be paid, is fair to tendering Preferred Stockholders" (ii) the Board had considered the analysis by PaineWebber, which had opined that the offering price was fair, and finally, (iii):

> The current range of market prices was among the factors in the Board of Directors' determination. See Section 6. The directors concluded that, based upon recent market prices of the Shares and in light of recent stock market trends, the premium of approximately 33% (which represents the approximate percentage difference between the Offer price of $55 per Share and the reported last sale price of the Shares on the NYSE on October 27, 1987 ($41.50)) was both reasonable from the Company's standpoint and fair to all of its stockholders.

While the quoted disclosure may be technically true, it fails to candidly disclose certain material facts relevant to the fairness of the price. Specifically, the "current range of market prices" was not simply "among the factors" considered by the Board.

Rather, current market prices were the primary, if not predominant, factor motivating both the Offer and the $55 offering price. The euphemistic references to "recent stock market trends," the "current range of market prices," and the "premium of approximately 33%" over $41.50, were not counterbalanced by any disclosure of (i) the fact that the $41.50 price at which PaineWebber and the directors had pegged the premium was the lowest price level at which the stock had traded in five years, or (ii) the fact that $55 represented only a 5% premium above the ($52.50) "precrash" price level. Although the role played by PaineWebber (particularly its fairness opinion) was given considerable prominence, the fact that PaineWebber's work was done over a single long weekend was not disclosed. That omission, in these circumstances, was also material.

Had the foregoing facts been disclosed, shareholders would have been given a more even-handed presentation of the economic merits of the Offer. The need for such a presentation would appear even more essential, because the directors had concluded that the Offer was fair, yet decided not to recommend that their shareholders tender into it.

The defendants argue (correctly) that it is common knowledge that on October 19, 1987, the stock market (and the price of the Preferred) declined precipitously. But what is not common knowledge, and what the directors were obliged to candidly disclose, was the role played by the market decline and the "post-crash" price levels in the directors' conclusion that $55 was a fair offering price. Those facts were exclusively within the CMC's directors knowledge and control, and they were material.

Disclosures Relating to the Directors Interest in the Success of the Offer

Finally, the Offer to Purchase does not adequately disclose that certain of CMC's directors had a potential conflict of interest by reason of their ownership of significant amounts of CMC's common stock. In this case an inherent conflict exists between the class of Preferred stock and the class of common. By decreasing the amount paid for the Preferred in the Offer, the directors correspondingly increase the amount of common shareholders' equity remaining in the corporation. Five of CMC's ten directors personally owned over 17.1% of CMC's common shares, and Odyssey Partners, of which [two directors] were general partners, owned 6.8% of CMC's common shares. The common stock holdings of the entire Schedule 13D group, when combined with the holdings of those directors, is 41%. A successful offer would benefit those directors by increasing the book value of their common stock by $3.5 million.[13]

By its discussion of the CMC directors' potential conflict, the Court does not intend to suggest that those directors, in approving the offer, necessarily acted improperly or placed their individual interests over those of the Preferred stockholders. The only point made here is that in these circumstances, the potential conflict of half of CMC's Board of Directors was a fact that should have been disclosed. The Preferred shareholders were entitled to know that certain of their fiduciaries had a self-interest that was arguably in conflict with their own, and the omission of the fact was material.

---

13. Further, a successful self-tender offer would eliminate the Preferred stock, and allow the directors to declare a dividend on the common stock alone. Presently, any dividend declared first be paid to the Preferred shareholders, and may only then be paid to the common shareholders.

The Claim of Inequitable Coercion

The plaintiff also contends that, independent of disclosure, the Offer must be enjoined as being wrongfully coercive.

The standard applicable to the plaintiff's claim of inequitable coercion is whether the defendants have taken actions that operate inequitably to induce the Preferred shareholders to tender their shares for reasons unrelated to the economic merits of the offer. Although the issue is not free from doubt, I conclude that the plaintiff has demonstrated a likelihood of ultimate success on the merits of his coercion claim.

The plaintiff argues that the Offer is inequitably coercive, because: (i) it was purposefully timed to coincide with the lowest market price for the Preferred since 1983, (ii) the offer occurs against the background of an announced Board policy of not paying dividends, despite CMC's present ability to do so, and (iii) CMC has announced that it intends to seek the delisting of the Preferred shares.

In these circumstances the coercion issue is not easy to decide. To be sure, the directors have timed the Offer to coincide with the lowest Preferred stock price levels since 1983. They have also made a business judgment (one that at this stage must be presumed valid) not to pay dividends on, or to redeem, the Preferred. Given those circumstances, Preferred stockholders may perceive, not unreasonably, that unless they tender, they may not realize any return on or value for their investment in the foreseeable future. In that sense the offer does have coercive aspects. And the coercion may be attributed, at least to some extent, to acts of the directors (namely, their timing of the Offer and their no-dividend policy) rather than to market forces alone.

If these were the only relevant circumstances (and if proper disclosure was made of all material facts), the Court would have difficulty concluding, at least on this preliminary record, that the Offer is inequitably coercive. In what sense do corporate directors behave inequitably if they cause the corporation to offer to purchase its own publicly-held shares at a premium above market, even if the market price is at an historic low? So long as all material facts are candidly disclosed, the transaction would appear to be voluntary. The only arguable inequity is that if the offer is successful, it may result in a decrease in the number and market value of the outstanding shares and in the number of shareholders. That state of affairs, in turn, would create the possibility that shares not tendered will be delisted and/or deregistered. However, that possibility and its disclosure in the offering materials, without more, has been held to be not wrongfully coercive.

In this case, however, the defendants have done more than simply acknowledge the possibility of delisting and deregistration; they have told the Preferred stockholders that CMC "*intends to request* delisting of the Shares from the NYSE." It is that disclosure which tips the balance and impels the Court to find that the Offer, even if benignly motivated, operates in an inequitably coercive manner.

CMC's directors are fiduciaries for the Preferred stockholders, whose interests they have a duty to safeguard, consistent with the fiduciary duties owed by those directors to CMC's other shareholders and to CMC itself. Those directors have disclosed that they intend to seek to eliminate a valuable attribute of the Preferred stock, namely, its NYSE listing. That listing is the source of that security's market value, and its elimination will adversely affect the interests of nontendering Preferred shareholders. On what basis are the defendants, as fiduciaries, entitled to do that? Defendants do not claim that they are obliged to seek delisting in order to protect a paramount interest of the corporation or an overriding interest of the common stock-holders. What they seem to argue is that the criticized disclosure is not coercive because it is not material, because if the criteria for listing are no longer met, the stock will be delisted automatically, irrespective of and without regard to any action of the directors.

That argument has two infirmities. First, it is inconsistent with the Offer to Purchase, which discloses that if the listing criteria are no longer met, the NYSE "would consider" delisting the shares. That disclosure does not say that delisting will be automatic. Second, if the defendants are correct in their argument that delisting will occur automatically as a matter of law, then they need not disclose that CMC "intends to request delisting." Such a disclosure is unnecessary and, therefore, misleading. The only apparent purpose of such a disclosure would be to induce share-holders to tender by converting a possibility of delisting into a likelihood or certainty. On that basis it must be concluded that the Offer is inequitably coercive.

QUESTIONS

1. Why did the issuer and the board of directors engage in the self-tender? Why was this motivation relevant?
2. What were the problems with the disclosure?
3. What was the problem with the fairness opinion?
4. Assume that the disclosures were properly made in accordance with the principles set forth by the court. How was economic coercion a basis to rule for the plaintiff?

The following case considers whether a merger is a redemption under the corporate charter. Consider the similarity in principle and form of analysis seen in *Rothschild International Corp. v. Liggett Group Inc.*

Rauch v. RCA Corp.
861 F.2d 29 (2d Cir. 1988)

MAHONEY, Circuit Judge:

Plaintiff Lillian Rauch appeals from a judgment of the United States District Court, dismissing her class action complaint challenging the propriety of a merger effected by defendants for failure to state a claim upon which relief can be granted. The district court held that Rauch's action was barred by Delaware's doctrine of independent legal significance. We affirm.

This case arises from the acquisition of RCA Corporation ("RCA") by General Electric Company ("GE"). RCA, GE and GE Sub, Inc. ("GE Sub"), a wholly owned Delaware subsidiary of GE, entered into an agreement of merger. Pursuant to the terms of the agreement, all common and preferred shares of RCA stock (with one exception) were converted to cash, GE Sub was then merged into RCA, and the common stock of GE Sub was converted into common stock of RCA. Specifically, the merger agreement provided that each share of RCA common stock would be converted into $66.50, each share of $3.65 cumulative preference stock would be converted into $42.50, and each share of $3.50 cumulative first preferred stock (the stock held by plaintiff and in issue here, hereinafter the "Preferred Stock") would be converted into $40.00. A series of $4.00 cumulative convertible first preferred stock was called for redemption according to its terms prior to the merger.

Plaintiff claimed that the merger constituted a "liquidation or dissolution or winding up of RCA and a redemption of the [Preferred Stock]," as a result of which holders of the Preferred Stock were entitled to $100 per share in accordance with the redemption provisions of RCA's certificate of incorporation, that defendants were in violation of the rights of the holders of Preferred Stock as thus stated; and that defendants thereby wrongfully converted substantial sums of money to their own use.

RCA's Restated Certificate of Incorporation, paragraph Fourth, Part I, provides in relevant part:

(c) The First Preferred Stock at any time outstanding *may be redeemed by the Corporation,* in whole or in part, *at its election,* expressed by resolution of the Board of Directors, at any time or times upon not less than sixty (60) days' previous notice to the holders of record of the First Preferred Stock to be redeemed, given as hereinafter provided, at the price of one hundred dollars ($100) per share and all dividends accrued or in arrears. . . .

It is clear that under the Delaware General Corporation Law, a conversion of shares to cash that is carried out in order to accomplish a merger is legally distinct from a redemption of shares by a corporation. Section 251 of the Delaware General Corporation Law allows two corporations to merge into a single corporation by adoption of an agreement that complies with that section. The RCA-GE merger agreement complied fully with the merger provision in question, and plaintiff does not argue to the contrary.

Redemption, on the other hand, is governed by sections 151(b) and 160(a) of the Delaware General Corporation Law. Section 151(b) provides that a corporation may subject its preferred stock to redemption "by the corporation at its option or at the option of the holders of such stock or upon the happening of a specified event." In this instance, the Preferred Stock was subject to redemption by RCA *at its election.* Nothing in RCA's certificate of incorporation indicated that the holders of Preferred Stock could initiate a redemption, nor was there provision for any specified event, such as the GE Sub-RCA merger, to trigger a redemption.

Plaintiff's contention that the transaction was essentially a redemption rather than a merger must therefore fail. RCA chose to convert its stock to cash to accomplish the desired merger, and in the process chose not to redeem the Preferred Stock. It had every right to do so in accordance with Delaware law. As the district court aptly noted, to accept plaintiff's argument "would render nugatory the conversion provisions within Section 251 of the Delaware Code."

Delaware courts have long held that such a result is unacceptable. Indeed, it is well settled under Delaware law that "action taken under one section of [the Delaware General Corporation Law] is legally independent, and its validity is not dependent upon, nor to be tested by the requirements of other unrelated sections under which the same final result might be attained by different means." *Rothschild Int'l Corp. v. Liggett Group,* 474 A.2d 133, 136 (Del.1984). The rationale of the doctrine is that the various provisions of the Delaware General Corporation Law are of equal dignity, and a corporation may resort to one section thereof without having to answer for the consequences that would have arisen from invocation of a different section.

Rothschild Int'l Corp. v. Liggett Group is particularly instructive. In that case, certain preferred shareholders of Liggett were entitled to a $100 per share liquidation preference under Liggett's certificate of incorporation. Liggett, however, undertook a combined tender offer and reverse cash-out merger (similar to the instant transaction) whereby Liggett became a wholly owned subsidiary of Grand Metropolitan Ltd., and the preferred shareholders in question received $70 per share. A preferred shareholder then brought a class action in which it claimed breach of contract and breach of fiduciary duty, asserting that the transaction was the equivalent of a liquidation of Liggett which entitled preferred shareholders to the $100 per share liquidation preference. The Delaware Supreme Court concluded, however, that "there was no 'liquidation' of Liggett within the well-defined meaning of that term" because "the reverse cash-out merger of Liggett did not accomplish a 'liquidation' of Liggett's assets." Accordingly, the Court held that the doctrine of independent legal significance barred plaintiff's claim.

The instant action presents a most analogous situation. Plaintiff claims that the GE Sub-RCA merger was, in effect, a redemption. However, there was no redemption within the well-defined meaning of that term under Delaware law, just as there had been no liquidation in *Liggett*. Thus, because the merger here was permitted by law, defendants legitimately chose to structure their transaction in the most effective way to achieve the desired corporate reorganization, and were subject only to a similar duty to deal fairly.

QUESTIONS

1. What is the common lesson in *Rauch* and *Rothchild*?
2. If a merger is not a redemption, what is a "redemption"?
3. What sort of a contract term might have protected the preferred shareholders' economic interest in the case of a merger?

4. MODIFICATION

The contractual rights or expectations of preferred stockholders may be subject to modification by charter amendment or defeasance by corporate transactions authorized by other provisions of corporation law. The rights and expectations of preferred stockholders are not etched in stone. Understanding this, preferred stockholders, like creditors, will seek maximum contractual protections against the possibility of adverse changes.

The following case involves a modification of the charter to eliminate the advantageous economic position held by the preferred stockholder. Consider the factual similarity and dissimilarity to *Goldman v. Postal Telegraph*, and consider the term or mechanism that could have protected the preferred stockholder.

Bove v. Community Hotel Corp.

249 A.2d 89 (R.I. 1969)

JOSLIN, Justice.

This civil action was brought in the superior court to enjoin a proposed merger of The Community Hotel Corporation into Newport Hotel Corp. Both corporations were organized under the general corporation law of [Rhode Island]. [The trial court] sitting without a jury decided the case on the facts appearing in the exhibits and as assented to by the parties in the pretrial order. The case is here on the plaintiffs' appeal from a judgment denying injunctive relief and dismissing the action.

Community Hotel was incorporated for the stated purpose of erecting, maintaining, operating, managing and leasing hotels. Its authorized capital stock consists of 6,000 shares of $100 par value six percent prior preference cumulative preferred stock, and 6,000 shares of no par common stock of which 2,106 shares are issued and outstanding. The plaintiffs as well as the individual defendants are holders and owners of preferred stock. At the time this suit was commenced, dividends on the 4,335 then-issued and outstanding preferred shares had accrued, but had not been declared, for approximately 24 years, and totaled about $645,000 or $148.75 per share.

Newport was organized at the instance and request of the board of directors of Community Hotel solely for the purpose of effectuating the merger which is the subject matter of this action. Its authorized capital stock consists of 80,000 shares of common stock, par value $1.00, of which only one share has been issued, and that to Community Hotel for a consideration of $10.

The essentials of the merger plan call for Community Hotel to merge into Newport, which will then become the surviving corporation. Although previously without assets, Newport will, if the contemplated merger is effectuated, acquire the sole ownership of all the property and assets now owned by Community Hotel. The plan also calls for the outstanding shares of Community Hotel's capital stock to be converted into shares of the capital stock of Newport upon the following basis: Each outstanding share of the constituent corporation's preferred stock, together with all accrued dividends thereon, will be changed and converted into five shares of the $1.00 par value common stock of the surviving corporation; and each share of the constituent corporation's no par common stock will be changed and converted into one share of the common stock, $1.00 par value, of the surviving corporation.

Consistent with the requirements of G.L. 1956, §7-5-3, the merger will become effective only if the plan receives the affirmative votes of the stockholders of each of the corporations representing at least two-thirds of the shares of each class of its capital stock.

The plaintiffs argue that the primary, and indeed, the only purpose of the proposed merger is to eliminate the priorities of the preferred stock with less than the unanimous consent of its holders.

It is true, of course, that to accomplish the proposed recapitalization by amending Community Hotel's articles of association under relevant provisions of the general corporation law would require the unanimous vote of the preferred shareholders, whereas under the merger statute, only a two-third vote of those stockholders will be needed. Concededly, unanimity of the preferred stockholders is unobtainable in this case, and plaintiffs argue, therefore, that to permit the less restrictive provisions of

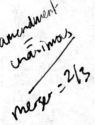

347

the merger statute to be used to accomplish indirectly what otherwise would be incapable of being accomplished directly by the more stringent amendment procedures of the general corporation law is tantamount to sanctioning a circumvention or perversion of that law.

The question, however, is not whether recapitalization by the merger route is a subterfuge, but whether a merger which is designed for the sole purpose of cancelling the rights of preferred stockholders with the consent of less than all has been authorized by the legislature. The controlling statute is §7-5-2. Its language is clear, all-embracing and unqualified. It authorizes any two or more business corporations which were or might have been organized under the general corporation law to merge into a single corporation; and it provides that the merger agreement shall prescribe "* * * the terms and conditions of consolidation or merger, the mode of carrying the same into effect * * * *as well as the manner of converting the shares of each of the constituent corporations into shares or other securities of the corporation resulting from or surviving such consolidation or merger*, with such other details and provisions as are deemed necessary." Nothing in that language even suggests that the legislature intended to make *underlying purpose* a standard for determining permissibility.

That a possible effect of corporate action under the merger statute is not possible, or is even forbidden, under another section of the general corporation law is of no import, it being settled that the several sections of that law may have independent legal significance, and that the validity of corporate action taken pursuant to one section is not necessarily dependent upon its being valid under another.

We hold, therefore, that nothing within the purview of our statute forbids a merger between a parent and a subsidiary corporation even under circumstances where the merger device has been resorted to solely for the purpose of obviating the necessity for the unanimous vote which would otherwise be required in order to cancel the priorities of preferred shareholders.

A more basic problem, narrowed so as to bring it within the factual context of this case, is whether the right of a holder of cumulative preferred stock to dividend arrearages and other preferences may be cancelled by a statutory merger. That precise problem has not heretofore been before this court, but elsewhere there is a considerable body of law on the subject. For illustrative purposes it is sufficient that we refer principally to cases involving Delaware corporations.

[In] *Federal United Corp. v. Havender*, 11 A.2d 331 (Del. 1940), the dissenting stockholders had argued that the proposed corporate action, even though styled a "merger," was in effect a recapitalization and was entitled to no different treatment. Notwithstanding that argument, the court did not refer to the preferred stockholder's right as "vested" or as "a property right in the nature of a debt." Instead, it talked about the extent of the corporate power under the merger statute; and it held that the statute in existence when Federal United Corp. was organized had in effect been written into its charter, and that its preferred shareholders had thereby been advised and informed that their rights to accrued dividends might be extinguished by corporate action taken pursuant thereto.

Delaware discarded "vested rights" as the test for determining the power of a corporation to eliminate a shareholder's right to preferred stock dividend accumulation, and to have adopted in its stead a standard calling for judicial inquiry into whether the proposed interference with a preferred stockholder's contract has been authorized by the legislature. The *Havender* approach is the one to which we subscribed as being the sounder, and it has support in the authorities.

The plaintiffs do not suggest that our merger statute will not permit in any circumstances a merger for the sole reason that it affects accrued, but undeclared, preferred stock dividends. Rather they argue that what should control is the date of the enactment of the enabling legislation, and they point out that in *Havender*, Federal United Corp. was organized and its stock was issued subsequent to the adoption of the statute authorizing mergers, whereas in this case the corporate creation and the stock issue preceded adoption of such a statute. That distinguishing feature brings into question what limitations, if any, exist to a state's authority under the reserved power to permit by subsequent legislation corporate acts which affect the preferential rights of a stockholder. More specifically, it raises the problem of whether subsequent legislation is repugnant to the federal and state constitutional prohibitions against the passage of laws impairing the obligations of contracts, because it permits elimination of accumulated preferred dividends by a lesser vote than was required under the law in existence at the time of the incorporation and when the stock was issued.

The mere mention of the constitutional prohibitions against such laws calls to mind *Trustees of Dartmouth College v. Woodward*, 17 U.S. 518 (1819), where the decision was that a private corporation charter granted by the state is a contract protected under the constitution against repeal, amendment or alteration by subsequent legislation. Of equal significance in the field of corporation law is Mr. Justice Story's concurring opinion wherein he suggested that application of the impairment clause upon acts of incorporation might be avoided if a state legislature, coincident with granting a corporate charter, reserved as a part of that contract the right of amendment or repeal. With such a reservation, he said, any subsequent amendment or repeal would be pursuant, rather than repugnant, to the terms of the contract and would not therefore impair its obligation.

Our own legislature was quick to heed Story's advice, and in the early part of the 19th century, when corporations were customarily created by special act, the power to alter, amend, or revoke was written directly into each charter. Later, when the practice changed and corporations, instead of being created by special enactment, were incorporated under the general corporation law, the power to amend and repeal was reserved in an act of general application, and since at least as far back as 1844 the corporation law [Section 7-1-13] has read in substance as it does today viz., "* * * The charter or articles of association of every corporation hereafter created may be amended or repealed at the will of the general assembly."

The terms of the preferred stockholder's contractual relationship are not restricted to the specifics inscribed on the stock certificate, but include also the stipulations contained in the charter or articles of association as well as the pertinent provisions of the general corporation law. One of those provisions is the reserved power; and so long as it is a part of the preferred shareholder's contract, any subsequent legislation enacted pursuant to it, even though it may amend the contract's original terms, will not impair its obligation in the constitutional sense. It is as if the stock certificate were inscribed with the legend "All of the terms and conditions hereof may be changed by the legislature acting pursuant to the power it has reserved in G.L.1956, s 7-1-13."

We conclude that the merger legislation, notwithstanding its effect on the rights of its stockholders, did not necessarily constitute an improper exercise of the right of amendment reserved merely because it was subsequent.

QUESTIONS

1. What was the business problem posed by the existence of the preferred stock?
2. What was the purpose of the merger?
3. In terms of the economic and business rationale of the transaction, what does it suggest when the board thought that it could get at least 67 percent of the vote of the preferred shareholders whose interests were purportedly undermined by the merger?
4. What are policy reasons for upholding the validity of the merger?

The following case considers the potential limitation on an attempt to modify the preference right or position of preferred stockholders. The questions concern whether the charter deals with the situation as a point of contract and, if not, whether such an attempt is or is not inequitable.

Gradient OC Master, Ltd. v. NBC Universal, Inc.
930 A.2d 104 (Del. Ch. 2007)

PARSONS, Vice Chancellor.

This dispute involves challenges by holders of two classes of senior preferred stock of ION Media Networks, Inc. ("ION" or the "Company") to an exchange offer being made to those stockholders as one of several transactions provided for under a Master Transaction Agreement ("MTA") to restructure the Company's ownership and capital structure. Defendants are ION, its directors, NBC Universal, Inc. ("NBCU") and Citadel Investment Group LLC and an affiliate, CIG Media, LLC, (collectively, "CIG"). ION, NBCU and CIG are parties to the MTA. Plaintiffs assert that the exchange offer violates Delaware's prohibition against coercive or misleading offers to stockholders and also improperly extracts value from minority shareholders for the benefit of a majority or controlling shareholder, namely, NBCU, CIG or both of them. The matter is presently before the Court on plaintiffs' motions for a preliminary injunction.

I conclude that plaintiffs have not shown a reasonable likelihood of success on the merits as to their claims for wrongful coercion based on, among other things, the elevation feature of the exchange offer, under which if less than 90% of the senior preferred shares participate in the exchange, preferred stock of NBCU and CIG junior to plaintiffs' stock will be elevated to subordinated debt with priority over plaintiffs' preferred shares.

Plaintiffs are a group of investors holding Cumulative Junior Exchangeable Preferred Stock, currently accruing dividends at 14 ¼% ("14 ¼% Preferred Stock" or "Preferred Stock") of ION.

ION is a network television broadcasting company that owns the largest television station group in the United States, operating approximately 60 television stations. In 1999, ION and NBCU's predecessor entered into an agreement whereby NBCU invested approximately $415 million in ION in exchange for 41,500 shares of 8% Series B convertible exchangeable preferred stock, warrants to purchase up to a total of over 32 million shares of Class A common stock, and registration rights under the Securities Act.

ION and NBCU entered into additional agreements to restructure NBCU's investment in the Company. NBCU acquired contractual provisions related to its preferred shares that required ION to obtain NBCU's consent before engaging in, among other things, certain financial transactions. NBCU also received an 18–month transferable call option that, if exercised, would trigger a sale of the rest of the Company and give NBCU a controlling block of Class A and B common stock and the right to designate a nominee to purchase those shares.

At some point, ION and NBCU determined that certain rules promulgated by the Federal Communications Commission ("FCC") would prohibit NBCU from exercising the call right, leading NBCU to seek a third party to which it could transfer the call right before it expired. NBCU and CIG engaged in discussions and negotiations with each other with a view toward proposing a comprehensive recapitalization transaction to ION, including a transfer of NBCU's call option to CIG. From NBCU's perspective, in addition to facilitating a transfer of the option, "a fundamental component of the transaction that ultimately was proposed with Citadel was to reduce the fixed claims or functional leverage on [ION's] balance sheet."

ION had a complex capital structure and was considered overly leveraged. As of March 31, 2007, the Company had [the following capital structure].

Author's Case Annotation: Capital Structure

Senior secured debt	$1,100m
14 1/4% Preferred Stock	$640m
9 3/4 % Series A Convertible Preferred Stock (the "9 3/4 % Preferred Stock")	$175m
11% Series B Convertible Exchangeable Preferred Stock (the "Series B Preferred Stock")	$706m

Note: Preferred stock amounts are aggregates of liquidation preference and accumulated dividends.

Under a previous refinancing of senior debt obligations, the Company was permitted to incur up to approximately $650 million of subordinated debt that could be available for use in a future recapitalization. In April, 2006, the Company retained UBS Securities LLC to advise it on financial strategies. In June, 2006, ION's Board created a special committee of independent directors to explore the Company's strategic options (the "Special Committee"). The following month, the Special Committee retained Lazard Frères & Co. LLC as its financial advisor and Pillsbury Winthrop as its legal advisor. In the fall of 2006, ION's management publicly announced that the Company's highly leveraged position was hampering their ability to progress and the Board needed to modify its capital structure to improve liquidity and reduce obligations.

The Senior Preferred Stock had mandatory redemption dates in November and December 2006. ION did not redeem the shares. As a result, the two classes of Senior Preferred Stock, including the 14 ¼% Preferred Stock, each elected two directors to the Board.

The Master Transaction Agreement

ION, NBCU, and CIG executed the MTA on or about May 3, 2007. The MTA summarizes the Company's agreement to an approach that would take ION private under the control of CIG or NBCU. The MTA contemplates several transactions. In general terms, NBCU assigns the call option to CIG and CIG exercises the option. A new call option is then issued from CIG to an affiliate of NBCU [to acquire CIG]. CIG lends $100 million to ION by purchasing newly issued notes. CIG tenders for the remaining shares of Class A common stock of ION at approximately $1.46 per share (the "Tender Offer"). The MTA also requires ION to commence "as soon as reasonably practicable" an Exchange Offer and Consent Solicitation ("Exchange Offer" or "Exchange") for exchanges of Senior Preferred Stock. An NBCU affiliate could exercise the call option to acquire majority control of CIG. Ultimately, the MTA preserves NBCU's ability to gain control of the Company through a new stockholder agreement between NBCU and CIG.

On May 4, CIG commenced the Tender Offer for the ION Class A common stock in accordance with the MTA. As of June 4, approximately 40.6 million shares, or 62.1% of the Class A common stock, had been tendered to CIG. By June 15, that number had increased to over 88%.

Author's Case Annotation: MTA and Exchange Offer Transactions

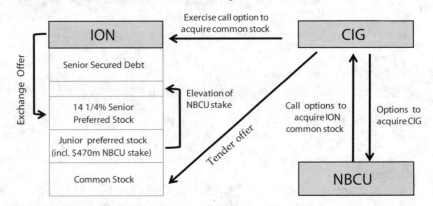

ION commenced the Exchange Offer and Consent Solicitation on June 8. In the Exchange Offer, ION is offering to exchange outstanding 14 ¼% Preferred Stock [for] newly-issued 11% Series A Mandatorily Convertible Senior Subordinated Notes due 2013 and, depending upon participation levels in the Exchange Offer, either newly issued 12% Series A–1 Mandatorily Convertible Preferred Stock or 12% Series B Mandatorily Convertible Preferred Stock. ION has conditioned the Exchange Offer upon the percentage of shares tendered. If more than 50% of the shares are tendered, each tendered share of 14 ¼% Preferred Stock will receive $7,000 principal amount of Series A Notes (subordinated debt) and $1,000 initial liquidation preference of the Series A–1 Convertible Preferred Stock, which would rank senior to any unexchanged Preferred Stock. If holders of 50% or less of the Senior Preferred Stock tender in the Exchange Offer, tendering holders will receive $7,500 principal amount of Series A Notes and $500 initial liquidation preference of Series B Convertible Preferred Stock, which would rank junior to any unexchanged Preferred Stock

("Minority Exchange Consideration"). The 14 ¼% holders who choose to participate in the Exchange also consent to amending the existing certificate of designations to eliminate restrictive covenants, such as ION's obligation to repurchase the 14 ¼% Preferred Stock upon a change of control, and all voting rights provided for in the original certificates.

[The transaction included a Contingent Exchange ("Contingent Exchange" or "Elevation") that would permit CIG and NBCU to exchange up to $470 million of their preferred stock for subordinated debt if less than 90 percent of Senior Preferred Stock participated in the exchange offer. The plaintiffs complain that this Elevation provision was an essential element of the coercive effect of the transaction.]

Likelihood of Success on the Merits

Plaintiffs argue that the Exchange Offer is coercive with respect to its terms. In particular, Plaintiffs argue that under Section 5.04(a) of the MTA, entitled "Contingent Exchange," if, at the close of the Exchange Offer, tendered shares are between 50 and 90 percent (*i.e.,* sufficient to be a majority of the shares but not for the Company to employ a short-form merger), the non-participating holders are required to give up the protective covenants present in the current Certificate of Designations ("CD") for the 14 ¼% Preferred Shares. Among the protections that would be eliminated are the requirement that ION redeem the shares upon a change of control and the voting rights to appoint Board directors triggered by, among other things, a failure to redeem the shares. Additionally, the Contingent Exchange triggers the Elevation of up to $470.6 million of NBCU and CIG holdings from junior preferred shares under the 14 ¼% Preferred Stock to subordinated debt above that stock in the Company's capital structure. The number of junior preferred shares so elevated is inversely proportional to the number of shares of 14 ¼% Preferred Stock tendered into the Exchange.

If tendered shares fall below 50% (*e.g.,* zero to minimal participation), closer to $470.6 million of NBCU and CIG holdings of junior preferred shares will be elevated to debt. Plaintiffs emphasized that the fairness opinion relied upon by the ION Board as to the MTA transactions in general, given by investment bank Houlihan Lokey Howard & Zukin ("Houlihan"), reports the enterprise value of ION to be between $1.61 to $2.01 billion. Before the Exchange Offer, the Company had $1.13 billion in senior secured debt. Thus, although the 14 ¼% Preferred Shares are currently within the enterprise value of the Company, the Elevation provided for in the Contingent Exchange would subordinate the 14 ¼% to such a degree that the exchange of NBCU and CIG shares would completely or substantially push the 14¼% shareholders "out of the money." Plaintiffs characterize their situation as one of a "prisoner's dilemma" of being forced to make a choice without knowing what choice is made by others where each others' choice directly affects the potential outcomes. Specifically, they contend:

> Here, Plaintiffs must choose between: (a) refusing to exchange and facing the devaluation caused by the NBC/CIG Elevation, or (b) participating in the Exchange and accepting its punitive redistribution of debt and stripped down preferreds, in the hope that over 90 percent of holders will also participate. Of course, this dilemma is increased exponentially by the possibility that 90 percent will not be reached, but more than 50 percent will. In such a case, non-participants face the doubly punitive

result of: (a) devaluation through the NBC/CIG Elevation, and (b) the stripping of all material rights from the Certificate governing their holdings.

In that regard, Plaintiffs argue that they are prevented from choosing the status quo and must select between two punishments in terms of loss of value in their securities.

Applicable legal principles to coercion claims

As a general rule, preferred shareholders' rights are primarily contractual in nature.[32] Therefore, those rights are governed broadly by the express provisions of the company's certificate of incorporation[33] and specifically through the document designating the rights, preferences, etc. of their special stock.[34] Where, however, a right asserted is not to a preference but rather a right shared equally with the common, the existence of such right and the scope of the correlative duty may be measured by equitable as well as legal standards.[35]

In that regard, this Court has recognized that preferred shareholders share the same right as common shareholders to be free from wrongful coercion in a stockholder vote.[36] In so holding, Delaware courts have determined that "the standard applicable to the [preferred shareholder's] claim of inequitable coercion is whether the defendants have taken actions that operate inequitably to induce the preferred shareholders to tender their shares for reasons unrelated to the economic merit of the offer."[37] In other words, the ordinary definition of "coercion," something akin to intentionally persuading someone to prefer one option over another is not the same as saying that the persuasion would so impair the person's ability to choose as to be legally actionable. The challenged conduct must be "wrongfully" or "actionably" coercive for a legal remedy to ensue.[39] Thus, an action is not coercive unless a shareholder is wrongfully induced to make a decision for reasons unrelated to merit. On the other hand, an action is "actionably coercive" if, in the context of a tender offer, it "threatens to extinguish or dilute a percentage ownership interest in relation to the interests of other stockholders."

In *In re General Motors Class H Shareholders Litigation*, 734 A.2d 611 (Del.Ch. 1999), Vice Chancellor Strine clarified the distinction between coercion and "wrongful" or "actionable" coercion. In that case, GM issued GMH stock, which represented

---

32. *Rothschild Int'l Corp. v. Liggett Group, Inc.*, 474 A.2d 133, 136 (Del. 1984).

33. *Id. See also Jedwab v. MGM Grand Hotels, Inc.*, 509 A.2d 584, 593 (Del.Ch. 1986) ("Generally, the provisions of the certificate of incorporation govern the rights of preferred shareholders, the certificate . . . being interpreted in accordance with the law of contracts, with only those rights which are embodied in the certificate granted to preferred shareholders.").

34. *Jedwab*, 509 A.2d at 593.

35. *Id.* at 593–94.

36. *Eisenberg v. Chicago Milwaukee Corp.*, 537 A.2d 1051, 1061 (Del.Ch. 1987).

37. *Id.*

39. As Chancellor Allen stated:

For purposes of legal analysis, the term "coercion" itself—covering a multitude of situations—is not very meaningful. For the word to have much meaning for purposes of legal analysis, it is necessary in each case that a normative judgment be attached to the concept ("inappropriately coercive" or "wrongfully coercive," etc.). But, it is then readily seen that what is legally relevant is not the conclusory term "coercion" itself but rather the norm that leads to the adverb modifying it.

[Quoting *Katz v. Oak Indus.*, 508 A.2d 873, 880 (Del.Ch. 1986)].

rights in equity and assets in the parent company, GM, but which tied dividends to the financial performance of Hughes Electronics, a GM subsidiary that consisted of Hughes Defense, Hughes Telecom, and Delco. In an effort to recapitalize, the GM board proposed and approved a spin off of Hughes Defense to Raytheon and, in doing so, transferred Delco into the parent GM. The transactions also included a $1 billion infusion of money by Raytheon into the remaining portion of Hughes Electronics [which post-transactions was diminished to only Hughes Telecom]. Upon approval of the transaction by shareholders, GMH shareholders would have economic interests [1] as direct stockholders in Raytheon, as the purchaser of Hughes Defense, [2] through a dividend interest in Hughes Telecom, as the holder of recapitalized GMH shares, and [3] through a tenuous economic interest in Delco, now a division of GM.

The recapitalization efforts needed majority approval from both the GM and the GMH shareholders. As part of the consent process, GM informed GMH holders that a vote to approve the transactions would have the effect of waiving any possible application of certain covenant amendments contemplating GMH remedies upon a recapitalization. The solicitation also disclosed that the transactions, as contemplated, were entitled to tax-free treatment but that, because of recently enacted federal tax legislation that would become effective after the closing of the transactions, a future recapitalization involving Hughes Defense, if consummated, would be subject to taxable gains.

The GMH shareholders alleged that they were actionably coerced by having to choose between giving up recapitalization covenants intentionally tied to an affirmative vote or blocking the transactions and squandering potentially enhanced values realized from those transactions. The GMH shareholders also alleged that the board actionably coerced them by disclosing that the Hughes recapitalization would receive favorable tax treatment, but that future transactions might not.

The court found no actionable coercion in the board's actions regarding the waiver of the recapitalization provision. First, the court noted that neither allegation stated a claim that the coercive actions were "unrelated to the merits of the Hughes Transactions." As the court quipped, "you can't have your cake and eat it too"; by alleging coercion, plaintiffs attempted to take the benefit of a company's recapitalization and, notwithstanding that benefit, insure their position by seeking, in addition, recapitalization covenant protection. However, "the opportunity to make this choice by vote carried with it a concomitant obligation on the part of the voters to accept responsibility for the outcome."[45]

Second, and perhaps more importantly, the court looked at the board's rationale for relating the covenant stripping to the transactions and determined that the "GMH stockholders had a free choice between maintaining their current status and taking advantage of the new status offered by the Hughes Transactions." In particular,

> The GM Board had no duty to structure the Hughes Transactions so as to trigger the Recap Provision, and thereby avoid asking the GMH stockholders to choose between the potential for a premium under the Recap Provision and the deal consideration.

---

45. Other cases have reached the same conclusion. *See, e.g., Katz v. Oak Indus.,* 508 A.2d 873, 881 (Del.Ch.1986) (upholding transaction that conditioned exchange offer to bondholders on receipt of exit consents).

> They were permitted to structure the deal as they did so long as they did not strong-arm the GMH stockholders into voting for it.
>
> Such strong-arming is absent here. In the event that the Hughes Transactions did not receive GMH stockholder approval, the GMH stockholders would have been in precisely the same position they were in before the vote.

A board's decision to construct a recapitalization without triggering contractual covenants is not, the court concluded, actionably coercive.

In making that determination, the court in *GM* focused on the *manner* in which the board used covenant stripping. In particular, the court held that a board's choices to formulate a business decision are given deference by the courts unless it impacts unfairly, or "strong-arms" the vote so as to force a shareholder, for reasons outside of the economic merit, to tender into the offer. The court concluded that the board's use of the covenant stripping did not amount to actionable coercion because the stockholders, if they chose not to tender, would still be in the same position they had been before the vote.

"Being in the same position," however, should not be read literally. A vote, by its nature, forces shareholders to suspend artificially the present circumstances in a snapshot economic situation. It is not, however, the same as suggesting that the economic world itself does not move forward. Keeping the shareholders in the "same" position, then, does not require an "identical" position, economic or otherwise. Instead, a shareholder is actionably coerced when he is forced into "a choice between a new position and a compromised position" for reasons other than those related to the economic merits of the decision.

Exit consents

I am not persuaded that the exit consents in the Exchange Offer are actionably coercive. Under the Exchange Offer, a holder of 14 1/4% Preferred Stock who decides to tender her shares also must provide an exit consent to the stripping of various covenants from the remaining 14 1/4% shares. If more than 50 percent of the 14 1/4% shares tender, the covenant stripping will take effect.

This allegation, as *In re General Motors* explains, manifests Plaintiffs' attempt to put one foot in a new bargain, and still keep the other foot in the previous game by hedging, through the related covenant protection, the original bargain. A majority of 14 1/4% shareholders can either take the offered exchange of debt, thus removing themselves from their originally bargained for position, or choose to hold on to their 14 1/4% Preferred Stock. Plaintiffs contend that the non-tendering shareholders are then placed in an economically disadvantaged position. Although linking the vote on the covenants to the decision to tender threatens to reduce economic protections to non-tendering holders, the shareholders, in the aggregate, are free to choose between accepting the new debt securities (by tendering one's shares), or staying in one's place (and refusing to tender). Should a majority of the 14 1/4% Preferred Stock choose to support the Company's decision to recapitalize in this manner, the elimination of the non-tendered shares' covenants is merely an effect of the reality that a majority of the 14 1/4% peers have disagreed with the non-tendering shareholders and concluded that accepting the Exchange Offer is in their best interest. The amendment of the CD for the 14 1/4% Preferred Stock by the holders of a majority of that class of stock is authorized by the CD.

ION's Board had no duty to structure these transactions in a way to trigger the contractual covenants. To suggest that the Board must fashion an imitative recapitalization or favor one group of shareholders over the overall benefit to the corporation here would contravene the fundamental principle that a board may freely make decisions that benefit ION as a whole. Thus, I provisionally conclude that ION's conditioning of a 14 ¼% Preferred Shareholder's acceptance of the Exchange on that shareholder's also providing a consent to delete certain covenants of the 14 ¼% Preferred Stock is not actionably coercive.

The Elevation provisions

I do not find the Elevation feature of the Exchange Offer actionably coercive.

The Contingent Exchange aspect of the Exchange Offer is an integral part of the economics of the exchange and is, broadly, one aspect of a larger Exchange Offer designed to delever ION over time. The Exchange Offer results initially in only a modest reduction of fixed claims and fixed charges against the Company. Over time and with maximum participation, however, mandatory conversion of the newly issued convertible securities would create a major benefit in terms of "deleveraging" the Company. This benefit also would inure to Plaintiffs and their class.

Defendants saw the Exchange Offer as part of a larger transaction designed to confer economic benefit on ION. Frederick Smith, a member of the ION Board and the Special Committee, expressed the view that, under the CIG/NBCU Proposal, "the Corporation's preferred stockholders would be offered a meaningful premium to incentivize participation in the proposed exchange offer" and provide an economic choice to participate. As a representative of NBCU explained, NBCU and Citadel intentionally "set up a structure where everyone in the capital structure would be incented to take a discount."

The Special Committee appreciated the economics of the Exchange Offer and sought to improve the premiums offered to the Senior Preferred Stock. "From the standpoint of the Special Committee, our goal was to negotiate the best transaction for the Company and to increase the likely participation in the exchange by improving the recoveries for the 14 ¼% Preferred Stock." The Special Committee analyzed anticipated levels of participation by the Preferred Stockholders as well as the integrated economic incentives structurally built into the proposed Exchange Offer. Investment banks provided to the Special Committee trading data, enterprise values, and valuations to assist them in trying to provide economic benefit to the 14 ¼% Preferred Shareholders. Before the Special Committee vote on May 1 and even on the day the MTA was approved, members of the Special Committee sought to negotiate better recovery values for the Preferred Shareholders. These few excerpts from the extensive negotiating history of the Exchange Offer and MTA are illustrative only. The evidence presented convinces me that all the parties recognized the economic aspects of the decision presented to the 14 ¼% Preferred Stock to either tender into the Exchange Offer or decline to do so and have the Elevation occur.

No party disputes that the Elevation, in part, was included as a deliberate attempt by NBCU and Citadel to induce tendering. Even Lazard recognized that "there is a significant likelihood that the Citadel/NBC exchange offer, if launched, would not be highly subscribed." The issue, however, is whether linking the Elevation to the shareholder's decision to tender "strong-arms" the vote in such a manner that Plaintiffs are precluded from making a decision on the economic merits of the offer. To use

Chancellor Allen's language in *AC Acquisitions,* does the Contingent Exchange aspect of the Exchange Offer prevent the Preferred Shareholders from making a decision in the sense that "no rational shareholder" could afford not to tender into the Company's offer? The Exchange Offer, while perhaps complicated, still preserves the ability of the Senior Preferred Shareholders to decide based on the economic merits of each alternative whether to tender their shares into the Exchange or retain them and endure the Elevation and possible covenant stripping.

Plaintiffs seemed to argue that, to use a "carrot and stick" analogy for inducements, a company may employ carrots or sticks in creating a security or other asset that it then offers to some or all of its stockholders, but may not as part of the same offer intentionally attach sticks or adverse aspects to a stockholder's decision to stay put, and not accept the offer. In oversimplified terms, Plaintiffs argue that a stockholder should have the right, as one of its options, to maintain the status quo. Based on my review of numerous coercion cases previously decided, I do not believe our law or the cases support such a sweeping proposition. Further, in the circumstances of this case, Defendants' actions in "linking" the Elevation provisions to the Exchange Offer and, specifically, to the situation in which significant numbers of Senior Preferred Shareholders reject the Exchange, appears to be logical and consistent with the legitimate objectives of ION to improve its capital structure and begin reducing its debt in terms of both fixed claims and fixed charges. Moreover, the result is that the 14 ¼% Preferred Stock must choose between at least two possible alternatives, both of which have pros and cons depending on each investors' views as to the future prospects for the Company. These are the types of risks and analyses sophisticated investors, like the holders of ION's Senior Preferred Stock appear to be, must deal with everyday.

Defendants aver that the Contingent Exchange portion of the overall transactions was inserted as a mechanical adjustment of their risk, based on the number of tendering 14 ¼% shares. Plaintiffs, then, challenge the Exchange Offer by presenting evidence they contend shows that NBCU and CIG arranged the transaction this way to strong arm the Preferred Shareholders into taking the Exchange or to reap a windfall, if they did not. I provisionally find that the evidence does not support so sinister an inference.

NBCU and Citadel included the Elevation in the Exchange Offer to control their risk in a transaction aimed at delevering ION. The risk of their bargain is directly tied to the degree of acceptance (or non-acceptance) of the Exchange Offer by the Senior Preferred Shares. Conversely, Defendants contend that the Elevation provision does not preclude Plaintiffs from making a decision rooted in the economic merits of the available alternatives and their view of ION's prospects after implementation of the MTA.

I also believe that Plaintiffs misinterpret the case law as it relates to the ability to "be in the same position." Merely choosing to remain in a position does not mean maintaining an equal and guaranteed economic position, particularly in the context of preferred shares. The ION Board, analogous to GM, informed the Preferred Stockholders that, should the Shareholders collectively approve the Exchange Offer, nontendering Shareholders should not expect to be in the same position because the Company will have begun to implement the process set forth in the Offer. Those simply are the realities the Senior Preferred Stockholders and the Company must contend with upon the successful closing of the Exchange Offer.

QUESTIONS

1. Explain the substance of the transaction here. What are the preferred shareholders getting and what are they giving up? Are they better off with the exchange?
2. Why did the court find that the elevation provision was valid?
3. What are legitimate coercion and actionable coercion? State the legal standard that determines this question.

5. BOARD REPRESENTATION —not required/necessary

Whether preferred stockholders have a right specific to board representation is a contractual matter. The right of preferred stockholders can be varied: For example, they may have no right at all; they may vote with common stockholders on same terms; they may have super voting rights; they may have the right to designate a specific number of board seats; or they may have a right that triggers only upon certain events, such as nonpayment of dividends. The issue is subject to contractual negotiations.

The following case addresses the issue of whether preferred stockholders can control a board installed by them due to dividend arrearage and whether there are limitations on the duration of the board's service.

Baron v. Allied Artists Pictures Corp.
337 A.2d 653 (Del. Ch. 1975)

BROWN, Vice Chancellor.

Plaintiff brought suit as a stockholder of the defendant Allied Artists Pictures Corporation, a Delaware corporation, (hereafter "Allied") to have the 1973 election of directors declared illegal and invalid and to have a master appointed to conduct a new election.

Plaintiff charges that the present board of directors of Allied has fraudulently perpetuated itself in office by refusing to pay the accumulated dividend arrearages on preferred stock issued by the corporation which, in turn, permits the preferred stockholders to elect a majority of the board of directors at each annual election so long as the dividend arrearage specified by Allied's certificate of incorporation exists. Defendants contend that the recent financial history and condition of the corporation has justified the nonpayment of the preferred dividend arrearages, at least to the present, and they further ask that the plaintiff's claims be dismissed because they constitute a purchased grievance.

Allied was originally started in the mid-1930's as Sterling Pictures Corporation and later changed its name to Monogram Films under which it gained recognition for many B-pictures and western films. In the early 1950's it changed its name to the present one. Around 1953, with the advent of television, it fell upon hard times. Being in need of capital, Allied's certificate of incorporation was amended in 1954 to permit the issuance of 150,000 shares of preferred stock at a par value of $10.00, with the dividends payable quarterly on a cumulative basis. The amended language of the certificate provides that the preferred shareholders are entitled to receive cash dividends "as and when declared by the Board of Directors, out of funds legally available for the purpose. . . ." The amended certificate further provides that

> in case at any time six or more quarterly dividends (whether or not consecutive) on the Preferred Stock shall be in default, in whole or in part, then until all dividends in default on the Preferred Stock shall have been paid or deposited in trust, and the dividend thereupon for the current quarterly period shall have been declared and funds for the payment thereof set aside, the holders of the Preferred Stock, voting as a class, shall have the right, at any annual or other meeting for the election of directors, by plurality vote to elect a majority of the Directors of the Corporation.

In addition, the amended certificate requires that a sinking fund be created as to the preferred stock into which an amount equal to ten percent of the excess of consolidated net earnings over the preferred stock dividend requirements for each fiscal year shall be set aside. From this sinking fund the preferred stock is to be redeemed, by lot, at the rate of $10.50 per share.

Thereafter, as to the preferred stock issued under the 1954 offering, regular quarterly dividends were paid through March 30, 1963. Subsequently, Allied suffered losses which ultimately impaired the capital represented by the preferred stock as a consequence of which the payment of dividends became prohibited by 8 Del.C. §170. Allied has paid no dividends as to the preferred shares since 1963. By September 1964 the corporation was in default on six quarterly dividends and thus the holders of the preferred stock became entitled to elect a majority of the board of directors. They have done so ever since.

As of December 11, 1973 election of directors, Kalvex, Inc. owned 52 per cent of the outstanding preferred stock while owning only 625 shares of Allied's 1,500,000 shares of common stock. Since the filing of the first action herein Kalvex has taken steps to acquire a substantial number of common shares or securities convertible into the same. Thus unquestionably Kalvex, through its control of the preferred shares, is in control of Allied, although its holdings are said to represent only 7 ½ percent of the corporation's equity.

Returning briefly to the fortunes of the corporation, in 1964 Allied was assessed a tax deficiency of some $1,400,000 by the Internal Revenue Service. At the end of fiscal 1963, it had a cumulative deficit of over $5,000,000, a negative net worth of over $1,800,000 and in that year had lost more than $2,700,000. As a consequence Allied entered into an agreement with the Internal Revenue Service to pay off the tax deficiency over a period of years subject to the condition that until the deficiency was satisfied Allied would pay no dividends without the consent of Internal Revenue.

Thereafter Allied's fortunes vacillated with varying degrees of success and failure which, defendants say, is both a hazard and a way of life in the motion picture and theatrical industry. Prior to fiscal 1973 there were only two years, 1969 and 1970, when its preferred capital was not impaired.

Starting with 1972, Allied's financial condition began to improve substantially. It acquired the rights to, produced and distributed the film "Cabaret," which won eight Academy Awards and became the largest grossing film in Allied's history up to that time. It thereafter took a large gamble and committed itself for $7,000,000 for the production and distribution of the film "Papillon." "Papillon" proved to be even a greater financial success than "Cabaret." For fiscal 1973 Allied had net income in excess of $1,400,000 plus a $2,000,000 tax carry-over remaining from its 1971 losses.

Presumably its financial situation did not worsen prior to the December 11, 1974 election of directors although unquestionably it has gone forward with financial commitments as to forthcoming film releases.

Throughout all of the foregoing, however, the Internal Revenue agreement, with its dividend restriction, persisted. Prior to the 1973 election the balance owed was some $249,000 and as of the 1974 election, one final payment was due, which presumably has now been made. Prior to the 1973 election, Allied was in default on forty-three quarterly preferred dividends totaling more than $270,000. By the time of the 1974 election, the arrearages exceeded $280,000.

The contractual right to elect a majority of the board continues until the dividends can be made current in keeping with proper corporate management, but that it must terminate once a fund becomes clearly available to satisfy the arrearages and the preference board refuses to do so. Plaintiff seeks to limit this requirement to a mere mathematical availability of funds. Allied's charter, and thus its contract with its preferred shareholders, does not limit the right merely until such time as a sufficient surplus exists, but rather it entitles the preferred shareholders to their dividends only "as and when declared by the Board of Directors, out of funds legally available for the purpose." This obviously reposes a discretion in Allied's board to declare preferred dividends, whether it be a board elected by the common or by the preferred shareholders.

The general rule applicable to the right to receive corporate dividends was succinctly stated by Justice Holmes in *Wabash Ry. Co. v. Barclay*, 280 U.S. 197, 203 (1930):

> When a man buys stock instead of bonds he takes a greater risk in the business. No one suggests that he has a right to dividends if there are no met earnings. But the investment presupposes that the business is to go on, and therefore even if there are net earnings, the holder of stock, preferred as well as common, is entitled to have a dividend declared only out of such part of them as can be applied to dividends *consistently with a wise administration of a going concern.*

Although one purpose of allowing the preferred to elect a majority of the board may be to bring about a payment of the dividend delinquencies as soon as possible, that should not be the sole justification for the existence of a board of directors so elected. During the time that such a preference board is in control of the policies and business decisions of the corporation, it serves the corporation itself and the common shareholders as well as those by whom it was put in office. Corporate directors stand in a fiduciary relationship to their corporation and its shareholders and their primary duty is to deal fairly and justly with both.

The determination as to when and in what amounts a corporation may prudently distribute its assets by way of dividends rests in the honest discretion of the directors in the performance of this fiduciary duty. Before a court will interfere with the judgment of a board of directors in refusing to declare dividends, fraud or gross abuse of discretion must be shown. And this is true even if a fund does exist from which dividends could legally be paid.

Plaintiff here appears to be asking that an exception be carved from these well established principles where the nonpayment of dividends and arrearages results in continued control by the very board which determines not to pay them. He asks for a ruling that a board of directors elected by preferred shareholders whose dividends are in arrears has an absolute duty to pay off all preferred dividends due and to return control to the common shareholders as soon as funds become legally available for that purpose, regardless of anything else. Thus, he would have the court limit the discretion given the board by the certificate of incorporation, and make the decision of pay arrearages mandatory upon the emergence of a lawful financial source even though the corporate charter does not require it. He has offered no precedent for such a proposition, and I decline to create one.

The established test for this is whether the board engaged in fraud or grossly abused its discretion. The mere existence of a legal source from which payment could be made, standing alone, does not prove either.

When the yearly hit-and-miss financial history of Allied from 1964 through 1974 is considered along with the Internal Revenue obligation during the same time span, I cannot conclude, as a matter of law, that Allied's board has been guilty of perpetuating itself in office by wrongfully refusing to apply corporate funds to the liquidation of the preferred dividend arrearages and the accelerated payment of the Internal Revenue debt. Thus I find no basis on the record before me to set aside the 1974 annual election and to order a new one through a master appointed by the court.

It is clear, however, that Allied's present board does have a fiduciary duty to see that the preferred dividends are brought up to date as soon as possible in keeping with prudent business management. This is particularly true now that the Internal Revenue debt has been satisfied in full and business is prospering. It cannot be permitted indefinitely to plough back all profits in future commitments so as to avoid full satisfaction of the rights of the preferred to their dividends and the otherwise normal right of the common stockholders to elect corporate management. While previous limitations on net income and capital surplus may offer a justification for the past, continued limitations in a time of greatly increased cash flow could well create new issues in the area of business discretion for the future.

Plaintiff's motion for summary judgment is denied. Defendants' motion for summary judgment is granted.

QUESTIONS

1. Absent contractual terms to the contrary, what principle trumps the plaintiff's argument that the preferred shareholders control the board even though they only have 7.5 percent of the company's equity?
2. Under the court's opinion, at what point is there a duty to pay dividends and thus eliminate the preferred stockholders' board seats?
3. How might the charter have been written to require the removal of the directors elected by the preferred stockholders even though the board continued to pay the dividend arrearage?
4. Does the case stand for the proposition that preferred stockholders cannot have an indefinite right to appoint board representation? Or is the court's suggestion of a limitation something that is tailored to the situation in the case?

6. VOTING

Preferred stocks may or may not come with voting rights, either on equal or different terms with common stockholders. Voting rights are a matter of contract. If dividends are not paid and there is continuing arrearage, many preferred stocks allow preferred stockholders a specially designated board seat or seats. Preferred stocks can also have voting rights with respect to corporate charter amendments if they affect the rights of preferred stockholders.

EXAMPLE

Goldman Sachs' Series G Preferred Stock

Section 8. Voting Rights.

    (a) General. The holders of Series G shall not have any voting rights except as set forth below or as otherwise from time to time required by law.

    (b) Class Voting Rights as to Particular Matters. So long as any shares of Series G are outstanding, in addition to any other vote or consent of stockholders required by law or by the Certificate of Incorporation, the vote or consent of the holders of at least 66 2/3% of the shares of Series G and any Voting Preferred Stock at the time outstanding and entitled to vote thereon, voting together as a single class, given in person or by proxy, either in writing without a meeting or by vote at any meeting called for the purpose, shall be necessary for effecting or validating:

    (i) Authorization of Senior Stock. Any amendment or alteration of the Certificate of Incorporation to authorize or create, or increase the authorized amount of, any shares of any class or series of capital stock of the Corporation ranking senior to the Series G with respect to either or both the payment of dividends and/or the distribution of assets on any liquidation, dissolution or winding up of the Corporation;

    (ii) Amendment of Series G. Any amendment, alteration or repeal of any provision of the Certificate of Incorporation so as to materially and adversely affect the special rights, preferences, privileges or voting powers of the Series G, taken as a whole; or

    (iii) Share Exchanges, Reclassifications, Mergers and Consolidations. Any consummation of a binding share exchange or reclassification involving the Series G, or of a merger or consolidation of the Corporation with another corporation or other entity, unless in each case (x) the shares of Series G remain outstanding or, in the case of any such merger or consolidation with respect to which the Corporation is not the surviving or resulting entity, are converted into or exchanged for preference securities of the surviving or resulting entity or its ultimate parent, and (y) such shares remaining outstanding or such preference securities, as the case may be, have such rights, preferences, privileges and voting powers, and limitations and restrictions thereof, taken as a whole, as are not materially less favorable to the holders thereof than the rights, preferences, privileges and voting powers, and limitations andrestrictions thereof, of the Series G immediately prior to such consummation, taken as a whole; *provided, however*, that for all purposes of this Section 8(b), any increase in the amount of the authorized Preferred Stock, or the creation and issuance, or an increase in the authorized or issued amount, of any other series of Preferred Stock ranking equally with and/or junior to the Series G with respect to the payment of dividends (whether such dividends are cumulative or non-cumulative) and/or the distribution of assets upon liquidation, dissolution or winding up of the Corporation will not be deemed to adversely affect the rights, preferences, privileges or voting powers of the Series G.

    If any amendment, alteration, repeal, share exchange, reclassification, merger or consolidation specified in this Section 8(b) would adversely affect the Series G and one or more but not all other series of Preferred Stock, then only the Series G and such series of Preferred Stock as are adversely affected by and entitled to vote on the matter shall vote on the matter together as a single class (in lieu of all other series of Preferred Stock).

If any amendment, alteration, repeal, share exchange, reclassification, merger or consolidation specified in this Section 8(b) would adversely affect the Series G but would not similarly adversely affect all other series of Voting Parity Stock, then only the Series G and each other series of Voting Parity Stock as is similarly adversely affected by and entitled to vote on the matter, if any, shall vote on the matter together as a single class (in lieu of all other series of Preferred Stock).

(c) Series G Voting Rights as to Particular Matters. In addition to any other vote or consent of stockholders required by law or by the Certificate of Incorporation, so long as at least 10,000 shares of Series G are outstanding, the vote or consent of the holders of at least 50.1% of the shares of Series G at the time outstanding, voting in person or by proxy, either in writing without a meeting or by vote at any meeting called for the purpose, shall be necessary for effecting or validating:

(i) Authorization or Issuance of Senior Stock. Any amendment or alteration of the Certificate of Incorporation to authorize or create, or increase the authorized amount of, any shares of any class or series of capital stock of the Corporation, or the issuance of any shares of any class or series of capital stock of the Corporation, in each case, ranking senior to the Series G with respect to either or both the payment of dividends and/or the distribution of assets on any liquidation, dissolution or winding up of the Corporation;

(ii) Amendment of Series G. Any amendment, alteration or repeal of any provision of the Certificate of Incorporation so as to affect or change the rights, preferences, privileges or voting powers of the Series G so as not to be substantially similar to those in effect immediately prior to such amendment, alteration or repeal; or

(iii) Share Exchanges, Reclassifications, Mergers and Consolidations. Any consummation of a binding share exchange or reclassification involving the Series G, or of a merger or consolidation of the Corporation with another corporation or other entity, unless in each case (x) the shares of Series G remain outstanding or, in the case of any such merger or consolidation with respect to which the Corporation is not the surviving or resulting entity, are converted into or exchanged for preference securities of the surviving or resulting entity or its ultimate parent, and (y) such shares remaining outstanding or such preference securities, as the case may be, have such rights, preferences, privileges and voting powers, and limitations and restrictions thereof as are substantially similar to the rights, preferences, privileges and voting powers, and limitations and restrictions of the Series G immediately prior to such consummation; *provided, however*, that for all purposes of this Section 8(c), the creation and issuance, or an increase in the authorized or issued amount, of any other series of Preferred Stock ranking equally with and/or junior to the Series G with respect to the payment of dividends (whether such dividends are cumulative or non-cumulative) and/or the distribution of assets upon liquidation, dissolution or winding up of the Corporation will not be deemed to adversely affect the rights, preferences, privileges or voting powers of the Series G.

The following cases in this section concern whether the charter provided preferred stockholders a vote with respect to the proposed transaction. In addition to the specific holdings in *Warner Communications v. Chris-Craft Industries, Inc.* and *Elliott Associates v. Avatex Corp.*, the two cases show the interplay between judicial interpretation of transaction documents and subsequent changes in market practice in response to advance predictable, uniform interpretations of commercial contract terms.

Warner Communications v. Chris-Craft Industries, Inc.
583 A.2d 962 (Del. Ch. 1989)

ALLEN, Chancellor.

Pending is a motion for judgment on the pleadings. Plaintiffs seek a determination that the related holders of Warner Communications Inc.'s Series B Variable Rate Cumulative Convertible Preferred stock ("Series B Preferred") are not entitled to a class vote upon a proposed merger among Warner, its controlling shareholder Time Incorporated (now renamed Time Warner Inc.) and TW Sub Inc., a wholly owned subsidiary of Time Warner.

Plaintiffs in this declaratory judgment action are the parties proposing the merger—Warner, Time and TW Sub, all of which are Delaware corporations. BHC, Inc. is the holder of the Series B Preferred stock. Plaintiffs generally will be referred to as Warner; Time Warner, for purposes of clarity, will be referred to as Time and the holders of the Series B Preferred will be referred to as BHC.

The merger in question is the proposed "back end" of a transaction, the first stage of which was a public tender offer for 51% of Warner's common stock for cash that closed on July 24, 1989. In that merger, the Series B Preferred stock would be cancelled and BHC as the holder of it would receive a new senior security, Time Series BB Convertible Preferred. Plaintiffs have stipulated that that substitution would adversely affect defendants.

I conclude that BHC has no right under the Warner certificate of incorporation to a class vote on the proposed merger.

The Series B Preferred was issued pursuant to an Exchange Agreement [in] 1983 among Warner, Chris-Craft and BHC. Under that Exchange Agreement, Warner obtained BHC preferred stock convertible into 42.5% of BHC's outstanding common stock. BHC obtained the entire issue, 15,200,000 shares, of Warner's Series B Preferred stock.

As provided in the certificate of designation creating the Series B Preferred, each share of that stock is entitled to a quarterly dividend equal to the greater of (a) $0.125 or (b) 200% of the regular quarterly dividend, if any, payable on a share of Warner common stock. Each share is convertible into common stock in accordance with a complex formula, and each carries the same voting rights as the common stock, except in the event that a dividend is in default. In that event, the Series B Preferred stock "voting as a class" elects three directors. Generally, however, [under Certificate of Designation, Section 3.1]:

> Except as otherwise by the Certificate of Incorporation or by law provided, the shares of Series B Stock and the shares of Common Stock . . . shall be voted together as one class.

[Sections 3.3(i) and 3.4(i)] provide the ground upon which the parties' ongoing battle is now fought.

Section 3.3(i) provides in pertinent part as follows:

> So long as any shares of Series B Stock shall be outstanding and unless the consent or approval of a greater number of shares shall then be required by law, (i) the affirmative vote or written consent of the holders of at least two-thirds of the total number of the then outstanding shares of Series B Stock and of any other series of Preferred Stock having the right to vote as a class on such matter, *voting as a class, shall be necessary to alter or change any rights, preferences or limitations of the Preferred Stock so as to affect the holders of all of such shares adversely.* . . .

In pertinent part, Section 3.4(i) provides as follows:

> So long as any shares of Series B Stock shall be outstanding and unless the consent or approval of a greater number of shares shall then be required by law, without first obtaining the consent or approval of the holders of at least two-thirds of the number of shares of the Series B Stock at the time outstanding, given in person or by proxy either in writing or at a meeting at which the *holders of such shares shall be entitled to vote separately as a class, the Corporation shall not (i) amend, alter or repeal any of the provisions of the Certificate of Incorporation or By-laws of the Corporation so as to affect adversely any of the preferences, rights, powers or privileges of the Series B Stock or the holders thereof.* . . .

Time and Warner have executed a merger agreement, which was amended and restated. That agreement contemplates a two-step transaction by which Time would acquire all of the outstanding stock of Warner. The first step was completed on July 24, 1989 when Time accepted for purchase 100 million shares of Warner common stock, representing approximately 50% of Warner's common stock, at $70 per share in cash.

Under the amended merger agreement, the tender offer is to be followed by a merger in which TW Sub will be merged into Warner which will survive as a wholly owned subsidiary of Time. The Warner common stock, other than that held by Time, will be converted into securities, cash or other property. The Warner Series B Preferred is to be converted into Time Series BB Preferred stock. The rights and preferences of the Time Series BB Preferred are set forth in a proposed form of certificate of designation.

Author's Case Annotation: Merger and Conversion

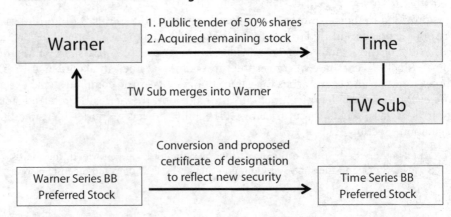

The parties have stipulated for the purposes of this motion that the holders of Warner Series B Preferred will be adversely affected by the back-end merger.

BHC contends that it is entitled to a class vote on the proposed merger under two distinct provisions of Warner's certificate of incorporation. First, defendants argue that Section 3.3(i) of the certificate of designation gives BHC the right to a class vote. It contends that Section 3.3(i) protects against *any corporate action* that alters or changes "any rights or preferences" of the preferred stock so as to adversely affect the preferred shareholders. The proposed merger, it says, will alter the rights of the Series B Preferred (and on this motion presumptively in an adverse way) by substituting a new security—Time BB Preferred–for the Series B Preferred. Thus, it concludes, Section 3.3(i) requires that BHC be afforded the opportunity to vote on that merger separately.

Second, defendants argue that Section 3.4(i) of the certificate of designation entitles BHC to a vote on the back-end merger because the Warner certificate of incorporation will admittedly be amended by the merger and necessarily so under Section 243 of the Delaware corporation law. That amendment they say—eliminating the provisions authorizing the Series B Preferred—will adversely affect BHC and will trigger the right to a class vote under Section 3.4(i).

In evaluating these contending positions, it should first be noted that the existence and extent of special stock rights are determined by reference to the issuer's certificate of incorporation; such rights are essentially contractual in nature. *Rothschild International Corp. v. Liggett Group, Inc.*, 474 A.2d 133, 136 (Del. 1984). In determining them, a court should apply the same techniques of contract interpretation generally applied to contractual disputes. Thus, the certificate of designation should be construed in its entirety, and an attempt should be made to reconcile all of the certificate's provisions "in order to determine the meaning intended to be given to any portion of it." While the effort is to arrive at the intended meaning of the words employed, it is generally said that rights or preferences over common stock should be clearly expressed and not presumed.

[Analysis of Section 3.4(i)]

Section 3.4(i) provides a right to a series vote (*i.e.*, the Series B Preferred voting alone) in the event of a charter amendment that amends, alters or repeals any provision of the certificate of incorporation so as to adversely affect the Series B Preferred or its holders.

Warner will be the surviving corporation in the proposed merger. Its charter will be amended in the merger. It is assumed that the substitution of the merger consideration for the Series B Preferred stock is damaging to defendants. Nevertheless, Section 3.4(i) does not grant a right to a series vote in these circumstances because the adverse effect upon defendants is not caused by an amendment, alteration or repeal of any provision of Warner's certificate of incorporation. Rather, it is the conversion of the Warner Series B Preferred into Time Series BB Preferred that creates the adverse effect. But the conversion of the Warner Series B Preferred into the Time BB Preferred does not depend to any extent upon the amendment of the Warner certificate of incorporation under Section 242 of the General Corporation Law [which authorizes amendments of the certificate of incorporation]. That conversion will occur pursuant to Section 251 of the statute which authorizes mergers and defines the steps necessary to effectuate a merger.

Given that the merger itself is duly authorized, the conversion of the Series B Preferred stock could occur without any prior or contemporaneous amendment to the certificate. Since the merger does contemplate the conversion of the Series B Preferred into the securities of another company, it is to be expected that the certificate would be amended to reflect the removal of these securities from the firm's capital structure. Section 243 requires such a step as a housekeeping matter, but that section does not require that amendment to be contemporaneous with the retirement of the stock and it surely does not make conversion of the stock dependent upon the amendment it contemplates.* Rather, the amendment contemplated is necessitated by the merger; such an amendment, like the conversion, flows from the merger and is not a necessary condition of it. Stated in terms of the language of Section 3.4(i), given the existence of the merger, the amendments of the certificate of incorporation can in no event themselves be said to "affect" BHC "adversely," even if one assumes, as I do on this motion, that the substitution of the Time BB Preferred stock for Warner Series B Preferred stock does have an adverse affect.

[Analysis of Section 3.3(i)]

I turn then to Section 3.3(i). It requires a class vote (the Series B stock voting with any other series of preferred stock that has a vote on the question presented) in order to: "alter or change any rights . . . of the Preferred stock so as to affect the holders of all such shares adversely." The central concern of Section 3.3(i) is action that would "alter or change" rights of the "Preferred Stock."

In addressing Section 3.3(i), it is analytically helpful to break down the universe of acts that might arguably "alter or change . . . rights of Preferred Stock" into two classes: amendments to a certificate of incorporation and other forms of acts, such as mergers, that might affect the holders of preferred stock.

At first blush, Section 3.3(i) appears to be principally directed to charter amendments, because under Delaware law, special stock rights and preferences are set forth in a corporate charter. Such rights must be stated in, or derivable in a manner clearly set forth in, the certificate of incorporation (8 *Del.C.* §151(a)) or set forth in a certificate of designation which, when effective (8 *Del.C.* §103), amends and becomes a part of the certificate of incorporation (8 *Del.C.* §151(g)).

Insofar as Section 3.3(i) does address charter amendments, the amendments that will follow the Warner-Time merger fail to trigger its provisions for the same reason that those amendments fail to trigger a series vote under Section 3.4(i): the amendments contemplated in the merger will not themselves adversely affect the preferred stock.

---

* Author's note: Section 243 concerns retirement of stock. As the court notes, it is a housekeeping provision. In its current form, it states: "If the certificate of incorporation prohibits the reissuance of such shares, or prohibits the reissuance of such shares as a part of a specific series only, a certificate stating that reissuance of the shares (as part of the class or series) is prohibited identifying the shares and reciting their retirement shall be executed, acknowledged and filed and shall become effective in accordance with §103 of this title. When such certificate becomes effective, it shall have the effect of amending the certificate of incorporation so as to reduce accordingly the number of authorized shares of the class or series to which such shares belong or, if such retired shares constitute all of the authorized shares of the class or series to which they belong, of eliminating from the certificate of incorporation all reference to such class or series of stock."

The pending motion may thus be seen to come down to the question whether the class vote contemplated by Section 3.3(i) can, in addition to being triggered by an amendment to the certificate of incorporation that "alters . . . rights . . . adversely," be triggered by other forms of transactions in which the interests of holders of the preferred—and arguably "the rights . . . of the Preferred Stock"—are adversely affected.

Will the Series B Preferred be altered or changed in the merger within the meaning of Section 3.3(i)? Concededly, the shares of that stock will be converted into a new security by operation of law in the merger. Did the parties that drafted Section 3.3(i) intend conversion of stock in a merger to be contemplated within the phrase "alter or change?" I cannot conclude, viewing the certificate of designation in its entirety, that there is even a reasonable likelihood that they did.

The draftsmen of this language—the negotiators to the extent it has actually been negotiated—must be deemed to have understood, and no doubt did understand, that under Delaware law the securities whose characteristics were being defined in the certificate of designation could be converted by merger into "shares or other securities of the corporation surviving or resulting from a merger or consolidation" or into "cash, property, rights or securities of any other corporation." 8 *Del.C.* §251(b). Those shares, for example, could be converted into a right to receive cash or other property in a merger and such a conversion would not entitle a holder of stock with a stated value upon liquidation to that value (*Rothschild, supra*); nor would such a cash out merger constitute a redemption of callable securities.

It is thus elementary that the possibility of a merger represents a possibility of the most profound importance to a holder of stock with special rights or preferences. *See generally* Richard Buxbaum, *Preferred Stock—Law and Draftsmanship*, 42 Calif. L. Rev. 243, 298-309 (1954). When one turns to the certificate of designation to ascertain whether the language of Section 3.3(i) was intended to incorporate changes effected through mergers, one is struck by two factors that together compel the conclusion that it was not. The first is the close similarity between the operative language of Section 3.3(i) and Section 242(b)(2) of the General Corporation Law. The second involves a comparison of the language of Section 3.3(i) with other sections of the certificate of designation in which the drafters of that document specifically and expressly treated the possibility of a future merger.

The language of Section 3.3(i) is closely similar to the language of Section 242(b)(2) of the corporation law statute governing amendments to a certificate of incorporation. That section creates a right to a class vote under certain circumstances. Section 242(b)(2) provides in pertinent part:

> The holders of the outstanding shares of a class shall be entitled to vote as a class upon a proposed amendment . . . if the amendment would . . . *alter or change the powers, preferences or special rights of the shares of such class so as to affect them adversely.*

The parallel language of Section 3.3(i), as quoted above, provides in pertinent part:

> the affirmative vote of at least two-thirds of the . . . outstanding shares of Series B Stock . . . shall be necessary *to alter or change any rights, preferences or limitations of the Preferred Stock so as to affect* the holders of all such stock *adversely.*

The parallel is plain. It is therefore significant, when called upon to determine whether Section 3.3(i) creates a right to a class vote on a merger, to note that the language of Section 242(b)(2) does not itself create a right to a class vote on a merger. The voting requirements for a merger are generally set forth in Section 251(c) of our corporation law statute. Under Section 251, unless a charter provision creates a right to a class vote, a merger is authorized by the company's shareholders when "a majority of the outstanding stock of the corporation entitled to vote thereon shall be voted for the adoption of the agreement [of merger]." 8 *Del.C.* §251(c). Unlike Section 242(b), Section 251 contains no class vote requirement.

Our bedrock doctrine of independent legal significance (*e.g., Rothschild, supra*) compels the conclusion that satisfaction of the requirements of Section 251 is all that is required legally to effectuate a merger. It follows, therefore, from rudimentary principles of corporation law, that the language of 242(b)(2), which so closely parallels the language of 3.3(i), does not entitle the holders of a class of preferred stock to a class vote in a merger, even if (as we assume here) the interests of the class will be adversely affected by the merger.

Since I take this legal conclusion to be the general understanding among corporation law specialists (*e.g.*, Buxbaum, 42 Calif. L. Rev. at 294, n.266), I can only conclude that it is extraordinarily unlikely that the drafters of Section 3.3(i), who obviously were familiar with and probably expert in our corporation law, would have chosen language so closely similar to that of Section 242(b)(2) had they intended a merger to trigger the class vote mechanism of that section.

[Analysis of Section 3.4(iii)]

This conclusion is further supported by a review of other provisions of the certificate of designation. These provisions demonstrate that the drafters were mindful of the effects a merger might have and shaped some special protections in light of the risks posed. The drafters did expressly address the possibility of a merger in connection with the very question of a class vote by the preferred and adopted the limited protection afforded by Section 3.4(iii):

> So long as any shares of Series B Stock shall be outstanding . . . without first obtaining the consent or approval of the holders of at least two-thirds of the number of shares of the Series B Stock at the time outstanding . . . the Corporation shall not . . . (iii) *be a party to any transaction involving a merger,* consolidation or sale of all or substantially all of the Corporation's assets *in which* the *shares of Series B Stock* either remain outstanding or *are converted into the right to receive equity securities of the* surviving, resulting or *acquiring corporation* (meaning the corporation whose securities are delivered in exchange for assets or securities of the Corporation) *unless such corporation shall have,* after such merger, consolidation or sale, *no equity securities either authorized or outstanding* (except such stock of the Corporation as may have been authorized or outstanding immediately preceding such merger or consolidation or such stock of the surviving, resulting or acquiring corporation as may be issued in exchange therefor) *ranking prior,* as to dividends or in liquidation, *to the Series B Stock or to the stock of the surviving, resulting or acquiring corporation issued in exchange therefor.*

Certificate of Designation, Section 3.4.

Thus, in Section 3.4(iii), the certificate of designation does specifically address the voting requirements of a corporate transaction that would "convert" the Series B

Preferred to the securities of another corporation and creates a right to a class vote in a subset of all such cases: when the "surviving, resulting or acquiring corporation" has no equity securities ranking prior to the Series B Preferred except any securities that ranked prior to it before the transaction. The parties agree that Section 3.4(iii) does not require a class vote here.

The only fair inference from Section 3.4(iii) is that it was intended to provide the only certificate-created requirement for a series or class vote upon a merger.

I recognize that this interpretation of Section 3.3(i) threatens to render it redundant in light of Section 3.4(i). An interpretation that gives an effect to each term of an agreement, instrument or statute is to be preferred to an interpretation that accounts for some terms as redundant. However, no plausible interpretation of Sections 3.3(i) and 3.4(i) and (iii) has been suggested that would accomplish that task here. Not only do I find implausible any interpretation of Section 3.3(i) that would extend its words to a merger in which the Series B Preferred was converted into another security, but such an interpretation—while giving Section 3.3(i) some room to operate—would render Section 3.4(iii) redundant. Thus, the problem of redundancy seems inescapable.

For these reasons, I conclude that the Warner certificate of incorporation does not afford to BHC, as the holder of the Series B Preferred stock, a right to vote upon the proposed Warner-Time merger as a separate class. Plaintiffs may submit a form of implementing order on notice.

QUESTIONS

1. According to the court, what was the cause of the preferred stockholder's economic injury? Why is the conceptualization of the cause of injury relevant?
2. Which provision of the certificate of designation did the court hold ultimately governed this situation? What legal doctrine drove the result in this case?
3. In what way does the court's interpretation of §3.3(i) make the provision therein redundant with §3.4(i)?
4. Is there a functional difference between §3.3(i) and §3.4(i)?

Elliott Associates v. Avatex Corp.
715 A.2d 843 (Del. 1998)

VEASEY, Chief Justice:

Defendant Avatex Corporation ("Avatex") is a Delaware corporation that has outstanding both common and preferred stock. Plaintiffs are all preferred stockholders of Avatex.

Avatex created and incorporated Xetava Corporation ("Xetava") as its wholly-owned subsidiary and announced its intention to merge with and into Xetava. Xetava is to be the surviving corporation. Once the transaction is consummated, Xetava will immediately change its name to Avatex Corporation. The proposed merger would cause a conversion of the preferred stock of Avatex into common stock of Xetava. The merger will effectively eliminate Avatex' certificate of incorporation, which includes the certificate of designations creating the Avatex preferred stock and setting forth its rights and preferences. The terms of the merger do not call for a class vote of these preferred stockholders. Herein lies the heart of the legal issue presented in this case.

Plaintiffs filed suit in the Court of Chancery to enjoin the proposed merger, arguing that the transaction required the consent of two-thirds of the holders of the First Series Preferred stock. Defendants responded with a motion for judgment on the pleadings, which the Court of Chancery granted, finding that the provisions governing the rights of the First Series Preferred stockholders do not require such consent.

The plaintiffs allege that, because of Avatex' anemic financial state, "all the value of Avatex is in the preferred stock." By forcing the conversion of the preferred shares into common stock of the surviving corporation, however, the merger would place current preferred stockholders of Avatex on an even footing with its common stockholders. In fact, the Avatex preferred stockholders will receive in exchange for their preferred stock approximately 73% of Xetava common stock, and the common stockholders will receive approximately 27% of the common stock.

The text of the terms governing the voting rights of the First Series Preferred Stock is set forth in the certificate of designations as follows:

> Except as expressly provided hereinafter in this Section (6) or as otherwise . . . required by law, the First Series Preferred Stock shall have no voting rights.
>
> . . .
>
> So long as any shares of First Series Preferred Stock remain outstanding, the *consent* of the holders of at least two-thirds of the shares of the *First Series Preferred Stock* outstanding at the time (voting separately as a class . . .) . . . *shall be necessary to permit, effect or validate* any one or more of the following: . . . (b) *The amendment, alteration or repeal, whether by merger, consolidation or otherwise,* of any of the provisions of the Restated Certificate of Incorporation or of [the certificate of designations] which would *materially and adversely affect any right, preference, privilege or voting power of the First Series Preferred Stock* or of the holders thereof. . .

Delaware law permits corporations to create and issue stock that carries no voting power. Professor Buxbaum, in his seminal article on preferred stock nearly 45 years ago, noted, among many other cogent observations, that: (a) statutes often permit alteration of preferred stock rights and preferences by merger;[11] (b) the merger may be with a "paper subsidiary created for that purpose with no independent business validity"; (c) "corporate articles [often] require consent of two-thirds (or a majority) of the preferred shareholders as a class for the consummation of any merger. . . ."; and (d) courts have struggled with "controls in the name . . . of 'fairness' and generally abandoned them [, which] is as it should be [since the] issue is one of corporate power."

This appeal reduces to a narrow legal question: whether the "amendment, alteration or repeal" of the certificate of incorporation is caused "by merger, consolidation or otherwise" thereby requiring a two-thirds class vote of the First Series Preferred stockholders, it being assumed for purposes of this appeal that their rights would be

---

11. Richard M. Buxbaum, *Preferred Stock—Law and Draftsmanship,* 42 Cal. L. Rev. 243, 303 (1954).

"materially and adversely" affected. The Court of Chancery answered this question in the negative. We disagree with its conclusion.

Relying primarily on *Warner Communications Inc. v. Chris-Craft Industries Inc.*, 583 A.2d 962 (Del.Ch. 1989), the Court of Chancery held that it was only the *conversion* of the stock as a result of the merger, and not the *amendment, alteration or repeal* of the certificate, that would adversely affect the preferred stockholders. It is important to keep in mind, however, that the terms of the preferred stock in *Warner* were significantly different from those present here, because in *Warner* the phrase "whether by merger, consolidation or otherwise" was not included. The issue here, therefore, is whether the presence of this additional phrase in the Avatex certificate is an outcome-determinative distinction from *Warner*.

The relevant statutory provisions are found in Sections 251(b) and 251(e) of the Delaware General Corporation Law ("DGCL"), which provide, in pertinent part:

§251. Merger or consolidation of domestic corporations.

* * *

(b) The board of directors of each corporation which desires to merge or consolidate shall adopt a resolution approving an agreement of merger or consolidation. The agreement shall state: (1) The terms and conditions of the merger or consolidation; (2) the mode of carrying the same into effect; (3) in the case of a merger, such amendments or changes in the certificate of incorporation of the surviving corporation as are desired to be effected by the merger, or, if no such amendments or changes are desired, a statement that the certificate of incorporation of the surviving corporation shall be its certificate of incorporation; (4) in the case of a consolidation, that the certificate of incorporation of the resulting corporation shall be as is set forth in an attachment to the agreement; (5) the manner of converting the shares of each of the constituent corporations into shares or other securities of the corporation surviving or resulting from the merger or consolidation and, if any shares of any of the constituent corporations are not to be converted solely into shares or other securities of the surviving or resulting corporation, the cash, property, rights or securities of any other corporation or entity which the holders of such shares are to receive in exchange . . . ; and (6) such other details or provisions as are deemed desirable. . . .

* * *

(e) In the case of a merger, the certificate of incorporation of the surviving corporation shall automatically be amended to the extent, if any, that changes in the certificate of incorporation are set forth in the agreement of merger.

In short, Section 251 of the DGCL describes three ways that a merger or consolidation can affect the certificate of a constituent corporation:

(1) *Section 251(b)(3) Amendments.* The merger agreement may call for amendments to the pre-existing certificate of the surviving corporation. 8 Del. C. 251(b)(3), (e).

(2) *Displacement and Substitution by Merger.* The merger can designate the certificate of one of the constituent corporations as the certificate of the surviving entity, and thereby render the certificate of every other constituent corporation a legal nullity. 8 Del. C. 251(b)(3).

(3) *Displacement and Substitution via Consolidation.* In the case of a consolidation, the certificate of the resulting corporation displaces and renders a legal nullity the certificate of every disappearing constituent corporation. 8 Del. C. 251(b)(4).

In speaking of the "amendment, alteration or repeal" of the Avatex certificate by "merger, consolidation or otherwise," the drafters must have been referring to some or all of the events permitted by Section 251. Therefore, Section 251 provides the relevant backdrop for the interpretation of the First Series Preferred voting rights.

Avatex argued below that *only* a Section 251(b)(3) Amendment to the surviving corporation's charter amounts to an "amendment, alteration or repeal" within the meaning of the provisions defining the voting rights of the preferred stockholders. These provisions would apply *only* in the circumstance (not present here) where Avatex survives the merger and its certificate is amended thereby. Since the proposed merger with Xetava does not contemplate any such amendments to the disappearing Avatex certificate, the argument goes, the transaction can go forward without a First Series class vote.

The difficulty with this reading is that it fails to account for the word *consolidation*, which appears in the phrase "by merger, consolidation or otherwise." A consolidation cannot entail a Section 251(b)(3) Amendment because in a consolidation there is no "surviving corporation" whose pre-existing certificate is subject to amendment. The resulting corporation in a consolidation is a completely new entity with a new certificate of incorporation.* All the certificates of the constituent corporations simply become legal nullities in a consolidation.

Although the transaction before us is not a consolidation, the drafters' use of the word *consolidation* is significant. They must have intended the First Series Preferred stockholders to have the right to vote on at least some mergers or other transactions whereby the Avatex certificate—and indeed, Avatex itself—would simply disappear. Consolidation, by definition, implicates the disappearance of all constituent corporations. Here, Avatex disappears, just as it would in a consolidation. Under the terms of the proposed merger, Xetava will be the surviving entity and, since Avatex will cease its independent existence, its certificate becomes a legal nullity, as defendants concede. In our view, this constitutes a repeal, if not an amendment or alteration. Thus, the proposed merger is potentially within the class of events that trigger First Series Preferred voting rights.

The first question is: What will happen as a result of the merger to the "rights, preferences, privileges or voting power" of the Avatex First Series Preferred stock as set forth in the existing Avatex certificate? They disappear when the preferred stockholders of Avatex become common stockholders of Xetava under its certificate that does not contain those protections. We assume that their elimination would affect the First Series Preferred stockholders adversely.

The second question is: What act or event will cause this adverse effect if the merger is consummated?

The First Series Preferred holders claim to have the right to a class vote only if (a) a transaction effects the "amendment, alteration or repeal" of the rights provided in the certificate, *and* (b) "any right, preference, privilege or voting power of the First Series Preferred" would thereby be materially and adversely affected. For example, plaintiffs make clear that the First Series Preferred would not have a class vote on mergers

---

* Author's note: In a consolidation, two entities combine to form a new entity: For example, A and B combine to form C, and thus post-transaction both predecessor companies no longer exist. In a merger, there is a surviving entity: A and B combine to form, and post-transaction either A or B is the surviving entity.

where they receive the same security in a new entity or are cashed out. The attributes of the First Series Preferred would be intact but for the merger or might be continued if the certificate of Xetava provided for separate classes of stock, guaranteeing to these holders those same attributes. In our view, the Court of Chancery misapplied *Warner's* holding that "the amendment contemplated [as a "housekeeping" measure post-merger] is necessitated by the merger [and the] amendment, like the conversion, flows from the merger and is not a necessary condition of it." This was the case in *Warner,* but is not here.

In our view, the merger does cause the adverse effect because the merger is the corporate act that renders the Avatex certificate that protects the preferred stockholders a "legal nullity." That elimination certainly fits within the ambit of one or more of the three terms in the certificate: *amendment* or *alteration* or *repeal.* The word *repeal* is especially fitting in this context because it contemplates a nullification, which is what defendants concede happens to the Avatex certificate.

Articulation of the rights of preferred stockholders is fundamentally the function of corporate drafters. Construction of the terms of preferred stock is the function of courts. This Court's function is essentially one of contract interpretation against the background of Delaware precedent. These precedential parameters are simply stated: Any rights, preferences and limitations of preferred stock that distinguish that stock from common stock must be expressly and clearly stated, as provided by statute. Therefore, these rights, preferences and limitations will not be presumed or implied. The other doctrine states that when there is a hopeless ambiguity attributable to the corporate drafter that could mislead a reasonable investor such ambiguity must be construed in favor of the reasonable expectation of the investor and against the drafter. This latter doctrine is not applicable here because there is no ambiguity.

In our view, the rights of the First Series Preferred are expressly and clearly stated in the Avatex certificate. The drafters of this instrument could not reasonably have intended any consequence other than granting to the First Series Preferred stock the right to consent by a two-thirds class vote to any merger that would result in the elimination of the protections in the Avatex certificate if the rights of the holders of that stock would thereby be adversely affected. The First Series Preferred stock rights granted by the corporate drafters here are the functional equivalent of a provision that would expressly require such consent if a merger were to eliminate any provision of the Avatex certificate resulting in materially adverse consequences to the holders of that security.

It is important to place what we decide today in proper perspective. The outcome here continues a coherent and rational approach to corporate finance. The contrary result, in our view, would create an anomaly and could risk the erosion of uniformity in the corporation law. The Court of Chancery was mindful of this concern in referring to our general observations that the courts should avoid creating enduring uncertainties as to the meaning of boilerplate provisions in financial instruments. To be sure, there are some boilerplate aspects to the preferred stock provisions in the Avatex certificate and those found in other cases. But one is struck by the disuniformity of some crucial provisions, such as the differences that exist when one compares the provisions in *Warner* with those presented here. That lack of uniformity is no doubt a function of (a) the adaptations by different drafters of some standard provisions; (b) negotiations by preferred stock investors seeking certain protections; (c) poor drafting; or (d) some combination of the above. The difference between the provisions in the Warner

375

certificate and the Avatex provisions are outcome-determinative because we find there is no reasonable interpretation of the Avatex certificate that would deny the First Series Preferred a class vote on an "amendment, alteration or repeal . . . by merger, consolidation or otherwise" of the protective provisions of the Avatex certificate.

The path for future drafters to follow in articulating class vote provisions is clear. When a certificate (like the Warner certificate or the Series A provisions here) grants only the right to vote on an amendment, alteration or repeal, the preferred have no class vote in a merger. When a certificate (like the First Series Preferred certificate here) adds the terms "whether by merger, consolidation or otherwise" and a merger results in an amendment, alteration or repeal that causes an adverse effect on the preferred, there would be a class vote. When a certificate grants the preferred a class vote in any merger or in any merger where the preferred stockholders receive a junior security, such provisions are broader than those involved in the First Series Preferred certificate. We agree with plaintiffs' argument that these results are uniform, predictable and consistent with existing law relating to the unique attributes of preferred stock.

The judgment of the Court of Chancery is reversed.

QUESTIONS

1. Under the plaintiff's theory, what was the purpose of the merger?
2. What is the significance of the term "consolidated" in the court's analysis?
3. What might have been the reason for the differences seen in *Warner* and *Elliott Associates* in the certificate provisions relating to class vote of preferred stockholders?
4. How does the court's opinion fit into the broader process in financial contracting where the importance and uniformity of boilerplate contract terms are given significant weight?

NOTES

1. The Delaware Supreme Court in *Waggoner v. Laster* (*supra* Chapter 4) noted that stock preferences must be "strictly construed." In footnote 46 of *Elliott*, the court disapproved of the term "strict construction." Instead, it approved an earlier formulation of the legal standard in *Rothschild Int'l Corp. v. Liggett Group* (*supra* this chapter), where the court wrote: "Preferential rights are contractual in nature and therefore are governed by the express provisions of a company's certificate of incorporation. Stock preferences must also be clearly expressed and will not be presumed."

Greenmont Capital Partners I, LP v. Mary's Gone Crackers, Inc.
2012 WL 4479999 (Del. Ch.)

PARSONS, Vice Chancellor.

This case presents a question about the interpretation of a Delaware corporation's certificate of incorporation. The corporation had authorized and issued common stock and two series of preferred stock, series A and series B. The plaintiff purchased series B preferred stock. Series B stockholders have special rights under the certificate of incorporation. The series B preferred have the right to a majority vote to validate any action that would "alter or change" the series B preferred stockholder's rights under the certificate. The certificate also grants series B preferred stockholders the right to a majority vote on any amendment to the certificate of incorporation. One action permitted by the certificate is an automatic conversion of the preferred stock into common stock upon a majority vote of the preferred shares. This certificate provision requires a majority vote of the series A and series B preferred voting together and does not afford the series B any special rights.

The corporation decided to seek an automatic conversion. Holders of a majority of the preferred shares, but not a majority of the preferred series B, voted in favor of the automatic conversion. After the purported conversion, the corporation's board voted to amend its certificate to eliminate reference to preferred stock. The plaintiff disputes the validity of the conversion and the subsequent certificate amendment. It maintains that a majority vote from the series B was required to validate the conversion because the conversion of the preferred stock into common stock effectively would deprive the series B preferred of the special rights they enjoyed under the certificate. According to the plaintiff, this action would "alter or change" its rights and the certificate requires a majority series B vote to validate such an action.

I rule in favor of the corporation and hold as a matter of law that the challenged conversion of preferred stock into common stock was a valid corporate action. I further conclude that the subsequent certificate amendment was valid because it occurred when no preferred shares remained outstanding and, thus, its validity was not contingent on a majority vote of the outstanding shares of series B preferred.

Greenmont Capital Partners I, LP invests in companies in the natural products industry. One of Greenmont's investments is in Series B Preferred shares in Mary's Gone Crackers ("MGC" or the "Company").

MGC produces and distributes organic and gluten-free baked goods. The Charter authorizes two classes of stock, Common and Preferred, and two series of the Preferred class, Series A and Series B. MGC authorized 65,000,000 shares: 37,522,485 Common; 15,028,444 Series A Preferred; and 12,449,071 Series B Preferred. The Common stock represents 58% of the total number of authorized shares and the Preferred represents 42%. Of the Preferred, Series A accounts for 55% and Series B accounts for 45%.

Greenmont owned 7,430,503 shares of the Series B Preferred. The Series B Preferred holders enjoy unique rights under the Charter. Article IV, Section D.2(b) lists twelve actions that must be approved by a majority of the Series B Preferred to have effect or to be valid. This Section, entitled Separate Vote of Series B Preferred (the "Voting Provision"), begins as follows:

> For so long as any shares of a series of Series B Preferred remain outstanding, in addition to any other vote or consent required herein or by law, the vote or written consent of the holders of at least a majority of the outstanding shares of the Series B Preferred shall be necessary for effecting or validating the following actions (whether by merger, recapitalization or otherwise):. . . .
>
> (i) Any amendment, alteration, repeal or waiver of any provision of the Certificate of Incorporation or the Bylaws of the Company (including any filing of a Certificate of Designation);

377

(ii) Any agreement or action that alters or changes the voting or other powers, preferences, or other special rights, privileges or restrictions of the Series B Preferred (including by way of a merger or consolidation);. . . .

The second Charter provision at issue in this dispute is Section D.5, entitled Conversion Rights. Subsection (*l*) to Section D.5 outlines procedures for an "Automatic Conversion." This subsection states:

Each share of Series Preferred shall automatically be converted into shares of Common Stock, based on the then-effective applicable Series Preferred Conversion Price, at any time upon the affirmative election of the holders of at least fifty-one percent (51%) of the then-outstanding shares of Series Preferred. . . .

On February 8, 2012, MGC solicited certain holders of Preferred to elect an automatic conversion of the Preferred into Common Stock under Section D.5. The Company limited its solicitation to holders of Preferred who indicated that they would support an automatic conversion; it did not solicit Greenmont. On February 17, MGC received written consent from at least 51% of the Preferred to convert Preferred into Common Stock. Later that same day, the MGC board voted to amend the Charter and filed an amended and restated Charter with the Delaware Secretary of State. The amended and restated Charter eliminates the provisions related to the Preferred.

Both parties assert that the Charter is plain and unambiguous and that there are no material facts in dispute. They ask the Court to declare as a matter of law whether the automatic conversion and subsequent Charter amendment violate the Charter or Delaware law.

In interpreting a corporate charter, the Court applies general principles of contract construction. A certificate should be construed in its entirety and the court "must give effect to all terms of the instrument, must read the instrument as a whole, and, if possible, must reconcile all provisions in the instrument." The existence and extent of special stock rights are contractual in nature and are determined by the issuer's certificate of incorporation.[9] The certificate must expressly and clearly state any rights, preferences, and limitations of the preferred stock that distinguish preferred stock from common stock.[10] This principle equally applies to construing the relative rights of holders of different series of preferred stock.[11]

Series B Preferred Shareholders' Right to Vote on the Conversion

I find that the Charter is unambiguous and that its language does not entitle the Series B Preferred holders to a series vote on the conversion of Preferred Stock into Common Stock. Under the Voting Provision, two elements must be present for Series B Preferred holders to have rights to a majority vote on a matter: (1) Series B Preferred must be outstanding; and (2) an enumerated action must be at issue.

The first clause of Section D.2(b) states: "For so long as any shares of a series of Series B Preferred remain outstanding." The parties do not dispute that when the Series Preferred were solicited to vote in favor of an automatic conversion, Series B

---

9. *Warner Commc'ns, Inc. v. Chris-Craft Indus., Inc.*, 583 A.2d 962, 966 (Del.Ch. 1989).
10. *Elliott Assocs., L.P. v. Avatex Corp.*, 715 A.2d 843, 852 (Del. 1998).
11. *See Avatex*, 715 A.2d at 852–53 ("Stock preferences must clearly be stated and will not be presumed.").

Preferred was outstanding. The second clause reads: "in addition to any other vote or consent required herein or by law." This language indicates that the provision grants Series B Preferred holders rights beyond any voting rights either found in the agreement or required by law. The next clause indicates what additional rights Series B Preferred holders have beyond their voting rights arising under the agreement or required by law. This clause provides that a majority vote of the outstanding Series B Preferred shares "shall be necessary for effecting or validating the following actions (whether by merger, recapitalization or otherwise)." Read together, these clauses compel the conclusion that what starts out broadly ("in addition to any other vote") finishes narrowly ("for effecting or validating the following actions"). Only the actions specified in the list of twelve enumerated actions require a majority vote of Series B Preferred in order to be valid.

Greenmont asserts that Section D.2(b)(ii) provides the enumerated action that grants it voting rights as to the automatic conversion. Section D.2(b)(ii) incorporates the following action into the Voting Provision: "Any agreement or action that alters or changes the voting or other powers, preferences, or other special rights, privileges or restrictions of the Series B Preferred (including by way of a merger or consolidation)." Notably, the drafters of the Charter included for a second time a reference incorporating action by merger. This presumably is in response to the Delaware Supreme Court's decision in *Elliott Associates, L.P. v. Avatex Corp.*

Here, the drafters appear to have attempted to take advantage of the safe harbor offered by *Avatex*. They included language in the introductory provision to incorporate actions by "merger, recapitalization or otherwise." While this language signals the intent to include the circumstance where a merger results in one of the enumerated actions, it does not touch on the disputed action here.

Section D.2(b)(ii) applies to "any agreement or action that alters or changes" the Series B Preferred's "voting or other powers, preferences, or other special rights, privileges or restrictions." The issue, therefore, is whether the automatic conversion of Series B Preferred into Common Stock "altered or changed" the Series B Preferred's powers, preferences, rights, privileges, or restrictions. This issue, in turn, requires a determination of what constitutes the Series B Preferred's "voting or other powers, preferences, or other special rights, privileges or restrictions." To answer this question, we look again to the language of the Charter. One group of rights provided for in the Charter is found in Section D.5 entitled Conversion Rights.

This Section contains subsection (*l*) which allows for an automatic conversion. The Automatic Conversion provision provides that the Preferred automatically may be converted into shares of Common Stock at any time upon the vote of 51% of the Preferred. The plain language of the Charter compels the conclusion that this automatic conversion is one of the "special rights, privileges or restrictions" created by the Charter. When contract language is plain and clear on its face, the Court will determine its meaning based on the writing alone. Because the Automatic Conversion provision exists on equal footing with the Voting Provision, an action taken under the Automatic Conversion provision cannot be seen to "alter or change" any of the Series B Preferred's "voting or other powers, preferences, or other special rights, privileges or restrictions." Rather than "alter or change" a right, the execution of an automatic conversion effectuates an existing right.

Greenmont asserts that this interpretation undermines the rights it bargained for in the Voting Provision. Notably, the Series A shareholders account for a majority of the Preferred shareholders. The Series A enjoy few benefits under the Charter and, therefore, could be expected to be more likely than the holders of Series B to vote for an automatic conversion.[22] The Series B's rights under the Charter, therefore, are somewhat dependent on the Series A's desire to remain holders of Preferred stock. Greenmont avers that it would not have bargained for such contingent rights and that an interpretation along those lines would be wrong. While Greenmont's interpretation makes sense, "its interpretation is not *reasonable* in light of the indisputably clear language of the contract." Instead, the plain language of the Charter indicates that the exercise of an automatic conversion would not alter or change the Series B Preferred's rights as those rights are defined in the Charter.

Greenmont further argues that this interpretation cannot be correct because an act that extinguishes the powers of the Series B Preferred cannot be interpreted as a "right" of that series. But, Greenmont cites no authority in support of its position. Delaware corporate law recognizes that the ability of holders of preferred stock to convert their shares into shares of common stock is a "right" of the preferred shareholders.[26] Nothing in the language of the Charter indicates that the Preferred shareholders' ability to convert their shares of Preferred Stock into shares of Common Stock under the Automatic Conversion provision is not a "right" of the Preferred shareholders. Indeed, the Automatic Conversion provision is contained in Section D.5 entitled "Conversion Rights."

This conclusion is consistent with the principle of Delaware corporation law that any rights or preferences of preferred stock must be expressed clearly.[27]

This conclusion is further supported by the fact that the drafters of the MGC Charter explicitly included one action identified elsewhere in the Charter as an enumerated action requiring a majority Series B Preferred vote under the Voting Provision. The Voting Provision includes a requirement for a majority Series B Preferred vote as to: "Any increase or decrease in the authorized number of shares of Common Stock or Preferred Stock." Had the drafters intended for the Automatic Conversion provision to be subject to an additional vote of a majority of the Series B Preferred, they could have listed it expressly in the Voting Provision as they did with the provision regarding an increase or decrease in authorized Common Stock. By expressly including Section B as an enumerated action under the Voting Provision, but not including Section D.5, the drafters implicitly excluded Section D.5.

Greenmont correctly emphasizes that the addition of the words "automatic conversion" to one of the twelve enumerated actions in Section D.2(b) is merely one way the drafters could have granted the Series B Preferred the right to a majority vote on any proposed automatic conversion. If the intent of the drafters was to include automatic conversion as an act requiring a majority Series B Preferred vote, however, then it was incumbent upon the drafters to make the Charter language precise in that

---

22. The Charter grants the Series A Preferred Stock preference over the Common Stock in receiving dividends and in receiving payment upon liquidation. The Series A also can elect one board member.

26. *See HB Korenvaes Invs., L.P. v. Marriott Corp.*, 1993 WL 257422 (Del.Ch. 1993) (considering the preferred shareholder plaintiffs' conversion rights).

27. *See Warner Commc'ns, Inc. v. Chris-Craft Indus., Inc.*, 583 A.2d 962, 967 (Del.Ch. 1989).

regard and to indicate such an intent clearly. As drafted, the Voting Provision does not grant this right. The dispositive question is not whether as a *result* of the vote in favor of automatic conversion the Series B Preferred's rights were altered or changed, but whether the act of the vote altered or changed their rights. The Automatic Conversion provision was included in the Series B Preferred's bundle of rights, privileges, and restrictions under the Charter and, thus, the act of at least 51% of the then-outstanding shares of Preferred in voting under Section D.5 to effect an automatic conversion did not alter or change those rights, privileges, and restrictions.

Series B Preferred Shareholders' Right to Vote on the Charter Amendment

I next must determine whether any Series B Preferred Stock remained outstanding at the time of the purported Charter amendment. If it did, then the Series B holders would have had the right to a majority vote on any Charter amendment under Section D.2(b)(i). If it did not, then the Series B holders would have no such right because the Voting Provision only applies "for so long as any shares of a series of Series B Preferred remain outstanding." At the time MGC amended the Charter, there were no Series B Preferred shares outstanding and, therefore, that series was not entitled to a separate series vote to validate the amendment.

Under the language of the Charter, a vote by a majority of the Preferred will automatically convert the Preferred into Common Stock. Section D.5(l)(ii) states: "Upon the occurrence of either of the events specified in Section D.5(l)(i) above, the outstanding shares of Series Preferred shall be converted automatically without any further action by the holders of such shares. . . ." In contrast, Section D.5(d) sets forth the "Mechanics of Conversion" in the context of an optional conversion of Preferred into Common Stock. The latter provision requires a Preferred holder to surrender its certificate in order for the conversion of its shares into Common Stock to be deemed to have been made. Notably, an optional conversion will be deemed to have been made at the close of business on the date the certificate is surrendered and "the person entitled to receive the shares of Common Stock issuable upon such conversion shall be treated for all purposes as the record holder of such shares of Common Stock *on such date.*" Because the automatic conversion provision states that the Series Preferred Stock shall be converted automatically, "whether or not the certificates representing such shares are surrendered to the Company," it follows that the automatic conversion also will be deemed to have been made on the date on which the holders of 51% of the Preferred voted to convert their shares into shares of Common Stock. In this case, the holders of at least 51% of the Preferred executed written consents to convert the then-outstanding Preferred Stock into Common Stock on February 17. Under the Charter, therefore, the class of Preferred was no longer outstanding as of that date.

MGC voted to amend the Charter later that same day. Therefore, the shareholder vote to amend the Charter took place when Common Stock was the only class of MGC stock outstanding. Because the Voting Provision only applies "for so long as any shares of a series of Series B Preferred remain outstanding," that provision did not apply to the Charter amendment.

For the foregoing reasons, I grant Defendant's Motion for Judgment on the Pleadings.

QUESTIONS

1. Why might the Series A shareholder vote for the automatic conversion, but the Series B preferred might not want to convert?
2. From the perspective of the Series B shareholder, was the certificate erroneously drafted in the sense that it did not express the subjective intent of the Series B shareholders? Was the certificate properly drafted as the bargained for understanding of all shareholders?
3. With the benefit of hindsight and with protecting the interest of the Series B shareholders, how should the certificate have been drafted to prevent automatic conversion?

C. FIDUCIARY DUTY

Since they are stockholders, preferred stockholders are owed fiduciary duty by the board. However, this proposition simply begs the question. Justice Felix Frankfurter's famous comment on fiduciary duty in *SEC v. Chenery Corp.*, 318 U.S. 80 (1949), is particularly apropos in determining the scope of fiduciary duty to preferred stockholders.

> But to say that a man is a fiduciary only begins the analysis; it gives direction to further inquiry. To whom is he a fiduciary? What obligations does he owe as a fiduciary? In what respect has he failed to discharge these obligations?

In the same way that creditors and stockholders have an inherent conflict, preferred shareholders and common shareholders do not have perfectly aligning interests. We should expect this to be the case since preferred stock is a hybrid instrument that has debt-like features. The cases in this section will illustrate the different kinds of situations where the conflict manifests. Harmonizing the fiduciary duties owed becomes complicated when the interests of preferred and common stockholders conflict.

This section presents the line of major Delaware cases addressing the nature of fiduciary duty to preferred stockholders as it relates to the interests of common stockholders. The focus here is exclusively Delaware case law because this body of case law as a whole illustrates the intricacy of the issues surrounding the nature of fiduciary duty to preferred stockholders. The cases are presented in chronological order to show the evolution of the doctrine of fiduciary duty to preferred shareholders in Delaware. The following is a roadmap of the broad issues.

- When common stock is bought out in a transaction, what are the board's fiduciary obligations to the preferred stockholders? The first three cases, *Dalton v. American Investment Co., Jedwab v. MGM Grand Hotels, Inc., In re FLS Holdings Inc. Shareholder Litigation*, as well as the last case, *LC Capital Master Fund, Ltd. v. James*, address this issue.
- How should a board allocate acquisition consideration between stockholders when the preferred stock contract does not specify an acquisition price? *Jedwab v. MGM Grand Hotels, Inc., In re FLS Holdings Inc. Shareholder Litigation,* and *LC Capital Master Fund, Ltd. v. James* address this issue.

3. What are the board's fiduciary obligations to preferred stockholders when the nature of their rights is defined in the corporate charter? *HB Korenaes Investments, L.P. v. Marriott Corp.*, and *LC Capital Master Fund, Ltd. v. James* address this issue.

4. When a board must make a decision on a specific corporate transaction, what are its fiduciary obligations to common stockholders and preferred stockholders when their interests conflict? *Orban v. Field*, *Equity-Linked Investors, L.P. v. Adams*, *In re Tradoes Inc. Shareholder Litigation*, and *LC Capital Master Fund, Ltd. v. James*, address this issue. Interestingly, these four cases involve venture capital investments in new or speculative companies.

Dalton v. American Investment Co.
490 A.2d 574 (Del. Ch. 1985)

BROWN, Chancellor.

This action is brought by certain preferred shareholders of American Investment Company. The suit charges that the individual defendants, in their capacity as the board of directors of American Investment Company ("AIC"), breached the fiduciary duty owed by them to the plaintiffs during the course of a merger whereby AIC was merged into Leucadia American Corp. In that merger, the common shareholders of AIC were eliminated from their equity position in the corporation at a price of $13 per share. However, the preferred shareholders of AIC were not cashed out, but were left as preferred shareholders of the corporation surviving the merger. Plaintiffs contend that AIC's board looked only to the interests of the common shareholders in seeking a merger partner for AIC and, by so doing, unfairly froze the preferred shareholders into the post-merger AIC as completely controlled by Leucadia. This is a decision after trial.

Plaintiffs own collectively some 220,000 shares of the total of some 280,000 shares of AIC's 5 ½% Cumulative Preference Stock, Series B. At the time of the events complained of, AIC had outstanding one other series of 5 ½% preferred stock consisting of some 81,000 shares. Immediately prior to the merger, AIC had slightly more than 5.5 million common shares outstanding. Thus, at the time of the merger the common stock comprised 94% of AIC's outstanding shares while the preferred stock constituted the remaining 6%.

This Series B preferred had a stated redemption and liquidation value of $25 per share. There was no provision for mandatory redemption of this preferred stock, but it carried with it an annual dividend rate of 5 ½% which was thus payable indefinitely. The prevailing interest rate in 1961 was approximately 4 ½% and thus, at the time, an annual dividend of 5 ½% guaranteed indefinitely no doubt appeared to be a good bargain.

Aside from operating the insurance companies, AIC was in the business of consumer finance. It borrowed money wholesale in order to lend it at retail rates through a chain of offices scattered throughout the country. It is my impression that consumer finance was the primary business of AIC during the 1970's.

The rising interest rates accompanying inflation began to put the squeeze on AIC. Its less than optimal bond rating hampered its efforts to obtain the long-term loans which it needed to conduct its consumer finance business and its earlier long-range financing procured in the previous days of lower interest rates was being gradually paid off with current funds. It became obvious that AIC needed either a merger or sale of assets to remain a viable company. As a result, following the 1977 resolution of the proxy contest, AIC retained the investment banking firm of Kidder, Peabody & Co. for the purpose of seeking out a prospective purchaser or merger partner.

Kidder, Peabody sent out many letters and pursued numerous merger candidates. Eventually, in 1978, Household Finance Corporation ("HFC") came forth with an offer to acquire all outstanding shares of AIC. The offer of HFC was $12 per share for the common stock and $25 per share for the two series of preferred stock. At the time Kidder, Peabody had valued AIC's common stock within a range of $9 to $11, and the $12 figure offered by HFC approximated the then book value of the common shares. At the $25 redemption and liquidation value, the price offered for the preferred shares represented their book value also. The preferred shares were trading for about $9 per share at the time.

This offer by HFC was approved as fair by Kidder, Peabody and was accepted by AIC's board. It was also approved overwhelmingly by AIC's shareholders, both common and preferred. However, the United States Department of Justice entered the picture and sought to prohibit the acquisition by HFC on antitrust grounds. Ultimately, the acquisition of AIC by HFC was enjoined by the federal courts and HFC's merger proposal was terminated.

Even before the appellate process concerning the HFC proposal had run its course, AIC's board authorized Kidder, Peabody to reactivate its efforts to find a merger partner for the company. This time, however, Kidder, Peabody was not given an exclusive right to do so, but rather the company also reserved the right to seek and entertain potential candidates on its own. In this endeavor the defendant Robert Brockmann, president of AIC and a member of its board, took the most active role.

It is significant to this decision to take note of three things in connection with this renewed effort to seek financial help for AIC, all of which necessarily permeated Brockmann's approach to the task. First, the HFC offer had tended to establish a range for the cost of acquisition by other interested parties by indicating a price in the vicinity of $12 per share for the common stock and by further indicating a total acquisition price in the vicinity of $75 million. Secondly, the fact that HFC's offer had compared favorably to the book value of AIC's shares provided Brockmann with the opportunity to suggest book value as the basis for any new offer, especially since the book value of AIC's common shares had increased during the interim even though its overall business outlook had continued to worsen. Thirdly, the offer of HFC to cash out the preferred shares at the $25 redemption and liquidation value had understandably come as somewhat of a surprise to the members of AIC's board. Since the preferred stock had been trading at less than $10 per share at the time, HFC's offer to cash out the preferred at $25 per share had been openly viewed by at least some of their number as a "Christmas present" for the preferred shareholders.

In his individual efforts to find a merger partner for AIC Brockmann adopted the approach of alluding to the book value of AIC's common shares as the basis on which an offer should be made. By that time, the book value of the common shares had increased to $13.50 per share. Brockmann was apparently careful to not ask for $13.50, or for any specific amount for the common shares even in his discussions with Leucadia, the eventual purchaser. He does concede, however, that by referring to the book value of AIC's stock he was attempting to establish a "floor" at which a potential purchaser would be inclined to commence its bidding.

In February 1980, Leucadia, a company also in the consumer finance business, submitted a written offer to AIC whereby it proposed to acquire all common shares of AIC for $13 per share. The proposal contained no offer for the preferred shares but rather it proposed to leave them in place. Later, presumably as a result of Brockmann's suggestion that something should be done for the holders of the preferred, Leucadia revised its proposal by offering to make available to AIC's preferred shareholders immediately following the merger a Leucadia debenture worth 40% of the face value of the preferred shares, with interest at 13%, which could be exchanged for the preferred shares. Still later, however, because of declining economic conditions, Leucadia withdrew its offer altogether.

In August, 1980, Leucadia reappeared. This time it offered $13 per share for all outstanding shares of AIC's common stock and offered further to increase the dividend rate on the preferred shares from 5 ½% to 7%. In addition, and again because of Brockmann's expression of concern for the preferred shareholders, Leucadia added a "sweetener" in the form of a sinking fund to redeem the preferred shares over a period of 20 years at the rate of 5% each year. Any such redemptions were to continue to be made by lot as provided by AIC's original preference designations, but subject, however, to the added proviso that any market purchases or other acquisitions of preferred shares made during a given year could be credited against the annual 5% redemption requirement.

Kidder, Peabody opined that this offer was fair to AIC and its shareholders, stressing the fairness of the price to the common (AIC was trading for $11 per share on the day prior to the announcement of the approval of the merger in principle) and the safety that the proposal would provide to the rights of the preferred. The board of AIC accepted the offer and, when put to the vote of the shareholders, it was overwhelmingly approved by AIC's common shareholders and was approved unanimously by the holders of the other series of preferred stock. However, the holders of the Series B preferred, including the plaintiffs, voted some 170,000 of the 280,000 Series B shares against the proposal. Nonetheless, with all shares being accorded an equal vote, the plan of merger was adopted and AIC was merged into Leucadia. The former common shareholders of AIC were cashed out at $13 per share. Leucadia became the owner of all of AIC's common stock while the preferred shareholders were continued on as shareholders of AIC, albeit at the increased dividend rate and with the added redemption and sinking fund provisions.

Finally, as of the time of the merger the market value of their Series B preferred was something less than $9 per share and there was no trading market for such shares. The holders of the preferred shares were entitled to appraisal rights so as to realize the value of their shares if they so chose. The plaintiffs did not seek such appraisal rights.

[Fiduciary Duty Claim]

[Plaintiffs contend that defendant] directors owed a duty of fair dealing to all shareholders of AIC, both the common and the preferred, in negotiating and agreeing to any plan of merger. They say, however, that the defendant directors violated this duty to the extent that it was owed to the preferred shareholders once the HFC proposal had aborted. They charge that the defendants did so following the cancellation of the HFC offer by discreetly seeking to channel the whole of any prospective purchase price toward the payment for the common shares of AIC alone, and to the deliberate exclusion of the preferred shares.

Plaintiffs suggest that what Brockmann and the other directors did was note that HFC had offered to pay a total of $75.7 million to acquire AIC, broken down into components of $66.5 million for the common ($12 per share x roughly 5.5 million shares) and $9.2 million for the total of the two series of preferred ($25 per share x some 361,000 shares). They say that simple arithmetic shows that AIC's 1980 book value of $13.50 for the common shares multiplied by the 5.5 million common shares outstanding worked out to approximately $75 million. Since it was not necessary for a potential acquirer to cash out the preferred shareholders in order to gain control of the company, and since the AIC board viewed the offer of HFC to purchase the preferred shares at their redemption value of $25 per share as having been a potential "Christmas present" to the preferred shareholders anyway, plaintiffs charge that what Brockmann did, with the board's ultimate approval, was to suggest the book value of the common stock as the starting point for any merger offer so as to assure that the whole of any new offer would go totally to the owners of the common shares.

Plaintiffs argue that even though they were minority preferred shareholders of AIC, they were nonetheless entitled to the protections of the fiduciary duty of fairness imposed upon those who were in a position to guide the fortunes of the corporation. Compare, *Rothschild International Corporation v. Liggett Group, Inc.*, 474 A.2d 133 (Del. 1984). They say that our law is well established that where the real and only purpose of a merger is to promote the interests of one class of shareholders to the detriment, or at the expense, of another class of minority shareholders, the duty to deal fairly with all shareholders is violated and the merger transaction itself is rendered improper.

Defendants argue that the rights of preferred shareholders are contract rights and that as against the rights of the common shareholders they are fixed by the contractual terms agreed upon when the class of preferred stock is created. Since the preferred shareholders had no contractual right to be bought out as part of the acquisition of AIC by Leucadia—either at par value or at any other price—defendants argue that the board of AIC had no fiduciary duty to bargain on their behalf in an effort to obtain a cash-out deal for them also.

Defendants argue that the record is completely devoid of any evidence that they actually solicited an offer from Leucadia for the common shares alone. In fact, they take the position that Leucadia's offer was unsolicited. They say that all that Brockmann did with regard to Leucadia was the same that he did with all other interested parties, namely, attempt to establish a "floor" for any offer by referring to the fact that HFC's offer had been for the equivalent of book value.

Defendants point out that the real reason for Leucadia's offer for the common shares only was the fact that as to Leucadia the preferred shares constituted "cheap debt", as Leucadia well appreciated. They point out that the cost of borrowing $9 million at an approximate 20% rate of interest in order to pay the preferred shareholders their liquidation value of $25 per share so as to eliminate a debt of the corporation carrying a 5 1/2% dividend rate would have made little economic sense.

I am satisfied that the answer to the plaintiffs' charges of breach of fiduciary duty lies somewhere between the legal positions advocated by the parties, and that it turns on the factual determination of whether or not Leucadia's offer was made in response to a solicitation by Brockmann and the other directors defendants. I find on the evidence that it was not, and accordingly I rule in favor of the defendants on this point.

I have no doubt that Brockmann and the AIC board were attempting to invite an offer of $13.50 for the common stock while at the same time they were seeking nothing specific for the preferred shares. One could scarcely reach any other conclusion. I am convinced also that they well suspicioned that if a third party offered anything near that amount for the common stock there would be little, if anything, offered for the preferred.

Given that Brockmann's approach of alluding to the book value of the common shares can be reasonably interpreted as a solicitation for an offer for the common shares only without a corresponding offer for the preferred, what the plaintiffs proceed to do in their argument is to then assume that the Leucadia offer was made in response to that solicitation and as a direct result of it. Because only if that were so can the plaintiffs establish that the predicament in which they now find themselves was caused by the conduct of the AIC directors, and only then would we reach the legal question of whether or not it was a breach of the fiduciary duty owed by the directors to the preferred shareholders for them to have engaged in such conduct.

The weakness in the plaintiffs' argument is making the factual assumption that because Brockmann's solicitation of an offer from Leucadia and the subsequent Leucadia offer crossed each other, the latter must have been a direct result of the former. It is the "but for" assumption. It is an argument that "but for" Brockmann's solicitation of an offer for the common stock alone with nothing sought for the preferred, Leucadia would likely have followed HFC's lead and proposed a buy-out of both classes of stock at a price of something less than $13 per share for the common and at a price either equating or approaching the liquidation value of the preferred. In addition to being speculative, such a proposition does not comport with the evidence.

The evidence indicates that the Leucadia offer was formulated and put forth by two of Leucadia's principle officers and shareholders, Ian Cumming and Joseph Steinberg. Steinberg in particular helped to structure the offer price. He has a background and experience in investment banking. The deposition testimony of Steinberg was admitted in evidence. It reveals that when asked how he arrived at the $13 per share figure which resulted in the total $72.2 million offer, Steinberg responded as follows:

> I reviewed the published financial data of AIC. I looked at the trading activity of the AIC stock. I looked up in the newspaper what other consumer finance companies were selling for. And I added to that my intuitive opinion of what it was worth. And I put that all into a hat and shook it up, and out came the price which we were eventually willing to pay after negotiating an overall deal with AIC.

As to Leucadia's reasons for not offering to cash out the preferred, the following colloquy appears:

Q. As the transaction ultimately took shape, a determination was made by Leucadia not to offer to cash out the preference stock of AIC in the merger transaction; is that right?
A. Yes.

387

Q. Why?

A. We regarded the preference stock as the equivalent of debt and an important consideration for us in being interested in American Investment was being able to leave in place all of the various long-term debt agreements of AIC. And we were advised by our attorneys that none of the provisions of any of the debt agreements or the preference stock agreement required that the stock be redeemed or debts paid off, and we did not see that it was to our advantage to prepay any debt or redeem any preference stock and were not interested in doing so and probably would not have been interested in the transaction at all if we have been required to prepay debt or redeem preference stock.

Finally, when asked to compare Leucadia's offer with the earlier HFC offer, Steinberg responded as follows:

A. Well, Household, I believe, was offering twelve dollars, and our offer was for thirteen on the common, and Household was prepared to redeem the preference stock at slightly over $25, and we were offering to increase the interest rate from 5 ½ to 7 and to establish a sinking fund where there was none before.

Q. Did you ever give consideration to offering twelve dollars for the common stock and redeeming the preference stock?

A. No.

Overall, Steinberg's testimony indicates that Leucadia had its own economic justification for not cashing out the preferred shareholders, that Leucadia was advised by its attorneys that it was not legally necessary that the preferred shares be bought out, and that Leucadia reached its decision to offer to purchase the common shares only for its own reasons and not because of anything said by Brockmann or anyone else on behalf of AIC.

Accordingly, I find on the evidence that Leucadia's offer was not made in direct response to a veiled solicitation by Brockmann. Rather, I find that the Leucadia offer was made by knowledgeable and experienced businessmen who chose to take advantage of an existing situation of which they were well aware for business reasons peculiar to the interests of their company. Thus, I cannot find that the terms of the merger which left the plaintiffs as continuing preferred shareholders of AIC were brought about as a result of any breach of fiduciary duty on the part of the defendant directors of AIC, even assuming without deciding that the conduct of Brockmann and the AIC board in seeking a merger partner in the manner they did would have constituted a breach of fiduciary duty owed to AIC's preferred shareholders.

For the reasons given, judgment will be entered in favor of the defendants.

no breach.

QUESTIONS

1. Why did Leucadia not want to make an offer for the preferred stock? How plausible is the given reason?
2. What is the legal question left unanswered in *Dalton*?
3. Does the board owe fiduciary duty to the preferred stockholders? If so, what exactly was the contour of that duty? In the context of this case, what exactly should the board have done?

Jedwab v. MGM Grand Hotels, Inc.
509 A.2d 584 (Del. Ch. 1986)

ALLEN, Chancellor.

MGM Grand Hotels, Inc. has entered into an agreement with Bally Manufacturing Corp. contemplating a merger between a Bally subsidiary and the Company. On the effectuation of such merger, all classes of the Company's presently outstanding stock will be converted into the right to receive cash.

Defendant Kirk Kerkorian individually and through Tracinda Corporation, which he wholly owns, beneficially owns 69% of MGM Grand's issued and outstanding common stock and 74% of its only other class of stock, its Series A Redeemable Preferred Stock. Mr. Kerkorian took an active part in negotiating the proposed merger with Bally and agreed with Bally to vote his stock in favor of the merger. Since neither the merger agreement nor the Company's charter contains a provision conditioning such a transaction on receipt of approval by a greater than majority vote, Kerkorian's agreement to vote in favor of the merger assured its approval.

Plaintiff is an owner of the Company's preferred stock. She brings this action as a class action on behalf of all owners of such stock other than Kerkorian and Tracinda and seeks to enjoin preliminarily and permanently the effectuation of the proposed merger. The merger is said to constitute a wrong to the preferred shareholders principally in that it allegedly contemplates an unfair apportionment among the Company's shareholders of the total consideration to be paid by Bally upon effectuation of the merger. Pending is plaintiff's motion for a preliminary injunction.

MGM Grand, through wholly-owned subsidiaries, owns and operates the MGM Grand Hotel-Las Vegas and the MGM Grand Hotel-Reno. The Company entered the hotel business in 1973, with the opening of its Las Vegas facility. That luxury hotel and casino now consists of some 2,800 guest rooms and a 62,500 square foot casino. The Las Vegas hotel was very profitable from the outset and in 1978 the Company opened its Reno hotel which was constructed on a similarly large scale.

In November 1980, tragedy struck at the MGM Grand Hotel-Las Vegas. That night a fire consumed the 25-story hotel and 84 lives were lost. The fire required the closing of the Las Vegas hotel for over 8 months and required almost total renovation of that facility. It gave rise as well to protracted litigation relating both to the personal injuries sustained in the fire and the loss of property by the Company. Hundreds of suits were brought against the Company seeking, in total, more than $650 million in compensatory damages and more than $2 billion in punitive damages. In addition, the Company was required to sue its property insurance carriers seeking recovery of losses occasioned by the fire.

Following the Las Vegas disaster there was a significant fall-off in the market value of MGM Grand's common stock. Closing the week of November 14, 1980, at 13 ¼, the price of the Company's common stock closed at 10 the following week and closed the week of December 12 at 7 ½.

Apparently in response to the reduced price of the Company's stock and to the risks to stockholders' investment represented by the fire-related litigation claims, [in] 1982, the Company publicly offered to exchange one share of common stock for one share of a new class of stock, the Series A Redeemable Preferred Stock. The offer extended to a maximum of 10 million shares of the Company's then outstanding 32,500,000 shares. The offering document stated that Mr. Kerkorian (who at that time controlled very slightly in excess of 50% of the issued and outstanding common stock) would tender into the offer that number of shares equal to the total numbered tendered by all other shareholders, but in no event would he tender less than 5 million shares.

terms of preferred

The preferred stock issued in connection with the exchange offer carries a cumulative $0.44 annual dividend (the same dividend paid with respect to the common stock both at the time of the exchange offer and now), is non-convertible, elects no directors unless dividends remain unpaid for six quarters, has a liquidation preference of $20 per share and carries a complex redemption right.

The redemption provisions require the Company to acquire each year a number of preferred shares determined by a formula set forth in the certificate designating the rights, preferences, etc. of the preferred. The Company, however, is required to redeem stock at $20 per share in any year only if it is unable privately to purchase, on the market or through a tender offer, the number of preferred shares required to be "redeemed" that year. In fact, during fiscal years 1982–84 the Company purchased a total of 766,551 shares of preferred stock on the open market at an average cost of $7.92 per share and has been required to redeem no shares at $20 per share.

The offering document explained the reasons for the exchange offer as follows:

> Prior to the announcement of the Exchange Offer, in management's opinion the earnings and possible future performance of MGM Grand were not being adequately reflected in the market price of the Common Stock. Accordingly, management decided that present stockholders should be given an opportunity to liquidate all or a portion of their Common Stock holdings in exchange for Preferred Stock. Assuming continued earnings of MGM Grand which are available for redemption of Preferred Stock, stockholders accepting the Exchange Offer who hold their Preferred Stock until their shares are called for redemption will receive $20 per share, without regard to future market fluctuations in the Common Stock. To the extent that MGM Grand has only minimal future net profits or has net losses, redemptions of Preferred Stock could extend over a significant number of years. . . . MGM Grand presently intends to satisfy its redemption obligations to the extent possible by acquiring Preferred Stock in the open market or otherwise so long as such stock can be acquired at a price of less than $20 per share. Accordingly, no assurance can be given as to whether any significant number of shares of Preferred Stock will ultimately be redeemed at the $20 per share redemption price.

Through the exchange offer, 9,315,403 common shares were exchanged, including 5 million shares by Mr. Kerkorian and his corporation, Tracinda.

On June 6, 1985, Tracinda and Kerkorian announced an intention to pursue a cash-out merger transaction that would eliminate the public common stockholders from the Company at $18 per share, but would leave the preferred stock in place. In response, the board of the Company created a special committee to review and evaluate such a proposal. The committee retained legal counsel and hired Bear Stearns & Co., Inc., to act as its financial advisor. While events mooted the Tracinda offer before Bear Stearns rendered a formal opinion on the proposed deal, its internal documents reflect the fact that its experts had apparently concluded by July 29 that the proposed offer at $18 per share was fair to the common stockholders from a financial point of view.

In August, 1985, the Drexel Burnham firm was engaged to explore alternatives to the Tracinda offer. That firm made a significant effort to instigate possible alternative deals—apparently some 50 firms were contacted, but the only indication of serious interest it apparently received was from Bally Manufacturing Corp.

In early November 1985, Kerkorian, Stephen Silbert, his principal legal advisor, and representatives of Drexel Burnham met with Robert Mullane, the chairman and chief executive officer of Bally to discuss Bally's interest. At that meeting Bally apparently ultimately took the position that it thought all of the Company's equity was worth $440 million and said it would be willing to make a cash offer at that price for all the Company's stock—common and preferred.

It seems agreed by all parties that Bally made a total price offer and had no real input into the way in which that consideration would be divided among classes of MGM Grand's stock, although its concurrence was obviously required. Kerkorian and Silbert had, however, discussed that question prior to the meeting, and Kerkorian had expressed the view that the common stock should get $18 a share since Tracinda had already announced an offer at that price.

Kerkorian, after discussions with his lawyer Silbert and with Drexel Burnham, apparently determined that $14 was the price that would be paid for the preferred. However, a $14 per share price for the outstanding preferred, when added to an $18 price for all the common stock, would result in a cash price in excess of $440 million for all of the Company's stock.* To solve this problem, Kerkorian agreed to take $12.24 per share for his common stock together with certain other property, including transfer of the exclusive rights to the name MGM Grand Hotels and certain contingent rights in litigation proceeds. This non-cash property has been the subject of an appraisal and, in part on the basis of that appraisal, Bear Stearns has opined that the total value of the consideration Kerkorian will receive for his common stock is less than $18 per share.

[The board ultimately approved the transaction. Bear Stearns rendered a fairness opinion concluding that "the aggregate consideration [to be] received by Tracinda and Mr. Kerkorian for their shares of Common Stock [on a per share basis] is less than the consideration per share to be received by the Public Shareholders of the Company's Common Stock . . ." and that "the price to be paid for the Preferred Stock . . . is fair from a financial point of view . . . ". At the shareholders' meeting, 77.5 percent of all of the issued and outstanding common stock voted in favor of the merger. The preferred stock had no right to vote on the merger.]

The main argument advanced by plaintiff is premised upon the assertion that the directors of a Delaware corporation have a duty in a merger transaction to negotiate and approve only a merger that apportions the merger consideration fairly among classes of the company's stock. To unfairly favor one class of stock over another is, on this view, a breach of the duty of loyalty that a director owes to the corporation and, by extension, that he owes equally to all of its shareholders.

Plaintiff compares the $18 per share price that the public common stockholders are to receive with the $14 per share into which the preferred stock is to be converted

---

* Author's note: Before the exchange offer creating the preferred stock, the common stock outstanding was 32.5 million shares. Of these shares, 9.3 million shares exchanged to preferred stock. At $18 per share, the merger consideration for the common stock would have been $417 million. At $14 per share, the merger consideration for the preferred stock would have been $130 million. Thus, the total merger consideration would have to have been $547 million.

and perceives an unfairness. Plaintiff offers an explanation of why this unfairness to the preferred resulted—an explanation that seems required by the fact that the controlling shareholder owns a greater proportion of the preferred (74%) than of the common stock (69%). That explanation posits that in apportioning the merger consideration, Kerkorian felt compelled to allocate $18 per share to the common in order to protect himself from possible lawsuits arising from persons who had purchased MGM Grand common stock after the market price for that stock had risen in response to Kerkorian's announcement of a forthcoming $18 cash out merger with Tracinda. Abandonment of that deal for another that would yield the common less, it is contended, would have exposed Kerkorian to charges of manipulation and to litigation. Thus, in allotting the proceeds of the merger among the Company's two classes of stock, plaintiff complains that Kerkorian sought to avoid a potential personal liability.

[Fiduciary Duty and Standard of Review]

Initially I address two preliminary although critical legal questions: first, whether, in these circumstances, defendants owe any fiduciary duties to the preferred at all and, second, what standard—entire fairness or business judgment—is appropriate to assess the probability of ultimate success.

Issue on the merits of claims alleged is first joined on the fundamental question whether the directors of MGM Grand owe *any* duty to the holders of the preferred stock other than the duty to accord to such holders the rights, powers and preferences set out in the certificate designating and defining the legal rights of the preferred.

Defendants contend there is no broad duty of fidelity owed to preferred stock if that duty is understood to extend beyond the specific contractual terms defining the special rights, preferences or limitations of the preferred. In support of its position on this point defendants cite such cases as *Rothschild International Corp. v. Liggett Group, Inc.,* 474 A.2d 133 (Del. 1984); *Wood v. Coastal States Gas Corp.,* 401 A.2d 932 (Del. 1979). Broadly speaking "preferential rights are contractual in nature and therefore are governed by the express provisions of a company's certificate of incorporation" *Rothschild,* 474 A.2d at 136. Defendants restate this accepted principle as meaning "all rights of preferred shareholders are contractual in nature". They then go on to argue (analogizing to the wholly contractual rights of bondholders—as to which no "fiduciary" duties extend) that the only duties directors have to preferred shareholders are those necessary to accord the preferred rights set out in their contract, i.e., the document designating the rights, preferences, etc., of their special stock.

The flaw in this argument lies in a failure to distinguish between "preferential" rights (and special limitations) on the one hand and rights associated with all stock on the other. At common law and in the absence of an agreement to the contrary all shares of stock are equal. Thus preferences and limitations associated with preferred stock exist only by virtue of an express provision (contractual in nature) creating such rights or limitations. But absent negotiated provision conferring rights on preference stock, it does not follow that no right exists. The point may be conclusively demonstrated by two examples. If a certificate designating rights, preferences, etc. of special stock contains *no* provision dealing with voting rights or *no* provision creating rights upon liquidation, it is not the fact that such stock has no voting rights or no rights upon liquidation. Rather, in such circumstances, the preferred stock has the same voting rights as common stock (8 *Del.C.* §212(a)); or the same rights to participate in the liquidation of the corporation as has such stock.

Thus, with respect to matters relating to preferences or limitations that distinguish preferred stock from common, the duty of the corporation and its directors is essentially contractual and the scope of the duty is appropriately defined by reference to the specific words evidencing that contract; where however the right asserted is not to a preference as against the common stock but rather a right shared equally with the common, the existence of such right and the scope of the correlative duty may be measured by equitable as well as legal standards.

With this distinction in mind the Delaware cases which frequently analyze rights of and duties towards preferred stock in legal (i.e., contractual) terminology (*e.g.*, *Wood v. Coastal States Gas Corp.*; *Rothschild International Corp. v. Liggett Group, Inc.*) may be made consistent with those cases that apply fiduciary standards to claims of preferred shareholders.

Accordingly, without prejudging the validity of any of plaintiff's liability theories, I conclude that her claim (a) to a "fair" allocation of the proceeds of the merger; (b) to have the defendants exercise appropriate care in negotiating the proposed merger and (c) to be free of overreaching by Mr. Kerkorian (as to the timing of the merger for his benefit) fairly implicate fiduciary duties and ought not be evaluated wholly from the point of view of the contractual terms of the preferred stock designations.

Assuming that plaintiff and the other preferred shareholders have a "right" recognized in equity to a fair apportionment of the merger consideration, what legal standard is to be used to assess the probability that a violation of that right will ultimately be proven. Plaintiff asserts that the appropriate test is one of entire or intrinsic fairness. That test is the familiar one employed when fiduciaries elect to utilize their power over the corporation to effectuate a transaction in which they have an interest that diverges from that of the corporation or the minority shareholders.

Our Supreme Court has made it quite clear that the heightened judicial scrutiny called for by the test of intrinsic or entire fairness is not called forth simply by a demonstration that a controlling shareholder fixes the terms of a transaction and, by exercise of voting power or by domination of the board, compels its effectuation. It is essential to show as well that the fiduciary has an interest with respect to the transaction that conflicts with the interests of minority shareholders. Speaking in the context of a parent dealing with a controlled but not wholly-owned subsidiary our Supreme Court has said:

> The basic situation for the application of the rule [requiring a fiduciary to assume the burden to show intrinsic fairness] is the one in which the parent has received a benefit to the exclusion and at the expense of the subsidiary.
>
> A parent does indeed owe a fiduciary duty to its subsidiary when there are parent-subsidiary dealings. However, this alone will not evoke the intrinsic fairness standard. This standard will be applied only when the fiduciary duty is accompanied by self-dealing—the situation when a parent is on both sides of a transaction with its subsidiary. Self-dealing occurs when the parent, by virtue of its domination of the subsidiary, causes the subsidiary to act in such a way that the parent receives something from the subsidiary to the exclusion of, and detriment to, the minority stockholders of the subsidiary.

Sinclair Oil Corporation v. Levien, 280 A.2d 717, 720 (Del. 1971).

As to what appears to be the material element of the negotiation of the Bally merger—the $440,000,000 cash price—Mr. Kerkorian had no conflicting interest of a kind that would support invocation of the intrinsic fairness test. With respect to total price, his interest was to extract the maximum available price. Moreover, as to the apportionment of the merger consideration between the two classes of the Company's stock, Mr. Kerkorian's interest again appears to create no significant bias on his part since his ownership of each class is not only great but substantially equal. Indeed, Kerkorian's ownership of the preferred is proportionately somewhat greater.

Thus, had Kerkorian apportioned the merger consideration equally among members of each class of the Company's stockholders (as distinguished from equally between classes of stock), then the fact of his substantially equivalent ownership of each class of stock would have supported invocation the business judgment rule. The fact that each class was treated differently would not itself require application of the intrinsic fairness test.

But Kerkorian directed the apportionment of merger consideration in a way that treated himself differently from other holders of common stock. He accorded to himself less cash per common share ($12.24) but, in the License Agreement, arrogated to himself the right to use or designate the use of the MGM Grand name and, under the Price Adjustment Agreement, he is to assume certain obligations and acquire certain rights with respect to pending property insurance claims of the Company.

Do these agreements create the possibility of a substantial conflict that would mandate the enhanced judicial scrutiny contemplated by the intrinsic fairness test? As to the License Agreement, I am persuaded the answer is no. I regard the subject matter of the license as of *de minimis* value in these circumstances. It was valued at $1.3 million by an independent appraisal firm. In the context of a cash price of $440 million for a company of which Kerkorian owns roughly 70% that amount would not appear to create a material conflict.

The Price Adjustment Agreement deals with an asset of MGM Grand that was doubtlessly difficult for Bally to value—insurance claims arising from the company's losses caused by the 1980 fire. Those claims have been in litigation for some time and apparently are complex. In the Price Adjustment Agreement Kerkorian removes the uncertainty that such claims create, by (1) guaranteeing that MGM Grand will recover $50 million on the claims treated, (2) undertaking to continue to supervise the litigation and (3) agreeing to pay one-half of the first $1,000,000 of legal fees and all such costs in excess of $1,000,000. In exchange for these undertakings Kerkorian receives the right to all amounts recovered by the Company on the claims in excess of $59.5 million.

[After analysis, the court concluded that the] maximum value of the contingent litigation rights would be approximately $25,000,000 or approximately $80 per share, when all shares, common and preferred, are included. I do not regard that amount as *de minimis*.

I conclude that, in apportioning that element of consideration wholly to his own shares to the exclusion of others Kerkorian was exercising power of a kind and in circumstances justifying invocation of the heightened standard of judicial review.

[Fairness Analysis]

I also conclude that, as to the claim of the preferred to an equal or fair share of the merger proceeds, the defendants are likely to meet the burden thus imposed upon them. It follows that plaintiff has failed to demonstrate a reasonable probability of success on this issue.

Contractual

First, it seems elementary that the preferred has no *legal* right to equivalent consideration in the merger. Neither the certificate of incorporation nor the certificate of designation of the preferred stock expressly creates such a right. Nor does it appear that such a right may be fairly implied from those documents when read in the light of the terms of the 1982 Exchange Offer. Nor do I perceive any basis to recognize an *equitable* right to mathematically equal consideration based upon the conduct of Kerkorian as a fiduciary.

As to a right of the preferred to have the total consideration fairly (as distinguished from equally) apportioned, the current record provides no persuasive basis to conclude that the allocation contemplated by the Bally merger is unfair.

Plaintiff's claim of unfairness in an apportionment of $18 per share to the common stockholders and $14 a share to the preferred involves a fundamental defect: it rests upon an invalid comparison. The pertinent comparison, if one is treating a right to fair apportionment among classes of stock, is between what those *classes* receive in the merger, on a per share basis, not between what the class of preferred receive per share and what the *public holders* of common stock are to receive.

The essential right plaintiff asserts is the right of the preferred to be treated as well as the common in the merger. There are now outstanding 22,803,194 common shares and 8,549,000 preferred. Thus, in all, there are 31,352,194 shares of MGM Grand stock. But when the total cash consideration—$440 million—is divided by the total number of shares, common and preferred, outstanding the result is $14.03 per share [= $440 million ÷ 31,352,194 shares].

But in addition to cash, Kerkorian will get other non-cash consideration that ought to be considered in comparing the financial treatment of the two classes of stock in the merger. If for these purposes we treat the value of the MGM Grand name as worth $1.3 million (its appraised value) and the value of contingent right to litigation proceeds as worth approximately $25 million, then it appears that the total value of the merger consideration is approximately $466.3 million. Dividing that number by 31,352,194 yields an average consideration per share for all stockholders of $14.87. Thus, if each preferred stockholder received the average consideration per share that all shareholders will receive, each preferred share would receive, on the foregoing assumption, not $14.00 but $14.87. In fact, the common stock *as a class* will not receive the $14.87 average for all shareholders but will receive total consideration (on the foregoing assumption) of $15.20 per share.

[Author's note: The $15.20 per share is important to understand because the court uses it as a benchmark in the analysis that follows. The assumptions in the calculation are total merger consideration of $466.3 million and the merger consideration actually paid to preferred stockholders of $14 per share. Since there were 8,549,000 preferred shares outstanding, the preferred stockholders would be allocated $119.7 million. This would leave $346.6 million for common stockholders. With 22,803,194 shares of common stock outstanding, the merger consideration to the common stock would be $15.20 per share.]

Given the fact that the preferred has no prospect for a future increment in dividends, no vote, and has historically tended to trade at a discount from the common, I cannot conclude that the $14 per share price (which represents a 6% discount from the $14.87 per share average value for all shares) is likely to be found not to be entirely appropriate.

Plaintiff might fairly say that the foregoing analysis does not meet the real thrust of her contention. That is, she would argue that the meaningful difference in the preferred's consideration is not between their $14 per share and the average to be received by all shares ($14.87 on the assumption set out above) but between $14 and $18 to be recovered by the *public holders* of the common stock. This difference—simply because it is materially larger—would be more difficult to justify.

But this comparison [is] invalid. It is true that the common as a class is not getting the average of all shareholders—$14.87 on my assumption concerning the value of the contingent litigation rights—but is getting $15.20 per share on that assumption. That difference ($0.33 per share), if it is to be justified, must be justified by reference to the difference in the legal claims and economic prospects of the two classes of stock.

The further difference—between $15.20 per share for the common as a class and the $18 per share that the public holders of common stock will receive need not be so justified in my opinion; it is clearly being funded entirely by Kerkorian personally. That is, the amount of the total increment to be received by the *public* holders of common stock over the average per share consideration to be received by the common stock as a class (7,064,021 public common shares x ($18.00 − $15.20) = $19,779,259) is supplied by Kerkorian, who has taken less for his common stock, even when the non-cash consideration is considered ($12.24 cash + $1.67 non-cash[10] = $13.91 per share). Thus, the amount per share that Kerkorian has given up ($15.20 − $13.91 = $1.29 per share) when multiplied by his total common stock holdings (15,739,173) equals $20,303,533 and more than fully funds the increment that the public common stockholders will receive over the average per share price to be received by common stockholders as a class.

Thus, if plaintiff is correct that Kerkorian sought to make sure the public common stockholders got $18 per share because he feared some potential liability if they got less, the rejoinder is that, to the extent the public holders of common are to receive more than all common stock as a class, Kerkorian paid for that benefit from his own pocket.

While the law requires that corporate fiduciaries observe high standards of fidelity and, when self-dealing is involved, places upon them the burden of demonstrating the intrinsic fairness of transactions they authorize, the law does not require more than fairness. Specifically, it does not, absent a showing of culpability, require that directors or controlling shareholders sacrifice their own financial interest in the enterprise for the sake of the corporation or its minority shareholders. It follows that should a controlling shareholder for whatever reason (to avoid entanglement in litigation as plaintiff suggests is here the case or for other personal reasons) elect to sacrifice some part of the value of his stock holdings, the law will not direct him as to how that amount is to be distributed and to whom.

---

10. That is, $25,000,000 value of contingent recovery + $1,300,000 value of MGM Grand name divided by 15,739,173 common shares owned by Kerkorian [= $1.67 per share].

QUESTIONS

1. To what extent does *Jedwab* clarify a board's fiduciary duty with respect to the allocation of merger consideration?
2. Why was it not inequitable to pay the preferred stockholders less than the public common stockholders?
3. In light of the events of the transaction, why might Kerkorian have felt compelled to give the public common stockholders $18 per share?

In re FLS Holdings Inc. Shareholder Litigation
1993 WL 104562 (Del. Ch. 1993)

ALLEN, Chancellor.

The present application is for an order under Chancery Court Rule 23(e) approving the settlement and dismissal of certain stockholder class action claims. The class is comprised of the holders of FLS Holdings, Inc. preferred stock, as of the date of a cash merger between FLS and Kyoei Steel Ltd., an unrelated third party. The claim asserted on behalf of the preferred is against the members of the board of directors of FLS and certain stockholders. The claim is that the price negotiated with Kyoei was not fairly allocated between the preferred stock and the common stock of FLS. The preferred had no right to vote for directors of FLS nor to vote on the merger.

The proposed settlement offers no additional consideration to the preferred. Rather the proponents of the settlement suggest that their efforts in bringing this suit resulted in some additional disclosures in the merger and resulted in some negotiating positions by the defendants that were more favorable to the preferred than would have been taken otherwise.

The proposal is objected to by members of the class holding approximately 20% of the preferred's claims. The objectors charge that the defendants breached duties to them in allocating the merger consideration between the common and preferred stock; that the settlement makes no serious effort to compromise those claims and that it should be rejected.

Those who would seek a court to settle and dismiss claims of absent class members must bear the burden to demonstrate that the proposed settlement is a fair compromise and represents adequate compensation for the claims to be released, considering the apparent strengths and weaknesses of those claims. The proponents of the settlement have not borne their burden on this motion. The motion will therefore be denied.

The 1988 Leveraged Buy-Out

FLS was formed in 1988 through a management affiliated leveraged buy-out of Florida Steel Company. The bankers and investors in this transaction were Goldman

Sachs, and Citibank. FLS purchased 84.5% of the outstanding common stock of Florida Steel for cash, through a tender offer at $50 per share.[1]

FLS had three classes of stock, Class A and Class B Common and Preferred Stock. Only the 500,000 shares of Class A common stock had voting rights. The Class A common shares were distributed as follows: Senior management of Florida Steel, 33.78%; Goldman Sachs, 45.56%; other FLS employees, 14.71%, other investors, 1.37%; Citicorp Capital Investors, 4.3%, Citicorp also held all 61,013 shares of Class B common.

FLS caused Florida Steel to merge with a wholly owned subsidiary of FLS, thereby converting each of the remaining publicly held shares of Florida Steel, into the right to receive one share of FLS preferred stock. Approximately 940,000 shares of Preferred Stock were issued in the back-end merger. The preferred stock had a liquidation preference of $53.33 per share, and a 17.5% dividend, payable in kind until February 1994 and in cash thereafter. As a result of the payment of dividends in kind since the buy-out, there are now 1,600,806 preferred shares outstanding, representing, at original issue prices, an investment of $80 million. The liquidation preference of these shares, including accrued but unpaid payable in kind dividends, is $94.7 million.

This LBO proved to be one of those that did not realize its investors' hopes. Operating results failed to meet expectations; the company incurred heavy losses. After earning net income of $3.04 million in 1990, FLS lost $8.9 million in 1991 and $24.2 million in 1992. By late 1991, FLS was in breach of certain financial covenants in its lending agreement. Its banks entered into agreements with FLS, waiving these breaches and agreeing to defer interest payments until December 1992. In return, FLS agreed to stop paying interest to its bondholders and to restructure the company. In sum, FLS was on the brink of insolvency. FLS management and Goldman Sachs began a world-wide search for potential buyers for the company and began to consider other options, such as filing for bankruptcy protection.

Negotiations to Sell FLS to Kyoei Steel [in 1992]

The highest offer obtained through these efforts was that of Kyoei Steel, Ltd., which approached Goldman Sachs informally and proposed buying all of FLS's common stock for $10 per share ($5 million), all of the preferred for $27 per share ($43.2 million), and repaying all FLS debt at 100 cents on the dollar. Goldman Sachs, who had been retained by the board to handle the matter, told Kyoei's negotiator, Peter Offerman of BT Securities, Inc., that Kyoei was being too generous to the preferred stock and not generous enough to the common stock.[2]

---

1. To finance the purchase, FLS borrowed $180 million from banks; issued $125 million in 14.5% subordinated debentures; and received $25 million in equity from its common stock owners, roughly $16.63 million in cash and shares of Florida Steel, and $8.33 million consisting of waivers by employees of rights under their employment agreements.

2. Let me add an interpretive observation: The negotiator for the board was in a tricky negotiation posture, given the effect that the negotiation might have on the interests of others not present—debt holders and preferred stock. These others might threaten to impede a transaction through court action. Thus the preferred strategy for a buyer would be to pay as high a proportion of the total selling price as possible, to the absent interest holders. So long as the common stock with whom he was negotiating would agree, then the best chance for a completed transaction is achieved in that way. Thus, a buyer in this position has an incentive to offer more than a fair share to the absent party. I mention this because seeing things in this way permits one to interpret the directors' negotiation positions as quite possibly the behavior of persons acting in a fair way despite the fact they were asking that the common be paid more and the preferred less.

Kyoei submitted a written proposal to FLS which doubled the offer for the common stock to $20 per share, ($10 million) while reducing the offer for the preferred stock to $24 per share ($38.4 million). This proposal called for paying all bank debt in full and debentures 95 cents on the dollar. This offer was contingent upon acceptance by 90% of the preferred stock and debenture holders, and apparently contemplated a tender offer for these securities.

Hand-written notes from meetings of the FLS leadership the next day suggest that it was concerned that the allocation between the preferred and common was unfair to the common, and therefore unfair to the directors and their affiliates. The notes state that FLS management discussed the fact that the preferred had "no options" because the common could "decide to sell or not to sell." Notes from an FLS staff meeting reflect concerns that if the transaction is not completed quickly the "preferred will get organized and 'want more'."

At the FLS Board Meeting, the question of the allocation between preferred and common stockholders was discussed and legal counsel reported that the allocation "must be fair." At a second board meeting, the amount of the offer for the equity as a whole was described as inadequate and the split between preferred and common as "not good." Representatives of Goldman Sachs proposed that FLS demand from Kyoei $60 million, with $20 million going to the common and $40 million to the preferred.

Kyoei extended a third offer to FLS, proposing to pay $12.4 million to the common and $38.4 million to the preferred. This offer contemplated a merger and no vote by the preferred stock would be required to complete the transaction.

Goldman continued to negotiate for a higher price for the common stock, apparently seeking $20 million. Eventually a compromise was negotiated, and both parties agreed to a merger between FLS and a wholly owned subsidiary of Kyoei, in exchange for the payment of 100% of the debts owed to banks and bondholders, $38.4 million to the preferred stock and $15 million to the common stock.

Upon completing its due diligence, however, Kyoei apparently discovered $24 million in higher than expected liabilities for environmental clean-up, settlement of a federal criminal and civil investigation, and additional pension costs. Offerman recommended that Kyoei not seek to reduce the price by the full $24 million. He predicted that if Kyoei attempted to do so, FLS would reject the entire deal and attempt a stand alone restructuring in which, in his estimation, the Preferred Stock would receive a substantial equity stake, worth approximately $40 million, while the common stock would receive an equity stake worth roughly $5-10 million.

FLS offered Kyoei a total price reduction of $12.8 million, with a $7.2 million reduction borne by the preferred and $5.6 borne by the residual risk bearing common stock. Kyoei rejected this offer and demanded a $15 million total reduction to which FLS agreed. The additional $2.2 million was deducted solely from the consideration to be paid to the preferred stock. A final further reduction of $400,000 was later agreed to and this amount was borne exclusively by the common stock. The final price received by the common stockholders therefore, was $9 million while the preferred received $29 million.

The common stockholders thus recouped 54% of their cash investment and 36% of their total investment (*i.e.,* including waivers of rights by management to deferred compensation) despite three years of losses that exceeded their equity investment. The preferred stock recouped 62% of the value of the Florida Steel common stock interests they surrendered in the 1988 backend merger. The preferred stockholders had, of course, a legal right to dividends payable in kind at a rate of 17.5%, and payable in cash beginning in 1994. This contracted for return on their investment, which the preferred stockholders earned for over three years, is difficult to value. What is clear, however, is that the proportionate claim of the preferred stock in FLS grew at a 17.5% annual rate, and its investment is greater than that represented by their original $47 million contribution at the time of the merger.

FLS was represented in its negotiations with Kyoei exclusively by directors who either owned large amounts of common stock, or were affiliates of Goldman Sachs and Citicorp. No independent adviser or independent directors' committee was appointed to represent the interests of the preferred stock who were in a conflict of interest situation with the common. The preferred stock did not have a right to vote on the transaction or on the allocation. An opinion was issued by an investment banker, after the merger agreement had been signed, concluding that the allocation was fair to the preferred.

FLS retained Salomon Brothers, Inc. to render an opinion as to the fairness of the Kyoei merger to the preferred stockholders, especially with regard to the fairness of the allocation between the preferred and common stock. FLS paid Salomon Brothers $400,000 for its work. To determine the fairness of the allocation, Salomon examined other transactions in which distressed companies were sold or restructured and the equity value of the company divided between the preferred and common stock. The record does not indicate whether the transactions examined involved arms-length bargaining between representatives of the preferred and common, or whether the common stock controlled these transactions, as in the present case.

Salomon's survey of other restructuring transactions showed that the median share of the total consideration paid to equity holders, received by preferred stockholders in restructurings, was 68.7%. The FLS preferred stock received 75.5% of the total consideration received by equity in the sale to Kyoei. Based upon this comparison, Salomon opined that the allocation of consideration between the preferred and common stock was fair to the preferred stock from a financial point of view.

The Value of the Claims Proposed to be Settled

In allocating the consideration of this merger, the directors, although they were elected by the common stock, owed fiduciary duties to both the preferred and common stockholders, and were obligated to treat the preferred fairly. *See Eisenberg v. Chicago Milwaukee Corp.*, 537 A.2d 1051, 1062 (Del.Ch. 1987); *Jedwab v. MGM Grand Hotels*, 509 A.2d 584, 593-94 (Del.Ch. 1986). That standard is, of course, a somewhat opaque one that, unless procedures are employed that are sufficient in themselves to give reasonable assurance of fairness, may require a reviewing agency to make a highly specific inquiry of the company and the transaction.

In preliminarily assessing plaintiffs' claim, I note first that here no mechanism employing a truly independent agency on the behalf of the preferred was employed before the transaction was formulated. Only the relatively weak procedural protection of an investment banker's *ex post* opinion, was available to support the position that the final allocation was fair. Plaintiffs' expert has also now opined that the allocation was fair to the preferred.

These opinions, while of some weight, in light of the other facts in the record, would not substantially assist in satisfying defendants' burden of showing that the allocation was fair. Defendants may very well meet their burden later in this litigation.

On this motion however, I conclude only that there is a substantial issue that is fairly litigable.

If this case proceeds to an adjudication of the merits of plaintiffs' claims, defendants will bear the burden of proving that the allocation was fair to the preferred.

Value of the Settlement to the Class

Plaintiffs and defendants claim that the settlement provides two benefits to the plaintiff class. First, plaintiffs obtained enhanced disclosure of the terms of the merger and the negotiations surrounding it, and a notice describing their rights to seek judicial appraisal of their shares under 8 *Del.C.* §262. Plaintiffs' claim that these disclosures are of material benefit to the class because class members may use the information in electing the appraisal remedy. Second, plaintiffs' claim that the settlement has produced an allocation of merger consideration which is more favorable to the preferred than it would have otherwise been. The more favorable allocation amounts to a claimed benefit of approximately $1.7 million.[4]

Improved disclosures may certainly prove beneficial to class members and may constitute consideration of a type which will support a settlement of claims. This court has often approved the settlement of very weak stockholder suits, typically involving claims that disinterested directors should be held liable for actions apparently protected by the business judgment rule. When such weak claims are presented, settlement in exchange for the minimal benefit represented by the adoption of therapeutic measures is one relatively cheap way of concluding worthless litigation on a voluntary basis. In the pending case, by contrast, the directors' conduct is subject to review by the standard of entire fairness. Plaintiffs' claims are of arguable merit and the therapeutic measures of the type offered in this case are scant consideration to support their surrender.

Had plaintiffs agreed to settle this litigation in exchange for the payment of $1.7 million to the plaintiff class, that payment would constitute substantial consideration for claims that have an absolute upward bound of $9 million and which, even assuming that they do have merit, are in all likelihood worth substantially less. In this case, however, plaintiffs' claim that the settlement has already conferred this benefit upon the plaintiff class is extremely problematic.

This case is different in a number of respects. Most fundamentally, the alleged benefit to the class consists not of an increased payment to the class, but of the defendants' (alleged) act of *refraining from reducing the allocation to the preferred by an additional $1.7 million*. On the evidence I find no basis to suppose that such restraint occurred or that the settlement of this litigation had anything to do with how that renegotiation proceeded. Focusing simply on the renegotiation, it *cost* the preferred $9.4 million. Perhaps there is a substantial benefit in there, but additional evidence will be necessary to persuade me of that fact.

The class claims are certainly litigable. Should plaintiffs be successful their claims could possibly be worth several million dollars. The consideration offered for the

---

4. The argument in favor of this cash benefit is dubious. Plaintiffs without any specific evidentiary support claim that when Kyoei demanded a $15 million price reduction and defendants acceded to reducing the price by that amount ($5.6m from common $9.4m from preferred) that but for this lawsuit the preferred would have been allotted an even greater portion of this burden.

release of the claims is extremely small, providing some therapeutic measures and no monetary benefit for the class. In addition, the refusal of a large holder of class claims to accept the settlement, combined with its desire to itself facilitate the adjudication of its rights, is, a factor I can properly take into account on this motion.

Though further litigation may well prove plaintiffs' claims to be groundless, that has yet to be done. The proponents of the settlement agreement have failed to meet their burden of establishing that the settlement provides the class with a fair consideration in exchange for the relinquishment of its claims. The court, applying its own business judgment, finds that the settlement is unfair and must be rejected.

QUESTIONS

1. What was the problem with the process used to negotiate and execute the deal with Kyoei?
2. Why did the court apply the entire fairness standard rather than the presumption of the business judgment rule? $ρ ⊂ b T$
3. Is the financial condition of FLS relevant to the legal or economic analysis? If so, how?

HB Korenaes Investments, L.P. v. Marriott Corporation
1993 WL 205040 (Del. Ch.)

ALLEN, Chancellor.

Plaintiffs claim that the proposed distribution of a special dividend to the common stockholders of Marriott Corporation consisting of securities representing a large part of the net worth of that company would, if accomplished, constitute a breach of duty owed to them as holders of Marriott's preferred stock. The transaction is to be voted upon by holders of common stock of the company at a forthcoming shareholders' meeting.

Plaintiffs are four institutional investors who between them have acquired more than 50% of Marriott's only presently issued class of preferred stock, the Series A Cumulative Convertible Preferred Stock. They bring this action seeking to enjoin the payment of the special dividend in question. Defendants include the corporation itself, and the ten individuals who serve as its board of directors. The board includes three members of the Marriott family, which together owns approximately 25.8% of the common stock of Marriott Corporation.

The special dividend was originally announced on October 5, 1992. It engendered controversy. Bondholders of the company objected quickly and with feeling. The proposal has subsequently been modified to assuage some, but not all, of those bondholders. As presently planned, and speaking very generally, if accomplished the transaction will have the effect of splitting Marriott Corporation into two companies. The first of these will be a spin-off company, Marriott International, Inc. which will hold Marriott's lodging, food services and facilities management and senior living services businesses.

The other will be the existing corporation, renamed Marriott Host Corporation, which will retain, either directly or through wholly owned subsidiaries, certain real

estate, and airport, toll road and stadium concessions as well as certain other properties. These assets, allegedly, comprise approximately 33% of Marriott's equity. More
importantly, however, Host will, directly and indirectly, retain responsibility for more
than 85% of Marriott's long-term bond obligations, while International will assume
only 15% of that liability.

This spin-off will be effectuated through the transfer of the spin-off assets to International (presently a wholly owned Marriott subsidiary), followed by a dividend to the
holders of Marriott's common stock of all of the stock of International. It is alleged that
in this spin-off most of Marriott's assets that generate a positive cash flow will be
transferred to International. The value of the assets to be transferred has not yet
been finally determined in the manner required by the certificate of designation
that defines the rights, etc. of the Series A Preferred Stock. The time set for that
valuation has not yet arrived.

The transaction will, of course, transform the capital structure of what is now
Marriott with several important effects upon the preferred and common stockholders.
Currently Marriott is obligated to pay annual dividends on the Series A Preferred
Stock before it may pay any dividend on its common stock. It has regularly paid
the preferred's dividend. On March 15, 1993, however, the company announced
for the first time that, following the special dividend, Host will indefinitely suspend
dividends on its preferred stock.

Moreover, Marriott has announced that dividends of $.07 per share will be paid on
the common stock of International, the same dividend as the common stock of Marriott currently earns. Thus, the transaction can be seen as enabling the common stockholders of Marriott to receive a dividend on their investment in Marriott without
satisfying the requirement that the preferred stockholders receive their preferred
dividends.

Thus, it has been the apparent expectation of all concerned that if and when the
proposed transaction is effectuated no dividends will be paid by Host Marriott on any
stock, but common stock dividends will be paid by International.

The proposed transaction is also said to constitute a breach of a fiduciary duty of
loyalty and care and of the contractual obligations of good faith and fair dealing.

Upon filing the complaint plaintiffs sought expedited treatment leading to a
preliminary injunction hearing prior to the Company's annual meeting then scheduled
for June 1993. This application was granted and discovery was authorized to commence without delay. Defendants moved to dismiss the complaint. That motion has
now been submitted to the court, while discovery continues. This is my decision on
certain aspects of the pending motion to dismiss the amended complaint.

I turn to Count I which asserts that the directors of Marriott owe the holders of
convertible preferred stock "fiduciary duties":

> to act only after receiving and considering all reasonably available material
> information, to act for their benefit, to exercise the highest standards of good faith
> and fair dealing, to act in a disinterested manner and to provide full disclosure of all
> material facts germane to any investment decision which Marriott calls upon
> shareholders to make.

Plaintiffs contend that each of these alleged duties are breached in the proposed
transaction.

The core of the loyalty theory is the claim that the transaction is designed to benefit common stockholders at the expense of the holders of preferred.

I assume for present purposes that plaintiffs can prove, insofar as the holders of preferred stock are concerned, that the proposed transaction is not, "for their benefit" but is for the benefit of the common stock only.

Defendants say that Count I fails to state a claim upon which relief might be granted, because with respect to the proposed transaction, they owe no duty of loyalty to the preferred stock, no duty to act "for their benefit." Thus, they assert that proof of any such purpose or any "unfair" effect would not justify the imposition of liability on fiduciary duty grounds. In so contending defendants assert that with respect to this matter at least, the relationship between the preferred and the issuer is contractual and where the contract between them governs the matter, questions of liability will be determined by contract principles.

Rights of preferred stock are primarily but not exclusively contractual in nature. The special rights, limitations, etc. of preferred stock are created by the corporate charter or a certificate of designation which acts as an amendment to a certificate of incorporation. Thus, to a very large extent, to ask what are the rights of the preferred stock is to ask what are the rights and obligations created contractually by the certificate of designation. *See, e.g., Rothschild International Corp. v. Liggett Group, Inc.,* 474 A.2d 133, 136 (Del. 1984). In most instances, given the nature of the acts alleged and the terms of the certificate, this contractual level of analysis will exhaust the judicial review of corporate action challenged as a wrong to preferred stock.

But the holder of preferred stock is not a creditor of the corporation. Such a holder has no legal right to annual payments of interest, as long term creditors will have, and most importantly has no maturity date with its prospect of capital repayment or remedies for default. In these respects the holder of preferred stock is in the exposed and vulnerable position *vis a vis* the board of directors that all stockholders occupy. Thus, it has been recognized that directors may owe duties of loyalty and care to preferred stock. For example, in a recent case a corporate board, elected by the common stock exclusively, negotiated and recommended to the common stock a cash merger (the preferred had been held to have no right to a class vote). Holders of preferred sued the directors asserting that the allocation of consideration between the common and the preferred was unfair. On a motion under Rule 23(e) to approve a proposed settlement it was held that, in the circumstances, the board had a burden to demonstrate that the apportionment of consideration that it negotiated and presented to the holders of common stock was not unfair to the preferred stock. *See In re FLS Holdings, Inc., Shareholders Litigation,* 1993 WL 104562 (Del.Ch. 1993) (Allen, C.).

In fact, it is often not analytically helpful to ask the global question whether (or to assert that) the board of directors does or does not owe fiduciary duties of loyalty to the holders of preferred stock. The question (or the claim) may be too broad to be meaningful. In some instances (for example, when the question involves adequacy of disclosures to holders of preferred who have a right to vote) such a duty will exist. In others (for example, the declaration of a dividend designed to eliminate the preferred's right to vote) a duty to act for the good of the preferred does not.[4] Thus, the question whether duties of loyalties are implicated by corporate action affecting

---

4. *Cf. Baron v. Allied Artists Picture Corp.,* 337 A.2d 653, 660 (Del.Ch. 1976).

preferred stock is a question that demands reference to the particularities of context to fashion a sound reply.

Of course even where a court concludes that contract principles govern the analysis, the need to address questions of ambiguity as to the scope of rights and duties under the certificate of designation may remain. The cognitive limitations of drafters, imperfect information and the nature of language itself assure that in contract law as well as fiduciary law, good faith disagreements about the nature of duty will arise. Indeed the contract doctrine of an implied covenant of good faith and fair dealing may be thought in some ways to function analogously to the fiduciary concept.

For purposes of this motion to dismiss I accept as true the contention of plaintiffs that the Marriott directors were not in any respect motivated to advance the economic interests of the preferred stock in proposing this transaction to the common stockholders. Beyond that, of course, I accept as true all of the factual allegations of the amended complaint.

Nevertheless, given the terms of the certificate of designation I conclude that the proposed transaction does not implicate or engage the directors' duty of loyalty but must be evaluated under the contractual law governing the special rights and preferences of the preferred. Count I of the amended complaint will therefore be dismissed.

In explaining this conclusion it is only necessary to demonstrate that the tailored terms of the certificate, which define the nature of the property owned, govern the propriety of the proposed transaction. Most important, in this connection, is the fact that the certificate of designation expressly contemplates the payment of a special dividend of the type here involved and supplies a device to protect the preferred stockholders in the event such a dividend is paid. Section 5 of the certificate, provides in part as follows:

> 5. *Conversion Rights.* The holders of shares of Convertible Preferred Stock shall have the right at their option, to convert such shares into shares of Common Stock on the following terms and conditions:'
>
> (a) Shares of Convertible Preferred Stock shall be convertible at any time into fully paid and nonassessable shares of Common Stock at a conversion price of $17.40 per share of Common Stock (the "Conversion Price").
>
> (e) The conversion Price shall be adjusted from time to time as follows: . . . (iv) *In case the Corporation shall, by dividend* or otherwise, *distribute to all holders of its Common Stock . . . assets* (including securities . . .), *the Conversion Price shall be adjusted* so that the same shall equal the price determined by multiplying the Conversion Price in effect immediately prior to the close of business on the date fixed for the determination of stockholders entitled to receive such distribution by a fraction of which the numerator shall be the current market price per share (determined as provided in subsection (vi) below) of the Common Stock on the date fixed for such determination less the then fair market value (as determined by the Board of Directors, whose determination shall be conclusive and shall be described in a statement filed with the transfer agent for the Convertible Preferred Stock) of the portion of the evidences of indebtedness or assets so distributed applicable to one share of Common Stock and the denominator shall be such current market price per share of the Common Stock, such adjustment to become effective immediately prior to the opening of business on the day following the date fixed for the determination of stockholder entitled to receive such distribution.

Thus, the legal obligation of the corporation to the Series A Preferred Stock upon the declaration and payment of an in-kind dividend of securities has been expressly treated and rights created. It is these contractual rights—chiefly the right to convert into common stock now or to gross-up the conversion ratio for future conversions—that the holders of preferred stock possess as protection against the dilution of their shares' economic value through a permissible dividend.

QUESTIONS

1. How did the spinoff transaction adversely affect bondholders and preferred stockholders?
2. What is the relationship between the preferred stock contract and fiduciary duty owed to preferred stockholders?
3. How did the conversion right defeat the claim that the board engaged in a transaction for the benefit of common stockholders only?

NOTES

1. In another opinion on the same case, *HB Korenvaes Investments, L.P. v. Marriott Corp.*, 1993 WL 257422 (Del.Ch.), the court addressed the claim that the suspension of dividends constitutes wrongful coercion designed to force plaintiffs to convert to common stock. The court rejected this argument and distinguished the case from *Eisenberg v. Chicago Milwaukee Corp.* 537 A.2d 1051 (Del.Ch. 1987).

> This court has on occasion enjoined as inequitable and inconsistent with an applicable fiduciary duty, corporate action designed principally to coerce stockholders in the exercise of a choice that the applicable certificate of incorporation, bylaws or statute confers upon them. *See, e.g., Eisenberg v. Chicago Milwaukee Corp.*, 537 A.2d 1051 (Del.Ch. 1987). These cases are premised upon the existence of a fiduciary duty on the part of the corporate directors with respect to the transaction under review. The last of them involved preferred stockholders to whom a tender offer had been extended by the Company. As an alternative holding this court held that a gratuitous statement by the Company concerning a plan to seek delisting of the preferred, constituted an inappropriate effort to coerce acceptance of the Company's offer. *See Eisenberg,* 537 A.2d at 1062. Plaintiffs rely upon this precedent to argue that the announcement of the discontinuation of preferred stock dividends has an analogous effect and is analogously a breach of duty.
>
> Plaintiffs are, I believe, incorrect in this. The critical differences between this case as it now appears and *Eisenberg* are several. First, that case was treated as a fiduciary duty case, not as a case involving, as this one does, the construction and interpretation of rights and duties set forth in the certificate of designation. In this instance Marriott has a right to suspend dividend payments and in the event that that should happen, the preferred's protections are in the contract and are several: most importantly, the dividends are cumulative and enjoy a liquidation preference; in addition, the redemption price is adjusted to include unpaid dividends; and prolonged suspension of dividends gives the preferred the right to elect two directors. Finally, the preferred may, in all events, be converted into common stock; and, as I construe the certificate, there is necessarily implied a restriction on the proportion of net worth that may be distributed by special dividend. These contractual protections are a recognition of the risk that dividends might not be paid currently. These protections are substantial. The correlative of the fact that

Marriott has a duty to respect them is the conclusion that it has a right to discontinue dividends when it observes them.

Secondly, unlike *Eisenberg* it cannot persuasively be urged, at this stage, that the discontinuation of dividends is not itself a prudent, business-driven decision. Thus, assuming that a corporation owes to the holders of its preferred stock the same implied duty of good faith that is present in every contractual relationship,[15] as I believe to be the case, the circumstances as they appear could not be construed as justifying the preliminary conclusion that the suspension of dividend payments is not a good faith business decision. Host is expected to have no net income, even though it will have substantial assets. Plaintiffs' suggestion that Host could, in the circumstances, borrow money to pay preferred dividends presents a classic business judgment issue; that such a possibility may exist does not constitute a persuasive argument that the suspension of dividend payments was itself undertaken in bad faith.

Thus, while the suspension of dividends may exert a powerful influence upon the decision whether holders of preferred stock will exercise rights to convert or not, I can see in that effect, at this time, no violation of any implied right to that degree of good faith that every commercial contractor is entitled to expect from those with whom she contracts.

Orban v. Field
1997 WL 153831 (Del. Ch. 1997)

ALLEN, Chancellor.

This is a stockholders' suit brought by certain holders of common stock of Office Mart Holdings Corp. ("Office Mart"). The suit arises out of a series of transactions culminating in a June 23, 1992 stock-for-stock merger between Office Mart and a subsidiary of Staples, Inc. The first of the transactions was a November 15, 1991 recapitalization in which, in exchange for forgiveness of principal and interest of outstanding notes, Office Mart creditors accepted a package of securities including common stock warrants and a new Series C Preferred stock. The second step was board action of May 1992 facilitating the exercise of certain warrants held by the holders of preferred stock. The concluding transaction was the merger with Staples. In that merger, various classes of Office Mart preferred stock were entitled to liquidation preferences that together exceeded the value of the consideration paid. Thus, the Office Mart common stock received no consideration in the merger. The merger

---

15. *See Merrill v. Crothall-American, Inc.,* 606 A.2d 96, 101 (Del. 1992) ("At common law the duty of fair dealing and good faith was deemed impliedly to be a part of contracts of every kind"); *Katz v. Oak Industries, Inc.,* 508 A.2d 873 (Del.Ch. 1986); *Pittsburgh Terminal Corp. v. Baltimore & Ohio R. Co.,* 680 F.2d 933, 941 (3d Cir. 1982) (holding that failing to notify convertible debenture holders of a special dividend prior to the record date, thereby frustrating their right to participate in the distribution through conversion violated an "implied covenant that neither party will do anything which will destroy . . . the right of the other party to receive the fruits of the contract"); E. Allan Farnsworth, *Farnsworth on Contracts* §7.17 (1990); *Restatement (Second) of Contracts* §205 (1981).

was an arm's-length transaction and it is not contended in this suit that the price paid by Staples was not a fair price or the best price reasonably available.

It is asserted that the Office Mart board breached its duty to the common stock by facilitating steps that enabled the holders of preferred stock to exercise warrants that enabled the preferred to overcome a practical power that the common held to impede the closing of the merger. This claim in essence asserts that the board, which was controlled by holders of preferred stock, exercised corporate power against the common and in favor of the preferred and, thus, breached a duty of loyalty to the common.

I conclude that there is no evidence upon which a fact finder could conclude that the board's actions in facilitating the exercise by holders of preferred stock of their legal rights to exercise warrants represented a disloyal act towards the common stock. Even assuming, as I do, that in facilitating the exercise of the warrants in these circumstances (where the warrants were used to overcome Mr. Orban's resistance to the merger) the board has a burden to establish either the reasonableness of its actions or its fairness, the record is, in my judgment, entirely consistent with that conclusion and wholly inconsistent with the opposite conclusion. [The defendants' summary judgment motion is granted.]

George Orban, the principal plaintiff in this action, founded Office Mart in 1987; served as its CEO until 1989; and as a director until March 1992. From 1987 to 1992, Office Mart developed and operated a chain of ten "WORKplace" office supply superstores in and around Tampa, Florida. The company was, however, never well capitalized. That fact became rather quickly apparent when the company sought to expand into the California market in 1988, from which it was forced to retreat.

Capital structure: Initially, the company was capitalized largely with equity in the form of voting preferred stock from institutional investors. Mr. Orban, who in this litigation, characterizes himself as a "venture capitalist," invested only approximately $15,000 in exchange for which he received all of the common stock. (Later other employees of the firm came to hold modest amounts of the common as well). The substantial capital came in several tranches from financial institutions. 2,422,750 shares of Series A preferred stock were issued in 1987 to raise $2,950,000 in initial capital. In May 1988, an additional $17,084,080 was raised by the private placement of 6,833,632 shares of Series B preferred stock.

All classes of equity voted together. Mr. Orban was the largest holder of common stock,[1] however, he held only 14.32% of the total voting power. Series A and Series B preferred stockholders held 22.59% and 63.18%, respectively, of the company's total voting rights. Both classes of preferred stock were convertible into common stock and entitled to vote on an as-converted basis, both had anti-dilution rights and possessed liquidation preferences payable in the event of a merger.[2] The common stock, of course, had no such rights.

---

1. Mr. Orban's 1,417,500 shares of common stock, purchased for less than $15,000, together with the 74,724 shares of common stock held by the other plaintiffs to this action, constituted 96% of the company's common stock. In addition to common stock, Mr. Orban held 82,500 shares of Series A preferred stock through an investment vehicle, Orban Partners.

2. In the event of a liquidation or merger, Series A shareholders would receive the return of their original investment and Series B shareholders would be entitled to recover their original investment and 9% interest, compounded annually, before any distributions could be made to common stockholders.

Continuing need for long term capital: Relatively early on, by June 1989, Office Mart's board was forced to conclude that it either had to find additional capital to pursue an aggressive growth strategy, or had to sell the company. At that point, Mr. Orban resigned as CEO and Stephen Westerfield agreed to assume the duties of CEO. Mr. Westerfield began taking steps to address these issues. The investment banking firm of Donaldson Lufkin & Jenrette was hired to assist in these efforts, but no potential investors or acquirors were identified and the financial position of the company continued to worsen.

Recognizing that it would be difficult for Office Mart to borrow necessary capital from commercial lenders, the company began to consider means to attract additional capital from the company's current investors. In April 1990, a group of Series B stockholders provided the company with a $5.2 million line of credit in consideration of the issuance by the company of its 13% secured notes and warrants to acquire 40% of the company's fully diluted equity shares, exercisable at a price of $1.39 per share. The notes matured in three years but could be prepaid at par plus accrued interest.

Office Mart began to draw down its credit facility shortly after its establishment. The company had difficulty from the beginning in meeting the interest payments on the debt. In order to ameliorate this situation, an agreement was reached with creditors pursuant to which the company's interest obligations were deferred, in consideration of the grant of additional common stock warrants. The warrants covered common stock equal to 1.75% of total equity for each quarter of interest deferred, for a maximum of up to 10.575% of total equity. Despite the credit facility and deferred interest agreement, Office Mart continued to have financial difficulties throughout 1991.

The recapitalization: On September 5, 1991, Mr. Westerfield recommended that a recapitalization plan be adopted in order to eliminate the debt burden on the company's balance sheet. During a telephone meeting, Mr. Westerfield expressed his opinion that the recapitalization was necessary for the company to continue as a going concern; the board approved a proposed recapitalization plan at that time.

The material elements of the recapitalization plan: First, a new senior, non-convertible Series C Senior Cumulative Redeemable Preferred Stock was created.[5] In exchange for 5.2 million shares of the Series C preferred stock and 2,136,976 new shares of common stock (equal to more than half of all then outstanding common stock and equal to 10% of the fully diluted equity of the company), the holders of the debt agreed to its cancellation and released the company from the repayment of the $5.2 million principal amount and $607,800 in accrued interest. Finally, the company reduced the exercise price on the warrants issued to the creditors from $1.39 to $0.75 per share.

Mr. Orban voted in favor of the recapitalization as a member of the Board and, subsequently, in his capacity as a Series A preferred stockholder.

---

5. In the event of a liquidation or merger of the company, the new Series C preferred stock would entitle its owners to receive an initial preference of $7.5 million and a secondary preference of $1.5 million to be paid only after $12 million had been distributed to the A and B preferred stockholders. After the satisfaction of the secondary preference, the remaining proceeds would first go to the A and B preferred stockholders in order to meet their still unpaid liquidation preferences. The common stockholders would not receive any distributions until all of these preferences had been satisfied in full.

As a result of the recapitalization plan, the following changes in the company's capital structure were to be made. As to Mr. Orban, his combined ownership of common and preferred stock was diluted from 13.27% to 2.54%. As to the common stockholders as a group, since the total number of shares of common stock outstanding had been increased from 1,548,411 to 3,685,387 shares, the percentage of voting power held by the holders of the pre-recap common was reduced from 14% to less than 3%. As to the former creditors, the recapitalization was structured to provide them with a potential for 50% voting interest in the company, with the Series A and B preferred stockholders now capable of voting 10.54% and 36.92% of the equity respectively, and with the remainder 3% voted by the common stockholders.

Here is where things get a little complicated: As mentioned above, the Class A and B preferred stockholders, but not the common stockholders, had anti-dilution rights. These rights were triggered by the creation and issuance of the new Series C stock. In order to have the recapitalization comply with the anti-dilution provisions, it would be necessary to increase the total authorized shares to over 55 million. Since Office Mart had only 25 million authorized shares of which 10.7 million were outstanding, this would require an amendment to the corporate charter which would be a nuisance, but not a practical problem since the institutions owning the vast preponderance of the Series A and B preferred stock could control the vote of all classes of stock. Instead of this step, however, the Board decided to *meet the anti-dilution obligation by proportionately reducing the number of shares of each class of stock outstanding*. As part of this plan, the Board asked Mr. Orban to surrender certificates for 874,708 of his common stock shares to the company for cancellation. Mr. Orban, however, delayed in complying and later refused to surrender the requested stock certificates. Office Mart's Board took no immediate action to remedy this problem which only became significant many months later when Office Mart and Staples entered into a merger agreement.

Acquisition discussions: Staples: The merger negotiations with Staples occurred quickly, beginning with discussions between Mr. Westerfield and the CEO of Staples, Thomas Stemberg. On February 20, Stemberg told Mr. Westerfield that Staples was interested in acquiring Office Mart. The deal was then quickly negotiated.

The material terms of the February 22 letter agreement: Office Mart would be acquired by Staples in a stock for stock transaction, providing Office Mart shareholders with substantially greater consideration: 1,093,750 shares of Staples common stock, valued at $35 million as of February 21.[10]

Staples demanded a contract clause requiring that each class of Office Mart stock approve the transaction with a 90% vote [which was required for favorable accounting and tax treatment].

On February 21 and 22, telephonic meetings were held by the Office Mart Board to discuss Staples' proposal. Mr. Orban was not involved in the discussions because he was in Europe at the time and could not be reached. The Board unanimously approved the proposed agreement. The Board concluded, based on two years of searching for an acquiror, that the proposal was superior to any other potential deals, in terms of the

---

10. As of February 22, the cumulative preferences of the Series A, B, and C preferred stock, equal to approximately $35,062,470, were greater than the merger consideration contemplated on that date.

amount of consideration received, and had the additional benefit that it would likely result in fewer employee lay-offs than would alternatives. Mr. Orban was present at a February 25 meeting of the Board when it ratified all of the actions taken in entering into the letter agreement. The minutes from that meeting state that the Board "unanimously agreed that the merger with Staples was in the Company's best interests and that the terms were fair."

[As a part of the merger negotiation, Staples required that] the parties had to agree upon a stock allocation date upon which to determine the proportionate distribution of the Staples shares to Office Mart stockholders. Due to the fact that the total consideration was of less value than the total preferred stock preferences, as of the date of the letter agreement, this issue was particularly important to the common stockholders. The common stockholders could only receive merger consideration if the value of the Staples shares exceeded $35,062,470—the total amount of preferences to which the preferred were entitled. (did not)

Dispute with Mr. Orban: In the interim between the letter agreement and the signing of the definitive merger agreement, Mr. Orban began to voice his objections to the deal in which the common stock would receive nothing. A dispute between the company and Mr. Orban, with regard to the pre-recapitalization stock certificates still held by Mr. Orban, provided him with a lever. As noted above, Staples conditioned its offer on the 90% approval of each class of Office Mart stock. The institutional investors who owned the preferred stock owned common stock or warrants sufficient to control a 90% vote, but because of the failure of the company to complete either the pro-rata reduction of outstanding shares or the increase in authorized stock necessary to fully satisfy the Series A and B anti-dilution rights, it was not clear that Mr. Orban did not still control more than 10% of the common stock. Thus, Staples became concerned that Mr. Orban could be able to vote more than 10% of the outstanding common stock against the merger since he had never returned the requested shares to the company for cancellation.[15]

In order to remedy this problem, members of the Board met with Mr. Orban. It is clear that negotiations ensued in which Mr. Orban attempted to extract a payment of $4 million from the company in exchange for his agreement to support the merger. The Board, however, was unwilling to enter into serious negotiations with Mr. Orban regarding the allocation of the merger consideration. Shortly after this meeting, Mr. Orban resigned from the Board.

Dilution of Mr. Orban's common stock interest: Instead of continuing negotiations with Mr. Orban, the Board removed the impediment to the closure of the transaction by facilitating the exercise of warrants to acquire common stock by the Series A and B stockholders.

Several steps were required to effectuate this readjustment of proportionate ownership. First, the company's certificate of incorporation had to be amended to increase the authorized common stock from 25 to 56 million and preferred stock shares from

---

15. In fact, Mr. Orban would have held more than 10% of the common stock, regardless of whether he had returned the pre-recapitalization certificates, unless the Series C preferred stockholders exercised a portion of their warrants to purchase common stock. But either the pro rata reduction in outstanding shares or an amendment authorizing the issuance of more shares was necessary to fully allow for the satisfaction of the anti-dilution rights.

15 to 16.175 million. Second, to compensate for the issuance of additional shares, the Board adjusted the conversion ratio of the Series A and B and proportionately increase the number of warrants held by the holders of Series C preferred.[18] Third, the Board proportionately reduced the exercise price of the warrants from $.75 to $.28726 in order to maintain the total exercise price of $6.4 million. Finally, the Board authorized the redemption of 2,089,714 shares held by Series C preferred stockholders, on a non-pro rata basis. In doing so, the company extended sufficient consideration to the Series C holders ($3,013,995) to enable them to exercise warrants to permit them, as a group, to hold more than 90% of Office Mart's outstanding common stock. The aggregate effect of these steps was to assure that Mr. Orban was entitled to vote less than 10% of the company's common stock.

The merger: When Office Mart and Staples entered into the definitive merger agreement on May 29, 1992, the agreement received the approval of 90% of each class of outstanding stock. The 1,093,750 shares of Staples common stock were worth a total of $31,992,188. That amount was used to allocate the merger proceeds to be distributed to each class of Office Mart stock in accord with the preferences of the preferred stockholders.

Since the merger consideration was insufficient to satisfy all of the contractual preferences of Office Mart's preferred stockholders, Mr. Orban and the other common stockholders received no proceeds. It might be noted, however, that Mr. Orban would have received no proceeds from the merger even if the recapitalization and related transactions had never occurred.

Mr. Orban filed this lawsuit challenging the fairness of the transactions which resulted in the dilution of his common stock interest in order to facilitate a merger in which only the preferred stockholders received consideration.

Analysis

Plaintiffs contend that the Board breached its fiduciary duty of loyalty to the common stockholders by facilitating the exercise of legal rights of preferred stockholders in transactions aimed at eliminating the leverage of the common stockholders by diluting their ownership interest below 10%.[23] The basic theory of Mr. Orban's case is that although the common stock was practically under water (i.e., valueless in a liquidation context) as of the spring of 1992, when evaluating the merger consideration in relation to the preferred stock preferences, *the pooling provision requiring a 90% approval vote of each class of stock gave Mr. Orban stock a certain value.* That value was destroyed when the Board took actions to assist the preferred stockholders to exercise their warrants, diluting the plaintiffs' common stock interest below 10%.

In response, defendants contend that the contested actions taken by the Board did not constitute any breach of fiduciary duty because they were legal and necessary to effectuate a merger in the best interest of the company. Further, defendants argue that the business judgment rule should apply to all of the challenged acts of the Board

---

18. To protect the right of Series C holders to exercise warrants sufficient to own 40% of the company in common stock, the company issued additional warrants entitling them to acquire 22,316,976 shares of common stock instead of only 8,547,906 shares.

23. There is no claim that the Board engaged in fraud or that the merger itself was not in the best interests of the corporation.

because the directors neither stood on both sides of the transactions nor received distinct personal benefits from such transactions. *See, e.g., Cede & Co. v. Technicolor, Inc.,* 634 A.2d 345, 362 (Del. 1993); *Aronson v. Lewis,* 473 A.2d 805, 812 (Del. 1984). According to defendants, all of the challenged acts of the Board were approved by a fully informed majority of disinterested directors and then ratified by an informed majority of the stockholders.

For purposes of this motion for summary judgment, I will assume that the business judgment rule is not applicable to the actions challenged by Mr. Orban's breach of fiduciary duty claim. Unquestionably in this instance the board of directors exercised corporate power—most pointedly in authorizing a non-pro-rata redemption of preferred shares for the purpose of funding the exercise by holders of preferred stock of warrants to buy common stock. That act was directed *against* the common stock who found themselves with a certain leverage because of the requirements for pooling treatment. A board may certainly deploy corporate power against its own shareholders in some circumstances—the greater good justifying the action—but when it does, it should be required to demonstrate that it acted both in good faith and reasonably. *See Unocal Corp. v. Mesa Petroleum Co.,* 493 A.2d 946 (Del. 1985). The burden is upon defendants, the party moving for summary judgment, to show that their conduct was taken in good faith pursuit of valid ends and was reasonable in the circumstances.

While such a test is inevitably one that must be applied in the rich particularity of context, it is not inconsistent with summary adjudication where no material facts are in dispute or disputed facts may be assumed in favor of non-movant. In my opinion, the record established, satisfies the defendants' burden.

As a preliminary matter, it is important to note that there is no evidence, or even remaining allegation, that the November recapitalization was part of a scheme to deprive the common stockholders of consideration in the subsequent merger. The recapitalization was legally effectuated by the Board, validly altering the existing ownership structure of the company. Certainly, when viewed as an isolated event, the recapitalization was fair, authorized appropriately, and if it were to be tested under a fairness test, it would satisfy that standard.

The subsequent conduct of the Board, while requiring a more involved analysis, was, in my opinion, fair as a matter of law as well.

Duty of loyalty: Dilution of Mr. Orban's common stock interest: Once Orban attempted to use a potential power to deprive the transaction of pooling treatment, the Board was inevitably forced to decide whether it would support the common stock's (Mr. Orban's) effort to extract value from the preferred position or whether it would seek to accomplish the negotiated transaction, which it believed to be the transaction at the highest available price.

Certainly in some circumstances a board may elect (subject to the corporation's answering in contract damages) to repudiate a contractual obligation where to do so provides a net benefit to the corporation. To do so may in some situations be socially efficient. *See, e.g.,* Richard Craswell, *Contract Remedies, Renegotiation, and the Theory of Efficient Breach,* 61 S. Cal. L. Rev. 629 (1988). But it would be bizarre to take this fact of legal life so far as to assert, as Mr. Orban must, that the Board had a duty to common stock to refrain from recognizing the corporation's legal obligations to its other classes of voting securities.

To resolve this situation, the Board decided not to negotiate with Mr. Orban, but rather to effectuate the transaction as intended, respecting the preferential rights of the preferred stockholders. In my opinion, it cannot be said that the Board breached a duty of loyalty in making this decision. Whereas the preferred stockholders had existing legal preferences, the common stockholders had no legal right to a portion of the merger consideration under Delaware law or the corporate charter. The Staples' transaction appeared reasonably to be the best available transaction. Mr. Orban's threat to impede the realization of that transaction by the corporation was thwarted by legally permissible action that was measured and appropriate in the circumstances.

Based on the foregoing, defendants' motion for summary judgment is granted.

QUESTIONS

1. What was the financial statement of the company at the time of the merger?
2. What was the total liquidation value for all of the preferred stock in relation to the merger consideration? What does this say about the value of the common stock?
3. What standard of review did the court apply? Why?
4. The board used corporate power to take an overtly hostile action against a major common shareholder. In what way was this action found to be not inequitable?
5. With respect to the equities of this case, did the court achieve the right result?

Equity-Linked Investors, L.P. v. Adams
705 A.2d 1040 (Del. Ch. 1997)

ALLEN, Chancellor.

The case now under consideration involves a conflict between the financial interests of the holders of a convertible preferred stock with a liquidation preference, and the interests of the common stock. The conflict arises because Genta Inc. is on the lip of insolvency and in liquidation it would probably be worth substantially less than the $30 million liquidation preference of the preferred stock. Thus, if the liquidation preference of the preferred were treated as a liability of Genta, the firm would certainly be insolvent now. Yet Genta, a bio-pharmaceutical company that has never made a profit, does have several promising technologies in research and there is some ground to think that the value of products that might be developed from those technologies could be very great.[1] Were that to occur, naturally, a large part of the "upside" gain would accrue to the benefit of the common stock, in equity the residual owners of the firm's net cash flows. But since the current net worth of the company would be put at risk in such an effort—or more accurately would continue at risk—if Genta continues to try to develop these opportunities, any loss that may eventuate will in effect fall, not on the common stock, but on the preferred stock.

---

1. Were one highly confident that all available information about those prospects was widely available and that non-public capital markets were highly efficient, one would be skeptical that a disjunction between liquidation value and management's envisioned long-term value could exist. Very good information about these research properties is not publicly available, however, and the market for bank loans or small private placements is surely imperfectly efficient. In all events the law admits of the possibility of such disjunction.

The Genta board sought actively to find a means to continue the firm in operation so that some chance to develop commercial products from its promising technologies could be achieved. It publicly announced its interest in finding new sources of capital. The holders of the preferred stock, relatively few institutional investors, were seeking a means to cut their losses, which meant, in effect, liquidating Genta and distributing most or all of its assets to the preferred. The contractual rights of the preferred stock did not, however, give the holders the necessary legal power to force this course of action on the corporation. Negotiations held between Genta's management and representatives of the preferred stock with respect to the rights of the preferred came to an unproductive and somewhat unpleasant end in January 1997.

Shortly thereafter, Genta announced that a third party source of additional capital had been located and that an agreement had been reached that would enable the corporation to pursue its business plan for a further period. The evidence indicates that at the time set for the closing of that transaction, Genta had available sufficient cash to cover its operations for only one additional week. A petition in bankruptcy had been prepared by counsel.

This suit by a lead holder of the preferred stock followed the announcement of the loan transaction. Plaintiff is Equity-Linked Investors, one of the institutional investors that holds Genta's Series A preferred stock. Equity-Linked also holds a relatively small amount of Genta's common stock, which it received as a dividend on its preferred. The suit challenges the transaction in which Genta borrowed on a secured basis some $3,000,000 and received other significant consideration from Paramount Capital Asset Management, Inc., a manager of the Aries Fund (together referred to as "Aries") in exchange for a note, warrants exercisable into half of Genta's outstanding stock, and other consideration. The suit seeks an injunction or other equitable relief against this transaction.

While *from a realistic or finance perspective,* the heart of the matter is the conflict between the interests of the institutional investors that own the preferred stock and the economic interests of the common stock, *from a legal perspective,* the case has been presented as one on behalf of the common stock, or more correctly on behalf of all holders of equity securities. The legal theory of the case, as it was tried, was that the Aries transaction was a "change of corporate control" transaction that placed upon Genta special obligations—"Revlon duties"—which the directors failed to satisfy.

While the facts out of which this dispute arises indisputably entail the imposition by the board of (or continuation of) economic risks upon the preferred stock which the holders of the preferred did not want, and while this board action was taken for the benefit largely of the common stock, those facts do not constitute a breach of duty. While the board in these circumstances could have made a different business judgment,[2] in my opinion, it violated no duty owed to the preferred in not doing so. The special protections offered to the preferred are contractual in nature. The corporation

---

2. *See Credit Lyonnais Bank Nederland, N.V. v. Pathe Communications Corp.,* 1991 WL 277613 at n.55 (Del.Ch.) (where foreseeable financial effects of a board decision may importantly fall upon creditors as well as holders of common stock, as where corporation is in the vicinity of insolvency, an independent board may consider impacts upon all corporate constituencies in exercising its good faith business judgment for benefit of the "corporation"); *Orban v. Field,* 1997 WL 153831 (Del.Ch.) (board breached no duty to "underwater" common by facilitating an arm's length merger over their objection that, as a practical matter benefitted voting preferred stock.).

is, of course, required to respect those legal rights. But, aside from the insolvency point just alluded to, generally it will be the duty of the board, where discretionary judgment is to be exercised, to prefer the interests of common stock—as the good faith judgment of the board sees them to be—to the interests created by the special rights, preferences, *etc.*, of preferred stock, where there is a conflict. *See Katz v. Oak Industries, Inc.,* 508 A.2d 873, 879 (Del.Ch. 1986). The facts of this case, as they are explained below, do not involve any violation by the board of any special right or privilege of the Series A preferred stock, nor of any residual right of the preferred as owners of equity.

That is the heart of this matter. But the case has been presented, not as a preferred stock case, but as a "Revlon" case. The plaintiff now purports to act as a holder of common stock. In effect, the plaintiff says: "Certainly the board can raise funds to try to realize its long-term business plan of developing commercial products from the company's research, (even though we holders of preferred stock are bearing the risk of it), but if the financing it arranges constitutes a 'change in corporate control,' then it must proceed in a way that satisfies the relevant legal test". Plaintiff argues that the board did not satisfy the relevant legal test because, it says, defendants did not search for the best deal. Specifically, the board did not ask the holders of the preferred stock what they would have paid for the consideration given by Genta to Aries. The preferred, plaintiff says, would have "paid more" and that *would have benefited the common or all equity*.

For the reasons set forth below, I conclude that the directors of Genta were independent with respect to the Aries transaction, acted in good faith in arranging and committing the company to that transaction, and, in the circumstances faced by them and the company, were well informed of the available alternatives to try to bring about the long-term business plan of the board. In my opinion, they breached no duty owed to the corporation or any of the holders of its equity securities.

The Company: Genta was started in 1988 by Dr. Thomas Adams who has served since as its CEO and Chairman. It is in the bio-pharmaceutical business with its principal facility in San Diego. It has three components. First, it owns various intellectual property rights with respect to a genetic research area known as "antisense". Its antisense activities involve research, development, and testing directed towards developing a treatment for certain cancers. It has developed no commercial products from its intellectual properties. Second, through a wholly owned subsidiary, JBL Scientific Inc., Genta manufactures generic chemicals, pharmaceuticals, and intermediate products used by bio-pharmaceutical companies, including its own antisense business. It has a positive cash flow. Thirdly, Genta owns a 50% interest in a joint venture with SkyePharma PLC, which is involved in the development of a new oral drug delivery technology. It has not yet produced a positive cash flow. Indeed, both the antisense and drug delivery products are still entirely at the development stage. The company has never made a profit and has expended almost $100 million on research, development, and overhead since its founding. While this sounds bleak, nevertheless, it is the case that some of its technologies, if they could be developed into marketable products, would be exceptionally useful and valuable.

Capital Structure: As of January 1997, the capital structure of Genta comprised 39,991,626 shares of common stock; 528,100 shares of Series A preferred stock; and 1,424 shares of Series C preferred stock outstanding. The original investment by the common stock had been about $58 million. The Series A preferred had originally invested $30 million. Something less than $10 million had been raised from later classes of preferred, much of which had subsequently been converted to common stock.

The Series A preferred stock was issued in 1993 at $50 per share. It carries a $50 per share liquidation premium ($30 million in total). It had a dividend paid in common stock for the first two years and earns a $5 per share cumulative dividend, payable if, as, and when declared for subsequent years. In the event of a "fundamental change," holders of Series A preferred stock would have an option to have their shares redeemed by the company at $50 per share, plus accrued dividends. Among events that would constitute a "fundamental change" would be a delisting of Genta stock on the Nasdaq. More important for this case, Genta was contractually obligated to redeem the Series A shares on September 23, 1996 with cash or common stock and, if common stock, to use its best efforts to arrange a public underwriting of the common stock. This obligation, and the factors which prevented the redemption from occurring, occasioned the long negotiation with the holders of the preferred stock discussed below.

In addition to the foregoing, the preferred had certain governance rights. For example, the holders were entitled to notice of board meetings and were to be given rights to inspect corporate books and visit and observe board meetings.

Chronic Financial Problems: The lack of a product that generates substantial positive cash flows, coupled with an active research and development agenda, has lead to a notable (later, a somewhat desperate) search for sources of new investment capital.

By the spring of 1996, it became quite apparent that as of September the company would have insufficient cash to redeem the preferred with cash and, that while common stock would be available, the company's good faith efforts to arrange a firm commitment underwriting of that stock would in all likelihood have no reasonable prospect of success. Genta's board retained Alex. Brown & Sons to advise and assist the company in dealing with its inability to provide either cash or an assured under-writing of its common stock. In addition, the company asked Alex. Brown to attempt to locate potential sources of equity financing for Genta and to participate in negotiations with SkyePharma.

Series A Committee Organized: In July 1996, plaintiff and five other investors holding Series A stock created the Series A Preferred Ad Hoc Committee to act as a bargaining agent with the company. The Committee was intensely interested in getting some return on the Series A and, no doubt, was interested in slowing or stopping the losses that the holders were implicitly realizing as the company continued to lose money.

At the first meeting between the committee and the company (July 1996), Alex. Brown proposed for discussion a three part restructuring. Two elements of that proposal involved the sale of the antisense and JBL businesses. The third part of the proposal involved the sale of a *controlling block* of Genta stock to SkyePharma, in exchange for SkyePharma's interest in the joint venture. Under this proposal, the obligation to the preferred stock would be satisfied and the common stock would continue to have an equity interest in Genta, which would continue to develop the intellectual property in the joint venture.

On August 19, 1996, the three part restructuring proposal was formally presented to the Series A committee by Alex. Brown. As discussed above, the plan included the sale or spin-off of the two businesses and the SkyePharma proposal, in which the Series A holders would convert their shares into a minority block of Genta's common stock, with SkyePharma becoming Genta's controlling shareholder. The proportionate interest of the pre-existing Genta common stockholders would be severely diluted as a result. The Series A holders did not accept this proposal.

The prospect of bankruptcy thus was discussed. According to a later Alex. Brown report to the Genta board, the Series A committee took the position that the preferred would "wait and see if [Genta would] run out of money and then get [delisted]. . . ." A delisting would give the preferred stock the legal right to the liquidation preference, allowing them to place the company into bankruptcy.

Multiple Track Investigations: During October, Alex. Brown continued to work on a restructuring proposal, scheduling a meeting for October 31 to update the Series A committee on its ongoing efforts. During this same period, Dr. Adams began new efforts to seek equity financing for the company. To assist in this search, LBC Capital Resources was retained and told that Genta was interested in raising between $10-12 million. Further, Dr. Adams informed LBC that the decision to seek equity financing, while continuing the restructuring negotiations, had the support of a majority of the board, but was opposed by two outside directors and Genta's Chief Financial Officer.

On October 22, Genta issued another press release concerning its financial position, which like the August press release, stated that Genta was "currently seeking additional capital." LBC solicited interest broadly. Of fifteen companies contacted, five responded. The five were Aries, Susquehanna, Promethian Investment Group, Cambridge Partners, and Loeb Partners. Dr. Adams arranged meetings with the latter three companies for October 31 and November 1.

Genta's worsening financial situation was widely recognized in the investment community. On November 14, Genta issued a Form 10-Q stating that:

> The Company will run out of its existing cash resources in December of 1996. Substantial additional sources of financing will be required in order for the Company to continue its planned operations thereafter. . . . If such funding is unavailable, the Company will be required to consider [various alternatives] . . . including, discontinuing its operations, liquidation or seeking protection under the federal bankruptcy laws.

On November 18, Genta's common stock price closed at $.31 per share. As a result, on November 19, Nasdaq announced that Genta's common stock would be delisted unless by December 3 it submitted a plan with respect to how it would comply with Nasdaq's listing requirements concerning net worth. Such a delisting would effectively bring to an end management's efforts to exploit the corporation's intellectual property.

On the LBC front, by the end of November, LBC was only pursuing negotiations with Aries because no other potential investors remained interested. A meeting of representatives from Genta and Aries was scheduled. In preparation for the meeting, Dr. Adams discussed with Mr. Mongiardo of LBC the potential impact of an equity investment on the rights of the Series A stockholders. Adams calculated that up to 60 million shares of common stock could be issued without triggering the "fundamental change" provision in the Series A designations which, if triggered, would obligate the company to repurchase such shares. In addition, prior to the meeting, LBC provided Dr. Rosenwald of Aries with requested information concerning the rights of the Series A holders and the effect that the potential delisting from Nasdaq would have on Genta.

Aries Proposal: Dr. Rosenwald presented the following financing proposal to Genta at the November 26 meeting. Aries would lend Genta between $5-6 million in exchange for a secured note plus securities consisting of a new class of preferred stock (special preferred stock with embedded alternative rights convertible into common stock at $.10 per share) and warrants to buy common stock at an exercise price of $0.10 per share. The letter setting forth this proposal stipulated that Aries's immediate control of the Genta board was a non-negotiable term of the proposed transaction.

Adams responded that Genta sought (1) a two tiered financing (i.e., some immediate cash infusion), (2) a higher exercise price on any warrants ($.25 per share) granted in consideration of the second tier financing, and (3) a more limited board presence, permitting Aries to designate only one director and two observers. Two days later, Aries agreed to the two tiered financing structure and a $0.20 second tranche exercise price for the warrants. It continued to insist upon a contract right to designate a majority of the board.

December Negotiations: On December 2, the Genta board met again to evaluate alternatives. At that meeting, Mr. Gineris of Alex. Brown was included in a discussion concerning the impact that a $6 million investment would have on the value of Genta's common stock if 6 million shares were granted as the consideration. Gineris expressed the view that such a financing would severely dilute the value of the common stock. Following the meeting, Alex. Brown prepared a report analyzing three financing proposals, two of which involved the sale of assets being considered as part of the restructuring plan, and the third involving a sale of 55%, a majority, of Genta's common stock for a $6 million investment. The report concluded that, on the terms assumed, the sale of equity was the least favorable proposal of those considered.

On December 3, the Series A committee made a further proposal to Genta that had three main components. First, Genta would sell JBL, placing all of the proceeds of the sale in escrow for the benefit of, and controlled by, the Series A shareholders. Second, Genta would sell its antisense assets, with the main part of the proceeds being paid to the Series A holders, and a portion of the proceeds being reserved for common stockholders in the event that certain milestones were reached. Third, Genta would sell control over the remainder of Genta to SkyePharma in exchange for $3 million in SkyePharma stock, to be distributed to the Series A holders, and a 29% interest in the joint venture, of which Genta's common stockholders would receive 20%. Any additional proceeds from the sale of residual assets were earmarked for the Series A holders as well.

Negotiations between Genta and Aries also continued throughout December. During the month, Mr. Mongiardo (1) informed Dr. Adams that Aries intended to continue the antisense business rather than sell it, (2) summarized LBC's attempts to find a potential investor, and (3) provided a draft letter, which was later presented to the board, stating a basis to conclude that Genta's value was between $58 and $184 million.

As of December 20, it had become apparent that Genta might be forced into bankruptcy if it did not fairly promptly effectuate one of the transactions on the table. Genta's bankruptcy counsel attended its December 20 board meeting at which the status of Genta's negotiations and the ongoing Nasdaq delisting proceedings were discussed. As expected, on December 21, Nasdaq denied Genta's request for continued listing, but the actual delisting was temporarily suspended until after a formal hearing could be held on January 23.

On December 24, Mr. Rosen, counsel to the Series A committee, wrote Dr. Adams a letter expressing frustration that Genta had not yet accepted the proposal that the preferred stock had put forward. In addition to stating that Dr. Adams was causing Genta to "crash and burn," Mr. Rosen stated that:

> Ad Hoc Committee will continue to try to bring about a resolution. However, if you wish to drive this bus into a canyon, no one can stop you. Just make sure you are alone when it happens.

On December 30, the Genta board received a formal presentation of the Aries proposal by Dr. Rosenwald. The board did not formally act at that time with respect to the proposal.

January 1997: Aries began performing due diligence activities in January, relying on statements that Genta intended to enter into a financing deal with Aries. The Genta board, however, continued analyzing its other options. On January 9, the Series A committee made its last proposal prior to the challenged transaction. By that date, it had become clear that the SkyePharma deal was unlikely to occur, and that proceeds from the sale of JBL would be insufficient to satisfy Genta's cash requirements. Thus, as part of this final proposal, the committee suggested that a portion of the Isis stock, which the Series A had proposed that they receive in a sale of the antisense assets, could be sold to take care of the cash shortage. In order to compensate the Series A holders for this loss of consideration, their final proposal contained a diminution in the common stockholder's percentage of the joint venture. If, as suggested, $1.5 million worth of Isis stock were sold, the common stockholders would not be entitled to any percentage of the remaining joint venture interest pursuant to the formula proposed by the committee. In addition to these proposals, the committee recommended that Genta initiate a prepackaged Chapter 11 bankruptcy.

On January 13, the Genta board met. It analyzed the most recent Series A proposal and the Aries and Wang proposals, as well as the consequences of a bankruptcy option. In the event of bankruptcy, the board concluded that the common stockholders would be likely to get no return on their investment. If the terms of the latest restructuring proposal were accepted, it was also likely that the common stockholders would receive zero value, based on calculations presented by Alex. Brown.

After the board meeting, Alex. Brown's Mr. Gineris sent Mr. Rosen a table reflecting his analysis. Gineris circled what in his judgment were the most likely scenarios on the table and wrote in comments reflecting his concern that such scenarios were "too punitive" to the common stock and would be unlikely to get stockholder approval. The Series A committee offered no amendment to the terms of their January 9 proposal.

On January 21, Genta's board members received several documents concerning the Aries deal to assist them in determining whether to approve that transaction. The packet of information distributed by Dr. Adams included the December 18 letter detailing LBC's efforts to find an equity investor, a two page letter from LBC concluding that the Aries deal was "fairer" than the restructuring proposal, a two page letter from Dr. Adams comparing the two proposals, and a stock information table. Board meetings were scheduled for January 26 and 28 to discuss these proposals.

On January 23, Genta and an Aries representative participated in the anticipated Nasdaq delisting hearing. As a result of the hearing, Nasdaq decided again to postpone the threatened delisting of Genta's stock. Genta was, however, informed that it would be delisted in the future unless it increased its net tangible assets and met other requirements.

As of the January 26 meeting, it had become clear that Genta had to complete a financing transaction rapidly, or else face bankruptcy. Recognizing that Genta would not have sufficient cash for its payroll due on February 1, Genta's bankruptcy lawyers had begun preparing the necessary papers to file for bankruptcy on January 29. At this juncture, faced with an imminent decision, Dr. Adams informed the board that he opposed the restructuring proposal in its present form. Further, Dr. Adams reported to the board that he had told Mr. Gineris that the current Series A proposal was unacceptable.

The Aries offer was set to expire as of January 28; the board had received no further restructuring proposals from the Series A committee; no firm offer from Ms. Wang was on the horizon; and bankruptcy was imminent. In this context, during the January 28 meeting, the board again reviewed the terms of each of the proposals before it made a decision concerning Genta's future.

Aries Transaction: On January 28, the Genta board unanimously approved the Aries transaction. According to plaintiff, the members of the Series A committee and Alex. Brown learned of this transaction for the first time when they read a press release disclosing the transaction on the following day.

Pursuant to a January 28 letter of intent, Genta and Aries agreed to enter into a two step financing on the following terms. The first step, which by the time of trial of this case had already occurred, involved Aries loaning Genta $3 million in cash. In exchange, Aries received convertible secured bridge notes with a $3 million face value, 7.8 million Class A warrants with a $.001 per share exercise price, and 12.2 million Class B warrants with a per share exercise price of $.55. The bridge notes are immediately convertible into 600,000 shares of Series D convertible preferred stock with a $10 stated value per share. In the event that Aries converts this preferred stock, Aries would receive 20 million shares of Genta common stock. Together the transaction offers Aries the right to acquire 40 million shares of Genta common stock—a controlling interest in the company.

In addition to this consideration in the form of debt and equity, Aries received an immediate contractual right to require the Genta board to cause a sufficient number of its designees to be added to the board so as to constitute a majority of the board. In the event that Aries does not satisfy its future obligations to raise additional capital (the second tier financing), however, this right will terminate. That is, pursuant to the terms of the second tranche of this financing, Aries has agreed to use its "best efforts" to arrange between $2.5 to $12 million in additional financing for Genta. If, within six months following the effective date of the agreement, Aries has not located at least $3.5 million of additional financing for the company, it will lose its right to designate a majority of the board. The agreement does not state the minimum terms upon which an acceptable financing can be made in order to satisfy Aries's obligation, but requires board approval and permits Genta to opt for alternative financing if it is available on preferable terms.

In addition to the financial terms of the deal, Aries represented to Genta that it did not intend to liquidate the company and would use its best efforts to continue Genta's antisense business. Aries did not make any representations or side agreements concerning the continued employment of Dr. Adams or other Genta board members.

To the contrary, the testimony is that Dr. Adams told Aries that it should consider hiring a new CEO.

Equity-Linked's March 3 Proposal: Immediately prior to the hearing in this action, Equity Linked delivered a proposal to Genta that offered to extend a $3.6 million loan to Genta on the same terms as those reflected in the Aries transaction. This offer appears to have been an attempt by plaintiff to demonstrate that it would have been willing to do the same deal on terms at least as favorable as those offered by Aries.

[Analysis]

The broad question is whether the foregoing facts constitute a breach of duty by the directors of Genta.

The legal theory that plaintiff advanced at trial does not really acknowledge the true nature of the financial conflict at the heart of the matter. Rather, plaintiff's trial theory acts as if plaintiff were simply like any other holder of *common stock* and sought a corrective order so that a higher price for the common could be achieved in a sale.

The claim now is that the board "transferred control" of the company and that in such a transaction it is necessary that the board act reasonably to get the highest price, which this board did not do. Plaintiff urges that the special duty recognized in *Revlon, Inc. v. MacAndrews & Forbes Holdings, Inc.,* 506 A.2d 173 (Del. 1986), arose here because (1) Aries has a contract right to designate a majority of the Genta board and (2) Aries acquired warrants that if exercised would give it the power to control any election of the Genta board. Thus, this transaction is seen as similar to the noted case of *Paramount Communications Inc. v. QVC Network Inc.,* 637 A.2d 34 (Del. 1993). Plaintiff claims that the board hid the fact that control might be for sale, instead of announcing it and creating price competition respecting it. In support of the assertion that the board could have done better for common stockholders, like themselves, plaintiff points to the litigation produced alternative proposal of the Series A preferred stock. The idea is that this alternative is financially a little better and that if the directors would have met their "Revlon duty" then, this or another better alternative would have come to light. In this way, plaintiff claims the interests of all holders of equity securities would have been better off because Genta would have gotten greater value.

"Revlon Duties" and a Change in Corporate Control: In *Paramount Communications, Inc. v. QVC Network Inc.,* the Delaware Supreme Court considered a series of cases dealing with the fiduciary duties of corporate directors when directors authorize a transaction that has the effect of changing corporate control. The most prominent of these was the 1986 opinion in *Revlon, Inc. v. MacAndrews & Forbes Holdings, Inc.* That case had been widely thought to announce special directorial duties in the event of a "sale" of the corporation. The specific character of that rule however was not entirely clear, but it was generally taken to be that in certain circumstances (loosely a "sale" of the company) directors must maximize the current value of the corporation's stock; they may not exercise a judgment to choose less when more is offered. But this broad generalization masks more questions than it answers. In fact the meaning of *Revlon*—specifically, when its special duties were triggered, and what those duties specifically required—were questions that repeatedly troubled the bench and the bar in the turbulent wake of the *Revlon* decision. Reasonable minds differed.

This existing uncertainty respecting the meaning of "Revlon duties" was substantially dissipated by the Delaware Supreme Court's opinion in *Paramount*. The case teaches a great deal, but it may be said to support these generalizations at least: (1) where a transaction constituted a "change in corporate control", such that the shareholders would thereafter lose a further opportunity to participate in a change of control premium, (2) the board's duty of loyalty requires it to try in good faith to get the best price reasonably available (which specifically means that the board must at least discuss an interest expressed by any financially capable buyer), and (3) in such context courts will employ an (objective) "reasonableness" standard of review (both to the process and the result!) to evaluate whether the directors have complied with their fundamental duties of care and good faith (loyalty). Thus, *Paramount* in effect mediates between the "normalizing" tendency of some prior cases and the more highly regulatory approach of others. It adopts an *intermediate level of judicial review* which recognizes the broad power of the board to make decisions in the process of negotiating and recommending a "sale of control" transaction, so long as the board is informed, motivated by good faith desire to achieve the best available transaction, and proceeds "reasonably."

With respect to the important question of when these duties are enhanced—specifically, the duty to try in good faith to maximize current share value and the duty to reasonably explore all options (i.e., to talk with all financially responsible parties)—the court's teaching ironically narrowed the range of Revlon duties, but did not make its application necessarily clearer. It narrowed the range of corporate transactions to which the principle of Revlon applies. That is, it explicitly recognized that where a stock for stock merger is involved, the business judgment of the board, concerning the quality and prospects of the stock the shareholders would receive in the merger, would be reviewed deferentially, as in other settings. The holding of *Paramount,* however, was that where the stock to be received in the merger was the stock of a corporation under the control of a single individual or a control group, then the transaction should be treated for "Revlon duty" purposes as a cash merger would be treated: there is no tomorrow for the shareholders (no assured long-term), the board's obligation is to make a good faith, informed judgment to maximize current share value, and the court reviews such determinations on a "reasonableness" basis, which otherwise they would not do. How this "change in control" trigger works in instances of mixed cash and stock or other paper awaits future cases.

Application of *Paramount* to the Aries Transaction: The questions that *Paramount* frames for this case are essentially two. First, is the Aries transaction a "change in corporate control" that triggers special directorial duties and that requires enhanced judicial review, under a reasonableness standard. Second, if it is, do the facts found, set forth above, constitute either (1) bad faith or insufficiently informed action or (2) unreasonable action given the type of transaction that was under consideration.

1. *Does the Aries transaction trigger special board duties?* I assume for purposes of deciding this case, without deciding, that the granting of immediately exercisable warrants, which, if exercised, would give the holder voting control of the corporation, is a transaction of the type that warrants the imposition of the special duties and special review standard of *Paramount*.

2. *What are the special duties that are triggered?* The duties that devolve upon the board when it approves a transaction having a change in corporate control effect

(Revlon duties)

423

(and here I mean specifically, as in *Paramount*, where corporate action plays a necessary part in the formation of a control block where one did not previously exist), is to take *special efforts to be well informed* of alternatives, and to approve only a transaction that seeks *reasonably* to maximize the *current value of the corporation's equity*. That is the gist of the Revlon state: to act reasonably to maximize current, not some future, value. (In other states, it is entirely up to the board to exercise judgment over what time-frame the corporation's resources are to be developed and how. *See Paramount Communications, Inc. v. Time Inc.*, 571 A.2d 1140 (Del. 1989)).

The enhanced information obligation, occasioned by the gravity of the triggering transaction, may be satisfied through an auction, through a "market check," or perhaps in other ways, but it is fundamental that the board's effort to be informed must be active and reasonable.

3. Have the director-defendants failed to reasonably attempt to advance the current interests (or value) of the holders of the corporation's equity securities? The board did not negotiate with the preferred stock with respect to a transaction of the kind it was attempting to find elsewhere. Thus the question: Did this violate the board's duty to be especially active and reasonable in searching for relevant information? Secondly, assuming, without deciding, that the March 3 proposal by the preferred stock was on better terms than the Aries deal—in that it offered a somewhat greater first tranche credit—has the board failed reasonably to maximize the current value of the firm's equity?

In my opinion, the answer to both of these questions is no.

[Did this violate the board's duty to be especially active and reasonable in searching for relevant information?]

Even though no offer was made to the preferred to permit them to acquire control, I cannot conclude that the board was not fully informed of the company's relevant alternatives (i.e., relevant to the board's good faith business plan) by the time it authorized the Aries transaction. The ultimate choice for the board was correctly understood. It was not between the Aries transaction and an alternative similar transaction at a "higher price" or on better terms, of which the board did not know because of its inattention (or otherwise). The real choice was between (1) a transaction that attempted to finance a future for the company in which products might be developed and brought to market, and (2) a transaction that treated the enterprise (perhaps correctly) as a failed effort and would therefore involve the sale of its assets and a distribution of the proceeds, largely if not entirely, to the preferred stock.[49] After a lot of effort the board saw this choice as the choice between accepting the Aries transaction, on one hand, which offered some prospect of further credit being raised, some bio-tech expertise being brought to bear by the investor, and some meaningful enhancement of the prospects of the company for survival, product development, and ultimate financial success, and, on the other hand, accepting the final, take it or leave it proposal of the Series A preferred stock, which meant that the common

---

49. It is not part of the court's responsibility to evaluate which course of action was wiser from the point of view of the convertible preferred or the common. I would have to accept the notion that the holders of the preferred stock are in the only position to say with authority what is in their best interest. Equally clearly, the common had an adverse interest to the preferred if the preferred didn't want (as they apparently did not want) to role the dice on the future.

would get essentially nothing and the corporation would never see the future benefit of the exploitation of its intellectual property.

The charge of failure to search appropriately for alternatives that would have been more beneficial to the owners of the company's equity securities is deeply unconvincing on the evidence. The evidence is completely inconsistent with the notion that some other (third) party, who was unknown, would have offered a better deal to Genta. The board, with the advice and assistance of professional advisors, had thoroughly explored that possibility. The more plausible supposition is that if the board had gone back to the Series A preferred stock once its deal with Aries was substantially negotiated, the preferred would likely have authorized a proposal like the one that the holders ultimately put forth in the litigation, which I will assume is in certain respects superior. Nevertheless, I conclude that the board's failure to afford the preferred stock an opportunity to meet or exceed the Aries proposal was quite reasonable in the circumstances (some reasonable minds may have thought it likely to be futile and wasteful).

The Genta board had been dealing with the preferred stock for some time in a rather intense way. The board knew, or had good reason to believe it knew, what *were* the business goals of the preferred with respect to its investment in Genta. The preferred quite certainly were interested in taking as much money out of Genta as possible, as soon as possible.

The various negotiations concerning the antisense business reflect one clear example of this. Management wanted to discuss an assignment of the intellectual property that the company possessed, but wanted to grant a non-exclusive license, so that the company itself, if it could find financing, could continue its research and development efforts. The Series A committee was unyielding. Any such step would limit the amount of cash that might be generated for distribution and, thus, was opposed.

Moreover, the Series A knew that management was looking for financing. There were press releases to that effect. Yet they were unwilling to put in more money. The preferred is of course not to be criticized for that. They have every right to send no good dollars after bad ones. Indeed, they had the right to withhold necessary consents to salvage plans unless their demands were satisfied. But when plaintiff now contends that the Genta board was required by fiduciary duty to the company's common stockholders to go back to the Series A preferred after finding an investor willing to do what the Series A sought to prevent, I cannot agree. Delaware law cannot sensibly criticize the Genta board of directors for recognizing the practical reality with which they were faced and acting on their permissible vision of their duty.

It was quite reasonable for the Genta board to conclude that, if the policy of the board was to try to find a way to finance further research and development in order to attempt to benefit the residual owners of the firm, that any proposal that transferred corporate control or potential control to the preferred stock was a highly dubious way to achieve *that goal*.

A bidding contest between the Series A and a new investor interested in developing Genta's intellectual property would be a poor way to attempt to maximize either the present value or some future value of the common stock in these particular circumstances that the Series A liquidation premium is greater than the liquidation value of the firm—but that the preferred stock has no legal right to force a liquidation. In that event, the preferred would have a bidding advantage and would use it to *deprive the common of their power to exploit the preferred that the common currently possesses.* Assume, for example, that the present value of the firm's prospects as a going concern would be only $9 million (net), which is also its liquidation value. Assume that in an open bidding contest, a well-informed bidder will offer *the company* something less than 3 million for a 51% interest (i.e., $9m + $3m = $12m divided by 2 = $6m; but since in liquidation the common stock would be worthless, the bidder would be unlikely to bid the maximum $6mm value on these assumptions). Assume such a $3m bid would permit the common stock some further opportunity to see a payoff in the company labs and in the marketplace. Now assume that a bidding contest occurs in which the preferred takes part. What will probably happen? The preferred's aim might be simply to liquidate the company and take all of the net proceeds and apply it to its preference. This will prevent its exploitation by the common and cut its losses. To accomplish that goal, the preferred could easily pay in an auction up to $21 million ($30 million liquidation preference minus present net liquidation value) because that amount would go into the company's treasury but could be immediately restored to the preferred when it exercised its voting power to cause the liquidation of the firm.

To generalize, the existence of a "below water" liquidation preference would allow the preferred to out bid an arm's length bidder for Genta's assets and defeat an attempt to exploit the company's properties (and not incidentally, an attempt to exploit the preferred in its current situation) for the benefit of the common stock. What the board did, in effect, was to try on behalf of the common to exploit the preferred—by imposing risks on them without proportionate opportunity for rewards. That the preferred is open to this risk legally, is a function of the terms of its security. I think it is perfectly permissible for the board to choose this course in these circumstances. To engage in a *Revlon* auction or otherwise allow the preferred to outbid a third party, would be to defeat this legitimate strategy.

While Aries does not offer complete assurance that it will be able to deliver on the board's long-term vision, its economic incentives are more aligned with its doing so than would be those of the holders of the Series A preferred stock. Aries would not have the conflict with the common that is created by the contractual right of the preferred to a liquidation preference. Thus, its incentives to achieve long-term value creation would be stronger.

[Assuming, without deciding, that the March 3 proposal by the preferred stock was on better terms than the Aries deal in that it offered a somewhat greater first tranche credit—has the board failed reasonably to maximize the current value of the firm's equity?]

If we assume that Genta's board was operating under the unusual gravitational pulls of planet Revlon, we must acknowledge that the board is supposed in such "sale of control" circumstances, to have the single aim of maximizing the present value of the firm's equity. That requirement is very clear when, for example, one bidder, offers an all cash deal and another offers all cash as well, but less money. It is tolerably clear when one bidder offers cash and another offers cash and widely traded securities, the package being worth less when measured by dependable markets. But what that requirement means in this setting, where (1) the transaction is not a merger or tender offer with a "price" per share at all, and (2) the transaction (or alternatives now advanced) are not otherwise easily reduced to a present value calculation, is not obvious. What *is* clear is that the Genta board was striving to maximize the possibility of the common stock participating in some "upside" benefit from the commercial development of the company's intellectual properties. It is clear too that the course it took to do that arguably was superior to an alternative in which the preferred acquired control, because the preferred had a financial incentive to liquidate the firm immediately, thus depriving the common of any current value.

Thus, unlike two competing cash transactions or transaction in which widely traded securities are offered, the alternatives that plaintiff poses are rich with legitimate, indeed unavoidable, occasions for the exercise of good faith business judgment. Where judgment is inescapably required, all that the law may sensibly ask of corporate directors is that they exercise independent, good faith and attentive judgment, both with respect to the quantum of information necessary or appropriate in the circumstances and with respect to the substantive decision to be made.

This principle has application here. The Genta board had a business goal of trying to maintain an equity participation for the common stock in its promising intellectual properties. It mattered to this strategy who was the controlling shareholder. While the Genta board hardly could (or at all events did not) negotiate binding provisions assuring that its goal would be obtained, it could and did exercise an informed good faith judgment concerning it. It took steps demonstrating its good faith efforts. First, it negotiated with Dr. Rosenwald for the second tranche of financing. Second, it received an undertaking from Dr. Rosenwald that he did not intend to liquidate the company and would try to develop the antisense business. Third, the economic incentives of Aries were inherently different than those of the Series A preferred stock and the board could recognize and depend to some extent on those differences. That is, the Series A inherently have some interest in protecting their liquidation preference. Aries, like other owners of only common, has an incentive to employ the remaining capital and that which can be raised, to commercially exploit Genta's properties.

Moreover, Aries did not simply offer money in exchange for potential control of Genta. It offered as well a good faith effort to raise additional financing and it offered a principal with considerable experience and expertise on the financing and operation of bio-technology firms. Even if one were to believe that the preferred stock's offer that came before trial should be accepted as a *bona fide* alternative to reach the company's long-term goal, there would be sufficient substantive differences between Aries's proposal and the only alternative that might have been available, to permit the judgment of the independent board to stand.

In short, the facts of this case clearly do not look like a situation in which, from the common stock's perspective, "there is no tomorrow," and the board ought not be recognized as having discretion to prefer what it sees as a "longer term value" over a higher present value. The court would have no basis to conclude that the immediate value of the common would in fact be greater had an alternative of the kind presented by the preferred somehow been put in place in January.

Thus, I conclude in the circumstances disclosed by the balance of the credible evidence, that the Genta board concluded in good faith that the corporation's interests were best served by a transaction that it thought would maximize potential long-run wealth creation and that in the circumstances, including the potential insolvency of the company and the presence of a $30 million liquidation preference, the board acted reasonably in pursuit of the highest achievable *present* value of the Genta common stock, by proceeding as it did.

Judgment will be granted for defendants and against plaintiff.

QUESTIONS

1. Why did the board reject Equity-Linked's offer in response to the Aries transaction?
2. What was the substance of the *Revlon* argument? And, why did the court reject the argument?
3. What might be the unstated policy preference of the court forming the basis of the explained rationale and the court's decision?

NOTES

1. The court wrote: "While the board in these circumstances could have made a different business judgment, in my opinion, it violated no duty owed to the preferred in not doing so." This comment foreshadowed the eventual demise of the Genta. Genta ultimately became a sad story of a failed investment. In a span of 24 years, it burned through $1.23 billion of shareholders' money, including the contribution of Equity-Linked Investors. On August 2, 2012, Genta filed for Chapter 7 bankruptcy liquidation. In the course of this decline, Genta experienced a series of setbacks in drug development and testing, resulting in a continued decline in share prices. To offset the decline in share prices, it engaged in a series of reverse stock splits. These reverse stock splits were: 1 for 10 (1997); 1 for 6 (2007); 1 for 50 (2009); 1 for 100 (2010); 1 for 50 (2011). Collectively, these stock splits constituted a 1 for 15 million reverse stock split (i.e., 15,000,000 = 10 x 6 x 50 x 100 x 50). The above opinion says that as of January 28, 1997, the company had 39,991,626 shares of common stock outstanding. In Genta's quarterly 10-Q filing, as of March 31, 2012, it reported 2.09 billion shares outstanding. These shares outstanding were achieved *with* the 1 for 15 million reverse stock splits. If these reverse stock splits had never occurred, this implies that Genta issued 31.35 quadrillion shares: This is the number 31,350,000,000,000,000.

   This situation occurs when a company desperately needs cash and each round of financing dilutes the original investors. A new investor will be reluctant to invest in a troubled company without proper pricing, resulting in the issuance of deeply discounted securities. In the case of Genta, the path from 40 million shares in 1997 to 31.35 quadrillion shares in 2012 is paved with a multiple series of dilutive stock issuances, each issuance more dilutive than the previous one. In Genta's case, let's assume that the 40 million shares were before the 1 for 10 reverse stock split in 1997 and that the common stock was worth $4 million (a generous assumption since the court noted that the company was "on the lip of insolvency and in liquidation" and was "worth substantially less than the $30 million liquidation preference of the preferred stock"). Assume that nothing else has changed by 2012 except the share dilution. The $4 million claim held by the original shareholders owning 40 million shares have been diluted down to a claim for $0.005 (a half a penny), which is calculated as: (40 million ÷ 31.35 quadrillion) × $4 million. In hindsight, it looks like Equity-Linked Investors made the right call in attempting to force liquidation before things got really bad.

In re Trados Inc. Shareholder Litigation
2009 WL 2225958 (Del. Ch.)

motion to dis~

CHANDLER, Chancellor.

This is a purported class action brought by a former stockholder of Trados Inc. for breach of fiduciary duty arising out of a transaction whereby Trados became a wholly owned subsidiary of SDL, plc. Of the $60 million contributed by SDL, Trados' preferred stockholders received approximately $52 million. The remainder was distributed to the Company's executive officers pursuant to a previously approved bonus plan. Trados' common stockholders received nothing for their common shares.

Plaintiff contends that this transaction was undertaken at the behest of certain preferred stockholders that desired a transaction that would trigger their large liquidation preference and allow them to exit their investment in Trados. Plaintiff alleges that the Trados board favored the interests of the preferred stockholders, either at the expense of the common stockholders or without properly considering the effect of the merger on the common stockholders. Specifically, plaintiff alleges that the four directors designated by preferred stockholders had other relationships with preferred stockholders and were incapable of exercising disinterested and independent business judgment. Plaintiff further alleges that the two Trados directors who were also employees of the Company received material personal benefits as a result of the merger and were therefore also incapable of exercising disinterested and independent business judgment.

Plaintiff has alleged facts sufficient, at this preliminary stage, to demonstrate that at least a majority of the members of Trados' seven member board were unable to exercise independent and disinterested business judgment in deciding whether to approve the merger. Accordingly, I decline to dismiss the breach of fiduciary duty claims arising out of the board's approval of the merger.

Before the merger, Trados developed software and services used by businesses to make the translation of text and material into other languages more efficient. Founded in 1984 as a German entity, Trados moved to the United States in the mid–1990s with the hope of going public, and became a Delaware corporation in March 2000. To better position itself for the possibility of going public, Trados accepted investments from venture capital firms and other entities. As a result, preferred stockholders had a total of four designees on Trados' seven member board. Each of the seven members of Trados' board at the time of the board's approval of the merger is named as a defendant in this action.

David Scanlan was the board designee of, and a partner in, Wachovia Capital Partners.

Lisa Stone was the board designee of Rowan Entities, transferees of Trados' preferred stock held by Hg Investment Managers. Stone was a director and employee of both Hg and the Rowan Entities.

Sameer Gandhi was a board designee of, and a partner in, several entities known as Sequoia.

Joseph Prang was also a board designee of Sequoia. Prang owned Mentor Capital.

Wachovia, Hg, Sequoia, and Mentor combined owned approximately 51% of Trados' outstanding preferred stock. Plaintiff alleges that these preferred stockholders desired to exit their investment in Trados.

Two of the three remaining director defendants were employees of Trados. Jochen Hummel was acting President of Trados from April 2004 until September or October 2004, and was also the Company's chief technology officer. Joseph Campbell was Trados' CEO from August 23, 2004 until the merger. The remaining Trados director was Klaus–Dieter Laidig.

In April 2004, the Trados board began to discuss a potential sale of the Company, and later formed a mergers and acquisitions committee, consisting of Stone, Gandhi, and Scanlan, to explore a sale or merger of Trados. Around the same time, the Company's President and CEO was terminated due to, among other issues, a perception by the rest of the board that Trados was underperforming. The board appointed Hummel as an interim President, but instructed him to consult with Gandhi and Scanlan before taking material action on behalf of the Company. In July 2004, Campbell was hired as the Company's CEO. Gandhi described Campbell as "a hard-nosed CEO whose task is to grow the company profitably or sell it." At the time Campbell joined Trados, however, the Company was losing money and had little cash to fund continuing operations. At a July 2004 meeting, Trados' board determined that the fair market value of Trados' common stock was $0.10 per share.

In June 2004, Trados engaged JMP Securities, an investment bank, to assist in identifying potential alternatives for a merger or sale of the Company. By July 2004, JMP Securities had identified twenty seven potential buyers of Trados, and contacted seven of them, including SDL. By August 2004, JMP Securities had conducted discussions with SDL CEO Mark Lancaster, who made an acquisition proposal in the $40 million range. Trados informed Lancaster that it was not interested in a deal at that price, and Campbell formally terminated JMP Securities in September 2004.

In July 2004, Scanlan expressed concern that the executive officers of the Company might not have sufficient incentives to remain with the Company or pursue a potential acquisition of the Company, due to the high liquidation preference of the Company's preferred stock. The board instructed Scanlan to develop a bonus plan to address these concerns. This led to the December 2004 board approval of the Management Incentive Plan (the "MIP"), which set a graduated compensation scale for the Company's management based on the price obtained for the Company in an acquisition.

Trados' financial condition improved markedly during the fourth quarter of 2004, in part due to Campbell's efforts to reduce spending and bring in additional cash through debt financing. By the time of the December 2004 board meeting, Trados had arranged to borrow $2.5 million from Western Technology Investment, with the right to borrow an additional $1.5 million.

Despite the Company's improved performance, the board continued to work toward a sale of the Company. In December 2004, Gandhi reported to Sequoia Capital that the Company's performance was improving, but that Campbell's "mission is to architect an M & A event as soon as practicable." At a February 2005 board meeting, Campbell presented positive financial results from the fourth quarter of 2004, including record revenue and profit from operations. As a result of its improved performance and the lack of an immediate need for cash, the board extended by six months the period during which it could obtain additional cash from Western Technology Investment.

In January 2005, SDL initiated renewed merger discussions with Campbell. Upon learning of SDL's interest, the Trados board expressed that it was not interested in any transaction involving less than a "60–plus" million dollar purchase price. Lancaster first discussed a transaction at $50 million, but later offered $60 million. At the February 2, 2005 meeting, the board instructed Campbell to continue negotiating with Lancaster under the general terms SDL proposed, including the $60 million price. In mid-February 2005, Campbell made inquiries with two other potential acquirers of Trados, but neither expressed any substantive interest.

In a theme that runs throughout his allegations, plaintiff alleges that there was no need to sell Trados at the time because the Company was well financed and experiencing improved performance under Campbell's leadership. For example, plaintiff contends that by February 2005 Trados was beating its revenue budget for the year, a trend that continued as Trados beat its revenue projections for the first quarter of 2005 and through the end of May 2005.

By February 2005, Campbell and Lancaster agreed to the basic terms of a merger at $60 million. Trados then re-engaged JMP securities, which plaintiff alleges acted as little more than a "go-between." In April 2005, SDL and Trados signed the letter of intent for the merger at the $60 million price.

The director defendants unanimously approved the merger, and on June 19, 2005 Trados and SDL entered into an Agreement and Plan of Merger. Of the $60 million merger price, approximately $7.8 million would go to management pursuant to the MIP, and the remainder would go to the preferred stockholders in partial satisfaction of their $57.9 million liquidation preference. Plaintiff alleges that the directors know both of these facts, and thus knew that the common shareholders would receive nothing in the merger. The merger was consummated.

Plaintiff alleges that Campbell and Hummel received benefits as a result of the merger. Campbell became a director of SDL and received $775,000 through the MIP, $1,315,000 in exchange for a non-compete agreement, and a $250,000 bonus. Campbell took $702,000 of his MIP compensation in SDL stock, and $73,000 in cash. Hummel became "SDL's general manager of Europe, the Middle East, and Asia (technology division)," and received $1,092,000 under the MIP, of which he took $436,800 in SDL stock and $655,200 in cash.

Analysis

Count I of the Complaint asserts a claim that the director defendants breached their fiduciary duty of loyalty to Trados' common stockholders by approving the merger. Plaintiff alleges that there was no need to sell Trados at the time because the Company was well-financed, profitable, and beating revenue projections. Further, plaintiff contends, "in approving the Merger, the Director Defendants never considered the interest of the common stockholders in continuing Trados as a going concern, even though they were obliged to give priority to that interest over the preferred stockholders' interest in exiting their investment."

Directors of Delaware corporations are protected in their decision-making by the business judgment rule, which "is a presumption that in making a business decision the directors of a corporation acted on an informed basis, in good faith and in the honest belief that the action taken was in the best interests of the company." The rule reflects and promotes the role of the board of directors as the proper body to manage the business and affairs of the corporation.

The party challenging the directors' decision bears the burden of rebutting the presumption of the rule. If the presumption of the rule is not rebutted, then the

Court will not second-guess the business decisions of the board. If the presumption of the rule is rebutted, then the burden of proving entire fairness shifts to the director defendants. A plaintiff can survive a motion to dismiss by pleading facts from which a reasonable inference can be drawn that a majority of the board was interested or lacked independence with respect to the relevant decision.

A director is interested in a transaction if "he or she will receive a personal financial benefit from a transaction that is not equally shared by the stockholders" or if "a corporate decision will have a materially detrimental impact on a director, but not on the corporation and the stockholders." The receipt of any benefit is not sufficient to cause a director to be interested in a transaction. Rather, the benefit received by the director and not shared with stockholders must be "of a sufficiently material importance, in the context of the director's economic circumstances, as to have made it improbable that the director could perform her fiduciary duties . . . without being influenced by her overriding personal interest. . . ."

"Independence means that a director's decision is based on the corporate merits of the subject before the board rather than extraneous considerations or influences." At this stage, a lack of independence can be shown by pleading facts that support a reasonable inference that the director is beholden to a controlling person or "so under their influence that their discretion would be sterilized."

Plaintiff's theory of the case is based on the proposition that, for purposes of the merger, the preferred stockholders' interests diverged from the interests of the common stockholders. Plaintiff contends that the merger took place at the behest of certain preferred stockholders, who wanted to exit their investment. Defendants contend that plaintiff ignores the "obvious alignment" of the interest of the preferred and common stockholders in obtaining the highest price available for the company. Defendants assert that because the preferred stockholders would not receive their entire liquidation preference in the merger, they would benefit if a higher price were obtained for the Company. Even accepting this proposition as true, however, it is not the case that the interests of the preferred and common stockholders were aligned with respect to the decision of whether to pursue a sale of the company or continue to operate the Company without pursuing a transaction at the time.

The merger triggered the $57.9 million liquidation preference of the preferred stockholders, and the preferred stockholders received approximately $52 million dollars as a result of the merger. In contrast, the common stockholders received nothing as a result of the merger, and lost the ability to ever receive anything of value in the future for their ownership interest in Trados. It would not stretch reason to say that this is the worst possible outcome for the common stockholders. The common stockholders would certainly be no worse off had the merger not occurred.

Taking, as I must, the well-pleaded facts in the Complaint in the light most favorable to plaintiff, it is reasonable to infer that the common stockholders would have been able to receive some consideration for their Trados shares at some point in the future had the merger not occurred.[36] This inference is supported by plaintiff's allegations that the Company's performance had significantly improved and that the

---

[36] On a motion to dismiss for failure to state a claim, I am required to draw all reasonable inferences in favor of the non-moving party. As a result, there are sometimes reasonable (even, potentially, more likely) inferences that must be passed over at this stage of the proceedings. For example, it would be reasonable to

Company had secured additional capital through debt financing. Thus, it is reasonable to infer from the factual allegations in the Complaint that the interests of the preferred and common stockholders were not aligned with respect to the decision to pursue a transaction that would trigger the liquidation preference of the preferred and result in no consideration for the common stockholders.[38]

Generally, the rights and preferences of preferred stock are contractual in nature.[39] This Court has held that directors owe fiduciary duties to preferred stockholders as well as common stockholders where the right claimed by the preferred "is not to a preference as against the common stock but rather a right shared equally with the common."[40] Where this is not the case, however, "generally it will be the duty of the board, where discretionary judgment is to be exercised, to prefer the interests of common stock—as the good faith judgment of the board sees them to be—to the interests created by the special rights, preferences, *etc.,* of preferred stock, where there is a conflict."[41] Thus, in circumstances where the interests of the common stockholders diverge from those of the preferred stockholders, it is *possible* that a director could breach her duty by improperly favoring the interests of the preferred stockholders over those of the common stockholders.[42] As explained above, the factual

---

infer from the allegations in the Complaint that pursing the transaction with SDL was in the best interest of the Company because it secured the best value reasonably available for the Company's stakeholders and did not harm the common shareholders because, in fact, there was no reasonable chance that they would ever obtain any value for their stock even absent the transaction. Nothing in this Opinion is intended to suggest that it would necessarily be a breach of fiduciary duty for a board to approve a transaction that, as a result of liquidation preferences, does not provide any consideration to the common stockholders.

38. Defendants do not argue that the board had an obligation to the preferred stockholders to pursue a transaction that would trigger the large liquidation preference of the preferred stock. Thus, it is reasonable to infer, at this stage, that one option would be for the Company to continue to operate without paying the large liquidation preference to the preferred, subject of course, to any other contractual rights the preferred stockholders may have had. Indeed, in a situation in which the liquidation preference of the preferred exceeded the consideration that could be achieved in a transaction, it would arguably be in the interest of the common stockholders not to pursue any transaction that would trigger the liquidation preference. It is also reasonable to infer that the preferred stockholders would benefit from a transaction that allowed them to exit the investment while also triggering their liquidation preference, something they did not have a contractual right to force the Company to do. Again, at this stage, I am required to make reasonable inferences in plaintiff's favor, even if there are other reasonable inferences that can be drawn from the alleged facts and that would result in dismissal of the Complaint.

39. *Jedwab v. MGM Grand Hotels, Inc.,* 509 A.2d 584, 594 (Del.Ch.1986) ("With respect to matters relating to preferences or limitations that distinguish preferred stock from common, the duty of the corporation and its directors is essentially contractual and the scope of the duty is appropriately defined by reference to the specific words evidencing that contract. . . .").

40. *Jedwab,* 509 A.2d at 594.

41. *Equity–Linked Investors, L.P. v. Adams,* 705 A.2d 1040, 1042 (Del.Ch.1997) (citing *Katz v. Oak Indus., Inc.,* 508 A.2d 873, 879 (Del.Ch.1986)).

42. *See Blackmore Partners, L.P. v. Link Energy LLC,* 864 A.2d 80, 85–86 (Del.Ch. 2004) ("The allegation that the Defendant Directors approved a sale of substantially all of [the company's] assets and a resultant distribution of proceeds that went exclusively to the company's creditors raises a reasonable inference of disloyalty or intentional misconduct. Of course, it is also possible to infer (and the record at a later stage may well show) that the Director Defendants made a good faith judgment, after reasonable investigation, that there was no future for the business and no better alternative for the unit holders. Nevertheless, based only the facts alleged and the reasonable inferences that the court must draw from them, it would appear that no transaction could have been worse for the unit holders and reasonable to infer, as the plaintiff argues, that a properly motivated board of directors would not have agreed to a proposal that wiped out the value of the common equity and surrendered all of that value to the company's creditors."). Defendants contend that *Blackmore Partners* can be distinguished from this case because "the Court in *Blackmore Partners* found that defendants

allegations in the Complaint support a reasonable inference that the interests of the preferred and common stockholders diverged with respect to the decision of whether to pursue the merger. Given this reasonable inference, plaintiff can avoid dismissal if the Complaint contains well-pleaded facts that demonstrate that the director defendants were interested or lacked independence with respect to this decision.

Plaintiff has alleged facts that support a reasonable inference that Scanlan, Stone, Gandhi, and Prang, the four board designees of preferred stockholders, were interested in the decision to pursue the merger with SDL, which had the effect of triggering the large liquidation preference of the preferred stockholders and resulted in no consideration to the common stockholders for their common shares. Each of these four directors was designated to the Trados board by a holder of a significant number of preferred shares. While this, alone, may not be enough to rebut the presumption of the business judgment rule, plaintiff has alleged more. Plaintiff has alleged that Scanlan, Stone, Gandhi, and Prang each had an ownership or employment relationship with an entity that owned Trados preferred stock. Scanlan was a partner in Wachovia; Stone was a director, employee and part owner of Hg; Gandhi was a partner in several entities referred to as Sequoia; and Prang owned Mentor Capital. Plaintiff further alleges that each of these directors was dependent on the preferred stockholders for their livelihood. As detailed above, each of these entities owned a significant number of Trados' preferred shares, and together these entities owned approximately 51% of Trados' outstanding preferred stock. The allegations of the ownership and other relationships of each of Scanlan, Stone, Gandhi, and Prang to preferred stockholders, combined with the fact that each was a board designee of one of these entities, is sufficient, under the plaintiff-friendly pleading standard on a motion to dismiss, to rebut the business judgment presumption with respect to the decision to approve the merger with SDL.

Defendants rely on *Orban v. Field*, 1997 WL 153831 (Del.Ch.), but that decision does not counsel in favor of dismissal at this stage of the litigation. In *Orban*, the Court was evaluating whether a board breached its duties where it "deployed corporate

---

favored creditors to whom they did not owe fiduciary duties over unit holders to whom they did owe fiduciary duties" and that plaintiff "does not, and cannot, allege that the Director Defendants favored anyone to whom they did not owe a fiduciary duty." As explained above, however, preferred stockholders are owed the same fiduciary duties as common stockholders when the right claimed by the preferred is "a right shared equally with the common." *Jedwab*, 509 A.2d at 594. If and when the interests of the preferred stockholders diverge from those of the common stockholders, the directors generally must "prefer the interests of common stock—as the good faith judgment of the board sees them to be—to the interests created by the special rights, preferences, *etc.*, of preferred stock." *Equity–Linked Investors*, 705 A.2d at 1042. Based on the allegations in the Complaint, it does not appear that the preferred stockholders had any contractual right to force a transaction that would trigger their liquidation preference. Moreover, the transaction with SDL was, under at least one reasonable inference that can be drawn from the Complaint, not in the best interest of Trados' common stockholders.

Defendants may be correct that the facts in *Blackmore Partners* are somewhat more "extreme" than those alleged in the complaint because the Court in *Blackmore Partners* found "a basis in the complaint to infer that the value of [the company's] assets exceeded its liabilities by least $25 million." *Blackmore Partners*, 864 A.2d at 85. The Court in *Blackmore Partners*, however, concluded, even in the absence of factual allegations that supported an inference of interest or lack of independence by the directors, that "the allegation that the Defendant Directors approved a sale of substantially all of [the company's] assets and a resultant distribution of proceeds that went exclusively to the company's creditors raises a reasonable inference of disloyalty or intentional misconduct." *Id.* at 86. Here, in contrast, there is an allegation that a majority of the board was interested in the decision to pursue the transaction; accordingly, the Court need not conclude that the decision to approve the transaction, of itself, raises "a reasonable inference of disloyalty or intentional misconduct."

power against its own shareholders" by "eliminating the leverage of the common stock-holders by diluting their ownership interest below 10%" in order to prevent the common stockholder from using his ability to block a transaction to extract value for his shares. The Court, in deciding to grant summary judgment in favor of defendants, asked whether defendants had met their burden "to show that their conduct was taken in good faith pursuit of valid ends and was reasonable in the circumstances." Although this inquiry was "inevitably one that must be applied in the rich particularity of context," the Court was still able to conclude, based on the evidence in the record, that the plaintiff's "threat to impede the realization of [the] transaction by the corporation was thwarted by legally permissible action that was measured and appropriate in the circumstances." In making this determination, the Court assumed that the business judgment rule did not apply to the challenged actions.

Here, in contrast, the issue on the motion to dismiss is whether plaintiff has rebutted the presumption of the business judgment rule. Unlike on a motion for summary judgment, I must accept the well-pleaded factual allegations in the Complaint as true. As explained above, those allegations, with the benefit of reasonable inferences, are sufficient, at this stage, to rebut the presumption of the business judgment rule. Unlike in *Orban,* I am unable, at this stage, to make determinations based on the record, such as that the board acted "both in good faith and reasonably." Those determinations must wait for another day.

Plaintiff has alleged facts that support a reasonable inference that a majority of the board was interested or lacked independence with respect to the decision to approve the merger. Accordingly, plaintiff has alleged sufficient facts to survive defendants' motion to dismiss the fiduciary duty claims based on the board's decision to approve the merger.

The motion to dismiss is denied with respect to the claim in Count I for breach of fiduciary duty arising out of the board's approval of the merger.

QUESTIONS

1. In what way is *Trados* distinguishable from *Orban*?
2. Why was the MIP necessary?
3. What kind of investors were the preferred stockholders?
4. In what way did the interest of preferred stockholders conflict with that of common stockholders?

LC Capital Master Fund, Ltd. v. James
990 A.2d 435 (Del. Ch. 2010)

STRINE, Vice Chancellor.

Plaintiff LC Capital Master Fund, a preferred stockholder of QuadraMed Corporation, seeks to enjoin the acquisition by defendant Francisco Partners II, L.P. of QuadraMed because the consideration to be received by the preferred stockholders of QuadraMed does not exceed the "as if converted" value the preferred were contractually entitled to demand in the event of a merger. That "as if converted" value was based on a formula in the certificate of designation governing the preferred stock, and gave the preferred the bottom line right to convert into common at a specified ratio (the "Conversion Formula") and then receive the same consideration as the common in the Merger. The plaintiff purports to have the support of 95% of the preferred stockholders in seeking injunctive relief and I therefore refer to the plaintiff as the preferred stockholders.

Based on certain contractual rights that the preferred had in the event that a merger did not take place, the preferred stockholders argue that the QuadraMed board of directors (the "Board") had a fiduciary duty to allocate more of the merger consideration to the preferred. Notably, the preferred stockholders do not argue that the Board breached any fiduciary duty owed to all stockholders; in particular, they do not claim that the board did not fulfill its fiduciary duty to obtain the highest value reasonably attainable, a duty commonly associated with *Revlon, Inc. v. MacAndrews & Forbes Holdings, Inc.*, 506 A.2d 173 (Del. 1986). Rather, the preferred stockholders contend that the preferred stock has a strong liquidation preference and certain non-mandatory rights to dividends that the Board failed to accord adequate value, and that as a result of these *contractual* rights, the QuadraMed Board owed the preferred a *fiduciary* duty to accord it more than it was contractually entitled to receive by right in a merger. The preferred stockholders seek to enjoin the Merger because of this supposed breach of duty.

I find that the preferred stockholders have not proven a reasonable probability of success on the merits of their fiduciary duty claim. Under Delaware law, a board of directors may have a gap-filling duty in the event that there is no objective basis to allocate consideration between the common and preferred stockholders in a merger. But, when a certificate of designations does not provide the preferred with any right to vote upon a merger, does not afford the preferred a right to claim a liquidation preference in a merger, but does provide the preferred with a contractual right to certain treatment in a merger, I conclude that a board of directors that allocates consideration in a manner fully consistent with the bottom-line contractual rights of the preferred need not, as an ordinary matter, do more. Consistent with decisions like *Equity–Linked Investors, L.P. v. Adams*, 705 A.2d 1040, 1042 (Del.Ch. 1997), and *In re Trados Incorporated Shareholder Litigation*, 2009 WL 2225958 (Del.Ch. 2009), once the QuadraMed Board honored the special contractual rights of the preferred, it was entitled to favor the interests of the common stockholders. By exercising its discretion to treat the preferred entirely consistently with the Conversion Formula the preferred bargained for in the Certificate, the QuadraMed Board acted equitably toward the preferred.

Factual Background

Under the terms of the challenged merger agreement, Francisco Partners will acquire QuadraMed at a price of $8.50 per share of common stock. The preferred stockholders will receive $13.7097 in cash in exchange for each share of preferred stock. The price for the preferred stock set forth in the Merger Agreement was pegged to the conversion right the Certificate granted to the preferred stockholders in the event of a merger. That conversion right allowed the preferred stockholders to convert their preferred shares into common shares and then to receive the same consideration as the common stock received in the merger. The conversion was determined by using the Conversion Formula of 1.6129 shares of preferred stock to one share of common stock. That is, in order to value the preferred stock, the merging parties agreed to simply cash out the preferred stock at the price the preferred stockholders would receive if they exercise their right to convert to common stock.

The preferred stockholders seek to enjoin the Merger on the grounds that the defendants breached their fiduciary duties of care and loyalty. But, the preferred stockholders do not allege that the defendants breached their *Revlon* duties as to *all* shareholders by approving a transaction that does not fully value QuadraMed as an entity. Instead, the preferred stockholders argue that the Merger consideration was unfairly allocated between the common and preferred stock. That is, the preferred stockholders do not challenge the overall adequacy of the Merger consideration. Rather, the preferred stockholders claim that they simply did not receive a big enough slice of the pie because the Board allocated the Merger consideration to the preferred stock on an "as-if converted" basis, which the preferred stockholders believe understates the value of their shares.

Requesting a preliminary injunction is the only means the preferred stockholders have to block the transaction because, per the Certificate, the preferred stock does not have the right to vote on a merger. The circumstances in which the preferred stock has voting rights are limited to: (1) if the Certificate were to be amended in a way "that materially adversely affects the voting powers, rights or preferences" of the preferred stockholders; (2) if any class of shares with ranking before or in parity with the preferred stock were to be created; and (3) if the company were to incur "any long term, senior indebtedness of the Corporation in an aggregate principal amount exceeding $8,000,000." Relatedly, if four quarterly dividends are in arrears, the preferred stockholders can elect two substitute directors.

The Certificate includes a number of other rights for the preferred stock that are arguably relevant to the current dispute. The preferred stock has a dividend right. This provides for the payment of a dividend of $1.375 per year, but it is to be paid only "when, as and if authorized and declared" by the Board.

The Certificate also provides a liquidation preference of $25 (plus accrued dividends) for each share of preferred stock. But, the Certificate does not afford the preferred stock a right to force a liquidation. The Certificate expressly provides that a merger does not trigger the preferred stock's liquidation preference.

The preferred stockholders also point out that the Certificate includes a mandatory conversion right that allows QuadraMed to force the preferred stockholders to convert into common shares. The preferred stockholders stress that this provision of the Certificate may only be used by QuadraMed to force conversion when the company's common stock hits a price of $25 per share, far above the $8.50 per common share Merger value. But, like the liquidation preference, the mandatory conversion provision does not have bite in a merger. That is, the Certificate does not provide that, in the event of a merger, the preferred stockholders must be converted at a formula that affords the preferred stockholders an implied common stock value of $25 per share.

To the contrary, in a merger, the preferred stockholders will receive either: (1) the consideration determined by the Board in a merger agreement; or (2) if the preferred choose, the right to convert their shares using the Conversion Formula into common shares and redeem the same consideration as the common stockholders. The bottom line right of the preferred stockholders in a merger, therefore, is not tied to its healthy liquidation preference or the company's mandatory conversion strike price—it is simply the right to convert the shares into common stock at the Conversion Formula and then be treated pari passu with the common.

Over the years, QuadraMed received expressions of interest from a number of potential acquirors. From 2008 to date, QuadraMed has been seriously considering a sale. From early on in this strategic process, the preferred stockholders demanded a high price, even $25, for their stock, apparently under the mistaken view that they had a right to their liquidation preference in the event of a merger. Initially, some bidders indicated an interest in either meeting the preferred stockholders' asking price—which would mean paying much more for the preferred stock than the common—or at least allowing the preferred stock to remain outstanding after the consummation of a merger. For example, Francisco Partner's first bid for QuadraMed, made in October 2008, offered to acquire the company at $11 per share of common stock and to allow the preferred stock to remain outstanding. And, a later bid, received August 31, 2009 from a bidder referred to as "Bidder D" in the proxy materials, proposed acquiring QuadraMed for $10.00 per share of common stock, and $25.00 par value for each share of preferred stock. By "par value," Bidder D seems not to have meant to offer the preferred stockholders $25 per share in current value but a security with the future potential of reaching that value. But this was perhaps not as clearly expressed as it could have been.

As the negotiations continued, moreover, both Francisco Partners and Bidder D revised their offers downward. After several months of negotiating, Francisco Partners submitted a revised offer of $9.50 per share of common stock, with the requirement that the preferred stock be cashed-out. In March 2009, the Board rejected this offer, and negotiations with Francisco Partners were suspended. And, after its initial approach, Bidder D made very plain its earlier position and explained that it "never intended to offer face value" for the preferred stock and was instead interested in paying $10 per share of common stock and reaching agreement with the holders of preferred stock on the terms of a debt instrument with a $25 face value, but a present value equal to $10 per share on an as-if converted basis. Therefore, the treatment of the preferred stock and common stock under Bidder D's initial proposal and under the Merger is not as different as at first appears.

In light of the various bids being made for the company, QuadraMed's outside counsel, Crowell & Moring, sent the QuadraMed Board a memorandum on September 1, 2009 addressing the legal issues relating to apportioning merger consideration between the common stock and preferred stock (the "September 2009 Memorandum"). In substance, the September 2009 Memorandum was Crowell & Moring's distillation of and update to a memorandum that Richards, Layton & Finger, QuadraMed's Delaware counsel, had prepared in June 2006. In 2006, while QuadraMed was in negotiations over a possible acquisition by a private equity firm, referred to as "Bidder B" in QuadraMed's proxy materials, Richards Layton authored a memorandum, dated June 22, 2006, that provided a general overview of the legal authority relevant to allocating merger consideration between common stock and preferred stock in a merger. The memorandum was addressed to counsel, Crowell & Moring, not the QuadraMed Board. Crowell & Moring's September 2009 Memorandum summarized Richards Layton's 2006 advice and discussed this court's April 2009 decision *In re Appraisal of Metromedia Int'l Group, Inc.*, 971 A.2d 893 (Del.Ch. 2009), which addressed the allocation of merger consideration between common and preferred stock in the context of an appraisal action.

The QuadraMed Board formed a special committee of independent directors (the "Special Committee") to evaluate the various bids. QuadraMed's Board is comprised of six individuals: Duncan James, William Jurika, Lawrence English, James Peebles, Robert Miller, and Robert Pevenstein (collectively, the "Special Committee members"). The Special Committee was comprised of Jurika, English, Peebles, Miller, and Pevenstein—that is, all of the Special Committee members except James, who was also QuadraMed's Chief Executive Officer. With the exception of Jurika, who owns over 650,000 shares of QuadraMed common stock, the Special Committee members hold a nominal amount of QuadraMed shares and in the money stock options. The preferred stockholders have not presented any evidence that these members' holdings of QuadraMed shares and options constitute a material portion of their personal wealth.

In early autumn 2009, after Bidder D's approach in August, QuadraMed's investment bankers shopped the deal. At this time, Francisco Partners made a second bid, offering $8.50 per share of common stock and requiring the cash-out of the preferred stock on an as-if converted basis, which yielded a value of $13.7097 per preferred share. Francisco Partners insisted on cashing out the preferred stock because it did not want to bear the risk of a voluntary conversion of the preferred stock into common stock after the Merger. The evidence also indicates that Francisco Partners wanted to increase QuadraMed's borrowing after the Merger, and therefore wanted to eliminate the preferred stock because the Certificate gives the preferred stock a right to vote on any incurrence of debt in excess of $8,000,000.

Because the preferred stockholders were demanding more consideration than the common stock, one of the questions before the Special Committee was what fiduciary duties it owed to the common stock and preferred stock when allocating the proposed Merger's consideration. The evidence indicates that the Special Committee carefully considered the duties it owed to both the preferred and common stockholders, and was concerned about any perception that it was favoring one class over the other. In a series of meetings, the Special Committee reviewed the bids, and at those meetings, QuadraMed's counsel informed the Special Committee that the Board could adopt a merger agreement that cashed out the preferred stockholders, and that if the Board respected the bottom line contractual rights of the preferred stockholders in a merger, it did not have to allocate additional value to the preferred stockholders. Indeed, Crowell & Moring said that the Board had to be careful about giving the preferred stockholders more unless there were special reasons to do so. Crowell & Moring also reported that Francisco Partner's counsel, Shearman & Sterling, had also reached the conclusion that a cash out of the preferred stock at closing was permissible under Delaware law, and that Francisco Partners would not insist on an "appraisal out" provision in the Merger Agreement so as to satisfy any concerns the Special Committee might have regarding the treatment of the preferred stock.

Meanwhile, Bidder D had been attempting to persuade the preferred stockholders to take a new debt security with a current value equal to what the common would receive but with a future upside. But, Bidder D found it "extremely difficult" to convince the holders of preferred stock to exchange their stock for a new debt security, and its bid foundered. Once Bidder D withdrew its offer on November 22, 2009, Francisco Partners became the only remaining bidder for QuadraMed. Although the Special Committee resisted cashing out the preferred stock for some time, the Committee eventually relented once it became clear that Francisco Partners would not do a deal that allowed QuadraMed's preferred stock to survive the Merger.

On December 7, 2009, a Special Committee meeting was held to consider approval of the Merger with Francisco Partners. At that meeting, Piper Jaffray, QuadraMed's financial advisor, presented an opinion that $8.50 per common share was fair to the common stockholders from a financial point of view. There was no separate opinion addressing the fairness of the Merger to the preferred stockholders. After deliberation, the Special Committee unanimously approved the Merger with Francisco Partners. From the meeting minutes, it appears that the Special Committee was wary of doing a deal that allocated more consideration to the preferred stock than to the common stock for two reasons: (1) shifting additional merger consideration to the preferred stock would cause the holders of common stock, who were the only stockholders who had a right to vote on the Merger, to vote against the transaction; and (2) there was no special reason to deviate from the Conversion Formula provided in the Certificate for allocating consideration to the preferred stock.

Legal Analysis

The contending arguments of the parties are starkly divergent. The preferred stockholders, pointing to the decisions of this court in *Jedwab v. MGM Grand Hotels, Inc.*, 509 A.2d 584 (Del.Ch. 1986), and *In re FLS Holdings, Inc. Shareholders Litigation*, 1993 WL 104562 (Del.Ch.), argue that the QuadraMed board had the duty to make a "fair" allocation of the Merger consideration between the common and preferred stockholders. To do this fairly, the preferred stockholders argue that the board had to set up some form of negotiating agent, with the duty and discretion to exert leverage on behalf of the preferred stockholders in the allocation process. This need, the preferred stockholders say, is heightened because of an unsurprising fact: the directors of QuadraMed own common stock and do not own preferred stock. Indeed, the preferred stockholders say, every member of the Special Committee owned common stock and one member, Jurika, owned over five million dollars worth. How, they say, could such directors fairly balance the interests of the preferred against their own interest in having the common get as much as possible? At the very least, the preferred imply, the QuadraMed Board should have charged certain directors with representing the preferred, and enabled them to retain qualified legal and financial advisors to argue for the preferred and to value the preferred based on its unique contractual rights and their economic value.

By contrast, the defendants say that the QuadraMed Board discharged any fiduciary obligation of fairness it had by: (1) fulfilling its *Revlon* obligations to all equity holders, including the preferred, to seek the highest reasonably available price for the corporation; and (2) allocating to the preferred the percentage of value equal to their bottom line right, in the event of a merger, to convert and receive the same consideration as the common. Given that the preferred stockholders had no contractual right to impede, vote upon, or receive consideration higher than the common stockholders in the Merger, the defendants argue that the Board's decision to accord them the value that the preferred were entitled to contractually demand in the event of a merger cannot be seen as unfair. That is especially so when the preferred bases its claim for a higher value entirely on contractual provisions that do not guarantee them any share of the company's cash flows if the company does not liquidate, and that do not even condition a merger on the payment of any accrued, but undeclared dividends. Indeed, because the QuadraMed Board honored all contractual rights belonging to the preferred, the defendants say it was the duty of the Board not to go further and bestow largesse on the preferred stock at the expense of the common stock.

The defendants cite *In re Trados Inc. Shareholder Litigation* and *Equity–Linked Investors, L.P. v. Adams* for the proposition that it was the Board's duty, once it had ensured treatment of the preferred in accord with their contractual rights, to act in the best interests of the common. To have added a dollop of crème fraiche on top of the merger consideration to be offered to the preferred would itself, in these circumstances, have amounted to a breach of fiduciary duty. Finally, the defendants argue that even if there is a case where directors might be found to be "interested" in a transaction simply because they own common stock and no preferred stock, this is not that case. For example, a sizable premium to the preferred of 10% to 20% would cause a reduction in the common stock price of approximately $1.30 to $2.60 per share. Because four of the five Special Committee members own very modest common stock stakes, this would reduce those Special Committee members' Merger take by, at most, several thousand dollars, an amount the preferred stockholders have done nothing to show is material to these directors.

The defendants have the better of the arguments. After reviewing the evidence, I perceive no basis to find that the directors sought to advantage the common stockholders at the unfair expense of the preferred stockholders. What the preferred stockholders complain about is that the directors did not perceive themselves as having a duty to allocate more Merger consideration to the preferred than the preferred could demand as an entitlement under the Certificate. Had the Board been advised properly and had the right mindset, the preferred stockholders say, they would have given weight to various contractual rights of the preferred, such as their liquidation preference rights, and determined that on the basis of those rights, they should get a higher share than the Certificate guaranteed they could demand. Ideally, in fact, the Board should have employed a bargaining agent on their behalf to vigorously contend for the proposition that the largest part of the roast should be put on the preferred stockholders' plate.

I admit that the preferred stockholders can point to cases in which broad language supporting something like a duty of this kind to preferred stockholders was articulated. In *FLS Holdings,* for example, Chancellor Allen found that:

> FLS was represented in its negotiations . . . exclusively by directors who . . . owned large amounts of common stock. . . . No independent adviser or independent directors' committee was appointed to represent the interests of the preferred stock who were in a conflict of interest situation with the common. . . . No mechanism employing a truly independent agency on behalf of the preferred was employed before the transaction was formulated. Only the relatively weak procedural protection of an investment banker's ex post opinion was available to support the position that the final allocation was fair.

Likewise, in *Jedwab,* Chancellor Allen said that directors owe preferred stockholders a fiduciary duty to "exercise appropriate care in negotiating a proposed merger" in order to ensure that preferred shareholders receive their "'fair' allocation of the proceeds of a merger."

A close look at those cases, however, does not buttress the preferred stockholders' arguments. Notable in both cases was the absence of any contractual provision such as the one that exists in this case. That is, from what one can tell from *FLS Holdings* and *Jedwab,* there was no objective contractual basis—such as the conversion mechanism here—in either of those cases for the board to allocate the merger consideration between the preferred and the common. In the absence of such a basis, the only protection for the preferred is if the directors, as the backstop fiduciaries managing the corporation that sold them their shares, figure out a fair way to fill the gap left by incomplete contracting. Otherwise, the preferred would be subject to entirely arbitrary treatment in the context of a merger.

The broad language in *FLS Holdings* and *Jedwab* must, I think, be read against that factual backdrop. I say so for an important reason. Without this factual context, those opinions are otherwise in sharp tension with the great weight of our law's precedent in this area. In his recent decision in *Trados,* Chancellor Chandler summarized the weight of authority very well:

> Generally the rights and preferences of preferred stock are contractual in nature. This Court has held that directors owe fiduciary duties to preferred stockholders as well as common stockholders where the right claimed by the preferred "is not to a preference as against the common stock but rather a right shared equally with the common." Where this is not the case, however, "generally it will be the duty of the board, where discretionary judgment is to be exercised, to prefer the interests of the common stock—as the good faith judgment of the board sees them to be—to the interests created by the special rights, preferences, etc., of preferred stock, where there is a conflict." Thus, in circumstances where the interests of the common stockholders diverge from those of the preferred stockholders, it is *possible* that a director could breach her duty by improperly favoring the interests of the preferred stockholders over those of the common stockholders.[44]

Notably, that summary relied heavily on decisions by Chancellor Allen, who authored both *Jedwab* and *Equity–Linked Investors*. Does the summary of *Trados* expose some inconsistency in our law?

No, not when Chancellor Allen's decision in *HB Korenvaes Investments, L.P. v. Marriott Corp.*, 1993 WL 205040 (Del.Ch.), is considered. In that case, a board took very aggressive action that was, objectively speaking, adverse to the interest of the preferred stockholders. The Marriott board agreed to a transaction that issued a large special dividend to the common stock and indefinitely suspended dividends on the preferred stock. The preferred stockholders then sought to enjoin the payment of the special dividend, arguing that Marriott's directors breached their fiduciary duties to the preferred stockholders by agreeing to the transaction. Chancellor Allen rejected that argument, finding that even on the assumption that the board had acted to advantage the common in the transaction, no breach of duty of loyalty claim was stated.

In explaining his holding, he first stated:

> Rights of preferred stock are primarily but not exclusively contractual in nature. The special rights, limitations, etc. of preferred stock are created by the corporate charter or certificate of designation which acts has an amendment to a certificate of

---

44. *Trados,* 2009 WL 2225958 (quoting *Jedwab,* 509 A.2d at 594, and *Equity–Linked Investors, L.P. v. Adams,* 705 A.2d 1040, 1042 (Del.Ch. 1997)).

incorporation. Thus, to a very large extent, to ask what are the rights of the preferred stock is to ask what are the rights and obligations created contractually by the certificate of designation. In most instances, given the nature of the acts alleged and the terms of the certificate, this contractual level of analysis will exhaust the judicial review of corporate action challenged as a wrong to preferred stock.

Chancellor Allen then noted that "it has been recognized that directors may owe duties of loyalty and care to preferred stock" where a lack of contractual rights renders "the holder of preferred stock [in an] exposed and vulnerable position vis-à-vis the board of directors."[50] In light of preferred stock's dual contractual and fiduciary protection, Chancellor Allen stated:

> In fact, it is often not analytically helpful to ask the global question whether (or to assert that) the board of directors does or does not owe fiduciary duties of loyalty to the holders of preferred stock. The question (or the claim) may be too broad to be meaningful. In some instances (for example, when the question involves adequacy of disclosures to holders of preferred who have a right to vote) such a duty will exist. In others (for example, the declaration of a dividend designed to eliminate the preferred's right to vote) a duty to act for the good of the preferred does not. Thus, the question whether duties of loyalties are implicated by corporate action affecting preferred stock is a question that demands reference to the particularities of context to fashion a sound reply.

Having framed the analysis thusly, Chancellor Allen then found that the fact that the certificate of designation considered the possibility of an in-kind dividend and gave the preferred certain rights in that context was dispositive of whether there was any fiduciary duty claim:

> Most important . . . is the fact that the certificate of designation expressly contemplates the payment of a special dividend of the type here involved and supplies a device to protect the preferred stockholders in the event such a dividend is paid. . . . [Therefore,] the legal obligation of the corporation to the Series A Preferred Stock upon the declaration and payment of an in-kind dividend of securities has been expressly treated and rights created. It is these contractual rights—chiefly the right to convert into common stock now or to gross-up the conversion ratio for future conversions—that the holders of preferred stock possess as protection against the dilution of their shares' economic value through a permissible dividend.

The reasoning of *Korenvaes* reconciles the doctrine. When, by contract, the rights of the preferred in a particular transactional context are articulated, it is those rights that the board must honor. To the extent that the board does so, it need not go further and extend some unspecified fiduciary beneficence on the preferred at the expense of the common. When, however, as in *Jedwab* and *FLS Holdings*, there is no objective contractual basis for treatment of the preferred, then the board must act as a gap-filling agency and do its best to fairly reconcile the competing interests of the common and preferred.

This case is much closer to *Korenvaes* than it is to *Jedwab*. Although the preferred stockholders make much of the fact that the Certificate does not mandate that the

---

50. *Korenvaes*, 1993 WL 205040 (citing *FLS Holdings*, 1993 WL 104562).

Board accord the preferred stockholders the same treatment as the common in a merger, the only right that the preferred stockholders extracted for themselves was to receive the same consideration they would have received if they had converted their shares per the Conversion Formula set forth in the Certificate. In a situation where the preferred have no mandatory right to annual dividends, no voting rights on a merger, and where the Certificate plainly provides that a merger is not a liquidation event triggering a right to receipt of accrued dividends and the liquidation preferences before the common is paid, it is difficult to fathom any duty on the part of the Quad-raMed Board to go further and allocate additional value to the preferred. To do so would seem inconsistent with Chancellor Allen's well-reasoned observation in *Equity–Linked Investors* that

> While the board in these circumstances could have made a different business judgment, in my opinion, it violated no duty owed to the preferred in not doing so. The special protections offered to the preferred are contractual in nature. The corporation is, of course, required to respect those legal rights. But . . . generally it will be the duty of the board, where discretionary judgment is to be exercised, to prefer the interests of common stock as the good faith judgment of the board sees them to be to the interests created by the special rights, preferences, *etc.*, of preferred stock, where there is a conflict.

This is not to say that the QuadraMed Board did not owe the preferred stockholders fiduciary duties in connection with the Merger. The Board certainly did. But those were the duties it also owed to the common. In the context of a sale of a company, those are the duties articulated in *Revlon* and its progeny; namely, to take reasonable efforts to secure the highest price reasonably available for the corporation. Notably, the preferred stockholders do not argue that the Board fell short of its obligations in this regard.[56] They simply want more of the proceeds than they are guaranteed

---

56. Therefore, in this decision, I need not confront what might be considered a much harder case. Imagine an issuance of preferred stock that had an absolute right to annual dividend payments of a large amount. The corporation's discounted cash flow ("DCF") valuation indicates that the corporation could pay those dividends. The certificate of designation, like the one here, only gives the preferred the right to convert based on a formula, and does not give the preferred the right to vote on a merger, nor does it treat a merger as an event implicating the preferred's right to a liquidation preference.

The corporation is valued fairly based on a DCF model in the merger. But, the conversion formula results in the preferred stockholders receiving a price for their shares that is lower than the discounted value of the dividends the preferred stockholders would be guaranteed to receive in the next five years. The board realizes this but chooses not to allocate more consideration to the preferred.

This hypothetical case is harder because the financial analysis undergirding the board's determination to proceed with the merger suggests that the corporation would have the financial capacity to pay the dividends to the preferred and that the certificate of designations would require that the board do so if the corporation remained as a going concern.

But remember that the preferred would not have bargained for, in the context of a merger, any contractual protection other than the bottom line right to be treated on as converted basis and the board would not have dishonored that protection. Under the reasoning of Chancellor Allen in *Korenvaes*, the board would not have owed any fiduciary duty of loyalty to somehow adjust upward the preferred stock's portion of the consideration. In that case, he sanctioned aggressive board action that clearly advantaged the common at the expense of the preferred. Because the preferred had bargained only for a limited right of protection in that context and the board has not deprived them of that protection, Chancellor Allen found that the board had no further duty and could take the action it did.

by the Certificate. But I do not believe that the Board acted wrongly in viewing itself as under no obligation to satisfy that desire.

To indulge such a notion would create great uncertainty and inefficiency for corporations seeking to engage in mergers and acquisitions. Having had the chance to extract more and having only obtained the right to demand treatment under the Conversion Formula that operates to allocate any consideration in a merger between the preferred and the common on a basis the preferred assented to in the Certificate, why should the preferred have the right to ask the Board to give them more? The preferred stockholders' view of what the Board should do if this notion is embraced exemplifies the problem. The preferred stockholders would have the Board consider as relevant to value facts such as the preferred stock's dividend rights, rights in the event of liquidation, and limited voting rights. These, the preferred shareholders say, should be taken into account. But, of course, if that is so, it is also necessary to take into account the fact that the common get to vote on a merger and the preferred do not, and that the common stockholders get to elect a majority of the Board even if dividends are not paid to the preferred stockholders, and the preferred get to elect two substitute directors. That is, the Board would have to "weigh" these soft contractual possibilities against each other and somehow value them. Realizing that this is not so easy, the preferred stockholders say they have a simple answer: just form two special committees, have each retain their own advisors, and go at it. They can cut up the pie, and, while they do it, the acquiror will, in their hypothetical world, wait patiently for the results.

As Chancellor Allen indicated in *Korenvaes,* there may be "particularities of context"—such as when there is no objective contractual basis to determine a fair allocation between the preferred and common stock in a merger—that may demand this approach. It is nonetheless difficult to fathom the utility or, more important, the fairness of requiring such an approach in a situation when the preferred have a contractual protection of which they can avail themselves. To accept the preferred stockholders' view is to, in essence, give them leverage that they did not fairly extract in the contractual bargain, a hold-up value of some kind that acts as a judicially imposed substitute for the voting rights and other contractual protections that they could have, but did not obtain in the context of a merger.

Another counterproductive consequence would result from accepting the preferred stockholders' arguments. For its entire history, our corporate law has tried to insulate the good faith decisions of disinterested corporate directors from judicial second-guessing for well-known policy reasons. The business judgment rule embodies that policy judgment. When mergers and acquisitions activity became a more salient and constant feature of corporate life, our law did not cast aside the values of the business judgment rule. Rather, to deal with the different interests manager-directors may have in the context of responding to a hostile acquisition offer or determining which friendly merger partner to seek out, our law has consistently provided an incentive for the formation of boards comprised of a majority of independent directors who could act independently of management and pursue the best interests of the corporation and its stockholders. This impetus also recognized that managers' incentives and the temptations they face, when combined with fallible human nature, make it advisable to have independent directors to monitor the corporation's approach to law compliance, risk, and executive compensation. Consistent with this viewpoint, it has been thought that having directors who actually owned a meaningful, long-term common stock stake was a useful thing, because that would align the interests of the independent directors with the common stockholders and give them a personal incentive to fulfill their duties effectively.

To hold that independent directors are disabled from the protections of the business judgment rule when addressing a merger because they own common stock, and not the corporation's preferred stock, is not something that should be done lightly. Corporate law must work in practice to serve the best interests of society and investors in creating wealth. Director compensation is already a difficult enough issue to address without adding on the need to ponder whether the independent directors need to buy or receive as compensation a share of any preferred stock issuance made by the corporation, for fear that, if they do not have an equally-weighted portfolio of some kind, they will not be able to impartially balance questions that potentially affect the common and preferred stockholders in different ways. Adhering to the rule of *Equity–Linked Investors*, *Trados*, and other similar cases, which hold that it is the duty of directors to pursue the best interests of the corporation and its common stockholders, if that can be done faithfully with the contractual promises owed to the preferred, avoids this policy dilemma. Admittedly, it does not solve for certain situations that directors might create themselves by authorizing multiple and sometimes exotic classes of common stock, situations that have led this court to, as a matter of necessity, consider the directors' portfolio balance, but it at least does not exacerbate the already complex challenge of compensating independent directors in a sensible way. And, given the unique nature of preferred stock and the often-fraught circumstances that lead to its issuance, our law should be chary to somehow suggest that otherwise independent directors should be receiving shares of this kind at the risk of facing being called "non-independent" or, worse, being deemed by loose reasoning to be "interested" and therefore somehow personally liable under the entire fairness standard for a merger allocation decision.

For the reasons discussed above, I refuse to enjoin the transaction. The preferred stockholders' motion is therefore denied.

QUESTIONS

1. In light of prior Delaware cases like *Rothschild International Corp. v. Liggett Group Inc*. (1984), why did the preferred stock not have a merger trigger tied to the liquidation preference?
2. What was the purpose of the mandatory conversion right held by QuadraMed, which would trigger upon the common stock reaching the share price of $25 per share?
3. Are the decisions in *Jedwab*, *FLS Holdings*, *HB Korenvaes*, *Trados*, and *LC Capital* consistent?
4. Your client is considering selling the company to an acquirer. The company has preferred and common stockholders. Explain Delaware law on the allocation of merger consideration between preferred and common stockholders.

D. CASE STUDY: WARREN BUFFETT'S INVESTMENT IN GOLDMAN SACHS

Goldman Sachs began underwriting securities in 1905, and in the ensuing century it became one of the most prominent full-service investment banks on Wall Street. Until 1999, it was operated as a private partnership. That year it did an initial public offering and became a publicly traded company. Since then, it has remained a highly success-ful company. However, during the financial crisis of 2008–2009, it experienced sig-nificant financial problems arising from the meltdown in the mortgage securities and related markets.

Background

After a long period of industry consolidation in the 1980s and 1990s, there were only five major, pure investment banks left: Goldman Sachs, Morgan Stanley, Merrill Lynch, Lehman Brothers, and Bear Stearns. These firms were "pure" investment banks because they were not affiliated with larger commercial banks. The combination of commercial and investment banking was made possible with the demise and repeal of the Glass-Steagall Act, a Depression-era statute that separated commercial banks and investment banks. Major investment banks had been acquired by and affiliated with larger commercial banks and depository institutions, such as Citigroup (formerly Salomon Smith Barney), UBS Warburg, Credit Suisse First Boston, and J.P. Morgan. By 2007, only five independent investment banks remained. By 2010, after the financial crisis, there would be only two firms left: Goldman Sachs and Morgan Stanley.

The activities of full-service investment banks can be broadly categorized into three categories: (1) investment banking, which is primarily mergers and acquisitions advisory services, and securities underwriting ("investment banking"); (2) asset man-agement and other securities services ("asset management"); and (3) trading and principal investments, including broker/dealer activities and proprietary trading ("trad-ing"). Investment banking and asset management are primarily fee-based businesses. The activity of investment banking can be risky, such as when a bank agrees to a firm commitment underwriting. M&A advisory work requires minimal capital, and the risks of underwriting can be managed through syndication and pricing. With respect to trading, an investment bank generates revenue in two primary ways: First, it charges commissions on trades executed for clients in its capacity as a broker; second, it takes proprietary trading positions as a dealer and principal in investments. The latter con-stitutes a large portion of net revenues from trading, and its activity is only possible with substantial support from the firm's capital and therefore puts that capital at risk. Proprietary trading and principal investment are the primary activities that led to the distress of major Wall Street firms.

The following charts provide composite data for the five investment banks before the financial crisis. These composite data do not incorporate 2008 data for Bear Stearns and Lehman Brothers because these two firms were acquired or filed for insolvency before they could file their 2008 10-Ks. Thus, 2008 data include only Goldman Sachs, Morgan Stanley, and Merrill Lynch.

The charts provide (1) composite net revenue segmentation of the business activities of the five investment banks, (2) their leverage ratios, and (3) their ROEs.

This data tells a compelling story. The business model of investment banks sig-nificantly evolved as the industry underwent a business cycle. From 1996 to 2000, the

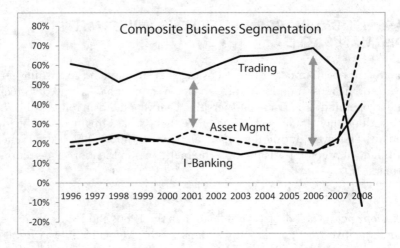

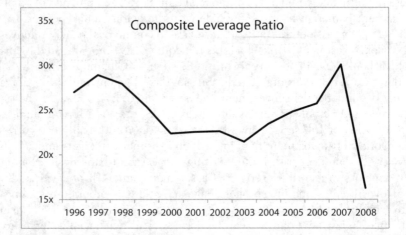

business mix of investment banking, asset management, and trading was relatively stable. These years marked a period of economic growth and the run up to the Internet-technology bubble. As expected, investment banks were highly profitable during this period as seen in the ROE in the range of 25 percent. During this period, there were also two major events in the industry. First was the 1998 merger of Citicorp and Travelers, which provided the model of post-Glass-Steagall universal financial services and cross-selling of various financial products under a single firm umbrella. Second was the 1999 conversion of Goldman Sachs from a private partnership to a public company. After the Internet bubble burst in 2000 and the September 11, 2001 terrorist attacks, profitability significantly declined as a result of the recession, and ROE hovered in the range of low teens, resembling the profitability levels of commercial banks. We also saw investment banking and asset management steadily decline as measured in terms of net revenue contribution in response to the slowing of investment activities during the recession, and trading became the prominent business activity of investment banks. This trend reached its apex in 2006 when trading contributed 69 percent of net revenue, as compared to 15 percent for investment banking and 16 percent for asset management.

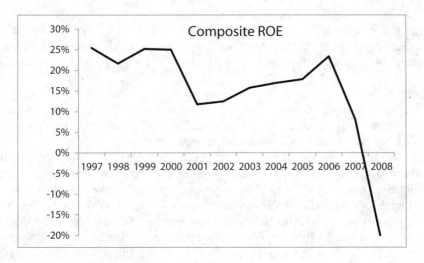

The focus on trading coincided with dramatically increasing leverage. Investment banks were not always so highly levered. The banks were seeking greater funding with short-term debt, as seen in the leverage ratios, as well as funding long-term capital with greater leverage, as seen in debt-to-equity ratios. From 2003 to 2007, the leverage ratio increased from approximately 21x to 30x. Although the leverage ratios were high in the 1990s as well, investment banks had diversified portfolios of business activities, with much of the net revenue coming from fees and commissions from investment banking and asset management, reducing the volatility of revenues and earnings from trading. Extreme leverage to fund primarily proprietary trading was a recent phenomenon. When a firm is highly leveraged and successful, its ROE tends to be higher. The influence of increasing leverage on ROE, which dramatically increased from the doldrums of the dot-com crash, the September 11 terrorist attacks, and subsequent recession—that is, until the industry collapsed under the weight of its leverage.

The increase in leverage was made possible by a crucial change in SEC regulation. Before 2004, the net capital requirement imposed by the SEC required that "no broker or dealer . . . shall permit its aggregate indebtedness to all other persons to exceed 1500 percent of its net capital."* This provided a definite, tangible limit on leverage. In 2004, the SEC changed the net capital rule and allowed investment banks to opt out of this restriction. The agency established a voluntary, alternative method of computing deductions to net capital for investment banks based on mathematical models to calculate net capital requirements for market and derivatives-related credit risk.** Given that these models were held by the firms themselves and the agency merely approves them for use, the change in the rule allowed great leeway and discretion in

---

* 17 C.F.R. §240.15c3-1(a)(1)(i) (2003). The rule also allows an alternative standard. *Id.* §240.15c3-1(a)(1)(ii). Aggregate indebtedness was defined as "the total money liabilities," subject to certain exclusions including collateralized indebtedness. *Id.* §240.15c3-1(c)(1). Net capital is net worth adjusted by certain items. *Id.* §240.15c3-1(c)(2).

** Alternative Net Capital Requirements for Broker-Dealers That Are Part of Consolidated Supervised Entities, Exchange Act Release No. 49,830, 69 Fed. Reg. 34,428, at 34,428 (June 21, 2004) (to be codified at 17 C.F.R. pts. 200 and 240) [hereinafter Alternative Net Capital Requirements].

setting the net capital levels. A significant consequence is, as the SEC noted, that a "broker-dealer's deductions for market and credit risk probably will be lower under the alternative method of computing net capital than under the standard net capital rule."***

Predictably, the leverage ratio of investment banks began to increase during 2004 and thereafter. During this time, the firms were also increasingly trading exotic securities, such as credit derivatives and collateralized debt obligations of asset-backed securities, for which there was no liquid market.

The data here is not surprising with respect to increasing leverage and reliance on debt to boost profitability. There is also a broader context of the evolutionary changes on Wall Street that took place over the past several decades. We see a business cycle: the economic boom of the 1990s, the technology crash of 2000, the September 11, 2001 terrorist attacks, and the economic slowdown of 2000 to 2002. The decline in the general economy at the turn of the century naturally led to a decline in revenue from asset management and investment banking. Profitability declined sharply in the period 2000 to 2002. The ROE was reaching levels of commercial banks and insurance companies, and not the high flying levels investment banks saw in the 1990s. At the same time, we also see that the capital markets were experiencing a period of declining yields on credit. Cheaper cost of credit incentivized leverage, which Wall Street firms took advantage of to boost profitability. The factors converged and in the subsequent years we experienced the evolution of the Wall Street business model.

An examination of Goldman Sachs reflects this narrative. The charts below provide (1) Goldman Sachs' net revenue segmentation of the investment bank's business activities, (2) its leverage ratio, and (3) its ROE.

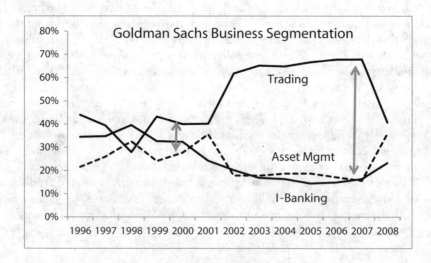

*** Alternative Net Capital Requirements, 69 Fed. Reg. at 34,428; *see id.* at 34,429 ("One commentator, however, questioned the use of models to the extent that it would lower broker-dealer capital requirements. . . .").

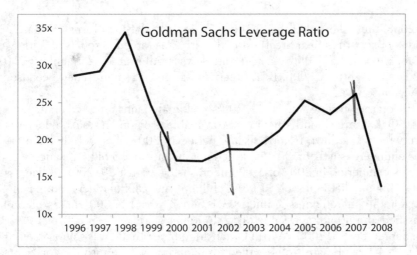

Goldman Sachs Leverage Ratio

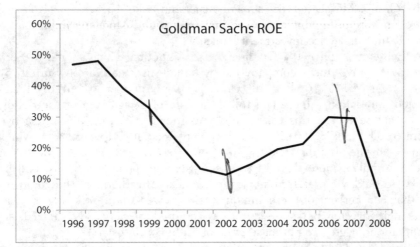

Goldman Sachs ROE

The trends shown in the data mirror the broader trends on Wall Street. The move away from a balance business mix to trading is even more pronounced for Goldman Sachs. When it was a private partnership before 1999, it was highly levered, but the business mix was diversified among three main lines of products and services. The result was an extraordinarily profitable firm as seen in the ROE figures hovering around 50 percent. Around the time of its IPO in 1999, the leverage ratio, debt-to-equity ratio, and ROE declined. A return to higher profitability was achieved by greater leverage and reliance on trading, which came to constitute approximately 70 percent of Goldman Sachs' net revenue.

Financial Crisis

In late 2006, Goldman Sachs began to realize that the residential real estate and mortgage securities markets were becoming distressed. It began shifting its risk away from mortgages and began to bet against the market. In 2007, this strategy yielded earnings of $4 billion on short-sales of mortgage securities, which more than offset the $1.5 to $2 billion losses from mortgage securities.

In 2008, the full brunt of the financial crisis hit Wall Street firms. In March 2008, a liquidity crisis struck Bear Stearns and the firm was forced to sell itself to JP Morgan Chase for $10 per share. Previously, the stock was trading at $172 in January 2007 and $93 as late as February 2008. Bear Stearns was forced to be rescued because it was effectively insolvent.

In the quarter ending August 29, 2008, Goldman Sachs reported on its unaudited Form 10-Q that three months' net income available to common stockholders was $810 million, which was down from the same period in 2007 of $2.8 billion. In the nine months ending August 29, 2008, it earned net income of $.3 billion, which was down from the same period in 2007 of $8.2 billion. As of August 29, 2008, it had assets of $1,081.8 billion, liabilities of $1,036.2 billion, and shareholders' equity of $45.6 billion. Of the shareholders' equity, $3.1 billion was 124,000 shares of preferred stock issued at a liquidation value of $25,000 per share.

On September 15, 2008, Merrill Lynch announced that it was selling itself to Bank of America, and Lehman Brothers filed for bankruptcy. The next day, on September 16, the U.S. government announced a multibillion dollar rescue of American International Group (AIG) and it took a major ownership stake. These events led to a global credit contagion, after which only Goldman Sachs and Morgan Stanley survived as independent, full-service investment banks.

On September 23, 2008, Goldman Sachs announced that it sold to Berkshire Hathaway, an investment company led by famed investor Warren Buffett, 50,000 shares of Series G 10 Percent Cumulative Perpetual Preferred Stock with $100,000 liquidation value. (The full certificate of designation of the Series G is attached at the end of this case study.) Additionally, Buffett received a five-year warrant to buy 43,478,260 shares of common stock at $115 per share, which was discounted to the prior day's closing stock price of $120.78 per share. Buffett agreed not to accumulate more than 14.9 percent stake in Goldman Sachs, and he was required to hold the preferred stock for five years. Furthermore, he could not sell more than 3.5 percent of the common stock received from exercising the warrants to any single investor. Berkshire Hathaway acquired the Series G preferreds and the warrants for an aggregate purchase price of $5 billion in cash.

The next day, Goldman Sachs also raised $5.75 billion through a public common stock issue.

The next day, on September 24, Goldman Sachs sold 4,675 million shares of common stock on the public market at a price of $123 per share, which produced proceeds of $5.75 billion.

On October 28, 2008, the U.S. government required Goldman Sachs to accept $10 billion in TARP funds.

In the fiscal year ending on November 28, 2008, Goldman Sachs reported on its audited Form 10-K that its net income available to common stockholders was $2.0 billion, which was down from $11.4 billion in 2007. It had assets of $884.5 billion, liabilities of $820.2 billion, and shareholders' equity of $64.4 billion. Of the shareholders' equity, preferred stock constituted $16.5 billion.

Aftermath

After 2009, it became clear that Goldman Sachs would weather the financial storm. Goldman Sachs paid off the capital issued to the U.S. government and Berkshire Hathaway.

On June 17, 2009, Goldman Sachs repaid the TARP funds by repurchasing preferred stock issued to the U.S. government for $10.04 billion. On July 22, 2009, Goldman Sachs repurchased the warrants on 12.2 million shares from the U.S. government for $1.1 billion.

On April 18, 2011, Goldman Sachs repaid Berkshire Hathaway by repurchasing the Series G preferred stock for $5.5 billion ($5 billion in face value and $500 million in dividends).

In March 2013, Goldman Sachs and Berkshire Hathaway amended the warrants deal so that Berkshire Hathaway did not acquire 43.478 million shares of Goldman Sachs. Instead, Berkshire Hathaway converted the warrants into shares equal in value to the difference between the exercise price and the average closing price for Goldman Sachs in the 10 trading days up to October 1, 2013.

In October 2013, Berkshire Hathaway exercised the warrants at $115 per share. The 10-day average trading price was $164.38 per share. Berkshire Hathaway got 13.1 million shares of common stock, making it the sixth largest external investor in Goldman Sachs. The warrants netted a profit of $2.15 billion.

QUESTIONS

1. In what way did the business model of investment banking firms contribute to their distress during the financial crisis?
2. Why did Goldman Sachs issue equity in September 2008? What was the effect of the preferred stock and common stock equity issuances in September and October 2008?
3. Review the certificate of designation of the Series G preferred stock, which is attached below. What are its most essential terms? What legal protections did Berkshire Hathaway get in the preferred stock?
4. In terms of the business deal, who got the better end of the deal?

* * *

Certificate of Designation of 10 Percent Cumulative Perpetual Preferred Stock, Series G of the Goldman Sachs Group, Inc.

THE GOLDMAN SACHS GROUP, INC., a corporation organized and existing under the General Corporation Law of the State of Delaware (the "Corporation"), in accordance with the provisions of Sections 103 and 151 thereof, DOES HEREBY CERTIFY:

The Securities Issuance Committee (the "Committee") of the board of directors of the Corporation (the "Board of Directors"), in accordance with the resolutions of the Board of Directors dated September 16, 2005 and September 29, 2006, the provisions of the restated certificate of incorporation and the amended and restated bylaws of the Corporation and applicable law, at a meeting duly called and held on September 29, 2008, adopted the following resolution creating a series of 50,000 shares of Preferred Stock of the Corporation designated as "10% Cumulative Perpetual Preferred Stock, Series G".

RESOLVED, that pursuant to the authority vested in the Committee and in accordance with the resolutions of the Board of Directors dated September 16, 2005 and September 29, 2006, the provisions of the restated certificate of incorporation and the amended and restated bylaws of the Corporation and applicable law, a series of Preferred Stock, par value $.01 per share, of the Corporation be and hereby is created, and that the designation and number of shares of such series, and the voting and other powers, preferences and relative, participating, optional or other rights, and the qualifications, limitations and restrictions thereof, of the shares of such series, are as follows:

Section 1. Designation. The distinctive serial designation of such series of Preferred Stock is "10% Cumulative Perpetual Preferred Stock, Series G" ("Series G"). Each share of Series G shall be identical in all respects to every other share of Series G.

Section 2. Number of Shares. The authorized number of shares of Series G shall be 50,000. Shares of Series G that are redeemed, purchased or otherwise acquired by the Corporation, or converted into another series of Preferred Stock, shall revert to authorized but unissued shares of Preferred Stock (*provided* that any such cancelled shares of Series G may be reissued only as shares of any series other than Series G).

Section 3. Definitions. As used herein with respect to Series G:

(a) "ByLaws" means the amended and restated bylaws of the Corporation, as they may be amended from time to time.

(b) "Business Day" means a day that is a Monday, Tuesday, Wednesday, Thursday or Friday and is not a day on which banking institutions

in New York City generally are authorized or obligated by law, regulation or executive order to close.

(c) "Certificate of Designations" means this Certificate of Designations relating to the Series G, as it may be amended from time to time.

(d) "Certification of Incorporation" shall mean the restated certificate of incorporation of the Corporation, as it may be amended from time to time, and shall include this Certificate of Designations.

(e) "Common Stock" means the common stock, par value $0.01 per share, of the Corporation.

(f) "Junior Stock" means the Common Stock and any other class or series of stock of the Corporation (other than Series G) that ranks junior

to Series G either or both as to the payment of dividends and/or as to the distribution of assets on any liquidation, dissolution or winding up of the Corporation.

(g) "Original Issue Date" means October 1, 2008.

(h) "Parity Stock" means any class or series of stock of the Corporation (other than Series G) that ranks equally with Series G both in the payment of dividends and in the distribution of assets on any liquidation, dissolution or winding up of the Corporation (in each case without regard to whether dividends accrue cumulatively or non-cumulatively). Without limiting the foregoing, Parity Stock shall include the Corporation's (i) Floating Rate Non-Cumulative Preferred Stock, Series A; (ii) 6.20% Non-Cumulative Preferred Stock, Series B; (iii) Floating Rate Non-Cumulative Preferred Stock, Series C; (iv) Floating Rate Non-Cumulative Preferred Stock, Series D; (v) Perpetual Non-Cumulative Preferred Stock, Series E; and (vi) Perpetual Non-Cumulative Preferred Stock, Series F.

(i) "Preferred Stock" means any and all series of preferred stock of the Corporation, including the Series G.

(j) "Voting Parity Stock" means, with regard to any matter as to which the holders of Series G are entitled to vote as specified in Section 8 of this Certificate of Designations, any and all series of Parity Stock upon which like voting rights have been conferred and are exercisable with respect to such matter.

(k) "Voting Preferred Stock" means, with regard to any matter as to which the holders of Series G are entitled to vote as specified in Section 8 of this Certificate of Designations, any and all series of Preferred Stock (other than Series G) that rank equally with Series G either as to the payment of dividends or as to the distribution of assets upon liquidation, dissolution or winding up of the Corporation and upon which like voting rights have been conferred and are exercisable with respect to such matter.

Section 4. Dividends.

(a) Rate. Holders of Series G shall be entitled to receive, on each share of Series G, out of funds legally available for the payment of dividends under Delaware law, cumulative cash dividends with respect to each Dividend Period (as defined below) at a per annum rate of 10% on (i) the amount of $100,000 per share of Series G and (ii) the amount of accrued and unpaid dividends on such share of Series G, if any (giving effect to (A) any dividends paid through the Dividend Payment Date (as defined below) that begins such Dividend Period (other than the initial Dividend Period) and (B) any dividends (including dividends thereon at a per annum rate of 10% to the date of payment) paid during such Dividend Period). Such dividends shall begin to accrue and be cumulative from the Original Issue Date, shall compound on each Dividend Payment Date (i.e., no dividends shall accrue on other dividends unless and until the first Dividend Payment Date for such other dividends has passed without such other dividends having been paid on such date) and shall be payable in arrears (as provided below in this Section 4(a)), but only when, as and if declared by the Board of Directors or the Committee (or another duly authorized committee of the Board of Directors) on each November 10, February 10, May 10 and August 10 (each, a "Dividend Payment Date"), commencing on November 10, 2008; *provided* that if any such Dividend Payment Date would otherwise occur on a day that is not a Business Day, such Dividend Payment Date shall instead be (and any dividend payable on Series G on such Dividend Payment Date shall instead be payable on) the immediately succeeding Business Day. Dividends payable on the Series G in respect of any Dividend Period shall be computed on the basis of a 360-day year consisting of twelve 30-day months. The amount of dividends payable on the Series G on any date prior to the end of a Dividend Period, and for the initial Dividend Period, shall be computed on the basis of a 360-day year consisting of twelve 30-day months, and actual days elapsed over a 30-day month.

Dividends that are payable on Series G on any Dividend Payment Date will be payable to holders of record of Series G as they appear on the stock register of the Corporation on the applicable record date, which shall be the 15th calendar day before such Dividend Payment Date (as originally scheduled) or such other record date fixed by the Board of Directors or the Committee (or another duly authorized committee of the Board of Directors) that is not more than 60 nor less than 10 days prior to such Dividend Payment Date (each, a "Dividend Record Date"). Any such day that is a Dividend Record Date shall be a Dividend Record Date whether or not such day is a Business Day.

Each dividend period (a "Dividend Period") shall commence on and include a Dividend Payment Date (other than the initial Dividend Period, which shall commence on and include the Original Issue Date of the Series G) and shall end on and include the calendar day next preceding the next Dividend Payment Date. Dividends payable in respect of a Dividend Period shall be payable in arrears on the first Dividend Payment Date after such Dividend Period.

Holders of Series G shall not be entitled to any dividends, whether payable in cash, securities or other property, other than dividends (if any) declared and payable on the Series G as specified in this Section 4 (subject to the other provisions of this Certificate of Designations).

(b) Priority of Dividends. So long as any share of Series G remains outstanding, no dividend shall be declared or paid on the Common Stock or any other shares of Junior Stock (other than a dividend payable solely in Junior Stock), and no Common Stock, Junior Stock or Parity Stock shall be purchased, redeemed or otherwise acquired for consideration by the Corporation, directly or indirectly (other than as a result of are classification of Junior Stock for or into other Junior Stock or of Parity Stock for or into other Parity Stock (with the same or lesser aggregate liquidation amount) or Junior Stock, or the exchange or conversion of one share of Junior Stock for or into another share of Junior Stock or of one share of Parity Stock for or into another share of Parity Stock (with the same or lesser per share liquidation amount) or Junior Stock) during a Dividend Period, unless all accrued and unpaid dividends for all past Dividend Periods, including the latest completed Dividend Period(including, if applicable as provided in Section 4(a) above, dividends on such amount), on all outstanding shares of Series G have been declared and paid in full (or declared and a sum sufficient for the payment thereof has been set aside for the benefit of the holders of shares of Series G on the applicable record date). The foregoing provision shall not restrict the ability of Goldman, Sachs & Co., or any other affiliate of the Corporation, to engage in any market-making or customer facilitation transactions in Junior Stock or Parity Stock in the ordinary course of its business or, in connection with the issuance of Junior Stock or Parity Stock, to engage in ordinary sale and repurchase transactions to facilitate the distribution of such Junior Stock or Parity Stock.

When dividends are not paid (or declared and a sum sufficient for payment thereof set aside for the benefit of the holders thereof on the applicable record date) on any Dividend Payment Date (or, in the case of Parity Stock having dividend payment dates different from the Dividend Payment Dates, on a dividend payment date falling within a Dividend Period related to such Dividend Payment Date) in full upon the Series G and any shares of Parity Stock, all dividends declared on the Series G and all such Parity Stock and payable on such Dividend Payment Date (or, in the case of Parity Stock having dividend payment dates different from the Dividend Payment Dates, on a dividend payment date falling within the Dividend Period related to such Dividend Payment Date) shall be declared pro rata so that the respective amounts of such dividends declared shall bear the same ratio to each other as all accrued and unpaid dividends per share on the Series G (including, if applicable as provided in Section 4(a) above, dividends on such amount) and all Parity Stock payable on such Dividend Payment Date (or, in the case of Parity Stock having dividend payment dates different from the Dividend Payment Dates, on a dividend payment date falling within the Dividend Period related to such Dividend Payment Date) bear to each other.

Subject to the foregoing, such dividends (payable in cash, securities or other property) as may be determined by the Board of Directors or the Committee (or another duly authorized committee of the Board of Directors) may be declared and paid on any securities, including Common Stock and other Junior Stock, from time to time out of any funds legally available for such payment, and the Series G shall not be entitled to participate in any such dividends.

Section 5. Liquidation Rights.

(a) **Voluntary or Involuntary Liquidation**. In the event of any liquidation, dissolution or winding up of the affairs of the Corporation, whether voluntary or involuntary, holders of Series G shall be entitled to receive for each share of Series G, out of the assets of the Corporation or proceeds thereof (whether capital or surplus) available for distribution to stockholders of the Corporation, and after satisfaction of all liabilities and obligations to creditors of the Corporation, before any distribution of such assets or proceeds is made to or set aside for the holders of Common Stock and any other stock of the Corporation ranking junior to the Series G as to such distribution, payment in full in an amount equal to the sum of (i) $100,000 per share and (ii) the accrued and unpaid dividends thereon (including, if applicable as provided in Section 4(a) above, dividends on such amount), whether or not declared, to the date of payment.

(b) **Partial Payment**. If in any distribution described in Section 5(a) above the assets of the Corporation or proceeds thereof are not sufficient to pay the Liquidation Preferences (as defined below) in full to all holders of Series G and all holders of any stock of the Corporation ranking equally with the Series G as to such distribution, the amounts paid to the holders of Series G and to the holders of all such other stock shall be paid *pro rata* in accordance with the respective aggregate Liquidation Preferences of the holders of Series G and the holders of all such other stock. In any such distribution, the "Liquidation Preference" of any holder of stock of the Corporation shall mean the amount otherwise payable to such holder in such distribution (assuming no limitation on the assets of the Corporation available for such distribution), including an amount equal to any declared but unpaid dividends (and, in the case of any holder of stock, including the Series G, on which dividends accrue on a cumulative basis, an amount equal to any accrued and unpaid dividends (including, if applicable, dividends on such amount), whether or not declared, as applicable), *provided* that the Liquidation Preference for any share of Series G shall be determined in accordance with Section 5(a) above.

(c) **Residual Distributions**. If the Liquidation Preference has been paid in full to all holders of Series G, the holders of other stock of the Corporation shall be entitled to receive all remaining assets of the Corporation (or proceeds thereof) according to their respective rights and preferences.

(d) **Merger, Consolidation and Sale of Assets Not Liquidation**. For purposes of this Section 5, the merger or consolidation of the Corporation with any other corporation or other entity, including a merger or consolidation in which the holders of Series G receive cash, securities or other property for their shares, or the sale, lease or exchange (for cash, securities or other property) of all or substantially all of the assets of the Corporation, shall not constitute a liquidation, dissolution or winding up of the Corporation.

Section 6. Redemption.

(a) **Optional Redemption**. The Corporation, at its option, subject to the approval of the Board of Governors of the Federal Reserve System, may redeem, in whole at any time or in part from time to time, the shares of Series G at the time outstanding, upon notice given as provided in Section 6(c) below, at a redemption price equal to the sum of (i) $110,000 per share and (ii) the accrued and unpaid dividends thereon(including, if applicable as provided in Section 4(a) above, dividends on such amount), whether or not declared, to the redemption date, *provided* that the minimum number of shares of Series G redeemable at any time is the lesser of (i) 10,000 shares of Series G and (ii) the number of shares of Series G outstanding. The redemption price for any shares of Series G shall be payable on the redemption date to the holder of such shares against surrender of the certificate(s) evidencing such shares to the Corporation or its agent. Any declared but unpaid dividends payable on a redemption date that occurs subsequent to the Dividend Record Date for a Dividend Period shall not be paid to the holder entitled to receive the redemption price on the redemption date, but rather shall be paid to the holder of record of the redeemed shares on such Dividend Record Date relating to the Dividend Payment Date as provided in Section 4 above. An exchange of Series G for Spinco Preferred (as defined in the Securities Purchase Agreement, dated as of September 29, 2008, between the Corporation and Berkshire Hathaway Inc. (the "SPA")) pursuant to Section 4.7 of the SPA, shall not be deemed to be a redemption for purposes of this Section 6.

(b) **No Sinking Fund**. The Series G will not be subject to any mandatory redemption, sinking fund or other similar provisions. Holders of Series G will have no right to require redemption of any shares of Series G.

(c) **Notice of Redemption**. Notice of every redemption of shares of Series G shall be given by first class mail, postage prepaid, addressed to the holders of record of the shares to be redeemed at their respective last addresses appearing on the books of the Corporation. Such mailing shall be at least 30 days and not more than 60 days before the date fixed for redemption. Any notice mailed as provided in this Subsection shall be conclusively presumed to have been duly given, whether or not the holder receives such notice, but failure duly to give such notice by mail, or any defect in such notice or in the mailing thereof, to any holder of shares of Series G designated for redemption shall not affect the validity of the proceedings for the redemption of any other shares of Series G. Notwithstanding the foregoing, if the Series G are issued in book-entry form through The Depository Trust Company or any other similar facility, notice of redemption may be given to the holders of Series G at such time and in any manner permitted by such facility. Each notice of redemption given to a holder shall state: (1) the redemption date; (2) the number of shares of Series G to be redeemed and, if less than all the shares held by such holder are to be redeemed, the number of such shares to be redeemed from such holder; (3) the redemption price; and (4) the place or places where certificates for such shares are to be surrendered for payment of the redemption price.

(d) **Partial Redemption**. In case of any redemption of part of the shares of Series G at the time outstanding, the shares to be redeemed shall be selected either *pro rata* or in such other manner as the Corporation may determine to be fair and equitable. Subject to the provisions hereof, the Corporation shall have full power and authority to prescribe the terms and conditions upon which shares of Series G shall be redeemed from time to time. If fewer than all the shares represented by any certificate are redeemed, a new certificate shall be issued representing the unredeemed shares without charge to the holder thereof.

(e) **Effectiveness of Redemption**. If notice of redemption has been duly given and if on or before the redemption date specified in the notice all funds necessary for the redemption have been deposited by the Corporation, in trust for the *pro rata* benefit of the holders of the shares called for redemption, with a bank or trust company doing business in the Borough of Manhattan, The City of New York, and having a capital and surplus of at least $50 million and selected by the Board of Directors, so as to be and continue to be available solely therefor, then, notwithstanding that any certificate for any share so called for redemption has not been surrendered for cancellation, on and after the redemption date dividends shall cease to accrue on all shares so called for redemption, all shares so called for redemption shall no longer be deemed outstanding and all rights with respect to such shares shall forthwith on such redemption date cease and terminate, except only the right of the holders thereof to receive the amount payable on such redemption from such bank or trust company, without interest. Any funds unclaimed at the end of three years from the redemption date shall, to the extent permitted by law, be released to the Corporation, after which time the holders of the shares so called for redemption shall look only to the Corporation for payment of the redemption price of such shares.

Section 7. Conversion. Holders of Series G shares shall have no right to exchange or convert such shares into any other securities.

Section 8. Voting Rights.

(a) **General**. The holders of Series G shall not have any voting rights except as set forth below or as otherwise from time to time required by law.

(b) **Class Voting Rights as to Particular Matters**. So long as any shares of Series G are outstanding, in addition to any other vote or consent of stockholders required by law or by the Certificate of Incorporation, the vote or consent of the holders of at least 66 2/3% of the shares of Series G and any Voting Preferred Stock at the time outstanding and entitled to vote thereon, voting together as a single class, given in person or by proxy, either in writing without a meeting or by vote at any meeting called for the purpose, shall be necessary for effecting or validating:

(i) **Authorization of Senior Stock**. Any amendment or alteration of the Certificate of Incorporation to authorize or create, or increase the authorized amount of, any shares of any class or series of capital stock of the Corporation ranking senior to the Series G with respect to either or both the payment of dividends and/or the distribution of assets on any liquidation, dissolution or winding up of the Corporation;

(ii) **Amendment of Series G**. Any amendment, alteration or repeal of any provision of the Certificate of Incorporation so as to materially and adversely affect the special rights, preferences, privileges or voting powers of the Series G, taken as a whole; or

(iii) **Share Exchanges, Reclassifications, Mergers and Consolidations**. Any consummation of a binding share exchange or reclassification involving the

Series G, or of a merger or consolidation of the Corporation with another corporation or other entity, unless in each case (x) the shares of Series G remain outstanding or, in the case of any such merger or consolidation with respect to which the Corporation is not the surviving or resulting entity, are converted into or exchanged for preference securities of the surviving or resulting entity or its ultimate parent, and (y) such shares remaining outstanding or such preference securities, as the case may be, have such rights, preferences, privileges and voting powers, and limitations and restrictions thereof, taken as a whole, as are not materially less favorable to the holders thereof than the rights, preferences, privileges and voting powers, and limitations and restrictions thereof, of the Series G immediately prior to such consummation, taken as a whole; *provided*, *however*, that for all purposes of this Section 8(b), any increase in the amount of the authorized Preferred Stock, or the creation and issuance, or an increase in the authorized or issued amount, of any other series of Preferred Stock ranking equally with and/or junior to the Series G with respect to the payment of dividends (whether such dividends are cumulative or non-cumulative) and/or the distribution of assets upon liquidation, dissolution or winding up of the Corporation will not be deemed to adversely affect the rights, preferences, privileges or voting powers of the Series G.

If any amendment, alteration, repeal, share exchange, reclassification, merger or consolidation specified in this Section 8(b) would adversely affect the Series G and one or more but not all other series of Preferred Stock, then only the Series G and such series of Preferred Stock as are adversely affected by and entitled to vote on the matter shall vote on the matter together as a single class (in lieu of all other series of Preferred Stock).

If any amendment, alteration, repeal, share exchange, reclassification, merger or consolidation specified in this Section 8(b) would adversely affect the Series G but would not similarly adversely affect all other series of Voting Parity Stock, then only the Series G and each other series of Voting Parity Stock as is similarly adversely affected by and entitled to vote on the matter, if any, shall vote on the matter together as a single class (in lieu of all other series of Preferred Stock).

(c) Series G Voting Rights as to Particular Matters. In addition to any other vote or consent of stockholders required by law or by the Certificate of Incorporation, so long as at least 10,000 shares of Series G are outstanding, the vote or consent of the holders of at least 50.1% of the shares of Series G at the time outstanding, voting in person or by proxy, either in writing without a meeting or by vote at any meeting called for the purpose, shall be necessary for effecting or validating:

(i) Authorization or Issuance of Senior Stock. Any amendment or alteration of the Certificate of Incorporation to authorize or create, or increase the authorized amount of, any shares of any class or series of capital stock of the Corporation, or the issuance of any shares of any class or series of capital stock of the Corporation, in each case, ranking senior to the Series G with respect to either or both the payment of dividends and/or the distribution of assets on any liquidation, dissolution or winding up of the Corporation;

(ii) Amendment of Series G. Any amendment, alteration or repeal of any provision of the Certificate of Incorporation so as to affect or change the rights, preferences, privileges or voting powers of the Series G so as not to be substantially similar to those in effect immediately prior to such amendment, alteration or repeal; or

(iii) Share Exchanges, Reclassifications, Mergers and Consolidations. Any consummation of a binding share exchange or reclassification involving the Series G, or of a merger or consolidation of the Corporation with another corporation or other entity, unless in each case (x) the shares of Series G remain outstanding or, in the case of any such merger or consolidation with respect to which the Corporation is not the surviving or resulting entity, are converted into or exchanged for preference securities of the surviving or resulting entity or its ultimate parent, and (y) such shares remaining outstanding or such preference securities, as the case may be, have such rights, preferences, privileges and voting powers, and limitations and restrictions thereof as are substantially similar to the rights, preferences, privileges and voting powers, and limitations and restrictions of the Series G immediately prior to such consummation; *provided, however*, that for all purposes of this Section 8(c), the creation and issuance, or an increase in the authorized or issued amount, of any other series of Preferred Stock ranking equally with and/or junior to the Series G with respect to the payment of dividends (whether such dividends are cumulative or non-cumulative) and/or the distribution of assets upon liquidation, dissolution or winding up of the Corporation will not be deemed to adversely affect the rights, preferences, privileges or voting powers of the Series G.

(d) Changes after Provision for Redemption. No vote or consent of the holders of Series G shall be required pursuant to Section 8(b) or (c) above if, at or prior to the time when any such vote or consent would otherwise be required pursuant to such Section, all outstanding shares of Series G (or, in the case of Section 8(c), more than 40,000 shares of Series G) shall have been redeemed, or shall have been called for redemption upon proper notice and sufficient funds shall have been deposited in trust for such redemption, in each case pursuant to Section 6 above.

(e) Procedures for Voting and Consents. The rules and procedures for calling and conducting any meeting of the holders of Series G (including, without limitation, the fixing of a record date in connection therewith), the solicitation and use of proxies at such a meeting, the obtaining of written consents and any other aspect or matter with regard to such a meeting or such consents shall be governed by any rules of the Board of Directors or the Committee (or another duly authorized committee of the Board of Directors), in its discretion, may adopt from time to time, which rules and procedures shall conform to the requirements of the Certificate of Incorporation, the Bylaws, and applicable law and the rules of any national securities exchange or other trading facility on which the Series G is listed or traded at the time. Whether the vote or consent of the holders of a plurality, majority or other portion of the shares of Series G and any Voting Preferred Stock has been cast or given on any matter on which the holders of shares of Series G are entitled to vote shall be determined by the Corporation by reference to the specified liquidation amount of the shares voted or covered by the consent (*provided* that the specified liquidation amount for any share of Series G shall be the Liquidation Preference for such share) as if the Corporation were liquidated on the record date for such vote or consent, if any, or, in the absence of a record date, on the date for such vote or consent.

Section 9. Record Holders. To the fullest extent permitted by applicable law, the Corporation and the transfer agent for the Series G may deem and treat the record holder of any share of Series G as the true and lawful owner thereof for all purposes, and neither the Corporation nor such transfer agent shall be affected by any notice to the contrary.

Section 10. Notices. All notices or communications in respect of Series G shall be sufficiently given if given in writing and delivered in person or by first class mail, postage prepaid, or if given in such other manner as may be permitted in this Certificate of Designations, in the Certificate of Incorporation or Bylaws or by applicable law. Notwithstanding the foregoing, if the Series G are issued in book-entry form through The Depository Trust Company or any similar facility, such notices may be given to the holders of Series G in any manner permitted by such facility.

Section 11. No Preemptive Rights. No share of Series G shall have any rights of preemption whatsoever as to any securities of the Corporation, or any warrants, rights or options issued or granted with respect thereto, regardless of how such securities, or such warrants, rights or options, may be designated, issued or granted.

Section 12. Replacement Certificates. The Corporation shall replace any mutilated certificate at the holder's expense upon surrender of that certificate to the Corporation. The Corporation shall replace certificates that become destroyed, stolen or lost at the holder's expense upon delivery to the Corporation of reasonably satisfactory evidence that the certificate has been destroyed, stolen or lost, together with any indemnity that may be reasonably required by the Corporation.

Section 13. Other Rights. The shares of Series G shall not have any rights, preferences, privileges or voting powers or relative, participating, optional or other special rights, or qualifications, limitations or restrictions thereof, other than as set forth herein or in the Certificate of Incorporation or as provided by applicable law.

IN WITNESS WHEREOF, THE GOLDMAN SACHS GROUP, INC. has caused this certificate to be signed by Elizabeth E. Beshel, its Treasurer, this 30th day of September, 2008.

7

DEBT INSTRUMENTS

Debt is a generic term for the form of financing arrangement characterized by the provision of credit. Debt is an important form of capital. The credit market is enormous, much bigger in total capitalization that the equity market. Most well-established, sophisticated corporate clients were, are, or will be borrowers. As between debt and equity, debt is the more senior security; it has priority in the right to payment and thus is the least risky financial instrument.

A. DEBT FINANCING

1. BASIC CHARACTERISTICS OF DEBT

The most important legal facet of debt is that it is the product of a contract. In this sense, debt is similar to preferred stock. Or, more accurately, preferred stock, as a corporate contract, is similar to debt with respect to the emphasis on contract rights, except that preferred stock arises out of (is enabled by) corporation law, has the rights of stock under corporation law subject to specific contractual rights, and thus is entitled to fiduciary duty even if that duty is complicated by the duty owed to common stockholders. Debt arises out of contract law. The creation from written financial contract raises two implications.

First, as a matter of general principle and outside of bankruptcy, courts and corporation law do not protect creditors much beyond the express terms of the credit contract and the implied good-faith adherence to them. Because debt arises out of contract law and is not enabled by corporation law, it does not generally benefit from the panoply of statutory and equitable protections of corporation law. Creditors are generally limited to the protections they negotiate in the financial contract. They have no voting power in matters of corporate governance; they are not owed fiduciary duty by the board of directors; and they do not partake in the management of the corporation, though they may have certain information rights. These are general principles only. Nuances to these principles are important, and this chapter explores them.

Second, since a credit transaction is a contract, freedom of contract suggests that transaction terms and types can vary greatly. Debt can be a private contract between the debtor and a single creditor, such as a bank loan. It can be registered and issued as a security to many bondholders as a public security issue. A creditor's primary protection rests on contract rights, and so the credit contract has a number of terms designed to protect the creditor, including protection against corporate debtor opportunism.

The terms in a credit transaction are many and varied. The two indispensable terms of a credit contract are: maturity, which is a fixed date of redemption generally unlike stock; and interest rate, the contractually defined charge for the provision of credit, which is considered "fixed" in the sense of a rate of return that is "defined and limited" as opposed to the variability of a residual claim. The possibility of the potential diversity and complexity of debt contracts can be seen by just considering the variations in maturity and interest rate.

Maturity. Short-term maturity typically matures within one year, but could be as long as a few years. Medium-term maturity typically matures within 5 to 10 years. Long-term maturity typically matures over 10 years.

Interest rate. Fixed interest rate is interest rate that is fixed as a percentage, *e.g.*, 7 percent of the face value of the bond. Floating interest rate is interest rate that is tied to some moving benchmark rate, *e.g.*, LIBOR plus 5 percent (the interest rate varies as LIBOR changes with time). A zero coupon bond is a bond where the interest charge and principal are paid as a bullet payment at maturity, *e.g.*, the bond is issued at $100 in Year 0 and in Year 10 the issuer pays $180 and retires the bond.

In addition to the above necessary terms, a debt issue may have some or all of these fairly common characteristics or attributes.

Priority. In addition to debt's priority over equity, there can be priorities among creditors. *Senior* debt is debt that is senior in priority of interest payment and liquidation to other debt. *Mezzanine* debt is debt that is in between the senior and junior debts in seniority. *Junior* debt is debt that is subordinate to both the senior and mezzanine debts in seniority.

Security interest. A bond may be secured by specific assets of the issuer, or it can be unsecured. This is the technical distinction between bonds (secured) and debentures (unsecured). Also, the creation of a security interest through a *sinking fund*, a fund that an issuer pays into periodically to secure payment of principal, is a common term in a bond transaction.

Convertibility. A bond may have a convertibility feature in which it can be converted at the option of the bondholder into an equity security, most typically common stock. The bond indenture will have a formula in which the bond will be converted into a specific number of common stock. The convertibility may be conditioned on some passage of time or occurrence of an event, or it may be unconditional up to maturity.

Redemption. A bond may be redeemed earlier than the maturity date by the issuer. An issuer may redeem a bond earlier because it no longer needs the financing, has cheaper financing options, or seeks to de-lever its balance sheet. If the bond is redeemable, it will state the price at which the issuer will redeem the bond.

Creditworthiness. Most significant debt instruments and their issuers are rated by credit rating agencies for creditworthiness. Creditworthiness is an assessment of the probability of default. A credit rating affects an issuer's cost of debt and the permissibility of certain regulated financial institutions to invest in the bonds. An investment grade bond will have a lower coupon rate and a greater pool of potential investors than a junk bond. For example, as of January 2011, the following were the prices and yields on a sample of corporate bonds.*

---

* Richard A. Brealey, Stewart C. Myers & Franklin Allen, Principles of Corporate Finance 65 (11th ed. 2014).

Issuer	Coupon (%)	Maturity	S&P Rating	Market Price (%)	Yield to Maturity (%)
Johnson & Johnson	5.15	2017	AAA	122.88	1.27
Walmart	5.38	2017	AA	117.99	1.74
Walt Disney	5.88	2017	A	121.00	2.07
Sun Trust Bank	7.13	2017	BBB	109.76	4.04
U.S. Steel	6.05	2017	BBB	97.80	6.54
American Stores	7.90	2017	B	97.50	8.49
Caesars Entertainment	5.75	2017	CCC	41.95	25.70

This table clearly shows that higher credit ratings have higher bond prices, resulting in lower yields (returns on the bond).

It goes without saying that creditors want the maximum rate of return along with the maximum contractual protections, and borrowers want the exact opposite. From these antipodal points of interest, the parties negotiate the terms of credit, which are found in the note or indenture. The terms of the credit reflect allocations of risk and return. The more contractual protections given to creditors (such as seniority or financial restrictions), the less return creditors will see, and vice versa. Terms and conditions allocate risk. The lawyer should understand these principles when negotiating credit contracts.

The following case explores the different natures of debt and equity. In most cases, the nature of the security is fairly obvious—e.g., it is a common stock or a bond. However, sometimes the nature is unclear due to unusual nomenclature, poor drafting of the financial contract, or hybrid qualities in the instrument. In these cases, courts consider the substance over form to determine the nature of the security.

Eliasen v. Itel Corp.
82 F.3d 731 (7th Cir. 1986)

POSNER, Chief Judge.

Three years ago Itel Corporation, which owned all the common stock plus 78 percent of the Class B debentures of the Green Bay & Western Railroad Company, sold the railroad. The owners of the remaining Class B debentures, who are the plaintiffs in this class action against Itel, claim to be entitled to share in the proceeds of the sale over and above the $1,000 face value of each debenture that they received when, in accordance with the terms of their debenture certificates, the debentures were repaid out of the proceeds of the sale. They argue that in refusing to honor their claim Itel has converted property that is rightfully theirs, in violation of both federal and state law under a variety of legal theories unnecessary to discuss. The district judge granted Itel's motion to dismiss, ruling that the debentures did not entitle the holders to more than $1,000 per debenture.

A debenture, as the word is normally used in the legal and financial communities of the United States, and as it was normally used a century ago as well, when the debentures involved in this suit were first issued, is a type of bond, specifically a bond unsecured by a lien. Ordinarily, when a corporation is sold, the proceeds above what is needed to pay off creditors, including bondholders—including therefore debenture holders—go to the shareholders, as the residual claimants to the corporation's assets. The plaintiffs argue that, contrary to the norm, the Class B debentures in the Green Bay & Western Railroad were intended to be the equivalent of shares of stock, while the shares of stock were intended to be the equivalent of debentures. They ask us to look behind the labels of these instruments to the economic reality.

Each debenture certificate is a contract between the railroad and the debenture holder, and parties to a contract can agree to use words in a nonstandard sense. But it does not help the plaintiffs' case that they are unable to direct us to any other instance in U.S. corporate history in which the word "debenture" has been used to denote an equity interest. Convertible debentures, that is, debentures convertible into stock upon the coming to pass of stated conditions, have by virtue of their conversion feature an equity hue; but the debentures issued by the Green Bay & Western Railroad are not convertible. A treatise gives an example of where the term "debenture" has been interpreted to mean preferred stock. But there is much less space between a conventional debenture and preferred stock than between a conventional debenture and common stock, since preferred stock normally is "maxed out" at its stated par value, just like the Class B debentures if Itel's interpretation is accepted.

To determine whether the interpretation is correct requires an examination of the history and terms of the securities. The Green Bay & Western Railroad was created, under a different name, in 1866. It went broke ten years later and again in 1888, emerging from the second bankruptcy exactly one century ago, in 1896, with a radically new capital structure. The first mortgagees, who had foreclosed on the railroad's property, received all the capital stock of the new company—25,000 shares with a par value of $100 each. The second mortgagees and old shareholders received the Class B debentures—7,000 debentures each with a face value, as we have said, of $1,000 [thus, the total face value of Class B debentures is $7 million]. They also received, in exchange for investing $600,000 of new money, 600 Class A debentures with a face value of $1,000 each. None of the three classes of securities specified either maturity dates or a fixed entitlement to income, and only the capital stock had voting rights.

Author's Case Annotation: Diagram of Restructuring Transaction

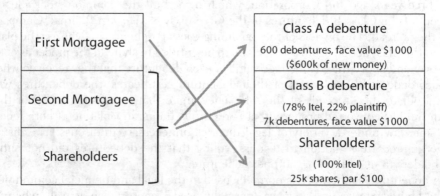

Although the debentures do not create a fixed entitlement to interest or dividends, they do provide for the allocation of any annual dividends that the board of directors decides to declare. The dividends are to go to the holders of the Class A debentures until those investors have received 2.5 percent of the face value of the debenture, then to the shareholders until they have received 2.5 percent of the par value of their stock, and then to the holders of the Class A debentures and the shareholders, pro rata, until the two groups have received a total of 5 percent of the face value of the Class A debentures and of the par value of the stock. Any money left after these distributions is to go to the holders of the Class B debentures. In simplest terms, then, the Class B debenture holders are entitled to any dividends that exceed what is necessary to give the shareholders and the Class A debenture holders 5 percent of the face amount of their securities.

Author's Case Annotation: Dividend Priority

1. Class A:	2.5% of face value
2. Shareholders:	2.5% par value
3. Class A and Shareholders:	Total of 5% of face/par values, pro rata
4. Class B:	Any remaining dividends

In the event of a sale or reorganization of the company, the Class B debenture certificate specifies the following distribution of the proceeds after payment of all liens and charges: the first $600,000 to the holders of the Class A debentures, the next $2.5 million to the shareholders, and either the rest—or the first $7 million of the rest—to the holders of the Class B debentures. Which it is the issue in this case.

Author's Case Annotation: Priority in a Sale

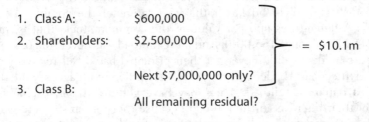

1. Class A:	$600,000	
2. Shareholders:	$2,500,000	= $10.1m
	Next $7,000,000 only?	
3. Class B:	All remaining residual?	

Each Class B debenture certificate states that the Green Bay & Western Railroad

certifies that this is one of a series of seven thousand of its Class B Debentures, in the sum of ONE THOUSAND DOLLARS each, aggregating in all the sum of Seven Million Dollars, *which sum of One Thousand Dollars will be payable to the bearer hereof* as follows: viz., only in the event of a sale or reorganization of the Railroad and property of said Company, and then only out of any net proceeds of such sale or reorganization which may remain after payment of any liens and charges upon such railroad or property, and after payment of Six Hundred Thousand Dollars to the holders of a series of Debentures known as Class A, issued or to be issued, by said Company, and the sum of Two Million Five Hundred Thousand Dollars to and among the stockholders of said Company. *Any such net proceeds remaining after such payments shall be distributed pro rata to and among the holders of this series of Class B Debentures.*

Itel argues that the first clause that we have italicized makes clear that the only entitlement of the holders of Class B debentures is to $1,000 per debenture. The plaintiffs argue that the last sentence in the quoted passage, which we have also italicized, makes clear that any proceeds from a sale over and above all liens and charges, $600,000 to the holders of the Class A debentures, and $2.5 million to the shareholders, go to the holders of the Class B debentures, making them in effect the equity owners of the railroad. On Itel's reading the shareholders have a debt-like claim to the par value of their stock (the $2.5 million) that is subordinate only to the other creditor interests, including the Class A debentures but excluding the Class B debentures, but they also have the normal equity interest, which comes into play after the Class B debenture holders are paid their $7 million.

The question of what happens after the Class B debenture holders receive the full face value of their debentures cannot arise unless at the time of sale or reorganization the net value of the company exceeds $10.1 million, the sum of the face or par values of the three classes of security. That happy eventuality must have seemed remote in 1896, for the debentures and other documents of the 1896 reorganization do not make clear provision for it. Nevertheless the presumption in 1896 as now was (is) that the residual, unprovided-for value of a corporation belongs to the shareholders rather than to the holders of debentures or other bonds. The first clause that we italicized in the Class B debenture reinforces the presumption, for it states flatly that the holder's right in the event of a sale or reorganization of the railroad is to receive the face amount of the debenture, $1,000. The sentence on which the plaintiffs rely can easily be read as merely specifying the mode of distribution among the Class B debenture holders in what must have seemed the likely event that the proceeds of the sale were insufficient to give them the full $7 million.

It is true that on Itel's interpretation the Class B debenture holders got very little in the reorganization. They got no right to any income unless the board of directors decided to declare a dividend larger than 5 percent of the combined face value of the Class A debentures and par value of the common stock, that is, more than 5 percent of $3.1 million ($155,000). And if the railroad was never sold or reorganized, the debenture holders would never get their principal back. But remember that the recipients of the Class B debentures were the junior mortgagees, and the share-holders, of a bankrupt railroad. They may have gotten little in exchange for the surrender of their interests in the railroad because those interests were worth little. The junior mortgagees had not been paid anything on their mortgages for the fourteen years preceding the reorganization. To the extent that these investors did not merely exchange their old interests for new ones but also contributed new value to the railroad, as they did, they were compensated by receiving Class A debentures. Those debentures were entitled to priority both in the distribution of the railroad's income and in the eventuality of a sale or reorganization. The new shareholders, having in their previous capacity as first mortgagees already foreclosed on the railroad, received both voting control and a bond-like entitlement to $2.5 million in the event that a sale or reorganization yielded net proceeds after all liens and charges of at least $3.1 million, plus (on Itel's interpretation) what must have seemed the remote possibility of an additional return should the railroad be sold and reorganized at a time when it had attained a net worth in excess of $10.1 million.

Itel's interpretation makes better economic sense than the plaintiffs' because it is more consistent with the creation and maintenance of proper incentives for operating the railroad in such a way as to maximize its value. (This is relevant because most commercial transactions are designed to be value-maximizing.) Only the shareholders had been given voting rights. Only the shareholders, therefore, could control the management of the corporation. If they had no right to any part of the gain from increasing the value of the corporation above $3.1 million, the level that would just cover their fixed entitlement to $2.5 million, they would have had little zeal for developing the railroad to the level it reached when it was sold in 1993. We do not know the sale price, because Itel sold the Green Bay & Western Railroad together with another railroad for a combined price of $64 million. The plaintiffs claim that $43 million is the *minimum* amount of the sale price fairly allocable to the Green Bay, which if so would entitle the Class B debenture holders, under the plaintiffs' theory of the case, to roughly $40 million. The plaintiffs, recall, own 22 percent of those debentures.

A corporate structure in which the bondholders, for that is what the plaintiffs think the shareholders are—holders of 25,000 bonds worth $100 apiece—have all the voting rights, and the shareholders, who are what the plaintiffs consider the Class B debenture holders to be, have no voting rights, is anomalous. And yet this inverted corporate structure would not be crazy if at the time it was created the possibility that the railroad would ever be worth at least $10.1 million was so remote that the shareholders, even if they were the residual claimants, would have no incentive to maximize the value of the railroad, beyond trying to create a cushion to protect their $2.5 million bond-like entitlement. Corporate indentures frequently shift voting rights to creditor groups when financial distress attenuates the shareholders' interests and makes the creditors the de facto residual claimants to the value of the corporation's assets. Throughout most of the history of the railroad it has been the Class B debenture holders who have been the real equity owners, because until the railroad attained a net value of $10.1 million (which for all we know has not yet occurred) any increase in value would enure to the benefit of those investors. But this is an argument for having given the Class B debenture holders the voting rights and hence control of the corporation, which the reorganization plan and the debenture certificates did not do. The only way to give the shareholders, who do control the corporation, a robust incentive to maximize the railroad's value is to give them an equity kicker above the Class B debenture holders' entitlement, and so the debenture contract can be presumed to have done this.

Another reason to doubt that the debenture holders received an equity interest is that the shareholders, being in control of the corporation as a consequence of their voting rights, could so easily circumvent that interest. Before a sale or reorganization of the railroad the value of the debentures would be depressed because the holders would have no right to force either a sale of the railroad or a declaration of dividends in an amount that would give any part of the railroad's income to the debenture holders. The owners of the stock could therefore buy up the debentures cheap, so that, when the railroad was sold, the stockholders (now also the debenture holders) would obtain the benefits of the equity interest nominally held, under the plaintiffs' interpretation, by the debenture holders. And indeed when Itel bought the railroad's common stock it also bought 78 percent of the Class B debentures.

Even if as we believe Itel has the better of the argument when consideration is limited to the text of the Class B debenture, should consideration be so limited? Since the debenture makes no explicit provision for the allocation of the net proceeds of sale above $10.1 million, and since the last sentence that we quoted from the debenture certificate, the sentence on which the plaintiffs pitch their case, provides at least some support for it, there is enough ambiguity to permit the consideration of extrinsic evidence, that is, evidence outside the text of the Class B debenture itself. Itel implicitly acknowledges this by pointing out that these debentures were issued in exchange for interests that probably had little value.

The plaintiffs point to a series of statements that the railroad made, some in the two cases that we discussed, some in other cases, others in submissions to the SEC and the ICC, which the plaintiffs construe as admissions that the Class B debenture holders are the residual owners of the railroad. So far as appears, however, these statements (contradicted, incidentally, by others, which do refer to the $7 million cap) were made at a time when the railroad was worth less than $10.1 million, so that the question of the entitlement to any surplus value above that was academic. In the 1940s, the market value of the Class B debentures was only $120, implying that the net worth of the railroad may have been as little as $3,940,000 ($0.6 million plus $2.5 million plus 7,000 x $120). If so, the Class B debenture holders were the real equity owners, because, had the railroad been sold then at that price, they would have received the entire net proceeds minus the $3.1 million reserved for the Class A debenture holders and the shareholders.

Despite what we have just said, the value of the railroad cannot be inferred directly from the market value of the Class B debentures. That market value would have been depressed by the inability of the debenture holders to force a sale or a distribution of income to them.

The plaintiffs presented no evidence of the value of the railroad at any of the times when the statements on which they rely were made, although it appears that as late as 1986 the railroad was worth no more than $8.4 million. Itel had acquired its interest in the railroad—100 percent of the common stock and 78 percent of the Class B debentures—in 1978 for a total of $8 million. (Because it had bought securities of the railroad rather than the railroad itself, its purchase did not trigger the entitlement of the debenture holders to be paid out.) The plaintiffs' claim that the railroad was sold for at least $43 million in 1993 appears to be grossly exaggerated. Itel had paid $61 million for the Fox River Valley Railroad, the railroad it sold together with the Green Bay & Western Railroad for $64 million in 1993.

Remarks, even considered statements, that the Class B debenture holders were the real equity owners of the Green Bay, made at the time when they *were* the real though not formal equity owners, are not highly probative of what their status would be if the residual value of the railroad rose above the face amount of those debentures. The plaintiffs want a trial but have cited no evidence that would rebut the presumption from the text and history and economic logic of the Class B debenture that it caps the holders' entitlement at $7 million. No jury would be permitted to speculate that this debenture was really a share of stock.

Affirmed.

QUESTIONS

1. Why is the plaintiff suing Itel since they both own the Class B debenture?
2. What was the economic logic of the restructuring and recapitalization that took place? Why did the first mortgagee, second mortgagee, and old shareholders get what they got in terms of the new securities in the restructured company?

3. Why was the Class B debenture created? What purpose did it have in the restructuring and recapitalization?
4. What is the significance of voting rights in determining who has the residual claim? What could potentially happen if economic rights and control rights are not properly aligned?
5. Judge Posner specifically identified a "hold up" problem caused by an inefficient arrangement of control rights. What is the nature of the "hold up" problem if in fact Class B debenture holders were the residual claimants but the shareholders had the voting rights with respect to a sale of the company?
6. What was the key drafting mistake with respect to the Class B debenture certificate? Propose the specific change in language to the certificate that would have avoided the confusion.

NOTES

1. With respect to voting rights, consider the following passage: "There is no law of nature that says residual cash-flow rights and residual control rights have to go together. For example, one could imagine a situation where the debtholder gets to make all the decisions. But this would be inefficient. Since the benefits of good decisions are felt mainly by the common stockholders, it makes sense to give them control over how the firm's assets are used." Richard A. Brealey, Stewart C. Myers & Franklin Allen, Principles of Corporate Finance 347 (10th ed. 2011).
2. Delaware General Corporation Law §221 provides that the certificate of incorporation may confer on bondholders the right to vote on corporate affairs and management. But the provision of voting rights in debt instruments would be unusual in circumstances where the corporation is not in financial distress.

2. CONFLICT BETWEEN CREDITORS AND SHAREHOLDERS

Creditors and shareholders have an inherent conflict of interest. In the most general respect, both desire that the firm does well so that they can be paid, but their preferences conflict upon a closer examination.

To understand this conflict, think about why a creditor is a creditor when she had the option to be an equityholder. A creditor is a person who has selected a particular, less risky spot in the order of priority among securityholders. A shareholder has selected a different, more risky spot. Creditors are only interested in being paid their interest and principal. That is the extent of their investment. Beyond getting paid, they do not care how profitable a firm is or is not. However, shareholders care greatly about the overall wealth generation because they are residual claimants and benefit only when all other claims are paid. These different interests create a conflict; creditors and equityholders will have different preferences on the corporation's management and investment strategies.

We can think about this conflict in more concrete terms. Assume this balance sheet: assets = 1,000, liabilities = 1,000, and equity = 0. The liability is a bond carrying an interest rate of 10 percent, with an annual interest payment of 100.

The firm is solvent and a going concern, but has no net profit (thus, shareholders are not being paid). As a matter of prospective business strategy, the firm is contemplating two strategies to generate operating profit, which is allocated to creditors and shareholders. The strategies have these probabilities and payouts:

	Strategy A			Strategy B	
Outcome	Probability of outcome	Expected value	Outcome	Probability of outcome	Expected value
200	25%	50	500	25%	125
150	50%	75	150	50%	75
100	25%	25	(100)	25%	(25)
	100%	**150**		100%	**175**

Strategy B is far riskier with a spread of potential outcomes of [+500, −100], as compared to Strategy A with a spread of [+200, +100]. On the other hand, Strategy B is more profitable than Strategy A. Compare the expected values U of the two strategies: $U_A = 150$ and $U_B = 175$.

From a bondholder's perspective, which strategy is preferred? Clearly, it is Strategy A. The bondholder has 100 percent chance of being paid interest, and 0 percent chance of having the principal be written down due to a loss. The bondholder has no downside. Strategy B is suboptimal for the bondholder because there is a 25 percent chance of not getting paid interest, and additionally the loss of 100 would reduce the assets on the balance sheet such that the bond principal is also threatened.

Compare this to the clear preference of diversified shareholders, who are thus risk neutral. They prefer Strategy B because it is more profitable. Under Strategy A, there is a 75 percent chance that shareholders will be paid (the outcomes of 200 and 150), but these payments are small (100 and 50 after payment to the creditors). Under Strategy B, there is still a 75 percent chance of getting paid, but these payments are 50 and 400 after payment of 100 to creditors. The poor outcome of (100) does not matter as much because there is limited liability and the decline in assets will come from the bondholders' claim on the assets since equity is 0.

This example shows that creditors and shareholders have an inherent conflict that manifests in negotiation over the terms of a credit contract in which creditors will seek to protect themselves against shareholder opportunism and risk-taking preferences. However, the creditor's power to contract for protection is limited because one party's concessions require counter-concessions from the counterparty. There is a sliding scale in which increased contract protection means lower return for the creditor.

———

The following case illustrates the conflict between shareholders and creditors when the corporation is operating in the "vicinity of insolvency." There, the divergent economic interests and incentives of shareholders and creditors is fully exposed, and as such there is a question of how the board should make corporate decisions given that creditors and shareholders seek different corporate actions.

Credit Lyonnais Bank Nederland, N.V. v. Pathe Comm'n Corp.
1991 WL 277613 (Del. Ch. 1991)

ALLEN:

At least where a corporation is operating in the vicinity of insolvency, a board of directors is not merely the agent of the [residual] risk bearers, but owes its duty to the corporate enterprise.

The possibility of insolvency can do curious things to incentives, exposing creditors to risks of opportunistic behavior and creating complexities for directors. Consider, for example, a solvent corporation having a single asset, a judgment for $51 million against a solvent debtor. The judgment is on appeal and thus subject to modification or reversal. Assume that the only liabilities of the company are to bondholders in the amount of $12 million. Assume that the array of probable outcomes of the appeal is as follows:

	Expected Value
25% chance of affirmative ($51 million)	$12.75
70% chance of modification ($4 million)	2.8
5% chance of reversal ($0)	0
Expected value of judgment on appeal	$15.55

Thus, the best evaluation is that the current value of the equity is $3.55 million [which is calculated as $15.55 million expected value of judgment on appeal—$12 million liability to bondholders]. Now assume an offer to settle at $12.5 million (also consider one at $17.5 million). By what standard do the directors of the company evaluate the fairness of these offers? The creditors of this solvent company would be in favor of accepting either a $12.5 million offer or a $17.5 million offer. In either event they will avoid the 75% risk of insolvency and default. The stockholders, however, will plainly be opposed to acceptance of a $12.5 million settlement (under which they get practically nothing). More importantly, they very well may be opposed to acceptance of the $17.5 million offer under which the residual value of the corporation would increase from $3.5 to $5.5 million. This is so because the litigation alternative, with its 25% probability of a $39 million outcome to them ($51 million − $12 million = $39 million) has an expected value to the residual risk bearer of $9.75 million ($39 million x 25% chance of affirmance), substantially greater than the $5.5 million available to them in the settlement. While in fact the stockholders' preference would reflect their appetite for risk, it is possible (and with diversified shareholders likely) that shareholders would prefer rejection of both settlement offers.

But if we consider the community of interests that the corporation represents it seems apparent that one should in this hypothetical accept the best settlement offer available providing it is greater than $15.55 million, and one below that amount should be rejected. But that result will not be reached by a director who thinks he owes duties directly to shareholders only. It will be reached by directors who are capable of conceiving of the corporation as a legal and economic entity. Such directors will recognize that in managing the business affairs of a solvent corporation in the vicinity of insolvency circumstances may arise when the right (both the efficient and the fair) course to follow for the corporation may diverge from the choice that the stockholders (or the creditors, or the employees, or any single group interested in the corporation) would make if given the opportunity to act.

QUESTIONS

1. In insolvency or the vicinity of insolvency, the shareholder may no longer have a residual claim because much of the equity value has been destroyed. In that case, if shareholders have control of the firm, they would be playing with other people's (creditors) money. What perverse incentives may this create?
2. Why should a director's fiduciary duty shift to creditors when the firm is in the vicinity of insolvency?

NOTES

1. In thinking about the implication of *Credit Lyonnais*, consider the following account of the conversations inside the Bear Stearns boardroom.* In 2008, Bear Stearns was collapsing due to toxic assets on its balance sheet, which essentially wiped out the equity in the firm. The firm was effectively insolvent. The Bear Stearns board was considering a $2 per share offer from JPMorgan Chase to rescue the company. Obviously, Bear Stearns shareholders, including Jimmy Cayne, the former CEO and prominent shareholder, wanted more money, and negotiation leverage was the "nuclear" option of filing for bankruptcy, which would harm the value of creditors' claims and also cause systemic disturbances in the greater financial system.

> For his part, Cayne was livid. At breakfast with Tese earlier that day, he had come to realize that blowing up the firm wouldn't do anyone any good. But now, upon hearing that JPMorgan deal was at $2 per share—meaning that his six million or so shares, which at their height had been worth more than $1 billion, would now be worth around $12 million—he was incensed. His finger moved back over the red ["nuclear"] button. He wondered if the firm's bondholders, who together held $70 billion of debt and who in a merger with JPMorgan would be made whole but in bankruptcy would be severely impaired, should be asked to make a contribution to the shrinking pie for shareholders. . . . As Cayne knew, the bondholders had by far the most to gain from a deal with JPMorgan. Whereas all through the week, the cost of insuring against a default in Bear Stearns debt had been increasing rapidly—the so-called credit default swaps—a deal with JPMorgan would transfer these obligations to JPMorgan's balance sheet and immediately make them worth 100 cents on the dollar.
>
> . . .
>
> The moment had come to seal the fate of Bear Stearns, the fifth-largest Wall Street securities firm. The lawyers walked the board through its fiduciary duties under Delaware law, which required them to consider their duty to creditors if they turned down the JPMorgan deal and opted for bankruptcy. Given that the choice was between nominal consideration for shareholders and 100 cents on the dollar for creditors or nothing for shareholders and pennies for creditors, Sullivan & Cromwell's advice for the board was that its fiduciary duties had shifted from shareholders to all the other stakeholders of Bear Stearns, among them creditors, employees, and retirees. . . .

---

* William D. Cohan, House of Cards: A Tale of Hubris and Wretched Excess on Wall Street 103-104, 108-109 (2010).

2. A more amusing anecdote on the different preferences for risk of shareholders and creditors is the story of Fred Smith and FedEx. In the early days of FedEx, the company was down to its last $5,000 in cash. Realizing that it would be unable to pay its fuel bills without more money, Fred Smith, the founder and CEO, took the money, went to Las Vegas, and played black jack against the casino. This is a recounting of the story by a founding executive of FedEx.**

> The loan guarantee from General Dynamics raised our hopes and increased our spirits, but also increased the pressure to finalize the private placement. We continued to be in desperate financial trouble, particularly with our suppliers. The most demanding suppliers when it came to payments were the oil companies. Every Monday, they required Federal Express to prepay for the anticipated weekly usage of jet fuel. By mid-July our funds were so meager that on Friday we were down to about $5,000 in the checking account, while we needed $24,000 for the jet fuel payment. I was still communing to Connecticut on the weekends and really did not know what was going to transpire on my return.
>
> However, when I arrived back in Memphis on Monday morning, much to my surprise, the bank balance stood at nearly $32,000. I asked Fred where the funds had come from, and he responded, "The meeting with the General Dynamics board was a bust and I knew we needed money for Monday, so I took a plane to Las Vegas and won $27,000." I said, "You mean you took our last $5,000—how could you do that?" He shrugged his shoulders and said, "What difference does it make? Without the funds for the fuel companies, we couldn't have flown anyway." Fred's luck held again. It was not much, but it came at a critical time and kept us in business for another week.

If FedEx was down to $5,000 in the checking account, it probably had unpaid creditors as well. Was it in the best interest of creditors that the shareholders of the firm gamble the last remaining funds in a desperate attempt to save the company? For whose interest did Fred Smith gamble the remaining funds?

3. In *In re Vision Hardware Group, Inc.*, 669 A.2d 671 (Del.Ch. 1995) (Allen, Ch.), the Chancery Court held that, when an insolvent company on the brink of bankruptcy merges with another company, the value of the debt is the dollar value of the legal claim that debt represented for the purpose of determining the appraisal value of dissenting shareholders under DGCL §262. Since insolvent companies would most likely have liabilities that are greater than equity under the balance sheet test of insolvency, this would imply that dissenting shareholders would get nothing in most appraisal proceedings. In *Vision Hardware*, the court held that the dissenting shares were worth "nuisance value no greater than the amount paid in fact" (which was $125,000), where the senior debtholders were paid approximately $44.395 million and subordinated debtholders and preferred stockholders got $2.65 million.

** Roger Frock, Changing How the World Does Business: Fedex's Incredible Journey to Success—The Inside Story 115 (2006).

B. BONDS AND INDENTURES

1. THE NATURE OF THE INDENTURE

Long-term debt instruments, characterized by maturities that are greater than 10 years, are most typically bonds and debentures. Under the Trust Indenture Act of 1939 (15 U.S.C. §77aaa *et seq.*), bonds are issued pursuant to an indenture. The statute sets forth the debt instruments required to be issued pursuant to an indenture. It applies only to debt instruments, and not to equity securities. A bond instrument is a contract between the issuer corporation and the bondholder specifying the term that the issuer owes the bondholder the amount of the credit. The indenture is attached to the bond, and it is a contract between the issuer corporation and the indenture trustee. It is a long, thick contract packed with boilerplate contract provisions defining the obligations of the issuer corporation, the rights and remedies of the bondholders, and the obligations of the trustee. The trustee's obligations are to administrate the bond terms and covenants, including the payment of interest and principal, as well as to monitor and enforce covenants and other indenture provisions on behalf of the bondholders. In this section, we will review some of the major provisions of bond indentures and case law analyzing them.

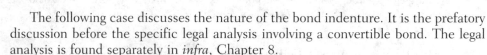

The following case discusses the nature of the bond indenture. It is the prefatory discussion before the specific legal analysis involving a convertible bond. The legal analysis is found separately in *infra*, Chapter 8.

Broad v. Rockwell International Corp.
642 F.2d 929 (5th Cir. 1981)

RANDALL, Circuit Judge.

Because the construction of the Indenture is basically a question of contract law, it is perhaps worthwhile to discuss briefly the way in which this type of contract operates, and the reasons why such contracts must be so long and detailed.

In part because of the differing treatment of debt and equity securities both by statute and at common law, debt securities are, to a much larger degree than is true of equity securities, creatures of contract law. The American Bar Foundation's *Commentaries on Indentures* make the following comments on the distinctions between long-term debt financing and equity financing:

> In general, funds needed for financing private corporate enterprises are obtained in exchange for interests of two essentially different kinds: (1) those of the "equity" owners or shareholders, whose securities represent certain rights of ownership, control and profit accompanied by a relatively greater risk of loss, and (2) those of the "lenders," who classically forego control and profit in return for periodic payments (interest and often sinking fund) without regard to profits and for repayment of principal at a fixed date, ahead of the equity owners.
>
> The most obvious and important characteristic of long-term debt financing is that the holder ordinarily has not bargained for and does not expect any substantial gain in the value of the security to compensate for the risk of loss. This is not true of a

debt security which is convertible into an equity security, and it is not entirely true of a debt security purchased for much less than its principal amount. With these exceptions, however, the significant fact, which accounts in part for the detailed protective provisions of the typical long-term debt financing instrument, is that the lender (the purchaser of the debt security) can expect only interest at the prescribed rate plus the eventual return of the principal. Except for possible increases in the market value of the debt security because of changes in interest rates, the debt security will seldom be worth more than the lender paid for it, provided he bought it at approximately its face amount. It may, of course, become worth much less. Accordingly, the typical investor in a long-term debt security is primarily interested in every reasonable assurance that the principal and interest will be paid when due.

The second fundamental characteristic of long-term debt financing is that *the rights of the holders of the debt securities are largely a matter of contract*. There is no governing body of statutory or common law that protects the holder of unsecured debt securities against harmful acts by the debtor except in the most extreme situations. Short of bankruptcy, the debt security holder can do nothing to protect himself against actions of the borrower which jeopardize its ability to pay the debt unless he takes a mortgage or other collateral or establishes his rights through contractual provisions set forth in the debt agreement or indenture.

Finally the long-term debt may be held by many holders, all of whom expect to be treated on a parity. Here, again, there is no body of law governing the procedures by which the holders of debt securities may take collective action. These procedures, as well as the mechanics of transfer and exchange of the securities, are matters of contract which are usually set out in the indenture and sometimes in the debt instrument. Thus the situation is quite unlike that involved in the issuance of stock where various substantive rights and procedural matters are in effect incorporated in the certificate of incorporation of the issuer by operation of the applicable corporation laws.

Commentaries at 1-2. As a result, the written contracts that govern the rights and obligations of debt securities are often long and complex, for those contracts attempt to anticipate and deal with in advance all possible contingencies that might call into question the operation of those rights and obligations. In the case of debentures, those contractual rights are set forth in a document that is separate from the debt instrument itself. That document, whose terms are incorporated by reference on the face of the debt instrument, is commonly called an indenture. The modern form of debenture indenture was originally adapted from a different form of negotiable security:

The first debt securities termed "debentures" did not involve a trustee. They were, in effect, promissory notes issued in quantity with no underlying indenture or comparable agreement. Prior to World War I, draftsmen were challenged with the task of creating debentures as to which all holders would be on a parity and protected by adequate covenants and which would nevertheless be negotiable. The solution was to take the corporate mortgage indenture form, delete the conveyancing and other provisions relating to the collateral, and insert covenants designed to protect the debentureholders. These protective covenants were designed to prevent the borrower from placing other creditors in a position senior to the debentureholders, indulging in excessive borrowing or otherwise jeopardizing its ability to meet the obligations on the debentures. Other provisions of an administrative nature remained much the same in a debenture indenture as those in a mortgage indenture. The result is a form of instrument which offers great flexibility for adaption to a particular transaction.

Commentaries at 7.

The debt represented by the debenture is typically not secured by specific assets of the issuer, and is frequently subordinated to senior indebtedness of the issuer. This feature distinguishes debentures from corporate bonds:

> There is no inherent or clearly established distinction between "bonds" and "debentures." . . . The terms "bond" and "debenture" came into use in the United States without any definite or consistent legal connotation and to some extent are still intermingled. Financial men refer to the "bond market" as including all forms of long-term debt securities. . . . (Under preferred usage), *"debenture" means a long-term debt security which is not secured*, and "bond" (except with respect to governmental or other public corporation securities) means a long-term debt security which is secured by a lien on some or all of the assets of the borrower. Most recent issues conform to this usage.

Commentaries at 7 n.3. Debentures are also distinguishable from long-term notes:

> There is no basic or historically established distinction between "debentures" and "notes." There has emerged, however, a clear and useful distinction in modern usage. According to this usage, in the area of long-term debt securities, a security is properly termed a "note" when it is not issued pursuant to an indenture and there is no indenture trustee. However, it may be, and usually is, issued to one or a few purchasers pursuant to a purchase or loan agreement which, in addition to provisions dealing with the terms of purchase, includes many of the contractual rights found in an indenture. In today's nomenclature *the security is properly termed a "debenture" when it is issued pursuant to an indenture and there is an indenture trustee.*

Commentaries at 8. These distinctions are, of course, merely generalizations; as such, they do not hold true in all cases. For example, long-term notes may be issued pursuant to an indenture, but without a trustee because they are to be purchased by a comparatively small number of institutional investors.

It is usually the case that the debentures of a given issue are held by a great number of parties, and for this reason it was found desirable, as the modern concept of debentures developed, that the indenture designate a corporate trustee to protect the rights of the many holders of the debentures and to perform certain ministerial tasks connected with the normal operation of the debentures. Thus, although the debts created by the debentures run directly from the issuer to the holders, the contractual rights conferred by the indenture run from the issuer to the trustee for the benefit of the holders of the debentures. In today's usage, then, a security is generally termed a "debenture" when it is a long-term unsecured debt security, issued pursuant to an indenture and with an indenture trustee.

The function of the trustee is explained by the historical context through which debentures developed:

> Even though the debenture indenture creates no lien, it was found desirable to retain the trustee. In fact, since 1939 a trustee has been required by the Trust Indenture Act for issues subject to registration under the Securities Act of 1933. The fact that the debenture indenture trustee does not hold title to, or have possession of, any property has caused some persons to regard its position as an anomaly and the title "trustee" a misnomer. As a matter of law, however, it is well established that the corpus of a trust may consist of contractual rights and that one who holds contractual rights for the benefit of others may be a trustee. Accordingly, the title "trustee" is appropriate in this situation because, although the debts created by the debentures run directly from the issuer to the holders, the contractual rights conferred by the indenture run from the issuer to the trustee for the benefit of the holders.

Apart from legal semantics, the role performed by the debenture indenture trustee is a practical necessity whenever there are any substantial number of holders of the debt securities. Some of the most useful functions customarily performed by the trustee are not performed in its capacity as trustee, but rather as transfer agent and paying agent. Nevertheless, the protection to debentureholders accorded by the pure trustee functions is of significant value.

Commentaries at 7-8.

[The court quotes the passage below discussing the nature of the debt contract.]

It is not surprising that corporate indentures are lengthy and complex. There is much that much be covered by the contract set forth in the indenture. But it is also true that much of what has to be covered is, or could be, virtually the same for all indentures. These are the provisions that are commonly referred to as "boiler-plate," e.g., provisions regulating the issuance, authentication, transfer and exchange of securities; provisions establishing the procedures for collective action by the security holders; and provisions prescribing the duties of the trustee. These, and certain others, are provisions which have been stated in many different ways in various indentures. Since there is seldom any difference in the intended meaning, such provisions are susceptible of standardized expression. The use of standardized language can result in a better and quicker understanding of those provisions and a substantial saving of time not only for the draftsmen but also for the parties and all others who must comply with or refer to the indenture, including governmental bodies whose approval of authorization or the issuance of the securities is required by law.

Commentaries at 2. Not least among the parties "who must comply with or refer to the indenture" are the members of the investing public and their investment advisors. A large degree of uniformity in the language of debenture indentures is essential to the effective functioning of the financial markets: uniformity of the indentures that govern competing debenture issues is what makes it possible meaningfully to compare one debenture issue with another, focusing only on the business provisions of the issue (such as the interest rate, the maturity date, the redemption and sinking fund provisions and the conversion rate) and the economic conditions of the issuer, without being misled by peculiarities in the underlying instruments.

QUESTIONS

1. Why is the indenture so long and complicated in its terms?
2. What is the relationship between boilerplate terms and uniformity of contract language? Is uniformity an end in itself or does it serve a higher purpose?
3. Section 302(a) of the Trust Indenture Act of 1939 provides that "indentures are commonly prepared by the obligor or underwriter in advance of the public offering of the securities to be issued." This is still true. Bond indentures are not typically negotiated in the sense of an actual arms-length negotiation between the investor bondholders and the issuing corporation. The typical public bond issue will involve many bond investors. The issuer provides the terms; investment banks underwrite the issue; and investors choose to invest or not. But in what more abstract way can it be said that there is a negotiation that goes on in every bond issuance even when the parties are not explicitly bartering for terms?

The following case discusses the nature of the bond indenture as a contract of adhesion.

Rudbart v. North Jersey District Water Supply Commission
605 A.2d 681 (N.J. 1992)

PER CURIAM

These consolidated class actions were brought on behalf of holders of notes issued by defendant North Jersey District Water Supply Commission ("Commission") to recover damages arising from an early redemption of the notes effected by newspaper notice. Plaintiffs' central claim was that notice by publication, although specifically provided for in the notes, was inadequate and unconscionable.

The Commission, a public corporation, operates and maintains a public water system serving northern New Jersey. The Commission authorized the issuance of $75,000,000 in new project notes to provide interim financing for a portion of the cost of constructing a new water-supply facility and to pay certain outstanding obligations. The Commission and its underwriters, one of which was defendant Fidelity, negotiated the terms of the notes; Fidelity also was designated as the indenture trustee and as registrar/paying agent for the notes. The underwriters agreed to purchase the notes at the discounted price of $73,800,000, intending to sell them on the secondary market at face value.

The project notes were issued on June 15, 1984. Issued in registered form, without coupons, in denominations of $5,000 or multiples thereof, the notes bore tax-free interest at the rate of 7 ⅞ per annum payable on June 15th and December 15th. The notes fixed a June 15, 1987, maturity date, but, as set forth in both the Commission's authorizing resolutions and the Official Statement offering the issue to the public, were subject to earlier optional redemption:

> The Notes are subject to redemption prior to maturity as a whole at the option of the Commission on 30 days published notice in a newspaper or newspapers of general circulation in the City of Newark, New Jersey and in the City of New York, New York on the dates and at the prices below:

Redemption Period (both dates inclusive)	Redemption Price (percent of par value)
June 15, 1986 to December 14, 1986	101 %
December 15, 1986 and thereafter	100 ½ %

> If on the date fixed for redemption sufficient monies are available to the Trustee to pay the redemption price plus interest accrued to the date of redemption, the Notes shall cease to bear interest and shall not be deemed to be outstanding from such date.

The back of each of the issued notes bore similar language.

In the summer of 1985, the Commission decided to redeem the notes prior to maturity. The Commission entered into an escrow deposit agreement with Fidelity, effective September 26, 1985, for the redemption of the notes on June 23, 1986. Among its other terms, the agreement provided for the Commission to deposit with Fidelity an escrow sum sufficient to pay the redemption price and interest until the redemption date, and for Fidelity to publish a notice of redemption in accordance with the note terms.

Although regular interest payments were mailed to registered noteholders on December 15, 1985, and June 15, 1986, neither those nor any other mailings informed the noteholders of the forthcoming early redemption. Fidelity did, however, provide the required notice by publication in *The Star-Ledger, The New York Times,* and *The Wall Street Journal* on May 23 and again on June 9, 1986. The June 3, 1986, issue of *Moody's Municipal & Government Manual* also contained the call notice.

As of December 15, 1986, the holders of approximately $10,000,000 of the notes still had not redeemed. A number of noteholders apparently made inquiries and complaints when they failed to receive their anticipated December 15, 1986, interest payments. Fidelity, at the Commission's request, mailed notice in early 1987 to those holders who had not yet redeemed, but declined the Commission's request to put the unredeemed funds in an interest-bearing account. The late-redeeming noteholders received the redemption price (101% of face value) and interest from June 15 to June 23, 1986, the date of redemption.

Plaintiffs filed separate actions on behalf of noteholders who allegedly had not learned of the redemption until after December 15, 1986. Plaintiffs demanded that they be paid interest at the 7 7/8% rate from June 23, 1986, until the dates that they submitted their notes for redemption or other appropriate relief.

Plaintiffs do not contend that the project notes are ambiguous, nor do they claim that the Commission or Fidelity committed fraud or violated federal or state securities laws. Ordinarily, then, contract law would make the terms of the notes fully binding on plaintiffs. That law, based on principles of freedom of contract, was well stated in *Fivey v. Pennsylvania Railroad,* 52 A. 472 (E. & A. 1902), in which the court enforced a release incorporated in a standard-form contract: "A party who enters into a contract in writing, without any fraud or imposition being practiced upon him, is conclusively presumed to understand and assent to its terms and legal effect."

If an agreement is characterized as a "contract of adhesion" however, nonenforcement of its terms may be justified on other than such traditional grounds as fraud, duress, mistake, or illegality. The essential nature of a contract of adhesion is that it is presented on a take-it-or-leave-it basis, commonly in a standardized printed form, without opportunity for the "adhering" party to negotiate except perhaps on a few particulars. We have previously defined "contract of adhesion" in just those terms: "a contract where one party * * * must accept or reject the contract * * *." Such a contract "does not result from the consent of that party." The distinct body of law surrounding contracts of adhesion represents the legal system's effort to determine whether and to what extent such nonconsensual terms will be enforced.

The project notes involved here unquestionably fit our definition of contracts of adhesion. They were presented to the public on standardized printed forms, on a take-it-or-leave-it basis without opportunity for purchasers to negotiate any of the terms.[1]

---

1. The Commission and the underwriters negotiated the terms of the notes. However, although the underwriters presumably sought to enhance the attractiveness of the offer to prospective purchasers, the record does not indicate whether the negotiation addressed the interests of individual noteholders with respect to the form of early redemption notice or otherwise. We thus reject defendants' suggestion that the noteholders had in fact negotiated the notice provision through the underwriters.

But the observation that the notes fit the definition of contracts of adhesion is the beginning, not the end, of the inquiry: we must now determine as a matter of policy whether to enforce the unilaterally-fixed terms of the notes.

factors to enforce K of adhesion

In determining whether to enforce the terms of a contract of adhesion, courts have looked not only to the take-it-or-leave-it nature or the standardized form of the document but also to the subject matter of the contract, the parties' relative bargaining positions, the degree of economic compulsion motivating the "adhering" party, and the public interests affected by the contract. Applying those criteria to the project notes, we find insufficient reason to invalidate the notice-by-publication term.

The three considerations that lead us to that conclusion derive primarily from the fact that the project notes were publicly-traded securities. First, no investor was under any economic pressure to buy the notes. The notes were not consumer necessities. Prospective investors could choose from a vast selection of alternative equity and debt investments, including bonds and notes with various call and notice provisions. They were not driven to accept the Commission's notes because of a monopolistic market or any other economic constraint. Accordingly, the Commission did not enjoy a superior bargaining position permitting it to dictate its own terms. In short, the principal justifications for invalidating terms of a contract of adhesion are simply not present in a fully open and competitive securities market. Professor Slawson has cogently explained that reality:

> What economists call "perfectly competitive markets" (the markets for commodities or corporate securities, for example) automatically balance supply and demand at a "market price," below which no buyer can hope to buy and above which no seller can hope to sell. A buyer for whom the products on such a market are essential buys them at prices and with other terms of sale that are adhesive, since he has no reasonable choice but to buy and, when he buys, no reasonable choice but to pay the prices and accept the other terms set by the market. Similarly, a seller for whom selling the product is essential sells at prices and other terms that are adhesive for him. But if the market is working free from improper influence, its lawmaking is legitimate. It is the mechanism through which society has implicitly chosen to enforce on buyers and sellers alike the prices and terms that meet the standards of supply and demand. Society has decided through its legitimate democratic processes that it wants those prices and terms imposed because theory teaches that they tend toward an optimum allocation of resources and are an incentive to efficiency. This decision serves as a standard of legitimacy, and since the contract is within this standard, it is legitimate and should be enforced.

Second, although securities are offered to the public on a take-it-or-leave-it basis, enforcement of their terms advances rather than contravenes well-established and important public policies. Securities are governed by Article 8 of the Uniform Commercial Code. The Legislature has mandated that terms incorporated in such instruments shall be effective "even against a purchaser for value and without notice." That provision, unique to investment securities and unlike the general Uniform Commercial Code principle that "a person 'knows' or has 'knowledge' of a fact when he has actual knowledge of it," is designed to provide certainty and stability in the marketing of securities.

The aim of Article 8 is to confer negotiability on securities; the statutory provisions should be implemented to ensure "the freedom of transferability which is essential to the negotiability of investment securities." Subjecting the terms of Article 8 securities to continual judicial determinations of fairness would seriously impair the reliability and transferability of such instruments.

Third, judicial review of the fairness of negotiable securities would be inconsistent with federal and state securities laws. Central to those statutes is the requirement of full disclosure of all material facts and the prohibition of fraudulent conduct in connection with the purchase or sale of securities. Both Congress and our Legislature have chosen to protect investors by assuring that they be given all materials necessary to make an informed decision; accordingly, the federal and state legislative schemes do not provide for governmental review—judicial or otherwise—of the risk, fairness, good sense, or other substantive qualities of the offered security. Introducing a judicial-fairness review would effectively reject those legislative judgments in favor of a view that full disclosure does not provide adequate protection to an investor. Similarly inappropriate is the Appellate Division's suggestion that terms of securities should be subject to a judicial-fairness review because the documents "are lengthy and difficult to understand." The forms of documents are dictated by, and their sufficiency is reviewable under, the securities laws.

[handwritten margin note: full disclosure = sufficient protection]

We are satisfied that in light of the considerations we have stated, the asserted unfairness of the notice provision is not sufficient to justify judicial intrusion. Notice by publication does not contravene or frustrate any legislative policy. Moreover, plaintiffs have not demonstrated any established judicial policy against contractual provisions for notice by publication.

We therefore conclude that although the project notes fit our literal definition of contracts of adhesion, plaintiffs are bound by the provision for notice by publication because of the unique policy considerations attendant on securities offerings.

QUESTIONS

1. Beyond the three specific reasons cited for the validity of the bond as a contract of adhesion, what is the overriding policy reason that is the basis for the court's holding that the notice provision, despite "asserted unfairness," was nevertheless valid?

2. DUTY OF THE INDENTURE TRUSTEE

In a registered bond offering, the Trust Indenture Act of 1939 ("TIA") (15 U.S.C. §§77aaa to 77bbbb) mandates the use of a trustee to administer the rights of bondholders. The statute was enacted to protect bondholders. Prior to its enactment, Congress found that bondholders were inadequately protected for several reasons: Obligor corporations failed to provide a trustee to protect and enforce bondholders' rights; trustees did not have adequate rights and powers; trustees and bondholders did not have adequate access to information.

The trustee is obligated to administer and monitor the indenture and the issuer's performance of the contract. The use of a trustee serves both the issuer's and the bondholder's purposes. From the perspective of the bondholder, using a trustee is a more efficient way to administer, monitor, and enforce the contract rather than to have these functions be performed by a potentially diffuse group of bondholders, each of whom may hold a small stake. Section 302(a) of the Trust Indenture Act of

1939 provides that a trustee is needed because: "(A) individual action by such investors for the purpose of protecting and enforcing their rights is rendered impracticable by reason of the disproportionate expense of taking such action, and (B) concerted action by such investors in their common interest through representatives of their own selection is impeded by reason of the wide dispersion of such investors through many States, and by reason of the fact that information as to the names and addresses of such investors generally is not available to such investors." With respect to monitoring the corporate issuer, shareholders and bondholders are in similar situations in that there are rational reasons why individual investors are not best placed to monitor or enforce their rights. The cost-benefit of active monitoring by a single shareholder or bondholder may be prohibitive. Bondholders are better served by a trustee hired to perform the administration, monitoring, and enforcement.

The use of a trustee also serves the issuer. The indenture is a contract between the issuer and the trustee, and the bondholder is an intended third-party beneficiary of this contract. The indenture contains the additional terms and conditions of the credit contract. The bondholder may enforce the credit contract directly against the issuer only under the terms and conditions set forth in the indenture. Similar to the way that the right of the shareholder to pursue direct actions against the corporation is limited in corporation law, the bondholder's right to pursue direct action against the issuer is typically limited for the same reason that we do not want to expose the issuer to multiple actions brought by numerous claimants from a potentially diffuse class of security holders. Rather, enforcement actions may be better channeled through a single person with that responsibility.

Trust Indenture Act of 1939, Section 315: Duties and Responsibilities of the Trustee

(a) Duties prior to default

The indenture to be qualified shall automatically be deemed (unless it is expressly provided therein that any such provision is excluded) to provide that, prior to default (as such term is defined in such indenture)—

(1) the indenture trustee shall not be liable except for the performance of such duties as are specifically set out in such indenture; and

(2) the indenture trustee may conclusively rely, as to the truth of the statements and the correctness of the opinions expressed therein, in the absence of bad faith on the part of such trustee, upon certificates or opinions conforming to the requirements of the indenture;

but the indenture trustee shall examine the evidence furnished to it pursuant to section 77nnn of this title to determine whether or not such evidence conforms to the requirements of the indenture.

(b) Notice of defaults

The indenture trustee shall give to the indenture security holders, in the manner and to the extent provided in subsection (c) of section 77mmm of this title, notice of all defaults known to the trustee, within ninety days after the occurrence thereof: Provided, That such indenture shall automatically be deemed (unless it is expressly provided therein that such

---

provision is excluded) to provide that, except in the case of default in the payment of the principal of or interest on any indenture security, or in the payment of any sinking or purchase fund installment, the trustee shall be protected in withholding such notice if and so long as the board of directors, the executive committee, or a trust committee of directors and/or responsible officers, of the trustee in good faith determine that the withholding of such notice is in the interests of the indenture security holders.

(c) Duties of the trustee in case of default

The indenture trustee shall exercise in case of default (as such term is defined in such indenture) such of the rights and powers vested in it by such indenture, and to use the same degree of care and skill in their exercise, as a prudent man would exercise or use under the circumstances in the conduct of his own affairs.

(d) Responsibility of the trustee

The indenture to be qualified shall not contain any provisions relieving the indenture trustee from liability for its own negligent action, its own negligent failure to act, or its own willful misconduct, except that—

(1) such indenture shall automatically be deemed (unless it is expressly provided therein that any such provision is excluded) to contain the provisions authorized by paragraphs (1) and (2) of subsection (a) of this section;

(2) such indenture shall automatically be deemed (unless it is expressly provided therein that any such provision is excluded) to contain provisions protecting the indenture trustee from liability for any error of judgment made in good faith by a responsible officer or officers of such trustee, unless it shall be proved that such trustee was negligent in ascertaining the pertinent facts; and

(3) such indenture shall automatically be deemed (unless it is expressly provided therein that any such provision is excluded) to contain provisions protecting the indenture trustee with respect to any action taken or omitted to be taken by it in good faith in accordance with the direction of the holders of not less than a majority in principal amount of the indenture securities at the time outstanding (determined as provided in subsection (a) of section 77ppp of this title) relating to the time, method, and place of conducting any proceeding for any remedy available to such trustee, or exercising any trust or power conferred upon such trustee, under such indenture.

Revised Model Simplified Indenture

Section 7.01: Duties of Trustee.

(a) If an Event of Default has occurred and is continuing, the Trustee shall exercise such of the rights and powers vested in it by this Indenture, and use the same degree of care and skill in their exercise, as a prudent person would exercise or use under the circumstances in the conduct of its own affairs.

(b) Except during the continuance of an Event of Default:

(1) The Trustee need perform only those duties that are specifically set forth in this Indenture and no others.

(2) In the absence of bad faith on its part, the Trustee may conclusively rely, as to the truth of the statements and the correctness of the opinions expressed

therein, upon certificates or opinions furnished to the Trustee and conforming to the requirements of this Indenture. However, the Trustee shall examine the certificates and opinions to determine whether or not they conform to the requirements of this Indenture.

(c) The Trustee may not be relieved from liability for its own negligent action, its own negligent failure to act or its own willful misconduct, except that:

(1) This paragraph does not limit the effect of paragraph (b) of this Section.

(2) The Trustee shall not be liable for any error of judgment made in good faith by a Trust Officer, unless it is proved that the Trustee was negligent in ascertaining the pertinent facts.

(3) The Trustee shall not be liable with respect to any action it takes or omits to take in good faith in accordance with a direction received by it pursuant to Section 6.05.

(4) The Trustee may refuse to perform any duty or exercise any right or power which would require it to expend its own funds or risk any liability if it shall reasonably believe that repayment of such funds or adequate indemnity against such risk is not reasonably assured to it.

(d) Every provision of this Indenture that in any way relates to the Trustee is subject to paragraphs (a), (b) and (c) of this Section.

(e) The Trustee shall not be liable for interest on any money received by it except as the Trustee may agree with the Company. Money held in trust by the Trustee need not be segregated from other funds except to the extent required by law.

The following cases discuss the duties of an indenture trustee. Under the Trust Indenture Act, the nature of the duty is different before and after default, and also there are equitable limitations. These cases outline the obligations and liability of the trustee.

Elliott Associates v. J. Henry Schroder Bank & Trust Co.
838 F.2d 66 (2d Cir. 1988)

ALTIMARI, Circuit Judge:

This appeal involves an examination of the obligations and duties of a trustee during the performance of its predefault duties under a trust indenture, qualified under the Trust Indenture Act of 1939 (the "Act"). The debenture holder alleged in its complaint that the trustee waived a 50–day notice period prior to the redemption of the debentures and did not consider the impact of the waiver on the financial interests of the debenture holders. The debenture holder alleged further that, had the trustee not waived the full 50–day notice period, the debenture holders would have been entitled to receive an additional $1.2 million in interest from the issuer of the debentures. The debenture holder therefore concludes that the trustee's waiver was improper and constituted a breach of the trustee's duties owed to the debenture holders under the indenture, the Act and state law.

Elliott Associates ("Elliott") was the holder of $525,000 principal amount of 10% Convertible Subordinated Debentures due June 1, 1990 (the "debentures") which were issued by Centronics Data Computer Corporation ("Centronics") pursuant to an indenture between Centronics and J. Henry Schroder Bank and Trust Company ("Schroder"), as trustee. Elliott's debentures were part of an aggregate debenture offering by Centronics of $40,000,000 under the indenture.

The indenture and debentures provided that Centronics had the right to redeem the debentures "at any time" at a specified price, plus accrued interest, but the indenture also provided that, during the first two years following the issuance of the debentures, Centronics' right to redeem was subject to certain conditions involving the market price of Centronics' common stock. To facilitate its right to redeem the debentures, Centronics was required to provide written notice of a proposed redemption to the trustee and to the debenture holders. Section 3.01 of the indenture required that Centronics give the trustee 50–day notice of its intention to call its debentures for redemption, "unless a shorter notice shall be satisfactory to the trustee." Section 3.03 of the indenture required Centronics to provide the debenture holders with "at least 15 days but not more than 60 days" notice of a proposed redemption.

At the option of the debenture holders, the debentures were convertible into shares of Centronics' common stock. In the event Centronics called the debentures for redemption, debenture holders could convert their debentures "at any time before the close of business on the last Business Day prior to the redemption date." Subject to certain adjustments, the conversion price was $3.25 per share. The number of shares issuable upon conversion could be determined by dividing the principal amount converted by the conversion price. Upon conversion, however, the debentures provided that "no adjustment for interest or dividends [would] be made."

Debenture holders were to receive interest payments from Centronics semi-annually on June 1 and December 1 of each year. Describing the method of interest payment, each debenture provided that:

> The Company will pay interest on the Debentures (except defaulted interest) to the persons who are registered Holders of Debentures at the close of business on the November 15 or May 15 next preceding the interest payment date. Holders must surrender Debentures to a Paying Agent to collect principal payments.

On March 20, 1986, Centronics' Board of Directors met and approved a complete redemption of all of its outstanding debentures and designated May 16, 1986 as the redemption date. On April 4, 1986—42 days prior to the redemption—Centronics' President, Robert Stein, wrote Schroder and informed the trustee that "pursuant to the terms of the Indenture, notice is hereby given that the Company will redeem all of its outstanding 10% Convertible Subordinated Debentures due June 1, 1990, on May 16, 1986."

On May 1, 1986, pursuant to section 3.03 of the indenture, Centronics gave formal notice of the May 16, 1986 redemption to the debenture holders. In a letter accompanying the Notice of Redemption, Centronics' President explained that, as long as the price of Centronics' common stock exceeded $3.75 per share, debenture holders would receive more value in conversion than in redemption. In the Notice of Redemption, debenture holders were advised that the conversion price of $3.25 per share, when divided into each $1,000 principal amount being converted, would yield 307.69 shares of Centronics common stock [i.e., $1,000 \div $3.25 = 307.69]. Based upon the April 30, 1986 New York Stock Exchange closing price of $5 ⅜ per share of

Centronics' common stock, each $1,000 principal amount of debenture was convertible into Centronics common stock having an approximate value of $1,653.83. Debenture holders were advised further that failure to elect conversion by May 15, 1986 would result in each $1,000 principal amount debenture being redeemed on May 16 for $1,146.11, which consisted of $1,000 in principal, $100 for the 10% redemption premium, and $46.11 in interest accrued from December 1, 1985 (the last interest payment date) to May 16, 1986 (the redemption date). Finally, the notice of redemption explained that accrued interest was not payable upon conversion:

> *No adjustments for Interest or Dividends upon Conversion.* No payment or adjustment will be made by or on behalf of the Company (i) on account of any interest accrued on any Debentures surrendered for conversion or (ii) on account of dividends, if any, on shares of Common Stock issued upon such conversion. Holders converting Debentures will not be entitled to receive the interest thereon from December 1, 1985 to May 16, 1986, the date of redemption. (emphasis in original).

On May 15, 1986, the last day available for conversion prior to the May 16, 1986 redemption, Centronics' common stock traded at $6 ⅝ per share. At that price, each $1,000 principal amount of debentures was convertible into Centronics' common stock worth approximately $2,038. Thus, it was clear that conversion at $2,038 was economically more profitable than redemption at $1,146.11. Debenture holders apparently recognized this fact because all the debenture holders converted their debentures into Centronics' common stock prior to the May 16, 1986 redemption.

Author's Case Annotation: Timeline of Notice

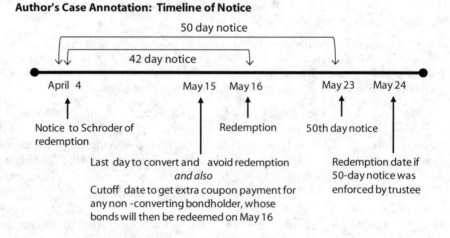

Elliott filed the instant action on May 12, 1986 and sought an order from the district court enjoining the May 16, 1986 redemption. Elliott alleged in its complaint that Schroder and Centronics conspired to time the redemption in such a manner so as to avoid Centronics' obligation to pay interest on the next interest payment date, i.e., June 1, 1986. Elliott alleged that, had it not been for the trustee's improper waiver, debenture holders would have been entitled to an additional payment of $1.2 million in interest from Centronics.

The parties stipulated to the facts, as summarized above. The district court granted Schroder and Centronics' motions to dismiss.

The central issue on this appeal is whether the district court properly held that the trustee was not obligated to weigh the financial interests of the debenture holders when it decided on March 12, 1986 to waive Centronics' compliance with section 3.01's 50–day notice requirement. We agree with the district court's conclusion that the trustee was under no such duty.

No such implied duty can be found from the provisions of the Act or from its legislative history. Indeed, section 315(a)(1) of the Act allows a provision to be included in indentures (which was incorporated into the indenture at issue here) providing that: the indenture trustee shall not be liable except for the performance of such duties [prior to an event of default] as are specifically set out in [the] indenture." Moreover, when the Act was originally introduced in the Senate by Senator Barkley, it provided for the mandatory inclusion of a provision requiring the trustee to perform its pre-default duties and obligations in a manner consistent with that which a "prudent man would assume and perform." However, the version of the Act introduced in the House of Representatives by Representative Cole excluded the imposition of a pre-default "prudent man" duty on the trustee. After extensive hearings on the House and Senate versions of the Act, during which representatives of several financial institutions expressed concern over the imposition of pre-default duties in excess of those duties set forth expressly in the indenture, Congress enacted the present version of section 315 of the Act. Thus, it is clear from the express terms of the Act and its legislative history that no implicit duties, such as those suggested by Elliott, are imposed on the trustee to limit its pre-default conduct.

In view of the foregoing, it is no surprise that we have consistently rejected the imposition of additional duties on the trustee in light of the special relationship that the trustee already has with both the issuer and the debenture holders under the indenture. As we [previously] recognized,

> An indenture trustee is not subject to the ordinary trustee's duty of undivided loyalty. Unlike the ordinary trustee, who has historic common-law duties imposed beyond those in the trust agreement, *an indenture trustee is more like a stakeholder whose duties and obligations are exclusively defined by the terms of the indenture agreement.*

We therefore conclude that, so long as the trustee fulfills its obligations under the express terms of the indenture, it owes the debenture holders no additional, implicit pre-default duties or obligations except to avoid conflicts of interest.

Our analysis here is therefore limited to determining whether the trustee fulfilled its duties under the indenture. As set forth above, section 3.01 requires that, when the company intends to call its debentures for redemption, it must provide the trustee with 50–day notice of the redemption, "unless a shorter notice shall be satisfactory to the trustee." Section 3.02 of the indenture sets forth the manner in which the trustee selects which debentures are to be redeemed when the company calls for a partial redemption. The American Bar Foundation's *Commentaries on Model Debenture Indenture Provisions* (1971) explains that "notice of the Company's election to redeem *all* the debentures need not be given to the Trustee since such a redemption may be effected by the Company without any action on the part of the Trustee. . . ." Thus, it appears that section 3.01's notice requirement is intended for the trustee's benefit to allow it sufficient time to perform the various administrative tasks in preparation for redemption. While compliance with a full notice period may be necessary in the event of partial redemption, the full notice may not be required in the event of a complete redemption. We find that, although the trustee may reasonably insist on the full 50–day notice in the event of a complete redemption, it nevertheless has the discretion to accept shorter notice when it deems such shorter notice satisfactory.

We affirm the judgment of the district court which dismissed Elliott's action.

QUESTIONS

1. What is a conversion price? What is its function in a convertible security?
2. The May 16th redemption date was probably not arbitrary. Why do you think the board of directors designated May 16 as the redemption date?
3. What are the predefault duties of an indenture trustee?
4. If the indenture trustee had a fiduciary duty or a duty of care to the bondholder, what should it have done?
5. The management of Centronics could have avoided this issue by still maintaining the redemption date of May 16. How?
6. Congress debated the issue of whether to impose a fiduciary or tort-like duty of care on the indenture trustee for the benefit of bondholders. What are the arguments for and against such a duty?

NOTES

1. In *Elliott Associates*, the court notes that there would be a cause of action if the indenture trustee engaged in a conflict of interest transaction resulting in injury to the bondholder. It relied on Learned Hand's opinion in *Dabney v. Chase National Bank*, 196 F.2d 668 (2d Cir. 1952), which provided:

> The duty of a trustee, not to profit at the possible expense of his beneficiary, is the most fundamental of the duties which he accepts when he becomes a trustee. It is a part of his obligation to give his beneficiary his undivided loyalty, free from any conflicting personal interest; an obligation that has been nowhere more jealously and rigidly enforced than in New York where these indentures were executed. "The most fundamental duty owed by the trustee to the beneficiaries of the trust is the duty of loyalty * * * In some relations the fiduciary element is more intense than in others; it is peculiarly intense in the case of a trust." We should be even disposed to say that without this duty there could be no trust at all.

In *Dabney*, while possessing knowledge of the issuer's insolvency, the trustee proceeded to collect personal loan obligations from the company to the detriment of other creditors the trustee was serving. The court held that the trustee's conduct constituted a breach of its obligation not to take an action which might disadvantage the debenture holders while providing itself with a financial advantage: that is, the trustee engaged in a conflict of interest giving rise to a cause of action.

Rudbart v. North Jersey District Water Supply Commission
605 A.2d 681 (N.J. 1992)

PER CURIAM

[This is the same case found in the prior portion of this chapter. Recall that the issuer, North Jersey District Water Supply Commission, decided to redeem the bonds prior to maturity as of June 23, 1986. Although regular interest payments were mailed to registered noteholders on December 15, 1985, and June 15, 1986, neither those nor any other mailings informed the noteholders of the forthcoming early redemption. Fidelity, the indenture trustee, provided the required notice by publication in various newspapers. However, it notified certain clients from its brokerage operation of the redemption and thus its clients were made personally aware of the redemption, which permitted them to redeem the bond and get the money earlier than some other bondholders who were unaware of the redemption. As of December 15, 1986, the holders of approximately $10 million of the notes still had not redeemed. After receiving a number of complaints, Fidelity mailed notice in early 1987 to those holders who had not yet redeemed, but declined the Commission's request to put the unredeemed funds it had received from the Commission to pay for redemptions in an interest-bearing account. The late-redeeming noteholders received the redemption price and interest up to June 23, 1986, the date of redemption, but no further interest. Bondholders sued. This portion of the opinion concerns the propriety of the actions of Fidelity in performing its duty as trustee.]

[The court finds] overwhelming inequity of allowing Fidelity to notify its customers of the redemption date while keeping the other investors in the dark and, as a result, perhaps benefiting from the use of the retained money. Because the trial court granted defendants' motion for summary judgment, we must grant to plaintiffs all the inferences that are favorable in the circumstances of this case.

Fidelity wore many hats with respect to this transaction. As an underwriter, it earned income (although it undoubtedly incurred a risk) by subscribing to a percentage of the notes for resale to its customers or for its own account. In addition, it served as an indenture trustee, which we take to mean that plaintiffs' money was to pass through Fidelity's hands as a stakeholder or escrow agent for the benefit of the noteholders. We believe that familiar principles of constructive trust apply to this latter function and entitle plaintiffs to at least a partial return of the interest earned on their money while it was retained by Fidelity.

In the circumstances of this case, there can hardly be any doubt that this was a highly unusual situation in which one of the defendants was aware that it was holding other people's money as a result of selective unfairness. Deposition testimony of Alex Williams, Executive Vice-President of Fidelity, revealed that the bank's investment department gave written or oral notice to its customers prior to the June 23, 1986 call date that the notes had been called. This notice was given whether or not those customers had safe-keeping accounts with the bank. Williams stated that Fidelity felt it would be "good business" to inform its customers. According to Williams, Fidelity took this action essentially because the bank wanted to sell new bonds to its customers, to continue good customer relations, and to insure that its customers received notice. Williams also expressed the opinion, in response to the questions of the bank's attorney, that Fidelity maintained the list of purchasers of the project notes in connection with its underwriting activities for the issuance of the notes. When asked if he could have obtained that information from the trust department, he speculated that the trust department would have said "it would have been a conflict of interest on their part. I don't know what they would have said because we didn't ask for it."

Charles Hoos, Senior Vice-President of Fidelity, testified that he was in charge of the corporate trust department and was aware that Fidelity had elected to give written notice of the redemption of the notes to customers of its investment department. Fidelity took the position that nothing in the record indicated that the personal notifications given by the investment department of the bank were in any way a result of the bank's position as trustee. It pointed to the deposition testimony of Fidelity's personnel that the investment department routinely telephones customers with respect to any major developments as to securities it sold. Fidelity took the position that the deposition testimony demonstrated that a "Chinese wall" existed between the trust department and the investment department that was kept intact during this transaction.

As trustee under the note issue (as well as in the other capacities) Fidelity presumably received significant fees for its responsibilities, which in part included protecting the rights of noteholders. In that fiduciary capacity, for which it was paid, Fidelity now insists that it had no obligation to notify any noteholders in any fashion other than by the method of publication as set forth in the Commission's resolution. On the other hand, Fidelity admits that in its capacity as a bank, its investment department, which also receives fees for its services, including protection of customers, apparently undertook to give special notice to its own customers past and potential, with no obligation to do so. Thus, Fidelity argues that it can demand the benefits of both worlds, but without any additional obligations, particularly toward those who did not purchase the notes through it.

We need not debate whether an indenture trustee may be held to any fiduciary duty beyond that spelled out in the trust agreement. It is one thing not to surcharge a trustee for such an omission; it is quite another to let a trustee profit unfairly from a lack of fair dealing with the beneficiaries of its trust. The fact is that Fidelity decided to notify selectively its own customers. It acted in a manner that exhibited at least a lack of fair dealing and possibly a lack of good faith. This is a compelling case in which to apply the fairness doctrine because Fidelity was aware of the noteholders' lack of notice but acted for only its own customers. Although Fidelity acted in multiple capacities it should not be allowed to assume duties with one hand and to reject them with the other to its own unjust enrichment.

In unjust-enrichment cases courts may presume that the parties "intended to deal fairly with one another [and will] employ the doctrine of *quantum meruit* or equitable remedies such as constructive or resulting trusts' in order to ensure that one party has not been unjustly enriched, and the other unjustly impoverished, on account of their dealings." That principle of fair dealing pervades all of our contract law. Although that principle will not alter the terms of a written agreement, allowing plaintiffs some portion of the return on their withheld funds does not in any sense alter the written terms of the agreement between these parties. Here, the bank knew or should have known that a large percentage of the noteholders would fail to receive notice of the early redemption, and knew exactly who they were. Nonetheless Fidelity did not take any steps to minimize the consequences of that failure, except to notify only its clients.

We can think of no fair reason, then, for holding that either defendant should be entitled to all of the income on plaintiffs' unredeemed funds. Surely, Fidelity recognized that it was a sound business practice and therefore fair dealing to assume that the customers to whom it sold a share of the notes should receive additional notice of the redemption. This multi-hatted trustee cannot simply pick and choose among those with whom it had contractual relationships without invoking the law's concern for "bringing about justice without reference to the intention of the parties." There might be a case in which administrative inconvenience in calculating interest to noteholders who straggle in might justify a denial of any interest. But this is not such a case. The sums involved here were, by the Commission's own account, described in depositions as "astronomical."

In short, this case was far from ripe for summary disposition. No affidavit before this Court has resolved the question of whether a profit was made on the unclaimed funds (once as high as $25,000,000). Clearly, if the Commission shared any of the benefits with Fidelity it should be required to disgorge that amount. The pleadings and the depositions set forth an actionable claim for some equitable share of any income earned on plaintiffs' funds.

The matter is remanded to the Law Division for further proceedings in accordance with this opinion.

QUESTIONS

1. Fidelity fulfilled the notice requirement under the indenture. What then is the problem?
2. What if Fidelity did not specially notify any individual bondholders? What result?
3. What was Fidelity's argument based on its "Chinese wall"? Why did the argument fail? In what way could a "Chinese wall" be a legitimate defense to not notifying bondholders?
4. On remand, what could be the range of remedies against Fidelity depending upon additional facts developed?

LNC Investments, Inc. v. First Fidelity Bank, N.A.
173 F.3d 454 (2d Cir. 1999)

SOTOMAYOR, Circuit Judge:

LNC Investments, Inc. and Charter National Life Insurance Company (collectively, "Bondholders") appeal from a judgment of the United States District Court dismissing their claims for breach of fiduciary duty, breach of contract and violation of §315(c) of the Trust Indenture Act of 1939 ("TIA") following a jury verdict in favor of First Fidelity Bank, United Jersey Bank and National Westminster Bank (collectively, "Trustees"). The Bondholders own bonds that were issued by a trust administered by the Trustees. The bonds were secured by aircraft that the trust purchased from Eastern Air Lines, Inc. ("Eastern") and then leased back to Eastern pursuant to a sale/leaseback transaction. In March 1989, Eastern filed for bankruptcy, while still in possession of the aircraft.

The Bondholders claim that the Trustees acted imprudently by waiting too long to move the bankruptcy court to lift the automatic bankruptcy stay or, alternatively, to order whatever other measures were necessary, possibly including the provision of additional security, to ensure that the Bondholders' interest in the collateral aircraft was adequately protected during the bankruptcy proceeding. The Bondholders argue that if the Trustees had moved earlier to lift the stay or for adequate protection, the bankruptcy court would have either lifted the stay and released the collateral to the Trustees, in which case the Trustees could have sold the aircraft for more than the bonds' value, or denied the motion, in which case the Bondholders' claims against Eastern's estate would have received superpriority over the claims of Eastern's other creditors.

On November 15, 1986, Eastern entered into a sale/leaseback transaction with a secured equipment trust ("Trust") created pursuant to an equipment indenture and lease agreement ("Trust Indenture" or "Indenture") between Eastern and defendant First Fidelity, the Indenture Trustee. The transaction called for Eastern to sell 110 used aircraft to the Trust, and for the Trust, in turn, to lease the same aircraft back to Eastern. The Trust issued three series of equipment trust certificates ("Bonds"), each in different initial principal amounts and with different interest rates and maturity dates, in order to raise the funds needed to purchase the aircraft. The three series of Bonds had a total principal value of $500,000,000. Under the Trust Indenture, Eastern promised to make lease payments to the Trust in amounts sufficient to pay the principal and the interest due on the Bonds as well as the expenses of the Trust. Title to the aircraft was to be held in trust as collateral for the Bonds. On February 13, 1987, in connection with the registration of the Bonds with the U.S. Securities and Exchange Commission, the Trust Indenture was amended to designate a separate Trustee for each series of Bonds and to redesignate First Fidelity as the collateral Trustee, which held title to the aircraft.

Author's Case Annotation: Schematic of Sale/Leaseback Transaction

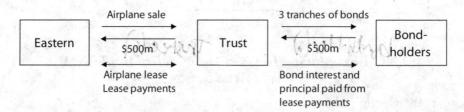

On March 9, 1989, while still in possession of the collateral aircraft, Eastern filed a voluntary petition in the United States Bankruptcy Court seeking protection under Chapter 11 of the United States Bankruptcy Code. Eastern's bankruptcy constituted an "Event of Default" under the Indenture. Upon an Event of Default, the Trustees were to "exercise such of the rights and powers vested in [them] by [the Trust Indenture], and use the same degree of care and skill in their exercise, as a prudent man would exercise or use under the circumstances in the conduct of his own affairs." Trust Indenture §9.02; *see also* TIA §315(c) ("The indenture trustee shall exercise in case of default (as such term is defined in such indenture) such of the rights and powers vested in it by such indenture, and . . . use the same degree of care and skill in their exercise, as a prudent man would exercise or use under the circumstances in the conduct of his own affairs."). Eastern's bankruptcy petition therefore triggered the Trustees' obligations of prudence under the Trust Indenture and the TIA.

Eastern's bankruptcy petition also triggered the automatic stay of §362(a) of the Bankruptcy Code, which prevented the Trustees from taking possession of the collateral aircraft. *See* 11 U.S.C. §362(a) ("A petition filed under section 301, 302, or 303 of this title . . . operates as a stay, applicable to all entities, of . . . any act to obtain possession of property of the estate or of property from the estate or to exercise control over property of the estate. . . ."). As of the date of Eastern's bankruptcy petition, there were 104 aircraft, with an appraised value of $681,800,000, remaining in the collateral pool, and the aggregate principal value of the outstanding Bonds was $453,765,000. The Trust was therefore oversecured by more than $228 million, or, in other words, it maintained an "equity cushion" in that amount. Over the course of the next twenty months, however, the market value of the aircraft decreased significantly as a result of various factors, including the Iraqi invasion of Kuwait in August 1990, which caused fuel prices to rise. As of November 9, 1990, the appraised value of the 67 aircraft remaining in the collateral pool, together with the funds set aside in a "cash collateral account" from the sales and leases of aircraft formerly in the collateral pool, totaled somewhere between $475,443,000 and $589,679,000.

On November 14, 1990, the Trustees filed a motion for adequate protection pursuant to §363(e) of the Bankruptcy Code, which requires a bankruptcy court to prohibit or condition a bankrupt party's use, sale or lease of property serving as collateral if such action is "necessary to provide adequate protection" of the creditor's interest in the collateral. The Trustees' motion sought protection of their interest in the collateral aircraft "in light of the rapid and constant deterioration of any equity cushion in the collateral aircraft." Before the bankruptcy court ruled on the Motion, however, Eastern announced that it would cease operations entirely. On the same day, January 18, 1991, the Trustees and Eastern's Chapter 11 trustee executed two stipulations providing for, among other things, Eastern's release to the Trustees of the remaining aircraft in the collateral pool and the majority of the funds set aside in the cash collateral account. On January 23 and 24, the bankruptcy court approved the stipulations releasing the collateral to the Trustees.

The Bondholders purchased second series and, in LNC's case, third series Bonds at various times between September 1989 and March 1994 [after the March 1989 filing of the voluntary bankruptcy petition]. The Bondholders subsequently brought suit against the Trustees alleging that the Trustees' delay in making the Motion was imprudent and deprived them of a substantial portion of the principal and accrued interest that they were entitled to under the Bonds. Had the Motion been made earlier, the Bondholders contend, one of two favorable outcomes would have resulted: (1) an order lifting the stay and permitting the Trustees to recover and sell the aircraft at a time when the aggregate commercially reasonable sale value of the aircraft was more than 150 percent of the principal amounts owed on the Bonds; or (2) an order denying the Motion on the ground that the Trust's interest in the aircraft was adequately protected, *i.e.,* by the existing equity cushion, in which case the Bondholders would have at least been entitled to superpriority distributions from Eastern's estate under §507(b) of the Bankruptcy Code in advance of Eastern's administrative creditors. Because the Motion was made too late, they argue, their claims did not receive

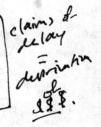

claims of delay = deprivation of §§.

superpriority status, and as a result, the Bondholders were left with only general unsecured claims, for which they will receive nothing from Eastern's estate. According to the Bondholders, a prompt motion to lift the stay or for adequate protection was "the only prudent course of action open to the Trustees upon the happening of an Event of Default," and the Trustees' failure to make the Motion earlier constituted a breach of their fiduciary and contractual duties under the Indenture and a violation of §315(c) of the TIA.

The Bondholders' claims against the Trustees were tried in a two-week bifurcated jury trial. After closing arguments in the liability stage, the district court instructed the jury on the "prudent man" standard applicable under the Indenture, §315 of the TIA and the common law of fiduciary duty. The court further instructed that "in order to succeed on their claims, plaintiffs must prove that the defendants' acts or omissions were not only imprudent, but were also a proximate cause of injury to them." The proximate cause instruction also included a reliance component, which stated that "if the plaintiffs did not rely on the defendants, then even if the defendants acted imprudently, plaintiffs have not suffered any injury as a result of the defendants' actions or inactions." [The Bondholders] objected to the reliance portion of the charge.

The jury ultimately returned a verdict finding that the Trustees had breached their duty of prudence, but that this breach did not proximately cause injury to the Bondholders. Based on the jury's findings, the district court entered judgment dismissing the Bondholders' complaint.

The district court's proximate cause instruction included the following reliance component:

> In considering whether the plaintiffs have suffered any damages, you must determine whether the plaintiffs have proved by a preponderance of the evidence that they relied upon the defendants. If the plaintiffs did not rely on the defendants, then even if the defendants acted imprudently, plaintiffs have not suffered any injury as a result of the defendants' actions or inactions. Similarly, if plaintiffs knew that the defendants were taking certain actions, knew all the facts and risks associated with those actions, and had the ability to correct them but chose not to, then you may find that those actions of the defendants did not cause the plaintiffs to suffer injury.
>
> In this regard, the plaintiffs need not show that they specifically expected or anticipated that the defendants would take any particular course of action. Rather, the plaintiffs must prove that they relied on the defendants to act prudently in general under the circumstances.

The Bondholders argue that this instruction was erroneous because it required a finding of reliance to establish causation. We agree. To whatever extent the Bondholders' knowledge of the Trustees' conduct is relevant to the Bondholders' claims, it is in relation to potential affirmative defenses and not as an element of causation, as to which the Bondholders have the burden of proof.

Reliance as an Element of Causation

The Trustees have identified no controlling authority—and we have found none—to suggest that reliance is required to establish causation in a breach of fiduciary duty or a breach of contract case.

The district court may have considered a reliance charge appropriate based on evidence that the Bondholders knew about the Trustees' alleged breaches of duty when they purchased the Bonds. The fact that the Bondholders purchased the Bonds knowing that the Trustees had not yet moved for adequate protection or to lift the stay, however, does not preclude a finding that they were injured by the Trustees' imprudence. The New York General Obligations Law §13-107(1) expressly permits a bondholder to sue an indenture trustee for breaches of duty that occur prior to his purchase of the bond, regardless of the bondholder's knowledge of these breaches.

The Bondholders specifically requested a jury instruction on §13-107(1) to counteract the reliance charge. We conclude that the district court erred in rejecting this request, particularly because the court admitted evidence at trial of the Bondholders' "specific knowledge relating to the value of the collateral aircraft, or whether the referenced applications [for relief from the stay and/or adequate protection] had been made by the indenture trustees." Without an instruction that the Bondholders acquired all claims of the prior holders irrespective of their knowledge of such claims, the reliance charge invited the jury to find no proximate causation simply on the basis of the Bondholders' pre-purchase knowledge of the Trustees' imprudence.

Affirmative Defenses

Although the Bondholders' knowledge or lack of reliance cannot defeat a finding of causation in this case, the Bondholders' knowledge of the Trustees' imprudence may be relevant to affirmative defenses such as waiver, estoppel or ratification. In fact, the district court denied the Trustees' request to charge the jury on ratification, acquiescence and estoppel, apparently on the ground that these defenses were subsumed within the reliance instruction. That ruling had the effect of misplacing the burden of proving these affirmative defenses. The reliance charge did not allocate this burden to the Trustees, but instead required the Bondholders to "prove by a preponderance of the evidence that they relied upon the [Trustees]." We therefore cannot treat the erroneous reliance charge as the functional equivalent of an instruction on affirmative defenses.

We note, moreover, that the criteria for application of affirmative defenses such as waiver and ratification are stringent. In order to establish that the Bondholders waived their objections to the Trustees' conduct, for example, the Trustees would have to demonstrate, among other things, that the Bondholders effected a "deliberate, informed abandonment of known rights." Similarly, to establish that the Bondholders ratified the Trustees' conduct, the Trustees would have to prove, among other things, that the Bondholders acted "with full knowledge of all material facts relating to the transaction." The Trustees could not carry their burden of establishing these defenses simply by proving that the Bondholders should not have purchased the Bonds knowing that the Trustees had not yet moved to lift the stay or for adequate protection. Under §13-107(1), the Bondholders' purchase of the Bonds vested in them all of the prior holders' claims or demands against the Trustees, "whether or not such claims or demands were known to exist." The Bondholders were therefore statutorily entitled to purchase the Bonds fully aware of the Trustees' alleged breaches of duty.

Furthermore, the Bondholders alleged a continuing breach of duty by the Trustees, *i.e.*, that the Trustees should have moved throughout the bankruptcy to safeguard the value of the collateral. The Bondholders' purchase of the Bonds with knowledge of the Trustees' past breaches therefore cannot by itself demonstrate that the Bondholders knew the Trustees would continue to act imprudently.

Nevertheless, the Trustees may be able to establish waiver, estoppel, ratification or similar affirmative defenses based on evidence other than or in conjunction with the Bondholders' pre-purchase knowledge of the Trustees' failure to make the Motion. We leave it to the district court on remand to determine whether the Trustees have proffered sufficient evidence to sustain the presentation of any affirmative defenses to the jury.

The judgment of the district court is vacated and the case remanded for a new trial.

QUESTIONS

1. Why would bondholders purchase bonds after Eastern filed for voluntary bankruptcy petition?
2. The trial court instructed the jury on the "prudent man" standard. In *Elliott Associates*, the trustee's duties were defined by contract with no additional duties beyond the avoidance of conflict of interest attached. What accounts for the different legal standards?
3. In what way are reliance and causation different? If the defendant was correct on the issue of reliance, why would the bondholders have lost the case?
4. What facts would support the trustee's affirmative defense based on reliance?

3. REPORTING REQUIREMENTS

The issuing corporation has periodic reporting obligations under the TIA, and accordingly this requirement is found in the indenture. Reporting information includes SEC filings and other negotiated information disclosure.

Trust Indenture Act of 1939,

Section 314(a): Reports by Obligor; Evidence of Compliance with Indenture Provisions

(a) Periodic reports. Each person who, as set forth in the registration statement or application, is or is to be an obligor upon the indenture securities covered thereby shall—

(1) file with the indenture trustee copies of the annual reports and of the information, documents, and other reports (or copies of such portions of any of the foregoing as the Commission may by rules and regulations prescribe) which such obligor is required to file with the Commission pursuant to section 13 or section 15(d) of the Securities Exchange Act of 1934; or, if the obligor is not required to file information, documents, or reports pursuant to either of such sections, then to file with the indenture trustee and the Commission, in accordance with rules and regulations prescribed by the Commission, such of the supplementary and periodic information, documents, and reports which may be required pursuant to section 13 of the Securities Exchange Act of 1934, in respect of a security listed and registered on a national securities exchange as may be prescribed in such rules and regulations;

(2) file with the indenture trustee and the Commission, in accordance with rules and regulations prescribed by the Commission, such additional information, documents, and reports with respect to compliance by such obligor with

the conditions and covenants provided for in the indenture, as may be required by such rules and regulations, including, in the case of annual reports, if required by such rules and regulations, certificates or opinions of independent public accountants, conforming to the requirements of subsection (e) of this section, as to compliance with conditions or covenants, compliance with which is subject to verification by accountants, but no such certificate or opinion shall be required as to any matter specified in clauses (A), (B), or (C) of paragraph (3) of subsection (c);

(3) transmit to the holders of the indenture securities upon which such person is an obligor, in the manner and to the extent provided in subsection (c) of section 313, such summaries of any information, documents, and reports required to be filed by such obligor pursuant to the provisions of paragraph (1) or (2) of this subsection as may be required by rules and regulations prescribed by the Commission; and

(4) furnish to the indenture trustee, not less often than annually, a brief certificate from the principal executive officer, principal financial officer or principal accounting officer as to his or her knowledge of such obligor's compliance with all conditions and covenants under the indenture. For purposes of this paragraph, such compliance shall be determined without regard to any period of grace or requirement of notice provided under the indenture.

The rules and regulations prescribed under this subsection shall be such as are necessary or appropriate in the public interest or for the protection of investors, having due regard to the types of indentures, and the nature of the business of the class of obligors affected thereby, and the amount of indenture securities outstanding under such indentures, and, in the case of any such rules and regulations prescribed after the indentures to which they apply have been qualified under this title, the additional expense, if any, of complying with such rules and regulations. Such rules and regulations may be prescribed either before or after qualification becomes effective as to any such indenture.

Revised Model Simplified Indenture

Section 4.02: SEC Reports.

The Company shall file with the Trustee within 15 days after it files them with the SEC copies of the annual reports and of the information, documents and other reports which the Company is required to file with the SEC pursuant to Section 13 or 15(d) of the Exchange Act. The Company will cause any quarterly and annual reports which it makes available to its stockholders to be mailed to the Holders. The Company will also comply with the other provisions of TIA Section 314(a). Delivery of such reports, information and documents to the Trustee is for informational purposes only and the Trustee's receipt of such shall not constitute notice or constructive notice of any information contained therein or determinable from information contained therein, including the Company's compliance with any of its covenants hereunder (as to which the Trustee is entitled to rely exclusively on Officers' Certificates).

Notes to Section 4.02

3. *Issuer No Longer A Reporting Company.* If the Company is not publicly-traded or ceases to be subject to the reporting requirements of the Exchange Act, many indentures add a

provision which requires the filing, with the Trustee, of the information, documents, and reports comparable to those required pursuant to Section 13 of the Securities Exchange Act of 1934 ("Exchange Act"), 15 U.S.C. §78m, in respect of a Security listed and registered on a national security exchange. *See* Note 2 to Sections 7.01/7.02. Such a provision might read:

> [In the event the Company is at any time no longer] (or) [If and so long as the Company is not] subject to the reporting requirements of Section 13 or 15(d) of the Exchange Act, the Company will prepare, in accordance with generally accepted accounting principles, (i) for the first three quarters of each fiscal year, quarterly financial statements substantially equivalent to the financial statements required to be included in a report on Form 10-Q under the Exchange Act, and (ii) on an annual basis, complete audited consolidated financial statements. The Company will provide such quarterly statements to the Trustee and Holders not later than [45] days after the end of each of the first three quarters of the fiscal year and annual reports not later than [90] days after the end of each fiscal year.

4. *Rule 144A Information.* Securities offered in a Rule 144A offering will have a paragraph requiring that the Company make information required under Rule 144A(d)(4) available during any period the Company is not subject to Section 13 or 15(d) of the Exchange Act. Such a provision might read:

> For so long as the Securities are Transfer Restricted Securities, the Company will continue to provide to Holders and to prospective purchasers of the Securities, the information required by Rule 144A(d)(4) under the Securities Act of 1933, as amended, and the Trustee shall make any such reports available to Securityholders upon request. In such event, such reports shall be provided at the times the Company would have been required to provide reports and had it continued to have been subject to the reporting requirements of Section 13 or 15(d) of the Exchange Act.

The following case concerns the obligation of the issuer to provide information to creditors. Such information is frequently in the form of SEC disclosures and filings.

UnitedHealth Group, Inc. v. Wilmington Trust Co.

548 F.3d 1124 (8th Cir. 2008)

MURPHY, Circuit Judge.

UnitedHealth Group (UHG) brought suit seeking a declaratory judgment that its failure to file timely reports with the Securities and Exchange Commission violated no duties owed to its noteholders. Wilmington Trust Company, as trustee for certain UHG notes, filed counterclaims asserting violations of the notes indenture, the Trust Indenture Act of 1939, and an implied covenant of good faith and fair dealing. The district court granted [summary] judgment in favor of UHG on all claims and counterclaims. We affirm.

The basic facts of this case are undisputed and relatively straightforward. On March 2, 2006, UHG publicly issued $850 million of 5.8% senior notes due March 15, 2036 (the notes). The notes were issued pursuant to an indenture entered into by UHG and the trustee. [The trustee] was charged with enforcing, as necessary, the indenture provisions against UHG. Throughout the life of the notes, UHG has made all required interest payments and the debt has continuously been rated investment grade.

As a publicly traded company, UHG is required to make periodic financial disclosures, including quarterly filings on SEC form 10-Q. *See* Securities and Exchange Act of 1934 (Exchange Act) §§13, 15(d). UHG came under public scrutiny in 2006 for backdating employee stock options by using the benefit of hindsight to assign option grant dates retroactively in order to reflect the most favorable historical market values. In response to public concerns about this practice, UHG formed a committee of independent directors to study its financial affairs. Because of this ongoing review, UHG failed to file its 2006 second quarter form 10-Q (2Q 10-Q) by its August 9 due date. Under such circumstances, SEC regulations require a delinquent filer to submit a form 12b-25 notification of late filing. UHG complied with this requirement on August 10. The company's 12b-25 filing explained the reasons for the delay and was accompanied by a 44 page appendix containing substantially the same information as the company would have included in a timely form 10-Q. A copy of this filing was forwarded to the trustee on August 14.

On August 25, 2006, a notice of default was sent to UHG on behalf of certain hedge funds which collectively owned more than twenty-five percent of the outstanding principal balance on the notes. The notice claimed that UHG's failure to file a timely 2Q 10-Q violated §504(i) of the trust indenture. That section reads as follows:

> So long as any of the Securities remain Outstanding, *the Company shall cause copies of all* current, quarterly and annual *financial reports* on Forms 8-K, 10-Q and 10-K, respectively, and all proxy statements, *which the Company is then required to file with the [Securities and Exchange] Commission pursuant to Section 13 or 15(d) of the Exchange Act to be filed with the Trustee* and mailed to the Holders of such series of Securities at their addresses appearing in the Security Register maintained by the Security Registrar, in each case, *within 15 days of filing with the Commission.* The Company shall also comply with the provisions of TIA §314(a).

At the very least, §504(i) requires that UHG forward to the indenture trustee copies of the company's required financial reports within fifteen days of actually filing such reports with the SEC. The notice of default claimed that §504(i) also imposed an affirmative duty to file timely reports with the SEC and that UHG's failure in that regard constituted a default under the indenture. The notice gave UHG sixty days to cure the default.

UHG filed this action against the trustee, seeking a declaratory judgment that it had not violated the terms of the indenture by failing to file a timely 2Q 10-Q. Shortly thereafter, the hedge funds caused a notice of acceleration to be served on UHG. The notice observed that UHG had not cured the alleged default under §504(i) and, based on that failure, demanded accelerated payment of the full principal amount of the notes. Wilmington Trust counterclaimed for breach of contract, violation of the Trust Indenture Act of 1939 (TIA) §314(a), and breach of an implied covenant of good faith and fair dealing.

UHG finally filed its 2Q 10–Q on March 6, 2007, almost seven months late. It simultaneously submitted an amended form 10–Q for the first quarter of 2006, a tardy form 10–Q for the third quarter of that year, and a form 10–K for the year ending December 31, 2006. The financial information contained in the 2Q 10–Q differed by less than one percent from the preliminary data which had accompanied the August form 12b–25 notice of late filing.

The district court granted summary judgment in favor of UHG on all claims and counterclaims. Wilmington Trust now appeals.

Here the basic facts are undisputed, and the outstanding issues are purely legal questions of contract interpretation and statutory construction.

Section 1306 of the indenture provides that its terms "shall be governed by and interpreted under the laws of the State of New York." Under New York principles of contract interpretation, "the words and phrases used by the parties must . . . be given their plain meaning."

Section 504(i) of the Indenture

Wilmington Trust argues that §504(i) of the indenture imposes an independent obligation on UHG to file timely SEC reports and, within fifteen days afterwards, to forward copies of such reports to the trustee. Under the Trust's interpretation, when UHG failed to file its 2Q 10–Q on time, it not only ran afoul of the Exchange Act and SEC regulations, but it also violated the indenture duties to its noteholders. UHG asserts that §504(i) imposes no independent obligation to make timely SEC filings. Rather, the provision merely requires the company to transmit to the trustee copies of whatever reports it *actually* files with the SEC. Based on this analysis UHG maintains that its indenture obligations were not even triggered until March 2007 when it finally filed its tardy 2Q 10–Q. Since the company forwarded a copy to Wilmington Trust within fifteen days of actual filing, UHG argues that it has not defaulted under the indenture.

Section 504(i), reduced to its essence, reads as follows: "the Company shall cause copies of . . . financial reports . . . which the Company is then required to file with the Commission pursuant to Section 13 or 15(d) of the Exchange Act to be filed with the Trustee . . . within fifteen days of filing with the Commission." Wilmington Trust argues that the plain meaning of the phrase "then required to file" imposes an independent obligation to file timely reports. Wilmington Trust correctly notes that the word "then" means "at that time." But for our purposes the word's placement and function within the sentence are just as important as its definition.

In §504(i) the phrase "then required to file" is part of a longer clause introduced by the relative pronoun "which." The antecedent of "which" is clearly and unambiguously the word "reports." Thus, as a simple matter of syntax, the phrase "then required to file" modifies the word "reports" and indicates *which* reports are subject to §504(i)'s terms. Just as clearly and just as unambiguously, the phrase "within fifteen days of filing with the Commission" modifies "shall cause . . . to be filed" and indicates *when* §504(i)'s command must be fulfilled. The plain meaning of §504(i) thus imposes only a relative time constraint: copies of the indicated reports must be forwarded to the trustee within fifteen days of actually filing them with the SEC. The clause imposes no absolute timetable or independent obligation to comply with the Exchange Act or SEC regulations. In fact, the plain language of §504(i) makes clear that any duty actually to file the reports is imposed "pursuant to Section 13 or 15(d) of the Exchange Act" and *not* pursuant to the indenture itself. The provision does not incorporate the Exchange Act; it merely refers to it in order to establish which reports must be forwarded.

Wilmington Trust also argues that New York law, while respecting the plain meaning of words and phrases, further requires that "primary attention must be given to the manifest purpose" of the parties. Wilmington Trust notes that in the Internet age, SEC filings are readily available online through the agency's EDGAR database. Based on this fact it maintains that a ministerial duty to forward copies of widely available reports would be meaningless and of no value to noteholders. The purpose of the provision, Wilmington Trust asserts, must therefore be to impose an independent obligation to file timely reports. Wilmington Trust ignores the origin of §504(i), however. As UHG points out, the language is derived from a Model Simplified Indenture drafted by the American Bar Association in 1983. *See* 38 Bus. Law. 741, 755 (1983). At the time the model provision was promulgated, the Internet did not exist as we know it today. The fact that §504(i) may be of slight value in the Internet age does not empower Wilmington Trust to impose unbargained for duties on UHG simply to breathe new relevance into an outdated provision.

UHG notes that another model indenture agreement *does* incorporate the SEC filing deadlines. A 1967 proposal prepared by the American Bar Foundation requires that an issuer "will . . . file with the Trustee, within 15 days after the Company is required to file the same, copies of the [reports]." This language differs from that of §504(i) in at least one critical respect: §504(i)'s fifteen day window opens when the company *actually* files its reports with the SEC, while the 1967 model's fifteen day window opens when the company is *required* to file regardless of when it actually does. The parties in this case are sophisticated and represented by teams of experienced attorneys. They could have chosen the 1967 ABF model over the 1983 ABA model, or they could have drafted their own language imposing a rigid timetable or explicitly incorporating SEC regulations. But, as the district court found, "this is not the agreement they made."

The precise issue in this case is a matter of first impression in the Eighth Circuit. It has recently been presented to three federal district courts and to a New York State trial court. Although none of the decisions of these courts is binding on us, we note that the three federal courts all concluded, on nearly identical facts, that similar indenture provisions did not impose independent obligations to file timely SEC reports.

In an unpublished opinion, the commercial division of the New York trial court reached the opposite conclusion. *Bank of N.Y. v. BearingPoint Inc.*, 2006 WL 2670143 (N.Y.Sup.Ct. 2006). The *BearingPoint* court rejected a debt issuer's argument that a similar indenture provision made "SEC filings optional under the Indenture." The court's analysis focused on the mandatory language of the indenture but did not distinguish between two distinct duties: one to file reports with the SEC in the first instance and another to forward copies of the reports to the trustee. More importantly, the court did not consider any timing issues and simply eliminated the phrase "within 15 days after it files such . . . reports . . . with the SEC," replacing it with a set of ellipses.

[Other federal] courts all considered and rejected *BearingPoint,* as did the district court in this case. They did so after coming to the same conclusion: the indenture provisions at issue imposed nothing more than the ministerial duty to forward copies of certain reports, identified by reference to the Exchange Act, within fifteen days of actually filing the reports with the SEC. As previously discussed, the clear and unambiguous language of the indenture in this case leads to the same conclusion. We therefore decline to follow *BearingPoint.*

Based on the plain meaning of §504(i), we hold that the indenture imposes no independent obligation to file timely SEC reports. UHG's delay in filing its 2006 2Q 10–Q—while potentially a violation of SEC regulations—did not constitute a default under the indenture. Since UHG did ultimately file with the SEC its "then required" reports and within fifteen days afterwards did transmit to the trustee copies of the same, it fulfilled its contractual duties.

TIA §314(a)

The Trust Indenture Act provides in part as follows:

> Each person who . . . is or is to be an obligor upon the indenture securities covered thereby shall: (1) file with the indenture trustee copies of the annual reports and of the information, documents, and other reports . . . which such obligor is required to file with the [Securities and Exchange] Commission pursuant to [§13] or [§15(d)] of [the Exchange Act]. . . .

TIA §314(a). The TIA therefore imposes on UHG a statutory obligation to provide copies of required SEC reports to the indenture trustee. The provision is obviously closely related to §504(i) of the indenture, and in fact §504(i) expressly incorporates the provisions of TIA §314(a).

Nevertheless, the TIA imposes no new obligations or duties and is actually *less* burdensome than §504(i) of the indenture insofar as it imposes no time constraints whatsoever. While the indenture creates a relative deadline of fifteen days after actual filing with the SEC, the TIA is completely silent as to when copies of SEC reports must be forwarded to the trustee. As was the case with §504(i) of the indenture, the TIA's reference to §§13 and 15(d) of the Exchange Act merely identifies *which* reports must eventually be forwarded to the trustee. It does not independently impose any particular timetable for filing nor does it incorporate the SEC's regulatory deadlines.

Wilmington Trust argues that a ministerial obligation without a corresponding duty to file timely reports is meaningless in today's world of instant Internet communication, particularly in light of the TIA's stated purpose to provide "adequate *current* information" to investors. *See* TIA §302(a)(4) (emphasis added). But the TIA was drafted in 1939. Under the circumstances of that era, the dissemination of "adequate current information" was certainly advanced by a ministerial duty to forward financial reports. What seems redundant in the 21st Century was once a critical mechanism for keeping investors informed as to a company's financial health. The development of more efficient electronic alternatives is no reason to expand UHG's duties under the TIA.

We conclude that TIA §314(a) requires only that debt issuers forward to their trustees copies of such reports as are actually filed with the SEC. Since UHG ultimately filed all required reports with the agency and promptly forwarded copies of the same to the trustee, the company violated no statutory duties under the TIA.

QUESTIONS

1. The issuer and bondholders can negotiate a term in which the indenture requires an independent obligation to provide information. However, from the issuer's perspective, what might be an objection to such a duty?
2. What is the policy rationale for interpreting TIA §314(a) as a ministerial function?

NOTES

1. Although the indenture was subject to New York law, the Eighth Circuit disapproved of a New York trial court's opinion in *Bank of N.Y. v. BearingPoint Inc.*, 2006 WL 2670143 (N.Y.Sup.Ct. 2006) that recognized an independent duty arising from the indenture. Subsequently, the New York Court of Appeals, in *Racepoint Partners, LLC v. JP Morgan Chase Bank, N.A.*, 928 N.E.2d 396 (N.Y. 2010), held that, citing *UnitedHealth Group, Inc. v. Wilmington Trust Co.*, the reporting requirement in the indenture was only a "ministerial function." Interestingly, the case involved notes issued by the Enron Corporation. In December 2001, in the wake of one of the largest accounting fraud scandals, Enron filed for bankruptcy. Thereafter, the plaintiffs bought approximately $1 billion of the notes from their holders. The plaintiffs then sued Chase Manhattan Bank, which was the indenture trustee, on a common law action for breach of contract. They argued that the *indenture* created a duty to file accurate reports with the SEC, which of course Enron did not. Plaintiffs claimed that Enron defaulted under the indenture agreement and that Chase Manhattan Bank, as indenture trustee, had actual knowledge of this default and that its failure to notify Enron and the noteholders of the default constituted breach of the agreement. The court held:

> It is clear therefore that indenture agreements containing the required delivery provisions pursuant to [TIA §] 314(a) refer to the Securities Exchange Act only to identify the types of report that should be forwarded to indenture trustees. They do not create contractual duties on the part of the trustee to assure that the information contained in any report filed is true and accurate. That is simply not the mission or purpose of the trustee or the contract under which it undertakes its duties.
>
> Of course, companies have a duty to file accurate reports with the SEC. That obligation, however, derives from the Securities Exchange Act, not from indenture agreements.
>
> Our holding that section 4.02 of the indenture agreement simply embodies a delivery requirement, and does not imply a duty on the part of the trustee to assure the filing of accurate reports or risk default, is consistent with the limited, "ministerial" functions of indenture trustees, and with the plain language of section 4.02, which states that "delivery of such reports, information and documents [filed with the SEC] to the Trustee is for informational purposes only." Plaintiffs' proposed interpretation, on the other hand, would require indenture trustees to review the substance of SEC filings, so as to reduce the risk of liability, greatly expanding indenture trustees' recognized administrative duties far beyond anything found in the contract.

2. Why might the plaintiffs in *Racepoint Partners* buy Enron bonds *after* the disclosure of the accounting fraud and the filing of bankruptcy? The plaintiffs clearly saw a

financial play of some sort. The bonds would have been steeply discounted in the market, and they must have had a strategy to extract more value from the bonds than they paid. Could one of the financial plays have been an anticipated lawsuit for damages against the indenture trustee Chase Manhattan Bank, which of course was solvent and had deep pockets? The court noted that "plaintiffs, as secondary holders of the notes, are vested with the claims and demands of the sellers [of the note]."

4. SINKING FUND PROVISION

Historically, a sinking fund was money accumulated by a debtor for the purpose of "sinking or wiping out" the debt. In a bond issue, the money is collected by the trustee from the issuer. The provision for a sinking fund must be found in the debt contract. The sinking fund is used to retire portions of the debt issue before maturity at a specified redemption price. It provides creditors with some assurance that the debt issue will be paid because it requires periodic repayment of debt prior to maturity.

A sinking fund can be satisfied through the deposit of cash. Indentures can also provide that the issuer may surrender securities in lieu of depositing cash; the issuer pays into the sinking fund by surrendering debt instruments constituting obligations against the issuer. From the perspective of creditors, the surrender of cash is preferable.

Commentaries on Model Debenture Indenture Provisions (American Bar Foundation, 1971), Simple Sinking Fund Provision

§12-1. Sinking Fund Payments.

As and for a Sinking Fund for the retirement of the Debentures, the Company will, until all the Debentures are paid or payment thereof provided for, deposit in accordance with §11-6, prior to _____ [here insert month and day at annual intervals or two months and days at semi-annual intervals] in each year, commencing with the year _____ to and including the year _____ (each such date being hereinafter referred to as a Sinking Fund Payment Date), an amount in cash sufficient to redeem on such Sinking Fund Payment Date $_____ principal amount of Debentures, at the Redemption Price set forth in §11-1 for redemption through the operation of the Sinking Fund. Each such Sinking Fund Payment shall be applied to the redemption of Debentures on such Sinking Fund Payment Date as herein provided. The Trustee shall, on or before the thirtieth day prior to such Sinking Fund Payment Date, select, in the manner provided in §11-4, the Debentures to be redeemed on the next Sinking Fund Payment Date and cause notice of the redemption thereof to be given in the name of and at the expense of the Company in the manner provided in §11-5. Such notice having been duly given, the redemption of such Debentures shall be made upon the terms and in the manner stated in §§11-7 and 11-8.

* * *

Indenture between Apple Inc. and The Bank of New York Mellon Trust Company, dated April 29, 2013

Section 1201. Applicability of Article.

The provisions of this Article XII shall be applicable to any sinking fund for the retirement of Securities of any series except as otherwise specified as contemplated by Section 301 for such Securities. The minimum amount of any sinking fund payment provided for by the terms of any series of Securities is herein referred to as a "mandatory sinking fund payment," and any payment in excess of such minimum amount provided for by the terms of such Securities is herein referred to as an "optional sinking fund payment." If provided for by the terms of any series of Securities, the cash amount of any sinking fund payment may be subject to reduction as provided in Section 1202. Each sinking fund payment shall be applied to the redemption of Securities of the series as provided for by the terms of such Securities.

Section 1202. Satisfaction of Sinking Fund Payments with Securities.

The Company (1) may deliver Outstanding Securities of a series (other than any previously called for redemption) and (2) may apply as a credit Securities of a series which have been redeemed either at the election of the Company pursuant to the terms of such Securities or through the application of permitted optional sinking fund payments pursuant to the terms of such Securities, in each case in satisfaction of all or any part of any sinking fund payment with respect to any Securities of such series required to be made pursuant to the terms of such Securities as and to the extent provided for by the terms of such Securities; provided that the Securities to be so credited have not been previously so credited. The Securities to be so credited shall be received and credited for such purpose by the Trustee at the Redemption Price, as specified in the Securities so to be redeemed, for redemption through operation of the sinking fund and the amount of such sinking fund payment shall be reduced accordingly.

Section 1203. Redemption of Securities for Sinking Fund.

Not less than 60 days (or such shorter period as shall be satisfactory to the Trustee) prior to each sinking fund payment date for any Securities, the Company will deliver to the Trustee an Officer's Certificate specifying the amount of the next ensuing sinking fund payment for such Securities pursuant to the terms of such Securities, the portion thereof, if any, which is to be satisfied by payment of cash and the portion thereof, if any, which is to be satisfied by delivering and crediting Securities pursuant to Section 1202 and will also deliver to the Trustee any Securities to be so delivered. Not less than 30 days prior to each such sinking fund payment date, the Securities to be redeemed upon such sinking fund payment date shall be selected in the manner specified in Section 1103 and the Company shall cause notice of the redemption thereof to be given in the name of and at the expense of the Company in the manner provided in Section 1104. Such notice having been duly given, the redemption of such Securities shall be made upon the terms and in the manner stated in Section 1106 and Section 1107.

5. "NO ACTION" PROVISION

The power of bondholders to file suit on behalf of themselves is limited. Indentures have a "no action" provision that limits the ability of the bondholder to bring suit against the issuer for breach of the indenture. Subject to exceptions the enforcement of the indenture is principally an obligation of the trustee who has the power to sue. The purpose of the "no action" provision is to limit individual bondholders from bringing individual suits. There is an efficiency consideration. Like shareholders in a corporation, bondholders may be many, which creates the risk of many meritless lawsuits. Under the indenture, the trustee has the duty to enforce the indenture, and a bondholder may bring an action against the issuer only if certain conditions set forth in the indenture are met.

Revised Model Simplified Indenture

Section 6.06, Limitation on Suits

A Securityholder may pursue a remedy with respect to this Indenture or the Securities only if:

(1) the Holder gives to the Trustee notice of a continuing Event of Default;

(2) the Holders of at least 25% in Principal amount of the Securities make a request to the Trustee to pursue the remedy;

(3) the Trustee either (i) gives to such Holders notice it will not comply with the request, or (ii) does not comply with the request within [15 or 30] days after receipt of the request; and

(4) the Holders of a majority in Principal amount of the Securities do not give the Trustee a direction inconsistent with the request prior to the earlier of the date, if ever, on which the Trustee delivers a notice under Section 6.06(3)(i) or the expiration of the period described in Section 6.06(3)(ii).

A Securityholder may not use this Indenture to prejudice the rights of another Securityholder or to obtain a preference or priority over another Securityholder.

Section 6.07, Rights of Holders to Receive Payment

Notwithstanding any other provision of this Indenture, the right of any Holder of a Security to receive payment of Principal and interest on the Security, on or after the respective due dates expressed in the Security, or to bring suit for the enforcement of any such payment on or after such respective dates, shall not be impaired or affected without the consent of the Holder.

Notwithstanding any other provision of this Indenture, the right of any Holder of a Security to bring suit for the enforcement of the right to convert the Security shall not be impaired or affected without the consent of the Holder.

Nothing in this Indenture limits or defers the right or ability of Holders to petition for commencement of a case under applicable Bankruptcy Law to the extent consistent with such Bankruptcy Law.

The following case concerns the difficulties bondholders face when there is a breach of the indenture, but the bondholder cannot muster sufficient level of support to pursue an action. It shows the potential for equitable relief from the "no action" provision.

Birn v. Childs Co.

37 N.Y.S.2d 689 (Sup. Ct. 1942)

WALTER, Justice.

[The court found that an issuer violated the sinking fund provision of the debenture when it delivered to the trustee unissued debentures rather than cash or marketable securities. The trustee accepted the delivery. The plaintiff gave the trustee written notice of a completed event of default, which was the failure to comply with an express term of the sinking fund provision. The plaintiff also made a written request upon the trustee to file suit against the issuer and afforded it a reasonable opportunity to do so. The trustee took the position that the sinking fund provision had been complied with, made no request for any indemnity, and did not file suit. The plaintiff then sued the issuer herself.]

I now come to the question of plaintiff's right to maintain the action in view of Section 6 of Article Five of the indenture, the text of which is quoted.

No holder of any debenture or coupon issued hereunder shall have any right to institute any suit, action or proceeding in equity or at law or otherwise for the enforcement of any covenant or remedy under this indenture or for the collection of any sum due from the Corporation under this indenture, or for the appointment of a receiver, unless such holder previously shall have given to the Trustee written notice of a completed event of default as hereinbefore provided; nor unless, also, the holders of at least twenty-five per cent. [25%] in principal amount of the debentures issued hereunder and then outstanding, shall have made written request upon the Trustee, and shall have afforded to it a reasonable opportunity to institute a suitable action, suit or proceeding in its own name; nor unless, also, they shall have offered to the Trustee security and indemnity satisfactory to it against the costs, expenses and liabilities to be incurred therein or thereby and the Trustee shall have refused or neglected to comply with such request within a reasonable time thereafter, and such notification, request and offer of indemnity are hereby declared, in every case, at the option of the Trustee, to be conditions precedent to the execution of the powers and trusts of this indenture for the benefit of the debenture holders, and to any action or cause of action or any other remedy hereunder. Provided, however, that nothing contained in this Article or elsewhere in this indenture or in the debentures or coupons shall affect or impair the obligation of the Corporation, which is unconditional and absolute, to pay the principal of the debentures to their respective holders or registered owners at the time and place in the debentures expressed or affect or impair the right of action, which is absolute and unconditional, of such holders or registered owners to enforce such payment.

This suit is one for the enforcement of a covenant of the indenture, the sinking fund provision, and is not one to enforce payment of the debentures or their coupons, and it thus falls within the scope of Section 6 of Article Five. All that is lacking, therefore, is that the request to the trustee to sue was not made by the holders of at least twenty-five percent [25%] of the debentures outstanding, and the question presented is whether or not because of that lack the suit must fail.

Restrictive or no-action clauses have been inserted in corporate mortgages and trust indentures for years. In so far as they prevent individual holders from getting special advantages for themselves and protect the rights and security of all holders as a class, and also in so far as they afford the trustee notice and an opportunity for examination, they serve a highly useful purpose and have been uniformity sustained, even though sometimes said to be not favored and to be strictly construed, but no case has been cited or found which holds that such a clause prevents such a suit as is here brought under such circumstances as are here disclosed.

We are here confronted with what I have found to be a breach of an express covenant to make specified payments or deliveries into a sinking fund created for the benefit of all holders of the outstanding debentures. Under the facts and the law as I find them to be the trustee should have brought the suit. It refused after notice and request to do so. Plaintiff has produced evidence which shows that, because the debentures are payable to bearer, it is difficult if not impossible for her even to locate other holders to the extent of twenty-five per cent of the total debentures outstanding, and she has framed her suit, not as one at law for damages payable to her for her own benefit, but as one in equity for the benefit of all holders. That the restrictive or no-action clause does not operate, under such circumstances, to prevent a court of equity from granting relief at the suit of a single holder was in effect held in *Ettlinger v. Persian Rug & Carpet Co.*, 36 N.E. 1055 (N.Y. 1894). The mortgage involved required that the request to the trustee to sue be made by a majority of the bondholders, and that provision was pressed upon the court in the briefs, and yet a suit by one bondholder was upheld.

Even if the indenture be regarded as going so far as by its terms to vest in the trustee alone the sole and exclusive right to enforce the sinking fund provision—the sole and exclusive title to any cause of action arising out of a breach thereof—the situation still is no different from the hosts of incidents in which beneficiaries of a trust are allowed to sue upon causes of action vested in the trustee upon a showing that the trustee unreasonably refuses to sue. Suits by stockholders in the right of their corporation upon causes of action vested in the corporation are the creatures and inventions of courts of equity. Equity also allows other beneficiaries to sue upon causes of action vested in their trustees when the trustee unreasonably refuses to sue. It sometimes is stressed that these restrictive or no-action clauses are matters of contract and that security holders must be held to their contract, but the contract, in its entirety, is one which gives rise to a trust, and upon the question of allowing a beneficiary to sue upon a showing of an unreasonable refusal of the trustee to sue I can perceive no difference between a trust based upon contract and one based on status or one arising by operation of law. In each instance the principle is the same, that equity will not permit a wrong to go unredressed because the trustee unreasonably refuses to sue.

Stating the same result in the terminology of contract rather than the terminology of equity and trusts, such limitation as the clause imposes upon the individual holder's right to sue is subject to the implied condition or covenant that the trustee will not unreasonably refuse to enforce any covenant of the indenture when a breach thereof is brought to its attention, whether it is brought to its attention by one holder or many, and when that implied condition or covenant is broken the limitation disappears.

Plaintiff is entitled to judgment directing Childs Company to pay to the trustee the sum of $423,000, in cash or outstanding debentures, to be held and disposed of by the trustee in accordance with the sinking fund provisions of the indenture.

QUESTIONS

1. In what way did the issuer breach the terms of the indenture? What is the problem with an unissued debenture as a contribution to the sinking fund?

2. What is the significance of the fact that the bonds were in bearer form? If the bonds were registered, could the plaintiff have sued?
3. What key factors permitted the plaintiff to sue even though the "no action" provision in the indenture was not satisfied? What is the holding of the case?

The following case illustrates the potential for relief from the "no action" provision due to improper action of the trustee in relation to the trustee's refusal to bring an action.

Rabinowitz v. Kaiser-Frazer Corp.
111 N.Y.S.2d 539 (NY Sup. 1952)

HART, Justice.

Defendant Kaiser-Frazer Corporation moves to dismiss the complaint on the grounds that the plaintiff has not legal capacity to sue.

This action was instituted against the three named defendants, Kaiser-Frazer, Bank of America and Graham-Paige Motors Corporation by the service of summons and verified complaint upon each of them.

The plaintiff is the original owner and holder of $10,000 in principal amount of 4% Convertible Debentures of Graham-Paige which were issued under an indenture with the Bank of America as trustee and has brought this action in behalf of himself and all other owners of such debentures similarly situated.

[Graham-Paige was engaged primarily in the production, distribution, and sale of automobiles and replacement parts. Upon the corporate formation of Kaiser-Frazer by a senior executive of Graham-Paige and others, Graham-Paige purchased 250,000 shares of common stock of Kaiser-Frazer. Graham-Paige and Kaiser-Frazer then entered into an agreement for joint use of a former bomber plant at Willow Run for the manufacture of automobiles and farm equipment. Under this agreement Graham-Paige was entitled to use one-third of Willow Run's automotive production facilities; Kaiser-Frazer the other two-thirds.]

In order to obtain its share of the needed capital to convert the Willow Run plant to automobile production and to obtain other working capital, Graham-Paige issued $11,500,000 of 4% Convertible Debentures due April 1, 1956, under an Indenture with Bank of America as trustee. Behind these debentures were pledged the Graham-Paige plant in Detroit, Michigan and the 250,000 shares of Kaiser-Frazer common stock.

Graham-Paige covenanted in said Indenture (Article "Third" relating to "Sinking Fund and Redemption of Debentures") that on or before April 1 of each year to and including April 1, 1956, so long as any of the debentures are outstanding, it would pay to the trustee, as and for a Sinking Fund for the retirement of the debentures, an amount in cash equal to 25% of its net earnings for the preceding calendar year.

Article Thirteenth of the Indenture also provided:

§13.01. Nothing in this Indenture shall prevent * * * any sale or conveyance, subject to the lien of this Indenture on the mortgaged and pledged property, of all or substantially all of the property of the corporation (Graham-Paige) to any other corporation * * *; provided, however, and the corporation covenants and agrees, that

(1) Any such * * * sale or conveyance shall be upon such terms as fully to preserve and in no respect to impair the lien of security of this Indenture * * *, and

(2) Upon any such * * * sale or conveyance, * * * the corporation to which all or substantially all the property of the Corporation shall be sold or conveyed shall execute with the trustee and record an indenture, satisfactory to the trustee, whereby the successor corporation shall expressly agree to pay duly and punctually the principal of and the interest and premium, if any, on the Debentures according to their tenure, and shall expressly assume the due and punctual performance and observance of all the covenants and conditions of this Indenture to be performed or observed by the Corporation.

§13.02. Upon any such * * * sale or conveyance * * * such successor corporation shall succeed to and be substituted for the Corporation with the same effect as if it had been named as the party of the first part (Graham-Paige) * * *.

By a contract dated December 12, 1946, Graham-Paige agreed to sell to Kaiser-Frazer all of its automotive assets in consideration of the issue to Graham-Paige of 750,000 shares of common stock of Kaiser-Frazer, of an agreement by Graham-Paige to pay Kaiser-Frazer $3,000,000 and by a debenture payment agreement between Graham-Paige and Kaiser-Frazer where under [Kaiser-Frazer] undertook to pay the interest on and the principal of the debentures of Graham-Paige then outstanding ($8,524,000).

The agreement (Article XI) specifically provides that Kaiser-Frazer shall not be required to pay the principal of any or all said 4% Convertible Debentures of Graham-Paige prior to the maturity date thereof (except for default in the payment of interest) and the debenture payment agreement of February 10, 1947, specifically provided (Article V) that except as therein provided Kaiser-Frazer does not "assume or agree to perform any of the promises, covenants, terms or conditions of the Indenture to be performed by" Graham-Paige and that neither the trustee under the indenture nor any debenture holder shall have any rights by virtue of such agreement and that the undertakings of Kaiser-Frazer are solely for the benefit of Graham-Paige and that they are limited to the making of Graham-Paige of the payments Kaiser-Frazer therein agreed to make.

It is significant to note that by virtue of the foregoing provisions Kaiser-Frazer specifically avoided any undertaking on its part to apply 25% of its annual net profits to the sinking fund of the debentures in accordance with the provisions of Article Third of the Debenture. It is this failure of Kaiser-Frazer to have assumed the obligations of the sinking fund and to have paid 25% of its annual profits into such fund which presents the crux of this case.

The complaint then proceeds to allege that the sale in question to the knowledge of Bank of America and Kaiser-Frazer constituted a conveyance of "all or substantially all" of the property of Graham-Paige and thereby terminated Graham-Paige's manufacturing and other activities in the automotive field; that Bank of America and Kaiser-Frazer knew or should have known that the sale as consummated would have the effect of depriving Graham-Paige of an opportunity to earn any moneys in the immediate or foreseeable future and would result in rendering nugatory the provisions in the indenture requiring Graham-Paige to make deposits in the sinking fund.

It is further alleged that by reason of the sale Bank of America was under a duty, as trustee, and within its powers under the terms of the indenture, to obtain from Kaiser-Frazer a supplemental indenture satisfactory in form to itself, whereby Kaiser-Frazer would expressly assume the performance of *all* the covenants and conditions of the indenture to be performed by Graham-Paige, particularly those provisions of the indenture (Article Third) relating to the "Sinking Fund and Redemption of Debentures"; that Bank of America failed or refused to perform its duties as trustee in this respect and thereby breached the trust indenture.

It is also alleged that Kaiser-Frazer is bound by the terms of the trust indenture despite its failure to execute a supplemental indenture to assume expressly the provisions relating to the "Sinking Fund"; that Kaiser-Frazer should have deposited with the trustee each year an amount in cash equal to 25% of its net earnings for the next preceding year; to wit, for the year 1947 the sum of $4,753,889.25 and for the year 1948 the sum of $2,590,524.50, making a total of $7,344,413.75, no part of which has been paid, and that Kaiser-Frazer is further obligated to the trustee for future sinking fund payments as provided in Article "Third" of the Indenture.

As of the date of this complaint there was outstanding $8,524,000 principal amount of the 4% Convertible Debentures of Graham-Paige.

It is also alleged that Graham-Paige made no deposit with the trustee of any part of its net earnings for the years 1947 and 1948; that there was a net income for the calendar year 1947 of $123,766.73 but for the calendar year 1948 Graham-Paige had a net loss of $3,391,113.36, and that Graham-Paige's manufacturing operations of the farm equipment business were closed early in 1949.

The complaint contains the following allegation: "This action and the relief herein sought are not for the remedies provided by the Indenture, this being an action invoking the inherent powers of this Court as a court of equity to declare, protect and preserve the rights of he debenture holders. No demand upon the Trustee to institute or prosecute this action is necessary, nor has such demand been made for the reason that the Trustee is a defendant herein and is liable to the plaintiff and other debenture holders similarly situated, for its own negligent and wilful misconduct with respect to the acts herein complained of, and would be demanding that the Trustee sue itself, and such demand would be entirely useless and futile."

The plaintiff alleges ownership of less than one-eighth of 1% of the outstanding debentures. The objection that plaintiff lacks the legal capacity to sue is predicated on the language of §8.08 of the Indenture which provides in substance that "no holder of any Debenture * * * shall have any right to institute any suit * * * unless such holder previously shall have given to the Trustee written notice of default * * * and unless also the holders of not less than 25% in aggregate principal amount of the Debentures then outstanding shall have made written request upon the Trustee to institute such action and the Trustee * * * shall have neglected or refused to institute any such action * * *."

The plaintiff urges that notwithstanding the presence of a "no action" clause, an individual bondholder has the right to bring a class action to protect his interests and the interests of all other bondholders of the same issue whenever the Indenture Trustee has acted in such a manner as to put itself in a position where it cannot faithfully and competently discharge its duty as a fiduciary. It seems to me that plaintiff's position is sound and is supported by such cases as *Ettlinger v. Persian Rug & Carpet Co.*, 36 N.E. 1055 (NY 1894); *Campbell v. Hudson & Manhattan R. Co.*, 277 A.D. 731 (N.Y.A.D. 1 Dept. 1951); *Birn v. Childs Co.*, Sup., 37 N.Y.S.2d 689 (Sup.Ct. 1942); *Buel v. Baltimore & O. S. Ry. Co.*, 53 N.Y.S. 749 (Sup.Ct. 1898). In *Ettlinger*, the incompetency of the trustee to act for the bondholders was predicated upon the trustee's absence from this country and his probable insanity. In *Birn*, the trustee's incompetency was based on its unreasonable refusal to sue. In *Buel*, the incompetency of the trustee was predicated upon its inconsistent position as trustee of conflicting trusts. In *Campbell*, where the trustee "renounced" or "abdicated" its function to sue, the Court made the following apposite statement: "All of those cases, and others like them, presuppose a trustee competent to act, and exercising its judgment in good faith respecting what is best for the bondholders as a whole concerning the matter in issue. If a trustee under such an indenture acts in bad faith, or, abdicating its function with respect to the point in question, declines to act at all, bondholders for themselves and others similarly situated may bring a derivative action in the right of the trustee, rather than in their own individual rights as bondholders. In that event they are not subject to the limitations of Article Seventh of the Indenture, which are not imposed on the trustee or on bondholders acting in the status of the trustee. This subject was considered lucidly, and the same result reached, by Justice Walter in *Birn v. Childs Co*. He said: 'That the restrictive or no-action clause does not operate, under such circumstances, to prevent a court of equity from granting relief at the suit of a single holder was in effect held in *Ettlinger v. Persian Rug & Carpet Co*.'"

Plaintiff's affidavit sets forth that subsequent to the date of the Indenture Bank of America made several loans to both Kaiser-Frazer and Graham-Paige which were enmeshed with the sale of the automotive assets of the latter to Kaiser-Frazer. The nature of these transactions was such as to create a conflict in the interests of Bank of America as trustee and Bank of America as a creditor of both Graham-Paige and Kaiser-Frazer. As trustee it was bound to protect the interests of the debenture holders and was charged with the duty of requiring Kaiser-Fraxer to assume the sinking fund provisions when the latter company acquired the automotive assets of Graham-Paige. On the other hand, as a bank creditor and in its self-interest Bank of America gave its express written consent to the terms of the Sales Agreement whereby Kaiser-Frazer delimited its undertakings with respect to the debentures so that it did not assume the obligations of the Sinking Fund provision of the Indenture. At the same time, in order to protect its own interests, in making a loan of $12,000,000 to Kaiser-Frazer, Bank of America required Kaiser-Frazer to amortize that loan to the extent of 25% of its annual net profits in addition to securing a mortgage on all of Kaiser-Frazer's property as well as on the property of Graham-Paige, the sale of which to Kaiser-Frazer was being contemplated and in the course of negotiation.

It seems to me that when Bank of America consented to Kaiser-Frazer's declination of assuming any of the provisions of the Indenture, including the sinking fund provisions, it placed itself in a position which was antagonistic to and in conflict with the interests of the debenture holders.

"A trustee cannot be permitted to assume a position inconsistent with or in opposition to his trust. His duty is single, and he cannot serve two masters with antagonistic interests."

The movant urges that under the circumstances of this case plaintiff's proper remedy is to have a new or substitute trustee appointed but such argument is untenable for the same reasons that the Court in *Ettlinger* rejected a similar contention. There the Court stated: "But the special term say that in such event a new trustee should have been appointed. That simply reproduces the same difficulty in another form, for a court would hardly remove a trustee without notice to him, and giving him an opportunity to be heard; and why should a new appointment be made, when any one of the bondholders can equally do the duty of pursuing the foreclosure? The court, in such an action, takes hold of the trust, dictates and controls its performance, distributes the assets as it deems just, and it is not vitally important which of the two possible plaintiffs sets the court in motion. The bondholders are the real parties in interest. It is their right which is to be redressed, and their loss which is to be prevented; and any emergency which makes a demand upon the trustee futile or impossible, and leaves the right of the bondholder without other reasonable means of redress, should justify his appearance as plaintiff in a court of equity for the purpose of a foreclosure."

In view of the foregoing it is my view that the "no action" clause involved in the case at bar is inoperative and inapplicable.

QUESTIONS

1. What may be the reasons why Kaiser-Frazer did not assume the sinking fund provision of the debenture?
2. According to the court, why might Bank of America have consented to the waiver of the sinking fund provision?
3. Is it sufficient to show that a trustee has had a credit transaction or other dealings with the issuer? What must be shown?

6. REDEMPTION PROVISION

An issuer cannot compel a bondholder to surrender the bond for cash payment before maturity, unless the indenture provides for a redemption right. A redemption provision gives the issuer the option to call back the debt and repay the principal at a time earlier than the maturity date. The indenture will provide for the terms including the redemption price required to be paid to the bondholders. The redemption price commonly includes a premium to the par value or the market value, which may have been required to entice the bondholders to subscribe a bond issue with a redemption right.

There are several business reasons why an issuer would want to redeem outstanding bonds. The issuer may need to renegotiate the terms of the bond for another business purpose, such as restrictions placed by financial covenants, but this may not be possible with bondholders in which case redeeming the bonds may be the only option. The issuer may need to delever the balance sheet. Interest rates may fall below the rate at which the issuer is paying on the bond, which would incentivize the issuer to refinance at lower rates.

The redemption may be unconditional, not subject to the occurrence of a contingency, or it may be subject to any defined contingency, such as the passage of a specific time. The redemption may also be restricted in other ways. One restriction may be that the debt cannot be financed by a cheaper debt issue. Under such a provision, a creditor is subject to redemption, but is protected when interest rates decline such that the issuer can refinance the debt with a cheaper issue.

The following case provides an example of a redemption provision in the indenture limiting the issuer's ability to refinance with cheaper debt. The case shows how business needs and financial transactions can complicate the interpretation of a seemingly clear redemption and refinancing provision in the indenture.

Morgan Stanley & Co. v. Archer Daniels Midland Co.

570 F. Supp. 1529 (S.D.N.Y. 1983)

SAND, District Judge.

This action arises out of the planned redemption of $125 million in 16% Sinking Fund Debentures by the defendant ADM Midland Company scheduled to take place on Monday, August 1st, 1983. Morgan Stanley & Company brings this suit under §§323(a) and 316(b) of the Trust Indenture Act of 1939, alleging that the proposed redemption plan is barred by the terms of the Indenture, the language of the Debentures, and the Debenture Prospectus. [Both parties moved for summary judgment.]

In May 1981, Archer Daniels issued $125,000,000 of 16% Sinking Fund Debentures due May 15, 2011. The [redemption provision in the indenture of the] Debentures state in relevant part:

The Debentures are subject to redemption upon not less than 30 nor more than 60 days' notice by mail, at any time, in whole or in part, at the election of the Company, at the following optional Redemption Price (expressed in percentages of the principal amount), together with accrued interest to the Redemption Date . . . , all as provided in the Indenture: If redeemed during the twelve-month period beginning May 15 of the years indicated:

Year	Percentage	Year	Percentage	Year	Percentage
1981	115.500	1988	110.075	1995	104.650
1982	114.725	1989	109.300	1996	103.875
1983	113.950	1990	108.525	1997	103.100
1984	113.175	1991	107.750	1998	102.325
1985	112.400	1992	106.975	1999	101.550
1986	111.625	1993	106.200	2000	100.775
1987	110.850	1994	105.425		

and thereafter at 100%; provided, however, that prior to May 15, 1991, the Company may not redeem any of the Debentures pursuant to such option from the proceeds, or in anticipation, of the issuance of any indebtedness for money borrowed by or for the account of the Company or any Subsidiary (as defined in the Indenture) or from the proceeds, or in anticipation of a sale and leaseback transaction (as defined in Section 1008 of the Indenture), if, in either case, the interest cost or interest factor applicable thereto (calculated in accordance with generally accepted financial practice) shall be less than 16.08% per annum.

The May 12, 1981 Prospectus and the Indenture pursuant to which the Debentures were issued contain substantially similar language. The Moody's Bond Survey of April 27, 1981, in reviewing its rating of the Debentures, described the redemption provision in the following manner:

The 16% sinking fund debentures are nonrefundable with lower cost interest debt before April 15, 1991. Otherwise, they are callable in whole or in part at prices to be determined.

516

The proceeds of the Debenture offering were applied to the purchase of long-term government securities bearing rates of interest below 16.089%.

ADM raised money through public borrowing at interest rates less than 16.08% on at least two occasions subsequent to the issuance of the Debentures [bringing in total proceeds of $136,955,500, and these instruments carried effective interest rates of less than 16.08%].

In the period since the issuance of the Debentures, ADM also raised money through two common stock offerings [bringing in total proceeds of $146,820,000].

Morgan Stanley bought $15,518,000 principal amount of the Debentures at $1,252.50 per $1,000 face amount on May 5, 1983, and $500,000 principal amount at $1,200 per $1,000 face amount on May 31, 1983. The next day, June 1, ADM announced that it was calling for the redemption of the 16% Sinking Fund Debentures, effective August 1, 1983. The direct source of funds was to be the two ADM common stock offerings of January and June, 1983.

Prior to the announcement of the call for redemption, the Debentures were trading at a price in excess of the $1,139.50 call price.

Discussion

Defendant's view of the redemption language is arguably supported by The American Bar Foundation's Commentaries on Model Debenture Indenture Provisions (1977), from which the boilerplate language in question was apparently taken verbatim. In discussing the various types of available redemption provisions, the Commentaries state:

> Instead of an absolute restriction [on redemption], the parties may agree that the borrower may not redeem with funds borrowed at an interest rate lower than the interest rate in the debentures. *Such an arrangement recognizes that funds for redemption may become available from other than borrowing,* but correspondingly recognizes that the debenture holder is entitled to be protected for a while against redemption if interest rates fall and the borrower can borrow funds at a lower rate to pay off the debentures.

We read this comment as pointing to the *source* of funds as the dispositive factor in determining the availability of redemption to the issuer—the position advanced by defendant ADM.

Morgan Stanley asserts that defendant's view would afford bondholders no protection against redemption through lower-cost borrowing and would result in great uncertainty among holders of bonds containing similar provisions. In its view, the "plain meaning" of the redemption bondholders of these bonds and the investment community generally, is that the issuer may not redeem when it is contemporaneously engaging in lower-cost borrowing, regardless of the source of the funds for redemption. At the same time, however, the plaintiff does not contend that redemption through equity funding is prohibited for the life of the redemption restriction once the issuer borrows funds at a lower interest rate subsequent to the Debenture's issuance. On the contrary, plaintiff concedes that the legality of the redemption transaction would depend on a factual inquiry into the magnitude of the borrowing relative to the size of the contemplated equity-funded redemption and its proximity in time relative to the date the redemption was to take place. Thus, a $100 million redemption two years after a $1 million short-term debt issue might be allowable, while the same redemption six months after a $20 million long-term debt issue might not be allowable.

This case-by-case approach is problematic in a number of respects. First, it appears keyed to the subjective expectations of the bondholders; if it *appears* that the redemption is funded through lower-cost borrowing, based on the Company's recent or prospective borrowing history, the redemption is deemed unlawful. The approach thus reads a subjective element into what presumably should be an objective determination based on the language appearing in the bond agreement. Second, and most important, this approach would likely cause greater uncertainty among bondholders than a strict "source" rule such as that adopted in *Franklin Life Insurance Co. v. Commonwealth Edison Co.,* 451 F.Supp. 602 (S.D.Ill. 1978).

After a thorough review of the record, we now grant the motion of defendant ADM for partial summary judgment on the contract claims.

The plaintiff's contract claims arise out of alleged violations of state contract law. Section 113 of the Indenture provides that the Indenture and the Debentures shall be governed by New York law. Under New York law, the terms of the Debentures constitute a contract between ADM and the holders of the Debentures, including Morgan Stanley. The relevant contract terms are printed on the Debentures and, by incorporation, in the Indenture.

We note as an initial matter that where, as here, the contract language in dispute is a "boilerplate" provision found in numerous debentures and indenture agreements, the desire to give such language a consistent, uniform interpretation requires that the Court construe the language as a matter of law. *See Sharon Steel Corp. v. Chase Manhattan Bank, N.A.,* 691 F.2d 1039, 1048–49 (2d Cir.1982); *cf. Broad v. Rockwell International Corp.,* 642 F.2d 929, 946–48 (5th Cir.) (en banc).

In *Franklin Life Insurance Co. v. Commonwealth Edison Co.,* the district court found, with respect to language nearly identical to that now before us, that an early redemption of preferred stock was lawful where funded directly from the proceeds of a common stock offering.

Morgan Stanley argues, however, that *Franklin* was incorrectly decided and should therefore be limited to its facts. We find any attempt to distinguish *Franklin* on its facts to be wholly unpersuasive. Commonwealth Edison, the defendant in *Franklin,* issued 9.44% Cumulative Preferred Stock in 1970. The stock agreement contained a redemption provision virtually identical to that at issue in this litigation. The prospectus announcing the preferred stock would be used primarily for interim financing of a long-term construction program. The construction program required an estimated expenditure of approximately $2.25 billion, of which $1.15 billion would have to be raised through the sale of additional securities of the company. In accord with this estimate, Commonwealth Edison's long-term debt increased from $1.849 billion at the end of 1971 to an amount in excess of $3 billion by the time of trial in 1978. All of this debt was issued at interest rates below 9.44%. In January of 1972, Commonwealth Edison announced its intention to redeem the preferred stock with the proceeds of a common stock issue.

Franklin Life Insurance brought suit, contending that the language of the redemption provision barred redemption where Commonwealth Edison had been borrowing at interest rates below 9.44%, and expected to continue borrowing at such rates in the near future. The district court rejected plaintiff's claims, and held that the redemption was lawful because the refunding was accomplished solely from the proceeds of the common stock issue. In adopting a rule that looked to the source of the proceeds for redemption, the court rejected a "net borrower" theory that would have examined the issuer's general corporate borrowing history. Thus, Edison's borrowing projections and the sizable anticipated increase in its long-term, lower-cost debt was irrelevant, given that the undisputed source of the redemption was the common stock issue.

Morgan Stanley contends nevertheless that *Franklin* was wrongly decided, as a matter of law, and that a fresh examination of the redemption language in light of the applicable New York cases would lead us to reject the "source" rule. In this regard, Morgan Stanley suggests a number of universal axioms of contract construction intended to guide us in construing the redemption language as a matter of first impression. For example, Morgan counsels that we should construe the contract terms in light of their "plain meaning," and should adopt the interpretation that best accords with all the terms of the contract. Words are not to be construed as meaningless if they can be made significant by a reasonable construction of the contract. Where several constructions are possible, the court may look to the surrounding facts and circumstances to determine the intent of the parties. Finally, Morgan Stanley urges that all ambiguities should be resolved against the party that drafted the agreement.

We find these well-accepted and universal principles of contract construction singularly unhelpful in construing the contract language before us. Several factors lead us to this conclusion. First, there is simply no "plain meaning" suggested by the redemption language that would imbue all the contract terms with a significant meaning.

Equally fruitless would be an effort to discern the "intent of the parties" under the facts of this case. It may very well be that ADM rejected an absolute no-call provision in its negotiations with the underwriters in favor of language it viewed as providing "greater flexibility." It is also clear, however, that neither the underwriters nor ADM knew whether such "flexibility" encompassed redemption under the facts of this case.

Finally, we view this as a most inappropriate case to construe ambiguous contract language against the drafter. The Indenture was negotiated by sophisticated bond counsel on both sides of the bargaining table. There is no suggestion of disparate bargaining power in the drafting of the Indenture, nor could there be. Moreover, even if we were to adopt this rule, it is not at all clear that ADM would be considered the drafter of the Indenture, given the active participation of the managing underwriter.

Because we find equitable rules of contract construction so unhelpful on the facts of this case, the decision in *Franklin* takes on added importance. While it is no doubt true that the decision in that case was a difficult one and in no sense compelled under existing law, we find the reasoning of the court thoroughly convincing given the obvious ambiguity of the language it was asked to construe. We also find the result to be a fair one. While *Franklin* was decided under Illinois law and is therefore not binding on the New York courts, we cannot ignore the fact that it was the single existing authority on this issue, and was decided on the basis of universal contract principles. Under these circumstances, it was predictable that *Franklin* would affect any subsequent decision under New York law. *Franklin* thus adds an unavoidable gloss to any interpretation of the redemption language.

Finally, we note that to cast aside the holding in *Franklin* would, in effect, result in the very situation the Second Circuit sought to avoid in *Sharon Steel*. In that case, the Court warned that allowing juries to construe boilerplate language as they saw fit would likely result in intolerable uncertainty in the capital markets. To avoid such an outcome, the Court found that the interpretation of boilerplate should be left to the Court as a matter of law. While the Court in *Sharon Steel* was addressing the issue of varying interpretations by juries rather than by the courts, this distinction does not diminish the uncertainty that would result were we to reject the holding in *Franklin*. Given the paramount interest in uniformly construing boilerplate provisions, and for all the other reasons stated above and in our prior Opinion, we chose to follow the holding in *Franklin*.

We note in this regard that the "source" rule adopted in Franklin in no sense constitutes a license to violate the refunding provision. The court is still required to make a finding of the true source of the proceeds for redemption. Where the facts indicate that the proposed redemption was indirectly funded by the proceeds of anticipated debt borrowed at a prohibited interest rate, such redemption would be barred regardless of the name of the account from which the funds were withdrawn. Thus, a different case would be before us if ADM, contemporaneously with the redemption, issued new, lower-cost debt and used the proceeds of such debt to repurchase the stock issued in the first instance to finance the original redemption. On those facts, the redemption could arguably be said to have been indirectly funded through the proceeds of anticipated lower-cost debt, since ADM would be in virtually the same financial posture after the transaction as it was before the redemption—except that the new debt would be carried at a lower interest rate. Here, by contrast, there is no allegation that ADM intends to repurchase the common stock it issued to fund the redemption. The issuance of stock, with its concomitant effect on the company's debt/equity ratio, is exactly the type of substantive financial transaction the proceeds of which may be used for early redemption.

QUESTIONS

1. In what way did the redemption provision protect the bondholders? In what way did it not protect them? In what way was Morgan Stanley harmed by the redemption?
2. One might think that issuers can use (or abuse) the holding in *Morgan Stanley* to substitute expensive debt for cheap debt through redemption and "cover its tracks," so to speak, by raising an equal amount of equity. However, what is the problem with this logic? Is it really in the issuer's best interest to do something like this?
3. The court rejects Morgan Stanley's attempt to invoke a number of contract interpretation rules, including: "plain meaning," "intent of parties," and contra proferentem. Why?
4. What are the efficiency arguments in favor of the "source" rule? In other words, why does the rule promote the goals of wealth maximization in corporate enterprises and the required smooth working of the capital markets?
5. If bondholders were concerned about the holding in *Morgan Stanley*—the adoption of the "source" rule—what contractual mechanism could be drafted into the indenture to solve the problem in their favor?
6. The court noted that prior to the call for redemption, the debentures were trading in excess of $1,139.50. What does this imply about the market's expectation of the direction of interest rates?
7. Here is a bond problem. The opinion stated that two of the debentures were issued under these terms: "On May 7, 1982, over a year before the announcement of the planned redemption, ADM borrowed $50,555,500 by the issuance of

$400,000,000 face amount zero coupon debentures due 2002 and $100,000,000 face amount zero coupon notes due 1992." Show that these zero coupon bonds had an effective interest rate of less than 16.08 percent as the court stated. What is the precise implied interest rate?

7. ASSET PROTECTION PROVISION

Creditors are ultimately concerned about whether the issuer will pay interest and principal. Key to this assessment is the assets of the corporation, since they generate the income necessary to pay interest and principal. Creditors are concerned about protection of the firm's assets. They can take security interest through a mortgage bond, which creates a mortgage interest in specific capital assets of the issuer. But many "bonds" are debentures, which are unsecured long-term debt. Outside of bankruptcy, creditors do not control the assets. Assets are in the control of the board and management, who are fiduciaries of the corporation and shareholders. — not CRs

Assets could be sold off, which would adversely affect the creditors' interest. Creditors will want the issuer to maintain the assets that were the basis for the provision of credit. On the other hand, issuers will not want to be tied down to a particular set of assets. Business conditions and circumstances may change. Certain assets may no longer fit with the company's strategy. Issuers will want a freer hand in managing the business including the purchase and disposal of assets.

Another problem for creditors is the possibility that at some point in the life of the bond, the issuer will merge with or consolidate into another entity. Through this process, the legal entity that owes the debt may disappear. Even if the issuer is the surviving entity, the merger may have adverse consequences on the issuer's ability to pay interest and principal. The merger may create a new capital structure where the creditor is now at a more disadvantageous position than before the merger; or the merger creates financial strains that diminish operating income. The creditors will not want these changes, but again the issuers seek transactions that create value for the corporation and its shareholders.

Creditors only expect to protect themselves from these types of situations through the contract. Creditors could ask for the proverbial moon: that is, they could attempt to lock-up all assets through a negative covenant or a security interest, but the issuer may push back and assert that the terms are too harsh. Creditors could prohibit any merger or consolidation, but the issuer may not agree to such a restrictive term. The credit contract can provide a compromise.

Revised Model Simplified Indenture: Article 5 "Successors"

Section 5.01. When Company May Merge, etc.
The Company shall not consolidate or merge with or into, or transfer all or substantially all of its assets to, any Person unless:

(1) either the Company shall be the resulting or surviving entity or such Person is a corporation organized and existing under the laws of the United States, a State thereof or the District of Columbia;

(2) if the Company is not the resulting or surviving entity, such Person assumes by supplemental indenture all the obligations of the Company under the Securities

---

and this Indenture, except that it need not assume the obligations of the Company as to conversion of Securities if pursuant to Section 10.17 the Company or another Person enters into a supplemental indenture obligating it to deliver securities, cash or other assets upon conversion of Securities; and

(3) immediately before and immediately after the transaction no Default exists.

The Company shall deliver to the Trustee prior to the proposed transaction an Officers' Certificate and an Opinion of Counsel, each of which shall state that such consolidation, merger or transfer and such supplemental indenture comply with this Article 5 and that all conditions precedent herein provided for relating to such transaction have been complied with.

Section 5.02. Successor Corporation Substituted.

Upon any consolidation or merger, or any transfer of all or substantially all of the assets of the Company in accordance with Section 5.01, the successor corporation formed by such consolidation or into which the Company is merged or to which such transfer is made shall succeed to, and be substituted for, and may exercise every right and power of, the Company under this Indenture and the Securities with the same effect as if such successor corporation had been named as the Company herein and in the Securities. Thereafter the obligations of the Company under the Securities and Indenture shall terminate except for (i) obligations the Company may have under a supplemental indenture pursuant to Section 10.17 and (ii) in the case of a transfer, the obligation to pay the Principal of and interest on the Securities.

* * *

Indenture between Apple Inc. and The Bank of New York Mellon Trust Company, dated April 29, 2013

Section 801. Company May Merge or Transfer Assets Only on Certain Terms.

The Company shall not consolidate with or merge with or into, or sell, transfer, lease or convey all or substantially all of its properties and assets to, in one transaction or a series of related transactions, any other Person, unless:

(1) the Company shall be the continuing entity, or the resulting, surviving or transferee Person (the "Successor") shall be a Person (if such Person is not a corporation, then the Successor shall include a corporate co-issuer of the Securities) organized and existing under the laws of the United States of America, any State thereof or the District of Columbia and the Successor (if not the Company) shall expressly assume, by an indenture supplemental hereto, executed and delivered to the Trustee, in form reasonably satisfactory to the Trustee, all the obligations of the Company under the Securities and this Indenture and, for each Security that by its terms provides for conversion, shall have provided for the right to convert such Security in accordance with its terms;

(2) immediately after giving effect to such transaction, no Default or Event of Default shall have occurred and be continuing; and

(3) the Company shall have delivered to the Trustee an Officer's Certificate and an Opinion of Counsel, each stating that such transaction and such supplemental indenture, if any, complies with this Indenture (except that such Opinion of Counsel need not opine as to clause (2) above).

> *Section 802. Successor Corporation Substituted.*
> The Successor shall succeed to, and be substituted for, and may exercise every right and power of, the Company under the Indenture, with the same effect as if the Successor had been an original party to this Indenture, and the Company shall be released from all its liabilities and obligations under this Indenture and the Securities.

The following case applies the successor obligor provision to a series of transactions in furtherance of a plan of liquidation. In addition to the specific holding, the court discusses the rule of boilerplate contract terms and the court's role in promoting efficiency in the capital markets.

Sharon Steel Corp. v. Chase Manhattan Bank, N.A.
691 F.2d 1039 (2d Cir. 1982)

WINTER, Circuit Judge:

This is an appeal by Sharon Steel Corp. and UV Industries, Inc., trustees of the UV Liquidating Trust (collectively the "UV Defendants") from grants of a directed verdict and summary judgment in favor of the Trustees of certain UV indentures ("Indenture Trustees") and intervening holders of debentures issued pursuant to certain of those indentures ("Debentureholders").

Background

Between 1965 and 1977, UV issued debt instruments pursuant to five separate indentures, the salient terms of which we briefly summarize. [These five debt obligations totaled an outstanding principal amount of approximately $123 million.]

The debentures, notes and guaranties are general obligations of UV. Each instrument contains clauses permitting redemption by UV prior to the maturity date, in exchange for payment of a fixed redemption price (which includes principal, accrued interest and a redemption premium) and clauses allowing acceleration as a non-exclusive remedy in case of a default. For example, the Manufacturer's Indenture states:

> *Remedies Cumulative and Continuing.* All powers and remedies given by this Article Six to the Trustee or to the Debentureholders shall, to the extent permitted by law, be deemed cumulative and not exclusive of any thereof or of any other powers and remedies available to the Trustee or the holders of the Debentures, by judicial proceedings or otherwise, to enforce the performance or observance of the covenants and agreements contained in this Indenture. . . .

[Each indenture] contains a "successor obligor" provision allowing UV to assign its debt to a corporate successor which purchases "all or substantially all" of UV's assets. [The Union Planters Lease Guaranty provides an exemplary "successor obligor" clause and it reads:]

> The Guarantor will maintain its corporate existence, will not dissolve or otherwise dispose of all or substantially all of its assets and will not consolidate with or merge into another corporation or permit one or more other corporations to consolidate with or merge into it; provided that the Guarantor may consolidate with or merge into

another corporation, or permit one or more other such corporations to consolidate with or merge into it, or sell or otherwise transfer to another such corporation *all or substantially all of its assets* as an entirety and thereafter dissolve, provided the surviving, resulting or transferee corporation, as the case may be, if it is not the Guarantor, shall expressly assume in writing all of the obligations of the Guarantor hereunder; provided, however, that neither the Company nor the Guarantor may dispose of *all or substantially all of its assets* to the other and may not consolidate with or merge into the other unless the Company and the Guarantor deliver to the Trustee and the County an opinion of counsel, satisfactory to the Trustee and the County, that the disposition, consolidation or merger, as the case may be, will not result in the merger of the Lease and Lease Guaranty Agreement or any provisions thereof, but that the Lease and Lease Guaranty Agreement and the provisions thereof will remain separate obligations of the transferee or consolidated or merged corporation which can be proved and scheduled separately in bankruptcy proceedings (as if the transfer, consolidation or merger had not taken place). The Guarantor will cause the Company to preserve and keep in full force and effect all licenses and permits necessary to the proper conduct of its business.

If the debt is not assigned to such a purchaser, UV must pay off the debt. While the successor obligor clauses [of the different indentures] vary in language, the parties agree that the differences are not relevant to the outcome of this case.

During 1977 and 1978, UV operated three separate lines of business. One line, electrical equipment and components, was carried on by Federal Pacific Electric Company ("Federal"). In 1978, Federal generated 60% of UV's operating revenue and 81% of its operating profits. It constituted 44% of the book value of UV's assets and 53% of operating assets. UV also owned and operated oil and gas properties, producing 2% of its operating revenue and 6% of operating profits. These were 5% of book value assets and 6% of operating assets. UV also was involved in copper and brass fabrication, through Mueller Brass, and metals mining, which together produced 13% of profits, 38% of revenue and constituted 34% of book value assets and 41% of operating assets. In addition to these operating assets, UV had cash or other liquid assets amounting to 17% of book value assets.

Author's Case Annotation: Breakdown of Business Units

	Federal	Oil & Gas	Mueller	Cash	TOTAL
Revenue	60%	2%	38%		100%
Operating profit	81%	6%	13%		100%
Book value of assets	44%	5%	34%	17%	100%
Operating assets	53%	6%	41%		100%

On December 19, 1978, UV's Board of Directors announced a plan to sell Federal. On January 19, 1979, the UV Board announced its intention to liquidate UV, subject to shareholder approval. On February 20, 1979, UV distributed proxy materials, recommending approval of (i) the sale of Federal for $345,000,000 to a subsidiary of Reliance Electric Company and (ii) a Plan of Liquidation and Dissolution to sell the remaining assets of UV over a 12-month period. The proceeds of these sales and the liquid assets were to be distributed to shareholders. The liquidation plan required "that at all times there be retained an amount of cash and other assets which the [UV Board of Directors] deems necessary to pay, or provide for the payment of, all of the liabilities, claims and other obligations . . ." of UV. The proxy statement also provided that, if the sale of Federal and the liquidation plan were approved, UV would effect an initial liquidating distribution of $18 per share to its common stockholders.

On March 26, 1979, UV's shareholders approved the sale of Federal and the liquidation plan. The following day, UV filed its Statement of Intent to Dissolve with the Secretary of State of Maine, its state of incorporation. On March 29, the sale of Federal to the Reliance Electric subsidiary for $345 million in cash was consummated. On April 9, UV announced an $18 per share initial liquidating distribution to take place on Monday, April 30.

On July 23, 1979, UV announced that it had entered into an agreement for the sale of most of its oil and gas properties to Tenneco Oil Company for $135 million cash. The deal was consummated as of October 2, 1979 and resulted in a net gain of $105 million to UV.

In November, 1979, Sharon proposed to buy UV's remaining assets. Another company, Reliance Group (unrelated to Reliance Electric), had made a similar offer. After a brief bidding contest, UV and Sharon entered into an "Agreement for Purchase of Assets" and an "Instrument of Assumption of Liabilities" on November 26, 1979. Under the purchase agreement, Sharon purchased all of the assets owned by UV on November 26 (*i.e.,* Mueller Brass, UV's mining properties and $322 million in cash or the equivalent) for $518 million ($411 million of Sharon subordinated debentures due in 2000—then valued at 86% or $353,460,000—plus $107 million in cash). Under the assumption agreement, Sharon assumed all of UV's liabilities, including the public debt issued under the indentures. UV thereupon announced that it had no further obligations under the indentures or lease guaranties, based upon the successor obligor clauses.

On December 6, 1979, in an attempt to formalize its position as successor obligor, Sharon delivered to the Indenture Trustees supplemental indentures executed by UV and Sharon. The Indenture Trustees refused to sign. Similarly, Sharon delivered an assumption of the lease guaranties to both Chase and Union Planters but those Indenture Trustees also refused to sign.

Discussion

Successor obligor clauses are "boilerplate" or contractual provisions which are standard in a certain genre of contracts. Successor obligor clauses are thus found in virtually all indentures. Such boilerplate must be distinguished from contractual provisions which are peculiar to a particular indenture and must be given a consistent, uniform interpretation. As the American Bar Foundation *Commentaries on Indentures* (1971) ("*Commentaries*") state:

> Since there is seldom any difference in the intended meaning [boilerplate] provisions are susceptible of standardized expression. The use of standardized language can result in a better and quicker understanding of those provisions and a substantial saving of time not only for the draftsman but also for the parties and all others who must comply with or refer to the indenture, including governmental bodies whose approval or authorization of the issuance of the securities is required by law.

Boilerplate provisions are thus not the consequence of the relationship of particular borrowers and lenders and do not depend upon particularized intentions of the parties to an indenture. There are no adjudicative facts relating to the parties to the litigation for a jury to find and the meaning of boilerplate provisions is, therefore, a matter of law rather than fact.

Moreover, uniformity in interpretation is important to the efficiency of capital markets. As the Fifth Circuit has stated:

> A large degree of uniformity in the language of debenture indentures is essential to the effective functioning of the financial markets: uniformity of the indentures that govern competing debenture issues is what makes it possible meaningfully to compare one debenture issue with another, focusing only on the business provisions of the issue (such as the interest rate, the maturity date, the redemption and sinking fund provisions in the conversion rate) and the economic conditions of the issuer, without being misled by peculiarities in the underlying instruments.

Broad v. Rockwell International Corp., 642 F.2d 929, 943 (5th Cir.). Whereas participants in the capital market can adjust their affairs according to a uniform interpretation, whether it be correct or not as an initial proposition, the creation of enduring uncertainties as to the meaning of boilerplate provisions would decrease the value of all debenture issues and greatly impair the efficient working of capital markets. Such uncertainties would vastly increase the risks and, therefore, the costs of borrowing with no offsetting benefits either in the capital market or in the administration of justice. Just such uncertainties would be created if interpretation of boilerplate provisions were submitted to juries sitting in every judicial district in the nation.

We turn now to the meaning of the successor obligor clauses. Interpretation of indenture provisions is a matter of basic contract law. As the *Commentaries* at 2 state:

> The second fundamental characteristic of long term debt financing is that the rights of holders of the debt securities are largely a matter of contract. There is no governing body of statutory or common law that protects the holder of unsecured debt securities against harmful acts by the debtor except in the most extreme situations . . . The debt securityholder can do nothing to protect himself against actions of the borrower which jeopardize its ability to pay the debt unless he . . . establishes his rights through contractual provisions set forth in the . . . indenture.

Contract language is thus the starting point in the search for meaning and Sharon argues strenuously that the language of the successor obligor clauses clearly permits its assumption of UV's public debt. Sharon's argument is a masterpiece of simplicity: on November 26, 1979, it bought everything UV owned; therefore, the transaction was a "sale" of "all" UV's "assets." In Sharon's view, the contention of the Indenture Trustees and Debentureholders that proceeds from earlier sales in a predetermined plan of piecemeal liquidation may not be counted in determining whether a later sale involves "all assets" must be rejected because it imports a meaning not evident in the language.

Sharon's literalist approach simply proves too much. If proceeds from earlier piecemeal sales are "assets," then UV continued to own "all" its "assets" even after the Sharon transaction since the proceeds of that transaction, including the $107 million cash for cash "sale," went into the UV treasury. If the language is to be given the "literal" meaning attributed to it by Sharon, therefore, UV's "assets" were not "sold" on November 26 and the ensuing liquidation requires the redemption of the debentures by UV. Sharon's literal approach is thus self-defeating.

The words "all or substantially all" are used in a variety of statutory and contractual provisions relating to transfers of assets and have been given meaning in light of the particular context and evident purpose. Sharon argues that such decisions are distinguishable because they serve the purpose of either shareholder protection or enforcement of the substance of the Internal Revenue Code. Even if such distinctions are valid, these cases nevertheless demonstrate that a literal reading of the words "all or substantially all" is not helpful apart from reference to the underlying purpose to be served. We turn, therefore, to that purpose.

Sharon argues that the sole purpose of successor obligor clauses is to leave the borrower free to merge, liquidate or to sell its assets in order to enter a wholly new business free of public debt and that they are not intended to offer any protection to lenders. On their face, however, they seem designed to protect lenders as well by assuring a degree of continuity of assets. Thus, a borrower which sells all its assets does not have an option to continue holding the debt. It must either assign the debt or pay it off. As the *Commentaries* state:

> The decision to invest in the debt obligations of a corporation is based on the repayment potential of a business enterprise possessing specific financial characteristics. The ability of the enterprise to produce earnings often depends on particular assets which it owns. Obviously, if the enterprise is changed through consolidation with or merged into another corporation or through disposition of assets, the financial characteristics and repayment potential on which the lender relied may be altered adversely.

Sharon poses hypotheticals closer to home in the hope of demonstrating that successor obligor clauses protect only borrowers: *e.g.*, a transaction involving a sale of Federal and the oil and gas properties in the regular course of UV's business followed by an $18 per share distribution to shareholders after which the assets are sold to Sharon and Sharon assumes the indenture obligations. To the extent that a decision to sell off some properties is not part of an overall scheme to liquidate and is made in the regular course of business it is considerably different from a plan of piecemeal liquidation, whether or not followed by independent and subsequent decisions to sell off the rest. A sale in the absence of a plan to liquidate is undertaken because the directors expect the sale to strengthen the corporation as a going concern. A plan of liquidation, however, may be undertaken solely because of the financial needs and opportunities or the tax status of the major shareholders. In the latter case, relatively quick sales may be at low prices or may break up profitable asset combinations, thus drastically increasing the lender's risks if the last sale assigns the public debt. In this case, for example, tax considerations compelled completion of the liquidation within 12 months. The fact that piecemeal sales in the regular course of business are permitted thus does not demonstrate that successor obligor clauses apply to piecemeal liquidations, allowing the buyer last in time to assume the entire public debt.

We hold, therefore, that protection for borrowers as well as for lenders may be fairly inferred from the nature of successor obligor clauses. The former are enabled to sell entire businesses and liquidate, to consolidate or merge with another corporation, or to liquidate their operating assets and enter a new field free of the public debt. Lenders, on the other hand, are assured a degree of continuity of assets.

Where contractual language seems designed to protect the interests of both parties and where conflicting interpretations are argued, the contract should be construed to sacrifice the principal interests of each party as little as possible. An interpretation which sacrifices a major interest of one of the parties while furthering only a marginal interest of the other should be rejected in favor of an interpretation which sacrifices marginal interests of both parties in order to protect their major concerns.

Of the contending positions, we believe that of the Indenture Trustees and Debentureholders best accommodates the principal interests of corporate borrowers and their lenders. Even if the UV/Sharon transaction is held not to be covered by the successor obligor clauses, borrowers are free to merge, consolidate or dispose of the operating assets of the business. Accepting Sharon's position, however, would severely impair the interests of lenders. Sharon's view would allow a borrowing corporation to engage in a piecemeal sale of assets, with concurrent liquidating dividends to that point at which the asset restrictions of an indenture prohibited further distribution. A sale of "all or substantially all" of the remaining assets could then be consummated, a new debtor substituted, and the liquidation of the borrower completed. The assignment of the public debt might thus be accomplished, even though the last sale might be nothing more than a cash for cash transaction in which the buyer purchases the public indebtedness. The UV/Sharon transaction is not so extreme, but the sale price paid by Sharon did include a cash for cash exchange of $107 million. Twenty-three percent of the sale price was, in fact, an exchange of dollars for dollars. Such a transaction diminishes the protection for lenders in order to facilitate deals with little functional significance other than substituting a new debtor in order to profit on a debenture's low interest rate. We hold, therefore, that boilerplate successor obligor clauses do not permit assignment of the public debt to another party in the course of a liquidation unless "all or substantially all" of the assets of the company at the time the plan of liquidation is determined upon are transferred to a single purchaser.

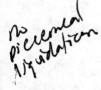

The application of this rule to the present case is not difficult. The plan of liquidation was approved by UV's shareholders on March 26, 1978. Since the Indenture Trustees make no claim as to an earlier time, *e.g.,* the date of the Board recommendation, we accept March 26 as the appropriate reference date. The question then is whether "all or substantially all" of the assets held by UV on that date were transferred to Sharon. That is easily answered. The assets owned by UV on March 26 and later transferred to Sharon were Mueller Brass, certain metals mining property, and substantial amounts of cash and other liquid assets. UV's Form 10-K and Sharon's Form S-7 state that Mueller Brass and the metals mining properties were responsible for only 38% of UV's 1978 operating revenues and 13% of its operating profits. They constitute 41% of the book value of UV's operating properties. When the cash and other liquid assets are added, the transaction still involved only 51% of the book value of UV's total assets.

Since we do not regard the question in this case as even close, we need not determine how the substantiality of corporate assets is to be measured, what percentage meets the "all or substantially all" test or what role a jury might play in determining those issues. Even when the liquid assets (other than proceeds from the sale of Federal and the oil and gas properties) are aggregated with the operating properties, the transfer to Sharon accounted for only 51% of the total book value of UV's assets. In no sense, therefore, are they "all or substantially all" of those assets. The successor obligor clauses are, therefore, not applicable. UV is thus in default on the indentures and the debentures are due and payable. For that reason, we need not reach the question whether the April Document was breached by UV.

We affirm [the] dismissal of Sharon's amended complaint and award of judgment to the Indenture Trustees and Debentureholders on their claim that the debentures are due and payable.

QUESTIONS

1. Sharon proposed to buy principally Mueller and assume the obligation of UV's debentures totaling approximately $123 million. Why? Analyze the deal between UV and Sharon. (Hint: In terms of deal analytics, Judge Winter characterized the UV-Sharon transaction as this: "Such a transaction diminishes the protection for lenders in order to facilitate deals with little functional significance other than substituting a new debtor in order to profit on a debenture's low interest rate.")
2. What is the consequence of the court's finding that UV and Sharon did not meet the "all or substantially all" term of the indenture?
3. What is the holding?
4. The core principle in *Sharon Steel* is the promotion of efficiency in the credit market. How? In other words, in what way do the legal principles in *Sharon Steel* reduce the cost of capital and promote wealth maximization? See *Kaiser Aluminum Corp. v. Matheson*, 681 A.2d 392, 398-399 (Del. 1996) (discussing importance of certainty in interpretation to standard provisions used in capital market transactions).
5. Why is adherence to a uniform interpretation and understanding of boilerplate so important?
6. At one point, Judge Winter suggests that uniform interpretation is more important than getting the interpretation right (see the comment "whether it be correct or not as an initial proposition" in the sentence after the citation to *Broad v. Rockwell International Corp.*). This is a striking comment. Explain why having a uniform "wrong" interpretation is better than having disparate interpretations in the market where on some occasions courts get the interpretation "right."

The following case tests the *Sharon Steel* principle. The court in *Sharon Steel* noted: "To the extent that a decision to sell off some properties is not part of an overall scheme to liquidate and is made in the regular course of business it is considerably different from a plan of piecemeal liquidation, whether or not followed by independent and subsequent decisions to sell off the rest." The question is whether a series of transactions can be considered a collective whole.

Bank of New York Mellon Trust Co., N.A. v. Liberty Media Corp.
29 A.3d 225 (Del. 2011)

HOLLAND, Justice:

Liberty Media Corporation ("LMC") and its wholly owned subsidiary Liberty Media LLC ("Liberty Sub," together with LMC, "Liberty") brought this action for declaratory and injunctive relief against the Bank of New York Mellon Trust Company, in its capacity as trustee. Liberty proposes to split off, into a new publicly traded company ("SplitCo") the businesses, assets, and liabilities attributed to Liberty's Capital Group and Starz Group (the "Capital Splitoff"). After Liberty announced the proposed splitoff of the businesses and assets attributable to its Capital and Starz tracking stock groups, Liberty received a letter from counsel for an anonymous bondholder.

In that letter, counsel for the bondholder stated that Liberty has pursued a "disaggregation strategy" designed to remove substantially all of Liberty's assets from the corporate structure against which the bondholders have claims, and shift those assets into the hands of Liberty's stockholders. Therefore, the bondholder contended that the transaction might violate the Successor Obligor Provision in the Indenture and threatened to declare an event of default. In response to that threat, Liberty commenced this action against the Trustee under the Indenture, seeking injunctive relief and a declaratory judgment that the proposed Capital Splitoff will not constitute a disposition of "substantially all" of Liberty's assets in violation of the Indenture.

The Capital Splitoff will be Liberty's fourth major distribution of assets since March 2004. The Trustee argues that when aggregated with the previous three transactions, the Capital Splitoff would violate a successor obligor provision in an indenture pursuant to which Liberty agreed not to transfer substantially all of its assets unless the successor entity assumed Liberty's obligations under the Indenture ("Successor Obligor Provision"). It is undisputed that, if considered in isolation, and without reference to any prior asset distribution, the Capital Splitoff would not constitute a transfer of substantially all of Liberty's assets or violate the Successor Obligor Provision.

The Court of Chancery concluded, after a trial, that the four transactions should not be aggregated, and entered judgment for Liberty. The Court of Chancery concluded that the proposed splitoff is not "sufficiently connected" to the prior transactions to warrant aggregation for purposes of the Successor Obligor Provision. The Court of Chancery found that "each of the transactions resulted from a distinct and independent business decision based on the facts and circumstances that Liberty faced at the time," and that each transaction "was a distinct corporate event separated from the others by a matter of years," and that these transactions "were not part of a master plan to strip Liberty's assets out of the corporate vehicle subject to bondholder claims."

We conclude that the judgment of the Court of Chancery must be affirmed.

Factual Backgrouund

For two decades, Liberty has enjoyed a dynamic and protean existence under the leadership of its founder and chairman, Dr. John Malone. Liberty emerged in 1991 from Tele–Communications, Inc. ("TCI"), then the largest cable television operator in the United States, when a threat of federal regulation led TCI to separate its programming assets from its cable systems. TCI formed Liberty and offered its stockholders the opportunity to exchange their TCI shares for Liberty shares. At the time, Dr. Malone was Chairman, CEO, and a large stockholder of TCI. After the exchange offer, Dr. Malone was also Chairman, CEO, and a large stockholder of Liberty.

In 1994, Bell Atlantic entered into merger discussions with TCI. Bell Atlantic insisted that Liberty's assets be part of any acquisition. To facilitate a transaction, TCI reacquired Liberty by merger. The discussions with Bell Atlantic broke down, but Liberty remained part of TCI.

In 1998, Dr. Malone convinced AT&T to acquire TCI by merger at a significant premium. In the transaction, both TCI and Liberty became wholly owned subsidiaries of AT&T. The agreement with AT&T allowed Liberty to operate autonomously, and Liberty's assets and businesses were attributed to a separate tracking stock issued by AT&T. Dr. Malone served as Liberty's Chairman.

While it was a subsidiary of AT&T, Liberty entered into the Indenture with the Trustee. From July 7, 1999 through September 17, 2003, Liberty issued multiple series of publicly traded debt under the Indenture, the proceeds of which totaled approximately $13.7 billion. Liberty has since retired or repurchased much of that debt. As of September 30, 2010, debt securities with a total balance of approximately $4.213 billion remained outstanding.

The Indenture includes a successor obligor provision. This provision prohibits Liberty from selling, transferring, or otherwise disposing of "substantially all" of its assets unless the entity to which the assets are transferred assumes Liberty's obligations under the Indenture (thereby releasing Liberty from its obligations). Section 801 of the Indenture ("Successor Obligor provision") provides, in pertinent part:

> [Liberty Sub] shall not consolidate with or merge into, or sell, assign, transfer, lease, convey or otherwise dispose of all or substantially all of its assets and the properties and the assets and properties of its Subsidiaries (taken as a whole) to, any entity or entities (including limited liability companies) unless:
>
> (1) the successor entity or entities . . . shall expressly assume, by an indenture (or indentures, if at such time there is more than one Trustee) supplemental hereto executed by the successor Person and delivered to the Trustee, the due and punctual payment of the principal of, any premium and interest on and any Additional Amounts with respect to all the Securities and the performance of every obligation in this Indenture and the Outstanding Securities on the part of [Liberty Sub] to be performed or observed . . . ;
>
> (2) immediately after giving effect to such transaction or series of transactions, no Event of Default or event which, after notice or lapse of time, or both, would become an Event of Default, shall have occurred and be continuing; and
>
> (3) either [Liberty Sub] or the successor Person shall have delivered to the Trustee an Officers' Certificate and an Opinion of Counsel [containing certain statements required by Section 801].

A failure to comply with the obligations imposed by Article Eight constitutes an "Event of Default."

The Indenture does not define the phrase "substantially all." Nor does the Indenture contain any covenants requiring Liberty to maintain a particular credit rating, a minimum debt coverage ratio, or a minimum asset-to-liability ratio. The Indenture does not contain any provision directly addressing dividends and stock repurchases, which are the corporate vehicles to effectuate a spinoff (stock dividend) and a splitoff (stock redemption).

In August 2001, AT&T split off Liberty to the holders of its publicly traded Liberty tracking stock. When Liberty re-emerged as a public company, it held a "fruit salad" of assets, consisting mainly of minority equity positions in public and private entities. For example, Liberty owned single-digit-percentage stakes in large public companies such as Sprint, Viacom, and Motorola. Liberty also owned large minority positions in private companies such as Discovery Communications. Most of Liberty's assets, except for a few controlled operating businesses, did not generate any cash flow.

The value of Liberty's holdings, which had been quite significant during the heady days of the internet bubble (recall that the Indenture was executed in 1999), fell significantly in 2000 and 2001 (the period leading up to the splitoff).

After the splitoff, Dr. Malone and the rest of Liberty's management team set out to build value at Liberty by rationalizing its investment portfolio. Put simply, Liberty wanted to use its minority investments to acquire controlling stakes in mutually supporting operating businesses that would generate cash flow. According to Dr. Malone,

> it was always obvious that the direction that the company needed to go—which was to—out of the cosmic dust, as it were, form some gravitational units that could then pull in these investment assets, monetize them and grow. It's always been a process of how do you convert from a portfolio of investments into a series of operating businesses.

Beginning in 2001, Liberty sought to own stakes in businesses that Liberty either controlled or saw a clear path to control. If Liberty did not control an asset and could not identify a path to control, then Liberty management evaluated all possible alternative uses for the asset. Over the ensuing decade, Liberty engaged in numerous transactions in pursuit of that overall strategy, frequently structuring its deals as swaps or exchanges to avoid triggering taxable events.

[LMI Transaction]

After separating from AT&T, Liberty looked first to build a cash-generating business in the area its management team knew best: cable television. Having sold the nation's largest cable provider to AT&T in 1999, Dr. Malone did not think it was feasible to make a comeback in the U.S. Instead, Liberty sought to expand, and consolidate, its international cable holdings.

By 2004, it was clear that creating an international cable business would require massive capital infusions that would need to be funded with additional debt. Liberty management determined that the most effective way to raise capital would be to move the international assets off Liberty's balance sheet and into a separate entity. That new entity could raise debt on its own, and the risks of international expansion would be borne "directly by those shareholders of Liberty Media who chose to do so, rather than by the company at large."

Thus, in 2004, Liberty spun off Liberty Media International, Inc. ("LMI"), which held Liberty's controlling interest in UGC and stakes in other international cable companies. Liberty also contributed to LMI Liberty's shares of News Corp. preferred stock, a 99.9% economic interest in 345,000 shares of ABC Family Worldwide preferred stock, and $50 million in cash.

Liberty management believed that the LMI spinoff would best serve both Liberty and the new entity:

> Creating a separate equity security will give existing Liberty Media shareholders and new investors the ability to concentrate their investment in either LMI, the remaining Liberty Media businesses, or both. We expect that this will increase the trading value of both securities, thereby reducing the discount in the current Liberty Media stock and creating better currencies for both entities to use in pursuit of acquisition activity. In addition, by their nature the LMI businesses can support higher levels of debt, which should generate higher equity returns.

The LMI spinoff was a significant transaction for Liberty. It removed $11.79 billion in assets (at book value) from Liberty's balance sheet, representing 19% of Liberty's total book value as of March 31, 2004—the date the Trustee contends should be used for purposes of determining what constituted "substantially all" of Liberty's assets. At the same time, Liberty avoided exposing itself to the massive borrowing that the international cable business required. If Liberty had retained the international assets and undertaken the transactions in which LMI later engaged, Liberty today would have an additional $21 billion in liabilities on its consolidated balance sheet, all senior to the public debt issued under the Indenture.

Notwithstanding the risks it faced, LMI has proved successful. The spun-off company, later renamed Liberty Global, Inc., is currently the largest cable operator outside of the United States. In 2009, Liberty Global reported assets (at book value) of $39.9 billion, total revenue of $11.1 billion, and operating income of $1.64 billion.

The Trustee views the LMI spinoff as the start of Liberty's disaggregation strategy. Commenting on the LMI spinoff in early 2005, Dr. Malone described it as "the first shoe to drop" and a "model we want to follow":

> That's what we continuously look for . . . opportunities to carve out if necessary other businesses that can go off and be part of a consolidation in their space, gain market power, improve profitability, appropriately use debt leverage, shelter taxes, or avoid corporate level taxes, and go on down the road in terms of maximizing shareholder value. . . . And that continues to be the plan today.

[Discovery Transaction]

Also during 2003 and 2004, Liberty management explored alternatives for Discovery, a cable channel that Liberty owned in partnership with Cox Communications and Advance/Newhouse. Although Discovery was performing well, Liberty owned less than 50% of the equity, lacked control, did not have a clear path to control, and was restricted by a stockholders agreement from selling or otherwise monetizing its position.

Consistent with its strategy of increasing minority positions into control positions, Liberty approached its partners in an effort to develop a path to control. When these efforts failed, Liberty attempted to explore plans for monetizing the business by selling it or taking it public. Liberty's partners were not interested in that alternative either.

With their preferred alternatives blocked, Dr. Malone and the Liberty management team decided to dividend Liberty's Discovery shares to its stockholders, thereby giving them a direct ownership interest in Discovery. Liberty management hoped that as a result of the distribution, Cox Communications and Advance/Newhouse "would perhaps ultimately see the benefit of a public vehicle for valuation and management motivation." To facilitate the distribution, Liberty created Discovery Holding Company, transferred to it Liberty's stake in Discovery, plus a small operating company called Ascent Media and $200 million in cash, and then spun off the new entity to Liberty's stockholders.

The Discovery spinoff removed from Liberty's balance sheet assets with a book value of $5.825 billion, representing 10% of Liberty's total book value as of March 31, 2004. After the spinoff, Liberty's securities lost their investment-grade rating. Moody's cited concern with "management's long-term strategic and financial vision for the company, and likely resultant credit protection levels." Moody's noted that "the rating could stabilize if management evidenced both the ability and willingness to maintain or improve the asset coverage that represents the primary source of credit protection levels at present."

Like LMI, Discovery prospered post-spinoff. In 2009, Discovery reported assets with a book value of $10.997 billion, revenues of $3.5 billion, and operating income of $1.24 billion.

The Trustee points to the Discovery spinoff as a continuation of Liberty's "disaggregation strategy." In its 2004 shareholder letter, Liberty management stated that:

> Since Liberty's inception 14 years ago, our overriding objective has been clear and consistent: to maximize the value of our shares. Over the years, we have accomplished this by executing three core strategies: owning businesses with significant built-in growth potential; making timely acquisitions that enable us to build on that growth potential and create new business lines; and actively managing our capital structure. In 2004, we introduced a fourth strategy of disaggregating businesses by distributing them to our shareholders. While this technique actually reduces the value of our shares, it also increases the wealth of our shareholders by giving them holdings in two companies instead of one.

Dr. Malone emphasized the disaggregation strategy in other public statements:

> The focus at Liberty has been figuring out how to rationalize the compliment of assets that we have, how to regain market share in those businesses that we think have that potential and how to avoid double or triple taxation as we attempt to exploit the underlying values of the assets. And that's led us kind of to voice a philosophy right now for Liberty, which is disaggregate in order to consolidate. . . .

[LEI Transaction]

The News Corp. swap gave Liberty an influential position in DirecTV. Consistent with its overall strategy, Liberty sought a path to control. In April 2008, Liberty purchased another 78.3 million shares of DirecTV for consideration of $1.98 billion in cash. Restrictions in the DirecTV certificate of incorporation, however, prohibited Liberty from acquiring more than 50% of DirecTV's equity unless Liberty offered to purchase 100% of the outstanding stock. To avoid triggering that provision, Liberty and DirecTV agreed that Liberty's equity ownership could exceed the 50% threshold, but Liberty's voting power would be capped at 48.5%. As a result of DirecTV's stock repurchase program, Liberty's equity ownership eventually climbed to 57%, although Liberty's voting power never exceeded 48.5%.

As 2008 wore on and the financial markets deteriorated, Liberty's management realized that financing to acquire the balance of DirecTV was not available. With the DirecTV charter provision otherwise blocking Liberty's path to control, Liberty management examined other potential alternatives. Ultimately, Liberty announced that it would split off its interest in DirecTV, along with certain other business, into a new entity called Liberty Entertainment, Inc. ("LEI"). Liberty and DirecTV then negotiated a transaction in which LEI would merge with DirecTV immediately after the splitoff. The splitoff and merger closed on November 19, 2009.

Liberty initially planned to split off all the assets attributed to the Entertainment Group, including the DirecTV stake, Starz, FUN Technologies, Inc., Liberty Sports Holdings, LLC, GSN, LLC and WildBlue Communications. Because Liberty management believed that DirecTV was undervaluing Starz and WildBlue in the merger negotiations, Liberty decided to retain those assets. Liberty management also considered the potential effect of the splitoff on bondholders. At that time, Dr. Malone stated that "we had to retain [the] cash and economic value of Starz in order to reassure the bondholders in Liberty that their interests were being protected." The Trustee cites this statement as evidence that Liberty knew its disaggregation strategy was approaching the "substantially all" limit. Dr. Malone and Liberty CEO Gregory Maffei testified at trial that they did not believe Liberty was legally required to hold back Starz and cash from the splitoff, but Liberty did so to protect itself during the height of the financial crisis and reassure bondholders and lenders.

The LEI splitoff removed from Liberty's balance sheet assets with a book value of $14.2 billion, representing 23% of Liberty's asset base as of March 31, 2004. The splitoff also removed roughly $2.2 billion in short-term debt that was attributable to LEI. DirecTV is now the world's leading provider of digital television entertainment services. In 2009, DirecTV reported assets with a book value of $18.26 billion, revenues of $21.57 billion, and operating profit of $2.67 billion. Dr. Malone served as Chairman of DirecTV until April 6, 2010.

The Proposed Capital Splitoff

In June 2010, Liberty announced the Capital Splitoff, in which Liberty proposes to split off the businesses allocated to its Capital and Starz Groups into SplitCo, a new public entity. SplitCo will own Starz Entertainment, Starz Media, Liberty Sports Interactive, Inc., the Atlanta Braves, True Position, Inc., and Liberty's interest in Sirius XM. The assets to be split off have a book value of $9.1 billion, representing 15% of Liberty's total assets as of March 2004. Dr. Malone is expected to serve as Chairman of the new entity's board, and Mr. Maffei is expected to serve as CEO.

After the Capital Splitoff, Liberty will hold the businesses attributed to Liberty's Interactive Group, consisting primarily of QVC, several e-commerce businesses (including Evite, Gifts.com, BuySeasons, and Bodybuilding.com), and minority equity stakes in Expedia, the Home Shopping Network ("HSN"), and Tree.com (which operates Lending Tree). All outstanding debt securities issued by Liberty will remain obligations of Liberty following the Capital Splitoff. Liberty's board analyzed Liberty's ability to service its outstanding debt after the splitoff, including debt at the QVC level and concluded that Liberty will have no difficulty servicing its debt.

Issue on Appeal

The parties dispute whether Liberty will breach the Successor Obligor Provision by disposing of substantially all its assets in a series of transactions. It is undisputed, however, that the Capital Splitoff, standing alone, does not constitute "substantially all" of Liberty's assets. The threshold question is, therefore, whether the Capital Splitoff should be aggregated with the prior spinoffs of LMI and Discovery and the splitoff of LEI.

The answer to that threshold question involves the construction of a boilerplate successor obligor provision in an indenture governed by New York law. That provision restricts Liberty's ability to dispose of "all or substantially all" of its assets unless the transferee assumes the Indenture debt. The question presented has not been addressed by the New York Court of Appeals, nor, to our knowledge, by any lower New York state court.

The Court of Chancery acknowledged that, as a theoretical matter, a series of transactions can be aggregated for purposes of a "substantially all" analysis. Indeed, the Successor Obligor Provision at issue recognizes that aggregation may occur. That Provision states that Liberty can comply with the Successor Obligor Provision only if "immediately after giving effect to such transaction *or series of transactions,* no Event of Default or event which, after notice or lapse of time, or both, would become an Event of Default, shall have occurred and be continuing." Courts applying New York law have determined that, under appropriate circumstances, multiple transactions can be considered together, *i.e.,* aggregated, when deciding whether a transaction constitutes a sale of all or substantially all of a corporation's assets.[9]   *piecemeal ⇒ liquidation scheme*

Sharon Steel Applied

In applying *Sharon Steel* to the facts of this case, the Court of Chancery carefully assessed whether the trial evidence demonstrated that Liberty had developed a plan or scheme to dispose of its assets piecemeal with a goal of liquidating nearly all its assets, or removing assets from the corporate structure to evade bondholder claims. The Court of Chancery made a legal conclusion that there was no basis in the trial record for such a determination.

The Court of Chancery's legal conclusion rests on its factual finding that aggregating the four transactions is not warranted because each transaction was the result of a discrete, context-based decision and not as part of an overall plan to deplete Liberty's asset base over time.

The Court of Chancery could have ended its analysis with the above-described application of the *Sharon Steel* holding to the facts of this case. The Court of Chancery decided, however, that the *Sharon Steel* opinion did not set forth a clear standard for determining when a series of transactions should be aggregated for purposes of a "substantially all" analysis. The Court of Chancery added a second layer of analysis, which it described as "doctrinal hindsight," to conclude that the *Sharon Steel* holding "fits within the step-transaction framework" and proceeded to apply that analytical framework to the facts of this case.

Step–Transaction Doctrine Applied

The Court of Chancery had previously applied the "step-transaction" doctrine in *Noddings Investment Group, Inc. v. Capstar Communications, Inc.,* 1999 WL 182568 (Del.Ch. 1999), *aff'd* 741 A.2d 16 (Del. 1999). In *Noddings,* the court was asked to determine whether a spinoff and merger could be considered together for purposes of an adjustment provision of a warrant governed by New York law. The Court of Chancery analyzed the facts under the "step-transaction" doctrine, which

> treats the "steps" in a series of formally separate but related transactions involving the transfer of property as a single transaction, if all the steps are substantially linked. Rather than viewing each step as an isolated incident, the steps are viewed together as components of an overall plan.

The step-transaction doctrine applies if the component transactions meet one of three tests. (1) Under the "end result test," the doctrine will be invoked "if it appears

---

9. *See Sharon Steel Corp. v. Chase Manhattan Bank, N.A.,* 691 F.2d 1039, 1051–52 (2d Cir.1982) (comparing assets acquired by successor corporation to assets held by debtor corporation one and a half years earlier, prior to two third-party asset sales, when determining whether successor corporation acquired "substantially all" of the debtor's assets).

that a series of separate transactions were prearranged parts of what was a single transaction, cast from the outset to achieve the ultimate result. [2] Under the "interdependence test," separate transactions will be treated as one if "the steps are so interdependent that the legal relations created by one transaction would have been fruitless without a completion of the series." [3] The "most restrictive alternative is the binding-commitment test under which a series of transactions are combined only if, at the time the first step is entered into, there was a binding commitment to undertake the later steps."

The Trustee argues that "*Sharon Steel* does not hold that a 'series of transactions' means a step-transaction." Moreover, the Trustee submits, "even if *Sharon Steel* fits within [the step-transaction framework] it does not follow that the Second Circuit intended to apply a step-transaction *requirement* for aggregating transactions under an indenture." The Trustee argues that "the fact that the Second Circuit never mentioned the step-transaction doctrine compels the conclusion that it did not intend to do so."

The Trustee also points to language in the American Bar Foundation's *Commentaries on Model Debenture Indenture Provisions* which shows that the evolution of the Successor Obligor Provision in this case does not incorporate the step-transaction doctrine. The Trustee notes that this Court and others have looked to the American Bar Foundation's *Commentaries on Model Debenture Indenture Provisions* as "an aid to drafting and construction" of common indenture language. Our examination of *Model Provisions and Commentary* leads us to conclude that the influence of the *Sharon Steel* decision on the Model provisions is more instructive and helpful than the absence of any reference to the step-transaction doctrine.

Boilerplate Provisions Require Uniform Interpretation

Successor obligor provisions in bond indentures consist of market-facilitating boilerplate language. Courts endeavor to apply the plain terms of such provisions in a uniform manner to promote market stability.[26] The Court of Chancery has previously noted that "boilerplate provisions" in indentures are "not the consequence of the relationship of particular borrowers and lenders and do not depend upon particularized intentions of the parties to an indenture." Therefore, in interpreting boilerplate indenture provisions, "courts will not look to the intent of the parties, but rather the accepted common purpose of such provisions."

The Trustee responds that although the Successor Obligor Provision at issue here is "boilerplate" (*i.e.,* was not the subject of specific negotiation between the parties), it is not the standard successor obligor provision boilerplate found in any of the various iterations of the model indenture. The Trustee and Liberty both acknowledge, however, that the "series of transactions" language in the Indenture is the result of a specific recommendation contained in the comments to the *Model Simplified Indenture,* which counseled draftsmen to give "serious consideration" to the risks posed by the "piecemeal" disposition of assets through "a series of transactions." The inclusion of the phrase "series of transactions" in the Indenture, the Trustee argues, broadened the meaning and scope of the Successor Obligor Provision. That argument is not persuasive.

---

26. *See Sharon Steel Corp. v. Chase Manhattan Bank, N.A.,* 691 F.2d at 1048 ("uniformity in interpretation is important to the efficiency of capital markets").

The "series of transactions" language first appeared in a comment to the *Model Simplified Indenture*,[29] published five months after the *Sharon Steel* decision. That comment cautions that "serious consideration must be given to the possibility of accomplishing *piecemeal, in a series of transactions,* what is specifically precluded if attempted as a single transaction." Liberty argues that the comment was designed to address the same concerns at issue in *Sharon Steel*. In support of that argument, it points to the fact that the *Revised Model Simplified Indenture,* promulgated in May 2000, contains the same commentary, but adds a citation to *Sharon Steel.* Accordingly, Liberty submits, the only fair conclusion to be drawn from the presence of "series of transactions" language in a post-*Sharon Steel* successor obligor provision (such as the one at issue here) is that the additional language is meant to underscore that a disposition of "substantially all" assets may occur by way of either a single transaction or an integrated series of transactions, as occurred in *Sharon Steel*. We agree.

Liberty's Indenture was executed many years after the Second Circuit's decision in *Sharon Steel.* There is no evidence in the record that the "series" language was included for any reason other than to clarify that the Successor Obligor Provision should be interpreted in the same manner as the one at issue in *Sharon Steel.* The trial testimony established—and the Trustee admits—that the Successor Obligor Provision was never a subject of negotiations between the parties in the case. Had the parties to the Indenture intended to create an asset disposition covenant with a broader scope than the standard, boilerplate successor obligor covenant, it was incumbent upon them to include it in a separate, negotiated covenant.

Liberty points out that at the time the Indenture was established, there were more rigorous model provisions available that explicitly required consideration of prior asset dispositions in determining the legal effect of a later disposition of any substantial part of an issuer's assets. For example, Sample Covenant 1 of Section 10–13 in the *Commentaries* states:

> Subject to the provisions of Article Eight, the Company will not convey, transfer or lease, any substantial part of its assets unless, in the opinion of the Board of Directors, such conveyance, transfer or lease, considered together with all prior conveyances, transfers and leases of assets of the Company, would not materially and adversely affect the interest of the Holders of the Debentures or the ability of the Company to meet its obligations as they become due.[35]

The Liberty Indenture contains no such provision. As the Court of Chancery also noted, there is also no covenant "requiring Liberty to maintain a particular credit rating, a minimum debt coverage ratio, or a minimum asset-to-liability ratio," and "the Indenture does not contain any provision directly addressing dividends and stock repurchases, which are the corporate vehicles to effectuate a spinoff (stock dividend) and a splitoff (stock redemption)." This Court has consistently held that the rights of bondholders and other creditors are fixed by contract. As the Court of Chancery properly recognized, it would be inconsistent with the concept of private ordering to expand the scope of the

---

29. *See* Section of Corporation, Banking and Business Law, American Bar Association, *Model Simplified Indenture,* 38 Bus. Law. 741, 791 (1983).

35. American Bar Foundation, *Commentaries on Model Debenture Indenture Provisions* §10–13, at 426–27 (1965).

Successor Obligor Provision by rewriting the Indenture contract to include by implication additional protections for which the parties could have—but did not—provide by way of a covenant separate and apart from the boilerplate successor obligor provision.

New York Law

In the context of the "substantially all" analysis under a boilerplate successor obligor provision in an indenture, and given the near absence of any authoritative New York case law, we conclude that the principles articulated in *Sharon Steel* are the proper basis for determining, under New York law, the nature and degree of inter-relationship that will warrant aggregation of otherwise separate and individual trans-actions as a part of a "series." In *Sharon Steel*, the Second Circuit determined that aggregation is appropriate only when a series of transactions are part of a "plan of piecemeal liquidation" and "an overall scheme to liquidate" and not where each trans-action stands on its own merits without reference to the others.

The Court of Chancery carefully considered and applied *Sharon Steel* to the facts before it, and concluded that the Capital Splitoff "is not sufficiently connected to the LMI and Discovery spinoffs or the [Entertainment] splitoff to warrant aggregating the four transactions." The Court of Chancery held:

> Following a consistent business strategy and deploying signature M & A tactics does not transmogrify seven years of discrete, context-specific business decisions into a single transaction. Liberty has engaged in acquisitions and divestitures as part of the regular course of its business. Liberty did not engage in an "overall scheme" to sell substantially all of its assets.

In support of that finding and legal conclusion—and without regard to the step-transaction doctrine—the Court of Chancery cited only the *Sharon Steel* decision as authority for its holding.

We conclude it is unnecessary to reach or decide whether the step-transaction doctrine and its three component tests would be adopted by the New York Court of Appeals as definitive New York law to determine whether to aggregate a series of transactions in a "substantially all" analysis. Given the Court of Chancery's factual findings, even if the Court of Chancery had not utilized "the three lenses of the step-transaction doctrine" as a doctrinal tool to "bring the picture into sharper focus," the legal conclusion in this case would have been the same under our independent reading of *Sharon Steel*.

The Trustee concedes that the Capital Splitoff, viewed in isolation, does not con-stitute a disposition of substantially all of Liberty's assets. On the facts of this case, the Court of Chancery properly held that aggregation is not appropriate. Accordingly, Liberty was entitled to a declaration that the Capital Splitoff does not violate the Successor Obligor Provision in the Indenture.

The judgment of the Court of Chancery is affirmed.

QUESTIONS

1. The trustee simply administers the indenture for the bondholders. It has no direct economic interest in the outcome of the case. Why did the trustee argue against the step-transaction doctrine in this case?

2. What were the business and economic rationales for Liberty to engage in these four transactions?

3. In light of the fact that the distribution of any asset economically harms bond-holders and that distributions routinely occur, what is the core prohibition in the successor obligor provision?

8. SUBORDINATION PROVISIONS

Within the class of debt instruments, there can be different priorities. Seniority is defined as priority in payment of interest and/or principal. Creditors can agree among themselves to hold senior debt or subordinated debt. The classes of priority can be finely divided. For example, subordinated debt can be further classified into senior subordinated debt and junior subordinated debt. All else being the same, the more subordinated the debt, the more interest payment the creditor should expect to negotiate and receive. The greater the contractual protection, the less risk the creditor is taking—therefore, the creditor should be receiving less than a subordinated cred-itor, all else being equal and absent specific circumstances to the contrary.

Commentaries on Model Debenture Indenture Provisions (American Bar Foundation, 1971), Covenant to Subordinate

§14-1. Agreement to Subordinate.

The Company covenants and agrees, and each Holder of Debentures, or any coupon, by his acceptance thereof, likewise covenants and agrees, that the indebtedness represented by the Debentures and the payment of the principal of (and premium, if any) and interest on each and all of the Debentures is hereby expressly subordinated, to the extent and in the manner hereinafter set forth, in right of payment to the prior payment in full of all Senior Debt. The term "Senior Debt" means indebtedness of the Company, whether out-standing on the date of execution of this Indenture or thereafter created, for money bor-rowed from banks, insurance companies and other financial institutions, unless in the instrument creating or evidencing such indebtedness it is provided that such indebtedness is not senior in right of payment to the Debenture.

§14-2. Distribution of Assets, etc.

Upon any distribution of assets of the Company upon any dissolution, winding up, liq-uidation or reorganization of the Company, whether in bankruptcy, insolvency, reorgani-zation or receivership proceedings or upon an assignment for the benefit of creditors or any other marshalling of the assets and liabilities of the Company or otherwise,

(a) the holders of all Senior Debt shall first be entitled to receive payment in full of the principal thereof (and premium, if any) and interest due thereon, or provision shall be made for such payment in case, before the Holders of the Debentures or coupons are entitled to receive any payment on account of the principal of (or premium, if any) or interest on the indebtedness evidenced by the Debentures;

(b) any payment by, or distribution of assets of, the Company of any kind or character, whether in cash, property or securities [optional insertion of "X" Clause], to which the

---

Holders of the Debentures or coupons or the Trustee would be entitled except for the provisions of this Article shall be paid or delivered by the person making such payment or distribution, whether a trustee in bankruptcy, a receiver or liquidating trustee or otherwise, directly to the holders of Senior Debt or their representative or representatives or to the trustee or trustees under any indenture under which any instruments evidencing any of such Senior Debt may have been issued, ratably according to the aggregate amounts remaining unpaid on account of the Senior Debt held or represented by each, to the extent necessary to make payment in full of all Senior Debt remaining unpaid after giving effect to any concurrent payment or distribution (or provision therefor) to the holders of such Senior Debt; and

(c) in the event that, notwithstanding the foregoing, any payment by, or distribution of assets of, the Company of any kind or character, whether in cash, property or securities [optional insertion of "X" Clause] shall be received by the Trustee or the Holders of the Debentures or coupons before all Senior Debt is paid in full, such payment or distribution shall be paid over to the holders of such Senior Debt or their representative or representatives or to the trustee or trustees under any indenture under which any instruments evidencing any of such Senior Debt may have been issued, ratably as aforesaid, for application to the payment of all Senior Debt remaining unpaid until all such Senior Debt shall have been paid in full, after giving effect to any concurrent payment or distribution (or provision therefor) to the holders of such Senior Debt.

The *Commentaries* explain that Clauses (b) and (c) of §14-2 requires that in a reorganization, any securities received by the holders of subordinated debt must be turned over to the holders of senior debt. However, some indentures contain an exception when mortgage bonds, preferred stock, or similar higher-class security is issued to the senior debtholder in a reorganization, and the subordinated debtholder receives common stock. The theory of the exception to the hand-over requirement is that this kind of a reorganization effectuates the subordination that already exists, and therefore turnover is not required. The Commentaries calls this exception by the unilluminating name "X" Clause.

One version of "X" Clause is the insertion after the phrase "whether in cash, property or securities" in Clauses (b) and (c) of Sample Provision §14-2 (see above grey shaded insertion slot) the following:

(other than securities of the Company as reorganized or readjusted or securities of the Company or any other corporation provided for by a plan of reorganization or readjustment the payment of which is subordinate, at least to the extent provided in this Article with respect to the Debentures, to the payment of all indebtedness in the nature of Senior Debt, provided that the rights of the holders of Senior Debt are not altered by such reorganization or readjustment)

The following case interprets the "X" Clause in the context of a potential ambiguity in the eye of a litigating party. The court notes that the contract was "poorly drafted" and yet "clear" (unambiguous from an interpretive perspective).

In re Envirodyne Industries, Inc.
29 F.3d 301 (7th Cir. 1994)

POSNER, Chief Judge.

This appeal arises out of an objection by creditors to a plan of reorganization filed by Envirodyne Industries, Inc., a Chapter 11 debtor. Envirodyne had three levels ("tranches," as they are called) of unsecured debt. One, the most senior, consisted of Senior Discount Notes. The plan called for the holders of these notes to receive notes of equivalent value in the reorganized firm. The next level consisted of 14% Senior Subordinated Debentures, and was junior to the Senior Discount Notes. The third level consisted of 13.5% Subordinated Notes and was junior to both the 14% notes (as we shall call them) and the Senior Discount Notes. The 13.5% notes had actually been issued before the Senior Discount Notes and the 14% notes (both issued in 1989 as part of a leveraged buyout of the company), but had been made subordinate to them by the indenture pursuant to which the 13.5% notes were issued. That indenture provided that in the event of a default, "all Superior Indebtedness" (defined to include the 14% notes, though issued later as we have said, together with the Senior Discount Notes)

> "shall first be paid in full before the Noteholders, or the Trustee, shall be entitled to retain any assets (other than shares of stock of the Company, as reorganized or readjusted or securities of the Company or any other corporation provided for by a plan of reorganization or readjustment, the payment of which is subordinated, at least to the same extent as the Notes, to the payment of all Superior Indebtedness which may at the time be outstanding)."

The plan of reorganization called for the distribution to the 14% noteholders of common stock worth $121 million in the reorganized firm in partial payment of their notes, the face amount of which was $200 million. The 13.5% noteholders, although owed $100 million, received only $20 million worth of stock, on the theory that by virtue of the subordination provision we quoted they were entitled to nothing until the holders of the Senior Discount Notes and the 14% notes received stock or other securities sufficient in value to satisfy their claims in full. The 13.5% noteholders objected to being subordinated in this fashion. They argued that the words "other than shares of stock in the Company" entitled them to be treated the same as the 14% noteholders if the distribution to creditors took the form of stock rather than new notes, as it has done. The bankruptcy judge rejected the objection and confirmed the plan. The 13.5% noteholders appealed to the district court, which affirmed the bankruptcy judge.

The parties agree that the parenthetical clause that is the focus of dispute is unambiguous. This use of the word "agree" may seem nonsensical, since the parties assign opposite meanings to the clause. But when opposing parties agree that the document whose meaning they dispute is not ambiguous, all they mean is that they are content to have its meaning determined without the help of any "extrinsic" evidence. What is unusual about this case is that the parties disagree about what counts as extrinsic evidence. The appellants argue that extrinsic evidence is everything except the Chicago Manual of Style, which they contend points unerringly to the interpretation that they favor. The 14% noteholders think that extrinsic evidence of the indenture's meaning would be testimony or documents concerning the intentions of the draftsmen of the indenture rather than scholarly literature on the purposes of the class of clause illustrated by the parenthetical clause in the indenture, such as the American Bar Foundation's *Commentaries on Model Debenture Indenture Provisions* (1971). They are surely right, though it hardly matters in this case, since the meaning of the clause is plain without regard to what the commentators have said about it.

The rule that bars the introduction of extrinsic evidence when a contractual provision is more or less clear "on its face" instantiates the broader principle that (with exceptions unnecessary to consider here) parol or extrinsic evidence is admissible to interpret but not to contradict or alter the written contract. If the written contract is clear without extrinsic evidence, then such evidence could have no office other than to contradict the writing, and is therefore excluded. The object in excluding such evidence is to prevent parties from trying to slip out of their clearly stated, explicitly assumed contractual obligations through self-serving testimony or documents—which, though self-serving, might impress a jury—purporting to show that the parties didn't mean what they said in the written contract. Contractual obligations would be too uncertain if such evidence were allowed. But dictionaries, treatises, articles, and other published materials created by strangers to the dispute, like evidence of trade usage, which is also admissible because it is also evidence created by strangers rather than by a party trying to slip out of a contractual bind, do not present a similar danger of manufactured doubts and are therefore entirely appropriate for use in contract cases as interpretive aids. Appropriate, and sometimes indispensable. It would be passing odd to forbid people to look up words in dictionaries, or to consult explanatory commentaries that, like trade usage, are in the nature of specialized dictionaries.

We cannot find a case actually discussing the admissibility of such materials, perhaps because it is thought obvious. Cases in which courts use them to interpret contractual or statutory provisions are legion; with reference to the ABF indenture commentaries alone, see *Sharon Steel Corp. v. Chase Manhattan Bank, N.A.,* 691 F.2d 1039, 1048-50 (2d Cir.1982); *Elliott Associates v. J. Henry Schroder Bank & Trust Co.,* 838 F.2d 66, 71-72 (2d Cir.1988).

The indenture in this case provides that the holders of the superior indebtedness are entitled to be paid in full before the 13.5% noteholders can receive any distribution other than (1) shares of stock in the reorganized firm, or (2) securities in the reorganized firm or any other firm created by the reorganization, payment of which is subordinated to the claims of the holders of the superior indebtedness. The appellants argue that the payment clause qualifies only (2), so if the distribution is of stock they are entitled to equal treatment with the holders of superior indebtedness. The 13.5% noteholders argue that the clause qualifies both (1) and (2). The appellants' argument is entirely grammatical and semantic. They say that the punctuation shows that the payment clause qualifies only (2) and that shares of stock, unlike dividends for example, are not "paid." We understand neither argument. It is commonplace to set off a series with commas and have a phrase at the end qualifying the entire series rather than the last entry in it. So one might say, "The man, or the woman, who is sitting on the bench." And if one doesn't "pay" stock, neither does one "pay" securities. The term "payment of" is used in the parenthetical clause as a synonym for "receipt of" or "entitlement to."

A better argument for the appellants is that if the draftsmen had wanted to subordinate all securities received by the junior creditors to the claims of the senior creditors, they easily could have said so clearly. It was not necessary to specify shares of stock and securities separately. Or they could have said "shares of stock and other securities" if they wanted to emphasize that there was no exception for stock. On balance the appellants have the better of the purely semantic argument. But their interpretation makes no sense once the context of the terminology being interpreted is restored.

The class of clause to which the parenthetical clause in this indenture belongs goes by the unilluminating name of "X Clause." Such clauses are common in bond debentures, although there is no standard wording. Without the clause, the subordination agreement that it qualifies would require the junior creditors to turn over to the senior creditors any securities that they had received as a distribution in the reorganization, unless the senior creditors had been paid in full. Then, presumably, if the senior creditors obtained full payment by liquidating some of the securities that had been turned over, the remaining securities would be turned back over to the junior creditors. The X Clause shortcuts this cumbersome procedure and enhances the marketability of the securities received by the junior creditors, since their right to possess (as distinct from pocket the proceeds of) the securities is uninterrupted.

The purpose of the clause bears no relation to the interpretation for which the appellants contend, under which the senior creditors' priority would depend entirely on the form of the distribution. The appellants concede that if the distribution took the form of new notes rather than of stock, the junior creditors would be subordinated. But if the distribution took the form of stock, they argue, the junior creditors would be pooled with the senior creditors, destroying the latter's seniority. We cannot understand why the *form* in which rights in the assets of the reorganized firm are allocated among the creditors should determine the creditors' priority—and specifically why a distribution in the form of stock should erase the priority of a senior class of creditors. To make priority depend on the form of distribution in this way would, moreover, give senior creditors an incentive to press for liquidation, contrary to the purpose of Chapter 11, since then there would be no distribution of stock and hence no chance for the junior creditors to achieve parity with the seniors.

The X Clause in this case was poorly drafted, but we think its meaning is clear: any securities, including stock, that the junior creditors receive in a reorganization are subordinated to the claims of the senior creditors. The judgment of the district court is therefore AFFIRMED.

QUESTIONS

1. If the court had been persuaded by the argument of the 13.5 percent noteholders, how much economic value would they have gained as a result of a favorable court ruling?

2. What does it mean when a contract like an indenture is said to be "unambiguous"? The X Clause in question "was poorly drafted" and confusing. In what way, then, is it still "unambiguous"?

3. Judge Posner concluded that "the meaning of the clause is plain without regard to what the commentators have said about it." But he goes on to defend the use of commentary in the interpretation of indentures. What might be the rationale for their use?

4. Redraft the X Clause in this case to make it clearer and in accordance with the holding of the case.

9. IMPLIED COVENANT OF GOOD FAITH AND FAIR DEALING

A bond is a financial contract. All contracts are said to have an implied covenant of good faith and fair dealing. *See Anthony's Pier Four v. HBC Assocs.*, 583 N.E.2d 806 (Mass. 1991) ("covenant of good faith and fair dealing is implied" in every contract, even "in contracts between sophisticated business people"); *Merrill v. Crothall-American, Inc.*, 606 A.2d 96, 101 (Del. 1992) ("At common law the duty of fair dealing and good faith was deemed impliedly to be a part of contracts of every kind"); *Gilbert v. El Paso Corp.*, 575 A.2d 1131, 1143 (Del. 1990) (acknowledging that "an implied covenant of good faith and honest conduct exists in every contract"); *Pittsburgh Terminal Corp. v. Baltimore & Ohio R. Co.*, 680 F.2d 933, 941 (3d Cir. 1982) (holding that a convertible bond has as a contract term an "implied covenant that neither party will do anything which will destroy . . . the right of the other party to receive the fruits of the contract"); Restatement (Second) Contracts §205 ("Every contract imposes upon each party a duty of good faith and fair dealing in its performance and its enforcement.").

That every contract has an implied covenant of good faith and fair dealing is unremarkable conceptually, but the hard issue is trying to define the contours of the implied contractual term in a debt contract. There is an inherent conflict between creditors and shareholders. Boards and management, who are fiduciaries of shareholders, can take actions that are in fact economically harmful to bondholders for the specific benefit of shareholders. Such actions are "intentional" in the tort sense of that word since boards and management, as sophisticated businesspersons, have that purpose in mind or at least know beforehand the adverse consequence of their actions on bondholders. Thus, the issue can be framed as the extent to which the implied covenant of good faith and fair dealing covers certain actions of the corporation that can be characterized as opportunistic at the expense of bondholders.

The following case arises out of one of the most famous LBOs in business history. The question is whether the bondholders have a legal right found in the implied covenant of good faith and fair dealing when the issuer took intentional action (the engagement of an LBO transaction) that it knew would economically harm the interest of bondholders.

Metropolitan Life Insurance Co. v. RJR Nabisco, Inc.
716 F. Supp. 1504 (S.D.N.Y. 1989)

WALKER, District Judge:

The corporate parties to this action are among the country's most sophisticated financial institutions, as familiar with the Wall Street investment community and the securities market as American consumers are with the Oreo cookies and Winston cigarettes made by defendant RJR Nabisco, Inc. The present action traces its origins to October 20, 1988, when F. Ross Johnson, then the Chief Executive Officer of RJR Nabisco, proposed a $17 billion leveraged buy-out ("LBO") of the company's shareholders, at $75 per share. Within a few days, a bidding war developed among the investment group led by Johnson and the investment firm of Kohlberg Kravis

545

Roberts & Co. ("KKR"), and others. On December 1, 1988, a special committee of RJR Nabisco directors, established by the company specifically to consider the competing proposals, recommended that the company accept the KKR proposal, a $24 billion LBO that called for the purchase of the company's outstanding stock at roughly $109 per share.

Plaintiffs allege, in short, that RJR Nabisco's actions have drastically impaired the value of bonds previously issued to plaintiffs by, in effect, misappropriating the value of those bonds to help finance the LBO and to distribute an enormous windfall to the company's shareholders. As a result, plaintiffs argue, they have unfairly suffered a multimillion dollar loss in the value of their bonds.[4]

Plaintiffs move for summary judgment against the company on Count I, which alleges a "Breach of Implied Covenant of Good Faith and Fair Dealing." RJR Nabisco moves for judgment on the pleadings on Count I in full.

Although the numbers involved in this case are large, and the financing necessary to complete the LBO unprecedented,[8] the legal principles nonetheless remain discrete and familiar. At the heart of the present motions lies plaintiffs' claim that RJR Nabisco violated a restrictive covenant—not an explicit covenant found within the four corners of the relevant bond indentures, but rather an *implied* covenant of good faith and fair dealing—not to incur the debt necessary to facilitate the LBO and thereby betray what plaintiffs claim was the fundamental basis of their bargain with the company. Plaintiffs ask this Court first to imply a covenant of good faith and fair dealing that would prevent the recent transaction, then to hold that this covenant has been breached, and finally to require RJR Nabisco to redeem their bonds.

RJR Nabisco defends the LBO by pointing to express provisions in the bond indentures that permit mergers and the assumption of additional debt. These provisions, as well as others that could have been included but were not, were known to the market and to plaintiffs, sophisticated investors who freely bought the bonds and were equally free to sell them at any time. Any attempt by this Court to create contractual terms *post hoc,* defendants contend, not only finds no basis in the controlling law and undisputed facts of this case, but also would constitute an impermissible invasion into the free and open operation of the marketplace.

Background

Metropolitan Life Insurance Co. ("MetLife") is a life insurance company. MetLife's assets exceed $88 billion and its debt securities holdings exceed $49 billion. MetLife alleges that it owns $340,542,000 in principal amount of six separate RJR Nabisco debt issues, bonds allegedly purchased between July 1975 and July 1988.

---

4. Agencies like Standard & Poor's and Moody's generally rate bonds in two broad categories: investment grade and speculative grade. Standard & Poor's rates investment grade bonds from "AAA" to "BBB." Moody's rates those bonds from "AAA" to "Baa3." Speculative grade bonds are rated either "BB" and lower, or "Ba1" and lower, by Standard & Poor's and Moody's, respectively. No one disputes that, subsequent to the announcement of the LBO, the RJR Nabisco bonds lost their "A" ratings.

8. On February 9, 1989, KKR completed its tender offer for roughly 74 percent of RJR Nabisco's common stock (of which approximately 97% of the outstanding shares were tendered) and all of its Series B Cumulative Preferred Stock (of which approximately 95% of the outstanding shares were tendered). Approximately $18 billion in cash was paid out to these stockholders. KKR acquired the remaining stock in the late April merger through the issuance of roughly $4.1 billion of pay-in-kind exchangeable preferred stock and roughly $1.8 billion in face amount of convertible debentures.

Some bonds become due as early as this year; others will not become due until 2017. The bonds bear interest rates of anywhere from 8 to 10.25 percent.

Jefferson-Pilot Life Insurance Co. has more than $3 billion in total assets, $1.5 billion of which are invested in debt securities. Jefferson-Pilot alleges that it owns $9.34 million in principal amount of three separate RJR Nabisco debt issues, allegedly purchased between June 1978 and June 1988. Those bonds, bearing interest rates of anywhere from 8.45 to 10.75 percent, become due in 1993 and 1998.

RJR Nabisco is a consumer products holding company that owns some of the country's best known product lines, including LifeSavers candy, Oreo cookies, and Winston cigarettes.

The bonds implicated by this suit are governed by long, detailed indentures, which in turn are governed by New York contract law. No one disputes that the holders of public bond issues, like plaintiffs here, often enter the market after the indentures have been negotiated and memorialized. Thus, those indentures are often not the product of face-to-face negotiations between the ultimate holders and the issuing company. What remains equally true, however, is that underwriters ordinarily negotiate the terms of the indentures with the issuers. Since the underwriters must then sell or place the bonds, they necessarily negotiate in part with the interests of the buyers in mind. Moreover, these indentures were not secret agreements foisted upon unwitting participants in the bond market. No successive holder is required to accept or to continue to hold the bonds, governed by their accompanying indentures; indeed, plaintiffs readily admit that they could have sold their bonds right up until the announcement of the LBO. Instead, sophisticated investors like plaintiffs are well aware of the indenture terms and, presumably, review them carefully before lending hundreds of millions of dollars to any company.

Indeed, the prospectuses for the indentures contain a statement relevant to this action:

> The Indenture contains no restrictions on the creation of unsecured short-term debt by [RJR Nabisco] or its subsidiaries, no restriction on the creation of unsecured Funded Debt by [RJR Nabisco] or its subsidiaries which are not Restricted Subsidiaries, and no restriction on the payment of dividends by [RJR Nabisco].

Further, as plaintiffs themselves note, the contracts at issue "do not impose debt limits, since debt is assumed to be used for productive purposes."

At least as early as 1982, MetLife recognized an LBO's effect on bond values. In the spring of that year, MetLife participated in the financing of an LBO of a company called Reeves Brothers. At the time of that LBO, MetLife also held bonds in that company.

A comprehensive memorandum, prepared in late 1985, evaluated and explained several aspects of the corporate world's increasing use of mergers, takeovers and other debt-financed transactions. That memorandum first reviewed the available protection for lenders such as MetLife:

> Covenants are incorporated into loan documents to ensure that after a lender makes a loan, the creditworthiness of the borrower and the lender's ability to reach the borrower's assets do not deteriorate substantially. *Restrictions on the incurrence of debt,* sale of assets, mergers, dividends, restricted payments and loans and advances to affiliates *are some of the traditional negative covenants that can help protect lenders in the event their obligors become involved in undesirable merger/takeover situations.*

The memorandum then surveyed market realities:

> Because almost any industrial company is apt to engineer a takeover or be taken over itself, *Business Week* says that investors are beginning to view debt securities of high grade industrial corporations as Wall Street's riskiest investments. In addition, *because public bondholders do not enjoy the protection of any restrictive covenants,* owners of high grade corporates face substantial losses from takeover situations, if not immediately, then when the bond market finally adjusts. . . . There have been 10-15 merger/takeover/LBO situations where, *due to the lack of covenant protection, [MetLife] has had no choice but to remain a lender to a less creditworthy obligor.* . . . The fact that the quality of our investment portfolio is greater than the other large insurance companies . . . may indicate that we have negotiated better covenant protection than other institutions, thus generally being able to require prepayment when situations become too risky . . . [However,] a problem exists. And *because the current merger craze is not likely to decelerate* and because there exist vehicles to circumvent traditional covenants, the problem will probably continue. Therefore, *perhaps it is time to institute appropriate language designed to protect Metropolitan from the negative implications of mergers and takeovers.*

Indeed, MetLife does not dispute that, as a member of a bondholders' association, it received and discussed a proposed model indenture, which included a "comprehensive covenant" entitled "Limitations on Shareholders' Payments." As becomes clear from reading the proposed—but never adopted—provision, it was "intended to provide protection against all of the types of situations in which shareholders profit at the expense of bondholders."

Apparently, that provision—or provisions with similar intentions—never went beyond the discussion stage at MetLife. MetLife's own documents articulate several reasonable, undisputed explanations:

> While it would be possible to broaden the change in ownership covenant to cover any acquisition-oriented transaction, *we might well encounter significant resistance in implementation with larger public companies* . . . With respect to implementation, we would be faced with the task of imposing a non-standard limitation on potential borrowers, *which could be a difficult task in today's highly competitive marketplace. Competitive pressures notwithstanding, it would seem that management of larger public companies would be particularly opposed to such a covenant since its effect would be to increase the cost of an acquisition* (due to an assumed debt repayment), a factor that could well lower the price of any tender offer (thereby impacting shareholders).

[These] documents set forth the background to the present action, and highlight the risks inherent in the market itself, for any investor. Investors as sophisticated as MetLife and Jefferson-Pilot would be hard-pressed to plead ignorance of these market risks. Those documents, after all, were not born in a vacuum. They are descriptions of, and responses to, the market in which investors like MetLife and Jefferson-Pilot knowingly participated.

Discussion

The indentures at issue clearly address the eventuality of a merger. [There is no express] restriction that would prevent the recent RJR Nabisco merger transaction. In their first count, plaintiffs assert that

> Defendant RJR Nabisco owes a continuing duty of good faith and fair dealing in connection with the contract [i.e., the indentures] through which it borrowed money

from MetLife, Jefferson-Pilot and other holders of its debt, including a duty not to frustrate the purpose of the contracts to the debtholders or to deprive the debtholders of the intended object of the contracts-purchase of investment-grade securities. In the "buy-out," the company breaches the duty [or implied covenant] of good faith and fair dealing by, *inter alia,* destroying the investment grade quality of the debt and transferring that value to the "buy-out" proponents and to the shareholders.

In effect, plaintiffs contend that express covenants were not necessary because an *implied* covenant would prevent what defendants have now done.

A plaintiff always can allege a violation of an express covenant. If there has been such a violation, of course, the court need not reach the question of whether or not an *implied* covenant has been violated. That inquiry surfaces where, while the express terms may not have been technically breached, one party has nonetheless effectively deprived the other of those express, explicitly bargained-for benefits. In such a case, a court will read an implied covenant of good faith and fair dealing into a contract to ensure that neither party deprives the other of "the fruits of the agreement." Such a covenant is implied only where the implied term "is consistent with other mutually agreed upon terms in the contract." In other words, the implied covenant will only aid and further the explicit terms of the agreement and will never impose an obligation "which would be inconsistent with other terms of the contractual relationship." Viewed another way, the implied covenant of good faith is breached only when one party seeks to prevent the contract's performance or to withhold its benefits. As a result, it thus ensures that parties to a contract perform the substantive, bargained-for terms of their agreement.

The appropriate analysis, then, is first to examine the indentures to determine "the fruits of the agreement" between the parties, and then to decide whether those "fruits" have been spoiled-which is to say, whether plaintiffs' contractual rights have been violated by defendants.

The American Bar Foundation's *Commentaries on Indentures* ("the *Commentaries*"), relied upon and respected by both plaintiffs and defendants, describes the rights and risks generally found in bond indentures like those at issue:

> The most obvious and important characteristic of long-term debt financing is that the holder ordinarily has not bargained for and does not expect any substantial gain in the value of the security to compensate for the risk of loss . . . The significant fact, *which accounts in part for the detailed protective provisions of the typical long-term debt financing instrument,* is that *the lender (the purchaser of the debt security) can expect only interest at the prescribed rate plus the eventual return of the principal.* Except for possible increases in the market value of the debt security because of changes in interest rates, the debt security will seldom be worth more than the lender paid for it . . . It may, of course, become worth much less. Accordingly, the typical investor in a long-term debt security is primarily interested in every reasonable assurance that the principal and interest will be paid when due. . . . Short of bankruptcy, *the debt security holder can do nothing to protect himself against actions of the borrower which jeopardize its ability to pay the debt unless he . . . establishes his rights through contractual provisions set forth in the debt agreement or indenture.*

This Court holds that the "fruits" of these indentures do not include an implied restrictive covenant that would prevent the incurrence of new debt to facilitate the recent LBO. To hold otherwise would permit these plaintiffs to straightjacket the company in order to guarantee their investment. These plaintiffs do not invoke an implied covenant of good faith to protect a legitimate, mutually contemplated benefit of the indentures; rather, they seek to have this Court create an additional benefit for which they did not bargain.

Although the indentures generally permit mergers and the incurrence of new debt, there admittedly is not an explicit indenture provision to the contrary of what plaintiffs now claim the implied covenant requires. That absence, however, does *not* mean that the Court should imply into those very same indentures a covenant of good faith so broad that it imposes a new, substantive term of enormous scope. This is so particularly where, as here, that very term—a limitation on the incurrence of additional debt-has in other past contexts been expressly bargained for; particularly where the indentures grant the company broad discretion in the management of its affairs, as plaintiffs admit; particularly where the indentures explicitly set forth specific provisions for the adoption of new covenants and restrictions; and *especially* where there has been no breach of the parties' bargained-for contractual rights on which the implied covenant necessarily is based. While the Court stands ready to employ an implied covenant of good faith to ensure that such bargained-for rights are performed and upheld, it will not, however, permit an implied covenant to shoehorn into an indenture additional terms plaintiffs now wish had been included.

Plaintiffs argue in the most general terms that the fundamental basis of all these indentures was that an LBO along the lines of the recent RJR Nabisco transaction would never be undertaken, that indeed *no* action would be taken, intentionally or not, that would significantly deplete the company's assets. Accepting plaintiffs' theory, their fundamental bargain with defendants dictated that nothing would be done to jeopardize the extremely high probability that the company would remain able to make interest payments and repay principal over the 20 to 30 year indenture term. Plaintiffs' submissions and MetLife's previous undisputed internal memoranda remind the Court that a "fundamental basis" or a "fruit of an agreement" is often in the eye of the beholder, whose vision may well change along with the market, and who may, with hindsight, imagine a different bargain than the one he actually and initially accepted with open eyes.

The sort of unbounded and one-sided elasticity urged by plaintiffs would interfere with and destabilize the market. And this Court, like the parties to these contracts, cannot ignore or disavow the marketplace in which the contract is performed. Nor can it ignore the expectations of that market—expectations, for instance, that the terms of an indenture will be upheld, and that a court will not, *sua sponte,* add new substantive terms to that indenture as it sees fit.[26] The Court has no reason to believe that the market, in evaluating bonds such as those at issue here, did not discount for the possibility that any company, even one the size of RJR Nabisco, might engage in an LBO

---

26. *Cf. Broad v. Rockwell,* 642 F.2d 929, 943 (5th Cir. 1981) ("A large degree of uniformity in the language of debenture indentures is essential to the effective functioning of the financial markets: uniformity of the indentures that govern competing debenture issues is what makes it possible meaningfully to compare one debenture issue with another, focusing only on the business provisions of the issue . . ."); *Sharon Steel Corporation v. Chase Manhattan Bank, N.A.,* 691 F.2d. 1039, 1048 (2d Cir.1982) (Winter, J.) ("Uniformity in interpretation is important to the efficiency of capital markets . . . The creation of enduring uncertainties as to the meaning of boilerplate provisions would decrease the value of all debenture issues and greatly impair the efficient working of capital markets.").

heavily financed by debt. That the bonds did not lose any of their value until the October 20, 1988 announcement of a possible RJR Nabisco LBO only suggests that the market had theretofore evaluated the risks of such a transaction as slight.

The Court recognizes that the market is not a static entity, but instead involves what plaintiffs call "evolving understandings." Just as the growing prevalence of LBO's has helped change certain ground rules and expectations in the field of mergers and acquisitions, so too it has obviously affected the bond market, a fact no one disputes.

To respond to changed market forces, new indenture provisions can be negotiated, such as provisions that were in fact once included in the 8.9 percent and 10.25 percent debentures implicated by this action. New provisions could include special debt restrictions or change-of-control covenants. There is no guarantee, of course, that companies like RJR Nabisco would accept such new covenants; parties retain the freedom to enter into contracts as they choose. But presumably, multi-billion dollar investors like plaintiffs have some say in the terms of the investments they make and continue to hold. And, presumably, companies like RJR Nabisco need the infusions of capital such investors are capable of providing.

Whatever else may be true about this case, it certainly does not present an example of the classic sort of form contract or contract of adhesion often frowned upon by courts. In those cases, what motivates a court is the strikingly inequitable nature of the parties' respective bargaining positions. Plaintiffs here entered this "liquid trading market," with their eyes open and were free to leave at any time. Instead they remained there notwithstanding its well understood risks.

In the final analysis, plaintiffs offer no objective or reasonable standard for a court to use in its effort to define the sort of actions their "implied covenant" would permit a corporation to take, and those it would not.[28] Plaintiffs say only that investors like themselves rely upon the "skill" and "good faith" of a company's board and management, and that their covenant would prevent the company from "destroying . . . the legitimate expectations of its long-term bondholders." Plaintiffs have failed to convince the Court that by upholding the explicit, bargained-for terms of the indenture, RJR Nabisco has either exhibited bad faith or destroyed plaintiffs' *legitimate,* protected expectations.

QUESTIONS

1. What is the court's holding? Under what circumstance can we have a valid argument based on the implied covenant of good faith and fair dealing?
2. If bondholders were not MetLife and Jefferson Pilot but were unsophisticated retail investors, would the fairness argument have prevailed? Is there a core philosophical basis upon which the decision rests? What is it?
3. What is the problem of recognizing arguments based on uncabined notions of "fairness" or "good faith" in bond contracts?

---

28. Under plaintiffs' theory, bondholders might ask a court to prohibit a company like RJR Nabisco not only from engaging in an LBO, but also from entering a new line of business—with the attendant costs of building new physical plants and hiring new workers—or from acquiring new businesses such as RJR Nabisco did when it acquired Del Monte.

4. The LBO transaction in RJR Nabisco also highlights the conflict between creditors and shareholders. MetLife and Jefferson Pilot, as investors in bonds, lost a lot of money when RJR Nabisco's bonds were downgraded. The LBO transaction destroyed value for creditors. Who captured some of the value?

5. Insurance companies are major investors in corporate bonds. Look up the financial statements of any public insurance company and you will see that a large portion of its assets are investment grade bonds. For example, as of December 31, 2011, The Hartford Financial Services Group, Inc. (NYSE: HIG), had total assets of $304.0 billion in assets, of which $134.9 billion were invested. In the investment portfolio, $83.1 billion were invested in bonds, of which at least $78.2 billion were investment grade (rated BBB or better), $31.4 were equities, and the remainder were other investments. Why would an insurance company invest mostly in investment grade bonds?

NOTES

1. When thinking about contract rights in securities, we should be mindful of this comment made in *Entel v. Guilden*, 223 F. Supp. 129, 131-132 (S.D.N.Y.1963): "One of the chief economic functions of a corporation, obviously, is to facilitate aggregations of capital. To further this function, there has developed a broad range of modes of investment within the corporate framework. Each such mode is a bundle of legal rights and duties; the market price for each bundle is no doubt determined at least in part by what the bundle contains. Thus, courts should act with conservatism in changing the content of any of these bundles in ways which would give the holders of some bundles less, and holders of other bundles more, than was bargained for in the marketplace."

C. RIGHTS OF CREDITORS

1. AMENDMENT AND COERCION

Like other contracts, bonds can be amended through the process of negotiation between bondholders and the issuer. The indenture restricts the ability of the trustee to amend the indenture without consent of bondholders.

Revised Model Simplified Indenture

Section 9.02, With Consent of Holders

The Company and the Trustee may amend this Indenture or the Securities with the written consent of the Holders of at least a majority in Principal amount of the Securities. However, without the consent of each Securityholder affected, an amendment under this Section may not:

   (1) reduce the amount of Securities whose Holders must consent to an amendment;

   (2) reduce the interest on or change the time for payment of interest on any Security;

   (3) reduce the Principal of or change the fixed maturity of any Security;

---

(4) reduce the premium payable upon the redemption of any Security [or change the time at which any Security may or shall be redeemed];

(5) make any Security payable in money other than that stated in the Security;

(6) make any change in Section 6.04, 6.07 or 9.02 (second sentence);

(7) make any change that adversely affects the right to convert any Security; or

(8) make any change in Article 11 that adversely affects the rights of any Securityholder.

The thrust of the negotiation for a substantive amendment is typically one directional. As long as the issuer is fulfilling its obligations, all is fine with bondholders (most of the time, except see cases like *Metropolitan Life Insurance Co. v. RJR Nabisco, Inc.*). It is the unusual case in which bondholders will want the issuer to concede something when the issuer has not defaulted. In such a case, the issuer will require some sort of consideration to renegotiate the terms at the behest of bondholders. More typically, the issuer initiates the renegotiation of terms. Issuers sometimes seek amendment to fit some business purpose, and such modification adversely affects bondholders. The indenture may place many limitations on the issuer for the protection of the bondholder. In due course, these limitations may prove to be too much. The issuer may be in danger of defaulting or has defaulted on the bond, and it seeks amendment of the terms to avoid default or bankruptcy, which neither party wants. The issuer may need to do a transaction, but the limitation in the bond practically precludes the transaction unless the bondholder agrees to amend the indenture. The situations are many.

The following case presents a similar circumstance seen in *Gradient OC Master, Ltd. v. NBC Universal, Inc.*, a case involving a claim of coercion on preferred stockholders by the issuer to facilitate an amendment of the charter. In this case, bondholders claimed that the issuer applied improper coercion to modify the indenture in an adverse way.

Katz v. Oak Industries Inc.
508 A.2d 873 (Del. Ch. 1986)

ALLEN, Chancellor.

A commonly used word—seemingly specific and concrete when used in everyday speech—may mask troubling ambiguities that upon close examination are seen to derive not simply from casual use but from more fundamental epistemological problems. Few words more perfectly illustrate the deceptive dependability of language than the term "coercion" which is at the heart of the theory advanced by plaintiff as entitling him to a preliminary injunction in this case.

Plaintiff is the owner of long-term debt securities issued by Oak Industries, Inc. In this class action he seeks to enjoin the consummation of an exchange offer and consent solicitation made by Oak to holders of various classes of its long-term debt. As detailed below that offer is an integral part of a series of transactions that together would effect a major reorganization and recapitalization of Oak. The claim asserted is in essence, that the exchange offer is a coercive device and, in the circumstances, constitutes a breach of contract.

[Background]

Oak manufactures and markets component equipments used in consumer, industrial and military products (the "Components Segment"); produces communications equipment for use in cable television systems and satellite television systems (the "Communications Segment") and manufactures and markets laminates and other materials used in printed circuit board applications (the "Materials Segment"). During 1985, the Company has terminated certain other unrelated businesses. As detailed below, it has now entered into an agreement with Allied-Signal for the sale of the Materials Segment of its business and is currently seeking a buyer for its Communications Segment.

Even a casual review of Oak's financial results over the last several years shows it unmistakably to be a company in deep trouble. During the period from January 1982 through September 1985, the Company has experienced unremitting losses from operations; on net sales of approximately $1.26 billion during that period it has lost over $335 million. As a result its total stockholders' equity has first shriveled (from $260 million on 12/31/81 to $85 million on 12/31/83) and then disappeared completely (as of 9/30/85 there was a $62 million deficit in its stockholders' equity accounts). Financial markets, of course, reflected this gloomy history.[2]

Unless Oak can be made profitable within some reasonably short time it will not continue as an operating company. Oak's board of directors, comprised almost entirely of outside directors, has authorized steps to buy the company time. In February, 1985, in order to reduce a burdensome annual cash interest obligation on its $230 million of then outstanding debentures, the Company offered to exchange such debentures for a combination of notes, common stock and warrants. As a result, approximately $180 million principal amount of the then outstanding debentures were exchanged. Since interest on certain of the notes issued in that exchange offer is payable in common stock, the effect of the 1985 exchange offer was to reduce to some extent the cash drain on the Company caused by its significant debt.

About the same time that the 1985 exchange offer was made, the Company announced its intention to discontinue certain of its operations and sell certain of its properties. Taking these steps, while effective to stave off a default and to reduce to some extent the immediate cash drain, did not address Oak's longer-range problems. Therefore, also during 1985 representatives of the Company held informal discussions with several interested parties exploring the possibility of an investment from, combination with or acquisition by another company. As a result of these discussions, the Company and Allied-Signal entered into two agreements. The first, the Acquisition Agreement, contemplates the sale to Allied-Signal of the Materials Segment for $160 million in cash. The second agreement, the Stock Purchase Agreement, provides for the purchase by Allied-Signal for $15 million cash of 10 million shares of the Company's common stock together with warrants to purchase additional common stock.

The Stock Purchase Agreement provides as a condition to Allied-Signal's obligation that at least 85% of the aggregate principal amount of all of the Company's debt

---

2. The price of the company's common stock has fallen from over $30 per share on December 31, 1981 to approximately $2 per share recently. The debt securities that are the subject of the exchange offer here involved (see note 3 for identification) have traded at substantial discounts.

securities shall have tendered and accepted the exchange offers that are the subject of this lawsuit. Oak has six classes of such long term debt.[3] If less than 85% of the aggregate principal amount of such debt accepts the offer, Allied-Signal has an option, but no obligation, to purchase the common stock and warrants contemplated by the Stock Purchase Agreement. An additional condition for the closing of the Stock Purchase Agreement is that the sale of the Company's Materials Segment contemplated by the Acquisition Agreement shall have been concluded.

Thus, as part of the restructuring and recapitalization contemplated by the Acquisition Agreement and the Stock Purchase Agreement, the Company has extended an exchange offer to each of the holders of the six classes of its long-term debt securities. These pending exchange offers include a Common Stock Exchange Offer (available only to holders of the 9 5/8% convertible notes) and the Payment Certificate Exchange Offers (available to holders of all six classes of Oak's long-term debt securities). The Common Stock Exchange Offer currently provides for the payment to each tendering noteholder of 407 shares of the Company's common stock in exchange for each $1,000 9 5/8% note accepted. The offer is limited to $38.6 million principal amount of notes (out of approximately $83.9 million outstanding).

The Payment Certificate Exchange Offer is an any and all offer. Under its terms, a payment certificate, payable in cash five days after the closing of the sale of the Materials Segment to Allied-Signal, is offered in exchange for debt securities. The cash value of the Payment Certificate will vary depending upon the particular security tendered. In each instance, however, that payment will be less than the face amount of the obligation. The cash payments range in amount, per $1,000 of principal, from $918 to $655. These cash values however appear to represent a premium over the market prices for the Company's debentures as of the time the terms of the transaction were set.

The Payment Certificate Exchange Offer is subject to certain important conditions before Oak has an obligation to accept tenders under it. First, it is necessary that a minimum amount ($38.6 million principal amount out of $83.9 total outstanding principal amount) of the 9 5/8% notes be tendered pursuant to the Common Stock Exchange Offer. Secondly, it is necessary that certain minimum amounts of each class of debt securities be tendered, together with consents to amendments to the underlying indentures.[4] Indeed, under the offer one may not tender securities unless at the same time one consents to the proposed amendments to the relevant indentures.

The condition of the offer that tendering security holders must consent to amendments in the indentures governing the securities gives rise to plaintiff's claim of breach of contract in this case. Those amendments would, if implemented, have the effect of removing significant negotiated protections to holders of the Company's long-term

---

3. The three classes of debentures are: 13.65% debentures due April 1, 2001, 10½% convertible subordinated debentures due February 1, 2002, and 11% subordinated debentures due May 15, 1998. In addition, as a result of the 1985 exchange offer the company has three classes of notes which were issued in exchange for debentures that were tendered in that offer. Those are: 13.5% senior notes due May 15, 1990, 9% convertible notes due September 15, 1991 and 11% notes due September 15, 1990.

4. The holders of more than 50% of the principal amount of each of the 13.5% notes, the 9% notes and the 11% notes and at least 66 2/3% of the principal amount of the 13.65% debentures, 10½% debentures, and 11% debentures, must validly tender such securities and consent to certain proposed amendments to the indentures governing those securities.

debt including the deletion of all financial covenants. Such modification may have adverse consequences to debt holders who elect not to tender pursuant to either exchange offer.

Allied-Signal apparently was unwilling to commit to the $15 million cash infusion contemplated by the Stock Purchase Agreement, unless Oak's long-term debt is reduced by 85% (at least that is a condition of their obligation to close on that contract). Mathematically, such a reduction may not occur without the Company reducing the principal amount of outstanding debentures (that is the three classes outstanding notes constitute less than 85% of all long-term debt). But existing indenture covenants prohibit the Company, so long as any of its long-term notes are outstanding, from issuing any obligation (including the Payment Certificates) in exchange for any of the debentures. Thus, in this respect, amendment to the indentures is required in order to close the Stock Purchase Agreement as presently structured.

Restrictive covenants in the indentures would appear to interfere with effectuation of the recapitalization in another way. Section 4.07 of the 13.50% Indenture provides that the Company may not "acquire" for value any of the 9 5/8% Notes or 11 5/8 % Notes unless it concurrently "redeems" a proportionate amount of the 13.50% Notes. This covenant, if unamended, would prohibit the disproportionate acquisition of the 9 5/8 % Notes that may well occur as a result of the Exchange Offers; in addition, it would appear to require the payment of the "redemption" price for the 13.50% Notes rather than the lower, market price offered in the exchange offer.

In sum, the failure to obtain the requisite consents to the proposed amendments would permit Allied-Signal to decline to consummate both the Acquisition Agreement and the Stock Purchase Agreement.

Plaintiff's claim that the Exchange Offers and Consent Solicitation constitutes a threatened wrong to him and other holders of Oak's debt securities[6] appear to be summarized in his Complaint:

> The purpose and effect of the Exchange Offers is [1] to benefit Oak's common stockholders at the expense of the Holders of its debt securities, [2] to force the exchange of its debt instruments at unfair price and at less than face value of the debt instruments [3] pursuant to a rigged vote in which debt Holders who exchange, and who therefore have no interest in the vote, *must* consent to the elimination of protective covenants for debt Holders who do not wish to exchange.

Plaintiff's claim is that no free choice is provided to bondholders by the exchange offer and consent solicitation. Under its terms, a rational bondholder is "forced" to tender and consent. Failure to do so would face a bondholder with the risk of owning a security stripped of all financial covenant protections and for which it is likely that there would be no ready market. A reasonable bondholder, it is suggested, cannot

---

6. It is worthy of note that a very high percentage of the principal value of Oak's debt securities are owned in substantial amounts by a handful of large financial institutions. Almost 85% of the value of the 13.50% Notes is owned by four such institutions (one investment banker owns 55% of that issue); 69.1% of the 9% Notes are owned by four financial institutions (the same investment banker owning 25% of that issue) and 85% of the 11% Notes are owned by five such institutions. Of the debentures, 89% of the 13.65% debentures are owned by four large banks; and approximately 45% of the two remaining issues is owned by two banks.

possibly accept those risks and thus such a bondholder is coerced to tender and thus to consent to the proposed indenture amendments.

[Analysis]

In order to demonstrate an entitlement to the provisional remedy of a preliminary injunction it is essential that a plaintiff show that it is probable that his claim will be upheld after final hearing; that he faces a risk of irreparable injury before final judgment will be reached in the regular course; and that in balancing the equities and competing hardships that preliminary judicial action may cause or prevent, the balance favors plaintiff.

I turn first to an evaluation of the probability of plaintiff's ultimate success on the merits of his claim. I begin that analysis with two preliminary points. The first concerns what is not involved in this case. This case does not involve the measurement of corporate or directorial conduct against that high standard of fidelity required of fiduciaries when they act with respect to the interests of the beneficiaries of their trust. Under our law—and the law generally—the relationship between a corporation and the holders of its debt securities, even convertible debt securities, is contractual in nature. *See* American Bar Foundation, *Commentaries on Indentures* (1971). Arrangements among a corporation, the underwriters of its debt, trustees under its indentures and sometimes ultimate investors are typically thoroughly negotiated and massively documented. The rights and obligations of the various parties are or should be spelled out in that documentation. The terms of the contractual relationship agreed to and not broad concepts such as fairness define the corporation's obligation to its bondholders.

Thus, the first aspect of the pending Exchange Offers about which plaintiff complains—that "the purpose and effect of the Exchange Offers is to benefit Oak's common stockholders at the expense of the Holders of its debt"—does not itself appear to allege a cognizable legal wrong. It is the obligation of directors to attempt, within the law, to maximize the long-run interests of the corporation's stockholders; that they may sometimes do so "at the expense" of others (even assuming that a transaction which one may refuse to enter into can meaningfully be said to be at his expense) does not for that reason constitute a breach of duty. It seems likely that corporate restructurings designed to maximize shareholder values may in some instances have the effect of requiring bondholders to bear greater risk of loss and thus in effect transfer economic value from bondholders to stockholders. But if courts are to provide protection against such enhanced risk, they will require either legislative direction to do so or the negotiation of indenture provisions designed to afford such protection.

The second preliminary point concerns the limited analytical utility, at least in this context, of the word "coercive" which is central to plaintiff's own articulation of his theory of recovery. If, *pro arguendo,* we are to extend the meaning of the word coercion beyond its core meaning—dealing with the utilization of physical force to overcome the will of another—to reach instances in which the claimed coercion arises from an act designed to affect the will of another party by offering inducements to the act sought to be encouraged or by arranging unpleasant consequences for an alternative sought to be discouraged, then—in order to make the term legally meaningful at all—we must acknowledge that some further refinement is essential. Clearly some "coercion" of this kind is legally unproblematic. Parents may "coerce" a child to study with the threat of withholding an allowance; employers may "coerce" regular attendance at work by either docking wages for time absent or by rewarding with a bonus such regular attendance. Other "coercion" so defined clearly would be legally relevant (to encourage regular attendance by corporal punishment, for example). Thus, for purposes of legal analysis, the term "coercion" itself—covering a multitude of situations—is not very meaningful. For the word to have much meaning for purposes of legal analysis, it is necessary in each case that a normative judgment be attached to the concept ("inappropriately coercive" or "wrongfully coercive", etc.). But, it is then readily seen that what is legally relevant is not the conclusory term "coercion" itself but rather the norm that leads to the adverb modifying it.

In this instance, assuming that the Exchange Offers and Consent Solicitation can meaningfully be regarded as "coercive" (in the sense that Oak has structured it in a way designed—and I assume effectively so—to "force" rational bondholders to tender), the relevant legal norm that will support the judgment whether such "coercion" is wrongful or not will, for the reasons mentioned above, be derived from the law of contracts. I turn then to that subject to determine the appropriate legal test or rule.

Modern contract law has generally recognized an implied covenant to the effect that each party to a contract will act with good faith towards the other with respect to the subject matter of the contract. The contractual theory for this implied obligation is well stated in a leading treatise:

> If the purpose of contract law is to enforce the reasonable expectations of parties induced by promises, then at some point it becomes necessary for courts to look to the substance rather than to the form of the agreement, and to hold that substance controls over form. What courts are doing here, whether calling the process "implication" of promises, or interpreting the requirements of "good faith", as the current fashion may be, is but a recognition that the parties occasionally have understandings or expectations that were so fundamental that they did not need to negotiate about those expectations. When the court "implies a promise" or holds that "good faith" requires a party not to violate those expectations, it is recognizing that sometimes silence says more than words, and it is understanding its duty to the spirit of the bargain is higher than its duty to the technicalities of the language. *Corbin on Contracts* §570.

It is this obligation to act in good faith and to deal fairly that plaintiff claims is breached by the structure of Oak's coercive exchange offer. Because it is an implied *contractual* obligation that is asserted as the basis for the relief sought, the appropriate legal test is not difficult to deduce. It is this: is it clear from what was expressly agreed upon that the parties who negotiated the express terms of the contract would have agreed to proscribe the act later complained of as a breach of the implied covenant of good faith—had they thought to negotiate with respect to that matter. If the answer to this question is yes, then, in my opinion, a court is justified in concluding that such act constitutes a breach of the implied covenant of good faith. *See Broad v. Rockwell International Corp.*, 642 F.2d 929, 957 (5th Cir. 1981).

Applying the foregoing standard to the exchange offer and consent solicitation, I find first that there is nothing in the indenture provisions granting bondholders power to veto proposed modifications in the relevant indenture that implies that Oak may not offer an inducement to bondholders to consent to such amendments. Such an implication, at least where, as here, the inducement is offered on the same terms to each holder of an affected security, would be wholly inconsistent with the strictly commercial nature of the relationship.

Nor does the second pertinent contractual provision supply a ground to conclude that defendant's conduct violates the reasonable expectations of those who negotiated the indentures on behalf of the bondholders. Under that provision Oak may not vote debt securities held in its treasury. Plaintiff urges that Oak's conditioning of its offer to purchase debt on the giving of consents has the effect of subverting the purpose of that provision; it permits Oak to "dictate" the vote on securities which it could not itself vote.

The evident purpose of the restriction on the voting of treasury securities is to afford protection against the issuer voting as a bondholder in favor of modifications that would benefit it as issuer, even though such changes would be detrimental to bondholders. But the linking of the exchange offer and the consent solicitation does not involve the risk that bondholder interests will be affected by a vote involving any- one with a financial interest in the subject of the vote other than a bondholder's interest. That the consent is to be given concurrently with the transfer of the bond to the issuer does not in any sense create the kind of conflict of interest that the indenture's prohibition on voting treasury securities contemplates. Not only will the proposed consents be granted or withheld only by those with a financial interest to maximize the return on their investment in Oak's bonds, but the incentive to consent is equally available to all members of each class of bondholders. Thus the "vote" implied by the consent solicitation is not affected in any sense by those with a financial conflict of interest.

In these circumstances, while it is clear that Oak has fashioned the exchange offer and consent solicitation in a way designed to encourage consents, I cannot conclude that the offer violates the intendment of any of the express contractual provisions considered or, applying the test set out above, that its structure and timing breaches an implied obligation of good faith and fair dealing.

One further set of contractual provisions should be touched upon: Those granting to Oak a power to redeem the securities here treated at a price set by the relevant indentures. Plaintiff asserts that the attempt to force all bondholders to tender their securities at less than the redemption price constitutes, if not a breach of the redemp- tion provision itself, at least a breach of an implied covenant of good faith and fair dealing associated with it. The flaw, or at least one fatal flaw, in this argument is that the present offer is not the functional equivalent of a redemption which is, of course, an act that the issuer may take unilaterally. In this instance it may happen that Oak will get tenders of a large percentage of its outstanding long-term debt securities. If it does, that fact will, in my judgment, be in major part a function of the merits of the offer (i.e., the price offered in light of the Company's financial position and the market value of its debt). To answer plaintiff's contention that the *structure* of the offer "forces" debt holders to tender, one only has to imagine what response this offer would receive if the price offered did not reflect a premium over market but rather was, for example, ten percent of market value. The exchange offer's success ultimately depends upon the ability and willingness of the issuer to extend an offer that will be a financially attractive alternative to holders. This process is hardly the functional equivalent of the unilateral election of redemption and thus cannot be said in any sense to constitute a subversion by Oak of the negotiated provisions dealing with redemption of its debt.

Accordingly, I conclude that plaintiff has failed to demonstrate a probability of ultimate success on the theory of liability asserted.

QUESTIONS

1. In what way is economic coercion consistent with the idea of freedom of contract?
2. What is the relationship between *Katz* and *Metropolitan Life*?
3. Does the holding advance or undermine the goal of wealth maximization? Explain.

2. FIDUCIARY DUTY

Shareholders are owed fiduciary duty. The board does not owe fiduciary duty to creditors, unless courts determine that the corporation is in a state of insolvency or near insolvency.

———————

The following case involves convertible bonds, which are bonds that can convert into common stock at the option of the bondholder. Because there is an equity link, these bonds are closer to equity than straight bonds.

Simons v. Cogan
549 A.2d 300 (Del. 1988)

WALSH, Justice:

This is an appeal from a decision of the Court of Chancery granting a motion to dismiss a class action brought by Louise Simons, a holder of convertible subordinated debentures, against the issuing corporation, Knoll International, Inc., its controlling shareholder, Marshall Cogan, and other related corporate constituents. Simons' complaint asserted claims based on violations of fiduciary duty [and] breach of indenture. In granting the motion to dismiss, the Court of Chancery determined that the issuing corporation and its directors do not owe a fiduciary duty to the debenture holders. We agree with the reasoning and holding of the Court of Chancery and accordingly affirm the judgment in all respects.

The transaction challenged in this case involves the merger of two related corporations, Hansac, Inc. and Knoll. The merger left Knoll, the surviving corporation, as the wholly owned subsidiary of Knoll Holdings. The merger caused the minority shareholders of Knoll to be eliminated through a $12 cash tender offer.

The merger resulted in the execution of a supplemental indenture which eliminated the right of Knoll's convertible debenture holders to convert their debentures into shares of its common stock. The supplemental indenture, which was executed by Knoll and the indenture trustee, provided that in lieu of the right to convert into the common stock of Knoll, the debentures would be convertible into $12.00 cash for each $19.20 principal amount of debenture. An additional supplemental indenture was also executed increasing the interest rate on the debentures from 8 ½ percent to 9 ⅞ percent per annum.

Simons filed a class action on behalf of the holders of Knoll's convertible debentures asserting as a primary cause of action that the defendants, in terminating the right to convert the debentures into the common stock of Knoll, breached a fiduciary duty to the debenture holders.

In order to determine whether a holder of a convertible debenture is owed a fiduciary duty by the issuing corporation and its directors we must begin our analysis with an examination of the nature of the interest or entitlement underlying a convertible debenture. A debenture represents a long term unsecured debt of the issuing corporation convertible into stock under certain specified conditions. A debenture is a credit instrument which does not devolve upon its holder an equity interest in the issuing corporation. Similarly, the convertibility feature of the debenture does not impart an equity element until conversion occurs.

> That a bond is convertible at the sole option of its holder into stock should no more affect its essential quality of being a bond than should the fact that cash is convertible into stock affect the nature of cash. Any bond, or any property, for that matter, is convertible into stock through the intermediate step of converting it to cash. . . . Case law indicates that a convertible debenture is a bond and not an equity security until conversion occurs.

In sum, a convertible debenture represents a contractual entitlement to the repayment of a debt and does not represent an equitable interest in the issuing corporation necessary for the imposition of a trust relationship with concomitant fiduciary duties.

Before a fiduciary duty arises, an existing property right or equitable interest supporting such a duty must exist. The obvious example is stock ownership. Until the debenture is converted into stock the convertible debenture holder acquires no equitable interest, and remains a creditor of the corporation whose interests are protected by the contractual terms of the indenture.

QUESTIONS

1. Bondholders are ordinarily not entitled to fiduciary duty. Why not?
2. Why does the convertibility of a bond, which has an equity-linked feature, not change the basic rule that bondholders are not owed fiduciary duty?

The following case addresses the issue of the board's fiduciary duty to creditors and the manner in which creditors can pursue such action. Recall that in *Credit Lyonnais Bank Nederland, N.V. v. Pathe Comm'n Corp.*, 1991 WL 277613 (Del.Ch. 1991), the Delaware Chancery Court held that "At least where a corporation is operating in the vicinity of insolvency, a board of directors is not merely the agent of the [residual] risk bearers, but owes its duty to the corporate enterprise." The Delaware Supreme Court subsequently opined on this principle.

N. Am. Catholic Educational Programming Found., Inc. v. Gheewalla
930 A.2d 92 (Del. 2007)

HOLLAND, Justice:

This is the appeal of North American Catholic Educational Programming Foundation, Inc. ("NACEPF") from a final judgment of the Court of Chancery that dismissed NACEPF's Complaint for failure to state a claim. NACEPF holds certain radio wave spectrum licenses regulated by the Federal Communications Commission ("FCC"). In March 2001, NACEPF, together with other similar spectrum license-holders, entered into the Master Use and Royalty Agreement (the "Master Agreement") with Clearwire Holdings, Inc.. Under the Master Agreement, Clearwire could obtain rights to those licenses as then-existing leases expired and the then-current lessees failed to exercise rights of first refusal.

The defendant are Rob Gheewalla, Gerry Cardinale, and Jack Daly (collectively, the "Defendants"), who served as directors of Clearwire at the behest of Goldman Sachs & Co. NACEPF's Complaint alleges that the Defendants, even though they comprised less than a majority of the board, were able to control Clearwire because its only source of funding was Goldman Sachs. According to NACEPF, they used that power to favor Goldman Sachs' agenda in derogation of their fiduciary duties as directors of Clearwire.

NACEPF is not a shareholder of Clearwire. Instead, NACEPF filed its Complaint as a putative *creditor* of Clearwire. The Complaint alleges *direct,* not derivative, fiduciary duty claims against the Defendants, who served as directors of Clearwire while it was either insolvent or in the "zone of insolvency."

We hold that the creditors of a Delaware corporation that is either insolvent or in the zone of insolvency have no right, as a matter of law, to assert direct claims for breach of fiduciary duty against the corporation's directors. Accordingly, the judgments of the Court of Chancery must be affirmed.

Facts

The Defendants were directors of Clearwire. The Defendants were also all employed by Goldman Sachs and served on the Clearwire Board of Directors at the behest of Goldman Sachs. NACEPF alleges that the Defendants effectively controlled Clearwire through the financial and other influence that Goldman Sachs had over Clearwire.

According to the Complaint, the Defendants represented to NACEPF and the other Alliance members [other spectrum license holders] that Clearwire's stated business purpose was to create a national system of wireless connections to the internet. Between 2000 and March 2001, Clearwire negotiated a Master Agreement with the Alliance, which Clearwire and the Alliance members entered into in March 2001. Under the terms of the Master Agreement, Clearwire was to acquire the Alliance members' ITFS spectrum licenses when those licenses became available. To do so, Clearwire was obligated to pay NACEPF and other Alliance members more than $24.3 million. The Complaint alleges that the Defendants knew but did not tell NACEPF that Goldman Sachs did not intend to carry out the business plan that was the stated rationale for asking NACEPF to enter into the Master Agreement, i.e., by funding Clearwire.

In June 2002, the market for wireless spectrum collapsed when WorldCom announced its accounting problems. It appeared that there was or soon would be a surplus of spectrum available from WorldCom. Thereafter, Clearwire began negotiations with the members of the Alliance to end Clearwire's obligations to the members. Eventually, Clearwire paid over $2 million to [other Alliance members] to settle their claims. These settlements left the NACEPF as the sole remaining member of the Alliance. The Complaint alleges that, by October 2003, Clearwire "had been unable to obtain any further financing and effectively went out of business."

NACEPF alleges that because, at all relevant times, Clearwire was either insolvent or in the "zone of insolvency," the Defendants owed fiduciary duties to NACEPF "as a substantial creditor of Clearwire," and that the Defendants breached those duties by:

(1) not preserving the assets of Clearwire for its benefit and that of its creditors when it became apparent that Clearwire would not be able to continue as a going concern and would need to be liquidated and (2) holding on to NACEPF's ITFS license rights when Clearwire would not use them, solely to keep Goldman Sachs's investment "in play."

In support of its claim that Clearwire was either insolvent or in the zone of insolvency during the relevant periods, NACEPF alleged that Clearwire needed "substantially more financial support than it had obtained in March 2001." The Complaint alleges Goldman Sachs had invested $47 million in Clearwire, which "represented 84% of the total sums invested in Clearwire in March 2001, when Clearwire was otherwise virtually out of funds."

After March 2001, Clearwire had financial obligations related to its agreement with NACEPF and others that potentially exceeded $134 million, did not have the ability to raise sufficient cash from operations to pay its debts as they became due and was dependent on Goldman Sachs to make additional investments to fund Clearwire's operations for the foreseeable future.

Additionally, in the Complaint, NACEPF alleges that, "by October 2003, Clearwire had been unable to obtain any further financing and effectively went out of business. Except for money advanced to it as a stopgap measure by Goldman Sachs in late 2001, Clearwire was never able to raise any significant money."

The Court of Chancery opined that insolvency may be demonstrated by either showing (1) "a deficiency of assets below liabilities with no reasonable prospect that the business can be successfully continued in the face thereof," or (2) "an inability to meet maturing obligations as they fall due in the ordinary course of business." The Court of Chancery also concluded that insolvency had been adequately alleged in the Complaint, for Rule 12(b)(6) purposes, for at least a portion of the relevant periods following execution of the Master Agreement.

Corporations in the Zone of Insolvency Direct Claims for Breach of Fiduciary Duty May Not Be Asserted by Creditors

In order to withstand the Defendant's Rule 12(b)(6) motion to dismiss, the Plaintiff was required to demonstrate that the breach of fiduciary duty claims set forth in Count II are cognizable under Delaware law. This procedural requirement requires us to address a substantive question of first impression that is raised by the present appeal: as a matter of Delaware law, can the *creditor* of a corporation that is operating within the *zone of insolvency* bring a *direct action* against its directors for an alleged *breach of fiduciary* duty?

It is well established that the directors owe their fiduciary obligations to the corporation and its shareholders. While shareholders rely on directors acting as fiduciaries to protect their interests, creditors are afforded protection through contractual agreements, fraud and fraudulent conveyance law, implied covenants of good faith and fair dealing, bankruptcy law, general commercial law and other sources of creditor rights. Delaware courts have traditionally been reluctant to expand existing fiduciary duties. Accordingly, "the general rule is that directors do not owe creditors duties beyond the relevant contractual terms."[25]

NACEPF argues that when a corporation is in the zone of insolvency, this Court should recognize a new direct right for creditors to challenge directors' exercise of business judgments as breaches of the fiduciary duties owed to them. This Court has never directly addressed the zone of insolvency issue involving directors' purported fiduciary duties to creditors that is presented by NACEPF in this appeal. That subject has been discussed, however, in several judicial opinions.[27]

The Court of Chancery noted that creditors' existing protections—among which are the protections afforded by their negotiated agreements, their security instruments, the implied covenant of good faith and fair dealing, fraudulent conveyance law, and bankruptcy law—render the imposition of an additional, unique layer of protection through direct claims for breach of fiduciary duty unnecessary. It also noted that "any benefit to be derived by the recognition of such additional direct claims appears minimal, at best, and significantly outweighed by the costs to economic efficiency." The Court of Chancery reasoned that "an otherwise solvent corporation operating in the zone of insolvency is one in most need of effective and proactive leadership—as well as the ability to negotiate in good faith with its creditors—goals which would likely be significantly undermined by the prospect of individual liability arising from the pursuit of direct claims by creditors." We agree.

Delaware corporate law provides for a separation of control and ownership. The directors of Delaware corporations have "the legal responsibility to manage the business of a corporation for the benefit of its shareholders owners." Accordingly, fiduciary duties are imposed upon the directors to regulate their conduct when they perform *that* function. Although the fiduciary duties of the directors of a Delaware corporation are unremitting:

> the exact cause of conduct that must be charted to properly discharge that responsibility will change in the specific context of the action the director is taking with regard to either the corporation or its shareholders. This Court has endeavored to provide the directors with clear signal beacons and brightly lined channel markers as they navigate with due care, good faith, a loyalty on behalf of a Delaware corporation and its shareholders. This Court has also endeavored to mark the safe harbors clearly.

In this case, the need for providing directors with definitive guidance compels us to hold that no direct claim for breach of fiduciary duties may be asserted by the creditors of a solvent corporation that is operating in the zone of insolvency. When a solvent corporation is navigating in the zone of insolvency, the focus for Delaware directors does not change: directors must continue to discharge their fiduciary duties to the corporation and its shareholders by exercising their business judgment in the best interests of the corporation for the benefit of its shareholder owners. Therefore, we hold the Court of Chancery properly concluded that the NACEPF Complaint fails to state a claim, as a matter of Delaware law, to the extent that it attempts to assert a

---

25. *See, e.g., Simons v. Cogan,* 549 A.2d 300, 304 (Del. 1988); *Katz v. Oak Indus., Inc.,* 508 A.2d 873, 879 (Del.Ch. 1986); *Production Res. Group v. NCT Group, Inc.,* 863 A.2d 772, 787 (Del.Ch. 2004).

27. *Credit Lyonnais Bank Nederland N.V. v. Pathe Commc'ns Corp.,* 1991 WL 277613 (Del.Ch.); *Production Resources Group, L.L.C. v. NCT Group, Inc.,* 863 A.2d 772 (Del.Ch. 2004).

direct claim for breach of fiduciary duty to a creditor while Clearwire was operating in the zone of insolvency.

Insolvent Corporations Direct Claims For Breach of Fiduciary Duty May Not Be Asserted by Creditors

It is well settled that directors owe fiduciary duties to the corporation. When a corporation is *solvent,* those duties may be enforced by its shareholders, who have standing to bring *derivative* actions on behalf of the corporation because they are the ultimate beneficiaries of the corporation's growth and increased value. When a corporation is *insolvent,* however, its creditors take the place of the shareholders as the residual beneficiaries of any increase in value.

Consequently, the creditors of an *insolvent* corporation have standing to maintain derivative claims against directors on behalf of the corporation for breaches of fiduciary duties. The corporation's insolvency "makes the creditors the principal constituency injured by any fiduciary breaches that diminish the firm's value." Therefore, equitable considerations give creditors standing to pursue derivative claims against the directors of an insolvent corporation. Individual creditors of an insolvent corporation have the same incentive to pursue valid derivative claims on its behalf that shareholders have when the corporation is solvent.

In *Production Resources Group, L.L.C. v. NCT Group, Inc.,* 863 A.2d 772 (Del.Ch. 2004), the Court of Chancery recognized that—in most, if not all instances—creditors of insolvent corporations could bring derivative claims against directors of an insolvent corporation for breach of fiduciary duty. In that case, in response to the creditor plaintiff's contention that derivative claims for breach of fiduciary duty were transformed into *direct* claims upon insolvency, the Court of Chancery stated:

> The fact that the corporation has become insolvent does not turn [derivative] claims into direct creditor claims, it simply provides creditors with standing to assert those claims. At all times, claims of this kind belong to the corporation itself because even if the improper acts occur when the firm is insolvent, they operate to injure the firm in the first instance by reducing its value, injuring creditors only indirectly by diminishing the value of the firm and therefore the assets from which the creditors may satisfy their claims.

Nevertheless, in *Production Resources,* the Court of Chancery stated that it was "not prepared to rule out" the *possibility* that the creditor plaintiff had alleged conduct that "might support" a *limited* direct claim.

To date, the Court of Chancery has never recognized that a creditor has the right to assert a *direct* claim for breach of fiduciary duty against the directors of an *insolvent* corporation. However, prior to this opinion, that possibility remained an open question because of the *dicta* in *Production Resources.*

Recognizing that directors of an insolvent corporation owe direct fiduciary duties to creditors, would create uncertainty for directors who have a fiduciary duty to exercise their business judgment in the best interest of the insolvent corporation. To recognize a new right for creditors to bring direct fiduciary claims against those directors would create a conflict between those directors' duty to maximize the value of the insolvent corporation for the benefit of all those having an interest in it, and the newly recognized direct fiduciary duty to individual creditors. Directors of insolvent corporations must retain the freedom to engage in vigorous, good faith negotiations with individual creditors for the benefit of the corporation. Accordingly, we hold that individual *creditors* of an *insolvent* corporation have *no right to assert direct* claims for breach of fiduciary duty against corporate directors. Creditors may nonetheless protect their interest by bringing derivative claims on behalf of the insolvent corporation or *any other* direct nonfiduciary claim, as discussed earlier in this opinion, that may be available for individual creditors.

QUESTIONS

1. What is the implication for bondholders that they do not have direct claims?
2. Is the line of cases from *Simons* to *Credit Lyonnais* to *Gheewalla* coherent? What is the common thread?
3. In what way does the recognition of the principle that creditors can be owed fiduciary duty seen in *Credit Lyonnais* and *Gheewalla* promote the goal of efficiency?

The following case addresses the question of whether a board breached its fiduciary duty to equityholders when it approved a sale of an insolvent company under terms that provided creditors all of the sale consideration.

Blackmore Partners, L.P. v. Link Energy LLC
2005 WL 2709639 (Del. Ch. 2005)

LAMB, Vice Chancellor.

Blackmore Partners L.P. instituted this action against Link Energy LLC and the members of its board of directors, alleging breaches of the defendants' fiduciary duties, arising out of a completed sale of Link's operating assets at a price likely to yield zero value to Link's equity owners. Following the conclusion of discovery, the defendants move for summary judgment. Construing all evidence in favor of the plaintiff, the court nevertheless concludes the defendants are entitled to the entry of judgment in their favor.

The facts of this case are largely uncontested. EOTT Energy Partners, L.P. filed for bankruptcy protection pursuant to Chapter 11 of the United States Bankruptcy Code. Link emerged from that reorganization as successor in interest to EOTT, planning to engage in the same business of purchasing, gathering, storing, transporting, processing and reselling crude oil, refined petroleum products, natural gas liquids, and other related products.

As part of the plan of reorganization, Link issued $104 million in senior unsecured 9% notes ("Notes"), in lieu of $235 million of 11% senior notes owed to a range of EOTT creditors. In addition, those same creditors received 95% of the newly issued common equity units in Link ("Units"). Three percent of the Units were distributed to the former holders of EOTT's common units, one of whom is the plaintiff in this case. While these exchanges resulted in a reduction in debt, Link remained relatively highly leveraged when it emerged from bankruptcy. In addition, Link had access to working capital through a credit facility with Standard Chartered Bank, which provided $290 million in funding until August 2004, subject to liquidity requirements waivable by that bank in its discretion.

The instrument governing the Notes contained a restrictive covenant requiring any purchaser of substantially all of Link's assets to assume the Notes. The provision was designed to ensure creditors that any such purchaser would honor the Notes, or at least ensure that the Note holders had a seat at the negotiating table in any post-bankruptcy acquisition of Link. In contrast to this power given to the Note holders, the Link operating agreement empowered the Link board of directors to authorize a sale of all or substantially all of Link's assets without a vote of the Unit holders.

Link was headed by CEO Thomas Matthews, who was joined on the board of directors by six persons appointed by EOTT's former note holders pursuant to EOTT's Restructuring Plan. Of the six additional directors, none except J. Robert Chambers (a managing director at Lehman Brothers, which held the same 19.1% share of both Units and Notes) had any affiliation or connection with any of EOTT's former note holders or with holders of the newly issued Notes.

The plan of operations devised by Link management hinged on its ability to attract a $100 million infusion of new equity into the company, which could be used to lower Link's debt levels and reduce its cost of credit. Link therefore entered the capital markets to search for an equity partner. Its efforts, however, were unsuccessful. Despite hiring Lehman Brothers to act as its financial adviser to assist the company in searching for new money, discussions failed with one investment group during the summer and early fall of 2003, and with another by February 2004.

Link attempted to improve its financial state by selling some non-strategic assets during its search for equity. All these efforts, however, were insufficient to offset losses caused by a worsening business environment. Thus, Link's board of directors determined to explore new ways of reducing the company's debt to the Note holders.

This determination, combined with threats by the provider of Link's credit facility to force the company into bankruptcy, caused Link to consider an acquisition offer by Plains All American Pipeline, L.P. of substantially all of the company's assets. The Link board of directors formed a Special Committee, consisting of all directors other than Matthews and Chambers to consider potential transactions. Plains initially appeared willing to assume the Notes as required by the bonds' restrictive covenant. If it had done so, the market value of the Notes, which were then trading at a discount, would have increased substantially as a result of Plains's substantially stronger credit rating. Plains ultimately made clear, however, that it would only assume the Notes upon a substantial, and probably prohibitive, discount to the purchase price for Link's assets. The company therefore began negotiating conditions under which the Note holders would be willing to waive their veto rights over potential transactions.

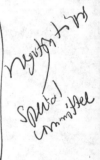

The [offer price] finally agreed upon after due diligence and negotiations between Link and Plains was $290 million. At the same time, Note holders agreed to waive the restrictive covenant, in return for a commitment by Link to repay the Notes at par plus accrued interest, and to pay the Note holders their proportionate share of up to $25 million from any funds remaining after the company wound up its affairs, but before any distribution to Unit holders. As the press release announcing the finalized deal made clear, the transaction at $290 million was likely to provide no recovery at all for Unit holders, given the demands of Link's debt and the deal struck with the Note holders.

Link announced that it was in advanced negotiations with a potential buyer, that sale proceeds would be used to retire the company's debt, and that Unit holders were likely to receive a minimal amount after the payment of all Link's liabilities, obligations, and contingencies. On the heels of that announcement, the market price of Link Units collapsed, dropping from over $5 to roughly $1. With the board of directors' agreement that the sale was the best available option for Link, the company's Special Committee met to consider the Plains transaction. At that meeting, the investment bank Petrie Parkman presented supporting information for its fairness opinion on the Plains transaction. The Special Committee also heard an update to the fairness opinion presented by Lehman Brothers to the board of directors. Upon a report by the board's counsel, and a full discussion of the Plains transaction, the Special Committee recommended the sale. The transaction closed on April 1, 2004, and Link has now begun the process of winding up operations.

The uncontroverted expert report of M. Freddie Reiss, introduced by defendants during discovery, examined Link's continued viability under three independent tests. The first of these techniques, the so-called "balance sheet test," is "concerned with the relative value of a company's equity." Under this test, a company's value can be determined either by individual asset valuation, in which each asset is valued on a going concern basis, or by business enterprise valuation, a more commonly used method which assumes that all assets are sold together, along with the business as a whole. The second technique used by Reiss is known as the "cash flow test," and examines whether a company can "reasonably meet its anticipated fixed (on-balance sheet and contingent) obligations as they become due."

Reiss came to the conclusion that Link was insolvent during the period relevant to this case. The fair value of the company's assets on a going concern basis was less than the fair value of the liabilities, which means that Link failed the individual asset valuation prong of the balance sheet test. After using two methods of business enterprise valuation, moreover, Reiss came to a negative figure for the value of Link's equity. Nor could Link meet its obligations as they became due, suffering from strained liquidity, negative cash flow, and operating losses. The plaintiffs have produced no evidence at all contradicting Reiss's report, or presented any evidence of their own suggesting that Link was not insolvent. The Reiss report, therefore, is the only piece of evidence in the record directly on point of Link's insolvency.

The plaintiff claims that Chancellor Allen's decision in *Orban v. Field*, 1997 WL 153831 (Del.Ch.), requires "that when a board approves a transaction that favors one corporate constituency over another, they lose, at least as an initial matter, the cloak of business judgment protection." But the plaintiff's reliance on *Orban* for the proposition that the company owed the Unit holders a higher duty of care in this case is misplaced.

It is doubtless true, as Chancellor Allen noted in *Orban,* that a board deploying corporate power against a class of shareholders must specially demonstrate that it acted reasonably and in good faith. But that duty, though important, is limited to circumstances where the board uses the very levers of corporate power against its own shareholders in order to achieve some purportedly higher end. In *Orban* itself, for example, the board did not simply make a business decision that hurt shareholders while repaying creditors, but engaged in an elaborate maneuver in which the defendant company intentionally diluted a major shareholder to a position where he was powerless to stop a merger favored by the directors. In the face of such overwhelming force, it was clearly appropriate for the court to require the board to demonstrate the reasonableness and good faith of its action on a full evidentiary record. And even in that case, the court eventually upheld the board's action as necessary in otherwise pressing circumstances.

This case stands in sharp contrast to *Orban*. The corporate action complained of here, though it did result in Unit holders being left with no residual value, did not involve the use of corporate power against a shareholder class in the sense of *Orban*. The defendants did not act "solely or primarily for the express purpose of depriving a shareholder of effective enjoyment of a right conferred by law." Crucially, the Unit holders, by charter, did not even retain the right to vote on the sale of substantially all of Link's assets. Thus, no extraordinary efforts were needed to secure approval, or to stop a vote, for no such approval or vote was necessary. In such a case, it seems plain that *Orban's* enhanced scrutiny does not apply. It is a test designed for different circumstances, ones raising the omnipresent specter of management entrenchment.

Even if one were to apply *Orban* to this case, however, the defendants meet the enhanced standard required by that case. Link was insolvent, teetering on the brink of bankruptcy. At any moment, the provider of its chief credit facility could have forced it into default. Business prospects were declining, reducing daily the amount of consideration the company could hope for in any non-bankruptcy alternative. Finally, no better transaction was available. These corporate interests are every bit as compelling as those that were served in *Orban*.

The plaintiff claims that the defendants violated their fiduciary duties to Unit holders by concentrating on the interests of creditors to the exclusion of their fiduciary duties to Unit holders. This claim fails on summary judgment. Under Delaware law, directors generally owe no fiduciary duties to creditors. In limited cases, however, such duties do arise. "Directors do not owe creditors duties beyond the relevant contractual terms absent 'special circumstances.'" Under long established precedent, one of those circumstances is insolvency, defined not as statutory insolvency but as insolvency in fact, which occurs at the moment when the entity "has liabilities in excess of a reasonable market value of assets held." When the insolvency exception arises "it creates fiduciary duties for directors for the benefit of creditors." The court, therefore, must first decide whether the company was insolvent at the time of the disputed transaction, and second whether the defendants discharged their duties to Link's Unit holders.

As to the first question, the plaintiff apparently concedes that the company was indeed insolvent as a matter of fact at the time of the Plains transaction. The plaintiff does not contradict expert testimony introduced by the defendants as to the insolvency of the company in the relevant period. The plaintiff is correct, of course, to say that having fiduciary duties to creditors does not excuse violations of fiduciary duty to Unit holders. During insolvency, the directors owe fiduciary duties to both the creditors and the Unit holders. But ultimately, the board of directors of an insolvent company may take into account the interests of creditors at the apparent expense of stockholders if, in doing so, the board meets its fiduciary duties to all relevant constituencies.

The plaintiff alleges that the business judgment rule's presumption of due care and good faith should be rebutted for two reasons. First, the plaintiff claims that the company's transaction with the Note holders was "wholly flawed" in part because Chambers was conflicted, therefore tainting board determinations. The claim that Chambers was conflicted rests primarily on the fact that Chambers was a managing director of Lehman Brothers, a holder of an equal percentage of both the Notes and the Units.[66]

The defendants here owe fiduciary duties to creditors because the company was insolvent. The choice between creditors and Unit holders in this case, therefore, does not present [a] clear conflict of interest. To the extent that a potential conflict of interest would arise by virtue of Chambers's membership on the board, there is no evidence of any other potential transaction that might have been better for Unit holders than the Plains transaction.

Nor would the court's determination change if the court were to conclude that Chambers was indeed conflicted. The protections of the business judgment rule may still insulate a board decision from challenge so long as a majority of the directors approving the transaction remain disinterested. Aside from the unsubstantiated allegations as to Chambers, the plaintiff makes no claims that any other directors were interested, and therefore a clearly independent majority of the board made the relevant decisions.

The defendants do not rely solely on the independent board majority to justify their approval of the Plains transaction. Rather, even though the Link board was not required to delegate its responsibilities to a special committee in this case, a special committee made up entirely of independent directors was indeed formed.

The plaintiff claims that the Special Committee was rendered inutile by the presence of Matthews and Chambers during meetings of the Committee. But Delaware law does not require that special committees be segregated from sources of vital information. Moreover, there is no evidence at all that Chambers or Matthews influenced the Special Committee, or acted as anything more than necessary sources of information. Nor does the record reveal the kind of secret or subversive communications between Chambers and Matthews. Even taking all the evidence in the light most favorable to the plaintiff, the court concludes that the Special Committee, created to reinforce the independence of a majority independent board, operated with sufficient independence to merit the cloak of business judgment protection.

QUESTIONS

1. Assume that the board allocated the $290 million price 90/10 between Notes and Units. What dollar value amount do the creditors give up to the Unit holders as compared to the actual transaction where the entire sales price went to the creditors?
2. Describe Lehman Brothers' role in this transaction.

---

66. It is unclear why Lehman's ownership of equal percentages of Notes and Units created a substantial conflict, at least as to the negotiation over whether to pay the Note holders more than was due to them by contract. Lehman would seem to gain no financial advantage from allocating the residue of the Plains transaction to Notes rather than Units. Because it owns the same percentage of both instruments, Lehman would receive the same amount of consideration no matter how any remaining value after satisfying Link's creditors was divided. At most, therefore, Lehman's dual ownership served to make it indifferent as to whether funds were distributed to the Unit holders or to the Note holders. The plaintiff also claims that Chambers was conflicted because Lehman Brothers issued a fairness opinion to the board in connection with the Plains transaction. But as the defendants note, Lehman's fairness opinion had nothing to do with the Note holder transaction. Rather, Lehman issued a fairness opinion relating to the entire Plains transaction.

3. The court notes in footnote 66 that Lehman Brothers could not have economically benefitted from the allocation decision because it owned equal amounts of Notes and Units. In what way could Lehman Brothers have had other incentives?
4. From a deal perspective, how could the transactional advisors, including Lehman Brothers, and the board have prevented ex ante this lawsuit in the transaction process? What would have been the downside to any attempt to prevent this lawsuit?

NOTES

1. In a prior proceeding on a motion to dismiss, the court held that there was a sufficient basis in the complaint to infer that the value of the LLC's assets exceeded its liabilities by a substantial amount and that the LLC was neither insolvent nor on the brink of bankruptcy. *Blackmore Partners, L.P. v. Link Energy LLC*, 864 A.2d 80 (Del. Ch. 2004). The court said the allegation that the directors approved a sale of substantially all of the assets and a resultant distribution of proceeds exclusively to the LLC's creditors raised an inference of disloyalty or intentional conduct.

D. BRIEF OVERVIEW OF BANKRUPTCY AND REORGANIZATION

The cases in the previous section involved situations where the corporation was financially troubled. In *Katz v. Oak Industries Inc.*, the corporation required restructuring and recapitalization, which meant that creditors were incentivized (coerced) to amend the terms in the bond. Under *N. Am. Catholic Educational Programming Found., Inc. v. Gheewalla*, creditors are owed fiduciary duty when the issuer is insolvent. The facts and circumstances of *Katz* and *Gheewalla* occurred outside the realm of bankruptcy, a formal legal process triggered by the filing of a bankruptcy petition. Outside of bankruptcy, the contracting parties are free to re-order their private ordering in response to changing circumstance, incentives, and bargaining power because a debtor-creditor relationship is the product of contract.

When private re-ordering through a voluntary workout is not an option for whatever reason, debtors and creditors have the option to pursue an action under the U.S. Bankruptcy Code and the auspice of the U.S. Bankruptcy Court. For the purpose of corporate financing which assumes a going concern (one does not finance the liquidation of a business enterprise), the most relevant portion of the Code is a Chapter 11 Reorganization.

The restructuring process—whether within or outside of bankruptcy—is a broad canvass. A restructuring can simply change the financial and legal terms of the credit contracts: for example, changing the maturity, interest rate, covenants, and conditions on credit contracts (*e.g., Katz v. Oak Industries Inc.*). A corporation may simply need relief from onerous yearly debt service, and changes in interest rate and maturities may do the trick. A financial restructuring may be more complex, requiring changes to the capital structure (*e.g., Gradient OC Master Ltd. v. NBC Universal, Inc.*). The terms of the debt may be restructured, and the company may also delever by converting some debt into equity or some other security. A restructuring can also be even more complex if the underlying business mix is also restructured. For example, a restructuring may require a change in the business strategy and plan of the company, and this change would require disposal of noncore or nonstrategic assets (*e.g.*, *HB Korenaes Investments, L.P. v. Marriott Corp.*). In a bankruptcy-facilitated restructuring, it occurs through reorganization under Chapter 11. Fundamentally, reorganization facilitates the process of changing a firm's debt obligations to convert the debtor's financial position from insolvency to solvency.

The Code sets forth the steps required for reorganization and discharge of obligations. Broadly speaking, the steps can be categorized into several important actions: filing of the bankruptcy petition, proposal of the plan of reorganization, and confirmation of the plan by the bankruptcy court. The entry into bankruptcy is the filing of the petition, and the exit out of bankruptcy is the confirmation of the plan of reorganization. A number of important activities and legal actions occur between entry and exit, including the continued operation of the business to preserve value.

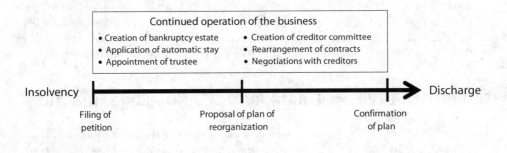

1. FILING PETITION AND AUTOMATIC STAY

The bankruptcy process begins upon the filing of a petition. The filing can be "voluntary" (Section 301) when a debtor files the petition. The decision to file for bankruptcy is a board decision. The filing can be "involuntary" (Section 303) when a creditor files the petition. Most bankruptcy petitions are voluntary. However, creditors are in many cases the driving force behind the voluntary petition due to the legal rights they wield that make continuing the business difficult: difficulties such as lawsuits, covenants that restrict financing or other business transactions, acceleration of maturity on debt, liens on assets, and seizure of collateral.

The filing of a petition triggers two important events. First, it creates by operation of law the bankruptcy estate. The estate holds the property of the debtor corporation (Section 541) including: (1) all legal or equitable interests of the debtor in property as of the commencement of the case; (2) any interest in property that the trustee recovers under the statute; (3) any interest in property preserved for the benefit of or ordered transferred to the estate under the statute; (4) proceeds, product, offspring, rents, or profits of or from property of the estate; and (5) any interest in property that the estate acquires after the commencement of the case. The creation of the bankruptcy estate transfers all assets and liability to the estate. Prebankruptcy claims against the debtor become claims against the estate.

Second, the filing of the petition triggers a hallmark feature of bankruptcy—the automatic stay. Section 362(a) provides that a petition "operates as a stay, applicable to all entities," of the following actions:

(1) the commencement or continuation, including the issuance or employment of process, of a judicial, administrative, or other action or proceeding against the debtor that was or could have been commenced before the commencement of the case under this title, or to recover a claim against the debtor that arose before the commencement of the case under this title;

(2) the enforcement, against the debtor or against property of the estate, of a judgment obtained before the commencement of the case under this title;

(3) any act to obtain possession of property of the estate or of property from the estate or to exercise control over property of the estate;

(4) any act to create, perfect, or enforce any lien against property of the estate;

(5) any act to create, perfect, or enforce against property of the debtor any lien to the extent that such lien secures a claim that arose before the commencement of the case under this title;

(6) any act to collect, assess, or recover a claim against the debtor that arose before the commencement of the case under this title;

(7) the setoff of any debt owing to the debtor that arose before the commencement of the case under this title against any claim against the debtor; and

(8) the commencement or continuation of a proceeding before the United States Tax Court concerning a tax liability of a debtor that is a corporation for a taxable period the bankruptcy court may determine or concerning the tax liability of a debtor who is an individual for a taxable period ending before the date of the order for relief under this title.

Section 362(d) permits secured creditors to petition the bankruptcy court to lift the stay for narrowly defined reasons: (1) for cause, including the lack of adequate protection of an interest in property of such party in interest; (2) with respect to property, the debtor does not have an equity in such property and such property is not necessary to an effective reorganization; (3) with respect to a single real estate asset, 90 days after filing if the debtor has not filed a plan of reorganization that has a reasonable possibility of being confirmed within a reasonable time or resumed monthly payments on the property; or (4) if a debtor is engaged in a fraudulent action to block a real estate foreclosure.

The automatic stay is otherwise broad. It applies to "all entities" and blocks creditors from attempting to collect on liabilities, including tax liability. Creditors must now work within the bankruptcy process under the auspice of the bankruptcy court to collect on the company's obligations to them. The automatic stay permits the debtor company to operate the business as a going concern, including spending funds and using collateral property subject to the bankruptcy process. Indeed, the policy behind the automatic stay is to shield the debtor from the uncontrolled individual efforts of creditors to recover against the debtor as the debtor becomes increasingly troubled (analogous to a "run on the bank"*). By managing the reorganization, the Code preserves the going concern value of the business.

When a petition is filed, the debtor company serves as the "debtor in possession" (DIP), defined as the debtor serving as the trustee of the bankruptcy estate. Since the DIP is the trustee, there is continuity of management as the prebankruptcy

---

* A "bank run" occurs when a mass of depositors literally run to the bank to demand their deposits, which are liabilities of the bank, due to fear that the bank will become insolvent, thus accelerating the insolvency or in some cases causing the insolvency.

management continues to manage the DIP. The DIP is responsible for taking care of the estate's property, examining the claims of creditors, furnishing information to relevant parties, and continuing the business to preserve or increase the value of the business. As an alternative to the DIP, a party in interest, typically a consortium of creditors, can petition to appoint a trustee in bankruptcy (TIB) (Section 1104(a)). The grounds for the appointment of a TIB is limited: (1) for cause, including fraud, dishonesty, incompetence, or gross mismanagement of the affairs of the debtor by current management, either before or after the commencement of the case; or (2) if such appointment is in the interests of creditors, any equity securityholders, and other interests of the estate.

Even without a formal opposition to the old management in control of the DIP, there may be tension since the old management was at the helm when the corporate ship ran aground (of course, that the management was at the helm does not necessarily mean that it caused the wreck, which may have been from decisions made by previous management or economic and business factors outside anyone's control). Management teams are sometimes replaced before or after filing, but this is not always the case. Various factors determine the decision to keep or replace management, including among others: risk and costs of old management, conflicting incentives among parties of interest, available opportunity to hire better management, and benefit to the business of continuity.

As soon as practicable, a committee of unsecured creditors is formed, and other committees may be formed such as a committee of equityholders. The major committee is the committee of unsecured creditors. Secured creditors often do not join a committee because they have secured interests, and thus their interests in the priority position often conflict with the interests of other parties in interest. A committee represents a major block of interest and formally engages in the bankruptcy process, including the right to move to convert the Chapter 11 reorganization process to a Chapter 7 liquidation. A committee may hire attorneys, accountants or other professionals to represent or perform services. It has the power to: (1) consult with the trustee or debtor in possession concerning the administration of the case; (2) investigate the acts, conduct, assets, liabilities, and financial condition of the debtor, the operation of the debtor's business and the desirability of the continuance of such business, and any other matter relevant to the case or to the formulation of a plan; (3) participate in the formulation of a plan, advise those represented by such committee of such committee's determinations as to any plan formulated, and collect and file with the court acceptances or rejections of a plan; (4) request the appointment of a TIB or examiner; and (5) perform such other services as are in the interest of those represented.

2. OPERATING AND RESTRUCTURING THE BUSINESS

The DIP continues to operate the business of the bankruptcy estate. The common mantra "cash is king," connoting the importance of cash flow in a firm's financial health, is no truer than in insolvency and bankruptcy. Cash is the lifeblood of an operating business, but it can be dissipated or squandered. The policy is to preserve value by continuing to operate the business during bankruptcy and this requires careful cash management. The Code restricts how the business operates and how it uses cash to protect the interests of creditors. The trustee may enter into transactions, including the sale or lease of property of the estate, "in the ordinary course of business" and spend cash accordingly (Section 363(c)(1)), but it is significantly restricted in the use of "cash collateral" which is secured or collateral interest in cash and cash equivalent held by another entity (Section 363(c)(2)). Businesses generate cash by selling products and spend cash on expenses. "Ordinary course" would not include business decisions like entering new businesses, shutting down businesses, or selling capital assets. The DIP must get court approval through a proceeding in which all parties of interest are heard.

The DIP can sell assets, subject to court approval (Section 363(b)). Asset sale is a common strategy when a company restructures its business model. Assets are rationalized, core assets are kept, and noncore assets are sold. Asset sales can also be part of a cash management strategy.

The Code gives the DIP a number of important powers to reorganize the business, and specifically to restructure contractual obligations. When engaging in business enterprise, a firm is bound by a myriad of legal contracts establishing the debtor-creditor relationship. An important facet of the reorganization is the re-ordering of executory contracts. An executory contract is one where the obligations of the contracting parties have not been fully performed such that a failure of either party to fulfill its obligation would be considered a material breach. Subject to the court's approval and certain significant exceptions, a trustee can elect to assume, reject, or assign any executory contract (Section 365).

If the DIP rejects a contract, it breaches the contract and the contracting party becomes a creditor with a "claim" against the estate. A claim is defined as a "right to payment, whether or not such right is reduced to judgment, liquidated, unliquidated, fixed, contingent, matured, unmatured, disputed, undisputed, legal, equitable, secured, or unsecured" (Section 101(5)). Like other claims, the contracting party's claim on a rejected executory contract will likely yield a pro rata distribution on the full value of the claim in bankruptcy. On the other hand, if the DIP assumes a contract, it binds itself post-petition to the obligation of the contract. The contract is fully enforceable, including enforcement of terms for prior default and cure, and damages are payable in full by the estate (Section 365). These protections assure the contracting party that, despite the bankruptcy petition, the assumed contract is fully protected in a way that other creditors are not in the pendency of the bankruptcy. Lastly, an assumed contract may also be assigned as would be the case in the course of ordinary business. Upon an assignment, the estate no longer has liability exposure on the contract.

The DIP has additional means to reorganize the contractual, property, and financial mix of the business. Bankruptcy is not like lightening striking without notice. To insiders and others close to the firm, the looming financial storm may be seen in the distant horizon. The imminent future may result in certain asset transfers before filing. However, the Code provides that certain transfers made within a specific window period before the filing of the petition are voidable. The trustee may avoid any

---

* For example, a trustee may not assume or assign any executory contract to make a loan, or extend other debt financing or financial accommodations, to or for the benefit of the debtor, or to issue a security of the debtor (Section 365(c)(2)). Although a debtor in bankruptcy can be assisted by preexisting contractual arrangements for financing, such as an open revolver, that can otherwise be assumed post-petition, they are by operation of law terminated.

transfer of an interest of the debtor in property: (1) to or for the benefit of a creditor; (2) for or on account of an antecedent debt owed by the debtor before such transfer was made; (3) made while the debtor was insolvent; (4) made on or within 90 days before the date of the filing of the petition or between 90 days and one year before the date of the filing of the petition, if such creditor at the time of such transfer was an insider; and (5) that enables such creditor to receive more than such creditor would receive if the case were a liquidation under Chapter 7, the transfer had not been made, and such creditor received payment of such debt to the extent provided by the provisions of this title (Section 547(b)).

The DIP has the power to avoid certain statutory liens. The trustee may avoid the fixing of a statutory lien on property of the debtor to the extent that such lien first becomes effective against the debtor when, among other situations: a petition is filed; the debtor becomes insolvent; and the debtor's financial condition fails to meet a specified standard (Section 545).

As seen in *Wieboldt Stores, Inc. v. Schottenstein, supra* Chapter 5, the DIP can also avoid a transfer if it is determined to be a fraudulent transfer. The trustee may avoid any transfer of an interest of the debtor in property, or any obligation incurred by the debtor, that was made or incurred on or within two years before the date of the filing of the petition, if the debtor voluntarily or involuntarily: (1) made such transfer or incurred such obligation with actual intent to hinder, delay, or defraud any entity to which the debtor was or became, on or after the date that such transfer was made or such obligation was incurred, indebted; or (2) received less than a reasonably equivalent value in exchange for such transfer or obligation, and (i) was insolvent on the date that such transfer was made or such obligation was incurred, or became insolvent as a result of such transfer or obligation; (ii) was engaged in business or a transaction, or was about to engage in business or a transaction, for which any property remaining with the debtor was an unreasonably small capital; (iii) intended to incur, or believed that the debtor would incur, debts that would be beyond the debtor's ability to pay as such debts matured; or (iv) made such transfer to or for the benefit of an insider, or incurred such obligation to or for the benefit of an insider, under an employment contract and not in the ordinary course of business (Section 548(a)(1)).

In addition to voidable preference, statutory liens, and fraudulent transfer, a bankruptcy court may apply the doctrine of equitable subordination. The court may subordinate for purposes of distribution all or part of a creditor's claim or interest or order that any lien securing such a subordinated claim be transferred to the estate (Section 510(c)). This power is based on equitable principles in which inside or outside creditors are deemed to have inequitably transferred or encumbered property or acquired an advantageous position. For example, an insider provided a loan to a business that was significantly undercapitalized; such a loan might be subordinated as equity rather than debt.

3. PLAN OF REORGANIZATION AND CONFIRMATION

The exit out of bankruptcy is a confirmation of a plan of reorganization. A plan must contain the following (Section 1123(a)):

(1) designate classes of claim and classes of interests;
(2) specify any class of claims or interests that is not impaired under the plan;

(3) specify the treatment of any class of claims or interests that is impaired under the plan;

(4) provide the same treatment for each claim or interest of a particular class, unless the holder of a particular claim or interest agrees to a less favorable treatment of such particular claim or interest;

(5) provide adequate means for the plan's implementation;

(6) provide for the inclusion in the debtor's corporate charter of a provision prohibiting the issuance of nonvoting equity securities, and providing, as to the several classes of securities possessing voting power, an appropriate distribution of such power among such classes, including, in the case of any class of equity securities having a preference over another class of equity securities with respect to dividends, adequate provisions for the election of directors representing such preferred class in the event of default in the payment of such dividends;

(7) contain only provisions that are consistent with the interests of creditors and equity securityholders and with public policy with respect to the manner of selection of any officer, director, or trustee under the plan and any successor to such officer, director, or trustee.

The DIP has the first opportunity to propose a plan of reorganization within an exclusive 120-day period. Any party of interest, including the committee of creditors, can thereafter propose a plan. The Code permits creditors to vote on the proposed plan. As a practical matter, the consent of creditors greatly facilitates the likelihood of the court confirming the plan, which is the exit out of bankruptcy. The plan of reorganization must designate classes of claims and interests and specify the treatment of each class. Creditors then vote by class. A class of claims is deemed to have accepted a plan if such plan has been accepted by creditors that hold at least two-thirds in amount, and more than one-half in number, of the allowed claims of such class held by creditors (Section 1126(c)). Typically, the committee of creditors is actively involved in the process of securing cooperation and consent.

A positive vote does not require unanimous consent of each creditor. The holdout and the holdup problems would be too great. However, dissenting creditors in a class have a basic protection mechanism. Unless an individual creditor consents, a dissenting creditor "will receive or retain under the plan on account of such claim or interest property of a value, as of the effective date of the plan, that is not less than the amount that such holder would so receive or retain if the debtor were liquidated under Chapter 7 of this title on such date" (Section 1129(a)(7)(ii)). Thus, the valuation floor of a creditor's claim in a Chapter 11 reorganization is the liquidation value in a Chapter 7 liquidation. This means that for a plan to be confirmable a reorganization must create value greater than a liquidation.

A confirmation does not require unanimous consent of each class of creditors. In a "cramdown," the plan is confirmed over the objection of a class of creditors, who are forced to proverbially swallow the deal. This is the force of bankruptcy. The Code provides protection, however. The court shall confirm the plan "if the plan does not discriminate unfairly, and is fair and equitable, with respect to each class of claims or interests that is impaired under, and has not accepted, the plan" (Section 1129(b)(1)). Fairness and equity are achieved by the "absolute priority rule" under which a plan cannot provide compensation to junior classes unless all of the senior classes either approve the plan or are fully compensated. Secured creditors are senior claimants and have priority. With respect to unsecured creditors, the plan must provide that each holder of a claim receive or retain value equal to the allowed amount of such claim, or else the holder of any junior claim or interest will not receive or retain under the plan (Section 1129(b)(2)(B)). The claims junior to the unsecured creditors are held by the former shareholders.

During the process of proposing a plan, valuation plays a crucial role. Recall that in *In re Vanderveer Estates Holding, LLC* in *supra* Chapter 2 and *In re Pullman Const. Indus., Inc.* in *supra* Chapter 3, the valuation of the bankruptcy estates' assets was an important factor in the consideration of the plan of reorganization. In a reorganization, the bankruptcy estate is still an operating business and policy favors preserving and enhancing value in a way that a reorganized postbankruptcy business would be greater in value than a liquidation of assets and liabilities. The allocation of value to each class of creditors depends on the valuation of the business assets, which, as discussed in *supra* Chapter 3, are subject to subjective judgment and a certain degree of uncertainty. As a result, the process of proposing and consenting to a plan involves the give-and-take of the negotiation process over a range of reasonable values.

Sometimes the negotiations with creditors occur before the initiation of bankruptcy but in anticipation of it. These bankruptcies are called "prepackaged" bankruptcies. The debtor corporation, in anticipation of insolvency requiring a bankruptcy filing, will begin the process of negotiating with major creditors. The terms and conditions of the plan of reorganization are anticipated and worked out before the actual filing. Since the reorganization process involves the costs associated with any judicial proceeding and business negotiations, including delays and disruptions to the business enterprise,* the purpose of a prepackaged bankruptcy is to speed up the reorganization process by negotiating with the major creditors ahead of filing. If negotiations with all creditors can be had, the bankruptcy filing would be unnecessary; there would be a restructuring of the business through private re-ordering. However, the bankruptcy process is still needed to force other creditors who would not be in favor of a voluntary workout. Bankruptcy is required to impose the reorganization on all.

The confirmation of the plan of reorganization is the exit out of bankruptcy. When the bankruptcy court confirms the plan, the plan of reorganization binds the debtor, creditors, and equityholders (Section 1141(a)). The confirmation of a plan vests all of the property of the estate in the debtor, and "the property dealt with by the plan is free and clear of all claims and interests of creditors [and] equity securityholders" (Section 1141(b)-(c)). The corporate debtor emerges out of bankruptcy bound to a confirmed plan, free and clear of prior obligations, and engages in business enterprise once again as a financially viable going concern.

E. CASE STUDY: MARRIOTT CORPORATION

This case study involves the Marriott Corporation, which engaged in a transaction where it spun off a newly created subsidiary to shareholders. Certain legal aspects of

---

* As discussed in *supra* Chapter 4, the cost of bankruptcy can be significant. Enron paid $757 million in legal and other professional fees, and the cost of resolving Lehman Brothers' bankruptcy are likely to reach $1.5 billion. The average direct cost of bankruptcy has been calculated to be about 3 percent of total book assets, and about 10 percent to 20 percent of pre-distress market value of the firm. The indirect costs are immeasurable: for example, the indirect costs associated with managing a bankruptcy, suboptimal business decisions made in the shadow of bankruptcy, and lost opportunities due to bankruptcy.

the spinoff involving holders of convertible preferred stock are studied in this book in *supra* Chapter 6 and in *infra* Chapter 8, providing excerpts of *HB Korenaes Investments, L.P. v. Marriott Corporation*, 1993 WL 205040 (Del.Ch.). This case study presents Marriott's business situation and the spinoff transaction's effect on Marriott's bondholders.

The Marriott Corporation was founded by J.W. Marriott, Sr., in 1927. It started as a food and beverage and restaurant business and operated as a private, family-owned company. In 1953, Marriott underwent an IPO and sold about one-third of its shares. In 1956, it opened its first hotel. As of 1992, the time of the spinoff transaction, the Marriott family owned about 25 percent of the company.

In the 1970s and 1980s, the company expanded its businesses significantly, including investments in real estate. Much of the expansion was financed with debt. These investments were in response to favorable tax laws, which expired in 1986. In 1990, several years before the spinoff transaction, the real estate market collapsed. As a result, Marriott's earnings and stock price declined significantly in that year. According to the chairman's letter to shareholders in the 1991 annual report, the company strategy was to reduce long-term debt to about $2 billion by the end of 1994 through increased cash flow and asset sales.

At the time of the spinoff, Marriott's core businesses were lodging and contract services. Lodging included sales of hotel rooms and food and beverages. Contract services included services related to reservations, franchises, and facilities management. The company had a large portfolio of hard assets, which were real estate, land, and travel plaza holdings.

The following are Marriott's financial and market data. Note that some financial information and data have been modified for the purposes here, the principal modification being the consolidation of certain line items into broader categories to simplify the presentation. However, the aggregate numbers are true.

INCOME STATEMENT

IN $ MILLIONS	1991	1990	1989
Revenue			
Lodging	4,379	3,942	3,546
Contract services	3,952	3,704	3,990
Total revenue	8,331	7,646	7,536
Operating expenses			
Lodging	(4,054)	(3,703)	(3,414)
Contract services	(3,799)	(3,590)	(3,818)
Total operating expenses	(7,853)	(7,293)	(7,232)
Operating profits			
Lodging	325	239	132
Contract services	153	114	172
Total operating profits	478	353	304
Nonoperating items			
Net gain on divestiture			227
Corporate expenses	(111)	(137)	(107)
Net interest expense	(222)	(136)	(130)
Income taxes	(63)	(33)	(117)
Net income	82	47	177
Earnings per share	$ 0.80	$ 0.46	$1.58

CASH FLOW STATEMENT

IN $ MILLIONS	1991	1990	1989
Operations			
Net income	82	47	181
Depreciation and amortization	272	208	186
Working capital adjustments	117	(40)	(35)
Other items	81	160	177
Total cash from operations	552	375	509
Investing			
Asset sales	84	975	1,390
Capital expenditures	(427)	(1,094)	(1,368)
Other items	(126)	(247)	(465)
Total cash from investing	(469)	(366)	(443)
Financing			
Issue of convertible preferred stock	195	-	-
Issue of debt	815	1,317	873
Repayment of long-term debt	(1,316)	(846)	(581)
Treasury stock, net of new issues	3	(270)	(239)
Dividend payments	(27)	(27)	(26)
Total cash from financing	(330)	174	27
Net cash flow	(247)	183	93

BALANCE SHEET

IN $ MILLIONS	1991	1990
Assets		
Current assets	1,023	1,428
Property and equipment	2,485	2,774
Assets held for sale	1,524	1,274
Other assets	1,368	1,450
Total assets	6,400	6,926
Liabilities		
Current liabilities	1,335	1,637
Other liabilities	1,197	1,284
Convertible subordinated debt	210	
Longterm debt	2,979	3,598
Total liabilities	5,721	6,519
Equity		
Convertible preferred stock	200	-
Common stock, issued 105.0m shares	105	105
Additional paid in capital	35	69
Retained earnings	583	528
Treasury stock, 9.5m shares and 11.4m	(244)	(295)
Total equity	679	407

LONGTERM DEBT

IN $ MILLIONS	1991	1990
Secured notes, 8.6%, maturing through 2010	527	175
Senior notes, 9.3%, maturing through 2001	1,323	1,198
Debentures, 9.4%, maturing 2007	250	250
Revolving loans, 5.3%, maturing through 1995	676	1,780
Other notes, 7.8%, maturing through 2015	193	209
Other adjustments	10	(14)
Total long-term debt	2,979	3,598

Source: Marriott Corporation, Harvard Business School Case 9-394-085, at p. 10 (April 28, 2006).

Note: All debt rated "Baa3" by Moody's and "BBB" by S&P.

SELECTED FINANCIAL DATA

IN $ MILLIONS	1991	1990	1989	1988	1987
Sales growth rate	9%	1%	14%	13%	26%
Capital expenditure	427	1,094	1,368	1,359	1,053
Earnings per share	$ 0.80	$ 0.46	$ 1.62	$ 1.59	$ 1.40
Dividends per share	$ 0.28	$ 0.28	$ 0.25	$ 0.21	$ 0.17
Interest cover ratio	1.5 x	1.4 x	2.6 x	3.3 x	4.7 x
Senior debt rating (Moody's)	Baa3	Baa2	A3	A3	A2
Share price	$ 16.50	$ 10.50	$ 33.38	$ 31.63	$ 30.00
Price/earnings ratio	21 x	23 x	21 x	20 x	21 x
Price/book ratio	3.3 x	2.4 x	5.5 x	4.8 x	4.4 x

Source: Marriott Corporation, Harvard Business School Case 9-394-085, at p. 14 (April 28, 2006).

On October 5, 1993, Marriott announced the spinoff transaction. Under the plan, Marriott would split into two independent companies. Marriott International ("International"), a newly created wholly owned company, would hold the management and services businesses, and Host Marriott ("Host") would include much of the hard assets such as real estate, airport and tollway concessions, and other capital-intensive businesses. International would constitute the most profitable and fastest growing business segments. Under the plan, Marriott intended to spinoff International by distributing all International stock as a dividend to Marriott's common stockholders. Thus, International would become an independent company directly owned by Marriott stockholders.

Marriott's proxy statement describes International's proposed business activities as follows:

> Pursuant to existing long-term management, lease and franchise agreements with hotel owners, and [similar] . . . agreements to be entered into with Host Marriott with respect to lodging facilities and senior living properties to be owned by Host Marriott, Marriott International will operate or franchise a total of 242 Marriott full service hotels, 207 Courtyard by Marriott hotels, 179 Residence Inns, 118 Fairfield Inns and 16 senior living communities. Marriott International will also conduct the Company's food and facilities management businesses, as well as the Company's vacation timesharing operations.

The assets retained by Host have a value of several billion dollars, but they will be burdened with substantial debt and a thin margin of cash flow after debt service.

Host Marriott will retain [ownership of] most of the Company's [Marriott's] existing real estate properties, including 136 lodging and senior living properties. Host Marriott will also complete the Company's existing real estate development projects and manage the Company's holdings of undeveloped real estate. Host Marriott will seek to maximize the cash flow from . . . its real estate holdings . . . Host Marriott . . . will also be the leading operator of airport and toll-road food and merchandise concessions in the U.S., holding contracts at 68 major airports and operating concessions at nearly 100 toll-road units.

At the time of the announcement, Stephen Bollenbach, the company's chief financial officer stated:

Net cash flow of Host Marriott will be used primarily to service and retire debt. The Company does not plan to pay dividends on its common stock . . . I am very comfortable with the way Host Marriott has been structured. I believe this approach represents the best way for Marriott shareholders to unlock the value of our long-term assets. Secondly, the transaction gives Host Marriott the staying power needed if the recovery is slower than anticipated in arriving. I am convinced Host Marriott has the financial means to meet all its obligations to employees, suppliers, lenders and other stakeholders."

The company anticipated that International would be highly profitable from its inception and well positioned for future growth. Compared to Host, International was believed to be the higher growth company. International was expected to pay common stockholders the same dividend that had been paid by the pre-transaction Marriott.

According to the facts in *HB Korenaes Investments, infra* Chapter 8, after the distribution International would have had assets of $3.048 billion, long-term debt of $902 million, and shareholders' equity of $375 million, according to *pro forma* balance sheet for the quarter ending March 26, 1993. Assuming the assets that it will hold, if International had been operated as a separate company in 1992, it would have had sales of $7.787 billion, earnings before interest and corporate expenses of $331 million, and net income of $136 million. Marriott's advisor, S.G. Warburg & Company, has estimated that in 1993 International would have sales of $8.210 billion, and EBIT of $368 million.

According to its *pro forma* balance sheet as of March 26, 1993, after the special dividend distribution of International, Host would have assets of $3.796 billion, long-term debt of $2.130 billion, and shareholders' equity of $516 million. Host's *pro forma* income statement for the fiscal year ending January 1, 1993, would reflect sales of $1.209 billion, earnings before corporate expenses and interest of $152 million, interest expense of $196 million, corporate expenses of $46 million, and a net loss of $44 million.

The following table summarizes the actual and pro forma financial data provided in *HB Korenaes Investments*.

Financials breakdown of Marriott's businesses

$ million	Marriott	International	Host
	As of Jan. 1, 1993	FY 1992	FY 1992
Sale	8,722	7,787	1,209
EBIT, before corp. expense	496	331	152
EBITDA	777		
Interest expense			196
Net income	85	136	–44
	As of Jan. 1, 1993	Pro forma Mar. 26, 1993	Pro forma Mar. 26, 1993
Assets	6,560	3,048	3,796
Longterm debt	2,732	902	2,130
Convertible preferred	200		
Shareholder equity		375	516
Market capitalization	2,600		

Note: It is not clear that Marriott should equal the sum of International and Host, probably not due to corporate expenses of the parent. Some discrepancies are due to timing differences. The court does not give the necessary financial information to accurately provide the complete financial picture.

There were several stated reasons for the spinoff. The principal rationale was a divestiture of disparate businesses. Each company would be able to focus on its business and provide "pure play" investment opportunities in hotel services management and real estate. The market may be able to better value pure business lines than a company with mixed, loosely connected businesses. Since International would be spunoff largely debt free, it would have financial flexibility to develop its business. With respect to Host, the market would value the company based on potential appreciation of its real estate portfolio rather than on expected earnings, which would drag down stock price of a holding company with mixed businesses. As a result, Host would not be under pressure for earnings growth, and instead it would attract investors who would be seeking appreciation in real estate values.

With respect to Marriott's long-term debt securities, none of them had "event risk" covenants in the event of certain specified events, such as mergers and acquisitions, restructuring, asset sales, and distribution of assets. At the end of the 1980s, approximately 30 percent of bonds had "event risk" covenants.* Recall that in *Metropolitan Life Insurance Co. v. RJR Nabisco, Inc.*, the bonds held by Metropolitan Life and Jefferson Pilot did not have such a covenant, which would have precluded RJR Nabisco from engaging in an LBO transaction. An event risk covenant can protect creditors by triggering legal protections such as immediate right to redemption.

---

* Kenneth Lehn & Annette B. Poulsen, *Contractual Resolution of Bondholder-Stockholder Conflicts in Leveraged Buyouts*, 24 J. L. & Econ. 645 (1991).

QUESTIONS

1. The spinoff transaction is simple in concept. Before the transaction, Marriott ("M") was held by shareholders. Marriott held two business units, International ("I") and Host ("H"). Accordingly, shareholders of M indirectly held H and I by ownership of M. After the spinoff transaction, shareholders directly held stocks in H and I. The assets were simply partitioned into formal entities. One way to look at this transaction is: M = I + H. Either pre-transaction or post-transaction, shareholders would ultimately own the same assets. What was Marriott's business strategy for increasing firm value (and therefore shareholder value) from this reshuffling of assets and ownership such that (M < H + I)?

2. With respect to bondholders, in what way is the spinoff transaction in Marriott similar to situations in *Metropolitan Life Insurance Co. v. RJR Nabisco, Inc.* and *Sharon Steel Corp. v. Chase Manhattan Bank, N.A.*?

3. What are some of the financial measures and indicators that would have concerned Marriott's creditors even before the spinoff?

4. Set aside any claims that the bondholders may have had under federal securities laws. Assess the merit of other potential claims that the bondholders may argue in this situation.

CHAPTER
8

CONVERTIBLE SECURITIES

Convertible securities are securities that give the holder an option to convert the security into some other security (most typically common stock). The typical convertible securities are bonds and preferred stocks, which are both senior to common stock. The holder of a convertible has an option to move down the order of priority to become a common stockholder. Convertible securities have specific uses that satisfy the needs of issuers and holders. A prominent use of convertible securities is in the field of venture capital where financial investors want the flexibility of having priority position relative to the common stock and at the same time the option to become a common stockholder when the invested company's value exceeds the value of the straight bond or preferred stock.

Convertible securities are creatures of contract. The financial contract provides the specific terms of conversion and, depending on how it is drafted, the extent to which the conversion right can be protected, altered, or negated.

A. CONVERTIBLE SECURITIES FINANCING

1. BRIEF INTRODUCTION TO CALL OPTION

A convertible security contains within it a call option. Options are a part of a family of financial instruments called derivatives, which are studied in greater depth in the next chapter. However, to understand convertible securities, some knowledge of a call option is needed.

A call option is a contract wherein an issuer sells for a premium an option giving the holder the right, but not the obligation (thus an option), to buy from the issuer a specified asset at a fixed exercise price before or on a specified maturity date. In the context of a convertible security, the security converts into common stock. With this in mind, assume that the exercise price is $100 and at maturity the common stock is worth $150 in the market. Clearly, the holder of the option should rationally exercise the option and buy the common stock for $100, which sells on the open market for $150. On the other hand, if the common stock sells on the market at $50, the holder would not rationally exercise the option and buy the stock for $100 since the common stock can be acquired on the market for only $50.

The profit and loss profile of a call option has a unique shape that is defined by the relationship between the market value of the asset price (common stock) and exercise price. Below is the profit profile of a call option.

Value of Call Option

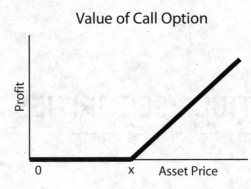

The option is "in-the-money" only when the asset price S exceeds the exercise price X. If S is less than X, the option will not be rationally exercised and so there will be no profit from exercising. The potential for profit is theoretically unlimited since S is not capped by any artificial boundary (this can be changed by contract, which could cap the potential upside by a defined amount). Here is a simple way to think about a call option: The holder of the option has a contractual right, but not an obligation, to purchase common stock at a fixed exercise price, and this option is profitable only if the value of the common stock is greater than the exercise price such that the holder can buy the common stock at a cheaper price through the conversion than the prevailing market price.

There is a direct relationship between a call option and a convertible security. The securityholder has a right to convert the security from debt or preferred stock into common stock at a contractually fixed conversion rate. The essential nature of this conversion right is a call option.

2. BASIC CHARACTERISTICS OF CONVERTIBLE SECURITIES

Convertible securities have two sets of rights. The first is a straight security defined as the right to an interest or dividend rate and the principal or liquidation value. Second, the security has an embedded call option in which the holder can acquire common stock at a fixed price.

Given these two sets of rights, the value of a convertible security is the combination of the value of the straight security and the value of the conversion right (the option).

Value of Straight Security

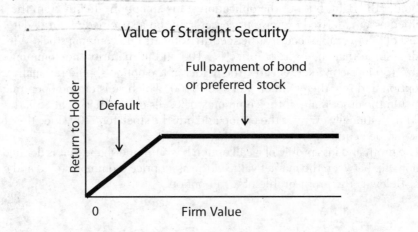

The accompanying graph shows that the value of the straight security is fixed by the interest rate and principal in the case of a bond, and the dividend and liquidation preference in the case of a preferred stock. This value declines only if the company defaults and cannot make the full payment on the fixed portion of the security. Otherwise, the return on the full payment of the bond or preferred stock is fixed by contract.

Value of Conversion

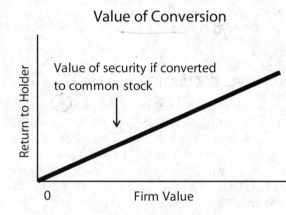

The graph presented here shows that, starting from zero value, the option value of the conversion increases without bound as the firm value increases. However, it is important to understand that only at a certain point does the option value equal the value of the straight bond. In other words, if the value of the straight security is 100 and the option value of the conversion is only 50, it would make no sense to convert the security into common stock. Only when the conversion value is greater than 100 would a security-holder be rational in converting the straight security into common stock.

Therefore, the value of the convertible security combines the above returns in a single security. This value can be depicted as shown in the following graph.

Value of Convertible Security

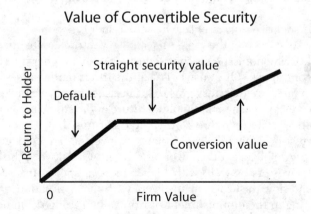

A variant of the convertible security is a bond or preferred stock with attached warrants. A warrant is an option, issued by the company, to purchase common stock at a fixed exercise price. There is an important distinction between an option and a warrant. An option transaction that does not involve the issuer does not result in the issuance of additional shares of common stock. If the holder of the option exercises against the seller, the latter must submit the shares of common stock, which if not owned must be purchased on the open market of shares already issued and trading in the market (only the issuing company can issue shares). On the other hand, if a holder of a warrant exercises against the issuer, the issuer issues stock to fulfill its obligation, which would increase the number of common stock outstanding. A bond or preferred stock with attached warrants is the issuance of two securities—a straight security plus an attached warrant—whereas a convertible security has both set of rights combined in a single security.

3. USES OF CONVERTIBLE SECURITIES

All else being the same, such as creditworthiness and terms, a convertible security has lower interest or dividend rate than a straight security. This is obvious since the convertible security has an equity-linked option that has value. Therefore, a bad reason for issuing convertible securities is that it is "cheaper" than straight debt securities. This is not so, because while the interest or dividend payments may be lower, the equity has a cost to the issuer. Ex post, if the company had to issue stock at a price much lower than market rates due to the conversion right, the issuance of stock would become very expensive. Like the value of all other securities, the convertible security is cheap to the issuer only if it has been overvalued by the investor and thus mispriced.

Another bad reason to issue convertible securities is that the issuance is considered a delayed, necessary equity issuance. The thought here is that the issuance of bond or preferred stock at a current "cheap" price is actually a necessary issuance of a more expensive common stock in the future. The problem with this rationale is that the conversion right is an option. It belongs to the holder, and the holder will only convert if the conversion makes economic sense, *i.e.*, the conversion price is cheap relative to the stock price to the holder at the time of conversion. The delayed common stock issuance may or may not occur, and so the issuance of convertible securities is an unreliable method of issuing common stock if the financing needs require a common stock issue.

A convertible security makes sense when the issuer is a more speculative firm, but not so risky or cash-starved in the mold of a startup venture capital investment. If the firm is more risky, why not issue straight securities with a higher interest or dividend rate to account for the risk? One answer is that the risk is hard to assess and thus hard to price at a fixed rate. Another answer is that the issuer may have uncertain cash flow or may prefer to preserve cash for anticipated future outlays. The issuer can make fixed income payments, unlike many venture capital startups, but it prefers to keep the payment of interest or dividends low. As long as investors are compensated through the equity link, they will accept the lower rate. Counterintuitively, the lower rate may actually benefit investors as well; with higher rates, a speculative enterprise has a higher risk of entering the "zone of insolvency." Such a situation creates perverse incentives resulting in the diminishment of firm value through common stockholder opportunism, the cost of which would deduct from the value of the straight security (*see supra* Chapter 7, *Credit Lyonnais Bank Nederland, N.V. v. Pathe Comm'n Corp.*).

Although the issuer is more risky, a higher interest or dividend rate may not be assessable or optimal in some circumstances. If so, the additional form of

590

compensation must come in the form of equity participation in the upside of the issuer. Why not simply issue common stock then? Common stock is the riskiest form of security, and thus it is the most expensive. A convertible security is cheaper than common stock. The conversion feature provides compensation to the holder, but is not a certain issuance of common stock. There is no common stock issuance if the firm does not realize its upside. From the investor's perspective, since the security-holder has an equity link, the risk of shareholder opportunism is reduced. Furthermore, if the firm increases in value, it enjoys the benefit of assuming a risk that was difficult to assess ex ante.

4. NATURE OF THE CONVERSION RIGHT

The right in a convertible security is the right to convert the bond or preferred stock into common stock based on a defined conversion ratio, which determines the conversion price at which a specific sum of bond or preferred stock is converted into one share of common stock. The conversion right must be precisely stated in the security instrument.

The ratio at which the convertible security is converted into common stock is called the conversion ratio. Consider, for example, an 8 percent bond with a face value of $1,000, maturing in 10 years. The bond can be converted into 25 shares of common stock, which is the conversion ratio. The conversion price is the value of the bond that the bondholder must surrender to acquire one share of common stock, which in this case is calculated as: $1,000/25 shares = $40.

Revised Model Simplified Indenture, Article 10 Conversion

Section 10.01. **Conversion right and conversion price**

A Holder of a Security may convert it into Common Stock at any time during the period stated in paragraph 9 of the Securities [text of which is provided below]. The number of shares issuable upon conversion of a Security is determined as follows: Divide the Principal amount to be converted by the conversion price in effect on the conversion date. Round the result to the nearest 1/100th of a share.

The initial conversion price is stated in paragraph 9 of the Securities. The conversion price is subject to adjustment in accordance with this Article.

A Holder may convert a portion of a Security if the portion is $1000 or a whole multiple of $1000. Provisions of this Indenture that apply to conversion of all of a Security also apply to conversion of a portion of it.

"Common Stock" means the Common Stock of the Company as such Common Stock exists on the date of this Indenture.

* * *

9. *Conversion.* A holder of a Security may convert it into Common Stock of the Company at any time before the close of business on [date]. If a Security is called for redemption, the holder may convert it at any time before the close of business on the Business Day prior to the redemption date (unless the redemption date is an interest record date in which event it may be converted through the record date). The initial conversion price is $_____ per share, subject to adjustment in certain events. In certain circumstances the right to convert a Security into

---

Common Stock may be changed into a right to convert it into securities, cash or other assets of the Company or another.

To determine the number of shares issuable upon conversion of a Security, divide the principal amount to be converted by the conversion price in effect on the conversion date. On conversion no payment or adjustment for interest will be made. The Company will deliver a check for cash in lieu of any fractional share.

To convert a Security a Holder must comply with Section 10.02 of the Indenture, which requires the Holder to (1) complete and sign the conversion notice on the back of the Security, (2) surrender the Security to a Conversion Agent, (3) furnish appropriate endorsements and transfer documents if required by the Paying Agent or Conversion Agent, (4) pay any transfer or similar tax if required, and (5) provide funds, if applicable, required pursuant to Section 10.02 of the Indenture. A holder may convert a portion of a Security if the portion is $1000 or a whole multiple of $1000.

B. TERMS AND RIGHTS OF CONVERTIBLE SECURITIES

1. ANTIDILUTION AND ANTIDESTRUCTION

Convertible securities typically have antidilution and antidestruction provisions that protect the holder from dilution and destruction of the conversion right through various transactions that increase the number of outstanding shares or distribute assets to common stockholders.

Revised Model Simplified Indenture, Article 10 Conversion

Section 10.06. **Adjustment for change in capital stock**

If the Company:

(1) pays a dividend or makes a distribution on its Common Stock in shares of its Common Stock;

(2) subdivides its outstanding shares of Common Stock into a greater number of shares;

(3) combines its outstanding shares of Common Stock into a smaller number of shares;

(4) makes a distribution on its Common Stock in shares of its capital stock other than Common Stock; or

(5) issues by reclassification of its Common Stock any shares of its capital stock,

then the conversion privilege and the conversion price in effect immediately prior to such action shall be proportionately adjusted so that the Holder of a Security thereafter converted may receive the aggregate number and kind of shares of capital stock of the Company that the Holder would have owned immediately following such action if the Security had converted immediately prior to such action.

Each adjustment contemplated by this Section 10.06 shall become effective immediately after the record date in the case of a dividend or distribution and immediately after the effective date in the case of a subdivision, combination or reclassification.

If after an adjustment a Holder of a Security upon conversion of it may receive shares of two or more classes of capital stock of the Company, the Board, acting in good faith, shall determine the allocation of the adjusted conversion price among the classes of capital stock. After such allocation, the conversion privilege and the conversion price of each class of capital stock shall thereafter be subject to adjustment on terms comparable to those applicable to Common Stock in this Article. The term "Common Stock" shall thereafter apply to each class of capital stock and the Company shall enter into such supplemental Indenture, if any, as may be necessary to reflect such conversion privilege and conversion price.

The adjustment contemplated by this Section 10.06 shall be made successively whenever any of the events listed above shall occur.

Section 10.07. Adjustment for rights issue

If the Company distributes any rights, options or warrants to all holders of its Common Stock entitling them for a period expiring within 60 days after the record date mentioned below to subscribe for or purchase shares of Common Stock at a price per share less than the current market price per share on that record date, the conversion price shall be adjusted in accordance with the following formula:

$$C^* = C \times \frac{O + \dfrac{N \times P}{M}}{O + N}$$

where:

C* = the adjusted conversion price.
C = the current conversion price.
O = the number of shares of Common Stock outstanding on the record date.
N = the number of additional shares of Common Stock subject to such rights, options or warrants.
P = the offering price per share of the additional shares.
M = the current market price per share of Common Stock on the record date.

The adjustment contemplated by this Section 10.07 shall be made successively whenever any such rights, options or warrants are issued and shall become effective immediately after the record date for the determination of stockholders entitled to receive the rights, options or warrants. If at the end of the period during which such rights, options or warrants are exercisable, not all rights, options or warrants shall have been exercised, the conversion price shall immediately be readjusted to what it would have been if "N" in the above formula had been the number of shares actually issued.

Section 10.08. Adjustment for other distributions

If the Company distributes to all holders of its Common Stock any of its assets (including, but not limited to, cash), debt securities or other securities or any rights, options or warrants to purchase assets, debt securities or other securities of the Company, the conversion price shall be adjusted in accordance with the following formula:

$$C^* = C \times \frac{M - F}{M}$$

where:

C* = the adjusted conversion price.

C = the current conversion price.

M = the current market price per share of Common Stock on the record date mentioned below.

F = the fair market value on the record date of the assets, securities, rights, options or warrants applicable to one share of Common Stock. Fair market value shall be determined in good faith by the Board, *provided* that the Company shall obtain an appraisal or other valuation opinion in support of the Board's determination from an investment bank or accounting firm of recognized national standing if the aggregate fair market value exceeds $[X] million.

The adjustment contemplated by this Section 10.08 shall be made successively whenever any such distribution is made and shall become effective immediately after the record date for the determination of stockholders entitled to receive the distribution.

This Section 10.08 does not apply to cash dividends or cash distributions paid in any fiscal year out of consolidated net income of the Company for the current fiscal year or the prior fiscal year, as shown on the books of the Company prepared in accordance with generally accepted accounting principles. Also, this Section does not apply to rights, options or warrants referred to in Section 10.07.

Section 10.09. Adjustment for common stock issue

If the Company issues shares of Common Stock for a consideration per share less than the current market price per share on the date the Company fixes the offering price of such additional shares, the conversion price shall be adjusted in accordance with the following formula:

$$C^* = C \times \frac{O + \dfrac{P}{M}}{A}$$

where:

C* = the adjusted conversion price.

C = the current conversion price.

O = the number of shares of Common Stock outstanding on the record date.

P = the aggregate consideration received for the issuance of such additional shares.

M = the current market price per share of Common Stock on the record date.

A = the number of shares of Common Stock outstanding immediately after the issuance of such additional shares.

The adjustment contemplated by this Section 10.09 shall be made successively whenever any such issuance is made and shall become effective immediately after the record date for the determination of stockholders entitled to receive such additional shares of Common Stock.

This Section 10.09 shall not apply to:

(1) any of the transactions described in Sections 10.07 and 10.08;

(2) the conversion of the Securities or the conversion or exchange of other securities convertible into or exchangeable for Common Stock;

(3) the issuance of Common Stock upon the exercise of rights, options or warrants issued to the holders of Common Stock;

(4) the issuance of Common Stock to the Company's employees under bona fide employee benefit plans adopted by the Board, and approved by the holders of Common Stock when required by law, but only to the extent that the aggregate number of shares excluded by this clause (3) and issued after the date of this Indenture shall not exceed 5% of the Common Stock outstanding as of the date of this Indenture;

(5) the issuance of Common Stock to stockholders of any Person that merges into the Company in proportion to their stock holdings of such Person immediately prior to such merger, upon such merger;

(6) the issuance of Common Stock in a bona fide public offering pursuant to a firm commitment underwriting; or

(7) the issuance of Common Stock in a bona fide private placement through a placement agent that is a member firm of the National Association of Securities Dealers, Inc. (except to the extent that any discount from the current market price shall exceed 20% of the then current market price).

Section 10.10. Adjustment for convertible securities issue

If the Company issues any securities, rights, options or warrants convertible into or exchangeable for Common Stock (other than the Securities or securities issued in transactions described in Sections 10.07, 10.08 and 10.09) for a consideration per share of Common Stock initially deliverable upon conversion or exchange of such securities less than the current market price per share on the date of issuance of such securities, the conversion price shall be adjusted in accordance with the following formula:

$$C^* = C \times \frac{O + \dfrac{P}{M}}{O + D}$$

where:

C^* = the adjusted conversion price.

C = the current conversion price.

O = the number of shares of Common Stock outstanding on the record date.

P = the aggregate consideration received for the issuance of such securities.

M = the current market price per share of Common Stock on the record date.

D = the maximum number of shares of Common Stock deliverable upon conversion or exchange of such securities at the initial conversion or exchange rate.

The adjustment contemplated by this Section 10.10 shall be made successively whenever any such issuance is made and shall become effective immediately after the record date for the determination of stockholders entitled to receive such securities, rights, options or warrants. If at the end of the period during which such securities, rights, options or warrants are convertible into or exchangeable for Common Stock, not all such securities, rights, options or warrants shall have been so converted or exchanged, the conversion price shall immediately be readjusted to what it would have been if "D" in the above formula had been the number of shares actually issued upon conversion or exchange.

This Section 10.10 shall not apply to:

(1) the issuance of convertible securities to stockholders of any Person that merges into the Company, or with a subsidiary of the Company, in proportion to

their stock holdings of such Person immediately prior to such merger, upon such merger;

(2) the issuance of convertible securities in a bona fide public offering pursuant to a firm commitment underwriting; or

(3) the issuance of convertible securities in a bona fide private placement through a placement agent that is a member firm of the National Association of Securities Dealers, Inc. (except to the extent that any discount from the current market price shall exceed 20% of the then current market price).

Section 10.11. Current market price

In Sections 10.07, 10.08, 10.09 and 10.10, the current market price per share of Common Stock on any date shall be the average of the Quoted Prices of the Common Stock for the five consecutive trading days selected by the Company commencing not more than 20 trading days before, and ending not later than, the earlier of (i) the date of such determination and (ii) the day before the "ex" date with respect to the issuance or distribution requiring such computation. The "Quoted Price" of a security shall be the last reported sales price of such security as reported by the New York Stock Exchange or, if the security is listed on another securities exchange, the last reported sales price of such security on such exchange which shall be for consolidated trading if applicable to such exchange, or as reported by the Nasdaq National Market System, or, if the security is neither so reported nor listed, the last reported bid price of the security. In the absence of one or more such quotations, the current market price shall be determined in good faith by the Board on the basis of such quotations as it considers reasonably appropriate. For the purposes of this Section 10.11, the term "ex" date, when used with respect to any issuance or distribution, shall mean the first date on which the security trades on such exchange or in such market without the right to receive such issuance or distribution.

Section 10.13. When no adjustment required

No adjustment need be made for a transaction referred to in Sections 10.06, 10.07, 10.08, 10.09 or 10.10 if Securityholders are permitted to participate in the transaction on a basis and with notice that the Board determines to be fair and appropriate in light of the basis and notice on which holders of Common Stock are permitted to participate in the transaction.

No adjustments need be made for rights to purchase Common Stock pursuant to a Company plan for reinvestment of dividends or interest.

No adjustment need be made for a change in the par value or no par value of the Common Stock.

To the extent the Securities become convertible into cash, no adjustment need be made thereafter as to the cash. Interest will not accrue on the cash.

Section 10.17. Reorganization of the company

If the Company is a party to a transaction subject to Section 5.01 or a merger that reclassifies or changes its outstanding Common Stock, the Person obligated to deliver securities, cash or other assets upon conversion of Securities shall enter into a supplemental indenture. If the issuer of securities deliverable upon conversion of Securities is an Affiliate of the surviving or transferee corporation, such issuer shall join in the supplemental indenture.

The supplemental indenture shall provide that the Holder of a Security may convert it into the kind and amount of securities, cash or other assets that such holder would have owned immediately after the consolidation, merger or transfer if the Security had been converted immediately before the effective date of the transaction. The supplemental indenture shall provide for adjustments that are as nearly equivalent as practicable to the adjustments provided for in this Article. The successor Company shall mail to Securityholders a notice briefly describing the supplemental indenture.

[If this §10.17 applies, §10.06 does not apply.]

EXAMPLE

New Stock Issue at Lower Price

Assume that a company issues new stock at a price lower than the current market price. The adjustment formula for this situation is in §10.09 of the Revised Model Simplified Indenture.

$$C^* = C \times \frac{O + \frac{P}{M}}{A}$$

where:

C^* = the adjusted conversion price.

C = the current conversion price.

O = the number of shares of Common Stock outstanding on the record date.

P = the aggregate consideration received for the issuance of such additional shares.

M = the current market price per share of Common Stock on the record date.

A = the number of shares of Common Stock outstanding immediately after the issuance of such additional shares.

Assume a $1,000 debenture with a conversion price of $20. The conversion ratio is 50, meaning that each debenture is entitled to 50 shares of common stock upon conversion. The company has 1,000 shares outstanding with a current market price of $20. Thus, at the conversion ratio of 50, the debenture converted into stock would be $1,000. The company issues 200 new shares at $15 per share. The adjusted conversion price would be:

$$C^* = \$20 \times \frac{1{,}000 \text{ shares} + \frac{\$3{,}000}{\$20}}{1{,}200 \text{ shares}} = \$19.167$$

The new conversion price is $19.167. Based on the $1,000 debenture, the conversion ratio is 52.174, meaning that each debenture is entitled to receive 52.174 shares of common stock upon conversion. The 2.174 shares is the adjustment for the fact that the company engaged in a dilutive transaction by selling discounted common stock.

Let's check the analysis formally. Assume that the company's sole liabilities are the debenture and that the company's stock price trades at book value per share. At preissue, assume the balance sheet is this:

Assets	21,000	Liabilities	1,000
		Equity	20,000

Shares outstanding	1,000
Book value per share	$ 20

At the conversion ratio of 50 shares, the conversion value is $1,000. When the company issues 200 shares at $15 per share for proceeds of 3,000, the new balance sheet is this.

Assets	24,000	Liabilities	1,000
		Equity	23,000

Shares outstanding	1,200
Book value per share	$ 19.167

The common stock offering is dilutive. The book value per share has been diluted to $19.167 per share. Based on the above formula, the conversion price adjusted to $19.167, resulting in a new conversion ratio of 52.174. If the debenture is converted, the holder would receive 52.174 shares of common stock. The total value of the conversion is $1,000 (= 52.174 × 19.167). The bondholder's conversion value has been protected from a dilutive common stock offering so long as the adjustment provision was drafted into the indenture.

The following cases analyze "antidestruction" provisions. The conversion right can be subject to defeasance through various corporate transactions. Antidestruction provisions are commonly found in convertible securities to protect the conversion right.

Wood v. Coastal States Gas Corp.

401 A.2d 932 (Del. 1979)

DUFFY, Justice:

This appeal is from an order dismissing the complaints in a consolidated class action filed by the owners of two series of [cumulative convertible preferred stock designated as "Series A" and "Series B"] in Coastal States Gas Corp. The suit is against Coastal, two of its subsidiaries and its chief executive officer. It is entirely between the owners of Coastal's preferred stock and the owners of its common stock.

A significant part of Coastal's business is the gathering, transporting and marketing of natural gas, all of which is conducted by a subsidiary, Coastal States Gas Producing Co. (Producing), also a defendant in this action. Producing, in turn, has a subsidiary, Lo-Vaca Gathering Co., another defendant, which supplies the gas to intrastate customers in Texas.

As a result of several factors associated with the "energy crisis" in the early 1970s, the wellhead price of natural gas increased significantly (from about 20¢ per 1000 cubic feet to about $2.00 for the same quantity) and Lo-Vaca was unable to honor its obligations to deliver gas to its customers at contract prices. In 1973, Lo-Vaca sought and obtained interim permission from the Railroad Commission of Texas to increase its rates; that authorization permitted Lo-Vaca to pass to its customers certain of its own cost increases. After the higher rates went into effect, a large number of Lo-Vaca industrial and municipal customers filed suits for breach of contract.

In December 1977, the Commission entered a final order denying Lo-Vaca's original petition for rate relief and, in effect, rescinding the interim order which had authorized the increase. The Commission then directed Lo-Vaca to comply with the contract rates and ordered Coastal, Producing and Lo-Vaca to refund the rate increment which had been charged to customers under the 1973 interim order. It is estimated that the refundable amount exceeds $1.6 billion which is about three times Coastal's net worth.

Given this state of affairs, with its obvious and enormous implications for a large section of Texas, settlement negotiations were undertaken and, eventually, a complex plan evolved.

[The litigation settlement agreement had two terms that are relevant to the issue in the case. First, Producing will be renamed "Valero Energy Corp." and be spun off from Coastal. Valero will consist principally of Producing's present gas utility pipeline and extraction plant operations, including Lo-Vaca, and a Texas retail gas distribution division of Coastal. Second, a trust for the benefit of the settling customers shall get 13.4 percent of the outstanding shares of the common stock of Valero.]

In addition, there will be a distribution by Coastal, in the form of an extraordinary dividend chargeable to earned surplus, to its common stockholders of the balance (86.6%) of the Valero common stock not transferred to the trust. Shareholders will receive one share of Valero for each share of Coastal common held at the time of the spin-off. It is this distribution which is at the center of this litigation between the preferred and common stockholders of Coastal. And Coastal's dividend history of annual payments to the preferred but none (with one exception) to the common suggests a reason for this. Coastal has paid regular quarterly dividends of $0.2975 per share on the $1.19 Series A and $0.4575 per share on the $1.83 Series B since each was issued. Only one dividend of $0.075 per share has been paid on the common in the last twenty years.

Coastal's Board of Directors unanimously approved the settlement. The Coastal management then submitted the plan for approval at a special meeting of its stockholders called for November 10.

Holders of the Series A and Series B preferred stock filed an action in the Court of Chancery to enjoin the special shareholders meeting. They alleged that the settlement plan breaches the "Certificate of the Designations, Preferences and Relative, Participating Optional or other Special Rights" (Certificate) of the Series A and Series B preferred stock. In essence, plaintiffs say that the plan violates their Certificate rights because the preferred will not receive any of the Valero shares, that is, the 86.6% to be distributed entirely to the Coastal common.

After a trial on the merits, the Vice Chancellor entered judgment for defendants. The Court determined that the spin-off of Producing and the distribution of Valero stock to the common stockholders of Coastal, is not a "recapitalization" within the meaning of the Certificate. (If it is, all parties concede that the preferred is entitled to participate in the distribution of the Valero shares.) The Vice Chancellor reasoned that a key phrase, "in lieu of," in the Certificate implies that the existing shares of Coastal common must be exchanged for something else before there is a "recapitalization" which creates rights in the preferred.

In pertinent part, the Certificate states:

(c)(5) [Conversion of Preferred Stock shall be subject to:] . . . In the event that the Corporation shall be *recapitalized*, . . . provision shall be made as part of the terms of such *recapitalization*, . . . so that any holder of . . . Preferred Stock may thereafter

> receive *in lieu of* the Common Stock otherwise issuable to him upon conversion of his . . . Preferred Stock, but at the conversion ratio stated in this Article . . . which would otherwise be applicable at the time of conversion, the same kind and amount of securities or assets as may be distributable upon such *recapitalization* . . . with respect to the Common Stock of the Corporation.

For most purposes, the rights of the preferred shareholders as against the common shareholders are fixed by the contractual terms agreed upon when the class of preferred stock is created. And, as to the conversion privilege, it has been said that the rights of a preferred shareholder are "least affected by rules of law and most dependent on the share contract." Richard M. Buxbaum, *Preferred Stock Law and Draftsmanship*, 42 Cal. L. Rev. 243, 279 (1954).

Our duty, then, is to construe the contract governing the preferred shares. In so doing, we employ the methods used to interpret contracts generally; that is, we consider the entire instrument and attempt to reconcile all of its provisions "in order to determine the meaning intended to be given to any portion of it."

This brings us to Section (c)(5) which plaintiffs contend is the heart of the matter. The short of it is that unless the plaintiffs can find something in this paragraph which, directly or by implication, prohibits Coastal from distributing the Valero stock to the holders of its common, without giving its preferred a right to participate therein (now or at the time of conversion), then, under our settled law, the preferred has no such right.

After noting that the "recapitalization" has no generally accepted meaning in law or accounting, the Vice Chancellor focused on the phrase, "in lieu of," as it appears in Section (c)(5) and concluded that, before the Section becomes applicable, the "Common Shares of Coastal must cease to exist and something (must) be given in lieu of them." Since the Coastal shares will continue in being after the spin-off, he concluded that the plan is not a recapitalization within the meaning of the Certificate.

Plaintiffs contend that Section (c)(5) is the key to analysis of the Certificate. They say that the settlement plan constitutes a "recapitalization" of the Coastal, which triggers the adjustment called for in that section.

Relying on the significant changes which the plan will effect in Coastal's capital structure, plaintiffs argue that there will be a recapitalization in fact and law.

Section (c)(5) contains what is typically considered to be "anti-destruction" language. Transactions listed therein a merger or consolidation, for example are the kind of events that will not merely dilute the conversion privilege by altering the number of shares of common but, rather, may destroy the conversion privilege by eliminating the stock into which a preferred share is convertible. We focus, however, on the preferred's claim of right if Coastal "shall be recapitalized."

At trial, both sides offered the testimony of experts as to what "recapitalization" means. [One expert] noted that there is not a precise or specific definition, but the term implies a "fundamental realignment of relationships amongst a company's securities" or a "reshuffling of the capital structure."

We agree with plaintiffs that the changes which the plan will bring to Coastal's financial structure are enormous. And it may be concluded that, collectively, these amount to a "reshuffling of the capital structure." But that is not the test. The critical question concerns what is said in the contract.

Section (c)(5) provides that in the event of "recapitalization" one of the provisions shall be that a holder of preferred may "thereafter" receive something. *When* he may receive it is clear: he may receive it "upon conversion" after the recapitalization has taken place. After that event, he may receive, not what he would have received *before* recapitalization; that was the common stock which was "otherwise issuable to him upon conversion." Certainly this clause is meaningless if the common share remains issuable to him *after* recapitalization. And so is the remainder of the paragraph which requires that the same conversion ratio be retained by distributing to the preferred, upon conversion, the "same kind and amount of securities or assets as may be distributable upon said recapitalization . . . with respect to the Common." The "same kind and amount" would be distributable to the common only if the common had been exchanged for something else. This was the situation the draftsman contemplated by the provision that the preferred "may receive" the "same kind and amount" of property "in lieu of the Common Stock."

Since the settlement plan does not include an exchange of the common and, given the added circumstances that the dividend or liquidated preference of the preferred is not threatened and that earned surplus is ample to support the distribution of the Valero shares to the common, the settlement plan does not include a recapitalization within the meaning of Section (c)(5).

Plaintiffs also argue that the settlement plan unjustly enriches the common shareholders at the expense of the preferred shareholders.

There is no contention that Coastal is in arrears on dividends payable to the preferred, nor is the Company in the process of dissolution. After the plan is implemented Coastal will have assets of more than $2.2 billion and a net worth of $477 million. But the significant fact is not what Coastal retains nor the extent of the "reshuffling." Any right of the preferred to participate in the Valero distribution must come from the Certificate. Because the contract is the measure of plaintiffs' right, there can be no recovery under an unjust enrichment theory independent of it.

QUESTIONS

1. Explain the significance of the term "in lieu of" in §(c)(5). What is the definition of a "recapitalization" in the drafted language of §(c)(5)?
2. What set of specific facts could have strengthened the preferred stockholder's argument to invalidate the settlement agreement or to participate in the spinoff? (Hint: see footnotes 12 and 13.)
3. Suppose drafters of the Certificate wrote §(c)(5) as follows: "In the event that the Corporation shall be recapitalized, . . . provision shall be made as part of the terms of such recapitalization, . . . so that any holder of . . . Preferred Stock may thereafter receive . . . the same kind and amount of securities or assets as may be distributable upon such recapitalization . . . with respect to the Common Stock of the Corporation." What would have been the outcome of the case? Is there an ambiguity? How might the court have attempted to resolve the ambiguity?
4. In what way was the plaintiff financially harmed? In what way could the plaintiff have participated in the spinoff of Valero without resorting to a lawsuit?

Lohnes v. Level 3 Communications, Inc.

272 F.3d 49 (1st Cir. 2001)

SELYA, Circuit Judge.

The primary issue raised in this appeal is whether the terms "capital reorganization" and/or "reclassification of stock," as used in a stock warrant, encompass a stock split. Warrantholder, Paul Lohnes, claims that a stock split effectuated by Level 3 Communications, Inc. triggered an antidilution provision in the warrant that automatically increased the number of shares of stock to which he was entitled. Level 3 resists this claim. The district court concluded that the language of the warrant could not reasonably be construed to encompass a stock split and, accordingly, granted Level 3's motion for summary judgment. We affirm.

[Through a series of transactions, Lohnes acquired] a warrant to purchase 8,541 shares of Level 3's common stock.

[Subsequently] Level 3's board of directors authorized a two-for-one stock split, to be effectuated in the form of a stock dividend granting common shareholders one new share of stock for each share held. The board set the record date as July 30, 1998. On July 20, Level 3 issued a press release announcing the stock split, but it did not provide Lohnes with personalized notice.

The split occurred as scheduled. Adhering to generally accepted accounting practices, Level 3 adjusted its balance sheet to account for the split by increasing its common stock account in the amount of $1,000,000 and reducing paid-in-capital by a like amount. These accounting entries had no net effect on either the retained earnings or the net equity of the company.

Despite the sharp reduction in the share price that accompanied the stock split, Lohnes paid no heed until approximately three months after the record date. When his belated inquiry revealed what had transpired, Lohnes contacted Level 3 to confirm that the stock split had triggered a share adjustment provision, thus entitling him to 17,082 shares (twice the number of shares specified in the warrant). Level 3 demurred on the ground that the warrant did not provide for any share adjustment based upon the occurrence of a stock split effected as a stock dividend.

Dissatisfied by Level 3's response, Lohnes exercised the warrant and received 8,541 shares of Level 3's common stock. He then sued Level 3 in a Massachusetts state court alleging breach of both the warrant and the implied duty of good faith and fair dealing.

The warrant at issue here contained a two-paragraph antidilution provision which, upon the occurrence of certain described events, automatically adjusted the number of shares to which the warrantholder would be entitled upon exercise of the warrant. In all, share adjustments were engendered by five separate contingencies: capital reorganization, reclassification of common stock, merger, consolidation, and sale of all (or substantially all) the capital stock or assets. However, the warrant did not explicitly provide for an adjustment of shares in the event of a stock split. Lohnes attempts to plug this lacuna by equating a stock split with a capital reorganization and/or a reclassification of stock. This argument brings the following paragraph of the antidilution provision into play:

> *Reorganizations and Reclassifications.* If there shall occur any capital reorganization or reclassification of the Common Stock, then, as part of any such reorganization or reclassification, lawful provision shall be made so that the Holder shall have the right

thereafter to receive upon the exercise hereof the kind and amount of shares of stock or other securities or property which such Holder would have been entitled to receive if, immediately prior to any such reorganization or reclassification, such Holder had held the number of shares of Common Stock which were then purchasable upon the exercise of this Warrant.

Building upon the premise that either "capital reorganization" or "reclassification of stock" encompasses a stock split, Lohnes concludes that Level 3's stock split activated the share adjustment mechanism set forth in the quoted paragraph.

Lohnes bears the burden of establishing the existence of a genuine issue of material fact. Given the circumstances of this case, the only way for him to succeed in this endeavor is by showing that one of the disputed terms ("capital reorganization" or "reclassification of stock") is shrouded in ambiguity, that is, that reasonable minds plausibly could reach opposite conclusions as to whether either term extended to stock splits.

Capital Reorganization

Since the warrant does not elaborate upon the meaning of "capital reorganization," we turn to other sources. Massachusetts law offers no discernible guidance.

Of interest is *Wood v. Coastal States Gas Corp.*, 401 A.2d 932 (Del. 1979). There, a corporation's preferred shareholders challenged a settlement that required the parent corporation to spin off a subsidiary and distribute a portion of the subsidiary's stock to the parent company's common shareholders. The preferred shareholders argued that the spin-off constituted a recapitalization, thereby triggering an antidilution adjustment in their stock certificates. The court rejected this argument, holding that the settlement plan did not constitute a recapitalization. This case suggests that the term "capital reorganization" is not so elastic as Lohnes claims, but it does not fully answer the question that we must decide.

Moving beyond the case law, the meaning of the term "capital reorganization" in common legal parlance seemingly belies Lohnes's ambitious definition. The preeminent legal lexicon defines "reorganization," in pertinent part, as a "general term describing corporate amalgamations or readjustments occurring, for example, when one corporation acquires another in a merger or acquisition, a single corporation divides into two or more entities, or a corporation makes a substantial change in its capital structure." *Black's Law Dict.* 1298 (6th ed. 1990). The first two prongs of this definition are clearly inapposite here. That leaves only the question of whether a stock split entails a "substantial change in [a corporation's] capital structure." We think not.

First and foremost, the accounting mechanics that accompany a stock split are mere window dressing. To be sure, a stock split effected through the distribution of shares in the form of a stock dividend results in an increase in the common stock at par account and an offsetting decrease in additional paid-in capital, but this subtle set of entries has no effect on total shareholder equity or on any other substantive aspect of the balance sheet. Because a stock split does not entail a substantial change in a corporation's capital structure, the unelaborated term "capital reorganization" cannot plausibly include a stock split effected as a stock dividend.

Reclassification of Stock

We turn next to the phrase "reclassification of stock." Two Massachusetts cases seem worthy of mention. In the first, a corporation took advantage of a new statute authorizing the issuance of preferred stock and amended its charter to divide its previously undifferentiated stock into common and preferred shares. *Page v. Whittenton Mfg. Co.,* 97 N.E. 1006 (Mass. 1912). The Massachusetts Supreme Judicial Court approved the corporation's actions. It held that a corporation could classify stock into common and preferred shares (providing preferred shareholders with cumulative dividends and a liquidation preference) so long as that classification was effected through a charter amendment.

In *Boston Safe Deposit & Trust Co. v. State Tax Comm'n,* 163 N.E.2d 637 (Mass. 1960), the court considered the tax implications of a reclassification of stock. The reclassification in question involved the partial substitution of redeemable, convertible, cumulative, nonvoting shares for nonredeemable, nonconvertible, noncumulative, voting shares. The court held that the reclassification constituted a taxable event under Massachusetts law.

Our reading of the Massachusetts cases leads us to conclude that the sine qua non of a reclassification of stock is the modification of existing shares into something fundamentally different. At the end of the day, the stockholders in *Page* held a different class of shares, while the stockholders in *Boston Safe* gained some privileges while losing the right to vote. Thus, *Page* and *Boston Safe,* respectively, illustrate two ways in which a security can be altered fundamentally: (a) by changing the class of stock, or (b) by modifying important rights or preferences linked to stock.

Stock splits effected as stock dividends do not entail any such fundamental alteration of the character of an existing security. For example, Level 3's stock split in no way altered its shareholders' proportionate ownership interests, varied the class of securities held, or revised any of the attributes associated with the stock. What is more, the stock split did not have a meaningful impact on either the corporation's balance sheet or capital structure. For those reasons, we perceive no principled basis on which to stretch the definition of "reclassification of stock" to encompass a stock split.

A rule promulgated by the Securities and Exchange Commission confirms our intuition. This rule extends the protections of the Securities Act of 1933 to shareholders who are offered securities in a business combination and are required to decide "whether to accept a new or different security in exchange for their existing security." SEC Rule 145. While the rule extends to reclassifications of stock, it explicitly exempts stock splits from the reclassification rubric. The upshot of this carve-out is unmistakable: the SEC does not consider shares received in conjunction with a stock split to constitute a "new or different security."

The Denouement

If more were needed—and we doubt that it is—the maxim *expressio unius est exclusio alterius* instructs that, "when parties list specific items in a document, any item not so listed is typically thought to be excluded." Here, the warrant's antidilution protection extended expressly to five designated contingencies: capital reorganizations, reclassification of the common stock, merger, consolidation, or sale of all (or substantially all) the capital stock or assets. Since nothing within the four corners of the warrant hints at additional contingencies, we apply this maxim and conclude that the parties intended stock splits to be excluded from the list of events capable of triggering the share adjustment machinery.

Lohnes is left, then, with his reliance on the principle of *contra proferentem*—the hoary aphorism that ambiguities must be construed against the drafter of an instrument. This reliance is mislaid. In order to invoke this principle, the proponent first must demonstrate that there is an ambiguity. Here, Lohnes has failed to show that the interpretation which he urges is, "under all the circumstances, a reasonable and practical one." Accordingly, we have no occasion to apply the principle of *contra proferentem*.

The Implied Covenant of Good Faith and Fair Dealing

Although the terms "capital reorganization" and "reclassification of stock," as they appear in the warrant, are inherently unambiguous and do not encompass stock splits, Lohnes mounts one further attack. He posits that Level 3 had a legal obligation, under the implied contractual covenant of good faith and fair dealing, to provide him with personalized, advance warning of the stock split. Lohnes further argues that Level 3 breached this obligation by failing to advise him specifically about the adverse impact that the stock split would have on the warrant if Lohnes did not exercise it before the record date. This argument lacks force.

Under Massachusetts law, every contract includes an implied duty of good faith and fair dealing. This implied covenant forbids a party from doing "anything which will have the effect of destroying or injuring the rights of the other party to receive the fruits of the contract."

The most prominent flaw in Lohnes's attempt to wield this club is that he misperceives the fruits of the bargain that he struck. After all, a warrantholder does not become a shareholder unless and until he exercises his purchase option. Consequently, a warrantholder's right to insist that the corporation maintain the integrity of the shares described in the warrant, if it exists at all, must be found in the text of the warrant itself. Put another way, the fruits of the contract were limited to those enumerated in the warrant.

An examination of the warrant reveals quite clearly that Level 3 was not contractually bound to provide Lohnes with individualized notice of the stock split. The warrant contained language stating that "until the exercise of this Warrant, the Holder shall not have or exercise any rights by virtue hereof as a stockholder of the Company." This disclaimer hardly could have been written more plainly.

In light of Lohnes's inability to show that a reasonable person plausibly could construe either "capital reorganization" or "reclassification of stock" to include stock splits, we conclude that these terms, as they appear in the warrant, were unambiguous and did not cover the contingency of a stock split effected as a stock dividend. It follows that the stock split in question here did not trip the warrant's antidilution provision. By like token, Level 3 did not breach the implied covenant of good faith and fair dealing by neglecting to give special notice beyond what the warrant itself required. The district court was correct in granting Level 3's motion for summary judgment.

QUESTION

1. Among other things, Lohnes claimed that he should have received personalized notice of the stock split (note that Level 3 provided a general notice of the stock

split). In what way could the plaintiff have prevented the financial harm to him if he was aware of the pending stock split?

NOTES

1. In an earlier opinion, *Cofman v. Acton Corp.*, 958 F.2d 494 (1st Cir. 1992), the First Circuit rejected the argument of warrant holders that they were entitled to the benefit of a stock price increase solely on the basis of a reverse stock split. A reverse stock split increases share price, and thus the warrant holder had reason to oppose an adjustment in the terms of the warrants. The warrants were issued in connection with a settlement in litigation, and they did not speak to any adjustments for a stock split and a reverse stock split. The court reasoned: "It defies common sense that [warrant holders] would have agreed that Acton could effectively escape the specified consequences of a rising market price by increasing the number of shares. And if Partnerships would not suffer from any increasing, it would follow, since a contract must be construed consistently, Restatement (Second) of Contracts, §205(5) (1981), Acton should not suffer from any decreasing." The court also seemed to distinguish the warrants as part of a litigation settlement agreement from financial instruments of the markets. In a footnote the court commented: "We do not pause over Partnership's sought analogy to convertible debentures, where the rule is that anti-dilution must be expressly stated. *Broad v. Rockwell International Corp.*, 642 F.2d 929, 940-45 (5th Cir. 1981) (en banc). These are formal, and complicated commercial structures, prepared with care for the general public. Purchasers have the bonds in any event. Here we have a simple agreement between individuals, not even assignable."

2. CONVERTIBILITY IN MERGER

Since the corporation that issued the convertible security may at some point engage in a business combination, the security instrument should provide for the disposition of the conversion right upon a merger, consolidation, or some other transaction with another corporation.

The following case analyzes the effect of a merger on the conversion right. One such situation is when the common stock contemplated in the conversion right would no longer exist as a result of the merger.

Broad v. Rockwell International Corp.
642 F.2d 929 (5th Cir. 1981) (en banc)

RANDALL, Circuit Judge:

This case turns on the construction of an indenture dated as of January 1, 1967. The Indenture governed the terms of $40,000,000 principal amount of 4⅞ Convertible Subordinated Debentures due January 1, 1987, which were issued by Collins in January 1967. United States Trust Company of New York [served] as Trustee under the Indenture.

The events that triggered this lawsuit occurred in the fall of 1973, when Rockwell International Corp. acquired Collins Radio Co. in a cash merger. The central question in the case is this: In what form did the conversion rights of the holders of the Debentures survive the merger under the terms of the Indenture?

David Broad sued Rockwell, Collins, the controlling persons of both, and the Trust Company, alleging that the defendants breached the terms of the Indenture. The district court granted a directed verdict in favor of the defendants, holding that the defendants' interpretation of the Indenture and their actions in accord with that interpretation were correct and nonactionable as a matter of state law.

We hold that the district court properly construed that document's provisions. We affirm.

In January 1967, Collins issued and sold to the public $40,000,000 aggregate principal amount of Debentures. The Debentures bore interest at the rate of 4⅞% per year and matured on January 1, 1987, unless sooner redeemed by Collins. They were convertible, at the option of the holders thereof, into the common stock of Collins ("Collins Common Stock"), which had a par value of $1 per share. The Debentures were offered to the public through an underwriting syndicate managed by two New York investment banking firms Kidder, Peabody & Co. and White, Weld & Co.

At the time the Debentures were marketed in 1967, Collins was a prosperous enterprise chiefly engaged in the development and production of radio communications and aircraft navigation equipment. During the period immediately before the offering of the Debentures, Collins Common Stock had traded on the New York Stock Exchange for approximately $60 per share. If a holder of Debentures were to choose to exercise his conversion privilege, Collins would issue to him, in exchange for his Debentures, one share of Collins Common Stock for every $72.50 principal amount of Debentures. This meant that conversion might become economically attractive if the market price of Collins Common Stock rose more than $12.50 over its market price of $60 per share at the time of the offering of the Debentures.

Beginning in its 1969 fiscal year, however, Collins suffered a series of economic reversals, manifested by declining sales and reduced income. In the midst of a generally declining stock market, Collins' fading fortunes did not go unnoticed: during the 1971 calendar year, Collins Common Stock never traded on the New York Stock Exchange at more than $21 per share, and in the fourth quarter of that year it was selling for as little as $9.75 per share. Collins was on the verge of bankruptcy. It was at that point, however, that Collins became affiliated with Rockwell.

In August 1971, Collins shareholders overwhelmingly approved the terms of an agreement by which Rockwell invested $35,000,000 in Collins, receiving in return two new series of Collins securities: preferred stock that was convertible into Collins class A common stock, and warrants to purchase additional class A common stock. As sole holder of the new issue of preferred stock, Rockwell also received, and soon exercised, the right to elect a majority of Collins' board of directors.

In August [1973], Rockwell made a tender offer for Collins Common Stock, offering the shareholders $25 cash per share tendered. As part of the offer, Rockwell disclosed that if the offer were successful, it intended to propose a merger of Collins into Rockwell at that same figure of $25 per share. The tender offer was successful, and Rockwell had acquired approximately 75% of the outstanding Collins Common Stock.

In accordance with the intentions it had stated prior to the tender offer, Rockwell with Collins duly entered into an Agreement and Plan of Merger (the "Merger Plan"), which provided that on the effective date of the merger, each holder of Collins Common Stock (other than Rockwell itself, of course) would receive $25 per share in cash upon surrender of the certificates evidencing such stock. The Merger Plan was approved by the vote of approximately 84.5% of the Collins Common Stock. The merger was effected on November 14, 1973, and from that date until the present Collins has operated only as an internal division of Rockwell.

The first significant activities of the Trust Company came in the fall of 1973 when the Trust Company was called upon to consider whether the terms of a proposed supplemental indenture to be executed by Rockwell, as successor by merger to the obligations of Collins under the Indenture, complied with the terms of the Indenture. Under that supplemental indenture, Rockwell would assume in full all of the obligations of Collins under the Indenture, including the obligation to pay interest, and eventually to repay the principal, on the outstanding Debentures until they either were redeemed or matured in 1987. With regard to the conversion feature of the Debentures, the proposed supplemental indenture provided that each holder of a Debenture would have the right to convert his Debenture into the amount of cash (not stock) that would have been payable to him under the Merger Plan had he converted his Debenture into Collins Common Stock immediately prior to the merger. In other words, a holder of Debentures could, at any time while his Debentures were outstanding, choose to convert them into exactly that which he would have received had he converted immediately before the merger and participated therein as a holder of Collins Common Stock. Because the holders of Collins Common Stock received no common stock in the merger, the holders of Debentures would have no right to convert into common stock either of Collins (who would have no more common stock) or of Rockwell after the merger. Rockwell's view of its post-merger obligations under the Indenture was shared by its counsel, and by Collins and Collins' counsel.

In order to determine whether the proposed terms of the supplemental indenture complied with the terms of the Indenture, the Trust Company engaged the New York law firm of Curtis, Mallet-Prevost, Colt & Mosle. Two partners in that firm John Campbell and John Marden undertook a review of the Indenture and the applicable law. Campbell and Marden took the position in September 1973 that a court might in the future find that the intent of the parties at the time the Indenture was executed was that *the right to convert into common stock would survive a merger of Collins into another company*, and that every holder of Debentures would have the right to convert his Debentures into common stock of the surviving company as long as the Debentures remained outstanding. Since the Indenture required that Rockwell assume all of Collins' obligations under the Indenture in the event of a merger, Campbell and Marden contended that Rockwell would be bound to agree in a supplemental indenture with terms providing for a conversion right of the Debentures into the common stock of Rockwell ("Rockwell Common Stock"), unless Rockwell could obtain the consent of each holder of Debentures that such a right could be extinguished. Furthermore, they contended, Rockwell's voting control of Collins prior to the merger imposed upon Rockwell and the directors of Collins a fiduciary obligation to the holders of Debentures.

On October 11, 1973, Rockwell sent a letter to the holders of the Debentures to notify them of the proposed merger between Rockwell and Collins. The text of the letter read as follows:

> Rockwell International Corporation ("Rockwell") has proposed the merger of Collins Radio Company ("Collins") into Rockwell. Pursuant to the terms of the proposed merger Rockwell would assume all of Collins obligations, including Collins obligations under the Indenture, dated as of January 1, 1967, relating to Collins 4⅞ Convertible Subordinated Debentures due January 1, 1987 (respectively the "Indenture" and the "Debentures").
>
> Rockwell and United States Trust Company of New York, the Successor Trustee under the Indenture (the "Trustee"), intend to execute a Supplemental Indenture to the Indenture on or about November 1, 1973. This Supplemental Indenture is to be effective on the effective date of the merger of Collins into Rockwell and will provide for the assumption by Rockwell of the due and punctual payment of the principal of and interest on the Debentures and the due and punctual performance and observance by Rockwell of all the terms, covenants and conditions of the Indenture. *The Supplemental Indenture does not alter or impair the rights accorded under the Indenture to holders of the Debentures and does not change the provisions of the Indenture.*
>
> With regard to the conversion rights of holders of the Debentures, counsel for Rockwell and counsel for Collins have each advised that *under Section 4.11 of the Indenture,* the Section that provides for the adjustment of conversion rights upon a merger or similar event, *a holder of a Debenture, upon effectiveness of the proposed merger, would have the right, until the expiration of the conversion right of such Debenture, to convert the Debenture into the amount of cash that would have been payable with respect to the number of shares of Collins Common Stock into which the Debenture could have been converted immediately prior to effectiveness of the proposed merger.* The current conversion price of $72.50 entitles the holder of a $1,000 Debenture to convert it into 13.79 shares of Collins Common Stock. Pursuant to the merger each share of Collins Common Stock outstanding immediately prior to the merger (other than those held by Rockwell) is to be converted into $25. *Thus, after the merger, a $1,000 Debenture will be convertible into $344.75 in cash.*
>
> *The Trustee has advised that it does not take a position with regard to this letter or the statements herein,* and that it has consulted with its counsel who confirmed that as Trustee it should not take a position with regard thereto.
>
> Neither the proposed merger nor the proposed Supplemental Indenture requires action by the Debentureholders. Upon effectiveness of the merger, the Debentures will represent indebtedness of Rockwell. You will not need to surrender or exchange your Debentures for new debentures.

On November 14, 1973, the merger was effected, and a supplemental indenture between Rockwell and the Trust Company was executed, effective as of November 1, 1973. The supplemental indenture provided that Rockwell would assume Collins' obligations on the Debentures. Specifically, it provided that after the merger, the holders of the Debentures had the right to convert the debentures into that which they would have received in the Merger Plan had they converted immediately before the merger's effective date. Rockwell has consistently interpreted this to mean that the Debentures could be converted into cash, but not into the common stock of either Rockwell or Collins; the conversion rate was $344.75 in cash for each $1000 in principal amount of Debentures surrendered.

Conversion Rights at Common Law and the Need for Contractual Antidilution Provisions

In the case at bar, there are specific portions of the Indenture that set out the rights of the holders of the Debentures, and the obligations of the Trustee and issuer, in the event that the issuer is merged into another company. Nonetheless, the common law's treatment of conversion rights upon merger is important in this case in two different respects. First, it must be determined whether the common law provides the holders of the Debentures with rights in addition to the rights that are set out in the Indenture. Second, an understanding of the common law's treatment of conversion rights upon merger explains the historical development of boilerplate contractual antidilution provisions of the sort found in the Indenture.

The American Bar Foundation's *Commentaries on Indentures* explain in brief the possible dangers to the conversion rights of the holders of debentures that might attend certain actions by the issuer of the debentures:

> The anti-dilution provisions are designed to preserve the value of the conversion privilege against diminution by certain voluntary corporate acts. For example, if the conversion price is $25 a share at a time when the common stock has a market value of $30 a share, the conversion right is clearly valuable. If the Company should then split its stock 3 for 1, the market price of its shares would be reduced to approximately $10 per share. Thus the value of the right to convert at $25 per share would have been virtually destroyed, by that voluntary corporate action, in the absence of appropriate protective provisions.
>
> Inasmuch as ownership of a convertible debenture does not give the holder the rights of a shareholder, the holder of a convertible debenture would have almost no protection against acts by the Company which would adversely affect the value of the common stock issuable on conversion, such as a split-up of shares, stock dividends, distribution of assets, issuance or sale of other convertible securities, issuance of options, issuance or sale of common stock at prices below the current conversion or market price, merger, sale of assets or dissolution and liquidation of the Company. Events of this type are customarily described as "diluting" the value of the conversion privilege, and *if protection is desired against such dilution, appropriate provisions must be included in the indenture.*

As justification for the phrase we have italicized above, the *Commentaries* cite *Parkinson v. West End Street Railway Co.*, 53 N.E. 891 (Mass. 1899) (per Holmes, J.).

Justice Holmes' decision in *Parkinson* was aptly cited by the authors of the *Commentaries* for the proposition that antidilution protection must be provided by contract if it is to be provided at all, for Parkinson holds that there is no such protection at common law. The plaintiff in *Parkinson* held Highland Street Railway bonds that were convertible into Highland's preferred stock. When West End Street Railway acquired Highland "subject to all (of Highland's) duties, restrictions, and liabilities," the existing holders of Highland's preferred stock received West End preferred stock or preemptive rights thereto in exchange for their Highland stock. West End refused, however, to convert the Highland bonds into West End preferred stock. The Massachusetts Supreme Court denied relief:

> (T)he contract does not prevent the corporation from consolidating with another in such a way as to make performance impossible, any more than it prevents the issue of new stock in such a way as to make performance valueless. . . . A consolidation which

makes no arrangement for furnishing stock in the new company, and which ends the existence of the old ones, as a general rule may be presumed to put an end to the right of bondholders to call for stock, not because the law has not machinery for keeping such a right alive, but because, not being bound to do so, it has made dispositions which manifestly take no account of it.

Thus, according to *Parkinson*, mergers may extinguish all conversion rights, absent explicit contractual provisions to the contrary.

Broad has cited no persuasive authority which would indicate that the common law of New York or of any other jurisdiction would provide any additional protection for his conversion rights upon merger, other than that protection which might be included in the Indenture. But the common law cases cited by the parties do shed light on the origin of and need for boilerplate antidilution provisions of the sort at issue here.

Holders of debentures were charged at common law with the knowledge that various voluntary corporate actions might dilute or even render nugatory the value of their debentures' conversion feature; because dilution was (at least constructively) within their contemplation when they purchased the security, there was no unfairness in denying the holders of debentures any compensation in the event of such dilution. But of course, even before the occurrence of a diluting event, this risk of dilution itself significantly diminished the value of the conversion feature. As Justice Holmes noted in *Parkinson*, however, the law does have machinery through which, if the parties so choose, the value of the conversion right may be protected. The draftsmen of indentures may guard against dilution through the insertion of any of three types of special contractual provisions.

The first and most drastic type of provision is the outright prohibition of certain types of voluntary corporate conduct. Such prohibitory covenants are more typically used to protect the value of the debt obligation represented by the debenture. But prohibitory covenants may also be used to protect the value of the conversion feature e.g., by means of an absolute ban on mergers. The efficacy of this means of antidilution protection must be balanced against the loss of business flexibility it means for the issuer. Some sorts of corporate conduct can be limited with little loss of flexibility, but other restrictions may so hamstring the company that they threaten its continued existence.

Happily, there are two less restrictive means of antidilution protection that do not bear such high costs in terms of business flexibility, as the following excerpt from the *Commentaries* indicates:

> In modern convertible debenture indentures it is virtually universal to provide some anti-dilution protection (that provides for the adjustment of the conversion price upon the taking of specific actions by the issuer that would cause the value of the conversion right to be diluted), usually in combination with provisions (requiring advance notice to the debentureholders of such acts), plus a provision for equitable adjustment in the event of a merger or other reorganization (in which the issuer is the surviving company). However, *adjustment of the conversion price by itself cannot provide the debentureholder with protection against all events which might substantially affect the conversion privilege*. For example, when the Company is to be merged into another corporation and the Company's common stock is to be replaced by convertible preferred stock or debentures of the surviving corporation, adjustment of the conversion price would not provide adequate protection. *Thus it is now customary*

> *to provide that the debentureholder will be given the right to convert his debentures into whatever securities are to replace the common stock of the Company.*

While the common law's treatment of conversion rights in the event of merger provides a useful background, and while various antidilution provisions promulgated by the American Bar Foundation and the commentators are useful for purposes of comparison, the resolution of this case ultimately turns upon our construction of the specific language in the Indenture under which the Debentures were issued in 1967.

The Meaning of Section 4.11 of the Indenture

The structure of the Indenture is fairly typical of convertible debenture indentures generally. As might be expected, there is an article of the Indenture devoted wholly to the conversion rights of the holders of the Debentures, and a section within that article which addresses the possibility of a merger of Collins with another company: Article Four of the Indenture is entitled "Conversion of Debentures," and the next-to-last section of that Article, Section 4.11, is described in the Indenture's table of contents as governing the "(c)ontinuation of the conversion privilege in case of a consolidation, merger or sale of assets." We note that there is no provision in the Indenture which explicitly mandates that the holders of the Debentures should have a continuing right to convert into common stock *after a merger*. Aside from his few arguments based on the language of Section 4.11, Broad basically argues his case by implication from more general language that is not specifically addressed to the merger context. But because Section 4.11 is more specifically addressed to the merger context than any other provision of the Indenture, we begin our discussion with that particular provision, to see if the language thereof clearly and unambiguously conveys the intent of the parties.

Section 4.11 provides, in pertinent part, as follows:

> In case of any consolidation of (Collins) with, or merger of (Collins) into, any other corporation . . . , the corporation formed by such consolidation or the corporation into which (Collins) shall have been merged . . . shall execute and deliver to the (Trust Company) a supplemental indenture . . . providing that the holder of each Debenture then outstanding shall have the right (until the expiration of the conversion right of such Debenture) to convert such Debenture into the kind and amount of shares of stock and other securities and property receivable upon such consolidation (or) merger . . . by a holder of the number of shares of Common Stock of (Collins) into which such Debenture might have been converted immediately prior to such consolidation (or) merger. . . .

Parsing this section into logical units, we note that it serves two purposes. First, it specifies what the Trust Company and Collins' successor must do in the event of a merger in which Collins is not the surviving company: they must execute a supplemental indenture that will formally provide for the conversion rights of the holders of Debentures after the merger. There is no question in this case but that Rockwell and the Trust Company complied with this directive.

The second part of Section 4.11 provides by its terms that after the merger, the holder of each Debenture shall have the right to convert that Debenture into something but what? It cannot be Collins Common Stock, for there will be no more of that after the merger. It therefore must be something else other than Collins

Common Stock. The *nature* of the "something else" into which the holder of a Debenture can convert his Debenture is specified by reference to what the holders of the Collins Common Stock received in the merger: he can convert into the kind of "shares of stock and other securities and property" that the holders of Collins Common Stock received as part of the Merger Plan. Thus, if the holders of Collins Common Stock had received Rockwell Common Stock in the merger in exchange for giving up their shares of Collins Common Stock, the holders of Debentures would have been entitled, at any time after the merger for so long as their Debentures were outstanding, to convert into Rockwell Common Stock. Alternately, if the holders of Collins Common Stock had received Rockwell debentures in exchange for their Collins Common Stock, the holders of the Debentures would have been entitled to convert into Rockwell debentures.

Broad suggests that the use of the conjunctive "and" in Section 4.11 ("shares of stock and other securities *and* property") means that in every instance of a merger, the holders of the Debentures would be entitled to receive all three types of property specified above. This might be a plausible construction, but for the fact that it would make meaningless the qualification to that phrase that follows immediately thereafter "receivable upon such consolidation (or) merger . . . by a holder of . . . shares of Common Stock of (Collins)." We decline to read Section 4.11 as a mandatory directive that any plan of merger between Collins and another company had to include provisions for the receipt by the holders of Collins Common Stock of both stock on the one hand, *and* other securities and property on the other. Had the parties to the contract wished to fashion such a bizarre provision, they certainly would have done so in a more explicit fashion.

Thus, the plain meaning of Section 4.11 is that after a merger, the *nature* of that "something else" into which the holders of Debentures are entitled to convert in lieu of Collins Common Stock is exactly equivalent to the nature of the "something" that the holders of Collins Common Stock received in the merger. No substantive limit or mandatory specification is provided in Section 4.11 as to what the holders of Collins Common Stock may receive in the merger; but whatever types of compensation the shareholders may receive in exchange for their Collins Common Stock, the holders of the Debentures are entitled to convert into each and all of those types.

In the case at bar, it is undisputed that the holders of Collins Common Stock received only cash in exchange for their shares; under the terms of the Merger Plan, they did not receive stock or any other type of property. Thus, the nature of the "something else" into which the holders of Debentures are entitled to convert in lieu of Collins Common Stock is *cash*—not Rockwell Common Stock, not other securities, and not other types of property besides cash.

But Section 4.11 also specifies the *quantity* of the "something else" into which the holders of the Debentures are entitled to convert after the merger. Like the nature of the "something else," the quantity of the "something else" is defined by reference to what the holders of Collins Common Stock received in the merger. Under Section 4.11, each holder of Debentures is entitled to convert each of his Debentures into that amount of the "something else" which was receivable under the terms of the Merger Plan "by a holder of the number of shares of Common Stock of (Collins) into which such Debenture might have been converted immediately prior to such . . . merger."

Thus, Section 4.11 gives us a formula for computing the quantity of the "something else." There are two variables in the formula: the conversion price of the Debentures immediately prior to the merger, and the quantity of the "something" received by the holders of Collins Common Stock in exchange for each share they surrendered as part of the Merger Plan. Section 4.11 directs that we first determine the number of shares of Collins Common Stock that a holder of Debentures would have been entitled to receive had he converted his Debentures immediately prior to the merger. As of the date of the merger, nothing had happened to trigger any of the conversion price adjustment provisions set out elsewhere in Article Four of the Indenture. Therefore, the conversion price originally specified when the Debentures were issued—$72.50— was still in effect at the time of the merger. At this conversion price, the Debentures were convertible immediately prior to the merger at the rate of 13.79 shares of Collins Common Stock per $1000 in principal amount of the Debentures surrendered.

The formula next provides that we take the quantity of the "something" that was received by the holders of Collins Common Stock in the merger in exchange for each share of Common Stock they surrendered ($25 cash), and multiply that "something" by the number of shares of Collins Common Stock into which the Debentures would have been convertible (13.79 shares per $1000 Debenture). The result is that each $1000 principal amount of Debenture is convertible into $344.75 cash (13.79 × $25).

Under the plain language of Section 4.11, then, we are compelled to the conclusion that Rockwell and the Trust Company correctly fulfilled their duties to execute a supplemental indenture providing for the post-merger conversion rights of the holders of Debentures; further, they correctly calculated those rights as specified by the terms of Section 4.11. Unless there is some compelling reason that we should not give the language of this Section its plain meaning, Broad's breach of contract claim must fail.

Reconciling Section 4.11 with the Remainder of the Indenture

Other arguments based on Article Four.—Broad next argues that the Indenture elsewhere provides an absolute, unabridgeable right to convert into Collins Common Stock at any time while the Debentures are outstanding. He first points to Section 4.01, which provides in pertinent part as follows:

> *Subject to and upon compliance with the provisions of this Article Four*, at the option of the holder thereof, any Debenture . . . may, at any time (while the Debentures are outstanding) be converted . . . into fully paid and non-assessable shares . . . of Common Stock of (Collins). . . .

Broad would have us read the "at any time" language as precluding the effect we would otherwise give to the language of Section 4.11.

In the first place, if there were any conflict between the above-quoted language of Section 4.01 and Section 4.11, the latter would control under principles of New York contract law, since of the two sections, Section 4.11 is more specifically addressed to the merger context. But in fact there is no conflict. Broad's suggested construction would make sense only if we were to ignore the introductory phrase of Section 4.01 "(s)ubject to and upon compliance with the provisions of this Article Four." Section 4.11 is part of Article Four, and Section 4.01, by its very terms, is explicitly made subject to that article. Thus, the "at any time" language of Section 4.01 is implicitly qualified by reference to Section 4.11 to mean "at any time except in the merger context, at which point Section 4.11 becomes applicable."

Broad makes a similar argument based on the language of Section 4.07, which provides in pertinent part as follows:

> (Collins) shall *at all times* reserve and keep available, free from pre-emptive rights, out of its authorized but unissued Common Stock, for the purpose of effecting the conversion of the debentures, the full number of shares of Common Stock *then issuable upon the conversion of all outstanding Debentures.*

We find no conflict. Even though not prefaced by the "subject to . . . the provisions of this Article Four" language, Section 4.07 by its terms only applies in those circumstances when the conversion right, if exercised, would result in the issuance of Collins Common Stock. The obligation to maintain sufficient shares of Collins Common Stock can have no meaning when there is no longer a conversion right into that stock. There is no such right after a merger in which Collins is not the surviving company. Under this interpretation, Sections 4.11 and 4.07 mesh perfectly.

It is also noteworthy that Article Four contains lengthy and complex provisions which mandate the adjustment of the conversion price upon specified conditions that would otherwise dilute the value of the conversion feature. *Nowhere* in Article Four, nor elsewhere within the four corners of the Indenture, is there any formula by which one could determine the ratio at which the Debentures would be converted into the surviving corporation's common stock. It would seem likely that such a formula would have been provided along with all the other conversion price adjustments, had the intent of the parties to the Indenture been that there should be an absolute right to convert into common stock of some sort, even in the event of a merger in which Collins and the Collins Common Stock would disappear.

Arguments based on Article Fourteen.—Section 14.01 provides in pertinent part as follows:

> Nothing in this Indenture shall prevent any consolidation or merger of (Collins) with or into any other corporation or corporations (whether or not affiliated with (Collins)) . . . ; provided, however, and (Collins) hereby covenants and agrees, that upon any such . . . merger, . . . the due and punctual payment of the principal of (and premium, if any) and interest on all of the Debentures, according to their tenor, and the due and punctual performance and observance of all the terms, covenants and conditions of this Indenture to be performed or observed by (Collins), shall be expressly assumed, by indenture supplemental hereto, satisfactory in form to the (Trust Company), executed and delivered to the (Trust Company) by the corporation formed by such consolidation, or by the corporation into which (Collins) shall have been merged. . . .

We begin by noting that the first phrase of this Section strongly supports the construction of the Indenture proffered by Rockwell and the Trust Company and accepted by the district court: if the Indenture provided an absolute right to convert into Collins Common Stock, there could be no completed merger of Collins into another company. The fact that Section 14.01 qualifies the entire Indenture evidences a strong and compelling intent of the parties that Collins should not be prevented from merging into another company by its obligations to the holders of the Debentures under the Indenture.

Broad's argument is based on the second clause of Section 14.01, which requires that the surviving corporation in a merger expressly assume "the due and punctual performance and observance of all the terms, covenants and conditions of this Indenture." He argues that this requires the surviving company to observe the covenants made by the issuer in Sections 4.01 and 4.07 the "at all times" covenants discussed above. Unfortunately for Broad, however, we have determined that those sections are not at all inconsistent with the interpretation we have placed on Section 4.11: in effect, Section 4.11 overrides those Sections. It is undisputed that Rockwell and the Trust Company did execute a supplemental indenture providing that Rockwell would observe all of those covenants applicable after the merger; likewise, it is undisputed that Rockwell has abided by those covenants, including the honoring of the debt obligation on the Debentures. Rockwell also stands ready to honor the conversion rights set out in the supplemental indenture, which have been adjusted pursuant to Section 4.11.

Section 14.02 provides in pertinent part as follows:

> In case of any such . . . merger, . . . and upon the execution by the successor corporation of an indenture supplemental hereto, as provided in Section 14.01, and upon compliance by such successor corporation with all applicable provisions of Section 4.11, such successor corporation shall succeed to and be substituted for (Collins). . . .
>
> In case of any such . . . merger, . . . such changes in phraseology and form (but not in substance) may be made in the Debentures thereafter to be issued as may be appropriate.

As stated above, Rockwell and the Trust Company did execute a proper supplemental indenture as provided for in Section 14.01, and they did comply with the applicable provisions of Section 4.11 in executing that supplemental indenture. Rockwell has properly succeeded to Collins' rights and obligations under the Indenture. Broad's arguments under Sections 14.01 and 14.02 must fail.

Arguments based on Article Thirteen.—Article Thirteen of the Indenture governs the circumstances in which the issuer and the Trustee can execute a supplemental indenture. Section 13.01, which is described in the Indenture's table of contents as specifying the "(p)urposes for which supplemental indentures may be entered into without consent of the Debentureholders," provides in pertinent part as follows:

> (Collins), when authorized by a resolution of its Board of Directors, and the (Trust Company), subject to the conditions and restrictions in this Indenture contained, may from time to time and at any time enter into an indenture or indentures supplemental hereto . . . for one or more of the following purposes:
>
> (a) *to make provision with respect to the conversion rights of holders of the Debentures pursuant to the requirements of Section 4.11*;
> (b) to evidence the succession of another corporation to (Collins), or successive successions, and the assumption by the successor corporation of the covenants, agreements and obligations of (Collins) pursuant to Article Fourteen;
> (c) to add to the covenants and agreements of (Collins) in this Indenture contained such further covenants and agreements thereafter to be observed, and . . . to surrender any right or power herein reserved to or conferred upon (Collins);
> (d) to cure any ambiguity or to correct or supplement any defective or inconsistent provision contained in this Indenture or in any supplemental indenture; and
> (e) to make such provisions with respect to matters or questions arising under this Indenture as may be necessary or desirable and not inconsistent with this

Indenture; *provided that such action shall not adversely affect the interests of the holders of any of the Debentures.*

The (Trust Company) is hereby authorized to join in the execution of any supplemental indenture authorized or permitted by the terms of this Indenture. . . .

Any supplemental indenture authorized by the provisions of this Section 13.01 may be executed by (Collins) and the (Trust Company) without the consent of the holders of any of the Debentures at the time outstanding, notwithstanding any of the provisions of Section 13.02.

We begin by noting that the first clause of this section reinforces our conclusions that Section 4.11 of the Indenture is intended to "make provision with respect to the conversion rights of holders of the Debentures" in the event of merger. Section 4.11, it will be recalled, requires in part that the surviving company in a merger execute a supplemental indenture in which is detailed the precise nature of the post-merger conversion rights of the holders of the Debentures, as calculated by the formula set out in Section 4.11.

Broad and the defendants have argued vigorously the question whether the last phrase in clause (e) of Section 13.01 modifies the entire section, or only clause (e). We agree with the defendants that under the most logical reading of Section 13.01, the phrase "provided that such action shall not adversely affect the interests of the holders of any of the Debentures" logically modifies only clause (e). Next, as we have noted before, Section 4.11 is the most specific recitation of the rights of the holders of the Debentures in the event of a merger; clause (a) of Section 13.01 ties in directly, and with equal specificity, to Section 4.11. Were there a conflict between those two provisions and the catch-all last phrase of clause (e) of Section 13.01, the former provisions would govern.

But more fundamentally, the execution of a supplemental indenture that complies with the directives of Section 4.11 does not "adversely affect the interests of the holders of any of the Debentures." The holders of Debentures have a legitimate interest only in those rights that are accorded them under the Indenture. Section 4.11 specifies what those rights are in the event of a merger; therefore, the execution of a supplemental indenture that complies with the requirements of Section 4.11 cannot be adverse to the legitimate interests of the holders of Debentures.

Broad also argues from the language of Section 13.02, despite the specific statement in Section 13.01 that a supplemental indenture required by Section 4.11 and clause (a) of Section 13.01 may be executed notwithstanding anything in Section 13.02. This statement in Section 13.01 should, and does, foreclose any arguments under Section 13.02.

But even under Section 13.02, which is described in the Indenture's table of contents as providing for the "(m)odification of Indenture with consent of holders of 66 2/3% in principal amount of Debentures," there is no help for Broad. Section 13.02 requires the permission of the holders of two-thirds of the Debentures before the issuer and the Trustee may execute a supplemental indenture that in any manner changes the rights and obligations of the parties to the Indenture or of the holders of the Debentures; certain types of alterations, including alterations of "the right to convert the (Debentures) into (Collins) Common Stock at the prices and *upon the terms provided in this Indenture*," are prohibited outright unless the Trustee and the issuer can obtain "the consent of the holder of each Debenture so affected." (Emphasis added.) Even were Section 13.02 applicable to those supplemental indentures that are required by Section 4.11 and clause (a) of Section 13.01, Section 13.02 would not prohibit that type of supplemental indenture, and neither would it require the consent of the holders of two-thirds or all of the Debentures: it is indisputable that one of the "terms provided in (the) Indenture" is Section 4.11 itself, and thus such a supplemental indenture does not *alter* the conversion rights of the holders of the Debentures. Rather, the supplemental indenture required under Section 4.11 merely evidences that all the requisite formalities for the clarification and protection of those rights have been complied with *i.e.*, that the formula set out in Section 4.11 has become applicable, and that the surviving company of the merger has formally accepted all the other obligations of, and been fully substituted for, the original issuer.

Our Conclusions With Respect to the Indenture

We conclude, after examining the entire Indenture in addition to those portions discussed specifically above, that the district court was correct in its conclusion that the Indenture is unambiguous. The intent of the parties is clearly evident from the four corners of the document. Section 4.11 fully and unambiguously sets out the conversion rights of the holders of the Debentures in the event of a merger in which Collins is not the surviving corporation: the holder of any outstanding Debenture is entitled to convert his Debenture into only that which he would have received had he converted it into Collins Common Stock immediately prior to the merger. On the facts of this case, that means a converting holder of a Debenture is entitled to receive $344.75 in cash for each $1000 in principal amount of the Debenture.

It is not the function of a court to rewrite a contract's terms in the process of "interpretation" to make them accord with the court's sense of equity. And yet, even were we inclined to do so, we are by no means certain that the outcome would be any different in this case.

Broad's persistent complaint has been that the Debentures' conversion feature was suddenly and arbitrarily liquidated, without permission or compensation. While the conversion feature has not technically been eliminated, since the holders of the Debentures retain the right to convert into $344.75 in cash for each $1,000 principal amount of Debentures, it is true that the merger did eliminate the possibility that the holders of the Debentures would benefit as a result of the future profitability of the Collins business, just as the merger eliminated that possibility for the holders of Collins Common Stock. A purchaser of Debentures, however, takes the risks inherent in the equity feature of the security, risks that are shared with the holders of Collins Common Stock. One of those risks is that Collins might merge with another company which is effectively the risk that any individual investor's assessment of the value of Collins Common Stock, based on Collins' prospects for the future, will be replaced by the collective judgment of the marketplace and the other investors in Collins who might vote in favor of the merger. This like the risk that Collins' future operations might be lackluster, with the result that conversion might never be economically attractive is simply a risk inherent in this type of investment.

The terms of the merger necessarily reflected the business prospects of Collins as of 1973. The fact that the initial high hopes that the holders of Debentures had for the equity securities of Collins hopes that were identical to those of the equity shareholders were defeated by the economic setbacks Collins suffered between 1967 and 1973 is not alleged in this lawsuit to be anyone's fault, least of all Rockwell's or the Trust Company's. When the market set the price of Collins Common Stock at less than $20, that price reflected the current aggregate judgment of the marketplace as to Collins' prospects for the future. The tendering shareholders, and those who gave up their shares in the merger, actually received a premium of roughly $5 per share over the market price a bonus of some 25%. The post-merger conversion terms mandated by Section 4.11 accorded the holders of the Debentures the benefit of that premium. They were accorded, as a result of the equity feature of the Debentures, the same treatment that the holders of Collins Common Stock received, and they received value based, in part, on Collins' prospects for the future. Insofar as the debt feature of the Debentures is concerned, they benefited by the merger in that the Debentures are now backed by a financially more secure corporation.

Based upon our interpretation of the Indenture, and without hesitation given the nature of convertible debentures, we affirm the judgment of the district court with regard to Broad's breach of contract claims.

QUESTIONS

1. As a way to manage the transaction, why didn't Rockwell solicit consents from the convertible debtholders?
2. In a merger or consolidation, what are the possible common stocks (as between the combining companies) that might be available post-transaction? Does §4.11 clearly cover these situations?
3. Try to redraft §4.11 to satisfy the needs of Collins and Rockwell.

3. NOTICE

Since a securityholder must exercise the conversion right, there is a question of when an issuer or a trustee must provide notice of some event or fact that would affect the conversion right.

———————————

The following cases discuss the obligation and duty of an issuer and a trustee to provide notice to convertible securityholders when their advantageous position in the conversion right would be adversely affected by some event or the issuer's action.

Van Gemert v. Boeing Co.
520 F.2d 1373 (2d Cir. 1975)

OAKES, Circuit Judge:

This appeal is from a judgment dismissing the amended complaint in a consolidation class action brought by nonconverting holders of The Boeing Company's "4½% Convertible Subordinated Debentures, due July 1, 1980." The gist of the complaint was that the appellants and their class had inadequate and unreasonable notice of Boeing's intention to redeem or "call" the convertible debentures in question and were hence unable to exercise their conversion rights before the deadline in the call of midnight, March 29, 1966. Their damage lay in the fact that the redemption price for each $100 of principal amount of debentures was only $103.25, while under the conversion rate of, at a minimum, two shares of common stock for each $100 of principal amount of debentures, the stock was worth $316.25 on March 29, 1966, the cut-off date for the exercise of conversion privileges, or within 30 days thereafter, $364.00. The named appellants number 56, and the total loss alleged is over $2 million.

The District Court held that Boeing complied with the notice provisions spelled out in the debentures and in the Indenture, between Boeing and The Chase Manhattan Bank (Chase), Trustee, and that it was required to do no more. We reverse and remand on the ground that there was an obligation on Boeing's part to give reasonably adequate notice of the redemption to the debenture holders, which obligation was not fulfilled in this instance.

A number of provisions in the debenture, the Indenture Agreement, the prospectus, the registration statement for the debentures and the Listing Agreement with the New York Stock Exchange (NYSE) dealt with the possible redemption of the debentures by Boeing and the notice debenture-holders were to receive of a redemption call so that they might timely exercise their right to convert the debentures into common stock rather than have their debentures redeemed at face value. The debentures themselves provided:

> The holder of this Debenture is entitled, at his option, at any time on or before July 1, 1980, or in case this Debenture shall be called for redemption prior to such date, *up to and including but not after the tenth day prior to the redemption date, to convert this Debenture* . . . at the principal amount hereof, or such portion hereof, into shares of Capital Stock of the Company . . .
>
> The Debentures are *subject to redemption* as a whole or in part, at any time or times, at the option of the Company, *on not less than 30 nor more than 90 days' prior notice, as provided in the Indenture*, at the following redemption prices (expressed in percentages of the principal amount) . . .
>
> This Debenture may be registered as to principal upon presentation at the office or agency of the Company, in the Borough of Manhattan, The City of New York, New York, . . .

The Indenture itself, a 113-page printed booklet, provides in Art. V, §5.02, as follows:

> In case the Company shall desire to exercise the right to redeem all or any part of the debentures, as the case may be, pursuant to Section 5.01, it shall publish prior to the date fixed for redemption a notice of such redemption at least twice in an Authorized Newspaper, the first such publication to be not less than 30 days and not more than 90 days before the date fixed for redemption. Such publication shall be in successive weeks but on any day of the week.
>
> [The indenture defines "Authorized Newspaper" as one published at least five days a week and of general circulation in the borough of Manhattan, N.Y.]

The Indenture also provided that debenture-holders who registered their bonds would receive notice by mail of any redemption call by the Boeing directors.

While the prospectus for the debenture issue did not refer to any registration rights, it did state that redemption could occur "on not less than 30 days' and not more than 90 days' published notice."

The NYSE Listing Agreement dated November 5, 1957, incorporated by reference into the listing application filed by Boeing in respect to the debenture issue, provided in Part III, Paragraph 4, as follows:

> The Corporation will *publish immediately to the holders* of any of its securities listed on the Exchange any action taken by the Corporation with respect to dividends or to the allotment of rights to subscribe or *to any rights or benefits pertaining to the ownership of its securities listed on the Exchange*; and will give prompt notice to the Exchange of any such action; and *will afford the holders of its securities listed on the Exchange a proper period within* which to record their interests and *to exercise their rights.* . . .

Section A10 of the NYSE "Company Manual" specifically defines what is meant by publicity in the Listing Agreement:

> Publicity: *The term "publicity,"* as used . . . below, and *as used in the listing agreement* in respect of redemption action, *refers to a general news release, and not to the formal notice or advertisement of redemption* sometimes required by provisions of an indenture or charter.
>
> *Such news release shall be made as soon as possible after corporate action which will lead to, or which looks toward, redemption* is taken . . . and shall be made by the fastest available means, i. e., telephone, telegraph or hand-delivery.
>
> To insure coverage which will adequately inform *the public*, the news should be released to at least *one or more newspapers of general circulation in New York City which regularly publish financial news*, or *to one or more of the national news-wire services* (Associated Press, United Press International), in addition to such other release as the company may elect to make.

Section A10 of the Company Manual also provides specifically that when a convertible security is to be redeemed, the news release must include the rate of conversion and the date and time when the conversion privilege expires. It further provides that in addition to the immediate news release the company must give notice immediately to the NYSE itself, so as to enable the NYSE to take any necessary action with respect to further trading in the security.

The Call and Its Circumstances Herein of the Notice Actually Given

On February 28, 1966, the Boeing board of directors authorized the president, vice president-finance or treasurer to call for redemption on a date to be selected by them or any one of them, all of the convertible debentures outstanding under the indenture of July 1, 1958. That same day a news release, headlining 1965 sales and net earnings, and referring to a contemplated stock increase, stock split and post-split dividends, mentioned that "(t)he company's management was also authorized to call for redemption at a future date all of the company's outstanding 4½ percent convertible subordinated debentures." This statement, which did not mention even the tentative dates for redemption and expiration of the conversion rights of debenture holders that had been settled upon, was released by the Boeing "News Bureau" nationally to the financial editors of the New York Times, the New York Herald-Tribune, the Wall Street Journal and other major national newspapers, in addition to the major wire services (Associated Press, United Press International and Dow Jones & Co.).

A short time after the February 28 board meeting, Boeing firmed up the key dates, complied with the indenture notice requirements and communicated to some extent with the Exchange proper. On March 2, 1966, at the home office in Seattle, at a meeting of Boeing officers, bankers and lawyers, it was decided to fix March 8 as the date for the first publication of the formal notice of redemption, April 8 as the redemption date and March 29 as the date for expiration of the conversion privilege. The second date for publication of the formal notice, March 18, was also fixed upon at this March 2 meeting, and Chase was notified to publish the redemption notice on those dates in all editions of the Wall Street Journal. All editions of the Journal carried the formal notices on March 8 and 18; the notices were in due form if not of extensive size. It is conceded by the appellants that the formal requirements of the Indenture were met by the Company and Trustee.

It was not until March 7, the day before the publication of the first formal notice of redemption, that the NYSE was itself notified of the firmed-up dates for redemption, conversion and notice. This was done by a telephone call from Company counsel in Seattle to the Exchange.

That Boeing did not issue any general publicity release, as that term is defined in Section A-10 of the New York Stock Exchange Company manual, concerning the call of the debentures during the period from March 1, through March 24, 1966.

There was, in short, no general news release as called for by the Listing Agreement as amplified in the Company Manual until on the eve of expiration of the conversion rights, March 25, 1966, it appeared that $10,849,300 face amount of debentures over one-half of those outstanding at that time remained unconverted. At that point Boeing issued a press release and then on March 28 the Company republished its earlier advertisement in all editions of the Wall Street Journal (Eastern, Mid-Western, Pacific Coast and South-West) and the New York Times, and additional advertisements were placed. This later action had what the court below termed a "dramatic and widespread rippling effect." Some $9,305,000 of debentures were converted on March 28 and 29. The ripples, however, had not spread to the appellants' class by the midnight deadline on the 29th; they literally went to sleep with $1.5 million of debentures that were worth $4 million if only converted.

It is true, however, and the court did properly find, that in addition to the publication of the two formal indenture notices, notices of the dates of the call and the expiration of the conversion privilege on March 29, 1966, were carried on the following services: NYSE ticker on March 8, 23, 24, 25, 26 and 28, 1966; NYSE Bulletin on March 11, 18 and 25, 1966; The Commercial and Financial Chronicle on March 14, 21 and 28, 1966; Standard & Poor's Bond Outlook on March 19, 1966; Standard & Poor's Called Bond Record on March 9, 11, 18 and 25, 1966; Moody's Industrials on March 11, 1966. Articles about these dates were also carried in the Seattle Post Intelligencer on March 25, 1966; the Seattle Times on March 27, 1966; and the Financial World on March 23, 1966; and the notice was also carried in the Associated Press Bond Tables published on one or more days in at least 30 newspapers published in major cities across the United States. But almost all of these notices or items were in fine print, buried in the multitude of information and data published about the financial markets and scarcely of a kind to attract the eye of the average lay investor or debenture holder. On March 9, 1966, the listing in the New York Times for the convertible debentures read, for example: "Boeing cv 4½ s 80." The change on March 10 was to "Boeing 4½ s 80 cld," giving the investor in Dubuque or Little Rock or Lampasas only 19 days to pick up this change and figure that "cld" meant "called." Proof of the inadequacy of these notices lies in the fact that, despite the dramatic disparity between the value of the debentures unconverted and the conversion stock, over one-half of the debentures outstanding on the date of the first notice remained unconverted until the general publicity release on the eve of expiration of the conversion privilege.

The Inadequacy of the Boeing Notice

The notice Boeing gave, we hold, had two deficiencies. First, Boeing did not adequately apprise the debenture holders what notice would be given of a redemption call. Investors were not informed by the prospectus or by the debentures that they could receive mail notice by registering their debentures, and that otherwise they would have to rely primarily on finding one of the scheduled advertisements in the newspaper or on keeping a constant eye on the bond tables. Second, the newspaper notice given by Boeing was itself inadequate.

The first factor we think highly significant. Many of the debenture holders might well have decided to register their bonds, had the significance of registration, or of the failure to register, been brought home in the materials generally available to the purchasers of the debentures. No detailed information as to notice was given on the face of the debentures, even in the fine print. The debentures stated simply:

> The debentures are subject to redemption, as a whole or in part, at any time or times, at the option of the Company, in not less than 30 nor more than 90 days' prior notice, as provided in the Indenture . . .

There was no indication that registration would mean that a debenture holder would receive mail notice. Nor was there any indication of the extent of newspaper notice to be provided either as to the papers that would be used or how often the notice would be published. Debenture holders were simply referred by the debenture, as well as by the prospectus, to the 113-page Indenture Agreement, which, to be sure, was available to debenture holders or prospective purchasers upon request, but which was not circulated generally with the warrants or debentures.

We have dwelt at length in the facts on the newspaper notice actually given. While it may have conformed to the requirements of the Indenture it was simply insufficient to give fair and reasonable notice to the debenture holders.

The duty of reasonable notice arises out of the contract between Boeing and the debenture holders, pursuant to which Boeing was exercising its right to redeem the debentures. An issuer of debentures has a duty to give adequate notice either on the face of the debentures, or in some other way, of the notice to be provided in the event the company decides to redeem the debentures. Absent such advice as to the specific notice agreed upon by the issuer and the trustee for the debenture holders, the debenture holders' reasonable expectations as to notice should be protected.

For less sophisticated investors (it will be recalled that warrants for the purchase of debentures were issued to all Boeing shareholders), putting the notice provisions only in the 113-page Indenture Agreement was effectively no notice at all. It was not reasonable for Boeing to expect these investors to send off for, and then to read understandingly, the 113-page Indenture Agreement referred to in both the prospectus and the debentures themselves in order to find out what notice would be provided in the event of redemption.

Boeing could very easily have run more than two advertisements in a single paper prior to the eleventh hour (March 28), at which time it issued its belated news release and advertised for the third time in the Wall Street Journal and for the first time in the

New York Times. Moreover, in the same period that the debentures were in the process of being redeemed, Boeing was preparing for its annual meeting (to be held April 24). Proxy materials were being prepared throughout March and were finally mailed sometime between March 24 and March 30. Management could readily have arranged the redemption dates and the proxy mailing so that notice of the redemption dates could have been included in the envelope with the proxy materials. Thus at no extra cost except that of printing brief notices, at least all Boeing shareholders would have received mail notice, and presumably a significant number of the plaintiff class owned Boeing common stock, as well as debentures, in 1966. Had Boeing attempted such mail notice, or mail notice to original subscribers, and also given further newspaper publicity either by appropriate news releases or advertising earlier in the redemption period, we would have a different case and reasonable and sufficient notice might well be found.

What one buys when purchasing a convertible debenture in addition to the debt obligation of the company incurred thereby is principally the expectation that the stock will increase sufficiently in value that the conversion right will make the debenture worth more than the debt. The debenture holder relies on the opportunity to make a proper conversion on due notice. Any loss occurring to him from failure to convert, as here, is not from a risk inherent in his investment but rather from unsatisfactory notification procedures. The debenture holder's expectancy is that he will receive reasonable notice and it is his reliance on this expectancy that the courts will protect. Had there been proper publication, a reasonable investor undoubtedly would have taken action to prevent the loss occurring to him.

Of course, it may be suggested that the appellee corporation itself was not the beneficiary of the appellants' loss; rather, the corporate stockholders benefited by not having their stock watered down by the number of shares necessary to convert appellants' debentures. But an award against Boeing will in effect tend to reduce pro tanto the equity of shareholders in the corporation and thus to a large extent those who were benefited, one might almost say unjustly enriched, will be the ones who pay appellants' loss.

QUESTIONS

1. If the notice met the formal requirements of the indenture, how did the court reach the conclusion that it was defective?
2. Is the court's analysis consistent with the emphasis on the contract terms to determine the rights and protections of creditors?

NOTES

1. In a subsequent opinion in the same case, the Second Circuit described *Van Gemert I* as: "We did find significant, however, the fact that the debentures did not explicitly set forth the type of notice which appellants could expect if Boeing decided to call the bonds. Without such a declaration, we held as a matter of law that appellants were entitled to expect that Boeing would employ a method of

notification reasonably calculated to inform the debenture holders of the call. In doing so, we merely applied the settled principle that in every contract there is an implied covenant that neither party shall do anything which will have the effect of destroying or injuring the right of the other party to receive the fruits of the contract. Simply stated, every contract contains the implied requirement of good faith and fair dealing. Boeing was found liable therefore because it breached its contract with appellants, and damages were awarded." *Van Gemert v. Boeing Co.*, 553 F.2d 812, 815 (2d Cir. 1977) (*Van Gemert II*).

Rudbart v. North Jersey District Water Commission
605 A.2d 681 (N.J. 1992)

PER CURIAM

[The defendant, a public corporation, issued redeemable debt whose indenture provided: "The Notes are subject to redemption prior to maturity as a whole at the option of the Commission on 30 days published notice in a newspaper or newspapers of general circulation in the City of Newark, New Jersey and in the City of New York, New York on the dates and at the prices below." If the notes had not been redeemed upon notice in the newspapers, the indenture provided: "the Notes shall cease to bear interest and shall not be deemed to be outstanding from such date." Although notice of redemption was published in *The Star-Ledger, The New York Times, The Wall Street Journal*, and *Moody's Municipal & Government Manual*, the plaintiff apparently was unaware of the redemption and thus his note lost its economic value. He relied on *Van Gemert* to argue that the notice was insufficient.]

We do not read *Van Gemert v. Boeing Co.*, 520 F.2d 1373 (2d Cir.) [*Van Gemert I*], relied on by plaintiffs, as holding that a court may properly invalidate a notice-by-publication term of a security. In *Van Gemert*, holders of Boeing's convertible debentures challenged as unreasonable the published notice given by Boeing of redemption of the debentures. Although the plaintiffs argued that the indenture agreement was "in the nature of a contract of adhesion" and thus any "unconscionable features * * * are unenforceable as a matter of policy," that court did not agree. Rather, it found that the newspaper notice was inadequate because the investors had not been adequately informed "by the prospectus or by the debentures" of the notice to be given. The court classified the limited scope of that holding in its later opinion after remand. *See* 553 F.2d 812 (1977) [*Van Gemert II*]. There the court stated that it had found "significant * * * the fact that the debentures did not explicitly set forth the type of notice [that the debenture holders] could expect" in the event of an early redemption, and accordingly had "held as a matter of law" what notice the debenture holders "were entitled to expect." *Id.* at 815. See also *Meckel v. Continental Resources Co.*, 758 F.2d 811 (2d Cir.1985), in which the same court described the *Van Gemert* holding as follows:

> Those debentures contained no indication as to the type of notice of redemption that was to be provided. It was the total lack of a notice provision in the debentures that we held necessary as a condition precedent to an imposition of a duty to provide "reasonable" notice.

As we have already noted, plaintiffs here do not dispute that the notes and the Official Statement fully disclosed that notice of redemption would be given by publication. If anything, *Van Gemert* suggests that such a fully disclosed term should be enforced.

QUESTIONS

1. Is the distinction made by the *Rudbart* court persuasive?
2. In reading *Van Gemert I*, *Van Gemert II*, and *Rudbart*, what are the essential lessons in drafting a redemption provision and executing a redemption?

Lorenz v. CSC Corp.
1 F. 3d 1406 (3d Cir. 1993)

COWEN, Circuit Judge.

The plaintiffs in these two related actions purchased convertible debentures issued by the defendant Baltimore and Ohio Railroad Company ("B&O"). The indenture trustee was defendant Chase Manhattan Bank. Plaintiffs allege that the defendants defrauded them from 1977 to 1986 by failing to disclose material information which would have enabled them to convert their debentures into B&O common stock and receive a lucrative dividend. Plaintiffs appeal the dismissal of their claims for breach of fiduciary duty [and] breach of the implied covenant of good faith and fair dealing. We will affirm.

The plaintiffs were holders of debentures in the B&O Railroad as of December 13, 1977. The debentures were convertible into B&O common stock at any time before maturing in the year 2010. To avoid Interstate Commerce Commission regulations hindering the development of non-rail assets owned by railroads, B&O devised a plan to segregate its rail and non-rail assets. Non-rail assets were transferred to a wholly owned subsidiary, Mid Allegheny Corporation ("MAC"), and MAC common stock was distributed as a dividend on a share-for-share basis to B&O shareholders. B&O sought to avoid the registration of its shares with the Securities and Exchange Commission ("SEC"), a time-consuming process which would have required appraisals of the transferred assets. Because B&O had few shareholders, the company thought that the SEC would issue a "no-action" letter excusing the registration of MAC stock. This plan would have been foiled if large numbers of B&O debentureholders exercised their conversion option in order to receive the MAC dividend.

To avoid this occurrence, B&O transferred its non-rail assets to MAC on December 13, 1977 and declared the dividend in MAC stock on the same date, without prior notice. As a result, the debentureholders could not convert their shares in time to receive the MAC dividend. Some of the debentureholders brought actions, later consolidated, under section 10(b) of the '34 Act against B&O. This suit is known as the *PTC/Guttmann* litigation. In 1978 and 1979, B&O and Chase Manhattan Bank entered into a series of letter agreements, whereby B&O agreed that if the *PTC/Guttmann* plaintiffs prevailed or obtained a settlement, debentureholders would be allowed to participate equally in that judgment or settlement regardless of whether they had converted their debentures.

The district court granted plaintiffs the opportunity to convert their debentures into shares and receive the MAC dividend plus dividend income accruing since December 13, 1977. The defendants were ordered to give notice to the debenture-holders of the district court's order. Defendants published notice of the remedy in the *New York Times* and *Wall Street Journal*. In a subsequent appeal, we held that the district court's remedy also included persons who held B&O debentures on December 13, 1977, converted them to B&O common stock, and subsequently sold the stock.

The plaintiffs in the present actions are those persons who are outside the scope of the *PTC/Guttmann* remedy. They held debentures on December 13, 1977 but subsequently sold them without having ever converted them into stock.

The district court dismissed plaintiffs' claims against the indenture trustee Chase Manhattan Bank for breach of the implied covenant of good faith and fair dealing, allegedly arising from the bank's failure to inform them of the MAC dividend, the letter agreements with B&O, and the *PTC/Guttmann* judgment. Because the indenture specifies that the liability of the trustee shall be determined under New York law, we will apply New York law.

The courts of New York consistently have held that the duties of an indenture trustee, unlike those of a typical trustee, are defined exclusively by the terms of the indenture. *Elliott Associates v. J. Henry Schroder Bank & Trust Co.*, 838 F.2d 66, 71 (2d Cir. 1988). The sole exception to this rule is that the indenture trustee must avoid conflicts of interest with the debentureholders.

The plaintiffs specifically claim that Chase Manhattan Bank violated the implied covenant of good faith and fair dealing which, under New York law, is contained in every contract. The implied covenant prohibits either party from doing anything which would prevent the other party from receiving the fruits of the contract. The covenant, however, cannot be used to insert new terms that were not bargained for. A covenant is implied only when it is consistent with the express terms of the contract.

An indenture is, of course, a contract. Unless the indenture trustee has deprived the debentureholders of a right or benefit specifically provided to them in the indenture, there is no violation of the implied covenant of good faith and fair dealing. *See Broad v. Rockwell Int'l Corp.*, 642 F.2d 929, 957-58 (5th Cir. 1981) (in banc) (applying New York law); *cf. Metropolitan Life Ins. Co. v. RJR Nabisco, Inc.*, 716 F.Supp. 1504, 1517-22 (S.D.N.Y. 1989) (no breach of implied covenant under New York law where corporation's incurrence of debt to fund leveraged buyout depleted the value of its debentures, as the indenture lacked any terms prohibiting the transaction). We therefore will consider whether the indenture in this case contains provisions which entitled the debentureholders to receive notice of the MAC dividend, the letter agreements with B&O, or any of the remedies in the *PTC/Guttmann* action.

The indenture contains no provisions which explicitly require the trustee to provide notice of any kind to the debentureholders. Plaintiffs cite two provisions which they claim implicitly require notice. First, the indenture states:

> The Indenture permits the amendment thereof and the modification or alteration, in any respect, of the rights and obligations of the Company and the rights of the holders of the Debentures . . . at any time by the concurrent action of the Company and of

the holders of 66 2/3 % in principal amount of the Debentures then outstanding affected by such amendment, modification or alteration (including, in the case of a modification of the terms of conversion of this Debenture into common stock of the Company or of payment of the principal of, or the premium or interest on, this Debenture, the consent of the holder hereof), all as more fully provided in the Indenture.

Plaintiffs claim that the letter agreements between B&O and Chase Manhattan Bank altered their rights under the Indenture. Those agreements provided that the debenture-holders would be allowed to participate equally in any judgment against B&O or any settlement regardless of whether they converted their debentures to common stock. Because the quoted language gives the debentureholders the right to vote regarding any change in their or the company's rights and obligations under the indenture, the plaintiffs argue that they were entitled to notice of the letter agreements.

Second, the indenture provides:

At any meeting at which there shall be a quorum the holders of the Affected Debentures shall have the power by resolution adopted as hereinafter provided:

(*a*) to authorize the Trustee to join with the Company in making any modification, alteration, repeal of or addition to any provision of this Indenture or of the Debentures, and any modification of or addition to the rights and obligations of the Company or the rights of the holders of the Debentures . . . under this Indenture or under the Debentures. . . .

The plaintiffs claim that the letter agreements between B&O and Chase Manhattan Bank were supplemental indentures which modified or added to their rights under the indenture. Because the debentureholders have the right to vote on whether to permit the indenture trustee and company to execute a supplemental indenture, the plaintiffs argue that they were entitled to notice.

Both provisions cited by plaintiffs provide debentureholders with the right to vote, and arguably therefore to receive notice, only if there is some modification of the debentureholders' rights or the company's obligations under the indenture. We agree with the district court that the letter agreements did not affect their rights under the indenture and cannot be characterized as supplemental indentures. The agreements pertained only to the scope of a possible remedy under the federal securities laws in the *PTC/Guttmann* litigation, in the event of a judgment against the defendant corporations or a settlement. The plaintiffs' contractual rights under the indenture itself, including rights regarding conversion of shares, were never modified.

It would have been advantageous for the plaintiffs to have been informed of the letter agreements and thus of potential violations of securities laws committed by B&O. However, so long as an indenture trustee fulfills its obligations under the express terms of the indenture, it owes the debentureholders no additional, implicit duties or obligations, except to avoid conflicts of interest. *Elliott Associates,* 838 F.2d at 71. There is no provision in the indenture which obligated the trustee Chase Manhattan Bank to inform the debentureholders that they possibly had rights against B&O under the federal securities laws. Because the bank did not deprive the plaintiff of any right under the indenture, the bank could not have breached the implied covenant of good faith and fair dealing.

Plaintiffs rely heavily on *Van Gemert v. Boeing Co.,* 520 F.2d 1373 (2d Cir. 1975) (*Van Gemert I*). In that case, debentures on their face required the company to provide notice before exercising its option to redeem them. The indenture provided that such notice could be by publication in a newspaper. The court concluded that because the debentures did not specify the kind of notice that would be provided, the debenture-holders were entitled to expect reasonable notice of the redemption call. Though the company complied with the terms of the indenture by publishing notice in a newspaper, the court held that it failed to provide fair and reasonable notice to the debentureholders. In a subsequent opinion, the court stated that the defendant was liable because it violated the implied covenant of good faith and fair dealing. *Van Gemert v. Boeing Co.,* 553 F.2d 812, 815 (2d Cir. 1977) (*Van Gemert II*).

Van Gemert indicates that when a debenture or indenture expressly requires notice, the implied covenant of good faith and fair dealing requires the defendant to provide notice which is reasonably calculated to enable the debentureholders to obtain the benefit of their contract. In the present case, however, the indenture does not have any provision which required the bank to provide notice regarding B&O's alleged violations of securities laws and the resulting litigation. To infer such a require-ment would, in effect, add a new term to the indenture, and the implied covenant can never be used for that purpose. The district court correctly dismissed the claims against Chase Manhattan Bank for breach of the implied covenant of good faith and fair dealing.

QUESTIONS

1. Did the settlement modify or alter the right of the convertible debtholders?
2. Suppose the debtholders were worried about not being informed by the trustee of important, relevant, or material information that is known by the trustee. Can a contract term be written to alleviate this concern?

4. PROTECTION OF CONVERSION RIGHT UPON DISTRIBUTION

The conversion right is contractually negotiated in a convertible security and thus is an express contractual term. However, this contractual term can be defeated if there is a distribution to common stockholders that is sufficient to deny the economic benefit of a conversion. The holder must have protection against such value-destroying distribution.

The following case analyzes the conversion right in the context of a spinoff of an asset to common stockholders. Consider what term or mechanism would protect the securityholder under these circumstances and whether such a provision can still be defeated in a corporate transaction.

HB Korenvaes Investments L.P. v. Marriott Corp.
1993 WL 257422 (Del. Ch. 1993)

ALLEN, Chancellor

In this action holders of Series A Cumulative Convertible Preferred Stock of Mar-riott Corporation seek to enjoin a planned reorganization of the businesses owned by that corporation. The reorganization involves the creation of a new corporate subsidiary, Marriott International, Inc., ("International"), the transfer to International of the greatest part of Marriott's cash-generating businesses, followed by the distribution of the stock of International to all of the holders of Marriott common stock, as a special dividend.

Plaintiffs assert that the proposed special dividend would leave the residual Marriott endangered by a disproportionate debt burden and would deprive them of certain rights created by the certificate of designation that defines the special rights, etc., of the preferred stock. More particularly, they claim that the distribution of the dividend will violate the provisions of Section 5(e)(iv) of the certificate of designation of the preferred stock. Section 5(e)(iv) is designed to protect the economic interests of the preferred stock in the event of a special dividend.

The Series A Cumulative Convertible Preferred Stock is Marriott's only outstanding issue of preferred stock. Plaintiffs are four institutional investors who have acquired more than 50% of the preferred stock.

Defendants assert that the reorganization, and more particularly the special dividend, constitutes a valid, good faith attempt to maximize the interests of Marriott's common stockholders. Marriott asserts the right to deal with the preferred stock at arm's length, to afford them their legal rights arising from the certificate of designation, but also to take steps not inconsistent with those rights to maximize the economic position of Marriott's common stock.

Pending is plaintiffs' motion for a preliminary injunction prohibiting the distribution of the special dividend.

I conclude that plaintiffs have not shown a reasonable likelihood of success with respect to those aspects of their claims that appear to state a claim upon which relief might be granted.

[Facts]

Marriott Corporation, as presently constituted, is in the business (1) of owning and operating hotels, resorts, and retirement homes, (2) of providing institutional food service and facilities management, and (3) of operating restaurants and food, beverage and merchandise concessions at airports, tollway plazas and other facilities. Its common stock has a present market value of approximately $2.6 billion. In December 1991 Marriott issued $200,000,000 face amount of convertible preferred stock bearing an 8¼% cumulative dividend [with a face value of $50], the stock owned by plaintiffs. Marriott has substantial debt, including Liquid Yield Option Notes with an accreted value of $228 million; and long-term debt of $2.732 billion. According to its proxy statement, the book value of Marriott's assets is $6.560 billion.

In the fiscal year ending January 1, 1993 Marriott's sales were $8.722 billion; earnings before interest, taxes, depreciation and amortization (EBITDA) was $777 million; earnings before interest and corporate expenses was $496 million; and net income was $85 million. Each common share has received an annual cash dividend of $0.28 per share and the preferred stock dividends have been paid over its short life.

The preferred stock is entitled to an 8¼% cumulative dividend and no more. It ranks prior to the common stock with respect to dividends and distribution of assets. It has in total, a face amount of $200,000,000 and that, plus the amount of any unpaid cumulated dividends, "and no more" is the amount of its liquidation preference. The corporation may, at its option, redeem any or all of the preferred stock after January 15, 1996, at prices set forth in the certificate.

The preferred stock is convertible at the option of the holder into common stock at a conversion price set forth in the certificate. Generally that means that every $50.00 face amount share of preferred stock may be converted into 2.87 shares of common stock. The certificate provides a mechanism to adjust the conversion price "in case the Corporation shall, by dividend . . . distribute to all holders of Common Stock . . . assets (including securities). . . ." Certificate of Designation §5(e)(iv).

There are no express restrictions on the payment of dividends other than the requirement that the quarterly dividend on the preferred must be paid prior to the distribution of dividend payments to common stock.

On October 5, 1992, Marriott announced a radical rearrangement of the legal structure of the Company's businesses. The restructuring was said to be designed to separate Marriott's "ownership of real estate . . . and other capital intensive businesses from its management and services businesses." The latter constitute Marriott's most profitable and fastest growing business segments. Following this transfer Marriott intends to "spin-off" this new subsidiary by distributing all its stock as a dividend to Marriott's common stockholders.

Marriott International

International is anticipated to be highly profitable from its inception and to be well positioned for future growth. It is expected to pay to its common stockholders the same dividend that has been paid to Marriott's common stock. Marriott's proxy statement describes International's proposed business activities as follows:

> Pursuant to existing long-term management, lease and franchise agreements with hotel owners, and [similar] . . . agreements to be entered into with Host Marriott with respect to lodging facilities and senior living properties to be owned by Host Marriott, Marriott International will operate or franchise a total of 242 Marriott full service hotels, 207 Courtyard by Marriott hotels, 179 Residence Inns, 118 Fairfield Inns and 16 senior living communities. Marriott International will also conduct the Company's food and facilities management businesses, as well as the Company's vacation timesharing operations.

According to its *pro forma* balance sheet for the quarter ending March 26, 1993, after the distribution (and assuming the Exchange Offer described below is effectuated) International will have assets of $3.048 billion, long-term debt of $902 million, and shareholders equity of $375 million.

Had International, with all the assets it will hold, been operated as a separate company in 1992, it would have had sales of $7.787 billion, earnings before interest and corporate expenses of $331 million and net income of $136 million. Marriott's adviser, S.G. Warburg & Company, has estimated that in 1993 International will have sales of $8.210 billion, and EBIT of $368 million.

Host Marriott

Marriott's remaining assets will consist of large real estate holdings and Marriott's airport and tollway concession business. Marriott will be renamed Host Marriott ("Host"). The assets retained by Host have a value of several billion dollars but will be burdened with great debt and produce little cash-flow after debt service.

Host Marriott will retain [ownership of] most of the Company's [Marriott's] existing real estate properties, including 136 lodging and senior living properties. Host Marriott will also complete the Company's existing real estate development projects and manage the Company's holdings of undeveloped real estate. Host Marriott will seek to maximize the cash flow from . . . its real estate holdings . . . Host Marriott . . . will also be the leading operator of airport and toll-road food and merchandise concessions in the U.S., holding contracts at 68 major airports and operating concessions at nearly 100 toll-road units.

Assuming the Exchange Offer is effectuated, after the special dividend Host will have, according to its *pro forma* balance sheet as of March 26, 1993, assets of $3.796 billion, long-term debt of $2.130 billion and shareholders' equity of $516 million. Host's *pro forma* income statement for the fiscal year ending January 1, 1993, would reflect sales of $1.209 billion, earnings before corporate expenses and interest of $152 million, interest expense of $196 million, corporate expenses of $46 million, and a net loss of $44 million.

Author's Case Annotation: Financials of Marriott's Businesses

$ million	Marriott	International	Host
	As of Jan. 1, 1993	FY 1992	FY 1992
Sale	8,722	7,787	1,209
EBIT, before corp. expense	496	331	152
EBITDA	777		
Interest expense			196
Net income	85	136	−44
	As of Jan. 1, 1993	Pro forma Mar. 26, 1993	Pro forma Mar. 26, 1993
Assets	6,560	3,048	3,796
Long-term debt	2,732	902	2,130
Convertible preferred	200		
Shareholder equity		375	516
Market capitalization	2,600		

Note: It is not clear that Marriott should equal the sum of International and Host, probably not due to corporate expenses of the parent. Some discrepancies are due to timing differences. The court does not give the necessary financial information to accurately provide the complete financial picture.

When he announced the spin-off transaction on October 5, 1992, Stephen Bollenbach, Marriott's Chief Financial Officer stated, with respect to the future of Host:

Net cash flow of Host Marriott will be used primarily to service and retire debt. The Company does not plan to pay dividends on its common stock . . . I am very comfortable with the way Host Marriott has been structured. I believe this approach represents the best way for Marriott shareholders to unlock the value of our long-term assets. Secondly, the transaction gives Host Marriott the staying power needed if the recovery is slower than anticipated in arriving. I am convinced Host Marriott has the financial means to meet all its obligations to employees, suppliers, lenders and other stakeholders."

Mr. Bollenbach reiterated this position two weeks later at a meeting of securities analysts.

If the special dividend is distributed, International and Host will formally constitute two separate corporate entities. They will, however, share a large number of relationships. International will have long-term agreements to manage many of Host's hotel properties and other real estate assets. International will have a right to share in the proceeds of some of Host's asset sales in lieu of receiving base management fees, as well as a right of first refusal in any sale of Host's airport and toll-road concessions.

International will extend a $630 million line of credit to Host's subsidiary Host Marriott Hospitality, Inc. ("HMH"). For ten years after the special dividend, International will have the right to purchase 20% of Host's common stock if any person acquires more than 20% or announces a tender offer for 30% or more of Host's common stock. The two companies will have common management, as Richard Marriott will be Host's Chairman and J.W. Marriott a director of Host, while both are simultaneously serving as directors of International. There will be a non-competition agreement between the two companies.

Bondholders' suits lead to modified transaction

Despite Mr. Bollenbach's assurances of October 5, Marriott's bondholders reacted strongly against the proposed special dividend. The transaction will of course remove very substantial assets and even more cash flow from their debtor and will, in the circumstances, substantially increase the risk associated with the bondholders' investment, or so it was thought.

Ten class-action lawsuits seeking to block the dividend were filed by various classes of bondholders. They have been consolidated in the United States District Court for the District of Maryland.

On March 11, 1993, Marriott reached a settlement with the bondholder class action plaintiffs. The settlement, if effectuated, would require Marriott to cause the Host subsidiary HMH to offer to exchange for existing bonds new bonds (Exchange Bonds) with a longer average maturity and bearing an interest rate 100 basis points higher than the existing bonds. The Exchange Bonds will include restrictive covenants that greatly limit opportunities for HMH to transfer cash to Host. Host's airport and toll road concession businesses, representing the preponderant part of its operating assets, and 40% of its cash-flow, will be transferred to a subsidiary of HMH. A $630 million credit line will be provided by International to HMH, but it cannot be drawn on to pay preferred dividends. One effect of the Exchange Offer, and the transfers it contemplates, is to restrict further Host's ability, as a practical matter, to pay dividends to the preferred stock.

Shortly after the Exchange Offer settlement Marriott announced for the first time that it was intended that, following the special dividend, Host would not pay dividends on its preferred stock. On March 15, 1993, Host announced in an S.E.C. filing that:

> It is the Company's present intention following the Distribution to declare dividends on its preferred stock only to the extent earnings equal or exceed the amount of such dividends. Since Host Marriott is expected to report book losses following the Distribution, this policy would lead to an indefinite suspension of dividends on the Company's preferred stock.

Plaintiffs' acquisition of preferred stock and short sales of common

Plaintiffs began for the first time to purchase substantial amounts of Marriott's preferred stock following the announcement of the special dividend.[8]

Plaintiff, Presidents and Fellows of Harvard College began purchasing preferred shares on October 30, 1992 and steadily accumulated shares for the next several months. Harvard held 480,300 preferred shares as of June 4, 1993, 83,000 of which were purchased after March 15, 1993. HB Korenvaes began a steady accumulation of preferred shares on October 6, 1992 and by June 4, 1993 held 408,000 preferred shares, 35,000 of which were purchased on March 17, 1993.

Since the preferred stock is convertible at the option of the holder into 2.87 shares of Marriott common stock and bears a dividend of 8¼% on its stated (liquidation) value of $50 per share, the market value of a share of preferred stock includes two possible components of value: the value of the conversion right and the value of the preferences. The presence of a presently exercisable conversion right will assure that the market value of the preferred will not fall below the market value of the security or property into which the preferred might convert, in this case 2.87 shares of common stock (less transaction costs of the conversion). The stated dividend, the dividend preference and the liquidation preference and other features of the preferred will ordinarily assure that the preferred trades at some premium to the value of the conversion right.

In this instance plaintiffs have acquired a majority of the shares of the preferred stock. Plaintiffs, however, did not simply acquire preferred stock. The record shows that each of the plaintiffs, except one, have hedged their risk by entering short sales contracts with respect to Marriott common stock. In this way plaintiffs have isolated their risk to that part of the preferred stock trading value represented by that stock's preference rights. Any change in the market price of the preferred stock caused by movement in the value of the underlying common stock will in their case be offset by change in the extent of their obligations under the short sales contracts.

Marriott common and preferred stock price changes

The prices of both Marriott common stock and Marriott preferred stock have increased substantially since the announcement of the special dividend. On the last trading day before the announcement of the transaction Marriott's common stock closed at $17.125 per share. The day of the announcement the price increased to $19.25 and by June 4, 1993 it had reached $25.75, for a total increase of approximately 50.3%.

The price of Marriott preferred stock closed on the last trading day before the announcement at $62.75, which represented a premium of $13.54 over the value of the 2.8736 common shares into which each preferred share could convert. The day of the announcement the preferred stock increased to $68.875. On June 4, 1993 the price of the preferred stock closed at $77.00 per share, an increase of 22.8% over the pre-announcement market price. The premium that the preferred

---

8. On October 7, 1992, plaintiff AKT purchased 140,500 preferred shares at prices ranging from $60.50 to $62.00. The next day AKT sold 14,000 preferred shares. AKT purchased an additional 50,000 shares on March 19, 1993 and 10,000 on March 29, 1993 after Marriott's March 15, 1993 announcement that Host would not pay dividends on the preferred.

stock commanded over the common into which it could convert (i.e., the market value of the preferences) however, had by June 4th, shrunk, to $3.00.

Thus while both common stock and preferred stock have experienced substantial increases in the market value of their securities, because of the impact of their hedging strategy, plaintiffs are in a different position than are non-hedged holders of preferred stock. The reduction of the premium at which the preferred stock trades has resulted in losses on their short sales, leading some plaintiffs, as of June 4, 1993, to net unrealized losses on their investments.

For example, plaintiff Harvard as of June 4, 1993 owned 480,300 shares of preferred stock, which were purchased for $33,580,108 and which had a market value on that day of $37,724,801. Thus, this plaintiff has an unrealized profit of $4,144,693 on its investment in the preferred stock. Harvard also entered into short sales of 1,338,300 shares of Marriott common stock, approximately 2.8 times the number of preferred shares it purchased. It received $30,949,383 on these short sales. The cost to cover these short sales, however, has increased to $34,609,056, or $3,659,673 more than was received on the sales, representing an unrealized loss in that amount. Thus, as of June 4, 1993, although the value of the preferred stock owned by this plaintiff has increased in value by over $4 million, the total value of its investment position has increased by only $485,020.

[Plaintiffs' Account]

Plaintiffs take a dark view. They see themselves being forced by defendants to relinquish their preferences at a time when defendants cannot call or redeem their stock. This coercion is arranged for them, plaintiffs say, because the Marriott family is motivated to assure its continuing control over Host following the spin-off. That such a concern exists is evidenced by certain internal Marriott documents as well as by the existence of certain agreements that will give International the right to purchase 20% of Host's stock in the event that any person acquires 20% or announces a tender offer for 30% of Host's shares.

Working from the premise that control over Host is very important to the Marriott family, plaintiffs point out that after the special dividend (*and after the adjustment of the preferred stock conversion rate that it will require*) [emphasis added] the preferred stock (if none of it is converted before the distribution) would be in a position to convert into more than 50% of the Host common stock. Thus, on this view, given the size of the special dividend, the existence of the conversion right transforms the preferred stock into a threat to Marriott family control of Host. The answer to this problem that plaintiffs say was hit upon was to force the preferred to convert into Marriott common stock before the record date for the special dividend. How could this be done? The principal means, according to plaintiffs, was to announce as early as the filing of Marriott's preliminary proxy on March 15, 1993 that Host would suspend dividends on the preferred stock indefinitely and would not reinstitute payment of the dividend until the Company's "earnings equal or exceed the amount of such dividends."

The scheme that plaintiffs detect has other elements (some of which may constitute independent wrongs). For example, in order to make post-distribution conversion less attractive, plaintiffs assert that defendants are intending to deviate from the conversion rate adjustment formula in the certificate of designation.

Plaintiffs' theory has another, more machiavellian aspect. According to plaintiffs, defendants knew in October 1992 that Host would not pay a dividend on its preferred stock, but withheld that information, and even implied the contrary in public statements. The first question that this assertion raises is the following: If knowledge of the discontinuation of dividends would promote the posited scheme to force conversions, why would defendants in October withhold knowledge of the planned suspension of dividends? This is where the plaintiffs' account gets machiavellian. According to plaintiffs, defendants understood that institutional investors would move into the preferred stock following the October 5 announcement and that these investors would hedge their position by short-selling Marriott common. Investors in this position (who isolate their risk in the preference rights) are, it is said, particularly sensitive to the "coercive" effect of a suspension of dividends. Therefore in delaying the announcement of the preferred dividend suspension defendants intended to cause these especially susceptible holders to move into the preferred stock before they sprang their trap.

Plaintiffs assert that the proposed transaction and the suspension of dividends constitute multiple violations of the contractual rights of the preferred stock. The most plausible of these allegations is the claim that the special dividend violates the certificate of designation because it distributes such a large proportion of the value of Marriott that the certificate of designation provision designed to protect the economic value of the preferred, in the face of a special dividend, cannot work.

[The Section 5(e)(iv) Claim]

I turn now to analysis of that which I regard as the centrally important certificate provision, Section 5(e)(iv). That section affords protection against dilution of the conversion component of the market value of the preferred stock by providing an adjustment to the conversion price when the corporation declares a dividend of assets, including securities. The principle that appears embedded in Section 5(e)(iv) is that when the assets of the firm are depleted through a special distribution to shareholders, the preferred will be protected by the triggering of a conversion price adjustment formula. Under Section 5(e)(iv) the number of shares into which the preferred can convert will be proportionately increased in order to maintain the value of the preferred's conversion feature. The principle seems clear enough; the realization of it will inevitably involve problems.

Section 5(e)(iv) of the certificate of designation requires Marriott, when effectuating a special dividend, to leave sufficient net assets in the corporation to permit that Section to function as intended to protect the pre-disposition value of the preferred stock.

The language of the certificate of designation is as follows:

5. *Conversion Rights*. The holders of shares of Convertible Preferred Stock shall have the right at their option, to convert such shares into shares of Common Stock on the following terms and conditions:

(a) Shares of Convertible Preferred Stock shall be convertible at any time into fully paid and nonassessable shares of Common Stock at a conversion price of $17.40 per share of Common Stock (the "Conversion Price").

* * *

(e) The Conversion Price shall be adjusted from time to time as follows:

(iv) *In case the Corporation shall, by dividend or otherwise, distribute to all holders of its Common Stock . . . assets* (including securities . . .), *the Conversion Price shall be adjusted* so that the same shall equal the price determined by multiplying the Conversion Price in effect immediately prior to the close of business on the date fixed for the determination of stockholders entitled to receive such distribution by a fraction of which the numerator shall be the current market price per share (determined as provided in subsection (vi) below) of the Common Stock on the date fixed for such determination less the then fair market value (as determined by the Board of Directors, whose determination shall be conclusive and shall be described in a statement filed with the transfer agent for the Convertible Preferred Stock) of the portion of the evidences of indebtedness or assets so distributed applicable to one share of Common Stock and the denominator shall be such current market price per share of the Common Stock, such adjustment to become effective immediately prior to the opening of business on the day following the date fixed for the determination of stockholders entitled to receive such distribution. (emphasis added).

Thus, stated simply, whenever Marriott distributes assets to its common stockholders this provision protects the value of the preferred conversion right by reducing the conversion price. Protection of this type may be important to the buyer of preferred stock and presumably its inclusion will permit an issuer to arrange the sale of preferred stock on somewhat more advantageous terms than would otherwise be available. What is intuitively apparent is that in a narrow range of extreme cases, a dividend of property may be so large relative to the corporation's net worth, that following the distribution, the firm, while still solvent, will not represent sufficient value to preserve the pre-dividend value of the preferred's conversion right.

Appended to this opinion are three hypothetical cases in which the Section 5(e)(iv) formula is employed. Case 1 involves a dividend of 40% of the issuing corporation's net asset value. Case 2 is a dividend of 90% of net asset value. Case 3 displays the consequences of a dividend of 95% of asset value. Given the assumptions of the examples (i.e. preferred conversion rights equal 9.1% of total pre-distribution value), only in the last case does the Section 5(e)(iv) formula fail to function.

* * *

The following three hypotheticals demonstrate how §5(e)(iv) operates to preserve the economic value of the conversion rights of the preferred when the company's assets are distributed as dividends to the common stockholders, and how at extreme levels it could fail.

Case I

Assume a company, Corporation Y, with $1 billion in assets and no debts. It has 10 million shares of common stock and 1 million shares of cumulative convertible preferred stock having a face amount and liquidation preference of $100 million. The preferred is convertible into common stock at a price of $100 face amount per common share or into 1 million common shares, in total. The certificate of designation contains a provision identical to §5(e)(iv).

Assume further that the capital markets operate efficiently and the common stock trades at [a] price reflecting Corporation Y's asset values on a fully diluted basis.

Under these assumptions at time T_1, Current Market Price ("CMP") is determined as follows:

$$\text{CMP} = \$1 \text{ billion} \times \frac{1}{11 \text{ million shares}} = \$90.9091 \text{ per share}$$

$$\text{Preferred Conversion Value} = 1 \text{ million shares} \times \frac{\$90.9091}{1 \text{ share}} = \$90,909,100$$

At time T_2 Corporation Y declares a dividend of assets with a fair market value of $400 million or $40 per outstanding common share, leaving the company with $600 million in assets.

The conversion price would be adjusted by the same formula as applies in Section 5(e)(iv):

$$\text{ACP} = \text{CP} \times \frac{\text{CMP} - \text{FMV}}{\text{CMP}}$$

where:

ACP = Adjusted Conversion Price
CP = Conversion Price
FMV = Fair Market Value
CMP = Current Market Price common stock

$$\text{ACP} = 100 \times \frac{\$90.9091 - \$40}{\$90.9091} = \$56.0000$$

The preferred would become convertible into 1,785,710 common shares,

$$\$100,000,000 \times \frac{1 \text{ common stock}}{\$56.0000} = 1,785,710^*$$

With an aggregate value of $90,908,900,

$$\$600,000,000 \times \frac{1,785,710 \text{ converted shares}}{11,785,710 \text{ common shares}} = \$90,908,900$$

---

*Author's note: The court's opinion stated that the quotient of $100 million divided by $56 is 1,785,870 shares. The stated quotient is a typographical error in the court's opinion. This has been corrected in the above. The quotient should be 1,785,710 shares as accurately reflected in the preceding sentence.

Thus in this case the anti-dilution provision of the certificate would serve to preserve the economic value of the preferred stock despite the diversion of 40% of Corporation Y's net worth out of the company.

Case II

Now assume alternatively that Corporation Y declares a special dividend to its common stockholders of $900 million of its assets or $90 per outstanding share.

The conversion price adjustment formula would work to adjust the conversion price from $100 to 1.00 per share:

$$\text{ACP} = \$100 \text{ x } \frac{\$90.9091 - \$90}{\$90.9091} = \$1.0000$$

The preferred would become convertible into 100,000,000 shares, (91% of all common stock) at T_2.

$$\$100,000,000 \text{ x } \frac{1 \text{ common share}}{\$1.0000} = 100,000,000 \text{ shares}$$

But the aggregate value of the preferred portion would remain unchanged at $90,909,091:

$$\frac{100,000,000 \text{ converted shares}}{110,000,000 \text{ common shares}} \text{ x } \$100,000,000 = \$90,909,091$$

Thus, on these assumptions, even if 90% of Corporation Y's assets are distributed to the common stockholders, the conversion value of the preferred is maintained at its pre-distribution level by the Section 5(e)(iv) gross-up provision.

Case III

When the special dividend is so large that insufficient equity remains in Corporation Y to maintain the value of the preferred upon conversion the gross-up provisions will fail to work. In such a situation the gross-up equation provides for a negative adjusted conversion price and is therefore meaningless.

For example: If Corporation Y declared a dividend of $950 million of its assets, the gross-up equation would give the following result:

$$\text{ACP} = \text{CP x } \frac{\text{CMP} - \text{FMV}}{\text{CMP}}$$

$$\text{ACP} = \$100 \text{ x } \frac{\$90.9091 - \$95.00}{\$90.9091} - (\$4.499)$$

Thus, a distribution of $950 million leaves only $50 million in assets in the corporation, making it impossible for the preferred to maintain its pre-distribution conversion value of $90.909 million. For that reason it also causes Section 5(e)(iv) to fail to work meaningfully.

* * *

In light of the mathematical effect demonstrated in the [above] appended examples, a court that must construe Section 5(e)(iv) is required to conclude that Marriott has voluntarily and effectively bound itself not to declare and distribute special dividends of a proportion that would deprive the preferred stockholders of the protection that that provision was intended to afford. In providing a mechanism to maintain pre-distribution value (putting to one side for the moment, how pre-distribution value is determined) the issuer impliedly but unmistakably and necessarily undertook to refrain from declaring a dividend so large that what is left in the corporation is itself worth less than the pre-distribution value of the preferred stock. No other interpretation of the certificate of designation gives the language of Section 5(e)(iv) its intended effect in all circumstances. Thus, were the facts of Case 3 the facts of this case, I would be required to find that the special dividend violated the rights of the preferred stockholders created by the certificate of designation.

Such a holding would not be inconsistent with those cases that hold that rights of preference are to be strictly construed. This strict construction perspective on the interpretation of certificates of designation has long been the law of this jurisdiction and others. While that principle does define the court's approach to construction and interpretation of the documents that create preferred stock, that principle does not excuse a court from the duty to interpret the legal meaning of the certificate of designation. Thus where the necessary implication of the language used is the existence of a right or a duty, a court construing that language is duty bound to recognize the existence of that right or that duty.

Plaintiffs have failed to introduce evidence from which it could be concluded at this time that it is reasonably probable that they will prevail on a claim that the special dividend violates Section 5(e)(iv).

(i) *The value that Section 5(e)(iv) intends to protect is the market value of the conversion feature at the time the board authorizes a special dividend transaction.*

The determination that Section 5 of the certificate creates by necessary implication an obligation on the part of the corporation to leave sufficient value in the corporation following a special dividend to permit the protections it creates to function with the intended effect, raises the further question, what value does Section 5 intend to protect. Plainly it is the value of the conversion feature, that is what all of Section 5 is about, but measured at what point in time?

On the last day of trading before the announcement of the special dividend, Marriott's common stock closed at $17.125. The preferred's *conversion feature*, (its right to convert into 11,494,400 common shares) had a value at that time of $196,842,000. Beginning the first trading day after the announcement of the special dividend, Marriott common stock rose greatly in price. By May 21, 1993, it had increased to approximately $26.00 per share and the value of the preferred's conversion right had increased to $298.5 million.

Plaintiffs' position is that this value, as effected by the prospect of the dividend attacked, is the value that must be left in the corporation.

I cannot accept this interpretation of what good faith adherence to the provisions of the certificate requires of Marriott. Section 5(e)(iv) operates to prevent the confiscation of the value of the preferred conversion right through a special dividend. By necessary implication it limits the board's discretion with respect to the size of special dividends. But that limitation is one that has its effect when it is respected by the board of directors at the time it takes corporate action to declare the dividend. If, when declared, the dividend will leave the corporation with sufficient assets to preserve the conversion value that the preferred possesses at that time, it satisfies the limitation that such a protective provision necessarily implies. That is, Section 5(e)(iv) does not, in my opinion, explicitly or by necessary implication grant the preferred a right to assurance that any increase in the value of their conversion rights following the authorization of a special dividend be maintained.

(ii) *Plaintiffs have failed to introduce evidence that establishes a reasonable probability of their proving that the net value remaining in Host after distribution of the special dividend is or is reasonably likely to be insufficient to maintain the pre-distribution value of the preferred's conversion right.*

In attempting to demonstrate that the special dividend will confiscate some part of their property, plaintiffs rely on the affidavit of Charles Wright, a certified public accountant. Mr. Wright states that following the special dividend the value of Host's equity will not exceed $200 million. This opinion is based upon analyses conducted by Wolfensohn, Inc. in October 1992, concerning the transaction as planned at that time. But the transaction of October 1992 reflected a very different financial structure than that now planned; it contemplated Host bearing substantially more debt than the transaction currently envisioned. Mr. Wright's conclusions are also based upon analyses conducted by S.G. Warburg, but under the assumption that the Exchange Offer will not be effectuated.

The later projections by Wolfensohn and S.G. Warburg, provide a different picture of Host's financial status than the earlier ones upon which Mr. Wright relies. On May 7, 1993, Wolfensohn provided Marriott's board with current valuations of Host and International. Wolfensohn concluded that, assuming the Exchange Offer closes, Host will have a total equity value of between $371 million and $556 million.

A discounted cash flow valuation of Host produced by Wolfensohn on April 20, 1993 and based on the assumption that the Exchange Offer will be effectuated, produced a range of values from $270 million (assuming a 14% discount rate; and a multiple of 7 times EBITDA) to $884 million (assuming a 12% discount rate and a multiple of 9 times EBITDA) with a middle case of $567 million (assuming a 13% discount rate and a multiple of 8 times EBITDA.)

S.G. Warburg's valuation of Host, dated May 6, 1993, estimated the trading value of Host, assuming the Exchange Offer closes, at $1.38 to $2.84 per share or an aggregate of $179 million to $368 million.

The lower end of S.G. Warburg's estimate of the likely range of trading values for Host stock falls below the $196.8 million that represents the value of plaintiffs' conversion rights prior to the announcement of the distribution. Unspecified assertions by plaintiffs' expert that "major assumptions used in the discounted cash flow analysis are inappropriate" and that companies used for comparison are not comparable to Host, do not, however, provide a basis upon which to conclude that it is more likely that Host's common stock will have a value in the lower end of this range of values rather than in the higher part. The mere possibility that this will be the case is not enough to support the grant of a preliminary injunction. I assume the shape of a graph of the probabilities of any of these values in the range being "correct" would form a bell shaped curve. That is to say it is more likely that, upon more exhaustive analysis or with a more definitive valuation technique, the intrinsic value of Host would be the mean number of these ranges rather than either expressed limit of them. These higher probability mean estimates are all in excess of $196 million.

Thus, I am unable to conclude that plaintiffs have shown a sufficient probability of demonstrating that the protective functions of Section 5(e)(iv) will be frustrated by the size of the special dividend to justify the issuance of an injunction preventing the effectuation of the planned reorganization of Marriott.

Plaintiffs have not shown that defendants have breached (or are about to breach) the agreed upon formula for implementing Section 5(e)(iv).

In its June 19, 1993 proxy statement, Marriott described the process that it intends to employ with respect to the operation of Section 5(e)(iv) of the certificate. After paraphrasing the certificate language quoted above, the proxy statement states:

> The Board currently intends to determine the "fair market value" of the Distribution, for purposes of this calculation, by ascertaining the relative, intrinsic values of Host Marriott and Marriott International (with reference to all factors which it deems relevant) and by designating the allocable portion of the Current Market Price attributable to Marriott International as the fair market value of the Distribution.

In this litigation defendants have amplified their proposed method for determining fair market value of the individual distribution. Marriott intends to first determine "with reference to all relevant factors" the "intrinsic values" of International and Host. Then the fraction of the value of a Marriott share represented by International would be determined by dividing International's "intrinsic value" by the sum of the intrinsic values of International and Host. This fraction would then be multiplied by the current trading value of Marriott to determine the fair market value (per share) of International and thus of the distribution. Therefore, the fair market value of the distribution (i.e., International) is treated by the board's proposed valuation method *as fraction of the market value of Marriott prior to the distribution* of the dividend. The premise of this methodology is the assertion that as long as Host common stock trades at some positive value, the fair market value of International for purposes of applying Section 5(e)(iv) must be less than the current market value of Marriott; the whole (Marriott) cannot be less than the sum of its parts (International plus Host).

Author's Case Annotation: Marriott's Calculation of International's FMV

$$FMV_{Int'l} = \frac{Int'l_{Intrinsic}}{Int'l_{Intrinsic} + Host_{Intrinsic}} \times Marriott_{Current\ Market}$$

Defendants claim that this method of determining fair market value is consistent with the certificate and that it reaches a determination of the fair market value of the distribution that can meaningfully be compared to the current market value of

Marriott. Indeed, they assert that any alternative technique which yields a value for International that is higher than the market value of Marriott must (as long as Host trades at a positive value) be faulty.

Plaintiffs contend that defendants' approach is inconsistent with the contract language. They say that it is designed to hide the fact that the special dividend is so large that the conversion price adjustment formula cannot work properly with respect to it.

Plaintiffs point out that the conversion price adjustment formula requires as a numerator the current per share market price of Marriott (determined over a 30-day period) less the *"then fair market value"* (expressed as a per share figure) of the assets distributed.[19] This number can be well estimated, it is claimed, by reference to the "when-issued" market which will, for a week or so before the distribution, establish a good proxy for the market value of the assets distributed. [Thus, plaintiffs would calculate the fair market value of International as: $FMV_{International}$ = International (market value of distribution "when issued" to shareholders).]

The possibility of different measuring periods (the certificate language contemplates that the current market value of Marriott be measured over a thirty day period commencing forty five days before the distribution) would introduce a possibility for the when issued market for International to be higher on any particular day than the value of Marriott common stock over the measuring period.

Plaintiffs claim that the method of determining the fair market value of International which defendants propose to employ is an attempt to manipulate Section 5(e)(iv), by artificially limiting the "fair market value" of the assets to be distributed (International's common stock) to a fraction of Marriott's total value despite the fact that Section 5(e)(iv) makes no mention of such a limitation. Plaintiffs rely on the language of the certificate which states explicitly that the board must determine the fair market value of the assets to be distributed, to support their argument that the board is required to determine this value without placing a ceiling on it of the value of Marriott.

In my opinion, Marriott's proposed technique for determining the values to employ in the contractual formula is one valid way to do what the company is contractually bound to do. It follows that this claim presents no grounds to justify the issuance of a preliminary injunction.

It is, of course, the case that plaintiffs' alternative technique might seem superior to some, in that it looks to a direct market measure of the value of the distribution. While that has appeal, it is also true that the different measuring times that this technique implies itself makes it possible that it would cause the adjustment formula to produce a negative number. Given the multiple factors that affect public securities markets, this could be true, even if far more equity were left in Host than the value of the preferred. Thus, there is good reason to reject plaintiffs' proposal even though it has appealing aspects.

---

19. I need not express a view as to whether the "then" is best read as (i) the time of the distribution (record date) or (ii) the time period during which the market value of Marriott stock is determined under the formula. In all events the "then fair market" is to be decided "by the Board of Directors, whose determination shall be conclusive," so long as made in good faith I would add.

Defendants' intended technique for estimating the "fair market value applicable to one share" would appear to serve the purpose of the section. As explained above, the equation is intended to operate to reduce the conversion price by the same percentage that the total assets of the company are being reduced. Assuming again that Host will have some positive net worth, it is clear that less than 100 percent of the assets of Marriott are being distributed. Therefore, in such a case the conversion price should be reduced by less than 100 percent. The method adopted by the company for determining applicable fair market value would, if fairly and competently applied, provide for the adjustment of the conversion price in a manner that effectuates the purposes of the clause. The certificate of course confers broad discretion on Marriott in implementing the formula of Section 5(e)(iv) and makes its choices "conclusive." While that grant may too imply a duty of commercial good faith, the facts adduced do not suggest that the employment of the formula by defendants has been other than in good faith.

Thus, I am unable to conclude that plaintiffs have shown a reasonable probability of success on the merits of their claim that the method of determining the fair market value of the assets to be distributed "applicable to one share of [Marriott] common stock", that defendants have announced they will employ, violates Section 5(e)(iv).

In light of the weaknesses of plaintiffs' claim, I cannot conclude that they have shown a likelihood of success on the merits. Therefore this claim cannot support the grant of the requested injunctive relief.

QUESTIONS

1. The plaintiffs purchased shares in the convertible preferred stock after the announcement of the transaction. They also hedged against the risk of fluctuations in the common stock price by shorting the stock, even though, if the transaction was value creating, the stock price should increase (and it did increase). In what way did the plaintiff seek to profit from their purchase of the convertible preferred stock?
2. The convertible preferred stockholders could have converted to common stock. Why did they not want to convert prior to the special distribution?
3. What is the court's legal theory that a distribution can be so large as to undermine the antidilution protection of §5(e)(iv)? In other words, §5(e)(iv) is silent as to permissible distribution; it simply provides for an adjustment of the conversion ratio. What is the theory that an improper action has been taken?
4. The plaintiffs and the defendant disagreed on the methods to value Marriott, Host, and International in the conversion adjustment formula. Describe the difference.

NOTES

1. An intuitive way to think about the effects of distribution is picturing the effects of a distribution on the balance sheet. The court references in the appendix three cases of distribution. In Case II, 90 percent of the assets were distributed to common shareholders, and the convertible preferred's claim on the assets is approximately 9 percent. The hypothetical company has no debt. Below is a pictorial representation of the distribution (note that the box areas are not to scale).

PERMISSIBLE

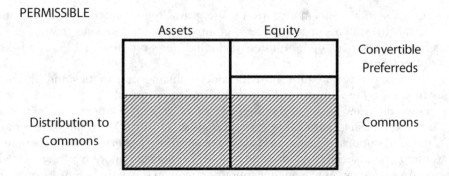

In Case III, 95 percent of assets are distributed to common shareholders. As a result, the claim of the convertible preferred stockholders is compromised.

IMPERMISSIBLE

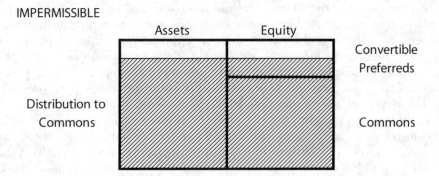

2. As the case referenced, the bondholders brought suit. *See, e.g., PPM America, Inc. v. Marriott Corp.*, 820 F.Supp. 970 (D.Md. 1993); *PPM America, Inc. v. Marriott Corp.,* 1993 WL 722257. Bondholders subsequently settled with Marriott. *See* Michael Dresser, *Marriott reaches accord with large bondholders over plan to split up 1 group balks, but analysts hail deal*, The Baltimore Sun (Mar. 12, 1993).

C. VENTURE CAPITAL

1. FINANCING NEW VENTURES

Venture capital (VC) is capital used by specialized financial intermediaries (VC firms) that help new and startup companies grow by seeding these firms with equity capital. The investment is typically more than money, and the VC firms provide advice and assistance at the broader board and executive level. VC firms are financial intermediaries because they aggregate capital contributions from various investors, and they invest and manage the investment fund and portfolio of companies on behalf of investors. The investors are varied and include insurance companies, banks, pension funds, sovereign funds, and high net worth individuals.

Related to venture capital is private equity. In the broadest terms, private equity is all investments that are not registered under the securities laws and thus cannot be resold in the public market. Private equity can have debt components to it despite the "equity" moniker. In a more narrow sense, private equity refers to a class of nonpublic capital investments managed by a group of investors looking for higher risk and private investment opportunities, including investors in VC, LBO, and distressed restructuring.

VC and private equity firms provide financing possibilities and alternatives in situations where capital is limited. Financing is one of the principal problems in launching a new business venture by an entrepreneur. If a new project is undertaken by an established corporation with sufficient resources, it would have a number of financing options, *e.g.*, internal funding or a variety of external funding options. For an entrepreneur seeking external funding, the options are more typically limited.

An entrepreneur's financing options depend on the nature of the business risk and the capital requirements. When the businesses are less risky and novel, the possibility of financing is greater.

If the venture is a small business with an established business model (see quadrant I of the accompanying chart), it can be funded by some combination of the entrepreneur's equity and small loans. The businesses are uncomplicated and fairly assessable. Debt financing is suitable because there is an expectation of recurring cash flow that services principal and interest. There is always unique business risk that a creditor would be undertaking, but the business model is proven. An example of this type of investment is a pizza restaurant. This business is uncomplicated and assessable, and while there is always unique risk of each business (*e.g.*, maybe the restaurant's pizza is not that good), the business model has been proven.

If the capital needs are much greater (see chart, quadrant II), it can be funded by large commercial loans, project financing through a combination of loans and bonds with a syndicate of lenders, or strategic partnerships with a corporation that has an interest in the project. Debt financing is suitable because there is an expectation of recurring cash flow. An example of this type of project could be the erection of cell-phone antenna towers, which require significant capital investment but, again, the business model revolving around cellphones has been tested.

Entrepreneurial Financing

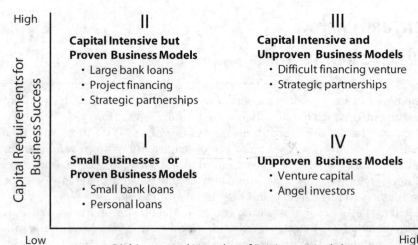

II
Capital Intensive but Proven Business Models
- Large bank loans
- Project financing
- Strategic partnerships

III
Capital Intensive and Unproven Business Models
- Difficult financing venture
- Strategic partnerships

I
Small Businesses or Proven Business Models
- Small bank loans
- Personal loans

IV
Unproven Business Models
- Venture capital
- Angel investors

Capital Requirements for Business Success (High / Low)

Riskiness and Novelty of Business Model (Low / High)

When the businesses are more risky and novel, the possibility and the options of financing are reduced. If the venture is a capital-intensive investment with a risky or unproven business model (see chart, quadrant III), there are funding difficulties. Debt financing is difficult because the amount of credit required is large, and the possibility that the venture cannot produce the necessary cash flow is high. There is a bit of a Catch-22 in these situations: In terms of creditworthiness, these projects may require "junk" (high-yield) debt, but the pricing at these levels may greatly increase the possibility of default. Some form of equity investment is required, but the list of potential investors would be smaller due to the required size of the investment. There are some venture capital firms that may have sufficient capital to deploy, but a consortium of such firms may be required to share the risk. Another typical way to fund these projects is to enter into a strategic partnership with a corporation with sufficient resources. An example of this type of investment is a new infrastructure project using new, unproven technology. Some biotech or pharmaceutical startups may also fit this profile (for example, *Equity-Linked Investors, L.P. v. Adams* in *supra* Chapter 6, the company ultimately went through $1.2 billion of shareholder money).

If the venture is a new or unproven business model and the required capital investment is not large (see chart, quadrant IV), this situation is ideal for VC investment. Equity is best when debt is infeasible. The amount of investment is smaller. This is important to manage a VC firm's risk. Since many investments are required in a portfolio to smooth out the risk in this type of investment activity, smaller investments facilitate this diversification strategy.

Since each investment in a startup venture is risky and speculative, VC firms expect many investments, if not most, to fail. Successful VC firms generate large returns from a minority of "home run" investments. Think of companies like Amazon, eBay, and Google: The VC investors that invested early in these companies made huge returns, and these returns would more than offset the many failed investments in the portfolio. VC firms therefore rely on "lumpy" returns on the investments in the portfolio, *i.e.*, a few investments may provide the majority of the return on the VC fund. The following table provides a simple illustration.

The VC firm made equal investments of $1,000 in six firms. Three of the firms (B, D, and E) are total failures. In investment C, the VC firm essentially gets its money back. Only two of the firms are considered a "success" in some form. If the VC firm's

	Investments	Returns				
COMPANIES	YEAR 0	YEAR 1	YEAR 2	YEAR 3	YEAR 4	YEAR 5
A	(1,000)	–	–	–	–	2,000
B	(1,000)	–	–	–	–	–
C	(1,000)	10	50	50	50	1,000
D	(1,000)	–	–	–	–	200
E	(1,000)	–	–	–	–	–
F	(1,000)	–	–	–	–	15,000
Total	(6,000)	10	50	50	50	18,200
Portfolio IRR	25%					

benchmark rate of return is 25 percent, even investment A is a failure since the IRR is 15 percent, and this return does not clear the 25 percent hurdle. Only investment F is a success, achieving a 72 percent IRR. Collectively, this portfolio of investments achieves the VC firm's benchmark rate of return of 25 percent.

Since many investments will ultimately be failures, a part of managing a portfolio of investments is to ration capital. Capital is limited, and thus VC firms actively shift capital away from failing investments to those with more promise. When they determine that a venture is failure, they want to quickly recover as much money as possible and deploy it to other investments. Obviously, in these situations the entrepreneurs who started the company would feel differently. Just as there is an inherent tension between creditors and equityholders, there is also an inherent tension between venture capitalists and entrepreneurs. Although inherent tension can be managed and success tends to align the interests, the tension is present whenever there are different classes of securityholders.

2. VALUATION

The valuation of startup firms is very difficult, if not impossible, to calculate in a way that results in highly reliable figures. There are no prior data to use as guidance in projecting future outcomes. Startups seek to enter unknown markets, create their own markets, or use unproven business models or technologies. Who can really predict the outcomes of these things? VC firms attempt to do so, and some firms may be quite good at picking winners, but the risk from each investment is high. These risks are minimized by a rigorous set of investment criteria, a key component of which is an assessment of the entrepreneur and the management team. If the entrepreneur and the management team are not good, then irrespective of how good the idea may be the chance of failure is high. Given these realities, how are investments valued?

The first step in this process is to understand the benchmark return that the VC firm seeks. Suppose that given the risks, the VC firm's target rate of return is 30 percent. The answer to the ultimate question ("yes" or "no") will depend on the expectation of the exit value. Consider an investment in which the entrepreneur seeks $5 million in equity. The exit, either an IPO or a sale of the company, is expected to be in six years. The VC firm's stake must be worth $24 million.

Initial investment:	$5 million
Target rate of return:	30%
Exit term:	6 years
Exit value required:	$24 million = $5 million $\times$ $(1 + 30\%)^6$

Valuation shows that the firm is expected to have a total value of $50 million in six years. Assume that the entrepreneur, the management, the business model, and the valuation have been vetted, and the VC firm is satisfied with the soundness of the business opportunity. The financial opportunity, which must also be sound, depends on the valuation. The VC firm must have $24 million of the firm worth $50 million in six years. This means that the $5 million investment must result in a purchase of 48 percent of the company, otherwise the VC firm will say "no." This is what we mean when we say that equity in a VC financing is expensive—the entrepreneur must give up 48 percent of the company to get the investment.

Once the VC firm and the entrepreneur agree on the investment, two different valuations are implied: a "post-money valuation" and a "pre-money valuation."

$$\text{Post Money Valuation} = \frac{\text{Investment Amount}}{\text{Percentage of Investor's Ownership}}$$

Pre Money Valuation = (Post Money Valuation) − (Investment Amount)

In the above, the post-money valuation is $10.4 million (= $5 million ÷ 48%), and the pre-money valuation is $5.4 million.

The above example shows that the negotiation with a VC firm over the financial terms revolves around the VC firm's target return and the anticipated exit valuation. Compare the above situation with these two cases:

Case 1: lower target return for VC
Target rate of return: 20%
Exit value required: $15 million = $5 million × $(1 + 20\%)^6$
Percent sale of company: 30% = $15 million ÷ $50 million

Case 2: higher exit valuation of company
Target rate of return: 30%
Exit value required: $24 million = $5 million × $(1 + 30\%)^6$
Percent sale of company: 24% = $24 million ÷ $100 million

A typical form of VC investment takes the form of a convertible preferred stock. The investment structure is schematized below.

Value of VC Convertible

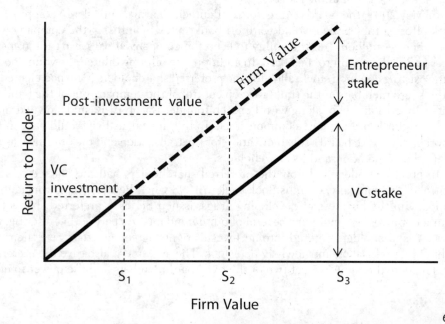

The VC firm invests equity of S_1. Since this is a preferred stock, the VC firm has a liquidation preference over the common stock, which is typically the entrepreneur. As long as the value of the firm is at S_1 or greater, the initial VC investment is protected. At a certain point S_2, the option value of the conversion becomes greater than the value of the straight preferred stock.

The above examples are based on one round of funding with a single VC firm negotiating with the entrepreneur. In many situations, a company will undergo several rounds of funding, often with different VC firms and sources of financing. The negotiation among the parties, much of which turns on the questions of rate of return and valuation, can become complicated.

3. PREFERRED STOCK IN VENTURE CAPITAL DEALS

A common financial instrument used to invest in a startup or young company is a convertible preferred stock with each series denoting a subsequent round of financing. Various issues may arise with respect to the rights of the convertible preferred stock and the issuing corporation or entrepreneur who holds the common stock.

The following case involves the recurring issue in venture capital investments of a potential change of control. Change of control can become serial, first experienced by the entrepreneur when the original "Series A" equity is issued, and then later experienced by earlier financiers during multiple rounds of financing. Dilution of control rights and economic claims is a reality of financing corporate enterprises, and particularly so for startups and young companies.

Fait v. Hummel
333 F.3d 854 (7th Cir. 2003)

TERENCE T. EVANS, Circuit Judge.

In May 2001, the board of directors of Pentech Pharmaceuticals, Inc. approved a stock offering they hoped would ward off bankruptcy by infusing the company with more than $4 million. But the ability to keep the company afloat wasn't the transaction's only selling point to the board. In addition, the offering diluted the voting power of the existing common stock, allowing the preferred shareholders (who had elected all of the board members at the time) to keep control of the company out of the hands of Fait—Robert Fait, who, along with Pentech founder Ragab El-Rashidy, owned more than two-thirds of Pentech's common stock. In this appeal, as Fait would have it, the power grab was the board's sole motivation for the transaction and the offering was not fair to the corporation and its shareholders.

In order to understand how the preferred shareholders had the chance to seize control of the company, we must look back to 1998 when Pentech, a pharmaceutical company in the business of developing drugs, issued Series A preferred shares to a number of investors, including several of our defendants. As part of that offering, the Series A shareholders entered into an investor rights agreement that gave them the right of first refusal on any newly issued stock. The agreement also gave the preferred shareholders the right to elect two of the five board members and the power to elect four of the five for a period of 2 years if Pentech violated certain covenants in the agreement.

The Series A shareholders took advantage of the latter provision in the fall of 2000 when an Illinois court agreed with the Series A shareholders' contention that Pentech had violated the rights agreement, giving the preferred shareholders the right to elect four of the five directors. They used their opportunity to replace Fait and another director elected by the common shareholders and then placed El-Rashidy on administrative leave from his duties as CEO. El-Rashidy resigned from the board of directors soon after and was not immediately replaced, leaving just four board members (all elected by the preferred shareholders) at the time of the offering-Dr. Bruce Ronsen and defendants James Lumsden, Albert Hummel, and Howard Myles.

On May 3, 2001, Ronsen, Hummel, and Myles voted unanimously to offer 4,220,921 shares of common stock for $1/share (because of his close ties to many of the Series A shareholders, Lumsden abstained). On the advice of Lumsden, the Series A shareholders exercised their right of first refusal and bought all of the available shares. Fait challenged the validity of the transaction, claiming it was unfair because it diluted the interest of the common shareholders and because the $1/share price was inadequate. He thinks Pentech would have been better off raising capital by taking on an investor, specifically Julphar Pharmaceuticals, Inc. Julphar had been discussing the possibility of buying up to $20 million worth of Series B preferred stock from Pentech, but the talks broke down. Fait claims the Pentech board gave up on the deal with Julphar prematurely because the May 3 offering gave the Series A shareholders a chance to achieve their true objective of retaining permanent control of Pentech. As such, he says the board should have had to prove that the offering was the best option for Pentech and that it was fair. The district court found in favor of the board after a 7-day bench trial, concluding that Fait had the burden of proving that the offering was not fair and that he did not meet that burden. Fait appeals that ruling.

Under Illinois law a director who receives a personal benefit from a corporate transaction has the burden of showing that the transaction was fair to the corporation, unless the transaction was approved by disinterested directors or shareholders with knowledge of all material facts.* Fait admits that the transaction was approved by a majority of the disinterested directors (as a Series A shareholder, Hummel benefitted from the offering, but Myles and Ronsen were disinterested). Instead, Fait argues that the interested directors should have borne the burden of proving the fairness of the offering because Myles and Ronsen did not have sufficient knowledge of all material

---

* Author's note: The Illinois statute, 805 ILCS 5/8.60(a), provides:

If a transaction is fair to a corporation at the time it is authorized, approved, or ratified, the fact that a director of the corporation is directly or indirectly a party to the transaction is not grounds for invalidating the transaction or the director's vote regarding the transaction; provided, however, that in a proceeding contesting the validity of such a transaction, the person asserting validity has the burden of proving fairness unless:

(1) the material facts of the transaction and the director's interest or relationship were disclosed or known to the board of directors or a committee of the board and the board or committee authorized, approved or ratified the transaction by the affirmative votes of a majority of disinterested directors, even though the disinterested directors be less than a quorum; or

(2) the material facts of the transaction and the director's interest or relationship were disclosed or known to the shareholders entitled to vote and they authorized, approved or ratified the transaction without counting the vote of any shareholder who is an interested director.

facts. Fait wants us to review the knowledge requirement *de novo,* but his argument ignores the fact that the district court's interpretation of the knowledge requirement was based on her factual findings, which we review only for clear error.

Although Illinois courts have rarely explored what constitutes "knowledge" in this context, some factors include whether the disinterested directors knew the market value of the proposed shares, whether they knew of the effects of the deal on the existing shareholders, and whether they knew of possible alternative sources of revenue. Myles and Ronsen knew all of that and more.

Fait admits that Myles had general knowledge of Pentech's financial condition but says that he should have had more specific information and done more independent research, especially as to an appropriate share price, before making his decision. Similarly, Fait argues that Ronsen, who has a doctorate in pharmacology, knew a lot about the drugs Pentech was developing but very little about the business side of the company. Fait also claims that any information Myles and Ronsen had about the transaction was tainted because it came from Lumsden and Hummel, who stood to gain financially if the offering went through.

Although Myles and Ronsen could have hired outside experts or done more research, both had sufficient knowledge to meet the requirements of 805 ILCS 5/8.60. Myles worked as an independent consultant for pharmaceutical medical device companies, so he was very familiar with the industry. In addition, he had spent nearly 5 years during two stints on the Pentech board, reviewed monthly reports on Pentech's financial condition, and frequently attended meetings and discussed Pentech's financial condition and options with other members of the board. Ronsen was equally well-informed. He voted for the offering after spending 7 years as Pentech's senior vice-president. During that time he was in charge of all of Pentech's daily operations, making him, as the district judge accurately noted, "personally familiar with Pentech's financial history and the value of its stock." In addition, both Myles and Ronsen had first-hand information about Julphar and other opportunities for outside investment. They knew about Pentech's dire financial situation, and they knew of the risks of trying to strike a deal with Julphar (which had never done business in the United States) or waiting for another outside investor. And although much of their information came from discussions with Lumsden and Hummel, they knew that their fellow board members had personal stakes in seeing the deal go through and were able to evaluate those conversations accordingly. Put together, Myles and Ronsen had knowledge of all material facts, leaving Fait with the burden to prove that the offering was not fair to the corporation.

Almost by his own admission, Fait cannot meet that burden. He fails to offer any experts or evidence to counteract the board's two expert witnesses, who testified that $1/share was a fair price. In fact, at oral argument, Fait was unable to offer a price he would have considered fair. In addition, neither side disputes that Pentech was experiencing serious financial problems, with bankruptcy (which would have left the common stock virtually worthless) a real possibility. Although Fait and the board disagreed about the best place to secure the capital they agree Pentech needed, the ultimate decision rested with the board as long as that decision was fair to Pentech, and Fait has not proven that it was not.

Because we find that Fait did not prove the transaction was unfair, we do not have to reach the issues he appeals regarding an appropriate remedy.

QUESTIONS

1. What circumstance led to the original investor and founder, Fait and El-Rashidy respectively, losing control of the company?
2. Is the potential for loss of control inevitable in subsequent negotiations for equity financing? What are the business considerations for the venture capital firm and the entrepreneur?
3. From the perspective of the venture capital firm, the company is without Fait and El-Rashidy. Is this good or bad? What does the venture capital firm do now?

The following two cases are recent cases in Delaware involving venture capital investments. They present different specific legal issues, but the core of the dispute involves the different financial and economic interests of the venture capital firm and the corporation or other securityholders.

SV Investment Partners, LLC v. ThoughtWorks, Inc.
7 A.3d 973 (Del. Ch. 2010)

LASTER, Vice Chancellor.

The plaintiffs are a group of affiliated investment funds and their advisor, SV Investment Partners, LLC (collectively, "SVIP"). In 2000, they purchased over 94% of the Series A Preferred Stock issued by the defendant ThoughtWorks, Inc. The amended and restated certificate of incorporation of ThoughtWorks dated granted the holders of the Preferred Stock the right to have their stock redeemed "for cash out of any funds legally available therefor" beginning five years after issuance. SVIP first exercised its redemption right in 2005.

ThoughtWorks does not have and cannot obtain the cash to redeem the Preferred Stock in full. Instead, each quarter, its board of directors (the "Board") carefully evaluates the Company's finances to determine (i) whether ThoughtWorks has surplus from which a redemption could be made, (ii) whether ThoughtWorks has or could readily obtain cash for a redemption, and (iii) whether a redemption would endanger the Company's ability to continue as a going concern. Over sixteen quarters, the Board has redeemed Preferred Stock on eight separate occasions. A total of 222,802 shares have been redeemed with a total value of $4.1 million.

SVIP objects to the Board's periodic approach. According to SVIP, the term "funds legally available" simply means "surplus." SVIP presented an expert at trial who opined that ThoughtWorks has surplus of $68 to $137 million. SVIP argues that while ThoughtWorks may not have cash or the ability to get it, it nevertheless has "funds legally available" and must redeem the Preferred Stock. Because ThoughtWorks has failed to do so, SVIP believes itself entitled to a judgment for the aggregate redemption price. As of April 5, 2010, that amount was $66,906,539.

SVIP's theory breaks down because the phrase "funds legally available" is not equivalent to "surplus." A corporation can have "funds" and lack "surplus," or have "surplus" and lack "funds." The binding constraint on ThoughtWorks' ability to redeem the Preferred Stock is a lack of funds and the concomitant risk that a significant redemption will render the Company insolvent. An unbroken line of decisional authority dating back to the late nineteenth century prohibits a corporation from redeeming shares when the payment would render the corporation insolvent. Even assuming that SVIP were correct and ThoughtWorks could be deemed to have "surplus," SVIP has not shown that ThoughtWorks has "funds legally available." Judgment is therefore entered in favor of ThoughtWorks and against SVIP.

Factual Background

The following factual findings have been made after a two-day trial. I also have relied on the factual findings made in a prior decision involving the parties, which are res judicata. *See ThoughtWorks, Inc. v. SV Inv. P'rs, LLC*, 902 A.2d 745 (Del.Ch. 2006) (the "*Working Capital Decision*").

Roy Singham founded ThoughtWorks in 1993. The Company describes itself as an information technology professional services firm that develops and delivers custom business software applications and provides related consulting services. Headquartered in Chicago, ThoughtWorks provides services to clients throughout the United States and, through subsidiaries, in various parts of the world. Singham owns approximately 94% of ThoughtWorks' common stock.

Singham created ThoughtWorks to establish "a prestige brand of outstanding talent" in the software consulting industry. To achieve this goal, he fostered a "secret sauce culture" that would appeal to the very best software developers, who, in his estimation, are ten to twenty times more productive than average software developers. ThoughtWorks places tremendous emphasis on recruiting elite professionals and providing them with challenging and intellectually stimulating work. The Company's employees, known as "ThoughtWorkers," are its most valuable asset.

The nature of ThoughtWorks' business makes for volatile cash flows. ThoughtWorks' engagements are typically short-term. Although some clients have engaged ThoughtWorks on multiple occasions over the years, each engagement typically lasts three to six months, does not automatically renew, and is subject to cancellation on as little as fifteen-days' notice. ThoughtWorkers arrive at the scene, solve the problem, and move on. As a result, ThoughtWorks' ability to forecast cash flows accurately is limited, and ThoughtWorks consistently failed to meet its forecasts every year through 2008.

Additionally, ThoughtWorks' business tends to be hyper-cyclical. In a downturn, clients terminate ThoughtWorks' contracts before laying off their own employees. In an upturn, clients engage ThoughtWorks before committing to new permanent hires. The business is also seasonal, largely due to ThoughtWorkers and clients taking holiday vacations. ThoughtWorks' slow period runs from November to January, causing the first calendar quarter to be a low point for cash flow.

Because of the volatility in its business, ThoughtWorks' management historically has tried to maintain a cash cushion that will enable the firm to ride out unexpected revenue shortfalls and seasonal lows. This is not to suggest that management has sought (much less been able) to amass a war chest. Rather, management prudently tries to keep some funds on hand so that checks don't bounce during a dry spell.

In 1999, ThoughtWorks began to consider an initial public offering. ThoughtWorks retained an investment bank, S.G. Cowen Securities, for advice. Having an existing venture capital investor was thought to enhance a new issuer's credibility.

ThoughtWorks and S.G. Cowen therefore prepared a confidential offering memorandum for a $25 million private equity investment.

SVIP received the offering memorandum and liked the ThoughtWorks opportunity. In contrast to the stereotypical dot-com concept, ThoughtWorks had a seven-year track record of revenue growth and profitability, and its customers consisted primarily of blue-chip, Fortune 1000 firms. While SVIP recognized that it was "paying a full valuation for the business," the firm believed that the deal could "provide attractive returns on reasonably (and comparatively) conservative exit assumptions." SVIP saw the "potential to achieve exceptional returns" if then-current market valuations held. As SVIP noted in its investment recommendation, ThoughtWorks "could be an early IPO in a market which has recently seen some extraordinary valuations."

When negotiating the terms of SVIP's investment, both SVIP and ThoughtWorks anticipated an IPO within a year or two. They also discussed redemption rights for SVIP in case no IPO materialized. The ThoughtWorks offering memorandum proposed a redemption right after seven years, with the payments made in twelve quarterly installments. SVIP countered with a redemption right after four years, then softened that demand to redemption after five years. ThoughtWorks proposed a two-year payout period. SVIP rejected that term. The parties compromised on a redemption right after five years, subject both to the legal availability of funds and to a one-year working capital carve-out.

On April 5, 2000, SVIP invested $26.6 million in ThoughtWorks in exchange for 2,970,917 shares of the Preferred Stock. Another 167,037 shares were purchased by eighteen individuals who are not parties to this action.

The Pertinent Terms of The Preferred Stock

The holders of the Preferred Stock are entitled to receive cumulative cash dividends at a rate of 9% per annum, compounded semi-annually and accruing semi-annually in arrears. In any liquidation, dissolution, or winding up of the Company, the Preferred Stock is entitled to a liquidation preference equal to the initial purchase price of $8.95 per share (adjusted for any stock dividends, splits, recapitalizations, or consolidations) plus all accrued and unpaid dividends, plus an amount equal to what the Preferred Stock would receive in liquidation assuming it were converted into common stock and shared ratably with the common.

Critically for the current case, Article IV(B), Section 4(a) of the Charter sets out the Preferred Stock's redemption right (the "Redemption Provision"). It states:

> On the date that is the fifth anniversary of the Closing Date . . . , if, prior to such date, the Company has not issued shares of Common Stock to the public in a Qualified Public Offering . . . each holder of Preferred Stock shall be entitled to require the Corporation to *redeem for cash out of any funds legally available therefor* and which have not been designated by the Board of Directors as necessary to fund the working capital requirements of the Corporation for the fiscal year of the Redemption Date, not less than 100% of the Preferred Stock held by each holder on that date. Redemptions of each share of Preferred Stock made pursuant to this Section 4 shall be made at the greater of (i) the Liquidation Price and (ii) the Fair Market Value (as determined pursuant to Section 4(e) below) of the Preferred Stock.

The Redemption Provision contains two limitations on the Company's obligation "to redeem for cash." First, the redemption can only be "out of any funds legally available therefor." Second, the provision excludes funds "designated by the Board of Directors as necessary to fund the working capital requirements of the Corporation for the fiscal year of the Redemption Date."

Article IV also addresses what happens if "funds of the Corporation legally and otherwise available for redemption pursuant to Section 4(a)" are "insufficient to redeem all the Preferred Stock required to be redeemed." In that event,

> funds to the extent so available shall be used for such purpose and the Corporation shall effect such redemption pro rata according to the number of shares held by each holder of Preferred Stock. The redemption requirements provided hereby shall be continuous, so that if at any time after the Redemption Date such requirements shall not be fully discharged, without further action by any holder of Preferred Stock, funds available pursuant to Section 4(a) shall be applied therefor until such requirements are fully discharged.

Charter art. IV(B), §4(d). The same provision states that "for the purpose of determining whether funds are legally available for redemption . . . , the Corporation shall value its assets at the highest amount permissible under applicable law" (the "Valuation Provision").

The Bubble Bursts and the IPO Is Abandoned

On March 10, 2000, the NASDAQ peaked at 5132.52 in intraday trading, having more than doubled in the preceding year. A year later, on March 9, 2001, the NASDAQ closed at 2,052.78, down 59.3%. Three years later, on March 10, 2003, the NASDAQ closed at 1,278.37. It rapidly became clear to everyone that an IPO was no longer a realistic possibility for ThoughtWorks in the near term.

ThoughtWorks Explores Ways to Redeem the Preferred Stock

In 2003, ThoughtWorks began considering internally how it might redeem the Preferred Stock. After an extensive analysis, ThoughtWorks general counsel Daniel Goodwin and CFO Eric Loughmiller concluded that ThoughtWorks likely could not pay approximately $43 million to redeem the Preferred Stock in April 2005. In October and November 2003, Singham presented the "Solving The Put Program" to the Global Operating Committee and the Board, identifying the redemption as one of ThoughtWorks' top three priorities.

ThoughtWorks informed SVIP in the summer of 2003 that it would not be able to meet the redemption obligation. During late 2003 and 2004, ThoughtWorks and SVIP discussed possible resolutions. In January 2005, ThoughtWorks engaged an investment bank, William Blair and Company, to seek debt financing to redeem the Preferred Stock. In the hope that financing could be obtained, SVIP agreed to postpone the earliest date the redemption payment would be due until July 5, 2005.

William Blair prepared a confidential information memorandum and distributed it to forty-five potential lenders. In April 2005, William Blair presented the lending proposals from potential lenders in a joint meeting with ThoughtWorks and SVIP. The results were disappointing. ThoughtWorks had hoped to secure at least $30 million in debt financing, but the largest proposal was for $20 million. With no ability to pay $43 million, ThoughtWorks formally offered to redeem all of the Preferred Stock for $12.8 million. SVIP rejected the offer.

Meanwhile, by demand letters sent by the various SVIP entities, SVIP exercised its redemption rights and requested immediate and full redemption effective July 5, 2005.

On July 1, 2005, the ThoughtWorks Board held a special meeting to consider the SVIP redemption demand. The Board focused on the working capital restriction and concluded that "funds required to fund the working capital requirements of the Company [were] an amount in excess of available cash on July 5, 2005." Because of the resulting lack of usable cash, the Board declined to redeem SVIP's shares of Preferred Stock.

After SVIP disagreed with ThoughtWorks' position, the Company filed a declaratory judgment action in this Court to obtain a determination that "it has the right, ongoing from year to year, to exclude necessary working capital from the funds available to pay the redemption obligation." *Working Capital Decision*, 902 A.2d at 752. This Court concluded that "the working capital set-aside applied only in fiscal year 2005, and, thus, ThoughtWorks must now redeem SVIP's preferred stock *to the extent funds are legally available therefor*." Id. at 754 (emphasis added). The Court noted that "the question whether ThoughtWorks has legally available funds under Delaware law to apply to its redemption obligation was not at issue in this action." A final order was entered July 25, 2006.

No Legally Available Funds

Shortly after this Court issued its final order, SVIP again exercised its redemption right. On August 3, 2006, SVIP demanded that ThoughtWorks redeem its Preferred Stock for $45 million, representing the aggregate redemption price at the time.

In response, the Board analyzed the extent to which the Company had "funds legally available" to make a redemption payment. The Board obtained legal advice from Freeborn & Peters LLP and financial advice from AlixPartners LLC. A Freeborn memorandum set out the process for the Board to follow:

> In declaring the amount of legally available funds for redemption, the Board must (a) not declare an amount that exceeds the corporation's surplus as determined by the Board at the time of the redemption, (b) reassess its initial determination of surplus if the Board determines that a redemption based on that determination of surplus would impair the Company's ability to continue as a going concern, thereby eroding the value of any assets (such as work in process and accounts receivable) that have materially lower values in liquidation than as part of a going concern, such that the value assumptions underlying the initial computation of surplus are no longer sustainable and the long term health of the Company is jeopardized, (c) exercise its affirmative duty to avoid decisions that trigger insolvency, (d) redeem for cash, (e) apply the amount declared pro rata to the Redeemed Stock, and (f) recognize the right of the Preferred Shareholders to a continuous remedy if the amount declared is not sufficient to satisfy in full the redemption obligation under the Charter.

At the August 24 meeting, the Board determined that ThoughtWorks had $500,000 of funds legally available and redeemed Preferred Stock in that amount.

In each of the subsequent sixteen quarters, the Board has followed the same process to determine the extent to which funds are legally available for redemptions. In each case, the Board has considered current financial information about the Company and consulted with its advisors. For example, in March 2010, AlixPartners advised the Board that ThoughtWorks' "net asset value" was in the range of $6.2 to $22.3 million, and its "cash availability"—net of the previously declared but still unpaid redemptions—ranged from approximately $1 million (in the worse of two downside cases) to approximately $3 million (in the base case). After deliberating, the Board determined that the Company had no funds legally available and "declared a redemption of Series A Preferred Stock in the amount of $0.00." The Board departed from AlixPartners' more bullish view after learning that a significant customer was falling behind in its payments and that the Company's "days sales outstanding" had increased during the prior quarter.

To date, through this quarterly process, ThoughtWorks has redeemed a total of $4.1 million of Preferred Stock. That equates to 222,802 shares, of which 214,484 are held by SVIP. SVIP has declined to submit its stock certificates for payment.

SVIP seeks a declaratory judgment as to the meaning of the phrase "funds legally available" and a monetary judgment for the lesser of (i) the full amount of Thought-Works' redemption obligation and (ii) the full amount of ThoughtWorks' "funds legally available."

Legal Analysis

Section 160 of the Delaware General Corporation Law (the "DGCL") authorizes a Delaware corporation to redeem its shares, subject to statutory restrictions. It provides, in pertinent part:

> (a) Every corporation may purchase, redeem, receive, take or otherwise acquire . . . its own shares; provided, however, that no corporation shall:
>
> > (1) Purchase or redeem its own shares of capital stock for cash or other property when the capital of the corporation is impaired or when such purchase or redemption would cause any impairment of the capital of the corporation, except that a corporation . . . may purchase or redeem out of capital any of its own shares which are entitled upon any distribution of its assets, whether by dividend or in liquidation, to a preference over another class or series of its stock . . . if such shares will be retired upon their acquisition and the capital of the corporation reduced in accordance with §§243 and 244 of this title.

"A repurchase impairs capital if the funds used in the repurchase exceed the amount of the corporation's 'surplus,' defined by 8 Del. C. §154 to mean the excess of net assets over the par value of the corporation's issued stock." *Klang v. Smith's Food & Drug Ctrs., Inc.*, 702 A.2d 150, 153 (Del.1997). "Net assets means the amount by which total assets exceed total liabilities." 8 Del. C. §154. Under Section 160(a)(1), therefore, unless a corporation redeems shares and will retire them and reduce its capital, "a corporation may use only its surplus for the purchase of shares of its own capital stock."

Section 160's restrictions on redemptions are intended to protect creditors. The statute seeks to accomplish this goal by prohibiting transactions that would redistribute to stockholders assets that were part of what nineteenth and early twentieth century common law jurists deemed a permanent base of financing upon which creditors were presumed to rely when extending credit. *See generally* Bayless Manning & James J. Hanks, Jr., *Legal Capital*, ch. 2 (3d ed. 1990) [hereinafter "Legal Capital"] (describing the development and theoretical underpinnings of "legal capital" as protection for creditors); *id*. at ch. 4 (describing the regulation of distributions to shareholders under the "legal capital" scheme). As a practical matter, the test operates roughly to prohibit distributions to stockholders that would render the company balance-sheet insolvent, but instead of using insolvency as the cut-off, the line is drawn at the amount of the corporation's capital.

Section 160(a) permits a Delaware corporation to redeem shares of stock. For ThoughtWorks, the Redemption Provision converts that authority into a mandatory obligation by granting SVIP the power "to require [ThoughtWorks] to redeem for cash out of any funds legally available therefor . . . not less than 100% of the Preferred Stock."

ThoughtWorks does not have and cannot raise sufficient funds to redeem "100% of the Preferred Stock." SVIP contends that under the circumstances, it is entitled to a judgment against ThoughtWorks for the full amount of the redemption price. SVIP argues that:

> It is common practice to include in . . . mandatory redemption provisions a phrase such as funds legally available, which simply means funds that carry no legal prohibition on their use. Under Delaware law, a corporation's surplus is legally available for the redemption of its stock. Surplus is the amount by which a corporation's net assets exceed its stated capital. . . . And here, ThoughtWorks promised in its Charter that for the purpose of calculating funds legally available for redemption it would value its assets at the highest legally permissible level. . . . At trial, SVIP's expert valued ThoughtWorks' assets to determine the amount of the company's surplus [using the three standard business valuation methodologies]. . . . The discounted cash flow ("DCF") method produced the lowest figure, but even this figure resulted in surplus in excess of the amount necessary to redeem all of the preferred stock. . . . On this basis, SVIP seeks a judgment in the amount of the redemption obligation, $64,126,770.

Equating "funds legally available" with "surplus" performs all of the work in SVIP's argument. With that move, SVIP converts a provision contemplating payment "for cash" into a formula based on an incorporeal legalism. This is a fallacy:

> One result of the perspective adopted by the legal capital scheme is that lawyers and judges often speak of making a distribution "out of surplus", or of "paying out the surplus" to shareholders. There is no special harm in this manner of speaking so long as the speaker and all their listeners are fully conscious that the statement is hash. "Surplus" and "deficit" are concepts invented by lawyers and accountants. They refer to an arithmetic balancing entry on a balance sheet, to the number that is the resultant of all the other numbers on the balance sheet and that is dictated by the basic mandate of the double entry book-keeping convention–that the left side and the right side must at all times balance. Distributions are never, and can never be, paid "out of surplus"; they are paid out of assets; surplus cannot be distributed-assets are distributed. No one ever received a package of surplus for Christmas. A distribution of assets will produce accounting entries that reduce assets and also reduce something on the right hand side of the balance sheet—often surplus—but that is quite another statement.

Legal Capital at 37-38. Rather than examining ThoughtWorks' assets to determine whether it has "funds" that are "available" and can be used "legally" for redemptions, SVIP seeks a judgment based on an accounting convention.

The Plain Meaning of "Funds Legally Available"

The plain meaning of "funds legally available" has more practical content. "A certificate of incorporation is viewed as a contract among shareholders, and general rules of contract interpretation apply to its terms." *Waggoner v. Laster*, 581 A.2d 1127, 1134 (Del. 1990).

Because the existence of surplus under Section 160 most commonly constrains a corporation's ability to pay dividends or redeem stock, "funds legally available" is colloquially treated as if synonymous with "surplus." The two concepts, however, are not equivalent. Black's Law Dictionary defines "funds" as follows:

> In the plural, this word has a variety of slightly different meanings, as follows: moneys and much more, such as notes, bills, checks, drafts, stocks and bonds, and in broader meaning may include property of every kind. Money in hand, assets, cash, money available for the payment of a debt, legacy, etc. Corporate stocks or government securities, in this sense usually spoken of as the "funds." Assets, securities, bonds, or revenue of a state or government appropriated for the discharge of its debts. Generally, working capital; sometimes used to refer to cash or to cash and marketable securities.

Non-legal dictionaries define funds (plural) as "available pecuniary resources," *Webster's New Collegiate Dictionary* 461 (1979), or "available money; ready cash," *American Heritage College Dictionary* 551 (1993). Each of these definitions focuses on cash, cash-equivalents, and other relatively liquid assets that could readily be used as a source of cash.

Black's Law Dictionary defines "available" as "suitable; useable; accessible; obtainable; present or ready for immediate use." Non-legal definitions of "available" include "present or ready for immediate use," *Webster's* at 77, and "[p]resent and ready for use; at hand; accessible," or "capable of being gotten; obtainable," *American Heritage* at 94.

Black's Law Dictionary defines "legal" as "conforming to the law; according to law; required or permitted by law; not forbidden or discountenanced by law; . . . lawful." Other definitions of "legal" include "conforming to or permitted by law or established rules," *Webster's* at 650, and "in conformity with or permitted by law," *American Heritage* at 774.

The phrase "funds legally available" therefore contemplates initially that there are "funds," in the sense of a readily available source of cash. The funds must both be "available" in the general sense of accessible, obtainable, and present or ready for immediate use, and "legally" so, in the additional sense of accessible in conformity with and as permitted by law. The Redemption Provision renders this usage of "funds" all the more clear by speaking in terms of redemption "for cash out of funds legally available therefor." The Redemption Provision thus directly links "funds" to the concept of "cash."

A corporation easily could have "funds" and yet find that they were not "legally available." *See Klang*, 702 A.2d at 154 (noting that balance sheet showed negative net worth, which prevented distribution of cash via self-tender prior to revaluation of assets). A corporation also could lack "funds," yet have the legal capacity to pay dividends or make redemptions because it had a large surplus. Under those circumstances, a corporation could still redeem shares in exchange for other corporate property. As an insightful monograph on legal capital explains,

> Occasionally, distributions are made in kind, as by parceling out security holdings or, to recall a famous World War II instance, through the distribution of warehouse receipts for whiskey. In special circumstances, a distribution may sometimes be made by distributing fractional undivided interests in a major asset, such as an oil well working agreement.

Legal Capital at 38.

Even within the narrow confines of the DGCL, the terms are not co-extensive. Section 160 authorizes shares to be redeemed out of capital "if such shares will be retired upon their acquisition and the capital of the corporation reduced in accordance with §§243 and 244." Under those circumstances, "legally available funds" extends beyond surplus to "capital." Section 170(a) authorizes dividends, which generally can be paid only out of surplus, to be paid alternatively "out of . . . net profits for the fiscal year in which the dividend is declared and/or the preceding fiscal year." 8 Del. C. §170(a). In that case, "legally available funds" extends to "net profits."

The common law has long restricted a corporation from redeeming its shares when the corporation is insolvent or would be rendered insolvent by the redemption.[3] Black-letter law recognizes that "the shareholder's right to compel a redemption is subordinate to the rights of creditors." 11 *Fletcher's Cyclopedia of the Law of Private Corporations* §5310.

> As against creditors of the corporation, preferred shareholders have no greater rights than common shareholders. They have no preference over them, either in respect to dividends or capital, and have no lien upon the property of the corporation to their prejudice, except where the statute provides otherwise. On the contrary, their rights, both in respect to dividends and capital are subordinate to the rights of such creditors, and consequently they are not entitled to any part of the corporate assets until the corporate debts are fully paid. Nor can the corporation give them any preference, either in respect to the payment of principal or dividends, which will be superior to the rights of creditors, unless by virtue of express statutory authority.

Id. §5297. Learned commentators similarly explain that the redemption right of a preferred stockholder cannot impair the rights of creditors and therefore cannot be exercised when the corporation is insolvent or would be rendered insolvent by the payment.[4]

---

3. *See, e.g., Vanden Bosch v. Michigan Trust Co.*, 35 F.2d 643, 644-45 (6th Cir. 1929) (rejecting preferred stockholder's claim that, when redemption right matured, she became a creditor to the extent of the redemption right; rather, her right remained inferior to that of the corporation's creditors); *Clapp v. Peterson*, 104 Ill. 26, 30 (Ill.1 882) (holding that validity of redemption depends on the "condition that the rights of creditors are not affected"); *Rider v. John G. Delker & Sons Co.*, 140 S.W. 1011, 1012 (Ky. 1911) ("It is only in cases where the corporation is solvent and the rights of creditors will not be injuriously affected thereby that agreements as to preferences among [stockholders] may be enforced."); *Hurley v. Boston R. Hldg. Co.*, 54 N.E.2d 183, 198 (Mass. 1944) ("It is an implied limitation upon the contract for the redemption of 'preferred stock' . . . that such contract for redemption cannot be enforced if the effect is to render the corporation insolvent"); *McIntyre v. E. Bement's Sons*, 109 N.W. 45, 47 (Mich. 1906) ("The promise of . . . a corporation to buy its own stock, if under any circumstances valid, must be considered as made, and accepted with the understanding that the shareholder may not, in face of insolvency of the company, change his relation from that of shareholder to that of creditor, escaping the responsibilities of the one and receiving the benefits of the other. To this rule there appears to be no exception."); *Topken, Loring & Schwartz, Inc. v. Schwartz*, 163 N.E. 735, 736 (N.Y. 1928) ("It has generally been held that no corporation can purchase its stock with its capital to the injury of its creditors. . . . Any agreement to purchase stock from a stockholder, which may result in the impairment of capital, will not be enforced, or will be considered illegal if the rights of creditors are affected.").

4. *See, e.g., Henry Winthrop Ballantine, Ballantine on Corporations* 510 (1946) ("As a general rule, however, an apparently definite promise [to redeem preferred stock] is subject to an implied legal restriction that it is not enforceable against the corporation if it will endanger the collection of the corporate debts, as where the corporation is insolvent at the time when [redemption] falls due or even if it has not become insolvent until the time when the [redemption] obligation is to be enforced."); Richard M. Buxbaum, *Preferred Stock-Law and Draftsmanship*, 42 Cal. L. Rev. 243, 264 (1954) ("A contract of compulsory redemption is interpreted to require redemption 'if the company is not insolvent or will not thereby become insolvent' (or harm creditors or impair capital).").

Delaware follows these principles. Since at least 1914, this Court has recognized that, in addition to the strictures of Section 160, "the undoubted weight of authority" teaches that a "corporation cannot purchase its own shares of stock when the purchase diminishes the ability of the company to pay its debts, or lessens the security of its creditors."

A corporation may be insolvent under Delaware law either when its liabilities exceed its assets, or when it is unable to pay its debts as they come due. *See, e.g., N. Am. Catholic Educ. Programming Found., Inc. v. Gheewalla,* 2006 WL 2588971 (Del.Ch. 2006), aff'd, 930 A.2d 92 (Del.2007). Although a corporation cannot be balance-sheet insolvent and meet the requirements of Section 160, a corporation can nominally have surplus from which redemptions theoretically could be made and yet be unable to pay its debts as they come due. The common law prohibition on redemptions when a corporation is or would be rendered insolvent restricts a corporation's ability to redeem shares under those circumstances, giving rise to yet another situation in which "funds legally available" differs from "surplus."

The Valuation Provision does not override these distinctions. It simply requires that when determining whether funds are legally available, ThoughtWorks must "value its assets at the highest amount permissible under applicable law." The provision recognizes that there could be situations, as in *Klang,* when ThoughtWorks could have "funds" on hand and yet could not satisfy applicable legal requirements, most obviously Section 160 of the DGCL. Under those circumstances, the Valuation Provision requires that ThoughtWorks re-value its assets "at the highest amount permissible under applicable law" in order to free "funds" for redemptions to the maximal extent permitted by law. The Valuation Provision does not create an obligation to redeem shares when no "funds" exist. Nor can the Valuation Provision trump other legal impediments to the use of funds for redemption, such as cash-flow insolvency, that cannot be addressed by re-valuing assets.

SVIP's claim depends on "funds legally available" being equivalent to "surplus." Because the two concepts differ, SVIP's claim fails as a matter of law. SVIP's claim also fails because it supposes that the existence of "surplus" is sufficient to establish conclusively a corporation's obligation to redeem shares, regardless of whether the corporation actually has funds from which the redemption can be made. "Funds legally available" means something different. It contemplates "funds" (in the sense of cash) that are "available" (in the sense of on hand or readily accessible through sales or borrowing) and can be deployed "legally" for redemptions without violating Section 160 or other statutory or common law restrictions, including the requirement that the corporation be able to continue as a going concern and not be rendered insolvent by the distribution.

The Amount of Funds Legally Available

The Redemption Provision obligates ThoughtWorks to redeem the Preferred Stock only to the extent it has funds legally available. If ThoughtWorks lacks sufficient funds to redeem 100% of the Preferred Stock, then "funds to the extent so available shall be used for such purpose and [ThoughtWorks] shall effect such redemption pro rata according to the number of shares held by each holder of Preferred Stock." Charter art. IV(B), §4(d). The Charter further provides that "the redemption requirements provided hereby shall be continuous, so that if at any time after the Redemption Date such requirements shall not be fully discharged, without further action by any holder of Preferred Stock, funds available pursuant to Section 4(a) shall be applied therefor until such requirements are fully discharged."

Under Delaware law, when directors have engaged deliberatively in the judgment-laden exercise of determining whether funds are legally available, a dispute over that issue does not devolve into a mini-appraisal. Rather, the plaintiff must prove that in determining the amount of funds legally available, the board acted in bad faith, relied on methods and data that were unreliable, or made a determination so far off the mark as to constitute actual or constructive fraud. *Klang*, 702 A.2d at 156.

The Valuation Provision requires that ThoughtWorks "value its assets at the highest amount permissible under applicable law." This language does not eliminate the need for judgment when determining "funds legally available." Judgment is inherently part of the valuation process, particularly when the necessary decisions encompass the corporation's ability to continue as a going concern. Nor does the Valuation Provision require this Court to mark ThoughtWorks' assets at the highest number a valuation expert can put on the Company while keeping a straight face. In *Klang*, the Delaware Supreme Court held that a corporation has the power to revalue its assets, rather than relying on book value, to show surplus for the purpose of making stock redemptions. The Delaware Supreme Court did not invite practitioners of the valuation arts to calculate speculative figures. The Court rather stated: "Regardless of what a balance sheet that has not been updated may show, an actual, though unrealized, appreciation reflects *real economic value that the corporation may borrow against or that creditors may claim or levy upon.*" A projection-driven discounted cash flow analysis may not reflect "real economic value" or bear any relationship to what a corporation might borrow or its creditors recover.

SVIP failed to prove at trial that the Board ever (i) acted in bad faith in determining whether ThoughtWorks had legally available funds, (ii) relied on methods and data that were unreliable, or (iii) made determinations so far off the mark as to constitute actual or constructive fraud. Rather than litigate these issues, SVIP instructed its expert, Laura Stamm, to value ThoughtWorks, and she did so utilizing the discounted cash flow, comparable companies, and comparable transaction methodologies. Based on these analyses, she valued ThoughtWorks' equity in the range of $68-$137 million. SVIP's counsel instructed Stamm that in light of the Valuation Provision, her valuation was equivalent to "funds legally available." She therefore opined that ThoughtWorks had sufficient "funds legally available" to redeem SVIP's Preferred Stock.

Stamm concededly did not consider the amount of funds ThoughtWorks could use for redemptions while still continuing as a going concern. She never considered how making an eight-figure redemption payment would affect ThoughtWorks' ability to operate and achieve the projections on which her analyses relied. She had no thoughts on how ThoughtWorks might raise the funds for such a redemption payment. Although defensible as a theoretical exercise, her opinion does not credibly address the issue of "funds legally available." It does not reflect "real economic value" or bear any relationship to what ThoughtWorks might borrow or its creditors recover. It offers no assistance in determining whether the Board acted in bad faith, relied on methods and data that were unreliable, or made determinations so far off the mark as to constitute actual or constructive fraud.

The factual record demonstrates that the Board has acted in the utmost good faith and relied on detailed analyses developed by well-qualified experts. For sixteen straight quarters, the Board has undertaken a thorough investigation of the amount of funds legally available for redemption, and it has redeemed Preferred Stock accordingly. On each occasion, the Board has consulted with financial and legal advisors, received current information about the state of the Company's business, and deliberated over the extent to which funds could be used to redeem the Preferred Stock without threatening the Company's ability to continue as a going concern. The Board's process has been impeccable, and the Board has acted responsibly to fulfill its contractual commitment to the holders of the Preferred Stock despite other compelling business uses for the Company's cash. This is not a case where the Board has had ample cash available for redemptions and simply chose to pursue a contrary course.

Most notably, the Board actively tested the market to determine what level of "funds" ThoughtWorks could obtain. A thorough canvass that included contacts with seventy potential funding sources generated a term sheet that would enable ThoughtWorks to borrow funds netting $23 million for redemptions, *if and only if* the "funds" were used to satisfy the entire obligation to the Preferred Stock. This proposal is the most credible evidence of the maximum funds legally available for a complete redemption of the Preferred Stock. There is no evidence that ThoughtWorks could obtain more funds for redemption or, importantly, that any third party would finance a partial redemption.

The Settled Commercial Expectations of Investors And Issuers

SVIP's plight is nothing new. The phrase "funds legally available" is not unique to the Charter. Those words or substantively identical variants customarily appear in charter provisions addressing dividends and redemptions.[5] Were these words omitted, a comparable limitation would be implied by law.[6] Authority spanning three different centuries adverts to and enforces limitations on the ability of preferred stockholders to force redemption. Delaware's restriction on a corporation purchasing its stock when doing so would impair capital dates from 1909. Faced with venerable and widely recognized impediments to mandatory redemption, investors have developed other ways to protect themselves and secure exit opportunities.

Most obviously, in lieu of preferred stock, investors can purchase convertible debt or straight debt with warrant coverage. Either combination provides the same potential equity upside as preferred stock, but carries the downside protection of a debt instrument's right to payment at a specified time, irrespective of the company's financial condition. *See* 1 Joseph W. Bartlett, *Equity Finance: Venture Capital, Buyouts, Restructurings and Reorganizations* §13.5, at 300 (2d ed. 1995) (explaining that a debenture with warrants "gets the holder to the same place as a convertible preferred"). SVIP's representative, Nicholas Somers, was aware of the differences between debt and equity and recognized that he could have invested using debt.

---

5. *See, e.g.,* National Venture Capital Association Model Term Sheet, at 6 ("The Series A Preferred shall be redeemable from funds legally available for distribution at the option of holders of at least [_____]% of the Series A Preferred commencing any time after [_____] at a price equal to the Original Purchase Price [plus all accrued but unpaid dividends].")

6. *HB Korenvaes Invs., L.P. v. Marriott Corp.,* 1993 WL 205040 (Del.Ch. 1993) (Allen, C.) (explaining that in light of legal limitations on a corporation's ability to make distributions to equity, preferred stock lacks rights enjoyed by creditors, like an unconditional right to periodic payments in the form of interest, and an unconditional right to capital repayment with concomitant remedies for default).

Although debt offers an alternative, there are many reasons why investors and issuers might want to structure a position as equity. Investors who take equity stakes often insist on additional protections, such as a springing right to board control. The National Venture Capital Association pointedly explains the rationale for such a provision in terms that apply to the current case:

> Due to statutory restrictions, it is unlikely that the Company will be legally permitted to redeem in the very circumstances where investors most want it (the so-called "sideways situation"), [so] investors will sometimes request that certain penalty provisions take effect where redemption has been requested but the Company's available cash flow does not permit such redemption—e.g., the redemption amount shall be paid in the form of a one-year note to each unredeemed holder of Series A Preferred, and the holders of a majority of the Series A Preferred shall be entitled to elect a majority of the Company's Board of Directors until such amounts are paid in full.

Another alternative, common in stockholders' agreements, allows a preferred stockholder to sell its security and "drag along" the remaining stockholders. "Drag along" rights, which effectively allow a preferred stockholder to sell the entire company to a third party without board involvement, are quite common. A similar but stronger provision requires the forced sale of the company to the preferred stockholder.

The existence of these and other widely utilized alternatives demonstrates at least two things. First, sophisticated investors understand that mandatory redemption rights provide limited protection and function imperfectly, particularly when a corporation is struggling financially. If a standard mandatory redemption provision offered a clear path to a large monetary judgment and concomitant creditor remedies, then so many alternatives likely would not have evolved. My interpretation of "funds legally available" thus fulfills the settled expectations of investors and issuers as evidenced by established commercial practice.

Second, SVIP easily could have protected its investment and avoided its current fate through any number of means. SVIP decided not to, and that choice was rational at the time. SVIP bought the Preferred Stock at the height of the dot-com mania from a technology firm with an established track record, real revenues, and actual earnings-all of which compared favorably with many issuers then embarking on over-subscribed and first-day-popping IPOs. Everyone involved anticipated that ThoughtWorks soon would go public at a multi-billion dollar valuation. Instead, the bubble burst. Now, with hindsight, SVIP understandably wishes it had additional rights, but "it is not the proper role of a court to rewrite or supply omitted provisions to a written agreement."

QUESTIONS

1. What is the purpose of a redemption provision in these kinds of investments?
2. If getting back its investment was SV Investment Partners' priority, it could have sought an investment in convertible debt. What is the likelihood that Thought-Works would have agreed to issue convertible debt?
3. In what way is "surplus" different from "funds legally available"?

NOTE

1. In the appeal of this case, *SV Investment Partners, LLC v. ThoughtWorks, Inc.*, 37 A.3d 205 (Del. 2011), the Delaware Supreme Court upheld the chancery court's decision on the factual record. It held that since "SVIP had failed to prove its case even under its own definition of 'legally available funds' [as being equivalent to surplus], we need not reach or address the issue of whether SVIP's definition is legally correct." *Id.* at 211-212. Presumably, then, the court also reserved the issue of whether the chancery court's definition of "funds legally available" was also correct.

Greenmont Capital Partners I, L.P. v. Mary's Gone Crackers, Inc.
2012 WL 4479999 (Del. Ch. 2012)

PARSONS, Vice Chancellor.

This case presents a question about the interpretation of a Delaware corporation's certificate of incorporation. The corporation had authorized and issued common stock and two series of preferred stock, series A and series B. The plaintiff, an investor, purchased series B preferred stock. Series B stockholders have special rights under the certificate of incorporation. Among other things, the series B preferred have the right to a majority vote to validate any action that would "alter or change" the series B preferred stockholder's rights under the certificate. The certificate also grants series B preferred stockholders the right to a majority vote on any amendment to the certificate of incorporation. One action permitted by the certificate is an automatic conversion of the preferred stock into common stock upon a majority vote of the preferred shares. This certificate provision requires a majority vote of the series A and series B preferred voting together and does not afford the series B any special rights.

The corporation decided to seek an automatic conversion. Holders of a majority of the preferred shares, but not a majority of the preferred series B, voted in favor of the automatic conversion. After the purported conversion, the corporation's board voted to amend its certificate to eliminate reference to preferred stock. The plaintiff disputes the validity of the conversion and the subsequent certificate amendment. It maintains that a majority vote from the series B was required to validate the conversion because the conversion of the preferred stock into common stock effectively would deprive the series B preferred of the special rights they enjoyed under the certificate. According to the plaintiff, this action, therefore, would "alter or change" its rights and the certificate requires a majority series B vote to validate such an action. Hence, the question before the Court is whether, under the terms of the certificate and Delaware law, the corporation had the power to implement the automatic conversion and the certificate amendment without the consent of the series B preferred.

I find that the execution of the challenged action, which was allowed under the certificate, did not alter or change the rights of a shareholder whose rights are defined by the certificate. For this reason, I rule in favor of the corporation and hold as a matter of law that the challenged conversion of preferred stock into common stock was a valid corporate action. I further conclude that the subsequent certificate amendment was valid because it occurred when no preferred shares remained outstanding and, thus, its validity was not contingent on a majority vote of the outstanding shares of series B preferred.

Plaintiff, Greenmont Capital Partners I, LP ("Greenmont") invests in companies in the natural products industry. One of Greenmont's investments is in Series B Preferred shares in Mary's Gone Crackers ("MGC" or the "Company").

Defendant MGC produces and distributes organic and gluten-free baked goods. The Charter authorizes two classes of stock, Common and Preferred, and two series of the Preferred class, Series A and Series B. MGC authorized 65,000,000 shares: 37,522,485 Common; 15,028,444 Series A Preferred; and 12,449,071 Series B Preferred. The Common stock represents 58% of the total number of authorized shares and the Preferred represents 42%. Of the Preferred, Series A accounts for 55% and Series B accounts for 45%.

At the time of the transactions in question here, Greenmont owned 7,430,503 shares of the Series B Preferred. The Series B Preferred holders enjoy unique rights under the Charter. Article IV, Section D.2(b) lists twelve actions that must be approved by a majority of the Series B Preferred to have effect or to be valid. This Section, entitled Separate Vote of Series B Preferred (the "Voting Provision"), begins as follows:

> For so long as any shares of a series of Series B Preferred remain outstanding, in addition to any other vote or consent required herein or by law, the vote or written consent of the holders of at least a majority of the outstanding shares of the Series B Preferred shall be necessary for effecting or validating the following actions (whether by merger, recapitalization or otherwise):. . . .

> (i) Any amendment, alteration, repeal or waiver of any provision of the Certificate of Incorporation or the Bylaws of the Company (including any filing of a Certificate of Designation);
> (ii) Any agreement or action that alters or changes the voting or other powers, preferences, or other special rights, privileges or restrictions of the Series B Preferred (including by way of a merger or consolidation);. . . .

The second Charter provision at issue in this dispute is Section D.5, entitled Conversion Rights. Subsection (l) to Section D.5 outlines procedures for an "Automatic Conversion." This subsection states:

> Each share of Series Preferred shall automatically be converted into shares of Common Stock, based on the then-effective applicable Series Preferred Conversion Price, at any time upon the affirmative election of the holders of at least fifty-one percent (51%) of the then-outstanding shares of Series Preferred. . . .

On February 8, 2012, MGC solicited certain holders of Preferred to elect an automatic conversion of the Preferred into Common Stock under Section D.5. The Company limited its solicitation to holders of Preferred who indicated that they would support an automatic conversion; it did not solicit Greenmont. On February 17, 2012, MGC received written consent from at least 51% of the Preferred to convert Preferred into Common Stock. Later that same day, the MGC board voted to amend the Charter and filed an amended and restated Charter with the Delaware Secretary of State. The amended and restated Charter eliminates the provisions related to the Preferred.

Greenmont filed this action on February 20, 2012 seeking a declaratory judgment that the automatic conversion and the related Charter amendment are unlawful, void, and prohibited. Greenmont moved for judgment on the pleadings and MGC cross-moved for the same. Both parties assert that the Charter is plain and unambiguous and that there are no material facts in dispute. They ask the Court to declare as a matter of law whether the automatic conversion and subsequent Charter amendment violate the Charter or Delaware law.

Greenmont maintains that, in addition to the 51% Preferred class vote required by the Automatic Conversion provision, the Voting Provision required a majority vote of the Series B Preferred holders for the automatic conversion to be valid. Plaintiff bases this argument on Section D.2(b)(ii) of the Voting Provision. This subsection requires a majority vote of Series B shares to effect "any agreement or action that alters or changes [the Series B Preferred's] voting or other powers, preferences, or other special rights, privileges or restrictions." Greenmont argues that the automatic conversion altered its rights, indeed completely eliminated them, and as such, was invalid without a Series B Preferred majority vote.

Plaintiff further disputes the validity of the purported Charter amendment because Section D.2(b)(i) requires approval by a Series B Preferred majority for any Charter amendment.

Defendant, MGC, argues that the automatic conversion did not trigger the Voting Provision and, thus, that the automatic conversion was valid as executed. Because the Automatic Conversion provision was one of the Series B Preferred shareholders' rights under the Charter, MGC argues, the exercise of that provision did not "alter or change" those rights. Rather, the Company asserts that the conversion constituted the exercise of a Charter term that always had been a right of the Series B Preferred under the Charter.

Defendant also maintains that the Charter amendment was valid as executed. MGC concedes that the Voting Provision provided for a Series B majority vote to validate a Charter amendment. Under MGC's reading of the Charter, however, upon receiving written consent of 51% of the Preferred to convert the Preferred into Common Stock, the Preferred automatically was converted into Common Stock and, thus, ceased to exist. The Voting Provision, however, only applies "for so long as any shares of a series of Series B Preferred remain outstanding." Because no Series B Preferred remained outstanding after the automatic conversion, MGC contends that the subsequent Charter amendment was valid even without a Series B Preferred majority vote.

Analysis

A motion for judgment on the pleadings will be granted if no material issue of fact exists and the moving party is entitled to judgment as a matter of law. No material facts are in dispute. Further, both parties contend that the Charter is unambiguous and that the Court, therefore, can rule as a matter of law.

In interpreting a corporate charter, the Court applies general principles of contract construction. A certificate should be construed in its entirety and the court "must give effect to all terms of the instrument, must read the instrument as a whole, and, if possible, must reconcile all provisions in the instrument." The existence and extent of special stock rights are contractual in nature and are determined by the issuer's certificate of incorporation.[9] The certificate must expressly and clearly state any rights,

---

9. *Warner Commc'ns Inc. v. Chris–Craft Indus., Inc.*, 583 A.2d 962, 966 (Del.Ch. 1989).

preferences, and limitations of the preferred stock that distinguish preferred stock from common stock.[10] This principle equally applies to construing the relative rights of holders of different series of preferred stock.[11] In interpreting an unambiguous certificate of incorporation, the court should determine the document's meaning solely in reference to its language without resorting to extrinsic evidence. Contract language is not ambiguous in a legal sense merely because the parties dispute what it means. To be ambiguous, a disputed contract term must be fairly or reasonably susceptible to more than one meaning.

Series B Preferred Shareholders' Right to Vote on the Conversion

I find that the Charter is unambiguous and that its language does not entitle the Series B Preferred holders to a series vote on the conversion of Preferred Stock into Common Stock. Under the Voting Provision, two elements must be present for Series B Preferred holders to have rights to a majority vote on a matter: (1) Series B Preferred must be outstanding; and (2) an enumerated action must be at issue. After the execution of the automatic conversion, I conclude that no enumerated action was at issue.

I start by considering the Charter language. The first clause of Section D.2(b) states: "For so long as any shares of a series of Series B Preferred remain outstanding." The parties do not dispute that when the Series Preferred were solicited to vote in favor of an automatic conversion, Series B Preferred was outstanding. Section D.2(b), therefore, is implicated. The second clause reads: "in addition to any other vote or consent required herein or by law." This language indicates that the provision grants Series B Preferred holders rights beyond any voting rights either found in the agreement or required by law. The next clause indicates what additional rights Series B Preferred holders have beyond their voting rights arising under the agreement or required by law. This clause provides that a majority vote of the outstanding Series B Preferred shares "shall be necessary for effecting or validating the following actions (whether by merger, recapitalization or otherwise)." Read together, these clauses compel the conclusion that what starts out broadly ("in addition to any other vote") finishes narrowly ("for effecting or validating the following actions"). Only the actions specified in the list of twelve enumerated actions require a majority vote of Series B Preferred in order to be valid.

Greenmont asserts that Section D.2(b)(ii) provides the enumerated action that grants it voting rights as to the automatic conversion. Section D.2(b)(ii) incorporates the following action into the Voting Provision: "Any agreement or action that alters or changes the voting or other powers, preferences, or other special rights, privileges or restrictions of the Series B Preferred (including by way of a merger or consolidation)." Notably, the drafters of the Charter included for a second time a reference incorporating action by merger. This presumably is in response to the Delaware Supreme Court's decision in *Elliott Associates, L.P. v. Avatex Corp.*[16] In *Avatex*, the Court provided a "path for future drafters." The Court held that language granting the

---

10. *Elliott Assocs., L.P. v. Avatex Corp.,* 715 A.2d 843, 852 (Del. 1998) (citing 8 *Del. C.* §151(a)).

11. *See also Avatex,* 715 A.2d at 852–53 ("Stock preferences must clearly be stated and will not be presumed.").

16. 715 A.2d 843 (Del.1998).

right to vote on an "amendment, alteration, or repeal" is not enough to provide preferred stockholders with the right to a class vote on a merger that leads to an amendment, alteration, or repeal of the certificate. A drafter must additionally indicate that the class vote applies when a merger results in an amendment, alteration, or repeal. One way to satisfy this requirement is by including the words "whether by merger, consolidation, or otherwise" in the appropriate provision in the certificate.

Here, the drafters appear to have attempted to take advantage of the safe harbor offered by Avatex. They included language in the introductory provision to incorporate actions by "merger, recapitalization or otherwise" and additionally in Section D.2(b)(ii) to include an alteration or change "by way of a merger or consolidation." While this language signals the intent to include the circumstance where a merger results in one of the enumerated actions, it does not touch on the disputed action here.

As noted, Section D.2(b)(ii) applies to "any agreement or action that alters or changes" the Series B Preferred's "voting or other powers, preferences, or other special rights, privileges or restrictions." The issue, therefore, is whether the automatic conversion of Series B Preferred into Common Stock "altered or changed" the Series B Preferred's powers, preferences, rights, privileges, or restrictions. This issue, in turn, requires a determination of what constitutes the Series B Preferred's "voting or other powers, preferences, or other special rights, privileges or restrictions." To answer this question, we look again to the language of the Charter. One group of rights provided for in the Charter is found in Section D.5 entitled Conversion Rights.

This Section contains subsection (l) which allows for an automatic conversion. As noted above, the Automatic Conversion provision provides that the Preferred automatically may be converted into shares of Common Stock at any time upon the vote of 51% of the Preferred. The plain language of the Charter compels the conclusion that this automatic conversion is one of the "special rights, privileges or restrictions" created by the Charter. When contract language is plain and clear on its face, the Court will determine its meaning based on the writing alone. Because the Automatic Conversion provision exists on equal footing with the Voting Provision, an action taken under the Automatic Conversion provision cannot be seen to "alter or change" any of the Series B Preferred's "voting or other powers, preferences, or other special rights, privileges or restrictions." Rather than "alter or change" a right, the execution of an automatic conversion effectuates an existing right.

Greenmont asserts that this interpretation undermines the rights it bargained for in the Voting Provision. Notably, the Series A shareholders appear to account for a majority of the Preferred shareholders. Further, the Series A enjoy few benefits under the Charter and, therefore, could be expected to be more likely than the holders of Series B to vote for an automatic conversion of Preferred Stock into Common Stock under Section D.5(l). The Series B's rights under the Charter, therefore, are somewhat dependent on the Series A's desire to remain holders of Preferred stock. Greenmont avers that it would not have bargained for such contingent rights and that an interpretation along those lines would be wrong. While Greenmont's interpretation makes sense, "its interpretation is not reasonable in light of the indisputably clear language of the contract." Instead, the plain language of the Charter indicates that the exercise of an automatic conversion would not alter or change the Series B Preferred's rights as those rights are defined in the Charter.

Greenmont further argues that this interpretation cannot be correct because an act that extinguishes the powers of the Series B Preferred cannot be interpreted as a "right" of that series. But, Greenmont cites no authority in support of its position. MGC counters that a conversion provision is indeed a "right" of preferred stock. Delaware corporate law recognizes that the ability of holders of preferred stock to convert their shares into shares of common stock is a "right" of the preferred shareholders.[26] Nothing in the language of the Charter indicates that the Preferred shareholders' ability to convert their shares of Preferred Stock into shares of Common Stock under the Automatic Conversion provision is not a "right" of the Preferred shareholders. Indeed, the Automatic Conversion provision is contained in Section D.5 entitled "Conversion Rights."

This conclusion is consistent with the principle of Delaware corporation law that any rights or preferences of preferred stock must be expressed clearly.[27] For example, in *Warner Communications, Inc. v. Chris–Craft Industries, Inc.*, the Court held that because the act of a merger, and not the subsequent act of a certificate amendment, was the act that adversely affected the plaintiffs, the following language in the certificate of designation did not provide the plaintiffs, a group of Series B Preferred stockholders, with the right to vote on the merger as a separate class: "Without first obtaining the consent or approval of the holders of at least two-thirds of the number of shares of the Series B Stock . . . the Corporation shall not (i) amend, alter or repeal any of the provisions of the Certificate . . . so as to affect adversely any of the preferences, rights, powers or privileges of the Series B Stock or the holders thereof. . . ." In *Warner*, the surviving corporation's certificate of incorporation would be amended in the merger. Also pursuant to the merger agreement, the plaintiffs' Warner Series B Preferred shares would be converted into new Time Series BB Preferred. Chancellor Allen found that the merger and the amendment were separate events: "Given that the merger itself was duly authorized, the conversion of the Series B Preferred Stock could occur without any prior or contemporaneous amendment to the certificate." He concluded, therefore, that the conversion of shares, not the certificate amendment, caused the adverse effect on the rights of the Series B stock. Because the certificate only provided for a Series B shareholder vote when an amendment adversely affected the Series B shareholder's rights, the Court held that the series was not entitled to a separate class vote on the merger.

This conclusion is further supported by the fact that the drafters of the MGC Charter explicitly included one action identified elsewhere in the Charter as an enumerated action requiring a majority Series B Preferred vote under the Voting Provision. Specifically, Section B of Article IV states that the number of authorized shares of Common Stock may be increased or decreased only after a vote of a majority of the stock of the Company. The Voting Provision includes a requirement for a majority Series B Preferred vote in Section D.2(b)(iii) as to: "Any increase or decrease in the authorized number of shares of Common Stock or Preferred Stock." Had the drafters intended for the Automatic Conversion provision to be subject to an additional vote of a majority of the Series B Preferred, they could have listed it expressly in the Voting Provision as they did with the provision regarding an increase or decrease in authorized Common Stock. By expressly including Section B as an enumerated action

---

26. *See HB Korenvaes Invs., L.P. v. Marriott Corp.*, 1993 WL 257422 (Del.Ch. 1993) (considering the preferred shareholder plaintiffs' conversion rights).

27. *See Warner Commc'ns, Inc. v. Chris–Craft Indus., Inc.*, 583 A.2d 962, 967 (Del.1989).

under the Voting Provision, but not including Section D.5, the drafters implicitly excluded Section D.5.[35]

Greenmont correctly emphasizes that the addition of the words "automatic conversion" to one of the twelve enumerated actions in Section D.2(b) is merely one way the drafters could have granted the Series B Preferred the right to a majority vote on any proposed automatic conversion. If the intent of the drafters was to include automatic conversion as an act requiring a majority Series B Preferred vote, however, then it was incumbent upon the drafters to make the Charter language precise in that regard and to indicate such an intent clearly. As drafted, the Voting Provision does not grant this right. The dispositive question is not whether as a result of the vote in favor of automatic conversion the Series B Preferred's rights were altered or changed, but whether the act of the vote altered or changed their rights. The Automatic Conversion provision was included in the Series B Preferred's bundle of rights, privileges, and restrictions under the Charter and, thus, the act of at least 51% of the then-outstanding shares of Preferred in voting under Section D.5 to effect an automatic conversion did not alter or change those rights, privileges, and restrictions.

Series B Preferred Shareholders' Right to Vote on the Charter Amendment

I next must determine whether any Series B Preferred Stock remained outstanding at the time of the purported Charter amendment. If it did, then the Series B holders would have had the right to a majority vote on any Charter amendment under Section D.2(b)(i). If it did not, then the Series B holders would have no such right because the Voting Provision only applies "for so long as any shares of a series of Series B Preferred remain outstanding." At the time MGC amended the Charter, there were no Series B Preferred shares outstanding and, therefore, that series was not entitled to a separate series vote to validate the amendment.

Under the language of the Charter, a vote by a majority of the Preferred will automatically convert the Preferred into Common Stock. Section D.5(l)(ii) states: "Upon the occurrence of either of the events specified in Section D.5(1)(i) above, the outstanding shares of Series Preferred shall be converted automatically without any further action by the holders of such shares. . . ." In contrast, Section D.5(d) sets forth the "Mechanics of Conversion" in the context of an optional conversion of Preferred into Common Stock. The latter provision requires a Preferred holder to surrender its certificate in order for the conversion of its shares into Common Stock to be deemed to have been made. Notably, an optional conversion will be deemed to have been made at the close of business on the date the certificate is surrendered and "the person entitled to receive the shares of Common Stock issuable upon such conversion shall be treated for all purposes as the record holder of such shares of Common Stock on such date." Because the automatic conversion provision states that the Series Preferred Stock shall be converted automatically, "whether or not the certificates representing such shares are surrendered to the Company," it follows that the automatic conversion also will be deemed to have been made on the date on which the holders of 51% of the Preferred voted to convert their shares into shares of

---

35. *Laster v. Waggoner,* 1989 WL 126670 (Del.Ch. 1989) (noting that the principle of statutory construction *expressio unius est exclusio alterius* applies with equal force in interpreting certificates of incorporation).

Common Stock. In this case, the holders of at least 51% of the Preferred executed written consents to convert the then-outstanding Preferred Stock into Common Stock on February 17, 2012. Under the Charter, therefore, the class of Preferred was no longer outstanding as of that date.

The automatic conversion occurred on February 17, 2012. MGC voted to amend the Charter later that same day. Therefore, as previously noted, the shareholder vote to amend the Charter took place when Common Stock was the only class of MGC stock outstanding. Because the Voting Provision only applies "for so long as any shares of a series of Series B Preferred remain outstanding," that provision did not apply to the Charter amendment.

Greenmont contends that this result is inconsistent with its subjective intent in purchasing its Series B Preferred stock. Indeed, Greenmont argues that the conversion and the amendment to the Charter are inextricably linked and that the conversion and amendment must be interpreted together, such that they collectively would be subject to the Voting Provision. Greenmont, however, cites no authority to support this proposition. To the contrary, Delaware case law generally requires that corporate acts be evaluated or considered independently as they occur. Just as the Court concluded that the stock conversion and subsequent certificate amendment in Warner were separate events, I consider the conversion and the Charter amendment here to have been separate and independent occurrences.

Plaintiff also asserts that Section 242(b)(2) of the Delaware General Corporation Law ("DGCL") requires a series vote on the Charter amendment because that amendment decreased the number of authorized shares of the Preferred class. Section 242(b)(2) provides in relevant part:

> The holders of the outstanding shares of a class shall be entitled to vote as a class upon a proposed amendment, whether or not entitled to vote thereon by the certificate of incorporation, if the amendment would increase or decrease the aggregate number of authorized shares of such class, increase or decrease the par value of the shares of such class, or alter or change the powers, preferences, or special rights of the shares of such class so as to affect them adversely. If any proposed amendment would alter or change the powers, preferences, or special rights of 1 or more series of any class so as to affect them adversely, but shall not so affect the entire class, then only the shares of the series so affected by the amendment shall be considered a separate class for the purposes of this paragraph.

For the reasons stated above, I conclude that no Preferred shares were outstanding at the time of the amendment.[44] Because Section 242(b)(2) only applies to the

---

44. *See Warner Commc'ns, Inc. v. Chris–Craft Indus., Inc.,* 583 A.2d 962, 970 (Del. 1989). In *Warner,* the Court determined that Section 242(b) did not require a class vote on a charter amendment that occurred after a merger had been effectuated under Section 251. In that case, the Court considered whether Section 3.3(i) of the charter, which contained language that paralleled the language in Section 242(b) of the DGCL, was intended to incorporate changes effected through mergers. The Court stated:

> Our bedrock doctrine of independent legal significance compels the conclusion that satisfaction of the requirements of Section 251 is all that is required legally to effectuate a merger. It follows, therefore, from rudimentary principles of corporation law, that the language of 242(b)(2), which so closely parallels the language of 3.3(i), does not entitle the holders of a class of preferred stock to a class vote in a merger. . . .

"holders of outstanding shares," it does not apply to the Charter amendment challenged in this case.

For the foregoing reasons, I deny Plaintiff's Motion for Judgment on the Pleadings and I grant Defendant's Motion for Judgment on the Pleading.

QUESTIONS

1. What percentage of the outstanding preferred stock did Greenmont own?
2. Why does the plaintiff not have a class right to vote on the conversion?
3. In what way is this reasoning of this case consistent with *Warner Communications, Inc. v. Chris-Craft Industries, Inc.*?

Id. (citation omitted). Just as the merger in *Warner* occurred independently of the charter amendment, so too in this case, the independent event of an automatic conversion under the Charter occurred before the Charter amendment. Section 242(b)(2), therefore, does not require a class vote on the disputed Charter amendment.

CHAPTER
9

DERIVATIVES

The derivative market experienced explosive growth in the 1990s, and is now a significant and permanent part of modern finance and capital markets. Yet, derivatives have been around for thousands of years. Consider this passage from Aristotle's *Politics*:

> There is the anecdote of Thales the Milesian and his financial device, which involves a principle of universal application, but is attributable to him on account of his reputation for wisdom. He was reproached for his poverty, which was supposed to show that philosophy was of no use. According to the story, he knew by his skill in the stars while it was yet winter that there would be great harvest of olives in the coming year; so, having a little money, he gave deposits for the use of all the olive-presses in Chios and Miletus, which he hired at a low price because no one bid against him. When the harvest-time came, and many were wanted all at once and of a sudden, he let them out at any rate which he pleased, and made a quantity of money. Thus he showed the world that philosophers can easily be rich if they like, but that their ambition is of another sort.

In the modern capital markets, derivatives are ubiquitous. There are a variety of derivative instruments, and innumerable number of assets or things that are the subject of the derivatives contracts. Although derivatives can be dizzyingly complex, there is nothing mysterious about the concept of a derivative. They are often as simple as Thales' option contract for olive presses. Indeed, virtually every adult has entered into a variant of a derivative contract—it is called insurance, which is essentially in the nature of a put option.

Derivatives can be used by speculators in the financial markets. This aspect of derivatives is not the focus of this chapter. Unlike equity and debt instruments, derivatives are not used principally to raise capital. However, derivatives play a substantial role in corporate governance and financial management. This chapter provides an overview of major classes of derivatives including futures and forwards, swaps, and options, and basic aspects of option valuation. It reviews two basic corporate uses of derivatives: (1) to compensate executives and employees through stock option grants, and (2) to manage or hedge risk.

A. BASIC CHARACTERISTICS OF DERIVATIVES

A derivative is a security instrument that derives its value from some other thing. In simple terms, it is a financial bet on the future value of a thing. The "thing" that determines the value of the derivative can be anything: plain vanilla derivatives can be tied to publicly traded stocks or bonds or market indices, but exotic derivatives can be tied to the weather, political developments, or other exotic securities. A derivative is fundamentally a financial bet on the future price of an asset or a thing. Like gambling, any form of betting has winners and losers with exactly offsetting gains and losses. Accordingly, a derivative transaction is always a zero sum transaction, meaning that a winner's gain of x is always matched by a loser's loss of x.

Derivatives can be complex for two reasons. First, while simple in the form of a contract, valuing a bet on the future value of a thing can be extremely complicated because, among other things, the value changes constantly over time. Second, derivatives can be complex because the value of the underlying asset or thing can be complex as well. The price of many underlying assets or things, such as commodities (*e.g.*, oil, soy, gold, pork bellies, etc.), interest rates (*e.g.*, LIBOR, prime, Treasuries, etc.), or financial or economic indices (*e.g.*, Dow Jones Industrial, S&P 500, Russell 2000) can be volatile. If the value of the underlying assets cannot be easily determined because they are unique or they do not have a liquid market from which a market price is easily determined, the derivative itself may be extremely complex and difficult to value.

Derivatives have some basic terminology that is used in the markets. We should know the following trading terms:

- *Long*: Long means the purchase of a security, derivative, or some asset. The long position is held by the buyer of the financial instrument or asset. For example, long on a call option means that the investor has bought a call option.
- *Short*: Short means the sale of a security, derivative, or some asset. The short position is held by the seller of the financial instrument or asset. For example, short the call means that the investor has written and sold a call option to the buyer (holder) and is now exposed to the risk of the option being called against him.

1. FORWARDS AND FUTURES

A basic derivative is a forward or futures contract. Both are contracts between two counterparties who agree to buy and sell an asset or a thing at a specific time in the future at a specific agreed price. Assets and things subject to a futures or forward contract are numerous: *e.g.*, commodities, indices, and securities. Unlike an option, a forward or future contract obligates the parties to execute the contract at the agreed upon maturity date, though the parties can settle by paying the cash difference rather than actually exchange the physical asset if agreed upon or permitted in the case of exchange-traded futures. The profit and loss of a forward or futures contract looks like this.

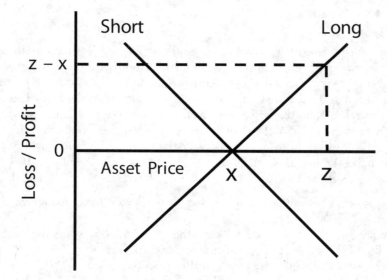

In the above diagram, the counterparties agreed to buy and sell the asset in the future at a price X. The long position gets to buy the asset at the price X at maturity. Clearly, there is a profit if at maturity the market price of the asset is greater than the agreed contract price Z. The profit is calculated as (Z − X) because the purchaser has the right to buy the asset at X, which is cheaper than the market price Z. There is a loss if the market price is lower than X. In this case, the long's loss is the short's profit. The short would have the right to sell an asset at X when the current market price is less than X. Notice that in a futures or forward contract, there is an obligation to perform on the contract at maturity, either in the form of sale and purchase of the underlying asset or thing, or payment of the cash difference between the contract price and the market price. This is not the case with options, which as the term connotes provides the holder the option, but not the obligation, to force the short to perform.

While forward and futures contracts operate under this same principle, they have important differences. A futures contract is a standardized, exchange-traded contract, meaning that contract terms and the underlying asset are standardized and set by the rules of an exchange, which is a marketplace where such contracts are publicly traded. A forward contract is a customized contract between two counterparties, without an exchange intermediary, with specific terms meeting the needs of the parties. It is not exchange traded, and therefore these contracts typically are unique to the parties.

2. SWAPS

Another type of a derivative is a swap. As the name suggests, a swap is an exchange of rights to different assets. A typical swap transaction involves the exchange of a variable interest rate debt instrument with a fixed interest rate debt instrument. A fixed interest rate debt instrument pays a fixed rate, for example 8 percent. A variable interest rate debt instrument pays an interest rate that varies depending on a defined contingency, such as the rate on U.S. Treasuries, or the prime interest rate, or the London Interbank Borrowing Rate (LIBOR): for example, LIBOR plus 5 percent where LIBOR will vary from day to day.

3. OPTIONS

A call option is a contract wherein an *issuer* (or *writer*) sells for a premium an option giving the *holder* the right, but not the obligation, to buy from the issuer a specified asset at a fixed strike price on or before a maturity date. A put option gives the holder the right to sell a specified asset to the issuer. At maturity, if the market value of this asset is worth less than the strike price X, the option is in-the-money and the holder profits since she has the right to sell the asset at a more expensive price than the current market value. If an option is out-of-the-money, the holder will not exercise the option and the loss is P.

An option is a contract, and there are only a few essential contractual terms:

- P represents the option premium paid by the holder to the issuer for the option right
- X represents the strike price, which is the agreed price at which the issuer will sell (call option) or buy (put option) the underlying asset
- T represents that maturity at which the option expires

An option transaction is a simple contract wherein for a premium P, the option issuer agrees to sell (call option) or buy (put option) an underlying asset at the strike price X at or before the maturity T. The holder has the right to buy (call option) or sell (put option) the underlying asset.

There are specific terminologies for options. An "American option" is the option to purchase the asset at any time up to the maturity, and a "European" option is the option to purchase the asset only at the maturity. Also, options are said to be "in-the-money," "at-the-money," or "out-of-the money."

- *In-the-money* means that if the option was exercised, it would result in a profit for the holder, which means: $S > X$ for a call option, and $S < X$ for a put option.
- *At-the-money* means that if the option was exercised, it would result in no profit for the holder or issuer, not including the option premium, that is: $S = X$.
- *Out-of-the-money* means that if the option was exercised, it would result in a loss for the holder and thus a rational holder would choose not to exercise the option. This means: $S < X$ for a call option, and $S > X$ for a put option.

The profit and loss profile of a call option has a unique shape. Below are the profiles for the long and short call positions.

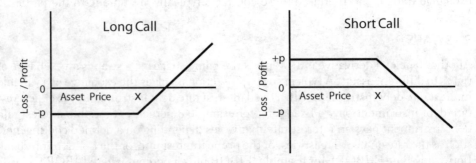

In the above diagrams, the holder of the call option (the long position) has paid the issuer an option premium of P. The option is in-the-money only when the asset price S

exceeds the strike price X. When the asset price $(S = X + P)$, the holder and the issuer are at breakeven. If the asset price exceeds this breakeven point, the holder will profit. His profit is theoretically unlimited since S is not capped by any artificial boundary. Notice that the issuer's profit and loss are mirror opposites. The issuer can only earn a maximum profit of P, and only if the option is "out-of-the-money" such that it would be irrational for the holder to exercise the option. The issuer is betting that the asset price will not increase past the strike price. The holder is betting that the asset price will increase and exceed the strike price. Time will tell who is right.

The profit and loss of the long and short positions of a put option are diagrammed below. Notice again the mirror opposite nature of the profit and loss for the issuer and the holder.

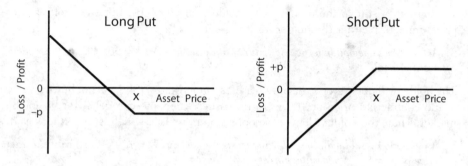

An interesting aspect of a put option is that it resembles an insurance policy. The holder of a put option is really purchasing insurance against the possibility that the value of a thing (asset) will decline. If the asset value declines from X to Y, the holder gains $(X - Y)$. Thus, put options can be used to hedge against the risk of an asset declining in value. This is the core principle of insurance.

Derivatives are zero-sum transactions. A counterparty's gain is precisely matched by the other's loss. If the long and the short option positions are transposed, we see that each counterparty's profit and loss profile is the mirror image of the other's (imagine a mirror running along the x-axis of the graph). The profit and loss lines for the long and the short are antipodes of each other.

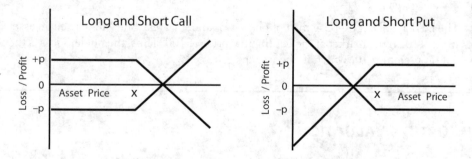

The above graphs show the zero sum nature of a derivative transaction. The long's gain is the short's loss, and vice versa.

EXAMPLE

Profit and Loss of Call Option Transactions

1. *A call option is sold with the following terms: P = 10 and X = 100. At maturity, the asset price is: S = 120. What is the holder's profit or loss?*

The option is in-the-money. The holder has the right to buy an asset worth 120 on the market for the contractual price of 100. She will exercise the option. The profit is 20 ($= 120 - 100$), less 10 paid in option premium. Thus, her net profit is 10 and the issuer's net loss is 10.

2. *Assume the same option terms. At maturity, the asset price is: S = 110. What is the holder's profit or loss?*

The option is still in-the-money. The holder's profit is 10, but the profit net of premium is 0. Neither the holder nor the issuer profits.

3. *Assume the same option terms. At maturity, the asset price is: S = 90. What is the holder's profit or loss?*

The holder will not exercise the option as it is "under water." She will not buy the asset at the contractual price of 100 from the issuer when she can get it for 90 in the market. Thus, the holder's loss is the option premium 10, which is the issuer's gain.

4. *A put option is sold with the following terms: P = 10 and X = 100. At maturity, the asset price is: S = 80. What is the holder's profit or loss?*

The option is in-the-money. The holder has the right to sell an asset worth 80 on the market for the contractual price of 100. She will exercise the option. The profit is 20 ($= 100 - 80$), less 10 paid in option premium. Thus, her net profit is 10 and the issuer's net loss is 10.

5. *Assume the same option terms. At maturity, the asset price is: S = 90. What is the holder's profit or loss?*

The option is still in-the-money. The holder's profit is 10, but the profit net of premium is 0. Neither the holder nor the issuer profits.

6. *Assume the same option terms. At maturity, the asset price is: S = 110. What is the holder's profit or loss?*

The holder will not exercise the option as it is "under water." She will not sell an asset worth 110 on the market at the contractual price of 100. Thus, the holder's loss is the option premium 10, which is the issuer's gain.

B. OPTION VALUATION

Lawyers will not be asked to calculate the value of options. It is not what they do. But business attorneys who work in complex transactions or sophisticated business environments should know the basic concepts of option valuation, at least enough to be conversant with the client at a basic level and to understand the determinants of option value, because these determinants will be identified in the derivatives contract. The math here is not difficult, but the concepts are.

1. PUT-CALL PARITY OF OPTIONS

Options are subject to a law of valuation called the put-call parity. This means that there is a relationship between the put and the call options. There is a mathematical relationship between the call option, put option, stock price, and strike price, which is the put-call parity.

$$S + P = C + \frac{X}{(1 + R)^T}$$

The put-call parity says that the stock price S plus the price of the put option P on an asset must equal the call option C on the asset plus strike price X discounted to present value.

The relationship in the put-call parity is intuitively seen by drawing the profit and loss profiles. If an investor owns stock (the underlying asset) and the long position on the put, the profit and loss profile of the combined position is seen below. To derive the combined position, transpose the stock and the put on top of each other and add up the gains and losses from each position. The resulting graph is seen in (S + P).

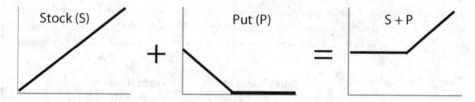

If an investor owns the discounted strike price and the long position on the call, the profit and loss profile of the combined position is seen below.

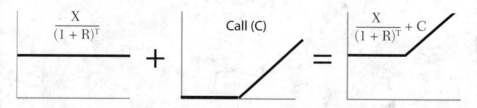

Why must the put-call parity hold? If it does not, an arbitrage opportunity occurs and an investor can make riskless profit by selling the overpriced option, and buying the underpriced option. As the above graphs show, the cash flows from the two positions, $C + \frac{X}{(1 + R)^T}$ and (S + P), are identical. Based on the Law of One Price, financial instruments with the same cash flow must be priced the same.

EXAMPLE

Arbitrage Enforcement of the Put-Call Parity

Assume that $S = \$31$, $P = \$2$, $C = \$1$, and $X/(1 + R)^T = \$32$. Assume that $T = 1$ year, and the risk-free rate $R = 6.25\%$. This means that the strike price $X = \$34$.

$$S + P = C + \frac{X}{(1 + R)^T}$$

$$31 + 2 = 1 + \frac{34}{(1 + 6.25\%)^1}$$

The put-call parity holds true at the price of $33 on each side of the equation. Assume now that $(S + P)$ is overpriced, and that it is actually trading at $35 (we don't know whether S or P or both are mispriced, but $(S + P)$ is trading higher than the opposite side of the put-call parity).

If an investor spots this error, can she earn a riskless profit? Yes. She should sell $(S + P)$, thus receiving $35, and use the funds to buy $(C + X/(1 + R)^T)$. She would purchase a call option for $1 and invest $32 at the risk-free rate, which would grow to $34 in one year at the rate of 6.25%. Note that there would be $2 remaining after these purchases.

The investor has sold the stock S and the put option P. Is the investor at risk if the stock price moves in any particular direction? No. She is perfectly hedged. Let's see why. Assume at maturity, the stock price S_m is either in-the-money or out-of-the-money as to the put option.

	Profit (Loss) at $S_m = 40$	Profit (Loss) at $S_m = 20$
Short position		
S (sold at $31)	(9) $= 31 - 40$	11 $= 31 - 20$
P (sold at $2)	2 $= 2 - 0$	(12) $= 20 + 2 - 34$
Net profit (loss)	(7)	(1)
Long position		
C (bought at $1)	5 $= 40 - 34 - 1$	(1) $= 0 - 1$
$X/(1 + R)^T$	2 $= 32 \times 6.25\%$	2 $= 32 \times 6.25\%$
Net profit (loss)	7	1

We see that by shorting $(S + P)$ and going long on $(C + X/(1 + R)^T)$, the investor is perfectly hedged. If $S_m = 40$, the investor loses (7) on the short position, but gains 7 on the long position. Similarly, if $S_m = 20$, the investor loses (1) on the short position, but gains 1 on the long position.

How does the investor achieve arbitrage if she is perfectly hedged? Recall that she shorted $(S + P)$ for $35, and it only took $33 to fund the long position $(C + X/(1 + R)^T)$. She has pocketed the $2 difference without any risk of losing it because the long position perfectly hedged the short position.

2. DETERMINANTS OF OPTION VALUE

The put-call parity states the economic relationship between the put and the call option on a common underlying asset. But it does not give us an independent means to value an option. The valuation of options and derivatives is perhaps the most difficult subject in financial economics because there is a great deal of high mathematics involved (the type of mathematics used in rocket science). We cannot cover the mathematics in this book, but we can gain an intuitive insight into the formal math using only basic arithmetic. Even the following stylized discussion using simple math can be difficult to follow, which illustrates how complex derivative valuation can be.

An option contract is legally simple. It is the right to buy (call option) or sell (put option) an asset for a fixed price by a maturity date. There are only several contract terms:

S = current price of the asset
X = strike price
P = writer's option premium
T = time

At any given point in time, the exercise value of an option is easy to calculate. The profit/loss of the holder of a call option is $V = \max[(S - X - P), -P]$. The issuer's profit/loss is $V = \min[(X - S + P), P]$. These mathematical expressions can be intimidating, but they are in fact quite simple.

EXAMPLE

Exercise Value of Options

On January 1, Issuer writes an option for a premium of $5 giving Holder the right to purchase one share of World's Best Co. Inc. for $100 by June 30 maturity. The current stock price is $80 per share.

What is the profit or loss for Issuer and Holder on March 31, three months before expiration of the option, for these stock prices?

Stock Price $S_{(March\ 31)}$	Issuer Profit & Loss $V = \min[(X - S + P), P]$	Holder Profit & Loss $V = \max[(S - X - P), -P]$
$80	$\min[(100 - 80 + 5), 5] = +5$	$\max[(80 - 100 - 5), -5] = -5$
$100	$\min[(100 - 100 + 5), 5] = +5$	$\max[(100 - 100 - 5), -5] = -5$
$120	$\min[(100 - 120 + 5), 5] = -15$	$\max[(120 - 100 - 5), -5] = +15$

Notice that the issuer can never make more money than the option premium, but the potential downside is theoretically infinite. The holder can never lose more money than the loss of the option premium paid to the issuer. The potential upside is theoretically infinite.

Assume that on March 31 the stock price is $120. Does this mean that the option has a value of $15?

No. It must be worth *more* than $15. If the option was exercise price on March 31, Holder profits by $15. But the option still has three months left until its maturity on June 30. The holders of options purchase the option precisely because it provides an option in the future. Three months of potential future upside must be compensated, meaning that it must be incorporated into the value of the option. Therefore, the value of the option on March 31 must be:

$$\text{Value} = \text{Exercise Value} + \text{Time Value}$$

Option value equals the exercise value only at maturity. Before maturity, there is always time value to consider. A bright elementary school graduate can calculate the exercise value. But how do we calculate the time value?

Option value depends on the interplay of six variables: the current stock price, the strike price, time to maturity, the volatility (variance) of the underlying stock price, the risk–free rate, and dividend yield. All else being equal, each factor affects option value. Because there are six variables, some of which move independently, the value of an option is a very challenging mathematical exercise. Option value fluctuates continuously until the maturity date at which point the exercise value equals the option value. This is why option pricing theory is so complex. Of the six variables, the most important factors affecting option value are: stock price S, strike price X, time to maturity T, and volatility. Let's think about this.

First, the value of the option increases as the strike price is closer to the stock price. For example, if the stock price is 100, a strike price on a call option of 150 increases the value of the option to 200.

Second, the value of the option increases as the maturity is further out in time. If the stock price is 100 and the strike price on a call option is 150, and if the maturity date is tomorrow, the option has little value because the stock price must increase by over 50 percent in one day to be in-the-money. But if the time to maturity is five years, the option has significant value because the stock need only increase in value by 8.5 percent per year for it to be in-the-money.

Third, what about volatility? Volatility means the propensity of the stock to move. Volatility and variance (*i.e.*, riskiness of the stock) are synonymous. The simple answer here is that as stocks become more risky, the option value increases. The intuition is that stocks that move significantly up and down have a better chance of hitting the strike price than a stock whose price moves horizontally.

We can intuit several simple rules. An increase in the following variables produces these changes to the long position on call and put options.

Increase in:	Effect on value of:	
	Call	Put
Stock price S	↑	↓
Strike price X	↓	↑
Time T	↑	↑
Volatility	↑	↑

Notice that both time T and volatility affect calls and puts the same way. This is intuitively obvious. The difference between the call and the put concerns the relationship between S and X, in both the movement of S and the relative distance between S and X.

The effects of time, stock price, and strike price on option value are easy to understand. However, volatility is a difficult concept. In previous chapters on finance and valuation, we saw that increased variance of cash flows *decreases* asset value, but increased riskiness of the stock *increases* option value. This is a key distinction between asset valuation and option valuation.

> In most financial settings, risk is a bad thing; you have to be paid to bear it. Investors in risky (high-beta) stocks demand higher expected rates of return. High risk capital investment projects have correspondingly high costs of capital and have to beat higher hurdle rates to achieve positive NPV [net present value].
>
> For options it's the other way around. As we have just seen, options written on volatile assets are worth more than options written on safe assets. If you can understand and remember that one fact about options, you've come a long way.[*]

We get an intuitive sense of the role of variance on option value. In the chart below, assume that the current stock price is S and the strike price is X. The call option is out-of-the-money. Assume two stocks, A and B, with different probability distributions. The price of stock A is less volatile, moving within a tight range. On the other hand, stock B is more volatile, moving within a broader range than stock A. From the perspective of the holder of two out-of-the-money call options on stocks A and B, why is an option on B more valuable?

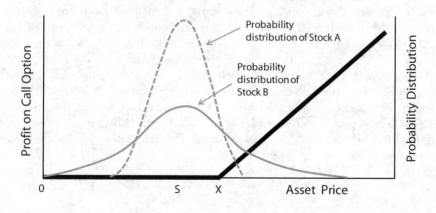

---

[*] Richard A. Brealey, Stewart C. Myers & Franklin Allen, Principles of Corporate Finance 557 (8th ed. 2006).

The intuition is that stocks that tend to move significantly to the downside (see stock B) also tend to move significantly to the upside. If the stock moves downward, the issuer does not incur more losses since he has already paid the option premium; on the other hand, a move to the upside has significant payoff.

Although an option is a simple contract, its valuation is no simple matter. A theory of valuation was elusive because the interplay among the six variables could not be captured. In 1973, Fischer Black and Myron Scholes solved the problem.* Their option pricing formula, called the Black-Scholes formula, is mathematically complex, but the solution is based on the simple principle that the payoff from an option can be replicated by a synthetic portfolio of stock and borrowing (assets and liabilities that can be readily valued). Since a riskless arbitrage opportunity cannot be sustained in a competitive market, the value of the synthetic portfolio must always equal the value of the option. Thus, if we can value the assets and liabilities at any given time, we can value the option.

3. EXAMPLE OF ARBITRAGE PRICING

It may be helpful to see a simplified option value calculation and how its determinants affect value, particularly as value relates to volatility. Assume that the current stock price $S = \$100$, strike price $X = \$130$, time period $T = 1$ year, borrowing rate $R = 5\%$, and no dividends or transaction costs. For simplicity, assume that the variance of the stock price moves ± 50 percent by maturity so that the spread of possible future share prices is $[S_u, S_d] = [\$150, \$50]$. At the strike price of $130, the option would be in-the-money only if the stock goes up by 50 percent. The option payoffs are calculated as $P = \max [0, S' - X]$ where S' is the share price at maturity. If the payoff is negative, meaning $X > S'$ at maturity, the option would not be exercised and so the payoff would be zero. The spread of possible option payoffs at maturity is $[(P_u = S_u - X), (P_d = S_u - X)] = [\$20, \$0]$.

Suppose the issuer wants to hedge this risk of the option being called against him. He must create a portfolio of stock and borrowing that replicates the option payoff. The hedge must be self-funding so that the purchase of the stock is funded externally by the option premium and borrowing. Based on these conditions, the issuer must purchase 1/5 share of common stock at the current price of $20 (= 1/5 of stock at price of $100 per share) to hedge the risk of an exercised option. This cost must be funded by $9.52 of borrowing, and $10.48 of option premium. Thus, the price of the option is $10.48. Why? Let's see how these figures are calculated.

These calculations assume that stock prices have a binomial distribution. Of course, stock prices typically take a distribution and the shape of this distribution is determined by the stock's volatility. The Black-Scholes option pricing formula takes this into account with complex mathematics. But the binomial assumption keeps the example simple. With this in mind, the calculation of the above values requires three steps.

---

* Fischer Black & Myron Scholes, *The Pricing of Options and Corporate Liabilities*, 81 J. Political Econ. 637 (1973).

Step 1: How many shares of stock must be bought to hedge the risk of the option? This is determined by the hedge ratio Δ, which is the spread of the possible option payoffs divided by the spread of the possible share prices:

$$\Delta = \frac{P_u - P_d}{S_u - S_d} = \frac{\$20 - \$0}{\$150 - \$50} = \frac{1}{5}$$

The issuer must buy 1/5 share of stock at the current price of $100. This $20 purchase must be funded by borrowing and the option premium.

Step 2: How much borrowing is required? The borrowing amount is the present value of the difference between the option payoff and the payoff from the 1/5 share at maturity:

$$\text{Borrowing} = \frac{(\Delta \times S_u) - P_u}{(1+R)} = \frac{(\Delta \times S_d) - P_d}{(1+R)} = \frac{(1/5 \times \$150) - \$20}{(1+5\%)} = \frac{(1/5 \times \$50) - \$0}{(1+5\%)} = \$9.52$$

Note that the borrowing is independent of the stock price movement. The up ($150) or down ($50) movement of the stock price does not matter.

Step 3: What is the option premium? The option premium is the value of the synthetic portfolio:

Option Value = Stock Value − Borrowing

Here, the option premium must be (1/5 x $100) − $9.52 = $10.48. The combined amount of borrowing ($9.52) and option premium ($10.48) exactly funds the issuer's purchase of the 1/5 share of stock ($20).

The value of the option equals the stock price minus borrowing. By replicating an option payoff from a synthetic portfolio of ordinary assets (stocks) and liabilities (borrowing), the issuer has hedged his exposure to the option risk. If this hedge is continuously maintained, the issuer has zero risk and so it is irrelevant whether the stock price goes up or down. Thus, we have a theoretical price for the option premium.

The synthetic portfolio value must equal the option value, lest there be a riskless arbitrage opportunity. Arbitrage is the simultaneous purchase and sale of securities that creates a riskless profit. Much of finance theory rests on the principle that market participants will ruthlessly exploit riskless arbitrage opportunities and so such opportunities are not sustainable. The possibility of arbitrage leads to the most fundamental principle of financial theory, the Principle of Absence of Arbitrage, which states that there is always a tradeoff between risk and reward because in the long term there are no unbounded riskless gains. The moment such opportunities are discovered, they will be exploited until they cease to exist. Thus, this process drives the market's Law of One Price. Arbitrage keeps prices of the same assets consistent in spite of the different ways in which these assets may be packaged.

In the option context, if the option price is mispriced (either higher or lower than the synthetic portfolio), an investor can always lock in a riskless profit by either selling the overpriced option or buying the underpriced option and hedging with the synthetic portfolio. We can prove this.

Assume a call option is mispriced one dollar higher than intrinsic value, *i.e.*, $11.48. An issuer could execute an arbitrage by selling the option at $11.48, borrowing $9.52 at a rate of 5 percent and then using the $21 in hand to buy 1/5 share of stock at $20. One dollar remains, which is invested at a risk-free 5 percent. At maturity, if the stock increases to $150, the call option is in-the-money and she owes the holder $20 and the lender $10. This $30 liability is matched exactly by the 1/5 share of a $150 stock she holds. The investor's profit is $1.05.

Now, if the stock price decreases to $50, the option is out-of-the-money and she owes the holder nothing but still owes $10 to the lender. This liability is matched by the 1/5 share of the $50 stock she holds. But her profit is still $1.05. By selling the mispriced option and hedging the exposure with the purchase of the fraction of the stock, she creates a riskless profit opportunity. Thus, the option value must equal the value of the replicating portfolio.

The variance of the stock price substantially affects option value. Assume that the stock price is less risky and moves ±35 percent rather than ±50 percent. At the strike price of $130 and per the above calculations, the option premium is $2.72. If the volatility is ±75 percent, the option value is now $22.86. The change in variance from ±35 to ±50 to ±75 percent results in an increase in option value from $2.72 to $10.48 to $22.86. *Thus, increased volatility of the underlying asset increases option value*.

Variance is important, but its direction is irrelevant in maintaining the hedge. This is an ingenious, Nobel Prize–winning insight by Black and Scholes: "If the hedge is maintained continuously, then the approximations mentioned above become exact, and the return on the hedged position is completely independent of the change in the value of the stock."* While an investor may take a position on an option because of a belief that the value of the underlying asset value will move one way or the other, that belief in the direction is not a variable in option pricing. At maturity, the option value is simply the exercise value of stock price minus the strike price. Before maturity, the variables of option value depend on the current exercise price, the time to maturity, and the variance of the underlying asset, but not any belief about where the stock price will ultimately be at maturity. The latter is simply the reason why one party will buy an option while another sells it. Without such differences of opinion, a liquid efficient market is impossible.

C. USES OF DERIVATIVES

1. EXECUTIVE STOCK OPTIONS

Stock options are a common form of executive and employee compensation. The basic idea of awarding stock options is that options incentivize executives and employees to increase the value of the corporation, and thereby increase the stock price. When the stock price increases, the value of a call option increases until at some point it becomes in-the-money. If the equity compensation is structured properly, the grant of options can better align the interests of employees (including senior executives) and the

---

* Black & Scholes, at 641.

corporation. Structured or executed improperly, the grant of options can at minimum not provide the optimal incentive structure and at worst constitute a giveaway of corporate assets.

The following cases illustrate the abuse of stock option grants through the manipulation of dates and private information by company insiders. In option valuation, the time and stock price movement are important variables in option value. These variables can be improperly manipulated by corporate insiders.

Ryan v. Gifford
918 A.2d 341 (Del. Ch. 2007)

CHANDLER, Chancellor.

On March 18, 2006, *The Wall Street Journal* sparked controversy throughout the investment community by publishing a one-page article, based on an academic's statistical analysis of option grants, which revealed an arguably questionable compensation practice. Commonly known as backdating, this practice involves a company issuing stock options to an executive on one date while providing fraudulent documentation asserting that the options were actually issued earlier. These options may provide a windfall for executives because the falsely dated stock option grants often coincide with market lows. Such timing reduces the strike prices and inflates the value of stock options, thereby increasing management compensation. This practice allegedly violates any stock option plan that requires strike prices to be no less than the fair market value on the date on which the option is granted by the board. Further, this practice runs afoul of many state and federal common and statutory laws that prohibit dissemination of false and misleading information.

After the article appeared in the *Journal*, Merrill Lynch issued a report demonstrating that officers of numerous companies, including Maxim Integrated Products, Inc., had benefited from so many fortuitously timed stock option grants that backdating seemed the only logical explanation. The report engendered this action.

Plaintiff Walter Ryan alleges that defendants breached their duties of due care and loyalty by approving or accepting backdated options that violated the clear letter of the shareholder-approved Stock Option Plan and Stock Incentive Plan ("option plans").

Maxim Integrated Products, Inc. is a technology leader in design, development, and manufacture of linear and mixed-signal integrated circuits used in microprocessor-based electronic equipment. From 1998 to mid–2002 Maxim's board of directors and compensation committee granted stock options for the purchase of millions of shares of Maxim's common stock to John Gifford, founder, chairman of the board, and chief executive officer, pursuant to shareholder-approved stock option plans filed with the Securities and Exchange Commission. Under the terms of these plans, Maxim contracted and represented that the exercise price of all stock options granted would be no less than the fair market value of the company's common stock, measured by the publicly traded closing price for Maxim stock on the date of the grant. Additionally, the plan identified the board or a committee designated by the board as administrators of its terms.

Ryan alleges that nine specific grants [of options to management] were backdated between 1998 and 2002, as these grants seem too fortuitously timed to be explained as simple coincidence. All nine grants were dated on unusually low (if not the lowest) trading days of the years in question, or on days immediately before sharp increases in the market price of the company.

As practices surrounding the timing of options grants for public companies began facing increased scrutiny in early 2006, Merrill Lynch conducted an analysis of the timing of stock option grants from 1997 to 2002 for the semiconductor and semiconductor equipment companies that comprise the Philadelphia Semiconductor Index. Merrill Lynch measured the aggressiveness of timing of option grants by examining the extent to which stock price performance subsequent to options pricing events diverges from stock price performance over a longer period of time. "Specifically, it looked at annualized stock price returns for the twenty day period subsequent to options pricing in comparison to stock price returns for the calendar year in which the options were granted." In theory, companies should not generate systematic excess return in comparison to other investors as a result of the timing of options pricing events. "If the timing of options grants is an arm's length process, and companies have [not] systematically taken advantage of their ability to backdate options within the [twenty] day windows that the law provided prior to the implementation of Sarbanes Oxley in 2002, there shouldn't be any difference between the two measures." Merrill Lynch failed to take a position on whether Maxim actually backdated; however, it noted that if backdating did not occur, management of Maxim was remarkably effective at timing options pricing events.

With regard to Maxim, Merrill Lynch found that the twenty-day return on option grants to management averaged 14% over the five-year period, an annualized return of 243%, or almost ten times higher than the 29% annualized market returns in the same period.

Plaintiff contends that all defendants breached their fiduciary duties to Maxim and its shareholders. The shareholder-approved 1983 Stock Option Plan and 1999 Stock Incentive Plan bound the board of directors to set the exercise price according to the terms of the plans. The 1999 plan allowed the board to designate a committee to approve the plans. Plaintiff alleges that from 1998 to 2002, the board actively allowed Maxim to backdate at least nine option grants issued to Gifford, in violation of shareholder-approved plans, and to purposefully mislead shareholders regarding its actions. As a result of the active violations of the plan and the active deceit, plaintiff contends that Maxim received lower payments upon exercise of the options than would have been received had they not been backdated. Further, Maxim suffers adverse effects from tax and accounting rules. The options priced below the stock's fair market value on the date of the grant allegedly bring the recipient an instant paper gain. At the time, such compensation had to be treated as a cost to the company, thereby reducing reported earnings and resulting in overstated profits. This likely necessitates revision of the company's financial statements and tax reporting. Moreover, Gifford, the recipient of the backdated options, is allegedly unjustly enriched due to receipt of compensation in clear violation of the shareholder-approved plans.

Defendants assert that plaintiff fails to state a claim for breach of fiduciary duty. This defense, stripped to its essence, states that in order to survive a motion to dismiss on a fiduciary duty claim, the complaint must rebut the business judgment rule. That is, plaintiff must raise a reason to doubt that the directors were disinterested or independent. Where the complaint does not rebut the business judgment rule, plaintiff must allege waste. Plaintiff here, argue the defendants, fails to do either. Further, there is no evidence that the defendants acted intentionally, in bad faith, or for personal gain.

The complaint here alleges bad faith and, therefore, a breach of the duty of loyalty sufficient to rebut the business judgment rule and survive a motion to dismiss. The business affairs of a corporation are to be managed by or under the direction of its board of directors. In an effort to encourage the full exercise of managerial powers, Delaware law protects the managers of a corporation through the business judgment rule. This rule "is a presumption that in making a business decision the directors of a corporation acted on an informed basis, in good faith and in the honest belief that the action taken was in the best interest of the company." Nevertheless, a showing that the board breached either its fiduciary duty of due care or its fiduciary duty of loyalty in connection with a challenged transaction may rebut this presumption. Such a breach may be shown where the board acts intentionally, in bad faith, or for personal gain.

Acts taken in bad faith breach the duty of loyalty. Bad faith may be shown where "the fiduciary intentionally acts with a purpose other than that of advancing the best interests of the corporation, where the fiduciary acts with the intent to violate applicable positive law, or where the fiduciary intentionally fails to act in the face of known duty to act, demonstrating a conscious disregard for his duties." Additionally, other examples of bad faith might exist. These examples include any action that demonstrates a faithlessness or lack of true devotion to the interests of the corporation and its shareholders.

Based on the allegations of the complaint, and all reasonable inferences drawn therefrom, I am convinced that the intentional violation of a shareholder approved stock option plan, coupled with fraudulent disclosures regarding the directors' purported compliance with that plan, constitute conduct that is disloyal to the corporation and is therefore an act in bad faith. Plaintiffs allege the following conduct: Maxim's directors affirmatively represented to Maxim's shareholders that the exercise price of any option grant would be no less than 100% of the fair value of the shares, measured by the market price of the shares on the date the option is granted. Maxim shareholders, possessing an absolute right to rely on those assurances when determining whether to approve the plans, in fact relied upon those representations and approved the plans. Thereafter, Maxim's directors are alleged to have deliberately attempted to circumvent their duty to price the shares at no less than market value on the option grant dates by surreptitiously changing the dates on which the options were granted. To make matters worse, the directors allegedly failed to disclose this conduct to their shareholders, instead making false representations regarding the option dates in many of their public disclosures.

I am unable to fathom a situation where the deliberate violation of a shareholder approved stock option plan and false disclosures, obviously intended to mislead shareholders into thinking that the directors complied honestly with the shareholder-approved option plan, is anything but an act of bad faith. It certainly cannot be said to amount to faithful and devoted conduct of a loyal fiduciary. Well-pleaded allegations of such conduct are sufficient, in my opinion, to rebut the business judgment rule and to survive a motion to dismiss.

Defendants contend that plaintiff's claim for unjust enrichment fails because there is no allegation that Gifford exercised any of the alleged backdated options and, therefore, Gifford did not obtain any benefit to which he was not entitled to the detriment of another. This defense is contrary both to the normal concept of remuneration and to common sense.

Unjust enrichment is "the unjust retention of a benefit to the loss of another, or the retention of money or property of another against the fundamental principles of justice or equity and good conscience." A defendant may be liable "even when the defendant retaining the benefit is not a wrongdoer" and "even though he may have received [it] honestly in the first instance."

At this stage, I cannot conclude that there is no reasonably conceivable set of circumstances under which Gifford might be unjustly enriched. Gifford does retain something of value, the alleged backdated options, at the expense of the corporation and shareholders. Further, defendants make no allegations that Gifford is precluded from exercising these options or that the options have expired. Thus, one can imagine a situation where Gifford exercises the options and benefits from the low exercise price. Even if Gifford fails to exercise a single option during the course of this litigation, that fact would not justify dismissal of the unjust enrichment claim. Whether or not the options are exercised, the Court will be able to fashion a remedy. For example, this Court might rely on expert testimony to determine the true value of the option grants or simply rescind them. Either way, Gifford's alleged failure to exercise the options up to this point does not undermine a claim for unjust enrichment Thus, I deny the motion to dismiss the unjust enrichment claim.

QUESTION

1. Why was backdating an option a bad-faith act by the defendants?

NOTES

1. Subsequently, the case settled for a $28,505,473 payment to the corporation by the defendants and their insurance carrier, $9,500,000 in plaintiff's attorney fees, plus other terms, and the court approved the settlement. *Ryan v. Gifford*, 2009 WL 18143 (Del.Ch. 2009).

Weiss v. Swanson
948 A.2d 433 (Del. Ch. 2008)

LAMB, Vice Chancellor.

Frederick Weiss challenges 22 option grants the company made between July 1996 and July 2005 pursuant to three stockholder-approved option plans. The plans set out the general terms by which options may be granted. Notably, the plans authorize the board of directors to approve grants made to directors. Thus, according to Weiss, the Director Defendants approved all option grants made to themselves. Weiss also alleges that the plans authorize the Compensation Committee to approve option grants made to officers.

Under Linear's stockholder-approved option plans, the administrators are authorized to grant options as part of a compensation system designed to "attract and retain the best available personnel" and "to provide additional incentive to Employees, Directors, and Consultants." Paragraph 9 of the [option plan] provides:

> The per Share exercise price shall be determined by the Administrator. In the case of a Non-statutory Stock Option intended to qualify as "performance-based compensation" within the meaning of Section 162(m) of the Internal Revenue Code, the per Share exercise price shall be no less than 100% of the Fair Market Value per Share on the date of grant.[7]

Thus, under the plans, the directors had full discretion to grant "in the money" options by setting exercise prices lower than the fair market value of Linear's stock price on the date of grant. The plans also provide that "the date of grant of an Option shall be, for all purposes, the date on which the Administrator makes the determination granting such Option, or such other later date as is determined by the Administrator."

Weiss alleges that from July 1996 to June 2005, the directors granted options that violated the purposes, intent, spirit, and objectives of these plans. Specifically, Weiss alleges that the Director Defendants knew the company's quarterly earnings releases were highly anticipated by Linear investors, and that Linear's stock was dramatically affected by these announcements.[9] Weiss claims that the directors had advance knowledge of the contents of the quarterly earnings releases, and used this information to time each of the 22 challenged grants on terms favorable to the defendants. According to the complaint, when the quarterly earnings release contained materially adverse information expected to drive down the market price of Linear's shares, the Director Defendants "bullet-dodged" the options, delaying their grant until after the release of the information. Conversely, when the quarterly earnings release contained material information expected to drive up the market price of Linear's shares, the Director Defendants allegedly "spring-loaded" the options, granting them just prior to the quarterly earnings release. Weiss also alleges that the Director Defendants never disclosed to stockholders that they timed option grants in this manner.

Weiss recognizes that granting and receiving spring-loaded and bullet-dodged options might be an appropriate exercise of business judgment in some circumstances. However, he asserts the Director Defendants' policy of timing options as alleged in this case was inconsistent with the expectations of the stockholders who approved the

---

7. "Fair Market Value" is defined as the closing bid price for Linear's stock. Thus, the 1996 Plan requires options intended to qualify under section 162(m) of the Internal Revenue Code to have an exercise price equal to the closing price of Linear's stock on the date the options are granted. Under section 162(m), compensation in excess of $1 million per year, including gains on stock options, paid to a corporation's five most highly compensated officers is tax deductible only if it is "performance-based," meaning it is given as an incentive for future performance, not as a reward for past performance. Options granted in the money allegedly do not meet this condition, and therefore are not eligible for treatment under section 162(m).

9. In support of his allegations that the quarterly earnings releases had a material effect on Linear's stock price, Weiss cites to a 2006 report by Merrill Lynch comparing the annualized 20-day returns from the dates of Linear's management stock option grants with investor calendar year annual returns. Weiss contends that the Merrill Lynch report found that between 1997 and 2002, the defendants realized returns for their option grants that exceeded investor returns by an average of 396%.

plans. Therefore, Weiss reasons, the defendants breached their fiduciary duties by authorizing, receiving, or (by abdication of duty) permitting grants not authorized by the stockholders. Weiss also contends that this timing policy harmed the corporation by artificially lowering the exercise price of the options, causing the company to receive too little money when the options are eventually exercised.

Weiss further alleges that the Director Defendants breached their fiduciary duties by causing Linear to issue the 1996 Proxy Statement, the 1998 Proxy Statement, the 2000 Proxy Statement, and the 2005 Proxy Statement without disclosing material information—namely, that options had been spring-loaded and bullet-dodged. Finally, Weiss brings a waste claim against the Director Defendants, and a claim for unjust enrichment against all the defendants.

The defendants contend that the complaint fails to state a claim against the Director Defendants for breach of fiduciary duty in connection with improper disclosures. The defendants note that under Delaware law, improper disclosure leads to a breach of fiduciary duty only when the disclosure is made in connection with a request for stockholder action. According to the defendants, Weiss has not identified any specific stockholder action connected to the disclosures.

This argument clearly lacks merit. Weiss alleges that the Director Defendants omitted that they would grant spring-loaded and bullet-dodged options from both the 1996 proxy statement seeking stockholder approval of the 1996 option plan and the 1998 proxy statement seeking stockholder approval of an amendment to the 1996 plan increasing the number of shares of common stock reserved for issuance. Weiss also alleges that in connection with proxy solicitations seeking reelection to Linear's board of directors, the Director Defendants made statements giving the impression that they had implemented the option plans in accordance with the plans' terms, when in fact they implemented a policy of timing grants that was not authorized under the plans. Therefore, Weiss has adequately pleaded a claim against the Director Defendants for breach of fiduciary duty based upon improper disclosures.

The defendants further argue that Weiss has not stated a claim for unjust enrichment as to any defendant because Weiss has not explained how the alleged timing of option grants enriched grantees. This argument is wholly without merit. Weiss posits that timing option grants ensures that the exercise price of a grantee's option is lower than it otherwise would be. Thus, upon exercise of the option, the grantee receives more value, and the company less, than he should.

The defendants argue that they have not been unjustly enriched as to options that remain unexercised. However, as the court stated in *Ryan v. Gifford*, 918 A.2d 341 (Del.Ch. 2007), this fact alone does not lead to a conclusion that there is no reasonably conceivable set of circumstances under which the defendants might be unjustly enriched. Indeed, the defendants retain something of value—the challenged options—at the expense of the corporation. Nothing suggests that the defendants are prevented from exercising their options once they fully vest. Thus, "one can imagine a situation where [the defendants] exercise the options and benefit from the low exercise price." Moreover, even if the defendants do not exercise any options at all, the court may still be able to fashion an appropriate remedy, such as repricing or rescinding the options. Thus, the motion to dismiss the unjust enrichment claim will be denied.

Waste has been defined as follows:

Roughly, a waste entails an exchange of corporate assets for consideration so disproportionately small as to lie beyond the range at which any reasonable person might be willing to trade. Most often the claim is associated with a transfer of corporate assets that serves no corporate purpose; or for which no consideration at all is received. Such a transfer is in effect a gift. If, however, there is any substantial consideration received by the corporation, and if there is a good faith judgment that in the circumstances the transaction is worthwhile, there should be no finding of waste, even if the fact finder would conclude *ex post* that the transaction was unreasonably risky.

The defendants argue that Weiss has failed to plead a claim for waste because he does not allege that the defendants should not have received any options, only that the option grants were excessive by some unarticulated amount. The defendants mischaracterize Weiss's allegations. Weiss alleges that the defendants should not have received any of the timed options at all, and that the grants were approved without any valid corporate purpose.

The court recognizes that a claim for waste must meet "an extreme test, very rarely satisfied by shareholder plaintiff." However, in this case, the court cannot conclude that there is no reasonably conceivable set of facts under which Weiss could prove a claim of waste. Therefore, Weiss has pleaded a claim for waste.

QUESTIONS

1. In what ways were "spring-loading" and "bullet-dodging" a breach of fiduciary duty and waste?
2. In both *Ryan* and *Weiss*, how were the plaintiffs able to successfully plead breach of fiduciary duty based on bad faith or faulty disclosure, unjust enrichment, and waste?

2. HEDGING

Derivatives have a Jekyll-Hyde duality about them. They can be used to increase one's exposure to risk, and thus they are instruments of financial speculation. The philosopher Thales, as described by Aristotle, was a speculator. How can derivatives be used to speculate? Derivatives increase the leverage in a transaction for the purchase of the underlying assets. The same amount of money that can be used to invest in the underlying asset can be used in a derivative transaction to control far greater quantities of the underlying asset. For example, the purchase of a share of stock may cost $100, but the same amount may be able to buy the purchase of a call option to purchase 10 shares of stock at the strike price of $110. If the stock price increases to $150, the profit on a single share is $50 (= $150—$100), but the profit on the call option is $400 (= ($150—$110) x 10 shares). The investors in a derivative transaction are exposing themselves to risks of the underlying assets as magnified by the greater quantity at stake.

Derivatives can also be used to hedge risk, which means to reduce or manage risk. How can derivatives be used to hedge? Derivatives can be used to sell unwanted risk to another. For example, the holder of a put option does not want downside risk in an asset, and thus she purchases a put option from the issuer who must now bear this risk. If the price of the asset decreases, she puts the asset to the option issuer who is obligated to buy the asset at the agreed strike price. Common insurance, such as auto or life insurance, is a special form of a put option used to mitigate risk from fortuitous events. If an auto policyholder had a valuable car that is reduced to scrap value due to an accident, she can put the car to the insurance company for an agreed value (*e.g.*, replacement value).

EXAMPLE

Foreign Currency Risk in a Cross-Border M&A Deal

This hypothetical is based on an experience in a real M&A transaction. A U.S. real estate company is interested in acquiring a UK real estate developer for £100,000,000. At the time of signing the acquisition agreement, the exchange rate between the pound sterling (£) and the U.S. dollar ($) is: $1.50 = £1.00. This means that $1.50 will buy £1.00 in London. At the time of the signing of the acquisition agreement, the consideration is expected to be $150,000,000.

At the time, the world currencies markets are volatile due to an Asian currency crisis. The U.S. company has to pay the acquisition consideration in pounds sterling at closing, but will not take place for several months. The deal is subject to currency risk. Suppose, for example, during this time the exchange rate moved to $1.60 = £1.00 (the dollar depreciates in value against the pound sterling). The consideration would be $160,000,000, or a $10 million (6.7%) increase in the budgeted cost of the acquisition. This is a real risk.

How can the U.S. company mitigate this risk?

It can hedge the risk by using derivatives. For example, it can buy a put option on the U.S. dollar. If the dollar decreases in value against the pound sterling, the U.S. company "wins" and it can apply the winnings against the increased cost of the acquisition. Or, the U.S. company can buy a call option on the pound sterling. If the pound sterling increases in value against the U.S. dollar, the U.S. company "wins." What are other potential derivative transactions that might work?

Why hedge the risk at all?

Risk is everywhere, and so the company could just "roll with it." But the U.S. company is not in the business of taking on foreign currency risk. Investment banks and currency speculators may desire this risk, but for other companies foreign currency may pose an unwanted risk. The company is in the business of taking risks in the real estate market. It wants insurance against a bad surprise just the way that ordinary people buy insurance against their property, health, and lives.

Note: In the real deal, the U.S. company chose not to hedge the currency risk because the purchase of financial insurance, which an investment bank would have provided, was considered too costly. Someone must be paid to bear the company's risk, and nothing is free in this world. The deal successfully closed anyway.

The following case shows the link between hedging and the fiduciary duty of care in the management of a company's business and affairs. It illustrates how derivatives can play an important part in the proper management of businesses.

Brane v. Roth
590 N.E.2d 587 (Ind. App. 1992)

RATLIFF, Chief Judge.

Directors appeal the award of $424,038.89 plus interest for shareholders in an action against them as directors of the LaFontaine Grain Co-op. We affirm.

This case involves a shareholders' action against the directors of a rural grain elevator cooperative for losses Co-op suffered in 1980 due to the directors' failure to protect its position by adequately hedging in the grain market. Approximately ninety percent of Co-op's business was buying and selling grain. The directors met on a monthly basis reviewing the manager's general report and financial reports prepared by the Co-op's bookkeeper. The directors also discussed maintenance and improvement matters and authorized loan transactions for Co-op. Requests for additional information on the reports were rare. The directors did not make any specific inquiry as to losses sustained in 1980.

The records show that Co-op's gross profit had fallen continually from 1977. After a substantial loss in 1979, Co-op's CPA, Michael Matchette, recommended that the directors hedge Co-op's grain position to protect itself from future losses. The directors authorized the manager to hedge for Co-op. Only a minimal amount was hedged, specifically $20,050 in hedging contracts were made, whereas Co-op had $7,300,000 in grain sales.

On February 3, 1981, Matchette presented the 1980 financial statement to the directors, indicating a net profit of only $68,684. In 1982, Matchette informed the directors of errors in his 1980 financial statement and that Co-op had actually experienced a gross loss of $227,329. The directors consulted another accounting firm to review the financial condition of Co-op. CPA Rex Coulter found additional errors in Matchette's 1980 financial statement, which increased the gross loss to $424,038. Coulter opined that the primary cause of the gross loss was the failure to hedge.

The court entered specific findings and conclusions determining that the directors breached their duties by retaining a manager inexperienced in hedging; failing to maintain reasonable supervision over him; and failing to attain knowledge of the basic fundamentals of hedging to be able to direct the hedging activities and supervise the manager properly; and that their gross inattention and failure to protect the grain profits caused the resultant loss of $424,038.89.

The directors contend that the trial court applied the wrong standard of care to their actions. The trial court utilized the standard of care set forth in Ind. Code §23-1-2-11. In 1980, Ind. Code §23-1-2-11 provided that a director shall perform his duties in good faith in the best interest of the corporation and with such care as an ordinarily prudent person in a like position would use in similar circumstances. The statute allows the director to rely upon information, reports, and opinions of the corporation's officers and employees which he reasonably believes to be reliable and competent, and public accountants on matters which he reasonably believes to be within such person's professional competence. A director has no liability if he meets this standard of care.

The directors argue in general that the trial court's decision is contrary to law because the shareholders failed to show proximate cause and specific damages. We remind them of the proper standard of review where the trial court made specific findings of fact and conclusions of law: we first must determine whether the evidence supports the findings, and then determine whether the findings support the judgment. The judgment of the trial court will be affirmed if we conclude that the specific findings support the judgment and are not clearly erroneous.

Under this standard of review, we find that there was probative evidence that Co-op's losses were due to a failure to hedge. Coulter testified that grain elevators should engage in hedging to protect the co-op from losses from price swings. One expert in the grain elevator business and hedging testified that co-ops should not speculate and that Co-op's losses stemmed from the failure to hedge.

Further evidence in the record supports the court's findings and its conclusions that the directors breached their duty by their failure to supervise the manager and become aware of the essentials of hedging to be able to monitor the business which was a proximate cause of Co-op's losses. Although the directors argue that they relied upon their manager and should be insulated from liability, the business judgment rule protects directors from liability only if their decisions were informed ones. *See Aronson v. Lewis*, 473 A.2d 805, 812 (Del. 1984) (business judgment rule is the presumption that directors acted on an informed basis, in good faith and in honest belief that the action taken was in the best interest of the company; the rule does not protect directors who have abdicated their functions or absent a conscious decision, failed to act; directors have a duty to inform themselves of all material information reasonably available to make their decision).

Here, the evidence shows that the directors made no meaningful attempts to be informed of the hedging activities and their effects upon Co-op's financial position. Their failure to provide adequate supervision of the manager's actions was a breach of their duty of care to protect Co-op's interests in a reasonable manner. The business judgment rule does not shield the directors from liability.

QUESTIONS

1. Does *Brane* stand for the proposition that a board must always hedge?
2. If not, how should a board view hedging strategy as a part of fulfilling its fiduciary duty?

NOTES

1. The precedential value of *Brane* was limited by the clearly erroneous standard of review upon the trial court's findings of facts. The case no longer has precedential value in Indiana in light of the new statute referenced in the opinion. In the opinion, the court noted that Ind. Code §23-1-2-11 was repealed and replaced by Ind. Code §23-1-35-1. The new statute preserved the standard of care ("the care an ordinarily prudent person in a like position would exercise under similar circumstances"), but the standard of liability requires a finding of "the breach or failure to perform constitutes willful misconduct or recklessness." Ind. Code §23-1-35-1(e). The court declined to apply the more restrictive standard of liability in Ind. Code §23-1-35-1

retroactively in this case. However, *Brane* suggests that a board's duty of care may implicate knowledge and use of derivatives in the management of a corporation.

3. CREDIT DERIVATIVES

Credit derivatives are a class of financial instruments that transfer credit risk from the protection buyer to the protection seller. Credit risk is the risk of diminution of the value of a debt obligation due to some adverse event. The credit derivative will contractually specify the nature of the adverse credit event, such as the occurrence of a default. The most common credit derivative is a credit default swap (CDS). Since the credit market is so large, the market for credit derivatives is also large and important.

CDSs and other swap and derivatives agreements use standardized agreements published by the International Swaps and Derivatives Association (ISDA) called the ISDA master agreement. These agreements provide the templates upon which a derivative contract is custom tailored to the needs of the contracting counterparties.

The following cases involve CDSs. The facts in these cases provide a sense of the business reasons for and situations necessitating the use of credit derivatives. With respect to the legal issues, these cases highlight the problem of clearly defining the credit event and other terms of the credit derivative. These cases involve the use and interpretation of the ISDA master agreement.

Eternity Global Master Fund Ltd. v. Morgan Guaranty Trust Co.
375 F.3d 168 (2d Cir. 2004)

Jacobs, Circuit Judge.

Eternity Global Master Fund Limited ("Eternity" or "the Fund") purchased credit default swaps ("CDSs" or "the CDS contracts") from Morgan Guaranty Trust Company of New York and JPMorgan Chase Bank (collectively, "Morgan") in October 2001. Eternity appeals from a final judgment entered in the District Court, dismissing with prejudice its complaint alleging breach of contract by Morgan in connection with the CDSs. The CDS contracts were written on the sovereign bonds of Argentina and would be "triggered" upon the occurrence of a "credit event," such that if Argentina restructured or defaulted on that debt, Eternity would have the right to put to Morgan a stipulated amount of the bonds for purchase at par value.

In late November 2001, the government of the Republic of Argentina, in the grip of economic crisis, initiated a "voluntary debt exchange" in which bondholders had the option of turning in their bonds for secured loans on terms less favorable except that the loans were secured by certain Argentine federal tax revenues. Eternity informed Morgan that the voluntary debt exchange was a credit event that triggered Morgan's obligations under the CDS contracts. Morgan disagreed.

We reverse the dismissal of the contract claim and remand for further proceedings.

On behalf of its investors, Eternity trades in global bonds, equities and currencies, including emerging-market debt. During the relevant period, Eternity's investment portfolio included short-term Argentine sovereign and corporate bonds. In emerging markets such as Argentina, a significant credit risk is "country risk," *i.e.,* "the risk that economic, social, and political conditions and events in a foreign country will adversely affect an institution's financial interests," including "the possibility of nationalization or expropriation of assets, government repudiation of external indebtedness, . . . and currency depreciation or devaluation." Credit risk can be managed, however. Banks, investment funds and other institutions increasingly use financial contracts known as "credit derivatives" to mitigate credit risk. In October 2001, in light of Argentina's rapidly deteriorating political and economic prospects, Eternity purchased CDSs to hedge the credit risk on its in-country investments.

A credit default swap is the most common form of credit derivative, *i.e.,* "a contract which transfers credit risk from a protection buyer to a credit protection seller." Protection buyers (here, Eternity) can use credit derivatives to manage particular market exposures and return-on-investment; and protection sellers (here, Morgan) generally use credit derivatives to earn income and diversify their own investment portfolios. Simply put, a credit default swap is a bilateral financial contract in which "a protection buyer makes periodic payments to . . . the protection seller, in return for a contingent payment if a predefined credit event occurs in the reference credit," *i.e.,* the obligation on which the contract is written.

Often, the reference asset that the protection buyer delivers to the protection seller following a credit event is the instrument that is being hedged. But in emerging markets, an investor may calculate that a particular credit risk "is reasonably correlated with the performance of [the sovereign] itself," so that (as here) the investor may seek to isolate and hedge country risk with credit default swaps written on some portion of the sovereign's outstanding debt.

In many contexts a "default" is a simple failure to pay; in a credit default swap, it references a stipulated bundle of "credit events" (such as bankruptcy, debt moratoria,[11] and debt restructurings) that will trigger the protection seller's obligation to "settle" the contract via the swap mechanism agreed to between the parties. The entire bundle is typically made subject to a materiality threshold. The occurrence of a credit event triggers the "swap," *i.e.,* the protection seller's obligation to pay on the contract according to the settlement mechanism. "The contingent payment can be based on cash settlement . . . or physical delivery of the reference asset, in exchange for a cash payment equal to the initial notional [*i.e.,* face] amount [of the CDS contract]." A CDS buyer holding a sufficient amount of the reference credit can simply tender it to the CDS seller for payment; but ownership of the reference credit prior to default is unnecessary. If a credit event occurs with respect to the obligation(s) named in a CDS, and notice thereof has been given (and the CDS buyer has otherwise performed), the CDS seller must settle. Liquidity in a secondary market increases the usefulness of a CDS as a hedging tool, though the limited depth of that market "can make it difficult to offset . . . positions prior to contract maturity."

The principal issue dividing the parties is whether the CDS contracts at issue are ambiguous in any material respect. "An ambiguity exists where the terms of a contract could suggest 'more than one meaning when viewed objectively by a reasonably intelligent person who has examined the context of the entire integrated agreement and

---

11. Generally speaking, a debt moratorium is "an order by a government making it lawful to defer payment of all or certain kinds of debts for a certain period of time beyond the original maturity, issued in order to prevent general bankruptcy or a collapse of credit by legally protecting debtors against their creditors in times of public danger."

who is cognizant of the customs, practices, usages and terminology as generally understood in the particular trade or business.'"

In this case, we assess ambiguity in the disputed CDS contracts by looking to (i) the terms of the three credit default swaps; (ii) the terms of the International Swaps and Derivatives Association's ("ISDA" or "the Association") "Master Swap Agreement," on which those swaps are predicated, (iii) ISDA's 1999 Credit Derivatives Definitions—which are incorporated into the disputed contracts; and (iv) the background "customs, practices, [and] usages" of the credit derivatives trade. Because customs and usages matter, and because documentation promulgated by the ISDA was used by the parties to this dispute, we briefly review some relevant background.

The term "derivatives" references "a vast array of privately negotiated over-the counter . . . and exchange traded transactions," including interest-rate swaps, currency swaps, commodity price swaps and credit derivatives—which include credit default swaps. A derivative is a bilateral contract that is typically negotiated by phone and followed by an exchange of confirmatory faxes that constitute the contract but do not specify such terms as events of default, representations and warranties, covenants, liquidated damages, and choice of law. These (and other) terms are typically found in a "Master Swap Agreement," which, prior to standardization efforts that began in the mid-1980s, "took the form of separate 15-to 25-page agreements for each transaction."

Documentation of derivatives transactions has become streamlined, chiefly through industry adherence to "Master Agreements" promulgated by the ISDA. In 1999, Eternity and Morgan entered the ISDA Multicurrency-Cross Border Master Agreement, which governs the CDS transactions disputed on appeal. Each disputed CDS also incorporates the 1999 ISDA Credit Derivatives Definitions, the Association's first attempt at a comprehensive lexicon governing credit derivatives transactions. Last year, due to the rapid evolution of "ISDA documentation for credit default swaps," the Association began market implementation of the 2003 Credit Derivatives Definitions, which evidently constitutes a work in progress.

Eternity's Global Master Fund is managed by HFW Capital, L.P., including its Chief Investment Officer, Alberto Franco. In 2001, Franco engaged Morgan to facilitate Eternity's participation in the Argentine corporate debt market. Fearing that a government debt crisis would impair the value of Eternity's Argentine investments, Franco sought to hedge using credit default swaps written on Argentine sovereign bonds. In October 2001, the Fund entered into three such contracts. Each CDS incorporated (i) the ISDA Master Swap Agreement, and (ii) the 1999 ISDA Definitions. The total value of the contracts was $14 million, as follows:

CDS Entry Date	Termination Date	Value
October 17, 2001	October 22, 2006	$2 million
October 19, 2001	December 17, 2001	$3 million
October 24, 2001	March 31, 2002	$9 million

Except as to value and duration, the terms were virtually identical, as follows:

(i) Eternity would pay Morgan a fixed periodic fee tied to the notional value of each respective credit default swap.

(ii) The swaps would be triggered upon occurrence of any one of four credit events—as defined by the 1999 ISDA Credit Derivative Definitions—with respect to the Argentine sovereign bonds: Failure to pay, Obligation Acceleration, Repudiation/Moratorium, and Restructuring.

(iii) Each CDS called for physical settlement following a credit event, specifically:

(a) Upon notification (by either party to the other) of a credit event, and confirmation via two publicly available sources of information (*e.g.,* the Wall Street Journal), and

(b) delivery to Morgan of the requisite amount of Argentine sovereign bonds,

(c) Morgan would pay Eternity par value for the obligations tendered.

Eternity entered into the swaps in reliance on Morgan's representations that it would provide access to a liquid secondary market that would enable the Fund to divest the contracts prior to termination.

The contracts at issue were signed in October 2001. By then, international financial markets had been speculating for months that Argentina might default on its $132 billion in government and other public debt. At an August 2001 meeting of bondholders in New York, Morgan acknowledged the possibility of a sovereign-debt default and advised that it was working with the Argentine government on restructuring scenarios. On October 31, 2001—after the effective date of the swap contracts at issue on this appeal—Morgan sent Eternity a research report noting that there was a "high implied probability of a restructuring" in which bondholders would likely receive replacement securities with a less-favorable rate of return. One day later, Argentine President Fernando de la Rua asked sovereign-bond holders to accept lower interest rates and longer maturities on approximately $95 billion of government debt.

On November 19, 2001, the Argentine government announced that a "voluntary debt exchange" would be offered to sovereign-bond holders. According to various public decrees, willing bondholders could exchange their obligations for secured loans that would pay a lower rate of return over a longer term, but that would be secured by certain federal tax revenues. So long as the government made timely payments on the loans, the original obligations would be held in trust for the benefit of Argentina; if the government defaulted, however, bondholders would have recourse to the original obligations, which were to "remain effective" for the duration of their life-in-trust. From late November through early December 2001, billions of dollars in sovereign bonds were exchanged for the lower-interest loans.

The complaint alleges that the debt exchange amounted to a default because local creditors had no choice but to participate, and that the financial press adopted that characterization. On November 8, 2001 Eternity served the first of three notices on Morgan asserting that the planned debt exchange was a restructuring credit event as to all three CDS contracts; but Morgan demurred.

On December 24, newly-installed interim President Adolfo Rodriguez Saa announced a public-debt moratorium. On December 27, Morgan notified Eternity that the moratorium constituted a credit event and subsequently settled the outstanding $2 million and $9 million credit default swaps (otherwise set to terminate on October 22, 2006 and March 31, 2002, respectively). According to Morgan, the third swap (valued at $3 million) had expired without being triggered, on December 17, 2001.

It is undisputed that the December 24 public-debt moratorium was a trigger of Eternity's outstanding swaps; in Eternity's view, however, the voluntary debt exchange had triggered Morgan's settlement obligations as early as November 8, 2001, as the Fund had been insisting throughout November and December of that year. In that same period, Eternity asked Morgan to liquidate the swaps on a secondary market. Notwithstanding Morgan's representations in February 2001 regarding the existence of a secondary market for the CDSs, it refused to quote Eternity any secondary-market pricing, though it did offer to "unwind" the contracts by returning the premiums Eternity had paid from October through November 2001.

Eternity alleges: (1) that the CDS contracts are valid agreements; (2) that the Fund satisfied its contractual obligations to Morgan, *i.e.*, paid its premiums; supplied the requisite notification and public information following the announcement of the voluntary debt exchange; and signaled its willingness to tender the necessary sovereign bonds; (3) that Morgan's refusal to settle the swaps was a breach of contract; and (4) that the Fund was damaged as a result of Morgan's breach—by the loss of the $3 million owed under the CDS that expired prior to the public-debt moratorium announced December 24, 2001, and by consequential damages arising from Morgan's refusal to settle the other swaps in November 2001.

The district court concluded that these pleadings were insufficient on the ground that the plain meaning of the CDS contracts conveyed the parties' unambiguous intention to exclude the voluntary debt exchange from the bundle of government actions that could qualify as a restructuring credit event. We disagree.

The question is whether at this stage it can be decided as a matter of law that the voluntary debt exchange was not a "restructuring credit event" covered by the Fund's CDS contracts with Morgan. Resolution of that issue turns on what the CDS contracts say. Under New York law, "the fundamental, neutral precept of contract interpretation is that agreements are construed in accord with the parties' intent." Typically, the best evidence of intent is the contract itself; if an agreement is "complete, clear and unambiguous on its face[, it] must be enforced according to the plain meaning of its terms." If the contract is ambiguous, extrinsic evidence may be considered "to ascertain the correct and intended meaning of a term" or terms. "Ambiguity exists where a contract term could suggest more than one meaning when viewed objectively by a reasonably intelligent person who has examined the context of the entire integrated agreement and who is cognizant of the customs, practices, usages and terminology as generally understood in the particular trade or business."

With respect to the CDS contracts at issue, certain intentions are unambiguous: Eternity and Morgan intended that a restructuring of Argentine sovereign debt would be a credit event triggering Morgan's obligations to settle the CDS contracts, and that the 1999 Definitions would govern whether a particular step taken by Argentina was a restructuring credit event. But resolution of the dispositive question—whether the parties intended that an event such as the voluntary debt exchange would qualify as a restructuring credit event—is not possible at this early stage of the litigation.

The 1999 ISDA Definition of "Restructuring" and the Terms of Argentina's Voluntary Debt Exchange

By their terms, Eternity's credit default swaps could be triggered by any of four credit events: Failure to Pay, Obligation Acceleration, Repudiation/Moratorium, and Restructuring. To flesh out these terms, Eternity and Morgan incorporated by reference the 1999 ISDA Credit Derivatives Definitions. Eternity concedes that

Argentina's voluntary debt exchange is a credit event *only* if it qualifies as a restructuring under §4.7 of the 1999 Definitions:

> "Restructuring" means that, *with respect to one or more Obligations, including as a result of an Obligation Exchange,* . . . any one or more of the following events occurs, is agreed between the Reference Entity or a Governmental Authority and the holder or holders of such Obligation or is announced (or otherwise decreed) by a Reference Entity or a Governmental Authority in a form that is binding upon a Reference Entity, and such event is not provided for under the terms of such Obligation in effect as of the later of the Trade Date and the date as of which such obligation is issued or incurred:
>
> (i) a reduction in the rate or amount of interest payable or the amount of scheduled interest accruals;
> (ii) a reduction in the amount of principal or premium payable at maturity or at scheduled redemption dates;
> (iii) a postponement or other deferral of a date or dates for either (A) the payment or accrual of interest or (B) the payment of principal or premium;
> (iv) a change in the ranking in priority of payment of any Obligation, causing the subordination of such Obligation; or
> (v) any change in the currency or composition of any payment of interest or principal.

ISDA, *1999 Credit Derivatives Definitions* §4.7(a) (1999) ("1999 Definitions"). The "obligations" relevant to Eternity's credit default swaps are Argentine sovereign bonds.

The basic terms of the voluntary debt exchange are undisputed. Presidential Decree 1387, released November 1, 2001, declares at Title II ("Reduction of the Cost of Argentine Government Debt"), Article 17:

> The MINISTRY OF ECONOMY is instructed to offer on *voluntary terms* the possibility of exchanging Argentine government debt for Secured Loans or Secured Argentine Government Bonds, provided that the collateral offered or the change in debtor allows the Argentine Government to obtain lower interest rates for the Argentine or Provincial Government Sector.

The class of "government debt" referred to in Article 17 includes the sovereign bonds on which the disputed CDS contracts are written. Thus holders of those bonds were eligible to participate in the government's exchange program.

Under Article 20 of Decree 1387, any exchange would be carried out

> at par value at a ratio of ONE (1) to ONE (1) in the same currency as the exchanged [originally held] obligation was denominated, *provided that the interest rate on the Secured Loan for which each government debt transaction is exchanged is at least THIRTY PERCENT (30%) less* than that established in the instrument submitted for exchange, per the terms of issue.

Under Article 22, the Ministry of the Economy was "authorized to appropriate funds belonging to the Nation," *i.e.,* certain federal tax revenues, "for up to the sum required to honor" the loans or other secured instruments for which any "original" sovereign-debt obligations would be exchanged.

On November 28, 2001, the Ministry of Economy issued Resolution 767 ("Government Debt"), which delineated the "exchange mechanism" contemplated in Decree 1387. Under Resolution 767, sovereign-debt holders would have until 3 p.m. on November 30, 2001 to submit "Offers of Exchange" to certain designated financial institutions. Between that date and December 3, the government would decide which offers it would accept, after which the bondholders so selected would have until December 7 to tender eligible securities. The exchanges would be "settled" on December 12, when former bondholders would receive the secured loans.

On December 12, the government approved (i) a "Secured Loan Agreement" to govern the new obligations, and (ii) a "Trust Agreement" governing the disposition of the original bonds. The Trust Agreement provides that any bonds exchanged for secured loans would be placed in trust for the benefit of the Republic of Argentina. The complaint alleges that as of December 6-7, 2001, holders of approximately $50 billion in Argentine sovereign debt had tendered their bonds.

Eternity contends that Argentina's voluntary debt exchange qualifies as a restructuring credit event in four ways: (i) as an obligation exchange under §4.9 of the 1999 Definitions that constituted a "restructuring" under §4.7; and even if not an obligation exchange, as an (ii) extension, and/or (iii) deferral, and/or (iv) subordination of the original obligations such that those obligations were restructured within the meaning of §4.7. Morgan counters, and the district court agreed, that the voluntary debt exchange was not a restructuring within the meaning of the CDS contracts because it was not an obligation exchange, nor did it affect the payment, value, or priority of the original obligations.

The voluntary debt exchange as an "Obligation Exchange"

Under the 1999 Definitions, an "Obligation Exchange" is "the *mandatory transfer* . . . of any securities, obligations or assets to holders of Obligations in exchange for such Obligations. When so transferred, such securities, obligations or assets will be deemed to be Obligations." *1999 Definitions, supra,* §4.9. Section 4.7 states that an "Obligation Exchange" can qualify as a restructuring, and further provides:

> *If* an Obligation Exchange has occurred, the determination as to whether one of the events described under Section 4.7(a)(i) to (v) has occurred will be based on a *comparison* of the terms of the Obligation immediately before such Obligation Exchange and the terms of the resulting Obligation immediately following such Obligation Exchange.

Thus *if* the voluntary debt exchange is an "Obligation Exchange," then it is a restructuring *if* the terms of the Secured Loans—as compared with the terms of the exchanged sovereign bonds—indicate that "one of the events [that constitutes a restructuring under §4.7] has occurred." Morgan concedes that such a comparison would show that the voluntary debt exchange was a restructuring credit event: The secured loans undeniably provide a lower return over a longer maturity than the original bonds, two features that qualify as restructuring occurrences under §4.7 (a)(i), (iii).

Morgan argues, however, that because §4.9 of the 1999 Definitions states that an "Obligation Exchange" is a "mandatory transfer" of one set of obligations for another, and because participation in the government's debt exchange program was "voluntary," a comparison of the two instruments is irrelevant.

The term "mandatory transfer" as it appears in §4.9 of the ISDA definitions is not self-reading, and is therefore ambiguous if it could suggest more than one meaning when viewed objectively, in the context of each CDS agreement and the "customs, practices, [and] usages . . . as generally understood" in the credit derivatives trade. Morgan makes the intuitively appealing argument that a "mandatory transfer" cannot be an exchange offered on "voluntary terms." The district court was persuaded by this argument, citing Black's Law Dictionary:

> Argentina's [voluntary debt] exchange program cannot qualify as "mandatory." Eternity made a choice. Along with "a substantial portion" of holders of those Argentine obligations, Eternity chose to exchange the obligations for lower-interest secured loans.. . . . Despite Eternity's attempt to argue that "mandatory" should be read to encompass situations that are "economically coercive," the plain meaning of the term "mandatory" does not permit such a finding. The term "mandatory" is defined by Black's Law Dictionary (7th Ed.1999) as "of, relating to, or constituting a command" or "required." The choice made by Eternity may have been unpalatable, but that does not make it mandatory.

A dictionary definition, however, does not take into account what "mandatory transfer" means in the context of a particular industry.

Eternity makes the less obvious but plausible argument that to credit-risk protection buyers such as itself, a "mandatory transfer" includes any obligation exchange achieved by "economic coercion," regardless of its classification as "voluntary" or "mandatory" by the initiating party. According to Black's, "economic coercion" is "conduct that constitutes improper use of economic power to compel another to submit to the wishes of one who wields it." Assuming that the government's debt exchange was economically coercive, "voluntary" participation by the "coerced" bondholders appears to resemble "mandatory" action. At the same time, from Argentina's perspective, the exchange may have been voluntary in fact, *i.e.*, the government may have had the intention to honor its debt obligations to nonparticipants without delay or reduction. But Argentina's characterization—which is self-serving—does not control, particularly when one considers Eternity's allegation that Morgan was an architect of the debt exchange. A proper interpretation of the CDS contracts must be drawn from the contract language and, where necessary, from other indicia of the parties' intent. Section 4.9 is silent as to whose perspective dictates whether an obligation exchange has occurred (*e.g.*, the issuer or the holder, or the investment press or community), and the parties' competing interpretations are plausible. We cannot resolve that ambiguity at this stage, as the district court took no submissions on the customs and usages of the credit derivatives industry, and the parties point us to no definitive source that resolves the difficulty.

We go on to consider Eternity's arguments that the government's debt exchange was a restructuring even if it was *not* an obligation exchange.

The effect of the voluntary debt exchange on Argentina's original debt obligations

Under the 1999 Definitions, a restructuring credit event occurs when any one of five enumerated events "occurs, is agreed [to] . . . or is announced" with respect to an "obligation" upon which a credit default swap is written. *1999 Definitions, supra,* §4.7(a). These include:

(i) a reduction in the rate of payable interest or principal on the obligation;
(ii) a postponement of payment on interest or principal; and
(iii) a subordination of the obligation that did not exist prior to the occurrence of the restructuring credit event.

Eternity contends that each of these three events "occurred" with respect to certain classes of Argentine sovereign bonds as a consequence of the government's voluntary debt exchange.

The district court held that "under the terms of the 'voluntary debt exchange,' the obligations submitted into the Trust ... themselves remained unchanged." That observation may be sound as far as it goes. But §4.7 provides that a restructuring results if any event defined in the section "occurs" with respect to "one or more obligations." Thus, the proper inquiry is whether the debt exchange caused a restructuring to occur with respect to *any* of the Argentine sovereign bonds. For the purpose of this analysis, it is useful to consider separately the impact of the debt exchange on obligations that were exchanged pursuant to the government's "voluntary" offer (participating obligations), and on those retained by sovereign-bond holders who elected to forgo the government's program (nonparticipating obligations). To negative the possibility that there was a restructuring credit event, it must be clear that none of the "events" described in §§4.7(a)(i)-(v) occurred with respect either to the participating obligations or to the nonparticipating obligations.

Participating Obligations

Participating obligations were ultimately deposited with the Central Bank of the Republic of Argentina pursuant to Article 23 of Presidential Decree 1387, issued November 1, 2001. Six weeks later, Presidential Decree 1646 approved both a Secured Loan Agreement to govern the terms of the loans that would replace the bonds tendered in the exchange, and a Trust Agreement that governed the status of obligations so tendered. Eternity contends that a restructuring credit event occurred with respect to tendered obligations because their terms were extended and/or payment was suspended for the duration of their life-in-trust.

Maturity Extension. On November 28, 2001 the Ministry of Economy promulgated Resolution 767 which defined the sovereign bonds eligible to participate in the voluntary exchange and, at Annex II, delineated the "exchange mechanism" for those securities, including the provision that "eligible Securities whose total or partial original maturity is prior to December 31, 2010 shall receive secured loans that will extend the average life *of the Eligible Security* by 3 years." Morgan does not directly respond to Eternity's contention that this wording extends the maturity of certain debt obligations within the class referenced in the disputed CDS contracts. This provision creates a question of fact as to whether the three-year extension constitutes a restructuring credit event under §4.7(iii) of the 1999 Definitions.

Suspension of Payment. Under the terms of the voluntary debt exchange (primarily laid down in Decree 1646), participating obligations were placed in trust. The Trust Agreement named Caja de Valores as trustee and provided that the government of Argentina would "acquire Participation Certificates in the ... Trust, the underlying assets of which are the Argentine government debt securities" that participated in the exchange. By virtue of its participation, the Republic of Argentina was the "Original Beneficiary" of the trust. Decree 1646 further provided that "for purposes of determining the outstanding amount of Argentine government debt or of determining the national debt ceiling, ... [tendered obligations] shall not be included in such calculations for so long as the Argentine Federal Government is the Beneficiary of any payments made in this regard." This provision implements Decree 1506, promulgated November 22, 2001, which amended Decree 1387 to provide that any obligations placed in trust pursuant to the voluntary debt exchange would be excluded from the calculation of Argentina's national debt. According to Decree 1506:

> Such an arrangement [was] called for because, even when securities subject to exchange are held [in the manner contemplated] . . . it is the Argentine Federal Government that is the beneficiary of the economic rights thereby granted, *with the liabilities thus becoming confused with the credits and offsetting same, inasmuch as the creditors of the ARGENTINE REPUBLIC can under no circumstances make simultaneous claims to credit rights that are granted by government securities in addition to those granted by Secured Loans substituting same.*

Eternity contends that these provisions suspended Argentina's liability on the bonds held in trust because (i) former bondholders could not enforce the original instruments while they were held in trust; and (ii) Argentina's role as both beneficiary and obligor on the trust assets suspended, at least temporarily, any enforceable legal obligation created by those debt instruments. We think that there is a question, at least on the present record, as to whether this trust mechanism constituted "postponement or other deferral of a date or dates for payment of those obligations," within the meaning of §4.7(a)(iii).

Morgan identifies three provisions of the Trust Agreement as support for its contention that the voluntary debt exchange did not affect Argentina's sovereign-debt obligations in any of the ways contemplated in §4.7. Two of the three provisions refer directly or indirectly to a Secured Loan Agreement, a copy of which has been furnished to us, apparently from a website; but Morgan's otherwise voluminous submissions do not include a translation into English. That omission frustrates a complete analysis because we are left to guess whether, given the Trust Agreement's repeated references to particular provisions of the Loan Agreement, the latter has any bearing on the debt obligations placed in trust.

Moreover, the language cited to establish the continued effectiveness of Argentine bonds placed in trust is indefinite. Under Section C of the Trust Agreement's "Whereas" clause:

> In accordance with the provisions of Article Ten of the Loan Agreement, an *essential condition* of same is that the Securities *remain effective,* with respect to both the economic and political rights of same, in such a manner that, under certain circumstances, their owners can recover fee simple thereof, all until such time as the Secured Loans have been settled. . . .

The economic and political rights of tendered obligations remain effective "in such a manner that, under certain circumstances" they can be recovered in fee simple. But it is wholly unclear what "such a manner" might mean on this record, or in what "circumstances" recovery would be allowed, or what it means for the bonds to "remain effective" when (under Decree 1506) they cannot be enforced by the former bondholders. In any case, it appears that tendered obligations "remain effective" only insofar as may be necessary to fulfill the contingency that former bondholders may one day have a right to reclaim their original obligations. Whether this qualified and contingent effectiveness constitutes a restructuring credit event is a question that cannot be resolved on the pleadings.

Finally, Morgan points to section 3.1 of the Trust Agreement, which directs the trustee to

> collect principal and interest *payments due* with respect to the Trust Assets and *pari passu* shall pay with such amounts *payments due* under the Participation Certificates

[held by the Republic of Argentina], until such time as the Participation Certificates are fully amortized, except upon the occurrence [of a default as defined in the Secured Loan Agreement].

The force of Morgan's argument is blunted by the absence of the Secured Loan Agreement; nonetheless, the quoted language begs the question: If, as Eternity contends, the government's legal obligation to make bond payments was suspended or postponed when Argentina became the trust beneficiary of assets on which it was obligated to pay, were any interest payments actually "due" on the original obligations?

Nonparticipating obligations

Eternity alleges that at some point during the voluntary debt exchange process, Argentina's Economy Minister announced that the "restructured loans held domestically will have the highest priority for payment." According to Eternity, this announcement "effectively" subordinated the original obligations to the secured loans, and was thus a credit event under §4.7, which includes "a change in the ranking in priority of payment of any Obligation, causing the subordination of such Obligation." *1999 Definitions* §4.7(a)(iv). Morgan disagrees, primarily on the ground that there is "no language in the Domestic Exchange that changes the rank in priority of payment on the existing Obligations."

Section 4.7(a)(iv) of the 1999 Definitions, which says that "subordination" is a reduction "in the ranking in priority of payment of any Obligation," does not in terms exclude policy declarations such as the one allegedly announced by Argentina's Economy Minister. True, "subordination" may denote more limited circumstances, such as a formal, contractual subordination of a particular debt. But that reading is not compelled by the wording of §4.7(a)(iv).

The ISDA promulgated a "Restructuring Supplement" to the 1999 Definitions in April 2001 which included §2.30(b) ("Pari Passu Ranking; Section 4.7(a)(iv)"), a provision that speaks directly to the definition of "subordination" under §4.7(a)(iv):

> For purposes of Section 4.7(a)(iv), "a change in the ranking in priority of payment of any Obligation, causing the subordination of such Obligation," means *only* the following: an amendment to the terms of such Obligation or other contractual arrangement pursuant to which the requisite percentage of holders of such Obligations ("Subordinated Holders") agree that, upon the liquidation, dissolution, reorganization or winding up of the Reference Entity, claims of holders of any other Obligations will be satisfied prior to the claims of Subordinated Holders. For the avoidance of doubt, the provision of collateral, credit support or credit enhancement with respect to any obligation will not, of itself, constitute a change in the ranking in priority of payment of any Obligation causing the subordination of such Obligation.

The Eternity/Morgan CDS contracts incorporate the 1999 Definitions, but do not appear to incorporate the Restructuring Supplement, which must be invoked specifically.[27] If the Supplement had been included, the subordination issue would likely be

---

27. The Supplement provides: "Any or all of the following definitions and provisions may be incorporated into a document by wording in the document indicating that . . . the document is subject to the 1999 ISDA Credit Derivatives Definitions (as published by the International Swaps and Derivatives Association, Inc. ('ISDA')), as supplemented by the Restructuring Supplement (the 'Definitions')." The Eternity/Morgan CDS contracts contain no such language.

settled (in Morgan's favor); but the version of §4.7(a)(iv) in use here is insufficiently clear as to whether subordination can be effected by policy statements such as the one cited by Eternity. Eternity and Morgan will have to resolve the issue in discovery or, if necessary, before a trier of fact.

QUESTIONS

1. What is the role of the ISDA form contract in this case and in the market generally?
2. What were the material ambiguities in the contract?

Deutsche Bank AG v. Ambac Credit Prods., LLC
2006 WL 1867497 (S.D.N.Y. 2006)

DENISE COTE, District Judge.

This is a dispute over a complex transaction between two sophisticated financial institutions. Although the instruments involved are somewhat abstruse, the central issue can be boiled down to a relatively straightforward question of contract interpretation: When was plaintiff Deutsche Bank AG ("DB") required to deliver a group of bonds to defendant Ambac Credit Products, LLC ("ACP")? DB claims that although the documents governing the disputed transaction set out a detailed timeline for delivery of the bonds, industry practice and other contractual provisions allowed for delivery well past the nominal deadline. Therefore, according to DB, ACP breached the contract when it refused to pay for the bonds DB tendered one month after the putative delivery date.

[DB filed this action, alleging breach of contract against ACP and Ambac Assurance Corporation ("AAC"). AAC is the parent company of ACP. AAC issues financial guarantees and loss indemnity policies, and AAC engages in credit derivative transactions. ACP does not have officers and employees distinct from the officers and employees of AAC. A bench trial was held. The court concludes that ACP did not breach its contract with DB, since it was under no obligation to pay for bonds that were not delivered in accordance with the contractual terms.]

Facts

The disputed transaction here is a species of credit derivative called a credit default swap ("CDS"). Credit derivatives are akin to insurance policies for holders of corporate bonds or other securities against downgrades in the credit of the issuing companies. They do this by transferring credit risk from a "protection buyer" to a "protection seller. A CDS is a common type of credit derivative in which the protection buyer makes a fixed payment to the protection seller in return for a payment that is contingent upon a "credit event"—such as a bankruptcy—occurring to the company that issued the security (the "reference entity") or the security itself (the "reference obligation"). The contingent payment is often made against delivery of a "deliverable obligation"—usually the reference obligation or other security issued by the reference entity—by the protection buyer to the protection seller. This delivery is known as the "physical settlement." Some CDS transactions, such as the one at issue here, are known as "portfolio" transactions, meaning they cover multiple reference entities and reference obligations.

CDS transactions are of relatively recent origin, having been developed in the mid-1990s. They are highly negotiated and are customarily based on standard terms published by the International Swaps and Derivatives Association, Inc. ("ISDA"). These terms may be modified for a particular transaction. At the time the transaction at issue here was executed, the 1999 ISDA Credit Derivatives Definitions ("1999 Definitions") provided the foundation for most CDS agreements.

The 1999 Definitions, which contemplate a transaction involving a single reference obligation, set out a highly detailed, carefully choreographed set of procedures to be followed if the reference entity experiences a credit event. First, pursuant to Section 3.3, either party may notify the other party of the credit event by means of an irrevocable Credit Event Notice, containing "a description in reasonable detail of the facts relevant to the determination that a Credit Event has occurred." Once the Credit Event Notice has been provided, the buyer of protection has 30 days to provide the seller with a Notice of Intended Physical Settlement ("NIPS"). Under Section 3.4, NIPS

> means an irrevocable notice from Buyer . . . to Seller that confirms that Buyer will settle the Credit Derivative Transaction and require performance in accordance with the Physical Settlement Method, and containing a detailed description of the type of Deliverable Obligations that Buyer reasonably expects to Deliver to Seller.

If a NIPS is not delivered within the 30-day window, the transaction terminates, and the buyer loses its ability to make any claim for credit protection. In the words of Section 3.4, the "thirtieth calendar day shall be the *Termination Date.*"

Assuming that a timely delivery of a NIPS has been made, the parties must settle the transaction within the Settlement Period, which is defined in Section 8.5 as:

> the number of Business Days specified as such in the related Confirmation or, if a number of Business Days is not so specified, the longest of the number of Business Days for settlement in accordance with *then current market practice* of any Deliverable Obligation being Delivered in the Portfolio, as determined by the Calculation Agent, in consultation with the parties.

The reference to "current market practice" allows the Calculation Agent to identify the delivery date that is customary for the securities that are at issue.

The final day of the Physical Settlement Period is known as the Physical Settlement Date, and under Section 8.1, it is the date on which the parties' obligations to each other come due:

> Buyer shall . . . on or prior to the Physical Settlement Date Deliver to Seller all or part of that portion of the Portfolio specified in the Notice of Intended Physical Settlement *and Seller shall pay to Buyer* that portion of the Physical Settlement Amount that corresponds to the portion of the Portfolio that Buyer has Delivered.

Thus, the seller's duty to pay is dependent on the buyer of protection's delivery of the securities identified in the NIPS.

Pursuant to Section 8.3, if delivery is completed by the Physical Settlement Date, the transaction ends. It provides that "If the entire portion of the Portfolio specified in the Notice of Intended Physical Settlement is Delivered on or before the Physical Settlement Date, the Physical Settlement Date shall be the *Termination Date.*"

Section 9.3(c)(ii), however, loosens the requirement that the buyer make delivery "on or prior to" the Physical Settlement Date:

> Buyer may continue to attempt to Deliver the whole of the Portfolio specified in the Notice of Intended Physical Settlement *for an additional five Business Days after the Physical Settlement Date.* Subject to Section 8.1 and to Sections 9.4, 9.5, 9.6 and 9.7, *if Buyer fails to Deliver any portion of the Portfolio specified in the Notice of Intended Physical Settlement on or prior to the date that is five Business Days after the Physical Settlement Date,* such failure shall not constitute an Event of Default and *such date shall be deemed to be the Termination Date.*

This provision creates a five-day grace period for the delivery of deliverable obligations to account for back-office delays in the procurement and delivery of securities. If, however, the buyer fails to make delivery within that five-day window, the transaction terminates, and the buyer loses its ability to make any claim for credit protection.

Thus, once a credit event occurs, the parties have a strictly controlled timeframe in which to act. A buyer of protection must first deliver a NIPS and then the securities within the time frames allowed, or lose the right to obtain payment from the protection seller. Similarly, assuming the buyer has performed its obligations, the seller of protection must be prepared to make the required payment associated with the credit event within a defined and relatively short period of time following a credit event.

The Triplets Transaction

In the transaction that is the subject of this lawsuit, DB, a large international bank headquartered in Germany, functioned as the protection buyer, and ACP functioned as the protection seller. The parties entered into a Master Agreement dated December 17, 1998, as well as a Schedule and Credit Support Annex (collectively, the "Master Agreement"). AAC also issued a Financial Guarantee Insurance Policy (the "Guarantee") unconditionally and irrevocably guaranteeing "any payment of the Cash Settlement Amount due from [ACP] to [DB] pursuant to the terms of any confirmation under the Master Agreement." The Schedule provides that the Master Agreement will "be governed by, and construed and enforced in accordance with, the laws of the State of New York without reference to its choice of law doctrine."

ACP and DB then entered into a Confirmation dated April 19, 2000 issued under the Master Agreement ("Confirmation") and relating to a CDS transaction known as "Triplets." Triplets involved a portfolio of 60 reference entities and reference obligations, including 7.375% Bonds due in 2027, issued by Solutia Inc. (the "Solutia Bonds"). DB agreed to pay ACP at regular intervals for the credit protection provided under the Confirmation. The Confirmation expressly incorporates the Master Agreement, the Schedule, and the 1999 Definitions, including the right of either the protection buyer or seller to serve a Credit Event Notice. It states that "in the event of any inconsistency between the Credit Derivatives Definitions and this Confirmation, this Confirmation will govern."

It was, in fact, necessary for the Confirmation to override certain provisions of the 1999 Definitions, since Triplets involved multiple reference entities and obligations, while the 1999 Definitions contemplated a single-name transaction. For example, under the 1999 Definitions, both completion of physical settlement and failure to adhere to the physical settlement timeline end the entire transaction. Here, however, the parties did not want the entire Triplets transaction to terminate upon the occurrence of a single credit event relating to a single reference entity, but to provide credit protection for a five-year term. Therefore, the Confirmation, which provides for an "Effective Date" of May 2, 2000, defines the "Termination Date" as "the later to occur of the Scheduled Termination Date and the final Physical Settlement date." The "Scheduled Termination Date" is listed as May 2, 2005.

The Solutia Credit Event and Physical Settlement

Solutia filed a bankruptcy petition in the Bankruptcy Court on December 17, 2003. Under the Confirmation, this filing constituted a credit event. As a result, DB delivered to ACP a Credit Event Notice and Notice of Publicly Available Information dated December 17, 2003, informing ACP of the Solutia bankruptcy. On January 16, 2004—the final date on which a NIPS could be delivered—DB sent ACP a NIPS, which stated in part:

> [DB] reasonably expects to deliver to [ACP] the following Deliverable Obligation: [Solutia Bonds]. Pursuant to the terms of the Credit Derivative Transaction, *[DB] will deliver such Deliverable Obligations for Physical Settlement,* with the total outstanding principal balance required under the terms of the Credit Derivatives Transaction as determined by the Final Price of the [Solutia Bonds], *on February 4, 2004* (the "Delivery Date"). On the Delivery Date, [ACP] will delivery to [DB] the amount required under the terms of the Credit Derivatives Transaction.

With this notice, DB chose the Delivery Date and triggered the duty of ACP to pay DB upon receipt of the Solutia Bonds. On February 2, DB sent ACP a letter confirming the terms of the Physical Settlement. The letter, which was revised on February 3, provides in relevant part:

> For purposes of clarifying the NIPS previously delivered to you, we hereby notify you that on the Delivery Date (as such term is defined in the NIPS) *[DB] reasonably expects to deliver to [ACP] a total of USD 8,771,000 in outstanding principal amount of the Deliverable Obligation* set forth in the NIPS. . . . Pursuant to the terms of the Credit Derivative Transaction, [DB] will deliver such Deliverable Obligations for Physical Settlement on the Delivery Date. *On February 4, 2004 (the Delivery Date), [ACP] is obligated to deliver to [DB] USD 8,771,000.*

Around February 4, ACP gave instructions to its custodian bank, the Bank of New York, to receive DB's delivery of Solutia Bonds. It also made a cash deposit of the Settlement Amount and instructed the Bank of New York to use the funds to pay for the Deliverable Obligation.

Early on February 4, ACP sent an e-mail to DB instructing it to contact [David Gleeson, an accountant for credit derivatives business line of Financial during the relevant period] to "confirm all details." [Kirk Ballard], an employee in the London Debt Securities Operations Group at DB, subsequently left a message for Gleeson. Later that day, [Peter] Campbell, the manager of Financial's treasury operations, and Gleeson returned the call. DB recorded the conversation; pursuant to regulatory requirements, all calls on "financial lines" are recorded.

Consistent with Ballard's statement that DB wanted to "make sure we got the details [of the settlement] clear," the parties confirmed the value and identity of the bonds, and the Bank of New York account number. During the conversation, which lasted just over a minute, Ballard mentioned that DB was "kind of short on . . . on the position [i.e., Solutia Bonds] at the moment—we're waiting for the bonds to come in on the other side." After confirming account numbers and a phone number, Ballard added, "Thanks, Pete. You should get those [the Solutia Bonds] in the next day or two." Campbell responded, "Okay, no problem."

Under Section 9.3(c)(ii) of the 1999 Definitions, DB was required to deliver the Solutia Bonds no later than February 11—five business days after the Delivery Date of February 4. Therefore, even if the call took place on February 9, Ballard's suggestion that the bonds would be delivered within a "day or two" was consistent with DB's obligations under the Confirmation.

At the time, both Ballard and Campbell had operational roles at their respective firms. Ballard was not authorized to enter into or substantively amend CDS transactions on behalf of DB. Likewise, Campbell, who oversaw the settlement of securities transactions, did not have the authority to enter into, substantively amend, or waive ACP's rights under contracts. There is no evidence indicating that either Ballard or Campbell believed that their brief, casual conversation altered DB or ACP's rights or obligations pursuant to the Confirmation. Ballard did not inform anyone else at DB about its substance. And after the conversation, there was no communication between DB and ACP regarding the Solutia Bonds for approximately four weeks.

DB did not make delivery on February 4 or even by February 11. DB had earmarked Solutia Bonds it was to receive around February 4 from JP Morgan Chase ("JPMC") and Credit Suisse First Boston ("CSFB") as the bonds it would deliver to ACP. The trades with JPMC were also CDS transactions; in that instance, DB was the protection seller. As of February 4, DB had not yet received the bonds due under these contracts, and it therefore possessed only about one-third of the Deliverable Obligation it was to provide to ACP. There is no evidence that DB made any effort to ensure that it received the Solutia Bonds from JPMC and CSFB in a timely manner. As a result, the bonds slowly rolled in over the month following the delivery date. Moreover, DB made no effort to substitute bonds owned and held by other parts of DB or to enter the market and try to obtain Soutia Bonds from other sources in order to make timely delivery to ACP. If it had entered into the market to try to obtain the bonds from other sources, it is not clear that it would have succeeded in doing so since it was difficult for CSFB to obtain Solutia Bonds during this period.

As it turned out, it took until March 4 before DB had the total amount of the Deliverable Obligation from JPMC and CSFB, and it tendered the Solutia Bonds to ACP on that same day. The Bank of New York refused the tender because on February 26 ACP had removed its instruction to accept the delivery. On February 26, an ACP executive with an expertise in CDS transactions and knowledge of the Triplets transaction learned for the first time that DB had failed to make a timely delivery of Solutia Bonds. She immediately understood that ACP might be "off risk" as a result of DB's default and took steps that led to the removal of the instructions to Bank of New York to pay DB. As described below, after confirming market practice, ACP made a final decision in April not to pay.

In July 2004, DB made a demand upon AAC, pursuant to the Guarantee, to pay the amount DB believed it was owed by ACP for the Solutia Credit Event. AAC refused to make such a payment.

The Parties' Expectations Regarding the Settlement Date

The parties' conversations and correspondence from the Delivery Date and the months that immediately followed it demonstrate that neither DB nor ACP believed that the Confirmation had established an open-ended delivery window. For example, on February 4, Jennifer Jillson, a member of DB's Bond and Equity Support group, sent e-mails to others within the company regarding DB's contracts for Solutia Bonds, including the Physical Settlement and the transaction with JPMC. She noted that the JPMC transaction was "settling today," that it was associated with a credit event, and as a result it was "important that the settlement [with JPMC] occurs." Also on February 4, ACP's Gleeson sent an e-mail in which he detailed the logistics of obtaining the $8,771,000 to pay DB, and noted that ACP would be "required to settle [the Solutia] credit event *today*."

In the three months that followed ACP's March 4 refusal to accept the Deliverable Obligation, representatives of DB and ACP engaged in multiple conversations regarding possible compromise arrangements that would not result in such a substantial loss for DB. In these conversations, DB urged ACP to accept the bonds on the basis of the longstanding relationship between the companies, and it threatened to cut off all business with Ambac if ACP stood by its decision. In none of these exchanges, however, did DB contend that ACP had been *contractually obligated* to accept the Solutia Bonds on March 4.

There is also no evidence that DB ever believed that Ballard's early February telephone conversation with ACP had given DB more leeway as to the Delivery Date. For 12 weeks after ACP's refusal, DB made *no mention* of the conference call, which it now alleges provided it with an indefinite extension of the Delivery Date. Indeed, shortly after ACP refused delivery of the bonds, Horn, a director of Deutsche Bank Securities, a subsidiary of DB, put together a timeline of salient events related to the Solutia credit event. Although the chronology includes nearly a dozen occurrences, the early February call is not among them. It appears, therefore, that at the time of the Physical Settlement, both DB and ACP understood the Confirmation to require delivery no later than February 11, or five business days after the Delivery Date of February 4.

Industry Practice

DB argues that even if the terms of the Confirmation appear to establish a firm delivery date, the common practice of those in the CDS industry at the time of the Triplets transaction was to be flexible with respect to the delivery of bonds and other obligations. The evidence, however, compels precisely the opposite conclusion.

[Holland West, a former partner at Shearman & Sterling LLP and former head of its global derivative, hedge fund, structured finance, and private equity practices], one of defendants' two expert witnesses testified that, in his experience working on hundreds of CDS transactions subject to the 1999 Definitions, no party ever discussed—much less agreed to—the possibility of allowing delivery of an obligation at any time during a multi-year portfolio transaction. Similarly, [Joseph Swain, a senior officer of Assured Guaranty Corporation], defendants' second expert, testified that he participated in hundreds of single-name and portfolio CDS transactions for Assured, and that he was unaware of even a single time that a protection buyer insisted that it could deliver a security after the delivery date. To the extent that a practice of leaving trades open until the bonds were delivered existed at all, Swain stated that it did not apply to transactions involving non-dealer protection sellers like ACP. Indeed, on two or three occasions, protection buyers asked Assured to accept late delivery of their obligations, and Assured consistently refused.

There is a compelling economic reason for parties to expect that delivery deadlines in a CDS transaction will be inflexible. In such transactions, the protection seller agrees to take on a precisely defined level of risk, for which it is paid an amount determined by its underwriting calculations. An open-ended delivery deadline would make such fine-tuned calculations difficult. As a result, a protection seller is highly unlikely to provide this sort of coverage without an express discussion of its parameters and the associated additional premium.

The evidence submitted by DB to rebut the testimony of defendants' experts is flimsy at best. DB relies primarily on its own employees' self-serving assertions that CDS market practice allows for sufficient time after a scheduled delivery date for the deliverable obligations to be obtained and transferred. These employees, however, identify only a handful of specific CDS transactions in which a deliverable obligation was accepted after it was due—and in none of these instances was a non-dealer like ACP a party.[10] DB's testimony from an expert who is not a DB employee is equally unavailing. [Lisa] Sloan, previously the chief administrative officer of M. Safra & Company, a hedge fund manager, testified that "market practice in late 2003 and 2004 in the bond market regarding bond trades and bond settlements was that the party receiving the bonds did not cancel the trade if delivery was not made on the scheduled settlement date." Although Sloan stated that "operations departments did not differentiate between the settlement of bond transactions related to derivatives and settlement of straightforward bond transactions," she was offered as an expert on the bond market, not on CDS transactions. Indeed, she admitted that she was not qualified to answer questions about such transactions. Therefore, her testimony is of minimal relevance here.

Moreover, there is a reason why market practices in the CDS and bond markets are not, in fact, identical. In typical corporate bond transactions, the buyer of the bond has chosen to make the purchase and begins to earn interest on the delivery date, regardless of when physical delivery actually occurs. In a CDS transaction, however, the protection seller does not want the bonds; it accepts them only because it must do so pursuant to the relevant confirmation. In such transactions, delivery is triggered by a credit event, which in most cases means that interest may have ceased to accrue.

Imposing a definite and tight timeframe for delivery has particular benefits for the seller of protection that do not pertain to the regular bond market. If the bond is one of those that is covered by many CDS transactions, as it appears may have been the case with the Solutia Bonds, then more bonds may be sought than are available in the market. When that happens, the buyer may be unable to obtain the bonds by the delivery date, relieving the seller entirely of its obligation to pay, or if the bonds are

---

10. Swain testified that this fact is of some significance. Dealers, such as banks and brokerage firms, usually engage in a high volume of CDS transactions, and may act as a buyer and seller of protection with respect to the same security. Non-dealers, however, typically engage in a much lower volume of transactions and do not act both as protection buyer and protection seller with respect to the same security. Therefore, industry practices for transactions between two dealers would not necessarily mirror those for transactions involving a non-dealer.

timely delivered, the intense bidding for those bonds may create a relatively inflated market price, allowing the credit seller to recover some of its loss by reselling the bonds quickly before the market price collapses.

And, most significantly, unlike ordinary bond transactions, CDS transactions are governed by detailed contracts that incorporate a fixed timetable for delivery. The evidence therefore clearly establishes that at the time of the Triplets transaction, it was the practice of the CDS marketplace to require compliance with physical settlement deadlines.

[Analysis]

Under New York law, to make out a claim for breach of contract, a plaintiff must establish "(1) the existence of an agreement, (2) adequate performance of the contract by the plaintiff, (3) breach of contract by the defendant, and (4) damages." *Eternity Global Master Fund Ltd. v. Morgan Guaranty Trust Co.,* 375 F.3d 168, 177 (2d Cir. 2004). Of course, if the conditions precedent to a defendant's duty to perform have not been met, breach is not possible.

Here, DB alleges that ACP failed to fulfill its contractual obligation under the Confirmation and 1999 Definitions to make payment in exchange for DB's delivery of the Solutia Bonds. ACP argues, in effect, that because DB did not deliver the deliverable obligation by February 4, or within the five-business-day grace period, it did not satisfy a condition precedent to ACP's duty to pay, and therefore a breach of contract claim cannot lie. The central question, then, is whether the Confirmation (read in conjunction with the Master Agreement and the 1999 Definitions) required DB to make delivery by the Delivery Date in order for ACP to be obligated to make payment, or whether it allowed for a longer delivery window, either by its explicit terms, or because of the customs and practices of the credit derivative marketplace.

Under New York law, the ultimate goal of contract interpretation is to construe agreements "in accord with the parties' intent." *Eternity Global,* 375 F.3d at 177. When interpreting a contract,

> words and phrases should be given their plain meaning, and the contract should be construed so as to give full meaning and effect to all of its provisions. An interpretation of a contract that has the effect of rendering at least one clause superfluous or meaningless is not preferred and will be avoided if possible.

When a transaction involves multiple writings that "are designed to effectuate the same purpose, [they] must be read together, even though they were executed on different dates and were not all between the same parties." If there are ambiguities in an agreement that cannot be resolved by reference to other cannons of contract interpretation, these "ambiguities are generally interpreted against the drafter."

DB contends that, by the terms of the Confirmation, it had until May 2, 2005 to deliver the Solutia Bonds—that is, more than one year later than the date on which it actually tendered the securities. The basis for this claim is the Confirmation's definition of "Termination Date" as "the later to occur of the Scheduled Termination Date and final Physical Settlement Date." According to DB, the earliest possible Termination Date under the Confirmation, then, is May 2, 2005, which is identified as the Scheduled Termination Date. DB further argues that this definition of Termination Date contradicts Section 9.3(c)(ii) of the 1999 Definitions, which states that if a buyer fails to deliver an obligation, the last day of the five-business-day window becomes the

Termination Date. According to DB, since terms in the Confirmation trump those in the 1999 Definitions, this effectively eliminates the requirement that the Deliverable Obligation be delivered within five days of the Physical Settlement Date.

To be sure, the Confirmation is drafted imperfectly and creates ambiguity regarding the interplay of the Termination Date and Physical Settlement Date, but under DB's interpretation of the documents, this ambiguity would all but swallow the agreement, creating many more problems than it resolves. The ambiguity stems from the fact that in the 1999 Definitions, Termination Date has two distinct meanings: It refers to the date on which protection for the single reference entity ends, and the date on which the entire transaction terminates. Because the 1999 Definitions address a single-obligation transaction, these two dates are the same, and a timely physical settlement (or failure to make timely delivery of a NIPS or an obligation) always ends not only the protection for a single reference entity, but also the entire transaction. Therefore, the 1999 Definitions do not differentiate between these two meanings of Termination Date. In a portfolio transaction, however, the buyer has purchased protection for multiple securities. So while both ACP and DB intended that a single physical settlement (or failure to deliver either a NIPS or bonds within the time allowed) would terminate protection for that obligation, they did not intend it to end the Triplets transaction altogether. The confusion here arises from the parties' failure to differentiate these two meanings of Termination Date and provide them with separate names.

Nonetheless, it is not difficult to discern the parties' intent by reading the Confirmation and the 1999 Definitions together, and by analyzing the context in which critical terms are used. Beginning with the Confirmation, it is clear that DB and ACP intended the Termination Date to define the end point of the entire transaction. It is for this reason that it is among the first three defined terms in the Confirmation, coming immediately after "Effective Date," the date on which the transaction begins. Thus, Triplets, with an Effective Date of May 2, 2000 and a Scheduled Termination Date of May 2, 2005, was designed to be a five-year transaction.

There is ample evidence that the parties anticipated that there could be many distinct physical settlements of individual securities on separate physical settlement dates within this five-year term. In the section regarding conditions to payment, for example, the Confirmation provides: "For the avoidance of doubt, Conditions to Payment may be satisfied more than once with respect to this Transaction; provided, however, that the Conditions to Payment may be satisfied only once with respect to each Reference Entity." Similarly, the Confirmation's definition of the Termination Date refers to the "*final* Physical Settlement Date," in recognition of the fact that there could be multiple physical settlement dates during the contract period. In other words, it is clear from the Confirmation that the parties aimed to create what were, in effect, 60 *separate* five-year CDS transactions documented with a single agreement. This allowed DB to retain coverage for the remaining reference obligations even after others had been physically settled.

DB attempts to create doubt about the parties' intent by pointing out that the Termination Date arises in the context of Section 9.3(c)(ii) of the 1999 Definitions, specifically the second sentence in which the consequences of a failure to make a timely delivery are spelled out. The first sentence of the Section establishes that the buyer can continue to make delivery attempts of the deliverable obligation for five business days after the Physical Settlement Date. The second sentence states that if the buyer fails to make delivery during this time, the fifth day after the Physical Settlement Date "shall be deemed to be the Termination Date." As DB correctly points out, this last phrase contradicts the definition of Termination Date laid out in the Confirmation, since on its face it would require the entire Triplets transaction to end if DB failed to deliver a single deliverable obligation within the five-day window.

DB's solution to this apparent contradiction, however, is based on an untenable reading of the Confirmation and the 1999 Definitions. DB argues that because, under Section 9.3(c)(ii), a failure to deliver causes the last day of the delivery window to become the Termination Date, "the Termination Date is therefore the last day that the bonds can be delivered under the Confirmation." And since the Confirmation states that the Termination Date can come no earlier than May 2, 2005, DB could not have been required to deliver the Solutia Bonds before that date. This argument is logically flawed. Just because the failure to deliver on the last permissible day can, in a single-obligation transaction, result in that day being deemed the Termination Date, it does not follow that the Termination Date is the last day on which an obligation can be delivered. Indeed, DB has pointed to no language in either the 1999 Definitions or the Confirmation indicating that Termination Date should have this meaning, and thereby extend the delivery period. While the second sentence of this section identifies the consequence of a delivery failure, the first sentence defines the duty, that is the period in which delivery must be made. A change in the consequences does *not* change the duty.

Pointedly, the Confirmation makes no change to Section 8.1 of the 1999 Definitions (which makes payment due upon delivery "on or prior to the Physical Settlement Date"), Section 8.5 (which defines the Physical Settlement Period), or the first sentence of Section 9.3(c)(ii) (which extends the Physical Settlement Date by five days). If DB had intended to expand the timetable for delivery, it would have modified terms affecting at least these sections of the 1999 Definitions. Simply put, the Confirmation does not reflect an intention to leave the delivery window open.

The better reading of the Confirmation's definition of Termination Date takes into account the fact that the parties intended to establish separate coverage for each of the 60 securities. As noted above, DB and ACP agree that physical settlement of one security was not intended to result in termination of the entire Triplets transaction. Indeed, DB had already been paid by ACP on eight separate Reference Entities that had been subject to credit events without triggering the termination of the Triplets contract. It is reasonable, then, to infer that a failure to make timely delivery of a single deliverable obligation was not meant to affect the coverage of the other securities. The issue therefore becomes what consequences flow from a failure to deliver securities within the five-day window established by Section 9.3(c)(ii).

DB takes the wholly implausible position that there are *no* consequences. It argues that under Section 9.3(c)(ii), untimely delivery would result in termination of the transaction; and because the Confirmation establishes that Triplets cannot end until May 2, 2005 at the earliest, that portion of Section 9.3(c)(ii) is overridden. According to DB's reading of the documents, then, the parties intended to permit either party to start the clock ticking through the delivery of a Credit Event Notice, to set a 30-day window in which to deliver a NIPS, and to establish a precisely negotiated physical delivery period based on market practice—but if DB failed to delivery either a NIPS or the bonds within the designated time, it would suffer no adverse consequences at all.

719

DB's interpretation is plainly wrong. In a single-security transaction governed by the 1999 Definitions, any failure to adhere to the detailed credit-event timeline results in the coverage for that security being terminated. There is no evidence that the parties to the Triplets transaction intended to take what was once a mandatory timeline and eviscerate it. The Confirmation explicitly acknowledges both parties' rights to start the timetable for delivery of a NIPS and the securities. With DB's reading, there is essentially no timetable, and ACP loses its right to trigger the countdown for delivery. Such a result should be avoided. Contracts should be read as a whole, with an eye toward giving effect to every provision. The best reading of the agreement, then, is that a failure to make timely delivery with respect to a single security terminates the credit protection with respect to that security, but not with respect the rest of the transaction.

This reading has several advantages. It accords with the intent of both parties.[12] It reflects their contemporaneous understanding of the operation of their contract. It makes commercial sense. And, as described below, it accords with industry practice.

When attempting to determine the parties' intent, courts look first to the contract itself. "If an agreement is complete, clear and unambiguous on its face, it must be enforced according to the plain meaning of its terms." *Eternity Global,* 375 F.3d at 177. If a contract is ambiguous, however, a court may look to extrinsic evidence "to ascertain the correct and intended meaning of a term or terms." The ambiguity need not appear on the face of the contract, but may exist if a term

> could suggest more than one meaning when viewed objectively by a reasonably intelligent person who has examined the context of the entire integrated agreement and who is cognizant of the customs, practices, usages and terminology as generally understood in the particular trade or business.

Here, as noted above, there is some ambiguity regarding the interpretation of the Termination Date. Although the Confirmation and 1999 Definitions alone would not support DB's position that the delivery window was to remain open until it obtained the necessary securities form other counterparties, DB claims that industry practice backs up this interpretation. In the context of a sale of goods, in order to affect contract interpretation, an industry practice must have "such regularity of observance in a place, vocation or trade as to justify an expectation that it will be observed with respect to the transaction in question." "It is not necessary for both parties to be consciously aware of the trade usage. It is enough if the trade usage is such as to justify an expectation of its observance." Those principles will be applied here.

Here, DB has utterly failed to show the existence of a market practice for credit default instruments that would have justified an expectation that it had an unlimited delivery window absent an express provision to that effect in the Confirmation. Its sole retained expert candidly admitted that she has no expertise whatsoever in the field of credit default obligations and did not disagree with any of the statements or analysis by ACP's expert, whose expertise within the field of credit default transactions was well established and unchallenged. At most, its own employees pointed to a handful of

---

12. In summation, plaintiff's counsel acknowledged that in drafting the Confirmation, DB had not anticipated how its change in the definition of Termination Date would impact the parties' rights when a security was not timely delivered.

isolated CDS transactions in which late delivery of a physical settlement obligation was accepted. In none of these transactions was a non-dealer a party, and their relevance is therefore marginal at best. ACP, on the other hand, has shown through compelling evidence that the firm practice in the CDS marketplace was to require that delivery occur according to the timetable to which the parties had agreed. Under these circumstances, DB could not reasonably have expected that ACP would accept delivery after February 11—and should have expected just the opposite.

Indeed, the evidence shows that DB itself understood in February 2004 that it had a firm obligation to deliver the Solutia Bonds by the date it identified in the NIPS it sent to ACP, or within the five-business-day window that followed. In March, April, and May, as executives in the companies discussed ACP's refusal to accept DB's late-tendered bonds, DB never took the position that ACP was contractually bound to accept them. In fact, in a candid internal communication, it conceded it had "no leverage . . . at all" in the negotiations.

QUESTIONS

1. What drafting error created the ambiguity in the "termination date"?
2. How did the court reason through the ambiguity?

Aon Fin. Prods. Inc. v. Société Générale
476 F.3d 90 (2d Cir. 2007)

SACK, Circuit Judge:

The plaintiffs, Aon Corp. and its subsidiary, Aon Financial Products, Inc. ("AFP", together "Aon"), brought suit seeking recovery in breach of contract against Société Générale ("SG") under a $10 million credit default swap agreement[1] between them dated March 8, 1999 (the "Aon/SG CDS contract").

The Aon/SG CDS contract provides that if a "Credit Event" occurs before the defined "Termination Date" of the agreement and Aon notifies SG of that Credit Event, then SG must pay Aon $10 million. Aon contends that a Credit Event occurred when the Government Service Insurance System ("GSIS"), an agency of the Philippine Government, defaulted on a surety bond that GSIS had issued to cover investments in a project with respect to which Bear Stearns International Limited ("BSIL") later made a loan. BSIL, in an effort to protect itself against the risk of GSIS defaulting on the bond, entered into a Credit Default Swap Agreement with Aon (the "BSIL/Aon CDS contract"). In a separate suit, the district court determined that a Credit Event occurred under the BSIL/Aon CDS contract when GSIS defaulted on the surety bond. *See Ursa Minor Ltd. v. Aon Financial Products, Inc.,* 2000 WL 1010278

---

1. "A credit default swap is the most common form of credit derivative, i.e., a contract which transfers credit risk from a protection buyer to a credit protection seller." *Eternity Global Master Fund Ltd. v. Morgan Guar. Trust Co. of N.Y.,* 375 F.3d 168, 171-72 (2d Cir. 2004).

(S.D.N.Y. 2000) ("*Ursa Minor*"). Aon argues that if a Credit Event occurred under the BSIL/Aon CDS contract, then a Credit Event also must have occurred under the Aon/SG CDS contract that is the subject of this suit, and that Aon therefore was entitled to payment thereunder. The issue on this appeal is whether a Credit Event occurred under any of the definitions set forth in the Aon/SG CDS contract such that SG's refusal to pay Aon constituted breach of contract. We disagree with the determination by the district court that a Credit Event occurred within the meaning of that term in the Aon/SG CDS contract, which prompted the court to grant the plaintiffs' motion for summary judgment and deny the defendant's motion for judgment on the pleadings. We therefore reverse the judgment of the district court and enter judgment in favor of SG.

This case arises out of one of a series of transactions related to the financing of a condominium complex in the Philippines. In 1999, BSIL agreed to loan Ecobel Land, Inc. ("Ecobel") $9.3 million to build the condominiums. Ecobel was obligated under this agreement to repay BSIL $10 million on March 7, 2000. As a condition precedent to that loan, BSIL required that Ecobel procure a surety bond from GSIS that guaranteed repayment of the full $10 million in the event that Ecobel defaulted on its loan. GSIS then purportedly transferred to BSIL as obligee a $10 million GSIS surety bond covering Ecobel's borrowings for the condominium project dated March 11, 1998, but apparently issued on February 5, 1999 (the "Surety Bond"), which listed Ecobel as principal and Philippine Veterans Bank as obligee.[2] Section 9 of the [Philippine] statute establishing GSIS states that "the government of the Republic of the Philippines . . . guarantees the fulfillment of the obligations of [GSIS] when and as they shall become due."

In order to protect itself against the risk of GSIS defaulting on the Surety Bond, BSIL entered into the BSIL/Aon CDS contract on February 4, 1999. According to the agreement, Aon promised to pay BSIL $10 million upon the occurrence of a "Credit Event," which the contract defined as a "Failure to Pay," that is, "the failure by [GSIS] to make, when due, any payments under the Obligations for whatever reason or cause."[4] The only "Obligation" referred to in the agreement was the Surety Bond. For this credit protection, BSIL paid Aon $425,000.

To reduce its own risk exposure, on February 9, 1999, Aon entered into a separate credit default swap agreement with SG (the "Aon/SG CDS contract"). In it, SG promised to pay Aon $10 million upon the occurrence of a "Credit Event," defined as one of five occurrences: a "Failure to Pay," a "Sovereign Event," a "Cross Default," a "Repudiation," or a "Restructuring." But whereas the BSIL/Aon CDS contract defined "Reference Entity," whose obligations were the subject of the swap, as GSIS and

---

2. As the *Ursa Minor* court explained, the nature of the Surety Bond and of BSIL's status as obligee thereunder was a matter of some dispute. The validity of the Surety Bond and of its assignment to BSIL is, however, not relevant to the issues on this appeal.

4. The document that defines "Credit Event," "Failure to Pay," and other relevant terms is known in the industry as the "confirmation." Parties to credit derivative swaps enter into a standard form "Master Agreement" created by the International Swaps and Derivatives Association, Inc. ("ISDA"), which governs the legal and credit relationship between the parties and other aspects of the agreement. Supplemental documents, such as confirmations, set forth economic terms and other transaction-specific modifications to the Master Agreement and other standard documents. The provisions of the BSIL/Aon CDS contract and the Aon/SG CDS contract that are at issue here are both contained in "confirmations," which incorporate materially similar versions of the ISDA Master Agreement.

any successors and assigns, the Aon/SG CDS contract defined "Reference Entity" as "Republic of Philippines and any successors." Similarly, while the "Reference Obligation," which was the subject of the BSIL/Aon CDS contract, was GSIS's $10 million Surety Bond, the "Reference Obligation" of the Aon/SG CDS contract was a $500 million Republic of Philippines treasury bond (coupon rate 8.875%, maturing on April 15, 2008). For the credit protection under the Aon/SG CDS contract, Aon paid SG $328,000, nearly $100,000 less than the amount that BSIL had paid Aon for protection under the BSIL/Aon CDS contract.

About one year later, in March 2000, Ecobel defaulted on its BSIL loan. On March 9, 2000, Bankers Trustee Company, Ltd. ("Bankers"), to whom BSIL had assigned its rights under the various agreements relating to the loan, notified Aon that it had received a letter from GSIS stating that it did not intend to pay Bankers on the bond because it had not been appropriately authorized on GSIS's behalf. Aon responded the following day that it would not pay Bankers under the BSIL/Aon CDS contract because GSIS's statement that it intended to refuse to honor the Surety Bond did not constitute a "Credit Event" under the BSIL/Aon agreement.

BSIL's assignees filed suit against Aon in the United States District Court (S.D.N.Y.) [which is the *Ursa Minor* litigation]. The district court granted summary judgment in the action in favor of the assignees. The court concluded that the BSIL/Aon CDS contract specifically defined "Credit Event" as a failure *by GSIS*, the Reference Entity, to pay under the Surety Bond "for whatever reason or cause," and that GSIS's default clearly satisfied that condition. The court concluded that Aon "bore the risk of non-payment by GSIS, for 'whatever reason or cause,' including a justifiable refusal to pay."

On April 8, 2000, more than two months before the district court's decision in *Ursa Minor,* Aon filed this action in the United States District Court (S.D.N.Y.) against SG, seeking payment of $10 million under the Aon/SG CDS contract. SG moved for judgment on the pleadings, arguing principally that Aon had failed to allege a breach of the Aon/SG CDS contract because GSIS was not included in the definition of "Republic of Philippines," the Reference Entity of the Aon/SG CDS contract, and GSIS's default therefore did not constitute a Credit Event for the purposes of that agreement.

In response, Aon moved for summary judgment, contending first that the finding in *Ursa Minor* that a Credit Event had occurred for the purposes of the BSIL/Aon CDS contract necessarily meant that a Credit Event had occurred for the purposes of the Aon/SG CDS contract. Aon argued that because both *Ursa Minor* and this litigation were based on the same "series of transactions" and "evidence regarding whether or not there was a failure to pay," and because SG was "in privity with Aon," SG was precluded from relitigating that factual issue. Aon urged the court to reject SG's argument "that the cases are distinct because the verbiage in the swap contracts in certain sections are slightly different" because the key issue, whether a "Credit Event" had occurred, was the same in both cases.

Second, Aon argued that SG was liable to Aon because a Credit Event occurred as a matter of law under the provision of the Aon/SG CDS contract defining a Credit Event as a "Sovereign Event" or a "Failure to Pay." In response to SG's argument that the GSIS default was not a Sovereign Event because the Republic of the Philippines and GSIS are separate entities, Aon asserted that the April 14, 2000, letter from the Philippine government refusing to honor its statutory guarantee of GSIS's obligations "did not deny that GSIS had authority to bind it [the Philippine government], . . . nor does it assert that the GSIS and the Philippine government are separate and distinct entities. . . ."

The district court denied SG's motion for judgment on the pleadings and granted Aon's counter-motion for summary judgment. The court decided that under the plain and unambiguous terms of the Aon/SG CDS contract, GSIS's default satisfied the definition of "Sovereign Event," and therefore constituted a Credit Event. *Aon Fin. Prods. & Aon Corp. v. Société Générale*, 2005 WL 427535 (S.D.N.Y. 2005) ("*Société Générale*"). The court concluded that the definition of "Sovereign Event," which includes "a condition . . . that has the effect of . . . causing a failure to honour any obligation relating to . . . the government of the Reference Entity . . . requires only that GSIS's act have the effect of causing a failure to honour an obligation *relating* to the Philippine government."

The court further concluded that Aon's March 22, 2000, letter notifying SG that GSIS had declined to make payment on the Surety Bond constituted sufficient notice of the Credit Event under the agreement. The court therefore granted Aon's motion for summary judgment and denied SG's motion for judgment on the pleadings.

Author's Note: Schematic of CDS Transactions and Separate Litigations

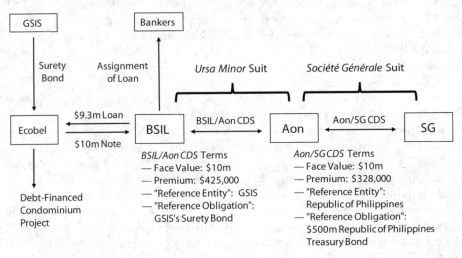

"Sovereign Event"

Credit default swaps are a method by which one party (the protection buyer) transfers risk to another party (the protection seller). In "emerging markets" such as the Philippines,

> protection buyers . . . can use credit derivatives to manage particular market exposures and return-on-investment; and protection sellers . . . generally use credit derivatives to earn income and diversify their own investment portfolios. Simply put, a credit default swap is a bilateral financial contract in which a protection buyer makes periodic payments to the protection seller, in return for a contingent payment if a predefined credit event occurs in the reference credit. . . .
>
> Often, the reference asset that the protection buyer delivers to the protection seller following a credit event is the instrument that is being hedged. But in emerging

markets, an investor may calculate that a particular credit risk is reasonably correlated with the performance of the sovereign itself, so that . . . the investor may seek to isolate and hedge country risk with credit default swaps written on some portion of the sovereign's outstanding debt.

Eternity Global Master Fund Ltd. v. Morgan Guar. Trust Co. of N.Y., 375 F.3d 168, 172 (2d Cir.2004).

CDS agreements are thus significantly different from insurance contracts. As *amicus* [by the ISDA] correctly points out, they "do not, and are not meant to, indemnify the buyer of protection against loss. Rather, CDS contracts allow parties to 'hedge' risk by buying and selling risks at different prices and with varying degrees of correlation." Aon bought from BSIL the risk of a "Credit Event" as defined by the BSIL/Aon CDS contract. With the Aon/SG CDS contract, Aon hedged the risk that it bought from BSIL by selling to SG the risk of a "Credit Event" as defined by the Aon/SG CDS contract. But the risk transferred *to* Aon and the risk transferred *by* it were not necessarily identical. The terms of each credit swap agreement independently define the risk being transferred.

To decide whether GSIS's failure to pay on the Surety Bond because GSIS took the position that it was not a legally binding obligation, an event that constituted a Credit Event as defined in the BSIL/Aon CDS contract, also constituted a "Credit Event" as defined in the Aon/SG CDS contract—the issue presently before us—we look first to the language of the contract. If it is unambiguous—which we think that it is—then "we are required to give effect to the contract as written."

The Aon/SG CDS contract defines "Credit Event" as a "Sovereign Event," which is

a condition which is created by or results from any act or failure to act by the government of the Reference Entity or any agency or regulatory authority thereof, including the central bank of the Reference Entity, that has the effect of declaring a moratorium (whether de facto or de jure) on, or causing a failure to honour any obligation relating to, or cancelling or generally causing material changes to the terms and conditions of, any obligation issued by the government of the Reference Entity or the central bank of the Reference Entity.

The contract defines "Reference Entity" as "Republic of Philippines and any successors." Thus, for purposes of our analysis, after redacting inapplicable language, the Aon/SG CDS Contract provides that an event is a "Sovereign Event" if it is "a condition . . . created by or resulting from any act or failure to act by the government of [the Republic of Philippines and any Successors] or any agency or regulatory authority [thereof] . . . that has the effect of . . . causing a failure to honour any obligation relating to . . . any obligation issued by the government of [the Republic of Philippines]."

The district court concluded that this definition "requires only that," to be a Credit Event, "GSIS's act has the effect of causing a failure to honour an obligation *relating* to the Philippine government." Similarly, Aon argues that "the contract . . . defines Sovereign Event as a failure to honor any obligation 'relating to . . . any obligation issued by the Reference Entity [i.e., the Philippine government].'" We disagree with Aon and the district court principally because we think that these interpretations ignore the crucial word "condition" at the outset of the definition. GSIS's failure to pay on the Surety Bond may well have been a failure to act, or an event, but surely it was not a "condition."

Put another way, Aon asks us to conclude that the GSIS *default on the Surety Bond* constituted (1) an act or failure to act by an agency of the Philippine government (GSIS), which (2) created a "condition," which had the effect of causing a failure of (3) *GSIS to honor its obligation, the Surety Bond,* (4) which obligation relates to an obligation of the Philippine government. But we do not think that the definition of Sovereign Event includes (a) the failure of a Philippine agency (GSIS) to honor its Surety Bond, thereby creating (b) a "condition" that in turn caused (c) the failure of the agency to honor the same Surety Bond, irrespective of whether the Surety Bond is an obligation that relates to an obligation of the Philippine government. The default was not a "condition" that caused the failure of GSIS to honor its obligation. Nor was it caused by an "act or failure to act by the Republic or its agency." It resulted from GSIS's decision that it was not legally bound to honor its putative obligation to pay. We do not think that GSIS's decision itself—its determination that it is not legally bound by the Surety Bond to pay—can be characterized as either "an act or failure to act" or as a "condition" within the ordinary meaning of those terms.

A literal reading of the Sovereign Event definition might suggest that the "act or failure to act" by the government of the Philippines that "had the effect of causing [the] failure [of GSIS] to honour" the Surety Bond was something other than the failure to pay on the Surety Bond itself. Hypothetically, for example, the "act" might have been the issuance of GSIS's letter to BSIL's assignees denying liability. Even if that were what Aon's complaint said, the argument would fail. The letter was, to be sure, an "act." But it did not *create* a separate "condition" which in turn *caused* the default on the Surety Bond.

Moreover, an "act or failure to act" in the context of a "Sovereign Event" seems to refer to such large-scale events as the restructuring of the Sovereign's—i.e., the government's—debt, taken in its capacity as a sovereign. The act of debt restructuring by a sovereign may well cause—indeed may be expected to cause—a general "condition" throughout the country (e.g., currency devaluation, restriction on exports of U.S. dollars, and the like) that in turn results in one or more defaults on one or more particular obligations against which an entity doing business with or within the country would want to protect itself. *Cf. Eternity Global,* 375 F.3d at 170 (addressing the operation of CDS contracts where "the government of the Republic of Argentina, in the grip of economic crisis, initiated a 'voluntary debt exchange'"). There was no such act or resulting condition here.

Aon points out that the *Ursa Minor* district court held that GSIS's default in March 2000 qualified as a Credit Event under the BSIL/Aon CDS contract. Indeed the court did so hold:

> The definition of "Credit Event" [in the BSIL/Aon CDS contract] specifically includes failure by GSIS to pay under the [Surety] Bond "for whatever reason or cause." Plaintiffs allege that GSIS's refusal to make payment under the Bond amounted to a Credit Event, that [Aon] was given proper notice and that [Aon's] refusal to pay constituted a default triggering Aon's obligations under the Guarantee.

The court then ruled against Aon because the GSIS default constituted a Credit Event, which the BSIL/Aon CDS contract defined as a "Failure to Pay," and because Aon "had an obligation to pay irrespective of the Bond's potential invalidity or enforceability with respect to GSIS." The *Ursa Minor* district court never addressed the possibility that the GSIS default may have been a "Sovereign Event"—under the BSIL/Aon CDS contract, let alone under the Aon/SG CDS contract before us. This is hardly surprising inasmuch as the BSIL/Aon CDS contract did not define "Credit Event" to include "Sovereign Event" as the Aon/SG CDS contract did.

Yet Aon contends that the *Ursa Minor* court's determination that a Credit Event occurred under the BSIL/Aon CDS contract necessarily means that a Credit Event occurred under the Aon/SG CDS contract. But it does not follow from the occurrence of a Credit Event as defined in one contract that there was a Credit Event as defined in the other. There is, as noted, no reason to assume that the risk transferred to Aon was precisely the risk that it transferred or sought to transfer to SG. And we can perceive of no basis for concluding that the district court's decision in *Ursa Minor* that there was a "Failure to Pay" Credit Event under the BSIL/Aon CDS contract implies that there was a "Sovereign Event" Credit Event under the Aon/SG CDS contract.

We therefore conclude that GSIS's default was not a "Sovereign Event" as that term is used in the Aon/SG CDS contract.

"Failure to Pay"

The district court considered only one of the five kinds of Credit Events referred to in the Aon/SG CDS contract—the Sovereign Event. Finding that there had been such a Credit Event under the terms of the Aon/SG CDS contract, the court declined to consider whether the events also constituted a "Failure to Pay," which is also one of the defined Credit Events under that agreement.

Apparently as a result of the district court's conclusion that a Sovereign Event had occurred, the parties devote little attention to the Failure to Pay issue in their briefs to us. But the parties amply presented arguments on that issue to the district court. In fact, there, the parties focused on the Failure to Pay language rather than the Sovereign Event provision upon which the district court eventually decided the motions. The interpretation of the unambiguous terms of a contract is, moreover, a matter of law that we may properly evaluate and decide ourselves.

As noted above, the Aon/SG CDS contract defines the "Reference Entity" as the "Republic of Philippines and any successors." Under the Aon/SG CDS contract, a *"Failure to Pay* means . . . the failure by the Reference Entity [*the Republic of Philippines* and any Successors] to make, when due, any payments equal to or exceeding the Payment Requirement (if any) under any Obligations." An "Obligation" under that agreement is: "With respect to the [Republic of Philippines], any obligation, (whether present or future, contingent or otherwise, as principal or surety or otherwise) for the payment or repayment of money." The Reference Obligation is identified as:

> Issuer/Borrower: Republic of Philippines
> Maturity: April 15, 2008
> Coupon. 8.8750%
> Original Issue Amount: USD 500,000,000

The Payment Requirement is "USD 5,000,000 or its equivalent in any other currency at the time of the Credit Event."

Aon argues that GSIS itself qualifies as the "Reference Entity" of the Aon/SG CDS contract, that is, that "Republic of Philippines" includes GSIS. GSIS's default on the Surety Bond, therefore, is a "Failure to Pay" by the Reference Entity on an Obligation of the Reference Entity. Aon contends that because the ISDA Credit Derivatives Definitions, incorporated into the Aon/SG CDS contract define "Sovereign" as "any state, political subdivision or government, or any agency, instrumentality, ministry, department or other authority (including, without limiting the foregoing, the central bank) thereof," the term "Republic of Philippines" must also include "any agency" of the state.[9] We disagree.

It is clear from the face of the Aon/SG CDS contract that "Republic of Philippines" does not include GSIS or other government agencies like it.[10] There is no language in the Reference Entity definition, or anywhere else in the agreement as we read it, suggesting that it does, or indicating that it incorporates the ISDA definition of "Sovereign." To incorporate that definition of "Sovereign" into the definition of "Reference Entity," we would expect the parties to use that word, "Sovereign," in the relevant portion of the contract. They did not. Rather, they use the words "Republic of Philippines." Where the contract uses the word "Sovereign," in the term "Sovereign Event," by contrast, the contract does clearly mean to incorporate the ISDA definition. "Sovereign Event" is the only term in the Aon/SG CDS contract that refers not only to the Reference Entity, but to "the Reference Entity or any agency or regulatory authority thereof, including the central bank of the Reference Entity."

If we were to credit Aon's argument as to the expansive meaning of "Republic of Philippines," it would follow that any CDS contract listing a sovereign nation as a Reference Entity will be incorporating the ISDA definition of "Sovereign" without using the term, or at least that the contract is ambiguous in that regard. We are given, and ourselves see, no reason to do so.

Instead, we look to Philippine law for guidance about the distinction between the Republic of the Philippines and its agencies and instrumentalities. Before the district court, SG offered uncontested expert evidence that, under Philippine law, GSIS is considered a juridical entity distinct from the Republic. We conclude that, as a matter of Philippine law, GSIS is a separate juridical entity from the Republic of the Philippines. As such, GSIS is not the "Republic of Philippines"; its obligations are not the Republic of the Philippines' obligations; and a failure by GSIS to make a payment on its obligations is not equivalent to the failure of the Republic of the Philippines to make a payment on its obligations.

To be sure, in the context of the argument that GSIS's failure to pay on the Surety Bond was a "Failure to Pay" as defined by the Aon/SG contract, Aon's assertion that the issue was decided by *Ursa Minor* appears to have more traction than when made in support of Aon's Sovereign Event argument. Although the *Ursa Minor* court did not address the question of whether a Sovereign Event had occurred—there was no such provision in the BSIL/Aon CDS contract—it *did* decide that there had been a "Failure to Pay" under that contract. Aon therefore argues that the *Ursa Minor* court's decision that there was a "Failure to Pay" under the BSIL/Aon CDS contract foreclosed the district court-and forecloses us-under principles of issue preclusion (or collateral estoppel) from deciding that there was no "Failure to Pay" under the Aon/SG CDS contract.

---

9. The Aon/SG CDS contract incorporates the 1991 ISDA Definitions (as supplemented by the 1998 Supplement). Both parties cite the 1999 ISDA Credit Derivatives Definitions, which *amicus* explains "replicate in relevant part" the 1991 ISDA Definitions as supplemented by the 1998 Supplement.

10. Aon does not dispute that GSIS, which it agrees is an "agency" of the Philippines, is a separate juridical entity from the Republic of the Philippines.

But even though the identical term "Failure to Pay" is used in both CDS agreements, and the *Ursa Minor* court decided that there was a Failure to Pay under the BSIL/Aon agreement, the term "Failure to Pay" has distinctly different meanings in the two agreements. Under the BSIL/Aon CDS contract, which defines "Reference Entity" as "GSIS and any Successors and assigns," and "Obligation(s)" as the Surety Bond, *"Failure to Pay* means . . . the failure by the Reference Entity [*GSIS* and any Successors and assigns] to make, when due, any payments under the Obligations [the Surety Bond] for whatever reason or cause." As discussed above, the Aon/SG CDS contract, by contrast, defines "Reference Entity" as *"Republic of Philippines* and any Successors." In that contract, *"Failure to Pay* means . . . the failure by the Reference Entity [*Republic of Philippines* and any Successors] to make, when due, any payments equal to or exceeding the Payment Requirement (if any) under any Obligations." Moreover, whereas the BSIL/Aon CDS contract defines "Obligation" as the Surety Bond, the Aon/SG CDS contract defines "Obligation" as "With respect to the Reference Entity [*Republic of Philippines*], any obligation (whether present or future, contingent or otherwise, as principal or surety or otherwise) for the payment or repayment of money." Thus, the Aon/BSIL agreement explicitly covers failure to pay *by GSIS* on the *Surety Bond,* while the Aon/SG agreement explicitly does not do so. It covers failure to pay *by the Republic of the Philippines* on obligations *of the Republic of the Philippines.*

We therefore conclude that neither the default, which constituted a Failure to Pay under the BSIL/Aon CDS contract, nor the Republic's failure to honor its alleged statutory obligation, constituted a Failure to Pay under the Aon/SG CDS contract. For the same reasons, neither event constituted a "Repudiation." They similarly do not satisfy the other definitions of Credit Event enumerated in the Aon/SG CDS contract.

As a matter of law and under the unambiguous language of the Aon/SG CDS contract, no Credit Event occurred thereunder and SG therefore did not breach that agreement by declining to pay Aon thereunder. We therefore reverse the judgment of the district court and enter judgment in favor of SG.

QUESTIONS

1. Why did Aon not hedge in precisely the same terms as the BSIL/Aon CDS?
2. The court notes that "CDS agreements are thus significantly different from insurance contracts." In what ways are CDS and traditional insurance different?

MODEL BUSINESS CORPORATION ACT

CHAPTER 6. SHARES AND DISTRIBUTIONS

Subchapter A: SHARES

§6.01. AUTHORIZED SHARES

(a) The articles of incorporation must set forth any classes of shares and series of shares within a class, and the number of shares of each class and series, that the corporation is authorized to issue. If more than one class or series of shares is authorized, the articles of incorporation must prescribe a distinguishing designation for each class or series and must describe, prior to the issuance of shares of a class or series, the terms, including the preferences, rights, and limitations, of that class or series. Except to the extent varied as permitted by this section, all shares of a class or series must have terms, including preferences, rights, and limitations that are identical with those of other shares of the same class or series.

(b) The articles of incorporation must authorize:

    (1) one or more classes or series of shares that together have unlimited voting rights, and

    (2) one or more classes or series of shares (which may be the same class or classes as those with voting rights) that together are entitled to receive the net assets of the corporation upon dissolution.

(c) The articles of incorporation may authorize one or more classes or series of shares that:

    (1) have special, conditional, or limited voting rights, or no right to vote, except to the extent otherwise provided by this Act;

    (2) are redeemable or convertible as specified in the articles of incorporation:

        (i) at the option of the corporation, the shareholder, or another person or upon the occurrence of a specified event;

        (ii) for cash, indebtedness, securities, or other property; and

        (iii) at prices and in amounts specified, or determined in accordance with a formula;

    (3) entitle the holders to distributions calculated in any manner, including dividends that may be cumulative, noncumulative, or partially cumulative; or

    (4) have preference over any other class or series of shares with respect to distributions, including distributions upon the dissolution of the corporation.

(d) Terms of shares may be made dependent upon facts objectively ascertainable outside the articles of incorporation in accordance with section 1.20(k).

(e) Any of the terms of shares may vary among holders of the same class or series so long as such variations are expressly set forth in the articles of incorporation.

(f) The description of the preferences, rights and limitations of classes or series of shares in subsection (c) is not exhaustive.

§6.02. TERMS OF CLASS OR SERIES DETERMINED BY BOARD OF DIRECTORS

(a) If the articles of incorporation so provide, the board of directors is authorized, without shareholder approval, to:

    (1) classify any unissued shares into one or more classes or into one or more series within a class,

    (2) reclassify any unissued shares of any class into one or more classes or into one or more series within one or more classes, or

    (3) reclassify any unissued shares of any series of any class into one or more classes or into one or more series within a class.

(b) If the board of directors acts pursuant to subsection (a), it must determine the terms, including the preferences, rights and limitations, to the same extent permitted under section 6.01, of:

    (1) any class of shares before the issuance of any shares of that class, or

    (2) any series within a class before the issuance of any shares of that series.

(c) Before issuing any shares of a class or series created under this section, the corporation must deliver to the secretary of state for filing articles of amendment setting forth the terms determined under subsection (a).

§6.03. ISSUED AND OUTSTANDING SHARES

(a) A corporation may issue the number of shares of each class or series authorized by the articles of incorporation. Shares that are issued are outstanding shares until they are reacquired, redeemed, converted, or cancelled.

(b) The reacquisition, redemption, or conversion of outstanding shares is subject to the limitations of subsection (c) of this section and to section 6.40.

(c) At all times that shares of the corporation are outstanding, one or more shares that together have unlimited voting rights and one or more shares that together are entitled to receive the net assets of the corporation upon dissolution must be outstanding.

§6.04. FRACTIONAL SHARES

(a) A corporation may:
 (1) issue fractions of a share or pay in money the value of fractions of a share;
 (2) arrange for disposition of fractional shares by the shareholders;
 (3) issue scrip in registered or bearer form entitling the holder to receive a full share upon surrendering enough scrip to equal a full share.

(b) Each certificate representing scrip must be conspicuously labeled "scrip" and must contain the information required by section 6.25(b).

(c) The holder of a fractional share is entitled to exercise the rights of a shareholder, including the right to vote, to receive dividends, and to participate in the assets of the corporation upon liquidation. The holder of scrip is not entitled to any of these rights unless the scrip provides for them.

(d) The board of directors may authorize the issuance of scrip subject to any condition considered desirable, including:
 (1) that the scrip will become void if not exchanged for full shares before a specified date; and
 (2) that the shares for which the scrip is exchangeable may be sold and the proceeds paid to the scripholders.

Subchapter B: ISSUANCE OF SHARES

§6.20. SUBSCRIPTION FOR SHARES BEFORE INCORPORATION

(a) A subscription for shares entered into before incorporation is irrevocable for six months unless the subscription agreement provides a longer or shorter period or all the subscribers agree to revocation.

(b) The board of directors may determine the payment terms of subscription for shares that were entered into before incorporation, unless the subscription agreement specifies them. A call for payment by the board of directors must be uniform so far as practicable as to all shares of the same class or series, unless the subscription agreement specifies otherwise.

(c) Shares issued pursuant to subscriptions entered into before incorporation are fully paid and nonassessable when the corporation receives the consideration specified in the subscription agreement.

(d) If a subscriber defaults in payment of money or property under a subscription agreement entered into before incorporation, the corporation may collect the amount owed as any other debt. Alternatively, unless the subscription agreement provides otherwise, the corporation may rescind the agreement and may sell the shares if the debt remains unpaid for more than 20 days after the corporation sends a written demand for payment to the subscriber.

(e) A subscription agreement entered into after incorporation is a contract between the subscriber and the corporation subject to section 6.21.

§6.21. ISSUANCE OF SHARES

(a) The powers granted in this section to the board of directors may be reserved to the shareholders by the articles of incorporation.

(b) The board of directors may authorize shares to be issued for consideration consisting of any tangible or intangible property or benefit to the corporation, including cash, promissory notes, services performed, contracts for services to be performed, or other securities of the corporation.

(c) Before the corporation issues shares, the board of directors must determine that the consideration received or to be received for shares to be issued is adequate. That determination by the board of directors is conclusive insofar as the adequacy of consideration for the issuance of shares relates to whether the shares are validly issued, fully paid, and nonassessable.

(d) When the corporation receives the consideration for which the board of directors authorized the issuance of shares, the shares issued therefore are fully paid and nonassessable.

(e) The corporation may place in escrow shares issued for a contract for future services or benefits or a promissory note, or make other arrangements to restrict the transfer of the shares, and may credit distributions in respect of the shares against their purchase price, until the services are performed, the note is paid, or the benefits received. If the services are not performed, the note is not paid, or the benefits are not received, the shares escrowed or restricted and the distributions credited may be cancelled in whole or part.

(f) (1) An issuance of shares or other securities convertible into or rights exercisable for shares, in a transaction or a series of integrated transactions, requires approval of the shareholders, at a meeting at which a quorum consisting of at least a majority of the votes entitled to be cast on the matter exists, if:

    (i) the shares, other securities, or rights are issued for consideration other than cash or cash equivalents, and

    (ii) the voting power of shares that are issued and issuable as a result of the transaction or series of integrated transactions will comprise more than 20% of the voting power of the shares of the corporation that were outstanding immediately before the transaction.

(2) In this subsection:

    (i) For purposes of determining the voting power of shares issued and issuable as a result of a transaction or series of integrated transactions, the voting power of shares shall be the greater of (A) the voting power of the shares to be issued, or (B) the voting power of the shares that would be outstanding after giving effect to the conversion of convertible shares and other securities and the exercise of rights to be issued.

    (ii) A series of transactions is integrated if consummation of one transaction is made contingent on consummation of one or more of the other transactions.

§6.22. LIABILITY OF SHAREHOLDERS

(a) A purchaser from a corporation of its own shares is not liable to the corporation or its creditors with respect to the shares except to pay the consideration for which the shares were authorized to be issued (section 6.21) or specified in the subscription agreement (section 6.20).

(b) Unless otherwise provided in the articles of incorporation, a shareholder of a corporation is not personally liable for the acts or debts of the corporation except that he may become personally liable by reason of his own acts or conduct.

§6.23. SHARE DIVIDENDS

(a) Unless the articles of incorporation provide otherwise, shares may be issued pro rata and without consideration to the corporation's shareholders or to the shareholders of one or more classes or series. An issuance of shares under this subsection is a share dividend.

(b) Shares of one class or series may not be issued as a share dividend in respect of shares of another class or series unless (1) the articles of incorporation so authorize, (2) a majority of the votes entitled to be cast by the class or series to be issued approve the issue, or (3) there are no outstanding shares of the class or series to be issued.

(c) If the board of directors does not fix the record date for determining shareholders entitled to a share dividend, it is the date the board of directors authorizes the share dividend.

§6.24. SHARE OPTIONS

(a) A corporation may issue rights, options, or warrants for the purchase of shares or other securities of the corporation. The board of directors shall determine (i) the terms upon which the rights, options, or warrants are issued and (ii) the terms, including the consideration for which the shares or other securities are to be issued. The authorization by the board of directors for the corporation to issue such rights, options, or warrants constitutes authorization of the issuance of the shares or other securities for which the rights, options or warrants are exercisable.

(b) The terms and conditions of such rights, options or warrants, including those outstanding on the effective date of this section, may include, without limitation, restrictions or conditions that:

    (1) preclude or limit the exercise, transfer or receipt of such rights, options or warrants by any person or persons owning or offering to acquire a specified number or percentage of the outstanding shares or other securities of the corporation or by any transferee or transferees of any such person or persons, or

    (2) invalidate or void such rights, options, or warrants held by any such person or persons or any such transferee or transferees.

(c) The board of directors may authorize one or more officers to (1) designate the recipients of rights, options, warrants, or other equity compensation awards that involve the issuance of shares and (2) determine, within an amount and subject to any other limitations established by the board and, if applicable, the stockholders, the number of such rights, options, warrants, or other equity compensation awards and the terms thereof to be received by the recipients, provided that an officer may not use such authority to designate himself or herself or any other persons the board of directors may specify as a recipient of such rights, options, warrants, or other equity compensation awards.

§6.25. FORM AND CONTENT OF CERTIFICATES

(a) Shares may but need not be represented by certificates. Unless this Act or another statute expressly provides otherwise, the rights and obligations of shareholders are identical whether or not their shares are represented by certificates.

(b) At a minimum each share certificate must state on its face:
   (1) the name of the issuing corporation and that it is organized under the law of this state;
   (2) the name of the person to whom issued; and
   (3) the number and class of shares and the designation of the series, if any, the certificate represents.

(c) If the issuing corporation is authorized to issue different classes of shares or different series within a class, the designations, relative rights, preferences, and limitations applicable to each class and the variations in rights, preferences, and limitations determined for each series (and the authority of the board of directors to determine variations for future series) must be summarized on the front or back of each certificate. Alternatively, each certificate may state conspicuously on its front or back that the corporation will furnish the shareholder this information on request in writing and without charge.

(d) Each share certificate (1) must be signed (either manually or in facsimile) by two officers designated in the bylaws or by the board of directors and (2) may bear the corporate seal or its facsimile.

(e) If the person who signed (either manually or in facsimile) a share certificate no longer holds office when the certificate is issued, the certificate is nevertheless valid.

§6.26. SHARES WITHOUT CERTIFICATES

(a) Unless the articles of incorporation or bylaws provide otherwise, the board of directors of a corporation may authorize the issue of some or all of the shares of any or all of its classes or series without certificates. The authorization does not affect shares already represented by certificates until they are surrendered to the corporation.

(b) Within a reasonable time after the issue or transfer of shares without certificates, the corporation shall send the shareholder a written statement of the information required on certificates by section 6.25(b) and (c), and, if applicable, section 6.27.

§6.27. RESTRICTION ON TRANSFER OF SHARES AND OTHER SECURITIES

(a) The articles of incorporation, bylaws, an agreement among shareholders, or an agreement between shareholders and the corporation may impose restrictions on the transfer or registration of transfer of shares of the corporation. A restriction does not affect shares issued before the restriction was adopted unless the holders of the shares are parties to the restriction agreement or voted in favor of the restriction.

(b) A restriction on the transfer or registration of transfer of shares is valid and enforceable against the holder or a transferee of the holder if the restriction is authorized by this section and its existence is noted conspicuously on the front or back of the certificate or is contained in the information statement required by section 6.26(b). Unless so noted or contained, a restriction is not enforceable against a person without knowledge of the restriction.

(c) A restriction on the transfer or registration of transfer of shares is authorized:

    (1) to maintain the corporation's status when it is dependent on the number or identity of its shareholders;

    (2) to preserve exemptions under federal or state securities law;

    (3) for any other reasonable purpose.

(d) A restriction on the transfer or registration of transfer of shares may:

    (1) obligate the shareholder first to offer the corporation or other persons (separately, consecutively, or simultaneously) an opportunity to acquire the restricted shares;

    (2) obligate the corporation or other persons (separately, consecutively, or simultaneously) to acquire the restricted shares;

    (3) require the corporation, the holders of any class of its shares, or another person to approve the transfer of the restricted shares, if the requirement is not manifestly unreasonable;

    (4) prohibit the transfer of the restricted shares to designated persons or classes of persons, if the prohibition is not manifestly unreasonable.

(e) For purposes of this section, "shares" includes a security convertible into or carrying a right to subscribe for or acquire shares.

§6.28. EXPENSE OF ISSUE

A corporation may pay the expenses of selling or underwriting its shares, and of organizing or reorganizing the corporation, from the consideration received for shares.

Subchapter C: SUBSEQUENT ACQUISITION OF SHARES BY SHAREHOLDERS AND CORPORATION

§6.30. SHAREHOLDERS' PREEMPTIVE RIGHTS

(a) The shareholders of a corporation do not have a preemptive right to acquire the corporation's unissued shares except to the extent the articles of incorporation so provide.

(b) A statement included in the articles of incorporation that "the corporation elects to have preemptive rights" (or words of similar import) means that the following principles apply except to the extent the articles of incorporation expressly provide otherwise:

    (1) The shareholders of the corporation have a preemptive right, granted on uniform terms and conditions prescribed by the board of directors to provide a fair and reasonable opportunity to exercise the right, to acquire proportional

amounts of the corporation's unisssued shares upon the decision of the board of directors to issue them.

(2) A shareholder may waive his preemptive right. A waiver evidenced by a writing is irrevocable even though it is not supported by consideration.

(3) There is no preemptive right with respect to:

    (i)   shares issued as compensation to directors, officers, agents, or employees of the corporation, its subsidiaries or affiliates:

    (ii)   shares issued to satisfy conversion or option rights created to provide compensation to directors, officers, agents, or employees of the corporation, its subsidiaries or affiliates;

    (iii) shares authorized in articles of incorporation that are issued within six months from the effective date of incorporation;

    (iv) shares sold otherwise than for money.

(4) Holders of shares of any class without general voting rights but with preferential rights to distributions or assets have no preemptive rights with respect to shares of any class.

(5) Holders of shares of any class with general voting rights but without preferential rights to distributions or assets have no preemptive rights with respect to shares of any class with preferential rights to distributions or assets unless the shares with preferential rights are convertible into or carry a right to subscribe for or acquire shares without preferential rights.

(6) Shares subject to preemptive rights that are not acquired by shareholders may be issued to any person for a period of one year after being offered to shareholders at a consideration set by the board of directors that is not lower than the consideration set for the exercise of preemptive rights. An offer at a lower consideration or after the expiration of one year is subject to the shareholders' preemptive rights.

(c) For purposes of this section, "shares" includes a security convertible into or carrying a right to subscribe for or acquire shares.

§6.31. CORPORATION'S ACQUISITION OF ITS OWN SHARES

(a) A corporation may acquire its own shares, and shares so acquired constitute authorized but unissued shares.

(b) If the articles of incorporation prohibit the reissue of the acquired shares, the number of authorized shares is reduced by the number of shares acquired.

Subchapter D: DISTRIBUTIONS

§6.40. DISTRIBUTIONS TO SHAREHOLDERS

(a) A board of directors may authorize and the corporation may make distributions to its shareholders subject to restriction by the articles of incorporation and the limitation in subsection (c).

(b) If the board of directors does not fix the record date for determining shareholders entitled to a distribution (other than one involving a purchase, redemption, or other acquisition of the corporation's shares), it is the date the board of directors authorizes the distribution.

(c) No distribution may be made if, after giving it effect:
   (1) the corporation would not be able to pay its debts as they become due in the usual course of business; or
   (2) the corporation's total assets would be less than the sum of its total liabilities plus (unless the articles of incorporation permit otherwise) the amount that would be needed, if the corporation were to be dissolved at the time of the distribution, to satisfy the preferential rights upon dissolution of shareholders whose preferential rights are superior to those receiving the distribution.
(d) The board of directors may base a determination that a distribution is not prohibited under subsection (c) either on financial statements prepared on the basis of accounting practices and principles that are reasonable in the circumstances or on a fair valuation or other method that is reasonable in the circumstances.
(e) Except as provided in subsection (g), the effect of a distribution under subsection (c) is measured:
   (1) in the case of distribution by purchase, redemption, or other acquisition of the corporation's shares, as of the earlier of (i) the date money or other property is transferred or debt incurred by the corporation or (ii) the date the shareholder ceases to be a shareholder with respect to the acquired shares;
   (2) in the case of any other distribution of indebtedness, as of the date the indebtedness is distributed; and
   (3) in all other cases, as of (i) the date the distribution is authorized if the payment occurs within 120 days after the date of authorization or (ii) the date the payment is made if it occurs more than 120 days after the date of authorization.
(f) A corporation's indebtedness to a shareholder incurred by reason of a distribution made in accordance with this section is at parity with the corporation's indebtedness to its general, unsecured creditors except to the extent subordinated by agreement.
(g) Indebtedness of a corporation, including indebtedness issued as a distribution, is not considered a liability for purposes of determinations under subsection (c) if its terms provide that payment of principal and interest are made only if and to the extent that payment of a distribution to shareholders could then be made under this section. If the indebtedness is issued as a distribution, each payment of principal or interest is treated as a distribution, the effect of which is measured on the date the payment is actually made.
(h) This section shall not apply to distributions in liquidation under chapter 14.

DELAWARE GENERAL CORPORATION LAW

§151. Classes and series of stock; redemption; rights

(a) Every corporation may issue 1 or more classes of stock or 1 or more series of stock within any class thereof, any or all of which classes may be of stock with par value or stock without par value and which classes or series may have such voting powers, full or limited, or no voting powers, and such designations, preferences and relative, participating, optional or other special rights, and qualifications, limitations or restrictions thereof, as shall be stated and expressed in the certificate of incorporation or of any amendment thereto, or in the resolution or resolutions providing for the issue of such stock adopted by the board of directors pursuant to authority expressly vested in it by the provisions of its certificate of incorporation. Any of the voting powers, designations, preferences, rights and qualifications, limitations or restrictions of any such class or series of stock may be made dependent upon facts ascertainable outside the certificate of incorporation or of any amendment thereto, or outside the resolution or resolutions providing for the issue of such stock adopted by the board of directors pursuant to authority expressly vested in it by its certificate of incorporation, provided that the manner in which such facts shall operate upon the voting powers, designations, preferences, rights and qualifications, limitations or restrictions of such class or series of stock is clearly and expressly set forth in the certificate of incorporation or in the resolution or resolutions providing for the issue of such stock adopted by the board of directors. The term "facts," as used in this subsection, includes, but is not limited to, the occurrence of any event, including a determination or action by any person or body, including the corporation. The power to increase or decrease or otherwise adjust the capital stock as provided in this chapter shall apply to all or any such classes of stock.

(b) Any stock of any class or series may be made subject to redemption by the corporation at its option or at the option of the holders of such stock or upon the happening of a specified event; provided however, that immediately following any such redemption the corporation shall have outstanding 1 or more shares of 1 or more classes or series of stock, which share, or shares together, shall have full voting powers. Notwithstanding the limitation stated in the foregoing proviso:

(1) Any stock of a regulated investment company registered under the Investment Company Act of 1940 [15 U.S.C. §80 a-1 et seq.], as heretofore or

hereafter amended, may be made subject to redemption by the corporation at its option or at the option of the holders of such stock.

(2) Any stock of a corporation which holds (directly or indirectly) a license or franchise from a governmental agency to conduct its business or is a member of a national securities exchange, which license, franchise or membership is conditioned upon some or all of the holders of its stock possessing prescribed qualifications, may be made subject to redemption by the corporation to the extent necessary to prevent the loss of such license, franchise or membership or to reinstate it.

Any stock which may be made redeemable under this section may be redeemed for cash, property or rights, including securities of the same or another corporation, at such time or times, price or prices, or rate or rates, and with such adjustments, as shall be stated in the certificate of incorporation or in the resolution or resolutions providing for the issue of such stock adopted by the board of directors pursuant to subsection (a) of this section.

(c) The holders of preferred or special stock of any class or of any series thereof shall be entitled to receive dividends at such rates, on such conditions and at such times as shall be stated in the certificate of incorporation or in the resolution or resolutions providing for the issue of such stock adopted by the board of directors as hereinabove provided, payable in preference to, or in such relation to, the dividends payable on any other class or classes or of any other series of stock, and cumulative or noncumulative as shall be so stated and expressed. When dividends upon the preferred and special stocks, if any, to the extent of the preference to which such stocks are entitled, shall have been paid or declared and set apart for payment, a dividend on the remaining class or classes or series of stock may then be paid out of the remaining assets of the corporation available for dividends as elsewhere in this chapter provided.

(d) The holders of the preferred or special stock of any class or of any series thereof shall be entitled to such rights upon the dissolution of, or upon any distribution of the assets of, the corporation as shall be stated in the certificate of incorporation or in the resolution or resolutions providing for the issue of such stock adopted by the board of directors as hereinabove provided.

(e) Any stock of any class or of any series thereof may be made convertible into, or exchangeable for, at the option of either the holder or the corporation or upon the happening of a specified event, shares of any other class or classes or any other series of the same or any other class or classes of stock of the corporation, at such price or prices or at such rate or rates of exchange and with such adjustments as shall be stated in the certificate of incorporation or in the resolution or resolutions providing for the issue of such stock adopted by the board of directors as hereinabove provided.

(f) If any corporation shall be authorized to issue more than 1 class of stock or more than 1 series of any class, the powers, designations, preferences and relative, participating, optional, or other special rights of each class of stock or series thereof and the qualifications, limitations or restrictions of such preferences and/or rights shall be set forth in full or summarized on the face or back of the certificate which the corporation shall issue to represent such class or series of stock, provided that, except as otherwise provided in §202 of this title, in lieu of the foregoing requirements, there may be set forth on the face or back of the certificate which the corporation shall issue to represent such class or series of stock, a statement that the corporation will furnish without charge to each stockholder who so requests the powers, designations, preferences and relative, participating, optional, or other special rights of each class of stock or series thereof and the qualifications, limitations or restrictions of such preferences and/or rights. Within a reasonable time after the issuance or transfer of uncertificated stock, the corporation shall send to the registered owner thereof a written notice containing the information required to be set forth or stated on certificates pursuant to this section or §156, §202(a) or §218(a) of this title or with respect to this section a statement that the corporation will furnish without charge to each stockholder who so requests the powers, designations, preferences and relative participating, optional or other special rights of each class of stock or series thereof and the qualifications, limitations or restrictions of such preferences and/or rights. Except as otherwise expressly provided by law, the rights and obligations of the holders of uncertificated stock and the rights and obligations of the holders of certificates representing stock of the same class and series shall be identical.

(g) When any corporation desires to issue any shares of stock of any class or of any series of any class of which the powers, designations, preferences and relative, participating, optional or other rights, if any, or the qualifications, limitations or restrictions thereof, if any, shall not have been set forth in the certificate of incorporation or in any amendment thereto but shall be provided for in a resolution or resolutions adopted by the board of directors pursuant to authority expressly vested in it by the certificate of incorporation or any amendment thereto, a certificate of designations setting forth a copy of such resolution or resolutions and the number of shares of stock of such class or series as to which the resolution or resolutions apply shall be executed, acknowledged, filed and shall become effective, in accordance with §103 of this title. Unless otherwise provided in any such resolution or resolutions, the number of shares of stock of any such series to which such resolution or resolutions apply may be increased (but not above the total number of authorized shares of the class) or decreased (but not below the number of shares thereof then outstanding) by a certificate likewise executed, acknowledged and filed setting forth a statement that a specified increase or decrease therein had been authorized and directed by a resolution or resolutions likewise adopted by the board of directors. In case the number of such shares shall be decreased the number of shares so specified in the certificate shall resume the status which they had prior to the adoption of the first resolution or resolutions. When no shares of any such class or series are outstanding, either because none were issued or because no issued shares of any such class or series remain outstanding, a certificate setting forth a resolution or resolutions adopted by the board of directors that none of the authorized shares of such class or series are outstanding, and that none will be issued subject to the certificate of designations previously filed with respect to such class or series, may be executed, acknowledged and filed in accordance with §103 of this title and, when such certificate becomes effective, it shall have the effect of eliminating from the certificate of incorporation all matters set forth in the certificate of designations with respect to such class or series of stock. Unless otherwise provided in the certificate of incorporation, if no shares of stock have been issued of a class or series of stock established by a resolution of the board of directors, the voting powers, designations, preferences and relative, participating, optional or other rights, if any, or the qualifications, limitations or restrictions thereof, may be amended by a resolution or resolutions adopted by the board of directors. A certificate which:

(1) States that no shares of the class or series have been issued;

(2) Sets forth a copy of the resolution or resolutions; and

(3) If the designation of the class or series is being changed, indicates the original designation and the new designation,

shall be executed, acknowledged and filed and shall become effective, in accordance with §103 of this title. When any certificate filed under this subsection becomes effective, it shall have the effect of amending the certificate of incorporation; except that neither the filing of such certificate nor the filing of a restated certificate of incorporation pursuant to §245 of this title shall prohibit the board of directors from subsequently adopting such resolutions as authorized by this subsection.

§152. Issuance of stock; lawful consideration; fully paid stock

The consideration, as determined pursuant to §153(a) and (b) of this title, for subscriptions to, or the purchase of, the capital stock to be issued by a corporation shall be paid in such form and in such manner as the board of directors shall determine. The board of directors may authorize capital stock to be issued for consideration consisting of cash, any tangible or intangible property or any benefit to the corporation, or any combination thereof. The resolution authorizing the issuance of capital stock may provide that any stock to be issued pursuant to such resolution may be issued in one or more transactions in such numbers and at such times as are set forth in or determined by or in the manner set forth in the resolution, which may include a determination or action by any person or body, including the corporation, provided the resolution fixes a maximum number of shares that may be issued pursuant to such resolution, a time period during which such shares may be issued and a minimum amount of consideration for which such shares may be issued. The board of directors may determine the amount of consideration for which shares may be issued by setting a minimum amount of consideration or approving a formula by which the amount or minimum amount of consideration is determined. The formula may include or be made dependent upon facts ascertainable outside the formula, provided the manner in which such facts shall operate upon the formula is clearly and expressly set forth in the formula or in the resolution approving the formula. In the absence of actual fraud in the transaction, the judgment of the directors as to the value of such consideration shall be conclusive. The capital stock so issued shall be deemed to be fully paid and nonassessable stock upon receipt by the corporation of such consideration; provided, however, nothing contained herein shall prevent the board of directors from issuing partly paid shares under §156 of this title.

§153. Consideration for stock

(a) Shares of stock with par value may be issued for such consideration, having a value not less than the par value thereof, as determined from time to time by the board of directors, or by the stockholders if the certificate of incorporation so provides.

(b) Shares of stock without par value may be issued for such consideration as is determined from time to time by the board of directors, or by the stockholders if the certificate of incorporation so provides.

(c) Treasury shares may be disposed of by the corporation for such consideration as may be determined from time to time by the board of directors, or by the stockholders if the certificate of incorporation so provides.

(d) If the certificate of incorporation reserves to the stockholders the right to determine the consideration for the issue of any shares, the stockholders shall, unless the certificate requires a greater vote, do so by a vote of a majority of the outstanding stock entitled to vote thereon.

§154. Determination of amount of capital; capital, surplus and net assets defined

Any corporation may, by resolution of its board of directors, determine that only a part of the consideration which shall be received by the corporation for any of the shares of its capital stock which it shall issue from time to time shall be capital; but, in case any of the shares issued shall be shares having a par value, the amount of the part of such consideration so determined to be capital shall be in excess of the aggregate par value of the shares issued for such consideration having a par value, unless all the shares issued shall be shares having a par value, in which case the amount of the part of such consideration so determined to be capital need be only equal to the aggregate par value of such shares. In each such case the board of directors shall specify in dollars the part of such consideration which shall be capital. If the board of directors shall not have determined (1) at the time of issue of any shares of the capital stock of the corporation issued for cash or (2) within 60 days after the issue of any shares of the capital stock of the corporation issued for consideration other than cash what part of the consideration for such shares shall be capital, the capital of the corporation in respect of such shares shall be an amount equal to the aggregate par value of such shares having a par value, plus the amount of the consideration for such shares without par value. The amount of the consideration so determined to be capital in respect of any shares without par value shall be the stated capital of such shares. The capital of the corporation may be increased from time to time by resolution of the board of directors directing that a portion of the net assets of the corporation in excess of the amount so determined to be capital be transferred to the capital account. The board of directors may direct that the portion of such net assets so transferred shall be treated as capital in respect of any shares of the corporation of any designated class or classes. The excess, if any, at any given time, of the net assets of the corporation over the amount so determined to be capital shall be surplus. Net assets means the amount by which total assets exceed total liabilities. Capital and surplus are not liabilities for this purpose. Notwithstanding anything in this section to the contrary, for purposes of this section and §§160 and 170 of this title, the capital of any nonstock corporation shall be deemed to be zero.

§155. Fractions of shares

A corporation may, but shall not be required to, issue fractions of a share. If it does not issue fractions of a share, it shall (1) arrange for the disposition of fractional interests by those entitled thereto, (2) pay in cash the fair value of fractions of a share as of the time when those entitled to receive such fractions are determined or (3) issue scrip or warrants in registered form (either represented by a certificate or uncertificated) or in bearer form (represented by a certificate) which shall entitle the holder to receive a full share upon the surrender of such scrip or warrants aggregating a full share. A certificate for a fractional share or an uncertificated fractional share shall, but scrip or warrants shall not unless otherwise provided therein, entitle the holder to exercise voting rights, to receive dividends thereon and to participate in any of the assets of the corporation in the event of liquidation. The board of directors may cause scrip or warrants to be issued subject to the conditions that they shall become void if not exchanged for certificates representing the full shares or uncertificated full shares before a specified date, or subject to the conditions that the shares for which scrip or warrants are exchangeable may be sold by the corporation and the proceeds thereof distributed to the holders of scrip or warrants, or subject to any other conditions which the board of directors may impose.

§157. Rights and options respecting stock

(a) Subject to any provisions in the certificate of incorporation, every corporation may create and issue, whether or not in connection with the issue and sale of any shares of stock or other securities of the corporation, rights or options entitling the holders thereof to acquire from the corporation any shares of its capital stock of any class or classes, such rights or options to be evidenced by or in such instrument or instruments as shall be approved by the board of directors.

(b) The terms upon which, including the time or times which may be limited or unlimited in duration, at or within which, and the consideration (including a formula by which such consideration may be determined) for which any such shares may be acquired from the corporation upon the exercise of any such right or option, shall be such as shall be stated in the certificate of incorporation, or in a resolution adopted by the board of directors providing for the creation and issue of such rights or options, and, in every case, shall be set forth or incorporated by reference in the instrument or instruments evidencing such rights or options. A formula by which such consideration may be determined may include or be made dependent upon facts ascertainable outside the formula, provided the manner in which such facts shall operate upon the formula is clearly and expressly set forth in the formula or in the resolution approving the formula. In the absence of actual fraud in the transaction, the judgment of the directors as to the consideration for the issuance of such rights or options and the sufficiency thereof shall be conclusive.

(c) The board of directors may, by a resolution adopted by the board, authorize 1 or more officers of the corporation to do 1 or both of the following: (i) designate officers and employees of the corporation or of any of its subsidiaries to be recipients of such rights or options created by the corporation, and (ii) determine the number of such rights or options to be received by such officers and employees; provided, however, that the resolution so authorizing such officer or officers shall specify the total number of rights or options such officer or officers may so award. The board of directors may not authorize an officer to designate himself or herself as a recipient of any such rights or options.

(d) In case the shares of stock of the corporation to be issued upon the exercise of such rights or options shall be shares having a par value, the consideration so to be received therefor shall have a value not less than the par value thereof. In case the shares of stock so to be issued shall be shares of stock without par value, the consideration therefor shall be determined in the manner provided in §153 of this title.

§160. Corporation's powers respecting ownership, voting, etc., of its own stock; rights of stock called for redemption

(a) Every corporation may purchase, redeem, receive, take or otherwise acquire, own and hold, sell, lend, exchange, transfer or otherwise dispose of, pledge, use and otherwise deal in and with its own shares; provided, however, that no corporation shall:

    (1) Purchase or redeem its own shares of capital stock for cash or other property when the capital of the corporation is impaired or when such purchase or redemption would cause any impairment of the capital of the corporation, except that a corporation other than a nonstock corporation may purchase or redeem out of capital any of its own shares which are entitled upon any distribution of its assets, whether by dividend or in liquidation, to a preference over another class or series of its stock, or, if no shares entitled to such a preference are outstanding, any of its own shares, if such shares will be retired upon their acquisition and the capital of the corporation reduced in accordance with §§243 and 244 of this title. Nothing in this subsection shall invalidate or otherwise affect a note, debenture or other obligation of a corporation given by it as consideration for its acquisition by purchase, redemption or exchange of its shares of stock if at the time such note, debenture or obligation was delivered by the corporation its capital was not then impaired or did not thereby become impaired;

    (2) Purchase, for more than the price at which they may then be redeemed, any of its shares which are redeemable at the option of the corporation; or

    (3) a. In the case of a corporation other than a nonstock corporation, redeem any of its shares, unless their redemption is authorized by §151(b) of this title and then only in accordance with such section and the certificate of incorporation, or

    b. In the case of a nonstock corporation, redeem any of its membership interests, unless their redemption is authorized by the certificate of incorporation and then only in accordance with the certificate of incorporation.

(b) Nothing in this section limits or affects a corporation's right to resell any of its shares theretofore purchased or redeemed out of surplus and which have not been retired, for such consideration as shall be fixed by the board of directors.

(c) Shares of its own capital stock belonging to the corporation or to another corporation, if a majority of the shares entitled to vote in the election of directors of such other corporation is held, directly or indirectly, by the corporation, shall neither be entitled to vote nor be counted for quorum purposes. Nothing in this section shall be construed as limiting the right of any corporation to vote stock, including but not limited to its own stock, held by it in a fiduciary capacity.

(d) Shares which have been called for redemption shall not be deemed to be outstanding shares for the purpose of voting or determining the total number of shares entitled to vote on any matter on and after the date on which written notice of redemption has been sent to holders thereof and a sum sufficient to redeem such shares has been irrevocably deposited or set aside to pay the redemption price to the holders of the shares upon surrender of certificates therefor.

§161. Issuance of additional stock; when and by whom

The directors may, at any time and from time to time, if all of the shares of capital stock which the corporation is authorized by its certificate of incorporation to issue have not been issued, subscribed for, or otherwise committed to be issued, issue or take subscriptions for additional shares of its capital stock up to the amount authorized in its certificate of incorporation.

§170. Dividends; payment; wasting asset corporations

(a) The directors of every corporation, subject to any restrictions contained in its certificate of incorporation, may declare and pay dividends upon the shares of its capital stock either:

    (1) Out of its surplus, as defined in and computed in accordance with §§154 and 244 of this title; or

    (2) In case there shall be no such surplus, out of its net profits for the fiscal year in which the dividend is declared and/or the preceding fiscal year.

If the capital of the corporation, computed in accordance with §§154 and 244 of this title, shall have been diminished by depreciation in the value of its property, or by losses, or otherwise, to an amount less than the aggregate amount of the capital represented by the issued and outstanding stock of all classes having a preference upon the distribution of assets, the directors of such corporation shall not declare and pay out of such net profits any dividends upon any shares of any classes of its capital stock until the deficiency in the amount of capital represented by the issued and outstanding stock of all classes having a preference upon the distribution of assets shall have been repaired. Nothing in this subsection shall invalidate or otherwise affect a note, debenture or other obligation of the corporation paid by it as a dividend on shares of its stock, or any payment made thereon, if at the time such note, debenture or obligation was delivered by the corporation, the corporation had either surplus or net profits as provided in (a)(1) or (2) of this section from which the dividend could lawfully have been paid.

(b) Subject to any restrictions contained in its certificate of incorporation, the directors of any corporation engaged in the exploitation of wasting assets (including but not limited to a corporation engaged in the exploitation of natural resources or other wasting assets, including patents, or engaged primarily in the liquidation of specific assets) may determine the net profits derived from the exploitation of such wasting assets or the net proceeds derived from such liquidation without taking into consideration the depletion of such assets resulting from lapse of time, consumption, liquidation or exploitation of such assets.

§173. Declaration and payment of dividends

No corporation shall pay dividends except in accordance with this chapter. Dividends may be paid in cash, in property, or in shares of the corporation's capital stock. If the dividend is to be paid in shares of the corporation's theretofore unissued capital stock the board of directors shall, by resolution, direct that there be designated as capital in respect of such shares an amount which is not less than the aggregate par value of par value shares being declared as a dividend and, in the case of shares without par value being declared as a dividend, such amount as shall be determined by the board of directors. No such designation as capital shall be necessary if shares are being distributed by a corporation pursuant to a split-up or division of its stock rather than as payment of a dividend declared payable in stock of the corporation.

§243. Retirement of stock

(a) A corporation, by resolution of its board of directors, may retire any shares of its capital stock that are issued but are not outstanding.

(b) Whenever any shares of the capital stock of a corporation are retired, they shall resume the status of authorized and unissued shares of the class or series to which they belong unless the certificate of incorporation otherwise provides. If the certificate of incorporation prohibits the reissuance of such shares, or prohibits the reissuance of such shares as a part of a specific series only, a certificate stating that reissuance of the shares (as part of the class or series) is prohibited identifying the shares and reciting their retirement shall be executed, acknowledged and filed and shall become effective in accordance with §103 of this title. When such certificate becomes effective, it shall have the effect of amending the certificate of incorporation so as to reduce accordingly the number of authorized shares of the class or series to which such shares belong or, if such retired shares constitute all of the authorized shares of the class or series to which they belong, of eliminating from the certificate of incorporation all reference to such class or series of stock.

(c) If the capital of the corporation will be reduced by or in connection with the retirement of shares, the reduction of capital shall be effected pursuant to §244 of this title.

§244. Reduction of capital

(a) A corporation, by resolution of its board of directors, may reduce its capital in any of the following ways:

   (1) By reducing or eliminating the capital represented by shares of capital stock which have been retired;

   (2) By applying to an otherwise authorized purchase or redemption of outstanding shares of its capital stock some or all of the capital represented by the shares being purchased or redeemed, or any capital that has not been allocated to any particular class of its capital stock;

   (3) By applying to an otherwise authorized conversion or exchange of outstanding shares of its capital stock some or all of the capital represented by the shares being converted or exchanged, or some or all of any capital that has not been allocated to any particular class of its capital stock, or both, to the extent that such capital in the aggregate exceeds the total aggregate par value or the stated capital of any previously unissued shares issuable upon such conversion or exchange; or

   (4) By transferring to surplus (i) some or all of the capital not represented by any particular class of its capital stock; (ii) some or all of the capital represented by issued shares of its par value capital stock, which capital is in excess of the

aggregate par value of such shares; or (iii) some of the capital represented by issued shares of its capital stock without par value.

(b) Notwithstanding the other provisions of this section, no reduction of capital shall be made or effected unless the assets of the corporation remaining after such reduction shall be sufficient to pay any debts of the corporation for which payment has not been otherwise provided. No reduction of capital shall release any liability of any stockholder whose shares have not been fully paid.

APPENDIX
C

REVISED MODEL SIMPLIFIED INDENTURE

Revised Model Simplified Indenture, 55 Business Lawyer 1115 (2000)
Ad Hoc Committee for Revision of the 1983 Model Simplified Indenture
American Bar Association.

INTRODUCTION

In 1983, *The Business Lawyer* published the Model Simplified Indenture,[1] which included both a form of indenture (the 1983 MSI) and a commentary (the 1983 Notes). The 1983 MSI and the 1983 Notes were promulgated with the hope that having a common form for the most standard provisions of indentures would reduce the need for significant negotiation of such provisions, and, in large part, the 1983 MSI accomplished that objective.

In 1995, a subcommittee on the Committee on Developments in Business Financing began work on a revision of the 1983 MSI. As did the 1983 MSI committee, the subcommittee's focus was on the non-covenant provisions of a "standard" convertible, subordinated indenture. Indentures are one of the most ancient of legal forms, and one of the secrets of their pervasiveness and continued utility is the ability of the form to change and adapt to new issues and areas of concern.[2] Although new indenture technology since 1983 has focused primarily on covenants, there have been enormous changes as well in other areas, particularly in subordination and trustee provisions. The 1999 Model Simplified Indenture (the Model Simplified Indenture) generally updates the 1983 MSI, with particular attention to those articles.

The subordination article presented a challenge to the subcommittee, as it does for lawyers negotiating such provisions. The increasing complexity of corporate capital structures and issues raised by the spate of bankruptcies and restructurings of the late 1980s and early 1990s have resulted in indentures containing an increased number of provisions, and provisions that are more elaborate than those generally found in indentures of the early 1980s. As with covenants, subordination provisions are therefore frequently the subject of fact-specific negotiations focused on the issuer, its capital structure, and the security purchasers' own requirements. This Model Simplified

---

1. 38 Bus. Law 741 (1983).
2. *See generally* Churchill Rodgers, The Corporate Trust Indenture Project, 20 Bus. Law. 551 (1965).

Indenture contains a fairly straightforward (read simplified) version of subordination provisions, such as might be found in a corporate indenture for a high credit rated issuer, rather than a more elaborate version such as would be found in unrated debt for a highly leveraged issuer. The best source of the current state of play for more elaborate subordination provisions will be recent indentures for comparable offerings.

As was the 1983 MSI, the new Model Simplified Indenture is accompanied by Notes. Because the Model Simplified Indenture and its Notes are designed to be used as a stand-alone resource, without requiring reference to the 1983 MSI and 1983 Notes, where the language of the 1983 Model Simplified Indenture and of the Model Simplified Indenture are essentially identical, the Notes to the Model Simplified Indenture are unchanged or have been updated solely for cross-references and the like. In other Notes to the Model Simplified Indenture we have tried to highlight particular areas of change between the 1983 MSI and this Model Simplified Indenture and to draw attention to new legal developments. Obviously, the seminal works for any lawyer attempting to understand the meaning and origin of particular provisions include the American Bar Foundation's *Commentaries on Indentures*,[3] and the basic background afforded by that work is not repeated in this draft.

This Model Simplified Indenture represents a variety of views, and, it is hoped, in the aggregate favors no particular party, whether issuer, trustee, or security holder. As a result, however, users should be aware that as to any particular provision, parties' positions may vary. In addition, the substantive positions taken in the Model Simplified Indenture do not necessarily represent the views of any individual member of the Committee. Lastly, it should be noted that changes to a form of provision contained in the 1983 MSI are not intended to be used as a frame of reference for evaluating or interpreting indentures which use the 1983 MSI provisions.

This project was begun in 1995, by the Ad Hoc Committee for Revision of the 1983 MSI, under the aegis of the Committee on Developments in Business Financing of the American Bar Association's Section of Business Law. In 1998, two other Committees joined the effort and helped push it to completion—the Committee on Trust Indentures and Indenture Trustees and the Business Bankruptcy Committee's Subcommittee on Trust Indentures. As a result, the number of contributors to the project was significant, and greatly improved the strength of the draft. Although we list everyone who contributed on the attached list, we want to thank in particular the following who provided significant assistance in the final drafting stages of the project: Hollace T. Cohen, Timothy C. Crane, Byran H. Hall, Harold L. Kaplan, J. Andrew Rahl, Jr., David Reynolds, Felicia Smith and Steven M. Wagner. Special cite-checking assistance was provided by Jo Christine Reed, Touro College, Jacob D. Fuchsberger Law Center ('01).

In addition, one person should get special recognition—Morey McDaniel. Morey, one of the principal drafters of the 1983 Model Simplified Indenture, is a nationally recognized expert on indentures and issues related to their interpretation and application, initiated this updating project, and provided his guidance, moral support and great learning throughout the drafting process. Those who worked on the project, and the greater legal community, owe Morey our debt of gratitude both for the 1983 MSI and for his continuing efforts to ensure that this evolution of the Indenture

---

3. American Bar Foundation, Commentaries on Indentures (1971).

form incorporates a thoughtful approach to the issues securityholders, issuers and trustees face under today's indentures.

> Ad Hoc Committee for
> Revision of the 1983
> Model Simplified Indenture
> Ruth E. Fisher, Chair
>
> Committee on Trust Indentures
> and Indenture Trustees
> Ben B. Floyd, Chair
> James Gadsden, Vice Chair
>
> Subcommittee on Trust Indentures
> James Gadsden, Chair

INDENTURE

UNIVERSAL BUSINESS CORPORATION

and

GREATER BANK AND TRUST COMPANY

_____ Trustee

Dated as of _____

$ _____

TABLE OF CONTENTS

ARTICLE 11 *Subordination*

ARTICLE 12 *Miscellaneous*

CROSS-REFERENCE TABLE

TIA Section	Indenture Section
310	
(a)(1)	7.10
(a)(2)	7.10
(a)(3)	N.A.
(a)(4)	N.A.
(a)(5)	N.A.
(b)	7.08; 7.10
(c)	N.A.
311	
(a)	7.11
(b)	7.11
(c)	N.A.

TIA Section	Indenture Section
312	
(a)	2.05
(b)	12.02
(c)	N.A.
313	
(a)	7.06
(b)(1)	N.A.
(b)(2)	7.06
(c)	7.06
(d)	7.06
314	
(a)(1)	4.02
(a)(2)	12.01
(a)(4)	4.03
(b)	N.A.
(c)	2.02; 7.02(b); 8.01(3)
(c)(1)	13.04
(c)(2)	13.04
(c)(3)	13.04
(d)	N.A.
(e)	4.03; 12.04
(f)	4.03
315	
(a)(1)	6.05; 7.01(b)(1)
(a)(2)	7.01(b)(2)
(b)	7.05; 12.01
(c)	7.01(a)
(d)(1)	7.01(b)
(d)(2)	7.01(c)(2)
(d)(3)	6.05; 7.01(c)(3)
(e)	6.09
316	
(a) (last sentence)	2.09
(a)(1)(A)	6.05
(a)(1)(B)	6.04
(a)(2)	N.A.
(b)	6.07
(c)	9.04
317	
(a)(1)	6.03
(a)(2)	6.10
(b)	2.04
318	
(a)	1.04

N.A. means not applicable.
Note: This Cross-Reference Table shall not, for any purpose, be deemed to be part of this Indenture.

ARTICLE 1
DEFINITIONS AND RULES OF CONSTRUCTION; APPLICABILITY OF THE TRUST INDENTURE ACT

Section 1.01. Definitions.

"Affiliate." Any Person controlling or controlled by or under common control with the referenced Person. *"Control"* for this definition means the power to direct the management and policies of a Person, directly or indirectly, whether through the ownership of voting securities, by contract, or otherwise. The terms "controlling" and "controlled" have meanings correlative to the foregoing.

"Agent." Any Registrar, Paying Agent or Conversion Agent.

"Board." The Board of Directors of the Person or any officer or committee thereof authorized to act for such Board.

"Business Day." A day that is not a Legal Holiday.

"Company." The party named as such above until a successor which duly assumes the obligations upon the Securities and under the Indenture replaces it and thereafter means the successor.

"Debt" means, with respect to any Person, (i) any obligation of such Person to pay the principal of, premium of, if any, interest on (including interest accruing on or after the filing of any petition in bankruptcy or for reorganization relating to the Company, whether or not a claim for such post-petition interest is allowed in such proceeding), penalties, reimbursement or indemnification amounts, fees, expenses or other amounts relating to any indebtedness, and any other liability, contingent or otherwise, of such Person (A) for borrowed money (including instances where the recourse of the lender is to the whole of the assets of such Person or to a portion thereof), (B) evidenced by a note, debenture or similar instrument (including a purchase money obligation) including securities, (C) for any letter of credit or performance bond in favor of such Person, or (D) for the payment of money relating to a capitalized lease obligation; (ii) any liability of others of the kind described in the preceding clause (i), which the Person has guaranteed or which is otherwise its legal liability; (iii) any obligation of the type described in clauses (i) and (ii) secured by a lien to which the property or assets of such Person are subject, whether or not the obligations secured thereby shall have been assumed by or shall otherwise be such Person's legal liability; and (iv) any and all deferrals, renewals, extensions and refunding of, or amendments, modifications or supplements to, any liability of the kind described in any of the preceding clauses (i), (ii) or (iii).

"Default." Any event which is, or after notice or passage of time would be, an Event of Default.

"Exchange Act." The Securities Exchange Act of 1934, as amended.

"Holder" or *"Securityholder."* A Person in whose name a Security is registered.

"Indenture." This Indenture as amended from time to time, including the terms of the Securities and any amendments.

"Officers' Certificate." A certificate signed by two Officers, one of whom must be the President, the Treasure or a Vice-President of the Company. See Sections 12.03 and 12.04.

"*Opinion of Counsel.*" Written opinion from legal counsel who is acceptable to the Trustee. See Sections 12.03 and 12.04.

"*Person.*" Any individual, corporation, partnership, joint venture, association, limited liability company, joint stock company, trust, unincorporated organization or government or other agency or political subdivision thereof.

"*Principal*" of a Security means the principal of the Security plus the premium, if any, on the Security which is due or overdue or is to become due at the relevant time.

"*Proceeding.*" A liquidation, dissolution, bankruptcy, insolvency, reorganization, receivership or similar proceeding under Bankruptcy Law, an assignment for the benefit of creditors, any marshalling of assets or liabilities, or winding up or dissolution, but shall not include any transaction permitted by and made in compliance with Article 5.

"*Representative.*" The indenture trustee or other trustee, agent or representative for an issue of Senior Debt.

"*SEC.*" The U.S. Securities and Exchange Commission.

"*Securities.*" The Securities described above issued under this Indenture.

"*Senior Debt.*" Debt of the Company whenever incurred, outstanding at any time except (i) Debt that by its terms is not senior in right of payment to the Securities, (ii) Debt held by the Company or any Affiliate of the Company, and (iii) Debt excluded by Section 12.09.

"*TIA.*" The Trust Indenture Act of 1939 (15 U.S.C. §§77aaa-77bbbb), as amended, as in effect on the date of this Indenture, except as provided in Sections 1.04 and 9.03.

"*Trust Officer.*" Any officer or assistant officer of the Trustee assigned by the Trustee to administer its corporate trust matters or to whom a matter concerning the Indenture may be referred.

"*Trustee.*" The party named as such above until a successor replaces it and thereafter means the successor. See also Section 11.14.

"*U.S. Government Obligations.*" Securities that are direct, noncallable, nonredeemable obligations of, or noncallable, nonredeemable obligations guaranteed by, the United States for the timely payment of which obligation or guarantee the full faith and credit of the United States is pledged, or funds consisting solely of such securities, including funds managed by the Trustee or one of its Affiliates (including such funds for which it or its Affiliates receives fees in connection with such management).

Section 1.02. **Other Definitions.**

Term	Defined in Section
"*Bankruptcy Law*"	6.01
"*Common Stock*"	10.01
"*Conversion Agent*"	2.03
"*Custodian*"	6.01
"*Defaulted Interest*"	2.13
"*Distribution*"	11.14
"*Event of Default*"	6.01
"*Junior Securities*"	11.13
"*Legal Holiday*"	12.06

Term	Defined in Section
"Notice"	12.01
"Officer"	12.09
"Paying Agent"	2.03
"Payment Blockage Period"	11.14
"Proceeding"	1.01
"Quoted Price"	10.11
"Registrar"	2.03
"Senior Debt Default Notice"	11.14
"Senior Debt Payment Default"	11.14

Section 1.03. Rules of Construction.

Unless the context otherwise requires:

(1) a term defined in Section 1.01 or 1.02 has the meaning assigned to it therein, and terms defined in the TIA have the meanings assigned to them in the TIA;

(2) an accounting term not otherwise defined has the meaning assigned to it in accordance with generally accepted accounting principles in the United States;

(3) "or" is not exclusive;

(4) words in the singular include the plural, and words in the plural include the singular;

(5) provisions apply to successive events and transactions;

(6) "herein," "hereof" and other words of similar import refer to this Indenture as a whole and not to any particular Article, Section or other subdivision; and

(7) "including" means including without limitation.

Section 1.04. Trust Indenture Act.

The provisions of TIA Sections 310 through 317 that impose duties on any Person (including the provisions automatically deemed included herein unless expressly excluded by this Indenture) are a part of and govern this Indenture upon and so long as the Indenture and Securities are subject to the TIA. If any provision of this Indenture limits, qualifies or conflicts with such duties, the imposed duties shall control. If a provision of the TIA requires or permits a provision of this Indenture and the TIA provision is amended, then the Indenture provision shall be automatically amended to like effect.

[Any reference to a requirement under the TIA shall only apply upon and so long as the Indenture is qualified under and subject to the TIA.]

ARTICLE 2
THE SECURITIES

Section 2.01. Form and Dating.

The Securities and the certificate of authentication shall be substantially in the form of Exhibit A, which is hereby incorporated in and expressly made a part of this Indenture. The Securities may have notations, legends or endorsements required by

Section 2.11, law, stock exchange rule, automated quotation system, agreements to which the Company is subject, or usage. Each Security shall be dated the date of its authentication.

Section 2.02. Execution and Authentication.

Two Officers shall sign the Securities for the Company by manual or facsimile signature.

If an Officer whose signature is on a Security no longer holds that office at the time the Security is authenticated, the Security is still valid.

A Security shall not be valid until an authorized signatory of the Trustee manually signs the certificate of authentication on the Security. The signature shall be conclusive evidence that the Security has been authenticated under this Indenture.

The Trustee shall authenticate Securities for original issue up to the amount stated in paragraph 4 of Exhibit A in accordance with an Officers' Certificate of the Company. The aggregate principal amount of Securities outstanding at any time may not exceed that amount except as provided in Section 2.07.

The Trustee may appoint an authenticating agent acceptable to the Company to authenticate Securities. An authenticating agent may authenticate Securities whenever the Trustee may do so. Each reference in this Indenture to authentication by the Trustee includes authentication by such agent. An authenticating agent has the same rights as an Agent to deal with the Company or an Affiliate.

Section 2.03. Agents.

The Company shall maintain an office or agency where Securities may be presented for registration of transfer or for exchange ("Registrar"), where Securities may be presented for payment ("Paying Agent") and where Securities may be presented for conversion ("Conversion Agent"). Whenever the Company must issue or deliver Securities pursuant to this Indenture, the Trustee shall authenticate the Securities at the Company's request. The Registrar shall keep a register of the Securities and of their transfer and exchange.

The Company may appoint more than one Registrar, Paying Agent or Conversion Agent. The Company shall notify the Trustee of the name and address of any Agent not a party to this Indenture. If the Company does not appoint another Registrar, Paying Agent, or Conversion Agent, the Trustee shall act as such.

Section 2.04. Paying Agent To Hold Money in Trust.

On or prior to each due date of the Principal and interest on any Security, the Company shall deposit with the Paying Agent a sum sufficient to pay such Principal and interest when so becoming due. The Company shall require each Paying Agent (other than the Trustee) to agree in writing that the Paying Agent will hold in trust for the benefit of Securityholders or the Trustee all money held by the Paying Agent for the payment of the Principal of or interest on the Securities, will notify the Trustee of any Default by the Company in making any such payment, and will comply with Article 11. While any such Default continues, the Trustee may require a Paying

Agent to pay all money held by it to the Trustee. The Company at any time may require a Paying Agent to pay all money held by it to the Trustee and to account for any funds disbursed by the Paying Agent. Upon complying with this Section, the Paying Agent shall have no further liability for the money delivered to the Trustee. If the Company or any Affiliate acts as Paying Agent, it shall segregate the money held by it as Paying Agent and hold it as a separate trust fund.

Section 2.05. Securityholder Lists.

The Trustee shall preserve in as current a form as is reasonably practicable the most recent list available to it of the names and addresses of Securityholders. If the Trustee is not the Registrar, the Company shall furnish to the Trustee, in writing at least 10 Business Days before each interest payment date and at such other times as the Trustee may request, a list in such form and as of such date as the Trustee may reasonably require of the names and addresses of Securityholders.

Section 2.06. Transfer and Exchange.

The Securities shall be issued in registered form and shall be transferable only upon surrender of a Security for registration of transfer. When a Security is presented to the Register with a request to register a transfer or to exchange them for an equal principal amount of Securities of other denominations, the Registrar shall register the transfer or make the exchange if its requirements for such transactions are met and the Security has not been redeemed. The Company may charge a reasonable fee for any registration of transfer or exchange but not for any exchange pursuant to Section 2.10, 3.06, 9.05 or 10.02.

All Securities issued upon any transfer or exchange pursuant to the terms of this Indenture will evidence the same debt and will be entitled to the same benefits under this Indenture as the Securities surrendered upon such transfer or exchange.

Section 2.07. Replacement Securities.

If the Holder of a Security claims that the Security has been lost, destroyed or wrongfully taken, then, in the absence of notice to the Company that the Security has been acquired by a protected purchaser, the Company shall issue a replacement Security. If required by the Trustee or the Company, an indemnity bond must be provided which is sufficient in the judgment of both to protect the Company, the Trustee and the Agents from any loss which any of them may suffer if a Security is replaced. The Company or the Trustee may charge the Holder for its expenses in replacing a Security.

Every replacement Security is an additional obligation of the Company.

Section 2.08. Outstanding Securities.

Securities outstanding at any time are all Securities authenticated by the Trustee except for those canceled by the Registrar, those delivered to it for cancellation and those described in this Section as not outstanding. A Security does not cease to be outstanding because the Company or an Affiliate holds the Security.

If a Security is replaced pursuant to Section 2.07, it ceases to be outstanding unless the Company receives proof satisfactory to it that the replaced Security is held by a protected purchaser.

If Securities are considered paid under Section 4.01, they cease to be outstanding and interest on them ceases to accrue.

Section 2.09. Treasury Securities Disregarded for Certain Purposes.

In determining whether the Holders of the required Principal amount of Securities have concurred in any direction, waiver or consent, Securities owned by the Company or an Affiliate shall be disregarded and deemed not to be outstanding, except that, for the purposes of determining whether the Trustee shall be protected in relying on any such direction, waiver or consent, only Securities which the Trustee knows are so owned shall be so disregarded. Securities so owned which have been pledged in good faith shall not be disregarded if the pledgee establishes to the satisfaction of the Trustee the pledgee's right to deliver any such direction, waiver or consent with respect to the Securities and that the pledgee is not the Company or any other obligor upon the Securities or any Affiliate of the Company or of such other obligor.

Section 2.10. Temporary Securities.

Until definitive Securities are ready for delivery, the Company may use temporary Securities. Temporary Securities shall be substantially in the form of definitive Securities but may have variations that the Company considers appropriate for temporary Securities. Without unreasonable delay, the Company shall deliver definitive Securities in exchange for temporary Securities.

Section 2.11. Global Securities.

The Company may issue some or all of the Securities in temporary or permanent global form. The Company may issue a global Security only to a depository. A depository may transfer a global Security only to its nominee or to a successor depository. A global Security shall represent the amount of Securities specified in the global Security. A global Security may have variations that the depository requires or that the Company considers appropriate for such a security.

Beneficial owners of part or all of a global Security are subject to the rules of the depository as in effect from time to time.

The Company, the Trustee and the Agents shall not be responsible for any acts or omissions of a depository, for any depository records of beneficial ownership interests or for any transactions between the depository and beneficial owners.

Section 2.12. Cancellation.

The Company at any time may deliver Securities to the Trustee for cancellation. The Paying Agent and Conversion Agent, if not the Trustee, shall forward to the

Trustee any Securities surrendered to them for payment or conversion. The Trustee shall cancel all Securities surrendered for registration of transfer, exchange, payment, conversion or cancellation and shall dispose of canceled Securities according to its standard procedures or as the Company otherwise directs. The Company may not issue new Securities to replace Securities that it has paid or which have been delivered to the Trustee for cancellation or that any Securityholder has converted.

Section 2.13. Defaulted Interest.

If the Company defaults in a payment of interest on the Securities ("Defaulted Interest") such Defaulted Interest shall cease to be payable to the Securityholder on the relevant record date and shall be paid by the Company, at its election, under either (1) or (2) below:

(1) The Company may pay the Defaulted Interest together with interest thereon to the Persons which are Securityholders on a subsequent special record date. The Company shall notify the Trustee of the amount of Defaulted Interest together with interest thereon to be paid and pay over such amount to the Trustee. The Trustee shall then fix a special record date and at the Company's expense shall notify Securityholders not less than 10 days prior to such special record date of the proposed payment, of the special record date, and of the payment date.

(2) The Company may make payment of Defaulted Interest together with interest thereon in any lawful manner not inconsistent with the requirements of any securities exchange or automated quotation system on which the Securities may be listed or designated for issuance. The Company shall give prompt notice to the Trustee and Securityholders that it intends to make payment pursuant to this Section 2.13(2) and of the special record date of the proposed payment, and of the payment date.

ARTICLE 3
REDEMPTION

Section 3.01. Notice to Trustee.

If Securities are to be redeemed, the Company shall notify the Trustee of the redemption date, the Principal amount of Securities to be redeemed and the provision of the Securities permitting or requiring the redemption.

The Company may reduce the Principal amount of Securities required to be redeemed pursuant to Paragraph Six of the Securities if it notifies the Trustee of the amount of the credit and the basis for it by delivery of an Officers' Certificate. If the reduction is based on a credit for redeemed, converted or canceled Securities that the Company has not previously delivered to the Trustee for cancellation, the Company shall deliver such Securities to the Registrar before the selection of securities to be redeemed.

The Company shall give each notice provided for in this Section at least 50 days before the redemption date unless a shorter period is satisfactory to the Trustee. If fewer than all the Securities are to be redeemed, the record date relating to such redemption shall be selected by the Company and given to the Trustee, which record date shall be not less than 15 days prior to the redemption date.

Section 3.02. Selection of Securities To Be Redeemed.

If less than all the Securities are to be redeemed, the Trustee shall select the Securities to be redeemed by a method that complies with the requirements, if any, of any stock exchange on which the Securities are listed and that the Trustee considers fair and appropriate, which may include selection pro rata or by lot. The Trustee shall make the selection from Securities outstanding not previously called for redemption. The Trustee may select for redemption portions of the Principal of Securities that have denominations larger than $1000. Securities and portions thereof selected by the Trustee shall be in amounts of $1000 or whole multiples of $1000. Provisions of this Indenture that apply to Securities called for redemption also apply to portions of Securities called for redemption.

Section 3.03. Notice of Redemption.

At least 30 days but not more than 60 days before a redemption date, the Company shall mail a notice of redemption to each Holder whose Securities are to be redeemed.

The notice shall state that it is a notice of redemption, identify the Securities to be redeemed and shall state:

(1) the redemption date;
(2) the redemption price;
(3) the conversion price;
(4) the name and address of the Paying Agent and Conversion Agent;
(5) that convertible Securities called for redemption may be converted at any time before the close of business on the Business Day immediately preceding the redemption date (unless the redemption date is also a record date for an interest payment, in which event they may be converted at any time through the redemption date);
(6) that Holders who want to convert Securities must satisfy the requirements for conversion set forth in the Securities;
(7) that Securities called for redemption must be surrendered to the Paying Agent to collect the redemption price;
(8) that, unless the Company defaults in making such redemption payment or the Paying Agent is prohibited from making such payment pursuant to the terms of this Indenture, interest on Securities (or portion thereof) called for redemption ceases to accrue on and after the redemption date; and
(9) list the CUSIP number of the Securities and state that no representation is made as to the correctness or accuracy of the CUSIP number, if any, listed in such notice or printed on the Securities.

At the Company's request, the Trustee shall give the notice of redemption in the Company's name and at its expense.

Section 3.04. Effect of Notice of Redemption.

Once notice of redemption is mailed, Securities called for redemption become due and payable on the redemption date at the redemption price. Upon surrender to the Paying Agent, such Securities shall be paid at the redemption price stated in the notice, plus accrued interest to the redemption price stated in the notice, plus accrued interest to the redemption date. Failure to give notice or any defect in the notice to any Holder shall not affect the validity of the notice to any other Holder.

Section 3.05. Deposit of Redemption Price.

On or before the redemption date, the Company shall deposit with the Paying Agent (or, if the Company or any Affiliate is the Paying Agent, shall segregate and hold in trust) money sufficient to pay the redemption price of, and accrued interest on, all Securities to be redeemed on that date other than Securities or portions of Securities called for redemption which have been delivered by the Company to the Registrar for cancellation. The Paying Agent shall return to the Company any money not required for that purpose because of conversion of Securities.

Unless the Company shall default in the payment of Securities (and accrued interest) called for redemption, interest on such Securities shall cease to accrue after the redemption date. Securities called for redemption shall cease to be convertible after the close of business on the Business Day immediately preceding the redemption date (unless the redemption date is also a record date for an interest payment, in which event they may be converted through the redemption date), unless the Company shall default in the payment of such Securities on the redemption date, in which event the Securities shall remain convertible until paid (together with accrued interest).

Section 3.06. Securities Redeemed in Part.

Upon surrender of a Security that is redeemed in part, the Company shall deliver to the Holder (at the Company's expense) a new Security equal in Principal amount to the unredeemed portion of the Security surrendered.

ARTICLE 4
COVENANTS

Section 4.01. Payment of Securities.

The Company shall pay the Principal of and interest on the Securities on the dates and in the manner provided in the Securities and this Indenture. Principal and interest shall be considered paid on the date due if the Paying Agent holds in accordance with this Indenture on that date money sufficient to pay all Principal and interest then due and the Paying Agent is not prohibited from paying such money to the Holders on such date pursuant to the terms of this Indenture.

The Company shall pay interest on overdue Principal at the rate borne by the Securities; it shall pay interest on overdue Defaulted Interest at the same rate to the extent lawful.

Section 4.02. SEC Reports.

The Company shall file with the Trustee within 15 days after it files them with the SEC copies of the annual reports and of the information, documents and other reports which the Company is required to file with the SEC pursuant to Section 13 or 15(d) of the Exchange Act. The Company will cause any quarterly and annual reports which it makes available to its stockholders to be mailed to the Holders. The Company will also comply with the other provisions of TIA Section 314(a). Delivery of such reports, information and documents to the Trustee is for informational purposes only and the Trustee's receipt of such shall not constitute notice or constructive notice of any information contained therein or determinable from information contained therein, including the Company's compliance with any of its covenants hereunder (as to which the Trustee is entitled to rely exclusively on Officers' Certificates).

Section 4.03. Compliance Certificate.

The Company shall deliver to the Trustee, within [105] days after the end of each fiscal year of the Company, a brief certificate signed by the principal executive officer, principal financial officer or principal accounting officer of the Company, as to the signer's knowledge of the Company's compliance with all conditions and covenants contained in this Indenture (determined without regard to any period of grace or requirement of notice provided herein).

Section 4.04. Notice of Certain Events.

The Company shall give prompt written notice to the Trustee and any Paying Agent of (i) any Proceeding, (ii) any Default or Event of Default, (iii) any cure or waiver of any Default or Event of Default, (iv) any Senior Debt Payment Default or Senior Debt Default Notice, and (v) if and when the Securities are listed on any stock exchange.

ARTICLE 5
SUCCESSORS

Section 5.01. When Company May Merge, etc.

The Company shall not consolidate or merge with or into, or transfer all or substantially all of its assets to, any Person unless:

(1) either the Company shall be the resulting or surviving entity or such Person is a corporation organized and existing under the laws of the United States, a State thereof or the District of Columbia;

(2) if the Company is not the resulting or surviving entity, such Person assumes by supplemental indenture all the obligations of the Company under the Securities and this Indenture, except that it need not assume the obligations of the Company as to conversion of Securities if pursuant to Section 10.17 the Company or another Person enters into a supplemental indenture obligating it to deliver securities, cash or other assets upon conversion of Securities; and

(3) immediately before and immediately after the transaction no Default exists.

The Company shall deliver to the Trustee prior to the proposed transaction an Officers' Certificate and an Opinion of Counsel, each of which shall state that such consolidation, merger or transfer and such supplemental indenture comply with this Article 5 and that all conditions precedent herein provided for relating to such transaction have been complied with.

Section 5.02. Successor Corporation Substituted.

Upon any consolidation or merger, or any transfer of all or substantially all of the assets of the Company in accordance with Section 5.01, the successor corporation formed by such consolidation or into which the Company is merged or to which such transfer is made shall succeed to, and be substituted for, and may exercise every right and power of, the Company under this Indenture and the Securities with the same effect as if such successor corporation had been named as the Company herein and in the Securities. Thereafter the obligations of the Company under the Securities and Indenture shall terminate except for (i) obligations the Company may have under a supplemental indenture pursuant to Section 10.17 and (ii) in the case of a transfer, the obligation to pay the Principal of and interest on the Securities.

ARTICLE 6
DEFAULTS AND REMEDIES

Section 6.01. Events of Default.

An "Event of Default" occurs if:

(1) the Company fails to pay interest on any Security when the same becomes due and payable and such failure continues for a period of [30] days;

(2) the Company fails to pay the Principal of any Security when the same becomes due and payable at maturity, upon redemption or otherwise;

(3) the Company fails to comply with any of its other agreements in the Securities or this Indenture and such failure continues for the period and after the notice specified below;

(4) the Company pursuant to or within the meaning of any Bankruptcy Law:

(A) commences a voluntary case,

(B) consents to the entry of an order for relief against it in an involuntary case,

(C) consents to the appointment of a Custodian of it or for all or substantially all of its property, or

(D) makes a general assignment for the benefit of its creditors;
or

(5) a court of competent jurisdiction enters an order or decree under any Bankruptcy Law that:

(A) is for relief against the Company in an involuntary case,

(B) appoints a Custodian of the Company or for all or substantially all of its property, or

(C) orders the liquidation of the Company, and the order or decree remains unstayed and in effect for 60 days.

The foregoing will constitute Events of Default whatever the reason for any such Event of Default, whether it is voluntary or involuntary, a consequence of the application of Article 11, or is effected by operation of law or pursuant to any judgment, decree or order of any court or any order, rule or regulation of any administrative or governmental body.

The term "Bankruptcy Law" means title 11 of the U.S. Code or any similar Federal or state law for the relief of debtors. The term "Custodian" means any receiver, trustee, assignee, liquidator or similar official under any Bankruptcy Law.

A Default under clause (3) is not an Event of Default until the Trustee or the Holders of at least [25]% in Principal amount of the Securities notify the Company and the Trustee of the Default and the Company does not cure the Default, or it is not waived, within [60] days after receipt of the notice. The notice must specify the Default, demand that it be remedied to the extent consistent with law, and state that the notice is a "Notice of Default."

Section 6.02. Acceleration.

If an Event of Default occurs and is continuing, the Trustee by notice to the Company, or the Holders of at least 25% in Principal amount of the Securities by notice to the Company and the Trustee, may declare the Principal of and accrued and unpaid interest on all the Securities to be due and payable. Upon such declaration the Principal and interest shall be due and payable immediately.

The Holders of a majority in Principal amount of the Securities by notice to the Company and the Trustee may rescind an acceleration and its consequences if the rescission would not conflict with any judgment or decree and if all existing Events of Default have been cured or waived except nonpayment of Principal or interest that has become due solely because of the acceleration.

Section 6.03. Other Remedies.

If an Event of Default occurs and is continuing, the Trustee may pursue any available remedy to collect the payment of Principal or interest on the Securities or to enforce the performance of any provision of the Securities or this Indenture.

The Trustee may maintain a proceeding even if it does not possess any of the Securities or does not produce any of them in the proceeding. A delay or omission by the Trustee or any Securityholder in exercising any right or remedy accruing upon an Event of Default shall not impair the right or remedy or constitute a waiver of or acquiescence in the Event of Default. All remedies are cumulative to the extent permitted by law.

Section 6.04. Waiver of Past Defaults.

The Holders of a majority in Principal amount of the Securities by notice to the Trustee may waive an existing Default and its consequences except:

(1) a Default in the payment of the Principal of or interest on any Security;
(2) a Default with respect to a provision that under Section 9.02 cannot be amended without the consent of each Securityholder affected; or
(3) a Default under Article 10.

Section 6.05. Control by Majority.

The Holders of a majority in Principal amount of the Securities may direct the time, method and place of conducting any proceeding for any remedy available to the

Trustee or exercising any trust or power conferred on the Trustee. However, the Trustee may refuse to follow any direction that conflicts with law or this Indenture, is unduly prejudicial to the rights of other Securityholders, or would involve the Trustee in personal liability or expense for which the Trustee has not received a satisfactory indemnity.

Section 6.06. Limitation on Suits.

A Securityholder may pursue a remedy with respect to this Indenture or the Securities only if:

> (1) the Holder gives to the Trustee notice of a continuing Event of Default;
> (2) the Holders of at least 25% in Principal amount of the Securities make a request to the Trustee to pursue the remedy;
> (3) the Trustee either (i) gives to such Holders notice it will not comply with the request, or (ii) does not comply with the request within [15 or 30] days after receipt of the request; and
> (4) the Holders of a majority in Principal amount of the Securities do not give the Trustee a direction inconsistent with the request prior to the earlier of the date, if ever, on which the Trustee delivers a notice under Section 6.06(3)(i) or the expiration of the period described in Section 6.06(3)(ii).

A Securityholder may not use this Indenture to prejudice the rights of another Securityholder or to obtain a preference or priority over another Securityholder.

Section 6.07. Rights of Holders To Receive Payment.

Notwithstanding any other provision of this Indenture, the right of any Holder of a Security to receive payment of Principal and interest on the Security, on or after the respective due dates expressed in the Security, or to bring suit for the enforcement of any such payment on or after such respective dates, shall not be impaired or affected without the consent of the Holder.

Notwithstanding any other provision of this Indenture, the right of any Holder of a Security to bring suit for the enforcement of the right to convert the Security shall not be impaired or affected without the consent of the Holder.

Nothing in this Indenture limits or defers the right or ability of Holders to petition for commencement of a case under applicable Bankruptcy Law to the extent consistent with such Bankruptcy Law.

Section 6.08. Priorities.

After an Event of Default any money or other property distributable in respect of the Company's obligations under this Indenture shall be paid in the following order:

First: to the Trustee (including any predecessor Trustee) for amounts due under Section 7.07;

Second: to holders of Senior Debt to the extent required by Article 11;

Third: to Securityholders for amounts due and unpaid on the Securities for Principal and interest, ratably, without preference or priority of any kind, according to the amounts due and payable on the Securities for Principal and interest, respectively; and

Fourth: to the Company.

The Trustee may fix a record date and payment date for any payment to Securityholders.

Section 6.09. Undertaking for Costs.

In any suit for the enforcement of any right or remedy under this Indenture or in any suit against the Trustee for any action taken or omitted by it as Trustee, a court in its discretion may require the filing by any party litigant in the suit of an undertaking to pay the costs of the suit, and the court in its discretion may assess reasonable costs, including reasonable attorneys' fees, against any party litigant in the suit, having due regard to the merits and good faith of the claims or defenses made by the party litigant. This Section does not apply to a suit by the Trustee, a suit by a Holder pursuant to Section 6.07 or a suit by Holders of more than 10% in Principal amount of the Securities.

Section 6.10. Proof of Claim.

In the event of any Proceeding, the Trustee may (and, if applicable, the trustee for or holders of Senior Debt may) file a claim for the unpaid balance of the Securities in the form required in the Proceeding and cause the claim to be approved or allowed. Nothing herein contained shall be deemed to authorize the Trustee or the holders of Senior Debt to authorize or consent to or accept or adopt on behalf of any Securityholder any plan of reorganization, arrangement, adjustment, or composition affecting the Securities or the rights of any Holder thereof, or to authorize the Trustee or the holders of Senior Debt to vote in respect of the claim of any Securityholder in any Proceeding.

Section 6.11. Actions of a Holder.

For the purpose of providing any consent, waiver or instruction to the Company or the Trustee, a "Holder" or "Securityholder" shall include a Person who provides to the Company or the Trustee, as the case may be, an affidavit of beneficial ownership of a Security together with a satisfactory indemnity against any loss, liability or expense to such party to the extent that it acts upon such affidavit of beneficial ownership (including any consent, waiver or instructions given by a Person providing such affidavit and indemnity).

ARTICLE 7
TRUSTEE

Section 7.01. Duties of Trustee.

(a) If an Event of Default has occurred and is continuing, the Trustee shall exercise such of the rights and powers vested in it by this Indenture, and use the same degree of care and skill in their exercise, as a prudent person would exercise or use under the circumstances in the conduct of its own affairs.

(b) Except during the continuance of an Event of Default:

(1) The Trustee need perform only those duties that are specifically set forth in this Indenture and no others.

(2) In the absence of bad faith on its part, the Trustee may conclusively rely, as to the truth of the statements and the correctness of the opinions expressed therein, upon certificates or opinions furnished to the Trustee and conforming to the requirements of this Indenture. However, the Trustee shall examine the certificates and opinions to determine whether or not they conform to the requirements of this Indenture.

(c) The Trustee may not be relieved from liability for its own negligent action, its own negligent failure to act or its own willful misconduct, except that:

(1) This paragraph does not limit the effect of paragraph (b) of this Section.

(2) The Trustee shall not be liable for any error of judgment made in good faith by a Trust Officer, unless it is proved that the Trustee was negligent in ascertaining the pertinent facts.

(3) The Trustee shall not be liable with respect to any action it takes or omits to take in good faith in accordance with a direction received by it pursuant to Section 6.05.

(4) The Trustee may refuse to perform any duty or exercise any right or power which would require it to expend its own funds or risk any liability if it shall reasonably believe that repayment of such funds or adequate indemnity against such risk is not reasonably assured to it.

(d) Every provision of this Indenture that in any way relates to the Trustee is subject to paragraphs (a), (b) and (c) of this Section.

(e) The Trustee shall not be liable for interest on any money received by it except as the Trustee may agree with the Company. Money held in trust by the Trustee need not be segregated from other funds except to the extent required by law.

Section 7.02. Rights of Trustee.

(a) The Trustee may rely on any document believed by it to be genuine and to have been signed or presented by the proper Person. The Trustee need not investigate any fact or matter stated in the document.

(b) Before the Trustee acts or refrains from acting, it may require an Officers' Certificate or an Opinion of Counsel. The Trustee shall not be liable for any action it takes or omits to take in good faith in reliance on the Officers' Certificate or an Opinion of Counsel. The Trustee may also consult with counsel on any matter relating to the Indenture or the Securities and the Trustee shall not be liable for any action it takes or omits to take in good faith in reliance on the advice of counsel.

(c) The Trustee may act through agents and shall not be responsible for the misconduct or negligence of any agent appointed with due care.

(d) The Trustee shall not be liable for any action it takes or omits to take in good faith which it believes to be authorized or within its rights or powers.

(e) Except in connection with compliance with TIA Section 310 or 311, the Trustee shall only be charged with knowledge of Trust Officers.

Section 7.03. Individual Rights of Trustee; Disqualification.

The Trustee in its individual or any other capacity may become the owner or pledgee of Securities and may otherwise deal with the Company or an Affiliate with the same rights it would have if it were not Trustee. Any Agent may do the same with like rights. However, the Trustee is subject to TIA Sections 310(b) and 311.

Section 7.04. Trustee's Disclaimer.

The Trustee shall have no responsibility for the validity or adequacy of this Indenture or the Securities, it shall not be accountable for the Company's use of the proceeds from the Securities and it shall not be responsible for any statement in the Securities other than its authentication.

Section 7.05. Notice of Defaults.

If a continuing Default is known to the Trustee, the Trustee shall mail to Securityholders a notice of the Default within 90 days after it occurs. Except in the case of a Default in payment on any Security, the Trustee may withhold the notice if and so long as a committee of its Trust Officers in good faith determines that withholding the notice is in the interests of Securityholders. [The Trustee shall mail to Securityholders any notice it receives from Securityholder(s) under Section 6.06, and of any notice the Trustee provides pursuant to Section 6.06(3)(i).]

Section 7.06. Reports by Trustee to Holders.

If required pursuant to TIA Section 313(a), within 60 days after the reporting date stated in Section 12.09, the Trustee shall mail to Securityholders a brief report dated as of such reporting date that complies with TIA Section 313(a). The Trustee also shall comply with TIA Section 313(b)(2).

A copy of each report at the time of its mailing to Securityholders shall be filed with the SEC and each stock exchange on which the Securities are listed.

Section 7.07. Compensation and Indemnity.

The Company shall pay to the Trustee from time to time reasonable compensation for its services, including for any Agent capacity in which it acts. The Trustee's compensation shall not be limited by any law on compensation of a trustee of an express trust. The Company shall reimburse the Trustee upon request for all reasonable out-of-pocket expenses incurred by it. Such expenses shall include the reasonable compensation and out-of-pocket expenses of the Trustee's agents and counsel.

The Company shall indemnify the Trustee against any loss, liability or expense incurred by it including in any Agent capacity in which it acts. The Trustee shall notify the Company promptly of any claim for which it may seek indemnity. The Company shall defend the claim and the Trustee shall cooperate in the defense. The Trustee may have separate counsel and the Company shall pay the reasonable fees and expenses of such counsel. The Company need not pay for any settlement made without its consent, which consent shall not unreasonably be withheld.

The Company need not reimburse any expense or indemnify against any loss or liability incurred by the Trustee through gross negligence, willful misconduct or bad faith.

To secure the Company's payment obligations in this Section, the Trustee shall have a lien prior to the Securities on all money or property held or collected by the Trustee, except that held in trust to pay Principal and interest on particular Securities.

Without prejudice to its rights hereunder, when the Trustee incurs expenses or renders services after an Event of Default specified in Section 6.01(4) or (5) occurs, the expenses and the compensation for the services are intended to constitute expenses of administration under any Bankruptcy Law.

Section 7.08. Replacement of Trustee.

A resignation or removal of the Trustee and appointment of a successor Trustee shall become effective only upon the successor Trustee's acceptance of appointment as provided in this Section.

The Trustee may resign by so notifying the Company. The Holders of a majority in Principal amount of the Securities may remove the Trustee by so notifying the Trustee and the Company. The Company may remove the Trustee if:

(1) the Trustee fails to comply with Section 7.10;
(2) the Trustee is adjudged a bankrupt or an insolvent;
(3) a receiver or public officer takes charge of the Trustee or its property; or
(4) the Trustee becomes incapable of acting.

If the Trustee resigns or is removed or if a vacancy exists in the office of Trustee for any reason, the Company shall promptly appoint a successor Trustee.

If a successor Trustee is not appointed and does not take office within 30 days after the retiring Trustee resigns, the retiring Trustee may appoint a successor Trustee at any time prior to the date on which a successor Trustee takes office. If a successor Trustee does not take office within [45] days after the retiring Trustee resigns or is removed, the retiring Trustee, the Company or, subject to Section 6.09, any Securityholder may petition any court of competent jurisdiction for the appointment of a successor Trustee.

If the Trustee fails to comply with Section 7.10, any Securityholder may petition any court of competent jurisdiction for the removal of the Trustee and the appointment of a successor Trustee. Within one year after a successor Trustee appointed by the Company or a court pursuant to this Section 7.08 takes office, the Holders of a majority in Principal amount of the Securities may appoint a successor Trustee to replace such successor Trustee.

A successor Trustee shall deliver a written acceptance of its appointment to the retiring Trustee and to the Company. Thereupon the resignation or removal of the retiring Trustee shall become effective, and the successor Trustee shall have all the rights, powers and duties of the Trustee under this Indenture. The successor Trustee shall mail a notice of its succession to Securityholders. The retiring Trustee shall promptly transfer all property held by it as Trustee to the successor Trustee, subject to the lien provided for in Section 7.07.

Section 7.09. Successor Trustee by Merger, etc.

If the Trustee consolidates, merges or converts into, or transfers all or substantially all of its corporate trust business to, another corporation, the successor corporation without any further act shall be the successor Trustee, if such successor corporation is eligible and qualified under Section 7.10.

Section 7.10. Eligibility.

This Indenture shall always have a Trustee who satisfies the requirements of TIA Sections 310(a)(1) and 310(a)(2). The Trustee shall always have a combined capital and surplus as stated in Section 12.09.

Section 7.11. Preferential Collection of Claims Against Company.

Upon and so long as the Indenture is qualified under the TIA, the Trustee is subject to TIA Section 311(a), excluding any creditor relationship listed in TIA Section 311(b). A Trustee who has resigned or been removed is subject to TIA Section 311(a) to the extent indicated.

ARTICLE 8
SATISFACTION AND DISCHARGE

Section 8.01. Satisfaction and Discharge of Indenture.

This Indenture shall cease to be of further effect (except as to any surviving rights of conversion, registration of transfer or exchange of Securities expressly provided for herein), and the Trustee, on demand of and at expense of the Company, shall execute proper instruments acknowledging satisfaction and discharge of this Indenture, when

(1) either
  (A) all Securities theretofore authenticated and delivered (other than (i) Securities which have been destroyed, lost or stolen and which have been replaced or paid as provided in Section 2.07 and (ii) Securities for whose payment money has theretofore been deposited in trust or segregated and held in trust by the Company and thereafter repaid to the Company or discharged from such trust, as provided in Section 8.04) have been delivered to the Trustee for cancellation; or
  (B) all such Securities not theretofore delivered to the Trustee for cancellation
    (i) have become due and payable, or
    (ii) will become due and payable at their stated maturity within one year, or
    (iii) are to be called for redemption within one year under arrangements satisfactory to the Trustee for the giving of notice of redemption by the Trustee in the name, and at the expense, of the Company, and the Company in the case of (i), (ii), and (iii) above, has deposited or caused to be deposited with the Trustee as trust funds in trust for the purpose an amount of money or U.S. Government Obligations sufficient to pay and discharge the entire indebtedness on such Securities not theretofore delivered to the Trustee for cancellation, for Principal and interest to the date of such deposit (in the case of

Securities which have become due and payable) or to the stated maturity or redemption date, as the case may be;

(2) the Company has paid or caused to be paid all other sums payable hereunder by the Company; and

(3) the Company has delivered to the Trustee an Officers' Certificate and an Opinion of Counsel, each stating that all conditions precedent herein provided for relating to the satisfaction and discharge of this Indenture have been complied with.

Notwithstanding the satisfaction and discharge of this Indenture, the obligations of the Company to the Holders under Section 4.01, to the Trustee under Section 7.07, and, if money or U.S. Government Obligations shall have been deposited with the Trustee pursuant to subclause (B) of Clause (1) of this Section, the obligations of the Trustee under Section 8.02 shall survive.

Section 8.02. Application of Trust Funds.

The Trustee or Paying Agent shall hold in trust, for the benefit of the Holders, all money and U.S. Government Obligations deposited with it (or into which such money and U.S. Government Obligations are reinvested) pursuant to Section 8.01. It shall apply such deposited money and money from U.S. Government Obligations in accordance with this Indenture to the payment of the Principal and interest on the Securities. Money and U.S. Government Obligations so held in trust (i) are not subject to Article 11 and (ii) are subject to the Trustee's rights under Section 7.07.

Section 8.03. Reinstatement.

If the Trustee or Paying Agent is unable to apply any money or U.S. Obligations in accordance with Section 8.01 by reason of any order or judgment of any court or governmental authority enjoining, restraining or otherwise prohibiting such application, then the Company's obligations under this Indenture and the Securities shall be revived and reinstated as though no deposit had occurred pursuant to this Article 8, until such time as the Trustee or Paying Agent is permitted to apply all such money or U.S. Government Obligations in accordance with Section 8.01; provided, however, that if the Company makes any payment of Principal of or interest on any Security following the reinstatement of its obligations, the Company shall be subrogated to the rights of the Holders of such Securities to receive such payment from the money or U.S. Government Obligations held by the Trustee or Paying Agent after payment in full to the Holders.

Section 8.04. Repayment to Company.

The Trustee and Paying Agent shall promptly turn over to the Company upon request any excess money or U.S. Government Obligations held by them at any time. All money or U.S. Government Obligations deposited with the Trustee pursuant to Section 8.01 (and held by it or a Paying Agent) for the payment of Securities subsequently converted shall be returned to the Company upon request.

The Trustee and the Paying Agent shall pay to the Company upon request any money held by them for payment of Principal or interest that remains unclaimed for two years after the right to such money has matured. After payment to the Company, Securityholders entitled to the money shall look to the Company for payment as unsecured general creditors unless an abandoned property law designates another Person.

ARTICLE 9
AMENDMENTS

Section 9.01. **Without Consent of Holders.**

The Company and the Trustee may amend this Indenture or the Securities without the consent of any Securityholder:

> (1) to cure any ambiguity, defect or inconsistency;
> (2) to comply with Section 5.01, 10.06 or 10.17; or
> (3) to make any change that does not adversely affect the rights of any Securityholder.

Section 9.02. **With Consent of Holders.**

The Company and the Trustee may amend this Indenture or the Securities with the written consent of the Holders of at least a majority in Principal amount of the Securities. However, without the consent of each Securityholder affected, an amendment under this Section may not:

> (1) reduce the amount of Securities whose Holders must consent to an amendment;
> (2) reduce the interest on or change the time for payment of interest on any Security;
> (3) reduce the Principal of or change the fixed maturity of any Security;
> (4) reduce the premium payable upon the redemption of any Security [or change the time at which any Security may or shall be redeemed];
> (5) make any Security payable in money other than that stated in the Security;
> (6) make any change in Section 6.04, 6.07 or 9.02 (second sentence);
> (7) make any change that adversely affects the right to convert any Security; or
> (8) make any change in Article 11 that adversely affects the rights of any Securityholder.

It shall not be necessary for the consent of the Holders under this Section to approve the particular form of any proposed amendment, but it shall be sufficient if such consent approves the substance thereof.

An amendment under this Section may not make any change that adversely affects the rights under Article 11 of any Senior Debt unless it consents to the change.

Section 9.03. **Compliance with Trust Indenture Act and Section 12.03.**

Every amendment to this Indenture or the Securities shall comply with the TIA as then in effect, so long as the Indenture and Securities are subject to the TIA. The Trustee is entitled to, and the Company shall provide an Opinion of Counsel and Officers' Certificate that the Trustee's execution of any amendment or supplemental indenture is permitted under this Article 9.

Section 9.04. Revocation and Effect of Consents and Waivers.

A consent to an amendment or a waiver by a Holder of a Security shall bind the Holder and every subsequent Holder of that Security or portion of the Security that evidences the same debt as the consenting Holder's Security, even if notation of the consent or waiver is not made on the Security. However, any such Holder or subsequent Holder may revoke the consent or waiver as to such Holder's Security or portion of the Security if the Trustee receives the notice of revocation before the date the amendment or waiver becomes effective. After an amendment or waiver becomes effective, it shall bind every Securityholder.

The Company may, but shall not be obligated to, fix a record date for the purpose of determining the Securityholders entitled to give their consent or take any other action described above or required or permitted to be taken pursuant to this Indenture. If a record date is fixed, then notwithstanding the immediately preceding paragraph, those Persons who were Securityholders at such record date (or their duly designated proxies), and only those Persons, shall be entitled to give such consent or to revoke any consent previously given or take any such action, whether or not such Persons continue to be Holders after such record date. No such consent shall be valid or effective for more than 120 days after such record date.

Section 9.05. Notice of Amendment; Notation on or Exchange of Securities.

After any amendment under this Article becomes effective, the Company shall mail to Securityholders a notice briefly describing such amendment. The failure to give such notice to all Securityholders, or any defect therein, shall not impair or affect the validity of an amendment under this Article.

The Company or the Trustee may place an appropriate notation about an amendment or waiver on any Security thereafter authenticated. The Company may issue in exchange for affected Securities new Securities that reflect the amendment or waiver.

Section 9.06. Trustee Protected.

The Trustee need not sign any supplemental indenture that adversely affects its rights.

ARTICLE 10
CONVERSION

Section 10.01. Conversion Right and Conversion Price.

A Holder of a Security may convert it into Common Stock at any time during the period stated in paragraph 9 of the Securities. The number of shares issuable upon conversion of a Security is determined as follows: Divide the Principal amount to be converted by the conversion price in effect on the conversion date. Round the result to the nearest 1/100th of a share.

The initial conversion price is stated in paragraph 9 of the Securities. The conversion price is subject to adjustment in accordance with this Article.

A Holder may convert a portion of a Security if the portion is $1000 or a whole multiple of $1000. Provisions of this Indenture that apply to conversion of all of a Security also apply to conversion of a portion of it.

"Common Stock" means the Common Stock of the Company as such Common Stock exists on the date of this Indenture.

Section 10.02. Conversion Procedure.

To convert a Security, a Holder must (1) complete and sign the conversion notice on the back of the Security, (2) surrender the Security to a Conversion Agent, (3) furnish appropriate endorsements and transfer documents if required by the Trustee or Conversion Agent, (4) pay any transfer or similar tax if required, and (5) provide funds, if applicable, required pursuant to the next paragraph. The date on which the Holder satisfies all such requirements is the conversion date. As soon as practicable, the Company shall deliver, or shall cause the Conversion Agent to deliver, upon the order of the Holder, a certificate for the number of full shares of Common Stock issuable upon the conversion and a check for any fractional share. The Person in whose name the certificate is registered shall be treated as a stockholder of record on and after the conversion date.

Any Security surrendered for conversion during the period from the close of business on the record date for any interest payment date to the close of business on the Business Day next preceding the following interest payment date shall be accompanied by payment, in New York Clearing House funds or other funds acceptable to the Company, of an amount equal to the interest otherwise payable on such interest payment date on the Principal amount being converted [; provided, however, that no such payment need be made if there shall exist at the conversion date a Default in the payment of interest on the Securities]. Notwithstanding Section 2.13, if a Holder has paid an amount equal to the interest otherwise payable in accordance with the preceding sentence and the Company thereafter defaults in the payment of interest on such interest payment date, such Defaulted Interest, together with interest thereon shall be paid to the Person who made such required payment no later than the payment date set in accordance with Section 2.13. Except as provided above in this Section 10.02, no payment or other adjustment shall be made for interest accrued on any Security converted or for dividends on any securities issued on conversion of the Security.

[Except as provided in the immediately preceding paragraph, the Company's delivery of the fixed number of shares of Common Stock into which a Security is convertible will be deemed to satisfy the Company's obligation to pay the Principal amount of the Security and all accrued interest (and original issue discount) that has not previously been (or is not simultaneously being) paid. The Common Stock is treated as issued first in payment of accrued interest (and original issue discount) and then in payment of Principal. Thus, accrued interest (and original issue discount) are treated as paid rather than cancelled.]

If a Holder converts more than one Security at the same time, the number of full shares issuable and payment pursuant to Section 10.03 upon the conversion shall be based on the total Principal amount of the Securities converted.

Upon surrender of a Security that is converted in part, the Trustee shall authenticate for the Holder a new Security equal in Principal amount to the unconverted Principal amount of the Security surrendered.

If the last day on which a Security may be converted is a Legal Holiday in a place where the Conversion Agent is located, the Security may be surrendered to the Company or the Conversion Agent on the next succeeding Business Day.

Section 10.03. Fractional Shares.

The Company shall not issue a fractional share of Common Stock upon conversion of a Security. Instead, the Company shall deliver a check for an amount equal to the current market value of the fractional share. The current market value of a fraction of a share shall be determined as follows: Multiply the current market price of a full share by the fraction. Round the result to the nearest cent.

The current market price of a share of Common Stock for purposes of this Section 10.03 shall be the Quoted Price of the Common Stock on the last trading day prior to the conversion date. In the absence of such a quotation, the Board shall determine the current market price in good faith on the basis of such information as it considers reasonably appropriate.

Section 10.04. Taxes on Conversion.

If a Holder of a Security converts it, the Company shall pay any documentary, stamp or similar issue or transfer tax due on the issue of shares of Common Stock upon the conversion. However, the Holder shall pay any withholding tax or any such tax that is due because the shares are issued in a name other than the Holder's name.

Section 10.05. Company to Reserve Common Stock.

The Company shall at all times reserve out of its authorized but unissued Common Stock or its Common Stock held in treasury enough shares of Common Stock to permit the conversion of the Securities.

All shares of Common Stock issued upon conversion of the Securities shall be fully paid and non-assessable and free of any preemptive or other similar rights.

The Company shall endeavor to comply with all securities laws regulating the offer and delivery of shares of Common Stock upon conversion of Securities and shall endeavor to list such shares on each national securities exchange on which the Common Stock is listed.

Section 10.06. Adjustment for Change in Capital Stock.

If the Company:

(1) pays a dividend or makes a distribution on its Common Stock in shares of its Common Stock;

(2) subdivides its outstanding shares of Common Stock into a greater number of shares;

(3) combines its outstanding shares of Common Stock into a smaller number of shares;

(4) makes a distribution on its Common Stock in shares of its capital stock other than Common Stock; or

(5) issues by reclassification of its Common Stock any shares of its capital stock, then the conversion privilege and the conversion price in effect immediately prior to such action shall be proportionately adjusted so that the Holder of a Security thereafter converted may receive the aggregate number and kind of shares of capital stock of the Company that the Holder would have owned immediately following such action if the Security had converted immediately prior to such action.

Each adjustment contemplated by this Section 10.06 shall become effective immediately after the record date in the case of a dividend or distribution and immediately after the effective date in the case of a subdivision, combination or reclassification.

If after an adjustment a Holder of a Security upon conversion of it may receive shares of two or more classes of capital stock of the Company, the Board, acting in good faith, shall determine the allocation of the adjusted conversion price among the classes of capital stock. After such allocation, the conversion privilege and the conversion price of each class of capital stock shall thereafter be subject to adjustment on terms comparable to those applicable to Common Stock in this Article. The term "Common Stock" shall thereafter apply to each class of capital stock and the Company shall enter into such supplemental Indenture, if any, as may be necessary to reflect such conversion privilege and conversion price.

The adjustment contemplated by this Section 10.06 shall be made successively whenever any of the events listed above shall occur.

Section 10.07. Adjustment for Rights Issue.

If the Company distributes any rights, options or warrants to all holders of its Common Stock entitling them for a period expiring within 60 days after the record date mentioned below to subscribe for or purchase shares of Common Stock at a price per share less than the current market price per share on that record date, the conversion price shall be adjusted in accordance with the following formula:

$$C' = C \times \frac{O + \frac{N \times P}{M}}{O + N}$$

where:
C' = the adjusted conversion price.
C = the current conversion price.
O = the number of shares of Common Stock outstanding on the record date.
N = the number of additional shares of Common Stock subject to such rights, options or warrants.
P = the offering price per share of the additional shares.
M = the current market price per share of Common Stock on the record date.

The adjustment contemplated by this Section 10.07 shall be made successively whenever any such rights, options or warrants are issued and shall become effective immediately after the record date for the determination of stockholders entitled to receive the rights, options or warrants. If at the end of the period during which such rights, options or warrants are exercisable, not all rights, options or warrants shall have been exercised, the conversion price shall immediately be readjusted to what it would have been if "N" in the above formula had been the number of shares actually issued.

Section 10.08. Adjustment for Other Distributions.

If the Company distributes to all holders of its Common Stock any of its assets (including, but not limited to, cash), debt securities or other securities or any rights, options or warrants to purchase assets, debt securities or other securities of the Company, the conversion price shall be adjusted in accordance with the following formula:

$$C' = C \ x \ \frac{M - F}{M}$$

where:

C' = the adjusted conversion price.

C = the current conversion price.

M = the current market price per share of Common Stock on the record date mentioned below.

F = the fair market value on the record date of the assets, securities, rights, options or warrants applicable to one share of Common Stock. Fair market value shall be determined in good faith by the Board, *provided* that the Company shall obtain an appraisal or other valuation opinion in support of the Board's determination from an investment bank or accounting firm of recognized national standing if the aggregate fair market value exceeds $[X] million.

The adjustment contemplated by this Section 10.08 shall be made successively whenever any such distribution is made and shall become effective immediately after the record date for the determination of stockholders entitled to receive the distribution.

This Section 10.08 does not apply to cash dividends or cash distributions paid in any fiscal year out of consolidated net income of the Company for the current fiscal year or the prior fiscal year, as shown on the books of the Company prepared in accordance with generally accepted accounting principles. Also, this Section does not apply to rights, options or warrants referred to in Section 10.07.

Section 10.09. Adjustment for Common Stock Issue.

If the Company issues shares of Common Stock for a consideration per share less than the current market price per share on the date the Company fixes the offering price of such additional shares, the conversion price shall be adjusted in accordance with the following formula:

$$C' = C \ x \ \frac{O + \dfrac{P}{M}}{A}$$

where:

C' = the adjusted conversion price.

C = the current conversion price.

O = the number of shares of Common Stock outstanding on the record date.

P = the aggregate consideration received for the issuance of such additional shares.

M = the current market price per share of Common Stock on the record date.

A = the number of shares of Common Stock outstanding immediately after the issuance of such additional shares.

The adjustment contemplated by this Section 10.09 shall be made successively whenever any such issuance is made and shall become effective immediately after the record date for the determination of stockholders entitled to receive such additional shares of Common Stock.

This Section 10.09 shall not apply to:

(1) any of the transactions described in Sections 10.07 and 10.08;

(2) the conversion of the Securities or the conversion or exchange of other securities convertible into or exchangeable for Common Stock;

(3) the issuance of Common Stock upon the exercise of rights, options or warrants issued to the holders of Common Stock;

(4) the issuance of Common Stock to the Company's employees under bona fide employee benefit plans adopted by the Board, and approved by the holders of Common Stock when required by law, but only to the extent that the aggregate number of shares excluded by this clause (3) and issued after the date of this Indenture shall not exceed 5% of the Common Stock outstanding as of the date of this Indenture;

(5) the issuance of Common Stock to stockholders of any Person that merges into the Company in proportion to their stock holdings of such Person immediately prior to such merger, upon such merger;

(6) the issuance of Common Stock in a bona fide public offering pursuant to a firm commitment underwriting; or

(7) the issuance of Common Stock in a bona fide private placement through a placement agent that is a member firm of the National Association of Securities Dealers, Inc. (except to the extent that any discount from the current market price shall exceed 20% of the then current market price).

Section 10.10. **Adjustment for Convertible Securities Issue.**

If the Company issues any securities, rights, options or warrants convertible into or exchangeable for Common Stock (other than the Securities or securities issued in transactions described in Sections 10.07, 10.08 and 10.09) for a consideration per share of Common Stock initially deliverable upon conversion or exchange of such securities less than the current market price per share on the date of issuance of such securities, the conversion price shall be adjusted in accordance with the following formula:

$$C' = C \times \frac{O + \dfrac{P}{M}}{O + D}$$

where:

C' = the adjusted conversion price.

C = the current conversion price.

O = the number of shares of Common Stock outstanding on the record date.

P = the aggregate consideration received for the issuance of such securities.

M = the current market price per share of Common Stock on the record date.

D = the maximum number of shares of Common Stock deliverable upon conversion or exchange of such securities at the initial conversion or exchange rate.

The adjustment contemplated by this Section 10.10 shall be made successively whenever any such issuance is made and shall become effective immediately after the record date for the determination of stockholders entitled to receive such securities, rights, options or warrants. If at the end of the period during which such securities, rights, options or warrants are convertible into or exchangeable for Common Stock, not all such securities, rights, options or warrants shall have been so converted or exchanged, the conversion price shall immediately be readjusted to what it would have been if "D" in the above formula had been the number of shares actually issued upon conversion or exchange.

This Section 10.10 shall not apply to:

(1) the issuance of convertible securities to stockholders of any Person that merges into the Company, or with a subsidiary of the Company, in proportion to their stock holdings of such Person immediately prior to such merger, upon such merger;

(2) the issuance of convertible securities in a bona fide public offering pursuant to a firm commitment underwriting; or

(3) the issuance of convertible securities in a bona fide private placement through a placement agent that is a member firm of the National Association of Securities Dealers, Inc. (except to the extent that any discount from the current market price shall exceed 20% of the then current market price).

Section 10.11. Current Market Price.

In Sections 10.07, 10.08, 10.09 and 10.10, the current market price per share of Common Stock on any date shall be the average of the Quoted Prices of the Common Stock for the five consecutive trading days selected by the Company commencing not more than 20 trading days before, and ending not later than, the earlier of (i) the date of such determination and (ii) the day before the "ex" date with respect to the issuance or distribution requiring such computation. The "Quoted Price" of a security shall be the last reported sales price of such security as reported by the New York Stock Exchange or, if the security is listed on another securities exchange, the last reported sales price of such security on such exchange which shall be for consolidated trading if applicable to such exchange, or as reported by the Nasdaq National Market System, or, if the security is neither so reported nor listed, the last reported bid price of the security. In the absence of one or more such quotations, the current market price shall be determined in good faith by the Board on the basis of such quotations as it considers reasonably appropriate. For the purposes of this Section 10.11, the term "ex" date, when used with respect to any issuance or distribution, shall mean the first date on which the security trades on such exchange or in such market without the right to receive such issuance or distribution.

Section 10.12. When De Minimis Adjustment May Be Deferred.

No adjustment in the conversion price need be made unless the adjustment would require an increase or decrease of at least 1% in the conversion price. All calculations under this Article shall be made to the nearest cent or to the nearest 1/100th of a share, as the case may be. Any adjustments that are not made shall be carried forward and taken into account in any subsequent adjustment.

Section 10.13. When No Adjustment Required.

No adjustment need be made for a transaction referred to in Sections 10.06, 10.07, 10.08, 10.09 or 10.10 if Securityholders are permitted to participate in the transaction on a basis and with notice that the Board determines to be fair and appropriate in light of the basis and notice on which holders of Common Stock are permitted to participate in the transaction.

No adjustments need be made for rights to purchase Common Stock pursuant to a Company plan for reinvestment of dividends or interest.

No adjustment need be made for a change in the par value or no par value of the Common Stock.

To the extent the Securities become convertible into cash, no adjustment need be made thereafter as to the cash. Interest will not accrue on the cash.

Section 10.14. Notice of Adjustment.

Whenever the conversion price is adjusted, the Company shall promptly mail to Securityholders a notice of the adjustment. The Company shall file with the Trustee a certificate from the Company's independent public accountants briefly stating the facts requiring the adjustment and the manner of computing it. The certificate shall be conclusive evidence that the adjustment is correct, absent mathematical error.

Section 10.15. Voluntary Reduction.

The Company may from time to time reduce the conversion price by any amount for any period of time if the period is at least 20 days and if the reduction is irrevocable during the period; *provided, however*, that in no event may the conversion price be less than the par value of a share of Common Stock.

Whenever the conversion price is reduced, the Company shall mail to Securityholders a notice of the reduction. The Company shall mail the notice at least 15 days before the date the reduced conversion price takes effect. The notice shall state the reduced conversion price and the period it will be in effect.

A reduction of the conversion price does not change or adjust the conversion price otherwise in effect for purposes of Sections 10.06 through 10.10.

Section 10.16. **Notice of Certain Transactions.**

If:

(1) the Company takes any action that would require an adjustment in the conversion price pursuant to Section 10.06, 10.07, 10.08, 10.09 or 10.10 and if the Company does not permit Securityholders to participate pursuant to Section 10.13;

(2) the Company takes any action that would require a supplemental indenture pursuant to Section 10.17; or

(3) there is a liquidation or dissolution of the Company, the Company shall mail to Securityholders a notice stating the proposed record date for a dividend or distribution or the proposed effective date of a subdivision, combination, reclassification, consolidation, merger, transfer, lease, liquidation or dissolution. The Company shall mail the notice at least 20 days before such date. Failure to mail the notice or any defect in it shall not affect the validity of the transaction.

Section 10.17. **Reorganization of the Company.**

If the Company is a party to a transaction subject to Section 5.01 or a merger that reclassifies or changes its outstanding Common Stock, the Person obligated to deliver securities, cash or other assets upon conversion of Securities shall enter into a supplemental indenture. If the issuer of securities deliverable upon conversion of Securities is an Affiliate of the surviving or transferee corporation, such issuer shall join in the supplemental indenture.

The supplemental indenture shall provide that the Holder of a Security may convert it into the kind and amount of securities, cash or other assets that such holder would have owned immediately after the consolidation, merger or transfer if the Security had been converted immediately before the effective date of the transaction. The supplemental indenture shall provide for adjustments that are as nearly equivalent as practicable to the adjustments provided for in this Article. The successor Company shall mail to Securityholders a notice briefly describing the supplemental indenture.

[If this Section 10.17 applies, Section 10.06 does not apply.]

Section 10.18. **Company Determination Final.**

Any determination that the Company or the Board must make pursuant to Section 10.03, 10.06, 10.07, 10.08, 10.09, 10.10, 10.11 or 10.13 is conclusive, absent mathematical error. Not later than the date of making any such determination pursuant to Section 10.06, 10.07, 10.08, 10.09, 10.10, 10.11 or 10.13, the Company shall deliver to the Trustee an Officers' Certificate stating the basis upon which such determination was made and, if pursuant to Section 10.06, 10.07, 10.08, 10.09 or 10.10, the calculations by which adjustments under such Sections were made.

Section 10.19. **Trustee's Disclaimer.**

The Trustee has no duty to determine when an adjustment under this Article should be made, how it should be made or what it should be. The Trustee has no duty to determine whether any provisions of a supplemental indenture under Section

10.06 or 10.17 are correct. The Trustee makes no representation as to the validity or value of any securities or assets issued upon conversion of Securities. The Trustee shall not be responsible for the Company's failure to comply with this Article. Each Conversion Agent other than the Company shall have the same protection under this Section as the Trustee.

ARTICLE 11
SUBORDINATION

Section 11.01. Securities Subordinated to Senior Debt.

The rights of Holders to payment of the Principal of and interest on the Securities is subordinated to the rights of holders of Senior Debt, to the extent and in the manner provided in this Article 11.

Section 11.02. Securities Subordinated in Any Proceeding.

Upon any Distribution in any Proceeding,

(1) any Distribution to which the Holders are entitled shall be paid directly to the holders of Senior Debt to the extent necessary to make payment in full of all Senior Debt remaining unpaid after giving effect to all other Distributions to or for the benefit of the holders of Senior Debt; and

(2) in the event that any Distribution is received by the Trustee before all Senior Debt is paid in full, such Distribution shall be applied by the Trustee in accordance with this Article 11.

Section 11.03. No Payment on Securities in Certain Circumstances.

The Company shall not, directly or indirectly (other than in capital stock of the Company) pay any Principal of or interest on, redeem, defease or repurchase any of the Securities (i) after any Senior Debt becomes due and payable, unless and until all such Senior Debt shall first be paid in full or (ii) after a Senior Debt Payment Default, unless and until such Senior Debt Payment Default has been cured, waived, or otherwise has ceased to exist.

During a Payment Blockage Period, no payment of any Principal of or interest on the Securities may be made, directly or indirectly, by the Company. Unless the Senior Debt in respect of which the Senior Debt Default Notice has been given has been declared due and payable in its entirety within the Payment Blockage Period, at the end of the Payment Blockage Period, the Company shall pay all sums not paid to the Holders during the Payment Blockage Period and resume all other payments on the Securities as and when due. Defaulted Interest shall be paid in accordance with Section 2.13. Any number of Senior Debt Default Notices may be given; provided, however, that as to any issue of Senior Debt (i) not more than one Senior Debt Default Notice shall be given within a period of any [366] consecutive days, and (ii) no specific act, omission or condition that gave rise to a default that existed upon the date of such Senior Debt Default Notice (whether or not such default applies to the same issue of Senior Debt) shall be made the basis for the commencement of any other Payment Blockage Period.

If any Distribution, payment or deposit to redeem, defease or acquire any of the Securities shall have been received by the Trustee at a time when such Distribution was prohibited by the provisions of this Section 11.03, then, unless such Distribution is no longer prohibited by this Section 11.03, such Distribution shall be received and applied by the Trustee for the benefit of the holders of Senior Debt, and shall be paid or delivered by the Trustee to the holders of Senior Debt for application to the payment of all Senior Debt.

Section 11.04. Subrogation.

The Holders shall not have any subrogation or other rights of recourse to any security in respect of any Senior Debt until such time as all Senior Debt shall have been paid in full. Upon the payment in full of all Senior Debt, the Holders shall be subrogated to the rights of the holders of Senior Debt to receive Distributions applicable to Senior Debt until all amounts owing in respect of the Securities shall be so paid. No Distributions to the holders of Senior Debt which otherwise would have been made to the Holders shall, as between the Company and the Holders, be deemed to be payment by the Company to or on account of Senior Debt.

If any Distribution to which the Holders would otherwise have been entitled shall have been applied pursuant to the provisions of this Article to the payment of Senior Debt, then the Holders shall be entitled to receive from the holders of such Senior Debt any Distributions received by such holders of Senior Debt in excess of the amount sufficient to pay all amounts payable on such Senior Debt to the extent provided herein.

Section 11.05. Obligations of the Company Unconditional.

This Article defines the relative rights of the Holders and holders of Senior Debt. Nothing in this Indenture is intended to or shall impair, as between the Company and the Holders, the obligation of the Company, which is absolute and unconditional, to pay to the Holders the Principal of and interest on the Securities as and when the same shall become due and payable in accordance with their terms, or is intended to or shall affect the relative rights of the Holders and creditors of the Company, other than the holders of Senior Debt, nor shall anything herein or in the Securities prevent the Trustee or any Holder from exercising all remedies otherwise permitted by applicable law upon default under this Indenture, subject to the rights, if any, under this Article 11, of the holders of Senior Debt in respect of any Distribution received upon the exercise of any such remedy. If the Company fails because of this Article to pay principal of or interest on a Security on the due date, the failure is still a Default. Upon any Distribution, the Trustee and the Holders shall be entitled to rely upon any order or decree made by any court of competent jurisdiction in which the Proceeding is pending, or a certificate of the liquidating trustee or agent or other Person making any Distribution for the purpose of ascertaining the Persons entitled to participate in such Distribution, the holders of Senior Debt and other Debt of the Company, the amount thereof or payable thereon, the amount or amounts paid or distributed thereon and all other facts pertinent thereto or to this Article 11.

Section 11.06. Trustee and Paying Agents Entitled to Assume Payments Not Prohibited in Absence of Notice.

The Trustee shall not at any time be charged with knowledge of the existence of any facts which would prohibit the making of any payment to or by the Trustee, unless and until a Trust Officer shall have received, no later than [ ] Business Day[s] prior to such payment, written notice thereof from the Company or from one or more holders of Senior Debt and, prior to the receipt of any such written notice, the Trustee, shall be entitled in all respects conclusively to presume that no such fact exists. Unless the Trustee shall have received the notice provided for in the preceding sentence, the Trustee shall have full power and authority to receive such payment and to apply the same to the purpose for which it was received, and shall not be affected by any notice to the contrary which may be received by it on or after such date. The foregoing shall not apply to any Affiliate of the Company acting as Paying Agent.

Section 11.07. Satisfaction and Discharge.

Amounts deposited in trust with the Trustee pursuant to and in accordance with Article 8 and not prohibited to be deposited under Section 11.03 when deposited shall not be subject to this Article 11.

Section 11.08. Subordination Rights Not Impaired by Acts or Omissions of the Company or Holders of Senior Debt.

No right of any holder of any Senior Debt established in this Article 11 shall at any time or in any way be prejudiced or impaired by any act or failure to act on the part of the Company or by any act or failure to act, in good faith, by any such holder, or by any failure by the Company to comply with the terms of this Indenture.

Section 11.09. Right to Hold Senior Debt.

The Trustee is entitled to all of the rights set forth in this Article 11 in respect of any Senior Debt at any time held by it to the same extent as any other holder of Senior Debt.

Section 11.10. No Fiduciary Duty of Trustee or Securityholders to Holders of Senior Debt.

Neither the Trustee nor the Holders owes any fiduciary duty to the holders of Senior Debt. Neither the Trustee nor the Holders shall be liable to any holder of Senior Debt in the event that the Trustee, acting in good faith, shall pay over or distribute to the Holders, the Company, or any other Person, any property to which any holders of Senior Debt are entitled by virtue of this Article or otherwise. Nothing contained in this Section 11.10 shall affect the obligation of any other such Person to hold such payment for the benefit of, and to pay such payment over to, the holders of Senior Debt.

Section 11.11. Distribution to Holders of Senior Debt.

Any Distribution otherwise payable to the holders of the Securities made to holders of Senior Debt pursuant to this Article shall be made to such holders of Senior Debt ratably according to the respective amount of Senior Debt held by each.

Section 11.12. Trustee's Rights to Compensation, Reimbursement of Expenses and Indemnification.

The Trustee's rights to compensation, reimbursement of expenses and indemnification under Sections 6.08 and 7.07 are not subordinated.

Section 11.13. Exception for Certain Distributions.

The rights of holders of Senior Debt under this Article do not extend (a) to any Distribution to the extent applied to the Trustee's rights to compensation, reimbursement of expenses or indemnification or (b) to (i) securities which are subordinated to the securities distributed to the holders of Senior Debt on terms no less favorable to the holders of Senior Debt than the provisions of this Article, or (ii) Distributions under any plan approved by the court in any Proceeding.

Section 11.14. Certain Definitions.

As used in this Article 11,

"*Distribution*" in any Proceeding means any payment or distribution of assets or securities of the Company of any kind or character from any source, whether in cash, securities or other property made by the Company, custodian, liquidating trustee or agent or any other person whether pursuant to a plan or otherwise.

"*Payment Blockage Period*" means the period beginning when a Senior Debt Default Notice is given to the Company and the Trustee and ending (a) when the default identified in the Senior Debt Default Notice is cured, waived or otherwise ceases to exist or (b) after [179 or fewer] days, whichever occurs first.

"*Senior Debt Default Notice*" means any notice of a default (other than a Senior Debt Payment Default) that permits the holders of any Senior Debt to declare such Senior Debt due and payable.

"*Senior Debt Payment Default*" means a default in the payment of any principal of or interest on any Senior Debt.

"*Trustee*" for purposes of this Article 11 includes any Paying Agent.

ARTICLE 12
MISCELLANEOUS

Section 12.01. Notices.

Any notice by one party to the other shall be in writing and sent to the other's address stated in Section 12.09. The notice is duly given if it is delivered in Person or sent by a national courier service which provides next Business Day delivery or by first-class mail.

A party by notice to the other party may designate additional or different addresses for subsequent notices.

Any notice sent to a Securityholder shall be mailed by first-class letter mailed to its address shown on the register kept by the Registrar. Failure to mail a notice to a Securityholder or any defect in a notice mailed to a Securityholder shall not affect the sufficiency of the notice mailed to other Securityholders.

If a notice is delivered or mailed in the manner provided above within the time prescribed, it is duly given, whether or not the addressee receives it.

If the Company mails a notice to Securityholders, it shall deliver or mail a copy to the Trustee and each Agent at the same time.

A "notice" includes any communication required by this Indenture.

Section 12.02. Communication by Holders with Other Holders.

Securityholders may communicate pursuant to TIA Section 312(b) with other Securityholders with respect to their rights under this Indenture or the Securities. The Company, the Trustee, and Registrar and anyone else shall have the protection of TIA Section 312(c).

Section 12.03. Certificate and Opinion as to Conditions Precedent.

Upon any request or application by the Company to the Trustee to take any action under this Indenture, the Company shall furnish to the Trustee:

(1) an Officers' Certificate stating that, in the opinion of the signers, all conditions precedent, if any, provided for in this Indenture relating to the proposed action have been complied with; and

(2) an Opinion of Counsel stating that, in the opinion of such counsel, all such conditions precedent have been complied with.

Section 12.04. Statements Required in Certificate or Opinion.

Each certificate or opinion with respect to compliance with a condition or covenant provided for in this Indenture shall include:

(1) a statement that each Person making such certificate or opinion has read such covenant or condition;

(2) a brief statement as to the nature and scope of the examination or investigation upon which the statements or opinions contained in such certificate or opinion are based;

(3) a statement that, in the opinion of such Person, the Person has made such examination or investigation as is necessary to enable such Person to express an informed opinion as to whether or not such covenant or condition has been complied with; and

(4) a statement as to whether or not, in the opinion of such Person, such condition or covenant has been complied with.

Section 12.05. Rules by Trustee and Agents.

The Trustee may make reasonable rules for action by or a meeting of Security-holders. Any Agent may make reasonable rules and set reasonable requirements for its functions.

Section 12.06. Legal Holidays.

A "Legal Holiday" is a Saturday, a Sunday or a day on which banking institutions are not required to be open. If a payment date is a Legal Holiday at a place of payment, payment may be made at that place on the next succeeding day that is not a Legal Holiday, and no interest shall accrue for the intervening period.

Section 12.07. No Recourse Against Others.

A director, officer, employee or stockholder, as such, of the Company shall not have any liability for any obligations of the Company under the Securities or the Indenture or for any claim based on, in respect of or by reason of such obligations or their creation.

Section 12.08. Duplicate Originals.

The parties may sign any number of copies, and may execute such in counterparts, of this Indenture. One signed copy is enough to prove this Indenture.

Section 12.09. Variable Provisions.

"*Officer*" means the President, any Vice-President, the Treasurer, the Secretary, any Assistant Treasurer or any Assistant Secretary of the Company.

The Company initially appoints the Trustee as Registrar, Paying Agent and Conversion Agent.

The first certificate pursuant to Section 4.03 shall be for the fiscal year ending on _____, 20_____.

The reporting date for Section 7.06 is _____ of each year. The first reporting date is _____.

The Trustee shall always have a combined capital and surplus of at least $_____ as set forth in its most recent published annual report of condition. The Trustee will be deemed to be in compliance with the capital and surplus requirement set forth in the preceding sentence if its obligations are guaranteed by a Person which could otherwise act as Trustee hereunder and which meets such capital and surplus requirement and the Trustee has at least the minimum capital and surplus required by TIA Section 310(a)(2).

In determining whether the Trustee has a conflicting interest as defined in TIA Section 310(b)(1), the following is excluded: Indenture dated as of January 1, 20_____; between the Company and Greater Bank and Trust Company, Trustee for the _____% Subordinated Debentures Due.

Senior Debt does not include:

(1) the debentures described in the preceding paragraph;

(2) the Company's _____% Convertible Subordinated Notes due _____, 20_____; and

(3) the Company's subordinated guarantee of the _____% Convertible Subordinated Debentures Due _____ of [Universal Overseas Finance Corporation].

The Securities are not senior in right of payment to the foregoing debt securities of the Company.

The Company's address is:

Universal Business Corporation
1 Commerce Plaza
New York, NY 10099
Facsimile No.:
[Attention: _____]

The Trustee's address is:

Greater Bank and Trust Company
Corporate Trust Department
500 Wall Street
New York, NY 10015
Facsimile No.:
[Attention: _____]

Section 12.10. Governing Law.

The laws of the State of _____ shall govern this Indenture and the Securities.

DATE: _____   UNIVERSAL BUSINESS CORPORATION

By: _____

Vice President

Attest:

_____

Assistant Secretary

DATE: _____   GREATER BANK AND TRUST COMPANY

By: _____

Trust Office
Vice President

Attest:

_____

Assistant Secretary

EXHIBIT A
(Face of Security)

No. _____ $ _____

UNIVERSAL BUSINESS CORPORATION

_____ % Convertible Subordinated Debenture Due

Interest Payment Dates: _____

Record Dates: _____

Universal Business Corporation promises to pay to _____
or registered assigns, the sum of _____ Dollars
on _____

    This Security is convertible and subordinated as specified on the other side of this Security. See the reverse and the Indenture referenced for additional provisions of this Security.

Dated: _____
Authenticated: _____

GREATER BANK AND TRUST
COMPANY
as Trustee
By: _____

Authorized Officer

UNIVERSAL BUSINESS
CORPORATION

By: _____

By: _____

[SEAL]

(Back of Security)

UNIVERSAL BUSINESS CORPORATION

_____% Convertible Subordinated Debenture Due _____

1. *Interest.* Universal Business Corporation ("Company"), a Delaware corporation, promises to pay interest on the principal amount of this Security at the rate per annum shown above. The Company will pay interest semiannually on _____ and _____ of each year. Interest on the Securities will accrue from the most recent date to which interest has been paid or, if no interest has been paid, from _____. Interest will be computed on the basis of a 360-day year of twelve 30-day months.

2. *Method of Payment.* The Company will pay interest on the Securities to the Persons who are registered holders of Securities at the close of business on the record date for the next interest payment date, except as otherwise provided herein or in the Indenture even though Securities are cancelled after the record date and on or before the interest payment date. Holders must surrender Securities to a Paying Agent to collect principal payments. The Company will pay Principal and interest in money of the United States that at the time of payment is legal tender for payment of public and private debts. However, the Company may pay Principal and interest by wire transfer or check payable in such money. It may mail an interest check to a record date holder's registered address.

3. *Agents.* Initially, Greater Bank and Trust Company ("Trustee"), 500 Wall Street, New York, NY 10015, will act as Registrar, Paying Agent and Conversion Agent. The Company may change any such Agent without notice. The Company or an Affiliate may act in any such capacity. Subject to certain conditions, the Company may change the Trustee.

4. *Indenture.* The Company issued the Securities under an Indenture dated as of _____ ("Indenture") between the Company and the Trustee. The terms of the Securities include those stated in the Indenture and those made part of the Indenture by the Trust Indenture Act of 1939 (15 U.S.C. §§77aaa-77bbbb) (the "Act"). The Securities are subject to all such terms, and Securityholders are referred to the Indenture and the Act for a statement of such terms. The Securities are unsecured subordinated general obligations of the Company limited to $_____ in aggregate principal amount.

5. *Redemption.* [The Securities may not be redeemed at the option of the Company prior to (date).] The Company may redeem all the Securities at any time or some of them from time to time after [(date)] [note this date should be at least two Business Days after the last interest payment date in the period described in the preceding sentence] at the following redemption prices (expressed in percentages of principal amount), plus accrued interest to the redemption date:

If redeemed during the 12-month period beginning _____, *Year Percentage Year Percentage*

The Company's right to redeem securities under this Section 5 may not be exercised if and for so long as the Company has failed to pay interest on any Security when the same becomes due and payable.

6. *Mandatory Redemption.* The Company will redeem $_____ principal amount of the Securities on _____ and on each _____ thereafter through _____ at a redemption price of 100% of principal amount, plus accrued interest to the redemption date.

The Company may reduce the principal amount of Securities to be redeemed pursuant to this paragraph by subtracting 100% of the principal amount (excluding premium) of any Securities that have been previously cancelled, that Securityholders have converted (other than Securities converted after being called for mandatory redemption), that the Company has delivered to the Trustee for cancellation or that the Company has redeemed other than pursuant to this paragraph. The Company may so subtract the same Security only once.

7. *Additional Optional Redemption.* In addition to redemptions pursuant to paragraph 6, the Company may redeem not more than $_____ principal amount of the Securities on _____ and on each _____ thereafter through _____ at a redemption price of 100% of principal amount, plus accrued interest to the redemption date.

8. *Notice of Redemption.* Notice of redemption will be mailed at least 30 days but not more than 60 days before the redemption date to each holder of Securities to be redeemed at his registered address.

9. *Conversion.* A holder of a Security may convert it into Common Stock of the Company at any time before the close of business on _____. If a Security is called for redemption, the holder may convert it at any time before the close of business on the Business Day prior to the redemption date (unless the redemption date is an interest record date in which event it may be converted through the record date). The initial conversion price is $_____ per share, subject to adjustment in certain events. In certain circumstances the right to convert a Security into Common Stock may be changed into a right to convert it into securities, cash or other assets of the Company or another.

To determine the number of shares issuable upon conversion of a Security, divide the principal amount to be converted by the conversion price in effect on the conversion date. On conversion no payment or adjustment for interest will be made. The Company will deliver a check for cash in lieu of any fractional share.

To convert a Security a Holder must comply with Section 10.02 of the Indenture, which requires the Holder to (1) complete and sign the conversion notice on the back of the Security, (2) surrender the Security to a Conversion Agent, (3) furnish appropriate endorsements and transfer documents if required by the Paying Agent or Conversion Agent, (4) pay any transfer or similar tax if required, and (5) provide funds, if applicable, required pursuant to Section 10.02 of the Indenture. A holder may convert a portion of a Security if the portion is $1000 or a whole multiple of $1000.

10. *Subordination.* The Securities are subordinated to Senior Debt as defined in the Indenture. To the extent provided in the Indenture, Senior Debt must be paid before the Securities may be paid. The Company agrees, and each Securityholder by accepting a Security agrees, to the subordination and authorizes the Trustee to give it effect.

11. *Denominations, Transfer, Exchange.* The Securities are in registered form without coupons in denominations of $1000 and whole multiples of $1000. The transfer of Securities may be registered and Securities may be exchanged as provided in the Indenture. The Registrar may require a holder, among other things, to furnish appropriate endorsements and transfer documents and to pay any taxes required by law. The Registrar need not exchange or register the transfer of any Security or portion of a Security selected for redemption. Also, it need not exchange or register the transfer of any Securities for a period of 15 days before a selection of Securities to be redeemed.

12. *Persons Deemed Owners.* Subject to Section 6.11, the registered holder of a Security may be treated as its owner for all purposes.

13. *Amendments and Waivers.* Subject to certain exceptions, the Indenture or the Securities may be amended, and any Default may be waived, with the consent of the holders of a majority in Principal amount of the Securities. Without the consent of any Securityholder, the Indenture or the Securities may be amended to cure any ambiguity, defect or inconsistency, to provide for assumption of Company obligations to Securityholders or to make any change that does not adversely affect the rights of any Securityholder.

14. *Successors.* When successors assume all the obligations of the Company under the Securities and the Indenture, the Company will be released from those obligations, except as provided in the Indenture.

15. *Satisfaction and Discharge Prior to Redemption or Maturity.* Subject to certain conditions, the Company at any time may terminate some or all of its obligations under the Securities and the Indenture if the Company deposits with the Trustee money or U.S. Government Obligations for the payment of Principal and interest on the Securities to redemption or maturity.

16. *Defaults and Remedies.* Subject to the Indenture, if an Event of Default, as defined in the Indenture, occurs and is continuing, the Trustee or the holders of at least 25% in Principal amount of the Securities may declare all the Securities to be due and payable immediately. Securityholders may not enforce the Indenture or the Securities except as provided in the Indenture. The Trustee may require indemnity satisfactory to it before it enforces the Indenture or the Securities. Subject to certain limitations, holders of a majority in Principal amount of the Securities may direct the Trustee in its exercise of any trust or power. The Trustee may withhold from Securityholders notice of any continuing Default (except a Default in payment of Principal or interest) if it determines that withholding notice is in their interests. The Company must furnish an annual compliance certificate to the Trustee.

17. *Trustee Dealings with Company.* Greater Bank and Trust Company, the Trustee under the Indenture, in its individual or any other capacity, may make loans to, accept deposits from, and perform services for the Company or its Affiliates, and may otherwise deal with the Company or its Affiliates, as if it were not Trustee, subject to the Indenture and the Act.

18. *No Recourse Against Others.* A director, officer, employee or stockholder, as such, of the Company shall not have any liability for any obligations of the Company under the Securities or the Indenture or for any claim based on, in respect of or by reason of such obligations or their creation. Each Securityholder by accepting a Security waives and releases all such liability. The waiver and release are part of the consideration for the issue of the Securities.

19. *Authentication.* This Security shall not be valid until authenticated by a manual signature of the Trustee.

20. *Abbreviations.* Customary abbreviations may be used in the name of a Securityholder or an assignee, such as: TEN COM (= tenants in common), TEN ENT (= tenants by the entireties), JT TEN (= joint tenants with right of survivorship and not as tenants in common), CUST (= Custodian), and U/G A (= Uniform Gifts to Minors Act).

The Company will furnish to any Securityholder upon written request and without charge a copy of the Indenture. Requests may be made to: Secretary, Universal Business Corporation, 1 Commerce Plaza, New York, NY 10099.

NOTES ON THE REVISED MODEL SIMPLIFIED INDENTURE

General

1. *General Principles of Construction of Indentures.* The rules of construction of indentures are well established. The courts emphasize the need for uniformity in the interpretation of agreements which control securities traded anonymously in the markets. Construction of indentures is uniquely a matter of law for the court. *See* Chemical Bank v. First Trust of N.Y. (*In re* Southeast Banking Corp.), 156 F.3d 1114, 1125 (11th Cir. 1998); Leverso v. Southtrust Bank, 18 F.3d 1527, 1534 (11th Cir. 1994); Sharon Steel Corp. v. Chase Manhattan Bank, N.A., 691 F.2d 1039, 1048 (2d Cir. 1982); Broad v. Rockwell Int'l Corp., 642 F.2d 929, 943 (5th Cir. 1981); Chemical Bank v. First Trust of N.Y., 93 N.Y.2d 178 (1999).

2. *Time Periods and Percentages.* The various time periods and percentages appearing in the Revised Model Simplified Indenture [RMSI or simply Model Simplified Indenture],[4] to the extent not prescribed by the Trust Indenture Act, 15 U.S.C. §§77aaa-77bbbb [hereinafter TIA], should be reviewed by prospective users of the Model Simplified Indenture in light of the conflicting interests of the particular parties. Certain of these periods and proportions are the subject of specific explanation in these notes (e.g., Note 5 to Section 6.01). Users may alter any of these figures, but it should be noted that there do exist interrelationships among some periods or percentages (appearing in different Sections of the Model Simplified Indenture) which are deliberate and should be considered in the alteration. For users' convenience, there is set forth below a list of the Sections containing time periods and percentages not prescribed by the TIA:

Sec.	2.12	Sec.	8.01(2)
	3.01 (last ¶)		8.04 (2nd ¶)
	3.02		9.02 (1st ¶)
	3.03 (1st ¶)		10.07 (1st ¶)
	4.02		10.09
	4.03		10.10 (1st ¶)
	6.01(1)		10.10 (2nd ¶)
	6.01(2)		10.13 (1st ¶)
	6.01(5)		10.13 (2nd ¶)
	6.01 (last ¶)		10.14
	6.02		11.03
	6.04		11.05
	6.06		11.06
	7.06		11.14
	8.01(1)		12.10

Security ¶¶ 1, 5, 6, 7, 8, 9, 11, 13, 14

---

4. All citations to the "Model Simplified Indenture" in this text refer to the Revised Model Simplified Indenture, unless otherwise noted. The 1983 version of this text is referred to as the "1983 MSI."

3. *Uniform Commercial Code*. The references to Article 8 of the Uniform Commercial Code ("U.C.C.") are to the 1994 Revision to that Article, which, although not yet adopted in every state, is contemplated to be so adopted.

4. *Guarantors*. The Model Simplified Indenture does not contain provisions which would be required if another entity were a guarantor of the Indenture.

Introductory Paragraphs

1. *Definitions*. The terms "Company," "Trustee" and "Securities" are defined in these paragraphs and further defined in Section 1.01. The definitions of those terms in Section 1.01 build on the definitions in the introductory paragraphs so that users need not repeat the Company's and Trustee's names and the title of the issue a second time in Section 1.01.

2. *Other Definitions*. Obviously, users will add additional defined terms as required for their particular transaction. Even common words may usefully be defined for a specific transaction. A defined term such as "Interest," for example, is frequently added to include items that may be virtue of the parties' negotiations be included in "Interest" (e.g., default interest). *Cf.* the definition of "Principal."

Section 1.01

1. *Affiliate*. This is the 1983 MSI definition; note although the Model Simplified Indenture does not automatically incorporate defined terms from the TIA (as did the 1983 MSI), this definition is set forth in TIA Rule 0-2, 17 C.F.R. §260.0-2 (1999). TIA Rule 0-2 defines as well the words "control," "controlling" and "controlled" which are repeated here. Because the definition of "affiliate" and therefore "control" may be key to covenants, both definitions may be subject to exceptions or clarifications for special fact situations.

2. *Agent*. The terms "Registrar," "Paying Agent" and "Conversion Agent" are defined in Section 2.03. *See* U.C.C. §8-407; *id.* §§8-401 to 8-406 (for the duties of Registrars). There is no comparable definition in the Model Indentures found in American Bar Foundation, Commentaries on Indentures (1971) [[hereinafter ABF Indenture Commentaries; or, if referring specifically to the Model Indentures found therein, cited as ABF Model Indentures].

3. *Board of Directors*. This definition is essentially the same as the one in the 1983 MSI, which itself was derived from the ABF Model Indentures. The reference to an "authorized" board committee maintains the ABF Indenture Commentaries' requirement (at 36) of compliance with applicable state law.

4. *Company*. Succession to the "Company," and successive successions, is provided for in Article 5 and Section 10.17. Each successive "Company" under Article 5 becomes an obligor on the Securities for payment and an obligor on the Indenture for other performance (although another "Company" may become obligor under Article 10—Conversion). In addition, while "Company" is deliberately broad enough to encompass non-corporate issuers, non-corporate users will find the Model Simplified Indenture adaptable, but not yet adapted, to their needs.

5. *Debt*. The definition of Debt was contained in Article 11 of the 1983 MSI and read "any indebtedness for borrowed money or any guarantee of such indebtedness."

The definition contained in this Section 1.01 is used in the definition of Senior Debt, and reflects Senior Debtholders' desire to have a broad definition which specifically includes, for example, common obligations to a lender under bank agreements (e.g. indemnification amounts, fees and expenses, letters of credit and capitalized leases). Conversely, in this definition or in the definition of Senior Debt there are frequently specific obligations carved out of the definition. *See* Note 11 below.

Note that as drafted, the parenthetical phrase in this definition of Debt, combined with the definition of Senior Debt and the provisions of the subordination article (Article 11), has the effect of authorizing the holders of Senior Debt to recover interest accruing on their claims after the filing of a bankruptcy petition by or against the Company from the distributions to the Securityholders unless specifically provided otherwise in Article 11. Holders of Senior Debt do not have as to their debt an allowable claim in the bankruptcy case for post-petition interest unless the creditor is oversecured or the estate is solvent (in which events the Senior Debt would have no need for recourse to the Securityholders' distributions). Applying the "Rule of Explicitness" in the construction of subordination contracts, most of the decided cases have held that the holders of Senior Debt are not entitled to recover post-petition interest from the distributions to subordinated creditors since it should be assumed that the claims of the holders of Senior Debt as to which they may seek subordination are limited to their allowable bankruptcy claims. *See In re* Time Sales Fin. Corp., 491 F.2d 841, 844 (3d Cir. 1974); First Fidelity Bank, N.A. v. Midlantic Nat'l Bank (*In re* Ionosphere Clubs, Inc.), 134 B.R. 528, 535 (Bankr. S.D.N.Y. 1991) (citation omitted); *In re* King Resources Co., 385 F. Supp. 1269, 1281 (D. Colo. 1974), *aff'd*, 528 F.2d 789, 791 (10th Cir. 1976); *In re* Kingsboro Mortgage Corp., 379 F. Supp. 227, 231 (S.D.N.Y. 1974), *aff'd*, 514 F.2d 400 (2d Cir. 1975). However, in *In re* Southeast Banking Corp., 156 F.3d 1114, 1125-26 (11th Cir. 1998), the circuit court held that the Rule of Explicitness has been superseded by Bankruptcy Code Section 510(a) and certified the question of the construction of the subordination provisions in the indentures to the New York State Court of Appeals. The New York State Court of Appeals, however, held that New York law recognized the Rule of Explicitness and found it applicable to the indentures in question. Chemical Bank v. First Trust, 93 N.Y.2d 178, 186 (1999).

Note as well that to the extent this definition of Debt is used in any financial covenants, it may be over-or-under-inclusive, depending on the intent of the financial covenant. For every covenant using the defined term Debt, the drafter must therefore carefully ascertain whether the definition must be adjusted in any respect.

6. *Default*. This definition is not contained in the ABF Model Indentures. It refers to an Event of Default as defined in Section 6.01, and also includes an event which would become an Event of Default after notice or passage of time.

7. *Officers' Certificate*. *See* Section 12.09 for the definition of "Officer." By reference to Section 12.09, it is intended that flexibility be afforded to users to expand the list of persons who qualify as officers. (Section 12.09 is used as a repository for other variations in the text, in order to avoid changes, fill-ins and re-numberings to the greatest extent possible). There is no provision in the Model Simplified Indenture for an engineer, accountant or other expert to give a certificate, as there is in the ABF Model Indentures, since such a provision accompanies negotiated covenants (which are not included in the Model Simplified Indenture).

8. *Principal*. The use of the term "principal" in the Model Simplified Indenture to include the "premium, if any" is intended to avoid the repetition of that phrase in many

separate provisions of the Indenture. "Principal," standing alone, is proper in almost all contexts (e.g., there is an immediate Event of Default under clause (2) of Section 6.01 if the Company fails to pay "principal" when due), and the premium is specifically excluded in those provisions (e.g., paragraph 6 of the form of Security) when required. While resort may always be had to the reference to "context" in the introductory clause of Section 1.03, it is hoped that each use of the term "principal" has been tested against the foregoing.

9. *SEC.* The ABF Model Indenture defines "Commission" to mean the SEC and any successor agency "performing the duties now assigned to [the SEC] under the Trust Indenture Act," i.e., under "the Trust Indenture Act of 1939, as in force at the date as of which this [indenture] was executed." While the SEC could by statute be consolidated or changed into some new or different agency, just as the TIA could be eliminated, combined into, or replaced by legislation, the Model Simplified Indenture does not deal with those possibilities.

10. *Securities.* The generic term "Securities" is used so that the Model Simplified Indenture can be utilized with respect to unsecured debt instruments of whatever formal appellation (notes, debentures, certificates, etc.). However, the Model Simplified Indenture is a closed-end indenture and contemplates a single series of debt instruments, in a specific aggregate maximum principal amount; it does not provide for multiple series of issues.

11. *Senior Debt.* The definition of Senior Debt is largely dependent on the definition of Debt. The Senior Debt definition is frequently highly negotiated. Among other issues to be considered is whether there are multiple tiers of "Senior Debt" with varying rights (e.g., "Designated Senior Debt" may have the sole right to invoke certain of the subordination provisions); and whether post-petition interest on such debt is to be included in such a definition. In addition, definitions of Senior Debt frequently provide that certain obligations shall in no event constitute Senior Debt, e.g., obligations to employees of the issuer (note this definition already incorporates an exclusion for Debt held by the Company and any of its affiliates); trade debt; preferred stock; obligations for taxes; capitalized lease obligations; and certain specified Debt, which varies with the issuer. The MSI calls for the last to be listed in Section 12.09, and Clause (iii) of this definition incorporates that exclusion by cross-reference. A definition of "Designated Senior Debt," if added, typically defines a class of institutional lenders to the Company as of the time that the Indenture is executed and is used where provisions of Article 11 provide different rights to that class (such as rights to invoke payment blockage provisions or to recover post-petition interest from the distributions to Securityholders). Note that this definition does not provide clarity as to how the Securities rank vis-a-vis Debt which is not "Senior Debt." If, for example, the issuer of the Security merges with another issuer which has several subordinated Debt issues outstanding, those issues are not likely to meet the definition of "Senior Debt." Unless this definition also excludes from "Senior Debt" any Debt which is subordinated to any other Debt (which usually accompanies an "anti-layering" covenant precluding the issuance of Debt subordinate to any other Debt and senior to the Securities), the relative priorities of the Securities over other Debt will be left to a determination in the particular circumstances.

12. *Subsidiary.* Since the term "subsidiary" may be used in different contexts with different definitions, and since those contexts frequently involve negotiated provisions, definition of the term has been omitted from this Section.

13. *TIA*. By virtue of this definition, the Trust Indenture Act of 1939 as in effect on the date of the Indenture is incorporated into the Indenture if the Indenture is qualified under and subject to the TIA. *See* Note 9 above; Notes 1 and 2 to Section 1.04; Note 2 to Sections 7.01 and 7.02.

14. *Trust Officer*. The MSI revises this definition to eliminate the listing of the Chairman and President as well as of any other officer or assistant officer assigned to administer corporate trust matters. The revision recognizes that the trust function is generally separate from other areas of most banks and responsibilities under the Indenture should be limited to those bank officers who are specifically authorized to administer Indentures. This is also consistent with the ethical walls now in place at most banks between the trading and trust administration departments, and the fact that information in one division of a large commercial bank may not—and often should not—filter to the trust area. *See* Note 9 to Section 7.02.

15. *U.S. Government Obligations*. This definition was previously contained in Section 8.01 of the 1983 MSI, and has been expanded to specify that qualifying obligations may not be subject to redemption or call, but may include funds consisting of government obligations (including funds for which the Trustee or one of its Affiliates receives fees).

Section 1.03

1. *GAAP*. Clause (2) contemplates generally accepted accounting principles as they exist at the time an accounting term is being construed. If an issuer is concerned that negotiated financial covenants (which must be added to the Model Simplified Indenture, if desired) have been structured on the basis of currently accepted accounting principles and that a future change in accounting principles may make those covenants too restrictive, clause (2) can be changed to lock onto accounting principles generally accepted at the date of the indenture. *See* James H. Fogelson, *The Impact of Changes in Accounting Principles on Restrictive Covenants in Credit Agreements and Indentures*, 33 BUS. LAW. 769, 777 (1978). Of course, that would impose upon the issuer the increasingly onerous obligation to restate subsequent years' financial statements, solely for indenture covenant purposes, on the basis of accounting principles otherwise no longer applied.

2. *And/Or*. Clause (3) eliminates the need for such awkward locutions as "and/or" and "A or B or both." *See* Bankruptcy Code, 11 U.S.C. §102(5).

3. *Successive Successors, Occurrences, etc.* Clause (5) is intended to underscore the intended application and re-application of definitional provisions like "Company" and "Trustee" in Section 1.01, and operating provisions like Sections 5.01 and 10.06, to successive obligors, fiduciaries, mergers, conversion adjustments, etc.

4. *Internal Reference*. The only addition to this Section from the comparable Section of the 1983 MSI is clause (6).

Section 1.04

1. *Automatic Incorporation*. This Section restates TIA Section 318(c), which provides that the provisions of TIA Section 310 to and including Section 317 that impose duties on any person (including provisions automatically deemed included unless the

indenture provides that they are excluded) are automatically deemed included in every qualified indenture, upon and for so long as it is qualified under the TIA. Notwithstanding the automatic incorporation, the Model Simplified Indenture sets forth most of the incorporated provisions as a matter of convenience. Note that to the extent TIA provisions are set forth in full in the Indenture they are not subject to amendment or repeal solely by virtue of the amendment or repeal of the comparable TIA provision. *See* Note 2 below. The last sentence, contained in brackets, should be used if it is the intent of the parties to continue TIA provisions (identified as such) only for so long as the Indenture is qualified under the TIA.

2. *Incorporated Law and Rules.* The TIA definition in Section 1.01 fixes the incorporated TIA to the statutory text in effect on the date borne by the Indenture. The effect is intended to be the same as long-form repetition, in conventional indentures, of provisions permitted or required by TIA Sections 310 to 317. The last sentence of this Section, however, provides for automatic conforming changes on the amendment of a portion of the TIA which is a required or permitted provision in the Indenture. Note this Section would continue the TIA in force, as then amended (to the extent described in the preceding sentence) if the TIA were repealed. *See* Note 2 to Sections 7.01 and 7.02. As to the possibility of change in the definition of certain indenture terms via rule-making under the TIA, see TIA Section 309(c): no such rule may affect the interpretation of an indenture previously qualified. *See* Note 2 to Sections 7.01 and 7.02.

Section 2.01

1. *The Form of Security.* This provision is slightly changed from the 1983 MSI to permit notations, etc. as required by the use of global securities, automated quotation systems or agreements to which the Company is subject. The approach of the Model Simplified Indenture is to utilize the form of Security (attached as Exhibit A) as the place, and the only place, where several of the substantive provisions of the Indenture appear. The first sentence of this Section is intended to effectuate that approach and to make clear that those provisions, although appearing only in the form of Security, are part of the Indenture.

2. *Format of the Security.* The phrase "substantially in the form of Exhibit A," appearing in the first sentence of this Section, is intended to allow for changes in format in the physical Securities, whether printed or lithographed or typed and whether or not framed in steel-engraved borders. The phrase is also intended to allow for corrections in the definitive Securities of errors in or omissions from Exhibit A.

Section 2.02

1. *Execution of Securities.* The signatures of two Company Officers are required in order to comply with certain stock exchange requirements for listing. *See* NEW YORK STOCK EXCHANGE LISTED COMPANY MANUAL ¶ 501.06 (1998) [hereinafter NYSE Listed Co. Manual]. It is understood that the signature of an Officer attesting to the Company's seal is one of the two acceptable for this purpose. Manual or (for the Company) facsimile signatures are both recognized as satisfactory.

2. *Continuing Validity.* The second paragraph of this Section embodies a requirement, and uses the language, of the NYSE Listed Co. Manual ¶ 501.06. It is recognized that individual Securities bearing proper signatures may be invalid for reasons wholly unrelated to the signature requirement.

3. *Certificate of Authentication.* What was formerly a certificate by the Trustee is, as can be seen on Exhibit A, to be a signature (like that of a stock transfer agent) evidencing authentication.

4. *Purpose and Effect of Authentication.* The ABF Indenture Commentaries (at 141) express the principal purposes of authentication as the following: identification of the Security with the Indenture; prevention of an overissue; and safeguarding against counterfeiting. As to the effect of authentication, see U.C.C. Section 8-208 (such a signature constitutes a warranty to a purchaser for value if the purchaser is without notice of a particular defect, that: the certificate is genuine, the person's participation in the issue of the security is within that person's capacity and the scope of its authority, and the person has reasonable grounds to believe the certificated security is in the form and within the amount the issuer is authorized to issue).

5. *Authenticating Agent.* While authentication is a principal responsibility of the Trustee, the capacity to appoint authenticating agents is preserved in the last paragraph of this Section if the Trustee chooses to use it, and authentication by an agent is treated as equivalent to authentication by the Trustee.

Section 2.03

1. *Registrar.* The 1983 MSI made a distinction between one registrar and one or more co-registrars, because only one definitive register of the names and addresses of Securityholders can be maintained, and that is done by the registrar. This distinction is eliminated in the Model Simplified Indenture.

2. *Exchange Requirements.* For Securities to be listed on the New York Stock Exchange, the Exchange still maintains the requirement for location of an office of the paying agent in Manhattan. *See%i NYSE Listed Co. Manual ¶ 601.01(B).*

Section 2.04

1. *Paying Agent to Comply with Article 11.* Note the addition, in the second sentence, of the requirement that the Paying Agent comply with Article 11. In Article 11, under Section 11.14, "Trustee" includes a Paying Agent.

Section 2.05

1. *Persons Deemed Owners.* The customary provision permitting the Company and the Trustee to recognize the registered holder of a Security as the owner for all purposes is found in paragraph 12 of the form of Security. The portion of the customary provision which disregards notice to the contrary is omitted from paragraph 12. As noted in the ABF Indenture Commentaries (at 191), the customary provision "may" exceed the boundaries of U.C.C. Sections 8-403 and 8-404. Some draftsmen may choose to leave out paragraph 12 on the theory that U.C.C. Section 8-207(a) already covers the point. *See* new Section 6.11 and Note 1 to Section 6.11 (discussing the

ability of beneficial holders to act for the owner of a Security in certain circumstances).

Section 2.06

1. *Rules for Transfer and Exchange*. Section 12.06 contemplates that the Registrar may make reasonable rules and set reasonable requirements for its functions. Compliance with such reasonable requirements is prescribed in this Section as a condition to registration of transfer or exchange.

2. *Transfer Fees*. The last sentence of the first paragraph of this Section is not intended to encourage the practice of charging fees to Securityholders but rather to protect issuers in the event that agency charges do become substantial. For Securities listed on the New York Stock Exchange, the Exchange forbids any such fee to be charged to Securityholders. *See* NYSE Listed Co. Manual ¶ 703.06(E).

3. *Same Debt*. The second paragraph of Section 2.06 is new. It makes express what had been implicit, that a Security issued on an exchange or transfer has the same characteristics as the Security surrendered.

Section 2.07

1. *Mutilated Securities*. The language "lost, destroyed, or wrongfully taken" is the language of U.C.C. Section 8-405, and a sufficient mutilation is treated as a destruction for U.C.C. purposes.

2. *Matured or Maturing Securities*. The language of the ABF Model Indentures, permitting payment of a matured or maturing Security (rather than issuance of a new Security which is then presented for payment), has been omitted on the assumption that such one-step payment would follow in any event.

3. *Protected Purchaser*. The 1983 MSI reference to a bona fide purchaser has been changed to "protected purchaser" in conformity with the term used in U.C.C. Section 8-303. *See also* Section 2.08, where the same change is made.

4. *Replacement Securities*. The ABF Indenture Commentaries (at 184-85) point out that the Indenture cannot discharge the obligation represented by a lost or stolen Security that comes into the hands of a bona fide (protected) purchaser. Therefore the last sentence of this Section provides that the total obligations of the Company are increased by the issuance of replacement Securities. As a practical matter, such increase is offset either by the destruction or unenforceability of the lost or stolen Security or by the indemnity furnished for the issuance of the substituted Security.

Sections 2.08/2.09

1. *Replaced Securities*. The intent of the second paragraph of this Section is to allow a determination, at any time, of the Securities then deemed to be outstanding. *See* Note 4 to Section 2.07. Note again the use of the term protected purchaser. *See* Note 3 to Section 2.07.

2. *Converted Securities*. There is no specification in these Sections that converted Securities are no longer outstanding, both because that does appear to be self-evident and because (i) paragraph 9 of the form of Security requires surrender of each Security

to a Conversion Agent in order to effect conversion; (ii) Section 2.12 requires the Conversion Agent to forward such Securities to the Trustee and further requires the Trustee to cancel such Securities; and (iii) this Section specifies that cancelled Securities are not outstanding.

3. *Securities Called for Redemption.* The only Securities which will cease to be outstanding on a redemption date if the Paying Agent has received funds sufficient to pay them are those Securities which are "payable on that date," i.e., those Securities as to which notice of redemption has been properly given. *See* Section 3.04.

4. *Securities Considered Paid.* Note 2 to Section 4.01 applies to this Section.

5. *Securities Held by the Company or an Affiliate.* According to the ABF Indenture Commentaries (at 42), the more usual practice is to include as outstanding those Securities which are owned by the Company and its Affiliates except for purposes of giving consents, waivers, etc.; but it is possible to exclude such Securities from the category of those outstanding. ABF Indenture Commentaries (at 42). The second sentence of Section 2.09 is new and reflects a common exception to the preceding sentence (prohibiting consents by the Company and its Affiliates), to the extent such Securities are held by a pledgee.

6. *Exit Consents.* Many bondholders object to issuers obtaining a consent to an amendment or a waiver where the Securities providing such consents or waiver are substantially simultaneously retired by the Company (an "exit consent"). If such an exit consent were to be prohibited, this would be a rational place to do so.

Section 2.11

1. *Global Securities.* Many securities, including securities sold in reliance on Rule 144A (17 C.F.R. §230.144A) under the Securities Act of 1933, 15 U.S.C. §§77a-77aa (the "1933 Act" or "Securities Act"), are generally issued in the form of global securities, i.e., securities are issued in the name of a depository (such as Depository Trust Company ("DTC")) and transfers among the beneficial owners of such securities are made by book-entry on the depository's books. If global securities are to be used, changes would also be made to the form of security to add appropriate legends and otherwise reflect that the security is a global security, and to add transfer provisions. *See* Note 1 to Section 2.01.

Section 2.12

1. *Destruction of Securities.* This Section is largely unchanged from the 1983 MSI, other than the change to permit the Trustee to dispose of canceled securities in accordance with its standard procedures. The Model Simplified Indenture, like the ABF Model Indentures, does not direct the Trustee to destroy securities surrendered to it. Destruction or other disposition of cancelled securities should be made the subject of a standing instruction from the Company to the Trustee, taking into account applicable document retention requirements and the Trustee's standard procedures.

Section 2.13

1. *Payees of Defaulted Interest*. On the date an interest payment is due, if not made, that interest becomes "Defaulted Interest." This Section 2.13 thereafter requires that defaulted interest be paid to Securityholders as of a special record date, as provided in this Section. The rights of persons who were registered holders of the Securities on the regular record date are therefore specifically overridden.

2. *Payment Methods*. This Section is a more detailed version of Section 2.12 of the 1983 MSI, placing more emphasis on the need to provide notice to Securityholders prior to the subsequent payment. Securityholders need prompt notice of record dates so that information can accurately be reflected in trading and valuations of securities.

3. *Interest on Defaulted Interest*. Assuming Section 4.01 requires the payment of interest on Defaulted Interest (as does the MSI), this Section needs to provide that such additional interest on Defaulted Interest is payable to the holders receiving the Defaulted Interest.

Article 3 Generally

1. *Scope of Redemption Right*. The parameters of the Company's redemption right are set forth in the form of security, rather than in Article 3.

2. *Issues Under Article 3*. Redemption provisions, like subordination provisions, are now more likely to be negotiated in light of specific facts relevant to an issuer than was true in 1983. Redemption provisions may include limitations on redemption where the funds used were obtained from less expensive financing, although there have been a series of cases growing out of such provisions where the issuer involved allegedly evaded the limitation illegally. *See, e.g.*, Shenandoah Life Ins. Co. v. Valero Energy Corp., No. 9032, 1988 Del. Ch. LEXIS 84, *25-*27 (Del. Ch. June 21, 1988); Morgan Stanley & Co. Inc. v. Archer Daniels Midland Co., 570 F. Supp. 1529, 1542-43 (S.D.N.Y. 1983). *See also* Texas-New Mexico Power Co. v. Jackson Nat'l Life Ins. Co., No. 4:95-CV-758-Y, 1997 U.S. Dist. LEXIS 5640 (N.D. Tex. Mar. 31, 1997) (discussing whether non-callable bonds could be redeemed because the proceeds to be used were received from "condemnation or eminent domain proceedings"). The Model Simplified Indenture does not provide language for such limitations.

Section 3.01

1. *Specification to the Trustee*. Since redemption may be effected under the mandatory, optional, or "additional optional" provisions of the form of Security, specification to the Trustee (in the required notice) appears appropriate. The ABF Model Indentures have no such requirement. *See also* Note 1 to Section 3.03.

2. *Securities To Be Credited*. Note this Section 3.01 (and Paragraph 6 of the Securities) permit converted Securities to be credited against the mandatory redemption amounts, if any. This is a term which may be negotiated out of the provision, in which event both this Section and Paragraph 6 should be modified.

3. *Notice Period*. The Model Simplified Indenture continues the provision specifying that notice of redemption shall be at least 50 days unless a shorter period is satisfactory to the Trustee. Note this provision may permit the manipulation of a

redemption date to force bondholders to convert just prior to an interest payment date, thus losing all accrued interest. *See, e.g.*, Elliott Assocs. v. J. Henry Schroder Bank & Trust Co., 655 F. Supp. 1281, 1287 (S.D.N.Y. 1987), *aff'd*, 838 F.2d 66 (2d Cir. 1998). Recommended changes to the conversion provisions (*see* Section 10.02 and Notes 1 and 2 to Section 10.02) can prevent that result.

Section 3.02

1. *Method of Selection.* The first sentence of this Section was changed from the 1983 MSI (which specified selection on a pro rata basis or by lot) to a formulation which gives the Trustee both clearly permissible methods and discretion if needed.

2. *Time of Selection.* The ABF Model Indentures provide for selection of Securities to be redeemed not more than 60 days prior to the redemption date. The Model Simplified Indenture, in specifying the methods of selection, adopts the approach of the ABF Model Indentures but prescribes a period of not more than 75 days since the notice of redemption may be given as early as 60 days before the redemption date.

3. *Notice to the Company.* The ABF Model Indentures also provide for a notice by the Trustee to the Company with respect to the Securities selected for redemption. The Model Simplified Indenture omits such a requirement since the Company can always make inquiry of the Trustee if it cares to do so.

Section 3.03

1. *Specification to the Securityholder.* While certain holders, particularly institutions, have expressed an interest in knowing whether redemption is being made pursuant to the mandatory, optional or "additional optional" provisions of the form of Security (among other reasons, to ensure that the redemption is permitted under the Indenture), the Model Simplified Indenture (like the ABF Model Indentures) does not require that such information be included among the statements in the redemption notice to Securityholders.

2. *Notice by Mail.* This Section is the first of several which prescribe notice by mail directly by Securityholders, without a parallel requirement of publication. Where notice by the Trustee is required under this and other Sections of the Indenture, the Trustee is required only to mail to Securityholders as they appear on the register of Securityholders. To the extent that the registered Securityholders are depositories or other nominees, it is their responsibility to transmit notices to their participants or beneficial owners.

3. *Timing of Conversion.* Note the timing of the conversion right (clause (5)) is to ensure a well-timed call for redemption does not require a holder to relinquish a full interest payment in order to convert. *See* Section 10.02 and Notes 1 and 2 to Section 10.02.

Section 3.05

1. *Funds Deposited for Redemption.* The requirement of deposit of moneys "sufficient" to pay the redemption price plus accrued interest is intended to import a

requirement that on the redemption date the Paying Agent be in possession of funds then available (i.e., funds cleared for its use) to pay for redemption and accrued interest.

2. *Interest After the Redemption Date; Conversion.* The form of Security previously was the only place which specified that interest on a Security called for redemption ceases to accrue on the redemption date; that language has been moved into Section 3.05. In addition, the effect on the conversion right is specified here, as well as the effect of a Default in paying a Security called for redemption on the redemption date.

Section 4.01

1. *Promise to Pay.* The Model Simplified Indenture defers to tradition in including in this Section a promise to pay that duplicates the promise to each Securityholder appearing in the form of Security. Inclusion of this separate promise running to the Trustee arose out of the need, prior to enactment of the TIA, to confer standing on the Trustee to enforce payment on behalf of the Securityholders. *See* Note 1 to Section 6.08.

2. *Payments Deemed to be Made.* By depositing with the Paying Agent a sum sufficient for the purpose (*see* Note 1 to Section 3.05), the Company is considered to have honored its obligation to pay principal and interest on the Securities, and those Securities cease to be outstanding. This Section makes clear that the Company must deposit an amount sufficient to pay all principal and interest due on the particular date, not (for example) just enough to pay principal and interest on Securities called for redemption if other amounts are due on the same date. As set forth in Section 2.04, each Paying Agent agrees to hold in trust all amounts so deposited.

3. *Interest on Overdue Payments.* While indentures generally provide that interest on overdue principal (and overdue interest, if lawful) will be computed at the pre-default rate, some users may consider this subject to be a matter for negotiation. If used, a penalty rate may better be placed in the Indenture than in the form of Security.

Section 4.02

1. *"Filing."* Assuming that TIA Section 314(a)(1), if applicable, were deemed satisfied, and the Trustee agreed, a "filing" might in the future include electronic transmissions to the Trustee.

2. *Reports by Company to Trustee and Securityholder.* TIA Section 314(a)(1) requires the Company to file its Exchange Act reports with the Trustee, but neither the SEC nor the stock exchanges require the Company to send Exchange Act reports or periodic shareholder reports to debtholders. The new sentence at the end of Section 4.02 requires the Company to mail quarterly and annual reports to Holders if made available to stockholders (whether by mail or otherwise), which is now a standard provision in most indentures. *Cf.* TIA §314(a)(3).

3. *Issuer No Longer a Reporting Company.* If the Company is not publicly-traded or ceases to be subject to the reporting requirements of the Exchange Act, many indentures add a provision which requires the filing, with the Trustee, of the information, documents, and reports comparable to those required pursuant to Section 13 of the Securities Exchange Act of 1934 ("Exchange Act"), 15 U.S.C. §78m, in respect of a

Security listed and registered on a national security exchange. *See* Note 2 to Sections 7.01/7.02. Such a provision might read:

> [In the event the Company is at any time no longer] (or) [If and so long as the Company is not] subject to the reporting requirements of Section 13 or 15(d) of the Exchange Act, the Company will prepare, in accordance with generally accepted accounting principles, (i) for the first three quarters of each fiscal year, quarterly financial statements substantially equivalent to the financial statements required to be included in a report on Form 10-Q under the Exchange Act, and (ii) on an annual basis, complete audited consolidated financial statements. The Company will provide such quarterly statements to the Trustee and Holders not later than [45] days after the end of each of the first three quarters of the fiscal year and annual reports not later than [90] days after the end of each fiscal year.

4. *Rule 144A Information*. Securities offered in a Rule 144A offering will have a paragraph requiring that the Company make information required under Rule 144A(d)(4) available during any period the Company is not subject to Section 13 or 15(d) of the Exchange Act. Such a provision might read:

> For so long as the Securities are Transfer Restricted Securities, the Company will continue to provide to Holders and to prospective purchasers of the Securities, the information required by Rule 144A(d)(4) under the Securities Act of 1933, as amended, and the Trustee shall make any such reports available to Securityholders upon request. In such event, such reports shall be provided at the times the Company would have been required to provide reports and had it continued to have been subject to the reporting requirements of Section 13 or 15(d) of the Exchange Act.

Section 4.03

1. *Reason for Compliance Certificate*. An annual certificate to this effect is required under TIA Section 314(a)(4).

2. *Contents of Compliance Certificate*. If the annual certification includes reference to a Default that occurred during the last fiscal year, it must also describe the status of the Default (i.e., continuing, cured or waived) at the time of certification. The Model Simplified Indenture, however, unlike the ABF Model Indentures, requires the inclusion in such certificate of the four recitals that derive from TIA Section 314(e) and are listed in Section 12.04.

3. *Timing of Compliance Certificate*. The suggested 105 day period is 15 days after the date an issuer required to file reports under the Exchange Act would be required to file its annual report on Form 10-K. This would therefore be at the end of the fifteen day period permitted under Section 4.02 for an issuer to provide copies of its reports to the Trustee.

Section 4.04

1. *New Covenant*. This covenant, which has no counterpart in the 1983 MSI, is designed to give prompt notice to the Trustee of events which are likely to affect the Securities. Note the Trustee's obligation to mail a notice to Securityholders of certain Defaults under Section 7.05.

Article 4 Further Covenants

1. *Techniques for Addition*. Where it is not practical to add covenants in full after Section 4.04, users might consider a single Section 4.05, to the general effect that "the Company shall perform each of the further covenants appearing in Appendix 1, which is part of this Article 4," with the text and related definitions of the several additional covenants set forth at length in an appendix attached to, and integrally a part of, the Indenture in the same manner as Exhibit A—the form of Security. In any event, users adding covenants should consider whether summary disclosure concerning any of such covenants should be set forth in the form of Security.

Section 5.01

1. *Scope*. It should be noted that this Section only applies to a transaction in which the Company consolidates or merges with or into another corporation or transfers or leases assets to another corporation.

2. *Non-Corporate Successors*. The ABF Model Indentures preclude the possibility of a non-corporate substituted obligor on the Securities by the combination of the traditional covenants (i) to preserve the obligor's corporate existence (which is omitted from the Model Simplified Indenture) and (ii) to limit consolidation, merger, or asset transfer only to "another corporation." The Model Simplified Indenture seeks to achieve the same effect by requiring a corporate successor in clause (1) of this Section. Given the rate of evolution in capital formation devices and the increased use of vehicles (such as joint ventures) for projects involving the possibility of a public borrowing, the likelihood, over the life of a long-term Security issue, of substituting a non-corporate obligor by asset transfer should not be discarded without thought. It should be remembered, nevertheless, that certain institutional investors (particularly life insurance companies) may be substantially disadvantaged if debt instruments in their portfolios become the obligations of non-corporate obligors.

3. *Foreign Successor Obligors*. The ABF Model Indentures also preclude consolidation, merger and asset transfer except to domestic corporations. The 1983 MSI stopped short of that prohibition; the Model Simplified Indenture returns to the ABF Model Indenture concept, which is more consistent with current practices. Note that because there is no clear practice on whether corporations formed under the laws of a territory of the United States should be included in clause (1) of Section 5.01, they are excluded unless the language of clause (1) is expressly modified. The note set forth immediately above applies as well to the possibility of foreign successor obligors.

4. *Triangular Transactions*. The Model Simplified Indenture takes the position that the basic obligations under the Securities should follow the initial obligor's assets (but see Notes 5 and 6 below). However, the exception to clause (2) of this Section recognizes the frequent pattern of merger into a subsidiary or vice versa, with the parent assuming subsequent obligations under Article 10—Conversions. The exception to clause (2) is also directed to the cash merger problems that were the subject of controversy in *Broad v. Rockwell Int'l Corp.*, 642 F.2d 929 (5th Cir. 1981).

5. *Any Series of Related Transactions*. In the context of asset disposition by transfer or lease, serious consideration must be given to the possibility of accomplishing

piecemeal, in a series of transactions, what is specifically precluded if attempted as a single transaction. Privately placed debt instruments frequently prohibit disposition of substantial assets (with a mathematical prescription of "substantial") in one or a series of related transactions. *See* Sharon Steel Corp. v. Chase Manhattan Bank, N.A., 691 F.2d 1039 (2d Cir. 1982).

6. *No Default*. Many indentures add, at the end of clause (3), a phrase similar to "and treating any Debt which becomes an obligation of the Company or of the resulting or surviving entity (if not the Company) as having been incurred at the time of such transaction."

7. *Opinion of Counsel*. At the end of the last paragraph of Section 5.01, many indentures carve out from the Opinion of Counsel any opinion regarding compliance with Section 5.01(3), or allow counsel to rely on representations of compliance under Section 5.01(3) contained in an Officers' Certificate. *See* Note 2 to Section 9.03.

Section 5.02

1. *Termination of the Obligations of the Prior Obligor*. Under the ABF Model Indentures, the prior obligor remains liable on the Securities. The 1983 MSI was similarly structured so that, whether or not the successor obligor properly assumes the obligations, the prior obligor (except in case of a merger or consolidation) is not released from its obligations to pay principal and interest on the Securities. Thus, if company A sold all of its assets to company B, which assumes all of A's liabilities, company A remained obligated to pay the Securities if B fails to do so. *See* Alleco Inc. v. IBJ Schroder Bank & Trust Co., 745 F.Supp. 1467 (D. Minn. 1989). The Model Simplified Indenture expressly releases the issuer, except for the specified obligations noted. *See also* form of Securities, Note 8.

Section 6.01

1. *Involuntary Defaults*. The ABF Model Indentures include, in the introductory clause to the default list, a lengthy parenthetical phrase which makes clear that Default is occasioned whether the occurrence "shall be voluntary or involuntary or be effected by operation of law." The ABF Indenture Commentaries (at 205) explain that this introductory material is intended to refute any argument that events resulting from *force majeure* are not to be treated as Defaults. The ABF Indenture Commentaries go on to say that some draftsmen feel this phrasology to be unnecessary, and the 1983 MSI took that view. The inclusion of language in the second paragraph of Section 6.01 to address this issue reflects the more common practice, not a change in view. *See* Chase Manhattan Bank v. Traffic Stream (BVI) Infrastructure Ltd., 86 F. Supp. 2d 244 (S.D.N.Y. 2000) (disscussion of involuntary defaults).

2. *Cross Defaults and Subsidiaries' Defaults*. The inclusion of cross-default provisions, and the drafting of such provisions, are matters for negotiation and are not addressed in the Model Simplified Indenture. Similarly, the extent to which subsidiaries of an issuing Company represent a major part of the credit upon which the Securityholders are relying, and should therefore be included (along with the Company) in clauses (4) and (5) of this Section 6.01, is left to negotiation.

3. *Custodian.* The particular language of clauses (4)(C) and (5)(B) of this Section is derived from 11 U.S.C. §303(h)(2).

4. *General Inability or Failure to Pay Debts as They Become Due.* Some current instruments include, among the specified defaults, the general inability or failure on the part of the Company to pay its debts as they become due. The Model Simplified Indenture omits this provision on the ground that it may be a disguised cross-default and bestows no obvious practical advantage on the Securityholders but, particularly in times of tight or expensive funds, it may inhibit the Company's ability to stretch its payables.

5. *Grace Periods.* Grace periods are by their nature arbitrarily selected. The Model Simplified Indenture retains 30 days as the grace period for Default in payment of interest but prescribes 60 days as the period of non-compliance with an indenture covenant after receipt of proper notice of the Default. The ABF Model Indentures use 30 days for both. Note that if there is a dispute as to whether a Default exists or not, the short period makes adjudication of the issue prior to the expiration of the cure period practically impossible, which is disadvantageous to the issuer. *See* Metropolitan Life Ins. Co. v. RJR Nabisco Inc., 906 F.2d 884, 892 (2d Cir. 1990) (court declined to toll cure period pending determination of whether default had occurred).

6. *Disclosure; Accounting Consequences.* An issuer that is subject to the reporting requirements of Section 13(a) or 15(d) of the Exchange Act must disclose material Defaults under an indenture to the SEC on Form 10-Q, Item 3—Defaults upon Senior Securities, and in its financial statements pursuant to Rule 4-08(c) under Regulation S-X, 17 C.F.R. §210.4-08(c) (1999). Certain events which are (e.g., bankruptcy) or may (e.g., acquisitions or dispositions which violate financial covenants) be Defaults under the Indenture may also be reported on Form 8-K. Further, if the maturity of a long-term debt issue may be accelerated because of a Default, the issuer may have to reclassify the issue as short-term debt until the Default is cured or waived. *See* Financial Accounting Standards Board [FASB], Statement of Financial Accounting Standards No. 78, *Classification of Obligations that Are Callable by the Creditor* (1983). Finally, if the consequences of Default may be material to investors, the issuer may have an obligation to provide "timely public disclosure" under Rule 10b-5 and other anti-fraud provisions and under applicable stock exchange policies. *See, e.g.,* NYSE Listed Co. Manual ¶ 202.05.

Section 6.02

1. *Percentage of Holders Required for Acceleration.* The ABF Model Indentures use a 25% figure in the analog to this Section but use only a 10% figure in the analog to the final paragraph of Section 6.01 (the percentage of Holders whose notice to the Company and the Trustee is requisite to the ripening of the specified Default). The Model Simplified Indenture uses 25% for both purposes.

2. *Accrued Interest.* The ABF Model Indentures do not specify that, upon acceleration, accrued interest as well as principal of the Securities shall become due and payable immediately. In part this may be because the ABF Model Indentures, or at least the ABF Indenture Commentaries, were written with coupon debentures in mind; the ABF Indenture Commentaries refer (at 218), in this connection, to the requirement that coupons be presented on the specified interest payment dates.

The Model Simplified Indenture, on the other hand, does specify acceleration of interest, presumably interest accrued to the date of declaration.

3. *Rescission of Acceleration*. The ABF Model Indentures, along with many current instruments, include a lengthy paragraph providing that after acceleration the holders of a majority in principal amount of the outstanding Securities may rescind the declaration and its consequences, subject to compliance by the Company with a set of conditions. The Model Simplified Indenture subsumes all such conditions within the phrase "cured or waived" in the final sentence of this Section. (The Model Simplified Indenture deliberately uses the same majority requirement for rescission of acceleration in this Section and for waiver in Section 6.04; the ABF Indenture Commentaries point out alternative possibilities (at 472-73).) *See also* Note 2 to Section 6.04.

4. *Relationship to Sections 6.04 and 6.05*. Although the holders of only 25% in principal amount of the Securities may accelerate upon an Event of Default, the Model Simplified Indenture does not attempt to create an impasse between a 25% minority and the majority. It is intended that the power of the majority, bestowed by Sections 6.04 and 6.05, shall in any event govern.

5. *Relationship to Article 11*. While a declaration of acceleration may make Principal and interest on the Securities immediately payable, no payment on the Securities may be made during the continuance of the circumstances provided for in Sections 11.02 and 11.03.

Section 6.03

1. *Available Remedies*. In authorizing the Trustee to "pursue any available remedy" for collection on the Securities or enforcement of the Indenture, the Model Simplified Indenture subsumes all of the customary phraseology: "actions, suits or proceedings," "at law or in equity," "under this Indenture or otherwise by law," etc. *Cf.* ABF Indenture Commentaries at 225-26. The provision that the Trustee may bring suit without having the Securities in its possession has been retained in the Model Simplified Indenture, although some may consider it unnecessary.

2. *Fraud claims*. The Indenture does not empower the Trustee to pursue claims which may be available to purchasers or sellers of Securities under state or federal securities laws or the common law for misrepresentations inducing them to purchase or hold the securities. *See* Central Bank of Denver, N.A. v. Deloitte & Touche, 928 P.2d 754, 758 (Colo. Ct. App. 1996); *cf.* Continental Bank, N.A. v. Caton, 1990 Fed. Sec. L. Rep (CCH) ¶ 95,623, at 97,922 (D. Kan. Aug. 6, 1990); *In re* Washington Pub. Power Supply Sys. Sec. Litig., 623 F. Supp. 1466, 1483-84 (W.D. Wash. 1985), *aff'd*, 823 F.2d 1349 (9th Cir. 1987). The Trustee's role is to enforce the rights arising under the Indenture and the Securities against the Company for the equal benefit of all Securityholders. For various reasons pursuing fraud claims may create a conflict for the Trustee in fulfilling that role. Fraud claims may be held by persons no longer holders of Securities who sold their Securities after the fraud was discovered as well as by persons who continue to hold Securities. Securityholders may have different rights depending on when they purchased their Securities and the extent to which they can prove reliance on the fraud. Recoveries by holders of fraud claims may prejudice collections by current holders. Lastly, securities fraud claims may be

subordinated to the claims upon the Securities of current holders under Section 510(b) of the Bankruptcy Code, thereby potentially raising adverse interests between fraud claimants and current Holders as to the desirability of or distributions in Proceedings. If a Trustee has the right to assert these claims against the Company and others such as the Company's accountants and investment bankers, it would also have to consider the extent to which it has an obligation to investigate whether such claims may exist. Existing procedures where such claims are pursued by individual or class actions by the injured parties do not appear to require changes to Indentures to change the party responsibility for pursuing such claims. *See also* Note 1 to Section 6.06.

Section 6.04

1. *Sequence of Events.* As is implicit in Note 3 to Section 6.02, the sequence of events is: first, Default under Section 6.01; second, acceleration under the first sentence of Section 6.02; third, waiver under this Section 6.04 or cure by the Company; and fourth, rescission under the last sentence of Section 6.02. Conceptually, waiver or cure is a precondition to rescission of acceleration.

2. *Effect of Waiver.* Unlike the ABF Model Indentures, the Model Simplified Indenture omits the traditional language to the effect that no waiver shall have an effect upon any unwaived occurrence or upon a repetition of the waived occurrence. As a practical matter, any waiver given under this Section should state the date as of which it speaks and specify that it has no effect on any occurrence not specifically waived. (An action rescinding acceleration, under the last sentence of Section 6.02, should be equally specific.)

3. *Waiver of Past Default vs. Approval of Supplemental Indentures.* The Model Simplified Indenture uses a majority provision for waiver of past Defaults but a two-thirds provision for consent to supplemental indentures. The ABF Indenture Commentaries point out alternative possibilities (at 472-73), and it is noted that some indentures covering debt securities to be offered under Securities Act Rule 415 have used a majority provision in both contexts. If the same percentage is used in both contexts, then those waiving a past Default will have the capacity, by consenting to a supplemental indenture, to effect what amounts to a permanent waiver.

Section 6.05

1. *Refusal by the Trustee.* The Model Simplified Indenture specifies three grounds for the Trustee's refusal to follow the directions of the holders of a majority of the Securities. *Cf.* ABF Indenture Commentaries at 237. In this connection, attention is drawn to Section 7.01(c), which relates to indemnities satisfactory to the Trustee. Upon receiving such indemnities, the Trustee may not refuse to follow a direction, otherwise unexceptionable, that might create liability for it in its capacity as Trustee, but the Model Simplified Indenture (unlike the ABF Model Indentures) specifies that the Trustee may refuse to follow a direction that would involve it in personal liability.

Section 6.06

1. *"No Action" Clauses.* No action clauses are strictly construed against the issuer and have been enforced in a variety of contexts in both federal and state courts. *See, e.g.,* Watts v. Missouri-Kansas-Texas R.R. Co., 383 F.2d 571, 575 (5th Cir. 1967); UPIC & Co. v. Kinder-Care Learning Ctrs., Inc., 793 F. Supp. 448, 454 (S.D.N.Y. 1992); Lichter v. Land Title Guarantee & Trust Co., 150 N.E.2d 70, 75 (Ohio Ct. App. 1957); *cf.* Cruden v. Bank, 957 F.2d 961, 968 (2d Cir. 1992) (clause strictly construed against *bondholders*). The clause applies, however, only to suits brought to enforce contract rights under the Indenture or the Securities, not to suits asserting rights arising under other laws. *See, e.g.,* McMahan & Co. v. Wherehouse Entertainment, Inc., 65 F.3d 1044, 1051 (2d Cir. 1995) (actions based on federal securities laws may not be precluded by the no-action clause); *accord* Kusner v. First Pa. Corp., 531 F.2d 1234, 1239 (3d Cir. 1976); Envirodyne Indus. Inc. v. Connecticut Mut Life Co. (*In re* Envirodyne Indus., Inc.), 174 B.R. 986, 992-93 (Bankr. N.D. Ill. 1994); Acacia Nat'l Life Ins. Co. v. Kay Jewelers, Inc., 610 N.Y.S.2d 209, 212 (App. Div. 1994). Actions to enforce the Indenture or Securities which are exceptions to the "no action" provisions are contained in Section 6.07. *See also* Notes 1 and 2 to Section 6.07.

Note that the introductory language requiring compliance prior to pursuing a remedy "with respect to this Indenture *or the Securities*" indicates merely that claims to enforce the contractual terms of the Securities (which may include rights incorporated from the Indenture) are likewise subject to the no-action clause (subject to the exclusion noted in the preceding paragraph). *See* UPIC Co. v. Kinder-Care Learning Ctrs., Inc., 793 F. Supp. 448, 455 n.8 (S.D.N.Y. 1992).

To aid the enforceability of this Section, paragraph 14 of the form of Security discloses the limitation on Securityholders' right to sue. *See* ABF Indenture Commentaries at 232-35. *See generally Conflict of Interests Between Indenture Trustee and Bondholders: Avoidance of "No Action" Clauses Prohibiting Bondholder Suits Against the Obligor,* 62 YALE L.J. 1097 (1953).

2. *Trustee's Indemnity.* Old "no-action" provisions, including the 1983 MSI, require, in addition to the notices and other requirements of this Section 6.06, that the Securityholders provide the Trustee with a satisfactory indemnity before the Trustee is required to bring action. The deletion of such a requirement here recognizes that the Trustee still may insist on indemnity as a condition of bringing action (*see* Sections 6.05 and 7.01(c)), but the Securityholders' failure to provide one does not block their ability to bring a suit or other action (provided the other provisions of Section 6.06 are met). In a circumstance where the Securities are unsecured, Securityholders may be hesitant to post an indemnity, because there is no easy means to recover from other holders any amounts expended under the indemnity.

3. *Securityholders' Derivative Suits.* The courts have traditionally denied standing to debtholders to bring derivative suits on behalf of a solvent corporation. Standing to bring such suits might nullify the effect of this Section. *See* John Coffee & Donald Schwartz, *The Survival of the Derivative Suit: An Evaluation and a Proposal for Legislative Reform,* 81 COLUM. L. REV. 261, 313 & n.277 (1981). *But see* Note, *Creditors' Derivative Suits on Behalf of Solvent Corporations,* 88 YALE L.J. 1299, 1300 & n.11 (1979).

4. *Shortening of Time Periods.* The 1983 MSI and ABF Model Indentures fixed the period of 60 days for a Trustee to respond to a request for action. Such a lengthy period is inconsistent with the exigencies of the modern world. A "pre-packaged" bankruptcy case can be taken from filing to confirmation of a plan in less than 60 days. The Model Simplified Indenture suggests that the 60 days be shortened to 15 or at most 30 days. It also provides a mechanism for the Trustee to further shorten the period by delivering a notice by which the Trustee declares that it will not comply with the request for action, clearing the way for the Holders to proceed.

5. *Notice to Securityholders.* An optional provision added to Section 7.05 requires the Trustee to notify other Securityholders of Securityholder notices it receives pursuant to Section 6.06 (which would include a notice under Section 6.06(4), and of a notice the Trustee provides under Section 6.06(3)(i)).

Section 6.07

1. *Exceptions to "No Action" Prohibition.* Section 6.07 contains the provision required by TIA Section 316(b) that a Securityholder have the right to sue directly to collect interest and Principal when due. Such suits, as well as actions to enforce conversion rights, are expressly exempted from the obligation to comply with Section 6.06.

2. *Securityholder's Right to Act as a Petitioning Creditor.* Consistent with Ninth Circuit opinion in *Grey v. Federated Group, Inc.* (*In re* Federated Group, Inc.), 107 F.3d 730 (9th Cir. 1997), the Model Simplified Indenture explicitly rejects, as wrongly decided, the cases holding that the "no-action" clause prevents a security-holder from acting as a petitioning creditor in a bankruptcy case. *See In re* Marcade Group, Inc., Case No. 92-B-43920, 1992 Bankr. LEXIS 2484 (Bankr. S.D.N.Y. Aug. 2, 1992); *In re* Iroquois Brands, Inc., No. 91-01018-H3-11, 1991 Bankr. LEXIS 1915, *6-*9 (Bankr. S.D. Tex. Mar. 7, 1991); *In re* Electro Audio Dynamics, Inc., Case No. 888 81406-20, 1989 Bankr. LEXIS 2755 (Bankr. E.D.N.Y. Sept. 25, 1989); *cf.* Envirodyne Indus., Inc. v. Connecticut Mut Life Co. (*In re* Envirodyne Indus., Inc.), 174 B.R. 986, 997 (Bankr. N.D. Ill. 1994) (holding that securityholders could act as petitioning creditors). Restating TIA Section 316(b), the first paragraph of Section 6.07 preserves the Securityholder's independent right to seek payment of the principal of and interest on his Security. A bankruptcy petition is simply another form of remedy to recover on the Securityholder's claim, if the other conditions for filing a petition exist. That right, like the right to file suit for the amounts due under the holder's Security, is not subject to the "no action" limitation on pursuit of remedies arising under the Indenture which necessarily affect all Securityholders. Section 6.07 does not empower a Securityholder to accelerate the principal of a Security, except by the means set forth in Section 6.02.

3. *Changes Affecting Mandatory Redemption Before Maturity.* As under TIA Section 316(b) the Model Simplified Indenture provides that a Securityholder's right to receive Principal and interest when due may not be impaired or affected without that holder's consent. It is recognized that this provision, like TIA Section 316(b), tends to frustrate consensual recapitalizations outside bankruptcy proceedings since Securityholders which do not consent to changes to payment or maturity terms are perceived by consenting Securityholders as benefiting (and even improving

their positions) because of the consenting Securityholders' concessions. Moreover, if there are enough non-consenting holders, or if the disparity in terms offered to consenting and non-consenting holders is too great, the recapitalization outside bankruptcy is likely to fail. *See* UPIC & Co. v. Kinder-Care Learning Ctrs., Inc., 793 F. Supp. 448, 453 (S.D.N.Y. 1992). *See generally* Mark J. Roe, *The Voting Prohibition in Bond Workouts*, 97 YALE L.J. 232 (1987). The percentage of Securityholders prescribed in Section 9.02 may, however, consent to an amendment of the Indenture to change or suspend the mandatory redemption provisions of the Securities, unless Section 9.02(4) provides otherwise. *See* ABF Indenture Commentaries at 309 (with respect to "sinking funds"); SECURITIES AND EXCHANGE COMMISSION, MANUAL OF THE TRUST INDENTURE ACT OF 1939, at 148 (1958) [hereinafter SEC TIA Manual].

Section 6.08

1. *Money or Property Held or Collected*. The introductory language of Section 6.08 is intended to clarify that the "waterfall" provisions apply: (i) regardless of who holds or collects the money or other property to be distributed (although in every instance, it must be either paid over to the Trustee or Paying Agent or otherwise segregated and clearly identified as property to be distributed in satisfaction of obligations under the Indenture (e.g., a payment pursuant to a confirmed plan in bankruptcy)); (ii) that it applies to money or other property; and (iii) that it applies after the occurrence of an Event of Default, regardless of when the money or other property has been collected or set aside for the distribution.

2. *Recovery on Proof of Claim*. *In re* Firstmark Corp., Case Nos. IP 89-1356-c, IP 92-176-C (S.D. Ind. June 22, 1992), enforced the trustee's rights to recover its fees and expenses from the securityholders' distributions through the operation of this Section of the indenture while refusing to enforce the "lien" granted to the trustee under Section 7.07. *See also* Blue-bird Partners v. First Fidelity Bank, 671 N.Y.S.2d 7, 11-12 (App. Div. 1998).

3. *Payment over to the Company*. Clause four of this Section is characterized by the ABF Indenture Commentaries (at 231) as "improper conformance to secured bond indenture precedents," on the ground that the Trustee for unsecured debentures cannot collect or hold any monies beyond the indebtedness and related expenses. The Model Simplified Indenture respectfully disagrees.

4. *Escheat*. The payment of any unused funds back to the Company is also related to the provisions of Section 8.04, pursuant to which unclaimed moneys held by the Trustee or any paying agent, in the administration of the Indenture, are paid back to the Company upon its request after two years. *See* Note 2 to Section 8.04. The intention of both provisions is to return funds to the Company, unless and until otherwise claimed. Obviously such provisions cannot change applicable state law, which generally prevents retention of such amounts by the issuer and requires payment over to the relevant state. *See, e.g.*, N.Y. ABAND. PROP. LAW §§300-306 (Consol. 1997); CAL. CIV. PROC. CODE §1516 (West 1997).

Section 6.09

1. *Undertaking for Costs.* Variance of the permissive provisions of TIA Section 315(e) in favor of the Trustee would run counter to an administrative position which may be summarized as follows: when the TIA permits the inclusion of indenture provisions, all other provisions not consistent with those provisions are excluded. *See* ABF Indenture Commentaries at 472; ALI, Federal Securities Code §1305 cmt. 2(b) (1980).

Section 6.10

1. *Revision Note.* This provision is a modified form of Section 6.09 of the 1983 MSI. Note that 11 U.S.C. §501(a) expressly authorizes the Trustee to file proofs of claim on behalf of the Securityholders, and TIA Section 317(a)(2), incorporated by reference into every qualified indenture, confers this power as well. Non-qualified indentures may wish to include a specific provision conferring such powers. *See* Sections 6.08 and 6.09 of the 1983 MSI.

Section 6.11

1. *Ability of Beneficial Owners to Act.* This provision is new and, together with the changes to Section 6.06, is intended to address the difficulties experienced in connection with directions to the Trustee in situations requiring immediate action. Two difficulties which beneficial holders of Securities and Trustees commonly face in situations with rapidly evolving events are that the time periods in Section 6.06 may be too long and it is difficult to obtain direction from the registered holder where there are several tiers of indirect ownership between the beneficial holder and the registered holder. For instance, an institutional holder may have its securities held by a custodian. That custodian may, in turn, be the customer of an institution which is a direct participant in a depository. The Trustee's records reflect that the depository is the registered holder. While wishing to respond to the direction of a beneficial holder, the Trustee will be concerned that it lacks Indenture protections if it follows direction from one or more entities which assert that they are beneficial holders but which are not registered Holders under the Indenture. Section 7.01(c)(3) provides exculpation to the Trustee only where it follows a direction "in accordance with a direction received by it in accordance with Section 6.05." New Section 6.11 makes a beneficial holder who complies with its provisions a Holder for the purposes of giving directions under Section 6.05 and otherwise exercising rights under Article 6. This Section does not otherwise vary the rule that the Holder is the "Person in whose name a Security is registered." (Section 1.01, definition of Holder). The registered Holder remains the party entitled to payment and notices. *See* Sections 2.13 and 3.03.

Sections 7.01/7.02

1. *Duties and Rights.* The Model Simplified Indenture proposes Section 7.01 to cover the Trustee's duties, while Section 7.02 governs the Trustee's rights. An

argument can be made that some "duties" are "rights" (*see, e.g.*, Section 7.01 (b)) and many indentures essentially combine these provisions.

2. *The TIA.* Several provisions of the Model Simplified Indenture are taken, more or less verbatim, from the TIA (see, e.g., tie sheet). Of course, Sections 310-317 of the TIA are deemed incorporated into every indenture required to be qualified under the TIA and need not, therefore, be set forth. *See also* Notes 1 and 2 to Section 1.03. Nonetheless, there are reasons to add (or not to add) such provisions.

First, there has been some discussion as to whether the TIA is necessary or even desirable. In July 1995, the Capital Markets Deregulation and Liberalization Act, H.R. 2131, 104th Cong. (1995) was introduced. Title IV of that proposed legislation contained a repeal of the TIA, and testimony before Congress included arguments by some parties that the increasing sophistication of the market for debt instruments, the ability and willingness of institutional debtholders to negotiate with issuers, and tensions between a Trustee's desire to protect itself and the debtholders' desire to make decisions and to pursue action raised issues about the TIA, including the role of the Trustee. H.R. 2131 did not pass, but a report of the *SEC's Task Force on Disclosure Simplification* (Mar. 5, 1996) <http://www.sec.gov/news/studies/smpl.txt> recommends that the SEC evaluate the continued effectiveness of the TIA. To the extent that mandatory TIA provisions were deemed desirable by a debtholder, it would be important to include them in the Indenture in the event of a repeal (or simplification or amendment) of the TIA. In addition, this would ensure that the provisions would be readily ascertainable and accessible. *Cf. Century Bonds Prove Effective Financing Tool for Three Big Independents*, PETROLEUM FIN. WK., Nov. 25, 1996 (Apache Corp., Anadarko Petroleum Corp., and Union Pacific Resources Group Inc. followed Walt Disney's lead and issued "century bonds" or 100-year notes in 1996); Craig Karmin & Charlene Lee, *First-Ever 1,000-Year Corporate Bond is Readied As Issuer Counts on Demand for Higher Yields*, WALL ST. J., Oct. 7, 1997, at C27 (1997 offering of bonds due the year 2997); *see also* Note 1 to Section 1.03.

Second, many of the mandatory provisions can be supplemented. In addition, there are certain provisions of the TIA which are explicitly optional and therefore should be included (in full text or by reference) if desired. *See, e.g.*, TIA §§311(b), 315(a), 315(b), 315(d), 315(e), 316(a)(1).

3. *Standard of Care.* Section 7.01(c) provides that the Trustee remains liable for its own negligent action or its own negligent failure to act, which is the standard set forth in TIA Section 315(d). To the extent the Indenture is not TIA qualified, the Trustee may insist on a change to "grossly negligent."

4. *Interest on Trust Funds.* The ABF Indenture Commentaries point out (at 260-61) that trust funds are not expected to be held by the Trustee for any significant period of time, and that it is therefore rare to find an agreement by the Trustee to pay interest. Unless otherwise negotiated and provided, trustees are therefore presumed to be entitled to hold funds in non-interest bearing accounts and to retain the benefit, e.g., of any float on the funds.

5. *Segregation of Indenture Funds.* The ABF Indenture Commentaries explain (at 260) that express permission for the Trustee to commingle funds held under the Indenture is customary and reflects case and statutory law on the subject. It is normal in trust law that beneficiary assets may not be commingled except in a common trust fund or where specifically permitted by the trust instrument. Such express permission

is necessarily subject (as the ABF Indenture Commentaries note) to applicable state or federal banking law and regulations.

6. *Pre-Default Duties of Trustee.* The Model Simplified Indenture does not alter the very limited duties imposed under the TIA upon the Trustee prior to a Default, and in that connection includes (in clause (b)(1) of Section 7.01) the protective provision permitted by TIA Section 315(a)(1). The law is well established that prior to an event of default, the trustee's duties are limited to those explicitly set forth in the indenture (the "Four Corners Rule"). The trustee assumes broader duties only after an event of default. *See* TIA §315(a)(1); *see also* Lorenz v. CSX Corp., 1 F.3d 1406, 1415 (3d Cir. 1993); Meckel v. Continental Resources Co., 758 F.2d 811, 816 (2d Cir. 1985). As noted in the 1983 MSI, a contrary position was considered by the Reporter for the Federal Securities Code, who concluded:

"It has been persuasively urged that extension of the 'prudent man' test for purposes of *ascertaining the occurrence of a default* . . . would be impracticable and prohibitively expensive in terms of increased trustees' fees."

ALI, Federal Securities Code, intro. at xl (1980). *See generally* Richard B. Schreiber & Thomas G. Wood, *Caveat Indenture Trustee: Avoiding the Expanding Scope of Sutton's Law,* 121 TRUSTS & ESTATES 48 (Jan. 1982). [When asked why he robbed banks, notorious 1930s felon Willie Sutton replied, "Because that's where the money is." Thus Sutton's Law of Litigation for plaintiffs: "When in doubt, sue the bank."]

7. *Additional Immunity for Trustee.* The ABF Model Indentures deliberately omit the provision, contained in paragraph (d) of Section 7.02, exempting the Trustee from liability for any action taken in good faith which it believes to be authorized or within its rights or powers. The Model Simplified Indenture respectfully disagrees with one of the premises in the ABF Indenture Commentaries (at 258), to the effect that this provision will encourage the Trustee to act in questionable circumstances. The provision is, of course, subject to the overriding provisions of the TIA.

8. *Trustee's Right to Obtain Indemnity.* The Model Simplified Indenture adds clause (4) to Section 7.01(c) and deletes clause 7.01(e) in the 1983 MSI. These changes have two purposes. First, placing the provision that the Trustee does not have to risk its own funds in (c) will limit the introduction to Section 7.01(c) and in fact every other provision of the Indenture by reason of Section 7.01(d). Although this is not explicitly provided for in the TIA, it has been this way in the ABF Model and sanctioned by the SEC in its TIA Manual (at 109-110). Secondly, the existing language in the 1983 MSI which implies that the Trustee has the right to receive a specific indemnity each time does not express the underlying concept here as well as does the ABF Model from which clause (4) was adopted.

9. *Extent of Trustee's Knowledge.* One of the current legal questions relating to corporate trust work is to what extent there may, should, or must be an ethical wall between the corporate trust department and other departments of the bank. The addition of clause (e) to Section 7.02 is a first attempt to permit such a wall and to provide some protection to a trustee which adopts appropriate measures. It also acknowledges that corporate trust officers need not (and often it would be inappropriate for them to) solicit information about the Company and its debt from other departments of the Bank. One may question whether the adoption of a wall and the resultant protection is consistent with the TIA; but with the growing judicial and regulatory acceptance of (and in some cases requirements for) such walls, the provision may be effective in at least some circumstance.

Section 7.03

1. *Ownership of "Securities" by the Trustee and Its Other Dealings with the Company*. At the time of the 1983 MSI, the note to this section noted the long-standing debate as to whether a Trustee should be prohibited from having other relationships with the Company. This issue was resolved in the Trust Indenture Reform Act of 1990, Pub. L. No. 101-550, 104 Stat. 2721, which amended TIA Section 310(b) to provide that a Trustee need not eliminate or avoid conflicts until a default arises under the Indenture.

Section 7.05

1. *Timing of Notice of Default*. The obligation to mail notice of Default arises only when the Default is known to the Trustee. If that knowledge comes too long after the Default occurs (whether during or after the prescribed 90-day period) to allow mailing of notice as a practical matter within the period prescribed, the Trustee needs, and can, only mail the notice with such promptness as meets the overriding standard of Section 7.01. As to the optional sentence in brackets, see Note 5 to Section 6.06.

Section 7.06

1. *Annual Report*. Although May 15 is the date as of which the Trustee reports on certain possible conflicting interests under TIA Section 310(b)(9), neither May 15 nor any other date is prescribed for the annual report required under TIA Section 313(a). The Model Simplified Indenture, therefore, like the ABF Model Indentures, allows selection of any date desired for the latter purpose.

2. *Notification of Listing*. So many new requirements outside the Indenture (*see, e.g.*, Note 4 to Section 9.04) become applicable upon listing on a stock exchange that the Model Simplified Indenture requires the Company to notify the Trustee of the occurrence of that event.

Section 7.07

1. *Trustee's Compensation*. The Model Simplified Indenture, like the ABF Model Indentures, specifies that the Trustee's compensation is not limited by other laws governing compensation of trustees of express trusts.

2. *Indemnity*. Trustee counsel have consistently been unhappy with the indemnity provisions of the 1983 MSI. They are fair enough for a claim when the Company is solvent, not in Default, and there is no conflict between the Company and the Trustee, but there are few claims in that situation. Claims against the Trustee are much more likely to arise in a Default or insolvency situation or where the Trustee and the Company are in conflict. In these situations the 1983 MSI provisions do not seem appropriate. One way to address this issue is to confine the indemnity provision in the Model Simplified Indenture to a single sentence. For example, "The Company shall indemnify the Trustee against any loss, liability or expense incurred by it, unless incurred by the Trustee through its own negligence or bad faith." Another is to try to craft more comprehensive provisions, but since various trustees tend to develop

their unique proprietary versions of this provision, the Model Simplified Indenture offers no detailed provision. Note that the exclusion of any indemnity obligation where the loss or liability is incurred by the Trustee as a result of gross negligence is a change from the 1983 MSI, which negated indemnity on negligence; gross negligence is the more common current standard in non-TIA indentures. Many believe that such an indemnity obligation is not inconsistent with or prohibited in TIA indentures by TIA Section 315 because exculpation from liability (the subject of TIA Section 315) is different from indemnity.

3. *Experts Retained by the Trustee.* The term "agents," whose expenses are reimbursable to the Trustee, is not used restrictively in this Section, nor are the expenses of agents the only expenses so reimbursable. Expenses of and for experts and other professionals such as appraisers, accountants and investment bankers are comprehended in the first paragraph of this Section.

4. *Cooperation in Defense of Claims.* The Model Simplified Indenture specifies that the Trustee may have separate counsel (for which the Company will pay) in the defense of any claim directed against the Trustee in its capacity as such. The requirement of cooperation by the Trustee with the Company in such defense is not inappropriate.

5. *Recovery from Collections.* The fourth paragraph of Section 7.07 should not be construed as permitting the Trustee's right to recovery of its fees and expenses to be defeated by designating collection as intended only to pay the Securityholders. *See, e.g.,* Bluebird Partners v. First Fidelity Bank, 671 N.Y.S.2d 7 (App. Div. 1998). It is intended to address the circumstances where, for example, a partial redemption of particular Securities has been called and the Trustee holds money intended for redemption of those identifiable securities, or where a check in payment of interest has yet to be deposited.

6. *Expenses of Administration in Bankruptcy.* The final paragraph of this Section has been added in the Model Simplified Indenture. While the Indenture provisions cannot predetermine the decision of a Bankruptcy Judge on the question, it is desirable to state the intention of the Company and the Trustee, at the time of entry into the Indenture, that compensation due to the Trustee for services rendered and expenses incurred after commencement of a proceeding in bankruptcy shall constitute expenses of administration, with their attendant priority in payment. Nothing in this Section, however, requires the Trustee to file an administrative claim.

Section 7.08

1. *Appointment of Successor Trustee.* Since the Company will have an ongoing relationship with any substituted Trustee, the Model Simplified Indenture (like the ABF Model Indentures) provides for the Company's appointment of a successor, in the first instance, when a vacancy or prospective vacancy arises. While some indentures only permit Securityholders to name a successor Trustee with the Company's consent, the Model Simplified Indenture (again like the ABF Model Indentures) recognizes the legitimacy of the Securityholders' choice in the matter. *See* the second sentence of the third paragraph of this Section.

2. *For Want of a Trustee, etc.* In those rare circumstances where no successor Trustee has accepted appointment properly and in timely fashion, the Model

Simplified Indenture permits the retiring Trustee, the Company or Securityholders to petition for the appointment of a successor Trustee. Note if a holder of less than 10% in principal amount of the Securities so petitions, it may be required to post an undertaking pursuant to Section 6.09.

Section 8.01

1. *Pre-Maturity Discharge.* Under the Model Simplified Indenture, pursuant to the terms of the Indenture itself, the Company may by proper deposit terminate all its obligations under the Indenture, with only specified exceptions. However, this falls short of full defeasance (along the municipal debt model) because the Company's obligations under Section 4.01—Payment of Securities is one of the exceptions. The intended consequence is that (assuming no obligations under covenants added to Article 4 are also added to the list of exceptions specified in this Section) all substantive obligations undertaken by the Company for the benefit of Securityholders will be terminated by a proper deposit except that, no matter how or with whom it makes its deposit in trust, under the Model Simplified Indenture the Company will retain the ultimate responsibility vis-a-vis the Securityholders to assure that they are paid. The difference in result between the second sentence of this Section and the second sentence of Section 4.01 appeared to the drafting committee to be justified in view of the difference in the time periods over which funds due to the Securityholders are likely to be held by a third party (albeit a fiduciary in both cases). *See also* Note 3 to this Section.

2. *Distinction from "Economic Defeasance."* In mid-1982 some corporate debt issuers made pre-maturity deposits to a separate grantor trust to ensure interest and Principal payments on certain outstanding debt although the governing indentures contained no provisions therefor. Christened "economic defeasance," this technique achieved instant popularity, but the resulting accounting treatment was promptly made the subject of a proposed moratorium by the FASB, in its Action Alert dated August 11, 1982, and the subject of a temporary bar (prospectively applied) by the SEC, in Financial Reporting Release No. 3, 25 SEC DOCKET. 1220 (Aug. 24, 1982), rescinded in Financial Reporting Release No. 15, 29 SEC DOCKET 544 (Dec. 22, 1983) in light of the FASB standards adopted. *See* FASB Statement No. 125, Accounting for Transfers and Servicing of Financial Assets and Extinguishments of Liabilities (June 1996).

3. *Applicable Period.* The Model Simplified Indenture, like the ABF Model Indentures, limits the possibility of termination by the Company of certain of its obligations under the Indenture (*see* Note 1 to this Section) to the last year prior to redemption or maturity. Users intending to list Securities and concerned about the 10-day limit imposed in the New York Stock Exchange listing requirements (*see* NYSE Listed Co. Manual ¶ 703.06(D)) should note that the obligation to pay is not discharged under the Model Simplified Indenture prior to the date payment is due.

4. *Governmental Securities.* The class of securities with which the deposit contemplated by this Section may be made is deliberately limited to direct obligations of the United States (including mutual funds comprised of such obligations), in order to remain as close as possible to a cash deposit. If such a deposit is in fact made, Securityholders should be notified at the time discharge takes place (since the rating of the

Securities may be expected to improve to reflect their government securities backing). In any event, the class of eligible U.S. government securities should not be broader than the definition of "government security" in Section 2(a)(16) of the Investment Company Act of 1940, 15 U.S.C. §§80a-1 to-64, in order to avoid any problem that might otherwise arise under Section 3(a)(3) of that Act. Note, under Section 8.02, that the Trustee is entitled to reinvest money or U.S. Government Obligations, but only in money and U.S. Government Obligations.

5. *Reasons for Early Deposit.* The Company may wish to discharge the Indenture prior to maturity in order to be relieved of covenants that have become too restrictive, to remove debt from its balance sheet, or to effect a voluntary liquidation. It may be motivated to utilize the opportunity for discharge under this Section because (i) the Securities are non-callable or are not callable at the time, (ii) the Securities are callable but the call premium is too expensive (as in the case of deep discount or zero coupon securities), or (iii) the government securities necessary for deposit can be purchased at a substantial discount. Occasionally, as well, circumstances arise in which the Company might prefer to "buy in" the Securities but some Securityholders refuse to sell except at a prohibitive price, or in which the market for Securities is illiquid and the Company faces the necessity of paying a substantial premium to obtain Securities to be credited at par against required sinking fund payments; discharge by early deposit may then become a very important alternative.

6. *Mechanics of Deposit.* The Model Simplified Indenture contemplates that book entry (by which ownership of government securities is most frequently maintained) to the Trustee's account will be sufficient to effect the deposit with the Trustee.

7. *Amount of Deposit.* The money and government securities to be deposited must, by their terms, provide for sufficient sums to pay the Principal and interest on the Securities at redemption or maturity and at all intervening interest payment dates. In that connection, non-callable securities are required so that there will be no reinvestment risk. To match the cash inflow more exactly with cash requirements, the Company may be able to purchase, from a government bond dealer, certificates or receipts evidencing interests in stripped government bonds (bonds whose unmatured coupons have been removed in whole or in part and sold separately) or in the coupons stripped from such bonds. Many indentures include a provision requiring a certificate of an independent accounting firm that the amount of the deposit is sufficient.

8. *Alternative of Full Defeasance.* The SEC Release cited in Note 2 to this Section applies, pending issuance of a final FASB standard, unless the Company is discharged from all obligations with respect to the Securities. (A proposed SFAS, circulated by the FASB under date of October 13, 1982, would treat debt as extinguished "when the debtor's obligation is satisfied and there is no continuing or contingent recourse to the debtor," and would include as an example: "the debtor satisfies the debt pursuant to a defeasance provision, thereby eliminating the debtor's obligation to the creditor.") Users of the Model Simplified Indenture desiring the ability to achieve full defeasance must, therefore, add a reference (in the introductory clause of the first sentence of this Section) to termination of the Company's obligations under the Securities and must also delete the reference to Section 4.01 from the list of Sections specified (in the first paragraph of this Section) as surviving despite the deposit. In connection therewith, such users should consider the prospective consequences of such procedure, both at the time of drafting the Indenture and again at the time of making the deposit. In particular, consideration might be given to (i) indemnifying the Trustee or arranging

for payment of any taxes that may be imposed on the deposited government securities or on the Principal and interest payments on such securities received by the Trustee and (ii) making disclosure to Securityholders of the occurrence of the deposit and the tax and other consequences thereof. Summary disclosure in the form of Security should also be considered.

9. *Effect of Other Debt Instruments*. In some cases negative pledge clauses in other instruments governing the Company's outstanding debt may prohibit an early deposit, which in certain respects resembles a pledge of cash collateral as security for an antecedent debt.

10. *Relationship to Article 11*. The deposit contemplated by this Section is effectively payment in full of the Securityholders. Therefore, it may only be made when permitted by the subordination provisions (*see* the second sentence of clause (2) of this Section), but once properly made is free of the rights of holders of Senior Debt bestowed under Article 11 (*see* the third sentence of Section 8.02).

Section 8.02

1. *Reinvestment*. New language has been added to make explicit the Trustee's right to reinvest funds deposited with it in trust for the Holders.

Section 8.04

1. *Unclaimed Money*. Money returned to the Company (after being held for unclaimed Principal or interest by a Paying Agent for two years) ceases to be money held in trust under Section 2.04. *See* Note 4 to Section 6.08.

2. *Application of TIA Sections 317(b), 316(b)*. Some have asserted that TIA Sections 317(b) and 316(b) impose a mandatory trust on all monies paid over to a paying agent and that money designated for payment to a holder (as opposed to excess funds) is never properly returned to an issuer, even in a situation where the money would become subject to abandoned property laws. If this argument is correct (about which this draft expresses no view) this Section should be revised to provide that money should instead be paid by the paying agent to the appropriate governmental entity in accordance with applicable abandoned property law.

Section 9.01

1. *Uncertificated Securities*. Clause (3) of this Section was included in the 1983 MSI to assure adaptability to the then proposed amendments to U.C.C. Article 8 (adopted in New York in 1982, as N.Y. U.C.C. LAW §§8-101 to -602 (Consol. 1984 & Supp. 1998)), and permit amendment of the Indenture to provide for delivery of uncertificated Securities but not to mandate the replacement of certificated Securities. Clause (3) could now be used to make changes required to issue global securities. *See* Section 2.11.

2. *Ambiguities, Inconsistencies and Non-Adverse Changes*. The ABF Model Indentures allow amendment to cure ambiguities or correct inconsistencies or defects provided there is no adverse effect on the interest of Securityholders. The Model Simplified Indenture separates the two portions of that provision in recognition of

the fact that it is frequently impossible to cure ambiguities or correct inconsistencies or defects without some minimal impact, which may be characterized as "adverse," upon the Securityholders. As to non-adverse changes which are unrelated to ambiguities or inconsistencies, the Model Simplified Indenture avoids the qualitative "materially adverse" which is found in some indentures and tends to engender thorny judgmental distinctions.

Section 9.02

1. *The Majority Requirement.* See Note 3 to Section 6.04.

2. *Additional Limitations.* The Model Simplified Indenture specifies that the limitations of this Section (and all of Sections 6.04 and 6.07) are non-amendable without the consent of all Securityholders, as is the case in the ABF Model Indenture. Note, however, TIA Section 3.16(b) permits holders of not less than 75% of the Securities to postpone interest payments for up to three years, and such a provision could be added here.

3. *Amendments Affecting Subordination.* In this Section the Model Simplified Indenture states the requirements for amendments of Article 11, whether they affect the Securityholders (see clause (8) of this Section) or the holders of Senior Debt (see the second paragraph of this Section). With respect to the holders of Senior Debt, consent must be given by the holders of that percentage of the Senior Debt issue which is prescribed by the terms of the issue. With respect to the Securityholders, no counterpart to clause (8) of this Section is mentioned in the ABF Indenture Commentaries, and users concerned that Securityholders withholding consent could some day impede negotiations for restructuring of debt might consider returning to the general 66-2/3% requirement.

4. *Amendments Affecting Redemption.* See bracketed language in Section 9.02(4) and Note 3 to Section 6.04.

5. *Non-Identical Securities.* The Model Simplified Indenture, like the ABF Model Indentures, does not preclude the Company from offering to increase the interest rate or reduce the conversion price or otherwise to provide a benefit only for Securityholders who consent to an amendment. *See In re* Magic Marker Corp., SEC No-Action Letter (July 30, 1971), *available in* 1971 SEC No-Act. LEXIS 1341. However, note that the SEC has taken the position that certain modifications to existing indentures may constitute the "offer" or "sale" of a new security and therefore must be registered under the 1933 Act unless exempt. *See, e.g.,* Bryant B. Edwards & Jon J. Bancone, *Modifying Debt Securities: The Search for the Elusive "New Security" Doctrine,* 47 BUS. LAW. 571, 572 (1992); Felicia Smith. *Applicability of the Securities Act of 1933 and the Trust Indenture Act of 1939 to Consent Solicitations to Amend Trust Indentures,* 35 HOW. L.J. 343, 349-51, 367-68 (1992). There may also be an issue of whether such consent solicitations violate state laws requiring the equal treatment of securityholders or prohibiting "vote buying."

Section 9.03

1. *Compliance of Supplemental Indentures with the TIA.* By virtue of TIA Section 309(e) the SEC's authority over an indenture ceases after that indenture has been

qualified. For that reason the SEC insists that every indenture have a provision to the same effect as this Section. *See* SEC TIA Manual at 157; *see also* IV LOUIS LOSS, SECURITIES REGULATION 1611 n.29 (3rd ed. 1990).

2. *Officers' Certificate and Opinion of Counsel.* The second sentence clarified that the Trustee is entitled to an Opinion of Counsel and Officers' Certificate as to any amendment or supplemental indenture, which states, *inter alia*, that the amendment or supplemental indenture may be executed by the Trustee pursuant to Article 9.

Section 9.04

1. *Effectiveness of Consents.* A consent given under the Model Simplified Indenture may and should prescribe the terms on which it will be "continuing," i.e., on which it may be used (e.g., until a given date or when joined in by the holders of a given percentage of Securities).

2. *Revocation of Consents.* While the Model Simplified Indenture provides that a subsequent Securityholder may revoke the consent given by his predecessor in interest, as a practical matter it may be extremely difficult to trace succession. The converse of this problem (*see* Note 3 to this Section) is that it may be extremely difficult to establish that revocation has not occurred.

3. *Effect of Accumulation of Securities by Depositories.* In recent years it has become the increasingly prevalent practice for Securities to be delivered to securities depositories and to be registered and held, as a block, in the names of the depositories' nominees. An adverse consequence of this practice is, as a practical matter, to preclude utilization of consents by Securityholders to effect amendment of indentures governing publicly-held debt issues. The reason for this may be summarized as follows: (i) it is the registered holders whose consent is required by the Company and the Trustee, since those holders are recognized as the owners of the Securities under paragraph 12 of the form of Security; (ii) the actual registered holders are the nominees for the depositories, who for these purposes may be treated as identical with the depositories; (iii) each depository holds Securities for the accounts of its participant broker-dealers (among others), who in turn hold the Securities for their own accounts, for the accounts of their customers, for the accounts of other broker-dealers for whom they perform clearing services, and for the accounts of customers of those other broker-dealers; (iv) transfers can take place at each level among these accounts, some with and some without the depository's knowledge; and (v) the depository, therefore, will not accept consent instructions from beneficial holders of Securities, or from those holders' broker-dealers, since the depository can at no time determine which among the Securities it holds are the subject of such instructions or whether a newly-received instruction adds to, duplicates or revokes any portion of an instruction previously received. Users of the Model Simplified Indenture might consider adding, either in this Section or at the end of Article 9, provisions authorizing the Company to fix a record date for purposes of determining Securityholders whose consents will be sought and also authorizing the Trustee to accept such consents if received within a specified period after the record date. This technique, which has been used under some indentures, allows the depositories to function in the consent process in the same manner as they have long functioned in the shareholder proxy solicitation process. Selection of the exact period after the record date during which consents will be

honored must balance the difficulties of reaching the large mass of Securityholders against the increasing likelihood that holders as of record date in the past will no longer own the Securities.

4. *Solicitation of Consents*. The SEC's Exchange Act Regulations 14A and 14C apply to the solicitation of consents or the taking action by consent, without a solicitation, in respect of a class of securities registered under Section 12 of that Act. Debt securities listed on a stock exchange, and convertible debt securities held of record by more than 500 persons at the end of any fiscal year of the issuer, must be registered under Section 12. If proposed amendments to an indenture would result in a sufficient change to create a "new security," the solicitation of consents to such amendments may also be deemed subject to registration under the Securities Act, in the absence of an exemption form registration under Section 3(a)(9) or otherwise. *See* Note 4 to Section 9.02.

Section 9.05

1. *Notice to Securityholder*. Once an amendment requiring Securityholders' consent becomes effective, the Model Simplified Indenture requires that the Company notify Securityholders. The ABF Model Indentures have no such requirement.

Section 10.01

1. *Conversion Privilege*. The conversion privilege in the Model Simplified Indenture is similar to that in other indentures: the Principal amount of the Securities is divided by the conversion price in effect on the conversion date, and the conversion price is subject to adjustment. A Security may be converted only in whole multiples of $1000 and into whole shares of Common Stock.

2. *Common Stock*. The term "Common Stock" is used throughout Article 10. The definition of Common Stock, as the form of such stock existing on the date of the Indenture, is deliberately used by the Model Simplified Indenture without the customary phrase "as it may be constituted from time to time." In the circumstances addressed by Section 10.17 and the last paragraph of Section 10.06, the "Common Stock" will necessarily be affected as a result of the transactions (and subsequent instruments) contemplated by such Sections. Further, this approach avoids the problem arising in certain reverse triangular cash mergers where (i) a new class of common stock is created and inherits the role of (but is not substituted for) the "Common Stock" into which conversions have been and must continue to be made, and (ii) the holders of the "Common Stock" receive cash or other property. *See also* Note 2 to Section 10.06 and Section 10.17.

3. *Section 16(b)*. Note recent authority indicating that the beneficial owner of a convertible instrument which as a result has the right to acquire 10% or more of an issuer's registered equity securities may be subject to Section 16(b) of the Securities Exchange Act of 1934, as amended. *See* Editek, Inc. v. Morgan Capital, L.L.C., 150 F.3d 830, 831-34 (8th Cir. 1998).

4. *Conversion After Default/Proceedings*. Some Trustees believe that conversion should not be permitted after a Default, or after the commencement of a Proceeding. As Securities are converted, the recovery generated on the Securities in the aggregate

is reduced which can leave the Trustee with lower amounts against which it can recoup fees, and prejudice Senior Debt to the extent the subordination provisions of Article 11 do not apply to the securities into which the Securities are converted.

Section 10.02

1. *Adjustment for Interest on Conversion.* The Model Simplified Indenture requires a Securityholder converting between an interest record date and an interest payment date to return the accrued interest to the Company (but see Note 2 below). The ABF Indenture Commentaries take no position on this subject, and the 1983 MSI took the position that interest need not be returned. *See* Notes 3 and 6 to the form of Security; *see also* Jamie Secs. Co. v. The Ltd., Inc., 880 F.2d 1572, 1573-77 (2d Cir. 1989); Elliott Assocs. v. J. Henry Schroder Bank & Trust Co., 655 F. Supp. 1281, 1284-87 (S.D.N.Y. 1987), *aff'd*, 838 F.2d 66 (2d Cir. 1988).

2. *Loss of Interest on Conversion.* Under paragraph 9 of the form of Security, Securityholders converting Securities, voluntarily or because of a well-timed call for redemption, lost all interest for the current interest period. That provision has come to be known by investors in convertible securities as the "screw clause." Such clauses are standard language in many indentures and can be invoked by issuers of convertible securities (via a timed call for redemption) to deny investors in such securities an entire interest payment. Generally, the market compromise is to ensure that the screw clause cannot operate for an interest period ending in the period during which the Security cannot be called (*see* form of Security, paragraph 5). *See* Notes 5 and 6 to Form of Security. For a discussion of the invocation of a "screw clause," see Gary Weiss, *Beware the Turn of the Screw*, BUS. WK., June 1, 1992, at 108. In addition, for cases where determinations were made regarding the effect of the "screw clause," see generally *Elliott Associates v. J. Henry Schroder Bank & Trust Co.*, 655 F. Supp. 1281 (S.D.N.Y. 1987), *aff'd*, 838 F.2d 66 (2d Cir. 1998); *Kardolac Industries Corp. v. Wang Labs Inc.*, 482 N.E.2d 386 (Ill. App. Ct. 1985).

3. *Deemed Payment of Interest.* Although the shares of Common Stock deliverable on conversion are generally determined by dividing the Principal amount of the Security by the conversion price (*see* Section 10.01), issuers may wish to claim that the delivery of shares of Common Stock satisfy not only the Principal but the accrued interest and original issue discount associated with the Security converted. The bracketed language would be inserted if the issuers wished to take this position. Note in that event the need to clarify that interest paid by a holder pursuant to the preceding paragraph of Section 10.02 is *not* satisfied, and the issuer must still, therefore, pay such amount.

Section 10.03

1. *Registration of Conversion.* The conversion of debt into equity is exempt from registration under Section 3(a)(9) of the Securities Act, provided the conversion of the debt is exchanged exclusively for another security (such as Common Stock). It is well-established that the Section 3(a)(9) exemption still is available where cash is paid in lieu of fractional shares. *See, e.g.*, Rule 152a promulgated under the Securities Act of 1933; *see also* Federated Communications Corp., SEC No-Action Letter (Dec. 8,

1975), *available in* 1975 SEC No-Act. LEXIS 2418; C.I.T. Fin. Corp., SEC No-Action Letter (Sept. 22, 1975), *available in* 1975 SEC No-Act. LEXIS 1947; Equimark Corp., SEC No-Action Letter (Mar. 28, 1973), *available in* 1973 SEC No-Act. LEXIS 1777. Note, however, that the further disposition of the equity by the Securityholder receiving such equity on conversion may well have to be registered. That obligation to register the disposition of equity securities, if applicable, is generally set forth in a separate agreement or is covered by the same registration statement in which the issuance of the Securities is registered. *See* Note 1 to Section 10.05.

2. *"Quoted Price."* Note the definition of "Quoted Price" in Section 10.11.

Section 10.05

1. *Compliance with Applicable Law and Listing Requirements.* Some indentures allow the Company to prohibit conversions, or at least to postpone delivery of the securities issuable on conversion, if registration or listing requirements are not met. The Model Simplified Indenture, like the ABF Indenture Commentaries (at 556), omits any such specific prohibition, and the implication is to the contrary. The parties may negotiate this provision to require either "best efforts" or another standard rather than "endeavor."

Section 10.06

1. *Allocation of Adjustments Among Separate Classes of Securities Issuable Upon Conversion.* The Model Simplified Indenture specifies that, if more than one class of capital stock is issuable upon conversion, adjustment of each class must be effected separately.

2. *Effect of Recapitalization.* The definition of "Common Stock", set forth in Section 10.01, is the Common Stock of the issuer on the date of the Indenture. Nonetheless, Section 10.06 makes clear that after an adjustment which changes the "Common Stock" to another class of capital stock, further adjustments to that class of capital stock, falls under, and are to result in the same adjustments contained in Article 10, as if that capital stock were "Common Stock." *See* Kaiser Aluminum Corp. v. Matheson, 681 A.2d 392, 396-97 (Del. 1996) (conversion provision used with respect to convertible preferred); *see also* Section 10.17.

Sections 10.07/10.08/10.09/10.10

1. *Algebraic Equations.* Indentures for convertible debt frequently state anti-dilution formulas in words. Consequently, a user must decipher the text to discern the underlying formulas. The Model Simplified Indenture eliminates that step by stating the formulas as algebraic equations.

2. *Anti-Dilution Formulas Generally.* The Model Simplified Indenture deliberately uses the market price adjustment formula prevalent in recent years in public offerings. Selection of any formula is arbitrary, and often a question of bargaining between the parties to the indenture. The formulas appearing in these Sections reflect the following principle: Securityholders receive stated interest and stockholders receive normal dividends; when stockholders are to receive something more, such as an

unusual distribution in kind or in cash, the Securityholders' conversion price should be adjusted. Parties to a proposed indenture may, of course, differ on what constitutes an "unusual" distribution. (It should be noted that these formulas do not make provision for adjustment upon the issuance of other convertible securities, cash dividends paid out of consolidated net income from the prior fiscal year, self-tender offers, or the exercise of other conversion rights.) For a justification of market price adjustment formulas, see generally David L. Ratner, *Dilution and Anti-Dilution: A Reply to Professor Kaplan*, 33 U. CHI. L. REV. 494 (1965-66). Note that many venture capital investors and other purchasers of private securities prefer a "conversion price" based formula (i.e., protection against issuance of Common Stock for less than the conversion price, even if at above the market price) on the theory that in the absence of a bona fide public market, the "market price" is not a meaningful concept and/or take the position that the securityholders should also be treated like Common Stockholders and therefore either "share" in dividends paid or receive a conversion price adjustment. *See* Note 4 below.

3. *Applicability and Effect of Conversion Formulas.* Section 10.07 sets out the formula for adjustment of the conversion price in the case of a conventional rights offering, where stockholders are issued rights entitling them for a limited period to subscribe for or purchase, pro rata, additional shares at a discount from the then current market price. Section 10.07 also provides for readjustment in the event that not all such rights, options, or warrants shall have been exercised.

Section 10.08 sets out the formula for adjustment in the case of other rights offerings and other distributions. If Section 10.08 rather than Section 10.07 applies to a rights offering, a greater downward adjustment of the conversion price, favorable to the Securityholders and adverse to the Company, may result because the two formulas do not operate in the same way. In a situation in which the Company has distributed substantial assets to its stockholders (for example, the spin-off of a major subsidiary), the application of Section 10.08 may thereafter materially increase the proportion of equity in the remaining company reserved for the Securityholders. For cases arising out of spin-offs, see *Prescott, Ball & Turben v. LTV Corp.*, 531 F. Supp. 213, 220 (S.D.N.Y. 1981) (spin-off of shares of a subsidiary is a dividend and not a capital reorganization requiring shares to be held apart for debtholders); *Pittsburgh Terminal Corp. v. Baltimore & Ohio Railroad Co.*, 680 F.2d 933, 936 (3d Cir. 1982); *HB Korenvaes Investments, L.P. v. Marriott Corp.*, 1993 Fed. Sec. L. Rep. (CCH) ¶ 97,773 at 97,740 (Del. Ch. July 1, 1993) (in providing conversion adjustment mechanism, issuer impliedly undertook to refrain from declaring a dividend so large that what is left in corporation is itself worth less than the pre-distribution value of the convertible security). It is intended that these conversion formulas, their applicability, and some of their possible variations be studies before use.

4. *Optional Adjustments to Conversion Price.* Sections 10.09 and 10.10 were not contained in the 1983 MSI. Section 10.09 sets out the formula for adjustment of the conversion price in the case of a below market price issuance of additional shares of Common Stock and Section 10.10 sets out the formula for adjustment of the conversion price in the case of an issuance of securities, rights, options or warrants convertible into or exchangeable for Common Stock. Both Sections except certain below market issuances in an effort to define a list of standard exceptions. Negotiation of these exceptions is appropriate. In many cases, below market issuances should only be treated as an adjustment event if the issuance was to an officer, director or affiliate.

5. *Optional Catch-All Provisions*. This form does not purport to include all conversion or adjustment mechanisms that are alive and well in the market. Indentures often contain other adjustment provisions. Set forth below is an example of an optional catch-all adjustment provision that may be appropriate in certain transactions and may properly be the subject of negotiation.

    No Dilution or Impairment. (a) If any event shall occur as to which the provisions of this Article 10 are not strictly applicable but the failure to make any adjustment would adversely affect the rights represented by this Indenture and the Securities in accordance with the essential intent and principles of this Article 10, then, in each such case, the Company shall appoint an investment banking firm of recognized national standing, or any other financial expert that does not (or whose directors, officers, employees, affiliates or stockholders do not) have a material direct or indirect financial interest in the Company or any of its subsidiaries, that has not been, and, at the time it is called upon to give independent financial advice to the Company, is not (and none of the directors, officers, employees, affiliates or stockholders of which are not) a promoter, director or officer of the Company or any of its subsidiaries, which investment banking firm shall give its opinion upon the adjustment, if any, that should be implemented in order to preserve, without dilution, the purchase rights represented by this Indenture and the Securities. Upon receipt of such opinion, the Company shall promptly mail a copy thereof to the holders of the Securities and shall make the adjustments described therein and in this Indenture.

    (b) The Company shall not, by amendment of its certificate of incorporation or through any consolidation, merger, reorganization, transfer of assets, dissolution, issue or sale of securities or any other voluntary action, avoid or seek to avoid the observance or performance of any of the terms of this Indenture, but will at all times in good faith assist in the carrying out of all such terms and in the taking of all such action as may be necessary or appropriate in order to protect the rights of the holders of the Securities against dilution or other impairment. Without limiting the generality of the foregoing, the Company (1) will take all such action as may be necessary or appropriate in order that the Company may validly and legally issue fully paid and nonassessable shares of Common Stock that are free of preemptive and other similar rights upon the conversion of the Securities from time to time outstanding and (2) will not take any action that would result in an adjustment of the conversion price if the total number of shares of Common Stock issuable after the conversion of all of the Securities would exceed the total number of shares of Common Stock then authorized by the Company's certificate of incorporation and available for the purpose of issue upon such conversion.

6. *Tax Consequences*. The tax consequences of non-cash distributions and conversion price adjustments are discussed in BORIS I. BITTKER & JAMES S. EUSTICE, FEDERAL INCOME TAXATION OF CORPORATION AND SHAREHOLDERS ¶¶ 7.20-7.23 (6th ed. 1998).

Section 10.11

1. *Determination of Current Market Price*. Section 10.11 sets forth the method and manner of determining the current market price per share of Common Stock for purposes of Sections 10.07, 10.08, 10.09 and 10.10. Section 10.11 provides for an averaging period of the minimum length reasonably required to prevent aberrations and manipulation of the market price, and permits the averaging period to terminate on the

record date or, if earlier, the day prior to the "ex" date. This gives the Company the flexibility to determine a starting date that will produce an acceptable current market price that accurately reflects the value of the issuance or the distribution. Section 10.11 (formerly Section 10.09 in the 1983 MSI) has been revised to prevent a circumstance where the current market price is less than the fair market value of the issuance or distribution, thus resulting in a negative adjusted conversion price, as discussed in *Harcourt Brace Jovanovich, Inc. v. Sun Bank National Ass'n*, No. 87-3985 (Fla. Cir. Ct. June 5, 1987), *available in part in* Mutual Shares Corp. et al., Amendment No. 1 to Schedule 13D Concerning *Harcourt Brace Jovanovich, Inc.* (July 8, 1987). For a further discussion of *Harcourt Brace Jovanovich* and a review of convertible indenture provisions providing for limitations on downward adjustment of the conversion price below a "reference market price," see generally Martin Riger, *A Conversion Paradox: Negative Anti-Dilution*, 44 BUS. LAW. 1243 (1989).

2. *Determination Where No Public Market*. In a situation where there is no active public market, the Board of Directors is to determine a current market price in good faith. Additional requirements applicable to such a determination may be appropriate. For example, the Board of Directors may be required to obtain a quotation from specified investment banks or accounting firms (*see, e.g.*, Section 10.08) or to obtain at least a specified number of quotations.

Section 10.13

1. *Participation in Transactions Otherwise Requiring Adjustment*. This Section provides for no adjustment of the conversion price if Securityholders are given notice of and allowed to participate in the transaction that would otherwise result in the adjustment. It is an approach that is different from those discussed in the ABF Indenture Commentaries, and was adapted by the 1983 MSI from institutional instruments and some convertible preferred stock provisions. In any circumstances, the tax implications of such participation will require careful exploration.

2. *Dividend Reinvestment Plans*. A dividend reinvestment plan where new shares are sold by the Company at a discount might be viewed as a continuous rights offering. However, this Section specifies that no adjustment is required for such a plan since, unlike a conventional rights offering, the right to participate in the plan is not transferable and has little or no independent or realizable value.

Section 10.14

1. *Computation of Adjustment*. Like the ABF Indenture Commentaries and the 1983 MSI, the Model Simplified Indenture requires an accountant's computation. Some indentures permit the Company itself to calculate any adjustment in the conversion price. In addition, under the Model Simplified Indenture, when there is an adjustment under Section 10.08 and the aggregate fair market value on the record date of the assets, securities, rights, or warrants being distributed exceeds $[X] million, the Company must obtain an appraisal or other valuation opinion in support of the Board of Directors' determination of fair market value from an investment bank or accounting firm of national standing.

2. *Publication of Notice*. In line with current practice (arising, presumably, from the *Boeing* case cited in Note 1 to Section 10.16), the Model Simplified Indenture requires notice of conversion price adjustments to be mailed to all Securityholders of record rather than simply to be published. *See* Note 2 to Section 3.03.

Section 10.15

1. *Voluntary Reduction*. In this Section, the Model Simplified Indenture formalizes, and places limits on, a privilege occasionally utilized by issuers. Notice of the reduction in the conversion price, and of the period of its effectiveness, must be given to Securityholders.

2. *Applicability; Limitations*. A voluntary, if temporary, reduction in conversion price may be considered by the Company when it desires to stimulate conversions but is unwilling or unable to undergo the optional redemption procedure. It may also be considered in connection with a call for redemption, but in that case the requirement in this Section for a period of at least 20 days could inhibit a multi-step, gradual reduction intended to reduce the conversion price only as far as necessary to induce the desired amount of conversions. For that reason, users may wish to consider deleting the 20-day limitation and reserving the right to make further reductions at any time during a period when a reduced conversion price is in effect.

3. *Relationship to Sections 10.06, 10.07, 10.08, 10.09 and 10.10*. Any reduced conversion price resulting under this Section is not subject to further adjustment, except voluntarily by the Company. The third paragraph of this Section is intended to cause the Company to continue to calculate adjustments from the pre-reduction price, and always to keep in effect the lower of (i) the reduced price, while it is in effect, or (ii) the adjusted pre-reduction price.

Section 10.16

1. *Notices*. The underlying purpose of the notice requirements of Section 10.16 is to afford Securityholders the opportunity to convert and participate in the distribution, combination or liquidation as stockholders rather than to continue to hold their Securities and receive a conversion price adjustment. No notice is required under this Section (i) if the Company elects under Section 10.13 to let Securityholders participate in the transaction, or (ii) if the transaction is so minor that any adjustment may be deferred under Section 10.12; notice is, however, required in the case of a stock dividend or a stock split. The Company may also be subject to notice requirements arising under SEC rules (such as Rules 10b-5 and 10b-17), under stock exchange and NASD policies (see NYSE Listed Co. Manual ¶ 204.12 and NAT'L ASS'N SEC. DEALERS' MANUAL (CCH) 1143-43.2) and under legal and equitable principles of general applicability. *See* Pittsburgh Terminal Corp. v. Baltimore & Ohio R.R. Co., 680 F.2d 933 (3d Cir. 1982) (failure to notify holders of convertible debentures of a proposed spin-off of shares of subsidiary); Van Gemert v. Boeing Co., 520 F.2d 1373 (2d Cir. 1975) (failure to give adequate notice to holders of convertible debentures in bearer form of call for redemption). *See generally* Andrew McDonald, *Theories of Liability Under Convertible Debenture Redemption Notice Requirements*, 44 FORDHAM L. REV. 817 (1976). If the Company has prepared a proxy or information statement

for stockholders describing the forthcoming transaction, it should consider sending that statement to Securityholders along with the notice required by this Section.

Section 10.17

1. *Triangular Transactions.* The "person obligated to deliver" upon conversion may be the parent of the new obligor upon the remainder of the Company's obligations under the Indenture. *See* Note 4 to Section 5.01. If the parent is not that "person" but is the issuer of the securities deliverable upon further conversions, the parent is required by the second sentence of this Section to join in the supplemental indenture for the protection of Securityholders.

2. *Cash Mergers.* Conversion into cash is specifically contemplated by this Section. The fourth paragraph of Section 10.13 provides that interest will not be accrued nor will subsequent adjustments be made after the cash merger date. *See also* Note 2 to Section 10.01. Note that in a cash merger, the holders of convertible securities lose their potential option premium. In light of the expectation of stock price appreciation, this provision can work an injustice, particularly for securities with a long remaining life.

Section 10.19

1. *Trustee's Non-Responsibility.* The Trustee's duties under the TIA, and therefore under the Model Simplified Indenture, relate only to the debt features of the Securities. The Trustee has no duty to monitor the Company's compliance with the terms of the conversion privilege. *See* Browning Debenture Holders' Comm. v. DASA Corp., 560 F.2d 1078, 1083-85 (2d Cir. 1977) (trustee had no duty to communicate to debentureholders an opinion regarding the fairness of a reduction in the conversion price proposed by management to induce debentureholders to consent to an amendment of the indenture). Section 6.07 prescribes that each Securityholder's right to sue to enforce the conversion privilege may not be impaired or affected without such holder's consent. *See also* Notes to Section 7.01.

Article 11 Generally

1. *Approach.* This article represents an attempt to simplify the complex form of subordination article such as that appearing in the ABF Model. It was comprehensively revised but with a view to retaining simple, short and clear language. The brevity of the provisions was accomplished in large part through the use of additional defined terms which are contained in new Section 11.14. The revision is intended to reduce the possibility of litigation related to the construction of subordination articles in indentures which has been generated by their turgid language. This Article 11 represents a fairly simple set of subordination provisions, such as might be found in an indenture for an issuer presenting no significant credit risk and a straightforward capital structure. The subordination provisions contained in indentures for issuers which do not have such a profile are generally more complex and are highly negotiated.

2. *Basis for Enforcing Subordination Provisions.* Due in part to the explicit recognition of the enforceability of subordination agreements added to the Bankruptcy Code

in 1978 (11 U.S.C. §510(a)), the enforceability of subordination agreements is universally accepted in the United States. The Article does not attempt to bolster its language by reference to the various theories of subordination discussed in the 1983 MSI, earlier case law and academic writing.

3. *Effect on Subordination of Changes in Senior Debt.* The ABF Indenture Commentaries recommend (at 572-73) a provision to the effect that holders of Senior Debt may extend, renew or change the Senior Debt without notice to or consent of Securityholders and without affecting the subordination of the Securities. The Model Simplified Indenture omits that provision because the Securities are subordinated to Debt of the Company "outstanding at any time" (unless expressly made not Senior—see "Senior Debt" definition in Section 1.01) regardless of when such Debt was incurred or how it may have changed since it was first incurred. To the extent that the Securityholders may be considered to have suretyship status (*see* RESTATEMENT (THIRD) OF SURETYSHIP AND GUARANTY §1 (1995)), a waiver of any suretyship defenses which may be available to the Securityholders by reasons of modifications to Senior Debt appears in Section 11.08.

4. *Cross-References.* See Note 5 to Section 6.02, Note 7 Section 8.01, and Note 3 to Section 9.02.

Section 11.01

1. *Agreement to Subordinate.* Express agreements to subordinate, such as the agreement set forth in this Section, furnish the basis for the contractual subordination provided for in Article 11, have uniformly been enforced by the courts, and, by facilitating correct analysis of the contractual rights involved, help assure continuance of such enforcement.

2. *Revision Note.* The changes to this Section from the 1983 MSI are intended to eliminate the implication that this Section operates independently of the remainder of Article 11 and gives the holder of Senior Debt rights to Distributions not expressly provided therein.

Section 11.02

1. *Effect of Subordination Provisions.* The subordinated debt evidenced by the Securities and the unsecured Senior Debt of the Company would each constitute a type of unsecured debt of the Company and would be proved on a parity in bankruptcy, without any priority of the Senior Debt over the subordinated Securities. However, express agreements such as those set forth in Sections 11.01, 11.02 and 11.03 "reallocate from the subordinated class to the senior class as much as is required to obtain for the latter the full equivalent in value of its claims." For an explanation of the mechanics of reallocation, see *In re* Imperial '400' National Inc., 2 SEC DOCKET 377, 381 (D.N.J. 1973). Note the comparable 1983 MSI provision stated that "holders of Senior Debt shall be entitled to receive payment in full in cash of the principal of and interest . . . before the Securityholders shall be entitled to receive any payment." This language led to suggestions that subordination operated as a "pour down" rather than a "pass up." "Pour down" erroneously suggests that Distributions should be made first to the holders of Senior Debt until they are paid in full, then to Holders of

subordinated debt. Subordination properly operates by distributions being made equally to the holders of Senior Debt and subordinated debt with the Holders of subordinated debt then being required to turn over their distributions to holders of Senior Debt to the extent necessary to pay Senior Debt in full. The effect of the difference is apparent in situations where there is other debt which is neither senior nor subordinated and in the right of the trustee for the subordinated debt to recover its fees and expenses from the distributions to the subordinated Securityholders prior to passing the distributions up to the holders of Senior Debt.

2. *Liquidations.* This Section applies to any liquidation, whether total or partial, voluntary or involuntary, and under whatever name (e.g., a "winding up"), in which a distribution is made to creditors.

3. *Post-Bankruptcy Interest.* The 1983 MSI specified that priority in right of payment would extend to interest accruing on Senior Debt even after the commencement of a bankruptcy proceeding; most indentures now include such post-petition interest expressly (if at all) in the definition of Debt or Senior Debt. *See* Notes 5 and 11 to Section 1.01.

4. *Cash, Securities, or Other Property.* This Section 11.02 replaces Section 11.03 of the 1983 MSI. One of the differences is the scope of the distributions which are expressly made subject to the claims of Senior Debtholders. The 1983 MSI provided holders of Senior Debt were entitled to receive payment in full, in cash; such holders now expressly want the right to receive as well securities or other property otherwise distributable to subordinated holders. *See* Note 1 to Section 11.13.

5. *Exclusion of Article 5 Events.* The definition of Proceeding (see Section 11.14) clarifies that if Article 5 applies to the transaction, and the issuer complies with the provisions of Article 5, distributions made in connection with that transaction are not subject to Section 11.02.

Section 11.03

1. *Changes.* This Section 11.03 replaces Section 11.04 of the 1983 MSI. The prohibition on payment, defeasance, redemption or repurchase is automatic and absolute on maturity of Senior Debt or on a payment default, unless the Senior Debt is paid in full in the first instance or the payment default is cured in the second instance. The revisions clarify that the prohibition applies to direct or indirect payments (which would include payments by controlled affiliates). Senior Debtholders in clause (i) of the first paragraph of this Section may want to specify that Senior Debt must have been paid in cash or cash equivalents. Subordinated holders in clause (ii) of the first paragraph may want to specify that the block applies only if the Payment Default continues beyond any applicable grace period in the instrument governing the terms of the Senior Debt.

2. *Prohibition of Payment During Default on Senior Debt; Applicable Conditions.* Prior Section 11.04 prohibited payments on the Securities or purchase of them while there was a Default on Senior Debt that permits the holders of Senior Debt to accelerate its maturity, but only if the Default was the subject of judicial proceedings or if the Trustee received notice of the Default from a specified person. The second paragraph of current Section 11.03 now prohibits payments or purchases on a non-Payment Default and express written notice to the Company and Trustee. The "fish or cut

bait" provision applies only to such Defaults, not to the Defaults noted in the first paragraph, which is the more standard structure in current indentures. (Note debt-holders will frequently negotiate with one another to have the trigger for the payment block be an Event of Default, rather than a Default.) In essence, the "fish or cut bait" provision of Section 11.03 represents an accommodation between the position of the holders of Senior Debt, who do not want payments to be made on the subordinated debt evidenced by the Securities while there is a continuing Default on Senior Debt and the position of the subordinated Securityholders, who do not want to be forced to accept a blockage of payments on the Securities, especially in a deteriorating situation, until the senior creditors decide, possibly after an extended period of time, that it is to the advantage of the senior creditors to accelerate the Senior Debt, initiate judicial proceedings, or take other actions to resolve the situation. This provision is included in Section 11.03 in view of the objectives stated in Note 1 to Article 11 generally. A blocking period approaching 180 days is typical for instruments requiring semi-annual interest payments. In the absence of appropriate limitations, the prohibition could prevent payment on the Securities for a long period of time even in a deteriorating situation. In fact, if the Default were a technical Default or a financial Default (such as failure to maintain a minimum net worth) on the Senior Debt rather than a Default in the payment of interest or Principal, the Company could, in the absence of appro-priate limitations, continue to amortize the Senior Debt for an extended period during which payment on the Securities was prohibited but no action was being taken by the holders of the Senior Debt to resolve the situation. To avoid notices that, by accident or design, string together consecutive payment block periods, the last sentence of the second paragraph provides there shall be only one payment block in any year, and that the same Default cannot be used for more than one block.

3. *Conversion of Securities*. Section 11.03 excepts from its prohibition the acqui-sition of Securities in exchange for capital stock of the Company. Thus, Securities may be converted into Common Stock during a period when Section 11.03 would prohibit payments on the Securities or acquisition of Securities in exchange for other types of property.

4. *Payment Over*. The payment over provision formerly contained in Section 11.06 of the 1983 MSI, which required Holders erroneously receiving distributions to hold them for the benefit of holders of Senior Debt, has been moved to this Section 11.03 and revised to apply only to distributions made to the Trustee. The reference to reco-vering from Holders has been deleted because such a right would not operate uni-formly on all Holders and is inconsistent with the principles of finality of transactions in securities. Assuming that a distribution has been made erroneously to the Holders, as a practical matter recovery will only be sought from the larger Holders since the expense of pursuing the smaller Holders is likely to be disproportionate to the amount to be recovered. In other contexts, the law has recognized the need for finality in securities transactions. 11 U.S.C. §546(e); Kaiser Steel Corp. v. Pearl Brewing Co. (*In re* Kaiser Steel), 952 F.2d 1230, 1240-41 (10th Cir. 1991).

Section 11.05

1. *Revision Note*. This provision is analogous to Section 11.09 of the 1983 MSI.

Section 11.06

1. *Specific Notice Required.* This Section replaces Section 11.12 of the 1983 MSI. That provision of the 1983 MSI provided that a Trustee or Paying Agent could continue to make payments on the Securities "until it receives notice of facts" that would cause a payment to violate Article 11. Trustees and Paying Agents now expressly want to eliminate any possibility that they will be deemed to have had notice and therefore generally require an express written notice to trigger the payment prohibition. A senior debtholder may also wish to add to this Section a provision requiring the Trustee to rely on a notice delivered by a Person representing itself as a holder of or representative for senior debt, e.g.:

> The Trustee shall be entitled to rely on the delivery to it of a written notice by a Person representing itself to be a holder of any Senior Debt (or a Trustee on behalf of, or other representative of, such holder) to establish that such notice has been given by a holder of such Senior Debt or a Trustee or representative on behalf of any such holder. In the event that the Trustee determines in good faith that any evidence is required with respect to the right of any Person as a holder of Senior Debt to participate in any payment or distribution pursuant to this Article, the Trustee may require such Person to furnish evidence to the reasonable satisfaction of the Trustee as to the amount of Senior Debt held by such Person, the extent to which such Person is entitled to participate in such payment or distribution and any other facts pertinent to the rights of such Person set forth in this Article and, if such evidence is not furnished to the Trustee, the Trustee may defer any payment to such Person pending judicial determination as to the right of such Person to receive such payment.

Section 11.08

1. *No Impairment.* This provision replaces Section 11.10 of the 1983 MSI. It adds the concept (previously implicit) that the actions or failures to act by a senior debtholder cannot impair a Senior Debtholder's right to enforce the subordination provisions. Many indentures give examples of actions (and failures to act) which will not affect the subordination provisions or liabilities or obligations under the Indenture.

Section 11.09

1. *Trustee's Right to Hold Senior Debt.* This provision restates the second paragraph of Section 11.12 of the 1983 MSI. Note, however, the Trustee's obligation to resign pursuant to TIA Section 310(b)(10) if the Trustee is a creditor of the issuer of the Securities and the Securities are in Default, the Trustee's duty to avoid conflicts of interest, and TIA Section 311.

Section 11.10

1. *No Fiduciary Duty.* This Section explicitly disclaims any fiduciary duties running from the Trustee to the Senior Debt holders by reason of any obligations which the Trustee undertakes to the Senior Debt holders through this Article. The Trustee's duties to the Senior Debt holders are only contractual. This avoids any possible

conflict of interest in the Trustee assuming fiduciary duties to two groups with adverse interests.

Section 11.12

1. *Clarification of Trustee's Rights.* This provision is contained in a separate Section since it applies to all of the provisions of the Article.

Section 11.13

1. *The "X Clause."* One exception to the payover provision (now contained in Section 11.02) is commonly found, namely the "X clause." The "X clause" (so named in the ABF Indenture Commentaries at 570-571) is generally written as an exception to the subordination provisions. In the 1983 MSI, Section 11.03, the X clause read:

> Until the Senior Debt is paid in full in cash, any distribution to which Securityholders would be entitled but for this Article shall be to holders of Senior Debt as their interests may appear, except that Securityholders may receive securities that are subordinated to Senior Debt to at least the same extent as the Securities.
>
> The Model Simplified Indenture moves this concept to this Section 11.13.

The X clause has been the subject of litigation in which judges have come to opposite results on their construction while each stating that the meaning of the clause is plain on its face and requires no resort to extrinsic evidence. In *In re* Envirodyne Industries, Inc., 29 F.3d 301, 305 (7th Cir. 1994), the Seventh Circuit found that the X clause in that case did not permit the subordinated creditors to retain any distributions until the senior creditors were paid in full. As drafted, this X Clause means that the holders of the Securities and the Trustee need not turn over to the holders of Senior Debt Distributions to the Securityholders (1) to the extent that the Distributions are applied to the Trustee's compensation, expenses or indemnification, (2) if the distribution to both holders of Senior Debt and Securityholders are securities and securities distributed to the Securityholders are subordinated to the securities distributed to the holders of Senior Debt or (3) the distributions are made under an approved plan in the Proceeding. All of these exceptions are subject to modification through negotiations among the parties involved in drafting the Indenture.

The first exception is important to assure that the Trustee's rights are preserved and is consistent with the general proposition that the Trustee's rights to payment are not subordinated (Section 11.12). The second exception (clause (b)(1)) recognizes that the rights of the holders of Senior Debt have been preserved if the securities received by the Holders are subordinated to securities to be distributed to Senior Debtholders to the same extent as was the subordinate debt to the Senior Debt. If Senior Debt were to receive preferred stock and the subordinated debt were to receive common stock, for example, where the preferred stock precluded distributions to common stockholders until the preferred stock was redeemed, the X clause would permit that distribution. Where all debt holders were to receive the same class of common stock, however, the common stock otherwise distributable to the subordinated holders would be distributed to Senior Debtholders until they were paid in full. *See, e.g., In re* Envirodyne Indus., Inc., 29 F.3d 301, 305 (7th Cir. 1994). (But see below.) The scope of the necessary subordination in exception (2) is a matter of negotiation and may require that there be no principal amortization on the securities distributed to the Securityholders until after the maturity of the securities distributed to the holders of Senior Debt.

The third exception (clause (b)(ii)) implements the accepted notion that, in bankruptcy, holders of Senior Debt will enforce their rights through the structuring of the distributions under the plan and Securityholders will be entitled to retain their distributions under the approved plan. In large part such provisions are the result of the perceived need in many bankruptcies to make some distribution to subordinated debt holders in order quickly to confirm a plan. Exception (3) may be, and not uncommonly is, expanded to permit the Securityholders to retain any common stock of the reorganized company received under a plan, even if the holders of Senior Debt also receive common stock (which does not have superior rights). The clause might also provide that the Securityholders may retain any Distribution they receive after the holders of Senior Debt receive property of a value equal to their claim, even if the property is a note rather than cash. *Cf.* 11 U.S.C. §1129(a)(10).

2. *"Junior Securities."* Many indentures define what will make a security one which is "subordinate to the same extent" as are the Securities. Such a definition could be added to Section 11.14 and might include language similar to the following: "(i) has a maturity, mandatory redemption obligation or put right, if any, longer than, or occurring after the final maturity date of, the Securities on the date of issuance of such capital stock or Debt, (ii) is unsecured, and (iii) by its terms or by law is subordinated in right of payment to Senior Debt outstanding on the date of issuance of such capital stock or Debt at least to the same extent as the Securities."

3. *"Senior Debt Payment Default."* Some definitions of Senior Debt Payment Default read "a default in the payment of any amount payable on any Senior Debt." This would obviously broaden the scope of the default to pick up other payment obligations to Senior Debt holders.

Section 12.01

1. *Notices.* The Model Simplified Indenture provides that all notices to Securityholders are to be given by overnight service or first class mail, and that a copy of each such notice is to be mailed to the Trustee and each Agent. Some users may wish to leave the choice of class of mail for such notices to the discretion of the Trustee and the Company. For example, the Trustee's annual mailing to Securityholders required in certain circumstances by TIA Section 313(a) may not warrant first class postage. Issuers and Trustees may also wish to consider the addition of permitting notices to be delivered by facsimile, e-mail and/or through the DTC LENS system. This Section has been revised from the 1983 MSI to make express an implicit concept, namely that all communications required under the Indenture are "notices" and are to be delivered in the manner set forth.

Section 12.02

1. *Communication with Holders.* This Section is unchanged from the 1983 MSI. *See* Notes 1 and 2 to Section 1.04, however; if the TIA is not applicable to the

Indenture, these provisions (or alternative provisions) should be set forth in full. *See also* Note 2 to Sections 7.01 and 7.02.

Section 12.03

1. *Certificates and Opinions*. This Section is unchanged from the 1983 MSI. Many indentures now combine Sections 12.03 and 12.04.

Section 12.04

1. *"No Default" Certification*. The text of this Section derives from TIA Section 314(e). Although each Officers' Certificate must cover satisfaction of all relevant conditions precedent to the particular proposed action, the Model Simplified Indenture does not require that such Certificate also cover the absence of any Default under the Indenture.

Section 12.05

1. *Use of Defined Terms*. The second sentence of this Section has been slightly modified in form, but not substance, by use of the defined term "Agent."

Section 12.06, 12.07, 12.08

1. *No Changes*. These Sections are unchanged from the 1983 MSI.

2. *"No Recourse" Clause*. The ABF Indenture Commentaries indicate (at 138, 244) that the no-recourse clause is unnecessary or inappropriate, at least where the issuer is a corporation. While each of the federal securities laws specifically provides against waiver of claims arising thereunder, the extent to which Securityholders may waive claims arising under state law will depend on state law. *See* Note, *The "No-Recourse" Clause in Corporate Bonds and Indentures*, 34 COLUM. L. REV. 107 (1934). The Model Simplified Indenture defers on this point to widespread practice. *See* Simons v. Cogan, 549 A.2d 300, 304-05 (Del. Ch. 1988) (claim against individuals sued for breach of indenture dismissed on basis of "no recourse" provision).

3. *Duplicate or Counterpart Indentures*. Regardless of how many copies of the Indenture are executed, it is intended that the production of any one of such copies will be sufficient to satisfy a best evidence rule.

Section 12.09

1. *Function*. It would be the best of all worlds for a draftsman if the final text of the Model Simplified Indenture could be used with only changes in names and addresses of the Company and Trustee, deletion of an unwanted clause or two in the Sections constructed with that in mind (for example, clause (1) of Section 5.01), and additions only in one place. While that aim is unattainable, it explains the potpourri found in this Section.

2. *Trustee's Capital and Surplus*. The second sentence of the fourth paragraph is new, and is meant to address the problem that arises when a corporate trust business is

sold. The business may be conducted in an Affiliate of the purchaser which may not meet the capital requirements itself but has a qualifying parent or Affiliate willing to guarantee its obligations.

3. *Exclusions from Senior Debt.* After listing the indebtedness excluded from Senior Debt, the Model Simplified Indenture suggests a specification of the other indebtedness (all or part of that listing) to which "the Securities are not senior in right of payment," in order to meet the requirements of any provisions in such other indebtedness similar to the first sentence of paragraph 10 of the form of Security. The objective is to avoid circular priorities. *See* Note 11 to Section 1.01. The parties should consider adding, as to each issue of excluded Debt, an indication of whether such Debt is subordinate to, or *pari passu* with, the Securities.

Section 12.10

1. *Governing Law.* If there is any concern that the renvoi doctrine may apply, a drafter may wish to add the phrase "without regard to principles of conflicts of law" at the end of this sentence. While there have been suggestions that a federal law of trusts might apply (in regard to certain obligations of federal agencies) in an indenture stated as being governed by New York law, and while it is undoubtedly true that both the TIA and the statute or regulation authorizing the performance of corporate trust powers by the Trustee cut across the application of this Section, the Model Simplified Indenture retains the traditional approach to choice of governing law. The interpretation of TIA provisions in an indenture is, of course, a matter of federal law, and some federal courts have recognized an implied right of action to enforce those provisions. *See* Zeffiro v. First Pa. Banking and Trust Co., 473 F. Supp. 201 (E.D. Pa.. 1979), *aff'd*, 623 F.2d 290 (3d Cir. 1980); Morris v. Cantor, 390 F. Supp. 817 (S.D.N.Y. 1975).

Signature Page

1. *Formalities.* The Model Simplified Indenture omits both a testimonium clause ("In witness whereof. . . .") and acknowledgments of signatures. If required, acknowledgments appropriate for filing in any jurisdiction can be added. An indenture governing unsecured debt is rarely required to be so filed. In deference to tradition, the Model Simplified Indenture does contemplate a seal and its attestation. Many instruments governing debt dispense with the formality of the seal.

Form of Security

1. *Seal.* The Company's seal is reproduced on the face of the Securities, pursuant to Section 2.02.

2. *Formalities.* The Model Simplified Indenture does not include the common express statements that (i) the provisions on the reverse form of Security are incorporated into the face of the Security and (ii) all terms defined in the Indenture have the same meaning in the form of Security. Both statements, however, are true regardless of the inclusion of such language. In addition, the Model Simplified Indenture varies from the 1983 MSI by including a sentence directing the holder to the reverse and to

the Indenture for a complete understanding of the provisions of the Securities. Note that the form of listed bonds must meet the formal requirements of the relevant stock exchange. *See, e.g.*, NYSE Listed Co. Manual ¶¶ 501.06, 501.12, 501.13, 502.00, 502.04.

3. *Interest on Debentures Cancelled After the Interest Record Date*. Paragraph 2 provides for payment of interest even though Securities are cancelled after the interest record date and on or before the interest payment date. This situation arises (i) if Securities are called before an interest record date for redemption after the record date but before or on the interest payment date, or (ii) if Securities are converted after the record date but before or on the payment date. *See* Note 2 to Section 10.02.

4. *Strict Enforcement of Redemption Provisions*. Securityholders generally insist on a period during which the Securities cannot be called, and then a call price on a premium to par (declining over time) to protect their yield. Exceptions to such provisions are generally strenuously negotiated and narrowly construed. *See, e.g.*, Texas-New Mexico Power Co. v. Jackson Nat'l Life Ins. Co., No. 4:95-CV-7584, 1997 U.S. Dist. LEXIS 5640 (N.D. Tex. Mar. 31, 1997).

5. *No Optional Redemption During Interest Default*. To avoid a situation where the Company fails to pay all interest due and payable then makes a call for redemption to force a conversion (at which point the Securityholder may lose all accrued interest), the Company's right to call an optional redemption is tolled for any period it has failed to pay all interest due.

6. *Timing of Optional Redemption Call*. It is critical, to avoid loss of interest *through* the period investors expect a convertible security to be non-callable, that the first redemption date be specified as the second *Business Day* after the interest payment date for the non-call period. Provided securities are convertible through the close of the Business Day prior to the redemption date (*see* form of Security, paragraph 9), this ensures a Securityholder will receive its interest payment and have one Business Day in which to convert prior to the redemption date. Note that even if the dates are properly aligned for the non-call period the issuer can force a conversion and loss of an interest payment after the non-call period under the Model Simplified Indenture (*see* Note 1 above), which is the current market practice. A securityholder converting after an interest record date but before an interest payment date will also be subject to the "wash" payment contemplated by Section 10.02 (*see* Note 1 to Section 10.02).

7. *Securities Credited Against Mandatory Redemption Requirement*. Pursuant to paragraph 6 of the form of Security, the Principal amount of Securities required to be redeemed in any year may be reduced by the principal amount of Securities cancelled or optionally redeemed and by the Principal amount of Securities converted *unless* those Securities were converted after having been called for a mandatory redemption.

8. *Disclosure of Principal Terms*. The form of Security included in the Model Simplified Indenture has been drafted to set forth in brief certain important terms in a place where they are readily accessible. *See* Van Gemert v. Boeing Co., 520 F.2d 1373, 1383 (2d Cir. 1975) (unreasonable for issuer to expect investors to send for, and then read and comprehend, a 113-page indenture); *see also* Note 1 to Article 4—Further Covenants, Note 6 to Section 5.01 and Note 8 to Sections 8.01.

9. *Conversion Price Adjustments*. Paragraph 9 summarizes the events which will result in conversion price adjustments. Any substantive changes in or additions to the

relevant Sections in Article 10 should also be reviewed against this paragraph to be sure that its text reflects such changes or additions.

10. *Successors*. Paragraph 14 reflects the revisions to Sections 5.01 and 5.02. *See* Note 1 to Section 5.02.

11. *Abbreviations*. Paragraph 20 is derived from the NYSE Listed Co. Manual ¶ 501.04.

12. *Availability of Indenture*. The boldface legend informs Securityholders how to obtain the Indenture, which includes the form of Security in larger size type.

INDENTURE FOR NOTES ISSUED BY APPLE INC.

Apple Inc.
as Issuer
and
The Bank of New York Mellon Trust Company, N.A.,
as Trustee

INDENTURE
Dated as of April 29, 2013

**CERTAIN SECTIONS OF THIS INDENTURE RELATING TO SECTIONS 310
THROUGH 318 INCLUSIVE, OF THE TRUST INDENTURE ACT OF 1939**

Trust Indenture Act Section	INDENTURE Section
Section 310(a)(1)	Section 609
(a)(2)	Section 609
(a)(3)	Not Applicable
(a)(4)	Not Applicable
(b)	Section 608
	Section 610
Section 311(a)	Section 613
(b)	Section 613
Section 312(a)	Section 701
	Section 702
(b)	Section 702
(c)	Section 702
Section 313(a)	Section 703
(b)	Section 703
(c)	Section 703
(d)	Section 703
Section 314(a)	Section 704
(a)(4)	Section 1004
(b)	Not Applicable

Trust Indenture Act Section	INDENTURE Section
(c)(1)	Section 102
(c)(2)	Section 102
(c)(3)	Not Applicable
(d)	Not Applicable
(e)	Section 102
Section 315(a)	Section 601
(b)	Section 602
(c)	Section 601
(d)	Section 601
(e)	Section 513
Section 316(a)	Section 101
(a)(1)(A)	Section 502, Section 511
(a)(1)(B)	Section 512
(a)(2)	Not Applicable
(b)	Section 508
(c)	Section 104
Section 317(a)(1)	Section 503
(a)(2)	Section 504
(b)	Section 1003
Section 318(a)	Section 107

NOTE: This reconciliation and tie shall not, for any purpose, be deemed to be a part of this Indenture.

TABLE OF CONTENTS

ARTICLE I DEFINITIONS AND OTHER PROVISIONS OF GENERAL APPLICATION

ARTICLE II SECURITY FORMS

ARTICLE III THE SECURITIES

ARTICLE IV SATISFACTION AND DISCHARGE

ARTICLE V REMEDIES

ARTICLE VI THE TRUSTEE

INDENTURE, dated as of April 29, 2013, between Apple Inc., a corporation duly organized and existing under the laws of the State of California (herein called the "Company"), and The Bank of New York Mellon Trust Company, N.A., a national banking association duly organized and existing under the laws of the United States, as Trustee (herein called the "Trustee").

RECITALS OF THE COMPANY

The Company has duly authorized the execution and delivery of this Indenture to provide for the issuance from time to time of its debt securities (herein called the "Securities"), to be issued in one or more series as in this Indenture provided.

All things necessary to make this Indenture a valid agreement of the Company, in accordance with its terms, have been done.

NOW, THEREFORE, THIS INDENTURE WITNESSETH:

For and in consideration of the premises and the purchase of the Securities by the Holders thereof, it is mutually agreed, for the equal and proportionate benefit of all Holders of the Securities or of any series thereof, as follows:

ARTICLE I
DEFINITIONS AND OTHER PROVISIONS OF GENERAL APPLICATION

Section 101. Definitions.

For all purposes of this Indenture, except as otherwise expressly provided or unless the context otherwise requires:

(1)   the terms defined in this Article I have the meanings assigned to them in this Article I and include the plural as well as the singular;

(2)   all other terms used herein which are defined in the Trust Indenture Act, either directly or by reference therein, have the meanings assigned to them therein;

(3)   all accounting terms not otherwise defined herein have the meanings assigned to them in accordance with GAAP;

(4) unless the context otherwise requires, any reference to an "Article" or a "Section" refers to an Article or a Section, as the case may be, of this Indenture;

(5) the words "herein," "hereof" and "hereunder" and other words of similar import refer to this Indenture as a whole and not to any particular Article, Section or other subdivision;

(6) "including" means including without limitation;

(7) "or" is inclusive;

(8) references to statutes are to be construed as including all statutory provisions consolidating, amending or replacing the statute referred to;

(9) when used with respect to any Security, the words "convert," "converted" and "conversion" are intended to refer to the right of the Holder or the Company to convert or exchange such Security into or for securities or other property in accordance with such terms, if any, as may hereafter be specified for such Security as contemplated by Section 301, and these words are not intended to refer to any right of the Holder or the Company to exchange such Security for other Securities of the same series and like tenor pursuant to Section 304, Section 305, Section 306, Section 906 or Section 1107 or another similar provisions of this Indenture, unless the context otherwise requires; and references herein to the terms of any Security that may be converted mean such terms as may be specified for such Security as contemplated in Section 301; and

(10) unless otherwise provided, references to agreements and other instruments shall be deemed to include all amendments and other modifications to such agreements and instruments, but only to the extent such amendments and other modifications are not prohibited by the terms of this Indenture.

"Act," when used with respect to any Holder, has the meaning specified in Section 104.

"Affiliate" means, with respect to any specified Person, any other Person directly or indirectly controlling or controlled by or under direct or indirect common control with such specified Person. For purposes of this definition, "control" when used with respect to any specified Person means the power to direct the management and policies of such Person, directly or indirectly, whether through the ownership of voting securities, by contract or otherwise; and the terms "controlling" and "controlled" have meanings correlative to the foregoing.

"Applicable Procedures" means, with respect to a Depositary, as to any matter at any time, the policies and procedures of such Depositary, if any, that are applicable to such matter at such time.

"Authenticating Agent" means any Person authorized by the Trustee pursuant to Section 614 to act on behalf of the Trustee to authenticate Securities of one or more series.

"Bankruptcy Law" has the meaning specified in Section 501.

"Board of Directors" means either the Board of Directors of the Company or any duly authorized committee of that Board of Directors.

"Board Resolution" means a copy of one or more resolutions certified by the Secretary or an Assistant Secretary of the Company to have been duly adopted by the Board of Directors and to be in full force and effect on the date of such certification and delivered to the Trustee.

"Business Day" means, when used with respect to any Place of Payment, unless otherwise specified as contemplated by Section 301, any day, other than a Saturday or Sunday, which is not a day on which banking institutions are authorized or obligated by law or executive order to close in that Place of Payment.

"Commission" means the U.S. Securities and Exchange Commission, from time to time constituted, created under the Exchange Act, or, if at any time after the execution of this Indenture such Commission is not existing and performing the duties now assigned to it under the Trust Indenture Act, then the body performing such duties at such time.

"Company" means the Person named as the "Company" in the first paragraph of this Indenture until a successor Person shall have become such pursuant to the applicable provisions of this Indenture, and thereafter "Company" shall mean such successor Person.

"Company Request" or "Company Order" means a written request or order signed in the name of the Company by an Officer of the Company (or any Person designated in writing by an Officer of the Company as authorized to execute and deliver Company Requests and Company Orders), and delivered to the Trustee.

"Corporate Trust Office" means the principal office of the Trustee at which, at any particular time, its corporate trust business shall be conducted (which office is located as of the date of this Indenture at The Bank of New York Mellon Trust Company, N.A., 400 South Hope Street, Suite 400, Los Angeles, California 90071, Attention: Corporate Trust Unit, or at any other time at such other address as the Trustee may designate from time to time by notice to the Holders).

"Covenant Defeasance" has the meaning specified in Section 1303.

"Custodian" has the meaning specified in Section 501.

"Default" means any event which is, or after notice or passage of time or both would be, an Event of Default.

"Defaulted Interest" has the meaning specified in Section 307.

"Defeasance" has the meaning specified in Section 1302.

"Depositary" means, with respect to Securities of any series issuable in whole or in part in the form of one or more Global Securities, a clearing agency registered under the Exchange Act that is designated to act as Depositary for such Securities as contemplated by Section 301.

"Event of Default" has the meaning specified in Section 501.

"Exchange Act" means the U.S. Securities Exchange Act of 1934 and any statute successor thereto, in each case as amended from time to time.

"Expiration Date" has the meaning specified in Section 104.

"GAAP" means generally accepted accounting principles in the United States as in effect from time to time.

"Global Security" means a Security that evidences all or part of the Securities of any series and bears the legend set forth in Section 202 (or such legend as may be specified as contemplated by Section 301 for such Securities).

"Holder" means a Person in whose name a Security is registered in the Security Register.

"Indenture" means this instrument as originally executed and as it may from time to time be supplemented or amended by one or more indentures supplemental hereto entered into pursuant to the applicable provisions hereof, including, for all purposes of this instrument and any such supplemental indenture, the provisions of the Trust

Indenture Act that are deemed to be a part of and govern this instrument and any such supplemental indenture, respectively. The term "Indenture" shall also include the terms of particular series of Securities established as contemplated by Section 301.

"interest" means, when used with respect to an Original Issue Discount Security which by its terms bears interest only after Maturity, interest payable after Maturity.

"Interest Payment Date" means, when used with respect to any Security, the Stated Maturity of an installment of interest on such Security.

"Internal Revenue Code" means the U.S. Internal Revenue Code of 1986, as amended from time to time.

"Maturity" means, when used with respect to any Security, the date on which the principal of such Security or an installment of principal becomes due and payable as therein or herein provided, whether at the Stated Maturity or by declaration of acceleration, call for redemption or otherwise.

"Notice of Default" means a written notice of the kind specified in Section 501.

"Officer" means the Chief Executive Officer, the Chief Financial Officer, the Corporate Treasurer, the Corporate Controller, or the General Counsel and Secretary, of the Company.

"Officer's Certificate" means a certificate signed by an Officer of the Company (or any Person designated in writing by an Officer of the Company as authorized to execute and deliver Officer's Certificates) and delivered to the Trustee.

"Opinion of Counsel" means a written opinion of counsel (who may be counsel for the Company) and which shall be reasonably acceptable to the Trustee. The counsel may be an employee of the Company. Opinions of Counsel required to be delivered under this Indenture may have qualifications customary for opinions of the type required.

"Original Issue Discount Security" means any Security which provides for an amount less than the principal amount thereof to be due and payable upon a declaration of acceleration of the Maturity thereof pursuant to Section 502.

"Outstanding" means, when used with respect to Securities, as of the date of determination, all Securities theretofore authenticated and delivered under this Indenture, except:

(1) Securities theretofore cancelled by the Trustee or delivered to the Trustee for cancellation;

(2) Securities for whose payment or redemption money in the necessary amount has been theretofore deposited with the Trustee or any Paying Agent (other than the Company) in trust or set aside and segregated in trust by the Company (if the Company shall act as its own Paying Agent) for the Holders of such Securities; provided that, if such Securities are to be redeemed, notice of such redemption has been duly given pursuant to this Indenture or provision therefor satisfactory to the Trustee has been made;

(3) Securities as to which Defeasance has been effected pursuant to Section 1302;

(4) Securities which have been paid pursuant to Section 306 or in exchange for or in lieu of which other Securities have been authenticated and delivered pursuant to this Indenture, other than any such Securities in respect of which there shall have been presented to the Trustee proof satisfactory to it that such Securities are held by a *bona fide* purchaser in whose hands such Securities are valid obligations of the Company; and

(5) Securities as to which any property deliverable upon conversion thereof has been delivered (or such delivery has been made available), or as to which any other particular conditions have been satisfied, in each case as may be provided for such Securities as contemplated in Section 301;

provided, however, that in determining whether the Holders of the requisite principal amount of the Outstanding Securities have given, made or taken any request, demand, authorization, direction, notice, consent, waiver or other action hereunder as of any date, (A) the principal amount of an Original Issue Discount Security which shall be deemed to be Outstanding shall be the amount of the principal thereof which would be due and payable as of such date upon acceleration of the Maturity thereof to such date pursuant to Section 502, (B) if, as of such date, the principal amount payable at the Stated Maturity of a Security is not determinable, the principal amount of such Security which shall be deemed to be Outstanding shall be the amount as specified or determined as contemplated by Section 301, (C) the principal amount of a Security denominated in one or more foreign currencies, composite currencies or currency units which shall be deemed to be Outstanding shall be the U.S. dollar equivalent, determined as of such date in the manner provided as contemplated by Section 301, of the principal amount of such Security (or, in the case of a Security described in clause (A) or (B) above, of the amount determined as provided in such clause), and (D) Securities owned by the Company or any other obligor upon the Securities or any Affiliate of the Company or of such other obligor shall be disregarded and deemed not to be Outstanding, except that, in determining whether the Trustee shall be protected in relying upon any such request, demand, authorization, direction, notice, consent, waiver or other action, only Securities which a Responsible Officer of the Trustee knows to be so owned shall be so disregarded. Securities so owned which have been pledged in good faith may be regarded as Outstanding if the pledgee establishes to the satisfaction of the Trustee the pledgee's right so to act with respect to such Securities and that the pledgee is not the Company or any other obligor upon the Securities or any Affiliate of the Company or of such other obligor.

"Paying Agent" means any Person authorized by the Company to pay the principal of or premium, if any, or interest on any Securities on behalf of the Company. The Company initially authorizes and appoints the Trustee as the Paying Agent for each series of the Securities.

"Person" means any individual, corporation, partnership, limited liability company, joint venture, association, joint-stock company, trust, unincorporated organization or government or any agency or political subdivision thereof or any other entity.

"Place of Payment" means, when used with respect to the Securities of any series, the place or places where the principal of and premium, if any, and interest on the Securities of such series are payable as specified as contemplated by Section 301.

"Predecessor Security" means, with respect to any particular Security, every previous Security evidencing all or a portion of the same debt as that evidenced by such particular Security; and, for the purposes of this definition, any Security authenticated and delivered under Section 306 in exchange for or in lieu of a mutilated, destroyed, lost or stolen Security shall be deemed to evidence the same debt as the mutilated, destroyed, lost or stolen Security.

"Redemption Date" means, when used with respect to any Security to be redeemed, the date fixed for such redemption by or pursuant to this Indenture.

"Redemption Price" means, when used with respect to any Security to be redeemed, the price at which it is to be redeemed pursuant to this Indenture.

"Regular Record Date" means, for the interest payable on any Interest Payment Date on the Securities of any series, the date specified for that purpose as contemplated by Section 301.

"Repayment Date" means, with used with respect to a Security to be repaid at the option of a Holder, the date fixed for such repayment by or pursuant to this Indenture.

"Responsible Officer" means, when used with respect to the Trustee, any officer within the corporate trust department of the Trustee, including any vice president, assistant secretary, senior associate, associate, trust officer, or any other officer associated with the corporate trust department of the Trustee customarily performing functions similar to those performed by any of the above designated officers who shall have direct responsibility for the administration of this Indenture and also means, with respect to a particular corporate trust matter, any other officer to whom such matter is referred because of such person's knowledge of and familiarity with the particular subject.

"Securities" has the meaning specified in the first recital of this Indenture and more particularly means any Securities authenticated and delivered under this Indenture.

"Securities Act" means the U.S. Securities Act of 1933 and any statute successor thereto, in each case as amended from time to time.

"Security Register" and "Security Registrar" have the respective meanings specified in Section 305.

"Special Record Date" means, for the payment of any Defaulted Interest, a date fixed by the Trustee pursuant to Section 307.

"Stated Maturity" means, when used with respect to any Security or any installment of principal thereof or interest thereon, the date specified in such Security as the fixed date on which the principal of such Security or such installment of principal or interest is due and payable.

"Subsidiary" means a corporation more than 50% of the outstanding voting stock of which is owned, directly or indirectly, by the Company or by one or more other Subsidiaries, or by the Company and one or more other Subsidiaries. For purposes of this definition, "voting stock" means stock which ordinarily has voting power for the election of directors, whether at all times or only so long as no senior class of stock has such voting power by reason of any contingency.

"Successor" has the meaning specified in Section 801.

"Trust Indenture Act" means the U.S. Trust Indenture Act of 1939 as in force at the date as of which this Indenture was executed; provided, however, that in the event the Trust Indenture Act of 1939 is amended after such date, "Trust Indenture Act" means, to the extent required by any such amendment, the Trust Indenture Act of 1939 as so amended.

"Trustee" means the Person named as the "Trustee" in the first paragraph of this Indenture until a successor Trustee shall have become such pursuant to the applicable provisions of this Indenture, and thereafter "Trustee" shall mean or include each Person who is then a Trustee hereunder, and if at any time there is more than one such Person, "Trustee" as used with respect to the Securities of any series shall mean the Trustee with respect to Securities of that series.

"U.S. Government Obligation" has the meaning specified in Section 1304(1).

"Vice President" means, when used with respect to the Company or the Trustee, any vice president, whether or not designated by a number or a word or words added before or after the title "vice president."

Section 102. Compliance Certificates and Opinions.

Upon any application or request by the Company to the Trustee to take any action under any provision of this Indenture, the Company shall furnish to the Trustee an Officer's Certificate stating that all conditions precedent, if any, provided for in this Indenture relating to the proposed action have been complied with and an Opinion of Counsel stating that in the opinion of such counsel all such conditions precedent, if any, have been complied with, except that in the case of any such application or request as to which the furnishing of such documents is specifically required by any provision of this Indenture relating to such particular application or request, no additional certificate or opinion need be furnished by the Company.

Every certificate or opinion with respect to compliance with a condition or covenant provided for in this Indenture (except for certificates provided for in Section 1004) shall include:

(1) a statement that each individual signing such certificate or opinion has read such covenant or condition and the definitions herein relating thereto;

(2) a brief statement as to the nature and scope of the examination or investigation upon which the statements or opinions contained in such certificate or opinion are based;

(3) a statement that, in the opinion of each such individual, he or she has made such examination or investigation as is necessary to enable him or her to express an informed opinion as to whether or not such covenant or condition has been complied with; and

(4) a statement as to whether, in the opinion of each such individual, such condition or covenant has been complied with.

Section 103. Form of Documents Delivered to Trustee.

In any case where several matters are required to be certified by, or covered by an opinion of, any specified Person, it is not necessary that all such matters be certified by, or covered by the opinion of, only one such Person, or that they be so certified or covered by only one document, but one such Person may certify or give an opinion with respect to some matters and one or more other such Persons as to other matters, and any such Person may certify or give an opinion as to such matters in one or several documents.

Any certificate or opinion of an Officer (or any Person designated in writing by an Officer of the Company as authorized to execute and deliver the Securities) may be based, insofar as it relates to legal matters, upon a certificate or opinion of, or representations by, counsel, unless such Officer (or any such Person designated in writing by an Officer of the Company as authorized to execute and deliver the Securities) knows, or in the exercise of reasonable care should know, that the certificate or opinion or representations with respect to the matters upon which such Officer's (or such Person's) certificate or opinion is based are erroneous. Any such certificate or Opinion of Counsel may be based, insofar as it relates to factual matters, upon a certificate or opinion of, or representations by, an Officer or Officers of the Company (or any Person or Persons designated in writing by an Officer of the Company as authorized to execute and deliver the Securities) stating that the information with respect to such factual matters is in the possession of the Company, unless such counsel knows, or in the exercise of reasonable care should know, that the certificate or opinion or representations with respect to such matters are erroneous. Counsel delivering an Opinion of Counsel may also rely as to factual matters on certificates of governmental or other officials customary for opinions of the type required.

Where any Person is required to make, give or execute two or more applications, requests, consents, certificates, statements, opinions or other instruments under this Indenture, they may, but need not, be consolidated and form one instrument.

Section 104. Acts of Holders; Record Dates.

Any request, demand, authorization, direction, notice, consent, waiver or other action provided or permitted by this Indenture to be given, made or taken by Holders may be embodied in and evidenced by one or more instruments of substantially similar tenor signed by such Holders in person or by an agent duly appointed in writing; and, except as herein otherwise expressly provided, such action shall become effective when such instrument or instruments are delivered to the Trustee and, where it is hereby expressly required, to the Company. Such instrument or instruments (and the action embodied therein and evidenced thereby) are herein sometimes referred to as the "Act" of the Holders signing such instrument or instruments. Proof of execution of any such instrument or of a writing appointing any such agent shall be sufficient for any purpose of this Indenture and, subject to Section 601, conclusive in favor of the Trustee and the Company, if made in the manner provided in this Section 104.

The fact and date of the execution by any Person of any such instrument or writing may be proved in any manner which the Trustee reasonably deems sufficient. Where such execution is by a Person acting in a capacity other than such Person's individual capacity, such certificate or affidavit shall also constitute sufficient proof of such Person's authority. The fact and date of the execution of any such instrument or writing, or the authority of the Person executing the same, may also be proved in any other manner which the Trustee deems sufficient.

The ownership of Securities shall be proved by the Security Register.

Any request, demand, authorization, direction, notice, consent, waiver or other Act of the Holder of any Security shall bind every future Holder of the same Security and the Holder of every Security issued upon the registration of transfer thereof or in exchange therefor or in lieu thereof in respect of anything done, omitted or suffered to be done by the Trustee or the Company in reliance thereon, whether or not notation of such action is made upon such Security.

The Company may set any day as a record date for the purpose of determining the Holders of Outstanding Securities of any series entitled to give, make or take any request, demand, authorization, direction, notice, consent, waiver or other action provided or permitted by this Indenture to be given, made or taken by Holders of Securities of such series; provided that the Company may not set a record date for, and the provisions of this paragraph shall not apply with respect to, the giving or making of any notice, declaration, request or direction referred to in the next paragraph. If any record date is set pursuant to this paragraph, the Holders of Outstanding Securities of the relevant series on such record date, and no other Holders, shall be entitled to take the relevant action, whether or not such Holders remain Holders after such record date; provided that no such action shall be effective hereunder unless taken on or prior to the applicable Expiration Date by Holders of the requisite principal amount of Outstanding Securities of such series on such record date. Nothing in this paragraph shall be construed to prevent the Company from setting a new record date for any action for which a record date has previously been set pursuant to this paragraph (whereupon the record date previously set shall automatically and with no action by any Person be cancelled and of no effect), and nothing in this paragraph shall be construed to render ineffective any action taken by Holders of the requisite principal amount of Outstanding Securities of the relevant series on the date such action is taken. Promptly after any record date is set pursuant to this paragraph, the Company, at its own expense, shall cause notice of such record date, the proposed action by Holders and the applicable Expiration Date to be given to the Trustee in writing and to each Holder of Securities of the relevant series in the manner set forth in Sections 105 and 106.

The Trustee may set any day as a record date for the purpose of determining the Holders of Outstanding Securities of any series entitled to join in the giving or making of (i) any Notice of Default, (ii) any declaration of acceleration referred to in Section 502, (iii) any request to institute proceedings referred to in Section 507(2) or (iv) any direction referred to in Section 511, in each case with respect to Securities of such series. If any record date is set pursuant to this paragraph, the Holders of Outstanding Securities of such series on such record date, and no other Holders, shall be entitled to join in such notice, declaration, request or direction, whether or not such Holders remain Holders after such record date; provided that no such action shall be effective hereunder unless taken on or prior to the applicable Expiration Date by Holders of the requisite principal amount of Outstanding Securities of such series on such record date. Nothing in this paragraph shall be construed to prevent the Trustee from setting a new record date for any action for which a record date has previously been set pursuant to this paragraph (whereupon the record date previously set shall automatically and with no action by any Person be cancelled and of no effect), and nothing in this paragraph shall be construed to render ineffective any action taken by Holders of the requisite principal amount of Outstanding Securities of the relevant series on the date such action is taken. Promptly after any record date is set pursuant to this paragraph, the Trustee, at the Company's expense, shall cause notice of such record date, the proposed action by Holders and the applicable Expiration Date to be given to the Company in writing and to each Holder of Securities of the relevant series in the manner set forth in Sections 105 and 106.

With respect to any record date set pursuant to this Section 104, the party hereto which sets such record dates may designate any day as the "Expiration Date" and from time to time may change the Expiration Date to any earlier or later day; provided that no such change shall be effective unless notice of the proposed new Expiration Date is given to the other party hereto in writing, and to each Holder of Securities of the relevant series in the manner set forth in Section 106, on or prior to the existing Expiration Date. If an Expiration Date is not designated with respect to any record date set pursuant to this Section 104, the party hereto which set such record date shall be deemed to have initially designated the 180th day after such record date as the Expiration Date with respect thereto, subject to its right to change the Expiration Date as provided in this paragraph.

Without limiting the foregoing, a Holder entitled hereunder to take any action hereunder with regard to any particular Security may do so with regard to all or any part of the principal amount of such Security or by one or more duly appointed agents each of which may do so pursuant to such appointment with regard to all or any part of such principal amount.

Section 105. <u>Notices, Etc., to Trustee and Company.</u>

Any request, demand, authorization, direction, notice, consent, waiver or Act of Holders or other document provided or permitted by this Indenture to be made upon, given or furnished to, or filed with,

(1) the Trustee by any Holder or by the Company shall be sufficient for every purpose hereunder if made, given, furnished or filed in writing (which may be by facsimile) to or with the Trustee at its Corporate Trust Office at the location specified in Section 101; or

(2) the Company by the Trustee or by any Holder shall be sufficient for every purpose hereunder (unless otherwise herein expressly provided) if in writing and mailed, first-class postage prepaid, to the Company addressed to the attention of the Secretary of the Company at the address of the Company's principal office specified in writing to the Trustee by the Company and, until further notice, at Apple Inc., 1 Infinite Loop, MS 301-4GC, Cupertino, California 95014, fax number: (408) 974-8530, Attention: Office of the General Counsel.

In addition to the foregoing, the Trustee agrees to accept and act upon notice, instructions or directions pursuant to this Indenture sent by unsecured e-mail, facsimile transmission or other similar unsecured electronic methods. If the party elects to give the Trustee e-mail or facsimile instructions (or instructions by a similar electronic method) and the Trustee in its discretion elects to act upon such instructions, the Trustee's understanding of such instructions shall be deemed controlling. The Trustee shall not be liable for any losses, costs or expenses arising directly or indirectly from the Trustee's reliance upon and compliance with such instructions notwithstanding such instructions conflict or are inconsistent with a subsequent written instruction. The party providing electronic instructions agrees to assume all risks arising out of the use of such electronic methods to submit instructions and directions to the Trustee, including without limitation the risk of the Trustee acting on unauthorized instructions, and the risk or interception and misuse by third parties.

Section 106. <u>Notice to Holders; Waiver.</u>

Where this Indenture provides for notice to Holders of any event, such notice shall be sufficiently given (unless otherwise herein expressly provided) if in writing and mailed, first-class postage prepaid, to each Holder affected by such event, at such Holder's address as it appears in the Security Register, not later than the latest date, if any, and not earlier than the earliest date, if any, prescribed for the giving of such notice. In any case where notice to Holders is given by mail, neither the failure to mail such notice, nor any defect in any notice so mailed, to any particular Holder shall affect the sufficiency of such notice with respect to other Holders. Any notice when mailed to a Holder in the aforesaid manner shall be conclusively deemed to have been received by such Holder whether or not actually received by such Holder. Where this Indenture provides for notice in any manner, such notice may be waived in writing by the Person entitled to receive such notice, either before or after the event, and such waiver shall be the equivalent of such notice. Waivers of notice by Holders shall be filed with the Trustee, but such filing shall not be a condition precedent to the validity of any action taken in reliance upon such waiver.

In case by reason of the suspension of regular mail service or by reason of any other cause it shall be impracticable to give such notice by mail, then such notification as shall be made with the approval of the Trustee shall constitute a sufficient notification for every purpose hereunder.

Where this Indenture provides for notice of any event to a Holder of a Global Security, such notice shall be sufficiently given if given to the Depositary for such Security (or its designee), pursuant to the Applicable Procedures of the Depositary, not later than the latest date, if any, and not earlier than the earliest date, if any, prescribed for the giving of such notice.

Section 107. Conflict with Trust Indenture Act.

If any provision of this Indenture limits, qualifies or conflicts with a provision of the Trust Indenture Act which is required under such Act to be a part of and govern this Indenture, the latter provision shall control. If any provision of this Indenture modifies or excludes any provision of the Trust Indenture Act which may be so modified or excluded, the latter provision shall be deemed to apply to this Indenture as so modified or to be excluded, as the case may be.

Section 108. Effect of Headings and Table of Contents.

The Article and Section headings herein and the Table of Contents are for convenience only and shall not affect the construction hereof.

Section 109. Successors and Assigns.

All covenants and agreements in this Indenture by the Company shall bind its successors and assigns, whether so expressed or not. All agreements of the Trustee in this Indenture shall bind its successors and assigns, whether so expressed or not.

Section 110. Separability Clause.

In case any provision in this Indenture or in the Securities shall be invalid, illegal or unenforceable, the validity, legality and enforceability of the remaining provisions shall not in any way be affected or impaired thereby.

Section 111. <u>Benefits of Indenture.</u>

Nothing in this Indenture or in the Securities, express or implied, shall give to any Person, other than the parties hereto and their successors hereunder and the Holders, any benefit or any legal or equitable right, remedy or claim under this Indenture.

Section 112. <u>Governing Law.</u>

This Indenture and the Securities shall be governed by, and construed in accordance with, the law of the State of New York.

Section 113. <u>Legal Holidays.</u>

In any case where any Interest Payment Date, Redemption Date, Repayment Date or Stated Maturity of any Security, or any date on which a Holder has the right to convert such Holder's Security, shall not be a Business Day at any Place of Payment, then (notwithstanding any other provision of this Indenture or of the Securities (other than a provision of any Security which specifically states that such provision shall apply in lieu of this Section 113)) payment of principal and premium, if any, or interest, or the Redemption Price or conversion of such Security, shall not be made at such Place of Payment on such date, but shall be made on the next succeeding Business Day at such Place of Payment with the same force and effect as if made on the Interest Payment Date, Redemption Date or Repayment Date, or at the Stated Maturity, or on such conversion date. In the case, however, of Securities of a series bearing interest at a floating rate based on the London interbank offered rate (LIBOR), if any Interest Payment Date (other than the Redemption Date, Repayment Date or Stated Maturity) would otherwise be a date that is not a Business Day, then the Interest Payment Date shall be postponed to the following date which is a Business Day, unless that Business Day falls in the next succeeding calendar month, in which case the Interest Payment Date will be the Business Day immediately preceding the scheduled Interest Payment Date. No interest shall accrue for the period from and after any such Interest Payment Date, Redemption Date, Repayment Date, Stated Maturity or conversion date, as the case may be, to the date of such payment.

Section 114. <u>No Recourse Against Others.</u>

No recourse shall be had for the payment of principal of, or premium, if any, or interest, if any, on any Security of any series, or for any claim based thereon, or upon any obligation, covenant or agreement of this Indenture, against any incorporator, shareholder, officer or director, as such, past, present or future, of the Company or any successor corporation of the Company, either directly or indirectly through the Company or any successor corporation of the Company, whether by virtue of any constitution, statute or rule of law or by the enforcement of any assessment of penalty or otherwise; it being expressly agreed and understood that this Indenture and all the Securities of each series are solely corporate obligations, and that no personal liability whatsoever shall attach to, or is incurred by, any incorporator, shareholder, officer or director, past, present or future, of the Company or of any successor corporation of the Company, either directly or indirectly through the Company or any successor corporation of the Company, because of the incurring of the indebtedness hereby authorized or under or by reason of any of the obligations, covenants or agreements contained in this Indenture or in any of the Securities of any series, or to be implied herefrom or therefrom; and that all such personal liability is hereby expressly released and waived as a condition of, and as part of the consideration for, the execution of this Indenture and the issuance of the Securities of each series.

Section 115. WAIVER OF JURY TRIAL.

EACH OF THE COMPANY AND THE TRUSTEE HEREBY IRREVOCABLY WAIVES, TO THE FULLEST EXTENT PERMITTED BY APPLICABLE LAW, ANY AND ALL RIGHT TO TRIAL BY JURY IN ANY LEGAL PROCEEDING AS BETWEEN THE COMPANY AND THE TRUSTEE ONLY ARISING OUT OF OR RELATING TO THIS INDENTURE OR THE SECURITIES.

Section 116. Submission to Jurisdiction.

The Company hereby irrevocably submits to the jurisdiction of any New York State court sitting in the Borough of Manhattan in the City of New York or any federal court sitting in the Borough of Manhattan in the City of New York in respect of any suit, action or proceeding arising out of or relating to this Indenture and the Securities, and irrevocably accepts for itself and in respect of its property, generally and unconditionally, jurisdiction of the aforesaid courts.

ARTICLE II
SECURITY FORMS

Section 201. Forms Generally.

The Securities of each series shall be in substantially such form or forms as shall be established by or pursuant to a Board Resolution or, subject to Section 303, set forth in, or determined in the manner provided in, an Officer's Certificate pursuant to a Board Resolution, or in one or more indentures supplemental hereto, in each case with such appropriate insertions, omissions, substitutions and other variations as are required or permitted by this Indenture, and may have such letters, numbers or other marks of identification and such legends or endorsements placed thereon as may be required to comply with applicable tax laws or the rules of any securities exchange or Depositary therefor or as may, consistently herewith, be determined by the Officer (or any Person designated in writing by an Officer of the Company as authorized to execute and deliver the Securities) executing such Securities, as evidenced by his or her execution thereof. If the form of Securities of any series is established by action taken pursuant to a Board Resolution, a copy of an appropriate record of such action shall be certified by the Secretary or an Assistant Secretary of the Company and delivered to the Trustee at or prior to the delivery of the Company Order contemplated by Section 303 for the authentication and delivery of such Securities. If all of the Securities of any series established by action taken pursuant to a Board Resolution are not to be issued at one time, it shall not be necessary to deliver a record of such action at the time of issuance of each Security of such series, but an appropriate record of such action shall be delivered at or before the time of issuance of the first Security of such series.

The definitive Securities shall be printed, lithographed or engraved or may be produced in any other manner, all as determined by the Officer (or any Person designated in writing by an Officer of the Company as authorized to execute and deliver the Securities) executing such Securities, as evidenced by his or her execution of such Securities.

Section 202. <u>Form of Legend for Global Securities.</u>

Unless otherwise specified as contemplated by Section 301 for the Securities evidenced thereby or as required by Applicable Procedures, every Global Security authenticated and delivered hereunder shall bear a legend in substantially the following form:

[*Insert, if applicable*—UNLESS THIS NOTE IS PRESENTED BY AN AUTHORIZED REPRESENTATIVE OF THE DEPOSITORY TRUST COMPANY, A NEW YORK CORPORATION ("<u>DTC</u>"), TO THE ISSUER OR ITS AGENT FOR REGISTRATION OF TRANSFER, EXCHANGE OR PAYMENT, AND ANY CERTIFICATE ISSUED IS REGISTERED IN THE NAME OF CEDE & CO. OR IN SUCH OTHER NAME AS IS REQUESTED BY AN AUTHORIZED REPRESENTATIVE OF DTC (AND ANY PAYMENT IS MADE TO CEDE & CO. OR TO SUCH OTHER ENTITY AS IS REQUESTED BY AN AUTHORIZED REPRESENTATIVE OF DTC), ANY TRANSFER, PLEDGE OR OTHER USE HEREOF FOR VALUE OR OTHERWISE BY OR TO ANY PERSON IS WRONGFUL INASMUCH AS THE REGISTERED OWNER HEREOF, CEDE & CO., HAS AN INTEREST HEREIN.

TRANSFERS OF THIS GLOBAL SECURITY SHALL BE LIMITED TO TRANSFERS IN WHOLE, BUT NOT IN PART, TO NOMINEES OF DTC OR TO A SUCCESSOR THEREOF OR SUCH SUCCESSOR'S NOMINEE AND TRANSFERS OF PORTIONS OF THIS GLOBAL SECURITY SHALL BE LIMITED TO TRANSFERS MADE IN ACCORDANCE WITH THE RESTRICTIONS SET FORTH IN THE INDENTURE REFERRED TO ON THE REVERSE HEREOF.]

[*Insert, if applicable*—THIS SECURITY IS A GLOBAL SECURITY WITHIN THE MEANING OF THE INDENTURE REFERRED TO HEREIN AND IS REGISTERED IN THE NAME OF A DEPOSITARY OR A NOMINEE THEREOF. THIS SECURITY MAY NOT BE EXCHANGED IN WHOLE OR IN PART FOR A SECURITY REGISTERED, AND NO TRANSFER OF THIS SECURITY IN WHOLE OR IN PART MAY BE REGISTERED, IN THE NAME OF ANY PERSON OTHER THAN SUCH DEPOSITARY OR A NOMINEE THEREOF, EXCEPT IN THE LIMITED CIRCUMSTANCES DESCRIBED IN THE INDENTURE.]

Section 203. <u>Form of Trustee's Certificate of Authentication.</u>

The Trustee's certificates of authentication shall be in substantially the following form:

This is one of the Securities of the series designated therein referred to in the within-mentioned Indenture.

Dated:

> The Bank of New York Mellon Trust
> Company, N.A.,
> as Trustee
>
> By: _____
> Authorized Signatory

ARTICLE III
THE SECURITIES

Section 301. <u>Amount Unlimited; Issuable in Series.</u>

The aggregate principal amount of Securities which may be authenticated and delivered under this Indenture is unlimited.

The Securities may be issued in one or more series. There shall be established in or pursuant to (a) a Board Resolution or pursuant to authority granted by a Board Resolution and, subject to Section 303, set forth, or determined in the manner provided, in an Officer's Certificate, or (b) one or more indentures supplemental hereto, prior to the issuance of Securities of any series:

(1) the title of the Securities of the series (which shall distinguish the Securities of the series from Securities of any other series);

(2) the limit, if any, on the aggregate principal amount of the Securities of the series which may be authenticated and delivered under this Indenture (except for Securities authenticated and delivered upon registration of transfer of, or in exchange for, or in lieu of, other Securities of the series pursuant to Section 304, Section 305, Section 306, Section 906, Section 1107 or Section 1405 and except for any Securities which, pursuant to Section 303, are deemed never to have been authenticated and delivered hereunder); <u>provided, however,</u> that the authorized aggregate principal amount of such series may from time to time be increased above such amount by a Board Resolution to such effect;

(3) the price or prices at which the Securities will be sold;

(4) the Person to whom any interest on a Security of the series shall be payable, if other than the Person in whose name that Security (or one or more Predecessor Securities) is registered at the close of business on the Regular Record Date for such interest;

(5) the date or dates on which the principal and premium, if any, of any Securities of the series is payable or the method used to determine or extend those dates;

(6) the rate or rates at which any Securities of the series shall bear interest, if any, or the method by which such rate or rates shall be determined, the date or dates from which any such interest shall accrue, or the method by which such date or dates shall be determined, the Interest Payment Dates on which

any such interest shall be payable and the Regular Record Date, if any, for any such interest payable on any Interest Payment Date, or the method by which such date or dates shall be determined, and the basis upon which interest shall be calculated if other than that of a 360-day year of twelve 30-day months, the right, if any, to extend or defer interest payments and the duration of such extension or deferral;

(7) the place or places where the principal of and any premium and interest on any Securities of the series shall be payable, the place or places where the Securities of such series may be presented for registration of transfer or exchange, the place or places where notices and demands to or upon the Company in respect of the Securities of such series may be made and the manner in which any payment may be made;

(8) the period or periods within which or the date or dates on which, the price or prices at which, the currency or currency units in which, and the terms and conditions upon which any Securities of the series may be redeemed, in whole or in part, at the option of the Company and, if other than by a Board Resolution, the manner in which any election by the Company to redeem the Securities shall be evidenced;

(9) the obligation or the right, if any, of the Company to redeem or purchase any Securities of the series pursuant to any sinking fund, amortization or analogous provisions or at the option of the Holder thereof and the period or periods within which, the price or prices at which, the currency or currency units in which, and the terms and conditions upon which any Securities of the series shall be redeemed or purchased, in whole or in part, pursuant to such obligation;

(10) if other than denominations of $2,000 and any integral multiple of $1,000 in excess thereof, the denominations in which any Securities of the series shall be issuable;

(11) if other than the Trustee, the identity of each Security Registrar and/or Paying Agent;

(12) if the amount of principal of or premium, if any, or interest on any Securities of the series may be determined with reference to a financial or economic measure or index or pursuant to a formula, the manner in which such amounts shall be determined;

(13) if other than the currency of the United States of America, the currency, currencies or currency units in which the principal of or premium, if any, or interest on any Securities of the series shall be payable and the manner of determining the equivalent thereof in the currency of the United States of America for any purpose, including for purposes of the definition of "Outstanding" in Section 101;

(14) if the principal of or premium, if any, or interest on any Securities of the series is to be payable, at the election of the Company or the Holder thereof, in one or more currencies or currency units other than that or those in which such Securities are stated to be payable, the currency, currencies or currency units in which the principal of or premium, if any, or interest on such Securities as to which such election is made shall be payable, the periods within which or the dates on which and the terms and conditions upon which such

election is to be made and the amount so payable (or the manner in which such amount shall be determined);

(15) if the provisions of Section 401 relating to the satisfaction and discharge of this Indenture shall apply to the Securities of that series; or if provisions for the satisfaction and discharge of this Indenture other than as set forth in Section 401 shall apply to the Securities of that series;

(16) if other than the entire principal amount thereof, the portion of the principal amount of any Securities of the series which shall be payable upon declaration of acceleration of the Maturity thereof pursuant to Section 502 or the method by which such portion shall be determined;

(17) if the principal amount payable at the Stated Maturity of any Securities of the series will not be determinable as of any one or more dates prior to the Stated Maturity, the amount which shall be deemed to be the principal amount of such Securities as of any such date for any purpose thereunder or hereunder, including the principal amount thereof which shall be due and payable upon any Maturity other than the Stated Maturity or which shall be deemed to be Outstanding as of any date prior to the Stated Maturity (or, in any such case, the manner in which such amount deemed to be the principal amount shall be determined);

(18) if other than by a Board Resolution, the manner in which any election by the Company to defease any Securities of the series pursuant to Section 1302 or Section 1303 shall be evidenced; whether any Securities of the series other than Securities denominated in U.S. dollars and bearing interest at a fixed rate are to be subject to Section 1302 or Section 1303; or, in the case of Securities denominated in U.S. dollars and bearing interest at a fixed rate, if applicable, that the Securities of the series, in whole or any specified part, shall not be defeasible pursuant to Section 1302 or Section 1303 or both such Sections;

(19) if applicable, that any Securities of the series shall be issuable in whole or in part in the form of one or more Global Securities and, in such case, the respective Depositaries for such Global Securities, the form of any legend or legends which shall be borne by any such Global Security in addition to or in lieu of that set forth in Section 202 and any circumstances in addition to or in lieu of those set forth in clause (2) of the last paragraph of Section 305 in which any such Global Security may be exchanged in whole or in part for Securities registered, and any transfer of such Global Security in whole or in part may be registered, in the name or names of Persons other than the Depositary for such Global Security or a nominee thereof;

(20) any addition to, deletion from or change in the Events of Default which applies to any Securities of the series and any change in the right of the Trustee or the requisite Holders of such Securities to declare the principal amount thereof due and payable pursuant to Section 502;

(21) any addition to, deletion from or change in the covenants set forth in Article X which applies to Securities of the series;

(22) the terms of any right to convert or exchange Securities of such series into any other securities or property of the Company or of any other corporation or Person, and the additions or changes, if any, to this Indenture with respect

to the Securities of such series to permit or facilitate such conversion or exchange;

(23) whether the Securities of the series will be guaranteed by any Person or Persons and, if so, the identity of such Person or Persons, the terms and conditions upon which such Securities shall be guaranteed and, if applicable, the terms and conditions upon which such guarantees may be subordinated to other indebtedness of the respective guarantors;

(24) whether the Securities of the series will be secured by any collateral and, if so, the terms and conditions upon which such Securities shall be secured and, if applicable, upon which such liens may be subordinated to other liens securing other indebtedness of the Company or any guarantor;

(25) whether the Securities will be issued in a transaction registered under the Securities Act and any restriction or condition on the transferability of the Securities of such series;

(26) the exchanges, if any, on which the Securities may be listed; and

(27) any other terms of the series (which terms shall not be inconsistent with the provisions of this Indenture, except as permitted by Section 901).

All Securities of any one series shall be substantially identical except as to denomination and except as may otherwise be provided in or pursuant to the Board Resolution referred to above or pursuant to authority granted by one or more Board Resolutions and, subject to Section 303, set forth, or determined in the manner provided, in the Officer's Certificate referred to above or in any such indenture supplemental hereto. All Securities of any one series need not be issued at one time and, unless otherwise provided in or pursuant to the Board Resolution referred to above and, subject to Section 303, set forth, or determined in the manner provided, in the Officer's Certificate referred to above or pursuant to authority granted by one or more Board Resolutions or in any such indenture supplemental hereto with respect to a series of Securities, additional Securities of a series may be issued, at the option of the Company, without the consent of any Holder, at any time and from time to time.

If any of the terms of the series are established by action taken pursuant to a Board Resolution, a copy of an appropriate record of such action shall be certified by the Secretary or an Assistant Secretary of the Company and delivered to the Trustee at or prior to the delivery of the Officer's Certificate setting forth the terms of the series.

Section 302. Denominations.

The Securities of each series shall be issuable only in registered form without coupons and only in such denominations as shall be specified as contemplated by Section 301. In the absence of any such specified denomination with respect to the Securities of any series, the Securities of such series shall be issuable in denominations of $2,000 and any integral multiple of $1,000 in excess thereof.

Section 303. Execution, Authentication, Delivery and Dating.

The Securities shall be executed on behalf of the Company by an Officer of the Company (or any Person designated in writing by an Officer of the Company as authorized to execute and deliver the Securities). The signature of any of these officers on the Securities may be manual or facsimile.

Securities bearing the manual or facsimile signatures of individuals who were at any time the proper officers of the Company shall bind the Company, notwithstanding that such individuals or any of them have ceased to hold such offices prior to the authentication and delivery of such Securities or did not hold such offices at the date of such Securities.

At any time and from time to time after the execution and delivery of this Indenture, the Company may deliver Securities of any series executed by the Company to the Trustee for authentication, together with an Officer's Certificate and a Company Order for the authentication and delivery of such Securities, and the Trustee in accordance with the Company Order shall authenticate and deliver such Securities. If the form or terms of the Securities of the series have been established by or pursuant to one or more Board Resolutions or pursuant to authority granted by one or more Board Resolutions as permitted by Section 201 and Section 301, in authenticating such Securities, and accepting the additional responsibilities under this Indenture in relation to such Securities, the Trustee shall be provided with, and, subject to Section 601, shall be fully protected in relying upon, an Opinion of Counsel stating,

(1) if the form of such Securities has been established by or pursuant to Board Resolution or pursuant to authority granted by one or more Board Resolutions as permitted by Section 201, that such form has been established in conformity with the provisions of this Indenture;

(2) if the terms of such Securities have been established by or pursuant to Board Resolution or pursuant to authority granted by one or more Board Resolutions as permitted by Section 301, that such terms have been established in conformity with the provisions of this Indenture; and

(3) that such Securities, when authenticated by the Trustee and issued and delivered by the Company in the manner and subject to any conditions specified in such Opinion of Counsel, will constitute valid and legally binding obligations of the Company enforceable in accordance with their terms, subject to (i) the effects of bankruptcy, insolvency, fraudulent conveyance, reorganization, moratorium and other similar laws relating to or affecting creditors' rights generally, (ii) general equitable principles and (iii) an implied covenant of good faith and fair dealing.

If such form or terms have been so established, the Trustee shall not be required to authenticate such Securities if the issue of such Securities pursuant to this Indenture will materially adversely affect the Trustee's own rights, duties or immunities under the Securities and this Indenture or otherwise in a manner which is not reasonably acceptable to the Trustee.

Notwithstanding the provisions of Section 301 and of the preceding paragraph of this Section 303, if all Securities of a series are not to be originally issued at one time, including in the event that the aggregate principal amount of a series of Outstanding Securities is increased as contemplated by Section 301, it shall not be necessary to deliver the Officer's Certificate, Board Resolution or supplemental indenture otherwise required pursuant to Section 301 or the Company Order and Opinion of Counsel otherwise required pursuant to this Section 303 at or prior to the authentication of each Security of such series if such documents are delivered at or prior to the authentication upon original issuance of the first Security of such series to be issued.

Each Security shall be dated the date of its authentication.

No Security shall be entitled to any benefit under this Indenture or be valid or obligatory for any purpose unless there appears on such Security a certificate of authentication substantially in the form provided for herein executed by the Trustee by manual signature, and such certificate upon any Security shall be conclusive evidence, and the only evidence, that such Security has been duly authenticated and delivered hereunder. Notwithstanding the foregoing, if any Security shall have been authenticated and delivered hereunder but never issued and sold by the Company, and the Company shall deliver such Security to the Trustee for cancellation as provided in Section 309, for all purposes of this Indenture such Security shall be deemed never to have been authenticated and delivered hereunder and shall never be entitled to the benefits of this Indenture.

Section 304. <u>Temporary Securities.</u>

Pending the preparation of definitive Securities of any series, the Company may execute, and, upon Company Order, the Trustee shall authenticate and deliver, temporary Securities which are printed, lithographed, typewritten, mimeographed or otherwise produced, in any authorized denomination, substantially of the tenor of the definitive Securities of such series in lieu of which they are issued and with such appropriate insertions, omissions, substitutions and other variations as the officers executing such Securities may determine, as evidenced by their execution of such Securities.

If temporary Securities of any series are issued, the Company will cause definitive Securities of such series to be prepared without unreasonable delay. After the preparation of definitive Securities of such series, the temporary Securities of such series shall be exchangeable for definitive Securities of such series upon surrender of the temporary Securities of such series at the office or agency of the Company in a Place of Payment for such series, without charge to the Holder. Upon surrender for cancellation of any one or more temporary Securities of any series, the Company shall execute and the Trustee shall authenticate and deliver in exchange therefor one or more definitive Securities of the same series, of any authorized denominations and of like tenor and aggregate principal amount. Until so exchanged, the temporary Securities of any series shall in all respects be entitled to the same benefits under this Indenture as definitive Securities of such series and tenor.

Section 305. <u>Registration, Registration of Transfer and Exchange.</u>

The Company shall cause to be kept at the Corporate Trust Office of the Trustee a register (the register maintained in such office and in any other office or agency of the Company in a Place of Payment being herein sometimes collectively referred to as the "<u>Security Register</u>") in which, subject to such reasonable regulations as it may prescribe, the Company shall provide for the registration of Securities and of transfers of Securities. The Trustee is hereby appointed "<u>Security Registrar</u>" for the purpose of registering Securities and transfers of Securities as herein provided.

Upon surrender for registration of transfer of any Security of a series at the office or agency of the Company in a Place of Payment for such series, the Company shall execute, and the Trustee shall authenticate and deliver, in the name of the designated transferee or transferees, one or more new Securities of the same series, of any authorized denominations and of like tenor and principal amount.

At the option of the Holder, Securities of any series may be exchanged for other Securities of the same series, of any authorized denominations and of like tenor and principal amount, upon surrender of the Securities to be exchanged at such office or agency. Whenever any Securities are so surrendered for exchange, the Company shall execute, and the Trustee shall authenticate and deliver, the Securities which the Holder making the exchange is entitled to receive.

All Securities issued upon any registration of transfer or exchange of Securities shall be the valid obligations of the Company, evidencing the same debt, and entitled to the same benefits under this Indenture, as the Securities surrendered upon such registration of transfer or exchange.

Every Security presented or surrendered for registration of transfer or for exchange shall (if so required by the Company or the Trustee) be duly endorsed, or be accompanied by a written instrument of transfer in form satisfactory to the Company and the Security Registrar duly executed, by the Holder thereof or such Holder's attorney duly authorized in writing.

No service charge shall be made for any registration of transfer or exchange of Securities, but the Company may require payment of a sum sufficient to cover any tax or other governmental charge that may be imposed in connection with any registration of transfer or exchange of Securities, other than exchanges pursuant to Section 304, Section 906, Section 1107 or Section 1405 not involving any transfer.

If the Securities of any series (or of any series and specified tenor) are to be redeemed in part, the Company shall not be required (A) to issue, register the transfer of or exchange any Securities of such series (or of such series and specified tenor, as the case may be) during a period beginning at the opening of business 15 days before the day of the mailing of a notice of redemption of any such Securities selected for redemption under Section 1103 and ending at the close of business on the day of such mailing, or (B) to register the transfer of or exchange any Security so selected for redemption, in whole or in part, except the unredeemed portion of any Security being redeemed in part.

The provisions of clauses (1), (2), (3) and (4) of this paragraph shall apply only to Global Securities:

(1) Each Global Security authenticated under this Indenture shall be registered in the name of the Depositary designated for such Global Security or a nominee thereof and delivered to such Depositary or a nominee thereof or custodian therefor, and each such Global Security shall constitute a single Security for all purposes of this Indenture.

(2) Notwithstanding any other provision in this Indenture, and subject to such applicable provisions, if any, as may be specified as contemplated by Section 301, no Global Security may be exchanged in whole or in part for Securities registered, and no transfer of a Global Security in whole or in part may be registered, in the name of any Person other than the Depositary for such Global Security or a nominee thereof unless (A) such Depositary has notified the Company that it is unwilling or unable or no longer permitted under applicable law to continue as Depositary for such Global Security, (B) there shall have occurred and be continuing an Event of Default with respect to such Global Security, (C) the Company so directs the Trustee by a Company Order or (D) there shall exist

such circumstances, if any, in addition to or in lieu of the foregoing as have been specified for this purpose as contemplated by Section 301.

(3) Subject to clause (2) above, and subject to such applicable provisions, if any, as may be specified as contemplated by Section 301, any exchange of a Global Security for other Securities may be made in whole or in part, and all Securities issued in exchange for a Global Security or any portion thereof shall be registered in such names as the Depositary for such Global Security shall direct.

(4) Every Security authenticated and delivered upon registration of transfer of, or in exchange for or in lieu of, a Global Security or any portion thereof, whether pursuant to this Section 305, Section 304, Section 306, Section 906, Section 1107 or Section 1405 or otherwise, shall be authenticated and delivered in the form of, and shall be, a Global Security, unless such Security is registered in the name of a Person other than the Depositary for such Global Security or a nominee thereof.

The Trustee shall have no obligation or duty to monitor, determine or inquire as to compliance with any restrictions on transfer imposed under this Indenture or under applicable law with respect to any transfer of any interest in any Security (including any transfers between or among Depositary participants or beneficial owners of interests in any Global Security) other than to require delivery of such certificates and other documentation or evidence as are expressly required by, and to do so if and when expressly required by the terms of, this Indenture, and to examine the same to determine substantial compliance as to form with the express requirements hereof.

Neither the Trustee nor any agent of the Trustee shall have any responsibility for any actions taken or not taken by the Depositary.

Section 306. <u>Mutilated, Destroyed, Lost and Stolen Securities.</u>

If any mutilated Security is surrendered to the Trustee, the Company shall execute and the Trustee shall authenticate and deliver in exchange therefor a new Security of the same series and of like tenor and principal amount and bearing a number not contemporaneously outstanding and shall cancel and dispose of such mutilated security in accordance with its customary procedures.

If there shall be delivered to the Company and the Trustee (1) evidence to their satisfaction of the destruction, loss or theft of any Security and (2) such security or indemnity as may be required by them to save each of them and any agent of either of them harmless, then, in the absence of notice to the Company or the Trustee that such Security has been acquired by a *bona fide* purchaser, the Company shall execute and the Trustee shall authenticate and deliver, in lieu of any such destroyed, lost or stolen Security, a new Security of the same series and of like tenor and principal amount and bearing a number not contemporaneously outstanding.

In case any such mutilated, destroyed, lost or stolen Security has become or is about to become due and payable, the Company in its discretion may, instead of issuing a new Security, pay such Security.

Upon the issuance of any new Security under this Section 306, the Company may require the payment of a sum sufficient to cover any tax or other governmental charge that may be imposed in relation thereto and any other expenses (including the fees and expenses of counsel to the Company and the fees and expenses of the Trustee and its counsel) connected therewith.

Every new Security of any series issued pursuant to this Section 306 in lieu of any mutilated, destroyed, lost or stolen Security shall constitute an original additional contractual obligation of the Company, whether or not the mutilated, destroyed, lost or stolen Security shall be at any time enforceable by anyone, and shall be entitled to all the benefits of this Indenture equally and proportionately with any and all other Securities of such series duly issued hereunder.

The provisions of this Section 306 are exclusive and shall preclude (to the extent lawful) all other rights and remedies with respect to the replacement or payment of mutilated, destroyed, lost or stolen Securities.

Section 307. <u>Payment of Interest; Interest Rights Preserved.</u>

Except as otherwise provided as contemplated by Section 301 with respect to any series of Securities, interest on any Security which is payable, and is punctually paid or duly provided for, on any Interest Payment Date shall be paid to the Person in whose name that Security (or one or more Predecessor Securities) is registered at the close of business on the Regular Record Date for such interest.

Any interest on any Security of any series which is payable, but is not punctually paid or duly provided for, on any Interest Payment Date (herein called "<u>Defaulted Interest</u>") shall forthwith cease to be payable to the Holder on the relevant Regular Record Date by virtue of having been such Holder, and such Defaulted Interest may be paid by the Company, at its election in each case, as provided in clause (1) or (2) below:

(1) The Company may elect to make payment of any Defaulted Interest payable on Securities of a series to the Persons in whose names the Securities of such series (or their respective Predecessor Securities) are registered at the close of business on a Special Record Date for the payment of such Defaulted Interest, which shall be fixed in the following manner. The Company shall notify the Trustee in writing of the amount of Defaulted Interest proposed to be paid on each Security of such series and the date of the proposed payment, and at the same time the Company shall deposit with the Trustee an amount of money equal to the aggregate amount proposed to be paid in respect of such Defaulted Interest or shall make arrangements satisfactory to the Trustee for such deposit prior to the date of the proposed payment, such money when deposited to be held in trust for the benefit of the Persons entitled to such Defaulted Interest as in this clause provided. Thereupon the Trustee in consultation with the Company shall fix a Special Record Date for the payment of such Defaulted Interest which shall be not more than 15 days and not less than 10 days prior to the date of the proposed payment and not less than 10 days after the receipt by the Trustee of the notice of the proposed payment. The Trustee shall promptly notify the Company of such Special Record Date and, in the name and at the expense of the Company, shall cause notice of the proposed payment of such Defaulted Interest and the Special Record Date therefor to be given to each Holder of Securities of such series in the manner set forth in Section 106, not less than 10 days prior to such Special Record Date. Notice of the proposed payment of such Defaulted Interest and the Special Record Date therefor having been so mailed, such Defaulted Interest shall be paid to the Persons in whose names the Securities of such series (or their respective Predecessor

Securities) are registered at the close of business on such Special Record Date and shall no longer be payable pursuant to the following clause (2).

(2) The Company may make payment of any Defaulted Interest on the Securities of any series in any other lawful manner not inconsistent with the requirements of any securities exchange on which such Securities may be listed, and upon such notice as may be required by such exchange, if, after notice given by the Company to the Trustee of the proposed payment pursuant to this clause, such manner of payment shall be deemed practicable by the Trustee.

Subject to the foregoing provisions of this Section 307, each Security delivered under this Indenture upon registration of transfer of or in exchange for or in lieu of any other Security shall carry the rights to interest accrued and unpaid, and to accrue, which were carried by such other Security.

In the case of any Security which is converted after any Regular Record Date and on or prior to the next succeeding Interest Payment Date (other than any Security whose Maturity is prior to such Interest Payment Date), interest whose Stated Maturity is on such Interest Payment Date shall be payable on such Interest Payment Date notwithstanding such conversion, and such interest (whether or not punctually paid or made available for payment) shall be paid to the Person in whose name that Security (or one or more Predecessor Securities) is registered at the close of business on such Regular Record Date. Except as otherwise expressly provided in the immediately preceding sentence, in the case of any Security which is converted, interest whose Stated Maturity is after the date of conversion of such Security shall not be payable. Notwithstanding the foregoing, the terms of any Security that may be converted may provide that the provisions of this paragraph do not apply, or apply with such additions, changes or omissions as may be provided thereby, to such Security.

Section 308. Persons Deemed Owners.

Prior to due presentment of a Security for registration of transfer, the Company, the Trustee and any agent of the Company or the Trustee may treat the Person in whose name such Security is registered as the owner of such Security for the purpose of receiving payment of principal of and premium, if any, and, subject to Section 307, any interest on such Security and for all other purposes whatsoever, whether or not such Security be overdue, and neither the Company, the Trustee nor any agent of the Company or the Trustee shall be affected by notice to the contrary.

Section 309. Cancellation.

All Securities surrendered for payment, redemption, registration of transfer or exchange or conversion or for credit against any sinking fund payment shall, if surrendered to any Person other than the Trustee, be delivered to the Trustee and shall be promptly cancelled by it. The Company may at any time deliver to the Trustee for cancellation any Securities previously authenticated and delivered hereunder which the Company may have acquired in any manner whatsoever, and may deliver to the Trustee (or to any other Person for delivery to the Trustee) for cancellation any Securities previously authenticated hereunder which the Company has not issued and sold, and all Securities so delivered shall be promptly cancelled by the Trustee. No

Securities shall be authenticated in lieu of or in exchange for any Securities cancelled as provided in this Section 309, except as expressly permitted by this Indenture. All cancelled Securities held by the Trustee shall be disposed of in accordance with its customary procedures. The Trustee shall provide the Company a list of all Securities that have been cancelled from time to time as requested by the Company.

Section 310. Computation of Interest.

Except as otherwise specified as contemplated by Section 301 for Securities of any series, interest on the Securities of each series shall be computed on the basis of a 360-day year of twelve 30-day months.

Section 311. CUSIP Numbers.

The Company in issuing any series of the Securities may use "CUSIP" or "ISIN" numbers and/or other similar numbers, if then generally in use, and thereafter with respect to such series, the Trustee may use such numbers in any notice of redemption with respect to such series; provided that any such notice may state that no representation is made as to the correctness of such numbers either as printed on the Securities of such series or as contained in any notice of a redemption and that reliance may be placed only on the other identification numbers printed on the Securities of such series, and any such redemption shall not be affected by any defect in or omission of such numbers.

Section 312. Original Issue Discount.

If any of the Securities is an Original Issue Discount Security, the Company shall file with the Trustee promptly at the end of each calendar year (1) a written notice specifying the amount of original issue discount (including daily rates and accrual periods) accrued on such Outstanding Original Issue Discount Securities as of the end of such year and (2) such other specific information relating to such original issue discount as may then be relevant under the Internal Revenue Code.

ARTICLE IV
SATISFACTION AND DISCHARGE

Section 401. Satisfaction and Discharge of Indenture.

This Indenture shall, upon Company Request, cease to be of further effect with respect to any series of Securities specified in such Company Request (except as to any surviving rights of registration of transfer or exchange of Securities of such series herein expressly provided for), and the Trustee, at the expense of the Company, shall execute proper instruments acknowledging satisfaction and discharge of this Indenture as to such series, when:

(1) either

    (A)   all Securities of such series theretofore authenticated and delivered (other than (i) Securities which have been mutilated, destroyed, lost or stolen and which have been replaced or paid as provided in Section 306 and (ii) Securities for whose payment money has theretofore been deposited in trust or segregated and held in trust by the Company and thereafter repaid to the Company or discharged from such trust, as provided in Section 1003) have been delivered to the Trustee for cancellation; or

(B) all such Securities of such series not theretofore delivered to the Trustee for cancellation

    (i)   have become due and payable, or

    (ii)   will become due and payable at their Stated Maturity within one year of the date of deposit, or

    (iii) are to be called for redemption within one year under arrangements satisfactory to the Trustee for the giving of notice of redemption by the Trustee in the name, and at the expense, of the Company,

and the Company, in the case of (i), (ii) or (iii) above, has deposited or caused to be deposited with the Trustee as trust funds in trust for such purpose money in an amount sufficient to pay and discharge the entire indebtedness on such Securities not theretofore delivered to the Trustee for cancellation, for principal and premium, if any, and interest to the date of such deposit (in the case of Securities which have become due and payable) or to the Stated Maturity or Redemption Date, as the case may be;

(2) the Company has paid or caused to be paid all other sums payable hereunder by the Company; and

(3) the Company has delivered to the Trustee an Officer's Certificate and an Opinion of Counsel, each stating that all conditions precedent herein provided for relating to the satisfaction and discharge of this Indenture as to such series have been complied with.

Notwithstanding the satisfaction and discharge of this Indenture, the obligations of the Company to the Trustee under Section 607 and, if money shall have been deposited with the Trustee pursuant to subclause (B) of clause (1) of this Section 401, the obligations of the Trustee under Section 402 and the last paragraph of Section 1003 shall survive such satisfaction and discharge.

Section 402. <u>Application of Trust Money.</u>

Subject to the provisions of the last paragraph of Section 1003, all money deposited with the Trustee pursuant to Section 401 shall be held in trust and applied by it, in accordance with the provisions of the applicable series of Securities and this Indenture, to the payment, either directly or through any Paying Agent (including the Company acting as its own Paying Agent) as the Trustee may determine, to the Persons entitled thereto, of the principal and premium, if any, and interest for whose payment such money has been deposited with the Trustee. All money deposited with the Trustee pursuant to Section 401 (and held by it or any Paying Agent) for the payment of Securities subsequently converted into other property shall be returned to the Company upon Company Request. The Company may direct by a Company Order the investment of any money deposited with the Trustee pursuant to Section 401, without distinction between principal and income, in (1) United States Treasury securities with a maturity of one year or less or (2) a money market fund that invests solely in short-term United States Treasury securities (including money market funds for which the Trustee or an affiliate of the Trustee serves as investment advisor, administrator, shareholder, servicing agent and/or custodian or sub-custodian, notwithstanding that (a) the Trustee charges and collects fees and expenses from such funds for services rendered and (b) the Trustee charges and collects fees and expenses for services rendered pursuant to this Indenture at any time) and from time to time the Company may direct the reinvestment of all or a portion of such money in other securities or funds meeting the criteria specified in clause (1) or (2) of this Section 402.

ARTICLE V
REMEDIES

Section 501. <u>Events of Default.</u>

Except as may be otherwise provided pursuant to Section 301 for Securities of any series, an "<u>Event of Default</u>" means, whenever used herein or in a Security issued hereunder with respect to Securities of any series, any one of the following events (whatever the reason for such Event of Default and whether it shall be voluntary or involuntary or be effected by operation of law or pursuant to any judgment, decree or order of any court or any order, rule or regulation of any administrative or governmental body):

(1) the Company defaults in the payment of any installment of interest on any Security of such series for 30 days after becoming due;

(2) the Company defaults in the payment of the principal of or premium, if any, on any Security of such series when the same becomes due and payable at its Stated Maturity, upon optional redemption, upon declaration or otherwise;

(3) the Company defaults in the performance of, or breaches any of its covenants and agreements in respect of any Security of such series contained in this Indenture or in the Securities of such series (other than a covenant or agreement, a default in the performance of which or a breach of which is elsewhere in this Section specifically dealt with or that has expressly been included in this Indenture solely for the benefit of a series of Securities other than that series), and such default or breach continues for a period of 90 days after the notice specified below;

(4) the Company, pursuant to or within the meaning of the Bankruptcy Law (as defined below):

(A) commences a voluntary case or proceeding;

(B) consents to the entry of an order for relief against it in an involuntary case or proceeding;

(C) consents to the appointment of a Custodian (as defined below) of it or for all or substantially all of its property;

(D) makes a general assignment for the benefit of its creditors;

(E) files a petition in bankruptcy or answer or consent seeking reorganization or relief;

(F) consents to the filing of such petition or the appointment of or taking possession by a Custodian; or

(G) takes any comparable action under any foreign laws relating to insolvency;

(5) a court of competent jurisdiction enters an order or decree under any Bankruptcy Law that:

(A) is for relief against the Company in an involuntary case, or adjudicates the Company insolvent or bankrupt;

(B) appoints a Custodian of the Company or for all or substantially all of the property of the Company; or

(C) orders the winding-up or liquidation of the Company (or any similar relief is granted under any foreign laws)

and the order or decree remains unstayed and in effect for 90 days; or

(6) any other Event of Default provided with respect to Securities of such series occurs.

The term "Bankruptcy Law" means Title 11, United States Code, or any similar federal or state or foreign law for the relief of debtors. The term "Custodian" means any custodian, receiver, trustee, assignee, liquidator or other similar official under any Bankruptcy Law.

A Default with respect to Securities of any series under clause (3) of this Section 501 shall not be an Event of Default until the Trustee (by written notice to the Company) or the Holders of at least 25% in aggregate principal amount of the outstanding Securities of such series (by written notice to the Company and the Trustee) gives notice of the Default and the Company does not cure such Default within the time specified in clause (3) after receipt of such notice. Such notice must specify the Default, demand that it be remedied and state that such notice is a "Notice of Default."

Section 502. Acceleration of Maturity; Rescission and Annulment.

If an Event of Default with respect to Securities of any series at the time Outstanding (other than an Event of Default specified in Section 501(4) or (5) with respect to the Company) occurs and is continuing, then in every such case the Trustee or the Holders of not less than 25% in aggregate principal amount of the Outstanding Securities of such series may declare the principal amount of all the Securities of such series (or, if any Securities of that series are Original Issue Discount Securities, such portion of the principal amount of such Securities as may be specified by the terms thereof), together with any accrued and unpaid interest thereon, to be due and payable immediately, by a notice in writing to the Company (and to the Trustee if given by Holders), and upon any such declaration, such principal amount (or specified amount), together with any accrued and unpaid interest thereon, shall become immediately due and payable. If an Event of Default specified in Section 501(4) or (5) with respect to the Securities of any series at the time Outstanding occurs, the principal amount of all the Securities of such series (or, in the case of any Security of such series which specifies an amount to be due and payable thereon upon acceleration of the Maturity thereof, such amount as may be specified by the terms thereof), together with any accrued and unpaid interest thereon, shall automatically, and without any declaration or other action on the part of the Trustee or any Holder, become immediately due and payable. Upon payment of such amount, all obligations of the Company in respect of the payment of principal and interest of the Securities of such series shall terminate.

Except as may otherwise be provided pursuant to Section 301 for all or any specific Securities of any series, at any time after such a declaration of acceleration with respect to the Securities of any series has been made and before a judgment or decree for payment of the money due has been obtained by the Trustee as hereinafter in this Article V provided, the Holders of a majority in aggregate principal amount of the Outstanding Securities of such series, by written notice to the Company and the Trustee, may rescind and annul such declaration and its consequences if:

(1) the Company has paid or deposited with the Trustee a sum sufficient to pay:
    (A)   all overdue interest on all Securities of such series,
    (B)   the principal of and premium, if any, on any Securities of such series which have become due otherwise than by such declaration of acceleration and any interest thereon at the rate or rates prescribed therefor in the Securities of such series,
    (C)   to the extent that payment of such interest is lawful, interest upon overdue interest at the rate or rates prescribed therefor in such Securities, and
    (D)   all sums paid or advanced by the Trustee hereunder and the reasonable compensation, expenses, disbursements and advances of the Trustee, its agents and counsel; and

(2) all Events of Default with respect to Securities of such series, other than the non-payment of the principal of Securities of such series which have become due solely by such declaration of acceleration, have been cured or waived as provided in Section 512.

No such rescission shall affect any subsequent default or impair any right consequent thereon.

Section 503. Collection of Indebtedness and Suits for Enforcement by Trustee.

The Company covenants that if (1) default is made in the payment of any interest on any Security when such interest becomes due and payable and such default continues for a period of 30 days or (2) default is made in the payment of the principal of or premium, if any, on any Security at the Maturity thereof, the Company will, upon demand of the Trustee, pay to it, for the benefit of the Holders of such Securities, the whole amount then due and payable on such Securities for principal and premium, if any, and interest and, to the extent that payment of such interest shall be legally enforceable, interest on any overdue principal and premium and on any overdue interest, at the rate or rates prescribed therefor in such Securities, and, in addition thereto, such further amount as shall be sufficient to cover the costs and expenses of collection, including the reasonable compensation, expenses, disbursements and advances of the Trustee, its agents and counsel.

If an Event of Default with respect to Securities of any series occurs and is continuing, the Trustee may in its discretion proceed to protect and enforce its rights and the rights of the Holders of Securities of such series by such appropriate judicial proceedings as the Trustee shall deem necessary to protect and enforce any such rights, whether for the specific enforcement of any covenant or agreement in this

Indenture or in aid of the exercise of any power granted herein, or to enforce any other proper remedy.

Section 504. Trustee May File Proofs of Claim.

In case of any judicial proceeding relative to the Company (or any other obligor upon the Securities), its property or its creditors, the Trustee shall be entitled and empowered, by intervention in such proceeding or otherwise, to take any and all actions authorized under the Trust Indenture Act in order to have claims of the Holders and the Trustee allowed in any such proceeding. In particular, the Trustee shall be authorized to collect and receive any moneys or other property payable or deliverable on any such claims and to distribute the same; and any custodian, receiver, assignee, trustee, liquidator, sequestrator or other similar official in any such judicial proceeding is hereby authorized by each Holder to make such payments to the Trustee and, in the event that the Trustee shall consent to the making of such payments directly to the Holders, to pay to the Trustee any amount due it and any predecessor Trustee under Section 607.

No provision of this Indenture shall be deemed to authorize the Trustee to authorize or consent to or accept or adopt on behalf of any Holder any plan of reorganization, arrangement, adjustment or composition affecting the Securities or the rights of any Holder thereof or to authorize the Trustee to vote in respect of the claim of any Holder in any such proceeding; provided, however, that the Trustee may, on behalf of the Holders, vote for the election of a trustee in bankruptcy or similar official and be a member of a creditors' or other similar committee.

Section 505. Trustee May Enforce Claims Without Possession of Securities.

All rights of action and claims under this Indenture or the Securities may be prosecuted and enforced by the Trustee without the possession of any of the Securities or the production thereof in any proceeding relating thereto, and any such proceeding instituted by the Trustee shall be brought in its own name as trustee of an express trust, and any recovery of judgment shall, after provision for the payment of the reasonable compensation, expenses, disbursements and advances of the Trustee, any predecessor Trustee under Section 607, its agents and counsel, be for the ratable benefit of the Holders of the Securities in respect of which such judgment has been recovered.

Section 506. Application of Money Collected.

Any money collected by the Trustee pursuant to this Article V shall be applied in the following order, at the date or dates fixed by the Trustee and, in case of the distribution of such money on account of principal or premium, if any, or interest, upon presentation of the Securities and the notation thereon of the payment if only partially paid and upon surrender thereof if fully paid:

FIRST: To the payment of all amounts due the Trustee under Section 607;
SECOND: To the payment of the amounts then due and unpaid for principal of and premium, if any, and interest on the Securities in respect of which or for the benefit

of which such money has been collected, ratably, without preference or priority of any kind (other than contractual subordination agreements pursuant to the Indenture), according to the amounts due and payable on such Securities for principal and premium, if any, and interest, respectively; and

THIRD: To the payment of the remainder, if any, to the Company.

Section 507. <u>Limitation on Suits.</u>

No Holder of any Security of any series shall have any right to institute any proceeding, judicial or otherwise, with respect to this Indenture, or for the appointment of a receiver, assignee, trustee, liquidator or sequestrator (or similar official) or for any other remedy hereunder, unless:

(1) Such Holder has previously given written notice to the Trustee of a continuing Event of Default with respect to the Securities of such series;

(2) the Holders of not less than 25% in aggregate principal amount of the Outstanding Securities of such series shall have made written request to the Trustee to institute proceedings in respect of such Event of Default in its own name as Trustee hereunder;

(3) such Holder or Holders have offered to the Trustee indemnity reasonably satisfactory to it against the costs, expenses and liabilities to be incurred in compliance with such request;

(4) the Trustee has failed to institute any such proceeding for 60 days after its receipt of such notice, request and offer of indemnity; and

(5) no direction inconsistent with such written request has been given to the Trustee during such 60-day period by the Holders of a majority in aggregate principal amount of the Outstanding Securities of such series;

it being understood and intended that no one or more of such Holders shall have any right in any manner whatever by virtue of, or by availing of, any provision of this Indenture to affect, disturb or prejudice the rights of any other of such Holders, or to obtain or to seek to obtain priority or preference over any other of such Holders (it being understood that the Trustee does not have an affirmative duty to ascertain whether or not such actions are unduly prejudicial to such Holders) or to enforce any right under this Indenture, except in the manner herein provided and for the equal and ratable benefit of all of such Holders.

Section 508. <u>Unconditional Right of Holders to Receive Principal, Premium and Interest and to Convert Securities.</u>

Notwithstanding any other provision in this Indenture, the Holder of any Security shall have the right, which is absolute and unconditional, to receive payment of the principal of and premium, if any, and, subject to Section 307, interest on such Security on the respective Stated Maturities expressed in such Security (or, in the case of redemption or repayment, on the Redemption Date or date for repayment, as the case may be, and, if the terms of such Security so provide, to convert such Security in accordance with its terms) and to institute suit for the enforcement of any such payment and, if applicable, any such right to convert, and such rights shall not be impaired without the consent of such Holder.

Section 509. <u>Rights and Remedies Cumulative.</u>

Except as otherwise provided with respect to the replacement or payment of mutilated, destroyed, lost or stolen Securities in the last paragraph of Section 306, no right or remedy herein conferred upon or reserved to the Trustee or to the Holders is intended to be exclusive of any other right or remedy, and every right and remedy shall, to the extent permitted by law, be cumulative and in addition to every other right and remedy given hereunder or now or hereafter existing at law or in equity or otherwise. The assertion or employment of any right or remedy hereunder, or otherwise, shall not prevent the concurrent assertion or employment of any other appropriate right or remedy.

Section 510. <u>Delay or Omission Not Waiver.</u>

No delay or omission of the Trustee or of any Holder of any Securities to exercise any right or remedy accruing upon any Event of Default shall impair any such right or remedy or constitute a waiver of any such Event of Default or an acquiescence therein. Every right and remedy given by this Article V or by law to the Trustee or to the Holders may be exercised from time to time, and as often as may be deemed expedient, by the Trustee or by the Holders, as the case may be.

Section 511. <u>Control by Holders.</u>

The Holders of not less than a majority in aggregate principal amount of the Outstanding Securities of any series shall have the right to direct the time, method and place of conducting any proceeding for any remedy available to the Trustee, or exercising any trust or power conferred on the Trustee, with respect to the Securities of such series; <u>provided</u> that

(1) such direction shall not be in conflict with any rule of law or with this Indenture, and
(2) the Trustee may take any other action deemed proper by the Trustee which is not inconsistent with such direction.

Section 512. <u>Waiver of Past Defaults.</u>

The Holders of not less than a majority in aggregate principal amount of the Outstanding Securities of any series may on behalf of the Holders of all the Securities of such series waive any past default hereunder with respect to such series and its consequences, except a default

(1) in the payment of the principal of or premium, if any, or interest on any Security of such series, or
(2) in respect of a covenant or provision hereof which under Article IX cannot be modified or amended without the consent of the Holder of each Outstanding Security of such series affected.

Upon any such waiver, such default shall cease to exist, and any Event of Default arising therefrom shall be deemed to have been cured, for every purpose of this Indenture, but no such waiver shall extend to any subsequent or other default or impair any right consequent thereon.

Section 513. <u>Undertaking for Costs.</u>

In any suit for the enforcement of any right or remedy under this Indenture, or in any suit against the Trustee for any action taken, suffered or omitted by it as Trustee, a court may require any party litigant in such suit to file an undertaking to pay the costs of such suit, and may assess reasonable costs against any such party litigant, in the manner and to the extent provided in the Trust Indenture Act; <u>provided</u> that neither this Section 513 nor the Trust Indenture Act shall be deemed to authorize any court to require such an undertaking or to make such an assessment in any suit instituted by the Company or the Trustee, a suit by a Holder under Section 508, or a suit by Holders of more than 10% in aggregate principal amount of the Outstanding Securities.

Section 514. <u>Waiver of Usury, Stay or Extension Laws.</u>

The Company covenants (to the extent that it may lawfully do so) that it will not at any time insist upon, or plead, or in any manner whatsoever claim or take the benefit or advantage of, any usury, stay or extension law wherever enacted, now or at any time hereafter in force, which may affect the covenants or the performance of this Indenture; and the Company (to the extent that it may lawfully do so) hereby expressly waives all benefit or advantage of any such law and covenants that it will not hinder, delay or impede the execution of any power herein granted to the Trustee, but will suffer and permit the execution of every such power as though no such law had been enacted.

Section 515. <u>Restoration of Rights and Remedies.</u>

If the Trustee or any Holder has instituted any proceeding to enforce any right or remedy under this Indenture and such proceeding has been discontinued or abandoned for any reason, or has been determined adversely to the Trustee or to such Holder, then and in every such case, subject to any determination in such proceeding, the Company, the Trustee and the Holders shall be restored severally and respectively to their former positions hereunder and thereafter all rights and remedies of the Trustee and the Holders shall continue as though no such proceeding had been instituted.

ARTICLE VI
THE TRUSTEE

Section 601. <u>Certain Duties and Responsibilities of Trustee.</u>

(1) Except during the continuance of an Event of Default with respect to any series of Securities,

    (A)   the Trustee undertakes to perform such duties and only such duties as are specifically set forth in this Indenture with respect to the Securities of such series, and no implied covenants or obligations shall be read into this Indenture against the Trustee with respect to such series; and

    (B)   in the absence of bad faith on its part, the Trustee may rely with respect to the Securities of such series, as to the truth of the statements and the correctness of the opinions expressed therein, upon certificates or opinions furnished to the Trustee and conforming to the requirements of this Indenture; but in the case of any such certificates or opinions which by any provision hereof are specifically required to be furnished to the Trustee, the Trustee shall be under a duty to examine the same to determine whether or not they conform to the requirements of this Indenture (but need not confirm or investigate the accuracy of mathematical calculations or other facts stated therein).

(2) In case an Event of Default with respect to any series of Securities has occurred and is continuing, the Trustee shall exercise such of the rights and powers vested in it by this Indenture with respect to the Securities of such series, and use the same degree of care and skill in their exercise, as a prudent person would exercise or use under the circumstances in the conduct of his or her own affairs.

(3) No provision of this Indenture shall be construed to relieve the Trustee from liability for its own negligent action, its own negligent failure to act, or its own willful misconduct, except that:

    (A)   this Section 601(3) shall not be construed to limit the effect of Section 601(1);

    (B)   the Trustee shall not be liable for any error of judgment made in good faith by a Responsible Officer, unless it shall be proved that the Trustee was negligent in ascertaining the pertinent facts;

    (C)   the Trustee shall not be liable with respect to any action taken or omitted to be taken by it in good faith in accordance with the direction of the Holders of a majority in aggregate principal amount of the Outstanding Securities of any series, determined as provided in Section 101, Section 104 and Section 511, relating to the time, method and place of conducting any proceeding for any remedy available to the Trustee, or exercising any trust or power conferred upon the Trustee, under this Indenture with respect to the Securities of such series; and

    (D)   no provision of this Indenture shall require the Trustee to expend or risk its own funds or otherwise incur any financial liability in the performance of any of its duties hereunder, or in the exercise of any of its rights or powers, if it shall have reasonable grounds for believing that repayment of such funds or adequate indemnity against such risk or liability is not reasonably assured to it.

(4) Whether or not therein expressly so provided, every provision of this Indenture relating to the conduct or affecting the liability of or affording protection to the Trustee shall be subject to the provisions of this Section 601.

Section 602. <u>Notice of Defaults.</u>

If a Default or an Event of Default occurs with respect to Securities of any series and is continuing and if it is actually known to the Trustee, the Trustee shall mail to each Holder of Securities of such series notice of the Default within 90 days after it is known to a Responsible Officer or written notice of it is received by a Responsible Officer of the Trustee. Except in the case of a Default in payment of principal of or interest on any Security, the Trustee may withhold the notice if and so long as a committee of its Responsible Officers in good faith determines that withholding the notice is not opposed to the interests of Holders of Securities of such series.

Section 603. <u>Certain Rights of Trustee.</u>

Subject to the provisions of Section 601:

(1)   the Trustee may conclusively rely and shall be fully protected in acting or refraining from acting upon any resolution, certificate, statement, instrument, opinion, report, notice, request, direction, consent, order, bond, debenture, note, other evidence of indebtedness or other paper or document believed by it to be genuine and to have been signed or presented by the proper party or parties;

(2)   if so requested by the Trustee, any request or direction of the Company mentioned herein shall be sufficiently evidenced by a Company Request or Company Order, and any resolution of the Board of Directors shall be sufficiently evidenced by a Board Resolution;

(3)   whenever in the administration of this Indenture the Trustee shall deem it desirable that a matter be proved or established prior to taking, suffering or omitting any action hereunder, the Trustee (unless other evidence be herein specifically prescribed) may, in the absence of bad faith on its part, conclusively rely upon an Officer's Certificate;

(4)   the Trustee may consult with counsel of its selection and the advice of such counsel or any Opinion of Counsel shall be full and complete authorization and protection in respect of any action taken, suffered or omitted by it hereunder in good faith and in reliance thereon;

(5)   the Trustee shall be under no obligation to exercise any of the rights or powers vested in it by this Indenture at the request or direction of any of the Holders pursuant to this Indenture, unless such Holders shall have offered to the Trustee security or indemnity reasonably satisfactory to it against the costs, expenses and liabilities which might be incurred by it in compliance with such request or direction;

(6)   the Trustee shall not be bound to make any investigation into the facts or matters stated in any resolution, certificate, statement, instrument, opinion, report, notice, request, direction, consent, order, bond, debenture, note, other evidence of indebtedness or other paper or document, but the Trustee, in its discretion, may make such further inquiry or investigation into such facts or matters as it may see fit, and, if the Trustee shall determine to make such further inquiry or investigation, it shall be entitled to examine the books, records and premises of the Company, personally or by agent or

attorney at the sole cost of the Company and shall incur no liability or additional liability of any kind by reason of such inquiry or investigation;

(7) the Trustee may execute any of the trusts or powers hereunder or perform any duties hereunder either directly or by or through agents or attorneys and the Trustee shall not be responsible for any misconduct or negligence on the part of any agent or attorney appointed with due care by it hereunder;

(8) the rights, privileges, protections, immunities and benefits given to the Trustee, including, without limitation, its right to be indemnified, are extended to, and shall be enforceable by, the Trustee in each of its capacities hereunder and to its agents;

(9) the Trustee shall not be liable for any action taken, suffered, or omitted to be taken by it in good faith and reasonably believed by it to be authorized or within the discretion or rights or powers conferred upon it by this Indenture;

(10) in no event shall the Trustee be responsible or liable for special, indirect, or consequential loss or damage of any kind whatsoever (including, but not limited to, loss of profit) irrespective of whether the Trustee has been advised of the likelihood of such loss or damage and regardless of the form of action;

(11) in no event shall the Trustee be responsible or liable for any failure or delay in the performance of its obligations hereunder arising out of or caused by, directly or indirectly, forces beyond its control, including, without limitation, strikes, work stoppages, accidents, acts of war or terrorism, civil or military disturbances, nuclear or natural catastrophes or acts of God, and interruptions, loss or malfunctions of utilities, communications or computer (software and hardware) services (it being understood that the Trustee shall use reasonable efforts which are consistent with accepted practices in the banking industry to avoid and mitigate the effects of such occurrences and to resume performance as soon as practicable under the circumstances);

(12) the Trustee shall not be deemed to have notice of any Default or Event of Default unless a Responsible Officer of the Trustee shall have actual knowledge thereof or unless written notice of any event which is in fact such a default shall have been received by the Trustee at the Corporate Trust Office of the Trustee, and such notice references the Securities and this Indenture; and

(13) The Trustee may request that the Company deliver a certificate setting forth the names of individuals and/or titles of officers authorized at such time to take specified actions pursuant to this Indenture.

Section 604. Not Responsible for Recitals or Issuance of Securities.

The recitals contained herein and in the Securities, except the Trustee's certificates of authentication, shall be taken as the statements of the Company, and the Trustee assumes no responsibility for their correctness. The Trustee makes no representations as to the validity or sufficiency of this Indenture or of the Securities. The Trustee shall not be accountable for the use or application by the Company of Securities or the proceeds thereof.

Section 605. <u>May Hold Securities.</u>

The Trustee, any Paying Agent, any Security Registrar or any other agent of the Company, in its individual or any other capacity, may become the owner or pledgee of Securities and, subject to Section 608 and Section 613, may otherwise deal with the Company with the same rights it would have if it were not Trustee, Paying Agent, Security Registrar or such other agent.

Section 606. <u>Money Held in Trust.</u>

Money held by the Trustee in trust hereunder shall, until used or applied as herein provided, be held in trust for the purposes for which they were received, but need not be segregated from other funds except to the extent required by law. The Trustee shall be under no liability for interest on any money received by it hereunder except as otherwise agreed with the Company.

Section 607. <u>Compensation and Reimbursement.</u>

The Company agrees

(1) to pay to the Trustee from time to time such reasonable compensation as shall be agreed to in writing between the Company and the Trustee for all services rendered by it hereunder (which compensation shall not be limited by any provision of law in regard to the compensation of a trustee of an express trust);

(2) except as otherwise expressly provided herein, to reimburse the Trustee upon its request for all reasonable expenses, disbursements and advances incurred or made by the Trustee in accordance with any provision of this Indenture (including the reasonable compensation and the reasonable expenses and disbursements of its agents and counsel), except any such expense, disbursement or advance as shall have been caused by its negligence or willful misconduct, and the Trustee shall provide the Company reasonable notice of any expenditure not in the ordinary course of business; and

(3) to indemnify the Trustee for, and to hold it harmless against, any loss, liability or expense incurred without negligence or willful misconduct on its part, arising out of or in connection with the acceptance or administration of the trust or trusts hereunder, including the reasonable costs and expenses of defending itself against any claim or liability in connection with the exercise or performance of any of its powers or duties hereunder.

The Trustee shall notify the Company promptly of any claim for which it may seek indemnity.

When the Trustee incurs expenses or renders services in connection with an Event of Default specified in Section 501(4) or (5), the expenses (including the reasonable charges and expenses of its counsel) and the compensation for the services are intended to constitute expenses of administration under any applicable federal or state bankruptcy, insolvency or other similar law.

The Trustee shall have a lien prior to the Securities as to all property and funds held by it hereunder for any amount owing it or any predecessor Trustee pursuant to this Section 607, except with respect to funds held in trust for the benefit of the Holders of Securities.

The provisions of this Section 607 shall survive the termination of this Indenture and the resignation or removal of the Trustee.

Section 608. <u>Conflicting Interests.</u>

If the Trustee has or shall acquire a conflicting interest within the meaning of the Trust Indenture Act, the Trustee shall either eliminate such interest or resign, to the extent and in the manner provided by, and subject to the provisions of, the Trust Indenture Act and this Indenture.

To the extent permitted by the Trust Indenture Act, the Trustee shall not be deemed to have a conflicting interest by virtue of being a trustee under this Indenture with respect to Securities of more than one series.

Section 609. <u>Corporate Trustee Required; Eligibility.</u>

There shall at all times be one (and only one) Trustee hereunder with respect to the Securities of each series, which may be Trustee hereunder for Securities of one or more other series. Each Trustee shall be a Person that is eligible pursuant to the Trust Indenture Act to act as such, has a combined capital and surplus of at least $50,000,000 and has its Corporate Trust Office in the Borough of Manhattan, The City of New York or any other major city in the United States that is acceptable to the Company. If any such Person publishes reports of condition at least annually, pursuant to law or to the requirements of its supervising or examining authority, then for the purposes of this Section 609 and to the extent permitted by the Trust Indenture Act, the combined capital and surplus of such Person shall be deemed to be its combined capital and surplus as set forth in its most recent annual report of condition so published. If at any time the Trustee with respect to the Securities of any series shall cease to be eligible in accordance with the provisions of this Section 609, it shall resign immediately in the manner and with the effect hereinafter specified in this Article VI.

Section 610. <u>Resignation and Removal; Appointment of Successor.</u>

No resignation or removal of the Trustee and no appointment of a successor Trustee pursuant to this Article VI shall become effective until the acceptance of appointment by the successor Trustee in accordance with the applicable requirements of Section 611.

The Trustee may resign at any time with respect to the Securities of one or more series by giving written notice thereof to the Company. If the instrument of acceptance by a successor Trustee required by Section 611 shall not have been delivered to the Trustee within 30 days after the giving of such notice of resignation, the resigning Trustee, at the expense of the Company, may petition any court of competent jurisdiction for the appointment of a successor Trustee with respect to the Securities of such series.

The Trustee may be removed at any time with respect to the Securities of any series by Act of the Holders of a majority in aggregate principal amount of the Outstanding

Securities of such series, upon written notice delivered to the Trustee and to the Company. If the instrument of acceptance by a successor Trustee required by Section 611 shall not have been delivered to the Trustee within 30 days after the giving of such notice of removal, the Trustee being removed, at the expense of the Company, may petition any court of competent jurisdiction for the appointment of a successor Trustee with respect to the Securities of such series.

If at any time:

(1) the Trustee shall fail to comply with Section 608 after written request therefor by the Company or by any Holder who has been a *bona fide* Holder of a Security for at least six months, or

(2) the Trustee shall cease to be eligible under Section 609 and shall fail to resign after written request therefor by the Company or by any such Holder, or

(3) the Trustee shall become incapable of acting or shall be adjudged bankrupt or insolvent or a receiver of the Trustee or of its property shall be appointed or any public officer shall take charge or control of the Trustee or of its property or affairs for the purpose of rehabilitation, conservation or liquidation,

then, in any such case, (A) the Company may remove the Trustee with respect to all Securities or (B) subject to Section 513, Holders of 10% in aggregate principal amount of Securities of any series who have been *bona fide* Holders of such Securities for at least six months may, on behalf of themselves and all others similarly situated, petition any court of competent jurisdiction for the removal of the Trustee with respect to all Securities and the appointment of a successor Trustee or Trustees.

If the Trustee shall resign, be removed or become incapable of acting, or if a vacancy shall occur in the office of Trustee for any cause, with respect to the Securities of one or more series, the Company shall promptly appoint a successor Trustee or Trustees with respect to the Securities of that or those series (it being understood that any such successor Trustee may be appointed with respect to the Securities of one or more or all of such series and that at any time there shall be only one Trustee with respect to the Securities of any particular series) and shall comply with the applicable requirements of Section 611. If a successor Trustee with respect to the Securities of any series shall be appointed by Act of the Holders of a majority in aggregate principal amount of the Outstanding Securities of such series delivered to the Company and the retiring Trustee, the successor Trustee so appointed shall, forthwith upon its acceptance of such appointment in accordance with the applicable requirements of Section 611, become the successor Trustee with respect to the Securities of such series and to that extent supersede the successor Trustee appointed by the Company. If no successor Trustee with respect to the Securities of any series shall have been so appointed by the Company or the Holders and accepted appointment in the manner required by Section 611, Holders of 10% in aggregate principal amount of Securities of any series who have been *bona fide* Holders of Securities of such series for at least six months may, on behalf of themselves and all others similarly situated, petition any court of competent jurisdiction for the appointment of a successor Trustee with respect to the Securities of such series.

The Company shall give notice of each resignation and each removal of the Trustee with respect to the Securities of any series and each appointment of a successor Trustee with respect to the Securities of any series to all Holders of Securities of such series in the manner provided in Section 106. Each notice shall include the name of the successor Trustee with respect to the Securities of such series and the address of its Corporate Trust Office.

Section 611. Acceptance of Appointment by Successor.

In case of the appointment hereunder of a successor Trustee with respect to all Securities, every such successor Trustee so appointed shall execute, acknowledge and deliver to the Company and to the retiring Trustee a written instrument accepting such appointment, and thereupon the resignation or removal of the retiring Trustee shall become effective and such successor Trustee, without any further act, deed or conveyance, shall become vested with all the rights, powers, trusts and duties of the retiring Trustee, but, on the request of the Company or the successor Trustee, such retiring Trustee shall, upon payment of its charges, execute and deliver a written instrument transferring to such successor Trustee all the rights, powers and trusts of the retiring Trustee and shall duly assign, transfer and deliver to such successor Trustee all property and money held by such retiring Trustee hereunder.

In case of the appointment hereunder of a successor Trustee with respect to the Securities of one or more (but not all) series, the Company, the retiring Trustee and each successor Trustee with respect to the Securities of one or more series shall execute and deliver an indenture supplemental hereto wherein each successor Trustee shall accept such appointment and which (1) shall contain such provisions as shall be necessary or desirable to transfer and confirm to, and to vest in, each successor Trustee all the rights, powers, trusts and duties of the retiring Trustee with respect to the Securities of that or those series to which the appointment of such successor Trustee relates, (2) if the retiring Trustee is not retiring with respect to all Securities, shall contain such provisions as shall be deemed necessary or desirable to confirm that all the rights, powers, trusts and duties of the retiring Trustee with respect to the Securities of that or those series as to which the retiring Trustee is not retiring shall continue to be vested in the retiring Trustee, and (3) shall add to or change any of the provisions of this Indenture as shall be necessary to provide for or facilitate the administration of the trusts hereunder by more than one Trustee, it being understood that nothing herein or in such supplemental indenture shall constitute such Trustees co-trustees of the same trust and that each such Trustee shall be trustee of a trust or trusts hereunder separate and apart from any trust or trusts hereunder administered by any other such Trustee; and upon the execution and delivery of such supplemental indenture the resignation or removal of the retiring Trustee shall become effective to the extent provided therein and each such successor Trustee, without any further act, deed or conveyance, shall become vested with all the rights, powers, trusts and duties of the retiring Trustee with respect to the Securities of that or those series to which the appointment of such successor Trustee relates; but, on request of the Company or any successor Trustee, such retiring Trustee shall duly assign, transfer and deliver to such successor Trustee all property and money held by such retiring Trustee hereunder with respect to the Securities of that or those series to which the appointment of such successor Trustee relates.

Upon request of any such successor Trustee, the Company shall execute any and all instruments for more fully and certainly vesting in and confirming to such successor Trustee all such rights, powers and trusts referred to in the first or second preceding paragraph, as the case may be.

No successor Trustee shall accept its appointment unless at the time of such acceptance such successor Trustee shall be qualified and eligible under this Article VI.

Section 612. <u>Merger, Conversion, Consolidation or Succession to Business.</u>

Any corporation into which the Trustee may be merged or converted or with which it may be consolidated, or any corporation resulting from any merger, conversion or consolidation to which the Trustee shall be a party, or any corporation succeeding to all or substantially all the corporate trust business of the Trustee, shall be the successor of the Trustee hereunder; <u>provided</u> that such corporation shall be otherwise qualified and eligible under this Article VI, without the execution or filing of any paper or any further act on the part of any of the parties hereto. In case any Securities shall have been authenticated, but not delivered, by the Trustee then in office, any successor by merger, conversion, consolidation or sale to such authenticating Trustee may adopt such authentication and deliver the Securities so authenticated with the same effect as if such successor Trustee had itself authenticated such Securities; and in case at that time any Securities shall not have been authenticated, any successor to the Trustee may authenticate such Securities either in the name of any predecessor hereunder or in the name of the successor to the Trustee; and in all such cases such certificates shall have the full force which it is anywhere in the Securities or in this Indenture provided that the certificate of the Trustee shall have.

Section 613. <u>Preferential Collection of Claims Against Company.</u>

If and when the Trustee shall be or become a creditor of the Company (or any other obligor upon the Securities), the Trustee shall be subject to the provisions of the Trust Indenture Act regarding the collection of claims against the Company (or any such other obligor)

Section 614. <u>Appointment of Authenticating Agent.</u>

The Trustee may appoint an Authenticating Agent or Agents with respect to one or more series of Securities which shall be authorized to act on behalf of the Trustee to authenticate Securities of such series issued upon original issue and upon exchange, registration of transfer or partial redemption thereof or pursuant to Section 306, and Securities so authenticated shall be entitled to the benefits of this Indenture and shall be valid and obligatory for all purposes as if authenticated by the Trustee hereunder. Wherever reference is made in this Indenture to the authentication and delivery of Securities by the Trustee or the Trustee's certificate of authentication, such reference shall be deemed to include authentication and delivery on behalf of the Trustee by an Authenticating Agent and a certificate of authentication executed on behalf of the Trustee by an Authenticating Agent. Each Authenticating Agent shall be acceptable to the Company and shall at all times be a corporation organized and doing business under the laws of the United States of America, any state thereof or the District of Columbia, authorized under such laws to act as Authenticating Agent, having a combined capital and surplus of not less than $50,000,000 and subject to supervision or examination by federal or state authority. If such Authenticating Agent publishes reports of condition at least annually, pursuant to law or to the requirements of said supervising or examining authority, then for the purposes of this Section 614, the combined capital and surplus of such Authenticating Agent shall be deemed to be its combined capital and surplus as set forth in its most recent report of condition so published. If at any time an Authenticating Agent shall cease to be eligible in accordance with the provisions of this Section 614, such Authenticating Agent shall resign immediately in the manner and with the effect specified in this Section 614.

Any corporation into which an Authenticating Agent may be merged or converted or with which it may be consolidated, or any corporation resulting from any merger, conversion or consolidation to which such Authenticating Agent shall be a party, or any corporation succeeding to all or substantially all of the corporate agency or corporate trust business of an Authenticating Agent shall be the successor Authenticating Agent hereunder, provided such corporation shall be otherwise eligible under this Section 614, without the execution or filing of any paper or any further act on the part of the Trustee or the Authenticating Agent.

An Authenticating Agent may resign at any time by giving written notice thereof to the Trustee and to the Company. The Trustee may at any time terminate the agency of an Authenticating Agent by giving written notice thereof to such Authenticating Agent and to the Company. Upon receiving such a notice of resignation or upon such a termination, or in case at any time such Authenticating Agent shall cease to be eligible in accordance with the provisions of this Section 614, the Trustee may appoint a successor Authenticating Agent which shall be acceptable to the Company and shall give notice of such appointment in the manner provided in Section 106 to all Holders of Securities of the series with respect to which such Authenticating Agent will serve. Any successor Authenticating Agent upon acceptance of its appointment hereunder shall become vested with all the rights, powers and duties of its predecessor hereunder, with like effect as if originally named as an Authenticating Agent. No successor Authenticating Agent shall be appointed unless eligible under the provisions of this Section 614.

The Company agrees to pay to each Authenticating Agent from time to time reasonable compensation for its services under this Section 614.

If an appointment with respect to one or more series is made pursuant to this Section 614, the Securities of such series may have endorsed thereon, in addition to the Trustee's certificate of authentication, an alternative certificate of authentication in the following form:

This is one of the Securities of the series designated therein referred to in the within-mentioned Indenture.

Dated: _____

The Bank of New York Mellon
Trust Company, N.A.,
As Trustee

By: _____

As Authenticating Agent

By: _____

Authorized Officer

ARTICLE VII
HOLDERS' LISTS AND REPORTS BY TRUSTEE AND COMPANY

Section 701. <u>Company to Furnish Trustee Names and Addresses of Holders.</u>

If the Trustee is not the Security Registrar, the Company shall cause the Security Registrar to furnish to the Trustee, in writing at least five Business Days before each Interest Payment Date and at such other times as the Trustee may request in writing, a list in such form and as of such date as the Trustee may reasonably require of the names and addresses of Holders of Securities of each series.

Section 702. <u>Preservation of Information; Communications to Holders.</u>

The Trustee shall preserve, in as current a form as is reasonably practicable, the names and addresses of Holders contained in the most recent list furnished to the Trustee as provided in Section 701 and the names and addresses of Holders received by the Trustee in its capacity as Security Registrar. The Trustee may destroy any list furnished to it as provided in Section 701 upon receipt of a new list so furnished.

The rights of Holders to communicate with other Holders with respect to their rights under this Indenture or under the Securities, and the corresponding rights and privileges of the Trustee, shall be as provided by the Trust Indenture Act.

Every Holder of Securities, by receiving and holding the same, agrees with the Company and the Trustee that neither the Company nor the Trustee nor any agent of either of them shall be held accountable by reason of any disclosure of information as to names and addresses of Holders made pursuant to the Trust Indenture Act.

Section 703. <u>Reports by Trustee.</u>

Within 60 days after each May 15, beginning in 2013, the Trustee shall transmit to Holders such reports concerning the Trustee and its actions under this Indenture as may be required pursuant to the Trust Indenture Act. The Trustee shall promptly deliver to the Company a copy of any report it delivers to Holders pursuant to this Section 703.

A copy of each such report shall, at the time of such transmission to Holders, be filed by the Trustee with each stock exchange and automated quotation system, if any, upon which any Securities are listed, with the Commission and with the Company. The Company will notify the Trustee when any Securities are listed on any stock exchange or automated quotation system or delisted therefrom.

Section 704. <u>Reports by Company.</u>

The Company shall file with the Trustee, and transmit to the Holders, such information, documents and other reports, and such summaries thereof, as may be required pursuant to the Trust Indenture Act. Delivery of such reports, information and documents to the Trustee is for informational purposes only and shall not constitute a representation or warranty as to the accuracy or completeness of the reports, information and documents. All required reports, information and documents referred to in this Section 704 shall be deemed filed with the Trustee and transmitted to the Holders at the time such reports, information or documents are publicly filed with the Commission via the Commission's EDGAR filing system (or any successor system). For purposes of clarification, the foregoing sentence does not impose on the Trustee any duty to search for or obtain any electronic or other filings that the Company makes with the Commission, regardless of whether such filings are periodic, supplemental or otherwise. The Trustee's receipt of such shall not constitute constructive notice of any information contained therein or determinable from information contained therein, including the Company's compliance with any of its covenants hereunder (as to which the Trustee is entitled to rely exclusively on Officer's Certificates).

ARTICLE VIII
CONSOLIDATION, MERGER AND SALE OF ASSETS

Section 801. <u>Company May Merge or Transfer Assets Only on Certain Terms.</u>

The Company shall not consolidate with or merge with or into, or sell, transfer, lease or convey all or substantially all of its properties and assets to, in one transaction or a series of related transactions, any other Person, unless:

(1) the Company shall be the continuing entity, or the resulting, surviving or transferee Person (the "<u>Successor</u>") shall be a Person (if such Person is not a corporation, then the Successor shall include a corporate co-issuer of the Securities) organized and existing under the laws of the United States of America, any State thereof or the District of Columbia and the Successor (if not the Company) shall expressly assume, by an indenture supplemental hereto, executed and delivered to the Trustee, in form reasonably satisfactory to the Trustee, all the obligations of the Company under the Securities and this Indenture and, for each Security that by its terms provides for conversion, shall have provided for the right to convert such Security in accordance with its terms;

(2) immediately after giving effect to such transaction, no Default or Event of Default shall have occurred and be continuing; and

(3) the Company shall have delivered to the Trustee an Officer's Certificate and an Opinion of Counsel, each stating that such transaction and such supplemental indenture, if any, complies with this Indenture (except that such Opinion of Counsel need not opine as to clause (2) above).

Section 802. <u>Successor Corporation Substituted.</u>

The Successor shall succeed to, and be substituted for, and may exercise every right and power of, the Company under the Indenture, with the same effect as if the Successor had been an original party to this Indenture, and the Company shall be released from all its liabilities and obligations under this Indenture and the Securities.

ARTICLE IX
SUPPLEMENTAL INDENTURES

Section 901. Supplemental Indentures Without Consent of Holders.

Without the consent of any Holders, the Company and the Trustee, at any time and from time to time, may enter into one or more indentures supplemental hereto, in form satisfactory to the Trustee, for any of the following purposes:

(1)   to add to the covenants for the benefit of the Holders of all or any series of Securities (and if such covenants are to be for the benefit of less than all series of Securities, stating that such covenants are expressly being included solely for the benefit of such series) or to surrender any right or power herein conferred upon the Company;

(2)   to evidence the succession of another Person to the Company, or successive successions, and the assumption by the successor corporation of the covenants, agreements and obligations of the Company pursuant to Article VIII;

(3)   to add any additional Events of Default for the benefit of the Holders of all or any series of Securities (and if such additional Events of Default are to be for the benefit of less than all series of Securities, stating that such additional Events of Default are expressly being included solely for the benefit of such series);

(4)   to add one or more guarantees for the benefit of Holders of the Securities;

(5)   to secure the Securities;

(6)   to evidence and provide for the acceptance of appointment hereunder by a successor Trustee with respect to the Securities of one or more series and to add to or change any of the provisions of this Indenture as shall be necessary to provide for or facilitate the administration of the trusts hereunder by more than one Trustee, pursuant to the requirements of Section 611;

(7)   subject to any limitations established pursuant to Section 301, to provide for the issuance of additional Securities of any series;

(8)   to establish the form or terms of Securities of any series as permitted by Section 201 and Section 301;

(9)   to comply with the rules of any applicable Depositary;

(10) to add to or change any of the provisions of this Indenture to such extent as shall be necessary to permit or facilitate the issuance of Securities in uncertificated form;

(11) to add to, change or eliminate any of the provisions of this Indenture in respect of one or more series of Securities; provided that any such addition, change or elimination (A) shall neither (i) apply to any Security of any series created prior to the execution of such supplemental indenture and entitled to the benefit of such provision nor (ii) modify the rights of the Holder of any such Security with respect to such provision or (B) shall become effective only when there is no Security described in clause (A)(i) Outstanding;

(12) to cure any ambiguity, to correct or supplement any provision of this Indenture which may be defective or inconsistent with any other provision herein;

(13) to change any other provision under this Indenture; <u>provided</u> that such action pursuant to this clause (13) shall not adversely affect the interests of the Holders of Securities of any series in any material respect;

(14) to supplement any of the provisions of this Indenture to such extent as shall be necessary to permit or facilitate the defeasance and discharge of any series of Securities pursuant to Section 401, Section 1302 and Section 1303; provided that any such action shall not adversely affect the interests of the Holders of Securities of such series or any other series of Securities in any material respect;

(15) to comply with the rules or regulations of any securities exchange or auto-mated quotation system on which any of the Securities may be listed or traded; and

(16) to add to, change or eliminate any of the provisions of this Indenture as shall be necessary or desirable in accordance with any amendments to the Trust Indenture Act, provided that such action does not adversely affect the rights or interests of any Holder of Securities in any material respect.

Section 902. <u>Supplemental Indentures With Consent of Holders.</u>

With the consent of the Holders of not less than a majority in aggregate principal amount of the Outstanding Securities of each series affected by such supplemental indenture (including consents obtained in connection with a tender offer or exchange for Securities), by Act of said Holders delivered to the Company and the Trustee, the Company and the Trustee may enter into an indenture or indentures supplemental hereto for the purpose of adding any provisions to or changing in any manner or elim-inating any of the provisions of this Indenture or of modifying in any manner the rights of the Holders of Securities of such series under this Indenture; <u>provided, however,</u> no such supplemental indenture shall, without the consent of the Holder of each Out-standing Security of such series affected thereby:

(1) change the Stated Maturity of the principal of, or any installment of principal of or interest on, any Security;

(2) reduce the principal amount of any Security or reduce the amount of the principal of an Original Issue Discount Security or any other Security which would be due and payable upon a declaration of acceleration of the Maturity thereof pursuant to Section 502, or reduce the rate of interest on any Security;

(3) reduce any premium payable upon the redemption of or change the date on which any Security may or must be redeemed;

(4) change the coin or currency in which the principal of or premium, if any, or interest on any Security is payable;

(5) impair the right of any Holder to institute suit for the enforcement of any such payment on or after the Stated Maturity thereof (or, in the case of redemption, on or after the Redemption Date);

(6) reduce the percentage in principal amount of the Outstanding Securities of any series, the consent of whose Holders is required for any such supplemental indenture, or the consent of whose Holders is required for any waiver (of

compliance with certain provisions of this Indenture or certain defaults here-under and their consequences) provided for in this Indenture;

(7) modify any of the provisions of this Section 902, Section 512 or Section 1005, except to increase any such percentage or to provide that certain other provisions of this Indenture cannot be modified or waived without the consent of the Holder of each Outstanding Security affected thereby; provided, however, that this clause shall not be deemed to require the consent of any Holder with respect to changes in the references to "the Trustee" and concomitant changes in this Section 902 and Section 1005, or the deletion of this proviso, in accordance with the requirements of Section 611 and Section 901(6); or

(8) if the Securities of any series are convertible into or for any other securities or property of the Company, make any change that adversely affects in any material respect the right to convert any Security of such series (except as permitted by Section 901) or decrease the conversion rate or increase the conversion price of any such Security of such series, unless such decrease or increase is permitted by the terms of such Security.

A supplemental indenture which changes or eliminates any covenant or other provision of this Indenture which has expressly been included solely for the benefit of one or more particular series of Securities, or which modifies the rights of the Holders of Securities of such series with respect to such covenant or other provision, shall be deemed not to affect the rights under this Indenture of the Holders of Securities of any other series.

It shall not be necessary for any Act of Holders under this Section 902 to approve the particular form of any proposed supplemental indenture, but it shall be sufficient if such Act shall approve the substance thereof.

After a supplemental indenture under this Section 902 becomes effective, the Company shall mail to the Trustee a notice briefly describing such supplemental indenture or a copy of such supplemental indenture and the Trustee shall mail such notice or supplemental indenture to Holders affected thereby. Any failure of the Company to mail such notice, or any defect therein, or any failure of the Company to mail such supplemental indenture, shall not in any way impair or affect the validity of any such supplemental indenture.

Section 903. Execution of Supplemental Indentures.

In executing, or accepting the additional trusts created by, any supplemental indenture permitted by this Article IX or the modifications thereby of the trusts created by this Indenture, the Trustee shall be entitled to receive, and, subject to Section 601, shall be fully protected in relying upon, an Officer's Certificate and an Opinion of Counsel stating that the execution of such supplemental indenture is authorized or permitted by this Indenture and that all conditions precedent in this Indenture to the execution of such supplemental indenture, if any, have been complied with. The Trustee may, but shall not be obligated to, enter into any such supplemental indenture which affects the Trustee's own rights, duties or immunities under this Indenture or otherwise.

Section 904. <u>Effect of Supplemental Indentures.</u>

Upon the execution of any supplemental indenture under this Article IX, this Indenture shall be modified in accordance therewith, and such supplemental indenture shall form a part of this Indenture for all purposes; and every Holder of Securities theretofore or thereafter authenticated and delivered hereunder shall be bound thereby.

Section 905. <u>Conformity with Trust Indenture Act.</u>

Every supplemental indenture executed pursuant to this Article IX shall conform to the requirements of the Trust Indenture Act.

Section 906. <u>Reference in Securities to Supplemental Indentures.</u>

Securities of any series authenticated and delivered after the execution of any supplemental indenture pursuant to this Article IX may, and shall if required by the Trustee, bear a notation in form approved by the Trustee as to any matter provided for in such supplemental indenture. If the Company shall so determine, new Securities of any series so modified as to conform, in the opinion of the Trustee and the Company, to any such supplemental indenture may be prepared and executed by the Company and authenticated and delivered by the Trustee in exchange for Outstanding Securities of such series.

ARTICLE X
COVENANTS

Section 1001. <u>Payment of Principal, Premium, if any, and Interest.</u>

The Company covenants and agrees for the benefit of each series of Securities that it will duly and punctually pay the principal of and premium, if any, and interest on the Securities of such series in accordance with the terms of the Securities and this Indenture. Principal and interest shall be considered paid on the date due if, on or before 11:00 a.m. (New York City time) on such date, the Trustee or the Paying Agent (or, if the Company or any of its Subsidiaries is the Paying Agent, the segregated account or separate trust fund maintained by the Company or such Subsidiary pursuant to Section 1003) holds in accordance with this Indenture money sufficient to pay all principal and interest then due.

The Company shall pay interest on overdue principal at the rate specified therefor in the Securities, and it shall pay interest on overdue installments of interest at the same rate to the extent lawful as provided in Section 307.

Notwithstanding anything to the contrary contained in this Indenture, the Company or the Paying Agent may, to the extent it is required to do so by law, deduct or withhold income or other similar taxes imposed by the United States of America or other domestic or foreign taxing authorities from principal or interest payments hereunder.

Section 1002. <u>Maintenance of Office or Agency.</u>

The Company will maintain in each Place of Payment for any series of Securities an office or agency where Securities of such series may be presented or surrendered for payment, where Securities of such series may be surrendered for registration of transfer or exchange, where Securities may be surrendered for conversion, and where notices and demands to or upon the Company in respect of the Securities of such series and this Indenture may be served. The Company will give prompt written notice to the Trustee of the location, and any change in the location, of such office or agency. If at any time the Company shall fail to maintain any such required office or agency or shall fail to furnish the Trustee with the address thereof, such presentations, surrenders, notices and demands may be made or served at the Corporate Trust Office of the Trustee; and such required office or agency in New York, New York shall be at an office of the Trustee located at 101 Barclay Street, Floor 4W, New York, New York 10286, Attention: Corporate Trust Administration. The Company hereby appoints the Trustee as its agent to receive all such presentations, surrenders, notices and demands.

The Company may also from time to time designate one or more other offices or agencies where the Securities of one or more series may be presented or surrendered for any or all such purposes and may from time to time rescind such designations; <u>provided, however,</u> that no such designation or rescission shall in any manner relieve the Company of its obligation to maintain an office or agency in each Place of Payment for Securities of any series for such purposes. The Company will give prompt written notice to the Trustee of any such designation or rescission and of any change in the location of any such other office or agency.

With respect to any Global Security, and except as otherwise may be specified for such Global Security as contemplated by Section 301, the Corporate Trust Office of the Trustee shall be the Place of Payment where such Global Security may be presented or surrendered for payment or for registration of transfer or exchange, or where successor Securities may be delivered in exchange therefor; and such Place of Payment with respect to a Global Security in New York, New York shall be at an office of the Trustee located at 101 Barclay Street, Floor 4W, New York, New York 10286, Attention: Corporate Trust Administration; <u>provided, however,</u> that any such payment, presentation, surrender or delivery effected pursuant to the Applicable Procedures of the Depositary for such Global Security shall be deemed to have been effected at the Place of Payment for such Global Security in accordance with the provisions of this Indenture.

Section 1003. <u>Money for Securities Payments to Be Held in Trust.</u>

If the Company shall at any time act as its own Paying Agent with respect to any series of Securities, it will, on or before each due date for the principal of or premium, if any, or interest on any of the Securities of such series, segregate and hold in trust for the benefit of the Holders of such Securities a sum sufficient to pay the principal and premium, if any, and interest so becoming due until such sums shall be paid to such Holders or otherwise disposed of as herein provided and will promptly notify the Trustee of its action or failure so to act.

Whenever the Company shall have one or more Paying Agents for any series of Securities, it will, no later than 11:00 a.m. (New York City time) on each due date for the principal of or premium, if any, or interest on any Securities of such series, deposit with a Paying Agent a sum sufficient to pay such amount, such sum to be held in trust for the Holders of such Securities entitled to the same, and (unless such Paying Agent is the Trustee) the Company will promptly notify the Trustee of its action or failure so to act.

The Company will cause each Paying Agent for any series of Securities other than the Trustee to execute and deliver to the Trustee an instrument in which such Paying Agent shall agree with the Trustee, subject to the provisions of this Section 1003, that such Paying Agent shall hold in trust for the benefit of Holders or the Trustee all money held by such Paying Agent for the payment of principal of or interest on the Securities and shall notify the Trustee in writing of any default by the Company in making any such payment.

The Company may at any time, for the purpose of obtaining the satisfaction and discharge of this Indenture or for any other purpose, pay, or by Company Order direct any Paying Agent to pay, to the Trustee all sums held in trust by the Company or such Paying Agent, such sums to be held by the Trustee upon the same trusts as those upon which such sums were held by the Company or such Paying Agent; and, upon such payment by any Paying Agent to the Trustee, such Paying Agent shall be released from all further liability with respect to such money.

Subject to any applicable abandoned property law, any money deposited with the Trustee or any Paying Agent, or then held by the Company, in trust for the payment of the principal of or premium, if any, or interest on any Security of any series and remaining unclaimed for two years after such principal, premium or interest has become due and payable shall be paid to the Company on Company Request, or (if then held by the Company) shall be discharged from such trust; and the Holder of such Security shall thereafter, as an unsecured general creditor, look only to the Company for payment thereof, and all liability of the Trustee or such Paying Agent with respect to such trust money, and all liability of the Company as trustee thereof, shall thereupon cease.

Section 1004. Statement by Officers as to Default.

The Company shall deliver to the Trustee within 120 days after the end of each fiscal year of the Company ending after the date hereof an Officer's Certificate signed by its principal executive officer, principal financial officer or principal accounting officer, stating whether or not, to the best knowledge of such officer, the Company is in default in the performance and observance of any of the terms, provisions and conditions of this Indenture (without regard to any period of grace or requirement of notice provided hereunder) and, if the Company shall be in default, specifying all such defaults and the nature and status thereof of which they may have knowledge.

Section 1005. Waiver of Certain Covenants.

Except as otherwise specified as contemplated by Section 301 for Securities of such series, the Company may, with respect to the Securities of any series, omit in any particular instance to comply with any term, provision or condition set forth in any covenant provided pursuant to Section 301(21), Section 901(1) or Section 901(8) for the benefit of the Holders of such series, if before the time for such compliance the Holders of at least a majority in aggregate principal amount of the Outstanding Securities of such series shall, by Act of such Holders, either waive such compliance in such instance or generally waive compliance with such term, provision or condition, but no such waiver shall extend to or affect such term, provision or condition except to the extent so expressly waived, and, until such waiver shall become effective, the obligations of the Company and the duties of the Trustee in respect of any such term, provision or condition shall remain in full force and effect.

ARTICLE XI
REDEMPTION OF SECURITIES

Section 1101. Applicability of Article.

Securities of any series which are redeemable before their Stated Maturity shall be redeemable in accordance with their terms and (except as otherwise specified as contemplated by Section 301 for such Securities) in accordance with this Article XI.

Section 1102. Election to Redeem; Notice to Trustee.

The election of the Company to redeem any Securities shall be evidenced by a Board Resolution or an Officer's Certificate or in another manner specified as contemplated by Section 301 for such Securities. In case of any redemption at the election of the Company of the Securities of any series (including any such redemption affecting only a single Security), the Company shall, at least 45 days prior to the Redemption Date fixed by the Company (unless a shorter notice shall be satisfactory to the Trustee), notify the Trustee of such Redemption Date, of the principal amount of Securities of such series to be redeemed and, if applicable, of the tenor of the Securities to be redeemed. In the case of any redemption of Securities (a) prior to the expiration of any restriction on such redemption provided in the terms of such Securities or elsewhere in this Indenture, or (b) pursuant to an election of the Company which is subject to a condition specified in the terms of such Securities or elsewhere in this Indenture, the Company shall furnish the Trustee with an Officer's Certificate evidencing compliance with such restriction or condition.

Section 1103. Selection by Trustee of Securities to Be Redeemed.

If less than all the Securities of any series are to be redeemed (unless all the Securities of such series and of a specified tenor are to be redeemed or unless such redemption affects only a single Security), the particular Securities to be redeemed shall be selected not more than 60 days prior to the Redemption Date, from the Outstanding Securities of such series not previously called for redemption, by lot or, in the case of Global Securities, pursuant to applicable Depositary procedures; provided that the unredeemed portion of the principal amount of any Security shall be in an authorized denomination (which shall not be less than the minimum authorized denomination) for such Security. If less than all the Securities of such series and of a specified tenor are to be redeemed (unless such redemption affects only a single Security), the particular Securities to be redeemed shall be selected not more than 60 days prior to the Redemption Date, from the Outstanding Securities of such series and specified tenor not previously called for redemption in accordance with the preceding sentence.

If any Security selected for partial redemption is converted in part before termination of the conversion right with respect to the portion of the Security so selected, the converted portion of such Security shall be deemed (so far as may be) to be the portion selected for redemption. Securities which have been converted during a selection of securities to be redeemed shall be treated by the Trustee as Outstanding for the purpose of such selection.

The Trustee shall promptly notify the Company in writing of the Securities selected for redemption as aforesaid and, in case of any Securities selected for partial redemption as aforesaid, the principal amount thereof to be redeemed.

The provisions of the three preceding paragraphs shall not apply with respect to any redemption affecting only a single Security, whether such Security is to be redeemed in whole or in part. In the case of any such redemption in part, the unredeemed portion of the principal amount of the Security shall be in an authorized denomination (which shall not be less than the minimum authorized denomination) for such Security.

For all purposes of this Indenture, unless the context otherwise requires, all provisions relating to the redemption of Securities shall relate, in the case of any Securities redeemed or to be redeemed only in part, to the portion of the principal amount of such Securities which has been or is to be redeemed. If the Company shall so direct, Securities registered in the name of the Company, any Affiliate or any Subsidiary thereof shall not be included in the Securities selected for redemption.

Section 1104. <u>Notice of Redemption.</u>

Notice of redemption shall be given by first-class mail, postage prepaid, mailed or otherwise in accordance with the Applicable Procedures not less than 30 nor more than 60 days prior to the Redemption Date (or within such period as otherwise specified as contemplated by Section 301 for Securities of a series), to each Holder of Securities to be redeemed, at such Holder's address appearing in the Security Register.

All notices of redemption shall identify the Securities to be redeemed and shall state:

(1) the Redemption Date;

(2) the Redemption Price (or the method of calculating such price);

(3) if less than all the Outstanding Securities of any series consisting of more than a single Security are to be redeemed, the identification (and, in the case of partial redemption of any such Securities, the principal amounts) of the particular Securities to be redeemed and, if less than all the Outstanding Securities of any series consisting of a single Security are to be redeemed, the principal amount of the particular Security to be redeemed;

(4) that on the Redemption Date the Redemption Price will become due and payable upon each such Security to be redeemed and, if applicable, that interest thereon will cease to accrue on and after said date;

(5) the place or places where each such Security is to be surrendered for payment of the Redemption Price;

(6) for any Securities that by their terms may be converted, the terms of conversion, the date on which the right to convert the Security to be redeemed will terminate and the place or places where such Securities may be surrendered for conversion;

(7) that the redemption is for a sinking fund, if such is the case; and

(8) if applicable, the CUSIP numbers of the Securities of such series; provided, however, that no representation will be made as to the correctness or accuracy of the CUSIP number, or any similar number, if any, listed in such notice or printed on the Securities.

Notice of redemption of Securities to be redeemed at the election of the Company shall be given by the Company or, at the Company's request (which may be rescinded or revoked at any time prior to the time at which the Trustee shall have given such notice to the Holders), by the Trustee in the name and at the expense of the Company. The notice, if sent in the manner herein provided, shall be conclusively presumed to have been given, whether or not the Holder receives such notice. In any case, failure to give such notice by mail or otherwise in accordance with the Applicable Procedures or any defect in the notice to the Holder of any Security designated for redemption as a whole or in part shall not affect the validity of the proceedings for the redemption of any other Securities.

Section 1105. Deposit of Redemption Price.

By no later than 11:00 a.m. (New York City time) on any Redemption Date, the Company shall deposit with the Trustee or with a Paying Agent (or, if the Company is acting as its own Paying Agent, segregate and hold in trust as provided in Section 1003) an amount of money sufficient to pay the Redemption Price of, and (except if the Redemption Date shall be an Interest Payment Date or the Securities of the series provide otherwise) accrued interest on, all the Securities which are to be redeemed on that date, other than Securities or portions of Securities called for redemption which are owned by the Company or a Subsidiary and have been delivered by the Company or such Subsidiary to the Trustee for cancellation. All money, if any, earned on funds held by the Paying Agent shall be remitted to the Company. In addition, the Paying Agent shall promptly return to the Company any money deposited with the Paying Agent by the Company in excess of the amounts necessary to pay the Redemption Price of, and accrued interest, if any, on, all Securities to be redeemed.

If any Security called for redemption is converted, any money deposited with the Trustee or with any Paying Agent or so segregated and held in trust for the redemption of such Security shall (subject to any right of the Holder of such Security or any Predecessor Security to receive interest as provided in the last paragraph of Section 307 or in the terms of such Security) be paid to the Company upon Company Request or, if then held by the Company, shall be discharged from such trust.

Section 1106. <u>Securities Payable on Redemption Date.</u>

Notice of redemption having been given as aforesaid, the Securities so to be redeemed shall, on the Redemption Date, become due and payable at the Redemption Price therein specified, and from and after such date (unless the Company shall default in the payment of the Redemption Price and accrued interest) such Securities shall cease to bear interest. Upon surrender of any such Security for redemption in accordance with said notice, such Security shall be paid by the Company at the Redemption Price, together, if applicable, with accrued interest to the Redemption Date; <u>provided, however,</u> that, unless otherwise specified as contemplated by Section 301, installments of interest whose Stated Maturity is on or prior to the Redemption Date will be payable to the Holders of such Securities, or one or more Predecessor Securities, registered as such at the close of business on the relevant Record Dates according to their terms and the provisions of Section 307; <u>provided further</u> that, unless otherwise specified as contemplated by Section 301, if the Redemption Date is after a Regular Record Date and on or prior to the Interest Payment Date, the accrued and unpaid interest shall be payable to the Holder of the redeemed Securities registered on the relevant Regular Record Date.

If any Security called for redemption shall not be so paid upon surrender thereof for redemption, the principal and premium, if any, shall, until paid, bear interest from the Redemption Date at the rate prescribed therefor in the Security.

Section 1107. <u>Securities Redeemed in Part.</u>

Any Security which is to be redeemed only in part shall be surrendered at a Place of Payment therefor (with, if the Company or the Trustee so requires, due endorsement by, or a written instrument of transfer in form satisfactory to the Company and the Trustee duly executed by, the Holder thereof or such Holder's attorney duly authorized in writing), and the Company shall execute, and the Trustee shall authenticate and deliver to the Holder of such Security without service charge, a new Security or Securities of the same series and of like tenor, of any authorized denomination as requested by such Holder, in principal amount equal to and in exchange for the unredeemed portion of the principal of the Security so surrendered.

ARTICLE XII
SINKING FUNDS

Section 1201. <u>Applicability of Article.</u>

The provisions of this Article XII shall be applicable to any sinking fund for the retirement of Securities of any series except as otherwise specified as contemplated by Section 301 for such Securities.

The minimum amount of any sinking fund payment provided for by the terms of any series of Securities is herein referred to as a "mandatory sinking fund payment," and any payment in excess of such minimum amount provided for by the terms of such Securities is herein referred to as an "optional sinking fund payment." If provided for by the terms of any series of Securities, the cash amount of any sinking fund payment may be subject to reduction as provided in Section 1202. Each sinking fund payment shall be applied to the redemption of Securities of the series as provided for by the terms of such Securities.

Section 1202. <u>Satisfaction of Sinking Fund Payments with Securities.</u>

The Company (1) may deliver Outstanding Securities of a series (other than any previously called for redemption) and (2) may apply as a credit Securities of a series which have been redeemed either at the election of the Company pursuant to the terms of such Securities or through the application of permitted optional sinking fund payments pursuant to the terms of such Securities, in each case in satisfaction of all or any part of any sinking fund payment with respect to any Securities of such series required to be made pursuant to the terms of such Securities as and to the extent provided for by the terms of such Securities; <u>provided</u> that the Securities to be so credited have not been previously so credited. The Securities to be so credited shall be received and credited for such purpose by the Trustee at the Redemption Price, as specified in the Securities so to be redeemed, for redemption through opera-tion of the sinking fund and the amount of such sinking fund payment shall be reduced accordingly.

Section 1203. <u>Redemption of Securities for Sinking Fund.</u>

Not less than 60 days (or such shorter period as shall be satisfactory to the Trustee) prior to each sinking fund payment date for any Securities, the Company will deliver to the Trustee an Officer's Certificate specifying the amount of the next ensuing sinking fund payment for such Securities pursuant to the terms of such Securities, the portion thereof, if any, which is to be satisfied by payment of cash and the portion thereof, if any, which is to be satisfied by delivering and crediting Securities pursuant to Section 1202 and will also deliver to the Trustee any Securities to be so delivered. Not less than 30 days prior to each such sinking fund payment date, the Securities to be redeemed upon such sinking fund payment date shall be selected in the manner spec-ified in Section 1103 and the Company shall cause notice of the redemption thereof to be given in the name of and at the expense of the Company in the manner provided in Section 1104. Such notice having been duly given, the redemption of such Securities shall be made upon the terms and in the manner stated in Section 1106 and Section 1107.

ARTICLE XIII
DEFEASANCE AND COVENANT DEFEASANCE

Section 1301. <u>Company's Option to Effect Defeasance or Covenant Defeasance.</u>

Unless otherwise provided as contemplated by Section 301, Section 1302 and Section 1303 shall apply to all Securities or each series of Securities, as the case may be, in either case, denominated in U.S. dollars and bearing interest at a fixed rate, in accordance with any applicable requirements provided pursuant to Section 301 and upon compliance with the conditions set forth below in this Article XIII; and the Company may elect, at its option at any time, to have Section 1302 and Section 1303 applied to any Securities or any series of Securities, as the case may be, pursuant to such Section 1302 or Section 1303, in accordance with any applicable requirements provided pursuant to Section 301 and upon compliance with the conditions set forth below in this Article XIII. Any such election to have or not to have Section 1302 and Section 1303 apply, as the case may be, shall be evidenced by a Board Resolution, Officer's Certificate or in another manner specified as contemplated by Section 301 for such Securities.

Section 1302. <u>Defeasance and Discharge.</u>

Upon the Company's exercise of its option, if any, to have this Section 1302 applied to any Securities or any series of Securities, as the case may be, or if this Section 1302 shall otherwise apply to any Securities or any series of Securities, as the case may be, the Company shall be deemed to have been discharged from its obligations with respect to such Securities as provided in this Section 1302 on and after the date the conditions set forth in Section 1304 are satisfied (hereinafter called "<u>Defeasance</u>"). For this purpose, such Defeasance means that the Company shall be deemed to have paid and discharged the entire indebtedness represented by such Securities and to have satisfied all its other obligations under such Securities and this Indenture insofar as such Securities are concerned (and the Trustee, at the expense of the Company, shall execute proper instruments acknowledging the same), subject to the following which shall survive until otherwise terminated or discharged hereunder: (1) the rights of Holders of such Securities to receive, solely from the trust fund described in Section 1304 and as more fully set forth in such Section 1305, payments in respect of the principal of and premium, if any, and interest on such Securities when payments are due, (2) the Company's obligations with respect to such Securities under Section 304, Section 305, Section 306, Section 1002 and Section 1003, (3) the rights, powers, trusts, duties and immunities of the Trustee hereunder and (4) this Article XIII. Subject to compliance with this Article XIII, the Company may exercise its option, if any, to have this Section 1302 applied to the Securities of any series notwithstanding the prior exercise of its option, if any, to have Section 1303 applied to such Securities.

Section 1303. <u>Covenant Defeasance.</u>

Upon the Company's exercise of its option, if any, to have this Section 1303 applied to any Securities or any series of Securities, as the case may be, or if this Section 1303 shall otherwise apply to any Securities or any series of Securities, as the case may be, (1) the Company shall be released from its obligations under any covenants provided pursuant to Section 301(21), Section 901(1) or Section 901(8) for the benefit of the Holders of such Securities and (2) the occurrence of any event specified in Section 501(3) and Section 501(6) shall be deemed not to be or result in an Event of Default, in each case with respect to such Securities as provided in this Section 1303 on and after the date the conditions set forth in Section 1304 are satisfied (hereinafter called "<u>Covenant Defeasance</u>"). For this purpose, such Covenant Defeasance means that, with respect to such Securities, the Company may omit to comply with and shall have no liability in respect of any term, condition or limitation set forth in any such specified Section, whether directly or indirectly by reason of any reference elsewhere herein to any such Section or by reason of any reference in any such Section to any other provision herein or in any other document, but the remainder of this Indenture and such Securities shall be unaffected thereby.

Section 1304. <u>Conditions to Defeasance or Covenant Defeasance.</u>

The following shall be the conditions to the application of Section 1302 or Section 1303 to any Securities or any series of Securities, as the case may be:

(1) The Company shall irrevocably have deposited or caused to be deposited with the Trustee (or another trustee which satisfies the requirements contemplated by Section 609 and agrees to comply with the provisions of this Article XIII applicable to it) as trust funds in trust for the purpose of making the following payments, specifically pledged as security for, and dedicated solely to, the benefits of the Holders of such Securities, (A) money in an amount, or (B) U.S. Government Obligations which through the scheduled payment of principal and interest in respect thereof in accordance with their terms will provide money in an amount, or (C) a combination thereof, in each case sufficient, in the opinion of an independent public accountant or financial advisor expressed in a written certification thereof delivered to the Trustee, to pay and discharge, and which shall be applied by the Trustee (or any such other qualifying trustee) to pay and discharge, the principal of and premium, if any, and interest on such Securities on the respective Stated Maturities, in accordance with the terms of this Indenture and such Securities. As used herein, "<u>U.S. Government Obligation</u>" means (x) any security which is (i) a direct obligation of the United States of America for the payment of which the full faith and credit of the United States of America is pledged or (ii) an obligation of a Person controlled or supervised by and acting as an agency or instrumentality of the United States of America the payment of which is unconditionally guaranteed as a full faith and credit obligation by the United States of America, which, in either case (i) or (ii), is not callable or redeemable at the option of the issuer thereof, and (y) any depositary receipt issued by a bank (as defined in Section 3(a)(2) of the Securities Act) as custodian with respect to any U.S. Government Obligation which is specified in clause (x) above and held by such bank for the account of the holder of such depositary receipt, or with respect to any specific payment of principal of or interest on any U.S. Government Obligation which is so specified and held; <u>provided</u> that (except as required by law) such custodian is not authorized to make any deduction from the amount payable to the holder of such depositary receipt from any amount received by the custodian in respect of the U.S. Government Obligation or the specific payment of principal or interest evidenced by such depositary receipt.

(2) In the event of an election to have Section 1302 apply to any Securities or any series of Securities, as the case may be, the Company shall have delivered to the Trustee an Opinion of Counsel stating that (A) the Company has received from, or there has been published by, the Internal Revenue Service a ruling or (B) since the date of this Indenture, there has been a change in the applicable

Federal income tax law, in either case (A) or (B) to the effect that, and based thereon such opinion shall confirm that, the Holders of such Securities will not recognize gain or loss for Federal income tax purposes as a result of the deposit, Defeasance and discharge to be effected with respect to such Securities and will be subject to Federal income tax on the same amount, in the same manner and at the same times as would be the case if such deposit, Defeasance and discharge were not to occur.

(3) In the event of an election to have Section 1303 apply to any Securities or any series of Securities, as the case may be, the Company shall have delivered to the Trustee an Opinion of Counsel to the effect that the Holders of such Securities will not recognize gain or loss for Federal income tax purposes as a result of the deposit and Covenant Defeasance to be effected with respect to such Securities and will be subject to Federal income tax on the same amount, in the same manner and at the same times as would be the case if such deposit and Covenant Defeasance were not to occur.

(4) The Company shall have delivered to the Trustee an Officer's Certificate to the effect that neither such Securities nor any other Securities of the same series, if then listed on any securities exchange, will be delisted as a result of such deposit.

(5) No Default or Event of Default with respect to such Securities or any other Securities shall have occurred and be continuing at the time of such deposit or, insofar as Sections 501(4) or 501(5) are concerned, at any time on or prior to the 90th day after the date of such deposit (it being understood that this condition shall not be deemed satisfied until after such 90th day).

(6) Such Defeasance or Covenant Defeasance shall not result in a breach or violation of, or constitute a default under, any other material agreement or instrument to which the Company is a party or by which it is bound.

(7) The Company shall have delivered to the Trustee an Officer's Certificate and an Opinion of Counsel, each stating that all conditions precedent with respect to such Defeasance or Covenant Defeasance have been complied with (in each case, subject to the satisfaction of the condition in clause (5)).

Before or after a deposit, the Company may make arrangements satisfactory to the Trustee for the redemption of Securities at a future date in accordance with Article XI.

Section 1305. Deposited Money and U.S. Government Obligations to Be Held in Trust; Miscellaneous Provisions.

Subject to the provisions of the last paragraph of Section 1003, all money and U.S. Government Obligations (including the proceeds thereof) deposited with the Trustee or other qualifying trustee (solely for purposes of this Section 1305 and Section 1306, the Trustee and any such other trustee are referred to collectively as the "Trustee") pursuant to Section 1304 in respect of any Securities shall be held in trust and applied by the Trustee, in accordance with the provisions of such Securities and this Indenture, to the payment, either directly or through any such Paying Agent (including the Company acting as its own Paying Agent) as the Trustee may determine, to the Holders of such Securities, of all sums due and to become due thereon in respect of principal and premium, if any, and interest, but money so held in trust need not be segregated from other funds except to the extent required by law.

The Company shall pay and indemnify the Trustee against any tax, fee or other charge imposed on or assessed against the U.S. Government Obligations deposited pursuant to Section 1304 or the principal and interest received in respect thereof other than any such tax, fee or other charge which by law is for the account of the Holders of Outstanding Securities; provided that the Trustee shall be entitled to charge any such tax, fee or other charge to such Holder's account.

Anything in this Article XIII to the contrary notwithstanding, the Trustee shall deliver or pay to the Company from time to time upon Company Request any money or U.S. Government Obligations held by it as provided in Section 1304 with respect to any Securities which are in excess of the amount thereof which would then be required to be deposited to effect the Defeasance or Covenant Defeasance, as the case may be, with respect to such Securities.

Section 1306. Reinstatement.

If the Trustee or the Paying Agent is unable to apply any money in accordance with this Article XIII with respect to any Securities by reason of any order or judgment of any court or governmental authority enjoining, restraining or otherwise prohibiting such application, then the obligations under this Indenture and such Securities from which the Company has been discharged or released pursuant to Section 1302 or Section 1303 shall be revived and reinstated as though no deposit had occurred pursuant to this Article XIII with respect to such Securities, until such time as the Trustee or Paying Agent is permitted to apply all money held in trust pursuant to Section 1305 with respect to such Securities in accordance with this Article XIII; provided, however, that (a) if the Company makes any payment of principal of or premium, if any, or interest on any such Security following such reinstatement of its obligations, the Company shall be subrogated to the rights, if any, of the Holders of such Securities to receive such payment from the money so held in trust and (b) unless otherwise required by any legal proceeding or any order or judgment of any court or governmental authority, the Trustee or Paying Agent shall return all such money and U.S. Government Obligations to the Company promptly after receiving a written request therefor at any time, if such reinstatement of the Company's obligations has occurred and continues to be in effect.

ARTICLE XIV
REPAYMENT AT THE OPTION OF HOLDERS

Section 1401. Applicability of Article.

Repayment of Securities of any series before their Stated Maturity at the option of Holders thereof shall be made in accordance with the terms of such Securities and (except as otherwise specified as contemplated by Section 301 for Securities of any series) in accordance with this Article XIV.

Section 1402. Repayment of Securities.

Securities of any series subject to repayment in whole or in part at the option of the Holders thereof will, unless otherwise provided in the terms of such Securities, be repaid at a price equal to the principal amount thereof and premium, if any, thereon, together with interest thereon accrued to the Repayment Date specified in or pursuant to the terms of such Securities. The Company covenants that on or before the Repayment Date it will deposit with the Trustee or with a Paying Agent (or, if the Company is acting as its own Paying Agent, segregate and hold in trust as provided in Section 1003) an amount of money sufficient to pay the principal (or, if so provided by the terms of the Securities of any series, a percentage of the principal) of, the premium, if any, and (except if the Repayment Date shall be an Interest Payment Date) accrued interest on, all the Securities or portions thereof, as the case may be, to be repaid on such date.

Section 1403. Exercise of Option.

Securities of any series subject to repayment at the option of the Holders thereof will contain an "Option to Elect Repayment" form on the reverse of such Securities. To be repaid at the option of the Holder, any Security so providing for such repayment, with the "Option to Elect Repayment" form on the reverse of such Security duly completed by the Holder (or by the Holder's attorney duly authorized in writing), must be received by the Company at the Place of Payment therefor specified in the terms of such Security (or at such other place or places of which the Company shall from time to time notify the Holders of such Securities) not earlier than 45 days nor later than 30 days prior to the Repayment Date. If less than the entire principal amount of such Security is to be repaid in accordance with the terms of such Security, the principal amount of such Security to be repaid, in increments of the minimum denomination for Securities of such series, and the denomination or denominations of the Security or Securities to be issued to the Holder for the portion of the principal amount of such Security surrendered that is not to be repaid, must be specified. The principal amount of any Security providing for repayment at the option of the Holder thereof may not be repaid in part if, following such repayment, the unpaid principal amount of such Security would be less than the minimum authorized denomination of Securities of the series of which such Security to be repaid is a part. Except as otherwise may be provided by the terms of any Security providing for repayment at the option of the Holder thereof, exercise of the repayment option by the Holder shall be irrevocable unless waived by the Company.

Section 1404. When Securities Presented for Repayment Become Due and Payable.

If Securities of any series providing for repayment at the option of the Holders thereof shall have been surrendered as provided in this Article XIV and as provided by or pursuant to the terms of such Securities, such Securities or the portions thereof, as the case may be, to be repaid shall become due and payable and shall be paid by the Company on the Repayment Date therein specified, and on and after such Repayment Date (unless the Company shall default in the payment of such Securities on such

Repayment Date) such Securities shall, if the same were interest-bearing, cease to bear interest. Upon surrender of any such Security for repayment in accordance with such provisions, the principal amount of such Security so to be repaid shall be paid by the Company, together with accrued interest and/or premium, if any, to (but excluding) the Repayment Date; provided, however, that, unless otherwise specified as contemplated by Section 301, installments of interest, if any, whose Stated Maturity is on or prior to the Repayment Date shall be payable (but without interest thereon, unless the Company shall default in the payment thereof) to the Holders of such Securities, or one or more Predecessor Securities, registered as such at the close of business on the relevant Record Dates according to their terms and the provisions of Section 307.

If the principal amount of any Security surrendered for repayment shall not be so repaid upon surrender thereof, such principal amount (together with interest, if any, thereon accrued to such Repayment Date) and any premium shall, until paid, bear interest from the Repayment Date at the rate of interest or yield to maturity (in the case of Original Issue Discount Securities) set forth in such Security.

Section 1405. Securities Repaid in Part.

Upon surrender of any Security which is to be repaid in part only, the Company shall execute and the Trustee shall authenticate and deliver to the Holder of such Security, without service charge and at the expense of the Company, a new Security or Securities of the same series, of any authorized denomination specified by the Holder, in a principal amount equal to and in exchange for the portion of the principal of such Security so surrendered which is not to be repaid.

* * *

This Indenture may be executed in any number of counterparts, each of which so executed shall be deemed to be an original, but all such counterparts shall together constitute but one and the same instrument.

[Signature page follows]

IN WITNESS WHEREOF, the parties hereto have caused this Indenture to be duly executed, all as of the day and year first above written.

APPLE INC.
By: /s/ Peter Oppenheimer
Name: Peter Oppenheimer
Title: Senior Vice President, Chief
     Financial Officer

THE BANK OF NEW YORK MELLON
TRUST COMPANY, N.A.,
as Trustee

By: /s/ R. Tarnas
Name: R. Tarnas
Title: Vice President

MODEL NEGOTIATED COVENANTS

Model Negotiated Covenants and Related Definitions
61 Business Lawyer 1439 (2006)
Committee on Trust Indentures and Indenture Trustees
ABA Section of Business Law*

INTRODUCTION

Negotiated covenants are the undertakings included in the indentures for debt securities where the investors in the securities are not satisfied to rely only on the issuer's promise to pay the principal of and interest on the securities when due. Similar to the covenants contained in bank loan agreements, the negotiated covenants protect the investors by limiting the issuer's right to take steps that may impair its ability to pay. Typically, the covenants limit the ability of the issuer to borrow money, grant liens on its assets, dispose of assets or make distributions to equityholders. The covenants address the variety of transactions that directly or indirectly have those economic effects.

The publication of model negotiated covenants is an outgrowth of a process that began in 1960 as the Corporate Indenture Project. That project was originated by the Committee on Developments in Business Financing of the Section of Business Law with encouragement from the Securities and Exchange Commission and important financial support from the American Bar Foundation.[1] The first Model Debenture Indenture Provisions were published in 1965 at the end of the bearer bond era. Recognizing the change in the market, the Model Debenture Indenture Provisions—All Registered Issue were published in 1967. Commentaries on the Model Debenture Indenture Provisions were published by the American Bar Foundation in 1971. Those forms, which include some negotiated covenants and commentary on those covenants have provided a drafting standard and authoritative guidance since that time.

The standard indentures provisions have updated twice. In 1983 a working group of the Committee on Developments in Business Finance of the Section of Business Law published the Model Simplified Indenture.[2] In 2000 the Committee on Developments in Business Finance, with contributions from members of the Committee on

---

* William J. Whelan, III, Cravath, Swaine & Moore LLP, New York, NY, Task Force Chair.
1. *See* Churchill Rodgers, *The Corporate Trust Indenture Project*, 20 Bus. Law. 551 (1965).
2. 38 Bus. Law. 741 (1983).

Trust Indenture and Indenture Trustees (which had been created as a committee of the Section of Business Law in the mid-1990s) published the Revised Model Simplified Indenture.[3] All the necessary terms for the issuance and exchange of the securities, appointment of the trustee and enforcement of remedies are fully elaborated in these models. The forms are simplified only by the omission of the negotiated covenants. The Model Negotiated Covenants are designed to integrate with the Revised Model Simplified Indenture to provide a complete drafting base for a corporate indenture.

Other efforts at standardization include a First Report on Uncertificated Debt Securities, System Credit Risk and Sample Uncertificated Debt Indenture prepared by an Ad Hoc Committee on Uncertificated Debt Securities which has not been widely implemented in the absence of market acceptance for uncertificated securities.[4] Modern indentures do incorporate terms reflecting the indirect holding system, principally through Depository Trust Company that is in near universal use for debt securities. The National Association of Bond Lawyers published a model municipal indenture in 2000 that includes fund mechanics and other aspects of municipal conduit indentures not found in corporate indentures.

The Model Simplified Indenture and the Revised Model Simplified Indenture expressly excluded from their scope the covenants negotiated with sub-investment grade issuers by the initial purchaser or underwriter on behalf of the ultimate investors in the securities. There have been significant developments in the covenants for such issues in the decades since the American Bar Foundation Indenture forms were published to address the variety of sophisticated transactions developed in the intervening period. Several law firms have prepared for their investment bank clients model covenants and commentary. The Task Force has prepared a set of the covenants that typically appear in indentures for high yield issuers with the necessary definitions and commentary on the issues that arise in connection with the negotiation and interpretation of the covenants. The commentaries also include citations to relevant court decisions.

Even if they are not adopted in substitution for various forms developed and currently used by the law firms for the investment banks that are principally responsible for the preparation of indentures, the model covenants and their commentary will be useful in highlighting issues to be considered by the representatives of issuers and other parties who become involved in the negotiation and interpretation of covenants. The material discussed in this article is for training and illustrative purposes only and does not purport to reflect appropriate covenants or definitions that should be used in any particular situation. With a few exceptions, the model covenants and definitions contained herein also do not purport to reflect a view what is and what is not "market" in high yield issues.

In this article, language that would actually appear in an indenture appears in regular, roman typeface. Commentary of the Task Force appears in italics and is clearly separated from the indenture text. Transaction specific details, such as financial ratios, to be inserted by the drafter are indicated by a bullet • or brackets [].

---

3. 55 Bus. Law. 1115 (2000).
4. 46 Bus. Law. 909 (1991).

TABLE OF CONTENTS

MODEL COVENANTS

MODEL DEFINITIONS

SECTION 1.01. DEFINITIONS

*"**Additional Assets**"* means:

(1) any property, plant or equipment, in each case that is not classified as a current asset under GAAP and is used in a Related Business;

(2) the Capital Stock of a Person that becomes a Restricted Subsidiary as a result of the acquisition of such Capital Stock by the Company or another Restricted Subsidiary; or

(3) Capital Stock constituting a minority interest in any Person that at such time is a Restricted Subsidiary;

provided, however, that any such Restricted Subsidiary described in clause (2) or (3) above is primarily engaged in a Related Business.

* *Commentary*

This definition is used in the Asset Disposition covenant, and identifies the type of assets in which the Company may reinvest the proceeds from an asset sale. Occasionally, depending on the Company's industry, clause (1) above may be expanded to include other long-term assets, such as licenses and other intellectual property or intangibles.

Alternative Example 1:

" . . . the Company may apply such Net Available Cash to . . . (B) acquire all or substantially all of the assets of an entity engaged in a Related Business; (C) acquire Voting Stock of an entity engaged in a Related Business from a Person that is not a Subsidiary of the Company; provided, that (x) after giving effect thereto, the Company or its Restricted Subsidiary owns a majority of such entity's Voting Stock and (y) such acquisition is otherwise made in accordance with this Indenture, including Section 4.05; or (D) make a capital expenditure or acquire other long-term assets that are used or useful in a Related Business."

This alternative removes any doubt that capital expenditures qualify as Additional Assets for purposes of reinvestment.

"***Affiliate***" of any specified Person means any other Person, directly or indirectly, controlling or controlled by or under direct or indirect common control with such specified Person. For the purposes of this definition, "control" when used with respect to any Person means the power to direct the management and policies of such Person, directly or indirectly, whether through the ownership of voting securities, by contract or otherwise; and the terms "controlling" and "controlled" have meanings correlative to the foregoing. For purposes of Section 4.05, Section 4.06 and Section 4.09 only, "Affiliate" shall also mean any beneficial owner of Capital Stock representing [5] [10]% or more of the total voting power of the Voting Stock (on a fully diluted basis) of the Company or of rights or warrants to purchase such Capital Stock (whether or not currently exercisable) and any Person who would be an Affiliate of any such beneficial owner pursuant to the first sentence hereof.

* *Commentary*

The term "Affiliate" is used throughout the covenants and definitions. In most cases, the term is intended only to reach those Persons that are in a "control" or "common control" relationship with the Company, but as is suggested by the introductory phrase of the final sentence of the definition, there are certain situations in which the covenants seek to regulate activities between the Company and significant stockholders, whether or not the stockholder would also be viewed to be in a control relationship.

"**Asset Disposition**" means any sale, lease, transfer or other disposition (or series of related sales, leases, transfers or dispositions) by the Company or any Restricted Subsidiary, including any disposition by means of a merger, consolidation, Sale/Leaseback Transaction or similar transaction or by way of the issuance of Capital Stock of a Restricted Subsidiary (each referred to for the purposes of this definition as a "**disposition**"), of:

(1) any shares of Capital Stock of a Restricted Subsidiary (other than directors' qualifying shares or shares required by applicable law to be held by a Person other than the Company or a Restricted Subsidiary);

(2) all or substantially all the assets of any division or line of business of the Company or any Restricted Subsidiary; or

(3) any other assets of the Company or any Restricted Subsidiary outside of the ordinary course of business of the Company or such Restricted Subsidiary (other than, in the case of clauses (1), (2) and (3) above,

(A) a disposition by a Restricted Subsidiary to the Company or by the Company or a Restricted Subsidiary to a Wholly Owned Subsidiary (including a Person that will become a Wholly Owned Subsidiary immediately following such Asset Disposition);

(B) for purposes of Section 4.06 only, (x) a disposition that constitutes a Restricted Payment (or would constitute a Restricted Payment but for the exclusions from the definition thereof) and that is not prohibited by Section 4.05 and (y) a disposition of all or substantially all the assets of the Company in accordance with Section 4.14;

(C) a disposition of assets with a fair market value of less than $500,000;

(D) a disposition of cash or Temporary Cash Investments; and

(E) the creation of a Lien (but not the sale or other disposition of the property subject to such Lien)).

* *Commentary*

This definition is used primarily in the Limitation on Sales of Assets covenant. It is broadly drafted and is intended to pick up any dispositions outside the ordinary course of business. The five exceptions in (A)—(E) are customary, and Companies occasionally request other exceptions or carve outs from this definition for dispositions that are reasonably foreseeable by the Company (and which are disclosed) at the time the Securities are issued. Exceptions are also commonly requested to allow for sales of accounts receivable and related assets in connection with securitization arrangements (as in clause (8) of Alternative Example 1 and clauses (9) and (10) of Alternative Example 2 below). Exception (B) above allows the Company to ignore the Asset Sale covenant so long as, in connection with the disposition, the Company has complied with either the Restricted Payments covenant or the Merger covenant in situations where they are applicable.

Alternative Example 1:

"'Asset Disposition' means:

(1) the sale, lease, conveyance or other disposition of any assets or rights; provided that the sale, conveyance or other disposition of all or substantially all of the assets of the Company and its Restricted Subsidiaries taken as a whole will be governed by the provisions of Section 4.07 and/or the provisions of Section 4.14 and not by the provisions of Section 4.06; and

(2) the issuance of Capital Stock in any of the Company's Restricted Subsidiaries or the sale of Capital Stock in any of its Restricted Subsidiaries.

Notwithstanding the preceding, the following items will not be deemed to be Asset Dispositions:

(1) *any single transaction or series of related transactions that involves assets having a fair market value of less than $• million or for Net Available Cash of less than $•;*

(2) *a transfer of assets between or among the Company and its Restricted Subsidiaries;*

(3) *an issuance of Capital Stock by a Subsidiary to the Company or to a Restricted Subsidiary of the Company;*

(4) *the sale or lease of equipment, inventory, accounts receivable or other assets in the ordinary course of business;*

(5) *the sale or other disposition of cash or cash equivalents;*

(6) *a Restricted Payment or Permitted Investment that is permitted by Section 4.05;*

(7) *any sale of Capital Stock in, or Indebtedness or other securities of, an Unrestricted Subsidiary;*

(8) *a transfer of accounts receivable, or participations therein, and related rights and assets in connection with any Receivables Facility;*

(9) *sales of property or equipment that has become worn-out, obsolete or damaged or otherwise unsuitable for use in connection with the business of the Company or any of its Restricted Subsidiaries;*

(10) *the license of patents, trademarks, copyrights and know-how to third Persons in the ordinary course of business; and*

(11) *the creation of security interests otherwise permitted by the indenture, including a pledge of assets otherwise permitted by the indenture."*

Alternative Example 2:

"'Asset Disposition' means any sale, transfer or other disposition (including by merger, consolidation or sale-and-leaseback transaction) of:

(1) *shares of Capital Stock of a Restricted Subsidiary of the Company (other than directors' qualifying shares) or*

(2) *property or assets of the Company or any of its Restricted Subsidiaries.*

Notwithstanding the foregoing, an Asset Disposition shall not include:

(1) *any sale, transfer or other disposition of shares of Capital Stock, property or assets by a Restricted Subsidiary of the Company to the Company or to any Restricted Subsidiary of the Company;*

(2) *any sale, transfer or other disposition of defaulted receivables for collection or any sale, transfer or other disposition of property or assets in the ordinary course of business;*

(3) *any isolated sale, transfer or other disposition that does not (together with all related sales, transfers or dispositions) involve aggregate consideration in excess of $• million;*

(4) *the granting in the ordinary course of business of any license of patents, trademarks, registrations therefore and other similar intellectual property;*

(5) *the granting of any Lien (or foreclosure thereon) securing Indebtedness to the extent that such Lien is granted in compliance with Section 4.08 herein;*

(6) *any sale, transfer or other disposition constituting a Permitted Investment or Restricted Payment permitted by Section 4.05;*

(7) *any disposition of assets or property in the ordinary course of business to the extent such property or assets are obsolete, worn-out or no longer useful in the Company's or any of its Subsidiaries' business;*

(8) *the sale, lease, conveyance or disposition or other transfer of all or substantially all of the assets of the Company as permitted by Section 4.14;*

(9) *sales of accounts receivable and related assets (including contract rights) of the type specified in the definition of "Qualified Securitization Transaction" to a Securitization Subsidiary; and*

(10) *transfers of accounts receivable and related assets (including contract rights) of the type specified in the definition of "Qualified Securitization Transaction" (or a fractional undivided interest therein) by a Securitization Subsidiary in a Qualified Securitization Transaction."*

The two alternatives do not differ substantially from the model covenant in any material respect. The model covenant has the benefit of including only transactions outside the ordinary course of business, thereby obviating the need for numerous exceptions for transactions that are clearly in the ordinary course of business for most companies. Alternative No. 1 specifically excludes the sale of Capital Stock of an Unrestricted Subsidiary—the theory behind that exclusion is that since the Unrestricted Subsidiary is not limited by the indenture in freely selling all its assets, the covenants should allow the Company the flexibility to structure a transaction as the sale of stock of the Unrestricted Subsidiary instead, since the economic effect on the holders will be the same.

"***Attributable Debt***" in respect of a Sale/Leaseback Transaction means, as at the time of determination, the present value (discounted at the interest rate borne by the Securities, compounded annually) of the total obligations of the lessee for rental payments during the remaining term of the lease included in such Sale/Leaseback Transaction (including any period for which such lease has been extended); provided, however, that if such Sale/Leaseback Transaction results in a Capital Lease Obligation, the amount of Indebtedness represented thereby will be determined in accordance with the definition of "Capital Lease Obligation."

"***Average Life***" means, as of the date of determination, with respect to any Indebtedness, the quotient obtained by dividing:

(1) the sum of the products of the numbers of years from the date of determination to the dates of each successive scheduled principal payment of or redemption or similar payment with respect to such Indebtedness multiplied by the amount of such payment by

(2) the sum of all such payments.

"***Board***" means the Board of Directors of the Company or any committee thereof.

"***Capital Lease Obligation***" means an obligation that is required to be classified and accounted for as a capital lease for financial reporting purposes in accordance with GAAP, and the amount of Indebtedness represented by such obligation shall be the capitalized amount of such obligation determined in accordance with GAAP; and the Stated Maturity thereof shall be the date of the last payment of rent or any other amount due under such lease prior to the first date upon which such lease may be terminated by the lessee without payment of a penalty. For purposes of Section 4.08, a Capital Lease Obligation will be deemed to be secured by a Lien on the property being leased.

* *Commentary*

The clause after the semi-colon in the first sentence of the foregoing definition allows the Company to treat the capital lease as maturing earlier than the actual end date of the lease if it can terminate the lease earlier than the end date without a penalty. This may help the Company in structuring the terms (including the maturity of) indebtedness incurred at a later date to refinance the capital lease.

"**Capital Stock**" of any Person means any and all shares, interests (including general or limited partnership interests, limited liability company interests or limited liability partnership interests), rights to purchase, warrants, options, participations or other equivalents of or interests in (however designated) equity of such Person, including any Preferred Stock, but excluding any debt securities convertible into such equity.

* *Commentary*

The foregoing definition is very inclusive, such that almost any instrument that is exercisable for or exchangeable into the equity security of a Person is considered Capital Stock. The ramifications of this treatment will be most profound in the Limitation on Restricted Payments covenant. The one notable exception in the definition is for convertible debt, regardless of ranking. Hence, the acquisition by a Company of its own convertible debt would not be a Restricted Payment, unless of course such debt fits within the definition of "Subordinated Obligation."

"**Change of Control**" means the occurrence of any one of the following:

(1) prior to the earlier to occur of (A) the first public offering of common stock of Parent or (B) the first public offering of common stock of the Company, the Permitted Holders cease to be the "beneficial owner" (as defined in Rules 13d-3 and 13d-5 under the Exchange Act), directly or indirectly, of a majority in the aggregate of the total voting power of the Voting Stock of the Company, whether as a result of issuance of securities of the Parent or the Company, any merger, consolidation, liquidation or dissolution of the Parent or the Company, or any direct or indirect transfer of securities by Parent or otherwise (for purposes of this clause (1) and clause (2) below, the Permitted Holders shall be deemed to beneficially own any Voting Stock of a Person (the "**specified person**") held by any other Person (the "**parent entity**") so long as the Permitted Holders beneficially own (as so defined), directly or indirectly, in the aggregate a majority of the voting power of the Voting Stock of the parent entity);

* *Commentary*

This first clause of the definition provides that, with respect to a Company that is not a public company, if a designated group of controlling shareholders (the so-called "Permitted Holders") fails to continue to own a majority of the outstanding Voting Stock of the Company, a change of control has occurred. The Permitted Holders will usually be the majority shareholder, if there is a single such shareholder, or a group of shareholders that at the time of the issuance of the Securities collectively own a majority of the Voting Stock of the Company. The underlying theory is that the Securityholders have made an investment decision based upon an evaluation of the skill and characteristics of the controlling shareholders and their managers at the time of the investment, and if such controlling shareholders fail to continue to hold that controlling position (which in a private company context is assumed to be a majority), then the Securityholders should be entitled to put their Securities back to the Company (typically at a price of 101% of principal).

(2) any "person" (as such term is used in Sections 13(d) and 14(d) of the Exchange Act), other than one or more Permitted Holders, is or becomes the beneficial owner (as defined in clause (1) above, except that for purposes of this clause (2) such person shall be deemed to have "beneficial ownership" of all shares that any such person has the right to acquire, whether such right is exercisable immediately or only after the passage of time), directly or indirectly, of more than 35% of the total voting power of the Voting Stock of the Company; provided, however, that the Permitted Holders beneficially own (as defined in clause (1) above), directly or indirectly, in the aggregate a lesser percentage of the total voting power of the Voting Stock of the Company than such other person and do not have the right or ability by voting power, contract or otherwise to elect or designate for election a majority of the Board (for the purposes of this clause (2), such other person shall be deemed to beneficially own any Voting Stock of a specified person held by a parent entity, if such other person is the beneficial owner (as defined in this clause (2)), directly or indirectly, of more than 35% of the voting power of the Voting Stock of such parent entity and the Permitted Holders beneficially own (as defined in clause (1) above), directly or indirectly, in the aggregate a lesser percentage of the voting power of the Voting Stock of such parent entity and do not have the right or ability by voting power, contract or otherwise to elect or designate for election a majority of the board of directors of such parent entity);

* *Commentary*

*The second described event is similar to the first, except that it applies in a public company context. Once the Company is public, the Permitted Holders are entitled to fall below 50% and in fact could fall all the way to zero in terms of percentage ownership, without triggering a change of control. A change of control under this prong occurs only if persons other than the Permitted Holders acquire (typically) "beneficial ownership" of 35% or more of the Voting Stock of the Company **and** the Permitted Holders own a lesser percentage **and** the Permitted Holders do not have the right, by contract or otherwise, to elect or designate a majority of the members of the Board. In situations where the Company has a parent corporation, the foregoing two prongs of the definition also requires an analysis of the stockholdings of the parent.*

Some have questioned whether it is fair to the Company to expand, as this definition does in clause (2) above, the definition of "beneficial ownership" beyond its common SEC meaning so that it includes having the right to acquire voting securities regardless of the duration of the exercise period of the option (the SEC rules only charge a person with beneficial ownership if such person's option to acquire the relevant securities is exercisable within 60 days of the relevant date of determination). (Most indenture forms follow the construct set out in the Model definition above.) While a Company may argue that no change of control occurs if a third party acquires an option, exercisable one year after the option grant, to purchase 35% of the Voting Stock of the Company, to date the market seems to have taken the opposite view. The theory is that a third party with such an option has the implicit power to direct the future policies of the Company, at least to such an extent that a creditor (i.e., the Securityholders) may wish to have an opportunity to reevaluate its investment in the Company.

An alternative to the multiple-trigger approach set forth above provides that if any third party (other than the Permitted Holders, if any) acquires a specified percentage of voting control (regardless of the holdings of the Permitted Holders), then a change of control has occurred. For example:

Alternative Example:

"( ) any 'person' (as such term is used in Sections 13(d) and 14(d) of the Exchange Act), other than one or more Permitted Holders, is or becomes the beneficial owner (as such term is defined in Rules 13(d)-3 and 13(d)-5 of the Exchange Act, except that for purposes of this clause (2) such Person shall be deemed to have 'beneficial ownership' of all shares that any such person has the right to acquire, whether such right is exercisable immediately or only after the passage of time), directly or indirectly, of more than 50% of the total voting power of the Voting Stock of the Company; provided that if such person is a group of investors which group includes one or more Permitted Holders, the shares of Voting Stock of the Company beneficially owned by the Permitted Holders that are part of such group shall not be counted for purposes of determining whether this clause ( ) is triggered;"

(3) [at any time after the first public offering of common stock of the Company or Parent, as the case may be,] individuals who on the Issue Date constituted the Board (together with any new directors whose election by such Board or whose nomination for election by the shareholders of the Company was approved by a vote of a majority of the directors of the Company then still in office who were either directors on the Issue Date or whose election or nomination for election was previously so approved or who were elected with the consent of the Permitted Holders) cease for any reason to constitute a majority of the Board of Directors then in office;

* Commentary

The foregoing event is designed to pick up the occurrence of a contested proxy fight where there may not be a change in ownership of the stock of the Company, but a new group of stockholders has gained control of the Board. The bracketed language is not included in all forms. Under some indentures, the foregoing provision is limited to changes that occur over a specified period of time. For example, the provision may provide that there is not a change of control unless the foregoing change in board membership occurs during any period of two consecutive years.

In some covenant forms, this provision is drafted to encompass situations in which the existing Board approves the election of new directors in the context of a threat of a proxy fight. For example:

"(3) the following individuals cease for any reason to constitute more than [two-thirds] [majority] of the number of directors then serving on the Board: individuals who, on the Issue Date, constitute the Board and any new director (other than a director whose initial assumption of the office is in connection with an actual or threatened election contest, including but not limited to a consent solicitation, relating to the election of directors of the Company) whose appointment or election by the Board or nomination for election by the Company's stockholders was approved by the vote of at least a majority of the directors then still in office or whose appointment, election or nomination was previously so approved or recommended";

(4) the adoption of a plan relating to the liquidation or dissolution of the Company; or

(5) the merger or consolidation of the Company with or into another Person or the merger of another Person with or into the Company, or the sale of all or substantially all

the assets of the Company (determined on a consolidated basis) to another Person other than (i) a transaction in which the survivor or transferee is a Person that is controlled by the Permitted Holders or (ii) a transaction following which (A) in the case of a merger or consolidation transaction, holders of securities that represented 100% of the Voting Stock of the Company immediately prior to such transaction (or other securities into which such securities are converted as part of such merger or consolidation transaction) own directly or indirectly at least a majority of the voting power of the Voting Stock of the surviving Person in such merger or consolidation transaction immediately after such transaction and in substantially the same proportion as before the transaction and (B) in the case of a sale of assets transaction, each transferee becomes an obligor in respect of the Securities and a Subsidiary of the transferor of such assets.

* *Commentary*

This final provision of the definition, which is included in most but not all indentures, may require a change of control offer even if the transaction complies with the Merger covenant. It addresses a transaction in which the Company is involved in a merger transaction in which the shareholders of the other company in the transaction become the majority shareholders of the surviving company. Assuming that there is no single shareholder (or group of shareholders) of the surviving company that would trip the 35% (or 50%) level after giving effect to the merger, this situation would not otherwise trigger a change of control under the second prong above. However, a transaction of such magnitude, where the Company has effectively been acquired, is a significant corporate event for the Company. Thus, this type of event is included in the change of control provisions of the indenture, even though no change of control (as the term may be commonly construed) actually occurs.

The exception described in clause (ii)(A) above, under some covenant forms, does not require that voting control be held in substantially the same proportion as it was prior to the transaction, so long as voting control is maintained in the aggregate by the original controlling group. Note also in the language above that voting control after the merger can be measured "directly or indirectly," so that if the parties use a subsidiary to effect the merger as opposed to completing a direct merger, no change of control would occur under this clause (5) if the shareholders of the pre-merger Company hold a majority of the voting securities of the survivor or the survivor's parent.

In clause (ii)(B), a sale of assets transaction will not be treated as a change of control if the Company sells the assets and takes back as consideration a majority voting position in the transferee. In such a case, the transferee becomes the "Company" by assuming the indenture obligations, but the transferor and its shareholders remain in control, so no change of control has occurred. In any other sale of assets transaction covered by the definition, control passes to the shareholder of the transferee, triggering the change of control offer. In 2000, a Minnesota court, applying New York law in interpreting a provision similar to clause (ii)(B) but which covered not only sales but also conveyances and transfers of all or substantially all the assets of the Company, concluded that the non-exclusive license by the Company of the Company's valuable patents was a "transfer" that, because of the relative value of the patents versus the Company's other assets, triggered the Company's obligation to make a change of control offer. U.S. Bank Nat'l Ass'n v. Angeion Corp., 615 N.W.2d 425 (Minn. 2000).

"*Consolidated Coverage Ratio*" as of any date of determination means the ratio of (x) the aggregate amount of Consolidated EBITDA for the period of the most recent four consecutive fiscal quarters ending at least 45 days prior to the date of such determination to (y) Consolidated Interest Expense for such four fiscal quarters; provided, however, that:

(1) if the Company or any Restricted Subsidiary has Incurred any Indebtedness since the beginning of such period that remains outstanding or if the transaction giving rise to the need to calculate the Consolidated Coverage Ratio is an Incurrence of Indebtedness, or both, Consolidated EBITDA and Consolidated Interest Expense for such period shall be calculated after giving effect on a pro forma basis to such Indebtedness as if such Indebtedness had been Incurred on the first day of such period; provided, however, that the pro forma calculation of Consolidated Interest Expense shall not give effect to any Indebtedness Incurred on the date of determination pursuant to Section 4.04(b);

(2) if the Company or any Restricted Subsidiary has repaid, repurchased, defeased or otherwise discharged any Indebtedness since the beginning of such period or if any Indebtedness is to be repaid, repurchased, defeased or otherwise discharged (in each case other than Indebtedness Incurred under any revolving credit facility unless such Indebtedness has been permanently repaid and has not been replaced) on the date of the transaction giving rise to the need to calculate the Consolidated Coverage Ratio, Consolidated EBITDA and Consolidated Interest Expense for such period shall be calculated on a pro forma basis as if such discharge had occurred on the first day of such period; provided, however, that the pro forma calculation of Consolidated Interest Expense shall not give effect to the discharge on the date of determination of any Indebtedness to the extent such discharge results from the proceeds of Indebtedness Incurred pursuant to Section 4.04(b);

(3) if since the beginning of such period the Company or any Restricted Subsidiary shall have made any Asset Disposition, Consolidated EBITDA for such period shall be reduced by an amount equal to Consolidated EBITDA (if positive) directly attributable to the assets which are the subject of such Asset Disposition for such period, or increased by an amount equal to Consolidated EBITDA (if negative), directly attributable thereto for such period and Consolidated Interest Expense for such period shall be reduced by an amount equal to the Consolidated Interest Expense directly attributable to any Indebtedness of the Company or any Restricted Subsidiary repaid, repurchased, defeased or otherwise discharged with respect to the Company and its continuing Restricted Subsidiaries in connection with such Asset Disposition for such period (or, if the Capital Stock of any Restricted Subsidiary is sold, the Consolidated Interest Expense for such period directly attributable to the Indebtedness of such Restricted Subsidiary to the extent the Company and its continuing Restricted Subsidiaries are no longer liable for such Indebtedness after such sale);

(4) if since the beginning of such period the Company or any Restricted Subsidiary (by merger or otherwise) shall have made an Investment in any Restricted Subsidiary (or any Person which becomes a Restricted Subsidiary) or an acquisition of assets, including any acquisition of assets occurring in connection with a transaction requiring a calculation to be made hereunder, which constitutes all or substantially all of an operating unit of a business, Consolidated EBITDA and Consolidated Interest Expense for such period shall be calculated after giving pro forma effect thereto (including the Incurrence of any Indebtedness) as if such Investment or acquisition had occurred on the first day of such period; and

(5) if since the beginning of such period any Person (that subsequently became a Restricted Subsidiary or was merged with or into the Company or any Restricted

Subsidiary since the beginning of such period) shall have made any Asset Disposition, any Investment or acquisition of assets that would have required an adjustment pursuant to clause (3) or (4) above if made by the Company or a Restricted Subsidiary during such period, Consolidated EBITDA and Consolidated Interest Expense for such period shall be calculated after giving pro forma effect thereto as if such Asset Disposition, Investment or acquisition had occurred on the first day of such period.

For purposes of this definition, whenever pro forma effect is to be given to an acquisition of assets, the amount of income or earnings relating thereto and the amount of Consolidated Interest Expense associated with any Indebtedness Incurred in connection therewith, the pro forma calculations shall be made in compliance with Article 11 of Regulation S-X, as determined in good faith by a responsible financial or accounting officer of the Company. If any Indebtedness bears a floating rate of interest and is being given pro forma effect, the interest on such Indebtedness shall be calculated as if the rate in effect on the date of determination had been the applicable rate for the entire period (taking into account any Interest Rate Agreement applicable to such Indebtedness if such Interest Rate Agreement has a remaining term in excess of 12 months). If any Indebtedness is incurred under a revolving credit facility and is being given pro forma effect, the interest on such Indebtedness shall be calculated based on the average daily balance of such Indebtedness for the four fiscal quarters subject to the pro forma calculation to the extent that such Indebtedness was incurred solely for working capital purposes.

* *Commentary*

In calculating the Company's Consolidated Coverage Ratio, the foregoing definition looks back over the preceding four fiscal quarters to give effect on a pro forma basis to the incurrence of the proposed indebtedness and any other incurrences or repayments of indebtedness as if such incurrences and repayments had occurred at the beginning of such period. Similarly, the definition gives the Company credit for Investments that have had the effect of adding Consolidated EBITDA during the course of the preceding four fiscal quarters, as well as subtracting Consolidated EBITDA that may have been attributable to a Restricted Subsidiary or line of business that may have been disposed of during the course of the year; again, those transactions are given pro forma effect as if they had occurred at the beginning of the four fiscal quarter period.

Please see the Commentary to Section 4.04(a) for a discussion of the provisos to clauses (1) and (2) above.

Article 11 of Regulation S-X generally permits adjustments only for items that are relatively certain to occur. For example, under that article, pro forma effect could not be given to cost savings that result from planned layoffs in connection with an acquisition unless the layoffs had been carried out and, even then, probably only if they were contemplated by the terms of the acquisition contract. The approach of tying permissible adjustments to Regulation S-X places some parameters around allowable adjustments, though significant room for management judgment as to what adjustments are consistent with the regulation remains.

Some covenant forms permit the Company to make pro forma adjustments to exclude the results of operations that have been discontinued (as defined under GAAP) during the relevant period. Such a formulation would permit the Company to exclude for the entire calculation period the costs of plants that were closed at any time since the beginning of the calculation period.

Alternative Example:

"'Consolidated Coverage Ratio' means the ratio of Consolidated EBITDA during the most recent four consecutive full fiscal quarters for which financial statements are available (the 'Four-Quarter Period') ending on or prior to the date of the transaction giving rise to the need to calculate the Consolidated Coverage Ratio (the 'Transaction Date') to Consolidated Interest Expense for the Four-Quarter Period. For purposes of this definition, Consolidated EBITDA and Consolidated Interest Expense shall be calculated after giving effect on a pro forma basis for the period of such calculation to:

(1) the incurrence of any Indebtedness or the issuance of any Preferred Stock of the Company or any Restricted Subsidiary (and the application of the proceeds thereof) and any repayment of other Indebtedness or redemption of other Preferred Stock (and the application of the proceeds therefrom) (other than the incurrence or repayment of Indebtedness in the ordinary course of business for working capital purposes pursuant to any revolving credit arrangement) occurring during the Four-Quarter Period or at any time subsequent to the last day of the Four-Quarter Period and on or prior to the Transaction Date, as if such incurrence, issuance, repayment, or redemption, as the case may be (and the application of the proceeds therefrom), had occurred on the first day of the Four-Quarter Period; and

(2) any Asset Disposition or other disposition or Asset Acquisition (including any Asset Acquisition giving rise to the need to make such calculation as a result of the Company or any Restricted Subsidiary (including any Person who becomes a Restricted Subsidiary as a result of such Asset Acquisition) incurring Acquired Indebtedness and also including any Consolidated EBITDA (including any pro forma expense and cost reductions calculated on a basis consistent with Regulation S-X under the Securities Act) associated with any such Asset Acquisition) occurring during the Four-Quarter Period or at any time subsequent to the last day of the Four-Quarter Period and on or prior to the Transaction Date, as if such Asset Sale or Asset Acquisition or other disposition (including the incurrence of, or assumption or liability for, any such Indebtedness or Acquired Indebtedness) had occurred on the first day of the Four-Quarter Period.

If the Company or any Restricted Subsidiary directly or indirectly guarantees Indebtedness of a third Person, the preceding sentence shall give effect to the incurrence of such guaranteed Indebtedness as if the Company or such Restricted Subsidiary had directly incurred or otherwise assumed such guaranteed Indebtedness.

For purposes of this definition, whenever pro forma effect is to be given to an Asset Acquisition, the amount of income or earnings relating thereto and the amount of Consolidated Interest Expense associated with Indebtedness incurred in connection therewith shall be based upon the reasonable good faith determination of the Chief Financial Officer of the Company.

In calculating Consolidated Interest Expense for purposes of determining the denominator (but not the numerator) of this Consolidated Coverage Ratio:

(1) interest on outstanding Indebtedness determined on a fluctuating basis as of the Transaction Date and which will continue to be so determined thereafter shall be deemed to have accrued at a fixed rate per annum equal to the rate of interest on this Indebtedness in effect on the Transaction Date;

(2) if interest on any Indebtedness actually incurred on the Transaction Date may option-ally be determined at an interest rate based upon a factor of a prime or similar rate, a Euro-currency interbank offered rate, or other rates, then the interest rate in effect on the Transaction Date will be deemed to have been in effect during the Four-Quarter Period; and

(3) notwithstanding clause (1) or (2) above, interest on Indebtedness determined on a fluctuating basis, to the extent such interest is covered by agreements relating to Hedging Obligations, shall be deemed to accrue at the rate per annum resulting after giving effect to the operation of these agreements."

The foregoing example employs the Regulation S-X formulation described above. In addition, note that the adjustments described in the immediately foregoing clauses (1) through (3) apply only to Consolidated Interest Expense as it is used in the denominator in calculating Consolidated Coverage Ratio, and not to Consolidated Interest Expense as it is added to Consolidated Net Income to arrive at Consolidated EBITDA, which is the numerator of the Ratio. Lastly, note that this example provides for pro forma adjustments to give effect to issuances and redemptions of preferred stock (dividends with respect to which are included in the calculation of Consolidated Interest Expense).

"Consolidated EBITDA" for any period means the sum of Consolidated Net Income, plus the following to the extent deducted in calculating such Consolidated Net Income:

(1) all income tax expense of the Company and its consolidated Restricted Subsidiaries;

(2) Consolidated Interest Expense;

(3) depreciation and amortization expense of the Company and its consolidated Restricted Subsidiaries (excluding amortization expense attributable to a prepaid oper-ating expense that was paid in cash in a prior period); and

(4) all other non-cash charges of the Company and its consolidated Restricted Subsidiaries (excluding any such non-cash charge to the extent that it represents an accrual of or reserve for cash expenditures in any future period);

in each case for such period. Notwithstanding the foregoing, the provision for taxes based on the income or profits of, and the depreciation and amortization and non-cash charges of, a Restricted Subsidiary shall be added to Consolidated Net Income to compute Consolidated EBITDA only to the extent (and in the same proportion, including by reason of minority interests) that the net income or loss of such Restricted Subsidiary was included in calculating Consolidated Net Income and only if a corresponding amount would be permitted at the date of determination to be dividended to the Company by such Restricted Subsidiary without prior approval (that has not been obtained), pursuant to the terms of its charter and all agreements, instruments, judgments, decrees, orders, statutes, rules and governmental regulations applicable to such Restricted Subsidiary or its stockholders.

* **Commentary**

The definition of Consolidated EBITDA is used in calculating the Company's debt coverage for purposes of the Limitation on Indebtedness covenant, and picks up the typi-cal items that would be included in such definition ("EBITDA" stands for "earnings before interest, taxes, depreciation and amortization"), but also typically entitles the Company to add back to net income other non-cash charges that it might have recognized in the relevant period. Often, covenant forms will provide for additional add-backs (including cash expenses) to income to recognize items that arguably have little bearing on the Company's ability to pay cash interest on its indebtedness in the future. Examples include charges/expenses relating to acquisitions, dispositions, restructurings or other events that occur infrequently. Covenant forms also sometimes provide that Consolidated EBITDA will be reduced by the amount of non-cash gains that were added in arriving at Consolidated Net Income, in order to get a more accurate measure of the Company's actual cash flow available for debt service. For example:

"'Consolidated EBITDA' means, with respect to any specified Person for any period, the Consolidated Net Income of such Person for such period plus:

(1) an amount equal to any extraordinary loss plus any net loss realized by such Person or any of its Restricted Subsidiaries in connection with an Asset Disposition, to the extent such losses were deducted in computing such Consolidated Net Income; plus

(2) provision for taxes based on income or profits of such Person and its Restricted Subsidiaries for such period, to the extent that such provision for taxes was deducted in computing such Consolidated Net Income; plus

(3) consolidated interest expense of such Person and its Restricted Subsidiaries for such period, whether paid or accrued and whether or not capitalized (including amortization of debt issuance costs and original issue discount, non-cash interest payments, the interest component of any deferred payment obligations, the interest component of all payments associated with Capital Lease Obligations, imputed interest with respect to Attributable Debt, commissions, discounts and other fees and charges incurred in respect of letter of credit or bankers' acceptance financings, and net of the effect of all payments made or received pursuant to Hedging Obligations), to the extent that any such expense was deducted in computing such Consolidated Net Income; plus

(4) depreciation, amortization (including amortization of goodwill and other intangibles but excluding amortization of prepaid cash expenses that were paid in a prior period) and other non-cash expenses (excluding any such non-cash expense to the extent that it represents an accrual of or reserve for cash expenses in any future period or amortization of a prepaid cash expense that was paid in a prior period) of such Person and its Restricted Subsidiaries for such period to the extent that such depreciation, amortization and other non-cash expenses were deducted in computing such Consolidated Net Income; minus

(5) non-cash items increasing such Consolidated Net Income for such period, other than the accrual of revenue in the ordinary course of business, in each case, on a consolidated basis and determined in accordance with GAAP."

For purposes of this example, "Consolidated Net Income" was defined to include losses from asset dispositions and extraordinary losses (see, the Commentary to clauses (4) and (5) of the definition of "Consolidated Net Income," below). Clause (1) of this example has the effect of adjusting for such losses. Therefore, under this alternative example, these charges are disregarded in calculating the Company's Consolidated Coverage Ratio, the same result as if the Model definitions of "Consolidated EBITDA" and "Consolidated Net Income" are used in tandem.

Note also that, in this example, the "interest" component (clause (3)) is narrower than the definition of Consolidated Interest Expense, which includes preferred stock dividends. Therefore, in calculating the Consolidated Coverage Ratio, preferred stock dividends are not added back to the numerator, but are added to the fixed charge measure (Consolidated Interest Expense) that comprises the denominator.

"Consolidated Interest Expense" means, for any period, the total interest expense of the Company and its consolidated Restricted Subsidiaries, plus, to the extent not included in such total interest expense, and to the extent incurred by the Company or its Restricted Subsidiaries, without duplication:

* *Commentary*

This definition is one on which a Company should devote significant attention. The high yield market has traditionally required a Company to take into account as interest expense not only cash interest expense but also non-cash interest expense. Nonetheless, there are many examples of indentures where some of the non-cash items below, which are not otherwise picked up as interest under GAAP, are not included in the definition of Consolidated Interest Expense.

    (1) interest expense attributable to Capital Lease Obligations;
    (2) amortization of debt discount and debt issuance cost;
    (3) capitalized interest;

* *Commentary*

Capitalized interest, which is typically interest on debt incurred to finance a construction project, is not "interest expense" under GAAP but rather is added to the basis of the project assets, thereby increasing depreciation or amortization expense in future periods. Whether or not capitalized interest is included in the definition of "Consolidated Interest Expense" is often negotiated. Arguably, capitalized interest is just a part of the cost of the asset being constructed and the covenants should not distinguish between the situation where the Company purchases the completed assets (and thus pays no capitalized interest) and where the Company constructs the asset (and pays interest on the Indebtedness incurred to finance construction).

    (4) non-cash interest expense;
    (5) commissions, discounts and other fees and charges owed with respect to letters of credit and bankers' acceptance financing;
    (6) net payments pursuant to Interest Rate Agreements;
    (7) dividends accrued in respect of all Preferred Stock held by Persons other than the Company or a Wholly Owned Subsidiary (other than dividends payable solely in Capital Stock (other than Disqualified Stock) of the Company); **provided, however,** that such dividends will be multiplied by a fraction, the numerator of which is one and the denominator of which is one minus the effective combined tax rate of the issuer of such Preferred Stock (expressed as a decimal) for such period (as estimated by the chief financial officer of the Company in good faith);

* *Commentary*

Preferred stock dividends, even if not related to Disqualified Stock, are often counted as part of consolidated interest expense. As a result, the ratio resembles more of a "fixed charge ratio" rather than a true interest coverage ratio. The foregoing clause also recognizes that since the dividend is not tax deductible to the Company (therefore making the dividend more expensive to the Company than a corresponding interest payment), the

Company should be required to include as interest expense a grossed-up amount of the dividend to reflect the lack of tax benefit. A good argument can be made, however, that a Company with substantial net operating loss carry forwards would be indifferent from a tax perspective to the payment of interest or dividends, and therefore should not be required to gross up its dividend payments to account for a lack of tax benefit that in fact is not relevant.

(8) interest incurred in connection with Investments in discontinued operations;

* *Commentary*

As noted above, some covenant forms allow a Company to give pro forma effect to the discontinuance of operations for purposes of calculating the Consolidated Coverage Ratio. In such cases, it would not make sense to include the foregoing item as part of interest expense. Many indentures do not, however, allow a pro forma calculation for the mere discontinuance (as opposed to actual disposition) of operations, in which case the Company should be charged, in calculating Consolidated Interest Expense, for any interest expense associated with such operations until they are in fact sold or the related debt is discharged.

(9) interest accruing on any Indebtedness of any other Person to the extent such Indebtedness is Guaranteed by (or secured by the assets of) the Company or any Restricted Subsidiary; and

(10) the cash contributions to any employee stock ownership plan or similar trust to the extent such contributions are used by such plan or trust to pay interest or fees to any Person (other than the Company) in connection with Indebtedness Incurred by such plan or trust.

* *Commentary*

Alternative Example:

"'Consolidated Interest Expense' means, with respect to any specified Person for any period, the sum, without duplication, of:

(1) the consolidated interest expense of such Person and its Restricted Subsidiaries for such period, whether paid or accrued, including amortization of debt issuance costs and original issue discount, non-cash interest payments, the interest component of any deferred payment obligations, imputed interest with respect to Attributable Debt, commissions, discounts and other fees and charges incurred in respect of letter of credit or bankers' acceptance financings, and net of the effect of all payments made or received pursuant to Interest Rate Agreements; plus

(2) the consolidated interest of such Person and its Restricted Subsidiaries that was capitalized during such period; plus

(3) any interest expense on Indebtedness of another Person that is Guaranteed by such Person or any of its Restricted Subsidiaries or secured by a Lien on assets of such Person or any of its Restricted Subsidiaries, whether or not such Guarantee or Lien is called upon; plus

(4) the product of (a) all dividends, whether paid or accrued and whether or not in cash, on any series of preferred stock of such Person or any of its Restricted Subsidiaries,

other than dividends on Capital Stock payable solely in Capital Stock of the Company (other than Disqualified Stock) or to the Company or a Restricted Subsidiary of the Company, times (b) a fraction, the numerator of which is one and the denominator of which is one minus the then current combined federal, state and local statutory tax rate of such Person, (expressed as a decimal), in each case, on a consolidated basis and in accordance with GAAP."

Clause (1) of the Alternative includes "imputed interest" on Attributable Debt. "Attributable Debt" is the debt equivalent of amounts payable under an operating lease arising out of a Sale/Leaseback transaction. Traditionally, high yield indentures do not restrict payments under operating leases. The reason for treating such an operating lease as debt and including the interest portion of the operating lease payments in Consolidated Interest Expense is that a Sale/Leaseback arguably is more akin to a financing rather than an ordinary course lease. Sometimes, the lease in a Sale/Leaseback constitutes a capitalized lease under GAAP, in which case the interest portion of the lease payment would constitute interest expense under either formulation of this definition. A significant number of indentures do not include this clause (1).

"Consolidated Leverage Ratio" as of any date of determination means the ratio of (x) the aggregate amount of Indebtedness of the Company and its Restricted Subsidiaries as of such date of determination to (y) Consolidated EBITDA for the most recent four consecutive fiscal quarters ending at least 45 days prior to such date of determination (the "**Reference Period**"); provided, however, that:

(1) if the transaction giving rise to the need to calculate the Consolidated Leverage Ratio is an Incurrence of Indebtedness, the amount of such Indebtedness shall be calculated after giving effect on a pro forma basis to such Indebtedness; provided, however, that the pro forma calculation of Indebtedness shall not give effect to any Indebtedness Incurred on the date of determination pursuant to Section 4.04(b);

(2) if the Company or any Restricted Subsidiary has repaid, repurchased, defeased or otherwise discharged any Indebtedness that was outstanding as of the end of the Reference Period or if any Indebtedness is to be repaid, repurchased, defeased or otherwise discharged on the date of the transaction giving rise to the need to calculate the Consolidated Leverage Ratio (other than, in each case, Indebtedness Incurred under any revolving credit agreement), the aggregate amount of Indebtedness shall be calculated on a pro forma basis; provided, however, that the pro forma calculation of Indebtedness shall not give effect to the discharge on the date of determination of any Indebtedness to the extent such discharge results from the proceeds of Indebtedness Incurred pursuant to Section 4.04(b);

(3) if since the beginning of the Reference Period the Company or any Restricted Subsidiary shall have made any Asset Disposition, the Consolidated EBITDA for the Reference Period shall be reduced by an amount equal to the Consolidated EBITDA (if positive) directly attributable to the assets which are the subject of such Asset Disposition for the Reference Period or increased by an amount equal to the Consolidated EBITDA (if negative) directly attributable thereto for the Reference Period;

(4) if since the beginning of the Reference Period the Company or any Restricted Subsidiary (by merger or otherwise) shall have made an Investment in any Restricted Subsidiary (or any Person which becomes a Restricted Subsidiary) or other acquisition of assets which constitutes all or substantially all of an operating unit of a business, Consolidated EBITDA for the Reference Period shall be calculated after giving pro forma effect thereto (including the Incurrence of any Indebtedness) as if such Investment or acquisition occurred on the first day of the Reference Period; and

(5) if since the beginning of the Reference Period any Person (that subsequently became a Restricted Subsidiary or was merged with or into the Company or any Restricted Subsidiary since the beginning of such Reference Period) shall have made any Asset Disposition, any Investment or acquisition of assets that would have required an adjustment pursuant to clause (3) or (4) above if made by the Company or a Restricted Subsidiary during the Reference Period, Consolidated EBITDA for the Reference Period shall be calculated after giving pro forma effect thereto as if such Asset Disposition, Investment or acquisition had occurred on the first day of the Reference Period.

For purposes of this definition, whenever pro forma effect is to be given to an acquisition of assets, the amount of income or earnings relating thereto and the amount of Consolidated Interest Expense associated with any Indebtedness Incurred in connection therewith, the pro forma calculations shall be made in compliance with Article 11 of Regulation S-X, as determined in good faith by a responsible financial or accounting officer of the Company. If any Indebtedness bears a floating rate of interest and is being given pro forma effect, the interest on such Indebtedness shall be calculated as if the rate in effect on the date of determination had been the applicable rate for the entire period (taking into account any Interest Rate Agreement applicable to such Indebtedness if such Interest Rate Agreement has a remaining term in excess of 12 months). If any Indebtedness is incurred under a revolving credit facility and is being given pro forma effect, the interest on such Indebtedness shall be calculated based on the average daily balance of such Indebtedness for the four fiscal quarters subject to the pro forma calculation to the extent such Indebtedness was incurred solely for working capital purposes.

* Commentary

This definition will not be used unless the leverage test is being employed in paragraph (a) of "Limitation on Indebtedness" in lieu of the coverage test. If this definition is used, the definition of "Consolidated Coverage Ratio" will not be used. The choice between whether the leverage test or the coverage test is contained in an indenture tends to be based on the issuer's industry and the expectations of the high yield market for issuers in that industry. The leverage test is more frequently employed, for example, for issuers in the media and telecommunications industries. See the discussion below.

"Consolidated Net Income" means, for any period, the net income of the Company and its consolidated Subsidiaries; provided, however, that there shall not be included in such Consolidated Net Income:

(1) any net income of any Person (other than the Company) if such Person is not a Restricted Subsidiary, except that:

(A) subject to the exclusion contained in clause (4) below, the Company's equity in the net income of any such Person for such period shall be included in such Consolidated Net Income up to the aggregate amount of cash actually distributed by such Person during such period to the Company or a Restricted Subsidiary as a dividend or other distribution (subject, in the case of a dividend or other distribution paid to a Restricted Subsidiary, to the limitations contained in clause (3) below); and

(B) the Company's equity in a net loss of any such Person for such period shall be included in determining such Consolidated Net Income;

* *Commentary*

Subsection (1) above allows the Company to include in "Consolidated Net Income" the net income of an Unrestricted Subsidiary or of any "investee" company (i.e., a minority interest investment or 50%-owned joint venture) only to the extent cash is actually received by the Company or one of its Restricted Subsidiaries. This limitation recognizes that the Company does not have free access to its attributable share of the net income of such entities and therefore it should not be entitled to a full credit for such net income, but only for the cash it actually receives.

The scope of the foregoing provision is sometimes drafted to include, in addition to entities that are not Restricted Subsidiaries, any Restricted Subsidiaries that are accounted for by the equity method of accounting (i.e., entities that have significant minority interests that could interfere with the Company's access to the cash of the Restricted Subsidiary). In addition, indentures will occasionally distinguish the treatment of investee companies and Unrestricted Subsidiaries. The theory is that the Company controls the timing of distributions of funds from Unrestricted Subsidiaries and could cause an Unrestricted Subsidiary to make a distribution for the sole purpose of increasing Consolidated Net Income during the measuring period for a debt incurrence. For example, an alternative approach to the foregoing is as follows:

"(A) the net income (but not loss) of any Person that is not a Restricted Subsidiary or that is accounted for by the equity method of accounting will be included only to the extent of the amount of dividends or distributions paid in cash to the specified Person or a Restricted Subsidiary of such Person;

(B) the net income (but not loss) of any Unrestricted Subsidiary will be excluded, whether or not distributed to the specified Person or one of its Subsidiaries";

(2) any net income (or loss) of any Person acquired by the Company or a Subsidiary in a pooling of interests transaction (or any transaction accounted for in a manner similar to a pooling of interests) for any period prior to the date of such acquisition;

* *Commentary*

Although pooling of interest accounting is no longer available in most acquisition transactions, it still is used in transactions involving persons under common control, so the clause remains in the Model definition.

(3) any net income of any Restricted Subsidiary if such Restricted Subsidiary is subject to restrictions, directly or indirectly, on the payment of dividends or the making of distributions by such Restricted Subsidiary, directly or indirectly, to the Company, except that:

(A) subject to the exclusion contained in clause (4) below, the Company's equity in the net income of any such Restricted Subsidiary for such period shall be included in such Consolidated Net Income up to the aggregate amount of cash actually distributed by such Restricted Subsidiary during such period to the Company or another Restricted Subsidiary as a dividend or other distribution (subject, in the case of a dividend or other distribution paid to another Restricted Subsidiary, to the limitation contained in this clause); and

(B) the Company's equity in a net loss of any such Restricted Subsidiary for such period shall be included in determining such Consolidated Net Income;

* *Commentary*

Similar to subsection (1) above, this subsection (3) assesses the Company's access to the net income (in the form of cash) of Restricted Subsidiaries. To the extent a Restricted Subsidiary is subject to restrictions (contractual or otherwise) on its ability to pay dividends to the Company, the Company does not get credit for the net income of that Restricted Subsidiary, except to the extent the Company receives cash from that Restricted Subsidiary. Often a Company will be able to negotiate clause (3)(A) to get credit for that position of a Restricted Subsidiary's net income that would have been permitted to be distributed, whether or not any cash was in fact distributed.

Practitioners need to keep the foregoing clause (3) in mind when negotiating the Limitation on Restrictions on Distributions from Restricted Subsidiaries covenant (Section 4.12). If a Company successfully negotiates for greater flexibility in that covenant with respect to a Restricted Subsidiary (e.g., broad dividend stoppers at the Subsidiary are permitted subject only to the discretion of a Company officer), then unless clause (3) above is simultaneously modified from the Model form, once the Restricted Subsidiary agrees to such a broad provision in a future debt instrument, clause (3) would exclude all or a portion of such Restricted Subsidiary's net income (and, ultimately, its EBITDA) in calculating Consolidated Net Income or Consolidated EBITDA. Occasionally, in strong markets, a Company is able to negotiate this clause (3) and Section 4.12 in tandem to achieve a more favorable result for the Company.

Alternative Example 1:

"(3) the net income of any Restricted Subsidiary during such period shall be excluded to the extent that the declaration or payment of dividends or similar distributions by such Restricted Subsidiary of that income is not permitted, directly or indirectly, by operation of the terms of its charter or any agreement, instrument, judgment, decree, order, statute, rule or governmental regulation applicable to that Subsidiary during such period, except that the Company's equity in a net loss of any such Restricted Subsidiary for such period shall be included in determining Consolidated Net Income";

Under the final clause of the Model definition and the foregoing alternative example, the Company is charged with the full amount of its equity in a loss at a Restricted Subsidiary, because the indenture allows the Company to make unlimited Investments in the Restricted Subsidiary, which could be used to fund the losses.

(4) any gain (or loss) realized upon the sale or other disposition of any assets of the Company, its consolidated Subsidiaries or any other Person (including pursuant to any sale-and-leaseback arrangement) which are not sold or otherwise disposed of in the ordinary course of business and any gain (or loss) realized upon the sale or other disposition of any Capital Stock of any Person;

* *Commentary*

This exclusion recognizes that asset sales and the associated gains and losses are one-time events that cannot be counted on to generate income to service debt in the future. This provision is sometimes drafted to exclude only the gain, and not any loss, from the sale or disposition of assets. In that case, such losses are generally added back in calculating

Consolidated EBITDA. Therefore, those losses do not reduce the Consolidated Coverage Ratio, but do reduce the restricted payments basket.

The provision may also be drafted to exclude from the calculation of Consolidated Net Income any provision for taxes realized in connection with such a disposition, and to exclude any gains (and any provision for related taxes) realized in connection with the disposition of any securities or the extinguishment of any debt. For example:

"any gain (but not any loss), together with any related provision for taxes on such gain (but not such loss), realized in connection with (a) any Asset Disposition or (b) the disposition of any securities by such Person or any of its Restricted Subsidiaries or the extinguishment of any Indebtedness of such Person or any of its Restricted Subsidiaries."

Note that in this example, the defined term "Asset Disposition" is used, rather than the more generic "sales outside the ordinary course" formulation. Therefore, adjustments under this provision will be subject to the various exclusions from the Asset Disposition definition.

(5) extraordinary gains or losses; and

* **Commentary**

Under some indentures, as in Alternative Example 1 below, only extraordinary gains, and not extraordinary losses, are excluded from the calculation of Consolidated Net Income. Like the previous example, such losses are generally added back in calculating Consolidated EBITDA, and therefore the extraordinary losses do not reduce the Consolidated Coverage Ratio, but do reduce the restricted payments basket. The provision may also be drafted to exclude any related provision for taxes relating to such a gain.

Alternative Example 1:

"any extraordinary gain (but not loss), together with any related provision for taxes on such extraordinary gain (but not loss)"

Alternative Example 2:

"any extraordinary gain or extraordinary loss together with any related provision for taxes and any one-time gains or losses (including those related to the adoption of new accounting standards) realized by the referent Person or any of its Restricted Subsidiaries during the period for which such determination is made"

Example 2 also excludes one-time gains and losses (often called "non-recurring" gains and losses). Unlike "extraordinary" items which are strictly limited under GAAP, "one-time" or "non-recurring" items are not defined under GAAP.

(6) the cumulative effect of a change in accounting principles;

* **Commentary**

This clause ensures that covenant calculations are not affected by changes in the accounting principles applied by the Company.

in each case, for such period. Notwithstanding the foregoing, for the purposes of Section 4.05 only, there shall be excluded from Consolidated Net Income any repurchases, repayments or redemptions of Investments, proceeds realized on the sale of Investments or return of capital to the Company or a Restricted Subsidiary to the extent such repurchases, repayments, redemptions, proceeds or returns increase the amount of Restricted Payments permitted under Section 4.05(a)(3)(D) thereof.

* *Commentary*

The exclusion in the final sentence of this definition ensures that a Company cannot double count certain transactions (realization events with respect to previously made Investments) in the calculation of the Company's Restricted Payment capacity. The Restricted Payments covenant explicitly includes (in Section 4.05(a)(3)(D)) a specific portion of the proceeds of such realization events in the calculation of the Restricted Payments basket, so that portion should not also be included in the calculation of Consolidated Net Income, which is in turn incorporated into the calculation of the Restricted Payments basket in Section 4.05(a)(3)(A).

"Credit Agreement" means the Credit Agreement to be entered into by and among, the Company, certain of its Subsidiaries, the lenders referred to therein, •, as Administrative Agent, •, as Syndication Agent, and •, as Documentation Agent, together with the related documents thereto (including the term loans and revolving loans thereunder, any guarantees and security documents), as amended, extended, renewed, restated, supplemented or otherwise modified (in whole or in part, and without limitation as to amount, terms, conditions, covenants and other provisions) from time to time, and one or more agreements (and related documents), including an indenture, governing Indebtedness incurred to Refinance, in whole or in part, the borrowings and commitments then outstanding or permitted to be outstanding under such Credit Agreement or one or more successor Credit Agreements.

* *Commentary*

The foregoing definition is fairly typical, and is notable for its breadth. The primary usage of this definition is in Section 4.04, where the first item of permitted Indebtedness, or Indebtedness that can be Incurred (regardless of whether a Company is then permitted to incur ratio debt), is Indebtedness that can be Incurred under a senior bank facility. Over time, this definition (and accordingly the scope of the permitted Indebtedness exception) has evolved in an issuer-friendly way so that the bank facility in place on the Issue Date of the high yield bonds can usually be replaced by any kind of subsequent debt, including a future senior secured, public high yield issuance. But practitioners ought to proceed with caution when interpreting older indentures, where the definition may not be as broad as it often is today. See, for example, Oaktree Capital Mgmt., LLC v. Spectrasite Holdings, Inc., No. Civ. A. 02-548 JJF, 2002 U.S. Dist. LEXIS 12761 (D. Del. Jun. 25, 2002), where the court focused on the phrase "or other non-convertible debt securities" located in the middle of an indenture's definition of "Credit Facility" to conclude that the issuer was not permitted to use the permitted debt exception for Credit Facility debt to issue convertible securities. The Model definition would permit such an issuance if it were used to refinance borrowings or commitments outstanding or permitted to be outstanding under the Credit Agreement (or any successor Credit Agreements).

"**Currency Agreement**" means any foreign exchange contract, currency swap agreement or other similar agreement with respect to currency values.

"**Disqualified Stock**" means, with respect to any Person, any Capital Stock which by its terms (or by the terms of any security into which it is convertible or for which it is exchangeable at the option of the holder) or upon the happening of any event:

(1) matures or is mandatorily redeemable (other than redeemable only for Capital Stock of such Person which is not itself Disqualified Stock) pursuant to a sinking fund obligation or otherwise;

(2) is convertible or exchangeable at the option of the holder for Indebtedness or Disqualified Stock; or

(3) is mandatorily redeemable or must be purchased upon the occurrence of certain events or otherwise, in whole or in part;

in each case on or prior to the first anniversary of the Stated Maturity of the Securities; provided, however, that any Capital Stock that would not constitute Disqualified Stock but for provisions thereof giving holders thereof the right to require such Person to purchase or redeem such Capital Stock upon the occurrence of an "asset sale" or "change of control" occurring prior to the first anniversary of the Stated Maturity of the Securities shall not constitute Disqualified Stock if:

(1) the "asset sale" or "change of control" provisions applicable to such Capital Stock are not more favorable to the holders of such Capital Stock than the terms applicable to the Securities contained in Section 4.06 and Section 4.07; and

(2) any such requirement only becomes operative after compliance with such terms applicable to the Securities, including the purchase of any Securities tendered pursuant thereto.

The amount of any Disqualified Stock that does not have a fixed redemption, repayment or repurchase price will be calculated in accordance with the terms of such Disqualified Stock as if such Disqualified Stock were redeemed, repaid or repurchased on any date on which the amount of such Disqualified Stock is to be determined pursuant to the Indenture; provided, however, that if such Disqualified Stock could not be required to be redeemed, repaid or repurchased at the time of such determination, the redemption, repayment or repurchase price will be the book value of such Disqualified Stock as reflected in the most recent financial statements of such Person.

* Commentary

The Company is afforded broad latitude in issuing its Capital Stock because of the junior status of equity. The foregoing definition is intended to identify and limit the issuance of certain types of stock that effectively do not follow this general rule of junior status. However, as described in the foregoing, capital stock is typically not "disqualified" solely as a result of change of control or asset sale repurchase obligations that may be applicable, though the limitations (if any) with respect to this feature differ from indenture to indenture. Common alternatives to the foregoing definition are as follows:

Alternative Example 1:

"'Disqualified Stock' means any Capital Stock that, by its terms (or by the terms of any security into which it is convertible, or for which it is exchangeable, in each case at the option of the holder of the Capital Stock), or upon the happening of any event, matures or is mandatorily redeemable, pursuant to a sinking fund obligation or otherwise, or redeemable at the option of the holder of the Capital Stock, in whole or in part, on or prior to the date that is 91 days after the date on which the Securities mature. Notwithstanding the preceding sentence, any Capital Stock that would constitute Disqualified Stock solely because the holders of the Capital Stock have the right to require the Company to repurchase such Capital Stock upon the occurrence of a change of control or an asset sale will not constitute Disqualified Stock if the terms of such Capital Stock provide that the Company may not repurchase or redeem any such Capital Stock pursuant to such provisions unless such repurchase or redemption complies with Section 4.05."

Note that the foregoing example does not include Capital Stock that is exchangeable for Indebtedness, but Example 2 below does.

Alternative Example 2:

"'Disqualified Stock' means any class or series of Capital Stock that, either by its terms, by the terms of any security into which it is convertible or exchangeable or by contract or otherwise, is or upon the happening of an event or passage of time would be required to be redeemed prior to the 91st day after the Stated Maturity of the Securities or is redeemable at the option of the holder thereof at any time prior to the 91st day after the Stated Maturity of the Securities, or is convertible into or exchangeable for debt securities at any time prior to the 91st day after the Stated Maturity of the Securities; provided that Capital Stock will not constitute Disqualified Stock solely because the holders thereof have the right to require the Company to repurchase or redeem such Capital Stock upon the occurrence of a change of control or an asset sale."

"GAAP" means generally accepted accounting principles in the United States of America as in effect as of the Issue Date, including those set forth in:

(1) the opinions and pronouncements of the Accounting Principles Board of the American Institute of Certified Public Accountants;

(2) statements and pronouncements of the Financial Accounting Standards Board;

(3) such other statements by such other entity as approved by a significant segment of the accounting profession; and

(4) the rules and regulations of the SEC governing the inclusion of financial statements (including pro forma financial statements) in periodic reports required to be filed pursuant to Section 13 of the Exchange Act, including opinions and pronouncements in staff accounting bulletins and similar written statements from the accounting staff of the SEC.

* Commentary

Not all covenant forms include the fourth clause. It is included here to make sure that in making calculations under the covenants, the Company cannot ignore specific SEC *staff guidance, particularly in the area of making pro forma calculations (such as in the Consolidated Coverage Ratio).*

A common alternative to this GAAP definition refers to GAAP "as in effect from time to time," and would allow the Company to avoid having to effectively keep two sets of books (issue date GAAP to moniter covenant compliance vs. current GAAP for financial reporting). Security analysts may also attempt to analyze covenant compliance on a current GAAP basis.

"Guarantee" means any obligation, contingent or otherwise, of any Person directly or indirectly guaranteeing any Indebtedness of any Person and any obligation, direct or indirect, contingent or otherwise, of such Person:

(1) to purchase or pay (or advance or supply funds for the purchase or payment of) such Indebtedness of such Person (whether arising by virtue of partnership arrangements, or by agreements to keep-well, to purchase assets, goods, securities or services, to take-or-pay or to maintain financial statement conditions or otherwise); or

(2) entered into for the purpose of assuring in any other manner the obligee of such Indebtedness of the payment thereof or to protect such obligee against loss in respect thereof (in whole or in part);

provided, however, that the term "Guarantee" shall not include endorsements for collection or deposit in the ordinary course of business. The term "Guarantee" used as a verb has a corresponding meaning. The term "Guarantor" shall mean any Person Guaranteeing any obligation.

"Hedging Obligations" of any Person means the obligations of such Person pursuant to any Interest Rate Agreement, Currency Agreement or any other swap or derivative transaction designed to hedge a business risk or exposure.

"Incur" means issue, assume, Guarantee, incur or otherwise become liable for; provided, however, that any Indebtedness of a Person existing at the time such Person becomes a Restricted Subsidiary (whether by merger, consolidation, acquisition or otherwise) shall be deemed to be Incurred by such Person at the time it becomes a Restricted Subsidiary. The term "Incurrence" when used as a noun shall have a correlative meaning. Solely for purposes of determining compliance with Section 4.04,

(1) amortization of debt discount or the accretion of principal with respect to a non-interest bearing or other discount security;

(2) the payment of regularly scheduled interest in the form of additional Indebtedness of the same instrument or the payment of regularly scheduled dividends on Capital Stock in the form of additional Capital Stock of the same class and with the same terms; and

(3) the obligation to pay a premium in respect of Indebtedness arising in connection with the issuance of a notice of redemption or the making of a mandatory offer to purchase such Indebtedness

will not be deemed to be the Incurrence of Indebtedness.

* *Commentary*

This definition is used in Section 4.04—Limitation on Indebtedness. Note that through its use, Indebtedness acquired in connection with an acquisition is also required to comply with the Limitation on Indebtedness covenant. Note also that a Company will be deemed to have "incurred" debt if it "otherwise becomes liable for" such debt—thus, if an obligation of a Company is recharacterized as debt from some other type of liability, one possible interpretation is the Company should test such an event as an incurrence of debt under the Limitation on Indebtedness covenant.

Note that in this definition, and in most indenture forms, accretion or original issue discount securities, and payment of interest through additional "pay-in-kind" or "PIK" securities, do not count as an incurrence of Indebtedness. However, since the economic effect of such accretion or PIK issuance is that a Company is in fact "borrowing" more money in order to meet its current interest expense, query whether this treatment is logical. For example, assume a Company takes advantage of a $100 million general debt basket in an indenture and issues OID notes yielding $100 million of gross proceeds. By the time those OID notes finish accreting to face amount, the Company might have $140 million of debt on its balance sheet. Securityholders that do not fully review all the terms in an indenture, and who may not be fully familiar with what is "market," might be surprised in a subsequent insolvency or bankruptcy proceeding to find themselves competing with a $140 million claim against the Company's assets, rather than the $100 million claim explicitly allowed by the Limitation on Indebtedness covenant.

"Indebtedness" means, with respect to any Person on any date of determination (without duplication):

> (1) the principal in respect of (A) indebtedness of such Person for money borrowed and (B) indebtedness evidenced by notes, debentures, bonds or other similar instruments for the payment of which such Person is responsible or liable;

* Commentary

Interest on Indebtedness is not Indebtedness (though some covenant forms include interest that is more than 30 days past due within the definition of Indebtedness, as in Alternative Example 1 to this definition presented below).

> (2) all Capital Lease Obligations of such Person and all Attributable Debt in respect of Sale/Leaseback Transactions entered into by such Person;

* Commentary

In some indentures, the foregoing provision does not include Attributable Debt.

> (3) all obligations of such Person issued or assumed as the deferred purchase price of property, all conditional sale obligations of such Person and all obligations of such Person under any title retention agreement (but excluding trade accounts payable arising in the ordinary course of business);

* Commentary

The foregoing provision is occasionally drafted to include obligations in respect of the deferred purchase price of services, as well as property, and to exclude, in addition to trade payables, other accrued expenses arising in the ordinary course of business.

> (4) all obligations of such Person for the reimbursement of any obligor on any letter of credit, bankers' acceptance or similar credit transaction (other than obligations with

respect to letters of credit securing obligations (other than obligations described in clauses (1) through (3) above) entered into in the ordinary course of business of such Person to the extent such letters of credit are not drawn upon or, if and to the extent drawn upon, such drawing is reimbursed no later than the tenth Business Day following payment on the letter of credit);

* *Commentary*

The parenthetical excludes ordinary course "trade" letters of credit that companies engaged in international trade often must post. These letters of credit are routinely drawn upon and promptly reimbursed by the account party, and are not commonly considered debt obligations. The reimbursement obligations on such letters of credit are not considered debt for purposes of the covenants unless they are not discharged within 10 business days. As demonstrated in Alternative Example 1 below, this exclusion is not included in all covenant forms.

(5) the amount of all obligations of such Person with respect to the redemption, repayment or other repurchase of any Disqualified Stock of such Person or and the amount of the liquidation preference of any Preferred Stock of any Restricted Subsidiary of such Person, the principal amount of such Capital Stock to be determined in accordance with this Indenture;

* *Commentary*

Clause (5) includes within the scope of the Indebtedness definition obligations in respect of Disqualified Stock of the Company and all Preferred Stock of the Company's Restricted Subsidiaries. The reason for including Preferred Stock of Restricted Subsidiaries is that such preferred stock has a claim to the assets and cash flow of the Restricted Subsidiaries that is prior to the claim of the Company as holder of the common equity of such Restricted Subsidiaries. If there are not subsidiary guarantees, the Securityholders' claim to the assets of Restricted Subsidiaries is indirect only; that is, through the Company's equity in the subsidiaries. If the high yield notes do not have the benefit of upstream guarantees from all Restricted Subsidiaries, from the perspective of the Securityholders, then the subsidiary Preferred Stock is therefore similar to debt.

(6) all obligations of the type referred to in clauses (1) through (5) of other Persons and all dividends of other Persons for the payment of which, in either case, such Person is responsible or liable, directly or indirectly, as obligor, guarantor or otherwise, including by means of any Guarantee;

* *Commentary*

Guarantees are Indebtedness (in most indentures (and in these Model definitions) they are also treated as Investments in the Person whose obligation is guaranteed).

(7) all obligations of the type referred to in clauses (1) through (6) of other Persons secured by any Lien on any property or asset of such Person (whether or not such obligation is assumed by such Person), the amount of such obligation being deemed to be the lesser of the value of such property or assets and the amount of the obligation so secured; and

(8) to the extent not otherwise included in this definition, Hedging Obligations of such Person.

Notwithstanding the foregoing, in connection with the purchase by the Company or any Restricted Subsidiary of any business, the term "Indebtedness" will exclude post-closing payment adjustments to which the seller may become entitled to the extent such payment is determined by a final closing balance sheet or such payment depends on the performance of such business after the closing; provided, however, that, at the time of closing, the amount of any such payment is not determinable and, to the extent such payment thereafter becomes fixed and determined, the amount is paid within 30 days thereafter.

The amount of Indebtedness of any Person at any date shall be the outstanding balance at such date of all unconditional obligations as described above; provided, however, that in the case of Indebtedness sold at a discount, the amount of such Indebtedness at any time will be the accreted value thereof at such time.

* *Commentary*

Alternative Example:

"'Indebtedness' means, with respect to any specified Person, any indebtedness of such Person, whether or not contingent:

(1) in respect of borrowed money;
(2) evidenced by bonds, notes, debentures or similar instruments or letters of credit (or reimbursement agreements in respect thereof);
(3) in respect of banker's acceptances;
(4) representing Capital Lease Obligations;
(5) representing the balance deferred and unpaid of the purchase price of any property, except any such balance that constitutes an accrued expense or trade payable; or
(6) representing any Hedging Obligations,

if and to the extent any of the preceding items (other than letters of credit and Hedging Obligations) would appear as a liability upon a balance sheet of the specified Person prepared in accordance with GAAP. In addition, the term 'Indebtedness' includes all Indebtedness of others secured by a Lien on any asset of the specified Person (whether or not such Indebtedness is assumed by the specified Person) and, to the extent not otherwise included, the Guarantee by the specified Person of any indebtedness of any other Person.

The amount of any Indebtedness outstanding as of any date will be:

(1) the accreted value of the Indebtedness, in the case of any Indebtedness issued with original issue discount; and
(2) the principal amount of the Indebtedness, together with any interest on the Indebtedness that is more than 30 days past due, in the case of any other Indebtedness."

The foregoing example is another common form of the "Indebtedness" definition. Note that in this example, "Attributable Debt" in respect of sale-leaseback transactions is not included within the scope of the definition. However, in cases such as this, the amount of Attributable Debt that is permitted to be incurred in connection with a Sale/Leaseback transaction is generally subject to the same Consolidated Coverage Ratio test as indebtedness by virtue of a separate covenant. Thus, the substantive result is the same, except that any applicable debt basket provided for in the Limitation on Indebtedness covenant would not be available for the incurrence of this type of obligation. Also note that this example includes certain specified items within the coverage of the "Indebtedness" definition only to the extent that they would be reflected as liabilities on a GAAP balance sheet.

In addition, this example does not include obligations in respect of the repurchase of capital stock. However, in covenant forms in which this alternative definition is used, the debt covenant specifically includes obligations in respect of Disqualified Stock within its coverage, so the ultimate result is largely the same (See Alternative Example 1 to Section 4.04).

"Interest Rate Agreement" means any interest rate swap agreement, interest rate cap agreement or other financial agreement or arrangement with respect to exposure to interest rates.

"Investment" in any Person means any direct or indirect advance, loan (other than advances to customers in the ordinary course of business that are recorded as accounts receivable on the balance sheet of the lender) or other extensions of credit (including by way of Guarantee or similar arrangement) or capital contribution to (by means of any transfer of cash or other property to others or any payment for property or services for the account or use of others), or any purchase or acquisition of Capital Stock, Indebtedness or other similar instruments issued by such Person. Except as otherwise provided for herein, the amount of an Investment shall be its fair market value at the time the Investment is made and without giving effect to subsequent changes in value.

For purposes of the definition of "Unrestricted Subsidiary," the definition of "Restricted Payment" and Section 4.05:

(1) "Investment" shall include the portion (proportionate to the Company's equity interest in such Subsidiary) of the fair market value of the net assets of any Subsidiary of the Company at the time that such Subsidiary is designated an Unrestricted Subsidiary, unless such Subsidiary, at the time of such designation, has total assets of $1,000 or less, in which case no Investment shall be deemed to occur as a result of such designation; provided, however, that to the extent the Investment resulting from such designation is treated by the Company as a Permitted Investment, then upon a redesignation of such Subsidiary as a Restricted Subsidiary, the Company shall first determine its portion (proportionate to its equity interest in such Subsidiary) of the fair market value of the net assets of such Subsidiary at the time of such redesignation and shall then determine how much of such portion, if any, it will treat as a net reduction in Investments under Section 4.05(a)(3)(D)(y); with respect to the balance of such portion, if (x) the aggregate amount of the Company's Permitted Investments in such Subsidiary made on or after the Issue Date that remain outstanding at the time of such redesignation exceed such balance, then the Company shall be deemed to have permanently used its Permitted Investment capacity to the extent of such excess and deemed to have fully repaid such Permitted Investment to the extent of such balance, and (y) such balance equals or exceeds such aggregate amount of Permitted Investments in such Subsidiary, then such aggregate amount of such Permitted Investments shall be deemed to have been fully repaid, and therefore no longer outstanding, as a result of and after giving effect to such redesignation; and

(2) any property transferred to or from an Unrestricted Subsidiary shall be valued at its fair market value at the time of such transfer, in each case as determined in good faith by the Board.

* *Commentary*

This definition is used in the definition of "Restricted Payments." Note that "Investment" includes the grant of a Guarantee (which also constitutes the incurrence of "Indebtedness"). Hence, if the issuer guarantees debt of another person (for example, a holding company), that grant constitutes both an Investment which must be tested under the Restricted Payments covenant as well as the incurrence of Indebtedness that must be tested under the Limitation on Indebtedness covenant.

The proviso at the end of the foregoing clause (1) recognizes that if the Company uses its Permitted Investment capacity to designate a Subsidiary as an Unrestricted Subsidiary (see definition of "Unrestricted Subsidiary"), it will get credit for the repayment of such Permitted Investments upon any redesignation of the Subsidiary as Restricted, but only if the Company's share of the Subsidiary's net assets at such time equal or exceed the amount of the Permitted Investments made in such Subsidiary during the time it was Unrestricted. If it does not, then the Company shall be treated as having permanently used its Permitted Investment capacity to the extent of the shortfall. To the extent the Company has used its Restricted Payment capacity under Section 4.05(a) at the time of the original designation of the Subsidiary as Unrestricted, then it must look to Section 4.05(a)(3)(D) to determine how much of that used capacity can be recovered upon the subsequent redesignation.

The foregoing definition of Investment sometimes incorporates a "catch all" that includes, in addition to the specifically enumerated items, all other items that would be classified as investments on a balance sheet prepared in accordance with GAAP. Investments by means of payment for property or services for the account or use of others is frequently not specifically enumerated, and the exclusion from the definition of "Investments" of advances to customers in the ordinary course of business that are recorded as accounts receivable on the balance sheet of the lender is not always provided.

The foregoing provision frequently includes additional language making clear that the acquisition of a person that holds an investment in another person will be deemed at the time of the acquisition to be an investment of the acquiror.

For example, the following is an alternative definition of Investment:

"'Investment' means, with respect to any Person, all direct or indirect investments by such Person in other Persons (including Affiliates) in the forms of loans (including Guarantees or other obligations), advances or capital contributions (excluding commission, travel and similar advances to officers and employees made in the ordinary course of business), purchases or other acquisitions for consideration of Indebtedness, Capital Stock or other securities, together with all items that are or would be classified as investments on a balance sheet prepared in accordance with GAAP. If the Company or any Subsidiary of the Company sells or otherwise disposes of any Capital Stock of any direct or indirect Subsidiary of the Company such that, after giving effect to any such sale or disposition, such Person is no longer a Subsidiary of the Company, the Company will be deemed to have made an Investment on the date of any such sale or disposition equal to the fair market value of the Capital Stock of such Subsidiary not sold or disposed of. The acquisition by the Company or any Subsidiary of the Company of a Person that holds an Investment in a third Person will be deemed to be an Investment by the Company or such Subsidiary in such third Person in an amount equal to the fair market value of the Investment held by the acquired Person in such third Person."

*"**Issue Date**"* means [insert date of closing of initial Securities offering].

*"**Lien**"* means any mortgage, pledge, security interest, encumbrance, lien or charge of any kind (including any conditional sale or other title retention agreement or lease in the nature thereof).

* *Commentary*

The definition of "Lien" sometimes includes a specific reference to options or agreements to grant a lien. For example:

"'Lien' means, with respect to any asset, any mortgage, lien, pledge, charge, security interest or encumbrance of any kind in respect of such asset, whether or not filed, recorded or otherwise perfected under applicable law (including any conditional sale or other title retention agreement, any lease in the nature thereof, any option or other agreement to sell or give a security interest in and any filing of or agreement to give any financing statement under the Uniform Commercial Code (or equivalent statute) of any jurisdiction)."

*"**Net Available Cash**"* from an Asset Disposition means cash payments received therefrom (including any cash payments received by way of deferred payment of principal pursuant to a note or installment receivable or otherwise and proceeds from the sale or other disposition of any securities received as consideration, but only as and when received, but excluding any other consideration received in the form of assumption by the acquiring Person of Indebtedness or other obligations relating to such properties or assets or received in any other non-cash form), in each case net of:

(1) all legal, title and recording tax expenses, commissions and other fees and expenses incurred, and all Federal, state, provincial, foreign and local taxes required to be accrued as a liability under GAAP, as a consequence of such Asset Disposition;

(2) all payments made on any Indebtedness which is secured by any assets subject to such Asset Disposition, in accordance with the terms of any Lien upon or other security agreement of any kind with respect to such assets, or which must by its terms, or in order to obtain a necessary consent to such Asset Disposition, or by applicable law, be repaid out of the proceeds from such Asset Disposition;

(3) all distributions and other payments required to be made to minority interest holders in Restricted Subsidiaries as a result of such Asset Disposition;

(4) the deduction of appropriate amounts provided by the seller as a reserve, in accordance with GAAP, against any liabilities associated with the property or other assets disposed in such Asset Disposition and retained by the Company or any Restricted Subsidiary after such Asset Disposition; and

(5) any portion of the purchase price from an Asset Disposition placed in escrow, whether as a reserve for adjustment of the purchase price, for satisfaction of indemnities in respect of such Asset Disposition or otherwise in connection with that Asset Disposition; provided, however, that upon the termination of that escrow, Net Available Cash will be increased by any portion of funds in the escrow that are released to the Company or any Restricted Subsidiary.

* *Commentary*

The foregoing definition is used in the asset sale covenant to specify the proceeds of asset sales that must be applied to the repayment of certain debt and the acquisition of certain assets according to the "waterfall" included in Section 4.06(a)(3)(A). It is intended to capture the cash available from a disposition after allowing for standard expenses and payment arrangements directly relating to the sale.

This example includes cash received from the sale of securities received as consideration, on the basis that securities are a common and generally liquid form of non-cash consideration. It is not uncommon, however, to include cash received from the sale of any non-cash assets received as consideration in an asset sale. It is also not uncommon for consideration received in the form of readily marketable cash equivalents, such as short-term treasury obligations, to be treated as cash for this purpose at the time they are received, regardless of when they are liquidated.

As demonstrated in the examples below, there is some variation among indentures in the enumerated expenses that are deducted in arriving at the net amount of cash the Company receives and has available to apply to debt repayment or the acquisition of additional assets.

Alternative Example 1:

"'Net Available Cash' means, with respect to any Asset Disposition, the proceeds thereof received by the Company or any Restricted Subsidiary in the form of cash or cash equivalents, including payments in respect of deferred payment obligations when received in the form of cash or cash equivalents (except to the extent that such obligations are financed or sold with recourse to the Company or any Restricted Subsidiary) net of (i) brokerage commissions and other fees and expenses (including, fees and expenses of legal counsel and investment bankers, recording fees, transfer fees and appraisers' fees) related to such Asset Disposition, (ii) provisions for all taxes payable as a result of such Asset Disposition, (iii) amounts required to be paid to any Person (other than the Company or any Restricted Subsidiary) owning a beneficial interest in the assets subject to the Asset Disposition, (iv) payments made to permanently retire Indebtedness where payment of such Indebtedness is secured by the assets or properties the subject of such Asset Disposition, and (v) appropriate amounts to be provided by the Company or any Restricted Subsidiary, as the case may be, as a reserve required in accordance with GAAP against any liabilities associated with such Asset Disposition and retained by the Company or any Restricted Subsidiary, as the case may be, after such Asset Disposition, including pension and other post-employment benefit liabilities, liabilities related to environmental matters and liabilities under any indemnification obligations associated with such Asset Disposition, until such time as such amounts are no longer or such reserve is no longer necessary (at which time any remaining amounts will become Net Available Cash to be allocated in accordance with Section 4.06.)"

Note the last sentence of the foregoing example, which provides that subsequent adjustments to reserves can give rise to additional Net Available Cash.

Alternative Example 2:

"'Net Available Cash' means the aggregate cash proceeds received by the Company or any of its Restricted Subsidiaries in respect of any Asset Disposition (including any cash received upon the sale or other disposition of any non-cash consideration received in any Asset Disposition), net of the direct costs relating to such Asset Disposition, including legal, accounting and investment banking fees, and sales commissions, and any relocation

expenses incurred as a result of the Asset Disposition, taxes paid or payable as a result of the Asset Disposition, in each case, after taking into account any available tax credits or deductions and any tax sharing arrangements, and amounts required to be applied to the repayment of Indebtedness, other than Senior Indebtedness, secured by a Lien on the asset or assets that were the subject of such Asset Disposition and any reserve for adjustment in respect of the sale price of such asset or assets established in accordance with GAAP."

Note that in this example, payments in respect of debt that is senior to the Securities and secured by the assets sold are not deducted in arriving at Net Available Cash. In addition, note that this example explicitly requires that taxes deducted from sale proceeds to arrive at net available cash be adjusted to account for possible tax benefits. In Energy Corp. of Am. v. MacKay Shields LLC, 91 Fed. Appx. 799 (4th Cir. 2003), the Company argued for an interpretation of the phrase "taxes paid or payable . . . (after taking into account any available tax credits . . . ") that would result in a very small amount of Net Available Cash, thus relieving the Company of any further obligation to use asset sale proceeds to repay debt or acquire new assets. The Fourth Circuit held that the Company was required to take into account all credits and deductions actually applied to reduce the actual tax obligation arising from the sale. This led to a smaller calculation to "taxes paid or payable" and therefore a greater amount of Net Available Cash that the Company needed to apply in accordance with the indenture.

"Net Cash Proceeds," with respect to any issuance or sale of Capital Stock or Indebtedness, means the cash proceeds of such issuance or sale net of attorneys' fees, accountants' fees, underwriters' or placement agents' fees, discounts or commissions and brokerage, consultant and other fees actually incurred in connection with such issuance or sale and net of taxes paid or payable as a result thereof.

"Obligations" means, with respect to any Indebtedness, all obligations for principal, premium, interest, penalties, fees, indemnifications, reimbursements and other amounts payable pursuant to the documentation governing such Indebtedness.

"Parent" means [the entity, if any, that owns a majority of the Voting Stock of the Company].

"Permitted Holders" means [identify those shareholders of the Company who control the Company on the Issue Date]. Except for a Permitted Holder specifically identified by name, in determining whether Voting Stock is owned by a Permitted Holder, only Voting Stock acquired by a Permitted Holder in its described capacity will be treated as "beneficially owned" by such Permitted Holder.

* *Commentary*

The second sentence of the foregoing definition is primarily designed to address situations where the term "affiliates" is used in the first sentence (e.g., "XYZ Corp and its affiliates"). To the extent an entity should at some time after the Issue Date cease to be an affiliate of the identified shareholder (and thereby cease to hold the Capital Stock in its "described capacity"), then the entity would cease to be a Permitted Holder by operation of the second sentence.

"Permitted Investment" means an Investment by the Company or any Restricted Subsidiary in:

(1) the Company, a Restricted Subsidiary or a Person that will, upon the making of such Investment, become a Restricted Subsidiary; provided, however, that the primary business of such Restricted Subsidiary is a Related Business;

(2) another Person if, as a result of such Investment, such other Person is merged or consolidated with or into, or transfers or conveys all or substantially all its assets to, the Company or a Restricted Subsidiary; provided, however, that such Person's primary business is, or following such Investment will be, a Related Business;

* *Commentary*

Clauses (1) and (2) involve Investments where the money invested stays within the "restricted group" of companies that are subject to the covenants of the Indenture (i.e., the Company and its Restricted Subsidiaries). For that reason, those investments are always permitted. In some variations on the approach to clause (1) above, "Permitted Investments" include Investments only in Restricted Subsidiaries that are guarantors or wholly owned subsidiaries, and they are not required to conduct a "Related Business" (but often indentures require Restricted Subsidiaries to be primarily engaged in a "Related Business"). In some such cases, Investments in Restricted Subsidiaries that are neither wholly owned nor guarantors are included within the scope of Permitted Investments only up to a specified cap. Restricting clauses (1) and (2) to Investments in guarantors may be problematic from the Company's perspective if the Company plans to operate in foreign countries through subsidiaries. Usually, foreign subsidiaries are not made guarantors because to do so would result in adverse U.S. tax consequences under the "deemed dividend" rationale of Section 951(a)(1)(B) of the Internal Revenue Code.

The following is an example of such an alternative approach to clauses (1) and (2) above:

"(A) any Investment in the Company or in a Restricted Subsidiary of the Company that is a Guarantor;

(B) any Investment in a Restricted Subsidiary of the Company that is not a Guarantor in an amount not to exceed $• million at any one time outstanding;

(C) any Investment by the Company or any Restricted Subsidiary of the Company in a Person, if as a result of such Investment:

(i) such Person becomes a Restricted Subsidiary of the Company that is a Guarantor; or

(ii) such Person is merged, consolidated or amalgamated with or into, or transfers or conveys substantially all of its assets to, or is liquidated into, the Company or a Restricted Subsidiary of the Company that is a Guarantor";

(3) cash and Temporary Cash Investments;

* *Commentary*

Highly liquid, short-term investment grade securities are almost always included as Permitted Investments for the Company.

(4) payroll, travel and similar advances to cover matters that are expected at the time of such advances ultimately to be treated as expenses for accounting purposes and that are made in the ordinary course of business;

(5) loans or advances to employees made in the ordinary course of business consistent with past practices of the Company or such Restricted Subsidiary;

* *Commentary*

The foregoing clause (5) is occasionally omitted from the definition of Permitted Investment and, in other cases, is included but capped at a specified amount (and, in any case, is now limited insofar as it extends to officers of the Company by restrictions in the Sarbanes-Oxley Act of 2002, Pub. L. No. 107-204, §402, 116 Stat. 745, 787 (codified at 15 U.S.C. §78m(k))).

(6) stock, obligations or securities received in settlement of debts created in the ordinary course of business and owing to the Company or any Restricted Subsidiary or in satisfaction of judgments;

(7) any Person to the extent such Investment represents the non-cash portion of the consideration received for (i) an Asset Disposition as permitted pursuant to Section 4.06 or (ii) a disposition of assets not constituting an Asset Disposition;

* *Commentary*

The foregoing clause (7) is designed to prevent the Company from inadvertently falling into a trap—the Company is allowed under the asset sale covenant to accept some noncash consideration in an asset sale. The covenant restricting Investments should not turn around and prevent such consideration.

Clause (ii) of the foregoing provision is occasionally not included.

(8) any Person where such Investment was acquired by the Company or any of its Restricted Subsidiaries (a) in exchange for any other Investment or accounts receivable held by the Company or any such Restricted Subsidiary in connection with or as a result of a bankruptcy, workout, reorganization or recapitalization with respect to such other Investment or accounts receivable or (b) as a result of a foreclosure by the Company or any of its Restricted Subsidiaries with respect to any secured Investment or other transfer of title with respect to any secured Investment in default;

* *Commentary*

The preceding provision, which effectively gives the Company the flexibility to recover value upon an event of default or insolvency with respect to certain other obligations owed to it, is not included in all forms. In some cases, a variation of clause (8) is included which includes within the definition of Permitted Investments certain Investments received in settlement of obligations arising in the ordinary course of business in the context of the bankruptcy of a customer, supplier or trade creditor. For example:

"any Investments received in compromise of obligations of such persons incurred in the ordinary course of trade creditors or customers that were incurred in the ordinary course of business, including pursuant to any plan of reorganization or similar arrangement upon the bankruptcy or insolvency of any trade creditor or customer";

Such an approach is of more limited scope than the provision in the model definition, which would include exchanges for Investments made outside of the ordinary course.

(9) any Person to the extent such Investments consist of prepaid expenses, negotiable instruments held for collection and lease, utility and workers' compensation, performance and other similar deposits made in the ordinary course of business by the Company or any Restricted Subsidiary;

*** Commentary***

The foregoing clause (9), which provides relief from the Limitation on Restricted Payments covenant for certain items that arise in the ordinary course of business and which are not Investments of the type the covenant is designed to restrict, is sometimes omitted, but the definition of "Investment" may not in fact cover some of the transactions described in the foregoing clause (9).

(10) any Person to the extent such Investments consist of Hedging Obligations otherwise permitted under Section 4.04;

(11) any Person existing on the Issue Date, and any extension, modification or renewal of any such Investments existing on the Issue Date, but only to the extent not involving additional advances, contributions or other Investments of cash or other assets or other increases thereof (other than as a result of the accrual or accretion of interest or original issue discount or the issuance of pay-in-kind securities, in each case, pursuant to the terms of such Investment as in effect on the Issue Date); and

*** Commentary***

The extension portion contained in the foregoing clause is not included in all indenture forms.

(12) Persons to the extent such Investments, when taken together with all other Investments made pursuant to this clause (12) outstanding on the date such Investment is made, do not exceed $● million.

*** Commentary***

Permitted Investments are excluded from the definition of Restricted Payments. These Permitted Investments are generally ordinary course types of Investments, such as accounts receivable (which are in effect investments in the customer), and advances to employees (which are investments in such persons). However, Permitted Investments also include any Investment that the Company makes in a Restricted Subsidiary or in a person that as a result of such Investment will become a Restricted Subsidiary. These are important provisions that permit the free flow of cash and assets between the Company and its Restricted Subsidiaries and is the quid pro quo for subjecting the Restricted Subsidiaries to the terms of the indenture. This is perhaps the most significant consequence of having distinctions between Restricted Subsidiaries and Unrestricted Subsidiaries (cash is not permitted to flow freely from the Company to an Unrestricted Subsidiary).

In addition to those listed in the example above, other covenant forms commonly identify other Investments as Permitted Investments, depending upon the circumstances of a particular Company. Common examples include baskets for Investments in joint venture or similar arrangements, baskets for foreign subsidiaries where such Investments are otherwise not generally permitted and carveouts for Investments in receivables subsidiaries or similar securitization vehicles.

"Permitted Liens" means, with respect to any Person:

(1) pledges or deposits by such Person under worker's compensation laws, unemployment insurance laws or similar legislation, or good faith deposits in connection with

bids, tenders, contracts (other than for the payment of Indebtedness) or leases to which such Person is a party, or deposits to secure public or statutory obligations of such Person or deposits of cash or United States government bonds to secure surety or appeal bonds to which such Person is a party, or deposits as security for contested taxes or import duties or for the payment of rent, in each case Incurred in the ordinary course of business;

(2) Liens imposed by law, such as carriers', warehousemen's and mechanics' Liens, in each case for sums not yet due or being contested in good faith by appropriate proceedings or other Liens arising out of judgments or awards against such Person with respect to which such Person shall then be proceeding with an appeal or other proceedings for review and Liens arising solely by virtue of any statutory or common law provision relating to banker's Liens, rights of set-off or similar rights and remedies as to deposit accounts or other funds maintained with a creditor depository institution; provided, however, that (A) such deposit account is not a dedicated cash collateral account and is not subject to restrictions against access by the Company in excess of those set forth by regulations promulgated by the Federal Reserve Board and (B) such deposit account is not intended by the Company or any Restricted Subsidiary to provide collateral to the depository institution;

* *Commentary*

The provision for liens imposed by law is sometimes written to be limited to such liens arising in the ordinary course of business and with respect to which any appropriate reserve or other provision required by GAAP has been made. For example:

"statutory mechanics', workmen's, materialmen's, operators' or similar Liens imposed by law and arising in the ordinary course of business for sums which are not yet due or are being contested in good faith by appropriate proceedings promptly instituted and diligently conducted and for which adequate reserves have been established or other provisions have been made in accordance with generally accepted accounting principles";

The permission for judgment liens included in this provision is often limited to judgments that do not result in an event of default. In addition, in some cases, there may be an allowance (often subject to a stated cap) for final, non-appealable judgment liens, to the extent the judgment does not result in an event of default.

(3) Liens for property taxes not yet subject to penalties for non-payment or which are being contested in good faith by appropriate proceedings;

* *Commentary*

This permitted lien is often limited to those with respect to which any appropriate reserve or other provision required by GAAP has been made. For example:

"(3) Liens for taxes, assessments or governmental charges or claims that are not yet delinquent or that are being contested in good faith by appropriate proceedings promptly instituted and diligently pursued; provided that any reserve or other appropriate provision as shall be required in conformity with GAAP shall have been made therefor";

(4) Liens in favor of issuers of surety bonds or letters of credit issued pursuant to the request of and for the account of such Person in the ordinary course of its business; provided, however, that such letters of credit do not constitute Indebtedness;

(5) minor survey exceptions, minor encumbrances, easements or reservations of, or rights of others for, licenses, rights-of-way, sewers, electric lines, telegraph and

telephone lines and other similar purposes, or zoning or other restrictions as to the use of real property or Liens incidental to the conduct of the business of such Person or to the ownership of its properties which were not Incurred in connection with Indebtedness and which do not in the aggregate materially adversely affect the value of said properties or materially impair their use in the operation of the business of such Person;

(6) Liens securing Indebtedness Incurred to finance the construction, purchase or lease of, or repairs, improvements or additions to, property, plant or equipment of such Person; provided, however, that such Liens may not extend to any other property owned by such Person or any of its Restricted Subsidiaries at the time the Lien is Incurred (other than assets and property affixed or appurtenant thereto), and the Indebtedness (other than any interest thereon) secured by such Lien may not be Incurred more than 180 days after the later of the acquisition, completion of construction, repair, improvement, addition or commencement of full operation of the property subject to the Lien;

* Commentary

The foregoing Permitted Lien for purchase money liens is sometimes limited to assets acquired in the ordinary course of business, and may apply only to liens on indebtedness incurred in compliance with the indenture. For example:

"(6) Liens created solely for the purpose of securing the payment of all or part of the purchase price of assets or property acquired or constructed in the ordinary course of business after the Issue Date; provided, however, that (A) the Indebtedness secured by such Liens shall have otherwise been permitted to be issued under this Indenture and (B) such Liens shall not encumber any other assets or property of the Company or any of its Restricted Subsidiaries";

In addition, the allowance for purchase money liens will sometimes state that indebtedness secured by the lien may not exceed the fair market value of the property (or the improvement) being financed.

(7) Liens to secure Indebtedness permitted under Section 4.04(b)(1).

* Commentary

The foregoing provision applies to Liens on any assets securing indebtedness under a Credit Agreement in the amount specified in Section 4.04(b)(1). Given the fact that the definition of "Credit Agreement" includes replacements and refinancings thereof, this provision permits Liens to be incurred under future credit facilities (or even indentures), so long as such indebtedness is incurred in compliance with the specified provision of the debt covenant.

(8) Liens existing on the Issue Date;

(9) Liens on property or shares of Capital Stock of another Person at the time such other Person becomes a Subsidiary of such Person; provided, however, that the Liens may not extend to any other property owned by such Person or any of its Restricted Subsidiaries (other than assets and property affixed or appurtenant thereto);

* Commentary

An alternative approach to the foregoing is as follows:

"(9) Liens on the assets or property of a Restricted Subsidiary of the Company existing at the time such Restricted Subsidiary became a Subsidiary of the Company and not

incurred as a result of (or in connection with or in anticipation of) such Restricted Subsidiary becoming a Subsidiary of the Company; provided, however, that (A) any such Lien does not by its terms cover any property or assets after the time such Restricted Subsidiary becomes a Subsidiary which were not covered immediately prior to such transaction, (B) the Incurrence of the Indebtedness secured by such Lien shall have otherwise been permitted to be issued under this Indenture, and (C) such Liens do not extend to or cover any other property or assets of the Company or any of its Restricted Subsidiaries";

(10) Liens on property at the time such Person or any of its Subsidiaries acquires the property, including any acquisition by means of a merger or consolidation with or into such Person or a Subsidiary of such Person; provided, however, that such Liens may not extend to any other property owned by such Person or any of its Restricted Subsidiaries (other than assets and property affixed or appurtenant thereto);

* Commentary

Sometimes clauses (9) and (10) will include the additional limitation that the liens in question cannot have been Incurred in contemplation of or in connection with the acquisition in question, although it is not entirely clear why such a limitation is necessary.

For example:

"(9) Liens on property or shares of Capital Stock of another Person at the time such other Person becomes a Subsidiary of such Person; provided, however, that such Liens are not created, Incurred or assumed in connection with, or in contemplation of, such other Person becoming such a Subsidiary; provided further, however, that such Liens may not extend to any other property owned by such Person or any of its Restricted Subsidiaries (other than assets and property affixed or appurtenant thereto);

(10) Liens on property at the time such Person or any of its Subsidiaries acquires the property, including any acquisition by means of a merger or consolidation with or into such Person or a Subsidiary of such Person; provided, however, that such Liens are not created, Incurred or assumed in connection with, or in contemplation of, such acquisition; provided further, however, that the Liens may not extend to any other property owned by such Person or any of its Restricted Subsidiaries (other than assets and property affixed or appurtenant thereto)";

(11) Liens securing Indebtedness or other obligations of a Subsidiary of such Person owing to such Person or a Wholly Owned Subsidiary of such Person;

(12) Liens securing Hedging Obligations so long as such Hedging Obligations relate to Indebtedness that is, and is permitted to be under the Indenture, secured by a Lien on the same property securing such Hedging Obligations; and

* Commentary

In some forms, the foregoing provision is drafted to apply to Interest Rate Agreements only, and not to all Hedging Obligations.

(13) Liens to secure any Refinancing (or successive Refinancings) as a whole, or in part, of any Indebtedness secured by any Lien referred to in the foregoing clause (6), (8), (9) or (10); provided, however, that:

(A) such new Lien shall be limited to all or part of the same property and assets that secured or, under the written agreements pursuant to which the original Lien arose, could secure the original Lien (plus improvements and accessions to, such property and assets or proceeds or distributions thereof); and

(B) the Indebtedness secured by such Lien at such time is not increased to any amount greater than the sum of (x) the outstanding principal amount or, if greater, committed amount of the Indebtedness described under clause (6), (8), (9) or (10) at the time the original Lien became a Permitted Lien and (y) an amount necessary to pay any fees and expenses, including premiums, related to such Refinancing.

* *Commentary*

In a subordinated or senior subordinated deal, if there is a definition of "Permitted Lien," it will almost always include a Permitted Lien securing Senior Indebtedness. Since the Securities are subordinated to all Senior Indebtedness, the holders are not disadvantaged by the Senior Indebtedness being secured. For example:

"Liens securing Senior Indebtedness of the Company or any Guarantor that was permitted by the terms of this Indenture to be incurred, and related Obligations";

Subordinated or senior subordinated deals may not have a definition of "Permitted Liens" because many such deals do not have a Limitation on Liens covenant (which is where such definition is used). The reason is that the subordinated debt holder does not typically care about the grants by the Company of any liens, whether "permitted" or not, unless they are granted for the benefit of any pari passu or junior indebtedness. For that reason, as long as a prohibition on granting liens on pari passu and junior indebtedness is included in such deals, either as a separate covenant or as part of the Limitation on Indebtedness covenant, there is then no reason to include a long list of "Permitted Liens" relating to unsubordinated indebtedness or to items that are not indebtedness at all.

Some senior note indentures also permit liens securing Indebtedness of non-guarantor subsidiaries for the same reason. Since that Indebtedness is already structurally senior to the Securities, securing such Indebtedness is not adverse to the holders of the Securities. For example:

"Liens securing Indebtedness of any Restricted Subsidiary (other than a Guarantor) that was permitted by the terms of this Indenture to be incurred, and related Obligations, which Liens encumber only assets of such Restricted Subsidiary."

The definition of Permitted Liens will often include additional security interests that are specific to the nature of the Company's business or financing arrangements, such as an exception for liens relating to securitization transactions. It may also include additional "general" types of liens in the nature of those listed in this example, such as the following:

"leases and subleases of real property which do not interfere with the ordinary conduct of the business of the Company or any of its Restricted Subsidiaries, and Liens securing the obligations (other than Indebtedness) of the Company or any of the Restricted Subsidiaries under any such leases and subleases of real property";

"any interest in or title of a lessor to any property subject to a Capital Lease Obligation permitted to be Incurred under this Indenture";

"Liens on property of an Unrestricted Subsidiary at the time that it is designated as a Restricted Subsidiary pursuant to the definition of "Unrestricted Subsidiary"; provided that such Liens were not incurred in connection with, or contemplation of, such designation";

"Liens arising from filing Uniform Commercial Code financing statements regarding leases";

"Liens on goods (and the proceeds thereof) and documents of title and the property covered thereby securing commercial letters of credit";

"Liens arising out of consignment or similar arrangements for the sale of goods entered into by the Company or any Restricted Subsidiary in the ordinary course of business in accordance with industry practice."

The definition of "Permitted Liens" may also include a basket for other liens, typically capped at either a specified dollar amount or at a specified percentage of the Company's consolidated tangible assets. For example:

"Liens securing Indebtedness, as measured by principal amount, which, when taken together with the principal amount of all other Indebtedness secured by Liens (excluding Liens permitted by clauses (1) though [(14)] above) at the time of determination, does not exceed [$• million] [•% of Consolidated Net Tangible Assets]."

The definition of "Permitted Liens" may also include a specific allowance for equal and ratable liens securing the Securities that may arise pursuant to the operation of the Limitation on Liens covenant (See Section 4.08).

Notwithstanding the foregoing, "Permitted Liens" will not include any Lien described in clause (6), (9) or (10) above to the extent such Lien applies to any Additional Assets acquired directly or indirectly from Net Available Cash pursuant to Section 4.06 For purposes of this definition, the term "Indebtedness" shall be deemed to include all Obligations in respect of such Indebtedness.

* Commentary

The final sentence of the definition is included to protect the Company from inadvertently violating the Limitation on Liens covenant, since "Indebtedness" as defined does not include premium, interest and other obligations in respect of Indebtedness, and yet they are typically secured to the same extent as principal in a secured debt transaction.

In drafting the foregoing definition, the drafter must determine whether the assets that are permitted to be subject to the liens should be limited (e.g., under clauses (9) or (10) only the asset acquired can be subject to the lien securing the purchase money debt) or whether the liens can apply to any assets of the Company (e.g., under clause (7) above, the Credit Agreement indebtedness could be secured by any assets of the Company or its Restricted Subsidiaries). In some transactions the exception for liens securing Credit Agreement debt will be limited to liens on accounts receivable and inventory (i.e., "working capital").

"Person" means any individual, corporation, partnership, limited liability company, joint venture, association, joint-stock company, trust, unincorporated organization, government or any agency or political subdivision thereof or any other entity.

"Preferred Stock," as applied to the Capital Stock of any Person, means Capital Stock of any class or classes (however designated) which is preferred as to the payment of dividends or distributions, or as to the distribution of assets upon any voluntary or involuntary liquidation or dissolution of such Person, over shares of Capital Stock of any other class of such Person.

* Commentary

Trust preferred securities would ordinarily be treated as Preferred Stock of the trust.

"Refinance" means, in respect of any Indebtedness, to refinance, extend, renew, refund, repay, prepay, purchase, redeem, defease or retire, or to issue other Indebtedness in exchange or replacement for, such indebtedness. "Refinanced" and "Refinancing" shall have correlative meanings.

"Refinancing Indebtedness" means Indebtedness that Refinances any Indebtedness of the Company or any Restricted Subsidiary existing on the Issue Date or Incurred in compliance with the Indenture, including Indebtedness that Refinances Refinancing Indebtedness; provided, however, that:

(1) such Refinancing Indebtedness has a Stated Maturity no earlier than the Stated Maturity of the Indebtedness being Refinanced;

(2) such Refinancing Indebtedness has an Average Life at the time such Refinancing Indebtedness is Incurred that is equal to or greater than the Average Life of the Indebtedness being Refinanced;

(3) such Refinancing Indebtedness has an aggregate principal amount (or if Incurred with original issue discount, an aggregate issue price) that is equal to or less than the aggregate principal amount (or if Incurred with original issue discount, the aggregate accreted value) then outstanding or committed (plus fees and expenses, including any premium and defeasance costs) under the Indebtedness being Refinanced; and

(4) if the Indebtedness being Refinanced is subordinated in right of payment to the Securities, such Refinancing Indebtedness is subordinated in right of payment to the Securities at least to the same extent as the Indebtedness being Refinanced;

* Commentary

Under some covenant forms, new debt used to refinance existing debt that is subordinated to the Securities must also have a final maturity that is after the final maturity of the Securities. For example:

"(4) if the Indebtedness being Refinanced is subordinated in right of payment to the Securities, such Refinancing Indebtedness has a final maturity date later than the final maturity date of, and is subordinated in right of payment to, the Securities on terms at least as favorable to the Holders of Securities as those contained in the documentation governing the Indebtedness being Refinanced";

provided further, however, that Refinancing Indebtedness shall not include (A) Indebtedness of a Subsidiary that Refinances Indebtedness of the Company or (B) Indebtedness of the Company or a Restricted Subsidiary that Refinances Indebtedness of an Unrestricted Subsidiary.

* Commentary

The reason for the final proviso above is that a Securityholder does not want to give a Company the ability, when incurring Refinancing Indebtedness, to disadvantage the relative claim of the Securityholders by replacing a competing claim against the Company's assets (i.e., the debt being refinanced) with a claim against the assets of a subsidiary of the Company, which claim would have structural superiority to the claims of the Securityholders. Similar considerations apply in (B) of the proviso—a Securityholder would not want the Company to have the unchecked ability to Incur debt to refinance debt of an Unrestricted Subsidiary, since the issuance of debt of the Unrestricted Subsidiary in the first place is not a transaction that is restricted by the indenture covenants.

Alternative Example:

""Refinancing Indebtedness" means Indebtedness of the Company or a Restricted Subsidiary issued in exchange for, or the proceeds from the issuance and sale or disbursement of which are used substantially concurrently to redeem or refinance in whole or in part, any Indebtedness of the Company or any Restricted Subsidiary (the "Refinanced Indebtedness") in a principal amount not in excess of the principal amount plus accrued interest, penalties and other costs of retiring the Refinanced Indebtedness so repaid or amended and the costs of issuance of such Refinancing Indebtedness (or, if such Refinancing Indebtedness refinances Indebtedness under a revolving credit facility or other agreement providing a commitment for subsequent borrowings, with a maximum commitment not to exceed the maximum commitment under such revolving credit facility or other agreement); provided that:

> *(1) the Refinancing Indebtedness is the obligation of the same Person as that of the Refinanced Indebtedness;*
> *(2) if the Refinanced Indebtedness was subordinated to or pari passu with the Securities, then such Refinancing Indebtedness, by its terms, is expressly pari passu with (in the case of Refinanced Indebtedness that was pari passu with), or subordinate in right of payment to (in the case of Refinanced Indebtedness that was subordinated to) the Securities at least to the same extent as the Refinanced Indebtedness;*
> *(3) the Refinancing Indebtedness is scheduled to mature either (a) no earlier than the Refinanced Indebtedness being repaid or amended or (b) after the maturity date of the Securities;*
> *(4) the portion, if any, of the Refinancing Indebtedness that is scheduled to mature on or prior to the maturity date of the Securities has an Average Life at the time such Refinancing Indebtedness is incurred that is equal to or greater than the Average Life of the portion of the Refinanced Indebtedness being repaid that is scheduled to mature on or prior to the maturity date of the Securities; and*
> *(5) the Refinancing Indebtedness is secured only to the extent, if at all, and by the assets, that the Refinanced Indebtedness being repaid or amended is secured."*

"Related Business" means any business in which the Company or any of the Restricted Subsidiaries was engaged on the Issue Date and any business related, ancillary or complementary to such business.

"Restricted Payment" with respect to any Person means:

> (1) the declaration or payment of any dividends or any other distributions of any sort in respect of its Capital Stock (including any payment in connection with any merger or consolidation involving such Person) or similar payment to the direct or indirect holders of its Capital Stock (other than (A) dividends or distributions payable solely in its Capital Stock (other than Disqualified Stock), (B) dividends or distributions payable solely to the Company or a Restricted Subsidiary and (C) pro rata dividends or other distributions made by a Subsidiary that is not a Wholly Owned Subsidiary to holders of a minority stake in the Capital Stock of such Subsidiary;

* **Commentary**

The parenthetical in clause (A) of the foregoing definition occasionally includes, in addition to Disqualified Stock, Preferred Stock.

Occasionally the question arises whether a payment made by a Company to a stockholder is made "in respect of its Capital Stock." In Health-Chem Corp. v. Baker, 737 F. Supp. 770 (S.D.N.Y. 1990), affirmed, 915 F.2d 805 (2d Cir. 1990), the Company was obligated in a settlement agreement to sell a former director's shares to a third party and turn over to the former director the sale proceeds as well as any deficiency in such proceeds as compared to a stipulated price for the shares. The court concluded that this was not a redemption of the shares by the Company and that the deficiency payment was not a payment to a current stockholder, but rather a settlement payment that did not reduce stockholders' equity. However, it is commonly understood (although sometimes specified in purported carveouts to the Restricted Payments definition) that reasonable compensation to members of the Board, customary financial sponsor management fees, and other such payments to persons who happen to be equity holders are not Restricted Payments.

> (2) the purchase, redemption or other acquisition or retirement for value of any Capital Stock of the Company held by any Person (other than by a Restricted Subsidiary) or of any Capital Stock of a Restricted Subsidiary held by any Affiliate of the Company (other than by a Restricted Subsidiary), including in connection with any merger or consolidation and including the exercise of any option to exchange any Capital Stock (other than into Capital Stock of the Company that is not Disqualified Stock);

* *Commentary*

The foregoing provision is sometimes limited to the purchase, etc., of the Company's capital stock only, and does not address the acquisition of capital stock of a subsidiary because an acquisition of such capital stock is an Investment, which is picked up in clause (4) below. However, since the definition of "Permitted Investments" (which are expressly excluded from clause (4) below) allows unlimited Investments in Restricted Subsidiaries, if the Securityholders are concerned about the ability of a Company to purchase minority interests from Affiliates of the Company (which might be viewed as a disguised dividend), then clause (2) should retain the concept as it appears in the model definition above. The foregoing clause (2) may also be drafted to restrict the acquisition of the stock of Restricted Subsidiaries from any person, as opposed to affiliates as set forth above, but this may be too restrictive, since Securityholders would normally view it as advantageous if the Company acquires minority interests from third parties—if a Restricted Subsidiary becomes wholly owned, then cash management between the Company and such Subsidiary becomes much easier for the Company. For example:

> "(2) the purchase, repurchase, redemption or other acquisition or retirement for value of any Capital Stock of the Company or any Restricted Subsidiary held by Persons other than the Company or a Restricted Subsidiary";

Advisors to a Company that is to be acquired in a leveraged buyout ought to keep in mind the court's holding in Alleco, Inc. v. IBJ Schroder Bank & Trust Co., 745 F. Supp. 1467 (D. Minn. 1989). While the actions of the Company and its controlling shareholder in that case were particularly egregious and designed to circumvent the indenture covenants, the decision is legally sound and would appear to have broad applicability. One common interpretation of the holding is that if the cash consideration to be paid to *stockholders in connection with a tender offer or merger is attributable to proceeds from indebtedness that is incurred by the acquisition vehicle or merger subsidiary immediately prior to the acquisition but in substance solely upon the creditworthiness and asset values of the Company, then notwithstanding the form of the transaction, the payment of such consideration is in substance a payment by the Company to acquire its Capital Stock for value and therefore a Restricted Payment. Presumably if the acquiror can supply an amount of cash from external sources (i.e., not based on the assets or cash flows of the Company) to pay the acquisition consideration to the existing shareholders, then it should be distinguishable from Alleco.*

(3) the purchase, repurchase, redemption, defeasance or other acquisition or retirement for value, prior to scheduled maturity, scheduled repayment or scheduled sinking fund payment of any Subordinated Obligations of the Company or any Subsidiary Guarantor (other than (A) from the Company or a Restricted Subsidiary or (B) the purchase, repurchase, redemption, defeasance or other acquisition of Subordinated Obligations purchased in anticipation of satisfying a sinking fund obligation, principal installment or final maturity, in each case due within one year of the date of such purchase, repurchase, redemption, defeasance or other acquisition); or

* *Commentary*

Unlike the foregoing example, other forms often do not exclude payments within the year prior to maturity or the applicable payment date from the definition. In addition, the foregoing provision is frequently drafted to include within its scope any subordinated indebtedness, rather than just that of the Company and the Guarantors. Other forms do not exclude purchases from the Company or a Restricted Subsidiary from the definition.

(4) the making of any Investment (other than a Permitted Investment) in any Person.

"Restricted Subsidiary" means any Subsidiary of the Company that is not an Unrestricted Subsidiary.

"Sale/Leaseback Transaction" means an arrangement relating to property owned by the Company or a Restricted Subsidiary on the Issue Date or thereafter acquired by the Company or a Restricted Subsidiary whereby the Company or a Restricted Subsidiary transfers such property to a Person and the Company or a Restricted Subsidiary leases it from such Person.

"Secured Indebtedness" means any Indebtedness of the Company secured by a Lien.

"Senior Indebtedness" means with respect to any Person:

(1) Indebtedness of such Person, whether outstanding on the Issue Date or thereafter Incurred; and

(2) all other Obligations of such Person (including interest accruing on or after the filing of any petition in bankruptcy or for reorganization relating to such Person whether or not post-filing interest is allowed in such proceeding) in respect of Indebtedness described in clause (1) above

unless, in the case of clauses (1) and (2), in the instrument creating or evidencing the same or pursuant to which the same is outstanding, it is provided that such

Indebtedness or other Obligations are [subordinate] [subordinate or pari passu] in right of payment to the Securities; provided, however, that Senior Indebtedness shall not include:

* Commentary

Generally, the drafter would use "subordinate" if issuing senior securities and "subordinate or pari passu" if issuing any type of subordinated securities.

(1) any obligation of such Person to the Company or any Subsidiary;

(2) any liability for Federal, state, local or other taxes owed or owing by such Person;

(3) any accounts payable or other liability to trade creditors arising in the ordinary course of business (including guarantees thereof or instruments evidencing such liabilities);

(4) any Indebtedness or other Obligation of such Person which is subordinate or junior in any respect to any other Indebtedness or other Obligation of such Person; or

* Commentary

Omit clause (4) if issuing junior subordinated securities.

(5) that portion of any Indebtedness which at the time of Incurrence is Incurred in violation of the Indenture.

* Commentary

Clause (5) above is central with respect to subordinated notes, as it effectively prevents indebtedness that is incurred in violation of the indenture from having the benefit of the indenture's subordination provisions.

As shown in the following examples taken from senior subordinated deals, alternative approaches to this definition commonly exclude additional types of obligations from the scope of "Senior Indebtedness."

Alternative Example 1:

"'Senior Indebtedness' means the principal of, premium, if any, and interest (including any interest accruing subsequent to the filing of a petition of bankruptcy at the rate provided for in the documentation with respect thereto, whether or not such interest is an allowed claim under applicable law) on any Indebtedness of the Company, whether outstanding on the Issue Date or thereafter created, incurred or assumed, unless, in the case of any particular Indebtedness, the instrument creating or evidencing the same or pursuant to which the same is outstanding expressly provides that such Indebtedness shall not be senior in right of payment to the Securities.

Notwithstanding the foregoing, 'Senior Indebtedness' shall not include:

(1) any Indebtedness of the Company to any of its Subsidiaries;

(2) Indebtedness to, or guaranteed on behalf of, any director, officer or employee of the Company or any of its Subsidiaries (including amounts owed for compensation);

(3) obligations to trade creditors and other amounts incurred in connection with obtaining goods, materials or services;

(4) Indebtedness represented by Disqualified Stock;

(5) any liability for taxes owed or owing by the Company;

(6) that portion of any Indebtedness incurred in violation of Section 4.04 (but, as to any such obligation, no such violation shall be deemed to exist for purposes of this clause (6) if the holder(s) of such obligation or their representative shall have received an Officers' Certificate of the Company to the effect that the incurrence of such Indebtedness does not (or, in the case of revolving credit indebtedness, that the incurrence of the entire committed amount thereof at the date on which the initial borrowing thereunder is made would not) violate such provisions of the Indenture);

(7) Indebtedness which, when incurred and without respect to any election under Section 1111(b) of Title 11, United States Code, is without recourse to the Company; and

(8) any Indebtedness which is, by its express terms, subordinated in right of payment to any other Indebtedness of the Company."

Note that in the foregoing example, obligations in respect of Disqualified Stock are specifically excluded, to prevent equity from receiving the benefits afforded senior indebtedness. In addition, non-recourse indebtedness and indebtedness to certain insiders are also excluded.

The language in clause (6) if Alternative Example 1 protects the interests of senior debt holders from losing the benefit of senior status by virtue of a breach of the debt covenant of which they are unaware and with respect to which they have taken certain actions.

Alternative Example 2:

""Senior Indebtedness" means:

(1) all Indebtedness of the Company outstanding under Credit Agreement and all Hedging Obligations with respect thereto;

(2) any other Indebtedness of the Company permitted to be incurred under the terms of the indenture, unless the instrument under which such Indebtedness is incurred expressly provides that it is on a parity with or subordinated in right of payment to the Securities; and

(3) all Obligations with respect to the items listed in the preceding clauses (1) and (2).

Notwithstanding anything to the contrary in the preceding, Senior Indebtedness will not include:

(1) any liability for federal, state, local or other taxes owed or owing by the Company;

(2) any intercompany Indebtedness of the Company or any of its Subsidiaries to the Company or any of its Affiliates;

(3) any trade payables; or

(4) the portion of any Indebtedness that is incurred in violation of the indenture."

In clause (2) of the foregoing example, the concept that indebtedness to related parties should not be considered senior to the Securities is expanded to include Affiliates (which is significantly broader in scope than "subsidiaries").

"Stated Maturity" means, with respect to any security, the date specified in such security as the fixed date on which the final payment of principal of such security is due and payable, including pursuant to any mandatory redemption provision (but excluding any provision providing for the repurchase of such security at the option of the holder thereof upon the happening of any contingency unless such contingency has occurred).

*"**Subordinated Obligation**"* means, with respect to a Person, any Indebtedness of such Person (whether outstanding on the Issue Date or thereafter Incurred) which is subordinate or junior in right of payment to the Securities or a Subsidiary Guaranty of such Person, as the case may be, pursuant to a written agreement to that effect.

*"**Subsidiary**"* means, with respect to any Person, any corporation, association, partnership or other business entity of which more than 50% of the total voting power of shares of Voting Stock is at the time owned or controlled, directly or indirectly, by:

(1) such Person;
(2) such Person and one or more Subsidiaries of such Person; or
(3) one or more Subsidiaries of such Person.

* *Commentary*

If an entity is not a Subsidiary of the Company under the foregoing definition (e.g., a 50%-owned joint venture), its activities are not governed by the covenants, although transactions between the Company and its Restricted Subsidiaries on the one hand and such other entity on the other hand will need to be evaluated for compliance with the covenants. High yield covenants typically distinguish between "Restricted" Subsidiaries, whose activities are governed by the covenants but which may, particularly if those Restricted Subsidiaries are wholly owned by the Company or are guarantors of the Securities, generally freely transact business with the Company, and "Unrestricted" Subsidiaries, which are not governed by the covenants but with which the Company does not have the benefit of freely transacting business. Rather, each transaction between a Company and its Restricted Subsidiaries on the one hand and an Unrestricted Subsidiary on the other must be tested for compliance with the covenants.

Practitioners should keep in mind that this distinction between "Restricted" and "Unrestricted" Subsidiaries makes sense in the context of high yield covenants, but may not make sense in the context of an investment grade covenant package. Thus, where a Company's creditworthiness improves to the point that the Company becomes investment-grade rated, the drafter of a new investment grade indenture would be well-advised to resist the temptation to use the Company's prior high yield indenture as a starting point, particularly the concepts of "Restricted" and "Unrestricted" Subsidiaries. If, however, the drafter does start with the high yield indenture and retains the notion of restricting the activities of Restricted Subsidiaries in the investment grade covenant but strips out the limitation on the ability of the Company to designate Unrestricted Subsidiaries (i.e., the Limitation on Restricted Payments covenant), on the theory that such a limitation does not appear in most investment grade transactions, the resulting indenture, read literally, might inadvertently allow the Company to designate all its Subsidiaries as "Unrestricted" and thereby put all of them beyond the reach of the investment grade indenture covenants.

*"**Temporary Cash Investments**"* means any of the following:

(1) any investment in direct obligations of the United States of America or any agency thereof or obligations guaranteed by the United States of America or any agency thereof and maturing within 180 days of the date of acquisition thereof;

(2) any investment in demand and time deposit accounts, certificates of deposit and money market deposits maturing within 180 days of the date of acquisition thereof issued by a bank or trust company which is organized under the laws of the United States of America, any State thereof or any foreign country recognized by the United States of America, and which bank or trust company has capital, surplus and undivided profits aggregating in excess of $100.0 million (or the foreign currency equivalent thereof) and has outstanding debt which is rated "A" (or such similar equivalent rating) or higher by at least one nationally recognized statistical rating organization (as defined in Rule 436 under the Securities Act);

(3) any investment in repurchase obligations with a term of not more than 30 days for underlying securities of the types described in clause (1) above entered into with a bank meeting the qualifications described in clause (2) above;

(4) any investment in commercial paper, maturing not more than 180 days after the date of acquisition, issued by a corporation (other than an Affiliate of the Company) organized and in existence under the laws of the United States of America or any foreign country recognized by the United States of America with a rating at the time as of which any investment therein is made of "P-1" (or higher) according to Moody's Investors Service, Inc. or "A-1" (or higher) according to Standard and Poor's Ratings Group;

(5) any investment in securities with maturities of 180 days or less from the date of acquisition issued or fully guaranteed by any state, commonwealth or territory of the United States of America, or by any political subdivision or taxing authority thereof, and rated at least "A" by Standard & Poor's Ratings Group or "A" by Moody's Investors Service, Inc.; and

(6) any investment in money market funds that invest substantially all their assets in securities of the types described in clauses (1) through (5) above.

* *Commentary*

Some indenture forms limit Temporary Cash Investments to dollar-denominated Investments. This definition should be reviewed against the actual cash management practices of the Company. It is sometimes inadvertently violated by the Company and, ironically, is occasionally too restrictive to accommodate the treasury services that are being cross-sold by the investment bank that is bringing the Securities to market.

"Unrestricted Subsidiary" means:

(1) any Subsidiary of the Company that at the time of determination shall be designated an Unrestricted Subsidiary by the Board in the manner provided below; and

(2) any Subsidiary of an Unrestricted Subsidiary.

The Board may designate any Subsidiary of the Company (including any newly acquired or newly formed Subsidiary) to be an Unrestricted Subsidiary unless such Subsidiary or any of its Subsidiaries owns any Capital Stock or Indebtedness of, or holds any Lien on any property of, the Company or any other Subsidiary of the Company that is not a Subsidiary of the Subsidiary to be so designated; provided, however, that either (A) the Subsidiary to be so designated has total assets of $1,000 or less or (B) if such Subsidiary has assets greater than $1,000, such designation would be permitted under Section 4.05.

The Board may designate any Unrestricted Subsidiary to be a Restricted Subsidiary; provided, however, that immediately after giving effect to such designation (A) the

Company could Incur $1.00 of additional Indebtedness under Section 4.04(a) and (B) no Default shall have occurred and be continuing. Any such designation by the Board of Directors shall be evidenced to the Trustee by promptly filing with the Trustee a copy of the resolution of the Board giving effect to such designation and an Officers' Certificate certifying that such designation complied with the foregoing provisions.

* *Commentary*

Other forms impose additional conditions on the right to designated subsidiaries as "unrestricted." The following is one example of a more restrictive definition:

"'Unrestricted Subsidiary' means any Subsidiary of the Company that is designated by the Board as an Unrestricted Subsidiary pursuant to a Board Resolution, but only to the extent that such Subsidiary:

(1) has no Indebtedness other than Non-Recourse Debt;

(2) is not party to any agreement, contract, arrangement or understanding with the Company or any Restricted Subsidiary of the Company unless the terms of any such agreement, contract, arrangement or understanding are no less favorable to the Company or such Restricted Subsidiary than those that might be obtained at the time from Persons who are not Affiliates of the Company;

(3) is a person with respect to which neither the Company nor any of its Restricted Subsidiaries has any direct or indirect obligation (a) to subscribe for additional Capital Stock of such Person or (b) to maintain or preserve such Person's financial condition or to cause such Person to achieve any specified levels of operating results;

(4) has not guaranteed or otherwise directly or indirectly provided credit support for any Indebtedness of the Company or any of its Restricted Subsidiaries; and

(5) has at least one director on its board of directors that is not a director or executive officer of the Company or any of its Restricted Subsidiaries and has at least one executive officer that is not a director or executive officer of the Company or any of its Restricted Subsidiaries.

Any designation of a Subsidiary of the Company as an Unrestricted Subsidiary shall be evidenced to the Trustee by filing with the Trustee a certified copy of the Board Resolution giving effect to such designation and an Officers' Certificate certifying that such designation complied with the preceding conditions and was permitted by Section 4.05. If, at any time, any Unrestricted Subsidiary would fail to meet the preceding requirements as an Unrestricted Subsidiary, it shall thereafter cease to be an Unrestricted Subsidiary for purposes of this Indenture and any Indebtedness of such Subsidiary shall be deemed to be incurred by a Restricted Subsidiary of the Company as of such date and, if such Indebtedness is not permitted to be incurred as of such date under Section 4.04, the Company shall be in default of such covenant. The Board of the Company may at any time designate any Unrestricted Subsidiary to be a Restricted Subsidiary; provided that such designation shall be deemed to be an incurrence of Indebtedness by a Restricted Subsidiary of the Company of any outstanding Indebtedness of such Unrestricted Subsidiary and such designation shall only be permitted if (1) such Indebtedness is permitted under Section 4.04, calculated on a pro forma basis as if such designation had occurred at the beginning of the four-quarter reference period; and (2) no Default or Event of Default would be in existence following such designation."

For purposes of this definition, "Non-Recourse Debt" is defined as follows:

"'Non-Recourse Debt' means Indebtedness:

(1) as to which neither the Company nor any of its Restricted Subsidiaries (a) provides credit support of any kind (including any undertaking, agreement or instrument that would constitute Indebtedness), (b) is directly or indirectly liable as a guarantor or otherwise, or (c) constitutes the lender;

(2) no default with respect to which (including any rights that the holders thereof may have to take enforcement action against an Unrestricted Subsidiary) would permit upon notice, lapse of time or both any holder of any other Indebtedness (other than the Securities) of the Company or any of its Restricted Subsidiaries to declare a default on such other Indebtedness or cause the payment thereof to be accelerated or payable prior to its stated maturity; and

(3) as to which the lenders have been notified in writing that they will not have any recourse to the stock or assets of the Company or any of its Restricted Subsidiaries."

Clauses (1) through (5) of the alternative definition of Unrestricted Subsidiary are intended to isolate the Unrestricted Subsidiary from the restricted group of companies so that a credit problem at or bankruptcy of the Unrestricted Subsidiary do not trigger defaults under debt of the restricted group or result in a bankruptcy of members of the restricted group. Clause (1) (and the definition of Non-Recourse Debt) ensures that a default on debt of the Unrestricted Subsidiary does not result in a cross-default under debt of the restricted group. Clauses (2) through (5) are designed to satisfy some of the separateness criteria that support an argument that the Unrestricted Subsidiary should not be substantively consolidated with its parent and sister companies in a chapter 11 proceeding, although various judicial approaches to substantive consolidation are still evolving. See, e.g., In re Owens Corning, 419 F.3d 195 (3d Cir. 2005), cert. denied sub nom., 126 S. Ct. 1910 (2006).

Sometimes, a particular Subsidiary or line of business may be prohibited from being designated as an Unrestricted Subsidiary, on the grounds that the particular business is an integral part of the credit story when the Securities are issued.

*"**Voting Stock**"* of a Person means all classes of Capital Stock of such Person then outstanding and normally entitled (without regard to the occurrence of any contingency) to vote in the election of directors, managers or trustees thereof.

*"**Wholly Owned Subsidiary**"* means a Restricted Subsidiary all the Capital Stock of which (other than directors' qualifying shares) is owned by the Company or one or more other Wholly Owned Subsidiaries.

SECTION 1.02. OTHER DEFINITIONS

Term	Defined in Section
"Affiliate Transaction"	4.09(a)
"Change of Control Offer"	4.07(b)
"Initial Lien"	4.08
"Offer"	4.06(e)
"Offer Amount"	4.06(e)(2)
"Offer Period"	4.06(e)(2)
"Purchase Date"	4.06(e)(1)
"Successor Company"	4.14(a)(1)

SECTION 1.03. INCORPORATION BY REFERENCE OF TRUST INDENTURE ACT

This Indenture is subject to the mandatory provisions of the TIA which are incorporated by reference in and made a part of this Indenture. The following TIA terms have the following meanings:

"Commission" means the SEC;

"indenture securities" means the Securities and the Subsidiary Guaranties;

"indenture security holder" means a Securityholder;

"indenture to be qualified" means this Indenture;

"indenture trustee" or "institutional trustee" means the Trustee, and

"obligor" on the indenture securities means the Company, each Subsidiary Guarantor and any other obligor on the indenture securities.

All other TIA terms used in this Indenture that are defined by the TIA, defined by TIA reference to another statute or defined by SEC rule have the meanings assigned to them by such definitions.

SECTION 1.04. RULES OF CONSTRUCTION

Unless the context otherwise requires:

(1) a term has the meaning assigned to it;

(2) an accounting term not otherwise defined has the meaning assigned to it in accordance with GAAP;

(3) "or" is not exclusive;

(4) "including" means including without limitation;

(5) words in the singular include the plural and words in the plural include the singular;

(6) unsecured Indebtedness shall not be deemed to be subordinate or junior to secured Indebtedness merely by virtue of its nature as unsecured Indebtedness;

(7) secured Indebtedness shall not be deemed to be subordinate or junior to any other secured Indebtedness merely because it has a junior priority with respect to the same collateral;

(8) the principal amount of any noninterest bearing or other discount security at any date shall be the principal amount thereof that would be shown on a balance sheet of the issuer dated such date prepared in accordance with GAAP;

(9) the principal amount of any Preferred Stock shall be (A) the maximum liquidation value of such Preferred Stock or (B) the maximum mandatory redemption or mandatory repurchase price with respect to such Preferred Stock, whichever is greater; and

(10) all references to the date the Securities were originally issued shall refer to the Issue Date.

LIMITATION ON INDEBTEDNESS

* *Commentary*

The limitation on the incurrence of indebtedness is designed to protect the Securityholders from the issuance by the Company of additional debt unless the Company has the demonstrated capacity (usually tested based upon a comparison of cash flow to interest expense) to service all its debt including the proposed new debt. This test is generally known as the "coverage" or "debt incurrence" test and the debt permitted to be so incurred is generally referred to as "ratio debt." If the Company does not have such demonstrated capacity, then it may not incur any additional debt except to the extent that it can take advantage of certain specified exceptions to the debt incurrence test that are available to the Company without regard to its debt-servicing capacity. This kind of permitted debt is often referred to as "permitted debt." A point to remember here is that this is a limitation on an incurrence of indebtedness; once incurred, the Company is permitted to leave that debt outstanding notwithstanding any subsequent deterioration in debt-servicing capacity. Also note that the fact that a particular item of debt constitutes "permitted debt" does not mean that interest on that debt can be ignored in calculations of the Consolidated Coverage Ratio.

SECTION 4.04. LIMITATION ON INDEBTEDNESS

(a) The Company shall not, and shall not permit any Restricted Subsidiary to, Incur, directly or indirectly, any Indebtedness; provided, however, that the Company [and its Restricted Subsidiaries] [and its Guarantors] shall be entitled to Incur Indebtedness if, on the date of such Incurrence and after giving effect thereto on a pro forma basis, no Default has occurred and is continuing and the Consolidated Coverage Ratio exceeds • to 1.0 [the Consolidated Leverage Ratio would be less than • to 1.0.] [if such Indebtedness is Incurred prior to •, 200•, • to 1.0, or • to 1.0 if such Indebtedness is Incurred thereafter].

* ***Commentary***

The foregoing is the basic debt incurrence test allowing for "ratio debt." If the Company on a trailing twelve month basis, and on a pro forma basis after giving effect to the incurrence of the proposed indebtedness, has enough cash flow (or "Consolidated EBITDA") in relation to its interest expense (typically a minimum ratio of 2 to 1 or higher), then the Company can incur such indebtedness. For example, assume the Company has outstanding $100 million of debt bearing interest at 5% per annum and has Consolidated EBITDA of $30 million for the trailing twelve months. Assume further that the Company wants to incur an additional $100 million in debt with an interest rate of 9%. With those numbers, pro forma Consolidated Interest Expense (assuming no other debt or preferred stock) would be $14 million. If the required minimum Consolidated Coverage Ratio is 2:1, the Company would be permitted to incur that additional debt; the Consolidated Coverage Ratio would be $30 million divided by $14 million or 2.14.

A related, but thorny question, arises when a Company proposes to Incur debt on a single day (e.g., to raise cash to consummate an acquisition transaction) where some of the debt is to be incurred pursuant to the ratio test and some pursuant to the permitted debt exceptions in paragraph (b) below. While some practitioners have struggled with the question whether the permitted debt portion should be taken into consideration in calculating the amount of debt that can be incurred under clause (a), the Model covenants and definitions make it clear, primarily in the Model Definitions of "Consolidated Coverage Ratio" and "Consolidated Leverage Ratio," but also in paragraph (d) below (which specifically acknowledges that debt can be divided and classified between paragraphs (a) and (b)), that in connection with any single or related incurrences, the Company can ignore the impact of the incurrence on the same date of debt under paragraph (b) in calculating the relevant ratio and must ignore the impact of the discharge on the same date of any debt to the extent discharged with proceeds of debt incurred under paragraph (b).

An alternative to the interest coverage test is a leverage test, which evaluates the relationship of the Company's consolidated debt to its trailing twelve month Consolidated EBITDA on a pro forma basis for the incurrence of such indebtedness. This test has typically been used for offerings in certain industries where companies are expected to experience high growth but generate limited free cash flow in the near term, such as for media, telecommunications and high tech companies.

An important item on which to keep focused in connection with the basic debt incurrence test, as well as the exceptions that follow, is whether the covenant allows Restricted Subsidiaries, as well as or instead of the Company, to issue the debt. If subsidiaries were allowed to issue such debt, substantial amounts of indebtedness could potentially be issued at a structurally superior level to the Securities. For this reason, ratio debt is frequently allowed to be incurred only by the Company and by subsidiaries who are guarantors of the Securities. It may also be appropriate to allow subsidiaries to incur ratio debt if the Securities are already contractually subordinated.

Some forms explicitly limit the issuance of Disqualified Stock. In the case of the Model Definitions, Disqualified Stock is included within clause (7) of the definition of "Indebtedness," and is therefore already included within the scope of the debt covenant. The debt covenant may also be drafted to explicitly restrict issuances of preferred stock by subsidiaries, payments with respect to which would be structurally senior to the Securities (to the extent the issuing subsidiary is not a guarantor). The Model Definition of "Indebtedness" already includes preferred stock of a Subsidiary, so no separate reference is required in the foregoing covenant.

Alternative Example 1:

"The Company will not, and will not permit any of its Restricted Subsidiaries to, directly or indirectly, create, incur, issue, assume, guarantee or otherwise become directly or indirectly liable, contingently or otherwise, with respect to (collectively, 'incur') any Indebtedness (including Acquired Debt), and the Company will not issue any Disqualified Stock and will not permit any of its Subsidiaries to issue any shares of preferred stock; provided, however, that the Company may incur Indebtedness (including Acquired Debt) or issue Disqualified Stock, if the Consolidated Coverage Ratio for the Company's most recently ended four full fiscal quarters for which internal financial statements are available immediately preceding the date on which such additional Indebtedness is incurred or such Disqualified Stock or preferred stock is issued would have been at least • to 1, determined on a pro forma basis (including a pro forma application of the net proceeds therefrom), as if the additional Indebtedness had been incurred or the preferred stock or Disqualified Stock had been issued, as the case may be, at the beginning of such four-quarter period."

The example above refers to "Acquired Debt," which is indebtedness of acquired or merged entities existing at the time they are acquired. This concept is effectively captured in the Model Definitions of "Incur" and "Indebtedness" included herein, and therefore no *separate reference is required in the Model covenant. The description of the pro forma adjustments in the foregoing example is addressed herein in the Model Definition of Consolidated Coverage Ratio.*

In addition, as in this example, language conditioning the incurrence of ratio debt on the absence of a default is not included in all forms.

(b) In addition to the foregoing paragraph (a), so long as no Default has occurred and is continuing, the Company and the Restricted Subsidiaries shall be entitled to Incur any or all of the following Indebtedness:

(1) Indebtedness Incurred [by the Company] pursuant to a Credit Agreement; provided, however, that, after giving effect to any such Incurrence, the aggregate principal amount of such Indebtedness then outstanding does not exceed the greater of (i) $• million less the sum of all principal payments with respect to such Indebtedness pursuant to Section 4.06(a)(3)(A) and (ii) the sum of (x) •% of the book value of the inventory of the Company and its Restricted Subsidiaries and (y) •% of the book value of the accounts receivables of the Company and its Restricted Subsidiaries;

* *Commentary*

Almost every high yield debt covenant contains an exception for the Company to incur bank debt. The exception may be constructed around the Company's borrowing base (inventory and accounts receivables) or it may be limited to a specified dollar amount. The example above also requires a reduction in the specified dollar level of debt permitted by this exception to the extent that the Company sells assets and uses the proceeds to permanently repay its Credit Agreement debt. The idea behind this requirement is that if a Company sells a portion of its assets and permanently reduces Credit Agreement debt from the proceeds, the Company no longer needs the full amount of the bank facility and consequently, the basket can be reduced. Otherwise, Securityholders would be faced with the diminution of the asset base that they could recover against in a bankruptcy, without a corresponding reduction in the Company's debt.

To the extent that subsidiaries are guarantors or obligors on credit facilities, they generally must be included within the scope of this permitted debt provision.

In some forms, this Credit Agreement debt provision will be divided into two separate clauses: one for revolving loans and one for term loans, with different limitations on each.

(2) Indebtedness owed to and held by the Company or a Restricted Subsidiary; provided, however, that (A) any subsequent issuance or transfer of any Capital Stock which results in any such Restricted Subsidiary ceasing to be a Restricted Subsidiary or any subsequent transfer of such Indebtedness (other than to the Company or a Restricted Subsidiary) shall be deemed, in each case, to constitute the Incurrence of such Indebtedness by the obligor thereon and (B) if the Company is the obligor on such Indebtedness, such Indebtedness is expressly subordinated to the prior payment in full in cash of all obligations with respect to the Securities;

* *Commentary*

The foregoing exception permits intercompany debt between the Company and Restricted Subsidiaries. Notice that the intercompany debt must not only be issued to the Company or a Restricted Subsidiary but it must remain with that person (or with another member of the same group). If the debt is transferred outside of the group to a third party, it no longer qualifies for this exception and is deemed to be incurred again at the time of transfer. The Company would in such a case need to identify another provision of this covenant that would allow it to incur such debt. In the event the Securities are guaranteed, clause (B) would typically be expanded to require that such debt of a guarantor be subordinated to payments in respect of the guarantee.

In many covenant forms, the foregoing would include an additional clause providing that, in the event that any Restricted Subsidiary which holds indebtedness of the Company or another Restricted Subsidiary is designated as an "Unrestricted Subsidiary," the designation would constitute an incurrence of Indebtedness subject to the other provisions of the debt covenant. Other covenant forms (including this one) provide in the definition of "Unrestricted Subsidiary" that a Restricted Subsidiary which is owed money by the Company or a Restricted Subsidiary may not designated as Unrestricted. In either case, the effect is to ensure that Indebtedness owed outside of the credit group is not assumed without satisfying the debt covenant.

(3) the Securities (other than any Additional Securities);

* Commentary

In the foregoing exception, Additional Securities that may be issued in an "add-on" deal at a subsequent time are excluded. Otherwise, there would be a loophole by which unlimited amounts of indebtedness could be issued under the indenture without satisfying the debt covenant. Although the indenture may contain the built-in mechanics for the issuance of Additional Securities, the Company is nonetheless required to find capacity to incur such Additional Securities through either its ratio test or through one of the other permitted debt exceptions to the covenant.

For purposes of the foregoing, Securities issued in an exchange offer for the Securities issued on the Issue Date are included within the definition of "Securities," and, hence, permitted, although often exchange securities will be explicitly mentioned in this provision.

(4) Indebtedness outstanding on the Issue Date (other than Indebtedness described in clause (1), (2) or (3) of this Section 4.04(b));

[(5) Indebtedness of a Restricted Subsidiary Incurred and outstanding on or prior to the date on which such Subsidiary was acquired by the Company (other than Indebtedness Incurred in connection with, or to provide all or any portion of the funds or credit support utilized to consummate, the transaction or series of related transactions pursuant to which such Subsidiary became a Subsidiary or was acquired by the Company); provided, however, that on the date of such acquisition and after giving pro forma effect thereto, the Company would have been able to Incur at least $1.00 of Indebtedness pursuant to Section 4.04(a);]

* Commentary

The acquisition of an entity that owes preexisting debt is an incurrence of indebtedness by the acquiror. The incurrence of debt under this clause is effectively tested by the basic debt coverage test. Therefore, if the debt coverage test is drafted to allow Restricted Subsidiaries to incur Indebtedness thereunder, this provision is unnecessary.

(5) Refinancing Indebtedness in respect of Indebtedness Incurred pursuant to Section 4.04(a) or pursuant to clause (3), (4) or (5) of this Section 4.04(b) or this clause (6); [provided, however, that to the extent such Refinancing Indebtedness directly or indirectly Refinances Indebtedness of a Subsidiary Incurred pursuant to clause (5), such Refinancing Indebtedness shall be Incurred only by such Subsidiary;]

* *Commentary*

To the extent a Company has outstanding debt, the indenture needs to permit the Company to refinance such debt at any time so that there is no potential for a default at the maturity of such indebtedness (similar to the notion that once incurred, the debt is always permitted). The requirements for the refinancing indebtedness are that the Company may not increase the principal amount (except to the extent needed to pay related costs, e.g., accrued interest, premium and other retirement costs), that the Company may not shorten the average life of the debt that is being refinanced and that debt may not be refinanced with more senior or structurally superior debt. In the case of indebtedness that was permitted by clause (5) (acquired subsidiary debt), the foregoing exception requires that such debt only be refinanced at that same subsidiary.

Note that this clause does not by its terms provide for refinancings of the credit facility debt incurred under clause (1). This does not mean, however, that bank indebtedness may not be refinanced under the indenture. The definition of "Credit Agreement" includes refinancings and replacements thereof; thus new bank or other debt may be incurred under clause (1) to replace existing bank debt, subject to the limitations on the amount set forth in clause (1).

(6) Hedging Obligations consisting of Interest Rate Agreements directly related to Indebtedness permitted to be Incurred by the Company pursuant to this Indenture;

* *Commentary*

Hedging Obligations are treated as debt primarily to create the potential for a cross acceleration default if the net costs of the hedging transactions are large and unpaid and here, secondarily, to make sure that the hedges are not speculative but designed to provide protection from specific business risks and exposures. In the example above, the carveout is limited to Interest Rate Agreements, though often it will include all Hedging Obligations (with appropriate limitations). For example:

> *"(6) Hedging Obligations that are incurred for the purpose of hedging interest rate risk with respect to any floating rate Indebtedness that is permitted by the terms of the indenture to be outstanding or for the purpose of fixing or hedging currency exchange risk in the ordinary course of business."*

(7) Indebtedness consisting of the Subsidiary Guaranty of a Subsidiary Guarantor and any Guarantee by a Subsidiary Guarantor of Indebtedness Incurred pursuant to Section 4.04(a) or pursuant to clause (1), (2), (3), (4), (6) or (9) of this Section 4.04(b);

(8) Indebtedness of the Company or any of its Restricted Subsidiaries represented by Capital Lease Obligations, mortgage financings or purchase money obligations, in each case, incurred for the purpose of financing all or any part of the purchase price or cost of construction or improvement of property, plant or equipment used in the business of the Company or such Restricted Subsidiary, in an aggregate principal amount, including all Refinancing Indebtedness incurred to refund, refinance or replace any

Indebtedness incurred pursuant to this clause, not to exceed $• million at any time outstanding; and

(9) Indebtedness [of the Company] in an aggregate principal amount which, when taken together with all other Indebtedness [of the Company] outstanding on the date of such Incurrence (other than Indebtedness permitted by clauses (1) through (9) of this Section 4.04(b) or Section 4.04(a)), does not exceed $• million.

* Commentary

Almost every high yield debt covenant contains a general basket—generally referred to as the "general debt basket"—that permits the Company, and sometimes its subsidiaries, to issue a specified amount of indebtedness, again without regard to whether the Company exceeds the specified minimum Consolidated Coverage Ratio or is under the maximum Consolidated Leverage Ratio that would permit it to issue ratio debt. This and other baskets are usually determined by selecting a relatively small dollar amount to which it supposed that the market will not object, or by reference to similarly situated issuers and the basket as a percentage of EBITDA or assets.

Covenant forms also commonly include an additional carveout for other ordinary course Indebtedness. For example:

"Indebtedness in respect of bid, performance or surety bonds issued for the account of the Company or any Restricted Subsidiary in the ordinary course of business, including guarantees or obligations of the Company or any Restricted Subsidiary with respect to letters of credit supporting such bid, performance or surety obligations (in each case other than for an obligation for money borrowed)";

In addition to the foregoing general exceptions to the debt incurrence test, the indenture will often contain additional exceptions that would apply to a specific Company or a specific subsidiary. Other somewhat typical exceptions are (i) Indebtedness arising from banks honoring checks drawn against accounts which have insufficient funds so long as the Indebtedness is repaid within two business days of incurrence; (ii) Indebtedness incurred in connection with letters of credit to provide security for workers' compensation claims and other insurance in the ordinary course of business; (iii) Indebtedness under indemnification, adjustment of purchase price or similar obligations in connection with asset dispositions. Many definitions of "Indebtedness," including the Model Definition, do not cover some or all of the foregoing items (i), (ii) and (iii) in the definition of "Indebtedness," so these exceptions may not be necessary.

(c) Notwithstanding the foregoing, the Company shall not Incur any Indebtedness pursuant to Section 4.04(b) if the proceeds thereof are used, directly or indirectly, to Refinance any Subordinated Obligations unless such Indebtedness shall be subordinated to the Securities to at least the same extent as such Subordinated Obligations.

* Commentary

The foregoing paragraph provides that if the Company is relying upon one of the permitted debt exceptions to incur debt rather than relying on the ratio test itself, the proceeds of which will be used to refinance subordinated debt, it can only refinance such subordinated debt with other subordinated debt. The Securityholders would lose the benefit of the "cushion" they had by virtue of having subordinated debt in the capital structure if that debt could be refinanced with pari passu or, even worse, senior debt. Some forms are less restrictive than the Model covenant, in that they only force the Company to refinance subordinated debt with new subordinated debt if the Company is relying on the permitted debt exception for Refinancing Indebtedness (clause (6) above). In those forms, if the Company is relying on another permitted debt exception (e.g., clause (1) for Credit Agreement debt), then the Company would not be precluded from refinancing the subordinated debt with pari passu or senior debt. The theory is that nothing prevents the Company from utilizing the Credit Agreement debt exception to incur senior debt for other purposes, so the Company should not be prevented from using it to refinance subordinated debt.

(d) For purposes of determining compliance with this Section 4.04, (1) in the event that an item of Indebtedness meets the criteria of more than one of the types of Indebtedness described herein, the Company, in its sole discretion, shall classify such item of Indebtedness at the time of Incurrence and only be required to include the amount and type of such Indebtedness in one of the above clauses and (2) the Company shall be entitled at the time of such Incurrence to divide and classify an item of Indebtedness in more than one of the types of Indebtedness described in paragraphs (a) and (b) above.

* *Commentary*

The foregoing paragraph clarifies for the Company that in connection with any individual incurrence of indebtedness, it does not need to identify a single exception that will permit the entire amount of such indebtedness. For instance, the Company could incur a portion of the indebtedness based upon the credit agreement exception, and could also incur a portion of such indebtedness pursuant to its general basket under clause (9). This form provides that once the Company has made the determination of which provision allows it to incur an item of indebtedness, it is bound by such determination so long as that indebtedness remains outstanding and may not subsequently reallocate the indebtedness to a different provision. Other covenant forms may not contain such a restriction and may allow the Company to re-classify some or all of its debt at future dates, with the result that as the Company begins to exceed its minimum Consolidated Coverage Ratio, the permitted debt baskets can be "emptied" and reallocated to ratio debt, thereby allowing the permitted debt baskets to be used again if and when the Company's credit statistics deteriorate at a later date.

[(e) Notwithstanding Section 4.04(a) or 4.04(b), the Company shall not Incur (1) any Indebtedness if such Indebtedness is subordinate or junior in ranking in any respect to any Senior Indebtedness, unless such Indebtedness is pari passu with or is expressly subordinated in right of payment to the Securities or (2) any Secured Indebtedness that is not Senior Indebtedness unless contemporaneously therewith the Company makes effective provision to secure the Securities equally and ratably with such Secured Indebtedness for so long as such Secured Indebtedness is secured by a Lien.]

* *Commentary*

The foregoing provision is bracketed because it is used only in senior subordinated note offerings. Clause (1) (referred to as the "anti-layering" clause) is designed to protect the relative priority of senior subordinated debt, in that the Company is not allowed to incur any debt that is contractually subordinated to any indebtedness unless the debt to be incurred is pari passu with the Securities or is subordinated to the Securities. In other words, this provision ensures that the Securities are in fact the most senior subordinated debt in the capital structure.

The equivalent provision in a senior note offering would read as follows:

"The Company will not, and will not permit any Subsidiary Guarantor to, incur any Indebtedness that is subordinated in right of payment to any other Indebtedness of the Company or such Subsidiary Guarantor, unless such Indebtedness is also subordinated in right of payment to the securities or the Subsidiary Guarantee of such Subsidiary Guarantor, as the case may be, on substantially identical terms."

This provision prevents the Company from incurring debt that is subordinated to senior debt (such as senior debt outstanding under the bank credit facility) unless that debt is also subordinated to the Securities. Thus, it ensures that the Securities are senior to all subordinated debt in the capital structure. While the anti-layering clause is very standard in senior subordinated note deals, a significant number of senior note deals do not have the foregoing provision.

Clause (2) prevents the Company from securing any indebtedness unless that indebtedness is senior indebtedness. If a Company were allowed to offer liens on assets to secure other senior subordinated indebtedness, that would in effect layer into the Company's capital structure a class of subordinated debt that is effectively superior to these senior subordinated notes by virtue of its direct access to certain assets through the enforcement of the security arrangements. Such an event would have a significant and adverse effect on the market price of the Securities.

LIMITATION ON RESTRICTED PAYMENTS

* **Commentary**

The Restricted Payments covenant is focused on limiting what the Company is allowed to do with cash or other assets that it may have generated from operations or otherwise. The general principle is that the Securityholders want to control the disposition of cash and other assets of the Company and its Restricted Subsidiaries and only allow them to exit the credit group under limited circumstances.

Note that asset acquisitions are not restricted by this covenant. Note also that acquisitions of capital stock of companies are not restricted by the Restricted Payments covenant if the target becomes a Restricted Subsidiary or is merged into the Company or a Restricted Subsidiary. See clauses (1) and (2) of the definition of "Permitted Investments."

SECTION 4.05. LIMITATION ON RESTRICTED PAYMENTS

(a) The Company shall not, and shall not permit any Restricted Subsidiary, directly or indirectly, to make a Restricted Payment if at the time the Company or such Restricted Subsidiary makes such Restricted Payment:

(1) Default shall have occurred and be continuing (or would result therefrom);

* *Commentary*

If the Company is in Default, it generally may not make any Restricted Payments, regardless of whatever other dividend-paying capacity it may have generated by operation of the following provisions.

(2) the Company is not entitled to Incur an additional $1.00 of Indebtedness under Section 4.04(a);

* *Commentary*

Clause 2 above requires that before the Company can make a Restricted Payment it must be in a position to incur indebtedness under its ratio debt incurrence test. If the Company is not healthy enough to meet the minimum threshold for incurring ratio debt (i.e., it doesn't have sufficient cash flow vis-a-vis interest expense or vis-a-vis its pro forma amount of debt), then it should not be making any Restricted Payments for the benefit of junior security holders.

(3) the aggregate amount of such Restricted Payment and all other Restricted Payments since the Issue Date would exceed the sum of (without duplication):

* *Commentary*

The amount that can be paid out by the Company as a Restricted Payment at any time is often referred to as the "dividend basket" or the "restricted payment basket." This basket will be increased or built-up from the Issue Date by the factors described below and will be reduced or depleted by the amount of Restricted Payments actually made from time to time from the Issue Date.

(A) 50% of the Consolidated Net Income accrued during the period (treated as one accounting period) from the beginning of the fiscal quarter immediately following the fiscal quarter during which the Issue Date occurs to the end of the most recent fiscal quarter ending at least 45 days prior to the date of such Restricted Payment (or, in case such Consolidated Net Income shall be a deficit, minus 100% of such deficit); plus

* *Commentary*

The general test for building up capacity to make Restricted Payments ("dividend-paying capacity") is based on the consolidated net income of the Company and Restricted Subsidiaries earned from the Issue Date. The fundamental principle of this covenant boils down to this:

to the extent that the Company has recognized, over the entire time period since the issuance of the Securities, positive net income, it is allowed to take 50% of that amount and pay it out as dividends or make other Restricted Payments.

The test period referred to in this clause is sometimes drafted to commence on the first day of the fiscal quarter during which the securities are issued and to end at the end of the most recent fiscal quarter for which internal financial statements are available, as opposed to the "45 day" requirement set forth above. The 45-day requirement incorporates a period of time when the Company's independent accountants typically would have reviewed and discussed the most recent quarterly results with the Company (whether or not such quarter includes the fiscal year end and the accountants are beginning their audit) and the Company would have published those results for Securityholders to see. Although there is no requirement that Consolidated Net Income, as used above, be audited, the accountants' review of the Company's financial results prior to their public filing with the SEC can result in adjustments to the reported results and provides a third-party evaluation of the Company's financial reporting.

In lieu of using a specified percentage of Consolidated Net Income as set forth above, indentures in some cases provide for an amount equal to cash flow (or Consolidated EBITDA) less some multiple of the Company's interest expense. Usually, the multiple exceeds 1 and is less than 2. Usually, this provision is found in indentures that have a leverage test for the incurrence of ratio debt (rather than a coverage test), such as in the case of certain media and high tech companies. For example:

"(A) (x) the aggregate Consolidated EBITDA (or, in the event such Consolidated EBITDA shall be a deficit, minus such deficit) accrued from the beginning of the fiscal quarter in which the Issue Date occurs to the most recent date for which financial information is available to the Company, taken as one accounting period, less (y) times Consolidated Interest Expense for the same period";

(B) 100% of the aggregate Net Cash Proceeds received by the Company from the issuance or sale of its Capital Stock (other than Disqualified Stock) subsequent to the Issue Date (other than an issuance or sale to a Subsidiary of the Company and other than an issuance or sale to an employee stock ownership plan or to a trust established by the Company or any of its Subsidiaries for the benefit of their employees) and 100% of any cash capital contribution subsequent to the Issue Date;

* Commentary

If the Company has raised equity proceeds since the original issuance of the Securities, other than proceeds from the issuance of Disqualified Stock, then it is entitled to receive a dollar-for-dollar credit to its dividend-paying capacity. Securityholders are willing to give credit to a Company for this purpose to the extent that the Company has raised the corresponding amount of cash in a bona fide third party equity transaction.

The exception included above for sales of stock to employee plans is omitted in some covenant forms. In addition, some forms include language limiting "cash contributions" to those that "constitute shareholders' equity of the Company in accordance with GAAP," or do not provide credit to Restricted Payments for cash contributions at all.

In most high yield indentures, Companies are given a limited right to use the proceeds of certain issuances of equity to redeem a portion of the outstanding Securities. Under some indentures, including the following example, any amount of equity proceeds used for such a redemption are not credited to the Company's restricted payments capacity.

"(B) 100% of the aggregate Net Cash Proceeds received by the Company either (x) as contributions to the common equity of the Company after the Issue Date or (y) from the issuance and sale of Capital Stock (other than Disqualified Stock) after the Issue Date, other than any such proceeds which are used to redeem Securities in accordance with [Optional redemption—Redemption with Equity Proceeds]";

(C) the amount by which Indebtedness of the Company is reduced on the Company's balance sheet upon the conversion or exchange (other than by a Subsidiary of the

Company) subsequent to the Issue Date of any Indebtedness of the Company convertible or exchangeable for Capital Stock (other than Disqualified Stock) of the Company (less the amount of any cash, or the fair market value of any other property, distributed by the Company upon such conversion or exchange); plus

* *Commentary*

To the extent that an Company's convertible indebtedness is actually converted or exchanged into Capital Stock, the Company is entitled to a dollar-for-dollar credit to the extent that the amount of indebtedness has been reduced on the Company's balance sheet.

In lieu of the foregoing formulation, in some indentures, credit is also given for the conversion of debt of Restricted Subsidiaries into the Capital Stock of the Company (other than Disqualified Stock). Some forms also allow credit for net cash proceeds received in respect of the issue or sale of convertible debt or convertible Disqualified Stock that has been converted into Capital Stock (other than Disqualified Stock). An example similar to the following would replace clauses (B) and (C) above:

Alternative Example 1:

"100% of the aggregate net cash proceeds received by the Company since the Issue Date as a contribution to its common equity capital or from the issue or sale of Capital Stock of the Company (other than Disqualified Stock) or from the issue or sale of convertible or exchangeable Disqualified Stock or convertible or exchangeable debt securities of the Company that have been converted into or exchanged for such Capital Stock (other than Capital Stock (or Disqualified Stock or debt securities) sold to a Subsidiary of the Company)"

Alternative Example 2:

"the aggregate net cash proceeds received after the Issue Date by the Company from any Person (other than a Subsidiary of the Company) for debt securities that have been converted into or exchanged for Capital Stock of the Company (other than Disqualified Stock) to the extent such debt securities were originally sold for cash, plus the aggregate amount of cash received by the Company (other than from a Subsidiary of the Company) at the time of such conversion or exchange";

(D) an amount equal to the sum of (x) the net reduction in the Investments (other than Permitted Investments) made by the Company or any Restricted Subsidiary in any Person resulting from repurchases, repayments or redemptions of such Investments by such Person, proceeds realized on the sale of such Investments, and proceeds representing the return of capital (excluding dividends and distributions) on such Investments, in each case received by the Company or any Restricted Subsidiary and (y) to the extent such Person is an Unrestricted Subsidiary, the portion (proportionate to the Company's equity interest in such Subsidiary) of the fair market value of the net assets of such Unrestricted Subsidiary at the time such Unrestricted Subsidiary is designated a Restricted Subsidiary; provided, however, that the foregoing sum shall not exceed, in the case of any Person or Unrestricted Subsidiary, the amount of Investments previously made (and treated as a Restricted Payment) by the Company or any Restricted Subsidiary in such Person or Unrestricted Subsidiary.

* *Commentary*

To the extent that the Company has, since the original issue date of the Securities, made an investment in a Person, and accordingly reduced the dividend basket, i.e., taken a dollar-for-dollar reduction in its dividend-paying capacity, it is entitled to replenish that capacity to the extent that it receives repayments of the Investment from such Person; however, the amount of such replenishment cannot exceed the amount by which the dividend-paying capacity was reduced in the first instance upon the making of such Investment. If the Person is an Unrestricted Subsidiary, then upon redesignating that Subsidiary as a Restricted Subsidiary, the Company gets credit in its dividend basket for the amount of the Company's share of the net assets of such Subsidiary. This add-back is also limited by the value of Investments (other than Permitted Investments) actually previously made in such Unrestricted Subsidiary. (See also the definition of "Investment.")

Alternative Example 1:

"to the extent not otherwise included in the Company's Consolidated Net Income, in the case of the disposition or repayment of any Investment constituting a Restricted Payment after the Issue Date, an amount equal to the lesser of the return of capital with respect to such Investment and the initial amount of such Investment, in either case, less the cost of the disposition of such Investment";

Note that the foregoing example deducts the expenses of the disposition of Investments from the amount that is credited to the Company's restricted payment capacity.

Alternative Example 2:

"to the extent that any Investment (other than a Permitted Investment) that was made after the Issue Date is sold for cash or otherwise liquidated or repaid for cash, the lesser of (i) the cash return of capital with respect to such Investment (less the cost of disposition, if any, and net of taxes) and (ii) the initial amount of such Investment."

Note that this alternative requires that the return of capital on the investment be made in cash.

Alternative Example 3:

"(D) the amount equal to the net reduction in Investments in Unrestricted Subsidiaries resulting from (x) payments of dividends, repayments of the principal of loans or advances or other transfers of assets to the Company or any Restricted Subsidiary from Unrestricted Subsidiaries or (y) the redesignation of Unrestricted Subsidiaries as Restricted Subsidiaries (valued in each case as provided in the definition of 'Investment') not to exceed, in the case of any Unrestricted Subsidiary, the amount of Investments previously made by the Company or any Restricted Subsidiary in such Unrestricted Subsidiary."

Indentures usually include either an additional dollar amount to be added to the credits set forth in (A) though (D) above in arriving at the total amount of the restricted payments basket or a dollar basket in clause (b) below.

(b) The provisions of Section 4.05(a) shall not prohibit:

* *Commentary*

The following four generic exceptions to the Restricted Payments covenant entitle the Company to make the following types of payments even if it is unable to incur additional indebtedness under the ratio test or it has been unable to generate sufficient dividend-paying capacity through net income and equity proceeds to make such payments under clause (a).

(1) any Restricted Payment (other than a Restricted Payment described in clause (1) of the definition of "Restricted Payment") made out of the Net Cash Proceeds of the substantially concurrent sale of, or made by exchange for, Capital Stock of the Company (other than Disqualified Stock and other than Capital Stock issued or sold to a Subsidiary of the Company or an employee stock ownership plan or to a trust established by the Company or any of its Subsidiaries for the benefit of their employees) or a substantially concurrent capital contribution; provided, however, that (A) such Restricted Payment shall be excluded in the calculation of the amount of Restricted Payments and (B) the Net Cash Proceeds from such sale or such capital contribution (to the extent so used for such Restricted Payment) shall be excluded from the calculation of amounts under Section 4.05(a)(3)(B);

* *Commentary*

The concept behind the foregoing exception is that the Securityholder is essentially indifferent to a transaction in which the Company makes a Restricted Payment with the proceeds of the issuance of capital stock (so long as it is not an issuance of Disqualified Stock). The one condition is that the Restricted Payment must occur substantially concurrently with the issuance of the new stock. One point that needs to be considered in connection with every exception to this covenant is whether or not the making of the specified Restricted Payment should be included or excluded in the calculation of the amount of Restricted Payments that have been made since the original issue date of the Securities. Another note about the foregoing exception is that while ordinarily the issuance of Capital Stock would increase the Company's dividend-paying capacity, if the Company uses such proceeds to effect a Restricted Payment permitted by the foregoing exception, then it is not entitled to double count the dollar amount of the proceeds of such equity offering by adding it to the dividend-paying capacity pursuant to Section 4.05(a)(3)(B).

(2) any purchase, repurchase, redemption, defeasance or other acquisition or retirement for value of Subordinated Obligations of the Company or a Subsidiary Guarantor made by exchange for, or out of the proceeds of the substantially concurrent sale of, Indebtedness of the Company or a Subsidiary Guarantor which is permitted to be Incurred pursuant to Section 4.04; provided, however, that such purchase, repurchase, redemption, defeasance or other acquisition or retirement for value shall be excluded in the calculation of the amount of Restricted Payments;

* *Commentary*

This exception again reflects the Securityholders' relative indifference to a transaction in which the Company acquires subordinated debt with the proceeds of other subordinated debt.

In some forms (as in this one), this provision does not specify that the Refinancing Indebtedness must be subordinated, but instead relies on the debt covenant itself or the definition of "Refinancing Indebtedness" to implement such requirement. However, not all forms give the Company the flexibility, as this form does, to use the proceeds of senior debt to refinance the subordinated debt, so long as the senior debt is incurred as ratio debt. Alternatively, the various restrictions on the Subordinated Obligations that may be used to refinance existing Subordinated Obligations are sometimes set out in detail in the covenant itself. For example:

Alternative Example 1:

"any redemption, repurchase or other acquisition or retirement of Subordinated Obligations of the Company in exchange for, or out of the net cash proceeds of a substantially concurrent issue and sale of, (1) Capital Stock (other than Disqualified Stock) of the Company to any Person (other than to a Subsidiary of the Company); provided, however, that any such net cash proceeds are excluded from clause 4.05(a)(3)(B) of this covenant; or (2) other Subordinated Obligations of the Company which (w) has no scheduled principal payment prior to the 91st day after the Stated Maturity of the Securities, (x) has an Average Life to Stated Maturity greater than the remaining Average Life to Stated Maturity of the Securities and (y) is subordinated to the Securities to at least the same extent as the Subordinated Obligations so purchased, exchanged, redeemed, acquired or retired";

(3) dividends paid within 60 days after the date of declaration thereof if at such date of declaration such dividend would have complied with this Section 4.05; provided, however, that at the time of payment of such dividend, no other Default shall have occurred and be continuing (or result therefrom); provided further, however, that such dividend shall be included in the calculation of the amount of Restricted Payments; or

* *Commentary*

This exception is intended to protect the Company who has declared a dividend at a time when it was entitled to do so under the covenant; thus the dividend can be paid on the dividend payment date even if, during the interim, the Company would otherwise have lost its capacity to pay such dividend (e.g., owing to an intervening net loss). This recognizes the fact that once declared, the dividend becomes an obligation of the Company under corporate law. However the exception is not available if, during the interim, a default unrelated to this particular dividend has otherwise occurred and continues (although some forms allow such a payment irrespective of an intervening default).

(4) so long as no Default has occurred and is continuing the repurchase or other acquisition of shares of or options to purchase shares of, Capital Stock of the Company or any of its Subsidiaries from employees, former employees, directors or former directors of the Company or any of its Subsidiaries (or permitted transferees of such employees, former employees, directors or former directors), pursuant to the terms of the agreements (including employment agreements) or plans (or amendments thereto) approved by the Board under which such individuals purchase or sell or are granted the option to purchase or sell, shares of such Capital Stock; provided, however, that the aggregate amount of such repurchases and other acquisitions shall not exceed $? in any

calendar year; provided further, however, that such repurchases and other acquisitions shall be excluded in the calculation of the amount of Restricted Payments.

* *Commentary*

This exception entitles the Company to acquire capital stock from its management under approved stock plans. This exception recognizes that many companies have management plans that entitle the management holder to put stock back to the Company upon death or retirement, and similarly many Companies have the right to purchase such stock from a member of management who retires or otherwise leaves the employment of the Company. In addition, in contrast to the example above, some forms allow these payments to be made regardless of the occurrence of an event of default, and some include such payments in the calculation of Restricted Payments.

Alternative Example:

( ) *"the purchase, redemption, retirement of Capital Stock of the Company held by officers, directors or employees or former officers, directors or employees of the Company or any of its Restricted Subsidiaries (or their transferees, estates or beneficiaries under their estates), upon or after their death, disability, retirement, severance or termination of employment or service; provided that the aggregate consideration paid for all such redemptions shall not exceed $* million during any fiscal year";*

Other examples of exceptions from the Restricted Payments covenants include:

( ) *"the redemption, repurchase, retirement, defeasance or other acquisition of Subordinated Obligation of the Company upon a Change of Control or Asset Disposition to the extent required by the agreement governing such Subordinated Obligation but only if the Company shall have complied with Section 4.07 or 4.06, as the case may be, and purchased all Securities validly tendered pursuant to the relevant offer prior to purchasing or repaying such Subordinated Obligation";*

This exception is sometimes included, particularly if the Company at the time the Securities are issued, has outstanding subordinated debt that includes an asset sale or change of control provision similar to Section 4.06 and 4.07. Purchasing subordinated debt pursuant to an asset sale or change of control offer under that subordinated debt would constitute a Restricted Payment under the indenture governing the Securities and, if the Company has insufficient restricted payment capacity or cannot incur ratio debt, would result in a default under the indenture. This provision would permit such a purchase to go forward provided that the Company has previously purchased all Securities tendered pursuant to the equivalent provisions of the indenture.

( ) *"the payment of any dividend (or any similar distribution) by a Restricted Subsidiary of the Company to the holders of its common Capital Stock on a pro rata basis";*

This provision permits a Restricted Subsidiary that is not wholly owned by the Company to pay pro rata dividends, but this is covered in the Model Definition of "Restricted Payment."

( ) *"dividends, other distributions or other amounts paid by the Company to [Holding Company] (a) in amounts equal to amounts required for [Holding Company] to pay franchise taxes and other expenses required to maintain its corporate existence and provide for other operating costs of up to $* per fiscal year";*

This provision is often included in indentures where there is a holding company of the Company that has no source of cash other than the Company and that is not included in the restricted group of companies (i.e., a dividend to it would be a Restricted Payment). It permits the Company to pay the basic operating expenses of that holding company.

It is not uncommon for an indenture to include an additional exception which allows additional Restricted Payments, regardless of form, to be made up to a maximum amount. Sometimes, this "general basket" provision is included as part of the restricted payments basket in paragraph (a) instead. If so, it can only be used if the Company is able to incur ratio debt. Furthermore, if there were losses in the past, such a general basket in paragraph (a) would be reduced by those losses.

It is also not uncommon to include a provision in connection with this covenant that provides for the determination of the amount of any Restricted Payments made other than in cash. For example:

"The amount of all Restricted Payments (other than cash) will be the fair market value on the date of the Restricted Payment of the asset(s) or securities proposed to be transferred or issued by the Company or such Restricted Subsidiary, as the case may be, pursuant to the Restricted Payment. The fair market value of any assets or securities that are required to be valued by this covenant will be determined by the Board whose resolution with respect thereto will be delivered to the trustee. The Board's determination must be based upon an opinion or appraisal issued by an accounting, appraisal or investment banking firm of national standing if the fair market value exceeds $* million. Not later than the date of making any Restricted Payment, the Company will deliver to the trustee an officers' certificate stating that such Restricted Payment is permitted and setting forth the basis upon which the calculations required by this "Restricted Payments" covenant were computed, together with a copy of any fairness opinion or appraisal required by the indenture."

LIMITATION ON SALES OF ASSETS

* *Commentary*

The limitation on sales of assets covenant does not prohibit a Company from effecting asset sales. Although the covenant requires sales of assets to be made at fair market value and that a large percentage of the consideration be received in cash, the main purpose of the covenant is to specify how the proceeds are to be used in the event that the Company does sell assets. The general concept is that the Company should not sell revenue-producing assets unless the proceeds are either reinvested in revenue-producing assets or used to repay debt (thereby saving interest expense), and long-term assets should not be sold to effectively provide working capital.

SECTION 4.06. LIMITATION ON SALES OF ASSETS AND SUBSIDIARY STOCK

(a) The Company shall not, and shall not permit any Restricted Subsidiary to, directly or indirectly, consummate any Asset Disposition unless

(1) the Company or such Restricted Subsidiary receives consideration at the time of such Asset Disposition at least equal to the fair market value (including as to

the value of all non-cash consideration), as determined in good faith by the Board, of the shares and assets subject to such Asset Disposition;

    (2) at least 80% of the consideration thereof received by the Company or such Restricted Subsidiary is in the form of cash or cash equivalents.

* *Commentary*

The percentage referred to above can range between 70% and 90% and is intended to make sure the Company has cash available to repay debt or invest in new assets. Indentures occasionally allow for consideration to be received in the form of additional capital assets, in the nature of those that could be purchased with cash proceeds pursuant to this covenant.

    (3) an amount equal to 100% of the Net Available Cash from such Asset Disposition is applied by the Company (or such Restricted Subsidiary, as the case may be)

    (A) first, to the extent the Company elects (or is required by the terms of any Indebtedness), to prepay, repay, redeem or purchase Senior Indebtedness or Indebtedness (other than any Disqualified Stock) of a Wholly Owned Subsidiary (in each case other than Indebtedness owed to the Company or an Affiliate of the Company) within one year from the later of the date of such Asset Disposition or the receipt of such Net Available Cash;

* *Commentary*

Some forms do not give the Company credit for complying with this covenant if it repays indebtedness of wholly owned subsidiaries that is not "Senior Indebtedness." As a general matter, such payments should be permissible to the extent that the indebtedness in question is structurally senior to the Securities.

    (B) second, to the extent of the balance of such Net Available Cash after application in accordance with clause (A), to the extent the Company elects, to acquire Additional Assets within one year from the later of the date of such Asset Disposition or the receipt of such Net Available Cash; and

    (C) third, to the extent of the balance of such Net Available Cash after application in accordance with clauses (A) and (B), to make an Offer to the holders of the Securities (and to holders of other [pari passu] Indebtedness designated by the Company) to purchase Securities (and such other [pari passu] Indebtedness) pursuant to and subject to the conditions of Section 4.06(b);

* *Commentary*

The bracketed phrases in the preceding paragraph entitle the Company to make simultaneous offers for other series of high yield, pari passu debt that may impose similar requirements on the Company to tender for such debt with the proceeds of asset sales. The drafter should make the appropriate modification to the Model covenant to conform to the ranking of the securities (e.g., "Senior Indebtedness" or "Senior Subordinated Indebtedness").

Alternative Example:

"To the extent of the balance of such Net Available Cash after application in accordance with clauses (A) and (B), the Company shall make an offer to all holders of Securities and all holders of other Indebtedness that is pari passu with the Securities containing provisions similar to those set forth in this Indenture with respect to offers to purchase or redeem with the proceeds of sales of assets to purchase the maximum principal amount of Securities and such other pari passu Indebtedness that may be purchased out of the Net Available Cash, subject to the conditions set forth below."

provided, however, that in connection with any prepayment, repayment or purchase of Indebtedness pursuant to clause (A) or (C) above, the Company or such Restricted Subsidiary shall permanently retire such Indebtedness and shall cause the related loan commitment (if any) to be permanently reduced in an amount equal to the principal amount so prepaid, repaid or purchased. Notwithstanding the foregoing provisions of this Section 4.06, the Company and the Restricted Subsidiaries shall not be required to apply any Net Available Cash in accordance with this Section 4.06(a) except to the extent that the aggregate Net Available Cash from all Asset Dispositions which are not applied in accordance with this Section 4.06(a) exceeds $*. Pending application of Net Available Cash pursuant to this Section 4.06(a), such Net Available Cash shall be invested in Temporary Cash Investments or applied to temporarily reduce revolving credit indebtedness.

* Commentary

The foregoing paragraph requires the permanent retirement of the indebtedness that is being repaid with asset sale proceeds. (This ties to the first exception in the debt covenant for Credit Agreement debt, which requires the dollar-for-dollar reduction in the permitted amount of Credit Agreement debt in connection with the repayment of any Credit Agreement debt with the proceeds of asset sales under paragraph (A) above.)

There are three "baskets" related to this covenant:

(1) The definition of Asset Disposition excludes de minimis dispositions.

(2) In the preceding paragraph, a second basket gives the Company an amount of asset sale proceeds that are forever excluded from the required application of proceeds. Some forms do not provide for this basket.

(3) When a tender has to be made for the Securities, the indenture includes another basket (paragraph (b) below) designed to allow the Company to defer launching the tender offer until a sufficiently large amount of such remaining proceeds (typically at least $5 or $10 million, depending on the size of the original offering) has accumulated as to justify the expense of making the tender offer.

The requirement as to the investment of Net Available Cash pending application pursuant to this covenant is common but varies from indenture to indenture. In the most flexible cases, some forms allow investment of such funds in any "Permitted Investment" or in any investment not prohibited by the indenture, although the fungiblity of cash is a subtle issue that is difficult for investors to monitor.

For the purposes of this Section 4.06(a), the following are deemed to be cash or cash equivalents: (1) the assumption of Indebtedness of the Company or any

Restricted Subsidiary (other than Subordinated Obligations) and the release of the Company or such Restricted Subsidiary from all liability on such Indebtedness in connection with such Asset Disposition and (2) securities received by the Company or any Restricted Subsidiary from the transferee that are promptly converted by the Company or such Restricted Subsidiary into cash.

* *Commentary*

In determining whether the requisite percentage of consideration has been received in cash, the indenture allows the Company to include as cash the amount of indebtedness in respect of which the Company is relieved of any repayment obligation, as well as securities received as consideration so long as they are promptly converted into cash.

There are various common approaches to the foregoing concept. The assumed indebtedness of the Company that may be treated as cash consideration under clause (1) of the foregoing provision is frequently limited to debt that is pari passu with or senior to the Securities, and obligations in respect of Disqualified Stock are often excluded.

Other forms give the Company credit for cash received to the extent any balance sheet liabilities are assumed by the transferee and from which the Company is released. However, such an approach allows the Company to discharge potentially short-term liabilities with the proceeds of the sale of long-life assets, which may not be in the interest of the Securityholders. In addition, there is some variability in forms regarding the assets received as consideration that may be treated as cash.

Alternative Example 1:

"For purposes of this provision, each of the following will be deemed to be cash: (1) any liabilities, as shown on the Company's or such Restricted Subsidiary's most recent balance sheet, of the Company or any Restricted Subsidiary (other than contingent liabilities and liabilities that are by their terms subordinated to the Securities or any Subsidiary Guarantee) that are assumed by the transferee of any such assets pursuant to a customary novation agreement that releases the Company or such Restricted Subsidiary from further liability and (2) any securities, notes or other obligations received by the Company or any such Restricted Subsidiary from such transferee that are contemporaneously, subject to ordinary settlement periods, converted by the Company or such Restricted Subsidiary into cash, to the extent of the cash received in that conversion."

Alternative Example 2:

"For the purposes of this Section 4.06(a), the following are deemed to be cash: (x) the assumption by the transferee of Indebtedness of the Company (other than Disqualified Stock of the Company and other than Indebtedness that is subordinated to the Securities) or Indebtedness of any Restricted Subsidiary and the release of the Company or such Restricted Subsidiary from all liability on such Indebtedness in connection with such Asset Disposition; (y) securities received by the Company or any Restricted Subsidiary from the transferee that are converted by the Company or such Restricted Subsidiary into cash within 20 days of the applicable Asset Disposition (to the extent of the cash received); and (z) any liabilities (as shown on the Company's or such Restricted Subsidiary's most

recent balance sheet) of the Company or any Restricted Subsidiary (other than contingent liabilities and liabilities that are by their terms subordinated to the Securities or any guarantee thereof) that are assumed by the transferee of any such assets pursuant to a customary novation agreement that releases the Company or any such Restricted Subsidiary from further liability."

    (b) In the event of an Asset Disposition that requires the purchase of Securities (and other [pari passu] Indebtedness) pursuant to Section 4.06(a)(3)(C), the Company shall purchase Securities tendered pursuant to an offer by the Company for the Securities (and such other [pari passu] Indebtedness) (the "Offer") at a purchase price of 100% of their principal amount (or, if other than the Securities, 100% of their principal amount or, in the event such other [pari passu] Indebtedness was issued with significant original issue discount, 100% of the accreted value thereof), without premium, plus accrued but unpaid interest (or, in respect of such other [pari passu] Indebtedness, such lesser price, if any, as may be provided for by the terms of such [pari passu] Indebtedness) in accordance with the procedures (including prorationing in the event of oversubscription) set forth in Section 4.06(c). If the aggregate purchase price of Securities (and any other [pari passu] Indebtedness) tendered pursuant to the Offer exceeds the Net Available Cash allotted to their purchase, the Company shall select the Securities and other [pari passu] Indebtedness to be purchased on a pro rata basis but in round denominations, which in the case of the Securities will be denominations of $1,000 principal amount or multiples thereof. The Company shall not be required to make an Offer to purchase Securities (and other [pari passu] Indebtedness) pursuant to this Section 4.06 if the Net Available Cash available therefor is less than $* million (which lesser amount shall be carried forward for purposes of determining whether such an Offer is required with respect to the Net Available Cash from any subsequent Asset Disposition).

    (c) Promptly, and in any event within 10 days after the Company becomes obligated to make an Offer, the Company shall deliver to the Trustee and send, by first-class mail to each Holder, a written notice stating that the Holder may elect to have his Securities purchased by the Company either in whole or in part (subject to prorating as described in Section 4.06(b) in the event the Offer is oversubscribed) in integral multiples of $1,000 of principal amount, at the applicable purchase price. The notice shall specify a purchase date not less than 30 days nor more than 60 days after the date of such notice (the "Purchase Date") and shall contain such information concerning the business of the Company which the Company in good faith believes will enable such Holders to make an informed decision and all instructions and materials necessary to tender Securities pursuant to the Offer, together with the information contained in clause (d)(3) below.

* *Commentary*

Some forms add further informational requirements at the end of the foregoing clause (c). The following is an example:

"(which at a minimum will include (A) the most recently filed Annual Report on Form 10-K (including audited consolidated financial statements) of the Company, the most recent subsequently filed Quarterly Report on Form 10-Q and any Current Report on Form 8-K of the Company filed subsequent to such Quarterly Report, other than Current Reports describing Asset Dispositions otherwise described in the offering materials (or corresponding successor reports), (B) a description of material developments in the Company's business subsequent to the date of the latest of such Reports, and (C) if material, appropriate pro forma financial information)"

(d) (1) Not later than the date upon which written notice of an Offer is delivered to the Trustee, the Company shall deliver to the Trustee an Officers' Certificate as to (A) the amount of the Offer (the "Offer Amount"), including information as to any other [pari passu] Indebtedness included in the Offer, (B) the allocation of the Net Available Cash from the Asset Dispositions pursuant to which such Offer is being made and (C) the compliance of such allocation with the provisions of Section 4.06(a) and (b). On or prior to the Purchase Date, the Company shall also irrevocably deposit with the Trustee or with a Paying Agent (or, if the Company is acting as its own Paying Agent, segregate and hold in trust) in Temporary Cash Investments, maturing on the last day prior to the Purchase Date or on the Purchase Date if funds are immediately available by open of business, an amount equal to the Offer Amount to be held for payment in accordance with the provisions of this Section 4.06(d)(1). If the Offer includes other [pari passu] Indebtedness, the deposit described in the preceding sentence may be made with any other paying agent pursuant to arrangements satisfactory to the Trustee. Upon the expiration of the period for which the Offer remains open (the "Offer Period"), the Company shall deliver to the Trustee for cancellation the Securities or portions thereof which have been properly tendered to and are to be accepted by the Company. The Trustee shall, on the Purchase Date, mail or deliver payment (or cause the delivery of payment) to each tendering Holder in the amount of the purchase price. In the event that the aggregate purchase price of the Securities delivered by the Company to the Trustee is less than the Offer Amount applicable to the Securities, the Trustee shall deliver the excess to the Company immediately after the expiration of the Offer Period for any purpose not prohibited by this Indenture.

* *Commentary*

Under some covenant forms, the excess amount referred to in the last sentence of the preceding paragraph must be applied only for one of the permitted purposes identified in (a)(3) above. While such an approach may be in the minority, it might be appropriate for situations where Securityholders expect significant deleveraging or reinvesting by the Company during the life of the Securities. If Securityholders have such an expectation, but the indenture nonetheless grants substantial latitude to the Company to deploy any proceeds that remain following the Offer, the Securityholders will be faced with the difficult choice between tendering Securities for an Offer price of par at a time when the Securities might be trading above par and not tendering Securities and hereby allowing any remaining of the Offer excess proceeds to be used by the Company to make Restricted Payments or Permitted Investments.

(2) Holders electing to have a Security purchased shall be required to surrender the Security, with an appropriate form duly completed, to the Company at the address specified in the notice at least three Business Days prior to the Purchase Date. Holders shall be entitled to withdraw their election if the Trustee or the Company receives not later than one Business Day prior to the Purchase Date, a facsimile transmission or letter setting forth the name of the Holder, the principal amount of the Security which was delivered for purchase by the Holder and a statement that such Holder is withdrawing his election to have such Security purchased. Holders whose Securities are purchased only in part shall be issued new Securities equal in principal amount to the unpurchased portion of the Securities surrendered.

(3) At the time the Company delivers Securities to the Trustee which are to be accepted for purchase, the Company shall also deliver an Officers' Certificate stating that such Securities are to be accepted by the Company pursuant to and in accordance

with the terms of this Section 4.06(d)(3). A Security shall be deemed to have been accepted for purchase at the time the Trustee, directly or through an agent, mails or delivers payment therefor to the surrendering Holder.

(e) The Company shall comply, to the extent applicable, with the requirements of Section 14(e) of the Exchange Act and any other securities laws or regulations in connection with the repurchase of Securities pursuant to this Section 4.06(e). To the extent that the provisions of any securities laws or regulations conflict with provisions of this Section 4.06(e), the Company shall comply with the applicable securities laws and regulations and shall not be deemed to have breached its obligations under this Section 4.06(e) by virtue of its compliance with such securities laws or regulations.

CHANGE OF CONTROL

* *Commentary*

The change of control covenant is designed to allow the Securityholder, upon the occurrence of certain events, to reevaluate the investment in the Company represented by the Securities. Upon the occurrence of such event, the Company is required to offer to purchase such Securities at a purchase price of 101% of the principal amount of such Securities. This is commonly referred to as a change of control "put."

In some instances, particularly in deals that are rated at the upper end of the high yield spectrum, indentures are drafted so that the change of control put is triggered only upon the occurrence of both a change of control transaction and a resulting adverse change in credit ratings.

Note that this provision does not entitle the Company to redeem the Securities at its election. As a result, if the Company is acquired in a transaction viewed as "credit positive" from a Securityholder's perspective, Securityholders may not tender (e.g., if the Securities trade at greater than 101% of principal amount, the Change of Control price). In such a situation, the Securities would remain outstanding unless the Company makes a tender offer for the Securities (at a higher price than 101%) and all Securities are tendered. In many situations, a tender will be accepted by a large percentage of outstanding Securityholders if the Company agrees to pay a "make-whole" premium equal to the discounted present value of (a) the redemption price on the first day on which the Company is entitled to redeem the Securities (which is typically the last day of year five for a 10 year note issue) and (b) all interest payments due until that earliest redemption date. The discount rate for this calculation is usually calculated to be the treasury rate (based on duration to the earliest redemption date) plus a margin of typically 50 to 100 basis points (.50% to 1.00%). In a small number of deals, the Company has the right to redeem the Securities upon a Change of Control at a "make whole" premium calculated in a similar fashion. This avoids the need to make a formal tender offer (and the resulting expense) and ensures that all Securities can be taken out upon a Change of Control (i.e., there will be no holdouts).

SECTION 4.07. CHANGE OF CONTROL

(a) Upon the occurrence of a Change of Control, each Holder shall have the right to require that the Company purchase such Holder's Securities at a purchase price in cash equal to 101% of the principal amount thereof plus accrued and unpaid interest, if any, to the date of purchase (subject to the right of holders of record on the relevant record date to receive interest on the relevant interest payment date), in accordance with the terms contemplated in Section 4.07(b). [In the event that at the time of such Change of Control the terms of the Senior Indebtedness of the Company restrict or prohibit the repurchase of Securities pursuant to this Section 4.07(a), then prior to the mailing of the notice to Holders provided for in Section 4.07(b) below but in any event within 30 days following any Change of Control, the Company shall (1) repay in full all such Senior Indebtedness or (2) obtain the requisite consent under the agreements governing such Senior Indebtedness to permit the repurchase of the Securities as provided for in Section 4.07(b).]

* *Commentary*

The bracketed language, for Securities that are subordinated, recognizes that the terms of senior debt may prohibit a Company from offering to purchase and purchasing subordinated debt. If that is the case, the covenant requires the Company, prior to making the offer to purchase the Securities, to either obtain the requisite consent from the senior lenders or refinance such senior debt. Some indentures do not contain such a requirement, but unless they also release the Company from making the Change of Control offer, it is not clear that the Company has any other option other than to refinance the Senior Indebtedness or to obtain such consent.

(b) Within 30 days following any Change of Control, the Company shall mail a notice to each Holder with a copy to the Trustee (the "Change of Control Offer") stating:

(1) that a Change of Control has occurred and that such Holder has the right to require the Company to purchase such Holder's Securities at a purchase price in cash equal to 101% of the principal amount thereof plus accrued and unpaid interest, if any, to the date of purchase (subject to the right of Holders of record on the relevant record date to receive interest on the relevant interest payment date);

(2) the circumstances and relevant facts regarding such Change of Control (including information with respect to pro forma historical income, cash flow and capitalization, each after giving effect to such Change of Control);

(3) the purchase date (which shall be no earlier than 30 days nor later than 60 days from the date such notice is mailed); and

(4) the instructions determined by the Company, consistent with this Section 4.07, that a Holder must follow in order to have its Securities purchased.

(c) Holders electing to have a Security purchased will be required to surrender the Security, with an appropriate form duly completed, to the Company at the address specified in the notice at least three Business Days prior to the purchase date. Holders will be entitled to withdraw their election if the Trustee or the Company receives not later than one Business Day prior to the purchase date, a facsimile transmission or letter setting forth the name of the Holder, the principal amount of the Security which was delivered for purchase by the Holder and a statement that such Holder is withdrawing his election to have such Security purchased.

On the purchase date, all Securities purchased by the Company under this Section 4.07 shall be delivered by the Company to the Trustee for cancellation, and the Company shall pay the purchase price plus accrued and unpaid interest, if any, to the Holders entitled thereto.

(d) Notwithstanding the foregoing provisions of this Section 4.07, the Company shall not be required to make a Change of Control Offer upon a Change of Control if a third party makes the Change of Control Offer in the manner, at the times and otherwise in compliance with the requirements set forth in Section applicable to a Change of Control Offer made by the Company and purchases all Securities validly tendered and not withdrawn under such Change of Control Offer.

(e) The Company shall comply, to the extent applicable, with the requirements of Section 14(e) of the Exchange Act and any other securities laws or regulations in connection with the repurchase of Securities pursuant to this Section 4.07. To the extent that the provisions of any securities laws or regulations conflict with provisions of this Section 4.07, the Company shall comply with the applicable securities laws and regulations and shall not be deemed to have breached its obligations under this Section 4.07 by virtue of its compliance with such securities laws or regulations.

* *Commentary*

Some forms include a provision requiring the Company to publicly announce the results of the offer to purchase on or shortly after the payment date for the tendered Securities.

LIMITATION ON LIENS

* *Commentary*

The Limitation on Liens covenant is intended to ensure that the Securities are not effectively subordinated to a material amount of secured debt or other secured obligations. The definition of "Permitted Liens" specifies which debt permitted to be incurred by the Indebtedness covenant can be secured and which other liens are permissible.

The Limitation on Liens covenant shown here is one that you would find in an offering of senior notes. In a senior subordinated note offering, this covenant is not necessary as long as the debt covenant includes the anti-layering protection arising from the Company's agreement not to grant any liens to secure other subordinated debt.

SECTION 4.08. LIMITATION ON LIENS

The Company shall not, and shall not permit any Restricted Subsidiary to, directly or indirectly, incur or permit to exist any Lien (the "Initial Lien") of any nature whatsoever on any of its properties (including Capital Stock of a Restricted Subsidiary), whether owned at the Issue Date or thereafter acquired, other than Permitted Liens, without effectively providing that the Securities shall be secured equally and ratably with (or prior to) the obligations so secured for so long as such obligations are so secured. Any Lien created for the benefit of the Holders of the Securities pursuant to the foregoing sentence shall provide by its terms that such Lien shall be automatically and unconditionally released and discharged upon the release and discharge of the Initial Lien.

* *Commentary*

Under some indenture forms, only Liens securing Indebtedness are prohibited. In addition, some forms will include a proviso to the effect that liens, in addition to Permitted Liens, may be incurred to secure indebtedness up to some specified principal amount notwithstanding the covenant. For example:

Alternative Example 1:

"provided, however, that the Company may Incur other Liens to secure Indebtedness as long as the amount of outstanding Indebtedness secured by Liens Incurred pursuant to this proviso does not exceed •% of consolidated net tangible assets, as determined on a consolidated balance sheet of the Company as of the end of the most recent fiscal quarter ending at least 45 days prior thereto."

In other indentures, such a general lien basket is included in the Permitted Lien definition—see the Commentary to that definition.

In addition, lien covenants often explicitly state that liens may not be granted in any income or profits from any property of the Company or its Restricted Subsidiaries, and that no such income or profits may be assigned. For example:

Alternative Example 2:

"The Company will not, and will not permit any of its Restricted Subsidiaries to, directly or indirectly, create, incur, assume or suffer to exist any Lien of any kind on any asset now owned or hereafter acquired, or any proceeds, income or profits thereon, or assign or convey any right to receive income therefrom, except Permitted Liens, unless all payments due under this Indenture are secured on an equal and ratable basis with (or, in the case of Subordinated Obligations, prior or senior thereto, with the same relative priority as the Securities shall have with respect to such Subordinated Obligations) the obligation so secured until such time as such obligations are no longer secured by a Lien."

Some lien covenants diverge from the "negative pledge" approach of the Model, and instead flatly prohibit any Liens except Permitted Liens.

Alternative Example 3:

The Company shall not, and shall not permit any Restricted Subsidiary to, directly or indirectly, incur or permit to exist any Lien (the "Initial Lien") of any nature whatsoever on any of its properties (including Capital Stock of a Restricted Subsidiary), whether owned at the Issue Date or thereafter acquired, other than Permitted Liens. Any Lien created for the benefit of the Holders of the Securities pursuant to the foregoing sentence shall provide by its terms that such Lien shall be automatically and unconditionally released and discharged upon the release and discharge of the Initial Lien."

LIMITATION ON AFFILIATE TRANSACTIONS

* *Commentary*

This covenant is designed to prevent the Company from circumventing the Restricted Payment covenant by disguising a dividend-like transaction in the form of a business transaction. Accordingly, the covenant requires the Company to ensure that the transaction is conducted on terms that are "arm's-length" and, depending upon the dollar amount involved in the transaction, that such terms are approved by the majority of disinterested directors and/or that such terms are determined to be fair to the Company in the opinion of an investment banking, appraisal or accounting firm of national standing.

This covenant takes on added significance when the Company is a private company that is controlled by one or a small group of shareholders. A Company that is publicly held is likely to be concerned about the fairness of affiliate transactions for reasons of corporate law and usually does not object to any significant degree to the terms of this covenant. A private company issuer is likely to request carveouts for fees paid to financial sponsors, for example, and for other transactions that are reasonably foreseeable. These exceptions should be kept to a minimum, since the effect of creating an exception may be to permit a transaction that may have terms that are not fair to the Company.

SECTION 4.09. LIMITATION ON AFFILIATE TRANSACTIONS

(a) The Company shall not, and shall not permit any Restricted Subsidiary to, enter into or permit to exist any transaction (including the purchase, sale, lease or exchange of any property, employee compensation arrangements or the rendering of any service) with, or for the benefit of, any Affiliate of the Company (an "**Affiliate Transaction**") unless:

(1) the terms of the Affiliate Transaction are no less favorable to the Company or such Restricted Subsidiary than those that could be obtained at the time of the Affiliate Transaction in arm's-length dealings with a Person who is not an Affiliate;

(2) if such Affiliate Transaction involves an amount in excess of $• million, the terms of the Affiliate Transaction are set forth in writing and a majority of the non-employee directors of the Company disinterested with respect to such Affiliate Transactions have determined in good faith that the criteria set forth in clause (1) are satisfied and have approved the relevant Affiliate Transaction as evidenced by a Board resolution; and

(3) if such Affiliate Transaction involves an amount in excess of $• million, the Board of Directors shall also have received a written opinion from an investment banking, appraisal or accounting firm of national standing, that is not an Affiliate of the Company, to the effect that such Affiliate Transaction is fair, from a financial standpoint, to the Company and its Restricted Subsidiaries or is not less favorable to the Company and its Restricted Subsidiaries than could reasonably be expected to be obtained at the time in an arm's length transaction with a Person who was not an Affiliate.

(b) The provisions of the preceding paragraph (a) shall not prohibit:

(1) any Investment (other than a Permitted Investment) or other Restricted Payment, in each case permitted to be made pursuant to Section 4.05 (but only to the extent included in the calculation of the amount of Restricted Payments);

* *Commentary*

The theory behind this first exception is that if the Company is allowed to pay a dividend that depletes its dividend basket, thereby sending assets completely out of the consolidated restricted group, the investor should be relatively indifferent if, rather than electing to pay a dividend, the Company elects to enter into some other kind of transaction (e.g., an Investment) with an Affiliate. Since Permitted Investments do not deplete the dividend basket, it is probably appropriate to test any such transactions involving an Affiliate under this covenant.

      (2) any issuance of securities, or other payments, awards or grants in cash, securities or otherwise pursuant to, or the funding of, employment arrangements, stock options and stock ownership plans approved by the Board;

* *Commentary*

Under some indenture forms, the exception in clause (2) will be stated more broadly. Alternative 1:

      (2) any employment agreements, consulting agreements, non-competition agreements, stock purchase or option agreements, collective bargaining agreements, employee benefit plans or arrangements (including vacation plans, health and life insurance plans, deferred compensation plans, stock loan programs, long term incentive plans, directors' and officers' indemnification agreements and retirement, savings or similar plans), related trust agreements or any similar arrangements, in each case in respect of employees, officers, directors or consultants and entered into in the ordinary course of business, any payments or other transactions contemplated by any of the foregoing and any other payments of compensation to employees, officers, directors or consultants in the ordinary course of business;

      (3) loans or advances to employees in the ordinary course of business consistent with the past practices of the Company or its Restricted Subsidiaries, but in any event not to exceed $● million in the aggregate outstanding at any one time;

* *Commentary*

Under the Sarbanes-Oxley Act, subject to certain limited exceptions, it is unlawful for an issuer to extend credit or arrange for the extension of credit in the form of a personal loan to any of its directors or executive officers.

      (4) the payment of reasonable fees to directors of the Company and its Restricted Subsidiaries who are not employees of the Company or its Restricted Subsidiaries;

      (5) any transaction with the Company, a Restricted Subsidiary or joint venture or similar entity which would constitute an Affiliate Transaction solely because the Company or a Restricted Subsidiary owns an equity interest in or otherwise controls such Restricted Subsidiary, joint venture or similar entity;

* *Commentary*

This exception in clause (5) permits transactions between the Company and its Restricted Subsidiaries. Also permitted are transactions with entities that may technically be Affiliates of the Company because they are controlled by the Company (e.g., 45%

voting stake), but otherwise should be viewed as a true third party (e.g., the remaining 55% voting stake is held broadly by Persons that are not Affiliates of the Company).

   (6) any transaction on arm's length terms with non-Affiliates that become Affiliates as a result of such transaction; and
   (7) the issuance or sale of any Capital Stock (other than Disqualified Stock) of the Company.

* Commentary

The theory behind the final exception is that the covenants should not impose restrictions on the ability on the Company to issue Capital Stock (other than Disqualified Stock, where, because of the types of extra terms (e.g. onerous redemption provisions) that are included in such instruments, there could be greater opportunity to include terms that may be unfair to the Company).

Among other common exceptions would be a provision that would "grandfather" transactions pursuant to contracts in effect at the time of the offering (and which in appropriate cases should generally be described in the offering document), as well as pursuant to amendments, renewals or extensions of such contracts that have terms not less favorable to the Company than those in the original contract.

LIMITATION ON THE SALE OR ISSUANCE OF CAPITAL STOCK OF RESTRICTED SUBSIDIARIES

* Commentary

This covenant is designed to protect Securityholders from transactions in which the Company that has a Wholly Owned Subsidiary, and thereby has complete control over the flow of cash between such subsidiary and the Company, sells a portion of the stock in such subsidiary such that minority shareholders are created in the subsidiary. The ensuing problem from the Securityholders' perspective is that, due to corporate law considerations in respect of minority stockholders, the Company loses its former flexibility in freely making Investments into and taking dividends out from such subsidiary.

One variation of this covenant is to make it apply only to common stock of subsidiaries that are wholly owned at the date of the offering of the Securities. High yield covenants do not normally limit an issuer from making future Investments in a Restricted Subsidiary that is less than wholly owned. As a result, an issuer that expects to create and control majority-owned subsidiaries in the future may reasonably question why it should be foreclosed from selling some stock of such a Restricted Subsidiary, such that it owns 60% rather than 70% of such Subsidiary. However, it is not unreasonable for investors to take the position that subsidiaries that are wholly owned on the date the Securities are issued should remain so, unless the issuer completely sells its interest in such subsidiary or, if it sells down below a majority interest, so long as the issuer's continuing Investment in such entity would comply with the Restricted Payments covenant (i.e. the issuer would be deemed to have made a new Investment at the point in time at which the subsidiary no longer constitutes a Subsidiary).

SECTION 4.10. LIMITATION ON THE SALE OR ISSUANCE OF CAPITAL STOCK OF RESTRICTED SUBSIDIARIES

The Company

(1) shall not, and shall not permit any Restricted Subsidiary to, sell, lease, transfer or otherwise dispose of any Capital Stock of any Restricted Subsidiary to any Person (other than the Company or a Wholly Owned Subsidiary), and

(2) shall not permit any Restricted Subsidiary to issue any of its Capital Stock (other than, if necessary, shares of its Capital Stock constituting directors' or other legally required qualifying shares) to any Person (other than to the Company or a Wholly Owned Subsidiary),

unless

(A) immediately after giving effect to such issuance, sale or other disposition, neither the Company nor any of its Subsidiaries own any Capital Stock of such Restricted Subsidiary; or

(B) immediately after giving effect to such issuance, sale or other disposition, such Restricted Subsidiary would no longer constitute a Restricted Subsidiary and any Investment in such Person remaining after giving effect thereto would have been permitted to be made under Section 4.05 if made on the date of such issuance, sale or other disposition.

For purposes of this Section 4.10, the creation of a Lien on any Capital Stock of a Restricted Subsidiary to secure Indebtedness of the Company or any of its Restricted Subsidiaries shall not be deemed to be a violation of this Section 4.10; provided, however, that any sale or other disposition by the secured party of such Capital Stock following foreclosure of its Lien will be subject to this covenant.

LIMITATION ON SALE/LEASEBACK TRANSACTIONS

* *Commentary*

This is a covenant that would typically only be found in a senior note offering. A sale leaseback transaction, where the Company sells an asset and immediately leases it back, is economically very similar to a secured financing, since the Company will receive sale proceeds (similar to loan proceeds) and will make rental payments over the life of the lease (similar to loan repayments). Thus, this covenant generally permits a Company to enter into Sale/Leaseback transactions so long as the Company has the ability to incur the related indebtedness represented by the lease obligation and would be able to incur the lien on the property securing the lease. However, since in a Sale/Leaseback transaction the asset is in fact sold and is therefore no longer part of the Company's consolidated assets following the sale (unlike a secured financing), this covenant contains the added requirement that the Company treat the sale proceeds as it would in connection with any other asset sale.

SECTION 4.11. LIMITATION ON SALE/LEASEBACK TRANSACTIONS

The Company shall not, and shall not permit any Restricted Subsidiary to, enter into any Sale/Leaseback Transaction with respect to any property unless:

(a) the Company or such Subsidiary would be entitled to (A) Incur Indebtedness in an amount equal to the Attributable Debt with respect to such Sale/Leaseback Transaction pursuant to Section 4.04 and (B) create a Lien on such property securing such Attributable Debt without equally and ratably securing the Notes pursuant to Section 4.08;

(b) the net proceeds received by the Company or any Restricted Subsidiary in connection with such Sale/Leaseback Transaction are at least equal to the fair market value (as determined by the Board of Directors) of such property; and

(c) the Company applies the proceeds of such transaction in compliance with Section 4.06.

LIMITATION ON RESTRICTIONS ON DISTRIBUTIONS FROM RESTRICTED SUBSIDIARIES

* *Commentary*

This covenant is designed to prevent the Company and its Restricted Subsidiaries from agreeing to any contractual limitation on the ability of the Restricted Subsidiaries to send cash and other assets, whether in the form of dividends or loans or other property transfers, to the Company. Obviously, to the extent that such contractual limitations were permitted, the Company could have substantially less ability to service its own debt, including the Securities. Generally the exceptions permitted below include those restrictions that are disclosed in the offering document to the extent they are material) and encumbrances that are contained in refinancing agreements and that are not more restrictive than those in the debt being refinanced.

Another consideration to take into account when more exceptions to this covenant are included is that to the extent that a subsidiary is contractually restricted from paying dividends to the Company, the definition of "Consolidated Net Income" excludes the income of such subsidiary from the Company's calculation of Consolidated Net Income. See the Commentary to clause (3) of such definition.

SECTION 4.12. LIMITATION ON RESTRICTIONS ON DISTRIBUTIONS FROM RESTRICTED SUBSIDIARIES

The Company shall not, and shall not permit any Restricted Subsidiary to, create or otherwise cause or permit to exist or become effective any consensual encumbrance or restriction on the ability of any Restricted Subsidiary to (a) pay dividends or make any other distributions on its Capital Stock to the Company or a Restricted Subsidiary or pay any Indebtedness owed to the Company, (b) make any loans or advances to the Company or (c) transfer any of its property or assets to the Company, except:

(1) with respect to clauses (a), (b) and (c),

(A) any encumbrance or restriction pursuant to an agreement in effect on the Issue Date;

(B) any encumbrance or restriction with respect to a Restricted Subsidiary pursuant to an agreement relating to any Indebtedness Incurred by such Restricted Subsidiary on or prior to the date on which such Restricted Subsidiary was acquired by the Company (other than Indebtedness Incurred as consideration in, or to provide all or any portion of the funds or credit support utilized to consummate, the transaction or series of related transactions pursuant to which such Restricted Subsidiary became a Restricted Subsidiary or was acquired by the Company) and outstanding on such date;

(C) any encumbrance or restriction pursuant to an agreement effecting a Refinancing of Indebtedness Incurred pursuant to an agreement referred to in clause (A) or (B) of this Section 4.12(1) or this clause (C) or contained in any amendment to an agreement referred to in clause (1) or (2) of this Section 4.12(1) or this clause (C); provided, however, that the encumbrances and restrictions with respect to such Restricted Subsidiary contained in any such refinancing agreement or amendment are no less favorable to the Securityholders than encumbrances and restrictions with respect to such Restricted Subsidiary contained in such predecessor agreements; and

(D) any restriction with respect to a Restricted Subsidiary imposed pursuant to an agreement entered into for the sale or disposition of all or substantially all the Capital Stock or assets of such Restricted Subsidiary pending the closing of such sale or disposition; and

(2) with respect to clause (c) only,

(A) any such encumbrance or restriction consisting of customary nonassignment provisions in leases governing leasehold interests to the extent such provisions restrict the transfer of the lease or the property leased thereunder; and

(B) restrictions contained in security agreements or mortgages securing Indebtedness of a Restricted Subsidiary to the extent of such restrictions restrict the transfer of the property subject to such security agreements or mortgages.

* *Commentary*

Often the debt incurrence covenant provides for future subsidiary borrowing arrangements. If such debt will necessarily contain dividend restrictions on the subsidiary issuer, the following is a possible exception to this covenant to accommodate this:

"any encumbrance or restriction contained in the terms of any Indebtedness Incurred pursuant to Section 4.04(b)(•) or any agreement pursuant to which such Indebtedness was issued if (x) either (i) the encumbrance or restriction applies only in the event of and during the continuance of a payment default or a default with respect to a financial covenant contained in such Indebtedness or agreement or (ii) the Board determines at the time any such Indebtedness is Incurred (and at the time of any modification of the terms of any such encumbrance or restriction) that any such encumbrance or restriction will not materially affect the Company's ability to make principal or interest payments on the Securities and any other Indebtedness that is an obligation of the Company and

(y) the encumbrance or restriction is not materially more disadvantageous to the holders of the Securities than is customary in comparable financings or agreements (as determined by the Board in good faith);"

Additional exceptions to clause (c) that can be found in some indentures include:

(x) any encumbrance or restriction on cash or other deposits or net worth imposed by leases, credit agreements, customer contracts or other agreements entered into in the ordinary course of business; and

(y) any encumbrance or restriction in customary form under joint venture agreements and other similar agreements;

SEC REPORTS

* *Commentary*

In the infancy of the high yield market, many Companies were able to avoid regular reporting to Securityholders and certainly often were able to avoid regular SEC reporting. Since most high yield note deals are ultimately held by less than 300 holders, Companies would automatically be relieved of any SEC reporting requirements beginning with respect to the fiscal year following the year in which the registration statement for the Securities became effective. It is now almost universally true in high yield indentures that the Company is required to make regular SEC reports to ensure the steady flow of readily accessible information for current holders and prospective holders. It is important in transactions involving foreign issuers to carefully draft the language to make sure that regardless of what they otherwise would be required to file under SEC rules for foreign issuers, they nonetheless file regular quarterly and annual reports that contain a management's discussion and analysis section similar to what would be required for domestic companies. Counsel should note that the covenant requires timely filing of SEC reports (vs. providing such reports to Security holders once the reports have been filed). Companies that have found themselves in restatement situations and thus unable to make their filings on a timely basis have been faced with technical default of this covenant. Securityholders would normally insist on the formulation set forth below, but there may be some room for negotiation.

SECTION 4.13. SEC REPORTS

Whether or not the Company is subject to the reporting requirements of Section 13 or 15(d) of the Exchange Act, the Company shall file with the SEC (subject to the next sentence) and provide the Trustee and Securityholders with such annual reports and such information, documents and other reports as are specified in Sections 13 and 15(d) of the Exchange Act and applicable to a U.S. corporation subject to such Sections, such information, documents and other reports to be so filed and provided at the times specified for the filings of such information, documents and reports under such Sections and containing all the information, audit reports and exhibits required for such reports. If at any time, the Company is not subject to the periodic reporting requirements of the Exchange Act for any reason, the Company shall nevertheless continue filing the reports specified in the preceding sentence with the SEC within the time periods required by such sentence unless the SEC shall not accept such a filing. The Company shall not take any action for the purpose of causing the SEC not to accept any such filings. In addition, the Company shall post such reports on its website within the time periods that would apply whether or not the Company is required to file those reports with the SEC.

At any time that any of the Company's Subsidiaries are Unrestricted Subsidiaries, then the quarterly and annual financial information required by the preceding paragraph shall include a reasonably detailed presentation, either on the face of the financial statements or in the footnotes thereto, and in "Management's Discussion and Analysis of Financial Condition and Results of Operations," of the financial condition and results of operations of the Company and its Restricted Subsidiaries separate from the condition and results of operations of the Unrestricted Subsidiaries of the Company.

In addition, the Company shall furnish to the Holders of the Securities and to prospective investors, upon the requests of such Holders, any information required to be delivered pursuant to Rule 144A(d)(4) under the Securities Act so long as the Securities are not freely transferable under the Securities Act.

Delivery of such reports, information and documents to the Trustee is for informational purposes only, and the Trustee's receipt of such shall not constitute constructive notice of any information contained therein or determinable from information contained therein, including the Company's compliance with any of its covenants hereunder (as to which the Trustee is entitled to conclusively rely exclusively on an Officers' Certificate).

* *Commentary*

The second paragraph is not found in all indentures, but consideration should be given to its inclusion if there is a likelihood that any significant operations will be conducted through Unrestricted Subsidiaries. The disclosure requirements of the SEC do not recognize the concepts of Restricted Subsidiaries and Unrestricted Subsidiaries (to be distinguished from Guarantor Subsidiaries and non-Guarantor Subsidiaries, for which special financial disclosure requirements are specified), and therefore a covenant that merely requires SEC-mandated disclosure may not adequately inform bondholders about the relative results of operations and financial condition of the restricted and unrestricted group.

MERGER AND CONSOLIDATION

* *Commentary*

The merger covenant is designed to ensure that the successor or survivor in any major transaction involving the Company, including the transferee of substantially all the assets of the Company, assumes the obligations with respect of the Securities. As for substantive requirements in connection with such transactions, the Model covenant requires that the Company on a pro forma basis be able to incur indebtedness under the debt incurrence ratio test and requires that there be no decrease in consolidated net worth as a result of the transaction. These substantive requirements arise because Securityholders want the Company to be financially healthy (as measured by the debt incurrence test) before it is entitled to engage in any significant merger transactions, and even if the Company is financially healthy, the Securityholders do not want the Company to re-leverage itself and reduce net worth as a result of the transaction. As a general rule, Securityholders reasonably expect some improvement in the Company's creditworthiness over the life of the Securities, as measured by debt ratios and an increase in net worth, and it would substantially and adversely impact the secondary trading value of Securities if the indenture permitted a reasonably healthy and de-leveraged Company to re-leverage itself as part of a merger transaction, particularly with a corporation that has a negative net worth. That being said, the net worth requirement is often omitted from a negotiated covenant, especially for issues in industries in which other participants are likely to have a negative net worth.

SECTION 4.14. MERGER AND CONSOLIDATION

The Company shall not consolidate with or merge with or into, or convey, transfer or lease, in one transaction or a series of transactions, all or substantially all its assets to, any Person, unless:

(1) the resulting, surviving or transferee Person (the "Successor Company") shall be a Person organized and existing under the laws of the United States of America, any State thereof or the District of Columbia and the Successor Company (if not the Company) shall expressly assume, by an indenture supplemental thereto, executed and delivered to the Trustee, in form satisfactory to the Trustee, all the obligations of the Company under the Securities and the Indenture; provided, that if the Successor Company is not a corporation, a corporate Wholly Owned Subsidiary that is a Restricted Subsidiary organized under the laws of the United States of America, any State thereof or the District of Columbia becomes a co-issuer of the Securities;

(2) immediately after giving effect to such transaction (and treating any Indebtedness which becomes an obligation of the Successor Company or any Subsidiary as a result of such transaction as having been Incurred by such Successor Company or such Subsidiary at the time of such transaction), no Default shall have occurred and be continuing;

(3) immediately after giving effect to such transaction, the Successor Company would be able to Incur an additional $1.00 of Indebtedness pursuant to Section 4.04(a);

(4) immediately after giving effect to such transaction, the Successor Company shall have Consolidated Net Worth in an amount that is not less than the Consolidated Net Worth of the Company immediately prior to such transaction; and

(5) the Company shall have delivered to the Trustee an Officers' Certificate and an Opinion of Counsel, each stating that such consolidation, merger or transfer and such supplemental indenture (if any) comply with the Indenture.

* *Commentary*

Some indenture forms add the following sixth requirement:

(6) the Company shall have delivered to the Trustee an Opinion of Counsel to the effect that the Holders will not recognize income, gain or loss for Federal income tax purposes as a result of such transaction and will be subject to Federal income tax on the same amounts, in the same manner and at the same times as would have been the case if such transaction had not occurred.

This extra requirement is relatively new and many indenture forms have yet to incorporate it. It is intended to make sure that as a result of the merger transaction, the holders do not recognize accelerated income on their investment resulting from a fundamental change in the security by virtue of the assumption by the survivor of the obligations of the Securities. In most cases, the opinion requirement is not an obstacle to structuring the merger transaction and provides some extra protection for Securityholders.

provided, however, that clauses (3) and (4) will not be applicable to (A) a Restricted Subsidiary consolidating with, merging into or transferring all or part of its properties and assets to the Company (so long as no Capital Stock of the Company is distributed to any Person) or (B) the Company merging with an Affiliate of the

Company solely for the purpose and with the sole effect of reincorporating the Company in another jurisdiction.

For purposes of this Section 4.14, the sale, lease, conveyance, assignment, transfer or other disposition of all or substantially all of the properties and assets of one or more Subsidiaries of the Company, which properties and assets, if held by the Company instead of such Subsidiaries, would constitute all or substantially all of the properties and assets of the Company on a consolidated basis, shall be deemed to be the transfer of all or substantially all of the properties and assets of the Company.

The Successor Company shall be the successor to the Company and shall succeed to, and be substituted for, and may exercise every right and power of, the Company under this Indenture, but the predecessor Company in the case of a conveyance, transfer or lease shall not be released from the obligation to pay the principal of and interest on the Securities.

* *Commentary*

The courts have variously conducted both quantitative and qualitative analyses in determining whether a transaction involves the disposition of "all or substantially all" of a company's assets, without establishing any bright-line standard under New York law. In Sharon Steel Corp. v. Chase Manhattan Bank, N.A., 691 F.2d 1039 (2d Cir. 1982), cert. denied, 460 U.S. 1012 (1983), the Company had engaged in a yearlong, piecemeal sale of its assets to various parties, culminating in a final sale of certain assets, representing 38% of operating revenues, 13% of operating profits and 51% of the net book value of total assets, to Sharon Steel, in connection with which Sharon Steel proposed to assume the obligations under the indenture. The indenture trustees took the position that this final sale was not the sale of all or substantially all the assets of the Company. Instead, they argued that the sales transactions over the course of the year had to be viewed as a voluntary liquidation of the Company, which under the indenture triggered a mandatory redemption of the securities at a premium. The court agreed with the trustees, saying that the quantity of the assets sold to Sharon Steel was not close to "all or substantially all." In contrast, in B.S.F. Co. v. Phila. Nat'l. Bank, 204 A.2d 746 (Del. 1964), the court held that the sale of subsidiary stock representing approximately 75% of the Company's consolidated assets did represent the sale of substantially all the Company's assets. See James Gadsden, All or Substantially All Assets, 13 Journal of Bankruptcy Law and Practice 85 (Nov.—Dec. 2004).

TABLE OF CASES

Principal cases are in bold type.

INDEX